North Pacific Ocean

MEXICO

Oahu **HAWAII**
Hawaii

Line Islands
Kiritimati

Line Islands

Marquesas Islands

FRENCH
Tuamotu Archipelago
Society Islands
Tahiti
POLYNESIA (FR)
Gambier Islands
Austral Islands

Pitcairn Islands (UK)

Easter

Pacific Ocean

POLITICAL ENTITIES
OF THE PACIFIC ISLANDS

Reprinted with permission from
The Center for Pacific Islands Studies
University of Hawaii at Manoa, by Manoa Mapworks, Inc. 1992

The solid lines surrounding island groups do not represent territorial boundaries.
Their sole purpose is to separate the islands by jurisdiction.

SOUTH PACIFIC ISLANDS LEGAL SYSTEMS

Contributors

Isaacus Adzoxornu
: *Faculty of Law, Victoria University of Wellington, New Zealand*

AH Angelo
: *Faculty of Law, Victoria University of Wellington, New Zealand*

Tony Deklin
: *Faculty of Management, University of Canberra, Australia*

Mary McCormick
: *Law Library, University of South Carolina, Columbia, South Carolina, U.S.A.*

John Nonggorr
: *Faculty of Law, University of Papua New Guinea*

Michael A. Ntumy
: *Faculty of Law, University of Papua New Guinea*

Bruce L. Ottley
: *College of Law, DePaul University, Chicago, Illinois, U.S.A.*

Don Paterson
: *Pacific Law Unit, University of the South Pacific, Port Vila, Vanuatu*

C. Guy Powles
: *Faculty of Law, Monash University, Melbourne, Australia*

Dhirendra K. Srivastava
: *Department of Law, City Polytechnic of Hong Kong*

Martin Tsamenyi
: *Faculty of Law, University of Tasmania, Hobart, Australia*

Jean G. Zorn
: *City University of New York, Law School, Queens College, Flushing, New York, U.S.A.*

Stephen A. Zorn
: *Pace University Law School, White Plains, New York, U.S.A.*

South Pacific Islands Legal Systems

MICHAEL A. NTUMY
General Editor

A H ANGELO
C. GUY POWLES
JEAN G. ZORN
STEPHEN A. ZORN
Editorial Committee

UNIVERSITY OF HAWAII PRESS • HONOLULU

© 1993 UNIVERSITY OF HAWAII PRESS
All rights reserved
Printed in the United States of America

98 97 96 95 94 93 5 4 3 2 1

Library of Congress Cataloging-in-Publication Data

South Pacific Islands legal systems / edited by Michael A. Ntumy.
    p.   cm.
    Includes bibliographical references.
    ISBN 0-8248-1438-X
    1. Law—Oceania.   I. Ntumy, Michael A.
KVC117.S68 1993
349.95—dc20   92-41464
[349.5]   CIP

University of Hawaii Press Books are printed on
acid-free paper and meet the guidelines for permanence
and durability of the Council on Library Resources

Contents

FOREWORD xiii
ACKNOWLEDGMENTS xv
INTRODUCTION xvii

PART ONE: THE PARLIAMENTARY MODEL

CHAPTER 1: THE COOK ISLANDS 3
Isaacus Adzoxornu and the Editorial Committee

- I. Dateline — 3
- II. Historical, Cultural, and Economic Survey — 3
- III. Sources of Law — 5
- IV. Constitutional System — 6
- V. Administrative Organization and Law — 10
- VI. International Obligations — 12
- VII. Revenue Law — 13
- VIII. Investment Law — 14
- IX. Welfare Law — 15
- X. Criminal Law — 15
- XI. Judicial Procedure — 16
- XII. Land and Natural Resources — 18
- XIII. Persons and Entities — 20
- XIV. Family Law — 20
- XV. Personal Property — 21
- XVI. Wills and Succession — 21
- XVII. Contracts — 21
- XVIII. Commercial Law — 22
- XIX. Torts — 22
- XX. Labor Law — 22
- XXI. Industrial and Intellectual Property Rights — 24
- XXII. Legal Education and Profession — 24
- XXIII. Research Guide — 24

CHAPTER 2: FIJI 26
Don Paterson and Stephen A. Zorn

- I. Dateline — 26
- II. Historical, Cultural, and Economic Survey — 27
- III. Sources of Law — 31
- IV. Constitutional System — 34
- V. Administrative Organization and Law — 43
- VI. International Obligations — 46
- VII. Revenue Law — 47
- VIII. Investment Law — 49
- IX. Welfare Law — 51
- X. Criminal Law — 52
- XI. Judicial Procedure — 53
- XII. Land and Natural Resources — 56
- XIII. Persons and Entities — 60
- XIV. Family Law — 60
- XV. Personal Property — 64
- XVI. Wills and Succession — 64
- XVII. Contracts — 65
- XVIII. Commercial Law — 66
- XIX. Torts — 67
- XX. Labor Law — 68
- XXI. Industrial and Intellectual Property Rights — 70
- XXII. Legal Education and Profession — 71
- XXIII. Research Guide — 72

CHAPTER 3: KIRIBATI — 75
Martin Tsamenyi
- I. Dateline — 75
- II. Historical, Cultural, and Economic Survey — 75
- III. Sources of Law — 77
- IV. Constitutional System — 79
- V. Administrative Organization and Law — 84
- VI. International Obligations — 85
- VII. Revenue Law — 86
- VIII. Investment Law — 86
- IX. Welfare Law — 87
- X. Criminal Law — 87
- XI. Judicial Procedure — 88
- XII. Land and Natural Resources — 89
- XIII. Persons and Entities — 91
- XIV. Family Law — 91
- XV. Personal Property — 93
- XVI. Wills and Succession — 93
- XVII. Contracts — 94
- XVIII. Commercial Law — 94
- XIX. Torts — 95
- XX. Labor Law — 96
- XXI. Industrial and Intellectual Property Rights — 97
- XXII. Legal Education and Profession — 98
- XXIII. Research Guide — 98

CHAPTER 4: THE REPUBLIC OF THE MARSHALL ISLANDS — 100
Jean G. Zorn
- I. Dateline — 100
- II. Historical, Cultural, and Economic Survey — 102
- III. Sources of Law — 103
- IV. Constitutional System — 106
- V. Administrative Organization and Law — 116
- VI. International Obligations — 118
- VII. Revenue Law — 119
- VIII. Investment Law — 120
- IX. Welfare Law — 121
- X. Criminal Law — 122
- XI. Judicial Procedure — 123
- XII. Land and Natural Resources — 126
- XIII. Persons and Entities — 131
- XIV. Family Law — 131
- XV. Personal Property — 133
- XVI. Wills and Succession — 133
- XVII. Contracts — 133
- XVIII. Commercial Law — 134
- XIX. Torts — 136
- XX. Labor Law — 137
- XXI. Intellectual Property Rights — 138
- XXII. Legal Education and Profession — 138
- XXIII. Research Guide — 139

CHAPTER 5: NAURU — 142
Tony Deklin
- I. Dateline — 142
- II. Historical, Cultural, and Economic Survey — 143
- III. Sources of Law — 144
- IV. Constitutional System — 146
- V. Administrative Organization and Law — 149
- VI. International Obligations — 150
- VII. Revenue Law — 151
- VIII. Investment Law — 151
- IX. Welfare Law — 151
- X. Criminal Law — 152
- XI. Judicial Procedure — 152
- XII. Land and Natural Resources — 152
- XIII. Persons and Entities — 154
- XIV. Family Law — 154
- XV. Personal Property — 155
- XVI. Wills and Succession — 155
- XVII. Contracts — 155
- XVIII. Commercial Law — 155
- XIX. Torts — 156
- XX. Labor Law — 156
- XXI. Industrial and Intellectual Property Rights — 156
- XXII. Legal Education and Profession — 156
- XXIII. Research Guide — 157

CHAPTER 6: NIUE 158
AH Angelo
    I. Dateline 158
    II. Historical, Cultural, and Economic Survey 158
    III. Sources of Law 159
    IV. Constitutional System 162
    V. Administrative Organization and Law 165
    VI. International Obligations 167
    VII. Revenue Law 168
    VIII. Investment Law 169
    IX. Welfare Law 169
    X. Criminal Law 169
    XI. Judicial Procedure 171
    XII. Land and Natural Resources 171
    XIII. Persons and Entities 173
    XIV. Family Law 173
    XV. Personal Property 175
    XVI. Wills and Succession 175
    XVII. Contracts 176
    XVIII. Commercial Law 176
    XIX. Torts 177
    XX. Labor Law 178
    XXI. Industrial and Intellectual Property Rights 178
    XXII. Legal Education and Profession 178
    XXIII. Research Guide 178

CHAPTER 7: NORFOLK ISLAND 180
Dhirendra K. Srivastava
    I. Dateline 180
    II. Historical, Cultural, and Economic Survey 180
    III. Sources of Law 182
    IV. Constitutional System 183
    V. Administrative Organization and Law 188
    VI. International Obligations 188
    VII. Revenue Law 188
    VIII. Investment Law 189
    IX. Welfare Law 190
    X. Criminal Law 190
    XI. Judicial Procedure 191
    XII. Land and Natural Resources 193
    XIII. Persons and Entities 195
    XIV. Family Law 195
    XV. Personal Property 197
    XVI. Wills and Succession 197
    XVII. Contracts 197
    XVIII. Commercial Law 198
    XIX. Torts 199
    XX. Labor Law 199
    XXI. Industrial and Intellectual Property Rights 200
    XXII. Legal Education and Profession 200
    XXIII. Research Guide 201

CHAPTER 8: PAPUA NEW GUINEA 202
John Nonggorr
    I. Dateline 202
    II. Historical, Cultural, and Economic Survey 202
    III. Sources of Law 205
    IV. Constitutional System 211
    V. Administrative Organization and Law 223
    VI. International Obligations 226
    VII. Revenue Law 227
    VIII. Investment Law 228
    IX. Welfare Law 229
    X. Criminal Law 230
    XI. Judicial Procedure 231
    XII. Land and Natural Resources 236
    XIII. Persons and Entities 242
    XIV. Family Law 242
    XV. Personal Property 243
    XVI. Wills and Succession 244
    XVII. Contracts 244
    XVIII. Commercial Law 245
    XIX. Torts 246
    XX. Labor Law 247
    XXI. Industrial and Intellectual Property Rights 249

XXII.	Legal Education and Profession	249
XXIII.	Research Guide	250

CHAPTER 9: PITCAIRN ISLAND 252
Dhirendra K. Srivastava

I.	Dateline	252
II.	Historical, Cultural, and Economic Survey	252
III.	Sources of Law	254
IV.	Constitutional System	255
V.	Administrative Organization and Law	258
VI.	International Obligations	258
VII.	Revenue Law	258
VIII.	Investment Law	259
IX.	Welfare Law	259
X.	Criminal Law	259
XI.	Judicial Procedure	260
XII.	Land and Natural Resources	261
XIII.	Persons and Entities	263
XIV.	Family Law	264
XV.	Personal Property	265
XVI.	Wills and Succession	265
XVII.	Contracts	265
XVIII.	Commercial Law	265
XIX.	Torts	266
XX.	Labor Law	266
XXI.	Intellectual Property Rights	267
XXII.	Legal Education and Profession	267
XXIII.	Research Guide	267

CHAPTER 10: SOLOMON ISLANDS 268
John Nonggorr

I.	Dateline	268
II.	Historical, Cultural, and Economic Survey	268
III.	Sources of Law	270
IV.	Constitutional System	272
V.	Administrative Organization and Law	279
VI.	International Obligations	281
VII.	Revenue Law	282
VIII.	Investment Law	282
IX.	Welfare Law	283
X.	Criminal Law	284
XI.	Judicial Procedure	284
XII.	Land and Natural Resources	286
XIII.	Persons and Entities	290
XIV.	Family Law	290
XV.	Personal Property	291
XVI.	Wills and Succession	291
XVII.	Contracts	292
XVIII.	Commercial Law	292
XIX.	Torts	292
XX.	Labor Law	293
XXI.	Industrial and Intellectual Property Rights	294
XXII.	Legal Education and Profession	294
XXIII.	Research Guide	295

CHAPTER 11: TOKELAU 296
AH Angelo

I.	Dateline	296
II.	Historical, Cultural, and Economic Survey	296
III.	Sources of Law	298
IV.	Constitutional System	299
V.	Administrative Organization and Law	303
VI.	International Obligations	305
VII.	Revenue Law	305
VIII.	Investment Law	306
IX.	Welfare Law	306
X.	Criminal Law	307
XI.	Judicial Procedure	307
XII.	Land and Natural Resources	307
XIII.	Persons and Entities	309
XIV.	Family Law	309
XV.	Personal Property	310
XVI.	Wills and Succession	311
XVII.	Contracts	311
XVIII.	Commercial Law	311
XIX.	Torts	312
XX.	Labor Law	312

XXI.	Industrial and Intellectual Property Rights	313
XXII.	Legal Education and Profession	313
XXIII.	Research Guide	313

CHAPTER 12: TONGA   315
C. Guy Powles

I.	Dateline	315
II.	Historical, Cultural, and Economic Survey	316
III.	Sources of Law	317
IV.	Constitutional System	319
V.	Administrative Organization and Law	325
VI.	International Obligations	326
VII.	Revenue Law	327
VIII.	Investment Law	328
IX.	Welfare Law	329
X.	Criminal Law	329
XI.	Judicial Procedure	330
XII.	Land and Natural Resources	332
XIII.	Persons and Entities	335
XIV.	Family Law	336
XV.	Personal Property	337
XVI.	Wills and Succession	337
XVII.	Contracts	337
XVIII.	Commercial Law	338
XIX.	Torts	339
XX.	Labor Law	339
XXI.	Industrial and Intellectual Property Rights	339
XXII.	Legal Education and Profession	340
XXIII.	Research Guide	340

CHAPTER 13: TUVALU   342
Martin Tsamenyi

I.	Dateline	342
II.	Historical, Cultural, and Economic Survey	342
III.	Sources of Law	344
IV.	Constitutional System	346
V.	Administrative Organization and Law	351

VI.	International Obligations	352
VII.	Revenue Law	352
VIII.	Investment Law	353
IX.	Welfare Law	353
X.	Criminal Law	354
XI.	Judicial Procedure	354
XII.	Land and Natural Resources	356
XIII.	Persons and Entities	357
XIV.	Family Law	357
XV.	Personal Property	358
XVI.	Wills and Succession	359
XVII.	Contracts	360
XVIII.	Commercial Law	360
XIX.	Torts	361
XX.	Labor Law	361
XXI.	Industrial and Intellectual Property Rights	362
XXII.	Legal Education and Profession	363
XXIII.	Research Guide	363

CHAPTER 14: VANUATU   365
Don Paterson

I.	Dateline	365
II.	Historical, Cultural, and Economic Survey	365
III.	Sources of Law	367
IV.	Constitutional System	369
V.	Administrative Organization and Law	375
VI.	International Obligations	377
VII.	Revenue Law	378
VIII.	Investment Law	379
IX.	Welfare Law	380
X.	Criminal Law	381
XI.	Judicial Procedure	381
XII.	Land and Natural Resources	384
XIII.	Persons and Entities	385
XIV.	Family Law	386
XV.	Personal Property	388
XVI.	Wills and Succession	388
XVII.	Contracts	388
XVIII.	Commercial Law	388
XIX.	Torts	391

XX.	Labor Law	391
XXI.	Industrial and Intellectual Property Rights	392
XXII.	Legal Education and Profession	393
XXIII.	Research Guide	393

CHAPTER 15: WESTERN SAMOA 395
C. Guy Powles

I.	Dateline	395
II.	Historical, Cultural, and Economic Survey	395
III.	Sources of Law	397
IV.	Constitutional System	400
V.	Administrative Organization and Law	408
VI.	International Obligations	410
VII.	Revenue Law	411
VIII.	Investment Law	412
IX.	Welfare Law	414
X.	Criminal Law	415
XI.	Judicial Procedure	415
XII.	Land and Natural Resources	418
XIII.	Persons and Entities	422
XIV.	Family Law	423
XV.	Personal Property	424
XVI.	Wills and Succession	424
XVII.	Contracts	425
XVIII.	Commercial Law	425
XIX.	Torts	427
XX.	Labor Law	427
XXI.	Industrial and Intellectual Property Law	428
XXII.	Legal Education and Profession	428
XXIII.	Research Guide	429

PART TWO: THE PRESIDENTIAL MODEL

CHAPTER 16: AMERICAN SAMOA 433
Mary McCormick

I.	Dateline	433
II.	Historical, Cultural, and Economic Survey	433
III.	Sources of Law	435
IV.	Constitutional System	436
V.	Administrative Organization and Law	443
VI.	International Obligations	445
VII.	Revenue Law	445
VIII.	Investment Law	446
IX.	Welfare Law	447
X.	Criminal Law	447
XI.	Judicial Procedure	449
XII.	Land and Natural Resources	452
XIII.	Persons and Entities	455
XIV.	Family Law	455
XV.	Personal Property	456
XVI.	Wills and Succession	456
XVII.	Contracts	457
XVIII.	Commercial Law	457
XIX.	Torts	458
XX.	Labor Law	459
XXI.	Industrial and Intellectual Property Rights	460
XXII.	Legal Education and Profession	460
XXIII.	Research Guide	460

CHAPTER 17: THE FEDERATED STATES OF MICRONESIA 462
Jean G. Zorn

I.	Dateline	462
II.	Historical, Cultural, and Economic Survey	463
III.	Sources of Law	466
IV.	Constitutional System	470
V.	Administrative Organization and Law	482
VI.	International Obligations	486
VII.	Revenue Law	487
VIII.	Investment Law	488
IX.	Welfare Law	492
X.	Criminal Law	493
XI.	Jurisdiction and Judicial Procedure	495

CONTENTS xi

XII.	Land and Natural Resources	498
XIII.	Persons and Entities	505
XIV.	Family Law	505
XV.	Personal Property	508
XVI.	Wills and Succession	508
XVII.	Contracts	509
XVIII.	Commercial Law	510
XIX.	Torts	512
XX.	Labor Law	513
XXI.	Industrial and Intellectual Property Rights	514
XXII.	Legal Education and Profession	514
XXIII.	Research Guide	515

CHAPTER 18: GUAM 518
Mary McCormick

I.	Dateline	518
II.	Historical, Cultural, and Economic Survey	518
III.	Sources of Law	519
IV.	Constitutional System	521
V.	Administrative Organization and Law	525
VI.	International Obligations	526
VII.	Revenue Law	526
VIII.	Investment Law	526
IX.	Welfare Law	527
X.	Criminal Law	527
XI.	Judicial Procedure	528
XII.	Land and Natural Resources	531
XIII.	Persons and Entities	532
XIV.	Family Law	532
XV.	Personal Property	535
XVI.	Wills and Succession	535
XVII.	Contracts	536
XVIII.	Commercial Law	536
XIX.	Torts	537
XX.	Labor Law	538
XXI.	Industrial and Intellectual Property Rights	538
XXII.	Legal Education and Profession	539
XXIII.	Research Guide	539

CHAPTER 19: THE COMMONWEALTH OF THE NORTHERN MARIANA ISLANDS 540
Bruce L. Ottley

I.	Dateline	540
II.	Historical, Cultural, and Economic Survey	541
III.	Sources of Law	542
IV.	Constitutional System	545
V.	Administrative Organization and Law	549
VI.	International Obligations	551
VII.	Revenue Law	551
VIII.	Investment Law	552
IX.	Welfare Law	552
X.	Criminal Law	553
XI.	Judicial Procedure	554
XII.	Land and Natural Resources	557
XIII.	Persons and Entities	559
XIV.	Family Law	559
XV.	Personal Property	561
XVI.	Wills and Succession	561
XVII.	Contracts	562
XVIII.	Commercial Law	562
XIX.	Torts	563
XX.	Labor Law	564
XXI.	Industrial and Intellectual Property Rights	565
XXII.	Legal Education and Profession	565
XXIII.	Research Guide	565

CHAPTER 20: THE REPUBLIC OF PALAU 567
Bruce L. Ottley

I.	Dateline	567
II.	Historical, Cultural, and Economic Survey	567
III.	Sources of Law	569
IV.	Constitutional System	571
V.	Administrative Organization and Law	575
VI.	International Obligations	577
VII.	Revenue Law	577

VIII.	Investment Law	578
IX.	Welfare Law	579
X.	Criminal Law	579
XI.	Judicial Procedure	580
XII.	Land and Natural Resources	584
XIII.	Persons and Entities	586
XIV.	Family Law	587
XV.	Personal Property	588
XVI.	Wills and Succession	588
XVII.	Contracts	589
XVIII.	Commercial Law	589
XIX.	Torts	590
XX.	Labor Law	591
XXI.	Industrial and Intellectual Property Rights	591
XXII.	Legal Education and Profession	591
XXIII.	Research Guide	591

PART THREE: THE FRENCH TERRITORIES

CHAPTER 21: NEW CALEDONIA 595
Michael A. Ntumy

I.	Dateline	595
II.	Historical, Cultural, and Economic Survey	596
III.	Sources of Law	599
IV.	Constitutional System	600
V.	Administrative Organization and Law	610
VI.	International Obligations	612
VII.	Revenue Law	613
VIII.	Investment Law	613
IX.	Welfare Law	614
X.	Land and Natural Resources	615
XI.	Legal Education and Profession	618
XII.	Customary Law	618
XIII.	Research Guide	620

CHAPTER 22: WALLIS AND FUTUNA 622
Michael A. Ntumy

I.	Dateline	622
II.	Historical, Cultural, and Economic Survey	622
III.	Sources of Law	623
IV.	Constitutional System	624
V.	Private Law	626
VI.	Criminal Law	627
VII.	Judicial Procedure	627
VIII.	Persons and Entities	628
IX.	Family Law	628
X.	Personal Property	630
XI.	Wills and Succession	630
XII.	Contracts	631
XIII.	Commercial Law	632
XIV.	Torts	633
XV.	Labor Law	633
XVI.	Industrial and Intellectual Property Rights	635
XVII.	Legal Education and Profession	635
XVIII.	Research Guide	635

CHAPTER 23: FRENCH POLYNESIA 637
Michael A. Ntumy

I.	Dateline	637
II.	Historical, Cultural, and Economic Survey	637
III.	Sources of Law	639
IV.	Constitutional System	639
V.	International Obligations	644
VI.	Legal Education and Profession	644
VII.	Research Guide	644

NOTES 645

Foreword

When the editors of this book approached me with a request to contribute a foreword, I was very happy to do so because the book illustrates some of the important legal developments that are taking place in the South Pacific. As Chief Justice of Papua New Guinea, I have been at the center of these developments in my own country. It therefore gives me great pleasure to be associated with the publication of an account of the developments that I have, by virtue of my office, helped to bring about.

For most of us in the South Pacific, it has been relatively few years since we achieved independence and, with that, the opportunity to develop our own legal systems. In that brief span, I have seen the courts, the legislatures, and the legal professions of the South Pacific island countries grow and come of age. We began, perhaps, as stepchildren of the past, with statutes and a sense of the common law borrowed from other nations, principally from our colonial powers. But we have gradually developed legal systems that we can truly refer to as our own. As the chapters in this book demonstrate, legal thought in the South Pacific has gathered its own momentum and is driven by two basic principles.

The first principle is the rule of law, the continuing importance of which is symbolized by the homegrown constitutions adopted by most of the island countries. To safeguard the freedoms and rights enshrined in these constitutions, the constitutions have been made the supreme law of the land, and the courts have been empowered to uphold the supremacy of the constitution. The second principle is the creation of a legal system and a common law (or an underlying law, as we call it in Papua New Guinea) that is attuned to the circumstances of our countries and their peoples. Judicial practice in many island countries reflects an awareness of the responsibility imposed by this principle. Notwithstanding problems of conceptual and doctrinal complexities, many countries have achieved some limited success in applying this principle. The lesson to be drawn from the limited success is the need for concerted collaborative efforts by the legislature (legislation and law reform) as well as the judiciary.

Turning the pages of this book, I am reminded that the courts in other South Pacific nations have struggled with many of the same problems that have confronted our National Court and Supreme Court here in Papua New Guinea. This shows clearly how very much we have to offer one another, if only we knew more about one another's systems of government and law, as well as the different judicial approaches to dispute settlement. In a very comprehensive and competent way, this book provides the relevant information that we need to learn about each other. In my opinion, it is an important and welcome addition to the library of every South Pacific judge and lawyer.

As I note the solidarity that can result from the knowledge of each other's legal systems, I hope that we will, in the near future, develop a system of circulating our statutes and judicial decisions among ourselves and that we in the judiciary will soon be citing one another's decisions—not as precedent, of course—but as guides to solving our common problems.

THE HONOURABLE SIR BURI KIDU
Chief Justice of Papua New Guinea

Acknowledgments

The research that laid the foundation for this volume and the preparation of the manuscript have taken four years of work and dedication. My job as general editor was made easier and more enjoyable by the extensive contributions of the editorial committee, the contributors, and everyone involved in the project.

The Asia Foundation has sponsored the project with a generous grant that covered the collection and distribution of materials to the contributors; the organization of field trips; a three-day workshop for the contributors in 1989 in Wellington, New Zealand; and the processing of the manuscript. Elizabeth White, then Area Director for the Pacific Region, Asia Foundation, was a constant source of moral and intellectual support. Heather Creech, then Law Librarian at the University of Papua New Guinea (UPNG), compiled a bibliography of legal materials on the South Pacific island jurisdictions. We also wish at this time to acknowledge the contributions of Joyce Kasokason, secretary at the Faculty of Law, UPNG, Eve Rannells, current Law Librarian at UPNG, and Agnes Montanari, a bilingual French lawyer.

From the first draft, the members of the editorial committee (Jean and Stephen Zorn, in particular, but with significant support from Guy Powles and Tony Angelo) have undertaken responsibility for a legal compendium that would be useful to Pacific judges, lawyers, lawmakers, and students. They read, edited, and updated the manuscript at each of its stages. The contributors and I entrusted them with the responsibility for making the whole as consistent, analytical, and accurate as possible. The contributors themselves met strict and sometimes inconvenient deadlines. To all of these individuals I am most grateful.

Because the law in the Pacific is difficult to obtain (which is one of the reasons that this volume will be useful), we depended on interviews and consultations with legal experts from various jurisdictions to supply us with missing information or to ensure that chapters are as accurate as possible. On behalf of all the contributors, I acknowledge with gratitude the assistance of Gilles Lucazeau, Attorney General of New Caledonia; Guy Agniel, Genevieve Phan, and Milena Bellini, all of Noumea; Edward King, formerly Chief Justice of the Federated States of Micronesia Supreme Court; Edwel Santos, Chief Justice of Pohnpei Supreme Court; Steve Skipton and Alan Burdick, the Federated States of Micronesia; Isikeli Mataitoga, Director of Public Prosecutions in Fiji; Jayand Prakash of the Attorney General's office in Fiji; D. J. Treadwell, legal adviser to the government of Pitcairn Island; Don Wright, senior legal counsel in the administration of Norfolk Island; Justice Fox, formerly of the Norfolk Island Supreme Court; Peter MacSporran of Melbourne; Sir Gavin Donne; and Roman Tomasic, of the Law Department, University of Canberra. Also acknowledged are the contributions of John Lynch, formerly Vice Chancellor of the University of Papua New Guinea, and Jacqueline Elliott, High Court Librarian, Canberra. There will, regrettably, be some who helped and whose names have been omitted. We offer them our apologies and our thanks.

Our thanks also go to Curtin University of Technology, Perth; University of Tasmania; Monash University; Victoria University of Wellington; and the University of Papua New Guinea for assisting the research project through either financial or material support to the contributors employed by them.

We thank the editorial staff of the University of Hawaii Press, particularly Pamela Kelley, Sally Serafim, Cheri Dunn, and Carolyn McGovern, for their cooperation, encouragement, and care during the production process. Finally, we thank all our secretaries and research assistants for enduring the pressure imposed by the enormity of the project.

MICHAEL A. NTUMY

Introduction

A comprehensive reference to the legal systems of the nations and territories of the South and Central Pacific has long been needed. This book is a major step toward meeting that need. Its objective is to provide an overview of the laws, legal structures, and governmental institutions of each of the states and territories of the region (Australia, New Zealand, and Hawaii are not considered directly because their systems have been sufficiently described elsewhere). The book is intended to serve lawyers and judges, legal scholars, officials of governmental and international organizations, businesspeople and others, both within and outside the region, who need information about the government and legal systems of the South and Central Pacific.

Information about the law of Pacific countries and territories is difficult to obtain, even in some cases within the jurisdiction. Thus, this book may be for some time the only and certainly the most accessible guide to the law of many of the countries in the region. Responding to the need for a more accessible source of information about Pacific legal systems, the general editor conceived the idea for this collection and, with financial assistance from the Asia Foundation, coordinated the four years of extensive and collaborative research that has led to its publication. Thirteen authors, each with considerable experience in Pacific law, worked on the book's twenty-three chapters. The manuscript was then further researched and extensively edited by the members of the editorial committee.

PLAN AND PURPOSE OF THE BOOK

The book is divided into three parts, corresponding roughly to major divisions in governmental structure among the Pacific states and territories. The first part includes those nations whose constitutional systems approximate a Westminster concept of cabinet government. Also included here are entities that remain territories of Australia, New Zealand, and the United Kingdom. The second part includes those states and territories whose constitutional arrangements exhibit closer ties to the American presidential model, with its emphasis on the separation of governmental functions and powers. The third part contains the current French territories.

The plan of the book reflects both the unity and diversity of law in the Pacific. The information about each country or territory is contained in a single chapter. To ensure as much consistency as possible in the presentation of the materials, each chapter covers similar topics in similar order, and major headings in all chapters are essentially identical. This arrangement should assist readers in systematically comparing the different legal systems. However, each chapter's subheadings vary somewhat, reflecting the diversity and uniqueness of each state or territory.

In order to keep footnotes to a minimum, secondary source materials are seldom footnoted but instead are collected in the Research Guide at the end of each chapter, and the book's debt to the authors of these works is hereby acknowledged. In addition, statutes are usually cited by name and (where a country or territory has adopted a code or compilation) by title or chapter number. Section numbers are used only where a particular section is being quoted.

The difficulty in obtaining primary legal materials (particularly statutes and judicial decisions) from many Pacific countries and territories is a reason for this book's existence. It is also the source of a caveat about the book's use. The contributors gathered primary material for their chapters, usually by visiting the jurisdictions, in 1988 and 1989. In many jurisdictions, there is no central depository for laws and statutes. It took ingenuity and patience to find everything. Since 1989, members of the editorial committee have traveled and corresponded to update the materials. Although the authors and editors have done their best to make each chapter as timely and authoritative as possible, new laws will have been enacted between the time when we were able to gather materials and the time the book goes to press, courts will have handed down new decisions, and, very occasionally, older statutes or cases will have come to light.

LAW AND LEGAL SYSTEMS OF THE PACIFIC

One purpose of this compendium is to aid Pacific legislators, lawyers, and judges who wish to become more familiar with the sometimes similar, sometimes diverse approaches that other Pacific states and territories have taken in developing their laws and legal systems. A feature common to most Pacific states and territories is the existence of a plural legal system. Customary law, laws and legal processes imported during the colonial era, and laws passed by local legislatures coexist, and all are changing to meet new circumstances. Each chapter of the book includes a summary, as complete and contemporaneous as possible, of the current state of the law in each country or territory. The remainder of this Introduction will draw some comparisons and contrasts.

CONSTITUTIONAL SYSTEMS OF THE PACIFIC

In the past three decades, the South and Central Pacific states and territories have attained varying degrees of autonomy, ranging from limited self-government to full independence. Autonomy brings with it the tasks of constructing stable governments and economies and devising new legal systems appropriate to the special circumstances of each country or territory.

Most islands in the region were colonized in the latter half of the nineteenth century, primarily by England, Germany, France, and the United States, which were vying for trading empires in the Pacific. With the exception of Tonga, which always retained significant autonomy, island societies began to regain their independence in the 1960s, with Western Samoa in 1962 the first to be recognized. For most, the road to independence was a gradual process of political development toward a Western model, and most adopted a governmental structure similar to that of their primary colonizing power. Only the Marshall Islands, which had been a United States dependency, elected to forgo the American presidential model in favor of a parliamentary system. Vanuatu, which had been a condominium jointly ruled by France and the United Kingdom, had to choose between the two systems, settling for a form of government and a legal system more akin to the English than the French example. But, whether Pacific nations have opted for a presidential or parliamentary system, each in its constitution has provided for checks on governmental power and for some degree of independence for the judicial branch.

Although all Pacific island societies had their own political systems long before colonization, few of those systems were organized on a scale that could form the basis for the political structure of a nation-state. Chiefs, members of the aristocracy, and other traditional leaders continue to play important leadership and advisory roles in the governing of most countries, but comparatively few constitutions give them a central role or extensive authority in the new governmental structure. Tonga and Western Samoa have maintained their highest traditional leaders as heads of state and have recognized chiefly status in other ways, but experience in both countries demonstrates that the nature of statehood alters the powers and duties associated with leadership in ways that are both significant and subtle.

Attempts have also been made in a number of other states or territories to create a formal role for chiefs in the national political process, but that role tends to differ from that which they traditionally fill. In Western Samoa, most of the seats in the Legislative Assembly are reserved for chiefs. In American Samoa, a chiefly title is a prerequisite for election to the Senate. In Fiji, the Great Council of Chiefs appoints the President and nominates twenty-four of the Senate's thirty-four members. Other countries have given more limited functions, sometimes primarily advisory, to chiefs. In the Marshalls, Palau, Vanuatu, and the Cook Islands, councils of chiefs have been created to advise the legislature or the executive. The Palauan council advises the President, but nothing requires the President to heed the council's advice. In Vanuatu, except in regard to customary land law, the council does not have the power to compel the legislature to submit bills to it, and the legislature is not required to amend bills of which the council disapproves. The Cook Islands' House of Arikis is also purely advisory. In the Marshalls, the authority of traditional leaders is potentially greater. The council may require the legislature to reconsider any bill affecting customary law or land tenure. Although the legislature need not amend the bill, it must at least go through the process of reconsideration.

With the exception of Niue, which is a state in free association with New Zealand, a prerequisite to independence for the South and Central Pacific states has been the adoption of a constitution that, in addition to laying out the structure of government, also includes a list of fundamental civil and political rights of individuals. Generally, government may not abrogate these rights or, as in the case of some of the rights guaranteed by the Papua New Guinea and Fiji and other constitutions, may abrogate them only under constitutionally prescribed circumstances. The adoption of a written constitution with a bill of rights and the decision to make the constitution the supreme law is a development consistent with constitutional theory long held in the United States and widely adopted in many of the nations born soon after World War II. The Pacific constitutions of the 1960s and 1970s were also influenced by the constitutional experiences of Asia and Africa and, of course, the provisions of the Universal Declaration of Human Rights and other international covenants.

Whether constitutional rule has successfully taken root throughout the Pacific probably cannot be assessed this early because one measure of such success is the longevity of the founding constitutions. Only a few of the Pacific island countries have made significant changes to their constitutions since independence. Fiji adopted a new constitution in 1990. Tuvalu has adopted a revised constitution, and the Cook Islands has made substantial changes. The Federated States of Micronesia (FSM) has made minor revisions, as the result of a constitutionally mandated ten-year review.

A better measure of the success of a constitutional system is the willingness of government to stay within the limits on governmental power set by the constitution, and the ability of courts and the people to keep government within these limits. The constitutions of a number of the independent Pacific states give the judiciary power to review acts of the legislature and the executive and to declare void any law or governmental action inconsistent with the constitution. In some states, such as the FSM, the Marshalls, and Vanuatu, the constitution itself contains guidelines about the way judicial review is to be conducted. The Constitution of the Marshalls, for example, instructs the judiciary to consider, in interpreting the constitution, decisions of courts in countries with similar constitutions and to adapt these decisions to the needs and circumstances of the Marshalls. In other states, such as Papua New Guinea, the courts have inferred the power of judicial review from the constitutions' supremacy clauses.

In some states, courts have declared statutes invalid, and other branches of government have complied with these decisions. But, so far, most courts have used their powers of judicial review sparingly. The extent to which courts will be willing to overturn major legislative or executive actions and the extent to which the other branches of government will comply with these decisions, even though the courts theoretically have the authority to require them to do so, remains to be tested.

THE JUDICIARY

The constitutions of Pacific island states generally establish a hierarchical system of trial and appellate courts with final appeal to the state's highest court. In a few states, notably Kiribati, Tuvalu, the Cook Islands, Nauru, and Niue, there is also a limited right of appeal to courts outside the country. In most states, immediately below the highest appellate court is a national court with unlimited original jurisdiction over criminal and civil matters as well as appellate jurisdiction over cases from the lower courts. Because of the relatively few experienced lawyers in the South Pacific, many countries have made their highest appellate court a division of the national trial court so that the same judges can serve on both. Most countries have had to call upon lawyers and judges from abroad to staff these courts. In 1980, with the appointment of Sir Buri Kidu as Chief Justice of the Supreme Court, Papua New Guinea became the first South Pacific island nation to appoint a citizen as Chief Justice of its highest court. In Fiji, as well, Chief Justice Sir Timoci Tuivaga is a citizen, and in 1992 the FSM named its first citizen Chief Justice. As the number of island lawyers increases, judiciaries will become increasingly homegrown.

Below the national trial courts in most Pacific jurisdictions are local courts with limited jurisdiction. In most countries, magistrates or judges of the lower courts need not be degree-qualified lawyers. A limited number of people have law degrees in these countries. But another reason for not requiring law degrees is that lay magistrates at the local or municipal level may better understand the customs and circumstances of their locality than would lawyers whose approaches are often influenced by imported legal concepts.

In a number of Pacific countries and territories, some lower courts have been designated as courts in which customary law rather than statute or common law is to be applied; in some cases these courts are also mandated to use customary dispute settlement processes, such as mediation and negotiation, in preference to adjudication. Vanuatu, the Solomons, and Papua New Guinea have established such courts. Customary courts in these countries have jurisdiction over minor civil and criminal matters. In Western Samoa, as in a few other jurisdictions, a special court has exclusive jurisdiction over all matters involving customary land and succession to chiefly titles. In Western Samoa, the Chief Justice or a judge of the Supreme Court is president of this court, but the other judges, including the deputy president, who presides at trials, are Samoan chiefs. Kiribati, Papua New Guinea, Tonga, and Tuvalu are also among the countries that have established courts with exclusive jurisdiction over customary land matters. In the case of the Land and Titles Court of Western Samoa and the Land Courts of Papua New Guinea, appeals to the common law courts are not allowed.

SOURCES OF LAW

The existence of special customary law courts points up the pluralistic nature of law in the Pacific. Many Pacific constitutions recognize both the imported law (in most such cases, the English common law) and customary law as sources for the development by the courts of an indigenous common law. The problem for the higher courts is threefold. They must decide what it means to receive English common law, what it means to recognize customary law, and how to balance the two.

Reception of Common Law

Although the Pacific states (with the exception of the French territories) have adopted English common law and equity, the wording of the relevant constitutional provisions (and, thus, the substance of the law that will, in fact, be applied by the courts) varies. At one extreme, the Papua New Guinea Constitution is very specific as to the source of law. It adopts the common law of England as at the date of independence, to the extent that such law does not conflict with the Constitution, statutes, or custom. In choosing the rules that will govern particular situations, Papua New Guinea courts feel themselves bound to apply the pre-independence decisions of English courts.

At the other extreme, the constitutions of Kiribati, Tuvalu, the FSM, and the Marshalls are silent as to the sources of the common law. In some countries, the legislature has filled the constitutional gap. In Tuvalu and Kiribati, for example, courts follow statutory rules for the reception of the common law. Courts of the FSM and the Marshalls have adopted the view that the absence of constitutional or statutory rules leaves them free to fashion a common law appropriate to the circumstances of the country, irrespective of the source of the rule, although they will refer to court decisions from countries with similar constitutions or common law systems. The FSM's national court, especially, tends to look first to decisions of courts in the United States.

The constitutions and courts of other Pacific states fall somewhere between these extremes. Many constitutions provide only that the courts should apply English common law and equity, a general prescription that the courts can interpret variously. Some courts still look first to England or the United States (or to the courts of the country that was the colonial power) for common law rules and principles; others are beginning to broaden the scope of their inquiry to include decisions of courts in other Commonwealth countries. The Supreme Court of Western Samoa, for example, has decided to treat the requirement that it should apply "English" law as though the word referred to a type of law rather than to the law's country of origin. The Western Samoa courts refer to court decisions from New Zealand and other Pacific countries as well as those from England. In the Solomons, on the other hand, the Constitution refers in general terms to "the principles and rules of common law and equity," but the courts seem to be narrowing this to mean the law and equity of England.

Because Pacific states and societies have considerably more in common with one another than with England, the United States, or other former colonial powers, the courts are likely over time to outgrow their reliance on cases decided elsewhere and to turn more frequently to their own customs and circumstances, and to one another, for appropriate rules and principles.

Recognition of Customary Law

In a number of the new Pacific nations, constitutions recognize that the development of a common law suited to the conditions of the country requires that the courts take into account not only the English common law, but also custom. Most constitutions provide that custom is to be a source of law, but some (such as those of the FSM, Fiji, Papua New Guinea, and the

Solomon Islands) give it a status superior to that of the imported common law. Others (for instance, Vanuatu's and Palau's) are ambiguous. The relationship between custom and statutes varies as well, with most constitutions providing that custom fails when it conflicts with statutory law and a few that custom overrides statutes in some circumstances. In Vanuatu, custom is made superior to statutes enacted prior to independence but is subject to statutes enacted after independence.

Whatever the status theoretically given to custom by the constitution or other laws, it will be important in shaping the indigenous common law of the country only to the extent that judges of the higher courts recognize and apply it. The new nations of the South and Central Pacific vary greatly in the extent to which their judges do this. Some Pacific legislatures have enacted statutes that set out the procedures for finding custom and the matters to which it may be applied. These statutes can be either expansive or limiting, depending on the nature of the statutes and the way the courts use them. In Papua New Guinea, for example, statutory guidelines restrict the application of customary law, particularly in criminal cases, whereas in Tuvalu the statute gives a broader scope to custom. In some countries, the rules of recognition characterize custom as a fact, which must be presented by the parties and proven; in others, it is characterized as law, which the court can find on its own.

A number of the Pacific nations and territories, such as American Samoa, have provided for the use in courts of assessors, persons who are familiar with the customary law, to sit in on cases with the judges and to assist them in finding and applying customary law. The Marshalls has a Traditional Rights Court, to which questions about the nature and applicability of customary law are sent from the common law courts. Although the use of assessors or special panels has the benefit of putting the common law court in touch with people with expert knowledge about custom, it also has a drawback. Since assessors are utilized only in those cases in which either the court or a party recognizes the existence of a customary law issue, other opportunities for the application of custom may be missed.

Whatever balance the courts might strike between customary law and the imported common law, both will be considerably changed by their application to the circumstances of the new nations and newly autonomous territories of the Pacific. The rules of the common law, developed for English society and culture, have a very different meaning and impact when transported to a different society and culture. Customary law, too, is changing to meet changing circumstances (much of what is considered custom today was not part of the customary law of one hundred or even fifty years ago). Moreover, common law courts use custom only as a source of rules, thereby separating the substantive rules from the customary dispute settlement processes within which they were developed. This separation of substantive from procedural customary norms will alter the meaning and the impact of the customary law.

LAND LAW

Land tenure may be the single most important substantive legal issue in the Pacific. Colonial practices in many of the islands resulted in either the direct confiscation of considerable areas of land or the conversion of land from customary tenure to a land titles system that permitted free alienation. In New Caledonia, for example, the ongoing political struggle for independence has often centered on the retrieval of land appropriated under the French administration. During the colonial period or at independence, many jurisdictions adopted constitutional or statutory provisions prohibiting the conversion of customary land to freehold tenure or the sale of that land to anyone other than its traditional holders. Territories and states that limit or totally prohibit sales of customary land to non-indigenes include Western Samoa, American Samoa, the Cook Islands, Tokelau, Fiji, Kiribati, Niue, Palau, Papua New Guinea, and Tuvalu. Territories and states that limit tenure conversion include Western Samoa, Kiribati, Papua New Guinea, the Cook Islands, Fiji, the Marshall Islands, and Niue.

In addition to providing shelter and subsistence, customary land can also provide an income for its owners. A number of Pacific countries are experimenting with ways to make customary land economically productive without destroying the bases of customary land tenure or permitting it to be freely alienated. For example, statutes in Fiji, American Samoa, Kiribati, Tuvalu, the Northern Marianas, Western Samoa, and the Cook Islands permit customary land to be leased for commercial purposes. In Tonga, all land is deemed to vest in the Crown; while land may not be sold, it may be leased or made subject to life mortgages. In Papua New Guinea, the development bank leases customary land and then sells the lease back to the traditional owners, an artificial legal device that allows the owners to use their leases as security for development loans.

Some countries have attempted not only to limit further conversions and sales of customary land but also to restore to citizen ownership freehold land that had been alienated to foreigners during the colonial period and to prevent additional sales of land to noncitizens. The Constitution of the Marshall Islands provides that land may be owned only by citizens or by corporations wholly owned by citizens, but the Constitution does not state what should be done about land that was sold to noncitizens before independence. The Solomon Islands Constitution goes further than that of the Marshalls. It not only provides that freehold titles may be held only by Solomon Islanders, but also contains a provision automatically converting all freeholds held by persons who are not Solomon Islanders into seventy-five-year leases. Other states and territories that prohibit the sale of fee simple interests to foreigners, or that require that all land be owned by indigenes, include Tonga, the Northern Marianas, and the FSM. Kiribati chose a slightly different route to reabsorb land that had been alienated; by statute, freehold lands can be sold only if the government is given the first option to purchase them. Western Samoa prohibits, without the prior consent of the government, the sale or lease for more than twenty years of freehold land to persons who are not resident citizens. Although statutes in Papua New Guinea prevent the alienation of customary land to anyone other than the government, Papua New Guinea is one of the few South Pacific countries whose constitution and statutes contain no significant limits on the alienation of freehold land to foreigners.

Conclusion

Whether in the process of decolonization or of nation building, the Pacific states and territories share the many common challenges of constructing governmental institutions and legal systems, developing economic resources, and providing for the people. There are many solutions to each of these challenges, and this volume demonstrates the diversity of approaches and range of options that are possible.

Michael A. Ntumy
Jean G. Zorn
C. Guy Powles

PART ONE

The Parliamentary Model

1. The Cook Islands

**ISAACUS ADZOXORNU
and the EDITORIAL COMMITTEE**

I. Dateline

600 A.D.	First evidence of Polynesian settlement, probably from the Marquesas via Tahiti.
1595	European contact begins.
1880s	A British protectorate declared on Rarotonga in October 1888.
1890	Establishment of the General Council.
1891	Elected federal Parliament and Supreme Court established.
1900	The Rarotongan Ariki petition New Zealand to annex the Cook Islands, and on June 11, 1901, the Cook Islands formally become part of New Zealand.
1946	The Cook Islands Amendment Act establishes a Legislative Council.
1957	Replacement of the Legislative Council with the Legislative Assembly.
1964	Resident Commissioner and all official members withdraw from Legislative Assembly. New Zealand Parliament grants a new Constitution to the Cook Islands.
1965	In the first general election for the Legislative Assembly, the Cook Islands party wins a substantial majority under the leadership of Albert Henry. The Constitution is amended to provide for the establishment of a House of Arikis.
1981	In the Constitution Amendment Act (No. 9) 1980–1981, the Legislative Assembly is renamed the Parliament and the number of parliamentary seats increased to twenty-four, with one member for each constituency throughout the Cook Islands. The amendment also provides for a bill of rights and a Court of Appeal.

II. Historical, Cultural, and Economic Survey

Prior to European contact, most of the islands now included within the boundaries of the Cook Islands were separate sociopolitical entities. The indigenous political systems were variations of a generally eastern Polynesian regime. Their characteristic feature was a system of hereditary chieftainship loosely based on the principle of primogeniture. Chieftainship was most highly developed on Rarotonga, although similar forms prevailed on the other Southern Islands. In the Northern Islands, chieftainship was less highly developed than in the south, chiefly power being largely constrained by other social groupings, such as councils of elders.

The arrival of English missionaries between 1821 and 1860 brought most of the islands under the sociospiritual control of the London Missionary Society. The gradual advance of Christianization in the Cook Islands profoundly altered the indigenous sociopolitical system. With the persuasion and encouragement of the missionaries, the chiefs of each island established legal codes covering most aspects of public and private law. These were administered by Ariki-appointed judges and police.

Largely as a result of the desire of European traders and planters to free themselves from the authority of the Ariki, and because of increasing concern about a possible French intrusion into the area, a British protectorate was declared on Rarotonga in October 1888. The protectorate, which became known as the Federation of the Cook Islands, included all the islands in the southern group. The protectorate oversaw the establishment of an elected federal Parliament, a Supreme Court, and a General Council made up of the Ariki, district judges, representatives of the lesser chiefs, and one representative of the European residents.

New Zealand annexed the Cook Islands in 1901, extending the boundaries to include the Northern Islands. In 1915, the New Zealand Parliament enacted the Cook Islands Act. While the act consolidated the laws of the Cook Islands, it made no mention of federal government. The period from 1915 to 1946 saw a concentration of power in the office of the Resident Commissioner and the New Zealand Minister of Island Territories. Self-government in the Cook Islands was largely restricted to Island Councils, which were relegated to an essentially advisory function.

The passage of the Cook Islands Amendment Act in 1946, which created the Cook Islands Legislative Council, was the first major step since New Zealand's annexation toward representative government in the Cooks. In 1958, the council was renamed the Legislative Assembly. It consisted of fourteen members elected by universal suffrage, seven members elected by Island Councils, one member elected by the European community, and five ex officio members, including the Resident Commissioner.

At the impetus of a 1960 United Nations resolution concerning non-self-governing territories, the New Zealand Parliament passed legislation in November 1964 granting a Constitution to the Cook Islands that took effect in 1965. The Cook Islands became a self-governing territory in "free association" with New Zealand. The Constitution called for twenty-two members of the Legislative Assembly to be elected by universal suffrage and a Cabinet of eight to be elected from the Assembly. Cook Islanders retained their New Zealand citizenship, which gave them the free right of entry into New Zealand. A High Commissioner appointed by New Zealand would represent the Queen, who remained Head of State. New Zealand assumed responsibility for external affairs and defense.

In 1965, the Constitution was amended to provide for the establishment of a House of Arikis (prominent chiefs). The House of Arikis is a consultative body, advising Parliament on matters relating to the people's welfare, customs, tradition, and land tenure.

On March 30, 1978, the Cook Islands party won its fifth successive election. However, this term in office was not long-lived. Three months later, party officeholders were impeached by the Chief Justice for electoral corruption. The Democratic party members who had been elected in March became the government. Thomas Davis became Premier, while Sir Albert Henry (leader of the Cook Islands party) and seven of his party colleagues were arraigned on corruption charges.

In 1981, the Legislative Assembly made substantial changes to the Constitution. Under the Constitution Amendment Act (No. 9) of 1980–1981, the Legislative Assembly was renamed the Parliament, and the Premier became the Prime Minister. The membership of Parliament was increased from twenty-two to twenty-four (later changed to twenty-five). The electoral boundaries were also revised to provide for constituencies with one seat each. A bill of rights was added to the Constitution, and a Court of Appeal was established.

None of the amendments was as politically sensitive as the extension of the parliamentary term from four to five years. This change alone sparked heated debate among the people of the Cook Islands. According to the Democratic party government, the primary reason for extending the term was to allow the government more time to consider pressing economic concerns without the distractions of campaigning and electioneering, but opponents of the amendment accused the government of wishing to extend its term because an extra year in office would qualify many members of Parliament for generous retirement payouts.

III. Sources of Law

The sources of Cook Islands law are its Constitution, statutes, the common law, and custom.

A. Constitution

The Constitution of the Cook Islands is the supreme law, and all acts of Parliament must conform to it (Constitution, Article 39). The Constitution grants to the High Court and Court of Appeals the power to interpret the Constitution and to determine the application and effect of its provisions (Article 60). By implication, therefore, the courts also have the power to strike down legislation that fails to comply with the Constitution.

Most articles of the Constitution may be amended by Parliament. To be effective, an amendment must be voted upon twice, with an interval of at least ninety days between the two votes, and must receive the votes of not less than two-thirds of the total membership of Parliament at each vote. The provisions of the Cook Islands Constitution Act 1964, establishing the Cook Islands' relationship of free association with New Zealand, and Article 2 of the Constitution, which declares the Queen of England to be the Cook Islands Head of State, may be amended only if, in addition to receiving the two-thirds assent of Parliament in two separate votes, it also receives the assent of two-thirds of the Cook Islands electorate (Constitution, Article 41). The Constitution has been amended a number of times **(see II Historical, Cultural, and Economic Survey)**.

B. Statutes

Acts passed by the Parliament of the Cook Islands constitute the major source of statutory law (Constitution, Article 39). Parliament may also declare acts of the Parliament of New Zealand applicable in the Cook Islands under Article 46 of the Constitution and the New Zealand Laws Act 1979. Also applicable to the Cook Islands are statutes of the United Kingdom defining the privileges, immunities, or powers of members of the House of Commons. Such statutes define the privileges, immunities, or powers of Cook Islands parliamentarians (Legislative Assembly Powers and Privileges Amendment Act 1979).

C. Custom

Although custom is recognized as a source of law, its legal significance is limited to certain matters. Section 422 of the Cook Islands Act 1915 provides that interests in customary land are to be determined by custom. While chiefly titles can be conferred on a person only in accordance with custom, custom is not expressly mentioned in statutes regulating marriage and divorce. Moreover, custom is defined very narrowly. The Cook Islands Act defines custom as "the ancient custom and usages of the Natives of the Cook Islands," thus precluding the courts from recognizing new or changed custom.

D. Common Law and Other Sources

Section 616 of the Cook Islands Act 1915 requires the courts to apply the rules of common law and equity, but does not stipulate that the decisions of English courts be followed exclusively. Thus, the Court of Appeal of the Cook Islands has found it appropriate to rely on Australian,

New Zealand, and English authorities.[1] In cases where there is a conflict between equity and the common law, the Judicature Act 1980–1981 provides that equity prevails.

IV. Constitutional System

A. Territory

The Cook Islands formally became part of New Zealand on June 11, 1901. In 1965 the Cook Islands became self-governing in free association with New Zealand, as provided in the Cook Islands Constitutional Acts (NZ) 1964 and 1965. New Zealand's responsibilities are limited to foreign affairs and defense (**see VI International Obligations**).

B. Nationality

Dual citizenship is a central feature of the relationship of New Zealand and the Cook Islands. Under the Cook Islands Constitution the people of the Cook Islands retain their New Zealand citizenship as previously provided by the New Zealand Citizenship Act 1948.

The Constitution does not contain provisions relating to Cook Islands citizenship. Instead, it provides at Article 76A for the status of permanent resident of the Cooks. Permanent residents include all persons who were born in the Cook Islands and who (1) have a parent who was a permanent resident at the date of the person's birth, (2) have a father who was a permanent resident at the date of the father's death, or (3) were adopted by a person who was a permanent resident at the date of the adoption. Persons may apply for permanent resident status, and Article 76A of the Constitution permits Parliament to prescribe the qualifications for applicants. The permanent resident status of anyone who obtained it by application may be revoked if that person is absent from the Cooks for longer than three years in circumstances indicating that the person has ceased to make his or her home in the Cooks.

C. Executive Government

Under Article 2 of the Constitution, the monarch of Great Britain is the Head of State of the Cook Islands. Article 12 vests the Queen of England with the "executive authority of the Cook Islands," which is exercised by a Queen's Representative. The Queen's Representative is appointed by the Queen for a three-year term (Article 3) and acts subject to the Constitution and on the advice of the Prime Minister and the Cabinet (Articles 4, 5, and 12). If the Queen's Representative is absent from the Cook Islands or unable to perform his or her duties, the Chief Justice acts as deputy Queen's Representative (Article 7).

Executive government lies with a Cabinet of ministers, comprising the Prime Minister and three to six other ministers, all of whom are elected members of Parliament. The Prime Minister, appointed by the Queen's Representative, is the member of Parliament commanding the confidence of the majority of the members. The other ministers are appointed on the advice of the Prime Minister (Constitution, Article 13).

All Cabinet decisions must be reported to the Queen's Representative and take effect only upon the approval of the Queen's Representative or, if the Queen's Representative does not act on the decision, then within four days from the date of the decision. If in the opinion of Cabinet the decision involves a matter of urgency, the Queen's Representative has only two days to give or withhold approval (Articles 18 and 19).

Article 22 of the Constitution establishes an Executive Council of the Cook Islands, consisting of the Cabinet and the Queen's Representative. Meetings of the Executive Council may be called by the Queen's Representative or the Prime Minister. The attendance of the Queen's Representative and at least three ministers is required for business to be transacted at a meeting. Although the Constitution does not explicitly say so, the major purpose of the Executive Council seems to be to enable Cabinet and the Queen's Representative to work out differences over Cabinet decisions. Under Article 25 of the Constitution, meetings of the Executive Council may be called to consider decisions of Cabinet that have been reported to the Queen's Representative. If, at the meeting, the Queen's Representative concurs in the decision, it takes effect. If the Queen's Representative does not concur, Cabinet may reconsider the decision and either reaffirm it or accept any amendments to it proposed by the Queen's Representative. In either case, it then takes effect. In its reconsideration, Cabinet may also decide to change the original decision in ways not suggested by the Queen's Representative. In that case, the new decision must be reported to the Queen's Representative for approval as if it were an original decision of Cabinet.

D. House of Arikis

Article 8 of the Constitution establishes a House of Arikis. The constitutional provisions are supplemented by the House of Arikis Act 1966 and its amendments. The House comprises up to fifteen ariki, one from each of the smaller islands and six from the more populous islands of Rarotonga and Palmerston. They are appointed by the Queen's Representative on nomination by the island they will represent. To be appointed, an ariki must be eighteen or older, usually domiciled in the Cooks, and, if the ariki has lived outside the Cooks at any time for three years or more, must have been resident in the Cooks for the three months preceding appointment. Each ariki serves a one-year term, which will be terminated earlier if the ariki fails to take the oath of allegiance to the Constitution or takes an oath of allegiance to a foreign state, does any act by which citizenship in another state becomes possible, resigns from the House, dies, ceases to be an ariki, ceases to be domiciled in the Cooks, fails to attend meetings of the House, becomes bankrupt, is convicted of an offense punishable by death or imprisonment for a year or more, is of unsound mind, or becomes a candidate for election to the Cook Islands Parliament.

The House of Arikis is ordinarily required to meet at least once every twelve months. The House has no legislating power. Its role is purely advisory. It is authorized to consider only such matters relating to the welfare of the people of the Cook Islands as may be submitted to it by Parliament and to express its opinion and make recommendations thereon. The House may also, on its own motion, make recommendations to Parliament on questions affecting the customs or traditions of the Cook Islands. The House lacks the power to advise on any bill concerning the imposition of taxes or the appropriation or expenditure of government funds unless Parliament requests that it do so.

E. Legislature

The Parliament of the Cook Islands is based on the Westminster model, although elements of the traditional Cook Islands political system are retained in the House of Arikis. Parliament consists of twenty-five members. Article 27 of the Constitution allows for both population and geographical factors by providing for representation of nearly all the islands in the Parliament, as well as a representative of Cook Islanders living overseas.

General elections to select the members of Parliament are held every five years, unless Parliament has been earlier dissolved by the Queen's Representative, in which case a general election must be held within three months after dissolution (Constitution, Article 37). Anyone who is a Commonwealth citizen or a permanent resident of the Cook Islands, has resided in the Cooks for the three months immediately preceding the election, and at some time has resided in the Cooks for a continuous period of at least twelve months is qualified to vote for a member of Parliament from his or her constituency. In addition, any Commonwealth citizen or permanent resident of the Cooks may qualify to vote for the member of Parliament representing the Overseas Constituency if the elector has been resident outside the Cooks for the three months preceding the election, has been absent from the Cooks for not more than three years, has an intention to return to the Cooks, and at some time has actually resided in the Cooks for not less than twelve months (Constitution, Article 28). Anyone qualified to elect members of Parliament may be a candidate for Parliament, unless he or she is bankrupt or has been convicted of a major offense (Constitution, Article 28B).

The power to make laws is conferred on the Parliament (Constitution, Article 39). Notwithstanding this, the government of the Cook Islands may request the Parliament of New Zealand to legislate for the Cook Islands (Constitution, Article 46). The Parliament of the Cook Islands may also declare acts of the Parliament of New Zealand applicable in the Cook Islands (New Zealand Laws Act 1979). Parliament may also delegate its law-making powers to any authorized person or body as it thinks fit. A product of such delegated power will not, however, qualify as an act of Parliament, but as a "regulation," "rule," or "bylaw."

Under Article 42 of the Constitution, any member of the Parliament may introduce any bill. A bill introduced into Parliament and every act passed must be in the Maori language as spoken in Rarotonga and also in the English language. However, Parliament may by resolution determine that only the English language be used, and, where there is conflict between the Maori version and the English version, the English version prevails. To be effective, bills must be assented to by the Queen's Representative, although either the Executive Council or Parliament can override a veto (Article 44).

F. Judiciary

The judicial system of the Cook Islands consists of a Court of Appeal, the High Court, and lesser courts established by acts of Parliament (Constitution, Part IV).

The High Court has original jurisdiction over all civil, criminal, and land matters, as well as appellate jurisdiction over lesser courts. It has three divisions: civil, criminal, and land (Constitution, Article 47). The judges of the High Court may serve in any of the divisions. The judges include the Chief Justice, who is appointed by the Queen's Representative on the advice of the Executive Council and Prime Minister, and as many other judges as the government may wish to appoint. Other judges are appointed by the Queen's Representative, acting on the advice of the Executive Council, Minister for Justice, and Chief Justice. A judge of the High Court must either have been a judge in New Zealand or elsewhere in the Commonwealth or have practiced as a barrister in New Zealand or elsewhere in the Commonwealth for at least seven years. Nonresident judges serve three-year terms; resident judges may serve until the age of seventy. The Queen's Representative may remove a judge from office due to inability to discharge the office or to misbehavior. In removing a judge, the Queen's Representative acts upon the recommendation of an investigatory tribunal appointed by the Queen's Representative. The current Chief Justice is also a judge of the New Zealand High Court.

A Court of Appeal of the Cook Islands was created in 1981 by the new Article 56 of the Constitution. Appeals from all divisions of the High Court are now heard by the Court of

Appeal. In the past, appeals were directed to the courts of New Zealand. Decisions of the Court of Appeal are final, except that certain matters may be appealed to the Queen in Council, with leave of the Court of Appeal or the Queen (Article 59). Cases that may be appealed as of right from the High Court to the Court of Appeal include cases that involve substantial questions about the interpretation, application, or effect of the Constitution; criminal cases in which the defendant has been sentenced to death or for a term in excess of six months or a fine of $200 or more; and civil cases in which the matter in dispute amounts to $400 or more. Other matters may be appealed with leave of the High Court or the Court of Appeal (Constitution, Article 60).

The judges of the Court of Appeal must include at least one person who has been a judge of a New Zealand court (and who acts as Chief Justice of the Cook Islands Court of Appeal) and the judges of the High Court. Additional judges may be appointed to the Court of Appeal by the Queen's Representative, so long as they fulfill the qualifications for being a High Court judge (Constitution, Article 56). The judges sit in panels of three to hear appeals. Appeals are decided by a majority vote of the panel. The panel that hears the appeal of a case may not include the judge who originally decided the case in the High Court (Constitution, Articles 57 and 58). The current Court of Appeal consists of the Chief Justice of the High Court and a number of other New Zealand judges. Most of the sittings of the court are in New Zealand.

The Constitution also provides, at Article 62, for lesser courts staffed by Justices of the Peace. These courts have jurisdiction over minor matters. Justices of the Peace are appointed by the Queen's Representative on the advice of the Executive Council. They are not required to have legal training. Appeals from decisions of a Justice of the Peace are to the High Court, which conducts a trial de novo.

G. Local Government

The Outer Islands Local Government Act 1988 applies to all islands of the Cook Islands except Rarotonga, Pukapuka, and Nassau. Where the act applies, local government is in the main vested in an Island Council. Membership of an Island Council consists of the following:

1. the Ariki of the island (if any);
2. a representative of the Aronga Mana (the council of chiefs) of the island, elected at a meeting chaired by the Chief Administrative Officer of the island;
3. the members of Parliament from the island; and
4. the elected members of the Island Council constituencies for each island.

Only elected members are entitled to vote at any meeting of an Island Council, although members belonging to the other categories have the right to speak and be heard at such a meeting. Each Island Council elects a Mayor and deputy mayor from its elected members. The Mayor (and in his or her absence, the deputy mayor) acts as the chairperson of the council and presides at its meetings. The Mayor is entitled to a deliberative vote, and in the event of a tie vote, is entitled to cast a tie-breaking vote.

The functions of an Island Council are the following:

1. to carry into effect and administer ordinances and bylaws applicable to the island;
2. to assist in the coordination of activities relevant to the economic and social development of the island;
3. to assist the government of the Cook Islands in the good rule and government of the island; and

4. to advise on or determine any matter, question, or dispute referred to it by any person or organization.

Island Councils have the power to make, alter, or revoke bylaws. Council bylaws reflect the customary law of the island. To be effective, a bylaw must be approved by Cabinet. Offenses against bylaws are punishable in the High Court or by a Justice of the Peace.

The Rarotonga Local Government Act 1988 regulates local government on the Island of Rarotonga. The act provides for the establishment of a Rarotonga Island Council, roughly similar in membership and powers to other Island Councils, and nine District Councils on the island. Each District Council consists of three elected members, one member of the Aronga Mana, and the member of Parliament for the district. A chairperson and a deputy chairperson are appointed from among the membership. The Rarotonga District Councils make recommendations on any matter to the Rarotonga Island Council, provide advice to the Island Council on matters affecting their districts, and perform such other functions as may be conferred upon them by enactment.

The revenue of Island Councils and District Councils come from monies appropriated by Parliament and from fees, services, charges, fines, contributions, subscriptions, rents, and other moneys paid pursuant to bylaws.

H. Human Rights

Section 8 of the Constitution Amendment Act 1980–1981 added human rights provisions to the Cook Islands Constitution. The following rights and freedoms are recognized and protected by Article 64:

1. the right to life, liberty, and security of person;
2. the right to equality before the law and the protection of the law;
3. the right of the individual to own property and the right not to be deprived of it;
4. freedom of thought, conscience, and religion;
5. freedom of speech and expression; and
6. freedom of peaceful assembly and association.

Article 64 imposes a duty on every citizen to ensure the enjoyment of these rights and freedoms by any other person. Every enactment or law is to be construed and applied in a manner that will not abrogate or infringe any other right or freedom. Particularly, no enactment or law should be construed or applied so as to, among other things, authorize or effect the arbitrary detention, imprisonment, or exile of any person; impose or authorize the imposition on any person of cruel and unusual treatment or punishment; deprive any person of the right to a fair hearing; deprive any person charged with an offense of the right to be presumed innocent; or deprive any person charged with an offense of the right to reasonable bail (Constitution, Article 65).

V. Administrative Organization and Law

A. Organization

Government administration in the Cook Islands is based on the New Zealand model. Although the number of public servants is smaller, the Cook Islands has approximately the same number of government departments as does New Zealand. While the government of the Cook Islands is endeavoring to place suitably qualified Cook Islanders in higher echelon positions, a considerable number of senior government officials are expatriates, mainly New Zealanders.

Statutory bodies include the Land Use Board, the Monetary Board, the Public Service Commission, and the Price Tribunal. There are also a number of state corporations, including the Cook Islands Development Bank, Cook Islands Tourist Authority, Cook Islands Broadcasting Corporation, and Waterfront Commission.

B. Public Service

The Cook Islands public service is regulated by Part VI of the Constitution and the Public Service Act 1975. Administration of the act is the responsibility of the Public Service Commissioner, subject to the control of the minister responsible for the public service. The Act sets out standards and procedures for the appointment, promotion, discipline, and dismissal of public servants.

The Public Service Commissioner is charged with the administration of the act and therefore is ultimately responsible for all appointments, promotions, transfers, terminations, and discipline of public servants (Constitution, Article 74B). The commissioner is appointed by the Queen's Representative acting on the advice of the Prime Minister. The commissioner must be a Commonwealth citizen or a permanent resident of the Cook Islands and may not be a member of Parliament or the holder of any other office in the public service. Commissioners serve four-year terms, which may be renewed. The Queen's Representative may suspend a commissioner from office for misbehavior or incompetence but must within seven days report the grounds of the suspension to Parliament. Parliament must then, within twenty-one days, either resolve to remove the commissioner from office or revoke the suspension (Constitution, Articles 73, 74, and 74A).

C. Public Finance and Audit

Article 67 of the Constitution establishes a government account that is free from taxation. The account is funded by taxes and other revenues raised or received by the government. Under Section 12 of the Public Moneys Act 1969, the account is to be kept at the National Bank of New Zealand at Rarotonga and at other banks as directed by the financial secretary. The account is administered by the Department of Treasury, which is under the control of the Minister of Finance. All expenditures in any financial year from the account or from any other public fund must have been authorized by an appropriation act and must be made in accordance with the statement of proposed expenditure for that financial year as approved by Parliament (Constitution, Article 70 and Public Moneys Act, Sections 22–25). The Audit Office of New Zealand is designated the auditor of the account and all other public funds or accounts, including accounts of all government departments and offices.

D. Review of Administrative Action

Review of administrative action may occur under the Commissions of Inquiry Act 1966, the Judicature Act 1980–1981 or the Ombudsman Act 1987.

Under Section 3 of the Commissions of Inquiry Act 1966, the Queen's Representative may, acting on the advice of the Executive Council, appoint people to a commission to inquire into and report on the administration of the government, the working of any existing law, or the conduct of officers in the service of the Crown. A commission so appointed has the power and status of the High Court. The commission may refer any disputed point of law arising in the course of an inquiry to the High Court.

Under Section 1 of the Judicature Act 1980–1981, jurisdiction is conferred upon the High Court to issue injunctions and writs of certiorari, mandamus, and prohibition. The court may award damages in lieu of injunction. This jurisdiction can be exercised to review administrative action.

Under the Ombudsman Act 1984, the Queen's Representative may appoint an ombudsman on the advice of the Prime Minister. The function of the Ombudsman is to investigate the actions of government departments or organizations and their officers, employees, or members.

The ombudsman may conduct investigations either on complaints made to him or her, or of his or her own motion. Also, parliamentary committees may refer matters to the ombudsman. However, the ombudsman cannot investigate decisions or recommendations:

1. if the Constitution or another act or regulation gives a right of appeal or review of that decision or recommendation;
2. of anyone acting as a trustee under the Trustee Act 1956;
3. of anyone acting as legal adviser to the Crown in relation to any proceedings; and
4. about members of the police who are the subjects of inquiries under the Police Act 1981, unless a complaint about them has been made to a superior officer and either the complaint has not been investigated or the complainant is dissatisfied with the result of the investigation.

VI. International Obligations

The status of the Cook Islands as an independent state capable of entering into international relations is controversial. When the Cook Islands became internally self-governing in free association with New Zealand in 1965, responsibility for external affairs and defense was vested in New Zealand. Section 5 of the Cook Islands Constitution Act 1964 provided that

> Nothing in this Act or in the constitution shall affect the responsibilities of Her Majesty the Queen in Right of New Zealand for the external affairs and defence of the Cook Islands, those responsibilities to be discharged after consultation by the Prime Minister of New Zealand with the Prime Minister of the Cook Islands.

This statement is considered to reserve legislative power to the New Zealand Parliament in matters of external affairs and defense of the Cook Islands.

However, in 1976, when the United States government sought the advice of the New Zealand government on the capacity and competence of the Cook Islands government to sign an agreement relating to the Peace Corps, the New Zealand response was

> In accordance with its constitutional status the Government of the Cook Islands has exercised and continues to exercise in the field of foreign relations attributes recognised in international law as attributes of a sovereign state. The Cook Islands Government is not restrained from initiating international reformations or countering agreements and there is no constitutional requirement for prior authority or approval from the Government of New Zealand.

In practice, the Cook Islands has entered into international arrangements. For example, the Cook Islands is a member of South Pacific Forum and the South Pacific Commission. Several countries—including Australia, Canada, France, Fiji, Germany, Republic of China, Norway, and South Korea—have their New Zealand representative accredited to the Cook Islands. A number of multilateral assistance agencies and bilateral donors deal directly with the Cook Islands. As further evidence of the Cook Islands' ability to conduct external relations, the government has commenced the licensing of fishing in its 200-mile exclusive economic zone. Fishing agreements have been concluded with Taiwan, Korea, and several Norwegian interests.

While the Cook Islands is dealt with as an independent legal personality by many members of the international community, some countries such as Japan do not recognize the Cook Islands as a sovereign state. They consider that the right to New Zealand citizenship particularly is inconsistent with the principle of independence. The free association status of the Cook Islands makes most countries, including Australia, reluctant to implement any sort of direct aid policy for the Cook Islands. The United States regards the Cook Islands as being constitutionally tied to New Zealand, due to the Cooks' free association status. The position of the United States may change now that it has asserted that the Federated States of Micronesia and the Marshall Islands, both of which are in free association with it, are sovereign and independent.

VII. Revenue Law

In an attempt to foster increased local investment, local company tax was reduced in 1980 from 35 to 20 percent. Special provision also exists for lower tax rates for companies involved in import substitution or which are export oriented. Under the Development Incentives Act 1977 approved companies pay tax at a levy of 5 percent with no distinction made between those with local and those with foreign ownership.

For natural persons, income tax is assessed on a sliding scale with rebates for a dependent wife and for children. Retirement contributions are not taxed. While no formalized double taxation agreement exists between the Cook Islands and any other country, an unofficial understanding does exist with New Zealand. Cook Islanders resident in New Zealand are given credit for tax paid in New Zealand, provided that it is not less than the amount that would be payable in the Cook Islands. However, New Zealand residents living in the Cook Islands for more than one month and less than fifteen months are liable for double taxation, pursuant to the Income Tax Act, whether the income is derived in the Cook Islands or overseas. The rationale is to prevent travel to and from the Cook Islands in order to retain a refund in both countries.

The Turnover Tax Act 1980 imposes a tax of 4 percent of gross revenue on retail sales and services and 1 percent of gross revenue on wholesale sales and services. Manufacturing and agricultural exports may be exempted.

To attract overseas companies, the Cook Islands enacted the Offshore Banking Act 1981 and the International Companies Act 1982. The Offshore Banking Act, administered by the Cook Islands Monetary Board, provides for the establishment and regulation of offshore banking facilities in the Cook Islands. Foreign banks established under the act do not pay income or other taxes earned on their international transactions, including their fees for managing trusts and holding companies or for acting as intermediaries for loans made between countries.

The International Companies Act 1982 established tax haven facilities in the Cook Islands. Offshore international companies registered under the act do not pay taxes. However, they are not entitled to establish an office or permanent presence in the country but must act through a trust company established under the Trustee Companies Act 1982. Companies whose beneficial ownership is in New Zealand or the Cook Islands are not permitted to register under the act.

The Currency Act provides for a system of currency and makes provision for coinage, legal tender, bank notes, and related matters. The unit of currency is the New Zealand dollar. The Currency Act provides in Section 5 that every transaction entered into in the Cook Islands shall be in Cook Islands currency.

VIII. Investment Law

The Cook Islands suffers from an adverse balance of trade. Imports amount to approximately four times the value of exports. The financing of imports is made possible primarily by aid from the New Zealand government and funds remitted by Cook Islands workers in New Zealand. The Cook Islands is still very much under the economic wing of New Zealand, and the close economic ties with New Zealand have, of course, been vital to the economic stability of the Cook Islands. Budgetary aid from New Zealand constitutes some 35 to 40 percent of government revenue. The bulk of exports, imports, and tourists flows between Auckland and Rarotonga.

Since the Cook Islands gained self-governing status in 1965, locally produced goods have had duty-free access to New Zealand markets under the South Pacific Regional Trade and Economic Cooperation Agreement (SPARTECA). SPARTECA also removed Australian tariff barriers for most products the Cook Islands can supply, although some nontariff barriers exist. While the Cook Islands' trade policy seeks to maintain and expand its New Zealand market, it is also placing emphasis on other markets. For instance, the markets of French Polynesia and American Samoa are targeted for the export of Cook Islands produce.

The Customs Tariff Act 1980 substantially reduces duties on imports into the Cook Islands. The high duties previously imposed on imports from countries other than New Zealand were relaxed to encourage competition and reduce prices.

The Cook Islands government encourages joint ventures, particularly in manufacturing. Most joint venture programs have been established with the aid of the Pacific Islands Industrial Development Scheme, which is controlled by the New Zealand government. The scheme provides financial assistance and incentives for New Zealand entrepreneurs who want to develop processing operations in the Pacific islands. The incentives include contributions toward feasibility studies and staff training costs.

The Cook Islands government, with the help of the Cook Islands Development Bank, evaluates the proposed ventures submitted by the Pacific Islands Industrial Development Scheme. The Cook Islands Development Bank, established in 1978, provides financing and advisory and technical services for persons engaged in economic development in the Cook Islands. The bank's sources of funding include the Asian Development Bank and the New Zealand government.

The Development Investment Act 1977 provides incentives to assist the development of business activities and enterprises in the Cook Islands. The act establishes the Monetary Board, which considers applications for incentives, sets registration conditions, and facilitates local investment in and ownership, management, and control of foreign enterprises.

IX. Welfare Law

The main welfare legislation consists of the Aged, Destitute and Infirm Persons Act 1966 and the Child Benefit Act 1978. The former provides pensions to Cook Islands residents above the age of sixty. Any person who was born in the Cook Islands or one of whose parents was a Cook Islands Maori and who has resided, either continuously or intermittently, in the Cooks for at least ten years is eligible for a pension. In addition, anyone who has resided, whether continuously or intermittently, in the Cook Islands for a total of twenty years is also eligible. A 1986 amendment fixed the pension at $60 per month. Pension applications are made to the Minister of Social Development.

The act also established a Destitute and Infirm Persons Relief Committee, to which applications for relief may be made. A *destitute* or *infirm* person is defined as "any person unable permanently to support himself by his own means or labour and includes persons with dependants where such dependants are unable through infirmity or age to support themselves by their own means."

Under the Child Benefit Act, parents may apply to the Chief Examiner of Child Benefits for benefits to be paid for the maintenance and education of children under the age of six. A "child" under the act includes "a step-child, an adopted child and any child who, though not a member of the applicant's family, is maintained as a member of that family." To be eligible, the child must have been born in the Cook Islands or to a mother temporarily absent from the Cook Islands at the time of its birth, or the child must have resided in the Cook Islands for not less than twelve months and must satisfy the Chief Examiner that he or she is likely to remain in the Cook Islands.

X. Criminal Law

The criminal law of the Cook Islands operates on the principle that there must be no crime or punishment except in accordance with law (Constitution, Article 64(1)(a)). The Crimes Act 1969 nevertheless preserves in Part III the right of defendants to invoke common law excuses or justifications in their defense. For example, infancy, insanity, or duress may exonerate an accused from criminal liability.

Part I of the Crimes Act 1969 deals with jurisdictional matters. The act applies to all offenses for which the offender may be proceeded against and tried in the Cook Islands and to all acts done or omitted in the Cook Islands.

Part IV of the act relates to participation in criminal offenses. Every person is a party to and guilty of an offense who actually commits the offense; aids or abets the commission of the offense; incites, counsels, or procures any person to commit the offense; or attempts to commit offenses.

Part V of the act deals with crimes against public order, including treason; inciting to mutiny; communicating secrets; sabotage; sedition; unlawful assembly and riot; fighting in public; being drunk in a public place; use of profane, indecent, or obscene language in a public place; disturbing public worship; carrying an offensive weapon; piracy; and dealing in persons.

Part VI deals with crimes affecting the administration of law and justice. Bribery and corruption of judicial and other public officers are prohibited, as are perjury and the making of false oaths, statements, and declarations. Also included in these offenses under Part VI are fabrication of evidence, conspiracy to bring a false accusation, conspiracy to defeat justice, and corruption of juries.

Part VII prohibits crimes against religion, morality, and public welfare. It prohibits blasphemous libel; distribution or exhibition of indecent matter; doing an indecent act in a public place; doing an indecent act with intent to insult or offend; and selling, printing, or distributing an indecent document. Prohibited sexual acts include rape, attempt to rape, incest, sexual intercourse with a girl under care or protection, sexual intercourse with a girl under the age of twelve years, and indecency with a girl under the age of twelve years. It is no defense to charge in relation to indecency with a girl under the age of twelve years that the girl consented or that the accused believed that the girl was over the age of twelve. Sexual intercourse with an idiot or imbecile woman or girl is also prohibited. So also is intercourse between a woman and a girl, a man and a boy, and a man and a man.

Crimes against public welfare include criminal nuisance, keeping a place of resort for homosexual acts, brothel keeping, living on the earnings of a prostitute, procuring sexual intercourse, accosting any person or loitering in a public place for the purpose of prostitution, neglect of the duty to bury or cremate any human remains, and improperly or indecently interfering with any dead human body. Witchcraft, sorcery, enchantment, and fortune telling are also prohibited.

Part VIII relates to crimes against the person. The major subcategories are neglect of duty to preserve life, murder, manslaughter, abortion, assault, bigamy, abduction, and kidnapping. Crimes against reputation come under Part IX. Property crimes prohibited under Part X include theft, robbery, extortion, fraud, and forgery. Part XI deals with threatening, conspiracy, and attempt to commit offenses.

XI. Judicial Procedure

A. Civil Procedure and Appeals

Civil procedure in the Cook Islands is regulated by the Judicature Act 1980–1981. Civil procedure of the High Court is such as the Court thinks in each case to be most consistent with natural justice and convenience. Parties to civil proceedings may be represented by a barrister or solicitor, or with the leave of the Court, by an agent. Generally, the Court has discretion to admit or reject evidence (Evidence Act 1968).

There is a general right of appeal to the High Court from lower courts and a limited right of appeal to the Court of Appeal from the High Court (see IV, F Judiciary). A notice of appeal will result in a stay of execution of the judgment appealed from unless a judge makes an order to the contrary (Judicature Act 1980–1981).

Where a question of constitutional interpretation arises for determination by the High Court, the Court may state a case on that question to the Court of Appeal for the latter's determination, which will then be binding on the High Court and the parties. The High Court may also order the removal of its interlocutory orders into the Court of Appeal.

The Court of Appeal has the power to amend any notice of appeal as it thinks fit and to make any order that ought to have been given or made in the High Court that the case on appeal requires.

B. Criminal Procedure

Criminal procedure is regulated primarily by the Criminal Procedure Act 1980–1981.

1. PRETRIAL PROCEDURES

Prosecutions of an offense may begin with an arrest of a defendant, which may be effected with or without a warrant. Defendants have the right to be informed promptly of the grounds of the arrest and the charges to be brought, to consult legal practitioners of their choice without delay, to be brought before a court as soon as possible, and in any case, not later than forty-eight hours after the arrest, and to be dealt with according to law.

2. BAIL

Everyone is bailable as of right who is charged with any offense for which the maximum punishment upon conviction is less than two years' imprisonment. Any offender who is not bailable as of right is bailable at the discretion of the court. The court may impose any condition it thinks fit where it grants bail. The terms of such a condition may be varied or may be revoked by the court. A breach of any condition may attract a warrant for the arrest of the offender; thereafter the offender is bailable only at the discretion of the court.

3. SEARCH AND SEIZURE

Search warrants may be issued by a judge, a Justice of the Peace, or the registrar for the search of any building, aircraft, ship, place, or premises, if there is reasonable ground for believing that there is in any such place any evidence, fruits, or implements of the offense.

4. TRIAL PROCEEDINGS

Defendants have the right to be present in court during the whole of the trial, unless a defendant's conduct interrupts and makes the continuance of the proceedings impracticable or unless the offense charged is punishable only by a fine.

5. TRIAL BY JURY

Until recently, jury trials were an entrenched aspect of Cook Islands criminal procedure. Offenses declared by the Judicature Act to be triable by a judge and a jury of twelve included most major offenses. In trials of all other offenses punishable by a term exceeding six months, defendants had the right to elect to be tried by either a judge sitting alone or a judge sitting with a jury. Recent amendments to the act have significantly reduced defendants' rights to a jury trial, and most cases are now heard by a judge alone.

The Juries Act 1968 provided that if a jury had deliberated for at least three hours and three-fourths of the jury indicated that there was no probability of a unanimous verdict, a three-fourths majority verdict was permitted. Judges could discharge juries that had deliberated for at least four hours and failed to agree on a verdict. In such an event, the court could order a new trial before a different jury.

6. EVIDENCE

Evidence in criminal trials is regulated by the Criminal Procedure Act 1980–1981, Part VII of the Cook Islands Act 1915, and the Evidence Act 1968. Under the Evidence Act, the spouse of a person charged with an offense is neither a competent nor a compellable witness for the prosecution unless the offense charged is bigamy, cruelty to a child, or an offense against the spouse, in which case a spouse is a competent but not a compellable witness. Confessional material may not be rejected on the ground that it was procured through a promise or threat or any other kind of inducement, if the judge is satisfied that the means of obtaining it were not likely to cause an untrue admission of guilt.

In sexual offense cases, the Evidence Amendment Act 1986–1987 provides that the complainant's evidence need not be corroborated and that a judge is not required to warn the jury as to the dangers of the absence of corroboration.

7. SENTENCING

The court may order a suspended sentence or may sentence an offender to serve a shorter term or pay a smaller fine than the one prescribed by any enactment. The court may also sentence an offender to pay a fine in addition to or instead of sentencing the offender to imprisonment, unless there is a provision in an enactment to the contrary. A corporation convicted of an offense punishable by imprisonment may be sentenced to pay a fine. In fixing the amount of a fine, the court must take into consideration the means of the offender.

A sentence of death may be imposed where any enactment requires it. A sentence of death is carried out by hanging and follows the procedure detailed in the Second Schedule to the Criminal Procedure Act 1980–1981.

8. APPEALS

Defendants may appeal against conviction or sentence. The general rules of appeals apply in criminal cases (**see XI, A Civil Procedure and Appeals**).

XII. LAND AND NATURAL RESOURCES

The land law of the Cook Islands derives from statutes, the common law, and custom. Before the colonial period, custom was the sole source of land law. Statutory law has, however, encroached upon custom so that that custom has ceased to be the only regime under which titles to or interests in land may be acquired.

A. Acquisition and Disposition of Interests in Land

All land in the Cook Islands is vested in the Crown. The Crown's title to land is without prejudice to any title vested in any person for an estate in fee simple, or title lawfully held in any person by virtue of custom or usage before the commencement of the Cook Islands Act 1915. The Crown may take land for a public purpose. However, Article 40 of the Constitution stipulates that adequate compensation must be paid within a reasonable time for any land taken by the Crown by compulsory process. The Crown may grant land in fee simple or grant leases, licenses, easements, or other limited estates, rights, or interests in any Crown land.

The Cook Islands Act 1915 (NZ) regulates the alienation of customary land. *Customary land* is defined as "land which being vested in the Crown is held by Natives or the descendants of Natives under Native customs and usages of the Cook Islands." Under Section 422 of the act, every title to and interest in customary land is to be determined according to the ancient customs and usage of the indigenes of the Cook Islands. Jurisdiction is conferred on the Land Division of the High Court to investigate titles to customary land and to determine the relative interests of owners (Section 421, Cook Islands Act). The Court may make an order in favor of a person or persons that operates to vest a legal estate in fee simple in the person or persons. The land then ceases to be customary land and becomes known as "native freehold land."

However, the act contains a general prohibition against the alienation or disposition of customary land. No will made by a Cook Island Maori is capable of having any force or effect with respect to his or her interest in customary land (Section 445 and Part XVI, Cook Islands Act). Even native freehold land may be alienated only by way of a lease, license, or easement, for a maximum term of sixty years, with a right of renewal in the alienee for one or more terms, and all such leases, licenses, or easements are subject to confirmation by the Land Division of the High Court. Also, under Section 31 of the Cook Islands Development Bank Amendment Act 1980, native freehold land may be mortgaged to the Cook Islands Development Bank as a security for a housing loan, but the mortgagee does not obtain freehold title to the land.

The Land (Facilitation of Dealings) Act 1970 enables not fewer than three persons owning native freehold land to apply to the Land Division of the High Court to be incorporated as a body corporate, which will have the power to occupy and manage the land as a plantation or farm, engage in mining or other operations on the land; use the land for the growing, felling, milling, or marketing of timber; or to conduct other enterprises on the land. Under Sections 22 and 24 of the act, a body corporate may mortgage or lease the land under the same conditions applicable to individuals mortgaging or leasing native freehold land.

B. Land Management and Use

Under the Land Use Act 1969, the Queen's Representative may, by zoning orders, establish in any island of the Cook Island zones of land to be used for recreation, tourist accommodation, residential purposes, industrial purposes, commercial purposes, agricultural purposes, or public works. Occupiers of land being considered for zoning may make objections or submissions to the Land Use Board.

The Conservation Act 1986–1987 provides for the conservation and protection of the environment and national resources, and the establishment of national parks and reserves. The act establishes a Conservation Service, with a council to carry out the functions of the service. The council consists of five members with a Director of Conservation as its chairperson.

The Territorial Sea and Exclusive Economic Zone Act 1977 declares sovereignty over the territorial sea and 200-mile exclusive economic zone of the Cook Islands. The act empowers the Queen's Representative and the Minister of Marine Resources to provide for the exploration, exploitation, conservation and management of the resources of the territorial sea and the exclusive economic zone. The Queen's Representative may regulate these activities in the territorial sea: the conduct of scientific research, the protection and preservation of the marine environment, the exploration and exploitation of the territorial sea for the production of energy from water, current, and winds; and the construction, operation, and use of artificial islands and other installations.

The Minister of Marine Resources determines, in respect of fisheries within the exclusive economic zone, the total allowable catch and the allowable catch for foreign fishing vessels. The minister is also empowered to grant, renew, vary, or revoke licenses for fishing in the exclusive economic zone.

The Ministry of Marine Resources Act 1984 complements these measures by establishing a Ministry of Marine Resources, whose primary objectives are the development, exploitation, management, and conservation of all living and nonliving resources found in waters under Cook Islands jurisdiction, and to exploit such resources in a manner that will ensure maximum benefits for the people of the Cook Islands.

XIII. Persons and Entities

Cook Islands law recognizes individuals and business entities such as business associations, corporations, and cooperative societies as legal persons that can own property, enter into contracts, sue, and be sued in their own right.

XIV. Family Law

A. Marriage

The minimum age at which one can marry in the Cook Islands is sixteen (Marriage Act 1973). However, consent can be obtained from a minor's parent or parents, or where such consent is refused, upon application to the High Court. Marriage of persons within certain degrees of consanguity is prohibited.

One of the parties to any intended marriage must give notice to the Registrar of Marriages. The registrar is required to issue a license authorizing the marriage not more than three days after notice of the intended marriage. Any person may lodge a caveat with any registrar against any person named in the caveat on the ground that a license should not have been issued. A judge of the High Court is empowered to inquire into the grounds of objection stated in a caveat and to discharge the caveat if the judge is of the opinion that the grounds relied on should not prevent the marriage. Damages will follow the making of a vexatious and unreasonable caveat.

Solemnization of marriages takes place before the registrar or an officiating minister, in the presence of two or more witnesses. The particulars of any marriage so solemnized are to be entered in a marriage register book and signed by the parties to the marriage, the officiating minister or registrar, and two witnesses.

B. Divorce

The High Court has jurisdiction to dissolve marriages entered into under the Marriage Act. To obtain a divorce, one of the parties must reside in the Cooks. Grounds for divorce include adultery, desertion, conviction for major criminal offenses, separation, and irreconcilable differences. The High Court may also declare statutory marriages annulled.

As part of divorce proceedings, the court may also order the payment of maintenance for the spouse or children and may make custody orders with respect to the children of the marriage.

C. Adoption

Statutory adoptions are regulated under the Cook Islands Act 1915. Jurisdiction is conferred on the High Court to make adoption orders on an application by the adopting parent or by the adopting parents jointly. Persons who may apply for adoption orders are limited to a European husband and his Cook Island Maori wife jointly, a Cook Island Maori husband and his European wife jointly, a European husband and his European wife jointly, and a European alone. The act does not regulate adoptions by Cook Islands Maoris, which are regulated instead by customary law.

A child to be adopted should be under the age of twenty-one. The applicant or one of the applicants is to be above the age of twenty-five and is to be at least twenty-one years older than the child. If the applicant is unmarried, he or she is to be thirty years older than the child. The consent of a child may be required if the child is above age twelve. Also the consent of the parent(s) of the child will be required unless the Court is satisfied that the child has been deserted or that the parent or parents are unfit to have the care and custody of the child. The effect of an adoption order made by the Court has the same effect as an order made under the Adoption Act 1955 of New Zealand.

XV. Personal Property

Individuals may own personal property and may dispose of it according to law. The New Zealand Chattels Transfer Act 1924 and the New Zealand Property Law Act 1952 regulate the disposition of interests in personal property.

XVI. Wills and Succession

The Wills Act 1837 (UK) applies in the Cook Islands by virtue of the Cook Islands Act 1915, except that no will made by a Cook Islands Maori has any force or effect with respect to his or her interest in land (**see XII, A Acquisition and Disposition of Interests in Land**). Also, no will made by a Cook Islands Maori is valid unless one of the attesting witnesses is a judge of the High Court or a Justice of the Peace.

The Cook Islands Act also provides that intestate succession to a deceased's estate is determined in accordance with the rules of customary law wherever applicable. Where customary law is not applicable, succession to a deceased's estate is determined according to the Wills Act. If the interest left by a deceased is in a native freehold land, the Land Division of the High Court has exclusive jurisdiction to determine who will succeed to that interest.

XVII. Contracts

Contractual transactions are regulated largely by the common law. Contract law is also affected by Section 645 of the Cook Islands Act 1915. The High Court has discretion to alter contracts made by Cook Islands Maoris. If the Court is of the opinion that a contract entered into by a Cook Islands Maori is oppressive, unreasonable, or improvident, it may either refuse to enforce it or may enforce it only to such an extent and on such terms as it thinks fit.

Another source of contract law is the Illegal Contracts Act 1987, which regulates contracts declared by the courts to be illegal. The act codifies the common law rules. An *illegal contract* is defined as "any contract that is illegal at law or in equity, whether the illegality arises from the creation or performance of the contract; and includes a contract which contains an illegal provision, whether the provision is severable or not" (Section 3). An illegal contract is of no effect, but the courts may grant relief by way of restitution, compensation, variation of the contract, or validation of the contract in part or in whole.

Section 7 of the act provides that if any provision of a contract constitutes an unreasonable restraint of trade, the court may delete the provision and give effect to the contract as amended, modify the provision, or declare the contract unenforceable.

XVIII. COMMERCIAL LAW

A. Consumer Protection

The Cook Islands has no separate legislation on consumer protection. The Control of Prices Act 1966 established a Price Tribunal with responsibility to fix prices for goods and services, investigate any complaints made or referred to the tribunal, keep under review trade practices and the prices of goods and services, and institute proceedings for offenses under the act.

B. Hire Purchase

Hire purchase transactions are regulated by the Hire Purchase Act 1986. Every hire purchase agreement or purchase on an installment plan must be in writing in the English or Maori language and must be executed, in the case of individuals, personally or by any person acting under a power of attorney. Where the purchaser is a partnership, the agreement must be executed by a person who has authority to execute it on behalf of the firm. Where the purchaser is a corporation, the execution must be done under the seal of the corporation or on its behalf by a person acting under its express or implied authority.

The act requires that every hire purchase agreement contain a description of the goods to which the agreement relates, specify the number of installments, the amount of each, the person to whom and the place at which the payments of installments are to be made, the date or the mode of determining the date on which each installment is payable, the full name and address of the vendor, and the method by which periodic balances are calculated on those balances. Each agreement must also set out on its first page the financial details of the transaction.

The act also contains provisions on terms and representations, liabilities of sellers' assignees, rights of purchasers, and repossession of goods.

XIX. TORTS

As with contract law, the common law is the basis for tort law in the Cook Islands. In practice few cases in tort are brought to the courts, as most disputes are resolved by customary dispute-settlement mechanisms such as conciliation and arbitration.

XX. LABOR LAW

Approximately 50 percent of the Cook Islands labor force is employed in the public service. About a quarter of the total workforce is engaged in manufacturing and commerce while the remainder is involved in agricultural production.

Successive Cook Islands governments have been concerned about the high proportion of the labor force employed in the public service. In the early 1980s a staffing freeze was imposed on the public service in an attempt to encourage the workforce into the private sector. The labor shortage, particularly of skilled workers and tradespeople, has been exacerbated by the emigration to New Zealand of younger workers.

Legislation controlling wages and hours of work follows New Zealand enactments and is administered by the Department of Trade, Labour and Transport. The Industrial and Labour Ordinance 1964 deals with management, industrial unions, industrial agreements, settlement of industrial disputes, workers' entitlements, health, welfare or safety, employment of women and children, and accommodation for workers.

An *industrial union* is defined in the ordinance as "any union of employers or workers registered under the Ordinance." Only registered unions may be parties to an industrial agreement, which may relate to or affect "industrial matters" only. An *industrial matter* is defined as "any matter affecting or relating to any work done or to be done by workers, or the privileges, rights and duties of any employer or workers." All industrial agreements must be registered, after which they become binding on the parties and on every member of the union. Provision exists for the variation or amendment of the terms of an industrial agreement during its life span.

Industrial disputes may be referred for settlement to the industrial relations officer. If the industrial relations officer is satisfied that an industrial dispute exists, he or she may appoint a conciliation committee consisting of an equal number of persons nominated by the union and the employer. The industrial relations officer and the conciliation committee must "endeavour to bring about a settlement of the dispute." If no voluntary settlement is reached, the dispute will be decided, subject to the approval of the industrial relations officer, by a majority decision of the members of the committee. Parties may appeal decisions of the committee or the industrial relations officer. Appeals are decided by an industrial magistrate whose determination is binding on the parties.

Part V of the ordinance deals with hours of work, holidays, minimum wages, rates of pay for overtime work, and wage protection in general. Unless overtime rates are paid, no worker is to be employed for more than forty hours in any one week or eight hours in any one day. Minimum wage rates are set by the government at the end of each calendar year.

Health, safety, and welfare of workers are regulated under Part VI of the ordinance. Employers must provide clean and safe work premises. Employment of women and children is regulated under Part VII of the ordinance. Women may not be required to work for six weeks after childbirth in any factory other than one in which only members of the same family are employed. It is also contrary to law to employ any woman to operate any machine in a factory without fully instructing her in the dangers associated with the machine and giving her sufficient training in work at the machine, or without putting her under the adequate supervision of a person who has a thorough knowledge and experience of the machine. A child under sixteen years of age may not be employed in any factory unless an employer obtains a certificate from the industrial relations officer certifying that the child is fit to be so employed. Also, a child cannot be employed between the hours of 6:00 P.M. and 7:00 A.M., or for any period in excess of the maximum of eight hours.

Compensation for industrial accidents is provided for under the Workers Compensation Ordinance 1964 and its amendments. Compensation is payable either to the worker or the worker's dependents where death results. Compensation is payable only if the injury to the worker incapacitates the worker for at least four days and prevents the worker from earning full wages at the work at which the worker was employed. Compensation is not payable if the injury was due to serious or willful misconduct by the worker, unless the injury results in death or serious or permanent disablement. Funds for industrial accident compensation are derived from compulsory insurance for workers by their employers.

XXI. Industrial and Intellectual Property Rights

There is no local legislation regulating industrial and intellectual property. The New Zealand Copyright Act 1963, Patents Act 1953, Designs Act 1953, and Trade Marks Act 1953 apply in the Cook Islands.

XXII. Legal Education and Profession

No tertiary institutions in the Cook Islands provide legal training. Most Cook Islands lawyers attended New Zealand universities. The Chief Justice of the High Court and the judges of the Court of Appeals are all judges of New Zealand courts (**see IV, F Judiciary**).

The Cook Islands legal profession is regulated by the Law Practitioners Act 1978. Under the act, two categories of people qualify for admission to practice law in the Cook Islands: (1) those who have been admitted to practice under New Zealand law and (2) those who in the opinion of the High Court have passed a suitable examination in law, have practiced law for not less than three years, and who are fit and proper persons.

The Law Practitioners Act also regulates the Cook Islands Law Society. Under Section 33 of the act, the society consists of any practitioners practicing in the Cook Islands on a regular or casual basis. The society is assigned the dual function of providing for the welfare of the profession and promoting and encouraging proper professional conduct among members of the profession.

XXIII. Research Guide

Carter, J. "Too Many Henrys Spoil the Cooks Broth," 50 *Pacific Islands Monthly (PIM)* 15 (March 1979).

Coppell, W. G. "New PM Describes the World as Seen from Rarotonga," 54 *PIM* 9 (August 1983).

Crocombe, R. G. "The Cook Islands: Fragmentation and Emigration," in R. G. Crocombe, ed. *Land Tenure in the Pacific*. 3d ed. Suva: University of the South Pacific, 1987.

———. *The Cook Islands 1820–1950*. Wellington: Victoria University of Wellington Press and Institute of Pacific Studies, University of the South Pacific, 1980.

———. "Focus on the Cook Islands: Problems with Progress," 57 *PIM* 41 (November 1986).

———. *Land Tenure in the Cook Islands*. Melbourne: Oxford University Press, 1964.

———. ed. *The Land Is for the People: Land and Society in the Cook Islands*. Suva: University of the South Pacific, 1987.

Frame, A. "The Cook Islands and the Privy Council," 14 *Victoria Univ. of Wellington Law Rev.* 311 (1984).

———. "The External Affairs and Defence of the Cook Islands: The 'Riddiford Clause' Considered," 17 *Victoria Univ. of Wellington Law Rev.* 141 (1987).

Garner-Williams, K. "Honolulu Far Away," 51 *PIM* 20 (March 1980).

Manarangi, A. "The Customary Settlement of Disputes in the Cook Islands," in C. G. Powles and M. Pulea, eds. *Pacific Courts and Legal Systems*. Suva: University of the South Pacific, 1988.

Mataio, T., and N. Tangaroa. "Role of Lay Adjudicators in Cook Islands," in C. G. Powles

and M. Pulea, eds. *Pacific Courts and Legal Systems*. Suva: University of the South Pacific, 1988.
Pacific Islands Yearbook, "Cook Islands." 15th ed. Sydney: Pacific Publications, 1984.
Population of the Cook Islands. New York: United Nations, 1983.
Roberts, M. "Economies of the Pacific," 58 *PIM* 33 (November 1987).
Rysary, P. "Cooks' Latest Extravaganza," 51 *PIM* 19 (July 1981).

2. Fiji

DON PATERSON AND STEPHEN A. ZORN

I. Dateline

1500 B.C.	First settlers (probably traveling by way of Vanuatu) reach the islands that come to be known as Fiji. Subsequently, migration both from Melanesia and Tonga (itself originally settled from Fiji) produce a culturally diverse society, with both Melanesian and Polynesian elements.
1100 A.D.	New wave of migration from Melanesia.
1643	First European sighting of Fiji, by Abel Tasman, Dutch explorer.
1760	Emergence of regional chiefdoms in Bau, Rewa, Cakaudrove, and Lau.
1774	First British sighting of Fiji, by Captain James Cook, navigator.
1803–1804	Beginning of the sandalwood and *bêche de mer* trades, the first European commercial activity in Fiji.
1830	Arrival of London Missionary Society lay teachers, followed in 1835 by European missionaries.
1855	Battle of Kaba, won by Maʻafu of Tonga, marks the beginning of significant Tongan and European influence in Fijian matters.
1858	First British Consul, W. T. Pritchard, arrives; expansion of European commercial interests in coconut oil trade.
1865	Formation of first Fijian central government, under Cabokau of Bau. This government collapses in 1867, but a successor, also headed by Cabokau, is formed in 1871.
1874	Offer by Cabokau to cede Fiji to Britain accepted, and on October 10, Deed of Cession signed; Fiji becomes British colony.
1875	Legislative Council, composed of Europeans appointed by Governor, established; first meeting of Bose Levu Vakaturaga, or Great Council of Chiefs,[1] the group called into being by the Governor to advise on matters affecting Fijians.
1879	First Indians arrive to serve as indentured laborers with right to remain in colony after ten years' indenture. Indentured laborers continue to arrive until 1916.
1881	Rotuma annexed by Great Britain; responsibility for administration given to British authorities on Fiji.
1904	Six elected European and two nominated Fijian[2] members named to the Legislative Council, beginning the system of communal (racial) representation.
1912	European settler representation added to Governor's Executive Council (Fijian representatives not added until 1944).
1914	European elected representation in Legislative Council increased to seven.
1929	Three elected Indian members added to Legislative Council (Fijian representation, now increased to three, continues to be nominated by the Great Council of Chiefs); number of European elected representatives reduced to six.
1937	Legislative Council reconstituted with five representatives of each ethnic group (plus official members appointed by the Governor).
1944	Establishment of separate Fijian administration to regulate Fijian village life. World War II reveals sharp difference in Army enlistment rates of Fijians, who generally volunteer, and Indians, who do not.

1946	Indian population exceeds that of Fijians for the first time (by 1966, Indians outnumber Fijians by a ratio of 6 to 5).
1963	Legislative Council reconstituted to provide for six members each from Fijian, Indian, and "general elector" (European, Chinese, and Mixed-race) communities.
1964	Introduction of "ministerial member" system, under which elected members of Legislative Council are given responsibility for groups of government departments.
1965	Fiji Constitutional Conference in London, attended by all eighteen nonofficial Legislative Council members, results in creation of full ministerial system and enlarged council of fourteen Fijians, twelve Indians, and ten "general electors" (Europeans, Chinese and others). Introduction of cross-voting system under which some seats are reserved for members of a specific ethnic group but elected by all registered voters.
1970	Fiji becomes independent country within the Commonwealth with written constitution establishing the Queen as Head of State, represented by a Governor General, and with elected House of Representatives and appointed Senate, and a ministry responsible to House of Representatives. Constitution provides for entrenchment of Fijian land rights.
1975	Constitutional Review Commission (all of whose members are British) recommends lower house of fifty-two members, of which twenty-seven would be elected from communal constituencies and twenty-five from a unified national roll, with no racial qualifications. Report is not acted upon.
1977	National Federation party (primarily Indian) wins largest number of seats in House of Representatives, but Governor General nonetheless appoints Ratu Mara, head of the Alliance party, as Prime Minister and promptly dissolves Parliament, resulting in new elections won by the (primarily Fijian) Alliance party.
1987	In April, Labour–National Federation party coalition wins election, with a parliamentary majority of twenty-eight, seven Fijians and twenty-one Indians. In May, military coup removes newly elected ministry. The Governor General, purporting to act under emergency powers, appoints new, Fijian-dominated ministry and dissolves Parliament. In October, second military coup establishes Republic and interim military government and abolishes the 1970 Constitution. In December, interim military government relinquishes power and is replaced by ministry appointed by President, the former Governor General.
1990	On July 25, a new Constitution is promulgated. Approved by the Bose Levu Vakaturaga, it gives indigenous Fijians political dominance over ethnic Indians and other races through a guaranteed majority in Parliament and continues the 1970 Constitution's provisions for entrenched status for land rights and certain other laws affecting ethnic Fijian interests.
1992	First elections under new Constitution.

II. Historical, Cultural, and Economic Survey

A. Political Status and History

The islands that now make up Fiji were initially settled from Melanesia; later, there were additional migrations of Melanesians, and invasions of Tongans in the precolonial period introduced Polynesian racial and cultural elements, especially in the eastern part of Fiji. Prior to European contact, most of Fiji was divided into small, often warring, social and political units, although strong regional chiefdoms had begun to emerge in the late eighteenth century, and the Tongan monarchy had established hegemony over parts of Fiji for short periods.

In the nineteenth century, increasing numbers of white settlers came to Fiji as traders, missionaries, beachcombers, plantation owners, and adventurers. The *bêche de mer* and sandalwood trades reached Fiji in 1803 and 1804, and the London Missionary Society began its activities in the islands in the 1830s.

In the 1850s, the pace of European settlement and commercial activity accelerated, and Fiji was visited by several American and French warships. In 1858, a British consul was appointed. The Vunivalu (principal chief) of Bau, Cabokau, who held authority over a considerable portion of Fiji, in cooperation with certain elements of the European population, formed national governments in 1865 and again in 1871. These governments, however, were unable to withstand a variety of pressures from dissident chiefs, European settlers, and foreign creditors. On October 10, 1874, a Deed of Cession was signed by Cabokau and twelve other high chiefs, ceding Fiji to Queen Victoria. On that date, Fiji became a British colony.

Initially, the colony was ruled directly by its Governor, although in 1875 the Governor appointed the Bose Levu Vakaturaga (Great Council of Chiefs) to advise on matters affecting Fijians. During the first half of the twentieth century, the government of Fiji moved toward democracy. In 1904, the Legislative Council, which since its inception in 1875 had been entirely composed of Europeans nominated by the Governor, was made more representative by the election of six Europeans and the nomination of two Fijian members by the Bose Levu Vakaturaga. In 1916 an Indian member of the Legislative Council was nominated by the Governor for the first time, and in 1929 provision was made for the election of Indian members. The Legislative Council was expanded in size until in 1963 it had a membership of thirty-eight—a nominated speaker, nineteen official members, and eighteen unofficial members comprising four elected and two nominated members each from the Fijian, Indian, and "general elector" (European, Chinese, and mixed-race) communities. In the 1963 election, women voted for the first time. In 1964 the Executive Council was enlarged and in effect became a Cabinet, with its members responsible for specific portfolios. In all these elections, each ethnic community voted from separate rolls.

On October 10, 1970, Fiji became an independent state. The Constitution, enacted by the British Privy Council, provided for the Queen to remain Head of State, represented by a Governor General, who was in most matters to act on the advice of ministers. Ministers were to be appointed by the Governor General on the advice of the Prime Minister, who in turn was the person considered by the Governor General as best able to command the support of the House of Representatives. The House of Representatives consisted of fifty-two members—twelve Fijian, twelve Indian, and three general elector members elected from communal rolls, and ten Fijian, ten Indian, and five general elector members elected from national rolls. The 1970 Constitution also provided for a nominated Senate comprising twenty-two members—eight nominated by the Bose Levu Vakaturaga, seven by the Prime Minister, six by the leader of the opposition, and one by the Council of Rotuma. From 1970 until 1987, the Alliance party, largely Fijian, was successful in elections, with the exception of the 1977 election, in which the primarily Indian National Federation party won a plurality of seats. However, the Governor General appointed the Alliance leader, Ratu[3] Sir Kamisese Mara, Prime Minister and promptly dissolved Parliament, leading to new elections won by the Alliance.

On May 14, 1987, after an election won by a Labour–National Federation party coalition, there was a military coup led by Lt. Col. Sitiveni Rabuka. The Governor General, Ratu Sir

Penaia Ganilau, declared a state of emergency, dissolved Parliament, and removed all ministers, replacing them with ministers nominated by himself. On October 1, 1987, the military again took control of the government, abolished the 1970 Constitution, and on October 7 declared Fiji a Republic, governed by an interim military government. The former Governor General agreed to act as President, and in December the interim military government returned control to Ratu Ganilau. As President, Ratu Ganilau appointed Ratu Mara Prime Minister.

On July 25, 1990, after considerable discussion within the Fijian community of the draft of a constitution, the President signed the Constitution of the Sovereign Democratic Republic of Fiji (Promulgation) Decree. The new Constitution confirms the status of Fiji as a Republic, with a President as Head of State and a Prime Minister, Cabinet, and Parliament. Fijians have a guaranteed majority in the House of Representatives, and the Senate has a membership consisting of twenty-four members appointed on the advice of the Bose Levu Vakuturaga, one appointed from Rotuma and nine appointed by the President from non-Fijian communities. Elections for this Parliament were held in May 1992, resulting in the appointment of Sitiveni Rabuka as Prime Minister.

B. Economic Survey

There are approximately 300 islands in the archipelago of Fiji, including many small, uninhabited islets. The two main volcanic islands, Viti Levu and Vanua Levu, account for about 87 percent of the country's total land area of 7,055 square miles. Only two other islands, Taveuni and Kadava, exceed 100 square miles in area. The whole group of islands (except for Rotuma) lies in a rectangle between 15 and 22 degrees south latitude and 175 degrees west and 175 degrees east longitude.

As of 1987, the total population was approximately 720,000, with ethnic Indians slightly outnumbering ethnic Fijians, and Chinese and Europeans as small minorities. Since 1987, however, many Indians, and in particular many professionals and businesspeople, have left Fiji. Indians are now less numerous than Fijians. In 1990, the population was estimated at 726,000, with the increase entirely attributable to the Fijian community.

Before 1800, Fijian communities were essentially self-sufficient, or at most interdependent within relatively localized trading networks. Since the arrival of Europeans in the nineteenth century, Fiji has been an export-dominated economy. The *bêche de mer* trade was especially active between 1828 and 1835, and again between 1842 and 1850. Beginning in 1858, trade in coconut oil became important, and German, American, and British commercial interests established themselves in the islands. Cotton, in response to the American Civil War, and sugar were established as export industries in the 1860s. As a result of land purchases and seizures by Europeans, virtually all the most fertile and accessible land had been alienated by the time of cession in 1874. Although more than 80 percent of all land remained in native Fijian ownership, most of this was economically marginal or worthless.

At the time of cession, the export economy of the new colony was weak. Copra and sugar seemed to have the greatest potential, but both required large numbers of laborers. Because the colonial administration was unwilling to compel Fijians to undertake this work, it approved the shipment of indentured laborers from India. These laborers were free to return to India at their own expense after five years, or after ten years they could elect to remain in Fiji or be returned at government expense. Many chose to stay on in Fiji after the ten-year period and eventually Indians formed approximately half the population. The importation of Indian laborers continued until 1916.

The sugar industry itself became increasingly dominated by a single company, Colonial Sugar

Refining Company of Australia. Over the half-century following cession, other agricultural exports declined in importance, and the economy became almost wholly dependent on sugar.

Beginning in the 1930s, gold mining and tourism emerged as significant economic sectors. By 1946, the gold industry accounted for more than 20 percent of Fiji's exports.

The economy in the postwar years has been based primarily on sugar and tourism. Between 1950 and 1970, exports increased by nearly 6 percent a year, and gross domestic product (GDP) per capita increased by 4.5 percent annually, even while population was growing at 2.5 percent annually.[4]

The sugar processing industry was nationalized shortly after independence. By 1983, gross national product (GNP) per capita was U.S.$1,790, compared to an average of U.S.$1,500 for middle-income developing countries.[5] In the 1980s, however, a series of economic reversals occurred; drought, hurricanes, and a collapse of the world sugar market combined to reduce average living standards. In the immediate aftermath of the 1987 coups, tourism fell off very sharply, and foreign investment declined. Moreover, an unknown but substantial number of business and professional men and women, almost all Indians, have left Fiji since the coups. Despite some recovery in sugar and tourism, the development of a new timber industry in recent years, and economic growth of 18 percent from 1989 to 1990, prospects for the economy in the near term remain uncertain.

The economy is highly dependent on trade. Exports account for roughly 35 percent of GDP, while imports are roughly 40 percent of GDP. The principal export is sugar (37 percent of the total), followed by gold and fish. Exports go primarily to the United Kingdom, Australia, and New Zealand, while imports are principally from Australia, New Zealand, and Japan. Tourism has been a source of considerable foreign exchange. Foreign aid is a relatively minor component of the economy, accounting for roughly 3 percent of GDP.

C. Cultural Survey

Before European contact, Fijian social organization was centered on the family, with several interrelated families forming a village. Families in a village typically traced their ancestry back through the male line to a principal male ancestor. Land was typically held communally, although individuals and families often had inheritable rights to particular plots for houses and gardens, and land tenure patterns differed from one area to another.

Cultural values included mutual aid, exercised by all members of the community, and the sharing of material goods within the community. When newcomers were admitted to a village, they were often required to pay tribute to the village chief, as the representative of the community. A distinction was often made between *taukei*, the original landowners, and *vulagi*, or "guests" who came from elsewhere and settled on the land with the original owners' permission.

These cultural and political patterns were not, however, static. People often moved to new land, formed new alliances, and developed new leadership and ceremonial ties in response to demographic or economic changes.

Two major changes appeared during the nineteenth century. First, Fijians became Christians, in the wake of substantial missionary activity by the London Missionary Society and others. In 1854, Cabokau, one of the most important chiefs, accepted a Wesleyan mission, marking the ascendancy of Christianity over the island of Viti Levu. Second, the foreign consuls, and after 1870 the British colonial government, established a system of indirect rule that in effect substantially increased the power of those persons recognized by the Europeans as chiefs.

In the postindependence period, these cultural elements have persisted within the Fijian community. The village is still central to Fijian life, although an increasing number of young people have moved to towns in search of employment. Christianity is still important; virtually all Fijians are active church adherents. And the authority of the chiefs has gained legal status in the 1990 Constitution, which explicitly recognizes the authority of the Bose Levu Vakaturaga.

The other major cultural element in Fiji is the Indian community. Most of the Indian immigrants were Hindus, from the Ganges plain and southern India, although a few thousand were Moslems and Sikhs from Punjab and Gujarat. Although the Indian immigrants have generally retained their religious ties, most caste distinctions have disappeared among Hindus.

Most areas of Fiji are either predominantly Fijian or predominantly Indian. Each group generally speaks its own language within its own community, and radio stations offer separate Fijian and Hindustani programs. Until recently, educational institutions were largely segregated along ethnic lines, and most voluntary social and economic organizations are uni-ethnic. Intermarriage between Fijians and Indians is very rare.

III. Sources of Law

A. Constitution

The 1990 Constitution states in Section 2 that it is the supreme law of Fiji, and that any law inconsistent with the Constitution is void. Subject to certain limitations, the High Court has jurisdiction under Sections 19 and 113 of the Constitution to hear any person's allegation that the Constitution is being contravened and that such person's interests are affected by the contravention. A similar provision of the 1970 Constitution, however, was rarely litigated, and most contested cases were decided in favor of the government's right to take action curtailing liberties.[6]

The Constitution includes guarantees of individual liberty that place limits on the power of Parliament to enact laws, and on the power of the executive to act, in contravention of the rights guaranteed. In addition, the Constitution, like its 1970 predecessor, entrenches certain legislation affecting Fijian rights, this legislation may be amended only with the concurrence of three-quarters of the Bose Levu Vakaturaga's nominees in the Senate.

The Constitution also sets out Fiji's overall structure of government. The Constitution may be amended by an act passed by an absolute majority in each House of Parliament. However, amendments affecting most substantive provisions, including human rights guarantees and protection of Fijian interests, require a two-thirds majority in each house, and amendments related to the role of the Bose Levu Vakaturaga's nominees in the Senate require the concurrence of at least three-fourths of those nominees.

B. Codes and Statutes

Fiji has no comprehensive code, although consolidated statutes, incorporating all amendments to date, must be published at periodic intervals, pursuant to the Revised Edition of the Laws Act 1971. The most recent compilation available was printed in 1987 and is up to date through December 31, 1985.[7] The annual revisions that were intended thereafter have not regularly been prepared. Legislation for 1986 is found in the Laws of Fiji (1986); for 1987 and subsequent years, decrees enacting laws have been published in the Royal Fiji Gazette (through September

1987), the Fiji Gazette (October to December 1987), and the Fiji Republic Gazette (December 1987 to the present). Prior to independence in 1970, the following statutory sources of law applied in Fiji:

1. ordinances of the Legislative Council of Fiji;
2. statutes of general application of the British Parliament in force in England on January 2, 1875 (when the Fiji Legislative Council was established), so far as the circumstances of Fiji and its inhabitants permitted and subject to any Fiji ordinance to the contrary; and
3. later statutes of the British Parliament specifically applied to Fiji—for example, the Marriage of British Subjects (Facilities) Act 1915 (UK) and the Copyright Act 1956 (UK).

The laws existing from before 1970 were, by the Order-in-Council that enacted the 1970 Constitution, continued in force, subject to anything to the contrary in that Constitution or subsequent acts of the Fiji Parliament. Postindependence acts of Fiji's Parliament are an additional source of statutory law.

As a result of the suspension of Parliament after the military coups in 1987, three other sources of law exist:

1. decrees issued by the Governor General during the period of emergency, from May 14, 1987, through September 1987;
2. decrees issued by the head of the interim military government, Commander Rabuka, from October 1987 to December 5, 1987; and
3. decrees issued by the President of the Republic of Fiji after December 5, 1987.

The Constitution of the Sovereign Democratic Republic of Fiji (Promulgation) Decree 1990 provides that the laws existing as of the date of the decree continue to apply, subject to anything to the contrary in the Constitution or in decrees promulgated after the coups in 1987. In addition, the President has authority, under Section 8 of the Promulgation Decree, to amend any existing law to bring it into conformity with the Constitution, without the need for any action by Parliament.

In a sedition case brought by the state against several Rotuman dissidents shortly after the declaration of the Republic in 1987,[8] Chief Justice Tuivaga held that all statutes in force immediately before the advent of the military government and the declaration of the Republic continued in full force thereafter, except as specifically repealed or amended by subsequent decrees. Accordingly, the pre-independence ordinances enacted by the Legislative Council and the pre-1987 statutes enacted by the Fiji Parliament still represent the bulk of legislation in force in Fiji.

An important feature of the constitutional system is the entrenchment, under Section 78 of the Constitution, of certain statutes relating to Fijian affairs and land ownership. Under Section 78, no amendment may be made to the following acts unless, in each case, the amendment is supported by at least eighteen of the twenty-four members of the Senate nominated by the Bose Levu Vakaturaga: Fijian Affairs Act, Fijian Development Fund Act, Native Lands Act, Native Lands Trust Act, Rotuma Act, Rotuma Lands Act, Banaban Lands Act, and Banaban Settlement Act. The same restriction applies to any other legislation that affects Fijian land, customs, or customary rights other than through amendment of the foregoing laws. In addition, no amendment may be made to the Agricultural Landlord and Tenant Act, which regulates dealings between Indian farmers and Fijian landowners, unless the amendment is supported by a two-thirds majority in each House of Parliament and by eighteen of the twenty-four Senate members nominated by the Bose Levu Vakaturaga. These entrenchment provisions, which largely parallel those in the 1970 Constitution,[9] insulate matters affecting Fijian land and custom from parliamentary action—even the action of a Parliament in which Fijians are guaranteed a majority.

C. Common Law

The 1990 Constitution makes no reference to common law. The Constitution does, however, establish the High Court as the successor to the pre-1987 Supreme Court, and, under Section 24 of the Supreme Court Act 1875 (Chapter 13), the rules of common law and equity that were in force in England as of January 2, 1875, continue in effect in Fiji "so far only as the circumstances of Fiji and its inhabitants and the limits of its jurisdiction permit and subject to any existing and future Acts of the Parliament of Fiji." Thus pre-1875 English common law remains theoretically relevant as a source of law.

In practice, Fijian courts have not been limited to English common law as precedent. Judicial decisions have routinely found persuasive value in courts of other Commonwealth countries, notably Australia and New Zealand. Although English common law remains a source of law for Fiji under the 1990 Constitution, Section 118 of the Constitution, which establishes a newly created Supreme Court as the final appellate court, eliminating the possibility of appeal to the Privy Council in London, will further erode the already limited precedential effect of modern English cases.[10]

Selected decisions of the Supreme Court and the Court of Appeal from 1875 through 1975 were published in the Fiji Law Reports by the Government Printer in Suva. From 1975, decisions have been issued in mimeographed or photocopied form by the Supreme Court and the Court of Appeal. A new series of Fiji Law Reports, covering the post-1975 period, is to be published beginning in 1992. Selected decisions from 1987 onward are published in *South Pacific Law Reports*.

D. Custom

Section 100 of the 1990 Constitution establishes Fijian custom as a primary source of law. Under that section, Fijian customary law has effect as part of the law of Fiji unless (1) an act of Parliament provides otherwise or (2) the particular custom, usage, or tradition is inconsistent with a statute or with the Constitution or is "repugnant to the general principles of humanity." Moreover, Section 100 mandates that, in enacting legislation, Parliament "shall have particular regard to the customs, traditions, usages, values, and aspirations of the Fijian people."

Section 100 of the Constitution also provides that decisions of the Native Lands Commission **(discussed in XII, B Fijian Land Tenure)** regarding customary ownership and use rights to Fijian land or matters relating to Fijian custom, usage, and tradition are not reviewable in any court of law.

These constitutional provisions represent a return to the pre-independence place of custom as a source of law. Under British regulations, a system of native Fijian courts had been established as early as 1876, staffed by Fijian magistrates and dealing with a wide range of matters at the village level. At independence, some of the Fijian Affairs Regulations were suspended or repealed, and the 1970 Constitution provided merely that Parliament could enact legislation for the recognition of custom, leading the courts to conclude that, under the 1970 Constitution and in the absence of specific legislation, custom had no legal status.[11] The recognition of custom in Section 100 of the 1990 Constitution explicitly reverses this decision.

IV. Constitutional System

A. Territory

Fiji is defined by the Interpretation Act as comprising all the islands lying between 15 and 22 degrees south latitude and between 175 degrees west and 175 degrees east longitude. Fiji includes also the island of Rotuma and its dependent islands, lying between 12 and 15 degrees of south latitude and between 175 and 180 degrees east longitude. The Marine Spaces Act 1977 (Chapter 158A) defines Fiji's internal waters, territorial sea, archipelagic waters, and exclusive economic zone in a manner consistent with the United Nations Convention on the Law of the Sea 1982.

B. Nationality and Citizenship

Under Section 22 of the Constitution, any person who was a citizen of Fiji as of October 6, 1987, retains that citizenship. This category includes virtually all Indians in Fiji, as well as many European, Chinese, and mixed-race persons. Under Sections 24 and 25 of the Constitution, persons born in Fiji after that date are citizens if either of their parents was a citizen at the time such person was born, but persons born outside Fiji are citizens only if their father is a citizen.

In addition, under Section 26 of the Constitution, registration as a citizen is available to (1) any woman who is or was married to a citizen and (2) any adult born outside Fiji any one of whose grandparents is or was a citizen. Registration is not automatic in these cases but is subject to exceptions or qualifications that may be prescribed in the interest of public policy or national security. In addition, the applicant must demonstrate his or her intention to be domiciled in Fiji. Any child adopted under Fiji adoption law by a citizen of Fiji has a right to be registered as a citizen.

For those not qualifying as automatic citizens or for registration under Section 26, Section 27 of the Constitution permits naturalization in the case of persons who have resided in Fiji either continuously for five years or continuously for twelve months and for five of the previous ten years and who can satisfy the government, among other things, that they

1. intend to be domiciled in Fiji;
2. have "been assimilated into the way of life of the people of Fiji"; and
3. are "capable of making useful contributions to the advancement, progress and well-being of Fiji."

Fiji does not permit dual citizenship. Any Fiji citizen acquiring citizenship of another country forfeits Fiji citizenship, and any applicant for registration or naturalization as a citizen must agree to renounce any other citizenship within twelve months following the granting of Fiji citizenship.

The Immigration Act 1971 (Chapter 88) provides for the issuance of residence and entry permits to non-Fiji citizens entering Fiji. By administrative direction, short-term visitors from many countries need not obtain visas prior to arrival. A visitor's permit, valid for up to four months, may be issued upon arrival, provided the visitor does not engage in a business or profession in Fiji, other than for a limited period in the pursuit of such person's non-Fiji business or profession, and does not behave "in a manner prejudicial to peace or good order."

Long-term residence permits may be issued to, among others, qualified professionals who intend to pursue their professions in Fiji; persons intending to invest a minimum of $F200,000 in businesses in Fiji; and persons who have been offered employment contracts in Fiji, but only if the job for which they have been hired cannot be filled locally.

C. Government

1. NATIONAL GOVERNMENT

Fiji is a sovereign independent state. From 1874 until 1970 it was administered as a British colony. From 1970 until 1987, it was an independent state with the Queen as Head of State, represented in Fiji by a Governor General, and with an elected House of Representatives and an appointed Senate. Since 1987, Fiji has been a Republic.

a. Head of State

From 1874 until 1970, the British monarch was Head of State of the country as a British colony, and after independence Queen Elizabeth II became Head of State of the independent state of Fiji, represented in Fiji by a Governor General who was generally required to act in accordance with the advice of the Cabinet or a minister.

In October 1987, Fiji was declared a Republic, and for a short period the army commander, Sitiveni Rabuka, was Head of State. But in December 1987, he relinquished that authority to Ratu Sir Penaia Ganilau, who had been Governor General; since that date, Ratu Ganilau has been President, a position confirmed by the Constitution of the Sovereign Democratic Republic of Fiji (Promulgation) Decree 1990. Under Section 31 of the 1990 Constitution, future Presidents are to be appointed by the Bose Levu Vakaturaga for five-year terms, with possibility of reappointment. The President is generally required to act in accordance with the advice of the Cabinet or a minister and to assent to any legislation enacted by Parliament.

b. Executive

After independence in 1970, the executive was composed of a Prime Minister and ministers appointed by the Governor General. The Prime Minister was appointed by the Governor General from among the members of the House of Representatives, and the ministers were appointed on the nomination of the Prime Minister. Ministers were to lose office if a vote of no confidence was passed in the House of Representatives.

Since the declaration of a Republic and the appointment of Ratu Ganilau as President in December 1987, the ministry has been appointed by the President. The President appointed Ratu Sir Kamisese Mara, who had been Prime Minister from independence until the 1987 elections, as the first Prime Minister of the Republic, and Ratu Mara's appointment was confirmed by the Constitution of the Sovereign Democratic Republic of Fiji (Promulgation) Decree 1990.

Under Section 83 of the 1990 Constitution, once elections for Parliament are held, the Prime Minister is to be appointed by the President from among the Fijian members of the House of Representatives. Following elections in May 1992, Sitiveni Rabuka was appointed Prime Minister. Other ministers are to be appointed by the President acting on the advice of the Prime Minister. A Prime Minister shall be removed from office by the President if the House of Representatives passes a no-confidence motion and may be removed if, following an election, the President determines that the Prime Minister will no longer command the support of a majority in the House. Ministers are to be appointed and removed from office by the President acting in accordance with the advice of the Prime Minister.

Section 85 of the Constitution provides for a Cabinet consisting of the Prime Minister, the

Attorney General, the minister responsible for defense and security matters, and other ministers as the Prime Minister designates. The Cabinet is collectively responsible for advising the President on those matters on which the President is required to act in accordance with the advice of the government.

c. Legislature

The 1970 Constitution provided for a Parliament of two houses: an elected House of Representatives and an appointed Senate. The House of Representatives comprised fifty-two members: twelve Fijian, twelve Indian, and three general elector members (elected from Fijian, Indian, and general elector rolls respectively), and ten Fijian, ten Indian, and five general elector members (elected from national rolls). The Senate comprised twenty-two members: eight nominated by the Bose Levu Vakaturaga, seven nominated by the Prime Minister, six nominated by the leader of opposition, and one nominated by the Council of Rotuma. The Senate had no power to initiate or to veto legislation, only the power to debate and delay it.

After the first military coup in May 1987, Parliament was dissolved, and laws were made in the following ways:

1. from May to September 1987, by emergency decrees of the Governor General;
2. from October to December 1987, by decrees of Commander Rabuka as head of the military government; and
3. after December 5, 1987, by decrees of the President.

The 1990 Constitution establishes a Parliament also consisting of an elected House of Representatives and an appointed Senate. Of the seventy members of the House of Representatives, thirty-seven are to be Fijians, of whom thirty-two are to be elected from rural provincial constituencies and five from urban electorates; twenty-seven are to be Indians, one a Rotuman, and five from other ethnic groups. The House is to be elected for a five-year term, subject to dissolution in the event of a vote of no confidence. Elections were scheduled to be held in May 1992.

The Senate is to consist of thirty-four members: twenty-four nominated by the Bose Levu Vakaturaga, one by the Council of Rotuma, and nine appointed by the President from other ethnic groups. Senators are to hold office for staggered four-year terms, unaffected by any dissolution. The assent of the Senate is required for all legislation except the following:

1. appropriations bills;
2. tax legislation and other money bills;
3. bills certified by the prime minister as "urgent," but not including constitutional amendments or matters relating to the entrenched legislation on Fijian land and Fijian affairs; and
4. any other bill (again, excluding constitutional amendments and entrenched legislation) that is passed in identical form by two successive sessions of Parliament, separated by at least six months, whether or not Parliament has been dissolved between the two sessions.

Section 21 of the Constitution requires Parliament to enact laws with the objective of promoting Fijian and Rotuman economic, social, educational, cultural, and traditional interests and mandates that the government enforce programs directed toward those interests, notwithstanding any apparent conflict with the human rights guarantees of Part II of the Constitution (see the discussion in this chapter in **IV, E Human Rights**).

d. Judiciary

The court structure of Fiji has four levels: Magistrates' Courts, the High Court (formerly the Supreme Court), the Fiji Court of Appeal, and the Supreme Court of Fiji. Prior to the declaration of a Republic in 1987, appeals had been possible to the Judicial Committee of the Privy Council in England.

In addition to these formal court structures, Section 122 of the Constitution provides for the establishment of Fijian courts having such jurisdiction and powers as Parliament may provide. Moreover, in Fijian villages the chiefs and in Indian villages the councils of elders exercise some disciplinary powers over members of the village in accordance with custom, but this process is neither part of the formal court structure nor subject to appeal to the courts.

(i) Magistrates' Courts and Small Claims Tribunal

Magistrates' Courts are established under the Magistrates' Courts Act 1944 (Chapter 14). Magistrates are appointed by the Judicial and Legal Services Commission, a body established by Section 123 of the Constitution, and are divided into three classes: (1) first-class or resident magistrates, who until recently were required to be qualified to practice as barristers and solicitors[12] and (2) second-class and (3) third-class magistrates, neither of whom have ever been required to be so qualified. The act also authorizes the appointment of justices of the peace, who may issue summonses, subpoenas, and search warrants but may not conduct trials or preliminary hearings.

Section 28 of the Magistrates' Courts Act specifically directs magistrates to promote reconciliation among litigants and to encourage and facilitate amicable settlement of disputes without proceeding to a judicial determination of the case, unless amicable settlement is clearly impossible.

In civil proceedings, the act, as amended by the Magistrates' Courts (Civil Jurisdiction) Decree 1988, provides that a resident magistrate has jurisdiction to hear all contract or tort claims where the amount claimed does not exceed $F15,000, and proceedings between landlord and tenant where the annual rental of property does not exceed $F2,000. If the amount in controversy exceeds these limits, the case may nonetheless be heard by a magistrate if the parties so agree. Second- and third-class magistrates have jurisdiction to try civil proceedings arising out of motor accidents where the amount claimed does not exceed $F1,000 and $F200 respectively.

The Small Claims Tribunal Decree 1991 established a new small claims tribunal for the informal determination of claims of up to $F2,000. Under the decree, such Tribunals are to consist of either a resident magistrate or a referee, who need not have legal qualifications, appointed by the minister. Small claims tribunals may not hear disputes involving title to or possession of land.

The decree contemplates an informal procedure; only if settlement efforts fail will the tribunal proceed to determine the case, and it is to decide "according to the substantial merits of the dispute," without being bound by technical rules of law. Lawyers may not represent clients before the tribunal, and appeals are permitted solely on the grounds that the tribunal exceeded its jurisdiction or that the proceedings were conducted by the referee in a manner that was unfair to the appellant and that prejudicially affected the result.

In criminal matters, the Penal Code 1944 (Chapter 17), as amended by the Electable Offences Decree 1988, provides that a resident magistrate has jurisdiction to try all offenses except treason, but certain serious offenses may, at the election of the accused, be tried in the High Court. Because a magistrate may not impose a sentence of more than five years' imprisonment, the Director of Public Prosecutions may choose to prosecute in the High Court in cases in which a longer sentence is sought.

A second-class magistrate has jurisdiction to deal with minor offenses specified in a schedule to the Penal Code, but may not impose a sentence of imprisonment exceeding one year or a fine exceeding $F200. Third-class magistrates have very restricted jurisdiction in criminal matters and may not impose a sentence of imprisonment exceeding six months or a fine exceeding $F100.

Under the Magistrates' Courts Act, appeals in civil proceedings from decisions of second- or third-class magistrates may be taken to a resident magistrate, and appeals from all decisions (including interlocutory matters) of a resident magistrate may be taken to the High Court. In addition, a magistrate may refer any question of law to the High Court.

Under the Criminal Procedure Code 1944 (Chapter 21), appeals from all decisions of all Magistrates' Courts in criminal proceedings lie to the High Court, except that there can be no appeal

1. against an acquittal without the approval of the Director of Public Prosecutions;
2. against a conviction for which the only penalty was a fine not exceeding $F10,000; or
3. against a conviction if the accused pleaded guilty, except as to the extent or legality of the sentence.

(ii) High Court

Sections 102–105 of the 1990 Constitution establish the High Court as Fiji's court of general jurisdiction, in place of the former Supreme Court. The High Court is to consist of the Chief Justice, appointed by the President on the advice of the Cabinet, and not more than eight other judges, appointed by the President after consultation with the Judicial and Legal Services Commission. Judges must have held high judicial office or have been admitted to practice for at least five years prior to appointment.[13] A judge of the High Court, other than the Chief Justice, may hold office until age sixty-five or resignation. Any judge may be removed by the President, acting on the advice of an ad hoc tribunal appointed by the President, for inability to perform the judge's functions or for misbehavior.

Under Section 111 of the Constitution, the High Court has general jurisdiction to hear and determine at first instance any civil or criminal proceedings. Sections 19 and 113 of the Constitution also authorize the Court to hear proceedings by any person claiming that the protections of fundamental rights and freedoms under Chapter II of the Constitution (discussed in **IV, E Human Rights**) have been contravened and that such person's interests are or are likely to be affected by such contravention. The High Court also has jurisdiction to hear appeals from and to supervise any civil or criminal proceedings before any subordinate courts.

(iii) Fiji Court of Appeal

The Fiji Court of Appeal, as established by Section 106 of the Constitution and, to the extent not inconsistent therewith the Court of Appeal Act 1949 (Chapter 12), consists of a judge other than the Chief Justice designated as president of the Court of Appeal, other Justices of Appeal the President may appoint after consultation with the Judicial and Legal Services Commission, and the judges of the High Court other than the Chief Justice. The first president of the Court of Appeal, a retired New South Wales judge, was appointed in 1992.

The Court of Appeal has jurisdiction, under Section 115 of the Constitution and the Court of Appeal Act, to hear appeals as of right

1. from final decisions of any court in any civil or criminal proceedings on questions of interpretation of the Constitution;
2. from final decisions of the High Court in the exercise of the Court's original jurisdiction in civil and criminal matters;
3. from final decisions of the High Court in proceedings relating to the fundamental rights and freedoms of individuals; and
4. from final decisions of the High Court in cases involving compulsory acquisition of property under Section 9(1) of the Constitution.

The court may also hear appeals in such other cases as may be prescribed by law. The Court of Appeal Act also provides for the court to hear appeals from any decision under the Matrimonial Causes Act.

In criminal proceedings, either a person convicted on a trial before the High Court or the state, in the case of an acquittal, may appeal on the following grounds:

1. as of right on any ground that involves a question of law alone;
2. with leave of the Court of Appeal or the trial judge, on any ground that involves a question of fact alone or a question of mixed law or fact;
3. on any other ground that appears to the court to be a sufficient ground of appeal; or
4. with the leave of the Court of Appeal, against a sentence unless it is fixed by law.

On appeal, the Court of Appeal may either order a new trial or reverse the decision of the court below.

(iv) Supreme Court of Fiji

The Supreme Court of Fiji is established by Section 118 of the 1990 Constitution as the final appellate court, replacing the Judicial Committee of the Privy Council. The Supreme Court comprises the Chief Justice as president of the Court, judges of the Supreme Court that the President may appoint after consultation with the Judicial and Legal Services Commission, and the Justices of Appeal. A judge of the Supreme Court may be appointed for one or more sessions of the Court or for a term not exceeding three years. At least three members of the Court must be present at any sitting.

Appeals to the Supreme Court from the Court of Appeal may be taken as of right from

1. decisions on any constitutional questions;
2. decisions in civil proceedings where the matter in dispute is $F20,000 or more, or involves a claim to property or a right of that value; and
3. in such other cases as may be prescribed by law.

Appeals may also be brought to the Supreme Court from the Court of Appeal with the leave of the Supreme Court

1. from decisions in civil proceedings where the question is one which, by reason of its great general or public importance or otherwise, ought to be submitted to the Supreme Court; and
2. in such other cases as may be prescribed by law.

The Supreme Court may also grant special leave to appeal from the decision of any court on any civil or criminal matter.

The Supreme Court is also required to issue advisory opinions on constitutional questions referred to it by the President. Decisions of the Supreme Court are final and binding on all courts in Fiji.

(v) Fijian Courts

Section 122 of the Constitution provides for the establishment of Fijian courts, having such jurisdiction as Parliament may specify. Such courts, though currently inoperative, have functioned in the past. The Fijian Affairs Act 1944 (Chapter 120) provides for the establishment of a Tikina Court in each *tikina*, or Fijian administrative unit,[14] presided over by a Fijian magistrate, with civil and criminal jurisdiction as prescribed by regulations. Prior to independence, the Fijian Affairs (Criminal Offences Code) Regulations authorized trial in Tikina Courts for a variety of minor offenses. These regulations were repealed before independence, and the Tikina Courts have not exercised criminal jurisdiction since that time. As of mid-1991, however, magistrates had again been appointed for the Tikina Courts, and the government intended these courts to operate in the near future.

The Fijian Affairs (Courts) Regulations, still in force, authorize the Tikina Courts to try civil matters between Fijians[15] where the amount in controversy does not exceed $F20 and to try Fijians for criminal offenses, under the Penal Code and other laws, where the maximum penalty does not exceed two months' imprisonment. These regulations also authorize provincial courts (**discussed in the next section**) to hear appeals from the Tikina Courts and to hear civil cases between Fijians where the amount in controversy does not exceed $F100. Under the regulations, proceedings in the Tikina Courts are open only to Fijians, while those in the provincial courts are open to the public generally. Both courts are to be conducted in the Fijian language.

Under the Fijian Affairs Act and the Fijian Affairs (Appeals) Regulations, appeals from Tikina Courts are permitted to the provincial court, comprising three members, of whom at least two must be Fijian magistrates and the third either a Fijian magistrate or a district officer. Appeals lie from the provincial courts to the High Court.

2. PROVINCIAL/LOCAL GOVERNMENT

Fiji is divided for administrative purposes into four districts—central, eastern, northern and western. In addition to these administrative districts, two cities (Suva and Lautoka) and seven towns (Ba, Labasa, Levuka, Nadi, Nausori, Savusavu, and Sigatoka) have been established. Each district, city, and town is governed by a council elected from common rolls and possessing powers set out in the Local Government Act 1972 (Chapter 125). The local government units are financed by government grants, user fees, and taxes on the unimproved value of land within their boundaries. The councils have general authority to act to promote the health, welfare, and convenience of their inhabitants and to provide housing and public utility services. They are responsible for maintenance of streets and drainage. A district council's authority may be extended to Fijian villages only with the approval of the Fijian Affairs Board, which will be described shortly.

3. FIJIAN AFFAIRS

For Fijians, an additional form of administration based on fourteen provinces was established by the Fijian Affairs Act 1944 (Chapter 120). Each province is governed by a provincial council that may make bylaws for the health, welfare, and good government of Fijians. The act establishes a hierarchy of institutions for the governance of Fijian affairs, including the Great Council of Chiefs, the Fijian Affairs Board, provincial councils, provincial courts, and Tikina Courts.

The Great Council of Chiefs, whose composition is specified in regulations, has generally included the Fijian members of the lower house of Parliament, representatives of the provincial councils, and both chiefs and commoners appointed by the Governor General (since 1987, the President). The council is responsible for choosing the President, making recommendations to the President regarding Fijian matters, nominating twenty-four of the thirty-four members of the Senate, and commenting on pending legislation or other matters that affect Fijian interests.

The Fijian Affairs Board consists of the Minister for Fijian Affairs, eight Fijian members of the lower house of Parliament, and two members of the Great Council of Chiefs. The board has authority to make regulations on Fijian matters and, in particular, to regulate the operation of the provincial councils and the Fijian courts. The councils, in turn, enact local regulations governing health, sanitation, and similar matters.

Executive authority under the act is in the hands of a *roko*, or Fijian provincial administrator, for each province and assistant rokos for each tikina. Historically, rokos and their assistants, traditionally known as *bulis*, were chosen by the colonial government from among those entitled to chiefly positions in the relevant areas. The system fell into disuse in the 1920s and 1930s but was revived following enactment of the act in 1944, although on the basis of larger, redefined tikinas that did not necessarily correspond to traditional boundaries.[16] After independence, the Fijian Affairs administration again was used inconsistently, but since 1987 there have been efforts to strengthen the system.

The Fijian Development Fund Act 1965 (Chapter 121) establishes a fund, financed principally through a levy on coconut and copra sales, that is intended to function as a kind of credit union. Each copra or coconut producer's account is credited with that person's applicable share of the levy, and the fund is empowered to make loans to any Fijian individual or group for economic development purposes.

In addition to the Fijian Affairs Act, separate administrative arrangements exist for Rotuma and the Banaban settlement on Rabi Island.

a. Rotuma

The Rotuma Act 1927 (Chapter 122) provides that all other Fiji legislation applies to Rotuma "only so far as the circumstances of the island and its inhabitants permit." The act establishes a separate District Officer's Court for Rotuma, with the district officer having both executive and judicial authority. The act also establishes the Council of Rotuma, composed of the customary chiefs of each of the seven Rotuma districts and one elected member from each district. The council has power to enact regulations for the self-government of the Rotuman community and to administer the Rotuman Development Fund, which is similar to the Fijian Development Fund.

b. Banaban Settlement

After the mining of phosphate deposits on Ocean (Banaba) Island, the inhabitants, ethnic Gilbert Islanders, were resettled by British authorities on Rabi Island in Fiji. The Banaban Settlement Act 1970 (Chapter 123) provides for the self-government of that community by an eight-member elected council of leaders. The council makes regulations for the peace, order, and good government of the Banaban community and administers the Rabi Island Fund, which is financed by payments from the British Phosphate Commissioners. The act also establishes the Rabi Island Tribunal, similar to the District Officer's Court for Rotuma. Certain Fiji legislation of otherwise general application does not apply on Rabi Island.[17]

The Banaban people also retain certain land and inheritance rights on their home island of Banaba, in Kiribati. These are discussed in **Chapter 3, Kiribati.**

D. Emergency Powers

Section 163 of the Constitution provides that the President may declare an emergency in the event of a threat to the security or economic life of Fiji. A presidential emergency decree automatically expires at the end of six months unless extended by action of Parliament.

While a state of emergency is in effect, the President may issue decrees and Parliament may pass laws inconsistent with any provision of the Constitution, if the decree or law states that the emergency requires it.

Moreover, Section 162 of the Constitution permits Parliament to enact laws that are inconsistent with the guarantees of personal rights and freedoms contained in Chapter II of the Constitution, provided that such legislation declares that it is being enacted in order to stop or prevent the following acts by a substantial body of persons, within or outside Fiji:

1. causing—or causing persons to fear—violence toward persons or property;
2. exciting disaffection against the President or the government;
3. promoting ill will or hostility between races or classes so as to cause violence;
4. procuring the alteration by unlawful means of anything established by law; or
5. acting in a manner prejudicial to the security of Fiji.

Section 162 is a broad grant of authority for legislation that may have the effect of suspending certain constitutional rights.

Since 1987, the government has enacted a number of broad emergency powers. The Internal Security Decree 1988, whose operation has been suspended, would have

1. prohibited the organization of quasi-military groups;
2. authorized preventive detention without criminal charges for up to two years;
3. suppressed the printing and distribution of publications deemed to be subversive;
4. authorized the minister to close places of public entertainment or schools; and
5. permitted the designation of "security areas" within which the government could impose curfews, requisition property, and exercise broad search and control powers.

The Fiji Intelligence Service Decree 1990 establishes a national intelligence organization with power to execute searches, install wiretaps, and intercept mail, subject to the approval of a Cabinet-level committee. The Suppression of Terrorism Decree 1991 authorizes broad emergency powers whenever at least three ministers agree that a "terrorist emergency" exists. The powers available to the government under the decree are similar, though more limited in geographic extent and time, to those authorized under the suspended Internal Security Decree.

The Public Safety Act 1920 (Chapter 19) and the Public Order Act 1969 (Chapter 20) provide that, if satisfied that an emergency that threatens the public safety exists or is likely to arise, or that there is or is likely to be significant interference with the supply or distribution of food, water, fuel, light, or health services, the President may make regulations

1. restricting access to certain areas;
2. regulating transport;
3. prohibiting the sale or consumption of alcohol;
4. restricting possession and use of firearms; and
5. prohibiting public meetings.

As a result of a sugar cane growers' strike in early 1991, the government enacted the Sugar Industry (Special Protection) (Amendment) (No. 3) Decree 1991 and the Protection of the National Economy Decree 1991. Under the first, any action interfering with cane growing, delivery, or processing is punishable by up to fourteen years' imprisonment. Under the second, the same penalty is extended to any action that harms the operation of any major industry, including not only sugar but also electricity supply, telecommunications, transport, aviation, tourism, mining, and copra production. Enforcement of the decrees was suspended, however, as part of a negotiated settlement of the sugar cane dispute.

E. Human Rights

Chapter II of the 1990 Constitution provides numerous guarantees of human rights, including protection

1. of the right to life;
2. of the right to personal liberty;
3. from slavery and forced labor;
4. from inhuman treatment;
5. from deprivation of property;
6. of privacy of the home and property;
7. to the secure protection of the law;
8. of freedom of conscience, expression, movement, assembly, and association;
9. from racial discrimination; and
10. of persons detained under emergency laws.

These rights, however, are generally qualified; they may be overridden by legislation enacted in the interest of defense or public safety, order, morality, or health, provided that such legislation is "reasonably justifiable in a democratic society." Any person who believes that any of the provisions of Chapter II have been contravened by government action directed against that person can apply to the High Court, which is authorized to make orders, issue writs, and give directions as it considers appropriate.

These qualified guarantees are, however, subject to the emergency provisions discussed above. Any action taken in accordance with Sections 162 and 163 of the Constitution need not be consistent with the human rights guarantees contained in Chapter II. In addition, under the Public Order Act, any public meeting may be banned if, in the view of a district officer or the Minister for Home Affairs, the meeting would not be in the interest of public safety and the maintenance of public order. This provision has been used in recent years to ban a number of public meetings. The Public Order Act also restricts freedom of speech by banning speech that incites racial antagonisms.[18]

The guarantees are also subject to the provisions of Section 21 of the Constitution, which authorizes Parliament to enact laws and the government to carry out programs favoring Fijian and Rotuman interests over other ethnic groups, notwithstanding the guarantees of Chapter II of the Constitution.

Freedom of the press is not separately recognized by the Constitution, even as a right subject to abridgement under the emergency powers provisions.

V. ADMINISTRATIVE ORGANIZATION AND LAW

A. Administrative Structure

The administrative organization of Fiji is not prescribed comprehensively in a single law. There is a public service, controlled by the constitutionally mandated Public Service Commission and regulated by the Public Service Decree 1990. The Constitution also provides for a judiciary largely appointed by a Judicial and Legal Services Commission, a police service controlled by the Police Service Commission and regulated by the Police Act 1965 (Chapter 85), and a number of independent offices, including the Director of Public Prosecutions, Auditor General, ombudsman and Supervisor of Elections. In addition, a number of quasi-independent statutory bodies are authorized by various statutes to perform various public functions.

B. Public Service

The public service is controlled, pursuant to Section 126 of the Constitution and the Public Service Decree 1990, by a Public Service Commission consisting of a chairman and not fewer than three nor more than five persons appointed by the President on the advice of the Prime Minister. The commission is responsible for reviewing the machinery of government, including the need for the creation of new ministries or departments. The commission also has responsibility for investigating, approving, and reviewing establishments; classifying and grading posts; and determining salaries and terms and conditions of employment other than those for senior personnel (these are set under the Higher Salaries Commission Act 1983 [Chapter 2A]); fostering efficiency and economy in the public service, prescribing training programs; providing suitable office accommodation; and providing or arranging for management consulting services. The commission is required to act in accordance with any policy directions from the minister.

The Public Service Commission is also authorized to make appointments to the public service and to remove and exercise disciplinary control over persons holding or acting in such offices. In selecting candidates for the public service, the commission is required by Section 127 of the Constitution to give preference, other things being equal, to citizens of Fiji who are suitably qualified, unless the Prime Minister has agreed that noncitizens may be selected, and to ensure that each ethnic community in Fiji receives fair treatment in the number and distribution of offices. Each level of each department is generally to include at least 50 percent Fijians and Rotumans. No appeal shall lie against decisions of the Public Service Commission concerning appointments, promotions, and transfers. Salaries for department heads and other executive officers, as well as for ranking executives of government-owned companies and statutory bodies, are determined by an independent commission established under the Higher Salaries Commission Act.

Fiji has a substantial military force, composed predominantly of Fijians.[19] These forces have served in numerous United Nations peacekeeping assignments and, since the 1987 coups, have been an important force in Fiji politics. The military forces are organized under the Fiji Military Forces Act 1949 (Chapter 81) and are responsible for the defense of Fiji and the maintenance of internal order. In the latter role, the jurisdiction of the military may overlap with that of the police.

C. Public Finance and Audit

Section 141 of the Constitution provides for a consolidated fund. No money may be withdrawn from the fund except pursuant to the Constitution or a statute or appropriation act passed by Parliament. The Minister for Finance is required each year to prepare estimates of revenue and expenditure for the coming financial year for approval by the Cabinet; these estimates, when approved, are included in an appropriation act. Under Section 144 of the Constitution, if an appropriation act for a financial year is not yet in effect, the Minister for Finance may authorize the withdrawal of money from the consolidated fund to carry on the government for up to the first four months of the financial year. The Finance (Control and Management) Act 1966 (Chapter 69) prohibits the government and statutory bodies from borrowing without specific legislative authorization.

Section 148 of the Constitution and the Audit Act 1969 (Chapter 70) provide for an Auditor General, who is not subject to direction or control by any other person, to examine all the public accounts of Fiji and report to the Minister for Finance.

D. Rule Making

No administrative procedure act or other general statutory provision regulates the manner in which regulations or subsidiary legislation are to be made in Fiji. The basic common law principle of ultra vires is applied by the courts to declare invalid any subsidiary legislation not authorized by legislation.[20]

E. Review of Administrative Action

1. OMBUDSMAN

The office of ombudsman was established by the 1970 Constitution and has been retained after the 1987 coups. Under Sections. 134–140 of the 1990 Constitution, the ombudsman has authority generally to investigate, on a complaint or on the ombudsman's own motion, the administrative functions of members of government departments, or of the police or prison service. However, the ombudsman may not investigate a complaint if there already exists a right of review or appeal to a tribunal established by law, or a right to bring proceedings in a court, unless such an action could not reasonably be expected. Nor may the ombudsman investigate if the action was taken by ministers or assistant ministers in the exercise of their own personal judgment, or if the complainant is not resident in Fiji or was not resident at the time of the action.

After investigation and after allowing the principal officer of the department or service and the person alleged to have taken the action in question an opportunity to comment on any allegations, if the ombudsman considers that the action was contrary to law, based wholly or partly on a mistake of law or fact, unreasonably delayed or otherwise unjust or manifestly unreasonable, then the ombudsman reports this opinion, with reasons, to the principal officer of the department or service. The ombudsman will also make appropriate recommendations and send a copy of the report to the Prime Minister and minister concerned.

If, after a reasonable time, the ombudsman considers that no adequate action has been taken on the report, the ombudsman may report to the Cabinet. As in other countries, the ombudsman has no power to take corrective or coercive action directly.

During the 1980s, the ombudsman generally investigated more than 400 complaints per year, principally involving the police, prison service, and courts. Of these complaints, some 10 to 15 percent were typically found to be justified.[21]

2. JUDICIAL REVIEW

The courts of Fiji follow general common law principles with regard to judicial review; accordingly, decisions of public officials may be reviewed on the ground of lack or excess of jurisdiction, breach of principles of natural justice, and errors of law or fraud. Even where the governmental act is one of discretion, the court may review procedural questions to ensure a fair hearing.[22]

The High Court also has jurisdiction, under Sections 19 and 113 of the Constitution, to hear allegations that any provision of the Constitution has been contravened, and that the interests of any person have been affected by such contravention. This power extends to a review of actions of public officials that violate the Constitution. The procedure for judicial review of administrative action under Sections 19 and 113 of the Constitution is prescribed by the High Court (Constitutional Redress or Relief) Rules 1990.[23] Under these rules, a constitutional challenge is heard in the first instance by a single High Court judge, and the Attorney General (or, in a criminal case, the Director of Public Prosecutions) has a right to intervene if not already a party.

F. Statutory Bodies

Fiji has a large number of government-owned corporations and statutory bodies that, while outside the formal structure of the public service, are responsible for significant economic and regulatory activity. Among the more important are the Fiji Electricity Authority, Civil Aviation Authority, Housing Authority, National Provident Fund, National Bank of Fiji, Fiji Broadcasting Commission, Ports Authority, Sugar Board, and Fiji Pine Ltd. Each such corporation or statutory body is governed by its own statute.

VI. International Obligations

A. Treaty Making

Treaties may be made by the Head of State or by ministers. Under the Constitution, as was the case under the prior 1970 Constitution, there is no requirement that international agreements be tabled in or ratified by Parliament.

B. Diplomatic Privileges

Fiji has adopted by legislation most of the articles of the Vienna Convention on Diplomatic Relations 1961 and the Vienna Convention on Consular Relations 1963. Under the Diplomatic Privileges and Immunities Act 1971 (Chapter 8) and the Consular Privileges and Immunities Act 1972 (Chapter 9), diplomatic staff, employees of international organizations, and bilateral and multilateral aid and technical assistance personnel are generally immune from suit and legal process for actions related to their official duties; they are also exempt from Fiji taxation of their offical salaries and allowances.

C. International Organizations

Fiji is a member of the United Nations, World Bank, International Monetary Fund, and Asian Development Bank and is the host of regional offices of the International Labor Organization, the United Nations Development Program and the World Health Organization.

Fiji is a member of the South Pacific Commission and the South Pacific Forum and hosts the secretariat of the forum (formerly the South Pacific Bureau for Economic Cooperation). Fiji is also a member of South Pacific Regional Trade and Economic Cooperation Agreement (SPARTECA), which is designed to allow the entry of certain goods from Pacific countries, including Fiji, into Australia and New Zealand on favorable terms.

Fiji was a member of the Commonwealth until 1987, when its membership was terminated. Following the 1992 elections, the government indicated it would seek readmission to the Commonwealth.

D. Reciprocal Enforcement of Judgments

The Reciprocal Enforcement of Judgements Act 1922 (Chapter 39) provides for the enforcement in Fiji of judgments obtained in courts of general jurisdiction in England, Ireland, or Scotland, and for the President to extend the application of the act to similar courts of other countries. The Foreign Judgements (Reciprocal Enforcement) Act 1935 (Chapter 40) provides for the enforcement in Fiji of civil judgments, other than those relating to matrimonial matters or decedents' estates,[24] obtained in superior courts of countries the President designates as providing substantial reciprocity of treatment for judgments of the Fiji High Court. These acts have been applied to the United Kingdom, Australia, New Zealand, the Solomon Islands, Kiribati, Tuvalu, Norfolk Island, Pakistan, India, Tonga, and Papua New Guinea.

E. Extradition

The Extradition Act 1972 (Chapter 23) provides that, if a person is found in Fiji who is accused or convicted of certain offenses in any country with which Fiji has an extradition treaty or in any Commonwealth country designated by the minister, that person may be arrested and returned to that country in accordance with the procedures prescribed by the act. Since 1987, certain Commonwealth countries, including the United Kingdom, have continued to comply with Fiji extradition requests, while others have maintained that a new bilateral extradition treaty must first be entered into before extradition proceedings may resume. Fiji and New Zealand signed such a treaty in 1991.

The offenses for which a person may be extradited are, in the case of a treaty, offenses that are designated by the treaty. In the case of a designated Commonwealth country, extraditable offenses are those described in a schedule to the act and punishable by imprisonment of twelve months or more, and which in either case would constitute offenses against the law of Fiji had they occurred in Fiji. Extradition will not be ordered, however, if the minister or the court determines that the offense in question is "political"; that the request for extradition is made for the purpose of prosecuting a person on account of race, religion, nationality, or political opinion; or if the person might be prejudiced on account of these factors in a trial in the country requesting extradition.

VII. REVENUE LAW

A. Individual Income Tax

Residents and nonresidents of Fiji are taxable, under the Income Tax Act 1974 (Chapter 201), on income from employment in Fiji. In addition, Fiji residents are taxed on their worldwide income, but income from non-tax-treaty countries is exempt from taxation in Fiji if taxed in the source country.

All resident individuals whose total income exceeds $F3,000 pay a "basic tax" of 2.5 percent on such excess. No deductions are allowed in computing basic tax. In addition, "normal tax" is levied at progressive rates, up to a maximum of 40 percent on taxable income exceeding

$F40,000. To reduce the tax burden on low-income persons, a rebate of $F255 is allowed against the sum of basic and normal tax liability.

In calculating taxable income for purposes of the normal tax, a married male taxpayer is allowed a deduction of $F750 for his wife, $F200 for each of the first three children, and $F130 for additional children or other dependents. An additional deduction of $F750 is allowed if either husband or wife is over age fifty-five. Deductions are also permitted for pension fund contributions, educational expenses, and interest on home mortgage loans.

Taxable income includes wages and certain fringe benefits, interest (but not the first $F400 annually of interest from savings institutions in Fiji), and a percentage of dividends received. Income tax is generally collected through withholding from wages, under a pay-as-you-earn system.

B. Company Tax

Companies pay basic tax of 2.5 percent plus normal tax at a rate of 35 percent (45 percent in the case of nonresident companies doing business in Fiji), calculated in each case on taxable income, after deductions for business expenses, depreciation, and certain specified contributions and allowances. Additional allowances and tax holidays may be provided as investment incentives (see **VIII Investment Law**). Effective in 1991, company tax is also levied on the income of government corporations and statutory bodies, which were previously tax exempt, and tax holidays expiring since 1990 have not been renewed.

C. Withholding Taxes

Dividends paid by Fiji companies to nonresidents are subject to 30 percent withholding tax, unless the rate is reduced by a tax treaty. A 5 percent withholding tax applies to dividends paid to Fiji residents. Royalties paid to nonresidents are subject to a 25 percent withholding tax. Interest paid to nonresidents, other than that paid by the government and statutory bodies or in respect of approved economic development projects, is subject to a 15 percent withholding tax. Both royalties and interest are subject to any tax treaty limitations.[25]

Fiji has entered into tax treaties with the United Kingdom, Australia, New Zealand, and Japan.

D. Wealth and Capital Gains Taxes

Fiji has no generally applicable taxes on property, wealth, or capital gains (other than municipal land rates), but gains arising from the sale of real property are treated as ordinary income. In addition, under the Land Sales Act 1974 (Chapter 137), a tax, at rates of 6 to 30 percent, is levied on gains, indexed for inflation, from transactions in real property, including profits from the sale of leases. The act does not apply to real property that has been occupied by the seller or the seller's family for at least twelve years, nor to property where the seller has made substantial improvements.

The Estate and Gift Duties (Amendment) Act 1985 abolished gift duties for gifts made after September 11, 1984, and abolished estate duty with respect to persons dying after that date. Previously, estates had been taxable at graduated rates of up to 40 percent, and gifts at rates of up to 30 percent.

E. Other Taxes

A hotel turnover tax on sums received by hotels for accommodation and refreshment and other items debited to a hotel guest was introduced by the Hotel Turnover Tax Act 1974 (Chapter 202). The turnover tax was extended by the Turnover Tax (Miscellaneous Services) Act 1983 (Chapter 202A), to apply to the provision of other services, such as acceptance of bets, hiring of videos, operation of night clubs and licensed premises, and provision of tickets for travel outside Fiji. The current rate of tax under both acts is 10 percent, except that overseas tickets are subject to a flat tax of $F15.[26] In addition, under the Airport Departure Tax Act 1986, a tax of $F10 is payable by a passenger embarking on an overseas flight from Fiji, other than children under sixteen and in-transit passengers.

F. Customs, Excise, and Stamp Duties

Stamp duties of the kind found in most Commonwealth countries are payable under the Stamp Duties Act 1920 (Chapter 205), and business license fees are payable for most trades and professions.

The Customs Act 1966 (Chapter 196) provides not only for the prohibition or restriction of the import or export of goods designated by the minister, but also for imposition of import duties. The government announced late in 1991 that tariffs, which average 40 percent of the value of imports, would be substantially reduced to encourage foreign investment.

No general sales tax is levied in Fiji, but certain goods grown or manufactured in Fiji—including cigarettes, matches, beer, sugar, and tobacco—are subject to excise duty at rates prescribed by the Excise Act 1955 (Chapter 199). The government has announced its intention to impose a value-added tax and to eliminate excise on most goods other than tobacco and alcohol.

VIII. INVESTMENT LAW

A. Foreign Investment Laws

Fiji has no comprehensive statute regulating foreign investment. The Economic Development Board Act 1980 (Chapter 221), as amended by the Economic Development Board (Amendment) Act 1986, creates a statutory body, the Fiji Trade and Investment Board, with the purpose of promoting and facilitating investment.

Under Part X of the Companies Act 1983 (Chapter 247), foreign companies doing business in Fiji (other than through an agent) must register with the Registrar for Companies and provide certain information.

Specific investment incentives are available for the tourism industry, under the Hotels Aid Act 1964 (Chapter 185), which authorizes cash grants of up to 7 percent of the cost of constructing tourism facilities or investment allowances for tax purposes of up to 55 percent of the cost, in addition to normally allowed depreciation. Incentives also exist for investments promoting economic development; such investments are eligible for tax holidays and accelerated depreciation allowances under the Income Tax Act.

The government has also established a program of "tax-free zones" for manufacturing and service enterprises that export at least 95 percent of their output. These enterprises are eligible for tax holidays of up to thirteen years; exemption from withholding tax on dividends, royalties, and interest; exemption from customs duty and licensing requirements with respect to imported inputs; and exemption from excise duty on products produced for export.

In 1989, Fiji acceded to the Multilateral Investment Guarantee Agency Convention, providing for World Bank-sponsored insurance of foreign investments in Fiji against political and currency risks.

B. Banking and Credit

The Banking Act 1983 (Chapter 212) provides that no banking business may be carried on in Fiji except by a financial institution licensed under the act. The licensing authority is the Reserve Bank. The act prohibits licensed financial institutions from making advances or allowing credit for a sum which is more than 25 percent of the issued capital and published reserves; making advances or allowing credit against the security of its own shares; making advances or allowing credit to any one person, without security, of more than 1 percent of its paid-up capital and published reserves; making advances or allowing credit to an employee exceeding one year's salary of that employee; engaging in wholesale or retail trading; acquiring shares in any financial, commercial, agricultural, industrial, or other undertaking to a value exceeding 25 percent of its paid-up capital and reserves; or purchasing land, except as necessary for conducting its business.

The Reserve Bank which was established under the Reserve Bank of Fiji Act 1983 (Chapter 210), has the sole right to issue currency and the responsibility to regulate the supply, availability, and international exchange of money; promote financial stability; and promote a sound financial structure and foster credit and exchange conditions conducive to the orderly and balanced development of the country. The board of directors comprises the governor of the Reserve Bank, the Permanent Secretary for Finance, and five other persons appointed by the minister. The minister may, after consultation with the board, issue to the Reserve Bank general written directives that are necessary to give effect to the economic policies of government. The bank must comply with these directives. The Reserve Bank is the banker and fiscal agent of the government and the depository of government funds.

The Reserve Bank supervises and controls licensed financial institutions; the bank may inspect their records at any time and investigate their operations.

A government-owned commercial bank, the National Bank of Fiji, is established by the National Bank of Fiji Act 1973 (Chapter 213). The board of directors comprises the Permanent Secretary for Finance, the chief manager of the National Bank and four other directors appointed by the minister. The bank is required to act in accordance with any general policy directions in the national interest given by the minister, to whom it must report annually. The repayment of all moneys deposited with the bank, with interest, is guaranteed by the government.

The Fiji Development Bank, which took over the assets and liabilities of the former Agricultural and Industrial Loans Board, is established by the Fiji Development Bank Act 1966 (Chapter 214). It is required to give special consideration and priority to the economic development of the rural and agricultural sectors of the economy, principally by lending to farmers.

The Credit Unions Act 1954 (Chapter 251) authorizes the registration of credit unions, which may be formed by fifteen or more persons resident in Fiji. Upon registration, a credit union becomes a body corporate with limited liability. The objectives of a credit union are to promote thrift among its members, receive the savings of its members, and make loans to members. For these purposes a credit union may receive money and invest in securities considered to be prudent investments for trustees. Loans may be made only to members and only for provident or productive purposes, and there is a statutory limit on the rate of interest that may be charged on such loans.

For a discussion of cooperative societies, see **XVIII, A Business Associations**.

C. Foreign Exchange Control

The Exchange Control Act 1952 (Chapter 211), prohibits a Fiji resident from making any payment outside Fiji without the permission of the Minister of Finance. The minister has delegated virtually all authority under the act to the Reserve Bank, and approval for most routine payments may be granted by commercial banks, acting under further delegation orders. Specific approval by the Reserve Bank is required for transactions exceeding $F50,000. The export from and import into Fiji of currency is generally prohibited by the Exchange Control Act, but subject to exceptions that may be designated by the minister. In practice, Fiji has maintained a generally open currency market, and transactions are handled routinely through commercial banks.

Capital repatriation is also subject to Reserve Bank approval, and direct investment abroad by Fiji residents is permitted only where benefits can be expected to accrue to Fiji within a relatively short period.

D. Export Restrictions

The Fruit Export and Marketing Act 1906 (Chapter 154) requires that all exporters of fruit, vegetables, trees, plants, shrubs, and roots, and their unmanufactured products be licensed by the Permanent Secretary for Primary Industries. The export of bananas is subject to special legislation, the Banana Export and Marketing Act 1960 (Chapter 155), which gives the Banana Marketing Board the exclusive right to purchase bananas for export and to export them.

E. Price Control

The Counter-Inflation Act 1973 (Chapter 73) establishes a comprehensive system of price control which has, by notice published in the Gazette, been applied to a wide variety of household necessities. The Prices and Incomes Board appointed under the act has power to fix maximum prices for any goods or services sold in Fiji, as well as to restrict or regulate the payment of salaries and other remuneration, company dividends, and rents. In practice, the board has largely limited its activity to regulating retail prices for foodstuffs, fuel, building and agricultural supplies, and household goods, although it has also issued orders limiting salary increases in the private sector.

IX. Welfare Law

The Fiji National Provident Fund Act 1966 (Chapter 217) establishes a national pension fund into which employers are required to pay contributions for each employee under age fifty-five at the rate of 14 percent of the remuneration paid to the employee, of which half is paid through payroll deductions from the employee's salary and half by the employer.

The moneys belonging to the fund are, subject to general direction by the minister, deposited in a bank or invested in accordance with the provisions of the Trustee Act. Moneys standing to the credit of an employee may be withdrawn if the employee has attained fifty-five years of age, has died, is physically or mentally incapacitated, is about to leave Fiji with no intention of returning, or (if a woman) has married.

The Fiji National Provident Fund Act authorizes the board to approve alternative provident funds or other schemes already in existence that provide pecuniary benefits of a value not less than the benefits provided by the act. Then employers may make payments to those schemes instead of to the fund.

Fiji has a government family assistance scheme, originally established to help destitute indentured Indian laborers, but later expanded to include all ethnic groups. The scheme is administered by the Social Welfare Department, which is authorized to pay benefits to a family in need because of unemployment, illness, old age, or the death or imprisonment of a wage earner.

The Employment Act 1965 (Chapter 92) and the public service regulations provide significant maternity benefits. Women civil servants are entitled to forty-two days' leave on full pay for each birth, an equal amount of paid leave for each of the first three children, and additional amounts of unpaid leave if desired.

The Fair Rents Act 1965 (Chapter 269) permits a tenant of residential premises in the cities of Suva and Lautoka to apply for a determination of the maximum rent payable, based on a percentage of the value of the dwelling, plus allowances for depreciation, improvements, and operating costs. The act also prohibits a landlord from evicting a tenant (other than for nonpayment of rent or other good cause) unless the landlord actually requires the dwelling as a personal residence, in which case the landlord must provide either a minimum of six months' notice to the tenant or alternative accommodation.[27]

X. Criminal Law

The Penal Code 1944 (Chapter 17) is a comprehensive statute that

1. provides for the allocation of criminal jurisdiction among the courts of Fiji;
2. provides general defenses to criminal liability, such as mistake of fact, bona fide claim of right, lack of intention, insanity, intoxication, immature age, compulsion, defense of person or property, previous acquittal or conviction, or execution of court orders;
3. prescribes sentences that may be imposed; and
4. defines the principal criminal offenses.

In most respects, the code is similar to criminal codes in effect in Commonwealth jurisdictions in the Pacific. The Penal Code explicitly preserves liability for common law crimes, as well as for those offenses enumerated in the statute.

Fiji retains the death penalty, but only for treason and genocide (murder motivated by ethnic, racial, or religious bias). The maximum penalty for murder, rape, arson, and other serious crimes is life imprisonment. The Dangerous Drugs Act (Amendment) Decree 1990 introduced a system of mandatory minimum sentences for narcotics offenses, but the courts have held that such sentences may nonetheless be suspended by the court.[28]

The Penal Code also permits corporal punishment of up to twelve strokes for males between ages seventeen and thirty-five who are convicted of certain violent crimes.

Under the Probation Act 1952 (Chapter 22), a court may order probation for one to three years in place of any sentence otherwise authorized under the Penal Code.

The Juveniles Act 1973 (Chapter 56) provides a separate system for dealing with offenders under age seventeen. Juvenile Courts (Magistrates' Courts sitting for the specific purpose of dealing with juvenile offenders) are directed to consider the welfare of the juvenile. They are authorized to order the removal of juveniles from "undesirable surroundings" and to make orders for maintenance, education, and training. No one under the age of fourteen may be imprisoned, and youths aged fifteen and sixteen may be imprisoned only if the court finds them so unruly or depraved that detention in a juvenile facility is inappropriate. In any event, detention in a juvenile facility may be ordered only if a juvenile is found guilty of certain violent offenses. Juvenile convictions cannot be taken into account in any criminal proceedings against a person aged twenty-one or over.

A Juvenile Court also has the power to make orders for the care, maintenance, education, and training of juveniles found to be in need of "care, protection and guidance," even if no offense has been proven, and to order probation for a juvenile, at the request of a parent or guardian, if the juvenile is found to be "beyond the control" of the parent or guardian.

XI. Judicial Procedure

A. Civil Proceedings

1. MAGISTRATES' COURTS

The procedure for civil proceedings in the Magistrates' Courts is regulated by the Magistrates' Courts Act 1944 (Chapter 14) and the Magistrates' Courts Rules made under that act. Civil proceedings begin with a writ or summons, which must contain the particulars of the claim. There is provision for interrogatories, and for discovery and production of documents before the hearing.

2. HIGH COURT

The procedure to be followed in civil proceedings at first instance in the High Court is now regulated by the High Court Rules adopted in 1988. These rules are very closely modeled on and provide procedures in all significant respects the same as those adopted in the High Court of England.

The Limitation Act 1971 (Chapter 35) prescribes statutes of limitations for various types of civil actions. Personal injury claims based on negligence, nuisance, or breach of duty have a three-year statute of limitations, while contract actions and other tort claims generally have a six-year limitation.

The Arbitration Act 1965 (Chapter 38) permits the parties to a dispute to agree to refer it to binding arbitration, whether or not court proceedings have already begun. The act also allows the parties to choose their own arbitrator or for the court to make the appointment. An arbitration award is final and will be enforced as if it were a final court judgment, unless a court finds "misconduct" on the part of the arbitrator or that the award was "improperly procured."

B. Criminal Proceedings

1. DIRECTOR OF PUBLIC PROSECUTIONS

The Director of Public Prosecutions, under Section 96 of the Constitution, is appointed by the Judicial and Legal Services Commission, with the approval of the Prime Minister, and has complete autonomy with respect to prosecutorial decisions.

Under Section 96 and the Criminal Procedure Code 1944 (Chapter 21), the director has overall responsibility for criminal prosecutions and the appointment of prosecutors. Specifically, the director has authority at any stage to discontinue proceedings by entering a nolle prosequi and, after a magistrate has committed a defendant for trial in the High Court, the director has power to investigate the case further and, if warranted, file an information, which is the basis for then proceeding in the High Court. The director also has power to determine which criminal cases, otherwise triable in the Magistrates' Courts under the Electable Offences Decree 1988, shall be tried in the High Court instead.

2. ARREST, SEARCH, AND BAIL

Under the Criminal Procedure Code 1944 (Chapter 21), a police officer may make an arrest either with a warrant issued by a magistrate, or without a warrant if the person arrested has actually committed an offense in the officer's presence or the officer has reasonable grounds for believing that the person has committed a "cognizable offence" (generally, a serious crime).[29] A private person may make an arrest of a person who actually commits a cognizable offense in the presence of the arresting person or whom the arresting person reasonably suspects of having committed a felony—if a felony has in fact been committed.

Apart from the search provisions contained in the various internal security and emergency powers statutes (**discussed in IV, D Emergency Powers**), the Criminal Procedure Code authorizes

1. the search without warrant of anyone validly arrested;
2. the search without warrant of vehicles, vessels, and packages found in public places, if there is reasonable suspicion that such a search will reveal the presence of stolen property or contraband; and
3. the search of any person or premises if a warrant has first been obtained from a magistrate or justice of the peace.

Persons arrested for any crimes except murder or treason may be released on bail pending trial, subject to conditions the magistrate may impose.

3. MAGISTRATES' COURTS

Only those crimes specified in the Electable Offenses Decree 1988 are triable in the High Court. All other cases are tried in the Magistrates' Courts, unless in a particular case the Director of Public Prosecutions determines otherwise. The procedure to be followed by the Magistrates' Court in criminal proceedings, as set out in the Criminal Procedure Code, is basically the same as that found in magistrates' courts in other South Pacific countries that were under British colonial control. Criminal proceedings are begun by a written complaint on oath by the complainant or, more usually, by a written charge by the police. Fiji courts will not necessarily exclude evidence obtained in an illegal search, even if the search violated the defendant's constitutional rights.[30] A statement or confession of the accused is not admissible unless the court is satisfied that it was made voluntarily, although since 1983 the courts have no longer been required to conduct full-scale evidentiary hearings to determine the voluntariness of such statements.[31]

Under Section 163 of the code, added in 1976, certain minor charges may be dismissed by the magistrate where there has been a reconciliation by way of customary compensation or apology.

4. HIGH COURT

The procedures provided by the Criminal Procedure Code for the hearing of criminal proceedings in the High Court are basically the same as for hearings in the Magistrates' Courts, except that High Court proceedings are commenced by an information lodged by the Director of Public Prosecutions, after a preliminary inquiry by a magistrate.

In criminal proceedings in the High Court, at least two lay assessors are present to advise the judge (in capital cases, at least four). When the case on both sides is closed, the judge sums up for the assessors and requires them to state their opinion. The judge then renders a decision, which is not required to conform to the opinions of the assessors; but if the judge disagrees with the majority of the assessors, the judge must give cogent reasons for doing so.[32]

C. Appellate Procedure

1. CIVIL PROCEEDINGS

The procedure for appeals from the Magistrates' Courts to the High Court in civil proceedings is set out in the Magistrates' Courts Rules. These require that written notice of intention to appeal be given to the other party and to the Magistrates' Court within seven days of the decision appealed against. The lodging of an appeal does not serve as a stay of execution unless the Magistrates' Court so directs.

In the exercise of its appellate jurisdiction in civil proceedings, the High Court is authorized by the Magistrates' Court Rules to hear the appeal on the basis of the record of the evidence in the Magistrates' Court, but it may allow or require new evidence. The High Court may make any order that the Magistrates' Court could have made or order the case to be reheard by a Magistrates' Court.

Procedures to be followed for appeals in civil proceedings from the High Court to the Court of Appeal are regulated by the Court of Appeal Act 1949 (Chapter 12) and by the Court of Appeal Rules made under that act. A notice of appeal must be lodged with the registrar of the Court of Appeal within twenty-one days from an interlocutory order or within six weeks from any other decision of the High Court. The Court of Appeal has limited power to receive new evidence that is not in the record.

The procedures for appeals from the Court of Appeal to the Supreme Court in civil proceedings are regulated by the Supreme Court Appeal Rules (No. 2) 1988. Notice of appeal as of right must be lodged within forty-two days from the date of judgment. When leave to appeal has to be sought, application for such leave must be made within forty-two days from the date of judgment and if leave is granted, the notice of appeal must be lodged within forty-two days from the granting of leave.

The hearing of the appeal will be conducted on the basis of the record; no new evidence can be adduced unless the court is satisfied that it could not by reasonable diligence have been available at the time of the hearing in the High Court. Nor can any grounds of appeal or objections that were not stated in the notice of appeal be argued in the Supreme Court. The decision of the Supreme Court is final.

2. CRIMINAL PROCEEDINGS

The procedure for appeal from a Magistrates' Court to the High Court in criminal proceedings is regulated by the Criminal Procedure Code. Appeals must be in the form of a petition signed by the appellant or the appellant's lawyer that must be lodged in the Magistrates' Court within twenty-eight days of the decision appealed from and contain a concise statement of the grounds of appeal.

The High Court may dismiss the appeal summarily if the appeal is brought on the grounds that the decision is unreasonable or cannot be supported on the evidence or that the sentence is excessive, if a judge of the High Court considers that there is nothing that could raise a reasonable doubt that the conviction was not right or that the sentence should be reduced. If the appeal is not dismissed summarily, the High Court may confirm, vary, or reverse the decision appealed from, or order a new trial. It may dismiss the appeal even though the appellants' contentions are upheld if the court considers that no substantial miscarriage of justice has occurred—that is, that the decision would have been the same even if the defect had not occurred.

Procedures for appeals in criminal proceedings from the High Court to the Court of Appeal are regulated by the Court of Appeal Act and the Court of Appeal Rules made under that act. The act requires that notice of appeal or notice of application for leave to appeal, where that is necessary, be lodged within thirty days of the date of conviction, stating precisely the question of law upon which the appeal is brought.

The procedures to be followed in appeals of criminal proceedings from the Court of Appeal to the Supreme Court are regulated by the Supreme Court Appeal Rules (No.2) 1988. These require that notice of application for leave to appeal to the Supreme Court be lodged within thirty days of the decision of the Court of Appeal, setting out concisely the grounds upon which the appellant intends to rely. The Supreme Court has power to review, modify, reverse, or affirm any decision. The decision of the Supreme Court is final.

XII. LAND AND NATURAL RESOURCES

A. Land Tenure and Administration

Land in Fiji falls into three basic categories: approximately 82 percent is customary or native land, 10 percent is freehold, and 7.5 percent is "State" land.[33]

Native land (the statutory term for customary land) is held under a system of land tenure established by the colonial administration early in the twentieth century, vesting ownership in *mataqali*, or kinship groups. Native land cannot be alienated except to the state, and the control of the use of native land is vested in the Native Land Trust Board, which is statutorily responsible for acting for the benefit of the Fijian owners. Native land that the board is satisfied is not beneficially occupied by the Fijian owners and not likely to be required by them for their use, maintenance, or support may be leased or licensed by the board.

Freehold titles, leases of state land and native land, and mining leases are registered under the provisions of the Land Transfer Act 1971 (Chapter 131), which adopts the Torrens title approach used in Australia, providing that the certificate of registration will generally be conclusive as to all interests in and charges on the land. Freehold and leasehold land is subject to taxation by local authorities but is not taxed by the central government.

State land consists of land sold to the state by Fijians, land without a Fijian claimant, and land all of whose Fijian owners have died. The State Lands Act 1945 (Chapter 132) provides that the government may sell or grant leases or licenses over such land.

B. Fijian Land Tenure

Land held on customary tenure, called native land, comprises about 82 percent of total land area of Fiji. The Native Land Act 1905 (Chapter 133) provides that native lands "shall be held by native Fijians according to native custom, as evidenced by usage and tradition" but in fact imposes a fairly uniform statutory framework, regardless of the customary practices in a locality.

Under this framework, virtually all native land is registered as being owned by a mataqali in communal title.[34] Under the act, a Fijian may lose membership in a mataqali for being away from the mataqali land for more than two years, except in the course of employment or in the case of a woman living with her husband.

Determinations as to what lands are held in customary tenure, and by whom, are to be made by the Native Lands Commission. In addition to one or more commissioners appointed by the Minister of Fijian Affairs, the commission consists of the roko of the province in which the land is situated, and also one or more assessors elected by the provincial council of that province. The commission may also determine disputes regarding the leadership of a mataqali. There is a right of appeal to an appeals tribunal, which consists of a chairman and two members all appointed by the minister, but under Section 100 of the Constitution decisions are not subject to review in a court of law. Fiji's courts have generally been reluctant to intervene in determining the merits of disputes over customary land. The courts see their role as merely ensuring that the procedures laid down by law have been followed.[35]

The Native Land Trust Act 1940 (Chapter 134) provides that native land will not be alienated by Fijian owners except to the state and will not be charged or encumbered by its Fijian owners. The act also provides that control of the use of all native land is vested in the Native Land Trust Board.

In general, the board divides Fijian land into "native reserves," or land thought to be required by Fijian communities for their own use, and nonreserve land, which is available for leasing. Leases may be granted only by the board, not directly by the landowning mataqali, and any dealings in the lease require the approval of the board.

Rents for native land leases are set every five years (regardless of the length of the lease), by reference to fair market value rents or, in the case of agricultural land, at 6 percent of the unimproved capital value of the land. The board may retain up to 25 percent of the rent to cover its own operating costs, and of the remaining 75 percent, 22.5 percent goes to chiefs at various levels and 52.5 percent to the mataqali as a whole.

1. ROTUMA

The Rotuma Lands Act 1959 (Chapter 138) provides statutory authority for the Polynesian style of customary landholding on Rotuma. Under the act, land may be held as

1. *hanua ne kainaga*, by a patrilineal descent group;
2. *hanua pau*, by a Rotuman individual; or
3. *hanua 'ne on tore*, roughly equivalent to a life estate shared among the first three generations of descendants of the owner of *hanua pau* land, with the last survivor again holding the land as *hanua pau*.

The act establishes a Rotuman Lands Commission to resolve disputes and prohibits the alienation of land on Rotuma to non-Rotumans.

2. BANABAN SETTLEMENT

Under the Banaban Lands Act 1965 (Chapter 124), all of Rabi Island is vested in freehold in the council of leaders established under the Banaban Settlement Act, as trustee for the benefit of the entire Banaban community. The council has power to allot land to members of that community and to lease out any land not so allotted. No allotted land may be transferred or leased to a non-Banaban.

The Banaban Lands Act also establishes a Land Court, composed of the officer appointed to the Rabi Island Tribunal under the Banaban Settlement Act, along with four assessors appointed by the council of leaders. The Land Court has power to resolve all disputes relating to land on Rabi Island and to determine questions of Banaban custom relating to land. No appeal is allowed against a decision of the Land Court.

The Native Land Act, the Native Land Trust Act, the Rotuma Lands Act, and the Banaban Lands Act are among the statutes that may be amended only with special majorities in Parliament, including concurrence of three-fourths of the senators nominated by the Bose Levu Vakaturaga, pursuant to Section 78 of the Constitution.

Banabans also retain land rights on their home island in Kiribati, as discussed in **Chapter 3**.

C. Government Taking of Land

The State Acquisition of Lands Act provides that, subject to the Constitution, the Minister of Lands, or a person or body authorized to acquire land compulsorily, may acquire any lands for any public purpose, either in fee simple or for a limited term, paying such compensation as may be agreed or as is determined in accordance with the terms of the act.

Public purpose is defined broadly by the act to include defense, public safety, public order, public morality, public health, town and country planning, or the use of any property to promote the public benefit.

Under Section 9 of the Constitution, property may be compulsorily acquired only if

1. reasonable notice of intention to take is given;
2. the acquiring authority applies to the High Court for an order authorizing the taking;
3. the High Court is satisfied that the proposed taking is for one of the public purposes defined by the act; and
4. the High Court determines the amount of compensation to be paid, unless agreement has been reached.

D. National Parks and Reserves

The National Trust for Fiji Act 1970 (Chapter 265) establishes the National Trust for Fiji as a body corporate with the objectives of promoting the preservation of lands, buildings, furniture, and pictures having historic, architectural, national, or aesthetic interest; protecting and augmenting the amenities of such lands and buildings; protecting animal and plant life; and providing access to and enjoyment by the public of these lands, buildings, and things.

To carry out these aims, the National Trust is given power to purchase, lease, or acquire any lands or buildings and to make investments and apply the income for the preservation of trust property or any particular purpose of the trust.

E. Forests

The Forests Act 1953 (Chapter 150) authorizes the Minister of Forests to declare any state land or private land leased to the state as a reserved forest. Any part of a reserved forest may be declared a sylvicultural area or a protected forest. With the consent of the Native Land Trust Board, the minister may declare that any native land is protected forest or a sylvicultural area.

When land has been declared a reserved forest or a sylvicultural area, no timber rights may be acquired to it without the consent of the Conservator of Forests, and when native land has been declared a protected forest, the Native Land Trust Board may not alienate it without such consent.

Under the Fiji Pine Decree 1990, the government established a wholly government-owned company, Fiji Pine Limited, to carry on forestry activities as successor to the former Fiji Pine Commission. The decree also establishes the Fiji Pine Trust to receive forestry income for the benefit of the Fijian owners of forest land. The trust holds all the shares of Fiji Pine Limited. The trustees, who are elected by the landowners and, in respect of state land, appointed by the Minister for Forests, are required to distribute net income to the landowners in proportion to the area of forest land made available to Fiji Pine Limited by each owner.

F. Agricultural Land

The Agricultural Landlord and Tenant Act 1966 (Chapter 270) regulates the rights of the owners of agricultural land, generally the Native Land Trust Board, representing the Fijian mataqalis; and the tenants of that land, who are mainly Indian cane farmers. The act provides that agricultural tenancies shall generally be for a term of thirty years. Tenancies shall not be terminated within that term except upon notice as specified in the act—and then only if the tenant has abandoned the land for a year or more, illegally subleases or subdivides the land, falls at least three months behind in rent payments, or fails to practice good husbandry, thereby materially prejudicing the interests of the landowner. The tenant, however, has no guaranteed right of renewal at the end of the thirty-year term.

The act also permits a person occupying and cultivating land to establish an agricultural tenancy by adverse possession for at least three years if the landowner has, within that time, taken no steps toward eviction.[36]

Rents must generally be paid in money, rather than a share of the tenant's production, and the amount of rent payable is set by agricultural tribunals appointed by the minister. Generally, rents are limited to 6 percent of the unimproved value of the land, and this value is reassessed at five-year intervals.

Subletting of agricultural land is permitted only on approval of the agricultural tribunal, and only for reasons such as ill health of the tenant or other inability to work the land.

G. Sugar Industry

Most aspects of the sugar industry are regulated by the comprehensive Sugar Industry Act 1984 (Chapter 206) and related legislation.[37] The government-owned Fiji Sugar Corporation has a monopoly on sugar milling and processing in Fiji. Under the act, a Sugar Cane Growers' Council is established to represent cane growers in dealing with the corporation. If, after a lengthy process of public inquiry and negotiations, the corporation and the council are unable to agree on terms for prices and quantities of cane to be delivered to the mills, the Sugar Industry Tribunal may make a master award governing the industry, fixing prices and assigning production quotas.

The act also regulates collective bargaining and industrial action in the sugar industry and in particular imposes mandatory cooling-off periods and mediation and arbitration procedures in case of work stoppages and nondelivery of cane by growers.

H. Copra Industry

The Coconut Industry Act 1965 (Chapter 152) and the Copra Industry Loans Act 1976 (Chapter 153) provide for a price-support loan fund, under which a grower's repayment obligation may be reduced when copra prices are low. In practice, loans to coconut growers are made through the Fiji Development Bank. The Coconut Industry Act also establishes a Coconut Board to regulate the industry, including setting production quotas and prices.

I. Fisheries

The Fisheries Act 1941 (Chapter 158) provides for the licensing of all persons carrying on the business of fishing and for the registration of all fishing vessels, except for foreign fishing vessels, which are regulated under the Marine Spaces Act 1977 (Chapter 158A), which defines Fiji's exclusive economic zone and authorizes the licensing of foreign fishing vessels.

The Fisheries Act also provides for the protection of customary fishing rights that have been registered by the Native Fisheries Commission by prohibiting the taking of fish, in areas where such customary rights exist, by anybody other than a Fijian entitled to such rights. The determination of native customary fishing rights is made by the commission, with appeal to an appeals tribunal consisting of three persons appointed by the Minister for Fijian Affairs.

XIII. Persons and Entities

Under the common law applying in Fiji, each living human being of whatever age has a separate legal identity. Legislation has provided, however, that children do not have legal capacity or power to undertake certain matters. For example, the Infants Relief Act (UK), adopted in Fiji, states that persons under the age of twenty-one do not have power to bind themselves absolutely by contracts unless the contracts are for necessaries or are beneficial contracts of service. Legal capacity to make a will is restricted by the Wills Act 1972 (Chapter 59) to persons aged eighteen or over, and legal capacity to marry is restricted by the Marriage Act 1968 (Chapter 50) to males aged eighteen or over or females aged sixteen or over. Legal capacity to vote at elections is restricted by Section 49 of the Constitution to persons aged twenty-one and over. The Penal Code provides that children under the age of ten are not criminally responsible for their conduct, and that children aged ten to twelve are criminally responsible for their conduct only if they know that their conduct was wrong.

Various legislation in Fiji provides for certain bodies of persons to be bodies corporate and have a legal identity that they would not have under common law. These entities include companies incorporated under the Companies Act, city and town councils incorporated under the Local Government Act, credit unions incorporated under the Credit Unions Act, and cooperative societies incorporated under the Co-operative Societies Act. Such bodies corporate have not only individual legal identity separate from their members but also perpetual existence until dissolved and the powers expressly or implicitly conferred by the incorporating statute.

XIV. Family Law

A. Marriage

The Marriage Act 1968 (Chapter 50) provides that the registrar-general, district registrars, Christian ministers, and other persons approved by the Registrar General as marriage officers for non-Christian religions may solemnize marriages in Fiji. Marriage may be contracted by males of eighteen and by females of sixteen, but the consent of the father—or, if he is dead or out of Fiji, the mother—must be given for the marriage of any person under twenty-one. If a parent unreasonably refuses consent or if both parents are incapacitated, dead, or out of Fiji, consent may be given by a district commissioner or magistrate. Customary marriage is not legally recognized, although most Indians in Fiji who have been legally married in a civil ceremony do not regard themselves as married until they have gone through a subsequent religious ceremony.[38] Polygamy is not legally sanctioned.

B. Divorce, Separation, and Annulment

The Matrimonial Causes Act 1968 (Chapter 51) provides that marriages are void if at the time of the marriage either party was lawfully married to some other person, both parties are within prohibited degrees of consanguinity, the consent of either party was not a real consent, either party was not of marriageable age, or the marriage was not in accordance with the legal requirements as to matters of form. A marriage is voidable, rather than void ab initio, if at the time of the marriage either party was incapable of consummating the marriage, of unsound mind or mentally defective, suffering from venereal disease, or, in the case of the wife, pregnant by a person other than the husband.

The grounds for dissolution of marriage are the following:

1. adultery (the ground cited in approximately half of all divorce actions);[39]
2. willful desertion, actual or constructive, for not less than two years;
3. willful and persistent refusal to consummate the marriage;
4. habitual cruelty;
5. commission of rape, sodomy, or bestiality;
6. habitual drunkenness or intoxication for not less than two years;
7. imprisonment for not less than three years for an offense whose maximum sentence is death or life imprisonment, or imprisonment for five years for any other offense;
8. conviction for attempted killing or infliction of grievous bodily harm on the petitioner;
9. habitual and willful failure to comply with a maintenance agreement for two years;
10. failure to comply with a decree for restitution of conjugal rights for not less than one year;
11. unsoundness of mind involving confinement in a mental institution for not less than five years;
12. continuous living apart for not less than five years without reasonable likelihood of resumption of cohabitation; and
13. absence for such period and in such circumstances as to provide reasonable grounds for presumption of death.

Courts are required by the Matrimonial Causes Act actively to encourage conciliation, and the courts generally refer parties to a divorce action to the Social Welfare Department for counseling. The courts will not terminate marriages unless satisfied that reconciliation efforts have failed.[40]

The worldwide trend toward no-fault divorce has yet to affect Fiji. A draft family law bill that would have introduced the no-fault concept was prepared before the 1987 coup but has not been acted upon.

A decree for dissolution cannot be sought within three years of the marriage, except in the cases of adultery; willful failure to consummate; or commission of rape, sodomy, or bestiality, unless this rule would impose exceptional hardship on the petitioner, or unless there has been exceptional depravity by the other party. Any petition for dissolution granted by the court becomes absolute after three months.

A decree for judicial separation may be made on any ground that is a ground for dissolution of marriage, except continuous living apart for not less than five years, and absence giving rise to presumption of death.

An order for maintenance and custody of the children of the marriage or for maintenance of the wife may be included in a divorce decree.

Petitions for nullity of marriage are heard and determined in the High Court, but petitions for dissolution and judicial separation are heard and determined in the Magistrates' Courts, subject to appeal to the High Court.

C. Maintenance

The Maintenance and Affiliation Act 1971 (Chapter 52) makes provision for separation, maintenance, and affiliation orders to be made by a Magistrates' Court. The act provides that a married woman may seek orders for separation, custody, and maintenance against her husband on the following grounds:

1. conviction for offenses against her person;
2. habitual drunkenness;
3. adultery;
4. desertion;
5. persistent cruelty to her or her children;
6. willful neglect to provide reasonable maintenance;
7. sexual intercourse while aware that he has a venereal disease; or
8. forcing the wife into prostitution.

The magistrate may request a probation officer to attempt to effect a reconciliation between the parties. Any order may be varied or discharged by a magistrate upon proof of change of circumstances.[41]

The Maintenance and Affiliation Act also provides that a single woman who is pregnant or has given birth to a child may apply to the Magistrates' Court for an order that the father of the child pay maintenance. Such an application must be made before the birth of the child, within twelve months after the child is born, within twelve months after the man has made provision for the child's maintenance, or within twelve months after the man returns to Fiji if he left within twelve months after the child's birth. Evidence of the complainant must be corroborated in some material respect. A maintenance order lasts until the child reaches sixteen years of age but may be varied from time to time.

The Maintenance (Prevention of Desertion and Miscellaneous Provisions) Act 1962 (Chapter 53) contains provisions to prevent men from leaving Fiji without making adequate provision for their wives or children. The Maintenance Orders (Facilities for Enforcement) Act 1922 (Chapter 54) and the Maintenance Orders (Reciprocal Enforcement) Act 1974 (Chapter 55) contain provisions for the enforcement and modification by Fiji courts of maintenance and support orders made outside Fiji, and vice versa. The provisions of these acts apply to orders obtained in the United Kingdom, Australia, Ireland, New Zealand, South Africa, Kiribati, the Solomon Islands, India, Tanzania, Canada, Tuvalu, Western Samoa, Nauru, and the state of California in the United States. Fiji is also a party to the International Convention on the Recovery of Maintenance Abroad.

D. Custody

The Matrimonial Causes Act provides that an order for the custody of any children of a marriage must be made when the marriage is dissolved, if the children are under age eighteen. Similarly, the Maintenance and Affiliation Act provides that an order for custody of children of a marriage may be made when a separation order is made under that act. The latter act also provides that if a single woman has applied to have a man adjudged the father of her child, the magistrate may make an order as to the custody of the child.

E. Adoption

The Adoption of Infants Act 1944 (Chapter 58) authorizes a married couple or an unmarried person to adopt an infant, provided at least one of the applicants is aged twenty-five or over and is at least twenty years older than the infant, or is aged twenty-one or over and is a relative of the infant. Although customary adoptions, without legal proceedings, are common in Fiji as elsewhere in the Pacific, such adoptions are not recognized in law. In 1978, an Adoption Review Committee recommended a new procedure, under which legal recognition could be given to Fijian customary adoption, but this recommendation has never been acted upon. Fewer than 100 adoptions a year are registered under the Adoption of Infants Act.[42]

The consent of the biological parents or guardians of the infant to a proposed adoption is required, unless such persons cannot be found; they are incapable of giving consent; their consent is unreasonably withheld; or the biological parent or guardian has abandoned, neglected, or persistently ill treated the infant, made no contribution to its maintenance for over five years, or persistently neglected or refused to contribute to the maintenance of the infant when liable to do so. A consent given by the biological mother earlier than six weeks after birth is not valid.

Before making an adoption order, the court is required to satisfy itself that every person whose consent is necessary has consented and understands the effect of an adoption order, that the adoption will be for the welfare of the infant, and that the applicant has not received any payment in consideration of the adoption except as the court has approved. The act also provides that an adoption order shall not be made if the sole applicant is a male and the infant is a female, unless there are special justifying circumstances, and that an adoption order shall not be made in favor of an applicant who is not resident in Fiji nor concerning an infant who is not resident. Regardless of when consent was given, an adoption order shall not be made until the infant has been continuously in the care and possession of the applicant for a probationary period of at least three consecutive months.

An adoption under the act extinguishes all parental rights and duties on the part of the natural parents and vests such rights and duties in the adopting parent. The adopted child is to be treated as the child of the adopting parent for purposes of inheritance.

F. Family Planning and Abortion

Under the Penal Code, abortion is a crime, punishable by up to seven years' imprisonment, unless "therapeutic," that is, if a doctor in good faith believes that failure to terminate the pregnancy would threaten the physical or mental health of the pregnant woman.[43] In practice, abortions are not performed except with the agreement of two physicians and a hospital medical superintendent, and a psychiatrist, in cases involving mental health.[44]

XV. Personal Property

No legislation in Fiji regulates in comprehensive terms the acquisition of interests in personal property, the effect of such interests, or the transfer of such interests.

The Property Law Act 1971 (Chapter 130), which is mainly concerned with real property, provides that debts and other choses in action may be assigned by written statement, if notice in writing is given to the person who is liable to pay.

The Bills of Sales Act 1879 (Chapter 225) regulates the way security can be given over chattels, including growing crops; the Indemnity, Guarantee and Bailment Act 1881 (Chapter 232) regulates the respective rights and responsibilities of those who give and receive goods on bailment.

Outside these areas, the extent of legal rights and obligations in relation to personal property is regulated by common law.

XVI. Wills and Succession

Fiji law does not, in general, recognize customary succession except in relation to native land. The Wills Act 1972 (Chapter 59) provides that any person aged eighteen years or over may make a will and by such will may dispose of all property belonging to that person or over which he or she has a power of appointment, and may appoint a guardian for minor children.

Generally, a will must be in writing and signed by the person making it or by some person acting in the presence and on the direction of the person making it. The signature is made or acknowledged in the presence of at least two witnesses. A bequest to a witness or the spouse of a witness is void but does not otherwise invalidate the will. Any alteration made to a will after execution is generally invalid.

Persons on active military, naval, or air service and mariners or seamen serving at sea are exempt from the normal legal requirements for the making of a will. Such persons, regardless of age, may make a will in written or spoken form, if it is clear that by so doing they intend to dispose of their property after death.

A will is automatically revoked by the subsequent marriage of the testator unless the will is expressly stated as made in contemplation of marriage. A will may also be revoked by a subsequent will or codicil executed as required by the act or by a written declaration of an intention to revoke the will executed as required by the act for a will, or the burning, tearing, or otherwise destroying the will by the testator or by someone else in his or her presence at his or her direction.

Under the Inheritance (Family Provision) Act 1939 (Chapter 61), a surviving spouse, if not left a minimum bequest of at least two-thirds of the income (though not the principal) of the decedent's net estate, may apply, on behalf of herself or himself and other dependents of the deceased, to the High Court for an award of "reasonable maintenance." The maximum allowable award under this provision is one-half of the income from the net estate if there are no dependents except the surviving spouse, and two-thirds of the income (to be shared by the spouse and dependents) if there are other dependents.

The British and Colonial Probates Act 1893 (Chapter 62) provides for the recognition by Fiji courts of any probate or letters of administration granted by a British court or "in any part of Her Majesty's dominions." If a national of certain countries dies outside Fiji leaving property in Fiji, that person's consul in Fiji may, under the Consular Conventions (Administration of

Estates) Act 1972 (Chapter 63), be authorized to represent the decedent's estate for purposes of dealing with the property.

If a person dies intestate, the Succession, Probate and Administration Act 1970 (Chapter 60) provides for the distribution of the property of that person. First, if the deceased is survived by a spouse, the spouse takes all tangible personal property and the lesser of $F2,000 or the value of the residuary estate. Second, as to the balance of the decedent's estate: (1) if the intestate leaves a spouse and no issue, the spouse takes one-half of the residuary estate and any surviving parents take the balance—but if neither parent survives, the spouse takes all; (2) if the intestate leaves a spouse and issue, the spouse takes one-third of the residuary estate and the issue take two-thirds of the residuary estate, distributed per stirpes; and (3) if the intestate leaves no spouse but does leave issue, then the issue take the whole of the residuary estate, distributed per stirpes. If the intestate leaves neither spouse nor issue, the act provides for parents, brothers and sisters, grandparents, uncles and aunts, in that order, to take the property. If there are no such surviving relatives, the property of an intestate escheats to the state.

The act provides expressly that children include both legitimate and illegitimate children, but an illegitimate child is not entitled to inherit from a father under the intestacy rules unless paternity has been admitted by or established against the father during his lifetime.

Application for probate to execute a will or for letters of administration to administer the property of a deceased intestate must be made to the High Court. The High Court Rules 1988 regulate who may make applications and the procedures to be followed.

If no provision is otherwise made for an executor or administrator of an estate, the Administrator General, acting as the public trustee under the Public Trustee Act 1968 (Chapter 64), may be appointed by the court.

XVII. Contracts

The legal principles regulating the making and the effect of contracts are provided generally by the principles of common law and equity. The legislature has intervened to make provisions only for particular aspects of contracts. The Property Law Act 1971 (Chapter 130) provides that a deed must be signed by the person to be bound thereby and must be attested by at least one person who is not a party. Sealing, formal delivery, and indenting of the deed are not necessary. The Indemnity, Guarantee and Bailment Act 1881 (Chapter 232) provides that no action shall be brought without written agreement signed by the person to be charged or some other person lawfully authorized

1. to charge any executor or administrator upon any promise to answer damages out of the executor's or administrator's own estate;
2. to charge any person upon any promise to answer for the debt, default, or miscarriage of another person; or
3. to charge any person (a) upon any agreement made in consideration of marriage, (b) upon any contract or sale of land tenements or hereditaments or any interest in them, or (c) upon any agreement that is not to be performed within one year from its making.

The act also provides that no action shall be brought to charge any person on account of any representation or assurance as to the character, credit, ability, trade, or dealings of another person so that the latter can obtain credit, unless the representation is in writing and signed by the person to be charged.

XVIII. Commercial Law

A. Business Associations

The Companies Act 1983 (Chapter 247) provides that any seven or more persons may form a public company, any two or more persons may form a private company, and a company may be limited by shares or by guarantee or may be a company of unlimited liability. To form a company, persons must subscribe their names to a memorandum setting out the name, registered office, objects of the company, and the contribution of each member and also to articles of association setting out the rules regulating the company.

A prospectus for an offering of shares in a company must contain the matters specified in a schedule to the act and must accompany every application for shares or debentures; a copy of the prospectus must be delivered to the registrar.

Every company must make an annual return to the registrar setting out the information specified in the act. Every company limited by shares or by guarantee and having a share capital must hold a meeting of members between one and three months after the commencement of business, and at least once a year thereafter. In addition, members holding not less than one-tenth of the paid-up capital of the company may require that a meeting be held, in addition to any power in the articles for the directors or others to call a general meeting of the company.

Companies may be wound up by the court, or voluntarily, or subject to the supervision of the court.

The Partnership Act 1910 (Chapter 248) provides that a partnership exists if persons are carrying on a business in common with a view to profit, unless they are registered as a company or incorporated in some other way. Every partner is deemed by the act to be an agent of the partnership, and a partner's actions in carrying on business as usual of the kind carried on by the partnership bind the other partners.

A partnership is automatically dissolved, subject to any agreement of the partners to the contrary,

1. when the fixed term for which it was entered into expires;
2. when the undertaking for which it was entered into is completed;
3. if any partner gives notice of an intention to dissolve the partnership; or
4. on the death or bankruptcy of any partner.

Fiji law does not provide for limited partnerships.

The Co-operative Societies Act 1947 (Chapter 250) provides that a society of at least ten members, which has as its object the promotion of the economic interests of its members in accordance with cooperative principles, or a society established to facilitate the operations of such society, may be registered under the act, with or without limited liability, by the Registrar of Cooperative Societies.

When registered, the society becomes a body corporate with power to do all things necessary for the purpose of its constitution. It may not make any loan to a nonmember, and it may deposit or invest its funds only in banks or other institutions approved by the registrar. Amendments to the bylaws of a registered society must be approved by the registrar, and its accounts must be audited by someone authorized by the registrar at least once a year.

A registered cooperative society may be dissolved by order of the registrar, after an inquiry or inspection of the society's affairs or after receiving an application by three-quarters of the members of the society.

B. Business Names

The Registration of Business Names Act 1923 (Chapter 249) requires registration for business names other than those of an individual, partnership, or company actually carrying on business in its own name. The courts have interpreted the act so as to create a partnership whenever two or more persons sign a registration statement.

C. Agency

The relationship of agency is regulated by the principles of common law and equity developed in England, which have not been codified or changed by Fiji legislation.

D. Sale of Goods and Consumer Protection

Sales contracts are governed by the Sale of Goods Act 1979 (Chapter 230). Under the act, sales by a merchant in the course of business result in an implied warranty of merchantability and, if the buyer has made known to the seller the particular purpose for which the goods are sought, an implied warranty of fitness for that purpose. These implied warranties may not be disclaimed by contract terms in consumer transactions and may be disclaimed in other types of transactions only if such a disclaimer is fair and reasonable in the circumstances, having regard for the relative bargaining position of the parties and other relevant factors. The act allows a buyer a reasonable opportunity to inspect goods before acceptance.

The Moneylenders Act 1938 (Chapter 234) provides for the licensing of lenders, restricts their advertising, and provides that a court may order the variation of a loan agreement where the interest charged is, in the court's view, excessive or the loan transaction is "harsh and unreasonable" or "substantially unfair." Section 22 of the act sets 12 percent annual interest as a prima facie standard for "excessive" rates. By regulation, all of the licensed commercial banks operating in Fiji have been exempted from these limitations.

The Consumer Council Act 1976 (Chapter 235) establishes the Consumer Council of Fiji to act as an advocate for consumers, with authority to hold inquiries, receive complaints, and—under the Small Claims Tribunal Decree 1991—represent consumers in small claims actions.

E. Insolvency

The Bankruptcy Act 1944 (Chapter 48) permits both voluntary and involuntary (that is, at the behest of creditors) bankruptcy actions, generally resulting in the court's appointing a receiver for the debtor's property. The act requires a meeting of creditors and a public examination of the debtor and permits a voluntary settlement, by way of a composition with creditors or a scheme of arrangement for the continuation of the debtor's business while debts are being repaid. If no such agreement is reached, the court may declare the debtor bankrupt and vest the debtor's property in a trustee for the benefit of the creditors. In most respects, the act is similar to those in force in the United Kingdom, Australia, New Zealand, and other Commonwealth jurisdictions.

XIX. Torts

The principles of liability in tort in Fiji are generally similar to those in other common law jurisdictions, and there has been relatively little intervention by Parliament. The role of statute has largely been to create areas of strict liability. The Occupiers' Liability Act 1968 (Chapter 33) sets out a statutory standard governing tort liability of owners and occupiers of premises, requiring such care as is reasonable in the circumstances. The act does not change common law rules limiting liability to trespassers.

The Compensation to Relatives Act 1920 (Chapter 29) permits wrongful death actions to be instituted by the spouse, parent, or child of a person killed, and the court has discretion to allocate any damages awarded among those relatives.

The Law Reform (Contributory Negligence and Tortfeasors) Act 1946 (Chapter 30) eliminates the common law defense of contributory negligence and replaces it with a comparative negligence standard; the court is authorized to reduce a plaintiff's damages "to such extent as the court thinks just and equitable having regard to the claimant's share in responsibility." The comparative negligence rule also applies to the wrongful death actions described above.

Under the State Proceedings Act 1951 (Chapter 24), the state has waived the defense of sovereign immunity in torts committed by government employees or agents, duties owed to government employees, and breach of common law duties to the owner or occupier of property. The act preserves sovereign immunity for actions of judges and harbor authorities, and wrongful death actions against members of the military forces, subject to certain limitations.

The Defamation Act 1971 (Chapter 34) provides for a privilege, applicable to "fair and accurate" newspaper reports and broadcasts of court and similar proceedings, public meetings, and information released by the government and certain charitable and commerical organizations. In addition, the common law defenses of truth and fair comment are recognized. Political figures have succeeded, however, in libel actions against local newspapers.[45]

XX. LABOR LAW

The Employment Act 1964 (Chapter 92) provides for the appointment of a Labour Advisory Board consisting of representatives of employers and employees and others to advise the Minister of Labour on matters concerned with labor and employment, and a Permanent Secretary and other officers and inspectors to assist in the administration of the act. The act applies both to private employers and to the public service, but not to the military, police, or prison services. The act

1. requires that employment contracts for more than six months be in writing;
2. prohibits summary dismissal except in certain circumstances;
3. prohibits deductions from wages other than for taxes, debts due to the employer, and deductions specifically authorized by the employee;
4. prohibits the employment of children under age twelve;
5. restricts employment of children under fifteen to casual daily work, with the child returning home each night;
6. prohibits employment of women and young persons in certain industrial jobs after 8:00 P.M. and before 6:00 A.M.; and
7. requires the provision of maternity leave and allowances, an adequate supply of pure water, and medical aid.

The National Training Act 1973 (Chapter 93) provides for the establishment of a training council appointed by the Minister of Labour and containing an equal number of employees' and employers' representatives. The council is empowered to provide and regulate appropriate training and apprenticeship standards for trades and industries. Trade tests have been developed and approved by the council, and it organizes training programs. Committees of the council have been formed to promote and oversee training programs in different occupations. Specific standards of skill and apprenticeship requirements have been prescribed under the act for the construction and metal trades and for printing, automotive, mechanical, and furniture-making occupations.

The Workmens' Compensation Act 1964 (Chapter 94) makes an employer liable to pay compensation on a prescribed scale for any accidental injury suffered by an employee arising out of and during employment. Compensation is payable notwithstanding that the worker was at the time of the accident acting contrary to any statutory or other regulation applicable to the employment, or to any orders given by the employer; however, there is no liability if the injury does not incapacitate the worker for at least three days from earning full wages, or if the injury was caused by the serious and willful misconduct of the worker. The act also provides for payment of compensation to a worker who is suffering from a work-related disease that causes disability or death. If an employee dies from a work-related injury or illness, the worker's dependents may obtain up to four years' salary as compensation; in the case of total disability, a worker is entitled to up to five years' salary.

If compensation is not paid by the employer, proceedings under the act can be brought by a worker in a Magistrates' Court to enforce payment. A judgment in common law proceedings is a bar to proceedings under the act, and a judgment in proceedings under the act is a bar to proceedings at common law.

The Industrial Associations Act 1941 (Chapter 95) and the Trade Unions Act 1964 (Chapter 96) provide for the registration by the administrator-general of organizations of employers and/or employees and of trade unions, provided their objects are not unlawful or in conflict with the acts. Once registered, an industrial association or a trade union becomes a body corporate, but neither it nor its officers or members are liable for any tortious act. Nor are they liable for any act done in furtherance of an industrial or trade dispute merely on the ground that such action induces a breach of contract of employment or interferes with the trade, business, or employment of another person. The Registrar of Trade Unions may suspend or cancel the registration of an industrial association or trade union on certain grounds specified in the acts, particularly that one of its objects has become unlawful, or that the group has willfully and after notice contravened any provision of the acts.

Under the acts, neither the employer nor any other person may make nonmembership in an industrial association or trade union a condition of employment.

A trade union is entitled under the Trade Unions (Recognition) Act 1976 (Chapter 96A) to be recognized as the collective bargaining agent for a group of employees if the union has the support of at least 50 percent of those employees. Recognized unions may have dues from their members deducted from members' wages and paid directly to the unions.

The Trade Disputes Act 1973 (Chapter 97) provides for the resolution of any dispute or difference between employers and employees or between groups of employees, except that such disputes in the sugar industry are not trade disputes unless the minister responsible so prescribes. The Permanent Secretary of Labour may endeavor to investigate the cause of the dispute or conciliate the parties, or the minister may appoint a board of inquiry. If a settlement cannot be reached, the minister may refer the dispute to the permanent arbitrator or to an arbitration tribunal with the consent of the parties or without their consent (1) if there is a strike or lockout that has been declared unlawful, (2) if the trade dispute involves an essential service or may jeopardize essentials of life of a significant part of the nation, or (3) if the dispute may endanger the public safety or life of the community. A strike or lockout may be declared unlawful by the minister if he or she is satisfied that all practicable means of reaching a settlement have been exhausted. Such a declaration may not remain in force for longer than a forty-two-day cooling-off period after the dispute is referred to the permanent secretary.

The Wages Council Act 1957 (Chapter 98) authorizes the Minister of Labour to establish wages councils in relation to any trade, industry, or occupation in Fiji. Such councils may make proposals to the minister for fixing the wages and the holidays for the trade, industry, or occupation, and the minister must either accept the proposals or refer them to the council for reconsideration with appropriate comments. A proposal accepted by the minister is embodied in a wages regulation order. Wages councils have been established for the hotel and catering trades, manufacturing, printing trades, road transport, saw milling, and the wholesale and retail trades. In mid-1991, the government announced that it would move away from the system of regulated wage fixing and toward unregulated collective bargaining between employers and groups of employees.

The Factories Act 1971 (Chapter 99) regulates conditions of employment to protect the health, safety, and welfare of people employed in factories and other industrial and construction sites, but not offices or retail premises. The act authorizes the appointment of inspectors with powers to inspect premises and make orders prohibiting the use of anything involving imminent danger of grave bodily injury. Inspectors can also apply to a Magistrates' Court for a prohibition order if a factory is operating without due regard to the safety, health, and welfare of persons employed in the factory. The minister is authorized to make regulations for the welfare, safety, and health of workers in factories and has in fact made a number of such regulations.

Similar but less extensive regulations apply to employment in wholesale and retail premises under the Shop (Regulation of Hours and Employment) Act 1964 (Chapter 100), which also prescribes mandatory shop-closing hours. These hours are subject to variation by actions of the city, town council, or township board in each municipality. The Sunday Observance Decree 1989 prohibits business and commercial activity, public entertainment and sporting events, and public meetings or processions on Sunday. The decree does not, however, apply to restaurants, tourist hotels, or a variety of essential services, nor does it prohibit participation in necessary agricultural work, religious activity, or picnics, barbecues, and other purely social gatherings. Activities otherwise prohibited by the decree may be carried on if a permit or exemption is obtained.

XXI. Industrial and Intellectual Property Rights

Copyright in Fiji is regulated by the Copyright Act 1956 (UK), which was extended to Fiji, subject to some modifications, by the Copyright (Fiji) Order-in-Council 1961. The British act's effect is also modified by the Copyright (Broadcasting of Gramophone Records) Act 1972 (Chapter 244), which provides that radio or television broadcasts by the Fiji Broadcasting Commission do not constitute breaches of copyright.

The Performers Protection Act 1966 (Chapter 243) prohibits the recording, filming, or broadcasting of any performance of acting, singing, playing music, dancing, or fire walking without the consent of the performers unless for private and domestic use and not for sale or any commercial purpose.

The Patents Act 1879 (Chapter 239) provides for patents to be granted to the inventors of any new manufacture or process of manufacture and any new methods of application or improvements of known processes. The grant of a patent confers the exclusive right of making, using, and selling the invention for a period of fourteen years. Application for a patent is made to the Administrator General, who issues a provisional certificate and requires public notification of the application. If there is no opposition to the application, the patent may be granted unless the invention is of no utility, is not a new invention, is not the invention of the applicant, or unless the application contains a willfully false statement. Patents issued in the United Kingdom may be registered in Fiji if there is no opposition and continue in force so long as the patent remains in force in the United Kingdom.

The Trade Marks Act 1933 (Chapter 240) provides for applications for registered trademarks to be made to the Administrator General and then advertised publicly. If there is no opposition, the trademark may be registered for a period of fourteen years, subject to renewal for further periods of fourteen years. Registration of a trademark confers on the proprietor the exclusive right to use it in connection with the goods for which it is registered.

Trademarks registered in the United Kingdom may be registered in Fiji on presentation of a certificate from the Comptroller General of the United Kingdom Patents Office.

The Merchandise Marks Act 1933 (Chapter 241) makes it an offense for a person to forge a trademark; falsely apply to goods a trademark or a similar mark calculated to deceive; make, have possession of, or dispose of any die or machine for the purpose of forging a trademark; make any false description of the quantity, weight, country of origin, mode of manufacture, composition, or ingredients of goods, or falsely state that the goods are the subject of an existing patent, privilege, or copyright.

XXII. Legal Education and Profession

The legal profession in Fiji as of 1987 comprised approximately 150 legal practitioners, mostly Indians. Since then, many of the Indian practitioners have left the country, and there is a shortage of legal personnel, especially within the government.

The profession is regulated by the Legal Practitioners' Act 1965 (Chapter 254). The act requires that any person wishing to practice law must be admitted to practice as a barrister and solicitor by the Chief Justice. The decision of the Chief Justice is not appealable.[46] The requirements for admission prescribed by the act include at least one year's practice on one's own account, study in the office of a barrister or solicitor, or a course of practical legal instruction approved by the Chief Justice. A law degree is also normally required for admission. The act generally requires applicants for admission who have not been practicing in Fiji to be citizens of a Commonwealth country and to have been admitted in the United Kingdom, Ireland, Australia, New Zealand, Papua New Guinea, Malaysia, Singapore, Sri Lanka, or Nigeria.[47] Admission pro hac vice is also available if the foreign practitioner appears with a person admitted to practice in Fiji.[48]

The Legal Practitioners' Act also establishes the Fiji Law Society and a disciplinary committee appointed by the Chief Justice from a panel nominated by the Law Society. Membership in the Law Society is mandatory. The disciplinary committee investigates complaints against barristers and solicitors, and if it finds the complaint justified, the committee may censure the offender, impose a fine, suspend from practice for a period not exceeding three years, or strike the practitioner's name off the roll. An appeal from a decision of the disciplinary committee lies to the Chief Justice.

Under the Barristers and Solicitors (Practice) Rules, lawyers may not advertise and may not, except in pro bono or legal aid matters, charge fees below those set out in regulations. Lawyers may not appear on behalf of companies or associations of which they are directors or salaried officers.

A. Legal Aid

Under the Legal Aid Act 1968 (Chapter 15), indigent criminal defendants and indigent parties in matrimonial proceedings may receive legal assistance. Once the registrar or clerk of the relevant court has certified a person as legally indigent, that person may choose to have the court appoint a lawyer or to receive a "legal aid certificate" authorizing the engagement of counsel directly. Lawyers taking legal aid cases receive payment, at prescribed rates below those prevailing in the commercial legal market, from the registrar of the High Court. There is no public solicitor's office or other agency generally providing legal representation to indigent persons, and the Legal Aid Act is used only to provide counsel in the most serious cases. Most indigent defendants in criminal cases—and virtually all poor litigants in civil cases—are not represented by counsel.[49]

B. Legal Education

Fiji has no law school, although the University of the South Pacific authorized the establishment of a regional law faculty. The Law Society undertakes refresher training programs for the profession. Students who wish to obtain a law degree have had to travel to Australia, New Zealand, or Papua New Guinea or outside the Pacific region, or enroll for an external law degree. The Pacific Law Unit of the University of the South Pacific, located in Vanuatu, provides an extension program for a certificate and diploma in legal studies for students in Fiji, as elsewhere in the university region.

XXIII. Research Guide

A. Official Materials

The 1990 Constitution has been published in a pamphlet edition by the Government Printer, Suva. Statutes and regulations in effect as of December 31, 1985, are collected in the fourteen-volume *Laws of Fiji*, 1985 edition, published by the Government Printer in 1987. In addition, there is an annual volume of Fiji laws for 1986. For the period from 1987 to the present, decrees of regulations are available only in the *Royal Fiji Gazette* (through September 1987), the *Fiji Gazette* (October–December 1987), and the *Fiji Republic Gazette* (from December 1987 onward). The Government Printer has also published a *General Index to the Laws of Fiji*, which is up to date as of May 1987.

Selected court judgments for the period 1875–1975 are available in the twenty-one-volume *Fiji Law Reports*. Judgments after 1975 in the Supreme Court and Court of Appeal, and after 1987 in the High Court, Fiji Court of Appeal, and Supreme Court, are available directly from the registrars of those courts. A virtually complete collection of judgments for 1975–1987 is also available in the Pacific Law Collection at the Michael Somare Library, University of Papua New Guinea. A new series of *Fiji Law Reports*, covering the post-1975 period, is being prepared by the Supreme Court registrar in Suva. In addition, digests and summaries of significant decisions are published in *Fiji Law Talk*, a quarterly digest issued by a committee headed by the Director of Public Prosecutions. Selected Fiji cases are also reported in *South Pacific Law Reports*, beginning in 1987.

A number of government agencies, including the Department of Law, the office of the ombudsman, and the Law Reform Commission, issue annual reports.

B. Books, Law Reviews and Journals, and Occasional Papers

An overall summary of available legal materials, up to date through 1985, is N. K. F. O'Neill, "Sources and Literature of the Law of Fiji," [1986] *Lawasia* 1.

1. CONSTITUTIONAL LAW AND HISTORY

Ali, A. "Fiji: The Arrival of the Communal Franchise," 1 *J. Pacific Studies* 20 (1975).
———. "Fiji: From Colony to Independence—Constitutional Changes 1874–1970," 10 *J. Constitutional and Parliamentary Studies* 27 (1976).
———. "Problems of Constitution-Making in Fiji," 4 *Pacific Perspective* 74 (1975).
Davidson, J. W. "Constitutional Change in Fiji," 1 *J. Pacific History* 165 (1966).
Ghai, Y, and J. Cottrell. *Heads of State in the Pacific*. Suva: Institute of Pacific Studies, 1990.
Hookey, J. F. "The Fiji Constitution of 1970," 1(2) *Melanesian Law J.* 38 (1971).
Islam, M. R. "The Proposed Constitutional Guarantee of Governmental Power in Fiji: an International Legal Appraisal," 19 *Calif. Western International Law J.* 120 (1989).
Mataitoga, I. "Constitution-Making in Fiji: The Search for a Practical Solution," 21 *Victoria University of Wellington Law Rev.* 221 (1991).
———. "Judicial Law Reform: Fijian Style," 12(1) *Pacific Perspective* 73 (1985).
Murray, D. J. "The Governor-General in Fiji's Constitutional Crisis," 13 *Politics* 230 (1978).
Premdas, R. "Constitutional Challenge: the Rise of Fijian Nationalism," 9(2) *Pacific Perspective* 30 (1980).
Vasil, R. K. "Communalism and Constitution-Making in Fiji," 45 *Pacific Affairs* 21 (1972).
Whitelaw, J. S. "Constitutional Change in Fiji," 74 *J. of the Polynesian Society* 503 (1965).

2. HUMAN RIGHTS

Aikman, H. "Public Order and the Bill of Rights in Fiji: *R. v Butadroga*," 11 *Victoria Univ. of Wellington Law Rev.* 169 (1981).
Johnson, M. "That Part of the New Fiji Constitution That Enables Them to Sweep Away All Those 'Guarantees,' " [August 1990] *Islands Business* 22.
Mataitoga, L. "Human Rights and the Supreme Court in Fiji: *Butadroga* Revisited," [1985] *New Zealand Law J.* 58.
Palmer, A. "State Ideology and National Security in Fiji," [1989] *Australasian Law Students J.* 45.

3. LAND AND CUSTOMARY LAW

France, P. *The Charter of the Land* (Melbourne: Oxford Univesity Press, 1969).
Kamikamica, J. N. "Fiji: Making Native Land Productive," in R. Crocombe, ed. *Land Tenure in the Pacific* (Suva: University of the South Pacific 3d ed., 1987).
Kamikamica, J. N., and T. L. Davey. "Trust on Trial: the Development of the Customary Land Trust Concept in Fiji," in Y. Ghai, ed. *Law, Politics and Government in the Pacific Island States*. Suva: University of the South Pacific, 1988.
Knox-Mawer, R. K. "Native Courts and Customs in Fiji," 10 *International & Comparative Law Q.* 642 (1961).
MacNaught, T. J. "Chiefly Civil Servants: Ambiguity in a District Administration and the Preservation of the Fijian Way of Life," 9 *J. Pacific History* 3 (1976).
Moynagh, M. "Land Tenure in Fiji's Sugar Cane Districts," 13 *J. Pacific History* 53 (1978).

O'Neill, N.K.F. "The Indigenous Fijians and the Fiji Legal System," 2 *Law & Anthropology* 405 (1987).
Rutz, H. J. "Fijian Land Tenure and Agricultural Growth," 49 *Oceania* 20 (1978).

4. THE 1987 COUPS

Brookfield, F. M. "The Fiji Revolution of 1987," [1988] *New Zealand Law J.* 250.
Dean, E., and S. Ritova. *Rabuka: No Other Way*. Sydney: Doubleday, 1988.
Ghai, Y. "A Coup by Any Other Name?" 2(1) *Contemporary Pacific* 11 (1990).
Hagan, S. "Race, Politics and the Coup in Fiji," 19(4) *Bull. of Concerned Asian Scholars* 2 (1987).
Harder, C. *The Guns of Lautoka*. Auckland: Sunshine Press, 1988.
Howard, M. C. "Fiji After the First Coup," 4(2) *South Pacific Forum* 180 (1987).
Islam, M. R. "The Recognition of the Revolutionary Regime of Fiji by Papua New Guinea," 16 *Melanesian Law J.* 75 (1988).
Kaplan, M. "The Coups in Fiji: Colonial Contradictions and the Post-Colonial Crisis," 8(3) *Critique of Anthropology* 93 (1988).
Kiwanuka, R. N. "On Revolution and Legality in Fiji," 37 *International & Comparative Law Q* 961 (1988).
Lal, B. V. *Power and Prejudice: The Making of the Fiji Crisis*. Wellington: New Zealand Institute of International Affairs, 1988.
Lawson, S. "Fiji's Communal Electoral System: a Study of Some Aspects of the Failure of Democratic Politics in Fiji," 23(2) *Politics* 35 (1988).
McLachlan, D. "The Fiji Constitutional Crisis of May, 1987: a Legal Assessment," [1987] *New Zealand Law J.* 175.
Ravuvu, A. *The Facade of Democracy: Fijian Struggles for Political Control 1830–1987*. Suva: Reader Pub., 1991.
Scarr, D. *Fiji: The Politics of Illusion*. Kensington: New South Wales University Press, 1988.

3. Kiribati

MARTIN TSAMENYI

I. Dateline

1000 B.C.	Austronesian-speaking people (probably from New Hebrides) settle the islands now comprising Kiribati.
1866	United Kingdom declares protectorate over Gilbert and Ellice Islands.
1883	British government enacts the Pacific Order-in-Council. Legislative authority over the islands vested in the High Commissioner, judicial power in the High Commissioner's Court for the Western Pacific.
1900	Banaba (Ocean Island) becomes part of the Protectorate of the Gilbert and Ellice Islands.
1916	Protectorate of the Gilbert and Ellice Islands transformed into a British Crown colony.
1919	Kiritimati Island becomes part of the colony.
1938–1939	United States claims jurisdiction over Canton and Enderbury Islands. In 1939, Britain and the United States reach an agreement for joint administration of the islands.
1962	The High Commissioner's Court for the Western Pacific reconstituted as the High Court for the Western Pacific. A resident judge and magistrates appointed to the colony.
1963	The Gilbert and Ellice Islands Order 1963 provides for an Executive Council.
1967	House of Representatives established.
1970	Legislative Council established.
1971	Under the Gilbert and Ellice Islands (Amendment) Order 1971, the government of the colony is separated from the High Commission for the Western Pacific. The office of Governor established in place of that of Resident Commissioner.
1974	The Gilbert and Ellice Island Order 1974 provides for a Council of Ministers and ministerial form of executive government and replaces the House of Representatives with a House of Assembly, or Maneaba.
1974–1975	Following a referendum in 1974, the Ellice and Gilbert Islands are made into separate colonies by the Gilbert Islands Order-in-Council 1975, which also provides a Constitution for the Gilberts.
1977	Internal self-government granted to the Gilberts.
1979	On July 12, Gilbert Islands become independent under a new Constitution as the Republic of Kiribati.

II. Historical, Cultural, and Economic Survey

Kiribati is a republic composed of thirty-three atolls lying astride the equator in the Central Pacific. The country consists of three main island groupings—the Gilberts proper, Phoenix, and Northern and Southern Line Islands. The national capital, Tarawa, is located on the island of Tarawa, where almost one third of the country's total population of more than 72,000 now reside, although in 1992 the government announced a plan to resettle up to 10 percent of the population on outlying islands. The total land area of Kiribati is about 700 square kilometers. Kiribati's noncontiguous exclusive economic zone (EEZ), covering 3.6 million square kilometers of the Pacific Ocean, is the second largest EEZ in the Pacific islands region. The citizens of Kiribati are known as i-Kiribati.

A. History and Culture

The islands of the Gilbert group have been inhabited for over 3,000 years by people of Micronesian culture. The Phoenix and Line Islands were never permanently inhabited until the period of British colonial rule in the 1880s. The first reported European visitors to the area were Spaniards seeking the fabled wealth of Terra Australis Incognita. Knowledge of the Central Pacific region developed rapidly after the establishment by the British government in 1788 of a penal colony in what is now Australia. In the late eighteenth and early nineteenth century, shipping in the region increased rapidly due to European trade with China and Australia and the development of a whaling industry.

Regular contact with Europeans began around 1840 with the whalers. Trading ships began to visit the islands regularly from 1850. Trade in coconut oil began about 1860, but by the 1870s this had given way to the sale of copra. Between 1860 and 1870, slave traders raided many of the islands and carried away some of the islanders to the South American guano mines and coffee plantations and to Fiji, Tahiti, Hawaii, and Queensland.

In 1882 the United Kingdom declared a protectorate over the Gilbert and Ellice Islands. Both were administered by a Resident Commissioner under the jurisdiction of the Western Pacific High Commission based first in Fiji and later in the Solomon Islands. The two protectorates became a Crown colony of the United Kingdom as the Gilbert and Ellice Islands Colony (GEIC), effective in January 1916.

As a matter of policy, the first colonial institutions in the Gilbert and Ellice Islands were closely modeled on traditional British colonial forms. In an attempt to secure some degree of uniformity, a high chief was made responsible for the good order of the islands. On all islands there was to be a British magistrate, who might act with a jury of kaubure (local government councillors). Only in the event of a murder conviction was reference to the Resident Commissioner mandatory. These structural changes to customary systems of political administration and justice had long-term effects on the Gilberts. In particular, the emergence of the magistrate as the dominant figure in island government was made inevitable by a combination of imperial policy and local perceptions and customs. The chief of the kaubure (local council) emerged as the executive agent of the magistrate. This system of law became increasingly anglicized during the period of British colonial rule, and the present political system of Kiribati grew out of these developments.

The Resident Commissioner, Charles Swayne, collected the laws of the islands, including those enforced by custom and the missions, and devised a common code for both the Gilbert and Ellice groups. Under this code, murder was punishable by death. Theft, assault, rape, adultery, drunkenness, damage to property, and more minor offenses were punished by terms of imprisonment, fines, and, for some second offenses, up to ten lashes.

A series of advisory and legislative bodies prepared the GEIC for self-government. As self-government approached, the controversial issue became whether the Ellice Islands should secede from the Gilbert Islands. In a referendum held in August and September 1974, over 90 percent of the Ellice Islanders favored separation from the Gilbert Islands. The main argument for separate status for the Ellice Islands was that the Gilbertese, comprising about 86 percent of the population of the GEIC, would dominate the Ellice Islanders at independence. This argument was reinforced by cultural differences between the two groups. The Ellice Islanders are predominantly Polynesians while the Gilbertese are Micronesians. Contrary to trends in decolonization in the 1960s and 1970s, the United Kingdom agreed to divide the Gilbert and Ellice Islands into the two separate colonies, which became the independent states of Kiribati and Tuvalu.

B. Economy

Before independence, the export economy of Kiribati was organized primarily around phosphate extraction. In 1975, for example, phosphates accounted for about 96.4 percent of total export earnings. However, the country's phosphate reserves were depleted by 1979, the year of independence, and as a result, the economic prospects of Kiribati became very bleak. At present, the only major exportable resources of Kiribati are the fisheries located in its EEZ.

III. Sources of Law

A. Constitution

The principal source of law in Kiribati is the Constitution. Any other law that is inconsistent with it is, to the extent of the inconsistency, void (Constituton, Chapter I, Section 2). The Constitution regulates human rights and fundamental freedoms, citizenship, the executive and legislative powers of the state, the judiciary, the public service, and state finance. The High Court of Kiribati is granted jurisdiction to provide relief to persons injured by acts in contravention of the Constitution (Chapter II, Section 17, and Chapter VI, Section 88).

The power to amend the Constitution is vested in the Kiribati legislature, called the Maneaba (which means traditional council of elders). A bill to amend the Constitution cannot be passed unless consideration of it is deferred, after its first reading, to the next meeting of the Maneaba and unless the bill is supported by a two-thirds vote of all the members. An act to alter the provisions on fundamental rights and freedoms (Chapter II of the Constitution) must be supported at a referendum by a two-thirds vote of all persons registered as voters in a general election (Constitution, Chapter V, Section 69). The provisions in Chapter IX of the Constitution relating to Banaba (Ocean Island) and the Banabans may be amended only after three readings in the Maneaba and two votes, at both of which the bill must receive the support of two-thirds of the members of the Maneaba and every member from Banaba (Chapter IX, Section 124).

B. Statutes

The second source of law in Kiribati is statutory. All actions of the Maneaba must be in the form of bills, which become acts when assented to by the President (Beretitenti). The Beretitenti may withhold assent only if, in his or her opinion, the bill, if assented to, would be inconsistent with the Constitution. Conflict between the Beretitenti and the Maneaba as to whether a bill is consistent with the Constitution is resolved by the High Court of Kiribati (Constitution, Chapter V, Section 66).

The Kiribati government is supporting a project to determine which of the legislation inherited from the United Kingdom is part of the law of Kiribati. One result of this project was the enactment in 1989 of the Laws of Kiribati Act, which declares what constitutes laws of Kiribati and the relationship among laws from different sources. Under the Laws of Kiribati Act, the Arbitration Act, and the Aircraft Security Act of the United Kingdom have been made applicable to Kiribati. As of mid-1991, steps had been taken to apply three other U.K. statutes: the Partnership Act, the Sale of Goods Act, and the Criminal Law and Procedure Act.

C. Common Law

The third source of law in Kiribati is common law. The Constitution contains no mention of common law, but Section 42 of the Magistrates' Courts Ordinance 1977, enacted two years before the effective date of the Constitution, required Magistrates' Courts to apply "the substance of the English common law and doctrines of equity" except where they conflicted with local circumstances. The Laws of Kiribati Act contains similar provisions.

D. Custom

Another source of law in Kiribati is customary law. In the preamble to the Constitution, the people of Kiribati pledge to cherish and uphold their customs and traditions. Section 5 of the Laws of Kiribati Act 1989 (based largely on Papua New Guinea's Customs Recognition Act) provides for the recognition and application of custom by the courts. In practice, customary law tends to be recognized and applied primarily in relation to criminal defenses, land, marriage, succession, adoption, and personal law generally.

The recognition of local custom by the Maneaba is illustrated by the Medical and Dental Practitioners (Amendment) Act 1981, which provides at Section 37 that "Nothing in this ordinance shall affect the right of I-Kiribati to practise in a responsible manner Kiribati traditional healing by means of herbal therapy, bone-setting and massage, and to demand and recover reasonable charges in respect of such practice." The only limitation on traditional medical practice is that the practitioner may not take or use any name, title, addition, or description likely to induce anyone to believe that he or she is qualified to practice medicine or surgery according to nontraditional methods. Other statutes, including the Native Land Ordinance, recognize custom for specific purposes.

Customary law is subject to the Constitution and statutes. The Magistrates' Courts Act provides at Section 42, "Nothing in this Ordinance shall deprive any magistrates' court of the right to observe . . . any local law or custom not being repugnant to natural justice, equity and good conscience, and not incompatible either directly or by necessary implication with any Ordinance or other law for the time being in force." The judiciary has interpreted this provision to mean that custom prevails over the common law.[1] The courts have generally been willing to apply custom, provided the existence of the custom can be established. For example, in *Ibeibe Tebwebwe v. R.*, the appellant raised as a defense to a murder conviction that custom had impelled him to fight the victim.[2] The appeal was dismissed on the grounds that evidence did not support the existence of this custom. If the appellant had established the existence of the custom, the court would have taken judicial notice of it.[3]

E. International Law

The Constitution is silent on the status of international law within the Kiribati legal system. The approach taken by most common law countries is that rules of international law embodied in treaties form part of the domestic law when such treaties have been implemented by acts of parliament. This approach has been adopted by Kiribati.

IV. Constitutional System

The Constitution of Kiribati came into existence at independence in 1979. The Constitution was conferred by the United Kingdom in that it is contained in United Kingdom Orders-in-Council. Kiribati is a sovereign democratic republic (Constitution, Chapter I, Section 1) with a popularly elected Beretitenti (President) who is both Head of State and head of government. The Beretitenti is responsible to the Maneaba, which may dismiss him or her.

A. Territory

Schedule 2 to the Constitution describes the territory of Kiribati as comprising thirty-three islands, together with all small islands, islets, rocks, and reefs depending on them. Kiribati has declared a 12-nautical-mile territorial sea under the Marine Zones (Declaration) Act 1983 in accordance with current international law.

B. Nationality and Citizenship

Chapter III of the Constitution governs citizenship. Kiribati citizenship may be acquired in four ways. The first relates to persons who are of i-Kiribati descent and who, before independence, were citizens of the United Kingdom and its colonies. They became citizens of Kiribati at independence if they were born in Kiribati or if they had a father who was born in Kiribati. People not of i-Kiribati descent were also eligible to become citizens at independence if they were born in Kiribati and were citizens of the United Kingdom and its colonies or if they had become British subjects while resident in Kiribati.

The second way Kiribati citizenship may be acquired covers persons born after independence. Everyone born in Kiribati becomes a citizen by birth unless their fathers are diplomatic agents and neither of their parents are citizens of Kiribati, or their fathers are citizens of a country with which Kiribati is at war, or they are not of i-Kiribati descent and they are registered as citizens of another country. Persons born outside Kiribati after independence are citizens if their fathers (or, if they are born out of wedlock, their mothers) are or would, but for their death, have been citizens of Kiribati.

The third form of citizenship is by application for registration as a citizen. This category includes people of i-Kiribati descent born before independence who did not become citizens at independence and women who, after independence, marry persons who are or become citizens of Kiribati. The Maneaba may make provision for other classes of persons to obtain citizenship by registration.

The Citizenship Ordinance provides a fourth way that citizenship may be obtained. A child adopted under any valid law in Kiribati is a citizen of Kiribati if the adoptive parent is a citizen of Kiribati. Also, persons of full age and capacity may apply to the Citizenship Commission to become Kiribati citizens by naturalization. To qualify for naturalization, the applicant must:

1. be ordinarily resident in Kiribati for a period of seven years immediately prior to the date of application;
2. intend to continue to reside in Kiribati;

3. be of good character;
4. be able to speak and understand Kiribati sufficiently for normal conversational purposes (unless prevented by physical or mental disability);
5. have respect for the customs and traditions of Kiribati;
6. have means of support;
7. have a reasonable knowledge and understanding of the rights, privileges, responsibilities, and duties of citizenship;
8. have renounced any other citizenship the person possesses; and
9. have taken and subscribed to the oath of allegiance.

The Citizenship Ordinance also provides for the loss or renunciation of Kiribati citizenship. A citizen who is not of i-Kiribati descent loses his or her nationality in the following circumstances:

1. obtaining the nationality or citizenship of another country by a voluntary act;
2. willfully exercising a right that is exclusive to nationals or citizens of another country;
3. taking an oath or making a declaration of allegiance to another country or to the sovereign or head of state of another country;
4. doing any act (other than marriage) by which the person becomes a national and citizen of another country;
5. serving in the armed forces of another country without the approval of the Beretitenti;
6. voting in a national, provincial, state, or local election, or accepting elective office, in another country.

Kiribati citizens who are of full age and full capacity may renounce their citizenship, but not unless the person already holds some other nationality or citizenship or the renunciation is for the purpose of obtaining some other nationality or citizenship. During time of war, citizenship may not be renounced without the prior consent of the responsible minister.

To a limited extent, the Constitution prohibits dual nationality for people who are not descendants of i-Kiribati. Any person not of i-Kiribati descent, who became eighteen years old before independence or became a citizen by birth and was also a national of some other country at independence, ceased to be a national of Kiribati after two years unless the other nationality was renounced or lost.

Deprivation of Kiribati citizenship is governed by the Citizenship (Amendment) Act 1986. A person not of i-Kiribati descent who became a citizen by adoption or naturalization may be deprived of citizenship if the minister in charge of citizenship is satisfied that it is in the public interest. An order by the minister to deprive someone of Kiribati citizenship is not justiciable.

C. Government

1. NATIONAL GOVERNMENT

a. Head of State

The Beretitenti is the Head of State and head of government (Constitution, Chapter IV, Section 30). The election of the Head of State is governed by Chapter IV of the Constitution and the Election of the Beretitenti Act, which provide for nomination by the Maneaba of three or four candidates from its members, followed by an election by the general electorate. On election, the Beretitenti vacates the electoral seat, but remains a member of the Maneaba as Beretitenti. A by-election is held to elect a new member of the Maneaba from the Beretitenti's district.

The Beretitenti serves a four-year term, and may be reelected twice. The term will be shortened if the Beretitenti resigns, or if a motion of no confidence is supported by an absolute majority in the Maneaba, the government is defeated in the Maneaba on an issue decided by the Beretitenti to be an issue of confidence, the Beretitenti ceases to be a member of the Maneaba, or the Maneaba determines, on the advice of qualified medical practitioners, that the Beretitenti is incapable of serving (Constitution, Chapter IV, Sections 33 and 34). If the Beretitenti vacates office because of a no-confidence vote or defeat on an issue of confidence, the Maneaba is dissolved and new general elections held, until which the executive functions of the government are performed by a Council of State consisting of the chair of the Public Service Commission, the Chief Justice, and the Speaker (Constitution, Chapter IV, Sections 35 and 49). Otherwise, the Kauoman-ni-Beretitenti (the Vice President, who is appointed by the Beretitenti) performs the duties of the office and may be confirmed as Beretitenti to fill out the remainder of the term (Constitution, Chapter IV, Section 35). If the Maneaba does not confirm the Vice President as Beretitenti, new elections for Beretitenti must be held before any bills can be considered (Section 35).

b. Executive

The Constitution vests executive authority collectively in the Cabinet (Constitution, Chapter IV, Section 45). The Cabinet consists of the Beretitenti, the Kauoman-ni-Beretitenti, and up to eight other ministers, all of whom are appointed from the Maneaba by the Beretitenti, who allocates portfolios (Constitution, Chapter IV, Sections 39 and 40). Ministers, as well as the Kauoman-ni-Beretitenti, vacate their positions by resignation or if they cease to be members of the Maneaba or are removed by the Beretitenti, if the office of Beretitenti changes hands, or if the government is defeated on a no-confidence vote or on a bill designated as a confidence issue (Constitution, Chapter IV, Section 41).

The Attorney General, who must be a lawyer, is also a Cabinet member and is appointed and may be removed only by the Beretitenti (Constitution, Chapter IV, Section 42). The Attorney General acts as the government's principal legal adviser and as director of prosecutions. A bill to deprive the Attorney General of Cabinet rank was defeated in the Maneaba in 1991.

c. Legislature

Chapter V, Section 52, of the Constitution establishes the Kiribati legislature, a single chamber known as the Maneaba ni Maungatabu (often translated as Great House of Assembly). The Maneaba has the power to make laws "for the peace, order and good government" of Kiribati (Constitution, Chapter V, Section 66).

The Maneaba consists of thirty-nine elected members in addition to the Beretitenti, a member nominated by the Rabi Island Council in Fiji to represent Banabans, and (if he or she is not an elected member) the Attorney General (Constitution, Chapter V, Section 53).

The Maneaba continues for four years after each general election, unless dissolved sooner (Constitution, Chapter V, Section 78). Members are elected from twenty-three electoral districts (some of which elect more than one member). Electors must be citizens, aged eighteen or older, and residents of the district in which they vote. Persons may not vote while serving a prison term of twelve months or more, if they are insane or of unsound mind, or if they have committed an election offense (Constitution, Chapter V, Section 64). Candidates for election must be at least twenty-one years old and citizens (Constitution, Chapter V, Section 55). Persons are disqualified from serving if they acknowledge adherence to any other state, are insane or of unsound mind, have been sentenced to death or are serving a prison sentence of twelve months or more, have committed election offenses, or hold public office or an office with responsibility for the conduct of elections (Constitution, Chapter V, Section 56).

Members serve until the next general election, unless they resign earlier, are continually absent from Maneaba sittings, cease to be citizens, are sentenced to death or imprisonment, become disqualified to serve, are the subject of a referendum in their district in which a majority of those entitled to vote in the referendum vote for removal, and unless the Maneaba is dissolved (Constitution, Chapter V, Sections 57–59). Dissolution of the Maneaba occurs when a vote of no confidence wins an absolute majority or a bill the Beretitenti has designated as a confidence issue is defeated in the Maneaba (Constitution, Chapter V, Section 78).

The Maneaba elects a Speaker from among persons who are not members of the Maneaba. A quorum is half the membership and, unless otherwise required, bills pass on a vote of a majority of members present and voting (Constitution, Chapter V, Sections 71–74). Members of the Maneaba may introduce bills, except financial bills, the introduction of which requires Cabinet sanction (Constitution, Chapter V, Section 68). All bills, other than those certified as urgent by the government, must be read at two separate meetings unless the Maneaba, by an absolute majority, vote to waive that requirement. The Constitution requires at Chapter V, Section 66 that the Beretitenti give assent to all bills but provides that the Beretitenti can withhold assent and return the bill if the Beretitenti believes that the bill is unconstitutional. If the Maneaba then refuses to amend the bill, the Beretitenti must either assent or refer the question of the bill's constitutionality to the High Court, whose decision is binding.

d. Judiciary

The Constitution and statutes provide for a judicial system consisting of Magistrates' Courts, a High Court, and a Court of Appeal.

(i) High Court

The High Court, established under Chapter VI, Section 80 of the Constitution, is a superior court of record. The Court has unlimited original jurisdiction, including original jurisdiction in constitutional matters (Constitution, Chapter VI, Section 88). The High Court also supervises lower courts. It may consist of the Chief Justice and as many other judges as statutes prescribe. The Chief Justice is appointed by the Beretitenti with the advice of Cabinet; other judges are appointed by the Beretitendi with the advice of the Chief Justice sitting with the Public Service Commission. Judges must have practiced law for five years or held judicial office in another country. They may be removed earlier than their appointed term only for cause (Constitution, Chapter VI, Section 81).

(ii) Court of Appeal

Chapter VI, Section 90 of the Constitution establishes a Court of Appeal, with appellate jurisdiction for civil, criminal, and constitutional cases that have been considered by the High Court, including, since a 1990 amendment to the Magistrates' Courts Ordinance, cases from the Land Courts. Constitutional cases that relate to the Banabans, however, are appealable directly to the Judicial Committee of the Privy Council in England. Judges of the Court of Appeal are the Chief Justice, who acts as president, other judges of the High Court, if any, and may also include temporary appointments of judges or lawyers from other countries. They may be removed only for cause (Constitution, Chapter VI, Sections 91 and 93).

(iii) Magistrates' Courts

There are twenty-four Magistrates' Courts (each consisting of three magistrates) hearing civil and criminal cases. Their jurisdiction is original and limited to civil cases where the amount of damages does not exceed A$3,000 and to criminal matters where the maximum punishment does not exceed five years' imprisonment and a fine of A$500. The Magistrates' Courts also have extensive original jurisdiction in a number of areas, including the probate of wills made by i-Kiribati, customary adoption, divorce, patrimony, and support. Another twenty-two Magistrates' Courts (each consisting of five magistrates) deal with disputes over land. These courts are informally called Land Courts. The Magistrates' Courts, established under the Magistrates' Courts Ordinance 1977, are courts of record, and have regional jurisdiction. Appeals from the magistrates' courts lie, in most civil and criminal matters, to a single judge of the High Court. In matters concerning land, divorce, and inheritance, appeals lie to the High Court's land division, which consists of a judge and two lands appeal magistrates.

2. LOCAL GOVERNMENT

The Local Government Act authorizes the Minister for Local Government to create local government councils. There are currently nineteen local councils, including town or urban councils. Local councils are composed of elected members who serve for three years. In addition, serving as ex officio members are members of the Maneaba for electoral districts the whole or part of which lie within the area of authority of the council, and, in rural areas, government medical officers resident in the area. The minister, after consultation with the council, may appoint additional persons to the councils.

The functions of the councils as set out in Part V of the Local Government Act include the prevention of crimes within their areas of authority and responsibility for agriculture, education, housing, health, trade, and commerce. The councils also have power to borrow money and raise revenue to finance their projects through the imposition of head taxes, land taxes, license fees, and rent.

D. Emergency Powers

Chapter II, Section 16 of the Constitution regulates the declaration of public emergencies. A public emergency is any period when Kiribati is at war or a proclamation under the Constitution declaring a public emergency is in force. The Constitution gives to the Beretitenti the power to declare that a state of public emergency exists and to make regulations for the emergency. This power is to be exercised in accordance with the advice of the Cabinet. A proclamation of public emergency, if not revoked, ceases to have effect three days after the date of publication unless the Maneaba approves it by resolution.

The Constitution allows certain human rights to be derogated from during periods of public emergency. These rights include the protection of personal liberty, the prohibition against forced labor, protection of privacy of home and property, freedom of conscience, freedom of expression, freedom of assembly and association, freedom of movement, and freedom from discrimination. Some limited protection is afforded by the Constitution to people detained during periods of public emergency.

E. Human Rights

The "fundamental rights and freedoms" protected by Chapter II of the Constitution are the following:

1. the right to life;
2. the right to personal liberty;
3. freedom from slavery and forced labor;

4. freedom from inhuman treatment;
5. freedom from deprivation of property;
6. the right to privacy of home and other property;
7. the right to the protection of the law;
8. freedom of conscience;
9. freedom of expression;
10. freedom of assembly and association;
11. freedom of movement;
12. freedom from discrimination on grounds of nationality, race, religion, and so on.

Significant limitations are imposed on the scope of these rights and freedoms in the interest of others or the public interest or during a public emergency. Jurisdiction to enforce the fundamental rights and freedoms is vested in the High Court (Constitution, Chapter II, Section 17).

V. Administrative Organization and Law

A. Organization

Kiribati's central government administration is divided into departments and ministries. The Beretitenti currently also supervises the Ministry of Foreign Affairs and the office of Secretary to the Cabinet. Other ministries include Finance, Natural Resources Development, Trade and Industry and Labour, Home Affairs, Education and Training, Communications, Works and Energy, Health and Family Planning, and the Ministry for the Line and Phoenix Group. The latter ministry is responsible for all government services on these island groups with the exception of natural resources, police, and customs. Each ministry is headed by a minister. The day-to-day operations of the ministries are the responsibilities of permanent secretaries appointed by the Beretitenti on the advice of the Public Service Commission.

In addition to the departments and ministries, there are also a number of statutory bodies. These bodies include the National Provident Fund, which administers the country's compulsory retirement fund; the Housing Corporation, which builds houses and gives loans for urban and rural housing; the Public Utilities Board, which provides power and water for South Tarawa; the Shipping Corporation, which provides domestic and international shipping services; Air Tungaru, which provides civil aviation services; the National Loans Board, which provides loans for local business; and the Broadcasting and Publications Authority, which provides national radio and newspaper services. Several of these entities—the Fishing Company, Air Tungaru, the shipping and shipyard facilities, and the Kiribati Oil Company—were, as of mid-1991, converted into government-owned companies, as a first step in a privatization process under which shares in government-owned enterprises will be sold to the general public.

B. Public Service

Government is the chief employer of labor in Kiribati; 70 percent of all employment is in government. Government employment is under the control of the Public Service Commission, which is regulated by Chapter VII of the Constitution.

The Public Service Commission is composed of a chairperson and four other commissioners. The members of the commission are appointed by the Beretitenti, with the advice of the Speaker of the Maneaba and the Chief Justice. Members of the Maneaba and public servants may not serve on the commission. Each commissioner is appointed for three years or for such lesser period as the Beretitenti specifies. The functions of the Public Service Commission include advising the Beretitenti about appointments to public offices, and the removal of and disciplinary control over persons in public office.

C. *Public Finance and Audit*

Chapter VIII of the Constitution regulates public finance. The main provisions can be summarized as follows:

1. No tax can be imposed or altered except by or under law.
2. All revenues of the government must be paid into a consolidated fund or into special funds established by the Maneaba.
3. All monies issued from the consolidated fund must be by authority of the Minister for Finance, who can approve only those expenditures authorized by an appropriations act.
4. Within sixty days after the commencement of every financial year, the Finance Minister must submit a budget to the Maneaba detailing estimates of government revenues and expenditures for that year. The expenditures contained in the budget are to be included in an appropriation bill that must be introduced in the Maneaba.

The Constitution provides at Chapter VII, Section 114 for the establishment of the office of the Director of Audit, whose duty is to audit the public accounts of Kiribati and all departments, offices, courts, and authorities of the government. An audit report must be submitted annually by the director to the Speaker of the Maneaba, who must lay it before the Maneaba. The Director of Audit is not subject to the direction or control of any other person or authority. The functions of the Director of Audit are supplemented by the Public Accounts Committee of the Maneaba established under chapter VII, Section 115 of the Constitution. The committee's three members are elected by the Maneaba from its members.

D. *Rule Making*

The law-making powers of the Maneaba may be delegated to any person or authority, which can make subordinate legislation. All statutory bodies have the power, within the limits of the legislation setting them up, to make subordinate legislation.

E. *Review of Administrative Action*

The exercise of the administrative functions of governmental bodies is limited by the Constitution, relevant statutes, and the common law, which provide generally that the exercise of government authority that directly affects individuals must comport with natural justice or due process. The courts have the power to review the actions of public bodies that impinge on legally recognized interests or that exceed the powers conferred on those bodies.

VI. INTERNATIONAL OBLIGATIONS

Contact with other nations has created for Kiribati certain international obligations in the form of treaties and membership of regional and international organizations. In force to implement these international obligations are several pieces of domestic legislation including the Consular

(Conventions) Act 1977, Diplomatic Privileges Act 1977, Extradition Act 1981, and Civil Aviation Act 1949.

Kiribati is a member of the South Pacific Forum, the Forum Fisheries Agency, the South Pacific Bureau for Economic Cooperation, the South Pacific Commission, the Economic and Social Commission for Asia and the Pacific, the Asian Development Bank, the British Commonwealth, and the United Nations.

Kiribati maintains no diplomatic representation overseas. Its Secretary of Foreign Affairs acts as a roving ambassador. The United Kingdom and Australia each have resident High Commissioners on Tarawa, while diplomats of some other countries, such as New Zealand, the United States, and Canada, who are located in neighboring capitals are accredited to Kiribati.

VII. Revenue Law

The bulk of government revenue is derived from export duties, fishing licenses, foreign aid, and taxation. Tax on the incomes and earnings of i-Kiribati is governed by the Income Tax Act 1990. The act provides for progressive individual income tax rates. Kiribati currently receives foreign aid from countries including Australia, the United Kingdom, Japan, and New Zealand, as well as from organizations such as the European Community and the United Nations Development Program. Kiribati is likely to remain heavily, and possible permanently, dependent on foreign development assistance. The small size of the market economy and the subsistence lifestyle of the majority of the people limit the amount of revenue derived from taxation. This is further limited by tax breaks to companies (**see VIII, A Investment**).

VIII. Investment Law

A. Investment

The loss of phosphate revenue since 1979 has critically reduced the economic viability of Kiribati. In response, the Kiribati government has created several legal incentives aimed at assisting the development of enterprises and investment as a whole.

In an effort to boost economic activity and employment and thereby to make Kiribati more financially self-reliant, the government is trying to attract foreign investment. Exemptions from taxation are used to promote industrial development. The Income Tax Act provides for up to five years' exemption from income tax for approved pioneer companies. The act also includes a number of incentives for investors, namely: (1) a low rate of taxation for private and public companies of 25 percent on net profits, (2) no capital gains tax or commodity sales taxes; and (3) a range of allowances to reduce the taxable income of these industries. These include a 50 percent depreciation allowance on plants and fittings in the first year and 25 percent on the reducing balance thereafter; a 25 percent depreciation allowance on buildings and ships in the first year and 10 percent on the reducing balance thereafter; the carrying forward indefinitely of losses on the previous year's operations; and a 75 percent deduction for interest on foreign loans and 100 percent on interest on local loans. General provisions under the Customs Act allow exemptions from import duty. The Protected Industries Act empowers the government to declare that the development of certain industries is in the public interest and to give incentives and protections to companies in these fields.

The government recognizes the significance of marine resources to the country. Special emphasis is devoted to tuna development and its exploitation by the country's domestic fleet as well as by licensed distant-water vessels (see **XII, E Agriculture, Forestry, Fisheries, and Mineral Resources**). Kiribati's bilateral fisheries agreements with Japan and the Republic of Korea, which have been in place since the late 1970s, have yielded a reliable and stable financial return each year. In 1985 Kiribati concluded a controversial tuna fisheries agreement with the Soviet Union, the first such agreement in the Pacific islands region. The Beretitenti responded to internal and foreign criticism of the agreement with the argument that it had been concluded out of economic necessity, as had the United States' agreement to trade grain with Russia.

B. Insurance

All insurance business is regulated by the Insurance Act 1981, which establishes the Kiribati Insurance Corporation and gives it exclusive rights to conduct on insurance business within Kiribati.

C. Financial Transactions

The Currency Ordinance provides that Australian dollar notes and coins and Kiribati coins constitute legal tender for all financial transactions within Kiribati.

IX. Welfare Law

There is no specific legislation dealing with welfare matters; however, provisions in legislation dealing with family law do address the welfare of children (see **XIV, C Custody and Maintenance**).

X. Criminal Law

Criminal offenses are contained in the Penal Code. Offenses are either felonies or misdemeanors. A felony is an offense that is punishable with imprisonment for three years or more. A misdemeanor is any other offense. The Magistrates' Courts can hear cases involving all misdemeanors and felonies carrying sentences of up to five years' imprisonment. All other felony cases are heard in the High Court. Any police officer may prosecute in the Magistrates' Courts at the direction of the Attorney General.

The Penal Code includes standard provisions for the protection of lives and bodies, homes and possessions. It includes provisions against corruption and abuse of office; for the administration of law and justice; and for crimes against morality, the person, and property. The section dealing with crimes relating to property includes the unusual provision of larceny of a tree. Section 272 of the Penal Code makes it an offense to steal, cut, break, uproot, destroy, or damage, with intent to steal the whole or any part of the tree, sapling, or shrub. Such a law is a reflection of land as the basis of status and wealth in Kiribati.

For those found guilty of criminal offenses in the Magistrates' Courts, sentencing may take a variety of forms. These include imprisonment, fines, corporal punishment of up to six strokes of a cane for male children under fourteen years or up to twelve strokes for male persons between fourteen and seventeen years, community service orders, suspended sentences, probation orders, binding over orders to keep the peace for a set period of time, deferred sentences to see if a person mends his or her ways, absolute or conditional discharge, residence orders, and police supervision for up to five years. Any person aggrieved by a conviction or order by a Magistrates' Court in a criminal case, in respect of any charge to which the defendant pleaded not guilty, may appeal to the High Court. No appeal lies against an order of acquittal except with the sanction of the Attorney General in writing.

The Extradition Act 1981 provides for the extradition of fugitive offenders to states with which Kiribati has extradition treaties and to designated Commonwealth countries. The act contains the internationally accepted exceptions to extradition such as political offenses and double criminality. A person extradited to Kiribati must be tried within six months of arrival.

XI. Judicial Procedure

A. Civil Procedure

1. MAGISTRATES' COURT

Civil procedure is regulated by the Magistrates' Courts Ordinance and the Magistrates' Courts Rules 1978. The procedure in civil cases is generally the same as that in the courts of other Commonwealth countries, except that, under Section 35 of the act, magistrates in civil and land cases are urged "as far as there is proper opportunity, [to] promote reconciliation . . . and encourage and facilitate settlement in an amicable way and without recourse to litigation of matters in difference between them."

Procedure in land cases and other customary matters before the Magistrates' Court is also contained in the Magistrates' Courts Rules 1978. Proceedings may be initiated by an applicant, either by asking the court to issue a summons or by attending the court and stating a claim. Alternatively, if there is no applicant, proceedings may be commenced by the court's own motion. The applicant and defendant may give evidence and call witnesses. If there is no applicant, the court itself may call such witnesses as it thinks fit. During the course of proceedings, the presiding magistrate may discuss with the other magistrates the custom applicable to the matter in issue. After hearing all the evidence and discussing the applicable customary law, the presiding magistrate summarizes the facts and the custom for the benefit of the court. The court's judgment is that of a majority of the magistrates on the panel.

2. HIGH COURT

Civil procedure before the High Court is regulated by the Western Pacific High Court (Civil Procedure) Rules 1964, which are generally in accord with U.K. and Commonwealth procedures.

B. Criminal Procedure

Procedures in criminal cases are regulated generally under Chapter II of the Constitution (the bill of rights), the Criminal Procedure Code 1977, and for Magistrates' Courts, under the Magistrates' Courts Rule 1978.

The High Court or the Magistrates' Court may, in its discretion, issue either a summons or a warrant to compel accused persons to appear before the court. If an accused fails to appear at the time and place appointed in the warrant, the court may issue a warrant for arrest of the accused.

Bail is readily available except for people charged with treason or murder. Bail may be granted with or without a surety. The amount of bail, which is fixed by the trial judge with due regard to the circumstances of the case, must not be excessive. Recognizance bail may also be granted.

The court may, at any stage of the trial, summon any person as a witness. All witnesses are examined on oath, and may be cross-examined and reexamined. At the end of the trial, judgment must be pronounced in open court and its substance explained.

The Magistrates' Courts Act makes some provision for customary legal process in criminal proceedings in Magistrates' Courts. It provides, at Section 35, "In criminal cases, a magistrates' court may promote reconciliation and encourage and facilitate the settlement in an amicable way of proceedings for common assault, or for any offense of a personal or private nature not amounting to felony and not aggravated in degree, on terms of payment of compensation or other terms approved by such court." If a settlement occurs, the magistrate may stay or terminate the criminal proceedings.

C. Appellate Procedure

Criminal and civil appeals are governed by the Civil Procedure Code. Every appeal petition must be in writing and contain the grounds upon which it is alleged the court erred. When it appears to the judge of the appellate court that the appeal ought to be allowed and the respondent gives notice of the intention not to oppose the appeal, the appeal may be summarily allowed without a hearing. Otherwise, the court hears the appeal and, after the hearing, the court may confirm, reverse, or vary the decision of the trial court or remit the matter to the trial court for rehearing.

XII. Land and Natural Resources

A. Land Tenure and Administration

Land is the basis of status and wealth in Kiribati. It is land that gives each individual true identity. Before the advent of colonial rule, land tenure was governed by customary law, which varied only slightly from island to island. The basis of the land tenure system was that land should remain forever in the family group. Custom, therefore, dictated restrictions over an owner's use of land, both during the owner's lifetime and in the disposal of the land after death. In this way, the landowner may be seen as a tenant for life of the land, which the owner effectively holds in trust for forthcoming generations.

British colonial rule disrupted the land tenure system in Kiribati. It became possible for foreigners to acquire land by sale or gift. Most of these lands have now been reabsorbed into i-Kiribati land holdings.

Today, land law aims to retain and enforce customary rules of land tenure. Interests and rights in land are governed by custom, modified and restricted to some extent by legislation, principally the Native Lands Ordinance and the Laws of Kiribati Act 1989.

B. Customary Land Tenure

The Native Lands Ordinance prohibits the sale or gift of native lands to non-natives. A native is any aboriginal inhabitant of Kiribati, and native land is land owned by natives. Native land may, however, be alienated to the Crown, a local government council, a registered cooperative society, the National Loans Board, and the National Housing Corporation.

Native land may be leased to non-natives. The Ordinance requires all leases of native lands to be registered. A lease or sublease of native land must be approved by the Minister of Lands, who cannot give approval unless satisfied that the terms of the lease are not disadvantageous to either party. The minister must also obtain confirmation from the Magistrates' Court of the district or island in which the land is situated that the land is the property of the lessor, that the lessor is not prohibited under the Native Lands Ordinance from alienating the land and that the lessor will be left with sufficient land for support. Leases cannot be granted for longer than ninety-nine years or for an area larger than 10 acres without the approval of the Minister for Lands.

Under the Non-Native Land (Restriction on Alienation) Act, non-native land cannot be alienated by sale, gift, lease or otherwise unless prior notice is given to the Minister for Lands, who may acquire the land for the Crown rather than permitting its alienation to a private individual. If the minister and the vendor are unable to agree on the purchase price, the land is deemed to have been acquired by compulsory process under the Crown Acquisition of Lands Act (see **XII, C Government Taking of Land**).

A unique aspect of land law in Kiribati is the practice of land reclamation, which developed from the fact that Kiribati is made up of small islands that require seawalls to be built to prevent erosion. The Foreshore and Land Reclamation Act provides that the foreshore, defined as the whole area of the beach below the high water mark, belongs to the Crown. The act also provides for the carrying out of land reclamation schemes. Land reclamation can be carried out by the government regardless of the ownership of the neighboring land. Compensation is paid to people whose lands may be affected by reclamation.

C. Government Taking of Land

The Constitution provides, at Chapter II, Section 8, that no land may be taken compulsorily unless for a public purpose, with reasonable justification for the hardship caused, and with provision for adequate compensation. The government may take private land under two statutes. The Neglected Lands Act allows the minister to purchase or acquire neglected lands for occupation by indigent persons or for use by local government. *Neglected land* is defined as land suitable for agricultural use that is not being fully and efficiently utilized for that purpose. An *indigent* is one who, in the opinion of a district administrative officer, has insufficient land for the support of him or herself and a family. In practice, in only two recorded instances has land been declared neglected.

Private land may also be acquired by the Crown under the Crown Acquisition of Lands Act as amended. Under the act, the minister may acquire, on behalf of the Republic, any land required for any public purpose. *Acquisition* is defined to include the acquisition of the freehold; the surrender of a lease, sublease or license; and the acquisition for a term of years. Compensation, as may be agreed upon or determined by the High Court, is payable to the owner and to any person with an interest in the land.

D. National Parks and Reserves

There is no legislation in force declaring national parks and reserves.

E. Agriculture, Forestry, Fisheries, and Mineral Resources

The climate of Kiribati does not encourage commercial agriculture. Copra is the only exported agricultural product. Other crops grown for domestic consumption include taro, bananas, breadfruit, and pawpaw. Livestock breeding for domestic consumption is small in scale.

The Mineral Development Licensing Act 1977 regulates mineral extraction. The act makes no express provision vesting property in minerals to the Crown. However, Section 3 provides that no person may conduct any reconnaissance for, prospect for, or mine any minerals except under a license. The act also preserves the customary rights of i-Kiribati to take minerals from their lands.

The Mineral Development Licensing Act also provides for the payment of royalties on minerals obtained by the holder of a mining license. The act draws a distinction between royalties derived from offshore operations or Crown lands and those derived from private lands. Royalties from the former categories are paid into the consolidated fund of the government. Royalties from the private lands are applied by the government to benefit those whose rights, interests, or welfare have been significantly affected by the mining operations.

Special legislation regulates phosphate mining on Banaba (Ocean Island). The (Banaba) Mining Ordinance prohibits mining on Banaba without a valid license from the government of Kiribati. The ordinance also provides for the payment of compensation by the Republic to any original owner or owners of land on Banaba subject to mining. This is consistent with the Constitution of Kiribati, which entrenches the rights of Banabans to their land. Under Section 119 of the Constitution, where the Republic has acquired any right or interest in land in Banaba from any Banaban for phosphate mining, the Republic is obliged to transfer that right or interest to the Banaban from whom it was acquired or to the heirs and successors upon completion of phosphate extraction. Also, no right or interest of a Banaban in land can be acquired by the government without agreement with the owner of the land.

At present, the only economic resources of commercial significance are fisheries located in Kiribati's exclusive economic zone. A host of laws regulate fishing and processing of fish within the waters of Kiribati. The Fisheries Ordinance 1977, as amended, prohibits fishing without a license by both local and foreign fishermen (**see VIII, A Investment**).

XIII. PERSONS AND ENTITIES

Individuals and business entities such as corporations, business associations, and cooperative societies constitute legal persons under the laws of Kiribati. They can own property, enter into contracts, sue, and be sued in their own right. Minors (people under twenty-one years) and the insane are not capable of entering into valid contracts.[4]

XIV. FAMILY LAW

In precolonial Kiribati, the family was the original cell of society. A woman was recognized as a man's companion, rather than his servant. Polygamy was rare, although every husband acquired a certain authority over women related to him. Divorce was by mutual consent. The growth of missions in Kiribati, particularly Catholic missions, led to a much more formalized attitude toward the institution of marriage. Today there is legislation covering all aspects of family law.

A. Marriage

Under the Marriage Act, all valid marriages must be solemnized by registered marriage celebrants, mostly priests and lay preachers. A marriage is void under five circumstances. The first is marriage between those related by blood and by affinity. The prohibited degrees of relationship set out in Schedule 1 to the act are very wide; they include the immediate family as well as spouses of the immediate family and grandparents. The second prohibition is on a marriage in which either party is under the age of sixteen years. The third is marriage between persons either of whom is still married to someone else. The fourth is marriage solemnized by a person not registered as a celebrant. Finally, a marriage is void in which either party marries under a false name.

If either party to an intended marriage is under the age of twenty-one years, a written consent of the father is required. If the father is dead, of unsound mind, or absent from the district, the mother or guardian may give the consent. The Registrar General may dispense with the requirements of parental consent when the person whose consent is required refuses to give it, and the Registrar General is satisfied that the refusal is perverse and not in the best interest of the applicant. Widows and widowers under the age of twenty-one years are exempt from the requirements of parental consent.

The Marriage Act also allows marriages by proxy when a person over the age of twenty-one and resident outside Kiribati wants to marry a person resident in Kiribati. An application to the Registrar General is required. A sworn affidavit that there is no impediment to the marriage is also required. All the requirements for a valid marriage also apply to marriage by proxy.

B. Divorce

Divorce between i-Kiribati is regulated by the Native Divorce Act, which provides that the grounds for divorce are adultery, desertion for three or more years, cruelty, failure to consummate, incurable insanity, epilepsy or venereal disease, marriage induced by duress or mistake, the parties' being within the prohibited degrees of consanguinity, and incompatibility.

Jurisdiction to dissolve marriages is vested in the Magistrates' Courts. A decree of divorce pronounced by the court is, in the first instance, only a decree nisi. The decree becomes absolute after review by the High Court. A certificate of divorce is issued after the dissolution of marriage.

C. Custody and Maintenance

The law governing custody and maintenance of children is contained in the Custody of Children Act, Native Lands Act, and Maintenance (Miscellaneous Provisions) Act. Under the Custody of Children Act, a court may, on application by or on behalf of any person, make orders with regard to the custody of any child and regulate the right of access to the child by the mother or father. The court also can discharge or vary a custody order at any time on application by one of the parents. Every parent is under obligation to maintain his or her children. A Magistrates' Court has power under the Native Lands Act to order that some of the property of a parent be set aside for the maintenance of his or her issue where the parent is preventing the issue from obtaining a livelihood from the land.

The Maintenance (Miscellaneous Provisions) Act provides for the maintenance of neglected persons and facilitates the enforcement in Kiribati of maintenance orders made in foreign countries. The courts may require the payment of maintenance if they are satisfied that a person has a legal or customary obligation to provide support and has willfully neglected to do so. Since, under custom, adult children are responsible for the care and support of their parents, the act applies to them as well as to the support by parents of minor children.

D. Adoption

The rules on adoption are contained in the Kiribati Lands Code and reflect Kiribati customary law. Adoption is permitted by a Magistrates' Court only if the court is satisfied that the adopting parent's issue or family will not suffer hardship as a result of the adoption. However, if the issue or family has neglected the parent, the courts would approve an adoption regardless of the economic consequences for the issue or family.

An adopted child is still entitled to inherit from the child's natural parents. In addition, the adopted child inherits from the adoptive parents as if he or she were their natural child.

XV. Personal Property

Kiribati law of property does not make substantial distinctions between personal property and real property. As a general rule, the owner of personal property is free to dispose of it subject to the obligations to maintain his or her next of kin and children (see **XVI, A Testate Succession**). Where the owner of personal property dies intestate, the personal property is treated as part of the estate of the deceased and is distributed according to the Lands Code.[5]

XVI. Wills and Succession

A. Testate Succession

The law on wills is contained in the Wills Act and the Lands Code. The Wills Act provides for choice of law to determine the validity of wills. As a general rule, a will is treated as having been properly executed if it conforms to the internal rules in the place of execution. The formalities of a valid will are contained in Section 10 of the Lands Code. A will must be written, and the testator must sign or make a mark on the will in the presence of two witnesses, who also sign the will. The two witnesses must not be beneficiaries under the will and must not be related to the testator. A verbal will can also be legally binding. The Lands Code provides that the court can consider a verbal will, providing it is properly witnessed, but once there is a written will, the court cannot consider verbal amendments to it.

The permissable terms of a will are also regulated by the Lands Code. As a general rule, every testator may dispose of property subject to the following rules of customary law:

1. In most parts of Kiribati, a parent can disinherit a child only if the child has been neglectful.
2. A testator may direct that his or her next of kin is to receive no share of the estate if that next of kin deliberately neglected the testator during the latter's lifetime.
3. However, a testator has complete authority over the disposal of any land he or she has bought or has received as a reward for work or in an exchange.

B. Intestate Succession

The Lands Code also governs intestate succession. If a person dies without leaving a valid will, the following rules, which are derived from customary law, apply to the distribution of the estate:

1. If a deceased male has more than one spouse, the eldest son of the first wife is appointed administrator. If there is no son by the first wife, the eldest daughter of the first wife becomes the administrator, but she may allow the first son of the second wife to be the administrator.
2. In some parts of the country, the issue of the first spouse receive the best land, after which the estate is shared equally among the issue of the other spouses. In other areas, the estate is distributed among the children irrespective of which spouse they come from.
3. In some parts of the country, the eldest son's share of the estate exceeds that of his brothers and the shares of the sons exceed those of the sisters. In other parts, all children of the deceased receive equal shares.
4. Where the deceased is issueless, immediate family or next of kin inherit the estate.

XVII. Contracts

The common law of England is the basis directly or indirectly of the contract law of Kiribati. There is also some customary law of contract. Custom still controls the ways transactions are entered into and carried out in village life.

XVIII. Commercial Law

A. Business Associations

The activities of business associations are regulated by the Companies Ordinance and the Companies Registration Ordinance. All companies, associations, syndicates, or partnerships consisting of more than twenty persons are required to be registered with the Registrar of Companies. Non-i-Kiribati can own companies without restriction.

A business association seeking incorporation must submit an application containing the following information:

1. certified copies of the organizing documents of the company;
2. a list of directors; and
3. the names and addresses of one or more persons resident in Kiribati authorized to accept on behalf of the company service of process or any notices required to be served on the company.

B. External Companies

Special provisions of the Companies Ordinance apply to external companies. An *external company* is defined as a body corporate formed outside Kiribati that has a branch, management, share registration, or an office in Kiribati. Within one month of the establishment of business in Kiribati, all external companies are required to register with the Registrar of Companies and to supply, in addition to the information required of domestic companies (see **XVIII, A Business Associations**), the addresses of their principal offices in their home countries, the nature of the business to be carried on in Kiribati, and the names and addresses of local managers.

Once registered, every external company is required to exhibit conspicuously, in every place it carries on business in Kiribati, the name of the company, the country in which it is incorporated, and the liabilities of the members. The company's local manager must be competent to be appointed manager of a local company under the Companies Ordinance, which prohibits minors and those convicted of any offense in connection with the promotion, formation, or management of a company. All the acts of a local manager of an external company bind the company unless the local manager has no authority to perform the act and the person with whom the manager deals has no constructive knowledge of the absence of authority.

C. Professional Bodies

The activities of some professional associations are regulated by legislation. These include medical and dental practitioners under the Medical and Dental Practitioners Ordinance, nurses and midwives under the Nurses and Midwives Ordinance, pharmacists under the Pharmacy and Poisons Ordinance, and traditional medical practitioners under the Medical and Dental Practitioners (Amendment) Act 1981.

D. Cooperative Societies

The formation and operation of cooperative societies are governed by the Co-operative Societies Ordinance, which requires all cooperative societies to be registered. The registration of a cooperative society renders it a body corporate with powers to hold property, enter into contracts, institute and defend suits and other legal proceedings, and perform all acts necessary for the purposes set out in its constitution.

E. Bills of Sale

The Bills of Sale Ordinance regulates all bills of sale, including assignments, transfer, declarations of trust, powers of attorney authority, or license to take possession of personal chattels and security for any debt and debentures. All bills of sale must be executed in the presence of and attested by at least one witness and be registered. Registration is effected by presenting to the registrar of the High Court the bill of sale with every schedule or inventory referred to in the bill, together with an affidavit stating the time of execution of the bill, its attestation, and a description of the residence and occupation of the persons making or giving the attestation.

XIX. TORTS

As with contract law, the English common law is the ultimate source of tort law in Kiribati. Decisions of the English courts, as well as those of other common law jurisdictions, are persuasive authority for the courts in Kiribati. Custom is also a source of tort law. However, judicial attitudes on the question of whether common law or customary law standards should be applied in tort cases is contradictory. In the late 1970s, judicial attitudes favored the application of common law standards. For example, in *Irata v. Bobu*, a slander case, the court applied the common law rules of torts.[6] In recent slander cases, however, the High Court has been more inclined to apply local custom.

XX. Labor Law

A. Employment

The main employers of wage labor include government, the copra plantations, and the missions. Matters relating to employment are governed by the Employment Act, which regulates the formalities of contracts of employment and the welfare of employees and sets minimum wages. It also provides for the appointment of a Commissioner of Labour to administer the act.

The Employment Act also regulates contracts entered into outside Kiribati for employment within Kiribati. If the employment laws of the place of origin are substantially the same as the relevant provisions of the Employment Act, the conditions for termination of the contract would be governed by Kiribati law. If the laws of the place of contract differ from those of Kiribati and any party has not fully complied with the terms of the contract, the portions of the contract not complied with are to be performed when the employee arrives in Kiribati. Thereafter, the Employment Act will apply as if the contract had been entered into in Kiribati.

The act also governs employment entered into in Kiribati for work outside Kiribati. With the exception of Nauru, which is regarded as territorial for this purpose, the maximum period of service under any such contract cannot exceed two years if the worker is not accompanied by family and three years if the worker is so accompanied. The maximum period for reengagement contracts cannot exceed twenty-one months if the worker is not accompanied by family and thirty-three months if the worker is so accompanied.

Special provisions of the Employment Act regulate and restrict the employment of women and children. With some exceptions, employers may not require women to work at night or in mining. The act prohibits the employment of children under fourteen, sets other minimum age limits for certain industries, and prohibits night work by children.

B. Trade Unions

Trade unions and collective action are regulated under the Industrial Relations Act 1977. Trade unions must be registered. A minimum of seven members is required to form a trade union. The act gives protection to trade unions and their members in pursuance of the objectives of the union. An agreement or combination of two or more persons to do or procure any action in contemplation or furtherance of a trade union dispute cannot be tried as a conspiracy. An action done in contemplation or furtherance of a trade dispute to induce some other person to break a contract of employment or an action that interferes with the trade, business, or employment of some other person is also not triable.

Trade unions or their officials can, however, be sued if they mishandle the property of the union. The members of a trade union can be prosecuted for riots, unlawful assembly, breach of the peace, sedition, or any offense against the state. An illegal or wrongful use of authority by a person in contemplation or furtherance of a trade dispute is also actionable. Picketing is permitted but picketing that is not peaceful is punishable as a crime.

Industrial relations in Kiribati are further regulated by the Industrial Relations Code, which requires all industrial disputes to be settled peacefully. It also prescribes the circumstances in which strike action may be used in the settlement of industrial disputes.

C. Workers' Compensation

I-Kiribati who suffer injury or death arising out of their employment are entitled to compensation under the Workers' Compensation Act. The act covers all persons who work under contracts of employment or apprenticeship, whether or not the contract complies with the Employment Act. Any provision of an employment contract in which an employee renounces his or her right to compensation for injury arising out of or in the course of employment is void.

Compensation is payable to the employee for any personal injury or accident arising out of and in the course of employment, including any accident or injury that occurs while the worker is traveling from or to work. The employer is not liable to pay compensation in four cases. The first is for an injury that incapacitates the employee for less than three days. The second is where the injury does not result in death or permanent incapacity and is attributable to the employee's serious and willful misconduct. The third is for incapacity or death resulting from deliberate self-injury. The final exception is for incapacity or death resulting from personal injury suffered in connection with another employment.

The amount of compensation for injury resulting in temporary or permanent incapacity depends on whether the injured employee needs ongoing care and whether the injury results in a partial or total incapacity. Compensation for death depends on the number of dependents. Awards may be determined in a negotiation between employer and employee. Failing agreement within fifteen days, the injured employee may ask the Magistrates' Court to set compensation.

XXI. Industrial and Intellectual Property Rights

A. Copyright

Copyright is protected under the Copyright Act. It is an offense for any person resident in Kiribati knowingly to make for sale or hire any infringing copy of a copyrighted work; distribute, let for hire, or by way of trade expose or offer for sale or hire any infringing copy of any such work; distribute infringing copies of any such work for trade or in a way that affects prejudicially the copyright owner, or by way of trade exhibit in public or import for sale or hire any infringing copy of such work. The act also prohibits the import of printed copies of literary, dramatic, or musical work made outside Kiribati that, if it had been published in Kiribati would have amounted to a breach of copyright. The owner of the copyright may give notice in writing to the minister in charge of copyright matters to request the classification of any such material as prohibited imports. The period of restriction may not exceed five years and cannot extend beyond the end of the period for which the copyright subsists.

B. Patents

Patent rights are protected under the Registration of U.K. Patents Act. This act extends to Kiribati the protection enjoyed by grantees of patents in the United Kingdom. Any person who is a grantee of a patent in the United Kingdom or any person deriving rights from such grantee may apply within three years from the date of issue of the patent to have it registered in Kiribati. All privileges and rights enjoyed by grantees of patents commence from the date of the patent in the United Kingdom and continue in force in Kiribati only so long as the patent remains in force in the United Kingdom.

C. Trademarks

Trademarks are protected under the Registration of U.K. Trade Marks Act. The act permits the registration in Kiribati of all trademarks protected under the laws of the United Kingdom. An application for registration of trademark in Kiribati is made to the Registrar of Trade Marks. The application must be accompanied by a certificate of the Comptroller General of the United Kingdom Patent Office giving full particulars of the registration in the United Kingdom. As with patents, there is a public register of trademarks.

D. Designs

Under the U.K. Designs Protection Act the registered proprietor of a design registered in the United Kingdom enjoys in Kiribati the same privileges and rights that the proprietary has in the United Kingdom. A person who infringes a copyright in a design is not liable to pay compensation to the registered proprietor if the person proves that at the time of the infringement he or she was not aware nor had any reasonable means of becoming aware of the existence of the registration.

XXII. Legal Education and Profession

Kiribati has no tertiary educational institutions. Academic studies, including legal studies, are undertaken overseas. The number of i-Kiribati in the legal profession is very small, about a half-dozen qualified lawyers in all. Most of these received their legal education from the University of Papua New Guinea or from universities in Australia and New Zealand. In the judiciary, only the Chief Justice and Registrar of the High Court have degrees in law.

As of mid-1991, two lawyers were in private practice in Kiribati. Private legal representation in the courts is often imported from overseas, usually from Fiji. Those who cannot afford overseas counsel resort to nonlawyer representatives, such as government administrative officers. To redress this situation, the government created the post of the Peoples' Lawyer to be filled by an experienced lawyer from overseas. The Peoples' Lawyer has the duty of providing legal representation to private individuals.

XXIII. Research Guide

Court decisions are available in the *Gilbert Islands Law Reports (G.I.L.R.)* for the pre-independence period and in the *Kiribati Law Reports* postindependence. A few selected decisions are printed in *South Pacific Law Reports*, beginning in 1987. The following articles are reasonably accessible and helpful.

Brechtefeld, N. "Lands Courts," in R. G. Crocombe, ed. *Land Tenure in the Atolls*. Suva: Institute of Pacific Studies, 1987.
Ietaake, T. "Land Taxation," in R. G. Crocombe, ed. *Land Tenure in the Atolls*. Suva: Institute of Pacific Studies, 1987.
Lambert, B. "Kiribati: Micro-individualism," in R. G. Crocombe, ed. *Land Tenure in the Pacific*. 3d ed. Suva: University of the South Pacific, 1987.

Lodge, M. "Kiribati Legal System," in C. G. Powles and M. Pulea, eds. *Pacific Courts and Legal Systems*. Suva: University of the South Pacific, 1988.

———. "Land Law and Procedure," in R. G. Crocombe, ed. *Land Tenure in the Atolls*. Suva: Institute of Pacific Studies, 1987.

Namai, B. "The Evolution of Kiribati Tenures," in R. G. Crocombe, ed. *Land Tenure in the Atolls*. Suva: Institute of Pacific Studies, 1987.

4. The Republic of the Marshall Islands

JEAN G. ZORN

I. Dateline

3000–500 B.C.	Micronesia, which includes the Marshall Islands, settled by people who probably originated in Southeast Asia.
1565	Micronesia claimed by Spain.
1800s	The islands visited by missionaries, traders, and whalers from Europe, Japan, the United States, and Russia. These nations, particularly Germany and Great Britain, dispute Spain's territorial claims.
1885	The dispute between Spain and Germany submitted to Pope Leo XIII, who grants Spain sovereignty over the Carolines but permits Germany to continue to use Micronesia as a naval and refueling station and gives Germany administrative control over the Marshalls.
1886	Germany annexes the Marshalls.
1920	The League of Nations mandates Micronesia to Japan as a class C mandate.
1944	U.S. forces capture Micronesia from the Japanese. U.S. Navy administers the islands under military rule.
1946	Evacuation by U.S. military of the residents of Bikini atoll; commencement of use of Bikini as a nuclear weapons testing site.
1947	By agreement dated July 18, the United Nations designates all Micronesian islands except Guam as the Trust Territory of the Pacific Islands, under U.S. administration. Of eleven trusteeships established under United Nations jurisdiction, this is the only one designated a "strategic trust" under joint oversight of U.N. Security Council and Trusteeship Council.
1949	Establishment by Trust Territory administration of an advisory Congress of the Marshall Islands, consisting of House of Iroij (members of the chiefly caste) and House of Assembly (elected representatives of localities).
1951	Administrative authority over the Trust Territory transferred by the president of the United States from the U.S. Navy to the secretary of the U.S. Department of Interior.
1958	Reorganization of Congress of the Marshall Islands into a unicameral legislature, with special seats reserved for iroij laplap (chiefs).
1965	In addition to the separate legislative bodies for each district, Trust Territory administration establishes a territorywide legislature, the Congress of Micronesia, an elected bicameral body. At first intended as merely advisory, the congress is later granted legislative powers, but its legislation is subject to U.S. veto, and the people of the Trust Territory are not given executive or judicial powers.

1967	The Congress of Micronesia creates Political Status Commission to begin negotiations with the United States on the future status of Trust Territory.
1968	Marshall Islands legislature renamed the Nitijela (a Marshallese term for a gathering of wise or powerful people).
1973	Believing that the Marshall Islands should seek independence as a state separate from other Trust Territory districts, the Nitijela establishes its own Political Status Commission to negotiate with the United States.
1975	Between July and November, representatives from the six districts of the Trust Territory meet in convention to draft a Micronesian Constitution. Representatives attend from Marshalls. Draft Constitution completed November 8.
1977	The United States agrees that the Marshall Islands Political Status Commission may participate in negotiations to dissolve Trusteeship. Marshall Islands Constitutional Convention elected and first session convened August 8.
1978	In April, United States and Trust Territory representatives agree to Hilo [Hawaii] Principles, establishing free association as guiding principle of future relationship of the United States with its former territories. In July 12 referendum, the Marshall Islands electorate votes against adoption of Micronesian Constitution. On December 21, Marshall Islands Constitutional Convention adopts draft Constitution for the Marshalls.
1979	In United Nations-observed referendum March 1, Marshall Islands Constitution approved by the people of the Marshalls by majority vote. Constitution takes effect May 1.
1982	Representatives of the governments of the United States, the Federated States of Micronesia, the Marshall Islands, and Palau sign Compacts of Free Association on October 1.
1983	On September 7, compact approved by majority vote (6,215 for, 4,509 against) of the people of the Marshalls in plebiscite observed by United Nations. On September 19, the Nitijela adopts Resolution No. 27 approving the compact.
1985–1986	Compact approved by Joint Resolution of U.S. Congress in December 1985 and signed by president of United States January 14, 1986. United States recognizes the Marshalls as an independent nation.
1986	United Nations Trusteeship Council approves Compact of Free Association May 26, by a vote of three to one. The effective date of the compact declared to be October 21. On November 3, president of United States, by proclamation, declares Trust Territory dissolved. United States and the Marshall Islands agree to a treaty under which United States will provide $220 million (later increased to $265 million) compensation for injuries to persons and property caused by U.S. nuclear testing.
1987	Except for financial and program grants, which remain under the U.S. Department of Interior, responsibility for the Marshalls transferred to U.S. Department of State. Office of the High Commissioner for the Trust Territory closed July 10.
1990	December 22, United Nations Security Council votes fourteen to one to dissolve the Trusteeship, thereby removing last barrier to international recognition of Marshalls' independence.

II. Historical, Cultural, and Economic Survey

The Republic of the Marshall Islands is part of the Micronesian archipelago, which occupies 3 million square miles in the western Pacific, between 1 and 12 degrees north of the equator. The Marshalls comprise thirty-four coral islands and atolls with a total land area of approximately 180 square kilometers and a population of about 43,000.

Although many Marshallese are employed in government jobs or in the service sector, most households still obtain a significant amount of their subsistence from traditional gardening and fishing, so the customary economic and social system is still influential. The people of the Marshalls are predominantly Micronesian, although the language of the Marshalls is different from those of neighboring islands with whom the Marshalls were linked in the Trust Territory of the Pacific Islands, and the traditional cultures of the various Micronesian regions differ in many significant respects.

Marshallese kin groups are organized into matrilineages, with land, ritual, and political rights residing in the matrilineage and under ultimate control of chiefs. Traditional Marshallese society is stratified, with rights and responsibilities differing depending upon whether one is a member of a royal or commoner lineage.

As a colony, the islands of Micronesia were ruled successively by Spain, Germany, Japan, and the United States. The Micronesians benefited little from any of their colonial rulers. The Spaniards focused primarily on conquest and religious conversion. Germany concentrated its attention on trade, copra production, and phosphate mining and paid Micronesian laborers very low wages for their work on the plantations and in the mines. Japan's economic development of the islands was more extensive, but its economic policies included the resettlement in western Micronesia of a substantial population of Japanese and Okinawans.

The interest of the United States in Micronesia has been primarily as a Pacific military installation. Especially in the early years of American occupation, economic development of the islands—where it occurred at all—tended to be an offshoot of U.S. military needs, rather than an end in itself. The Marshalls were especially the object of U.S. military interest, with several islands serving as missile ranges and nuclear test sites; the consequences of this use were the forced emigration of the inhabitants from these islands and continuing reports of widespread radiation-caused illnesses. In the 1960s, the United States introduced a program of political development based on an American model and began to make substantial financial contributions to the Trust Territory. However, funding primarily went to wages for government employment and welfare programs, rather than to economic development projects that might have led to significant economic growth. The Marshalls were closed to U.S. private investment until the mid-1960s and to third-country investment until the mid-1970s. Although the Republic of the Marshall Islands is politically independent, it remains economically dependent on the United States and other aid-giving nations; because of its small size and lack of an industrial base, it is likely to remain so.

Despite the inroads of colonialism and the introduction of political institutions modeled on those of the western democracies, the traditional culture of the Marshalls continues to be reflected in the political structures adopted by the new nation. In 1967, the locally elected legislature of the Trust Territory (the Congress of Micronesia) established a Political Status Commission to negotiate with the United States for the termination of Trusteeship status. In 1973, the Marshall Islands district legislature (called the Nitijela, for the traditional councils of elders who advised the chiefs) established its own Political Status Commission to engage separately in the independence negotiations, and in 1977 the Marshall Islands Constitutional Convention was convened. The Constitution of the Republic of the Marshall Islands was ratified and the Marshalls became self-governing in 1979. In addition to the Nitijela, an elected unicameral legislature that elects the president of the Marshalls, the Constitution provides for an advisory council of chiefs (the Council of Iroij).

Although self-governing by 1979, the Marshalls did not become independent until 1986. Many Marshallese desired full political independence by the 1970s, but they also recognized that economic underdevelopment (in large part caused by the United States' Trusteeship policies) would require continuing financial reliance on the United States. Nor was the United States willing entirely to sever its relationship with Micronesia, believing that U.S. national security interests necessitated a continuing presence. Thus, independence negotiations proceeded slowly, even after the concept of free association as the basis for a continuing relationship between the United States and an independent Marshallese republic was adopted at meetings between the United States and representatives of the Trust Territory governments in Hilo, Hawaii, in 1978.

Under the Compact of Free Association, which took effect in 1986, the Marshalls attained autonomous political status and continuing economic support from the United States, but the United States retained authority over national defense and, to a limited extent, foreign affairs **(see VI International Obligations)**. Independence for the Marshalls was approved by the United Nations Trusteeship Council in 1986, but the Security Council, whose approval was also required, did not formally take up the matter until 1990. In the interim, a number of nations, including the United Kingdom and the Soviet Union, did not recognize the Marshalls as fully sovereign and independent. However, with the vote of the Security Council in 1990 to end the Trusteeship, the independence of the Marshalls is now internationally accepted.

During negotiations with the United States for an end to the Trusteeship, the peoples of the Trust Territory were determining whether they would form one or several nations and what the governing structure of such nations would be. The impetus toward separatism came from several sources. First, the cultural diversity of the peoples of the Trust Territory and the vast geographical distances separating the islands militated against the creation of a unitary state. Moreover, the differential treatment the districts had received from the United States under the Trusteeship—and were likely to receive after independence—deprived them of a sense of common purpose. Most importantly, Micronesia's long experience of colonialism has left its peoples with a deep distrust of centralized power and a consequent bias in favor of decentralization. As a result, the former Trusteeship has divided itself into three independent nations and a commonwealth—the Republic of the Marshall Islands, the Republic of Palau, the Federated States of Micronesia, and the Commonwealth of the Northern Marianas.

III. SOURCES OF LAW

A. Constitution

The Marshall Islands Constitution is by its terms the "supreme law of the Marshall Islands" (Article I, Section 1). At Article I, Sections 1 and 2, the Constitution provides that all judges and other public officers are bound by the Constitution, that all legislative and executive instruments, as well as court or agency decisions, have the force of law only if made pursuant to it, and that any law inconsistent with it is void.

The Constitution recognizes other sources of law subsidiary to it, including legislation, treaties and compacts, customary law, and the decisional law of Marshall Islands courts. Article I, Section 3 of the Constitution provides that responsibility for interpreting the Constitution resides ultimately with the judiciary. In interpreting and applying the Constitution, courts may consider but are not bound by decisions of courts of other countries having constitutional provisions similar to those under review. The courts are to adapt these decisions "to the needs of the Marshall Islands, taking into account the Constitution as a whole and the circumstances in the Marshall Islands from time to time" (Article I, Section 3(1)). The Constitution is to be construed "to achieve the aims of fair and democratic government, in the light of reason and experience" (Article I, Section 3(2)). In carrying out this constitutional responsibility, the courts will be making new law for the Marshalls, whether they intend to or not.

Many of the provisions of the Constitution may be amended by a vote of two-thirds of the total membership of the Nitijela (the legislature) followed by a majority of the votes cast in a referendum open to all qualified voters (Constitution, Article XII). However, certain provisions (the Supremacy Clause; the Bill of Rights; the provisions protecting traditional rights; the principles underlying the makeup of the Nitijela; or any change in the composition, method of selection, or tenure of any of the governmental institutions or officers that are established by the Constitution) may be amended only if submitted to the people by a constitutional convention and approved by two thirds of the votes cast in a referendum open to all qualified voters. The Nitijela is also required to report every ten years on the advisability of amending the Constitution or of calling a referendum on that issue.[1]

B. Legislation

Legislation is of three kinds: provisions of the Trust Territory Code; laws enacted by the Nitijela when it was the Marshall Islands district legislature prior to May 1, 1979 (the effective date of the Constitution); and laws of the Nitijela enacted after the effective date.

Laws of the Trust Territory and laws enacted by the Nitijela prior to the effective date, to the extent that they are consistent with the Constitution, continue to be in force until repealed or revoked (Constitution, Article XIII).

The Marshall Islands Revised Code (MIRC), published in 1988, contains all such legislation still in effect, as well as laws enacted by the Nitijela subsequent to the effective date. Each act is given a chapter in the Code, and related chapters are grouped into titles. Acts are referred to here by name, title number, and chapter number.

C. Treaties and Compacts

Article V of the Constitution makes the Cabinet responsible for conducting the foreign affairs of the Marshalls, whether by treaty or otherwise, but treaties must be approved by the Nitijela, and no treaty has the force of law in the Marshalls until so approved. The government of the Marshalls has entered into a number of international agreements, but the Compact of Free Association remains its most significant treaty obligation (see **VI International Obligations**).

D. Custom

The Constitution not only makes a place in the new political system for the customary norms of the people of the Marshall Islands, but to some extent also brings traditional political leaders into the new system (see **IV, C (1) National Government**). However, both the norms and the institutions are changed by their presence in a new legal entity.

Under the Constitution, substantive customary law is defined at Article XIV as "any custom having the force of law in the Marshall Islands." Customary law enters the formal legal system in two ways, through court decisions and through legislation. First, Articles X and XIII provide that all law (including customary law) existing on the effective date remains in force, unless amended or repealed. These provisions, in essence, require the courts to apply custom whenever applicable. The Constitution suggests, however, that custom will not apply if a contrary statute exists, since amendment and repeal can occur indirectly or implicitly, as well as directly and explicitly. It also implies that custom is frozen at the effective date of the Constitution and that the courts may not take later unofficial modifications to custom into account. The Marshall Islands High Court, however, has held that the Court can take judicial notice of new local custom when it is firmly established, generally known, and peacefully and fairly uniformly acquiesced in by those whose rights are affected.[2]

Second, Article X of the Constitution empowers the Nitijela to declare by act the customary law. Such declarations may "supplement the established rules of customary law," a provision that suggests that, in declaring custom, the Nitijela may modify it or take into account that custom changes to meet changing social needs and circumstances. Prior to the second reading of any bill that declares custom, the Nitijela must establish with the Council of Iroij (a council of traditional leaders) a joint committee and must afford the committee a reasonable opportunity to report on the bill. The Nitijela has scarcely used this declaratory power, although an interest in utilizing and supporting traditional practices is evident in a number of acts. An example is the provision of the Local Government Act (4 MIRC, Chapter 1) regarding consensus elections (**see IV, C, 2 Legislature**), but that legislation was not designated as a bill to declare custom and a joint committee did not meet on it.

The Constitution leaves somewhat uncertain the relation between customary law and the Bill of Rights. Article X provides that "Nothing in Article II [the Bill of Rights] shall be construed to invalidate the customary law or any traditional practice concerning land tenure or any related matter." This may mean that customary law generally overrides the Bill of Rights or that only those customs and traditional practices relating to land tenure do so.

E. Common Law

Neither the Constitution nor the Judiciary Act 1983 (27 MIRC, Chapter 2) gives explicit guidance to the courts on the development of the common law. One could argue by analogy to the Article I provisions on constitutional interpretation (**see III, A Constitution**), that, in the development of the common law as well, the courts should treat the decisions of foreign courts (including those of the United States and the Trust Territory) as persuasive but not binding, and that the common law should be adapted to the needs and circumstances of the Marshall Islands. In addition, as discussed earlier (**III, B Legislation**), Articles X and XIII of the Constitution suggest that the courts should apply customary law whenever applicable.

The Trust Territory Code provided that American common law, as expressed in the American Law Institute's *Restatements* or as generally understood and applied in the United States, would be the common law of the Trust Territory (1980 1 TTC 103). The *Restatements* are attempts by American legal scholars to codify the common law. Since the common law of each American state differs, the *Restatements* contain either the rule adopted by the majority of the states or the rule that the scholars drafting the *Restatements* prefer. If the Trust Territory courts used the *Restatements*, they were in effect deciding cases by applying a civil code rather than by common law. This provision does not appear in the Marshall Islands Revised Code, suggesting that it has been repealed and that the courts of the Marshall Islands are free to develop an indigenous common law.

IV. Constitutional System

In drafting its Constitution, the Republic of the Marshall Islands became one of the few former colonies to adopt a governmental structure different from that of the colonial power. Although the United States has a system under which the executive and legislature are each popularly elected, the Marshalls has chosen a quasi-parliamentary form of government, in which the president and ministers are chosen by the legislature from among its members and serve at the pleasure of the legislature.

The Procedure and Jurisdiction Committee of the Constitutional Convention explained its reasons for proposing a parliamentary system:

> Surprising as it may seem, the main reason is that this system is closest to the actual political experience of the Marshall Islands people. Although, for the last 30 years, they have been governed under a system based on the separate physical identity of the legislative and executive branches of government, the democratically elected representatives of the people have served only in the legislative branch. The Marshall Islands have never been governed under a system where the head of the executive branch, also, was democratically elected.[3]

The Constitution modifies the parliamentary model. Some of its modifications seem based upon United States precedents and others upon Marshallese custom. Although the Constitution does not provide for a separation of the executive and legislative branches of government as complete as does the United States Constitution, it does limit the development of undue power in any branch through regularly scheduled elections, the power of the legislature to pass a vote of no confidence in the Cabinet, the power of the President to dissolve the legislature, and the power of the judiciary to review and void governmental acts that conflict with the Constitution.

A. Territory

The Constitution does not define the geographical territory of the Republic. The Marine Zones (Declaration) Act 1984 (33 MIRC, Chapter 2) defines the internal and archipelagic waters, the territorial sea, and the exclusive economic zone of the Republic. The act establishes the low water line of the reefs as a baseline and provides that waters on the landward side of the reefs are internal and archipelagic waters of the Republic, and that the territorial sea of the Republic extends 12 nautical miles seaward from the reefs.

The sovereignty of the Republic includes the airspace over its territorial land and sea, the seabed and subsoil under them, and the resources contained in them. A contiguous zone extends 24 nautical miles seaward from the baseline, and the Republic has within the contiguous zone all rights necessary to prevent infringements of its laws and regulations relating to customs, immigration, and sanitation.

The Republic claims an exclusive economic zone extending 200 nautical miles seaward from the baseline. The Republic's rights over the exclusive economic zone include the exploration, exploitation, conservation and management of natural resources, the production of energy, and all other rights conferred or recognized by international law.

The Republic has asserted a claim to Wake Island, currently a U.S. possession.

B. Nationality and Citizenship

Citizens of the Marshall Islands include all persons who immediately before the effective date of the Constitution were citizens of the Trust Territory, if they or either of their parents have customary land rights. Persons born on or after the effective date are citizens if, at their date of birth, either of their parents is a citizen or if they are born in the Marshall Islands and are not at birth entitled to be or become a citizen of any other country (Constitution, Article XI).

Persons may become citizens by registration if they have customary land rights, or have been resident in the Marshalls for not less than three years and are the parents of a citizen, or if they are of Marshallese descent and their application should be granted in the interests of justice (Constitution, Article XI).

The Citizenship Act 1984 (43 MIRC, Chapter 4) provides that any noncitizen adopted by a citizen acquires citizenship on the date of the adoption, and that citizenship may be obtained by naturalization by any adult who has resided in the Marshalls for five years immediately prior to the date of application, is domiciled in the Republic, is of good character, is able to speak and understand Marshallese, has an understanding and respect for the customs and traditions of the Marshalls, has the means to support himself or herself and his or her dependents, has a reasonable knowledge and understanding of the Constitution, and has renounced prior citizenship.

Citizenship will be lost by any adult who voluntarily obtains the citizenship of another country without Cabinet approval. Citizenship that was obtained by registration or naturalization may be lost on grounds of concealment of a material fact in applying for citizenship; advocacy of the overthrow of the government by unlawful means; or commission of espionage, sabotage, or sedition against the government. Under the compact, Marshallese enjoy essentially unrestricted entry to the United States. In 1989, the Marshalls inaugurated a plan to sell citizenship to foreigners, promising them easy entry into the United States, but the U.S. government responded that naturalized Marshallese would have to establish five-year residency in the Marshalls before the United States would admit them.

C. Government

The Republic of the Marshall Islands has adopted a quasi-parliamentary form of government. Legislative power is vested in the Nitijela, a unicameral legislature named for the traditional councils of elders who advised the chiefs.

Executive power is vested in the Cabinet, which is chosen by the Nitijela from among its members.

Judicial power is independent of both the legislature and the executive, and judges may declare acts of the legislature and the executive void if they do not comply with the Constitution. In addition, a council of traditional leaders, the Council of Iroij, can make recommendations to the Cabinet and the Nitijela.

1. NATIONAL GOVERNMENT

a. Head of State

The President is declared by Article V of the Constitution to be Head of State, but it is a purely honorary position. The Cabinet is responsible for the general direction and control of the government, the conduct of foreign affairs, and national security.

b. Executive

The executive authority of the Marshall Islands is vested by Article V of the Constitution in the Cabinet, whose members are collectively responsible to the Nitijela.

The powers, functions, duties, and responsibilities of the Cabinet include general direction and control of the government, recommending to the Nitijela legislative proposals necessary or desirable to carry out Cabinet policies, accounting to the Nitijela for public expenditures, the conduct of foreign affairs (but no treaty has the force of law until acted upon by the Nitijela) and of security (but no armed force may be raised or stationed in the Marshalls in peacetime except by legislation passed by the Nitijela), and the powers of reprieve and pardon.

The Cabinet is also vested with the responsibility to establish and maintain hospitals and other institutions designed to help the people of the Marshalls maintain an adequate standard of living and enjoy their legal rights, and to serve their economic, social, and cultural welfare. The Cabinet may exercise these powers and duties collectively or by delegation to individual ministers or other officers but shares responsibility collectively.

Article V of the Constitution provides that a new Cabinet is formed at the first meeting of the Nitijela after each general election or after a President has vacated his or her seat in the Nitijela or tendered his or her resignation. The Nitijela elects the President by secret ballot from among the members of the Nitijela. The President then selects from six to ten other members of the Nitijela to form a Cabinet. If a Cabinet of at least six members cannot be formed within seven days after a President has been chosen, the Nitijela holds a new election for President.

The President allocates portfolios among the ministers, and may reallocate them at any time (**see V, A Organization**). If there are fewer than ten ministers, the President may nominate additional members to the Cabinet. A minister may resign from Cabinet office and must vacate it if his or her appointment as a minister is revoked by the President or if he or she vacates a seat in the Nitijela for any reason other than the dissolution of the Nitijela. If Cabinet vacancies bring the total of ministers below six, the President must fill the vacancies within thirty days. If the President fails to do so, he or she will be deemed to have resigned.

A motion of no confidence in the Cabinet may be made by any four backbenchers and must be voted upon no sooner than five days and no later than ten days after notice of the motion has been given. If the motion is carried by a majority of the total membership of the Nitijela, the President is deemed to have tendered his or her resignation, in which case the Nitijela must proceed to elect a new President within fourteen days. If a new President is not elected in this time, the tender of the President's resignation lapses. If a vote of no confidence fails or lapses, notice of a new vote of no confidence may not be brought for ninety days.

The President chairs Cabinet meetings. Four members of the Cabinet constitute a quorum, and the decision of the Cabinet on any matter is taken by the members present at a meeting at which there is a quorum. Decisions of the Cabinet take effect when signed by the President. The Constitution does not specify voting requirements. Notice of each meeting is to be given to every minister, and to the Chief Secretary, the Attorney General, and the Secretary of Finance. The Chief Secretary has the right to attend meetings and to speak on any matter under consideration.

The President does not have the power (as does a President in a presidential system) to veto bills passed by the Nitijela; the President's only power over the Nitijela is the limited power to dissolve the Nitijela, forcing a new general election.

c. Legislature

Article IV of the Constitution provides for a thirty-three-member unicameral legislature, the Nitijela, and sets out the districts from which members are to be elected and the number of members from each district. The Nitijela may, by act, vary its total membership, the number or geographic boundaries of electoral districts, or the number of members from any district. But it may do so only after reviewing a report that states whether it is desirable to change the composition of the Nitijela. Such a report must be prepared every ten years.

The apportionment of electoral districts is to be based primarily on the principle of equal representation, but geographical features, community interests, the boundaries of administrative and traditional areas, means of communication, and the mobility and density of the population may also be taken into account.

Elections to the Nitijela are by secret ballot. All citizens of the Marshall Islands who are eighteen years of age or older and who are not certified insane, serving a sentence of imprisonment, or on parole or probation for a felony are eligible to vote. Persons may vote either in the electoral district where they reside or in the district where they have customary land rights. Any questions concerning the right to vote in an election or the qualifications of candidates for the Nitijela are referred to the High Court (Constitution, Article V; Elections and Referenda Act 1980, 2 MIRC, Chapter 1).

General elections are held every four years, but the Nitijela may be dissolved by the President and an election held earlier if two motions of no confidence in the Cabinet have lapsed or if, thirty days after the election of a President, no Cabinet has been appointed. The President's power to dissolve the Nitijela lapses after thirty days. A general election must be held within seven weeks after dissolution.

Article IV of the Constitution provides that candidates for the Nitijela must be eligible voters at least twenty-one years old and permits candidates to stand in a district other than that in which they reside. Employees of the public service must resign their employment if elected. If the seat of a member of the Nitijela becomes vacant for any reason other than the dissolution of the Nitijela, a special election to fill the vacant seat is held in the district. A member's seat may be declared vacant if the member ceases to possess the qualifications for membership, dies, resigns, is absent without leave for twenty consecutive sitting days, or accepts appointment to any other office (except the Cabinet) compensated by public funds.

The Nitijela meets in regular session, beginning on the first Monday in January and lasting at least fifty days. Sessions must be extended upon notice that a motion of no confidence will be called or that an election of a President and appointment of a new Cabinet is required. Special sessions must be called after each general election and may be called by any ten backbenchers, provided that they represent at least four districts and that at least 120 days have elapsed since the end of the preceding session. Although the petition calling for a special session must set forth the "matters of urgent public business" to be considered (Constitution, Article IV, Section 10(3)), other matters may be taken up as well. Special sessions must last at least thirty days.

The Nitijela makes its own rules for the conduct of its proceedings, but the Constitution requires that the rules ensure that all points of view are heard. A quorum is half the membership. Except where the Constitution otherwise requires, decisions are by a majority of the votes of members present, and no decision may be taken on an evenly divided vote. Any member may introduce a bill, and any member may require a roll-call vote, unless on an issue where the Constitution requires a secret ballot. No bill may be passed until it has been read three times. A bill does not become law until it has passed the Nitijela and been certified by the Speaker (who must, prior to certification, submit to the Council of Iroij any bills that involve customary law).

The first order of business of the Nitijela after each general election is election of the Speaker and Vice Speaker. Meetings of the Nitijela are chaired by the Speaker, in the Speaker's absence by the Vice Speaker, and in the absence of both by a member chosen by the Nitijela. If both the Speaker and the Vice Speaker are unable to perform their duties between sessions, the Clerk of the Nitijela (a public service officer) may appoint a backbencher as interim Speaker. The Legislative Procedure Act 1968 (3 MIRC, Chapter 3) provides that the Speaker and the chairs of committees have the power to compel the appearance before meetings of the Nitijela or its committees of witnesses and documents.

Article IV of the Constitution permits the Nitijela to hold in contempt any member who has acted contrary to the Constitution, an act relating to the official business of the Nitijela, or the rules of the Nitijela. The punishment for contempt by a member is limited to suspension for ten sitting days. Nonmembers may be punished only under an act and by the High Court. Members of the Nitijela are privileged from arrest, except for felonies, during a session and while going to or returning from a session. The Nitijela and its members are immune from liability for any vote, statement, publication, or other act done as part of the official business of the Nitijela. The Speaker and other officers are also immune from liability for the conduct of the business of the Nitijela.

Bills relating to the compensation of the President, ministers, the Speaker, Vice Speaker, and members of the Nitijela must be supported by a committee report that takes into account the general level of incomes in the community, the cost of living, nature of the office, qualifications of the persons affected, freedom of these persons to engage in other occupations, and any other relevant conditions.

d. Council of Iroij

The governmental system prescribed by the Constitution is largely nontraditional, but the Constitution makes room for the participation in government of traditional leaders, although "not necessarily in a traditional manner or solely with respect to their traditional functions."[4]

The Council of Iroij (Iroij are chiefly lineages) is one of the ways that the presence of traditional leaders in the government is institutionalized. The council's function is advisory. It has no authority over either the Nitijela or Cabinet and no power to veto legislation or ministerial acts.

The Constitution (Articles III and X) gives four functions to the council:

1. it may consider any matter of concern to the Marshall Islands and express an opinion on that matter to Cabinet;
2. it may request the reconsideration by the Nitijela of any bill affecting customary law, traditional practice, or land tenure;
3. it may have any other functions that are conferred on it by the Nitijela; and
4. when the Nitijela is considering the passage of a bill that declares the customary law, a joint committee of the Nitijela and the council must report on the matter to the Nitijela before the bill's second reading.

The council's advisory function with respect to the Cabinet is very broad; the council is not limited to advice on matters relating to customary law but may speak on any matter of concern to the Marshalls. The Cabinet, however, is not required to follow the council's advice. The council's advisory function with respect to the Nitijela is theoretically more narrow, limited to customary law and land matters. This power could be quite sweeping, however, because every act of the Nitijela affects custom in some way, and Article III of the Constitution gives the council the power to decide which bills affect custom.

Under Article III, the Nitijela must reconsider any bill returned to it by the council but need not follow the council's advice. The council receives every bill the Nitijela passes, and the Speaker must delay certification of bills for one week to give the council time to decide whether the bill should be reconsidered. If the council requests reconsideration, the Nitijela must reconsider the bill. To aid in the Nitijela's reconsideration, the council may include its "observations" when it resubmits the bill. In addition, "for the purpose of endeavoring to reach agreement about the content of the bill" (an aim that sounds more like traditional government by consensus than like a parliamentary system), the Speaker, in consultation with the chairperson of the council, may arrange for a joint conference between members of the Nitijela and council (Constitution, Article III). Although the council can require reconsideration, the Nitijela is free after reconsideration either to amend the bill or to reaffirm its support for the bill without amendment.

The council's role in relation to bills that declare customary law is limited to membership on a joint committee that is given a "reasonable opportunity" to report on the bill to the Nitijela (Constitution, Article X). The ultimate decision as to what form the bill will take and whether to pass it is up to the majority vote of the Nitijela. To date, no legislation has been passed conferring other functions on the council. Lynch reports that, up to 1983, "the public involvement of the Council of Iroij in the governance of the Marshalls [was] minimal."[5]

The council is composed of twelve "eligible persons"—five from the Ralik (western or sunset) chain of atolls and islands and seven from the Ratak (eastern or sunrise) chain (Constitution, Article III). The selection of members combines traditional and new criteria. An eligible person is an Iroij chief or the equivalent, who must be qualified to vote in general elections and may not be a member of the Nitijela. If there are more eligible persons in a district than seats on the council, the member from that district is chosen every year, either by agreement of the eligible persons or, if that is not possible, by the Nitijela. If there is no eligible person in a district, the council, taking customary law and traditional practice into account, selects as the member from that district a person who has family ties to the person who would have been the member. The Constitution also recognizes that custom can change. If individuals or a group come to have rights and obligations analogous to those of Iroij leaders, they become eligible persons. Any question as to the right of a person to be a member is to be determined by the High Court.

The chair of the council, who presides at its meetings, is selected by majority vote in a secret ballot. If the chair and the vice chair are unavailable, the oldest living member presides.

The council meets whenever the Nitijela is in session and for as long thereafter as it needs to review bills. A quorum is half the membership; there is no provision in the Constitution as to the number of votes needed to take action. Council members may appoint deputies to represent them at meetings they cannot attend. Council members are immune from liability for their votes, statements, publications, or any other action taken as part of the official business of the council.

e. Judiciary

Article VI of the Constitution provides that the judiciary is independent of the executive and the legislature. That article establishes a Supreme Court, High Court, Traditional Rights Court and whatever District Courts, Community Courts, or other subordinate courts may be prescribed by law.

(i) High Court and Supreme Court

The Supreme Court is the highest appellate court. Appeals lie of right to the Supreme Court from final decisions of the High Court; the Supreme Court also has the discretion to take appeals from final decisions of other courts. Two or more Supreme Court judges must concur in any appeal (Constitution, Article VI; Judiciary Act 1983, 27 MIRC, Chapter 2).

The High Court is both a trial court with original jurisdiction and an appellate court for cases from subordinate courts. If a judge of the High Court determines that a case involves a substantial question of law as to the interpretation of the Constitution or any other matter of public importance, the judge may convene a panel of three judges (some of whom may be drawn, if the membership of the High Court is insufficient, from the Supreme Court) to decide the case. In addition, the High Court may, on its own motion or on the application of a party to the proceedings, remove to the Supreme Court any question about the interpretation or effect of the Constitution. (Constitution, Article VI).

Article VI of the Constitution and the Judiciary Act together establish the membership, appointment, and removal of Supreme Court and High Court judges. The Supreme Court consists of a Chief Justice and two associate justices, and the High Court of a Chief Justice and such associate judges as may from time to time be designated. Judges of the Supreme Court and High Court are appointed by the Cabinet, acting on the recommendation of the Judicial Service Commission and with the approval of the Nitijela. Marshallese judges hold office during good behavior and until the age of seventy-two, but a judge who is not a citizen of the Marshall Islands may be appointed for a term of one or more years. Article VI stipulates that "judges must be persons qualified by education, experience and character to discharge judicial office," suggesting that they should but need not necessarily be lawyers. Judges may be removed from office only by a two-thirds vote of the total membership of the Nitijela and only on the grounds of clear failure to discharge the duties of office or treason, bribery, or other high crimes.

(ii) District Courts and Community Courts

The Nitijela has, in the Judiciary Act, established a District Court, which has original jurisdiction, concurrently with the High Court, in civil cases where the property involved does not exceed $5,000 (with some exceptions, including cases adjudicating interests in land) and in criminal cases involving offenses for which the maximum penalty does not exceed a fine of $2,000 or imprisonment for a term of three years or both. The District Court also has appellate jurisdiction over decisions of Community Courts.

The District Court consists of a presiding judge and such number of associate judges as is determined by the Judicial Service Commission. Judges are appointed by the Judicial Service Commission for terms of ten years and may be removed from office on the same grounds as High Court justices may be removed. The presiding judge must be either an attorney licensed to practice in the Marshall Islands or a person who has been an associate judge for at least five years. Associate judges must be admitted to practice as trial assistants. Each District Court has jurisdiction throughout the entire Republic, although the Chief Justice of the High Court may assign District Court judges to different geographical areas.

The Judiciary Act also establishes a Community Court for each local government area. A Community Court has original jurisdiction, concurrent with the High Court and District Court, in its local government area over civil cases where the amount claimed or value of the property involved does not exceed $100 (with some exceptions, including cases involving interests in land) and in criminal cases for which the maximum penalty does not exceed a fine of $200 or imprisonment for six months or both.

Each Community Court consists of a presiding judge and such number of associate judges as is determined by the Judicial Service Commission. Judges are appointed by the commission for terms of up to four years and may be removed for cause. A Community Court judge need not have legal training or experience. In appointing Community Court judges, the commission may consider the wishes of the people of the local government area.

Where there is concurrent jurisdiction, a case may be removed to the higher court on motion of a party or on the request of the higher court. Similarly, the higher court may determine that a case is better heard in the lower court.

A District Court or a Community Court may, at the request of a party to a dispute, conduct informal hearings in an effort to obtain an amicable settlement. The settlement, when written by the judge and signed by the parties, has the same effect as a judgment of the court. A settlement may be reached even though for an amount that would put the case beyond the usual jurisdiction of the District or Community Court.

(iii) Traditional Rights Court

The jurisdiction of the Traditional Rights Court is ancillary to proceedings pending in the other courts. The Traditional Rights Court's jurisdiction may be invoked "as of right" by a party to a pending proceeding, but only if the court hearing the case certifies that a "substantial question has arisen within the jurisdiction of the Traditional Rights Court" (Constitution, Article VI). Or a judge of the High Court may appoint one or more assessors to sit with the High Court at trial and advise him in regard to customary law or traditional practice but not to participate in the determination of the case (Judiciary Act).

The Traditional Rights Court determines questions relating to customary titles, land rights, or other legal interests depending wholly or partly on customary law or traditional practice (Constitution, Article VI). In addition, the Traditional Rights Court has jurisdiction when the government exercises its right of eminent domain. Before making an order relating to compensation for a compulsory taking of private property, the High Court must refer the matter to the Traditional Rights Court for advice on "whether compensation for land rights is just" (Constitution, Article II).

In eminent domain cases under Article II, the opinion of the Traditional Rights Court is merely advisory, although the High Court is required to give substantial weight to its opinion. In other customary law cases under Article VI, the High Court is required not only to give substantial weight to the opinion of the Traditional Rights Court but also to deem the Traditional Rights Court's determination binding if the certifying court concludes that justice so requires. (It is unclear whether this provision intends the determination to be binding only upon the certifying court or binding precedent for later cases, including those before the Traditional Rights Court. Given that it is the certifying court that decides whether the determination will be binding, the latter interpretation seems more likely.)

The Traditional Rights Court is not given jurisdiction over a number of issues where one might have expected its expertise to be sought. Thus, it is the High Court, not the Traditional Rights Court, that settles controversies about membership of the Council of Iroij. And it is the Nitijela, with advice from the council, but not from the Traditional Rights Court, that declares customary law (Constitution, Articles III and X).

The Constitution, Article VI, provides for the membership of the Traditional Rights Court to consist of panels of three or more judges, selected so as to include fair representation of all classes of customary land rights and, within those guidelines, for the membership and rules of the Traditional Rights Court to be determined by the High Court. The High Court's rules provide for a total membership on the Traditional Rights Court of twelve judges—four iroij, four alab and four dri jerbal (i.e., chiefs and leaders of the major groups holding customary land rights). Five are from the Ralik chain and seven from the Ratak chain. Appointments are for five years. Judges do not need legal degrees. They must be citizens of the Marshall Islands, thirty years of age or older, and knowledgeable in the customs and traditions of the Marshall Islands.

2. LOCAL GOVERNMENT

The Constitution, at Articles I and IX, provides that the people of every populated atoll or island have the right to a local government that operates in accordance with law. Local governments are given the power to make ordinances for their areas, to the extent that such ordinances do not conflict with any act, executive instrument, or the Constitution. In 1980, the Nitijela passed the Local Government Act (4 MIRC, Chapter 1), which provides that local governments are bodies corporate that may acquire, hold, and dispose of property and may sue and be sued. The act is an amalgam of customary and new forms of government. On the one hand, it requires each local government to have a written constitution that provides for an elected legislature, an executive committee, a head of government, and a staff. On the other hand, elections to the local government's legislative council and to the executive may be either by ballot or by consensus. Elections by consensus are overseen by a certifying officer, who holds election meetings at which the officer should attempt to achieve a decision by consensus. There must be at least two meetings, and more may be held if the officer determines that they are necessary. Should the certifying officer decide that additional meetings are unlikely to result in consensus in a reasonable time, or if the chief electoral officer decides that, because of geography, number of electors, or other reasons, election by consensus is impracticable, an election by ballot may be held instead.

The Elections and Referenda Act (2 MIRC, Chapter 1) provides that the qualifications for voting for local government candidates are the same as those for elections to the Nitijela (**see IV, C (1) National Government**) and that candidates for local government must be eligible voters who have registered to vote in the local government area for which they are candidates. Local government councils may set additional qualifications for their candidates.

The Local Government Act stipulates that the Cabinet include a minister with responsibility for local government affairs. The act also establishes a department to maintain continuing oversight over the operations of local governments, coordinate relations between each local government and the central government, and arrange training for local government staffs. The department also includes a local government advisor. The act establishes a local government fund. The Nitijela authorizes payments into the fund, disbursements from which may be made only with the consent of the Secretary of Finance. Local governments may raise additional revenues by imposing taxes on beer and liquor consumption. If the operations of a local government endanger the health, safety, or economic well-being of a local government area, the Cabinet may suspend the local government and appoint an administrator or receiver.

D. Emergency Powers

The Emergencies Act 1979 (7 MIRC, Chapter 11) authorizes the Cabinet (or, if the Cabinet cannot be convened, the President) to declare a state of emergency when a grave emergency exists endangering life, health, or property. A state of emergency lapses after ten days, if the Nitijela is in session or after thirty-one days if the Nitijela is not in session, unless it has in the meantime been confirmed by the Nitijela, in which case it may remain in force for up to twelve months. In the absence of a resolution by the Nitijela, a state of emergency may be extended by the issuance of a new proclamation. When a state of emergency is in force, the Cabinet (or President) may promulgate whatever orders are necessary to ensure the safety of life, health, and property of the community, including the advancement of monies from the general fund. However, the Constitution does not authorize the issuance of any order that would suspend or limit the Bill of Rights and, in the absence of constitutional authority, no statute may do so.

E. Human Rights

Article II of the Marshall Islands Constitution (the Bill of Rights) protects the civil rights of individuals as against their government. Article II includes detailed explanations of each right, most of which summarize the long history of decisions of American courts interpreting the U.S. Constitution's Bill of Rights. Although these explanations were probably intended to clarify the constitutional grant of rights (and some of them do), many of them are understandable only in the light of a full reading of the relevant U.S. judicial decisions and applicable only in the American context. Article II provides that no right (either those enumerated or any other right retained by the people) may be denied or abridged and that any provision of the Bill of Rights may be invoked in litigation either as a defense or as a basis for obtaining relief.

The rights addressed in the Marshall Islands Constitution are as follows:

1. freedom of thought, speech, press, religion, assembly, association, and petition;
2. freedom from slavery and involuntary servitude;
3. freedom from unreasonable search and seizure;
4. right to due process and fair trial;
5. freedom from government takings of land rights or private property, unless for just compensation and for a public use;
6. freedom from cruel and unusual punishment;
7. right to habeas corpus;
8. freedom from ex post facto laws and bills of attainder;
9. no quartering of soldiers without consent;
10. no imprisonment for debt;
11. no conscription except in time of war and right to conscientious objection;
12. right to equal protection under the law;
13. right to personal autonomy and privacy;
14. right to invoke the judicial process and right to vote;
15. right to health, education, and legal services; and
16. right to responsible and ethical government.

The first fourteen of the enumerated rights are in the U.S. Constitution, either expressly or by judicial interpretation. As such, they reflect the individualistic values of a free market society; they are all limitations on governmental power. Except for Article II, Section 5, relating to the government's power of eminent domain (**see XII Land and National Resources**), they tend to follow American models closely, with no particular modifications to make them applicable to the special circumstances and culture of the Marshalls. Experience and the people of the Marshall Islands will determine whether they are appropriate to a society in which government's major role will be to provide services rather than to order the market, in which kin group relations take precedence over individualism and in which deference to rank carries its own dignity. In this connection, it should be noted that Article X of the Constitution seems to permit the Bill of Rights to be abridged by customary law and traditional practices relating to land tenure, but perhaps not by customary law and traditional practices relating to other matters (**see III, D Customs**).

The last two of the enumerated rights do differ significantly from the Bill of Rights in the American Constitution. Rather than limitations on the power of government, they are aspirations for the government to use its power for the public good. Article II states that the government is not required immediately to offer the services promised in Sections 15 and 16, but "to take every step reasonable and necessary" to provide them. Although it will be difficult to protect these rights judicially, Article II permits suits to be brought to enforce them.

V. Administrative Organization and Law

A. Organization

Under Article V of the Constitution, the Cabinet generally directs and controls the government of the Marshall Islands. The President must, as soon as practicable after taking office, nominate for appointment as ministers not fewer than six nor more than ten members of the Nitijela and allocate portfolios among them. The constitutionally required portfolios are Finance, Foreign Affairs, Communications and Transportation, Resources and Development, Social Welfare, and Public Works. Statutes add additional responsibilities. The Local Government Act, for example, requires that one minister have responsibility for local government (see IV, C (2) Local Government). In addition, by statute, the Nitijela has created a number of government offices, departments, agencies, and corporations.

The President is authorized, by the Commissions of Inquiry Act 1986 (6 MIRC, Chapter 3) to appoint commissions of inquiry to investigate and report on any matter having to do with the administration of any department of the government, the conduct of any member of the public service, or any matter about which an inquiry is, in the President's opinion, in the interest of the public safety, national security, or welfare. Commissioners have broad powers to issue summons and to obtain information under oath.

B. Public Service

The Constitution, Article VII, provides for a public service that comprises all government employees. The Public Service Commission Act 1979 (5 MIRC, Chapter 1) establishes a Public Service Commission, consisting of a chair and two other members appointed for terms of up to three years (with eligibility for reappointment) by the Cabinet with the approval of the Nitijela. At least two of the members must be citizens, and no member may serve concurrently in the Nitijela or in other public service employment.

The Public Service Commission is the employing authority for the public service, appoints all public service employees, sets the terms and conditions of their employment, and has general oversight and control of all departments and offices. The commission is responsible to the Cabinet, except that it acts independently in all matters relating to decisions about individual employees. In establishing conditions of employment, the commission must take into account the need for efficient staff; the need to provide employment, varied careers, and adequate advancement for citizens; and the need to further the government's economic and social policies.

There are three constitutional offices in the public service—the Chief Secretary, the Attorney General, and the Secretary of Finance (Constitution, Article VII). All are appointed by the Public Service Commission, but the commission must consult the President and obtain the concurrence of the Cabinet before appointing a Chief Secretary or an Attorney General, and no public service employee may appeal appointments to these offices.

The Chief Secretary heads the public service and is chief administrative and advisory officer of the government. The Chief Secretary is responsible to the Cabinet for the general direction of the work of all departments and offices (including public corporations and statutory authorities) and is entitled to sit in on Cabinet meetings. The Attorney General (who must have the same qualifications as High Court judges) heads the Justice Department; advises on legal matters referred by the Cabinet, the President, or any minister; is responsible for instituting prosecutions and for seeing to it that the laws are executed. In performing these functions, the Attorney General is independent of Cabinet. The Secretary of Finance heads the Finance Department and advises the Minister of Finance. The Secretary is also responsible for the preparation of annual accounts.

C. Public Finance and Audit

Article VIII of the Constitution lays down a number of rules intended to promote fiscal responsibility. No taxes may be imposed and no public money expended unless authorized by law. All taxes and other revenues received by the government must be paid into a general fund, unless a statute specifies another fund established for a specific purpose. No money may be withdrawn from any fund unless authorized by an appropriations act. The Secretary of Finance submits to the Nitijela annually an accounting of the prior year's revenues and expenditures and a proposed budget for the next year. Bills on all matters pertaining to the budget must originate in the Cabinet. No public money may be expended without Cabinet approval. The Secretary of Finance reports to the Cabinet on the financial implications of any proposal for public expenditure.

Unlike other constitutional officers (who are appointed by the Public Service Commission), the Auditor General is nominated by the Speaker, approved by the Nitijela, and appointed by the President. An Auditor General serves, during good behavior, until retirement. The duties of the Auditor General include auditing the funds and accounts of all branches, offices, corporations, and authorities of government and reporting annually to the Nitijela. In carrying out these duties, the Auditor General is not subject to Cabinet or any other authority but acts independently (Constitution, Article VIII). The Nitijela has provided in the Auditor General's Compensation Act 1980 (3 MIRC, Chapter 3) and Auditor General (Duties, Functions and Powers) Act 1986 (3 MIRC, Chapter 9) that the Auditor General must be either a certified public accountant or a person with extensive accounting experience. The acts require the Auditor General to submit audits of government funds to the Nitijela twice a year, instead of once, as provided in the Constitution. The Auditor General has extensive powers in the conduct of audits so as to prevent fraud and waste, including protection of whistle-blowers, access to confidential information, subpoena powers, and penalties for persons who fail to provide information.

The Nitijela has enacted a variety of additional safeguards to prevent fraud or waste in the expenditure of public funds. The Department of Finance Act 1979 (11 MIRC, Chapter 8) establishes a department to administer all revenue, fiscal, and procurement functions. The Over-Expenditure and Over-Obligation of Appropriated Funds Act 1977 (11 MIRC, Chapter 9) makes personally liable anyone who authorizes or expends government funds in excess of authorized amounts. The Procurement Code 1988 (44 MIRC, Chapter 1) establishes a Procurement Policy Office, directly responsible to the Chief Secretary, to promulgate regulations concerning government supplies, services, and construction contracts and to audit and monitor the implementation of its regulations.

D. Rule Making

Under the Administrative Procedure Act 1979 (6 MIRC, Chapter 1) every agency, board, commission, department, or office of the government is authorized to adopt rules that set out the general course and method of its operations and set forth the nature and requirements of its formal and informal procedures. Prior to the adoption, amendment, or repeal of any rule, the agency must give at least thirty days' notice by posting the notice in various government offices and having it read over Marshallese radio. Notices must be in both English and Marshallese. The agency must afford all interested persons reasonable opportunity to comment on proposals and must consider these comments fully, but need conduct public hearings only if requested by the Nitijela or any other government agency.

The act permits any interested person to petition an agency to adopt, amend, or repeal a rule. Within fifteen days thereafter, the agency must either deny the petition, giving in writing its reasons for the denial, or convene a public hearing on the petition, and notify the petitioner of its action within the following fifteen days. A party who alleges that an agency rule, or its threatened application, would impair the party's legal rights and privileges may bring an action in the High Court for a declaratory judgment as to the validity or applicability of the rule.

E. Review of Administrative Action

The Administrative Procedure Act provides that any party whose legal rights have been directly and adversely affected by agency action is entitled to an agency hearing. All parties to the hearing must receive reasonable notice of the time, place, and nature of the hearing; the legal authority and jurisdiction under which it is being held; the statutes and rules involved; and a short and plain statement of the issues. All parties must have an opportunity to respond and present evidence and argument on the issues, and findings of fact must be based exclusively on the evidence and on matters officially noted. Generally, the rules of evidence of the High Court must be followed, although when it is necessary to obtain information that is not admissible under these rules, the evidence may be presented, provided that it is of a type commonly relied upon by reasonably prudent persons in the conduct of their affairs. Final decisions must be in writing and contain findings of fact and conclusions of law, separately stated. If a majority of the officials of the agency who are to render the final decision in a contested case have not heard the case or read the record, and if they intend to render a decision adverse to a party other than the agency, they must submit their proposed decision to the parties and give them the opportunity to file exceptions and to present briefs and oral arguments.

A person who has exhausted all the administrative remedies the agency provides and who is aggrieved by the outcome of a hearing is entitled to judicial review by the High Court. The review is confined to the record of the agency hearing, although parties may petition to present additional evidence, if it is material and if there were justifiable reasons why it was not presented at the hearing. The court does not substitute its judgment for that of the agency as to questions of fact but may reverse or modify the agency decision if it finds that substantial rights of the petitioner have been prejudiced because the agency action violates the Constitution or a statute; exceeds the agency's statutory authority; was made upon unlawful procedure; was affected by other error of law; was clearly erroneous in view of the reliable evidence in the record; or was arbitrary, capricious, or characterized by abuse of discretion (Administrative Procedure Act 1979).

VI. International Obligations

The Constitution, Article V, makes the Cabinet responsible for conducting the foreign affairs of the Marshalls, although all treaties must be approved by the Nitijela. The major international obligation of the Marshalls is the Compact of Free Association between the Marshalls and the United States, which became effective in 1986. Under the compact, Section 311, the United States has assumed "full authority and responsibility for security and defense matters in or relating to the Marshall Islands." The compact permits the United States to retain military bases in the Marshalls for fifteen years from the compact's effective date. Further, although the compact recognizes the capacity of the Marshalls to enter into treaties and other international agreements, the Marshalls must consult with the United States in the conduct of foreign relations and must refrain from actions determined by the United States to be incompatible with its authority over security matters (Sections 121, 123, 313). In return, the United States serves as the Marshalls' primary source of financial support for fifteen years from the compact's effective date and provides the Marshalls with numerous programs and infrastructural services during that period. Most provisions of the compact may be earlier terminated by mutual agreement, unilaterally by the United States on six months' notice, and unilaterally by the Marshalls after a plebiscite and on three months' notice (Sections 441, 442 and 443). If the compact were terminated by mutual agreement, the parties could agree to a continuation of economic aid from the United States. If the compact were terminated by the United States, many of its financial responsibilities would nevertheless continue for fifteen years from the effective date. If terminated by the Marshalls, the authority of the United States over the Marshalls' security and defense would continue for the same period (Sections 451, 452, 453).

The government of the Marshalls adopted into law the Vienna Convention on Diplomatic Relations by means of the Diplomatic Privileges and Immunities Act 1988 (3 MIRC, Chapter 14). The Republic is a member of the United Nations, the South Pacific Forum, the Asian Development Bank, and other international and regional bodies.

VII. Revenue Law

The United States provides a major portion of the government revenues of the Marshall Islands, pursuant to obligations created by the Compact of Free Association. The major sources of taxation are wages and salaries, business revenues, and imports. There is a tax of 8 percent on the first US $11,000 and 12 percent on amounts over US $11,000 of all wages and salaries, except that the tax on noncitizen employees of contractors of U.S. military agencies is 5 percent. Persons earning less than US $5,000 are allowed a US $1,000 deduction (Income Tax Act 1979, 11 MIRC, Chapter 1). Businesses earning less than US $2,000 per year in gross revenues are exempt from taxation. Between US $2,000 and US $10,000 in gross revenues per year, the tax is US $80, and on gross revenues above US $10,000, the tax is 3 percent (Income Tax Act). There are also taxes on most imports, under the Import Duties Act 1984 (11 MIRC, Chapter 5).

In 1987, the Nitijela passed the Foreign Attorneys Tax Act (11 MIRC, Chapter 4), requiring that any attorney who is not a citizen of the Marshall Islands and whose principal place of business is outside the Marshall Islands, must pay a tax amounting to 10 percent of the fee received by him or her for services rendered, whether inside or outside the Marshall Islands, in relation to land situated in the Marshall Islands, a tort or offense committed in the Marshall Islands, any contract or suit relating to the Marshall Islands, or any action or proceeding relating to the Marshall Islands. Failure to pay the tax results in recovery of the amount of tax due plus an amount equal to 200 percent of the amount of tax in default and suspension of the attorney from practice in the Marshalls. The act applies to contracts existing at its effective date to the extent that payments are outstanding.

VIII. INVESTMENT LAW

The Nitijela has created a number of executive agencies and public corporations to aid in investment and economic development. Chief among these are the Office of Planning and Statistics, Foreign Investments Advisory Board, Marshall Islands Development Authority, Kwajalein Atoll Development Authority, and the Marshall Islands Development Bank.

The Office of Planning and Statistics, created by the Planning Act (10 MIRC, Chapter 1), is an advisory body to the Cabinet and is responsible for formulating national and local development goals and objectives, reviewing and making recommendations on programs of the executive departments, coordinating foreign assistance granted to the government for development, reviewing and making recommendations on annual and long-term budget proposals, compiling statistical data, coordinating and mobilizing government resources to implement development plans, and presenting development plans to the Nitijela. The chief planner, who heads the office, is appointed by the Public Service Commission.

The Foreign Investments Advisory Board was created by the Foreign Investments Advisory Board Act 1987 (10 MIRC, Chapter 5). The board has potentially conflicting roles, in that it both promotes foreign investment and licenses foreign investors. The seven-member board consists of the Secretary of Resources and Development, the Secretary of Foreign Affairs, the Chief Secretary, the Secretary of Finance, the Secretary of Interior and Outer Islands Affairs, and two other persons appointed by the President. The chief planner serves as secretary of the board. The board may examine and report on all foreign investments within the country, make recommendations for foreign investment priorities, recommend a system of foreign investment incentives, examine applications for intended foreign investments, and advise the government on the administration needed to facilitate economic development. In carrying out these functions, the board is supposed to promote foreign investment.

No noncitizen may acquire any interest in or carry on any business in the Marshalls without first having submitted an application for a foreign investment license to the board. The board reviews applications to determine the economic need for the business, the degree to which the investment will increase exports and decrease imports, the investment's contribution to the economic well-being of the country, and its potentially adverse effect on existing social and cultural values and customs. Recommendations of the board are submitted to the Cabinet, which acts in its sole discretion. As part of its responsibility for supervision of ongoing foreign investment, the board may revoke licenses if a business is engaging in activities detrimental to the social, economic, and cultural well-being of the country; if it is violating the law; or if its license is found to have been obtained on the basis of false information. The penalty for doing business without a license, for obtaining a license by fraud or misrepresentation or for failure to comply with the terms and conditions of a license is a fine of up to US $10,000 and/or imprisonment of up to one year.

The Marshall Islands Development Authority was created by the Marshall Islands Development Authority Act 1984 (10 MIRC, Chapter 6) as a public corporation with a nine-member board, consisting of the Ministers of Resources and Development, Finance, Interior and Outer Islands Affairs, and Public Works; the Chief Secretary; the chief planner; and three members appointed by Cabinet from the private sector. The authority was empowered to conduct, on behalf of the government, businesses of social and economic importance (including, according to the act, tourism, poultry farming, and piggeries). It was intended to be self-supporting and to contribute profits (as defined in the act) to the general fund.

The Marshall Islands Development Bank has taken over many functions of the Development Authority. The bank, which was established by the Marshall Islands Development Bank Act 1988 (10 MIRC, Chapter 8), is a corporation with authorized capital of US $10 million, raised through share subscriptions. Profits from its activities go to shareholders, rather than to the government's general fund. The managing director of the bank is appointed by the Cabinet. The board of directors consists of the managing director and four to six additional members, appointed by the Cabinet for three-year terms. The bank's primary function is to promote the development and expansion of the Marshalls economy by providing loans and guarantees to enterprises operating in the Marshalls; identifying investment opportunities; supplying technical, managerial, and financial consulting to enterprises; and managing or taking part in the management or supervision of such enterprises. The funds of the Marshall Islands Development Authority have been transferred to the bank.

The Kwajalein Atoll Development Authority, established under the Kwajalein Atoll Development Authority Act 1985 (10 MIRC, Chapter 7), is funded primarily by payments made by the United States under the Compact of Free Association, Sections 321 and 323, which provide compensation for U.S. military uses of Kwajalein. The authority is a public corporation, with a five-member board of directors appointed by the President and made up of the following: the minister with responsibility for Kwajalein, one member of the Kwajalein delegation in the Nitijela (nominated by consensus of the delegation), the Mayor of the Kwajalein Atoll local government, the president of the Chamber of Commerce for Ebeye Island (where many Kwajalein refugees live), and one member nominated by majority decision of the rest of the board. The authority's primary functions are to develop and implement social and economic development programs for the inhabitants of Kwajalein, including a plan to develop other available islands in the atoll for human habitation. For these purposes, the authority may develop and itself carry on agriculture, fisheries, tourism, animal husbandry, and other industries. The authority may buy and sell land and may borrow. The authority is intended to make a profit from its enterprises. It must conduct its enterprises using sound business practices, and its programs and activities must be consonant with overall Marshall Islands development plans and objectives.

Commercial banks may operate in the Marshalls only if they have obtained a license issued by the Commissioner of Banking under the Banking Act 1987 (17 MIRC, Chapter 1).

IX. Welfare Law

The Bill of Rights (Constitution, Article II) provides that the government "recognizes the right of the people to health care, education and legal services" and obliges the government "to take every step reasonable and necessary to provide these services." In addition, Article V, Section 1, of the Constitution makes the Cabinet responsible for establishing and maintaining such institutions and services as are reasonable and necessary for the public health; to enable the Marshallese people to enjoy educational opportunities, an adequate standard of living, and their legal rights; and to serve the people's economic, social and cultural welfare.

Laws relating to public health provide for immunization programs, compulsory reporting of communicable diseases, disaster assistance, and the establishment of a Health Care Revenue Fund (Public Health Safety and Welfare Act, 7 MIRC, Chapter 1; School Immunization Act 1981, 7 MIRC, Chapter 4; Disaster Assistance Act 1987, 7 MIRC, Chapter 10; Communicable Diseases Prevention and Control Act 1988, 7 MIRC, Chapter 15; Health Care Revenue Fund Act 1986, 7 MIRC, Chapter 3).

The Health Services Act 1983 (19 MIRC, Chapter 1) and the Board of Nurse Examiners Act 1984 (19 MIRC, Chapter 2) create boards to establish qualifications, examinations, and other licensing requirements for persons working in medicine, surgery, dentistry, nursing, and related health services.

Education in the Marshalls is not compulsory, and a large proportion of the population has no more than a primary school education. To provide the possibility of tertiary education to as many students as possible, the Scholarship Assistance Act 1979 (14 MIRC, Chapter 1) creates a scholarship assistance fund administered by the Marshall Islands Scholarship Grant and Loan Board, composed of five members appointed by the Cabinet. The board provides grants and loans for scholastic programs that are on a priority list set by the Cabinet to applicants who demonstrate the ability to complete the program and who cannot pay the costs. Recipients must agree to return to the Marshall Islands within six months after completion of the program and to reside there for a period of not less than one year for every two years that were funded.

X. Criminal Law

The Criminal Code (31 MIRC, Chapter 1) classifies a felony as an offense punishable by imprisonment for more than one year. All other offenses are misdemeanors. Every person who commits an offense—or who aids, abets, counsels, commands, induces, or procures the commission of an offense—is punishable as a principal. Every person who, after an offense has been committed, knowingly aids the offender, is classified as an accessory and is punishable by up to one-half the maximum fine or prison term prescribed for the principal (except that, if the maximum term is life imprisonment, an accessory may be imprisoned for up to ten years). Any person who unlawfully attempts to commit a crime is punishable by up to one-half the maximum fine or prison term that may be imposed for the offense (except that, if the crime is first-degree murder, the offender may be imprisoned for thirty years, and if the crime is second-degree murder, the offender may be imprisoned for not less than thirty months nor more than thirty years).

No person judged insane by competent medical authority can be convicted of a crime. Children under the age of ten are conclusively presumed to be incapable of committing a crime. Children between ten and fourteen are conclusively presumed to be incapable of committing any crime except murder and rape, in which case the presumption is rebuttable. The statute of limitations on all Code crimes, except murder, is three years. The statute of limitations is tolled if the offender cannot be found or has left the Republic, so that process cannot be served.

An action may be made a crime either by the Criminal Code (which contains a list of offenses and the maximum penalty for each), by other statutes, or by generally respected native custom. The penalty for customary offenses may not exceed six months' imprisonment or a US $100 fine or both.

Before imposing or suspending sentence, the court may receive evidence on the character of the defendant, including evidence about prior convictions. Under Section 61 of the Code, "due recognition of the customs of the inhabitants of the Republic" must be given in sentencing. Instead of or in addition to the fines or imprisonment set out in the Code, the court may direct that the offender reside within a specified area for a period up to the maximum imprisonment that could be imposed for the offense. The court may also order an offender to pay restitution or compensation to the victim or the government. Instead of imprisonment, the court may order that the offender perform hard labor or work on a public project. The court may suspend the sentence it has imposed, on such terms as to good behavior and such other conditions as the court thinks proper. A condition of a suspended sentence may include the requirement that the offender be placed on probation. Any person convicted of a crime may be pardoned or paroled by the Cabinet on whatever terms it deems best. There is no capital punishment in the Marshalls.

XI. Judicial Procedure

The Judiciary Act 1983 (27 MIRC, Chapter 2) provides that the Supreme Court may make rules governing its practice and procedure and, subject to any act, may make rules of evidence for any court. The Judiciary Act permits the High Court to make rules regulating its civil and criminal procedure, as well as the size, membership, and procedures of the Traditional Rights Court. Although the act does not specify the source of rules for the District and Community Courts, it suggests that Community Courts will be more informal than other courts. Both the Supreme Court and the High Court have issued rules of procedure, and these have been supplemented or later amended by statute. The rules of the Supreme Court and High Court are very similar to the Federal Rules of the United States.

The High Court has also issued rules for hearings before the Traditional Rights Court. Such hearings are to be held, in the first instance, before panels of three judges, representing each of the three major Marshallese traditional landholding classes. A reasonable attempt should be made to assign to a panel judges from the chain of islands in which the land with which the case is concerned is situated. Parties are permitted to make opening and closing statements to the panel and to present witnesses and other evidence. The court may question any of the witnesses and may require that additional witnesses and evidence be presented. The High Court has imposed relatively formal rules of procedure upon the Traditional Rights Court, including the requirement that the rules of evidence applicable in the High Court apply to the Traditional Rights Court. Decisions are by majority vote. Hearings may also be held jointly with the trial court, if the High Court, the Chief Judge of the Traditional Rights Court, or the presiding judge of the panel assigned to the case thinks this would be in the best interests of justice and economy. In a joint hearing, the rules of procedure are those of the trial court.

A. Civil Procedure

The Civil Procedure Act (29 MIRC, Chapter 1) supplements rules made by the courts. It permits an action to proceed where a party is absent from the Marshalls and has not appeared, provided that the defendant has been personally served. In cases other than those concerning divorce, annulment, or adoption, if a defendant who was not personally served appears at any time within one year from final judgment, the court must set aside the judgment.

There is a twenty-year statute of limitations on the enforcement of judgments. The statute of limitations is two years on actions for assault and battery, false imprisonment, or slander; actions against police or process servers; actions for medical malpractice; and actions for personal injury or wrongful death. Actions against the personal representative of a deceased person must be brought within two years of the representative's appointment. All other actions must be commenced within six years after accrual. The statute is tolled for persons who were minors, insane or imprisoned when the cause of action first accrued.

The Evidence Act 1986 (28 MIRC, Chapter 1) applies to judicial proceedings in every court (presumably including the Traditional Rights Court and Community Courts). In general, the act is a simplified and streamlined version of the U.S. Federal Rules of Evidence. The simplicity of the act does away with the confusion found in many established codes. For example, instead of the complicated hearsay rules of other statutes, the act provides simply that evidence must in all cases be direct, explaining that, if evidence refers to a fact that could be seen, the evidence must be given by a witness who saw that fact. Rules as to relevance, proof of the existence and contents of documents, burden of proof, presumptions, estoppel, and privileges are similarly streamlined and made intelligible.

The act includes special rules relating to customary law. Evidence as to any transaction by which a right or custom was created, modified, recognized, asserted, or denied is admissible to show the existence (or nonexistence) of the custom, as is evidence of particular instances in which the right or custom was claimed, recognized, or exercised or in which its exercise was disputed, asserted, or departed from. The opinions of experts as to the existence of custom are also admissible, and, for this purpose, experts are defined broadly as persons who would be likely to know of the existence of the custom.

Under the Arbitration Act 1980 (30 MIRC, Chapter 3) parties may choose to have their disputes arbitrated rather than tried in the courts. The High Court is required to send to arbitration any dispute covered by a written agreement to arbitrate. The act permits parties to choose their own arbitrators and procedures but provides rules for when an agreement is silent. Thus, if the agreement does not stipulate a method for choosing arbitrators, the High Court appoints two or more arbitrators from a list compiled by the parties or, if the parties cannot agree on a list, the Court nominates the arbitrators. Awards are by majority decision in writing of the arbitrators. The High Court may vacate an award only if it was procured by corruption or fraud, an arbitrator was corrupt, the rights of a party were substantially prejudiced by the misconduct of an arbitrator (including refusal to postpone a hearing when sufficient cause was shown or refusing to hear material evidence), or an arbitrator exceeded his or her powers.

B. Criminal Procedure

Any person accused of committing an offense punishable by imprisonment of three years or more may be tried by a jury of four persons, under the Jury Trial Act (27 MIRC, Chapter 5). The state and the defendant are each entitled to two peremptory challenges. A juror must be a citizen, eighteen years or older, and must have resided in the Marshalls for one year immediately prior to jury service. A juror must be able to read, write, speak, and understand either Marshallese or English. He or she may not have been convicted of a crime punishable by imprisonment for more than one year and may not be incapable of being an efficient juror by reason of mental or physical infirmities.

Except in cases authorized in the Criminal Procedure Code (32 MIRC, Chapter 1), no arrest of any person may be made without first obtaining a warrant, which will be issued by a court or the clerk of courts upon a complaint stating facts sufficient to show probable cause to believe or strongly suspect that the person named in the complaint has committed an offense. Arrest without a warrant is authorized by the Criminal Procedure Code where an offense has been committed and the offender is trying to escape, where the offender is in the act of committing an offense, where a police officer has reasonable grounds to believe that a person has committed an offense, or where a police officer finds persons under circumstances that justify a reasonable suspicion that they have committed or are about to commit a felony. For offenses where the penalty is not more than a US $100 fine or six months' imprisonment, a summons may be issued in place of a warrant. A Community Court may issue an oral order in place of either a warrant or a summons.

Force as necessary to compel submission may be used by an arresting officer upon a person who attempts to escape. A police officer or a person entering premises to make an arrest for an offense committed in his or her presence may enter the premises forcefully but must first announce loudly and in a local language that he or she is making an arrest.

During an arrest, the arresting officer may search and seize from the offender's person and from the premises where the arrest was made (to the extent that the premises are in the control of the arrested person) any offensive weapons and any fruits or evidence of the offense. Otherwise, search and seizure may occur only with a warrant issued by a court or the clerk of courts and only if the official is satisfied that grounds for the search exist or that there is probable cause to believe they exist.

The search warrants of every court except Community Courts must be in writing. Warrants may be issued only for property whose possession is unlawful, such as weapons or evidence or tools of a crime. In executing a warrant, a police officer may force entrance, but only after loudly stating the purpose of the entry in a language understood in the locality. No sentence may be set aside for an error in issuing a search warrant unless the reviewing court determines that the error prejudiced the defendant.

Upon arrest, a person must be tried without unnecessary delay. An arrested person has the following rights:

1. to meet with counsel, family members, or an employer;
2. to send a message to those persons;
3. to be released or charged within twenty-four hours;
4. to be informed that he or she has these rights and to be advised of the right to remain silent;
5. to have counsel present during police questioning; and
6. to have the services of the Public Defender without charge.

Evidence obtained in violation of these rights is inadmissible. In addition, every defendant in a criminal case is entitled

1. to have in advance of trial a copy of the charge,
2. to consult counsel before trial and have a representative of defendant's own choosing defend him or her at trial,
3. to have additional time to prepare a defense if the defense would otherwise be prejudiced,
4. to have material witnesses present at trial,
5. to give evidence on his or her own behalf (but may not be required to do so), and
6. to have proceedings interpreted.

A person arrested for murder in the first degree may be released on bail by any judge authorized to sit on the Supreme Court. Any other arrested person is entitled as a matter of right to be released on bail before conviction, and any court or official authorized to issue warrants may fix the bail. Bail should be set promptly; if possible, the amount of bail should be on the arrest warrant. The amount of bail is determined by the court or official fixing it and should guarantee the continuing presence of the accused, taking into account the nature and circumstances of the offense, the weight of the evidence, and the accused's financial ability and character. For any offense punishable by not more than a fine of US $100 or six months' imprisonment, the arrested person may be released on personal recognizance instead of bail.

Upon a written request, accompanied by a copy of the indictment, judgment of conviction, or similar document, the Cabinet will have arrested and delivered up to the executive authority of another government any person charged with treason, felony, or other crime who has gone from that jurisdiction to the Marshalls. The accused may ask for a hearing before a court to contest the legality of the arrest, but neither Cabinet nor the court may inquire into the guilt or innocence of the accused.

C. Appellate Procedure

The Judiciary Act 1983 (27 MIRC, Chapter 2) provides that any appellate tribunal may affirm, modify, set aside, or reverse the decision appealed from or may remand the case with directions for a new trial or for the entry of judgment. The findings of fact of the High Court in cases tried by it shall not be set aside by the Supreme Court unless clearly erroneous, but in all other cases the appellate court may review the facts as well as the law. In a criminal case, the appellate tribunal may set aside a conviction or commute, reduce, or suspend a sentence but may not institute a conviction or increase a sentence. Execution of judgment pending appeal will be stayed only upon order of the appellate court or, for cause shown, the trial court. Generally, either party has a right to appeal, except that, in a criminal case, the government of the Marshall Islands may appeal only when a statute has been held invalid (Civil Procedure Act, 29 MIRC, Chapter 1).

XII. Land and Natural Resources

A. Land Tenure and Administration

During the colonial period, much land in the Marshalls was alienated from local ownership to be used for expatriate settlement and businesses, administrative centers, military bases, and weapons testing sites. While the laws of the Republic contain no provisions requiring the return of alienated land, Section 13 of the Real and Personal Property Act (24 MIRC, Chapter 1) provides that land in the Marshalls may be owned only by citizens or by corporations wholly owned by citizens.

Each of Micronesia's successive colonial rulers tried, to one extent or another, to convert the form of land tenure by Micronesians from customary group rights to individual freeholds. This attempted change was least advanced, however, in the Marshalls, so that most of the land still owned by Marshallese is held under customary tenure. In its support of customary law, the Constitution is strongest in relation to land rights and to the titles of traditional leaders. The equal attention paid to land and titles is not surprising, since land and rank are inextricably mixed in customary law. The main aspects of authority left to traditional leaders after the changes wrought during the colonial period are their powers to decide who can use and transfer customary land and who will hold traditional titles.

The privileging by the Constitution of customary land law occurs in several ways. The Constitution provides, at Article X, that nothing in Article II (the Bill of Rights) invalidates the customary law or any traditional practice concerning land tenure or related matters. In the Bill of Rights itself, customary land tenure is explicitly mentioned as a protected interest, and in the Constitution's general grants of authority over customary law to both the Council of Iroij and the Traditional Rights Court, land rights are specifically mentioned (Articles II, III and VI). Article X of the Constitution further affirms customary land tenure rules by providing that customary land may not be alienated or otherwise disposed of without the approval of the traditional leader who represents all persons having an interest in the land.

The Nitijela has also shown an interest in protecting customary tenure. The Nitijela has used its constitutional power to declare customary law only in relation to customary land rights and the power of traditional leaders over land. The Customary Law (Restoration) Act 1986 (39 MIRC, Chapter 2) declares null and void a decision of the Trust Territory court that, by applying rules adopted by the Japanese administration, would have undermined the powers of traditional leaders over land matters.[6]

The High Court has, to some extent, supported customary land rights, for example in its unwillingness to accept without question the determinations as to land ownership made by various boards and commissions set up during the U.S. administration. The High Court has held that Article X and Article VI, Section 4, of the Constitution entitle all Marshallese to have their land rights determined by customary process. Thus, where the land rights of commoners are in dispute, the High Court's Rules of Civil Procedure require that the parties attempt to obtain a decision of the iroij laplap (the paramount chief) before filing in the High Court. If the land rights of chiefs and chiefly lineages are in contest, the High Court also requires that the parties attempt to reach a settlement by customary means.[7] However, by placing substantive and procedural due process limitations on the powers of chiefs over land, the High Court is changing the nature of traditional land tenure (see **XII, B Customary Land Tenure**).

Because registration and surveying (particularly of land alienated during the colonial period for which recompense is now claimed) have caused numerous problems for the government and for land claimants, statutes pay particular attention to achieving certainty in land registration. The Land Surveyors Registration Act (19 MIRC, Chapter 3) establishes a board composed of the Surveyor General, the Chief Engineer, the Chief of Lands and Surveys, and three members appointed by Cabinet, to license and regulate land surveyors. The Real and Personal Property Act (24 MIRC, Chapter 1) provides for surveying of boundaries and for a fine of up to US $100 or imprisonment not exceeding one year, for the defacement or alteration of boundary markers. The clerk of the High Court maintains a land register, and no transfer of an interest in land, other than a lease for a term not exceeding one year, is valid against any subsequent good faith purchaser of the interest unless recorded. In keeping with this policy of achieving certainty of titles, the High Court has held that professional surveys of land boundaries are conclusive evidence, and the Court will not refer disputes of boundary lines to be decided in customary proceedings, as it does with other disputes concerning customary land rights.[8]

The power to mortgage land is limited. The Constitution provides, at Article X, that, unless customary law permits otherwise, no mortgage of customary land is valid without the approval of the responsible traditional leaders, acting as representatives for the community. The Real Property Trust Instruments Act 1987 (24 MIRC, Chapter 2) permits the Marshall Islands Housing Authority, the Marshall Islands Development Bank, or any other public corporation or authority approved by the Cabinet to lend money taking land as security. Upon foreclosure, the land may be sold at public auction. The act does not require that the purchaser be a Marshallese citizen or a member of the landholding group. Furthermore, Section 14 provides that the act prevails over any contrary law. If the act were held to prevail over the prohibition in the Real and Personal Property Act on land ownership by noncitizens, then foreigners could obtain land in the Marshalls by buying it at foreclosure sales. The Real Property Mortgage Act 1987 (24 MIRC, Chapter 3) permits the mortgaging of leasehold (but not of ownership or traditional land rights) interests. All such mortgages must be registered with the clerk of the High Court; failure to register does not affect the mortgage's validity, but makes it subordinate to registered mortgages. Mortgaged property may be sold upon foreclosure, but the purchaser is buying merely the leasehold interest.

Under the Planning and Zoning Act 1987 (10 MIRC, Chapter 2), zoning is delegated to municipalities. The local government councils of Majuro Atoll, Kwajalein Atoll, and any others from time to time designated by the Minister for Local Government must have a planning commission, consisting of the Mayor, two other members of the local government council, and two local landowners appointed by the council. The planning commissions advise the councils in matters relating to land and water use and zoning.

B. Customary Land Tenure[9]

Throughout most of the Marshalls, the customary land tenure systems of the precolonial era reflected the hierarchical structure of traditional Marshallese society. In theory, all land belonged to the iroij (or ruling) matrilineages and was worked by the kajur (or commoner) matrilineages. The iroij laplap (or paramount chief) could in theory redistribute land rights at will. In practice, land probably did sometimes change hands due to war or other events, and an iroij laplap might on occasion arbitrarily take land away from a lineage or household. But for the most part, because rulers depend on the goodwill of their subjects, a kajur lineage could expect to work the land it had inherited and to pass it on within the lineage, so long as the chiefs received an adequate share of the produce of the land.

Lineages, each of which was administered by an alab (or lineage elder), tended to allocate to each household within the lineage a narrow strip of land, running from the ocean to the lagoon side of the atoll, so that each would have access to farming, fishing, and foraging land available on the atoll. Within households, certain plots of land or rights to certain products could be allocated by a father to his children or could be obtained as gifts upon marriage or adoption.

Successive colonial authorities intended to abolish chiefly and alab authority over land in Micronesia and to convert land tenure to individual ownership (under the German administration, patrilineal inheritance was also encouraged), but these efforts were not very successful in the Marshalls. Colonialism and economic change have, however, had an impact on traditional land tenure systems. The abolition of warfare ended one way in which land was acquired, and the importation by the courts of fairness requirements (both procedural and substantive) into the dealings of iroij laplap with subordinate matrilineages has circumscribed what was once the chief's absolute authority over land. For example, the High Court has refused to permit an iroij laplap to take land away from a commoner who had voted against him in an election, holding that the right to inherited lands may be terminated only on good cause shown by clear and convincing evidence.[10]

C. Government Taking of Land

Public lands are defined in the Public Lands and Resources Act (9 MIRC, Chapter 1) as lands that were owned or maintained by the Japanese government during the Japanese administration and such other lands as the government has acquired or may hereafter acquire for public purposes. However, this provision was enacted under the Trusteeship and, although it has not been modified or repealed, probably does not represent contemporary Marshallese sentiment as to which lands ought to be considered public or government land. Under the Japanese, government-owned land included not only land purchased from Marshallese by the colonial administration but also all purportedly "unused and ownerless" land. "The arbitrary assumption of state title by the Japanese government over land classified as 'unused' was never accepted by the Micronesian people, who regarded all lands and coastal water as being the rightful property of one group or another, irrespective of the intensity or otherwise of use."[11] Nor did the Marshallese agree that land purchases by successive colonial administrations gave the government fee simple title to land that, under customary land law, could not be permanently alienated.

Under the Trusteeship, little was done to return land alienated by the Germans and Japanese to customary owners. During World War II, the American military took over more land without compensation. After the War, the Trusteeship administration (not the Marshallese) decided which lands would remain the property of the administration and which would be returned to prewar owners. The Trusteeship established commissions to determine the ownership of land in the Marshalls, but the work of the commissions was hampered by the wartime destruction of many records and the preference of the Trusteeship authorities for titles granted by the Germans and Japanese over customary land rights, so that many titles are still in dispute. More recently, the Marshall Islands High Court has held that, unlike the Trust Territory courts, it does not consider the findings of these administrative commissions res judicata and will not accept their determinations unless, after inquiry, it is satisfied that due process requirements were observed.[12]

Pursuant to the provision in the Bill of Rights that land may not be acquired by the government other than for just compensation and for a public purpose, the Nitijela has spelled out in detail in the Land Acquisition Act 1986 (9 MIRC, Chapter 2) the procedures for government acquisition of lands, which include preparation by the government of studies justifying compulsory acquisition, notice to all persons interested (including traditional leaders), and review by the High Court and the Traditional Rights Court. The Bill of Rights also requires that land may be taken only if no alternative means to accomplish the purpose exists, that any taking must be preceded by an order of the High Court (which itself must give substantial weight to an opinion of the Traditional Rights Court) establishing the lawfulness of the taking and the fairness of the compensation, and that compensation must include the granting of reasonably equivalent land rights for subsistence and additional payments for those who must then live in circumstances requiring higher levels of support.

A trust fund has been established, funded by the U.S. government, for money that is to be distributed to owners of the lands, water, and airspace of Kwajalein Atoll. The Secretary of Finance oversees distributions from the fund in accordance with agreements between the Marshallese government and the owners (**see also XIX Torts,** for discussion of the Nuclear Claims Tribunal).

D. National Parks and Reserves

There is, in the 1988 edition of the Code, no legislation relating to national parks and reserves.

E. Agriculture, Forests, and Fisheries

Copra is the Marshalls' major agricultural export. The Copra Stabilization Board is empowered to manufacture, process, purchase, sell, and ship copra and its by-products, as well as to engage in research and development of copra production, in order to ensure a continuing market for copra and an economically producible commodity. The board, a public corporation owned 25 percent by the Marshall Islands Development Bank and 75 percent by the government, has a board of directors consisting of the Secretary of Finance, the chair of the Marshall Islands Development Bank, the chair of the Nitijela Committee on Resources and Development, and a copra buyer and a copra processor appointed by the Chief Secretary (Copra Stabilization Board Act 1976, 8 MIRC, Chapter 1). No person or corporation may purchase copra for export unless licensed by the Cabinet, which may also determine the agencies through which copra is exported. No license is required, however, for the export of products manufactured from copra (Business Regulations Act, 20 MIRC, Chapter 1).

The Endangered Species Act 1975 (8 MIRC, Chapter 5) forbids the export (except for subsistence food or for traditional uses) of indigenous plants and animals that, in the determination of the Secretary of Resources and Development, are in danger of extinction.

The Marine Resources Act (33 MIRC, Chapter 1) prohibits fishing by means of explosives, poisons, or chemicals and sets limits on the size and number of turtles, sponges, and mother-of-pearl shells that may be taken. The Marine Resources (Trochus) Act 1983 (33 MIRC, Chapter 3) prohibits the taking of trochus, except during open seasons declared by the Cabinet by persons with customary law rights to fish or under a fishing license.

Licenses for trochus and other fish are issued under the Marine Resources Authority Act 1988 (33 MIRC, Chapter 4), which also establishes the Marine Resources Authority as a public corporation to manage and control the exploitation of marine resources. The authority is governed by a board of directors, consisting of the Ministers of Resources and Development, Foreign Affairs, and Interior and Outer Islands Affairs, and two other members appointed by the President. The authority's powers and duties extend throughout the exclusive economic zone and include implementing a conservation and management program; issuing fishing licenses and licenses for the exploitation of the seabed and subsoil; negotiating foreign fishing agreements; participating in fishing programs through stock ownership, partnerships, joint ventures, or otherwise; and making regulations respecting conservation and management, the operation of fishing vessels, fishing licenses, foreign fishing, and other activities. The Marine Resources Authority Act makes it unlawful for a foreign fishing vessel to operate in the exclusive economic zone unless in accordance with a valid license issued under the act and, if in waters under the jurisdiction of a local government, in accordance with a fishing license issued by that local government as well.

F. Other Natural Resources

The National Environmental Protection Act 1984 (35 MIRC, Chapter 1) establishes the National Environmental Protection Authority, a public corporation whose membership consists of a chair and four other members (two of whom must have experience in environmental concerns, one of whom must have skill in environmental management, and one of whom represents the general public) appointed by the President. The members serve for life unless removed by the President for cause.

The authority's primary purpose is to preserve and improve the quality of the environment. The act gives the authority all powers necessary or convenient for carrying out this goal, including the power to make regulations with respect to drinking water; pollutants; pesticides and other chemicals; hazardous waste; and the preservation of important historical, cultural, and natural sites. In addition, the authority is to formulate policies and regulations for the efficient use and conservation of land, other natural resources, fisheries, and soil. All governmental departments must, in all proposals that may have an environmental impact, include an environmental impact assessment.

The Marshalls are atolls, low-lying coral islands subject to erosion and, as a result of the diminution of the ozone layer, disappearance. The Coast Conservation Act 1988 (33 MIRC, Chapter 5) appoints a Director of Coast Conservation, subject to the National Environmental Protection Authority, responsible for managing and conserving the coastal zone (defined as the area within 25 feet landwards of the high water line and 200 feet seawards of the low water line). The director was required to submit by 1991 a plan for conservation and management of the zone, taking into account both conservation of the coastline and preservation of cultural sites. The plan was to include guidelines to be used in determining the suitability of particular development activities (defined as any activity likely to alter the physical nature of the coast in any way). Thereafter, no person may engage in any development activity in the zone unless he or she has obtained a permit from the director. The director may attach conditions to any permit, and may require any applicant for a permit to submit an environmental impact assessment.

Culture is a natural resource, and a number of acts, including the Natural Environmental Protection Act and the Coast Conservation Act, call for its protection. In particular, the Language Commission Act 1983 (39 MIRC, Chapter 1) establishes a commission to investigate and recommend to the government methods of preserving and encouraging the use of the Marshallese language. The commission is composed of persons appointed by the Cabinet with the concurrence of the Nitijela. The commissioners must be well versed in the Marshallese language and culture or have specialized knowledge of linguistics.

XIII. Persons and Entities

The age of majority is eighteen (Domestic Relations Act, 26 MIRC, Chapter 1), although a woman may be married at sixteen with her parents' consent (see XIV, A Marriages), and a criminal defendant who is sixteen or over may be treated as an adult "if, in the opinion of the court, his physical and mental maturity so justifies" (Juvenile Procedure Act, 26 MIRC, Chapter 3, Section 2). The term *person* is not defined in the Code, but corporations, business associations, and partnerships seem to be able to sue and be sued and to hold and deal in property.

XIV. Family Law

Registers of births, marriages, and deaths are maintained throughout the Marshall Islands. The birth of every child must be registered by the registrar for the atoll on which the child is born. If a child is born out of wedlock, whether statutory or customary, no person may be required to give information as to its father, and the registrar may not enter in the register the father's name except at the joint request of the mother and the person acknowledging himself to be the father. The death of every person and the cause of death must be registered by the registrar for the atoll in which the death occurred. All statutory marriages must be registered by the registrar of the atoll where the marriage took place, but marriages contracted between citizens according to recognized customary practice need not be registered (Births, Deaths and Marriages Registration Act 1988, 26 MIRC, Chapter 4).

A. Marriage

The Code recognizes as valid both marriages contracted between citizens in accordance with recognized customs and marriages contracted pursuant to statute (Births, Deaths and Marriages Registration Act). In order to contract a valid statutory marriage, the male must be eighteen or older and the female sixteen or older (and, if between sixteen and eighteen, her parents' approval is necessary), the marriage may not be between two parties within the prohibited degrees of kinship by statute or customary law, and the parties may not be married to anyone else at the time. Statutory marriages must be performed by a registrar, an ordained minister, a judge of the High Court or District Court, or any person authorized by law to perform marriages (Births, Deaths and Marriages Registration Act).

B. Divorce, Separation, and Annulment

Marriages may be annulled or divorces obtained either in accordance with local custom or in accordance with the Domestic Relations Act (26 MIRC, Chapter 1), regardless of the form under which the marriage was entered into. When an annulment or divorce has been effected in accordance with custom, and its validity is disputed by anyone, any party may bring an action in the High Court for a decree confirming it. The High Court will enter this decree upon a finding that the annulment or divorce is valid in accordance with recognized custom. Proceedings for statutory annulment or divorce may be brought in any Community or District Court within whose jurisdiction either party has resided for three months, or in the High Court.

Grounds for statutory annulment are anything existing at the time of marriage that makes it illegal and void or voidable, under either common or customary law. Grounds for declaring a marriage illegal and void include bigamy, incest, age, or taking part in the ceremony with no intent to marry. Grounds for declaring a marriage voidable include insanity, intoxication, force, and fraud. No annulment will be granted unless one of the parties has resided in the Marshalls for the three months immediately before the filing of the petition. The Domestic Relations Act provides that a court may refuse to grant an annulment if the parties continued to cohabit after the obstacle to the validity of the marriage ceased. The High Court has suggested that continued cohabitation would convince it to uphold a voidable marriage but would have no bearing on a void marriage, because these obstacles to the validity of the marriage are "so strongly embedded in public opinion."[13]

Grounds for statutory divorce are adultery, cruel treatment, neglect and personal indignities, willful desertion continued for at least a year, habitual intemperance, the sentencing of either party to imprisonment for three years or more, insanity, leprosy, separation for two consecutive years, or willful neglect by the husband to provide suitable support for his wife. To bring a divorce action, one of the parties must have resided in the Marshalls for the two years immediately preceding the filing of the complaint. No statutory divorce may be granted if the ground for the divorce has been forgiven by the injured party. Forgiveness may be shown by express proof or by the voluntary cohabitation of the parties with knowledge of the fact, but forgiveness is revoked if the party forgiven again commits a like act or is "guilty of conjugal unkindness sufficiently habitual and gross to show that the conditions of forgiveness have not been accepted in good faith" (Domestic Relations Act).

C. Custody and Support

The Domestic Relations Act provides that the court may make such orders concerning custody of minor children, child support, support of either party, and disposition of their property as justice and the best interests of all concerned require. The act contains reciprocal legislation so that support orders may be pursued in and from other jurisdictions and so that the laws of the Marshalls are uniform with those of other states.

D. Adoption

Children may be adopted in accordance with either local custom or the Domestic Relations Act. When an adoption has been effected in accordance with custom and its validity is disputed by anyone, the act entitles any party to bring an action in the High Court for a decree confirming the adoption. The High Court will enter this decree on a finding that the adoption is valid in accordance with recognized custom.

XV. Personal Property

Questions of the ownership of personal property are matters of customary or common law. The Real and Personal Property Act (24 MIRC, Chapter 1) applies to agreements intending to give rights in personal property as security for the performance of obligations. It obliges both the debtor and the creditor to exercise their rights in the property in good faith and limits the creditor's power to foreclose. The creditor may foreclose after the debtor has been in default for twenty days, if the agreement so provides, but only after forty days if the agreement contains no twenty-day provision, and in any case only after notice to the debtor and an opportunity to cure. Creditors may take possession of foreclosed property without judicial intervention unless this would occasion a breach of the peace.

XVI. Wills and Succession

To be enforceable, a will must have been made in conformity either with the Probate Code (25 MIRC, Chapter 1) or with customary law. Presumably, customary law alone governs in cases of intestacy, since the code contains no intestacy provisions. Under customary law, a person may choose to bequeath items of personal property to named beneficiaries, and a father may grant parcels of land to his children, but most land would, subject to approval of the iroij laplap (the chief of the landholding lineage), remain in the matrilocal household, under the ultimate responsibility of the matrilineage.

Wills made under the Probate Code must be made by persons of sound mind, eighteen years or older. A written will must be executed by the testator and at least two witnesses. If a witness is interested, the will is not invalidated, but the witness cannot take any property left to him or her under the will, unless at least two disinterested witnesses also signed. A holographic will may be made without any witness, but the handwriting must be that of the testator and must be proven by two witnesses. An oral will may be made only by a person in imminent peril of death and is valid only if the maker does then die of the peril. An oral will must be made in the presence of two disinterested witnesses, can dispose only of personal property worth no more than US $1,000, and cannot displace an existing written will.

XVII. Contracts

Contracts, other than those relating to the sales of goods or real property, are matters of customary or common law. Cases involving contract disputes will probably be decided by the courts using a mixture of common law principles, primarily those of American courts, and substantive customary law (see III, E Common Law).

XVIII. COMMERCIAL LAW

A. Sales of Goods

The law relating to sales of goods is codified in the Sale of Goods Act 1986 (23 MIRC, Chapter 1). A contract of sale may be either written or oral or may be implied from conduct, but a contract of sale is enforceable only if the buyer has accepted part of the goods or paid part or all of the price, or if there exists written evidence of the contract that is signed by the party to be charged. Acceptance by the buyer occurs when he or she does any act in relation to the goods that recognizes the existence of the contract. The price in a contract of sale may be fixed by the contract, left to be fixed in a manner agreed, determined by course of dealing of the parties, or—if not determined by any of the foregoing—a reasonable price. Whether a contract provision is a condition (the breach of which permits repudiation of the contract) or a warranty (the breach of which gives rise only to a claim for damages) depends upon the construction of the contract and not upon what the provisions are called. However, a buyer may elect to treat any breach of a condition by the seller as a breach of warranty; if the buyer has accepted the goods, then such breach must be treated as a breach of warranty.

The act contains no implied warranties of merchantability, unless the goods are sold by description or sample. If the goods are sold by sample, there is an implied condition that the goods will correspond to the sample, and that they are free from any defect rendering them unmerchantable that would not be apparent upon reasonable inspection of the sample. If the goods are sold by description from a seller who deals in goods of that kind, there is an implied condition that the goods are merchantable. There is no implied warranty of fitness, unless the buyer has described the intended use to the seller and shown that he or she relies on the seller's judgment.

The Sale of Goods Act maintains the antiquated concept of title, which most jurisdictions in the United States have discarded. Title passes, according to the act, when the parties intended that it did. Intent is determined by the terms of the contract, the conduct of the parties, and the circumstances. Unless a different intention appears, the act presumes that title passes when the contract is made, if it is unconditional; when the goods are in a deliverable state and the buyer has notice thereof, if the seller has promised to do something to the goods before delivering them; when the buyer signifies approval of the goods or after a reasonable time, if the goods were delivered on approval; and, when the goods are appropriated to the contract, if the contract is for future or unascertained goods. Goods are appropriated to the contract when the seller delivers them to a carrier or bailee. Risk of loss passes with title, except that risk lies with the party at fault. A buyer acquires no title in goods unless the seller had title, but a buyer acquires a good title if the buyer bought in good faith and without notice from a seller with voidable title.

The place of delivery of goods is the seller's place of business, unless the contract provides otherwise. Where the contract authorizes or requires that the seller send goods to the buyer, delivery to the carrier is deemed to be delivery to the buyer. Acceptance by the buyer occurs when the buyer intimates to the seller that the buyer has accepted the goods, when the buyer does any act in relation to the goods that is inconsistent with the seller's ownership, or if the buyer retains the goods without intimating to the seller that the buyer has rejected them. If goods that the buyer has not examined are delivered to the buyer, the buyer is not deemed to have accepted them until he or she has had a reasonable opportunity to examine them.

The seller's major remedy is an action for the price. If the buyer wrongfully refuses to accept, the seller may maintain an action for damages, measured by the difference between the contract price and the market price. The buyer's remedy for nondelivery is damages, also measured by the difference between the contract price and the market price. In an action for nondelivery, the court may also award specific performance. The buyer's remedy for breach of warranty does not include rejection of the goods, but the buyer may set off against the price damages for the breach, measured by the difference between the value of the goods as delivered and the value they would have had.

B. Corporations

Private corporations (both profit and nonprofit) are formed by submission for Cabinet approval of articles of incorporation providing information as to the corporate name, its principal office, proposed duration, purposes, powers, capitalization, names of incorporators, number and names of directors (which cannot be less than three) and officers, provisions for management, provisions for voting, disposition of financial surplus, provisions for liquidation, and procedure for amendment of articles and bylaws (Corporations, Partnerships and Associations Act, 18 MIRC, Chapter 1). The act requires the submission of organization documents to the Registrar of Corporations in the Office of the Attorney General, who receives as well all other certificates or documents required to be filed by the act or by regulations. Members of nonprofit corporations have the right to inspect the books and accounts of corporations of which they are members. Shareholders of business corporations do not have that right under the act, but the registrar may order any corporation to produce its books and accounts, and the Cabinet may order an audit of the accounts of any corporation. The registrar also has the power, when the registrar deems it in the public interest, to convene a special meeting of the members, directors, or officers of any corporation. Violations of the act or regulations may be enjoined, and the attorney general may seek other relief as well.

The High Court seems to be deciding cases involving Marshall Islands corporations using an amalgam of U.S. corporate law principles and Marshallese custom. Thus, it held an action of the board of directors of the Kwajalein Atoll Corporation invalid on the ground that the board was dominated by a member with an interest in the outcome. The Court found that the domination stemmed from the inability of persons of lesser traditional rank on a board to disagree with a member who is an iroij laplap.[14]

C. Business Regulation

A business license is required of any person, partnership, corporation, or association engaged in importing or exporting; securities dealing; insurance; hotel operation; the practice of law, medicine, dentistry, accounting, or professional consulting; the operation of commercial shipping; a trading or travel agency; or a small business. Licenses are issued by the Secretary of Finance for renewable terms of one year. The Secretary of Finance may refuse to issue a license or may revoke a license if satisfied that it is in the public interest to do so, and a person aggrieved by a refusal or revocation may petition the High Court within thirty days. Willful operation without a valid license is a misdemeanor. In addition, the license fee is increased by 10 percent for each month in default, up to a maximum of 100 percent. License fees are prescribed by statute (Business Licenses Act 1983, 20 MIRC, Chapter 2).

Under the Unfair Business Practices Act (20 MIRC, Chapter 3), it is unlawful to use a combination of capital in order to create or carry out restrictions in trade or commerce, limit or reduce production or increase the price, prevent competition, fix prices, or discriminate in price between different purchasers of the same goods. Contracts or agreements attempting to do any of the above are void, and violators of these provisions are guilty of a misdemeanor and liable for a fine of US $50 to US $5,000. Injured parties may bring civil actions in the High Court and recover treble damages.

D. Consumer Protection

The Consumer Protection Act (20 MIRC, Chapter 4) makes it unlawful to engage in the following unfair or deceptive acts in the conduct of trade:

1. passing off goods or services as those of another;
2. causing likelihood of confusion or of misunderstanding as to the source of goods or services;
3. representing that used goods are new;
4. misrepresenting the standard or quality of goods or services;
5. disparaging the goods or services of another by false statements;
6. advertising goods or services with the intent not to sell them as advertised or with a supply that is insufficient to meet public demand;
7. making false statements about the reasons for price reductions; or
8. engaging in any other conduct that creates the likelihood of confusion or is unfair or deceptive to consumers.

Willful violations of the act may result in civil fines of up to US $1,000 per violation. The Attorney General may bring civil proceedings to enjoin the above activities, and violations of an injunction are punishable by civil fines up to US $10,000. Corporations that have violated the act may have their corporate franchise revoked. Injured parties may sue in the High Court and receive the greater of actual damages or US $100; the Court may, in addition, award punitive damages. If the unlawful act has caused similar injury to numerous persons, class actions may be brought.

In 1975, finding that in numerous instances merchants, in monopoly or near-monopoly situations, were charging excessive prices, the Nitijela enacted the Price Control Act (10 MIRC, Chapter 11) providing for the appointment of a Price Control Board, which may declare price controls whenever it finds that the retail prices of essential items are unreasonably high. The board is composed of five members who must be citizens and residents of the Marshalls, appointed by the Chief Secretary with the advice and consent of the Nitijela. The act states that retail prices that do not exceed 130 percent of the direct cost paid by the retailer are not unreasonably high.

XIX. Torts

Tort law is a customary and common law matter. Tort law cases were decided by the Trust Territory courts in accordance with the American Law Institute's *Restatement of Torts* or the general rules of U.S. jurisdictions. Today, the courts are free to fashion tort principles that accord with the conditions and customs of the Marshall Islands (**see III, E Common Law**).

In a wrongful death action, the court may award damages not exceeding US $100,000, proportional to the pecuniary injuries to the persons for whose benefit the action was brought (which persons may be only the surviving spouse, children, and next of kin). In the death of a child, the damages awarded to a parent (or one who stands in the place of a parent pursuant to customary law) may include an amount for pain and suffering (Civil Procedure Act, 29 MIRC, Chapter 1).

Under a 1986 treaty, the United States has provided $220 million (later raised to $265 million) in compensation for medical problems and land damage caused to the residents of Bikini, Eniwetok, Rongelap, Utirik, and other atolls by U.S. nuclear testing. Payments are to be allocated by the Nuclear Claims Tribunal, composed of three judges appointed by the government of the Marshall Islands. The Nuclear Claims Tribunal Act 1987 (42 MIRC, Chapter 1) establishes not only the tribunal to hear claims, but also local distribution authorities to receive and distribute funds provided to any particular atoll. The act also establishes an Office of Public Advocates to assist claimants, Office of the Defender of the Fund to defend claims against the fund, and mediation officers familiar with customary law to try to effect amicable settlements of claims. The act contains rules for processing, mediating, and arbitrating claims seeking compensation, challenging the fairness of proposed redistribution schemes or the administration of those schemes, or challenging the determinations of local distribution authorities.

XX. Labor Law

The minimum wage for every employee of the government or of private employers is US $1.50 per hour. The penalty for paying below the minimum wage is a fine up to US $1,000 or, in default, imprisonment up to six months (Minimum Wage Act 1986, 16 MIRC, Chapter 4). A board of inquiry (consisting of four members appointed by the Cabinet with the approval of the Nitijela) was established in 1983 to investigate the cost of living and working conditions in the Marshalls, and to make recommendations with regard to minimum wages, working hours and overtime, dangerous work, and minimum ages for employment (Labor [Minimum Conditions] Inquiry Act 1983, 16 MIRC, Chapter 5).

A manpower training program has been established under the direction of a board of supervisors consisting of the Secretaries of Resources and Development, Social Services, Education, and Public Works, the chair of the Public Services Commission, and two persons from the private sector appointed by the Minister for Resources and Development. The board establishes priorities for business training programs, administers a fund to finance the programs, oversees the programs and selection of trainees, and gives loans to persons who have completed training courses so that they may set themselves up in businesses (Industries Development Act 1981, 10 MIRC, Chapter 3).

The government has established a social security system covering all employees, including employees of the government (Social Security Act 1987, 15 MIRC, Chapter 1). Employee contributions are a graduated percentage (from 3 percent prior to June 30, 1990, rising to 6 percent after June 30, 2000) of the first US $2,000 of covered earnings. Employers contribute equal amounts per employee. Benefits (which are calculated as a percentage of covered earnings, so that persons who earned more will obtain more) include old age benefits (defined as commencing at age sixty), disability insurance, and surviving spouse and children annuities.

It is the purpose of the Marshallese government to give preference in employment to Marshallese residents (Protection of Resident Workers Act, 16 MIRC, Chapter 1). To this end, the Labor Division employment service operates free public employment offices throughout the Marshalls. The act prohibits employers from hiring nonresidents for longer than ninety days unless the employer has filed with the employment service an application stating the number of nonresident workers desired, and their occupational qualifications and wages. The application will be granted only if the employment service is unable to fill the jobs with qualified resident workers. Employers who violate the act are subject to fines up to US $2,000 and/or imprisonment up to six months. The Nonresident Workers (Fee) Act 1987 (16 MIRC, Chapter 2) requires an employer of nonresident workers to pay to the government a fee equal to US $0.25 for every hour of work performed by each nonresident worker.

XXI. Intellectual Property Rights

The 1988 edition of the Code does not contain legislation relating to trademarks, copyright, or patent protection.

XXII. Legal Education and Profession

There is no law school in the Marshalls. In 1986, there were an estimated twenty-one attorneys practicing full-time in the Marshalls, about one for every 1,750 people. Since this figure includes government lawyers, the actual number of lawyers available to handle legal matters for individuals would be lower. Although few Marshallese have law degrees, a number have experience as trial assistants, having practiced as such during the Trusteeship and since independence. The Judiciary Act 1983 (27 MIRC, Chapter 2) charges the High Court, subject to the approval of the Supreme Court, with regulating the admission, prescribing the rules of conduct of, and disciplining persons practicing before the courts.

The Bill of Rights (Constitution, Article II) recognizes the right of the people to legal services. Under Section 15 of the Bill of Rights, the government obligates itself to take every step reasonable and necessary to provide these services. The Office of the Public Defender has been established (Public Defender Act 1979, 5 MIRC, Chapter 3) to provide legal defense and representation in criminal proceedings to all persons in the Republic upon request. The Chief Public Defender must be a lawyer, admitted to practice in any common law jurisdiction, but the act does not require that other counsel in the office be lawyers. A legal aid office has also been established, under the Legal Aid Office Act 1984 (37 MIRC, Chapter 1) to furnish legal services to any Marshallese citizen who is unable to afford legal services or to find qualified counsel. The services include legal advice and counseling, drafting documents, and representing parties in civil actions. The office also represents criminal defendants when ordered by a court to do so. The chief legal aid officer must be a lawyer, but other counsel in the office may be either lawyers or trial assistants.

The judges of the Supreme Court and High Court need not be lawyers, but they must have (according to the Constitution, Article VII) the education and experience necessary to exercise their judicial functions. At present, the Chief Justices of both courts are noncitizens, as are the judges of the Nuclear Claims Tribunal. There has been considerable turnover of expatriate judges, and allegations of attempts by the Nitijela to influence decisions of the courts and the tribunal. The presiding judge of the District Court must be either a lawyer or a person who has been a judge of that court for at least five years. The other judges of the District Court may be persons who were admitted to practice as trial assistants. The judges of the Community Courts and Traditional Rights Court are expected to be versed in custom and therefore need not be lawyers or trial assistants.

The Lawyers Fees (Regulation and Control) Act 1986 (20 MIRC, Chapter 7) empowers the Minister of Justice to prescribe maximum fees that lawyers may charge their clients. At present, the regulations apply only to contingent fees and provide that for claims other than contractual or debt recovery matters, the contingent fee may not exceed 40 percent on the net (after subtracting the lawyer's disbursements) of the first US $1,000 recovered, 30 percent on the next US $2,000, 20 percent on the next US $47,000, 15 percent on the next US $50,000, 7.5 percent on the next US $50,000, 5 percent on the next US $500,000, and 2.5 percent on any amount over US $1,000,000. In contractual and debt recovery cases, the contingent fee may not exceed 30 percent on the first US $5,000 recovered, 20 percent on the next US $20,000, 15 percent on the next US $75,000, and the above rates on amounts over US $100,000. In addition, foreign lawyers are subject to a special tax on income (see **VII Revenue Law**).

XXIII. Research Guide

A. Statutes and Cases

The Marshall Islands Constitution and statutes have been collected in the Marshall Islands Revised Code (referred to in this chapter as the Code or MIRC), which was published in 1988. The code contains those laws of the Trust Territory that are still in effect, those laws enacted by the Nitijela prior to the effective date of the Constitution that are still in effect, and all laws enacted by the Nitijela through 1988 (see **III, B Legislation**). The Code is arranged in titles and chapters by subject matter. It was published in looseleaf volumes so that legislation enacted after 1988 can be inserted in the volumes.

Laws of the Trust Territory were collected in the Trust Territory Code, but any Trusteeship statute still in effect is in the Marshall Islands Revised Code.

The High Court and Supreme Court issue written decisions. To date, these have not been published, although then Chief Justice John C. Lanham collected some of his High Court decisions in a mimeographed volume he titled *Selected Decisions (and Digests of Decisions) of the High Court of the Republic of the Marshall Islands, April 1982–March 1985*. Copies of this volume and of other decisions of these courts may be available from the clerk of the court.

B. Law, Culture, and Politics of the Marshalls

Armstrong, A. J. "The Island Nations of the Pacific Basin: Their Emerging Independence and Regionalism," in R. Rosendahl, ed. *Current Legal Aspects of Doing Business in the Pacific Basin.* Chicago: American Bar Association, 1987.

Bowman, A. "Judicial Seminars in Micronesia," 9 *Univ. of Hawaii Law Rev.* 533 (1987).

Callies, D., and C. Johnson. "Legal, Business and Economic Aspects of Cobalt-Rich Manganese Crust Mining and Processing in the Republic of the Marshall Islands." East-West Center and University of Hawaii, Honolulu, 1989. Mimeo.

Crocombe, R. G., and A. Ali. *Politics in Micronesia.* Suva: University of South Pacific, Institute of Pacific Studies, 1983.

Dunlap, T. P. "Marshallese Property Law: A Clash Between Native Customs and Western Law," 52 *California State Bar J.* 500 (1977).

Hooper, A., et al. *Class and Culture in the South Pacific.* Suva and Auckland: University of South Pacific and University of Auckland, 1987.

JK (Joan King) Report on Micronesia. Monthly Newsletter, Kolonia, Pohnpei.

Kahn, E. J., Jr. "Customs, Courts and Castes," in E. J. Kahn, Jr., *A Reporter in Micronesia*. New York: Norton, 1966.

King, S. "Remedies for Civil Wrongs: A Pacific Perspective," 9 *Univ. of Hawaii Law Rev.* 13 (1987).

Lundsgaarde, H. *Land Tenure in Oceania*. Honolulu: University of Hawaii Press, 1974.

Mason, L. "The Marshall Islands: Tenures from Subsistence to Star Wars," in R. G. Crocombe, ed. *Land Tenure in the Atolls*. Suva: Institute of Pacific Studies, University of the South Pacific, 1987, 1–27.

McGrath, W., and W. Scott Wilson. "The Marshall, Caroline and Mariana Islands: Too Many Foreign Precedents," in R. G. Crocombe, ed. *Land Tenure in the Pacific*. 3d ed., Suva: University of the South Pacific, 1987, 190.

Neas, M. "Land Ownership Patterns in the Marshall Islands," 85 *Atoll Research Bull.* 17 (1961)

Powles, C. G., and M. Pulea, eds. *Pacific Courts and Legal Systems*. Suva: University of the South Pacific, 1988.

Tobin, J. "Land Tenure in the Marshall Islands," 11 *Atoll Research Bull.* (1956).

Trust Territory of the Pacific Islands, Office of. *First Land Management Conference*. 2 vols. 1966.

———. Office of the High Commissioner. *Land Tenure Patterns: Trust Territory of the Pacific Islands*. 1958.

C. Development of the Compact of Free Association and the Constitution

Armstrong, A. J. "The Emergence of the Micronesians into the International Community: A Study of the Creation of a New International Entity," 5 *Brooklyn J. of International Law* 207 (1979).

———. "The Negotiations for the Future Political Status of Micronesia," 74 *American J. of International Law* 689 (1980).

———. "Strategic Underpinnings of the Legal Regime of Free Association: The Negotiations for the Future Political Status of Micronesia," 7 *Brooklyn J. of International Law* 179 (1981).

Armstrong, A. J., and H. L. Hills. "The Negotiations for the Future Political Status of Micronesia (1980–1984)," 78 *American J. of International Law* 484 (1984).

Burdick, A. "The Constitution of the Federated States of Micronesia," 8 *Univ. of Hawaii Law Rev.* 419 (1986); also in Y. Ghai, ed. *Law, Politics and Government in the Pacific Island States*. Suva: University of the South Pacific, 1988.

Comment. "International Law and Dependent Territories: The Case of Micronesia," 50 *Temple Law Q.* 58 (1976).

Hirayasu, N. "The Process of Self-Determination and Micronesia's Future Political Status under International Law, 9 *University of Hawaii Law Rev* 487 (1987).

Hughes, D., and S. Lingenfelter. *Political Development in Micronesia*. Columbus: Ohio State University, 1974.

Isenberg, M. D. "Reconciling Independence and Security: The Long Term Status of the Trust Territory of the Pacific Islands," 7 *UCLA Pacific Basin Law J.* 210 (1985).

Lynch, C. J. "The 1979 Constitution of the Marshall Islands—A Hybrid?" 61 *Parliamentarian* 230 (1980).

———. "Traditional Leadership in the Constitution of the Marshall Islands." Working Papers Series, Pacific Islands Studies, Center for Asian and Pacific Studies, Social Science Research Institute, University of Hawaii, 1984.

Macdonald, J. R. "Termination of the Strategic Trusteeship: Free Association, the United Nations and International Law," 7 *Brooklyn J. of International Law* 235 (1981).

Meller, N. *Constitutionalism in Micronesia.* Honolulu: Institute for Polynesian Studies, Brigham Young University, 1985.

———. "On Matters Constitutional in Micronesia," 20 J. *Pacific History* 83 (1987).

Quentin-Baxter, A. "The Constitutions of Niue and the Marshall Islands: Common Traits and Points of Difference," in P. Sack, ed. *Pacific Constitutions.* Canberra: Australian National University, 1982.

Van Dorn, W. G., Jr. "The Compact of Free Association: An End to the Trust Territory of the Pacific Islands," 5 *Boston Univ. International Law* 213 (1987).

5. Nauru

TONY DEKLIN

I. Dateline

1798 British Captain John Fearn makes first European contact with Nauru.
1887 Reichschancellor approves incorporation of Nauru into Imperial German Protectorate.
1888 Official incorporation of Nauru into the protectorate. Prohibition of importation and use of firearms and ammunition on Nauru. Commissioner puts all chiefs under arrest and weapons are surrendered. German government grants exclusive right to export phosphate to Jaluit Gesellschaft.
1900 New Zealander Albert Ellis, working for London firm of J. T. Arundel & Company, discovers phosphate on Nauru and Ocean Island.
1905 Right to exploit phosphate transferred to Pacific Phosphate Company. Laborers recruited from Gilbert, Caroline, and Ellice Islands, and later from China.
1906 Phosphate mining begins.
1914 Britain declares war on Germany. H.M.A.S. *Melbourne* visits Nauru, but possession by Australia is not formalized.
1915 Shares held by German subjects in Pacific Phosphate Company vested in Public Trustee as Custodian of Enemy Property.
1917 German stock sold by public auction to large British shipping firm, Elder, Dempster and Company, for £600,000. All German rights of royalty and right of transfer of mining concession abrogated by war, and Pacific Phosphate Company's rights to phosphate now based on British conquest and occupation of Nauru.
1919 Nauru Agreement, providing for joint administration of the island, signed by United Kingdom, Australia, and New Zealand.
1920 Purchase Agreement signed by King George V, granting to Australia, New Zealand, and United Kingdom rights of Pacific Phosphate Company to Nauru phosphate; League of Nations mandate over Nauru granted to Great Britain.
1921 Australian administrator assumes de facto control of administration of Nauru.
1922 Australian government, in response to criticisms voiced by Permanent Mandate Commission of League of Nations, issues statement that mining of phosphate is not detrimental to natives' interests. Public Trustee assigns German royalty rights to British Phosphate Commissioners.
1927 Permanent Mandate Commissioners express to Australia concern about separating judiciary from executive.
1942 Japanese forces occupy Nauru.
1943 1,200 Nauruans, two-thirds of population, deported to Truk.
1945 Japanese surrender Nauru to Australian occupation forces. Surviving deportees return.
1947 Nauru declared a United Nations Trust Territory, administered by Australia.
1950 United Nations Visiting Mission recommends that Council of Chiefs be given increased responsibility in legislation, especially budget appropriation.
1951 U.N. Trusteeship Council supports Nauruans' claim for political advancement. Nauru Local Government Ordinance enacted. First elections under universal suffrage held.

1962 U.N. General Assembly votes 80 to zero to give independence to Nauru.
1964 Nauruans ask Australia for transfer of legal ownership of phosphate deposits to them. Nauruans reject their resettlement on Curtis Island near Queensland.
1966 Trusteeship Council resolution calls on Australia to grant independence to Nauru by January 31, 1968. Legislative Council formed and elections held.
1967 Partnership agreement signed by Nauru local government council and governments of Australia, New Zealand, and United Kingdom.
1968 Elections for Legislative Assembly held; Nauru Independence Constitution adopted by Legislative Assembly; legal and political independence thereby achieved.
1971 Customs and Adopted Laws Act passed, recognizing customary law of Nauruans.
1992 Nauru Local Government Council abolished and Nauru Island Council formed.

II. Historical, Cultural, and Economic Survey

Nauru, a single raised atoll surrounded by reefs, has an area of 8 square miles and, at low tide, a circumference of 12 miles. The plateau rises to some 213 feet above sea level at its highest point. Lying some 26 miles south of the equator at 166 degrees 55 minutes east longitude, Nauru is not a part of any archipelago and is fairly remote from any other islands in the Pacific. Its nearest neighbors are Ocean Island, 165 miles to the east, and Kiribati and Tuvalu, some 400 miles to the northeast.

Nauru is one of the smallest independent states in the Pacific, with a present population of under 10,000, of which 7,000 are Nauruans, who ethnically are Micronesians. The remainder are temporary residents consisting mainly of families of contract officers and indentured tradesmen and laborers employed in the public service and phosphate industry. The principal groups among these temporary residents are Indians, Filipinos, and Europeans, primarily employed in administrative and technical positions and Chinese and Kiribatis, primarily employed as tradesmen and laborers.

Nauruans have their own language, although English is used for official purposes. Most Nauruans are Christians, belonging either to the Nauru Congregational church, the Roman Catholic church, or the Nauru Independent church.

A. Political History

The Nauruan traditional political system was characterized by an elaborate hierarchy of chiefly authority. The political system introduced by the German, British, and Australian administrations during their respective colonial periods took advantage of this chiefly system, using chiefs to advise and sometimes assist in the administration of matters concerning Nauruans.

The development of Nauru's current political and legal system has been shaped by a number of forces: Nauru's traditional chiefly politics; the beachcombers preceding 1888; the German administration in the period from 1888 to 1920; the British administration during which Australia played the main role from 1921 to 1947; the Australian administration from 1947 until 1968, when Nauru became independent; and the Nauruans themselves since independence.

B. Legal History

The cornerstone of the traditional legal system was the authority of the chiefs to maintain order in their communities, and successive colonial administrations relied on this system to maintain their own rule and enforce their regulations. Hence in 1921 chiefs were given power to deal with minor offenses for which fines did not exceed five shillings; the paramount chief dealt with offenses for which the fines were as high as twenty shillings.

The law introduced by the colonial authorities was statutory, consisting primarily of legislation from Germany and later Australia applied by the administering authority and, during Australia's administration, ordinances made by the Administrator.

The Nauruan legal system is, therefore, characterized by a duality of the traditional customary law and the introduced law. Customary law is primarily concerned with land ownership and inheritance, while introduced law applies in other areas.

C. Economy

Before the exploitation of phosphate on the island, Nauruans had a rich subsistence agriculture that supplied all the normal needs of the Nauruans. The coconut tree played a vital role in the subsistence agriculture; every part of the tree had a use in the Nauruan community. This reliance on subsistence agriculture has been replaced almost entirely by the cash economy generated and maintained by the phosphate industry. In Nauru, Nauruans now depend on imported foods and other necessities, and a few Nauruans live in Australia and other countries.

Before the discovery of phosphate, copra was the main source of income for Nauru. Copra production was introduced by the Germans when they took possession of the island as part of the Marshall Islands protectorate in the early 1880s. With the emphasis on phosphate, copra received less and less attention from both the people of Nauru and the administering authorities. Copra is now nonexistent as a cash crop.

The discovery of phosphate in 1900 by Albert Ellis, a New Zealander who worked for a London firm that was exploring for phosphate in the Pacific, made Nauru the richest among the small islands in the Pacific. The subsequent exploitation of phosphate, first by the British Phosphate Company and then by a consortium of British, New Zealand, and Australian governments' representatives, has been the backbone of Nauru's economy up to the present.

Nauruans by and large depend for their living on the royalties they receive from phosphate mining. Excluding Australia and New Zealand, Nauruans have the highest per capita income in the Pacific. The monies from the phosphate mining have been invested abroad as well as locally. For example, in the middle of the city of Melbourne, Australia, is a multistory office complex called Nauru House.

Nauru has its own airline, Air Nauru, which flies to some ten countries and territories. Recently the Nauru government has taken steps to invest in the tourism industry throughout the Pacific, including airlines in Australia and a hotel in Fiji.

Apart from phosphate, there is no other major source of revenue on Nauru. The main prospect lies with fishing, but Nauruans have not yet given serious attention to developing a viable fishing industry.

III. SOURCES OF LAW

The laws applicable on Nauru are derived from four sources: the Constitution, legislation, the common law, and custom.

A. Constitution

The Nauru Constitution was adopted in 1968 by a constitutional convention created by the Legislative Assembly. The Constitution provides, in Article 2, that it is "the supreme law of Nauru," and that any "law inconsistent with [the] *Constitution* is, to the extent of the inconsistency, void." Under Article 84, the Constitution may be altered by Parliament. Most constitutional provisions may be amended by a vote of two-thirds of the entire membership of Parliament. An interval of at least ninety days must pass between the introduction of the proposed constitutional amendment and the vote. However, the amendment of certain constitutional provisions requires both a two-thirds absolute majority in Parliament and a two-thirds majority in a referendum of all qualified voters. These entrenched provisions are set out in Schedule 5 to the Constitution and include, besides Schedule 5, the rules on amending the Constitution and the supremacy clauses, provisions on the following:

1. fundamental rights and freedoms;
2. election of the president;
3. executive authority of Cabinet;
4. establishment and powers of Parliament;
5. duties of the Speaker;
6. government financial matters;
7. automatic citizenship;
8. the major transitional provisions; and
9. Article 93, which maintains in force the 1967 Partnership agreement.

B. Legislation

Nauruan legislation is of four kinds. First are acts of the Nauru Parliament passed since independence in 1968. Second are various forms of subordinate legislation including regulations made under various acts of Parliament. The power to make these is delegated by various enabling acts.

Third, pre-independence legislation that was in force immediately before Independence Day has been adopted under Section 85 of the Constitution. Colonial legislation was known as ordinances, and these continue to be called such. Finally, Section 4 of the Customs and Adopted Laws Act 1971 adopts certain statutes of general application in force in England on January 31, 1968.

C. Common Law

The Customs and Adopted Law Act 1971 adopts both the common law and principles of equity in force in England on January 31, 1968, to the extent that such common law and equity are consistent with the circumstances of Nauru. Since then, the Nauru Supreme Court has developed its own case law, notably in the field of criminal law; most cases that reach the Supreme Court are criminal cases. The Criminal Code of Queensland, Australia, as in force on July 1, 1921, still applies in Nauru.

D. Customary Law

The Constitution of Nauru does not expressly provide for recognition of customs and traditions of the people of Nauru as a source of law. This omission is partially filled by the Custom and

Adopted Laws Act 1971, which directs the courts of Nauru to give effect to customs and usages of Nauruans, to the extent that these are not limited or repealed by legislation. The act provides that Nauruan custom, unless limited or changed by statute, is effective to regulate all dealings in land, all transfers of Nauruans' personal property by gift or succession, and "any matters affecting Nauruans only." The act, however, explicitly abolishes any custom that permits a person to take or deal with another person's property without the consent of the latter person or that permits parents to be deprived of custody of their children without the parents' consent. Arguments that the Constitution may include, by implication, customary law have recently been dismissed by the Supreme Court, which held that customary law has effect only to the extent that it is applied by ordinance or statute.

IV. Constitutional System

A. Territory

The Constitution does not define Nauru's territory, which is described here in **II Historical, Cultural, and Economic Survey**. The Interpretation Act 1971 defines Nauru as the island and its territorial waters, which extend 12 miles from the edge of the reef at low tide.

B. Citizenship

Article 71 of the Constitution provides that persons born before independence who were members of the "Nauruan community" as defined in the pre-independence Nauruan Community Ordinance of 1956–1966, are citizens of Nauru. In addition, under Article 72, anyone born after independence both of whose parents are Nauruan citizens is automatically a citizen. Anyone born after independence one of whose parents is a Nauruan citizen and the other is a Pacific Islander (a term also defined in the Nauruan Community Ordinance) is a citizen if neither parent has, within seven days of birth, declared the child not to be a Nauruan citizen. Citizenship is also granted automatically to persons born in Nauru who have no other nationality. Women married to Nauruan citizens are entitled to Nauruan citizenship.

Parliament is given wide discretion to grant citizenship to persons who are not eligible for automatic citizenship and to deprive persons (other than automatic citizens) of their citizenship for any reason. Parliament may deprive any person, including automatic citizens, of citizenship if that person has become a citizen of another country other than by marriage.

C. Government

Article 1 of the Constitution provides that Nauru is an independent republic. The country is known as the Republic of Nauru. The Constitution establishes a parliamentary form of government, with a President and Cabinet at its head.

The structure of the government reflects the separation of power doctrine in that there are executive, legislative, and judicial branches.

1. HEAD OF STATE

The Constitution does not create a separate office of Head of State. The position, however, seems to be implicit in Article 16 of the Constitution, which creates the office of President, and this is confirmed by the practice of treating the President as Head of State.

The President is elected by Parliament from among the elected members of Parliament (Constitution, Article 16). The qualifications for a candidate for the presidency are therefore those prescribed for members of Parliament (see IV, C., (3) Legislature). The President, however, is the most important authority in the constitutional system, as legislation tends over time to vest more power in the office. In addition, the President has power to appoint and dismiss ministers, to assign portfolios, to preside at Cabinet meetings (Constitution, Articles 9, 22, and 23), to exercise emergency powers (Articles 77 and 78), and to grant pardons or lessen or remit sentences (Article 80).

2. EXECUTIVE

The executive power of the Republic is vested in the Cabinet, which is given authority for what the Constitution terms "the general direction and control of the government of Nauru" (Article 17). The Cabinet comprises the President and four or five ministers appointed by the President, all of whom must be members of Parliament (Article 19). The Cabinet regulates its own procedure and appoints one of its members to act as President whenever the President is unable to act (Articles 21 and 22).

Ministers cease to hold office when a new President is elected, when removed by the President, or when they resign or cease to be members of Parliament (Article 20). The Cabinet is collectively responsible to Parliament, which has the power to remove the Cabinet and President through a vote of no confidence in the Cabinet collectively. If such a vote has the support of at least one-half of the total number of members of Parliament, a new election of the President is held. If Parliament fails to choose a new President within seven days, Parliament itself is dissolved (Article 24).

3. LEGISLATURE

The national legislature of the republic, the Parliament, consists of eighteen members, each of whom must be a citizen of Nauru and at least twenty years of age. In addition, no person can be a member of Parliament if he or she is bankrupt or insolvent, is insane, has been convicted of an offense punishable by death or a prison term of one year or more, or holds a prescribed office in the Nauru government or in a statutory corporation (Constitution, Articles 26–31). The organization of Parliament is similar to that of the Westminster system. Parliament elects one of its members to be Speaker. The Speaker cannot be a Cabinet member (Articles 34–35).

Elections to Parliament are held every three years, or sooner if the President dissolves Parliament or if Parliament is unable to choose a President after a no-confidence vote (Articles 24 and 41). Any Nauruan citizen at least twenty years old is eligible to vote (Article 29).

An individual member forfeits his or her seat if he or she ceases to be qualified, resigns, is absent without leave for two months, or ceases to be a citizen of Nauru (Article 32). The Constitution gives to the Supreme Court of Nauru the power to determine the rights of persons to be and remain members of Parliament (Article 36).

The general power to make laws for the peace, order, and good government of Nauru is vested in Parliament by Article 27. A quorum is half the total number of members of Parliament, and a bill passes if agreed to by a majority of the members present and voting (Articles 45 and 46). A bill becomes law on the date the Speaker certifies the vote (Articles 45–47). The Constitution gives extra territorial effect of any law so made (Article 27).

Parliament may make its own rules regarding the privileges and immunities of its members, Parliamentary committees, and the conduct of its business (Articles 37–38).

4. JUDICIARY

The Constitution establishes the Supreme Court of Nauru as a superior court and permits subordinate courts to be established by law (Articles 48 and 56).

a. Supreme Court

The Supreme Court consists of a Chief Justice and other judges, if any, as determined by law (Article 49). No other judges have been appointed. Judges of the Supreme Court are appointed by the President and must have been entitled to practice as a barrister or solicitor in Nauru for at least five years. A judge must retire at the age of sixty-five unless this age limit is extended by law (Articles 49–50). Judges may be removed for cause by a vote of two-thirds of the entire number of members of Parliament (Article 51).

The Constitution vests in the Supreme Court original jurisdiction to determine any question relating to the interpretation or effect of any provision of the Constitution. The President or a minister, acting with Cabinet approval, may refer to the Supreme Court for an advisory opinion any question that has arisen or may arise in Cabinet concerning the effect or interpretation of the Constitution (Article 55).

Parliament may provide for an appellate division of the Supreme Court, consisting of two or more judges and may provide that appeals from the decisions of the Supreme Court may be taken to a court of another country (Article 57).

Under the Courts Act 1972, each Supreme Court judge, if there are more than one, may exercise the full jurisdiction of the Supreme Court. The act also establishes the positions of the registrar and deputy registrar of the Supreme Court. The duties of the registrar are as prescribed by the rules of court or as determined by the Chief Justice. The act appears to prefer the English system to those of either Australia or New Zealand, although both the latter countries have been involved as much as Great Britain, if not more, in the development of modern Nauru.

b. District Court

The Courts Act also establishes a District Court, composed of a resident magistrate and not fewer than three lay magistrates. The qualifications for appointment as resident magistrate are the same as those for appointment as a judge of the Supreme Court. Lay magistrates must have qualifications of a pleader before they can be appointed. Both the resident magistrate and the lay magistrates are appointed by the President after consultation with the Chief Justice. No lay magistrates have yet been appointed.

The jurisdiction of the District Court in civil matters covers any claim in either contract or tort not exceeding $A3,000.

The act does not appear to give substantive criminal jurisdiction to the District Court; it may well be that because of the small size of the community, matters of a criminal nature can be best left to the Supreme Court.

c. Family Court

The Nauru Family Court was established by the Family Court Act 1973. The court consists of the resident magistrate and other members appointed by the President. This specialist court has specific jurisdiction under the Maintenance Ordinance 1959–1967 and the Adoption of Children Ordinance 1965–1967. The proceedings of the Family Court are not open to the public, in order to safeguard the confidentiality of family matters of the parties.

D. Emergency Powers

Article 77 of the Constitution provides that, if the President is satisfied that a grave emergency threatening the security or economy of Nauru exists, the President may declare a national emergency. The state of emergency lapses if not approved by Parliament within seven days, if Parliament is sitting, or otherwise within twenty-one days. Once approved by Parliament, the state of emergency may extend for up to twelve months and may be further extended by additional declarations. During a national emergency, the President may make orders that appear to the President to be reasonably required, notwithstanding that such orders may be inconsistent with the Constitution's fundamental rights provisions or with any law (Article 78). Any person detained under an Article 78 order must, within three months, be brought before an advisory board—consisting of the Chief Justice, a person nominated by the Chief Justice, and a person nominated by Cabinet—which shall determine whether there is sufficient cause for detention (Article 79).

E. Human Rights

Part II of the Constitution guarantees to "every person in Nauru" protection of certain "fundamental rights and freedoms of the individual," including the right to life, liberty, and security of the person; the enjoyment of property; the protection of the law; freedom of conscience, expression, peaceful assembly and association; and respect for private and family life (Article 3).

Part II also contains limitations on that protection, however, "designed to ensure that the enjoyment of these rights and freedoms by any person does not prejudice the rights and freedoms of other persons or the public interest" (Article 3). Thus, the right to life is limited, in Article 4, by the lawful use of force to defend persons or public property, make a lawful arrest or prevent an escape, or put down riot or insurrection. Similarly, a person's liberty may be denied, under Article 5, in execution of a court's sentence upon conviction, to bring a person before a court, upon reasonable suspicion that a person has committed a crime; to cure diseases and addictions; to prevent the spread of disease; or to ensure the education or welfare of a minor. Article 5, however, requires that a detained person be promptly informed of the reasons for the detention. The other rights enumerated in Part II (most of which are similarly limited, explained, and supported) include

1. freedom from forced labor;
2. freedom from torture and inhuman or degrading punishment;
3. the right not to be compulsorily deprived of property, except for a public purpose and on just terms;
4. freedom from search of persons or property or of entry onto property without consent;
5. conviction only for offenses defined by law; and
6. freedom of thought and religion, including the freedom to change religious beliefs, to worship alone or with others, and to manifest and propagate one's beliefs.

Freedoms and rights conferred by Part II are enforceable by the Supreme Court.

V. Administrative Organization and Law

A. Public Service

The political and legal responsibility for governing Nauru is conferred by the Constitution on the Cabinet, which consists of the President and his ministers. But, as is usual in the Westminster model, that responsibility is carried out in practice by a public service of which the Chief Secretary is the head under the Constitution (Article 68). The Chief Secretary is appointed by the Cabinet and also functions as secretary to the Cabinet (Article 25).

The Chief Secretary has the power both to appoint persons to positions in the public service and to discipline and remove members of the public service (Article 69). The Constitution also provides that decisions of the Chief Secretary can be challenged through appeals to a public service appeals board, consisting of the Chief Justice as chair, a person appointed by the Cabinet, and a representative chosen by public servants (Article 70).

The public service of Nauru is governed by the Public Service Act 1962–1979. The service comprises permanent and temporary officers, who in turn are divided into three divisions. The first division consists essentially of departmental heads, the second division covers middle-ranked officers, and the rest come under the third division.

The administration of the public service is entrusted to a Public Service Commissioner whose main function is to advise the responsible minister on all matters pertaining to the administration of the act. The commissioner is appointed by the minister.

The Public Service Act 1962–1979 states that only Nauruans are eligible for appointment. Nauruan is defined in the Interpretation Act 1971.

B. Public Finance

Articles 58 and 59 of the Constitution limit the government's use of tax revenues and other monies raised or received in Nauru. All such monies must be deposited in funds from which they can be withdrawn only in accordance with an appropriations law prepared by Cabinet and enacted by Parliament. Cabinet must present estimated revenue and expense accounts to Parliament annually.

Article 66 of the Constitution provides for a Director of Audit, who is a member of the public service, but who may be removed from office only for cause by a vote of two-thirds of the entire membership of Parliament.

The salaries of the Supreme Court judges, the clerk of Parliament, and the Director of Audit must be set by law and cannot be lowered during their terms of office (Constitution, Article 65).

VI. International Obligations

Being an independent state, Nauru has the capacity to handle its own international affairs. Its status as a "special" member of the Commonwealth of Nations does not entitle it to representation at the meetings of Commonwealth heads of government but does give Nauru access to all other Commonwealth committees and organizations.

Nauru has developed a number of bilateral relationships, principally with Australia, New Zealand, the United States, and Japan.

On the regional level, Nauru is a member of the South Pacific Conference, South Pacific Forum, and the United Nations Economic and Social Council for Asia and the Pacific (ESCAP).

Even though Nauru is not a member of the United Nations, it has ratified a number of international conventions.

Several countries, including Australia, have diplomatic representatives resident on Nauru. Their normal diplomatic immunities are provided for by the Diplomatic Privileges and Immunities Act 1976.

VII. Revenue Law

Part VI of the Constitution provides that no tax may be raised except as prescribed in a law recommended to Parliament by the Cabinet. To date, no income tax law has been enacted in Nauru. Under the Foreign Trusts, Estates and Wills Act 1972, any foreign will submitted to probate in Nauru does not have tax or duties attached. But the Succession, Probate and Administration Act 1976 confers power on the Chief Justice to determine such fees for the probate of wills, including foreign wills, as the Chief Justice considers necessary.

The revenue earned by the Nauru government from the phosphate industry makes it unnecessary for the government to levy any substantial taxation on its people.

VIII. Investment Law

Article 83 of the Constitution vests the right to mine phosphate in the Republic of Nauru. As required by Article 62 of the Constitution, the Nauru Parliament has set up long-term investment funds in preparation for the time when the phosphate mines are exhausted. Over 60 percent of the revenue earned from phosphate exports is paid into these funds.

The main legislation providing the vehicle for government investment of phosphate royalties and other earnings is the Nauru Phosphate Royalties Trust Act 1968–1991, which establishes a state corporation with a board of directors appointed by the government. The Trust has invested a considerable portion of the phosphate earnings in Australian real property and other overseas investments.

Banking and insurance businesses are carried on by privately owned corporations, organized under the Corporation Act 1972. Separate legislation regulates insurers and banks. The only such corporations carrying on business in Nauru are the Bank of Nauru and the Nauru Insurance Corporation, both owned by the government.

Under the Government Loans Act 1972, the government can enter into an agreement with any financier to raise loans. The responsibility is given to the Finance Minister in particular to secure any loan—but only on order in writing from the Cabinet.

There is no substantial foreign investment since the phosphate mine was finally purchased by the Nauru Phosphate Corporation in 1970.

IX. Welfare Law

While substantial royalties are received by landowners, the amounts are not evenly spread among the 7,000 Nauruans. Because what is received does filter down through extended families, a welfare system has not been considered necessary.

The government of Nauru does pay the cost of health and education services for Nauruans who go overseas, particularly to Australia, to obtain these services. Nauruan children attending school overseas are sponsored by the government. These services appear to be given on the basis of political and administrative considerations, rather than because of any requirement of law. No general social security legislation exists.

Both education and health care on the island are provided free by the government. Education is compulsory for children between the ages of six and seventeen.

X. Criminal Law

Nauru has adopted the Queensland Criminal Code as the main legislation governing offenses on the island. (For a discussion of the definition of crimes and sentencing under the code, see **Chapter 8, Papua New Guinea**. Papua New Guinea has also adopted the Queensland code.) The Supreme Court accordingly relies on the decisions of the Queensland Supreme Court and other Australian courts in interpreting the code. The code is fairly comprehensive and thus replaces the areas of offense previously governed by the common law.

The other source of criminal law is the custom and tradition of the people of Nauru. As pointed out above (**III, D Customary Law**), the courts are directed under the provisions of the Customs and Adopted Laws Act 1972 to recognize these customs and traditions.

XI. Judicial Procedure

The Courts Act 1972 provides for English to be used as the language of the Supreme Court, but in the District Court it is left to the discretion of the magistrate to choose either English or Nauruan as the language of the court. The act also gives the Chief Justice the power to make rules of court for purposes of the act.

Rules of civil and criminal procedure are provided in the Civil Procedure Act 1972 and the Criminal Procedure Act 1972, respectively. These two laws provide the normal procedural protections for parties in civil and criminal actions.

This procedural protection in criminal cases is guaranteed to a large extent by the right to the protection of the law guaranteed by the Constitution of Nauru. Section 10(2) of the Constitution requires, for example, that a charge be heard within a reasonable time by an independent and impartial court.

XII. Land and Natural Resources

A. Land Tenure and Administration

The total area of Nauru is 8.25 square miles. Approximately two-thirds of this is phosphate-bearing land. A small portion of land near the shore has comparatively fertile soil, and most Nauruans reside there.

The island is owned by Nauruans, and land is therefore regulated by custom with exception of a few small allotments held by the Nauru government, Phosphate Commission, and missions. Each plot of land is owned by a family, whether or not it is waste or vacant. Title to land, which once passed matrilineally, is now dealt with largely by will and, in intestacy, by family agreement or, in lieu of agreement, according to law.

Two systems of title are recognized by Nauru law: titles under customary tenure recognized by customary law; and titles under noncustomary tenure that were governed, prior to independence, by the Lands Ordinance 1921–1968. Freehold title to any land cannot be transferred to anyone but a Nauruan. A breach of this provision carries an imprisonment term of up to six months. The act also voids any sale, transfer, lease, or grant of any estate or interest in any land in Nauru without prior consent in writing of the President of Nauru. The language of the relevant provisions is broad enough to cover virtually any form of transaction, including transfers, mortgages, leases, and any other form of interest in land. The Supreme Court has held that devises by will, however, are not covered by the act.

The validity of titles and other interests granted under previous legislation is retained by the act.

The act also vests in the minister the power to direct a public officer to execute any necessary lease instrument on behalf of minority owners who refuse consent with respect to a portion of land that the minister has requested be leased to the state for public purpose, where the majority of the owners have consented. In such a case of compulsory acquisition, the Constitution requires payment of just compensation.

Because most land in Nauru is owned under custom, customary law plays a greater role in land matters than do statutes. The power to determine questions of ownership of customary titles is vested in the Nauru Lands Committee, established by the Nauru Lands Committee Act 1956–1963. Under that act, the committee may consider any question relating to the identification of portions of land, ownership, and distribution of the estates of deceased owners.

The German administration kept records of land ownership in Nauru, and the Australian administration set up a land registration book in 1928. The Nauru Lands Committee uses these as official records to ascertain formal title holders.

The Supreme Court of Nauru has supervisory jurisdiction over the committee. Anyone aggrieved by a decision of the committee has twenty-one days to appeal to the Supreme Court. The court has declined where an appeal is after this deadline.

B. Other Resources

1. MINERALS

The main natural resource that has been exploited economically is phosphate; the legal basis for the exploitation has often been asserted to lie in the tripartite agreement of 1920. Recent research, however, shows that, under German law, title to the phosphate was always in the Nauruan landowners. The Nauruan Constitution recognizes this position, leaving title to the phosphate with the landowners while giving the state only the right to mine.

2. FISHERIES

The other natural resource of some significance is fisheries. Fishing channels and reefs are owned by individual families. Rights pertaining to these fisheries are governed by customary law.

The people of Nauru have not been pressed to resort to legislation either to protect these natural resources or to allow their exploitation economically, perhaps because the relative wealth brought by the phosphate industry has satisfied their financial needs.

3. AGRICULTURE

The coastal land below the coral plateau is comparatively rich, but agriculture has been not an important source of revenue.

Traditionally, the coconut has been the most useful tree. It provided Nauruans food and building materials and had much significance in other aspects of the Nauruan culture. A copra industry was well developed during the German period of administration but waned after World War I, when the phosphate industry began.

Usufructuary rights over customary land for agricultural purposes are still by and large determined by the customary law.

There is hardly any husbandry industry in Nauru. The Animals Act 1982 prohibits import of animals into Nauru, particularly "any female dog; or any male dog which has not been rendered permanently incapable of procreation."

XIII. Persons and Entities

No legislation specifically covers the age of majority. However, the Interpretation Act 1971 indicates in its definition of *young person* that, for practical legal purposes, the age of majority is eighteen. The Constitution defines *person* as including a body corporate or politic.

The formation and operation of companies are governed by the Corporation Act 1972. The act provides for the formation of trading and holding corporations by anyone who subscribes to a memorandum and complies with registration requirements. The Partnership Act 1976 deals with partnerships.

XIV. Family Law

The solemnization of marriage, its invalidation and dissolution, and custody and guardianship are governed by statute.

A. Formation of Marriages

The main statute governing the formation of marriage through formal solemnization is the Births, Deaths and Marriages Ordinance 1957. Part IV of the ordinance, dealing with marriages, sets down the requirements to be satisfied by the parties to a marriage, the person authorized to solemnize the marriage, and the powers and duties of the registrar. A male who is to marry has to prove that he is eighteen years or over, and, if under eighteen, he has to have written consent of his parents; a female must prove that she is sixteen years of age or over, and, if under sixteen, she also needs the written consent of her parents. The parties must not come within the prohibited degrees of consanguinity or affinity. Two Nauruans who are to marry must also produce a certificate signed by both the head chief and the secretary of the Nauru council that the council has consented to the marriage.

B. Dissolution of Marriages

Matters relating to dissolution of marriages are dealt with by the Matrimonial Causes Act 1973. The act prohibits dissolution of a marriage during the first three years after a marriage is solemnized. A marriage may be dissolved when there is an irretrievable breakdown or following a judicially recognized separation of the parties.

A marriage can also be declared void if one of the parties is already married at the time of the formalization of the marriage; or voidable if there is duress, mistake of fact about the identity of a party to the marriage, or the inability of a party to consummate marriage.

Before any order for dissolution of marriage is made, the court has the statutory obligation to ensure that the welfare of any children of the marriage are properly and adequately cared for by seeing that satisfactory arrangements are made.

XV. Personal Property

Personal property is governed by both customary law and case law. There is no sales of goods legislation.

Personal property at common law includes leaseholds. Under the Lands Act 1976, leaseholds can be mortgaged or used in any other way for purposes of security as long as certain restrictions (for example, leasing to Nauruans only) in the act are observed.

XVI. Wills and Succession

The main Nauruan legislation governing administration of a person's property upon death is the Succession, Probate and Administration Act 1976. The act applies only to wills and estates of persons dying after the act came into effect in 1976. The act governs administration of estates only; legislation concerning the form and content of wills and the rules of intestate succession is found in United Kingdom statutes made applicable to Nauru, including the Wills Act 1837, Wills Act Amendment Act 1852, and Wills Act 1963.

Wills made by Nauruans, and intestate succession to Nauruans' property is generally left to be decided by Nauruan customary law, consistent with the requirements of the Customs and Adopted Laws Act, 1971.

XVII. Contracts

Under the Customs and Adopted Laws Act 1971, contract law in Nauru is based on English case law as at January 31, 1968.

The Supreme Court of Nauru does hear civil claims, but there have not been many such cases. The Supreme Court, however, does provide the means for development of case law on contracts in Nauru.

XVIII. Commercial Law

Nauruan business life is governed by both case law and legislation. The main source of case law is contract law. There is no sale of goods act. The Bills of Sale and Bills of Exchange statutes of England apply by virtue of the Custom and Adopted Laws Act 1971.

The two important pieces of legislation that govern business transactions are the Registration of Business Names Act 1976 and the Corporation Act 1972.

All business firms carrying on business in Nauru are required to register with the office of the register of business names. The 1976 act requires an applicant to inform the registrar of the name of the business, general nature of the business, and names of the partner or partners of the business. A corporation operating under a business name that is not its corporate name is required to register under the act.

Banking activities are regulated by the Banking Act 1975. Any bank wishing to carry on banking business on Nauru has to be both registered and granted license to operate.

XIX. Torts

Tort law is governed by English case law, as a result of the adoption of the English common law as at January 31, 1968, by the Customs and Adopted Laws Act 1971. By virtue of the same act, the limitation of actions statutes of England apply in Nauru.

The Republic Proceedings Act 1972 makes the Republic liable in tort as if it were a private person for acts or omissions committed by its servants in their official capacities, subject to certain qualifications.

XX. Labor Law

No specific legislation covers the general relationship between employers and their employees in Nauru. The major aspect of labor relations covered by legislation is compensation for accidental injuries suffered by workers during the course of their employment, under the Workers Compensation Ordinance 1956. Under the ordinance, an employee who sustains injury or suffers death in the course of employment (which includes traveling to attend a technical training school) is entitled to be compensated by the employer. But the act also absolves an employer of liability where injury is self-inflicted or in disobedience of an order of the employer.

The act sets out the procedural requirements for making a claim. The claimant must give notice as soon as practicable, and any claim for compensation needs to be made within six months of the date of the accidental injury or death. If the employer does not make an effort to settle the claim within fourteen days after having been served with the notice of the claim, the injured worker may apply to the Supreme Court of Nauru to hear the matter. In a case where a claimant dies leaving dependents behind, compensation may be paid to the dependents. Otherwise the right to compensation is not assignable.

XXI. Industrial and Intellectual Property Rights

The Patents Register Act 1973 gives the person to whom a certificate is issued the right to use the patent right in Nauru for an invention registered in the principal country where the invention was made.

XXII. Legal Education and Profession

The right to practice law on Nauru is governed by the Legal Practitioners Act 1973. Under the act, any person wishing to practice law may apply to the Chief Justice by lodging a petition with the registrar of the Supreme Court. The registrar is required to send a copy of the petition to the minister responsible for legal matters. After considering the petition and taking into account any comments from the minister, the Chief Justice decides whether to allow the petitioner to practice. A successful petitioner is admitted to practice as both a barrister and solicitor.

The act requires that a person seeking admission be twenty-one years of age. The person also must have been admitted as a barrister or solicitor or both in England, Ireland, Australia, or New Zealand; or must have a degree in law from any university approved by the minister in consultation with the Chief Justice. The registrar of the Supreme Court is required to keep a roll of all those who have been admitted to practice as barristers and solicitors on Nauru.

Under the act, certain persons who have completed a course of training approved by the Chief Justice may be admitted by the Chief Justice as "pleaders." It would appear that these pleaders act as paralegals, since the act does not require them to have formal legal qualifications that are essential for those seeking admission as barristers and solicitors.

The legal profession is very small and relatively new.

XXIII. Research Guide

Bhalla, "Nauru: A Central Pacific Parliamentary Democracy," 64 *Parliamentarian* 127 (1983).
Charters, "The Mandate over Nauru Island," *British Year Book of International Law*, 1923–1924.
Commonwealth of Australia. *Report to the League of Nations on the Administration of Nauru.* 17 December 1920 and passim to 1940.
Commonwealth of Australia. *Report to the General Assembly of the United Nations on the Administration of the Territory of Nauru.* 1947–8 to 1965–6.
Connell, H. B., "After Five Completed Years of Independence," *Australia's Neighbours*, April–June 1974.
Dakin, "The Story of Nauru," *Walkabout*, March 1935.
Davidson, J. W. "Current Development in the Pacific: The Republic of Nauru," 3 *J. of Pacific History* 145 (1968).
Ellis, *Ocean Island and Nauru* Sydney: Angus and Robertson, 1936.
———. "Rehabilitation of Nauru and Ocean Island," 80 *New Zealand J. of Agriculture*, 1950.
Government of Nauru. *Acts.* Nauru: Government Printer, published annually from 1968.
———. *Nauru Corporation Legislation.* Nauru: Government Printer.
Hughes, "The Political Economy of Nauru," *Economic Record*, December 1964.
Inder, "Independence Comes to Tiny Nauru—But What Now?" *Pacific Islands Monthly* (March 1968) 30.
James, "The Wealth of Nauru," *New Nation Magazine*, December 1925.
Keke, "Land Tenure and Administration in Nauru," in C. G. Powles and M. Pulea, eds. *Pacific Courts and Legal Systems.* Suva: University of the South Pacific, 1988.
Kraus, N. L. H. *Bibliography of Nauru, Western Pacific.* (Honolulu, 1970).
Pittman, G. A. *Nauru: The Phosphate Island.* Melbourne: Longman 1959.
Tate, "Nauru, Phosphate and the Nauruans," 14 *Australian J. of Politics and History* 177 (1968).
Varsanyi, "Independence of Nauru," 7 *Australian Lawyer* 161 (1968).
Viviani, N. *Nauru: Phosphate and Political Progress.* Honolulu: University of Hawaii Press, 1970.
Wedgewood, "Report on Research Work in Nauru Island, Central Pacific," 6 *Oceania* No. 4; 7 *Oceania* No. 1 (1936).

6. Niue

AH ANGELO

I. Dateline

1000 A.D.	First evidence of settlement, probably by people from Samoa.
1500	Migration from Tonga; Niuean language and customs at this time strongly reflect Tongan influences.
1774	First European landing on Niue, by British explorer Captain James Cook.
1830	First contact with Christian missionaries.
1863	Peruvian slavers land and take many male islanders.
1900	British protectorate status granted.
1901	Niue annexed to New Zealand as part of Cook Islands.
1904	Separate administration for Niue and Island Council established.
1960	Island Council replaced by elected Legislative Assembly.
1974	Niueans choose status of self-government in free association with New Zealand.

II. Historical, Cultural, and Economic Survey

Niue is a self-governing state, in free association with New Zealand.

A. History

The early settlement and population of Niue was probably first from Samoa and later from Tonga and the Cook Islands. The first contact with Europeans was on June 20, 1774, when British explorer Captain James Cook visited the island.

In the 1830s and early 1840s, the London Missionary Society made unsuccessful attempts to missionize the island. In 1846, a Niuean trained in Samoa as a missionary landed, and by 1854 the island was almost totally Christianized.

In 1863, a Peruvian slaving vessel took more than 100 men off the island, and in 1869 about 90 persons of both sexes were kidnapped and taken to Tahiti.

Niueans first elected a king in 1876, and his successor petitioned Queen Victoria to make Niue a protectorate of the British Crown. That petition was granted in 1900, giving Niue its first real contact with European laws. On June 11, 1901, Niue was annexed to New Zealand by an Order-in-Council and a proclamation that provided for Niue to be administered by the New Zealand government as part of the Cook Islands. The Cook and Other Islands Government Act Amendment Act 1903 (NZ) placed Niue under separate administration. By the Cook Islands Amendment Act 1957 (NZ), the Island Council that had exercised limited home-rule powers was replaced by the Niue Assembly. Representatives from each of the island's villages were elected to the Assembly. The Resident Commissioner served as President. The Cook Islands Act 1915 (NZ) applied to Niue until 1966, when the *Niue Act* 1966 (NZ) was passed, delegating some of the powers of the Resident Commissioner to the Legislative Assembly and introducing a representative system of government.

In 1971, under the Niue Amendment Act 1971 (NZ), the Resident Commissioner became responsible to the Niue executive committee. Until October 19, 1974, the Niue Assembly could make laws only on matters not reserved to New Zealand by the Niue Act. On that date, under the Niue Constitution Act 1974 (NZ), the current self-governing status of Niue was fully recognized.

B. Culture and Economy

Niue is a raised coral atoll situated at approximately 19 degrees south latitude and 170 degrees west longitude, about 400 kilometers east of Tonga and 560 kilometers southeast of Samoa. The land area is 258 square kilometers, and the highest point above sea level is 65 meters. The island is covered in vegetation, but cultivation is difficult because of the lack of soil.

The indigenous people of Niue are Polynesian. As of January 1, 1989, approximately 2,000 people were living in Niue; approximately three times that number of Niueans were living in New Zealand.

The government of New Zealand provides the bulk of fiscal resources to the government of Niue (a grant of NZ$10 million in the 1988–1989 fiscal year). The rest of the economy consists of small local production, principally agricultural and including passion fruit, lime, honey, coconut, and handicrafts. All exports are agricultural. For all goods above subsistence level, Niue depends on imports, which come mainly from New Zealand. There is a once-monthly shipping service for cargo only and an air service from Auckland, New Zealand.

The transport available in Niue is a great barrier to the export of agricultural products and the development of tourism. The existing airport would need upgrading to accommodate night flights or the runway would need extension before Niue could provide the standard air services for the region and could make the island readily accessible.

The Niue public service of 600 employs 80 percent of the available workforce. The bulk of the remaining 20 percent work on private plantations.

III. Sources of Law

The sources of law, in order of priority, are the Constitution, statutes, regulations, common law of England, and custom.

A. Constitution

The Constitution of Niue is found in the Niue Constitution Act 1974 (NZ) in the First and Second Schedules, which contain a Niuean and an English language version, respectively. Under Article 23(4) of the Constitution, both languages are equally authentic.

The Constitution came into force on October 19, 1974. The Niue Constitution Act 1974 (NZ), in which it is embodied, is law for both New Zealand and Niue. The Constitution itself is both the supreme law of Niue (see Section 4(1)) and, to a limited degree, effective as statute law for New Zealand.

Under Article 35 of the Constitution, any bill to change the Constitution or the Niue Constitution Act 1974 (NZ) must receive the affirmative votes of at least two-thirds of the total membership of the Niue Assembly at both the second and third readings of the bill. The third reading vote must take place at least thirteen weeks after the preceding vote; after the final vote, the bill must in addition receive the approval by referendum of, in most cases, two-thirds of the votes validly cast. In respect of a few provisions, change to the Constitution requires the support of only a majority of the votes validly cast.

In October 1990, the Niue Assembly established a select committee to review the 1974 Constitution. The committee's report, tabled in the Assembly in 1991, recommended amendments that would merge the High Court and the Land Court, establish a Court of Appeal, repeal the requirement that the Chief Justice comment on certain bills presented to the Assembly, and tighten requirements for electors and candidates for the Assembly. None of these amendments can take effect until the amendment procedures described above are completed. As of late 1991, amending legislation had not yet been introduced in the Assembly.

Article 36 of the Constitution provides that no act of New Zealand made after October 19, 1974, becomes part of the law of Niue without the request and consent of the Niue Assembly. No New Zealand regulations made after that date are part of the law of Niue unless they are made under an act extended to Niue and were requested and consented to by the Niue Assembly.

Any statute or regulation inconsistent with the Constitution is invalid by virtue of Article 28 of the Constitution. The Niue Constitution Act 1974 (NZ) is not expressly declared to be supreme law for Niue but is, under Article 35 of the Constitution, given entrenchment equal to that of the Constitution itself.

The Niue Constitution Act 1974 (NZ) is not entrenched as a matter of New Zealand law, but Section 8 of the act envisages that no unilateral legislative action by New Zealand should change the relationship between Niue and New Zealand.

New Zealand has retained a constitutional responsibility for citizenship, external affairs, and defense. In addition, under the Niue Constitution Act 1974 (NZ), New Zealand has an obligation to provide to Niue "necessary economic and administrative assistance," some court facilities, and the base for the Niue public service. These provisions are also part of Niue law but may be repealed with respect to Niue by decision of the Niue Assembly alone. In other words, the Constitution provides for self-government with a unilateral option of independence.

B. Statute Law

The statutes that apply in Niue include the following:

1. acts of the New Zealand Parliament extended to Niue before 1974 that have not been repealed by the Niue Assembly since 1974;
2. Niue ordinances (pre-1974); and
3. acts of the Niue Assembly (post-1974).

The Niue Act 1966 (NZ), the principal New Zealand statute establishing substantive rules of law for Niue, is a substantial statute of more than 800 sections. It deals with those matters of the executive and legislative government of Niue not covered by the Constitution and also contains a substantial number of provisions relating to the Constitution and the operation of the High Court of Niue.

Subject to section 677 of the act, the acts of the Parliament of New Zealand in force in Niue have the same force as the pre-1974 ordinances of the Niue Island Council or the post-1974 acts of the Niue Assembly. About thirty statutes of New Zealand are in force in Niue by virtue of their express extension to Niue in the Niue Act 1966 (NZ). Other New Zealand statutes extended to Niue by the act are not mentioned expressly; for example, the law of Niue on limitation of actions is "the same as that which is in force for the time being in New Zealand." Therefore, the Limitation Act 1950 of New Zealand is Niue law, although that act is not expressly mentioned in the Niue Act 1966 (NZ).

Article 36 of the Constitution, as indicated above, requires that any application of a New Zealand act to Niue as a result of New Zealand legislation after 1974 be requested and consented to by resolution of the Niue Assembly, and that the New Zealand act declare that the request and consent procedure was followed. However, in the case of the limitation law and others whose extension to Niue is not express, New Zealand would not be legislating for Niue but would simply be legislating for New Zealand. Such New Zealand statutes become the law of Niue by virtue of Section 706 of the Niue Act 1966 (NZ) and not by virtue of any action of the New Zealand Parliament vis-à-vis Niue. Further, the "in force for the time being" formula used in the Niue Act 1966 (NZ) is a familiar one within the Commonwealth, and its meaning is well settled; the operation of any law by virtue of such a provision is an exercise of the legislative sovereignty of the state whose law "for the time being" is to be applied and not of the legislative authority of the state that is "receiving" or applying the law.

In certain limited cases a change in New Zealand law directly affects Niue law. For example, in domestic relations law, New Zealand's repeal of the Matrimonial Proceedings Act 1963 (NZ) in 1980 meant that the parallel jurisdiction in domestic relations matters that existed for the Supreme Court [now High Court] of New Zealand and the High Court of Niue no longer exists, and that jurisdiction is now solely in the High Court of Niue.

In addition to the applicable New Zealand statutes, there are approximately 100 statutes of the Niue legislature.

C. Subordinate Legislation

Subordinate Legislation in Niue may be made under the Constitution or under any statute in force in Niue. The power to make subordinate legislation is typically a power granted to the Cabinet to make regulations. All regulations must be laid before the Assembly within twenty-eight days after promulgation. There is very little Niue-enacted subordinate legislation, but a substantial body of New Zealand regulations and rules are part of the law of Niue. Significant among these are the High Court Rules and regulations made under New Zealand statutes that are specifically extended to Niue.

By virtue of Section 51 of the Niue Act 1966 and the Village Council Ordinance 1966, the village councils of Niue may make bylaws.

In 1991, all the New Zealand and Niue statutes and regulations in force in Niue as of August 1990 were published in a five-volume set, incorporating all amendments through August 1990. Periodic updating of this compilation is authorized by the Reprint of Statutes Act 1991.

D. Common Law

The final direct source of law for Niue is found in Section 672 of the Niue Act 1966 (NZ), which provides that the law of England as it existed on January 14, 1840, if not inconsistent with the act or inapplicable to the circumstances of Niue, is in force in Niue. In addition, certain British and imperial statutes in force in Niue on January 1, 1967, continue to apply. These statutes, however, have not been definitely identified, and their number is in any event very small.

E. Custom

Custom is not a direct source of law; however, the Constitution and other enactments of Niue place some emphasis on customary values and practices. In particular, Section 296 of the Niue Act 1966 states that judicial notice is to be taken of "Niuean custom so far as it has the force of law" under the Niue Act. Although the provision indicates a general intention, it provides no information about Niuean custom. What is critical is to know in what circumstances custom has the force of law. Much of Niuean life is in fact governed by custom, but outside of the land system very little of that custom is formally recognized by the law. To the extent that custom and tradition contradict the law, the custom or tradition will not be legally recognized. The land system and its governance by customary rules are entrenched in the Constitution and provided for specifically in the Niue Amendment Act (No. 2) 1968 (NZ). That same act, however, expressly invalidates adoptions of children that are made according to Niuean custom.

IV. Constitutional System

A. Territory

Niue's territory includes the land area of the island of Niue, a territorial sea of 12 nautical miles from a statutory baseline, and an exclusive economic zone for fishing that extends jurisdiction for a further 188 nautical miles. The relevant rules for the sea boundaries are found in the Territorial Sea and Exclusive Economic Zone Act 1978.

B. Citizenship, Entry, and Residence

As a consequence of the Niue Constitution Act 1974 (NZ) and the Citizenship Act 1977 (NZ), persons born in Niue or descended from persons born in Niue are New Zealand citizens and have a right to New Zealand passports. There is neither a separate Niuean citizenship nor a Niue passport. The right to New Zealand citizenship, with the associated right to move freely to and from New Zealand, is a major factor in the current political arrangement between Niue and New Zealand.

Under the above acts, New Zealand citizenship flows from birth in Niue or descent. Citizenship by descent is available for one generation only. A discretionary grant of citizenship is possible (but not often made) on the basis of marriage to a New Zealand citizen, residence in Niue, or employment in the Niue public service.

The Entry, Residence and Departure Act 1985 of Niue provides expressly that New Zealand citizens, persons born in Niue, and permanent residents of Niue are beyond the range of the substantive provisions of the act. As a result, no legislation deals with the entry, residence, and departure of those persons. Other persons may be classified as prohibited immigrants if they have certain physical or mental illnesses, represent a public security risk, have criminal records, or have overstayed as visitors. A visitor may enter Niue for thirty days with any valid passport and onward travel documentation. All immigrants require a permit.

C. Government

1. NATIONAL GOVERNMENT

   a. Head of State

   The Head of State of Niue is the sovereign of New Zealand, at present Her Majesty Queen Elizabeth II, who is represented in relation to Niue by the Governor General of New Zealand, under Article 1 of the Constitution of Niue, the Constitutional Provisions Act 1982, and the Letters Patent of 1983 for the Office of the Governor General of New Zealand. In practice, the

Queen and the Governor General have little to do with Niue, and executive authority is generally exercised on behalf of Her Majesty by the Cabinet of Niue.

The right of the monarch, under British constitutional law, to advice and information about government is provided by the ministers in the Niue Cabinet. In matters involving the New Zealand government, where there is a duty on the New Zealand government—such as economic and administrative assistance, external affairs and defense, and citizenship—Her Majesty would also be entitled to advice from the relevant New Zealand minister in addition to the Niue minister.

b. Executive

The executive power of Niue is exercised by the Cabinet, which comprises the Premier and three other members of the Niue Assembly.

(i) Premier

The Premier is a member of the Niue Assembly elected by the Assembly at its first meeting after a general election or whenever the office of Premier is vacant. Election is by an absolute majority of the members present and voting at the particular meeting of the Assembly. The Premier's office becomes vacant if the Premier ceases to be a member of the Assembly, resigns, or is deemed under a constitutional provision to have tendered a resignation. Another minister may be appointed as acting Premier when necessary by the Speaker, who acts on the request of the Cabinet.

(ii) Cabinet

The Cabinet consists of the Premier and three other members of the Niue Assembly nominated by the Premier. The Cabinet has a quorum of three and is collectively responsible to the Assembly.

Under Article 2 of the Constitution, the four members of the Cabinet "have the general direction and control of the executive government of Niue."

c. Assembly

The Niue Assembly, established under Section 16 of the Constitution, consists of fourteen members elected from village constituencies and six at-large elected members. The Speaker of the Assembly is elected by the members at the Assembly's first meeting after a general election. The clerk of the Assembly is a member of the Niue public service. Where there is no person qualified and available to perform the function of the Speaker, the clerk performs all of the functions necessary to enable meetings of the Assembly to be held.

The conduct of the Assembly is governed by the Constitution and the standing orders of the Assembly. A bill becomes law if it has been discussed in the Assembly and formally approved on three readings at which a minimum of ten members are present. All bills introduced into the Assembly and all acts of the Assembly are written in both Niuean and English.

In addition to the basic procedure of three readings of a proposal made by any member of the Assembly, particular restrictions relate to legislative proposals in designated subject areas. No bill concerning fiscal or financial matters may proceed without the recommendation or consent of the Premier. Any proposal affecting criminal behavior, criminal process, evidence, extradition, status, or the courts of general jurisdiction may proceed only after the Chief Justice has had an opportunity to comment on the legal, constitutional, and policy issues raised by that bill. In a similar vein, proposals affecting the Niue public service require the Assembly to have before it a report by the Niue Public Service Commission before proceeding to debate the bill.

No bill relating to Niuean customary land may proceed unless a commission of inquiry has been set up to consider the matter and has reported to the Assembly.

The privileges and immunities of the members of the Assembly and its officers are established by Article 24 of the Constitution. The Speaker and the officers of the Assembly are not subject to the jurisdiction of any court in respect of their duties in the Assembly, and neither the Speaker nor any member may be made subject to court proceedings in respect of anything said in the Assembly or any of its committees.

d. Judiciary

(i) *High Court and Court of Appeal*

The High Court of Niue is the court of general jurisdiction for Niue. The High Court consists of a Chief Justice and other judges and commissioners. No judicial officer is required to have legal qualifications. There is presently only one judge, the Chief Justice, a legally qualified person with professional judicial experience in the New Zealand judicial service. The commissioners of the High Court are local lay judges, and the bulk of the cases in the High Court are heard by them.

At the lowest level in the system are the Justices of the Peace. Two of them acting together have the same jurisdiction as a commissioner of the High Court. Where cases are heard by a commissioner or two Justices of the Peace, appeal may be made to a judge of the High Court. From the High Court there is, under Article 51 of the Constitution, appeal as of right to the Court of Appeal of New Zealand. Exceptionally and as a prerogative matter, appeals may be heard from Niue courts by the Judicial Committee of the Privy Council sitting in London.

The Chief Justice and judges of the High Court are appointed by the Governor General on the advice of the Cabinet. A judge of the High Court may be removed by the Governor General acting on the advice of the Cabinet given in accordance with a resolution of the Assembly. Justices of the Peace are appointed by the Cabinet for a period designated in their warrants of appointment. The justices, as lay officers, are unremunerated. They may be removed from office only by the Cabinet acting with the Chief Justice's recommendation. The salary of a judge or commissioner may not be reduced during the term of office. Judges and commissioners of Niuean courts leave office at the expiration of their term of office or on reaching age sixty-eight.

(ii) *Land Court and Land Appellate Court*

The Land Courts of Niue are established in Part III of the Constitution. The specific jurisdiction of the Land Court, however, is set out in Sections 47 and 48 of the Niue Amendment Act (No. 2) 1968 (NZ). Those sections grant to Land Courts exclusive jurisdiction in all matters relating to Niuean land, which is defined in Section 2 of the same act as being "land in Niue vested in the Crown but held by Niueans according to the customs and usages of Niue." As very little land in Niue is Crown land, the jurisdiction of the Land Court relates to virtually all of Niue.

The Land Court has a Chief Judge, and other judges and commissioners may be appointed by the Cabinet. The judges of the Land Court may be removed from office only by the Cabinet acting in accordance with a resolution of the Assembly. The Land Appellate Court hears appeals from the Land Court and is the final court of appeal in all matters within the jurisdiction of the Land Court.

The Land Appellate Court is composed of the Chief Judge and other judges of the Land Court of Niue and the Chief Judge and other Judges of the Maori Land Court of New Zealand.

Two judges constitute a quorum, and every decision requires the concurrence of at least two judges.

2. LOCAL GOVERNMENT

Government at a local level is provided by village councils elected under the Village Councils Ordinance 1967 and Section 50 of the Niue Act 1966 (NZ). A village council has power to make bylaws.

D. Emergency Powers

A proclamation of emergency may be made by the Cabinet. A proclamation, which is valid for one month, gives the Cabinet the power to make regulations that override all legislation other than the Constitution. A proclamation of emergency must be communicated to the Niue Assembly at its next meeting, and any regulations expire after fourteen days unless continued by resolution of the Assembly.

E. Human Rights

There is no provision in the Constitution for fundamental rights. Article 31, however, refers specifically to the rules of due process, and Article 31 also requires comment by the Chief Justice on any proposed amendment to the existing laws that may affect basic legal rights.

The main protection of human rights is in the Niue Act 1966 (NZ) and in particular in Parts V and VI, which set out the principal criminal offenses for Niue. Section 68 of the Niue Act 1966 (NZ) incorporates into the law of Niue the English common law rules on the writ of habeas corpus.

The International Covenant on Civil and Political Rights, the International Covenant on Social and Economic Rights, and the Convention for the Elimination of All Forms of Discrimination Against Women have been ratified (by New Zealand) in respect of Niue, and, although those treaties have not expressly been made law of Niue by legislation, there is substantial compliance with their requirements. The absence of specific legislative action in Niue may be explained by the existence, at the time of ratification, of law in force in Niue that was already consistent with the international obligations arising under these treaties.

V. Administrative Organization and Law

A. Organization

The government of Niue is led by the Premier and the three other Cabinet ministers, all four of whom are members of the Legislative Assembly. The functioning of executive government at the ministerial or departmental level is basically untrammeled by legislative requirement, nor is there yet a range of statutory bodies performing governmental or quasi-governmental functions.

B. Public Service

The Niue Public Service Commission is a key institution in the Niue constitutional scheme. As of January 1989, 601 persons were employed in the Niue public service, of whom 21 were overseas officers. Because the total Niuean workforce is only about 750 people, the role of the Niue public service is central to contemporary life in Niue.

Employment in the Crown service of Niue as a salaried employee is governed by the Niue Public Service Commission. The permanent head of the Niue public service and the chief administrative officer of the government of Niue is the secretary to the government, who is appointed by the commission after consultation with the Premier and concurrence of the Cabinet. The Niue Public Service Commission is made up of three persons, two of whom are members of the New Zealand State Services Commission. The quorum of the commission is two, and at least two members must concur in every decision of the commission. The Commission has general oversight and control of the Niue public service and determines the terms and conditions of employment of public servants. The commission also is responsible for the appointment of public servants and their promotion and discipline.

The commission is responsible to the Cabinet and must inform and advise the Cabinet on matters relating to the public service as necessary. The commission also reports to the Assembly from time to time as circumstances require.

Under Section 665 of the Niue Act 1966 (NZ), the commission may make regulations for the Niue public service. In addition to its right to be consulted by the Assembly on any law that would affect the Niue public service, the commission has a constitutionally entrenched duty to promote adequate advancement for Niueans with special skills, to provide reasonable opportunities for employment in Niue for Niueans and to bear in mind the employment opportunities and levels of remuneration available in New Zealand and the need to act consistently with government economic and social policy, given the key role of the public service in the Niue political and economic setting.

C. Public Finance and Audit

The government is required under Part IV of the Constitution to obtain parliamentary approval for taxation, expenditure, and borrowing (see the Government Loans Act 1980).

An appropriation act is required to authorize the expenditure of public money for each financial year. The Cabinet is responsible for the supervision of government expenditure and is accountable to the Assembly for public expenditure.

Under Article 60 of the Constitution, the auditing of the Niue government account is carried out by the Audit Office of New Zealand. The audit is conducted at least once a year and presented by the Audit Office to the Speaker of the Niue Assembly for presentation to the Assembly.

D. Rule Making

The power to make subordinate legislation is vested in various bodies both by the Constitution and statutes. The most common power is one vested in the Cabinet to make regulations.

The Niue Public Service Commission is empowered under the Constitution to make regulations for the public service, and the rules of the High Court and the Land Court are made by regulation by the Cabinet. The rules of the Land Appellate Court are made, however, by act of the Niue Assembly. The village councils also have power to make bylaws, all of which have to be approved by the Cabinet.

The regulation-making power is governed by the Regulations Ordinance 1967, but this power has been exercised very rarely in Niue since self-government in 1974.

E. Review of Administrative Action

The law deals specifically with misuse of and thus severely limits access to official information. Access to official information is generally considered a privilege, to be granted by the person in charge of the relevant information. Specific access in the context of litigation would be possible by an order for discovery under the Crown Proceedings Act 1950 (NZ) but would be subject to being withheld on the ground of Crown privilege. The common law of Niue on Crown privilege (see Crown Proceedings Act 1950 and Section 321 of the *Niue Act 1966* (NZ)) cannot be stated with certainty but would most likely follow the New Zealand cases, which allow no absolute privilege and permit the court to view the information and decide whether privilege is properly claimed.

The primary controls on administrative action are by virtue of the prerogative writs of certiorari, mandamus, prohibition, and injunction on the civil side, and the writ of habeas corpus in the case of unlawful imprisonment and detention. The courts' jurisdiction over civil writs is the same as that possessed and exercised for the time being by the High Court of New Zealand. In New Zealand, the law relating to those remedies has been considerably developed in recent years and made more flexible by statutory provisions, principally by the Judicature Amendment Act 1972 (NZ). The common law of England on these matters has been extended to Niue by that New Zealand legislation and the judicial practice under it.

There is no ombudsman in Niue, but Nuie's Commissions of Inquiry Ordinance 1968 enables the Cabinet to set up a commission of inquiry to investigate government administrative matters, disasters, and conduct of civil servants. Any such commission has the power and status of a High Court judge.

The government of Niue may be sued under the Crown Proceedings Act 1950 (NZ), as adopted by Section 321 of the Niue Act 1966 (NZ).

VI. International Obligations

A. Treaties and Conventions

Section 6 of the Niue Constitution Act 1974 (NZ) states that "nothing in this Act or in the Constitution shall affect the responsibilities of Her Majesty the Queen in right of New Zealand for the external affairs and defence of Niue." Niue is not a party to any treaty or convention, leaving the exercise of such external relations matters to New Zealand. No constitutional provision prevents Niue's entering into international treaties on its own behalf, although other states may regard its constitutional relationship with New Zealand as ambiguous and therefore may prefer to conclude a treaty with New Zealand rather than with Niue. Nevertheless, Niue frequently represents itself at international conferences and in particular, has separate representation in a number of regional organizations.

Entering into international relationships is a prerogative of the executive; there is no requirement for consideration of the treaty proposals by the legislature. However, no treaty becomes domestic law unless it is implemented by statute.

B. Diplomatic Privileges

The Consular Privileges and Immunities Act 1971 (NZ) and the Diplomatic Privileges and Immunities Act 1968 (NZ) are Niue law and make the Vienna Conventions on those matters part of the law of Niue. The only foreign government represented in Niue is that of New Zealand.

The New Zealand Representative Act 1981 of Niue extends to the government of New Zealand the same privileges and immunities as a sending state under the Diplomatic Privileges and Immunities Act 1968 (NZ). The office staff and documents of the New Zealand representative in Niue receive the same privileges and immunities as those of a diplomatic mission.

C. Reciprocal Enforcement and Extradition

The enforcement of civil judgments is mutual between New Zealand and Niue and completed by filing a memorial of judgment in the relevant court, pursuant to Sections 95 and 126 of the Niue Act 1966 (NZ). No other legislation provides for the enforcement of foreign judgments. The rules of Niue are therefore the English common law rules, which require that the judgment be the final judgment of a foreign court with jurisdiction in the matter and that the judgment be for a liquidated sum of money. Such a judgment will be enforced simply by suit on the judgment debt, provided that the original judgment is not tainted by fraud and was not given in breach of the rules of natural justice, and that its enforcement would not be against the public policy of Niue.

On the criminal side, a special regime exists regarding the return of offenders from Niue to New Zealand and the Cook Islands. The offender is returned on the basis of a foreign-issued warrant. Once that warrant has been authenticated by a judge of the High Court of Niue, the Niue Act 1966 (NZ) requires that the offender be returned unless the High Court is of the opinion that the return would cause undue hardship or would otherwise be unjustifiable or inexpedient. The return to Niue of offenders who are found in New Zealand follows an identical procedure.

In respect of other jurisdictions, the applicable law is found in Section 320 of the Niue Act 1966 (NZ), which provides that the Extradition Act 1965 (NZ) is Niue law and also provides a number of adaptations of that law to Niue circumstances. Restrictions on extradition include requirements that the offense is not of a political character and that the accused will not be proceeded against or prejudiced on account of race, religion, nationality, or political opinion.

The Fugitive Offenders Act 1881 (UK) is also in force in Niue. That act provides that, where a person accused of having committed an offense in one part of the Commonwealth has left that area and is found in another part of the Commonwealth, the person can be apprehended and returned to the part of the Commonwealth where the offense was committed. The phrase "part of the Commonwealth" is defined in the Fugitive Offenders Amendment Act 1976 (NZ) to include any country that is a member of the Commonwealth.

VII. Revenue Law

The principal method of taxation is a levy on personal and corporate income, administered under the Income Tax Ordinance 1961. Income derived from primary production is free of tax up to the first $NZ5,000 per year. The corporate rate of tax is a flat rate of 30 percent, and all other income is subject to tax at a rate of 10 percent on the first $NZ5,000, increasing to a maximum rate of 50 percent on income above $NZ35,000 per year. Payment of income tax by employees is administered through a pay-as-you-earn scheme, with deduction by employers.

The Customs Act 1966 (NZ) is Niue law, and duties are levied under that act in accordance with the Niue Customs Tariff Act 1982. Goods from New Zealand and the Cook Islands are imported free into Niue by virtue of Section 656 of the Niue Act 1966 (NZ). Niue also derives income from fees paid for the exploitation of commercial fishing rights by foreign vessels in the exclusive economic zone under the Territorial Sea and Exclusive Economic Zone Act 1978 and from fees paid under the Film and Public Entertainment Act 1979, Mining Act 1977, and Air Travel Tax Act 1980.

VIII. INVESTMENT LAW

Until 1991, Niue had promulgated no legislation in the areas of offshore banking, insurance, and investment, although the Income Tax Ordinance 1961 does contain a provision concerning determination of the assessable income of overseas insurance companies. The *Income Tax Ordinance* 1961 also provides relief from double taxation for persons who have income not derived in Niue that has already been taxed. No double taxation agreements have been made as yet.

In 1991 the Development Investment Bill was introduced, providing both for the regulation of foreign investment in Niue and for a comprehensive set of investment incentives. The bill gives the Cabinet the right to review and approve investment proposals and amends the Income Tax Ordinance to provide for the granting of tax concessions by the Cabinet.

IX. WELFARE LAW

The Constitution, Section 61, places a duty on the Cabinet to provide all necessary services for public health in Niue, to provide public schools and educational opportunities for the people in Niue, and to do all else that it considers necessary to "provide a reasonable standard of living for the people of Niue and to secure their economic, social, and cultural welfare." Education is compulsory between the ages of five and fourteen years, and free public schooling is provided at primary and secondary levels. Health care, which is free to Niueans, is provided to others at government-fixed scheduled rates.

A small old-age pension is available to persons of sixty years and over who have lived in Niue for at least 10 years. Permanent employees of the Niue public service are required to join the government retirement scheme, which is run in conjunction with the New Zealand government. Although not part of the law of Niue, the relevant statute is the New Zealand Government Superannuation Fund Act 1956 (NZ). Under this scheme, the Niue Public Service Commission pays into the fund an amount equal to 10 percent of the employee's wages, one-half of which is deducted by the employer from the employee's wages. The fund pays benefits on death, at sixty years of age, and on permanent incapacity. The benefits include payment on death or monthly pension and limited lump sum rights.

There is no accident compensation law in Niue, and industrial, traffic, and accident injuries will be compensated, if at all, under the English common law relating to personal injury.

X. CRIMINAL LAW

Offenses are created by a large number of Niue enactments, of which the most important are Part V of the Niue Act 1966 (NZ); the Aviation Crimes Ordinance 1973; and the fishing offenses specified by the Niue Fish Protection Ordinance 1958, Territorial Sea and Exclusive

Economic Zone Act 1978, and Sunday Fishing Prohibition Act 1980. The Liquor Act 1975, Niue Transport Ordinance 1965, and Misuse of Drugs Act 1975 (NZ) denominate other criminal offenses.

The provisions of the Niue Act 1966 (NZ) that set out the substantive criminal law follow a predictable Western European criminal code pattern. The provisions in the act are direct successors to those in the Cook Islands Act 1915 (NZ), which, in turn, were directly related to the criminal code of New Zealand.

Section 239 of the Niue Act 1966 (NZ) provides that "No person shall be proceeded against for any criminal offence at common law." There is therefore in Niue no criminal offense without clear legislative provision.

Nothing in the criminal law provisions of the Niue Act 1966 (NZ) is specifically Niuean, and the range of offenses would be found with little variation in most jurisdictions in the world. They include homicide, various lesser assaults, property damage, sexual offenses and crimes against indecency, theft, forgery, gaming, counterfeiting, breach of the peace, disorderly conduct, drunkenness, prostitution and animal trespass. The most serious offenses are murder, manslaughter, and rape. The punishments range from imprisonment for life in the case of conviction for murder, to a maximum $NZ10 fine for obstructing a public place or willful trespass on land.

All the common law rules as to justification, excuse, or defense to any charge are preserved by Section 238 of the Niue Act 1966 (NZ). No person under ten years of age may be convicted of an offense, and no person between the ages of ten and fourteen years may be convicted unless it is proved the person knew the act or omission was wrong or contrary to law. Sentences of imprisonment are served in Niue but may in the case of a sentence for six months or more be ordered by the Cabinet to be served in a New Zealand prison. A person liable to a term of imprisonment for any offense may be sentenced to pay a fine not exceeding $NZ200 instead of the period of imprisonment.

The court with jurisdiction in criminal offenses is the High Court of Niue. Where the offense charged is punishable by imprisonment for a term of more than five years, the judge must sit with assessors; where the offense charged is punishable by a lesser term or only by a fine, the judge may sit alone. Where a judge sits without an assessor the maximum term of imprisonment to which an offender may actually be sentenced, regardless of the maximum punishment prescribed by law for the offense, is twelve months.

Where the court sits with assessors, the judge will appoint six from a list drawn up by the Cabinet and published in the *Niue Island Gazette*. Failure to serve as an assessor without reasonable excuse is a contempt of court. The assessors are paid allowances as fixed by the judge at the trial. An assessor may be removed on a challenge by a prosecutor, the accused, or the court. No conviction may be entered in a case heard by a judge and assessors unless the judge and at least four of the assessors agree to convict. The fixing of the sentence is in the sole discretion of the judge.

No person may be arrested without warrant, and a person must be told at the time the reason for the arrest. Prosecution is commenced by an information in writing, laid by a constable or any other person as prosecutor, and in general an arrested person may be released on bail, unless the offense involves a risk to private citizens or public order.

A search warrant is required for the police to enter premises in search of property. The court has the power in any criminal trial to enter a conviction without sentence or to grant a discharge without conviction. The prerogative of mercy is exercised by the Governor General, and, in cases where the punishment is imprisonment for a term of less than one year or a fine not exceeding $NZ100, the powers of pardon and remission may be exercised by the Cabinet.

The court additionally has the power to order the payment of compensation for loss or damage flowing from the offense in any case where a conviction is entered. The power to withdraw a criminal prosecution is vested, by Section 283 of the Niue Act 1966 (NZ), in the Cabinet.

XI. JUDICIAL PROCEDURE

A. Civil and Criminal Procedure

The rules of the High Court of Niue were originally promulgated as the Rules of the High Court 1916 under the Cook Islands Act 1915 (NZ). The rules are brief and contain approximately fifteen pages of text and fifteen pages of forms. Civil process is typically commenced "by way of action" with the filing of a statement of claim with the registrar, and then the issue by the registrar of a summons to the defendant to appear to answer the claim. No pleadings other than the statement of claim are required. Proceedings not commenced by statement of claim are begun by oral motion in court or by filing a brief application with the registrar.

A commissioner has jurisdiction where the amount claimed does not exceed $NZ500, or where the offense charged is punishable by fine only or by imprisonment for a term not exceeding one year. A commissioner and two Justices of the Peace sitting together may, if there is a guilty plea, give judgment in any case of an offense punishable by a term of ten years' imprisonment or less. The sentence in such a case is subject to confirmation by the Chief Justice.

Criminal proceedings are begun by the laying of an information before the High Court. Appeals from the judgment of a commissioner may be appealed to a judge of the High Court within twenty-one days of judgment. Every such appeal is by way of rehearing.

B. Land Court

Procedural matters are found in the Niue Land Courts Rules 1969. The rules are brief, containing about fifteen pages of text and six of forms. Proceedings are commenced by application in the Land Court and notice of appeal in the Land Appellate Court. The application must be delivered to the registrar. At least fourteen days' notice of the hearing of an application must be given in the *Niue Island Gazette*, and three days' notice of the date of the commencement of the sitting of the court at which the application is to be heard must be given to the parties.

XII. LAND AND NATURAL RESOURCES

A. Land Tenure and Administration

The question of land is one of the most basic and important ones in Niue. The land tenure system is still principally based on custom, and the existing laws—the Niue Amendment Act (No. 2) 1968 (NZ) and the Land Ordinance 1969—both reflect that fact. They reserve the use of the land exclusively to Niueans. Although the land is "vested in the Crown," the mangafaoa, or family unit, holds the land for and on behalf of all its members. From each family unit a trustee, or Leveki Mangafaoa, is appointed to act on behalf of the family in respect of land. Any one individual may have rights in a number of land-owning groups. Title to Niuean land is determined "according to the custom and usages of the Niuean people," by ascertaining and declaring the mangafaoa of the land by reference to the common ancestor thereof or by any other means. The common ancestor may be the father or grandfather of the claimant. How far back one needs to go in order to determine the common ancestor depends on the nature of evidence produced by the claimant. The genealogy records held in the Department of Justice are vital in assisting the determination of title.

As another illustration of the importance of land, Article 33 of the Constitution provides that the Niue Assembly may not proceed with any bill if it concerns customary title to Niuean land, alienation of Niuean land, purchase or acquisition of Niuean land for any public purpose, or the constitution or jurisdiction of the Land Court or the Land Appellate Court, unless it has before it a copy of a commission of inquiry report investigating the legal, constitutional, and policy issues raised by the bill.

B. Government Taking of Land

Under Section 462 of the Niue Act 1966 (NZ), land may be occupied by the government, by order of the Cabinet, and cultivated and managed on behalf of the Leveki Mangafaoa or the owners or those interested in the land. The Cabinet may do all things necessary to develop the land and may retain revenue derived from the business for later expenditure in management of the business. The Cabinet may expend sums necessary to carry on the business and also make advances to the Leveki Mangafaoa or Niuean beneficiaries out of the Cabinet's share. Money expended or advances made are treated as a charge on the land. In this way land can be developed where otherwise it would not be.

The Cabinet may take title to land for the Crown for any public purpose, under Section 11 of the Niue Amendment Act (No. 2) 1968 (NZ). Where land is taken under this power the land or rights concerned vest absolutely in the Crown. Where the land or interest involved is occupied and already used for a public or private purpose, then the prior written consent of the trustee, or owner, or the Niue Assembly is required. The owners of land taken under Section 11 are entitled to compensation, and where an offer of compensation is not accepted, the amount will be assessed and awarded by the Land Court. The Niue Amendment Act 1968 (NZ) also provides that the Crown may acquire land for public purpose by private negotiation.

C. National Parks and Reserves

Section 44 of the Land Ordinance 1969 provides for the setting aside of Niuean land as a reservation for

> the common use of the residents of a village, or a Church or other group or institution for such purposes as a burial ground, fishing ground, village site, landing place, place of historic interest, source of water supply, Church site, building site, recreation ground, bathing place or any other specified purpose whatsoever.

Before an order is made under Section 44, the interest of the mangafaoa must be taken into account.

There are no specific laws relating to agriculture, forests, and fisheries other than the Niue Fish Protection Ordinance 1965, Territorial Sea and Exclusive Economic Zone Act 1978, and Sunday Fishing Prohibition Act 1980. Other natural resources are covered by the Wildlife Ordinance 1972 and the Mining Act 1977. The latter act vests in the Crown title to all minerals on or under the surface of Niue. Prospecting for minerals and the exploitation of minerals is also governed by the Mining Act. The only exception concerns matters dealt with in the Atomic Energy Act 1945 (NZ).

XIII. Persons and Entities

Under Section 692(1) of the Niue Act 1966 (NZ), the Minors' Contracts Act 1969 (NZ), as in force on October 19, 1974, is in force in Niue. That act provides that married minors generally have the same contractual capacity as a person of full age. Most contracts entered into by minors over eighteen years of age have effect as though the minor were of full age, but contracts entered into by minors under eighteen years of age are enforceable on behalf of the minor but unenforceable against the minor.

Partnerships are regulated by the Partnership Act 1908 (NZ), as in force at October 19, 1974. The act is in force in Niue by virtue of Section 697 of the Niue Act 1966 (NZ). The Partnership Act sets out matters relating to the law of partnerships and covers the nature of partnerships, relations of partners to persons dealing with them and to one another, and dissolution of partnerships.

XIV. Family Law

A. Marriage

The requirements for a valid marriage in Niue are that the parties not be within the prohibited degrees of consanguinity and affinity, that the marriage take place in the presence of a marriage officer and at least two other witnesses, that two days' notice of marriage be given, that the parties to the marriage be of age, and, in the case of minors, that they have the consent of at least one parent.

Section 515 of the Niue Act 1966 (NZ) says that the prohibited degrees of consanguinity and affinity for Niue are the same as those for the time being in New Zealand. First-cousin marriages are permitted in New Zealand.

A marriage officer may not solemnize a marriage if the husband is under the age of eighteen or the wife under the age of fifteen. If the husband is over eighteen but under twenty-one, or the wife is over fifteen but under nineteen, the marriage officer may not solemnize the marriage of those parties without the consent of one parent of each of the parties; dispensation of parental consent may be obtained from the judge of the High Court.

The common law rules relating to husband and wife are substantially amended by the Niue Act 1966 (NZ). Section 707 of the act abolishes the English common law's concept of the husband and wife as a single economic and legal union and also provides that, other than in cases of intestate succession, marriage confers no property rights on one party in respect of the property of the other. The legal capacity of a married woman is the same as that of an unmarried woman. For the purposes of jurisdiction in matrimonial causes, the domicile of a married woman who is a minor is determined as if she were an adult.

B. Divorce

Divorce jurisdiction in Niue is vested in the High Court. Jurisdiction in divorce proceedings requires that either the petitioner or respondent be domiciled in Niue. Grounds for divorce include the following:

1. adultery by the respondent;
2. desertion for three years or more;

3. habitual drunkenness or drug addiction;
4. conviction for certain criminal offenses;
5. conviction for murder;
6. a respondent of unsound mind who is unlikely to recover;
7. the existence of a separation agreement that has been in force for at least three years; and
8. the petitioner and respondent's living apart without likelihood of reconciliation for not less than seven years.

The order of the High Court of Niue in a case of divorce is final, and there is no right of appeal. At the time of making a divorce decree the High Court may order a husband to pay maintenance for the future upkeep of his former wife as long as she remains unmarried or to pay a lump sum to his former wife. Custody orders with respect to children of the marriage may also be made at the time of the making of a divorce decree.

The High Court has jurisdiction to make maintenance orders as between husband and wife and as between parent and child. Maintenance includes lodging, clothing, education, and medical services. A child, for purposes of a maintenance order, is any person under the age of sixteen.

C. Custody

Under Section 692(1) of the Niue Act 1966 (NZ), the Guardianship Act 1968 (NZ), as in force at October 19, 1974, is in force in Niue. The Guardianship Act makes a distinction between *custody*, which is the right to possess and care for a child, and *guardianship*, which is both custody and the right to control the upbringing of the child. The act defines *child* as a person under age twenty.

In respect of guardianship, the act provides that both the mother and father of a child will be the child's guardians. The mother retains sole guardianship rights where she is not married to the father or is separated from the father before the child was conceived and in either case was not living with the father when the child was born. In such cases, the father may nevertheless apply to the court to be appointed as guardian in addition to or instead of the mother. Guardianship rights terminate when the child reaches age twenty or marries under that age.

Custody orders may be made by the court under the Guardianship Act, on application of the father, mother, stepparent, or guardian of the child, or any other person with leave of the court. Custody orders are subject to any conditions that may be prescribed by the court and may not generally be made or have effect after the child reaches age sixteen.

The Guardianship Act also makes provision for the court, on application by a parent who does not have custody of child, to grant that parent rights of access to the child. The Court may also grant access rights to other parties related to the child. In all matters of guardianship, custody, and access, the key principle of the Guardianship Act is that the welfare of the child is the first and paramount consideration.

D. Adoption

Sections 91 to 101 of the Niue Amendment Act (No. 2) 1968 (NZ) provide a statutory regime for adoption in Niue. That system declares invalid any adoption by Niuean custom. Adoption orders are made by the Land Court on application by the would-be adoptor (who does not have to be Niuean or domiciled in Niue) in respect of a person under the age of twenty-one years, who also does not have to be Niuean and does not have to be domiciled in Niue.

No adoption will be made unless the statutory age differential exists between the applicant and the adoptive child and in the case of a sole applicant unless certain statutory requirements are complied with, such as age differential and sex of the child. A child over the age of twelve must consent to the adoption. The consent of the biological parents of the child is also required.

Under both the law of New Zealand and Niue, any adoption order made under this statute has the same effect as an adoption order made under the Adoption Act 1955 (NZ). That is to say, the relationship of the adopted child to the adoptive parent is deemed for all legal purposes to be that of a natural parent to natural child.

Under Section 100 of the Niue Amendment Act (No. 2) 1968 (NZ) the Land Court may vary or discharge an adoption order on the application of an adoptive parent or an adoptive child, regardless of whether the adoption was made in Niue or not, when it was made, whether the adopted person is in Niue, or whether the adoptive parent is domiciled in Niue. Any application for discharge for an adoption has to be approved by the Cabinet and that approval will not be given unless the adoption order was made by mistake as to a material fact, in consequence of a misrepresentation to the court making the order, or as to any person concerned.

XV. Personal Property

Under Section 700 of the Niue Act 1966 (NZ), the Property Law Act 1952 (NZ), as in force at October 19, 1974, is in force in Niue. The act deals with a wide range of subjects in real and personal property—for example, general rules affecting property, insurance of real and personal property, powers and conditions of sale, deeds, covenants, mortgages, leases, easements, and apportionment. To the extent not superseded by the Property Law Act, the rules of the common law as to personal property apply.

XVI. Wills and Succession

It is critical to distinguish the rights of the deceased in Niuean land from his or her rights to any other property. In respect of succession to Niuean land, rights are determined by custom, and disputes settled in the Niue Land Court. No will may be made by a Niuean in respect of Niuean land. Concerning other property, a Niuean may make a will, provided the will is in compliance with the Wills Act 1837 (UK) and the Wills Amendment Act 1852 (UK). One of the attesting witnesses must, under Section 489 of the Niue Act 1966 (NZ), be a judicial officer, a solicitor of the High Court of New Zealand, or a court registrar of Niue.

Intestate distribution of property other than Niuean land is generally governed by the Administration Act 1969 (NZ), which is made part of the law of Niue by Section 680 of the Niue Act 1966 (NZ). If a decedent does not leave a will disposing of personal property, Section 490 of the Niue Act 1966 (NZ) provides that the successors and their shares are determined in accordance with Niuean custom. Only where there is no relevant custom will the law apply "as if the deceased were a European"—that is, in accordance with the ranking of successors and sharing arrangements found in the Administration Act 1969 (NZ). In such cases, the order of successors is surviving spouse, children, parents, grandparents, and siblings.

XVII. Contracts

The Niue Act 1966 (NZ), Section 711, provides that any court has discretion to refuse to enforce a contract made by a Niuean if the court regards the contract as oppressive, unreasonable, or improvident. The exception to this rule is a contract for the alienation of Niue land that has been confirmed by the Land Court.

Section 710 of the act provides that no promise in writing made by a person is invalid only because the consideration for the promise does not appear in writing, and Section 712 provides that no security given by a Niuean over property is enforceable without the leave of the High Court.

Under Section 701 of the Niue Act 1966 (NZ), the Sale of Goods Act 1908 (NZ), as in force at October 19, 1974, applies in Niue. This act covers the formation, effect, and performance of the contract, the rights of the unpaid seller, and actions for breach of contract.

The Price Control on Imported Goods for Resale in Niue Act 1975 controls prices on imported goods resold in Niue and sets up a price control board for the purpose.

XVIII. Commercial Law

A. Businesses

A variety of acts cover incorporation of specific types of entities in Niue. The Incorporated Societies Act 1908 (NZ), as in force at October 19, 1974, applies in Niue by virtue of Section 690 of the Niue Act 1966 (NZ). The act provides for the incorporation of societies that are not established for pecuniary gain. Provision is made for the rules of the society, application for incorporation, conferring of body corporate status, name of the society, contracts made by the society, annual financial statements, and dissolution. Incorporation in Niue is also possible under the Charitable Trusts Act 1957 (NZ), as in force at October 19, 1974, under Section 683A of the Niue Act 1966 (NZ). The act provides that trustees of trusts established for charitable purposes may apply for incorporation. The act sets out the procedure for incorporation and makes provision for schemes for certain charitable trusts.

The Industrial and Provident Societies Act 1908 (NZ), as in force at October 19, 1974, is in force in Niue by virtue of Section 691 of the Niue Act 1966 (NZ). This act provides for the registration, rules, and other proceedings of industrial and provident societies.

The Business Licences Ordinance 1961 provides for the licensing of businesses. *Business* is defined broadly, and the act deals with the procedure for licensing any person who wishes to carry on any business and with the nature and scope of the license.

The Niue Hours of Business Ordinance 1965 provides for the fixing of hours of business and prohibits trading outside regular hours. Some businesses are regulated in Niue. For example, under Section 21 of the Niue Act 1966 (NZ), no person may practice medicine or surgery in Niue unless that person is registered as a medical practitioner under the Medical Practitioners Act 1968 (NZ), holds a certificate issued by the Medical Council of New Zealand, or is a graduate of the Fiji School of Medicine who is an employee of the Niue public service.

Generally it is unlawful to import, manufacture, and sell intoxicating liquor in Niue. There are certain rules on Niuean antiquities, such as a prohibition on the export of antiquities without first having offered them for sale to the government.

B. Banking and Credit

Banking is restricted, by Section 726 of the Niue Act 1966 (NZ), to those entities licensed by statute. Under the Banking Act 1986, the Westpac Bank operates a branch in the principal town, Alofi. No bank may issue banknotes in Niue. The currency is regulated by the Decimal Currency Act 1964 (NZ) and is therefore the notes and coins of New Zealand. There is no exchange control law. Sections 207–211 of the Niue Act 1966 (NZ) provide for offenses relating to forgery and counterfeit coin.

The Credit Restriction Ordinance 1971 restricts and controls the granting of credit in Niue. The act deals with dishonesty by receivers of goods from traders and borrowers, acts and omissions of agents regarding credit, and exemptions in cases of emergency.

C. Judgment Debts

Sections 88–95 of the Niue Act 1966 (NZ) set out the rules for execution of judgments. Writs of sale may be caused to be issued by persons to whom money is payable under a judgment of the High Court. Writs of possession may be issued in respect of land and chattels owing to a person under a judgment of the High Court. The writs are issued by the registrar.

Where, under a judgment of the High Court, payment of a sum of money is due, a charging order may be made by the Court against the property of the person who owes the money.

The act also contains provisions for the issue of judgment summonses by creditors to recover debts, damages, or sums of money owing. The court may order the judgment debtor to pay the amount of the debt, but only after the Court is satisfied that the debtor is able to pay the debt, or that the liability was incurred by fraud, or that the debtor has removed property to avoid paying the debt.

Judgments of the High Court can be enforced in the Supreme Court of New Zealand.

Sections 96–100 of the Niue Act 1966 (NZ) deal with absconding debtors. A defendant may be arrested and imprisoned for up to three months where, in an action before the High Court, the plaintiff proves that he or she has a good cause of action and that the defendant is likely to abscond and that such action will materially prejudice the plaintiff's case. A defendant may give security that he or she will not leave Niue.

Where the action is for a penalty at the suit of the Crown, it is unnecessary to show material prejudice to the Crown's case. In those cases, the security to be given is that any sum recovered against the defendant will be paid, or the defendant will be sent to prison.

D. Securities and Negotiable Instruments

The law on these matters is found in the Bills of Exchange Act 1908 (NZ). This act, as in force at October 19, 1974, applies in Niue by virtue of Section 682 of the *Niue Act 1966* (NZ). The act sets out the law on bills of exchange—for example, the capacity and authority of parties, consideration of a bill, general duties of the holder, and discharge of bills. There are also provisions for checks drawn on banks and promissory notes.

XIX. TORTS

The rules relating to torts are those of the English common law for the time being. Those rules have been little affected by legislation in Niue. The Deaths by Accidents Compensation Act

1952 (NZ) is Niue law; it provides for the survival of causes of action in the field of torts. Defamation is actionable without proof of actual damage and the common employment rule in the field of vicarious liability is abolished. The common law rule by which a husband was responsible for the torts of his wife has been abolished by Section 707 of the Niue Act 1966 (NZ).

XX. Labor Law

There is no labor legislation specifically for Niue, and the common law regulating employer and employee relationships is therefore relevant. The only substantial employer is the Niue Public Service Commission, whose rules and determinations provide the industrial regime for all civil servants. Effectively the *Niue Public Service Manual*, which sets out in considerable detail the terms and conditions of employment of Niue civil servants, provides the rules governing most workers in Niue.

XXI. Industrial and Intellectual Property Rights

The main intellectual property laws of Niue are all New Zealand statutes. The Trade Marks Act 1953 (NZ), Patents Act 1953 (NZ), Merchandise Marks Act 1954 (NZ), Designs Act 1953 (NZ), and Copyright Act 1962 (NZ), as in force at October 19, 1974, apply in Niue in the same manner, in all respects as if Niue were for all purposes a part of New Zealand.

Although the New Zealand legislation applies in Niue, no separate administrative structure is in place, with the consequence that the New Zealand administrative structures in intellectual property also operate for Niue, so that the registration of a patent or trademark for Niue would have to be done in New Zealand. Any copyright, patent trademark, or design held in New Zealand is, by virtue of these provisions, also a protected property right in Niue.

The Merchandise Marks Act 1954 (NZ) provides for certain goods to bear a mark of origin and provides for the offense of false trade descriptions.

XXII. Legal Education and Profession

The one practicing lawyer in Niue works within the government service and is not a Niuean. A Niuean lawyer practicing in New Zealand travels to Niue from time to time to represent litigants and provide legal advice to the public. New Zealand lawyers have a right of audience in the High Court of Niue, as do other agents with the leave of that Court.

XXIII. Research Guide

Angelo, A. H., ed. *Niue: Its Constitution, Statutes and Subsidiary Legislation.* 5 vols. Alofi, Niue: 1991.
Chapman, T. *The Decolonisation of Niue.* Wellington: Victoria University Press, 1976.
Kalauni, S., L. Haioti, and T. Johns. "Adjudicators as Members of the Community in Niue," in C. G. Powles and M. Pulea, eds. *Pacific Courts and Legal Systems.* Suva: University of the South Pacific, 1988.
———. "The Public Defender: Niue's Experience," in Powles and Pulea.

———. "Written and Unwritten Law in Niue," in Powles and Pulea.
Land Tenure in Niue. Suva: Institute of Pacific Studies, 1977.
"Report of the Niue Review Group" (Wellington, 1986, Unpublished).
Tongatule, I. P. "Niue National Report: Mixed Civil and Customary Jurisdictions in Developing Countries." Paper presented at Congress of International Academy of Comparative Law, University of Sydney and Monash University, Australia, 1986.

7. Norfolk Island

DHIRENDRA K. SRIVASTAVA

I. Dateline

1774	Captain James Cook makes first European sighting of the island and names it after Duke of Norfolk.
1788	Lieutenant Philip Gidley King lands with fifteen convicts and nine civil and military personnel to form the first penal settlement.
1789	Norfolk Island is administered as dependency of colony of New South Wales.
1814	Penal settlement is closed and Norfolk Island abandoned.
1825	Norfolk Island is reoccupied for settlement of the worst criminals; no free settlers are allowed; Norfolk Island is again administered as dependency of New South Wales.
1844	The act for the annexation of Norfolk Island to Van Diemen's Land comes into effect, and Norfolk Island is administered from Hobart.
1852	Bishop Wilson of Van Diemen's Land recommends that the penal settlement be closed. Norfolk Island is suggested as home for Pitcairn Islanders.
1856	All convicts removed. All 194 Pitcairners leave Pitcairn Island and arrive on Norfolk Island. By an Order-in-Council, Norfolk Island is severed from Tasmania (until 1853, Van Diemen's Land) and proclaimed a separate settlement under jurisdiction of Governor of New South Wales.
1857	Proclamation of laws and regulations by Governor Denison of New South Wales. Executive power vested in Chief Magistrate and two councillors.
1858–1863	Many Pitcairners return to Pitcairn.
1901	Commonwealth of Australia established; Norfolk Island to be administered by Governor of state of New South Wales.
1903	Executive Council set up, with two elected members and four appointed by Governor.
1913	Norfolk Island becomes a territory of Australia.
1957	Norfolk Island Act (Aust.) passed; elected council of eight retained in an advisory role.
1960s	Norfolk Island attains prominence as a tax haven.
1977	Norfolk Island Council's appeal to U.N. Committee on Decolonization to prevent Norfolk Island's integration into Australia is rejected.
1979	Norfolk Island Act passed, providing for establishment of elected Legislative Assembly.

II. Historical, Cultural, and Economic Survey

Norfolk Island is an external territory of the Commonwealth of Australia. It is a small volcanic island, 8 kilometers by 5 kilometers, lying 29 degrees south latitude and 168 degrees east longitude in the South Pacific Ocean. The island is 1,676 kilometers from Sydney and 1,063 kilometers from Auckland. Its total land area is 35 square kilometers. According to the census of June 30, 1986, the island's population was 2,367, including 1,428 permanent residents, 549 temporary residents, and 390 tourists.

A. Political and Legal History

The recorded history of Norfolk Island began with its sighting in 1774 by Captain James Cook. The island was then uninhabited, but some historians suggest that Polynesians may have been its earlier settlers.

On February 7, 1788, when the island began to be used as a penal colony, the first recorded residents arrived from England. They consisted of male and female prisoners and civil and military personnel. The period between 1788 and 1814 was marked by attempts by some convicts to take the island by force, shortages of food, problems such as drinking and ill health, and general unrest. Because of the expense in its upkeep, its distance from Sydney, and the lack of safe anchorage, the island was abandoned in 1814.

After a hiatus of eleven years, Norfolk Island was reoccupied in July 1825, again as a British penal colony. New cultivation programs were implemented, handsome buildings at Kingston and Longridge erected, and roads constructed. But these improvements in the landscape sharply contrasted with the severity of the penal system. The island was again abandoned in 1855. Meanwhile the people of Pitcairn Island (descendants of the H.M.S. *Bounty* mutineers and their Tahitian women) were suffering from scarcity of food and water and were looking for a new home. On the instructions of the British government, the entire community of Pitcairn—194 men, women, and children—left Pitcairn Island for Norfolk, where they arrived on June 8, 1856. Many Pitcairners returned to Pitcairn Island in 1858 and 1863, but the majority stayed on in Norfolk. Forty-six percent of the population still consists of the descendants of Pitcairners.

Norfolk Island was administered as part or as a dependency of the colony of New South Wales from 1789 to 1814 and 1825 to 1844 and as part of the dependency of Van Diemen's Land (later Tasmania) from 1844 to 1855. Norfolk Island, including its settlement of Pitcairners, became a distinct and separate colony in the British Empire, but the same individual who was Governor of New South Wales was appointed Governor of Norfolk Island. On July 1, 1914, Norfolk Island became a territory of Australia and has continued as such since then. Norfolk Island has, however, achieved a considerable measure of self-government under the Norfolk Island Act 1979, now the principal act governing Norfolk Island.

The Norfolk Island Act 1913 established the island as an Australian territory. The Governor General of Australia was empowered to make ordinances for the peace, order, and good government of Norfolk Island. The act abolished the island's Executive Council and replaced it with an elected advisory council of eight members. The High Court of Australia was made the final appellate court. Subject to the act, all laws, rules, and regulations in force were to continue in force unless altered or repealed. Although Norfolk Island became a territory of the Commonwealth of Australia, the acts of the Australian federal Parliament (except the Norfolk Island Act 1913) were not to apply in Norfolk Island unless specifically extended to Norfolk Island.

The Norfolk Island Act 1913 was repealed and replaced by the Norfolk Island Act 1957, which gave the islanders a greater say in running their affairs. The act created the Norfolk Island Council, with limited executive powers, and the Office of the Administrator, appointed by the Governor General.

Under the Norfolk Island Act 1963, judges of the Federal Court of Australia can be appointed to the Supreme Court of Norfolk Island. In 1964 the Norfolk Island Council was enlarged to eight elected members with an elected President and the Administrator as ex officio chairman.

The Australian Parliament passed the Norfolk Island Act 1979, which confers wide powers on the Legislative Assembly created under the act, establishes an executive of the Westminster type, and delineates the jurisdiction of the Supreme Court.

B. Culture

The foundation of Norfolk Island's society was laid on the beliefs and customs brought by the descendants of the *Bounty* mutineers. The islanders speak English, but their language has considerable Tahitian influence.

C. Economy

Subsistence agriculture was the mainstay of Norfolk Island's economy until World War II. Even today, subsistence farming produces Kentia palm seed, cereals, vegetables, and fruits. Norfolk Island's waters are rich in fish and adequately meet local needs. There is a program to improve the health of livestock and the quality of meat, but local demand exceeds supply. Norfolk Island exports a large quantity of Kentia palm seed. The seed of the Norfolk pine is also exported.

From 1960 onward, Norfolk Island experienced a rapid growth in the tourist industry, which now provides employment to half of the population.

Since 1979, Australia has ceased to supplement Norfolk Island's recurrent budget, but the Australian government does provide funds to maintain the airport, meteorological station, the Office of the Administrator, historic buildings at Kingston and Arthur Vale, and the National Park. Australia has also agreed to share the cost of establishing central sewerage and water systems. Norfolk Island residents are entitled to medical benefits in Australia. Australia is responsible for defense.

Customs duty continues to be the largest single item of locally raised revenue. There is no income tax on income derived in Norfolk Island.

III. Sources of Law

The main sources of law are legislation and English common law and equity.

A. Statute Law

Prior to December 23, 1913, English law and laws promulgated by the Governor of Norfolk Island or New South Wales or enacted by the legislature of New South Wales or Tasmania applied. Before Norfolk Island became a territory of Australia, its then-existing laws were consolidated. Certain new laws were enacted by the Governor of New South Wales and came into effect on December 24, 1913. Under the Norfolk Island Act 1979, the legislation now applicable consists of the following:

1. laws proclaimed by the Governor of New South Wales on December 24, 1913, and still in force when the Norfolk Island Act 1979 was passed;
2. Commonwealth acts that expressly extend to Norfolk Island and the statutory rules made thereunder;

3. ordinances made by the Governor General between 1914 and 1979;
4. ordinances made by the Governor General under the Norfolk Island Act 1979;
5. regulations, bylaws, proclamations, declarations, and notices made or issued under the laws and ordinances referred to in 1, 3, and 4 above.
6. imperial acts and Orders-in-Council;
7. acts passed by the Legislative Assembly of Norfolk Island created under the 1979 act;
8. regulations, rules, and bylaws made under acts passed by the Legislative Assembly; and
9. adopted statutes and statutory provisions of some Australian states and the Australian Capital Territory.

Many titles to land still depend on the legal position before December 24, 1913.

Although the Commonwealth Parliament is the supreme legislative body for Norfolk Island, the island's own Legislative Assembly is the most important source of statutory laws. Its formal legislative power is virtually unlimited.

As for matters not covered by specific laws, the statutes in force in England on July 25, 1828, continue to apply so far as "the same can be applied."

Because the Commonwealth Parliament has plenary legislative power, in the case of an inconsistency between an applicable Commonwealth law and a law passed by the Legislative Assembly, the Commonwealth law will prevail to the extent of the inconsistency.

B. Common Law and Equity

Initially, Norfolk Island received the English common law on its establishment as part of the colony of New South Wales in 1789. In 1828, specific provisions were made in the Australian Courts Act 1828 (Imperial) for the reception of common law as in force in England on July 25, 1828, subject to its being appropriate. That position has been affirmed by the Judicature Ordinance 1960 of Norfolk Island, which is still in force.

While the qualification "so far as they are applicable" gives the courts powerful means to limit the adoption of English common law and equity, the principles and rules of English common law and equity remain by far the most important source of law that has not been codified—for example, laws relating to contracts, torts, and sale of goods.

C. Custom

From the time Pitcairners settled on the island, the British government followed a policy of noninterference with their practices. Yet there is no specific mention of custom as a source of law under the Norfolk Island Act 1979. Certain legislation, however, such as the Public Reserves (Animals) Act 1983, Commons and Public Reserves Ordinance 1936, Absentee Landowners Levy Ordinance 1976, and Protection of Movable Cultural Heritage Act 1985, codifies customary rights and obligations.

IV. Constitutional System

A. Legal Status

The Norfolk Island Act 1913 unequivocally declared that Norfolk Island is a territory under the authority of the Commonwealth of Australia. That position was not altered by the 1957 act.[1]

The islanders have expressed discontent with the position taken by the Australian courts. On various grounds, they stress that Norfolk Island is not an Australian territory, but rather a dependency of Australia or a British Crown colony, or a separate and independent state. Recently Mr. John Brown, the President of the Legislative Assembly, said that Norfolk Island was pushing toward independence. In December 1991, the islanders rejected an Australian government proposal to include them in Australian federal elections.

B. Immigration and Residency

The Australian Constitution provides that the federal Parliament can make laws with respect to immigration. Schedule 3 of the Norfolk Island Act 1979 also confers power on the island's Legislative Assembly to make laws on immigration. Since 1922, Norfolk Island has had its own laws dealing with immigration and has not been subject to Commonwealth legislation. Under the Immigration Act 1980, the power to refuse or grant entry permits is exercised by a member of the government of Norfolk Island subject to a right of appeal to the Australian minister.

Visitors' permits are ordinarily granted for up to thirty days. Temporary entry permits are sought by people intending to take up employment or research and are usually given for one year or less. General entry permits are granted to people who have a special relationship to Norfolk Island; they are usually valid for five years and six months and are further renewable.

The Immigration Act declares that certain categories of persons are considered residents of Norfolk Island. These categories include persons born when one of their parents was a resident. If a parent of a person born in Norfolk Island becomes a resident before that child reaches age eighteen, that child (subject to certain provisions) becomes a resident at the same time as the parent. A British subject who holds a general entry permit may apply to be declared a resident of Norfolk Island, provided he or she is ordinarily resident in Norfolk Island, has been resident for at least five years during the seven years immediately preceding the application, and intends to continue to reside ordinarily in Norfolk Island.

Norfolk Islanders are Australian citizens under the Australian Citizenship Act 1948.

C. Government

As noted earlier, the Commonwealth Parliament has given considerable autonomy to the islanders under the Norfolk Island Act 1979. That act sets out the structure of the government, providing for an elected Legislative Assembly with executive and legislative powers.

1. HEAD OF THE TERRITORY

Her Majesty the Queen is the Head of State of the Commonwealth of Australia, of which Norfolk Island is a territory. The Commonwealth of Australia, however, exercises its authority to govern Norfolk Island through an Administrator appointed by the Governor General.

2. EXECUTIVE

The Norfolk Island Act 1979 states that the Administrator of the Territory shall administer the government of the Territory under the authority of the Commonwealth. In exercising the powers and functions of the office, the Administrator is required to act in accordance with the advice of the Executive Council in relation to certain matters or the instructions of the Australian Territories Minister.

The Executive Council advises the Administrator on all matters relating to the government. It consists of the persons for the time being holding certain specified executive offices, determined by the Legislative Assembly and appointed by the Administrator on the advice of the Legislative Assembly. Except in exceptional circumstances, the Administrator may not terminate their appointments unless so advised by the Legislative Assembly.

3. LEGISLATURE

The Norfolk Island Act 1979 confers wide powers on the Norfolk Island Legislative Assembly. The Assembly has power, with the assent of the Administrator or the Governor General, to make laws for the peace, order, and good government of the territory. In general, the Assembly has power to legislate on all matters other than defense, foreign policy, currency, and state acquisition of property. On the other hand, the Australian Parliament has plenary power to make laws for the government of any territory. Indeed, the Commonwealth has legislated on certain matters falling within the competence of the Legislative Assembly, including the Liquid Fuel Emergency Act, Biological Control Act 1984, Fisheries Licences Levy Act, and Registration of Deaths Abroad Act 1984.

The Legislative Assembly consists of nine members who are elected for a term of not more than three years. At the first meeting after a general election, the members elect one of their number to be President and another to be Deputy President of the Legislative Assembly. A member of the Legislative Assembly may resign office by a signed writing delivered to the President or, if there is no President or the President is absent, to the Administrator. Where a casual vacancy occurs in the office of a member of the Legislative Assembly less than two years and nine months after the first meeting of the Assembly, an election must be held for the purpose of filling the vacant office for the remainder of the term of office.

A person is qualified to be a candidate for election to the Legislative Assembly if at the date of nomination the person has attained the age of eighteen years, is entitled to vote at elections of members of the Legislative Assembly, has been ordinarily resident within the Territory for a period of five years immediately preceding the date of nomination or satisfies statutory requirements relating to residence, and does not have any of the statutory disqualifications.

The voting system for the election of the members of the Legislative Assembly is unique. The Legislative Assembly Regulations 1983 provide that each voter has as many votes as the total number of vacancies but cannot give more than four votes to any one candidate. All votes carry equal value, and the highest scoring candidates are elected.

The Legislative Assembly is required to meet at least once every two months. If that does not happen, the Administrator may convene a meeting to ensure compliance with that requirement even though no request to convene a meeting was made by the members of the Assembly.

The President, the Deputy President, or, if they both are absent, a member elected by the Legislative Assembly, presides over a meeting of the Assembly. At a meeting of the Assembly, five members constitute a quorum. Questions are decided by a majority of the votes of the members present and voting. The member presiding has a deliberative vote only, and in the event of an equal number of votes on each side, the question is defeated.

Every proposed law passed by the Legislative Assembly must be presented to the Administrator for assent. The Administrator may give or withhold assent to the proposed law or reserve it for the Governor General's pleasure. Alternatively, the Administrator may return the proposed law to the Legislative Assembly with amendments.

Where a proposed law has been reserved by the Administrator for the Governor General's pleasure, the Governor General may give or withhold assent or return the proposed law with amendments. If the Governor General returns it with amendments, the Legislative Assembly must consider the amendments recommended by the Governor General and present the proposed law again to the Administrator for assent with or without amendments. The Governor

General may, within six months after the Administrator's assent to a proposed law, disallow that law or part of it.

4. JUDICIARY

Norfolk Island has inherited the English common law system. The courts exercising jurisdiction in Norfolk Island are the High Court, Federal Court, and Family Law Court of Australia and the Supreme Court and the Court of Petty Sessions of Norfolk Island.

a. Court of Petty Sessions

The Court of Petty Sessions is a court of record exercising jurisdiction under the Petty Sessions Ordinance 1960. Its powers may be exercised by the Chief Magistrate or any three other magistrates. The ordinance provides that the court has jurisdiction over offenses punishable on summary conviction or where the only penalty is a fine.

The powers of the court also include jurisdiction to deal with and impose punishments for contempt of the court; to impose punishments and penalties as provided by any law; and to award costs in all matters brought before the court. The court also determines civil claims in matters that do not exceed $A10,000.

The court also exercises jurisdiction over some offenses punishable under Australian legislation, such as the Crimes Act 1914 (Commonwealth). By virtue of the Family Law Act 1975 (Commonwealth), which has been extended to Norfolk Island, the court has jurisdiction in family matters to grant ancillary relief, but it has no power to grant principal relief. Thus it cannot entertain proceedings for declaring the validity of a marriage or granting a decree of dissolution or nullity of marriage. Matrimonial causes may not be instituted in the court unless at least one of the parties is at that time ordinarily resident within the Territory.

b. Supreme Court

The Supreme Court is a court of record and consists of a Chief Judge and such other judges as are appointed by the Governor General. The Court has two regular sittings annually, in spring and fall. It may also sit in New South Wales, Victoria, or the Australian Capital Territory to hear and determine noncriminal matters if the Court is satisfied that this would not be contrary to the interests of justice.

The Court is the highest judicial authority in Norfolk Island, with unlimited original civil and criminal jurisdiction and appellate jurisdiction from the judgments of inferior courts. It also determines constitutional matters.

The Court may also grant a mandamus or an injunction and may appoint a receiver by an interlocutory order in all cases in which it appears to be just or convenient to do so. The Court, however, has no power to deal with family law matters.

c. High Court and Federal Court

Under the Supreme Court Ordinance, the High Court of Australia may grant special leave to appeal from any judgment (whether final or interlocutory) of the Supreme Court of Norfolk Island.

Under the Federal Court of Australia Act 1976, the Federal Court has jurisdiction to hear appeals from a judgment of the Supreme Court of Norfolk Island. The appellate jurisdiction of the Federal Court is exercised by a full court containing three or more judges.

The Australian High Court has jurisdiction in some cases to hear and determine appeals from decisions of the Federal Court both in civil and criminal matters.

Only a few cases have gone to the High Court or the Federal Court, and criminal cases in particular are generally disposed of promptly by the Norfolk Island Supreme Court.

d. Family Court

The Family Law Act 1975 (Commonwealth) created the Family Court of Australia, a specialist federal court to deal with family matters. Its jurisdiction extends to all matters covered by the act, including dissolution, adoption, marriage, guardianship, custody, and maintenance. The act has been extended to Norfolk Island.

e. Coroner's Inquests

Under the Coroners Ordinance 1927, coroners carry out judicial investigations into cases of unexplained deaths or deaths caused in suspicious circumstances. They also hold inquests into the causes and origins of any fire that damaged or destroyed property and conduct inquiries into the whereabouts of missing persons.

f. Trial by Jury

The Juries Ordinance 1960 provides for trial by jury for criminal offenses prosecuted in the Supreme Court. Juries are not generally used in civil cases.

D. Emergency Powers

No direct provisions deal with emergency powers, but the Norfolk Island Act 1979 declares that the Governor General may make an ordinance without introducing it into the Legislative Assembly if it appears to the Governor General that urgency or special circumstances exist. The Governor General may also make an ordinance where it appears to the Governor General that no provision or insufficient provision has been made for the expenditure of funds out of the public accounts for the purposes of the government of Norfolk Island.

E. Human Rights

The Norfolk Island Act 1979 does not specifically confer any human rights on the islanders except that the Legislative Assembly cannot make a law for the acquisition of property otherwise than on just terms. Some important rights have been conferred, however, under other statutory provisions.

The Court of Petty Sessions Ordinance 1960 provides that a person taken into custody for an offense without a warrant must be brought before the court as soon as practicable. If it is not practicable to bring the person before the court within twenty-four hours the person must be discharged after entering into recognizance unless the offense appears to the police officer to be serious. The Criminal Law Ordinance 1960 protects persons from being tried or punished more than once for the same conduct.

Some Australian statutes, such as the Sex Discrimination Act 1984, Human Rights and Equal Opportunity Commission Act 1986, Affirmative Actions (Equal Employment for Women) Act 1986, and Racial Discrimination Act 1984, all of which extend to Norfolk Island, confer a number of basic human rights.

V. Administrative Organization and Law

Norfolk Island is administered by an Administrator appointed by the Australian Governor General. During any vacancy in the office of the Administrator, the Governor General may appoint an acting Administrator. The Governor General also appoints a deputy administrator. The Executive Council of the island advises the Administrator on all matters relating to the government of the island. The Administrator appoints executive members on the advice of the Legislative Assembly. The executive members hold ministerial positions and are in charge of their departments. The chief administrative officer is appointed by the Administrator in accordance with recommendation of the Legislative Assembly.

The Public Service Ordinance 1979 established a Public Service Board, consisting of the administrator (who is the chairman), chief administrative officer, an officer of the public service elected by its members, and two independent members appointed from the community by the Legislative Assembly. The Public Service Board deals with matters of appointment, promotion, and transfer of officers and other related matters. An officer or employee who is dissatisfied with a decision of the chief administrative officer that directly affects him may appeal to the board, which may affirm, vary, or reverse the decision.

Several other boards and tribunals exercise quasi-judicial functions. These include the Norfolk Island Building Board, Employment Tribunal (established under the Employment Act 1988), Hospital Board, Licensing Board, Immigration Council, Social Service Board, and Museum Board. The Building Board, constituted under the Building Ordinance 1967, examines applications for erection of new dwellings, alteration or extension to existing dwellings, and upgrading of tourist accommodation. The Licensing Board, appointed under the Liquor Licensing Ordinance 1960, deals with applications for the issue, renewal, and transfer of licenses for the supply or serving of liquor in public places.

In most cases where a person is aggrieved by the decision of an administrative tribunal, the applicant may appeal to the Court of Petty Sessions.

VI. International Obligations

Since Norfolk Island is a territory of Australia, it has no right to engage in international relations; however, not all international conventions ratified by Australia apply to Norfolk Island. While some Australian acts passed to implement international conventions apply to the full extent (for example, the Designs Act 1906, Copyright Act 1968, and Trade Marks Act 1955), others apply to only a limited extent. The Foreign Judgments (Reciprocal Enforcement) Ordinance allows a judgment creditor to apply to the Supreme Court of Norfolk Island to have a foreign judgment registered.

VII. Revenue Law

The main sources of revenue in Norfolk Island include customs duty, financial institutions levy, absentee landowner's levy, public works levy, and duty on checks.

A. Income Tax

Until 1973, Norfolk Island was used as a tax haven by Australian companies and businessmen. That was stopped by extending the Australian Income Tax Assessment Act 1936 to Norfolk

Island. But Norfolk Island residents and companies wholly owned by them are still exempt from tax on income derived from sources in Norfolk Island or outside Australia.

B. Customs Duty

Import duties are payable on certain goods brought into Norfolk Island. Under the Customs Ordinance 1913, the rates of duty vary from item to item, and some goods are not subject to any duty.

C. Financial Institutions Levy

Under the Financial Institutions Levy Act 1985, a levy is imposed at the rate of 0.2 percent on receipts of any registered bank or financial institution.

D. Absentee Landowners Levy

Under the Absentee Landowners Ordinance, 1976, an annual levy is imposed on all land owned in fee simple by persons absent from Norfolk Island on the levy date, at a rate of 4 percent of the unimproved value of the land. Where an absentee is nonetheless a Norfolk Island resident, that person must pay only 25 percent of the amount otherwise payable but in no case more than $A250. Certain institutions, such as scientific and religious institutions, and persons are not liable to pay the levy.

E. Public Works Levy

Under the Public Works Levy Ordinance 1976, every person who is ordinarily resident in Norfolk Island and has attained the age of eighteen years is liable to pay $A100 to the Administrator as "public works levy" on a levy day. Where a person is not ordinarily resident in Norfolk Island, the levy payable may be reduced. Where one or more persons were dependents of a person, the amount of levy is reduced by $A10 for each dependent. The amount of levy is also reduced for low-income persons.

F. Checks Duty

The Cheques Duty Act 1983 imposes a duty of twenty cents on every check payable at a branch in Norfolk Island unless drawn by the Commonwealth, the Administrator, a body established for public purposes under an enactment, or an organization or body declared to be exempt.

VIII. INVESTMENT LAW

A. Foreign Investment

Norfolk Island's foreign investment policy is subject to the Foreign Takeovers Act 1975 (Commonwealth). Proposals by foreign investors to acquire substantial shareholdings (other than a nontrading company whose assets are less than $A1,000) must be reported to the Treasurer. The Fisheries Act 1952 (Commonwealth) also applies. At present, negotiations are underway with Japanese investors to exploit the vast fisheries resources of the island. Foreign investors do not enjoy a tax holiday in Norfolk Island.

B. Imports

Foreign goods can be imported into Norfolk Island subject to compliance with statutory requirements. Under the Customs Ordinance 1913, import duties are payable for certain types of goods brought into the island. The Dangerous Drugs Ordinance 1927 prohibits the importation of any dangerous drugs without a license, and various statutes prohibit or restrict the importation of certain plants and animals.

C. Insurance

Insurance is regulated under the Insurance Contracts Act 1984 (Commonwealth), which extends to Norfolk Island. Section 21 of the act imposes a duty of disclosure on persons obtaining insurance, but only of matters the insured knows are relevant to the decision of the insurer whether to accept the risk and on what terms, or of matters a reasonable person in the circumstances could be expected to know are relevant. Where a person failed to answer, or gave an obviously incomplete or irrelevant answer to a question included in a proposal, the insurer is deemed to have waived compliance with the duty of disclosure in relation to the matter.

The act, however, does not apply to reinsurance, health, marine, workers' compensation, or third-party motor vehicle insurance. The Insurance (Agents and Brokers) Act 1984 (Commonwealth) and the Life Insurance Act 1945 (Commonwealth) have also been extended to Norfolk Island.

IX. Welfare Law

Norfolk Island has its own social security schemes, which are not as extensive as the Australian programs. Under the Social Services Act 1980 of Norfolk Island, benefits are payable to eligible aged, invalid, and widowed residents or residents who have care, custody, and control of an orphaned or handicapped child. Originally benefits were paid at 75 percent of their Australian equivalent. The rates went up to 78 percent in 1982. By the Social Services (Amendment) Act 1985, the retail price index was made the basis of biannual adjustment of the rates of benefit. There is no provision for unemployment benefits.

X. Criminal Law

The provisions of the Crimes Act 1900 of New South Wales as amended before December 16, 1936, apply as law of Norfolk Island, subject to the modifications prescribed by the Criminal Law Ordinance 1960 of Norfolk Island. The Police Offences Ordinance 1933 punishes a variety of petty offenses not included in the Crimes Act.

Under the Crimes Act, a person convicted of murder or rape may be sentenced to death. A person committing a felony or misdemeanor may be sentenced to imprisonment or fined or awarded other punishments prescribed under the New South Wales Act or the Criminal Law Ordinance. Sentences of whipping or irons can still be given in certain cases.

Other kinds of orders, such as restitution orders, compensation orders, and cancellation of driving license, may be made. Cumulative sentences can also be given and outstanding charges taken into account in passing a sentence in special cases. The court also possesses power to discharge or vary conditions of recognizance.

XI. Judicial Procedure

A. Civil Procedure

The rules of civil procedure for the Court of Petty Sessions are set out in the Court of Petty Sessions Ordinance 1960 (as amended by the Court of Petty Sessions Amendment Act). The rules of procedure in a civil action before the Supreme Court are similar to those applied in the Supreme Court of the Australian Capital Territory.

1. COURT OF PETTY SESSIONS

The Court of Petty Sessions Amendment Act (No. 2) 1988 gives the Court of Petty Sessions jurisdiction to determine civil claims in respect of matters that do not exceed $A10,000. The court does not have jurisdiction to hear actions in which title to land or the validity of a devise, bequest, or limitation under a will or settlement is in question. The court may grant leave for the removal of a civil action to the Supreme Court.

2. SUPREME COURT

Subject to the Supreme Court Ordinance 1960, the practice and procedure of the Supreme Court is to be governed by the Rules of the Supreme Court (Amending) 1964 of Norfolk Island. Those rules adopt the rules of court of the Supreme Court of the Australian Capital Territory with some modifications.

In every civil case the trial is held without a jury, unless it appears just to the Supreme Court to hold the trial with a jury. Unless the parties agree to the contrary, testimony at the trial is given orally in open court. At the trial, proof may be given by affidavit of the service of any document. Any defect or error in any proceedings in the Court may be corrected by the Court at any time during the course of the trial.

B. Criminal Procedure

The procedure for criminal trials in Norfolk Island is largely governed by the Court of Petty Sessions Ordinance 1960, Supreme Court Ordinance 1960 and Criminal Law Ordinance 1960.

1. COURT OF PETTY SESSIONS

The Court of Petty Sessions Ordinance states that a criminal proceeding may be commenced by an information laid before a magistrate. Where an information is laid before a magistrate, the magistrate may issue a summons or a warrant of arrest for the person alleged to have committed an offense.

a. Indictable Offenses

Where a person charged with an indictable offense against whom a summons has been issued does not appear before the court, the court may issue a warrant for the arrest of that person. A person taken into custody without a warrant must be brought before the court as soon as practicable or within twenty-four hours unless the offense is of a serious nature. A person charged with an indictable offense, but one not punishable by death or imprisonment for life, may at any stage of the committal proceedings plead guilty. The court may accept or reject the plea. Where the court accepts the plea, it may deal with the matter summarily and finally dispose of the charge and other incidental matters, or it may commit the accused to a sitting or sittings of the Supreme Court. Where the Court rejects the plea, the proceedings before the Court must continue as if the plea had not been made. After all the evidence for the prosecution and the defense has been taken, the court may, depending upon the evidence, either discharge the accused or commit him to take his trial before the Supreme Court.

A person charged with a capital offense cannot be admitted to bail except by order of the Supreme Court or a judge of the Supreme Court. But a person committed for trial for an offense the maximum punishment for which is imprisonment or fine may be admitted to bail by the Court of Petty Sessions.

b. Offenses Punishable Summarily

Where a date for hearing of an offense punishable summarily has been fixed and the defendant attends the court but the informant does not appear, the court may either dismiss the information or adjourn the hearing to some other day. On the other hand, where the defendant does not appear at the appointed day of hearing, the court may proceed ex parte to hear and determine the case. Where both parties appear either personally or by counsel, solicitor, or agent, the court proceeds to hear and determine the information.

2. SUPREME COURT

The procedure before the Supreme Court is largely governed by the rules of the Supreme Court of the Australian Capital Territory and the Supreme Court Ordinance 1960, which states that an indictable offense triable before the Supreme Court must be prosecuted by information in the name of the Administrator or another person appointed for that purpose by the Governor General. The procedure in admission of oral testimony and evidence by affidavit are similar to those in a civil case.

C. Appellate Jurisdiction

Under the Court of Petty Sessions Ordinance 1960, where a party has been fined $A10 or sentenced to imprisonment for any term by the Court of Petty Sessions, that party has a right to appeal to the Supreme Court. In civil cases, there is a right of appeal where the judgment given by the Court of Petty Sessions involves $A100 or more. In other cases, the Supreme Court may grant special leave to appeal where the Court is of the opinion that granting of leave would be in the public interest. Under the Federal Court of Australia Act 1976, the Federal Court may hear and determine appeals from judgments of the Supreme Court. The appellate jurisdiction of the Federal Court is exercised by a full court consisting of three judges. The High Court has jurisdiction to hear appeals from decisions of the Federal Court, in both civil or criminal matters. The High Court also exercises appellate jurisdiction under the Supreme Court Ordinance 1960 to hear appeals from any judgment (whether final or interlocutory) of the Supreme Court in civil matters.

A person convicted on indictment before the Supreme Court may appeal to the full court of the High Court against the conviction on the ground that the case involves a question of law. In other cases the appellant cannot appeal without leave of the Supreme Court or the High Court.

In family matters, appeals from the Court of Petty Sessions of Norfolk Island lie to a single judge of the Family Court and an appeal from a decree of a single judge lies to a full court of that court (Family Law Act 1975 [Commonwealth]). An appeal from a decree of a full court of the Family Court, under the Family Law Act, lies to the High Court by special leave of the High Court or upon a certificate of the full court that an important question of law or public interest is involved. Thus, a family matter arising in the Court of Petty Sessions may eventually end up in the High Court of Australia.

XII. Land and Natural Resources

A. Land Tenure and Administration

Norfolk Island's total land area is about 3,500 hectares—1,700 freehold, 1,010 Crown leasehold, and 745 in roads, commons, and reserves. After the first settlement in 1789, grants of land were made to nonconvicts and convicts who had completed their sentences. Norfolk Island's present land titles, however, are derived from freehold grants made to Pitcairners in 1856. Up to a 50-acre block was granted to the head of each family. If a male married, he was granted a 25-acre block. No official record has been kept of early dealings in or transfers of land carried out. Reports by two commissions of inquiry, sent to Norfolk Island in 1855 and 1896, still provide the basic data for land searches.

1. SYSTEMS OF TITLE

The legal basis of land ownership is to be found in the Titles of Land Ordinance 1913. Section 1 of the act provides for a system of deed registration. Until recently defects in title could not be cured by adverse possession. This position has now been changed by the Limitation of Actions (Real Property) Act 1988. Now, an action by the Crown to recover the land cannot be maintained later than thirty years after the time the Crown became first entitled to bring the action. For persons other than the Crown, the period of limitation is twelve years.

2. CONVEYANCING

The common law rules of conveyancing apply as modified by the Conveyancing Ordinance 1913. Section 4(1) of the ordinance requires the parties to any sale, mortgage, lease, or any other transaction relating to land (or their duly constituted attorneys) to appear before the Registrar of Lands. The registrar is to see that the appropriate forms are filled out and executed.

B. The Commonwealth's Power to Acquire Property

Under the Australian Constitution, the Australian Parliament generally has power to acquire property from any state or person for any purpose in respect of which the Parliament has power to make laws but must do so on "just terms." This limitation of "just terms" does not, however, apply to acquisition of territorial property; the Australian Parliament under the Constitution has plenary, unqualified, and unlimited power to acquire territorial property without conceding just terms. However, compensation is required to be paid for land compulsorily acquired by the minister under the Crown Lands Ordinance 1913.

C. Crown Lands

The law relating to the Crown lands is largely governed by the Crown Lands Ordinance 1913.

1. WASTE LANDS

Under the Crown Lands Ordinance, the power of leasing or authorizing the occupation or use of the waste lands of the Crown can be exercised by the Governor General or the minister. But alienation of such lands can be made only by the Governor General.

2. CROWN LEASES

The Governor General or the minister may approve sale by auction of, or tender for, lease of any Crown lands. Ordinarily no lease will be granted in respect of a greater area than 1 acre for building or business purposes or 25 acres for cultivation and grazing purposes. Notwithstanding any lease, all pine trees remain the property of the Crown. The Governor General or the minister may attach other conditions to a lease. If a lessee becomes the holder of a freehold or another leasehold interest in Norfolk Island, the lease may be forfeited. The term of any lease cannot exceed twenty-eight years. Further, no lease can be assigned, sublet, or mortgaged without the approval of the Governor General or the minister.

3. COMPULSORY ACQUISITION OF LAND BY THE CROWN

Section 28 of the Crown Lands Ordinance authorizes the minister to acquire or resume any land for a variety of public purposes. Section 30 states that, subject to any covenants or conditions contained in any grant or lease reserving the right of resumption of land for public purposes, compensation shall be paid on land acquired or resumed under the ordinance, and such compensation shall be assessed in the prescribed manner.

D. Commons and Public Reserves

Under the Commons and Public Reserves Ordinance 1936, part of Norfolk Island's land has been reserved for a variety of purposes including forestry, grazing, and recreation. All commons and reserves are under the control of the Administrator. The Administrator may declare any Crown land to be a common or public reserve. A lease cannot be granted of any portion of a common or public reserve. However, an area of land may be excised from the commons or the public reserves and a lease of that portion thereafter granted.

E. National Park, Botanic Garden, and Historic Places and Buildings

Under the National Parks and Wildlife Conservation Act 1975 (Commonwealth), an area of 460 hectares has been proclaimed for the National Park and an area of 0.6 hectare for the Botanic Garden. The principal act relating to the National Park and the Botanic Garden is the Norfolk Island National Park and Botanic Garden Act 1984.

Although Norfolk Island's total land area is only 35 kilometers, there are many historic places and buildings of interest. The Australian government has spent a considerable amount of money on the maintenance and upkeep of old stone buildings.

F. Agriculture, Forests, and Fisheries

Norfolk Island has a subtropical climate that favors grazing and crop cultivation. A number of factors, however, restrict the extent of farming, including the porous soils that make it difficult to store water in earth dams. At the time of its discovery, Norfolk Island was a dense and largely impenetrable jungle, of which pine was an important component. The pine has assumed great importance; some of the huge pines that predate the penal settlement days are revered as historic monuments. Fish is plentiful, but the exportation of fish is subject to strict regulations.

The future of the island lies in the conservation of its waters, soils, pastures, forests, plants, and fish. The laws are not adequate to achieve that purpose. However, the Water Assurance (Easements) Act 1989 was recently passed to ensure purity of groundwater. The act empowers the administration to acquire, either by agreement or compulsorily, from a person who has an interest in land a sewerage easement on that land.

The Timber Licenses Ordinance 1913 makes it an offense to cut, obtain, or remove green timber or to collect pine cones or seeds for sale or export on or from any Crown land without a license or authority, or to willfully destroy or damage any sapling or tree on any Crown land. A person cutting any pinewood or hardwood or obtaining any pinewood or hardwood from any Crown land is required to pay royalty.

XIII. Persons and Entities

A. Legal Capacity

The Age of Majority Act 1980 provides that, except in certain cases, a person attains full age for all purposes of the law of Norfolk Island at the age of eighteen years.

Persons who are insane or lunatic lack legal capacity and suffer a variety of disabilities. The law relating to insane persons in Norfolk Island is governed mainly by the Lunacy Ordinance 1932, which, subject to modifications, applies the Lunacy Act 1898 of New South Wales (the 1898 act has since been repealed in New South Wales).

Under the Companies Act 1985, a corporation has the same powers as a natural person of full age and capacity. The Companies Act provides that persons who desire the incorporation of a company must lodge the memorandum and the articles (if any) of the proposed company with the registrar together with other necessary documents. The consequences of incorporation of a company are that it (1) is capable of performing all the functions of a body corporate; (2) is capable of suing and being sued; (3) has perpetual succession; and (4) has power to acquire, hold, and dispose of property.

B. Names

A person may carry on business under a business name either alone or in association with other persons (for example, as a partner). A business name must be registered under the Business Names Ordinance 1976, unless it consists merely of the names of each person associated in carrying on the business.

XIV. Family Law

In matters of family law, the islanders are largely governed by the Australian law. The two most important Australian Acts, namely the Marriage Act 1961 (Commonwealth) and the Family Law Act 1975 (Connonwealth), have been extended to Norfolk Island.

A. Marriage

The Marriage Act requires that a marriage must be solemnized by or in the presence of an authorized celebrant. But a marriage is not invalid by reason only that the person solemnizing it was not authorized, if either party to the marriage believed that that person was lawfully authorized. Parties intending to marry must give notice in writing of the intended marriage not earlier than six months and not later than one month before the date of marriage. The act states that the marriageable age for males is eighteen years and for females sixteen years. A male who has attained the age of sixteen or a female who has attained the age of fourteen may be permitted by a judge or a magistrate to marry a person of marriageable age. Where a party is a minor (under eighteen years of age), his or her marriage generally cannot be solemnized without the consent of the parents, guardians, or a magistrate or judge. A marriage is void where

1. either of the parties is, at the time of the marriage, lawfully married to some other person;
2. the parties are within a prohibited relationship;
3. by reason of Section 48, the marriage is not a valid marriage;
4. the consent of either of the parties is not a real consent because (a) it was obtained by duress or fraud, (b) one party is mistaken as to the identity of the other party or as to the nature of the ceremony performed, or (c) one party is mentally incapable of understanding the nature and effect of the marriage ceremony; or
5. either of the parties is not of marriageable age.

B. Divorce, Separation, and Annulment

Under the Family Law Act, irretrievable breakdown of marriage is the sole ground for dissolution of marriage. To establish irretrievable breakdown, it must be proved that the parties have separated and have lived apart for not less than twelve months. But the court will not grant a decree of dissolution of marriage if it is satisfied that there is a reasonable likelihood of cohabitation being resumed.

C. Custody and Maintenance

The Family Law Act provides that, in general, each of the parents of a child who has not attained the age of eighteen years is a guardian of the child, and parents have joint custody of the child. It is the object of the provision concerning child maintenance that "children receive a proper level of financial support from their parents." Their obligation may continue even after the child has attained the age of eighteen years.

D. Adoption

Under the Adoption Ordinance 1932, an unmarried person or two spouses may be jointly authorized by the court to adopt a child. There are certain restrictions on who may adopt children. The ordinance prohibits making an adoption order if the applicant is less than twenty-five years of age or fewer than twenty-one years older than the infant to be adopted unless they are within the prohibited degrees of consanguinity or, being of the same sex, are of the same blood. The court may refuse to authorize an adoption where the sole applicant is a male and the infant to be adopted is a female, except in exceptional circumstances. An adoption requires consent in writing of every parent or guardian of the infant to be adopted and of every person who has custody of the infant or is liable to contribute to the support of the infant. In suitable cases the court may dispense with the requirement for written consent. The court will make an adoption order only if it is satisfied that such an order will be for the welfare of the infant to be adopted. Where an infant has been adopted, its ties are severed with the earlier family and new rights created in the adoptive family. An adopted child has the same rights of inheritance as if he or she were born to the adopter or adopters and ceases to have any right of succession to any real or personal property of its natural parent or parents.

XV. Personal Property

Norfolk Island does not have its own sale of goods legislation. The transfer of property under a contract of sale is governed by the common law. However, the Sale of Goods (Vienna Convention) Act 1987 gives effect within Norfolk Island to the United Nations Convention on Contracts for the International Sale of Goods, adopted at Vienna on April 10, 1980.

Several Australian statutes, particularly the Trade Practices Act 1974 (Commonwealth), drastically change the common law principles to suit the needs of today's consumer-oriented society. But the Trade Practices Act has not been extended to Norfolk Island, nor has Norfolk Island modified its own laws to regulate sale of goods, loans, and mortgages in the same way Australian States and internal Territories have done.

XVI. Wills and Succession

In Norfolk Island much of the law relating to wills and succession is governed by statutes. The Wills Ordinance 1973 provides that a person may, by will, devise, bequeath, or dispose of any real or personal property. A will is not valid unless it is in writing, signed by the testator or by another person in the testator's presence and according to the testator's direction, and witnessed by two or more persons. An alteration in a will to be valid must also be executed with the same formalities as a will. A gift to an attesting witness or the witness's spouse is invalid. A person cannot make a valid will unless he or she is at least eighteen years of age and is of sound mind. Where a person marries after having made a will, the earlier will is revoked unless it was made in contemplation of that marriage.

A will may be revoked by the testator by a subsequent valid will or by executing a revocation document with the same formalities required for a will.

An executor is appointed by the court by a grant of probate to administer the estate of a person who died leaving a will. An administrator is appointed by the court in the case of a person dying intestate, that is, without leaving a will.

XVII. Contracts

In the field of contracts, Norfolk Island has taken much of its law from England. By far the most important source of contract law is English common law (including principles of equity). All statutes and laws made under statutes, rules, and principles of common law and equity not inconsistent with any statute in force on July 25, 1828, were adopted in Norfolk Island subject to their circumstantial applicability and some other conditions.

Under the Creditors' Remedies Ordinance 1929, if a plaintiff can show the Supreme Court or the Court of Petty Sessions that he or she has a good cause of action for a certain sum of money and that the defendant is about to leave the jurisdiction of the court and the action will be defeated unless the defendant is forthwith apprehended, the court may order the defendant to be arrested and held to bail for a sum, specified in the order and not exceeding the amount claimed in the action.

The Mercantile Ordinance 1959 provides that a bill of sale does not create a security interest in the goods sold unless it is in accordance with the prescribed form, sets forth the consideration for which it is given, specifies the conditions to which it is subject, and is registered under the ordinance.

XVIII. Commercial Law

A. Sales of Goods

Whereas the Australian Parliament and state legislatures in Australia have passed laws affecting the underlying common law principles and offering protection to the consumer, there is little legislation of that kind in the contract law applicable to Norfolk Island.

Sales are mainly governed by common law principles, although some aspects of leases of land are regulated by statutory provisions. The Conveyancing Ordinance 1913 requires registration of sales, mortgages, and leases. Any agreement to grant a lease for more than five years may be ineffective by virtue of the Land (Subdivision) Ordinance 1967. A transfer, conveyance, or other instrument providing for the subdivision of land does not have any force or effect unless and until the subdivision is approved by the appropriate persons, and the court and a plan of the subdivision is registered.

B. Partnerships

There is no partnership legislation applying to Norfolk Island. Consequently the common law principles are applied to determine disputes concerning a partnership or its partners.

C. Regulated Businesses

A number of businesses and professions are regulated and require a license or registration. These include apiarists, auctioneers, butchers, surveyors, persons importing "dangerous drugs," persons selling poisonous and dangerous substances, teachers at public schools, persons selling liquor, electrical contractors, and persons or firms selling food.

D. Banking

Under the Constitution, the Australian Parliament has power to make laws with respect to currency, coinage, and legal tender; banking other than state banking; state banking extending beyond the limits of the state concerned; the incorporation of banks; and the issue of paper money. Various Parts of the Commonwealth Banking Act 1959 apply to Norfolk Island. Two Australian banks operate in Norfolk Island.

E. Negotiable Instrument

The Bills of Exchange Ordinance 1961 applies to bills of exchange, checks, and promissory notes. This ordinance is very similar to the Bills of Exchange Act 1909 (Commonwealth), which was modeled on the English Act of 1882. The Cheques and Payment Orders Act 1986 (Commonwealth), which specifically deals with checks, has been extended to Norfolk Island.

XIX. Torts

The English common law continues to be the main source for dealing with tort cases. Some British and Australian acts have been reenacted with minor changes of names, dates, and so forth. Some common law principles have been given statutory force.

The Law Reform (Miscellaneous Provisions) Ordinance 1971 states that, on the death of a person, all causes of action subsisting against or vested in that person survive against the estate, or for the benefit of the estate, except causes of action for defamation, seduction, adultery, or inducing a wife to remain apart from her husband. Section 9 provides that a husband is not liable for his wife's torts and antenuptial obligations. Part IV of the ordinance deals with proceedings against and contributions between joint tort-feasors. Section 15 provides that, where a person suffers damage as the result of partly his or her own fault and partly the fault of another person, the damage recoverable will be reduced with regard to the degree of fault of the claimant. This provision changed the earlier common law rule of contributory negligence, that a plaintiff whose acts contributed to the plaintiff's injury could not claim damages from the defendant. The ordinance also abolishes the defense of common employment allowed under the common law.

At common law, death of either party extinguishes a cause of action. Under the Law Reform (Miscellaneous Provisions) Ordinance 1971, such an action may nonetheless continue after death, or the beneficiaries of the estate of the deceased may if they wish pursue a wrongful death action under the Law Reform (Fatal Injuries) Ordinance 1971.

XX. Labor Law

In the area of labor law, the most important legislation is the Employment Act 1988. Australia is a member of the International Labor Organization and several other United Nations specialized agencies are concerned with labor and related matters. Some of the conventions ratified by Australia have been extended to Norfolk Island.

The Employment Act 1988 protects workers in a number of ways. Section 11 states that where a contract provision is less favorable to an employee than the terms and conditions of employment specified in the act, the provision is deemed to have been varied so as to be consistent with the act. The act prescribes minimum rates of pay and conditions for employment of children. The act also states that an employee may refuse to work outside the working hours; requires employers to pay employees' wages at least each fourteenth day; requires pay for public holidays; enjoins an employer to give at least seven clear days' written notice of termination of employment or pay the amount the employee was entitled to be paid for the week before termination; declares that every employee has a rest period of at least twenty-four continuous hours in every week; and provides that, where an employee is required by law or the employer to wear safety equipment or special clothing or footwear, the employer must provide them free of charge.

Part III of the act contains elaborate schemes for compensation for work-related accidents. Where an employee dies, a dependent of the employee is entitled to compensation. If an employee suffers incapacity, the employer is required to pay periodic compensation. Section 39 requires an employer to obtain and maintain an approved policy of insurance or indemnity for the full amount of the employer's liability to pay compensation. Section 49 requires employers and manufacturers to maintain a safe working environment.

The act establishes the Employment Conciliation Board, which has three members. An aggrieved person may lodge a complaint with any member of the board concerning:

1. noncompliance with a provision of a written contract entered into in pursuance of the act;
2. noncompliance with the minimum terms and conditions of employment specified in this act;
3. noncompliance with any other provision of this act; or
4. any other matter in relation to employment.

The board must try to resolve a complaint by conciliation and must take steps to effect an amicable settlement; it is not bound by the rules of evidence. After dealing with the complaint, the board is required to issue a certificate setting out the result of that dealing.

The act further establishes the Employment Tribunal, which consists of five members. A person who remains aggrieved by the complaint to which the certificate of the Employment Conciliation Board relates may apply in writing to the tribunal for an inquiry. The tribunal is not bound by the rules of evidence, but must act according to equity, good conscience, and the substantial merits of the case without regard to technicalities and legal forms.

A person who is aggrieved by a determination, or order of the tribunal may apply to the Court of Petty Sessions for a review of the determination or order. The court's hearing and determining an application under the act is not bound by the rules of evidence. The court can make an order setting aside or varying the determination or order or confirming the determination, or it can make an order it thinks fit. An order made by the Court of Petty Sessions is final except on questions of law. The court may, however, refer a question of law to the Supreme Court for its opinion.

XXI. Industrial and Intellectual Property Rights

In this field, all the relevant Australian acts have been extended to Norfolk Island. These include the Patents Act 1952, Trade Marks Act 1955, Designs Act 1906, and Copyright Act 1968. Their application to Norfolk Island was considered necessary to enable Australia to fulfill its international obligations under the various conventions relating to these subjects.

XXII. Legal Education and Profession

A person admitted to practice in the Supreme Court of the Australian Capital Territory or the Federal Court of Australia is allowed to practice in the Supreme Court of Norfolk Island. There are no such formal requirements for practice in the Court of Petty Sessions.

Norfolk Island has no law schools. Some islanders have obtained legal qualifications from Australia or New Zealand, but they are not practicing as lawyers on Norfolk Island. A few Australian practitioners are resident on Norfolk Island.

Local magistrates and magistrates are appointed from the magistracy of the Australian Capital Territory. The Chief Magistrate is from Canberra; he visits Norfolk Island twice every year. At present there are five resident magistrates in Norfolk Island. The Supreme Court usually has two judges—the Chief Judge and another judge.

XXIII. Research Guide

Copies of legislation in force after December 24, 1913, may generally be obtained from the Legal Branch, Administration of Norfolk Island, Kingston, Norfolk Island. Copies of statutes passed by the Commonwealth Parliament for Norfolk Island can be obtained from the Australian Government Publishing Service. Until 1940, Norfolk Island ordinances were printed in the Australian *Commonwealth Gazette*. Some of the legislative materials of the early periods can be found in the Historical Records of New South Wales and the *Hobart Town Gazette*.

The decisions of the Supreme Court are not published in any law report. Photocopies of some decisions are available from the Legal Branch in Norfolk and can also be found in the Supreme Court Library of New South Wales.

A. Official Publications

Norfolk Island Administrator. *Annual Reports*, 1914–1915 through 1986–1987.
Norfolk Island. *Government Gazette*, 1937 to date.

B. Laws and Regulations

Acts and Regulations. Norfolk Island Legislative Assembly 1979 to date.
The Laws of Norfolk Island 1914–1964 in Force on 1st January 1965. Canberra: Commonwealth Government Printer.

C. Books, Journals, Yearbooks, and Reports

Currey, C. H. "An Outline of the Story of Norfolk Island and Pitcairn's Island, 1788–1857." *Journal and Proceedings of the Royal Australian Historical Society* 44, pt. 6 (1958).
Hoare, M. *Norfolk Island: An Outline of Its History: 1774–1987*. 4th ed. Brisbane: University of Queensland Press, 1988.
Nobbs, Christopher. *Which Future for Norfolk Island?* Norfolk Island: Norfolk Marketing, 1983.
The Winds of Change—Norfolk Island 1950–1982. Suva: Institute of Pacific Studies, University of the South Pacific, 1983.

8. Papua New Guinea

JOHN NONGGORR

I. Dateline

25,000 B.C.	Earliest evidence of settlement in New Guinea region.
8000 B.C.	Rising sea level separates New Guinea from Australia, eventually differentiating their cultures.
6000 B.C.	New wave of Austronesian migration from Southeast Asia; first evidence of domestication of pigs.
1512	First European sighting of New Guinea, by Portuguese explorer Antonio d'Abreu.
1873	London Missionary Society starts first European settlement in Papua New Guinea, at Port Moresby.
1884	Britain declares a protectorate over southeastern New Guinea. Germany annexes northeastern New Guinea and grants a charter to the New Guinea Company to administer the colony.
1888	Britain formally annexes southeastern New Guinea, naming the colony British New Guinea.
1899	German government takes over the New Guinea Company's administrative role in northeastern New Guinea.
1901	Britain transfers British New Guinea to the new Commonwealth of Australia.
1905	Australia formally accepts control of British New Guinea and renames it Papua.
1914	Australian army takes control of German New Guinea. Military administration lasts until May 1921.
1919	New Guinea becomes a mandate of the League of Nations, administered by Australia. Its administration and laws remain separate from those of Papua.
1921	Civil administration by Australia begun under mandate.
1942	ANGAU, Australian army unit, administers both territories during World War II.
1945	Australia establishes a single civilian administration of the two territories.
1973	Papua New Guinea gains self-governing status.
1975	Papua New Guinea becomes an independent nation.

II. Historical, Cultural, and Economic Survey

Papua New Guinea is an independent nation. Geographically, it consists of the eastern half of the island of New Guinea and over 1,400 smaller islands and archipelagoes, including New Britain, New Ireland, and Bougainville. Papua New Guinea lies to the north of Australia and shares a border in the west with the Indonesian province of Irian Jaya. Its land area is 462,840 square kilometers.

Papua New Guinea's population is more than 3.5 million people. They make up many distinct ethnic and cultural groups and speak over 740 different languages. About 75 percent of the people live in rural areas, where subsistence farming is their main occupation. Major cash crops include coffee, copra, and cocoa. The two main industries are mining and logging.

A. History

Humans have lived in Papua New Guinea for at least 25,000 years. The earliest migrations, from Southeast Asia, brought people similar to those who settled in Australia. A later migration, perhaps 8,000 to 10,000 years ago, brought the people who subsequently spread out across the South Pacific. This second migration was also responsible, apparently, for the introduction of agricultural techniques still widely used in the country, including domestication of the pig and cultivation of taro and other root crops.

In 1512, Portuguese explorer Antonio d' Abreu made the first European sighting of the island of New Guinea. Almost two centuries later, several European groups attempted to settle there, but tropical disease drove them away. The first lasting settlement was in 1873, when two missionaries from the London Missionary Society established a mission station in Port Moresby, where they were joined by more missionaries, explorers, and traders. In the northern part of the island, a number of Germans opened trading stations during the same period. The separate influences by individuals and companies of the northern and southern parts of eastern New Guinea led to separate developments in these areas.

In 1884, the British government, under an agreement with Germany that related to British and German interests in Africa as well, divided the eastern part of New Guinea. Britain annexed the southern part, calling it British New Guinea, while Germany annexed the northern part, naming it German New Guinea.

On November 6, 1884, Commodore Erskine of the British Navy raised the flag in Port Moresby, declaring the area a British protectorate. Formal annexation followed on September 4, 1888. In 1906, the Australian government assumed control and renamed the territory Papua.

In German New Guinea, the involvement of the German government was at the initiative of Die Neu Guinea-Kompagnie (New Guinea Company), which was associated with a private bank, the Disconto Company, headed by Adolf Von Hansman. Von Hansman saw New Guinea as a second Java and sought to exploit it economically.

The New Guinea Company was formed by private financiers to set up plantations. In 1888, the German imperial government granted a charter to the company to administer German New Guinea. The charter gave the company rights over the area for an indefinite period. The imperial government maintained control of foreign relations and the administration of justice, as well as a vague right of control over the indigenous people.

World War I and the defeat of the German empire changed control of German New Guinea. Australian forces landed near Kokopo in East New Britain on September 12, 1914, and after a brief resistance the German forces surrendered three days later. German New Guinea was administered by the Australian military for the next seven years. In 1919, it became a mandate territory of the League of Nations under Australian administration, although Australian civil administration did not actually begin until 1921.

Following the invasion of Rabaul on January 21, 1942, by the Japanese, a military administration was again established. The Australian New Guinea Unit (ANGAU) was formed to carry out operations and civil administrative functions. ANGAU administered the two territories until a civil administration was reestablished in 1945.

The two territories were then administered by the Commonwealth of Australia as the Territory of Papua and New Guinea. This arrangement continued until self-government in 1973, when the name of the territory was changed to Papua New Guinea, followed by independence in 1975.

B. Legal Development

The laws that applied to pre-independence Papua New Guinea are somewhat complicated, due largely to the colonization of the country by two powers. They can best be examined by looking at the different periods of the colonial era.

1. 1884–1945

a. British New Guinea (Papua)

When Commodore Erskine of the British Navy proclaimed British New Guinea a domain of Her Majesty Queen Victoria in 1884, English imperial acts applied. In 1888, a local Legislative Council was established that exercised some legislative power. The Courts and Laws Adopting Ordinance 1888 was passed by the local legislature, adopting (subject to a number of exceptions) the laws of Queensland as the laws of British New Guinea; and later, by Sections 3 and 4 of the Courts and Laws Adopting Ordinance (Amended) 1889, English law (comprising English statutes in force in Queensland on September 17, 1888, and the rules of common law and equity of England applying from time to time) was made the basic law. When British New Guinea came under the control of the Commonwealth of Australia, the Papua Act 1905, which changed the territory's name to Papua, provided for the laws previously in force to continue to apply.

b. German New Guinea

German law applied to German New Guinea during the period between 1888 and 1914 after the German imperial government granted the imperial charter to the New Guinea Company. The company had legislative powers over all matters excepting a few areas where legislative power was retained by the imperial government. During and after World War I, German law continued to apply, until 1921, when this northern part of New Guinea was made a League of Nations mandate. Under the mandate, Australia was given legislative power, which Australia used to enact the Laws Repeal and Adopting Ordinance 1921, repealing German law and replacing it with English law, comprising English statutes applying in Queensland at the commencement of the act and the common law existing in England on May 9, 1921.

2. 1945–1975: PAPUA AND NEW GUINEA

After World War II, the territories of Papua and New Guinea were administered jointly by Australia; the laws applying were English laws, imported mostly through the Australian state of Queensland, and laws made by the local legislative councils. Most law applying in both territories was the same, but in a few cases, certain legislation applying in former German New Guinea did not apply to Papua, and certain legislation applying in Papua did not apply in former German New Guinea. Two examples were the Native Administration Regulations (New Guinea) and the Native Regulations (Papua), which applied to New Guinea and Papua respectively.

Immediately prior to independence, the applicable laws in Papua New Guinea included English imperial acts, certain Queensland acts, Australian Commonwealth enactments expressly adopted, and laws made by the local legislative council and later the pre-independence House of Assembly.

3. LOCAL CUSTOM

Throughout the colonial period, there were no courts in which customary law was applied by indigenous adjudicators, and until 1963 the role of custom in the courts was uncertain. In New Guinea, the Laws Repeal and Adopting Ordinance 1921–1923 provided for limited recognition of custom. No similar statute existed for Papua, although the courts did occasionally recognize custom and were required to do so where customary land rights were involved.[1] The enactment of the Native Customs (Recognition) Act 1963 that still applies today made more elaborate provisions for the recognition and application of custom in Papua New Guinea.

III. Sources of Law

Since independence on September 16, 1975, the laws applying in the Independent State of Papua New Guinea are (in order of superiority) the Constitution, the organic laws, acts of the National Parliament, emergency regulations, provincial laws, certain adopted pre-independence laws, and the "underlying law" (the term adopted in Papua New Guinea's constitution which was intended to refer to the indigenous common law, incorporating custom and to the extent not inconsistent with statutes or custom, the adopted English common law).

A. Constitution

The Constitution of the Independent State of Papua New Guinea, adopted on independence, was a product of the work of the Constitutional Planning Committee, which held consultations throughout the country from 1973 to 1975. It is the supreme law. The Constitution itself asserts this superiority under Section 11:

> This Constitution and the Organic Laws are the Supreme Laws of Papua New Guinea . . . [and] all acts (whether legislative, executive or judicial) that are inconsistent with them are, to the extent of the inconsistency, invalid and ineffective.

Section 10 of the Constitution states that all other laws are to be read and construed subject to the Constitution. However, Section 10 has been held to provide a rule of construction only, rather than a rule of substantive law.[2]

The Constitution begins with a statement of the national goals and directive principles, which are nonjusticiable, followed by provisions for the important organs of government and government instrumentalities; the laws of the country; and the establishment and functions of several constitutional offices including the Ombudsman Commission, the Public Prosecutor, the State Solicitor, the Public Solicitor, the Auditor General, and a Leadership Code. The Constitution makes detailed provision for the three branches of government—the Parliament and its law making powers; the executive, headed by a Governor General and a National Executive Council; and the judiciary, vested with wide powers to develop an indigenous jurisprudence.

Since independence, Parliament has not looked closely at the working of the Constitution. A number of recommendations by the Constitutional Review Committee for the amendment of several provisions of the Constitution have not even been debated. The courts have also come under criticism for failing to develop the constitutional laws as well as the underlying law in accordance with the constitutional mandate.[3] In 1991, however, amendments of provisions relating to no-confidence votes in Parliament have been passed.

B. Organic Laws

Organic laws are laws made by Parliament as specifically authorized by the Constitution. Section 12 of the Constitution defines an organic law as "a law made by Parliament that is . . . for or in respect of a matter provision for which is expressly authorized by this Constitution." Section 12 also provides for the manner of altering organic laws. Organic laws can be altered only by another organic law or by the alteration of the Constitution. However, if an organic law covers a subject or contains provisions that are authorized to be contained in an act of Parliament, the provisions can be altered in the same way as can an act.[4] Further, organic laws, though in a special position as regards prescribed majority votes for their amendment, are, like other legislation, to be read and construed subject to the Constitution. The court has accordingly held that "to the extent that an Organic Law is unauthorized by the Constitution or is inconsistent with it, it is invalid."[5]

Organic laws have been passed on provincial governments, the electoral process, an ombudsman commission, and electoral boundaries. Provincial government constitutions have also been given organic law status by Section 13 of the Organic Law on Provincial Government (Chapter 1). However, the constitutionality of that status is questionable, as the Constitution does not provide for it.

C. Acts of Parliament

Section 100 of the Constitution gives the national Parliament the mandate to "make laws having effect within and outside the Country, for the peace, order and good government of Papua New Guinea and the welfare of the People." The section further states "Acts of Parliament, not inconsistent with the Constitutional Laws, may provide for all matters that are necessary or convenient to be prescribed for carrying out and giving effect to this Constitution." Acts of Parliament are made by Parliament in exercise of these constitutional powers.

D. Provincial Laws

Provincial governments established under Part VIA of the Constitution have power to legislate in areas designated by the Organic Law on Provincial Government (Chapter 1). Section 20(1) of the Organic Law provides that "Within the limits allowed or imposed by this Organic Law and the other National Constitutional Laws, a provincial legislature has full legislative power to make laws for the peace, order and good government of the province."

The legislative power shared by the national Parliament with the provincial legislatures falls into three categories. The first are in the area referred to as "primary provincial competence." These include the licensing of mobile traders (other than banks) and places of public entertainment; control of primary schools and education other than curriculum; regulation of the sale and distribution of alcoholic liquor; construction and operation of housing (other than state-owned housing); libraries, museums, and cultural centers; regulating sporting activities; exercising certain powers in relation to village courts; and, subject to a number of limitations, operating local, community, and village governments and other local governments, excluding taxation.

The organic law provides, under Section 26(d), that "the National Parliament has no power to make an Act of the Parliament on a subject or subjects" under this category. However, Section 26(2) allows the national Parliament to make a law in the area if a provincial government has not made "an exhaustive law on it." It is not clear whether the national Parliament can make a law in this area under the proviso if some provincial governments have made exhaustive laws and others have not. The subsection refers to "a" provincial government, which could mean that the national Parliament may make laws applying to the provinces that have not made an exhaustive law on the subject. But more importantly, these provisions may offend Section 100 of the Constitution, which states that "Nothing in any Constitutional Law enables or may enable the Parliament to transfer permanently, or divest itself of legislative power."

The second area allowed for provincial legislative activity is described by the organic law as the "concurrent field" where both the national legislature and a provincial legislature can legislate. The areas covered by this provision include community and rural development; primary school curricula; agriculture and stock; fishing and fisheries; health and public works; trade and business; commercial and industrial investment and development; vocational, technical, and high schools; gambling, lotteries, and games of chance; tourism; transportation and transportation facilities; town planning; land and land development; forestry; wildlife protection; parks and reserves; family and marriage laws (laws relating to divorce and other matrimonial proceedings and to custody of children); courts and tribunals (other than village courts and their jurisdiction); communications and mass media; wharves and harbors; aviation; labor and employment; research and training institutions; marketing; and renewable and nonrenewable natural resources. The imposition of taxation is excluded.

In these areas, the national legislature can make laws in matters of national interest only. A provincial legislature can legislate on these areas, but its legislation must not be inconsistent with national legislation.

The third area of legislative activity for provincial governments is described as the "unoccupied legislative field." Section 33 of the organic law states that "If the National Parliament has not made an exhaustive law, applying in a province, on any subject, the provincial legislature may make a law, not inconsistent with any Act of Parliament on that subject." It provides further that if an act of Parliament is later passed that conflicts with the provincial law in the area, the provincial law is ineffective to the extent of the inconsistency.

Provincial laws generally have effect only within the boundaries of the province. However, the organic law declares, under Section 14, that "Full faith and credit shall be given throughout Papua New Guinea to laws, the public acts and records and the judicial proceedings of all provinces." This section says nothing more than that provincial acts are to be respected by persons outside the province.

The provincial constitutions are given the status of organic laws by the Organic Law on Provincial Government. The legal effect of this organic law status given to the provincial Constitutions by another organic law is doubtful, in the light of Section 12 of the national Constitution, which declares that an organic law must specifically be authorized by the national Constitution.

E. Adopted Statutes

On independence the legislative slate was wiped clean, and the Constitution brought into force only a few pre-independence laws. Section 20(3) of the Constitution declares that "Certain pre-Independence statutes are adopted and shall be adopted, as Acts of Parliament and subordinate enactments of Papua New Guinea, as prescribed by schedule 2." The adopted statutes are subject to the same constitutional limitations as acts of Parliament.[6] The adopted enactments fall into two categories: first are the laws passed by the pre-independence House of Assembly, and second are the "adopted" or "received" legislation from Australia and England. Three statutes, one an Australian Commonwealth act, the Papua New Guinea Independence

Act 1975, and two pre-independence House of Assembly acts—the Statute Law Revision (Independence) Act 1975 and the Laws Repeal Act 1975—repealed all pre-independence laws existing immediately prior to independence. The repeal and adoption process during the period immediately preceding independence was not as tidy as expected. There are still difficulties in tracing the applicable law on, for instance, admiralty jurisdiction.[7]

Following the repeal of all pre-independence legislation, the Constitution took effect on independence with provisions adopting several pre-independence laws. The term *pre-independence law* is defined as certain enactments of the pre-independence House of Assembly and a number of statutes (in most cases single sections) from Australia and England.

F. Underlying Law

The underlying law is the term adopted by the framers of the Papua New Guinea Constitution to refer to the indigenous common law, which is to incorporate custom and the adopted English common law. The Constitution specifies that an act of Parliament declares and provides for the development of the underlying law. In the meantime, with Papua New Guinea custom and the principles and rules of common law and equity, to the extent the latter are not inconsistent with statutes or custom, are to be the underlying law.

The Constitution, to create an indigenous jurisprudence, gives both Parliament and the courts responsibility for developing an underlying law for the country. The Constitution authorizes Parliament to enact legislation declaring the underlying law. The Law Reform Commission, which was established to assist in this task, prepared draft legislation in 1975, but Parliament has not yet acted to provide for the underlying law. Until Parliament acts, the temporary rules contained in Schedule 2 apply. These direct the courts to develop the underlying law by looking to custom, the principles and rules of common law and equity, and decisions of the National Court and Supreme Court.

1. CUSTOM

The Constitution declares, under Schedule 2.1, that "custom is adopted, and shall be applied and enforced as part of the underlying law." Custom is given precedence over the common law. Accordingly, some judges have stated that, when one is seeking to apply the underlying law, custom must be considered first.[8] The custom to be applied must, however, meet certain criteria—it must be consistent with statutory law and it must not be repugnant to the general principles of humanity.

Custom is defined by Schedule 1.2 of the Constitution to mean "the customs and usages of indigenous inhabitants of the country existing in relation to the matter in question at the time when and the place in relation to which the matter arises, regardless of whether or not the custom or usage has existed from time immemorial." An act of Parliament was to make further provision for the pleading and application of custom. The Customs Recognition Act (Chapter 19), a pre-independence act later amended, is now treated as serving the purpose. This act makes further provisions on custom generally and its application to criminal and civil cases in particular. It also addresses the manner in which conflicts of custom are to be resolved.

a. Recognition of Custom

Section 6 of the Customs Recognition Act provides that "native custom shall be recognized and enforced by, and may be pleaded in, all courts" subject to similar qualifications as those stipulated under the Constitution, that the custom to be applied must not be repugnant to the general principles of humanity; inconsistent with any statutory law, and that their recognition and enforcement would not result in injustice or be against the public interest; [and] in a case involving the welfare of a child under the age of sixteen years, its recognition or enforcement would not be in the best interest of the child.

b. Criminal Cases

The courts are not to take custom into account in criminal cases except to determine the existence of a state of mind of a person; the reasonableness of an act, default, or omission by a person; the reasonableness of an excuse; in accordance with another law, whether to proceed to conviction of a guilty party; the penalty (if any) to be imposed on a guilty party; or whether not taking the custom into account will cause an injustice to be done to a person (Section 7).

c. Civil Cases

The application of custom in civil cases is also restricted. It can be applied to determine the following:

1. the ownership over or in connection with customary land, including rights of hunting or gathering;
2. the ownership or rights in the sea or reef or lake, including rights of fishing;
3. the ownership by custom of rights to water;
4. the devolution of interests in customary land;
5. trespass by animals;
6. marriage, divorce, or the right to the custody or guardianship of infants under a customary marriage;
7. a transaction the parties intend should be (or which justice requires should be) regulated by custom;
8. the reasonableness of an act, default, or omission by a person;
9. the existence of a state of mind of a person; or
10. whether not taking custom into account will do an injustice to a person.

d. Guardianship

In deciding questions relating to guardianship and custody of infants and adoption, the courts are required to take full account of custom.

e. Conflict of Custom

If there is conflict as to which of two or more systems of custom should prevail, and the court is not satisfied as to what evidence to apply, the court is required to consider all the circumstances and may adopt the custom that the justice of the case requires. If the court is unable to do this, it may apply the rules of common law and equity.

f. Recognition in Specific Acts

A number of acts recognize custom for specific purposes. These include the Marriage Act (Chapter 280), recognizing customary marriages; Wills, Probate and Administration Act (Chapter 291), preserving customary succession rules; Local Courts Act (Chapter 41), empowering local courts to certify the dissolution of customary marriages; Village Courts Act (Chapter 44), setting up the village court system to resolve disputes applying custom; Land Dispute Settlements Act (Chapter 45), introducing customary means of resolving land disputes; and Business Groups Incorporation Act (Chapter 144), recognizing customary groups and allowing them to carry on business in accordance with custom.

The express application of custom by the courts has been negligible. The courts have given a number of reasons for not applying custom more frequently. One reason is that in Papua New Guinea there are many customary groups, and therefore it is difficult to decide which custom to apply.[9] The customs of the people are not written rules that the courts can ascertain and apply, lawyers appearing in court do not argue custom, and the courts do not have the resources to carry out research into custom on their own.[10] The argument that the customs of the people are not rules implies that the common law does consist of rules that the court can readily ascertain, which may not be entirely correct. Nevertheless, the Constitution has made custom a part of the laws of the country, and therefore the customary rules are "law." The court's list of practical limitations reveals the limited commitment of the government, the legal profession, and the courts to developing the indigenous jurisprudence that the Constitution calls for.

Other reasons for the court's unwillingness to apply particular customs include their "repugnancy" to the general principles of humanity and their inconsistency with specific statutes.[11]

2. COMMON LAW AND EQUITY

The Constitution adopts the principles and rules of common law and equity, to the extent they are not inconsistent with statutes or custom, as part of the underlying law to "assist" in the development of an indigenous jurisprudence. The applicable rules of common law and equity are to be those existing in England on September 16, 1975, the date of Papua New Guinea's independence (Constitution, Schedule 2.2(3)). The common law and equity principles to the Constitution are adopted as unaffected by statutory modifications in England.[12] A controversial issue relates to the status of a decision of a competent court of England handed down after September 16, 1975, abolishing a common law rule and creating a new one, varying an existing rule, or developing a new rule. One view on the question is that English decisions handed down after independence, whether they vary, abolish, or replace a principle after the independence date, do not form part of the common law received into Papua New Guinea. This view[13] has been supported by academic commentators.[14] The opposing view, urged strongly by Kapi, Dep. C.J., is that excepting those postindependence English decisions that develop new principles, any case from a competent English court correcting an error and declaring what the common law has always been are part of the law of Papua New Guinea.[15] However, considering the spirit of the Constitution as a whole, and more particularly the purpose of Schedule 2, the preferable view is that English decisions made after independence are not binding but only of persuasive value on Papua New Guinea courts. The argument itself demonstrates the artificiality of adopting for Papua New Guinea a foreign law at an arbitrary date and suggests again the need for the development of an indigenous jurisprudence.

3. DEVELOPMENT OF UNDERLYING LAW

The National and the Supreme Courts are vested with the responsibility to develop the underlying law by Schedule 2.3 of the Constitution, which states,

> If in any particular matter before a court there appears to be no rule of law that is applicable and appropriate to the circumstances of the country, it is the duty of the National Judicial System, and in particular of the Supreme Court and the National Court, to formulate an appropriate rule as part of the underlying law.[16]

In this task, the courts are required to consider the national goals and directive principles and the basic social obligations contained in the Constitution; the basic rights provisions of the Constitution; analogies drawn from relevant statutes and custom; legislation and relevant decisions of the courts of any country that in the opinion of the court have legal systems similar to that of Papua New Guinea; relevant decisions of courts exercising jurisdiction in or concerning all or part of the country at any time; and the circumstances of the country prevailing from time to time. The courts have used the power to develop new principles of the underlying law in a number of cases.[17] If a question arises in another court that would involve the development of a new principle of law, the other court is to refer the matter to the Supreme Court for its decision. The courts are required to ensure that, with due regard to the need for consistency, the underlying law develops as a coherent system in a manner appropriate to the circumstances of the country from time to time, except in so far as it would not be proper to do so by judicial act.

IV. Constitutional System

A. Territory

Section 2 of the Constitution declares the territory of Papua New Guinea to consist of the land area, internal waters, and territorial sea that were known as Papua New Guinea before independence.

B. Nationality and Citizenship

The provisions for citizenship under Part IV of the Constitution were taken from the recommendations of the Constitutional Planning Committee. The three ways in which citizenship was conferred on independence continue to apply today as well. The first category of citizens are automatic citizens, the second are citizens by descent, and the third group are citizens by naturalization.

Automatic citizens, who attained citizenship automatically on independence, include persons who were born in Papua New Guinea before independence with two grandparents born in the country or an adjacent area; or persons who were born outside the country before independence but with two grandparents born in the country, and who were registered as citizens within one year of independence. If the person in the latter case held another citizenship, the person was to renounce it and make a declaration of loyalty. The expression "adjacent area" includes the Solomon Islands, Irian Jaya, and the Torres Straits islands. The bulk of the population of Papua New Guinea assumed citizenship under this provision.

Persons who assumed citizenship by descent are those who had one parent who was a citizen or if dead would have become a citizen if living on the date of independence. Acquisition of citizenship in this manner is provided under Section 66 of the Constitution. Where a person in this category is born in the country, the citizenship is automatic. Where the person is born outside the country, he or she is required to be registered on birth in Papua New Guinea to acquire citizenship.

Citizenship by naturalization applies to persons not qualifying under the first two categories as provided under Section 67. They must meet the following qualifications:

1. continuous residence in Papua New Guinea for a period of not less than eight years;
2. good character;
3. intention to reside permanently in the country;
4. ability to speak or understand pidgin, motu, or another vernacular of the country;
5. respect for the customs and cultures of the country;

6. self-sufficiency such that the person is unlikely to be or become a charge on public funds;
7. reasonable knowledge and understanding of the rights, privileges, and responsibilities of citizenship;
8. renunciation of other citizenship; and
9. declaration of loyalty.

All questions or applications for citizenship are considered by a Citizenship Advisory Committee established under the Citizenship Act (Chapter 12). This committee's functions, as provided under the Constitution, include advising the Minister for Foreign Affairs on these matters. The minister is not bound to follow the committee's decision, but if the minister departs from the advice of the committee, a person affected by it or the committee can request for disclosure of the reasons, and Parliament then decides on the matter.

A person can lose citizenship automatically under certain circumstances—for instance, if a person takes up the nationality of another country. Provision is also made for regaining citizenship. A person who lost citizenship as a consequence of marriage, for example, may apply to regain citizenship.

C. Government

1. NATIONAL GOVERNMENT

a. Head of State

The executive branch of the national government has a Head of State, who acts on almost all matters only on the advice of the National Executive Council (NEC) or other prescribed body or authority. The NEC is for practical purposes, as reflected by Section 86(2) of the Constitution, the head of the executive.

The Constitution retains the Queen of England as the Head of State, represented by a Governor General. The decision to create the office of the Head of State was made by the preindependence government. The Constitutional Planning Committee (CPC) recommended against having the English monarch as Head of State. The CPC perceived this to be in line with the whole purpose of independence, to sever Papua New Guinea from its colonial past. The government disagreed with the CPC proposals that either the Prime Minister or the Speaker perform the functions. The government at that time argued the necessity of having as Head of State a figurehead separate from the government to perform ceremonial functions and ensure continuity of the executive during intervals when there is an election or before a new government takes over.

Provisions for the appointment and removal of the Head of State are contained in Part V of the Constitution. The person appointed as Governor General must be a citizen who is qualified to be a member of Parliament and is a mature person respected by the community. The term of office of the Governor General is six years. If for any reason the office is vacant, the Speaker of the national Parliament is to be acting Governor General. In the event of a vacancy in both the offices of Head of State and Speaker, the Chief Justice is to be the acting Governor General.

Section 92 permits the Governor General to resign by writing to the Queen; the resignation takes effect when the Queen, on the advice of the NEC, accepts it. The dismissal of the Governor General may be done (under Section 93 of the Constitution) by the Queen on the advice of the NEC. The NEC may decide on its own or the Parliament may decide by an absolute majority vote. No specific reasons are required for the decision to dismiss. If the Governor General is ill, the Speaker of Parliament, after receiving medical advice from two registered medical practitioners, may recommend to Parliament his or her dismissal. The Governor General may be suspended from office (under Section 94) for refusing or failing to act on advice or acting contrary to advice, or because of a pending investigation for dismissal. In 1991, the then-Governor General, Sir Serei Eri, refused to execute the necessary documents to implement a decision of a leadership tribunal dismissing a minister for corruption. The NEC advised the Queen to dismiss the Governor General under Section 93, but the crisis was defused when the Governor General resigned.

b. Executive

The National Executive Council (NEC), comprising the ministers making up the Cabinet, is headed by the Prime Minister. The Prime Minister is appointed by Parliament. The procedures followed in Parliament for the appointment of the Prime Minister are nonjusticiable.[18] The Prime Minister selects the other ministers, who must all be members of the Parliament. The Minister for Justice also becomes the Attorney General if he or she is a lawyer. The Secretary for the Department of Justice (who must be a lawyer) becomes the Attorney General if the Minister for Justice is not a lawyer. The number of ministers is limited by the Constitution to a minimum of six and a maximum of one-quarter of the members of Parliament.

The function of the NEC, as provided by the Constitution, is to be responsible for the executive government of the country. The functions of individual ministers are determined by the Prime Minister. A minister would normally be appointed to be the political head of a department, although this has not always been the case, as a minister could also be appointed to assist another minister.

The Prime Minister can be dismissed by the Governor General if a successful motion of no confidence is brought against him or her in Parliament or if certified by two doctors to be medically unfit. Other ministers can also be dismissed by the Head of State on the advice of the Prime Minister.

The ministers who make up the NEC are, under Section 141 of the Constitution, "collectively answerable to the people through the Parliament, for the proper carrying out of the executive government of Papua New Guinea and for all things done by or under the National Executive."

This collective responsibility to be answerable to the people means that as political heads of their departments, they are entitled to be briefed and kept generally informed of the affairs of the respective departments, but they do not have the power to control and direct the heads of government departments or other persons.[19]

Among the more controversial provisions of the Constitution have been those permitting motions of no confidence. These provisions, Sections 142(5)(a) and 145, permit the Head of State to dismiss the Prime Minister if Parliament passes a motion of no confidence. Since independence numerous motions of no confidence have been introduced, and several have been passed. The use of this procedure has created great instability affecting politics, administration, and the private sector. There have been calls for reforms and Parliament in 1991 amended the Constitution, changing the period following an election during which a no-confidence motion is prohibited from six months to eighteen months.

c. Legislature

The national Parliament is an elective legislature, subject to the constitutional laws, with unlimited powers of law making. Where Parliament does exercise its powers—for instance, in enacting legislation—the courts cannot intrude into its area of authority.[20] However, the Constitution is supreme over Parliament, and laws made by Parliament must therefore be consistent with the Constitution.

Section 100 of the Constitution states that "Nothing in any constitutional law enables or may, . . . enable the Parliament to transfer permanently, or divest itself of, legislative power." This provision may render unconstitutional some aspects of sharing of legislative power with provincial governments.

The Constitution provides for a single-chamber legislature consisting of three types of representatives: (1) representatives from "open" electorates, all of which are intended to be roughly equal in population; (2) representatives from the provincial electorates; and (3) a maximum of three nominated members.

The provincial electorate system was created before independence. Provincial members require a minimum educational qualification. This was intended, in the pre-independence House of Assembly, to ensure that the majority of members of those electorates would be white, as not many indigenous people then had the required educational qualification. The Constitution did not retain this educational requirement, because of the constitutional provisions on equality and right to stand for public office. The idea of the provincial electorate itself was retained mainly to increase the number of representatives, especially for the less populated provinces. There have, however, been calls for the provincial constituencies to be abolished.

The provisions for nominated members are not fully laid out. The Constitution merely states in Section 100, "The Parliament may, from time to time, by a two-thirds absolute majority vote, appoint a person (other than a member) to be a nominated member of Parliament." No further provision is made on the duration of appointment and on whether or not the qualifications of elected members are applicable to nominated members as well. There has been no nominated member in the national Parliament since independence.

To be eligible for election to Parliament, a person must fulfill a number of qualifications. Section 103 of the Constitution requires that the person must be over twenty-five years of age when nominated to contest an election and must have been in the electorate "or have resided in the electorate for a continuous period of two years preceding his nomination or for a period of five years at any time." The courts have held that the residential requirements apply to both actual and "constructive residence," the latter "implying an available residence from which the claimant has not debarred himself from returning."[21] After the last three national elections, numerous electoral petitions have been brought in the courts alleging that certain winning candidates were not residentially qualified under this provision; reforms have been advocated that would do away with this qualification.

Section 103 also stipulates that an elected member becomes disqualified to hold office if of unsound mind, if under sentence of death or imprisonment for more than nine months, or if otherwise disqualified under the Constitution. The Constitution does not prevent a person from running and being a member again, for instance after serving a sentence.[22] There are no provisions for disqualification of a member declared bankrupt, which is instead treated as a matter of misconduct in office under the Leadership Code. Further, it has been held that a member of Parliament has a right to resign, thereby terminating a Leadership Code investigation against him or her.[23]

A member of Parliament holds office for five years, the normal life of Parliament. Parliament can, however, be dissolved and a general election called if, during the last twelve months of its life, a successful vote of no confidence is brought against the Prime Minister, or if the Prime Minister has raised for vote a question of confidence and is defeated. Parliament at any time can dissolve itself by an absolute majority vote. By-elections can also be called if an elected member dies or is disqualified.

The Organic Law on National Elections (Chapter 1) is administered by the electoral commission that is established under that organic law. It provides rules for the conduct of elections and also sets out the manner and conditions for challenging election results in the National Court. An election petition must comply with all the conditions precedent set by the organic law.[24] Electoral boundaries are decided by Parliament in accordance with recommendations from a boundaries commission, an independent body.

The offices of Speaker and Deputy Speaker are created by the *Constitution* under Sections 107 and 108, and their functions are

> subject to and in accordance with the Constitutional Laws, the Acts of Parliament and the Standing Orders of the Parliament, for upholding the dignity of the Parliament, maintaining order in it, regulating its proceedings and administering its affairs and for controlling the precincts of the Parliament as defined by or under an Act of Parliament.

All members in Parliament are entitled to introduce bills, petitions, or other motions and to vote on any matter; except as otherwise required by a constitutional law or standing order, a vote on any matter is decided by a majority of members present and voting. The quorum is one-third of the number of seats in Parliament.

The Constitution provides in Section 115 an elaborate list of privileges for members of Parliament. Everything done, said, or omitted to be done in Parliament carries no criminal or civil liability. Outside Parliament, a member is also privileged in respect of, first "the exercise of his powers or the performance of his functions, duties or responsibilities as such," and second, acts or things said or done under the authority or order of the Parliament. Third, members of Parliament are free from arrest for civil debts during meetings of the Parliament and for the three days before and after meetings if they are either traveling to or returning from them.

The administration of Parliament is the responsibility of the Speaker and the clerk of Parliament. The Constitution, in Section 132, establishes a parliamentary service separate from the public service. The parliamentary service is responsible for serving Parliament and ministers of the National Executive Council.

d. Judiciary

The Constitution, Section 158, provides that "the judicial authority of the people is vested in the National Judicial System" and "[i]n interpreting the law the courts shall give paramount consideration to the dispensation of justice." Sections 160 and 163 establish, respectively, the Supreme Court and the National Court, and Section 172 provides for the establishment of other courts by acts of Parliament. Pursuant to this authority, there are four lower courts: the District Courts under the District Courts Act (Chapter 40), the Local Courts under the Local Courts Act (Chapter 41), the Local Land Courts under the Land Dispute Settlement Act (Chapter 45), and the Village Courts under the Village Court Act (Chapter 44).

The Constitution maintains a separation of powers of the three arms of government. One of these arms of government cannot usurp the powers of the other. Thus, it has been held that a law requiring a court to convict an accused without a hearing is an invasion by the legislature of the judicial power vested exclusively in the National Judicial System.[25]

(i) National Court

The National Court consists of a Chief Justice, Deputy Chief Justice, and such number of additional judges as may be prescribed by Parliament. Currently, the National Court has fourteen judges, including the Chief Justice and Deputy. The Chief Justice is appointed by the Head of State on the advice of the National Executive Council after consultation with the Minister for Justice. The other judges are appointed by the Judicial Services Commission established by the Constitution.

The Chief Justice is, under Section 169(3) of the Constitution, also responsible for the organization and administration of the National Court and the Supreme Court. The Chief Justice acts as Head of State when both the Speaker of the national Parliament and the Head of State are absent for any reason.

A judge may be either a citizen or noncitizen. In the case of a citizen appointed as a judge, he or she must have held a law degree for at least six years and have practiced for at least four years. A noncitizen must have at least five years' practical experience in Papua New Guinea or in a country with a similar legal system. A serving judge in a country with a similar legal system can also be appointed. To maintain the impartiality of judges and to put them out of reach of undue influences, they may be removed by a tribunal appointed by the Judicial Services Commission. The Chief Justice may be removed only by a tribunal appointed by the National Executive Council. Grounds for the removal of judges are limited to mental or physical infirmity, misbehavior, or breach of the Leadership Code.

The National Court has, under Section 155(2) of the Constitution, an unlimited jurisdiction. It has an inherent power to review the exercise of judicial authority by inferior courts or tribunals and powers to enforce the constitutional laws except when the Supreme Court is exercising these powers. The National Court also has jurisdiction to hear appeals from the Local Courts and District Courts. In addition to its appellate jurisdiction, the National Court reviews decisions of the lower courts and has held that, even where a statute purports to prohibit appeals, its review power is not affected, nor can an act of Parliament limit its power of review.[26]

The original jurisdiction of the National Court in criminal and civil cases is unlimited. It can hear all matters. However, in practice, because of the prohibitive cost of litigation in the National Court, only serious criminal cases and major civil cases exceeding the jurisdictional limits of the District Courts come to the National Court.

Appeals from the National Court are heard by the Supreme Court. In accordance with Section 4 of the Supreme Court Act (Chapter 37), appeals lie as of right on questions of law or of a combination of fact and law and only by leave of the Supreme Court on questions of fact alone. The National Court can also reserve a legal question for the opinion of the Supreme Court—for instance, on a question involving constitutional interpretation.

(ii) Supreme Court

The jurisdiction of the Supreme Court may be divided into three categories. First, it has an original jurisdiction. The Constitution, under Section 18, vests in the Supreme Court the sole power to decide a question relating to the interpretation or application of a provision of a constitutional law. A constitutional law question arising in another court, unless the matter is trivial, vexatious, or irrelevant, is referred to the Supreme Court. Although the Constitution does not expressly provide that the courts can hold statutes unconstitutional, the courts have inferred that they have the power to do so.[27]

Section 19 of the Constitution confers an advisory jurisdiction on the Supreme Court. On application by one of the prescribed authorities, the Supreme Court can give its opinion on a question concerning the interpretation or application of a provision of a constitutional law, including questions relating to the validity of a law. However, the Supreme Court will not consider hypothetical questions.[28] The National Court has ruled that the question as to whether the Defamation Act 1963 conflicts with Section 46 of the Constitution on the right to freedom of expression was too "vexatious" and possibly "trivial" to be referred to the Supreme Court.[29]

Authorities that can refer a question for advice include the national Parliament; Head of

State acting with the advice of the National Executive Council; law officers, including the Secretary for Justice, Public Solicitor, and Public Prosecutor; Law Reform Commission; ombudsman commission; Speaker of the national Parliament; and the leader of the opposition.[30]

Secondly, the Supreme Court has an appellate jurisdiction. It is the final court of appeal of Papua New Guinea, doing away with the appeals to the High Court of Australia and the Privy Council that were used before independence. The Supreme Court, when hearing an appeal, is normally constituted of three judges sitting together presided over by the Chief Justice or the next senior judge. The Supreme Court has wide powers under Section 16 of the Supreme Court Act to make orders; affirm, reverse, or modify judgments; give the judgment that ought to have been given at first instance; remit the case in whole or in part for rehearing; or order a new trial. The Supreme Court is the final court of appeal in Papua New Guinea. Hence, where an appeal is decided by the Supreme Court, it has been held that another constituted Supreme Court cannot review the decision of an earlier one.[31]

The third area of jurisdiction of the Supreme Court is its power of judicial review under Section 155(2) of the Constitution. A particularly important area of this jurisdiction is the enforcement of the basic right provisions of the Constitution. The Supreme Court shares this jurisdiction with the National Court and the District Court.

(iii) District Courts

The District Courts are presided over by Magistrates, Grades III–V. Each grade of magistrate has jurisdictional limits on the amount of fine or length of imprisonment in criminal cases and the amount of money that can be awarded in civil claims. Grade V Magistrates, for example, have jurisdiction in civil cases to award damages or compensation of up to K10,000 (Kina). Each District Court can hear only cases arising in its district area.[32]

In criminal cases, the District Court has jurisdiction over all summary offenses and has power to hear specified indictable offenses. The District Court also hears committal proceedings in serious criminal offenses triable in the National Court.

In civil cases, the District Court has power to hear "all personal actions in law or equity." It has no jurisdiction, however, in the following areas under Section 21 of the District Court Act:

1. actions over land, except in making temporary orders on possession of land;
2. disputes over wills and settlements;
3. trademark infringements and actions for illegal arrests, false imprisonment, or malicious prosecution; and
4. seduction or breach of promise to marry.

The procedure and other rules relating to the proceedings of the District Court are prescribed under the District Court Act. Appeals lie to the National Court.

(iv) Local Courts

The Local Courts are presided over by Magistrates Grade I and II. They sit alone in trials, but there is provision for assistant magistrates to sit with a magistrate to advise the latter on custom.

The Local Courts have jurisdiction to hear all summary or simple criminal offenses and small civil claims. In criminal cases, they have power to levy fines of up to a maximum of K100 or imprisonment for a period not exceeding six months and an order of compensation not exceeding K200, or they can make a combination of these orders. In respect of a number of summary offenses, the Local Courts' jurisdiction is concurrent with the District Courts. Where the jurisdiction is concurrent, before hearing a summary offense, a Local Court must first certify that it is expedient that the case be heard in the Local Court. If there is no certification, the decision of the Local Court is a nullity.[33] This certification is separate from the defendant's right to elect the District Court to hear his or her case.

Local Courts have power to order damages or compensation under Section 15 of the Local Court Act to a maximum monetary limit of K1,000. Further, Local Courts do not have jurisdiction to hear offenses committed more than three months before the hearing, except where the defendant had disappeared so that the complainant had no reasonable opportunity to serve the complaint.[34]

Local Courts were established for particular localities to apply custom and deal with customary claims. The courts are required to attempt to mediate a dispute; if mediation fails, they can adjudicate on the matter. The Local Courts have jurisdiction to certify a customary divorce but not to order a divorce. Appeals from the Local Court lie to the National Court.

(v) Land Courts

Land Courts, which are not strictly part of the national judicial system, were established under the Land Dispute Settlement Act (Chapter 45) to resolve disputes relating to customary land. The act requires mediation as a first step and provides for the appointment of land mediators who are normally village elders. If mediation fails, the dispute is then referred to a Local Land Court. Presided over by a Local Court magistrate, this court will attempt again to mediate the dispute first, failing which it can adjudicate. A Land Court is not bound by formal procedure. It can make orders in accordance with the custom of the disputing parties.

Appeals from the Local Land Court lie to a Provincial Land Court magistrate, who is often a senior magistrate of the District Court. The act intended no appeal, but the National Court has held that a decision or act of the Land Court can be challenged by way of judicial review in the National Court.

(vi) Village Courts

Village Courts were established in 1974, by the Village Court Act (Chapter 44), as a "peoples' court" to be conducted by the people in their own community, applying local custom. Magistrates of the Village Courts are therefore chosen from among the people that the court serves, and each must be familiar with local custom.

Village Courts are set up by the Minister for Justice for particular localities, with jurisdiction in both criminal and civil matters arising in the locality. Where a matter involves two parties from different Village Court areas, a joint sitting can take place. Village Courts have been established throughout the country in rural areas, as well as in some urban settlement areas.

The criminal jurisdiction of Village Courts is limited to the offenses listed in the Village Court Regulations, covering such matters as injury to persons, damage to property, stealing, breach of the peace, slander and insulting language, breaking of customary rules, carrying offensive weapons, sorcery, and breach of local government council rules. The Village Courts can impose fines of up to K200 and order community work for up to six months. They do not have power to impose prison sentences except if a person disobeys a Village Court order.

The Village Courts have power to hear all civil matters arising under custom. The amount of compensation they can award is limited to K1,000, except that in matters relating to bride price, compensation claim for a death, or child custody matters, there is no set limit. On land matters, they can only make temporary orders. The Land Courts have jurisdiction to determine ownership of customary land.

The procedure in these courts is informal. The act requires that magistrates attempt first to mediate disputes; only if mediation fails to produce a settlement should the magistrates adjudicate the dispute. They are not required to observe procedural rules; however, they must observe the natural justice requirement that the magistrates presiding must not have an interest in the matter and that the parties must both be present in the hearing. The act further provides that the Village Court must apply customary law, even when that conflicts with an act of Parliament. A court clerk, a person with some basic education, advises the magistrates on their jurisdiction and keeps records of orders they make.

Appeals from a Village Court lie to a supervising magistrate, who is a Local Court or District Court magistrate. The supervising magistrate can also review a decision of a Village Court on his own initiative. The supervising magistrate also has the general duty of supervising and advising the Village Courts on how best to perform their tasks.

2. PROVINCIAL GOVERNMENT

A provincial government system was strongly recommended by the Constitutional Planning Committee in its final report on a Constitution for Papua New Guinea. The two main reasons for this recommendation were a desire to open up the decision-making process to the people and a conscious effort to decentralize the large bureaucracy concentrated in Port Moresby. Despite the strong recommendations, the government did not favor the inclusion in the Constitution of provisions for the establishment of provincial governments, so no such provision was made in the Constitution adopted on independence. This led to secession threats in parts of the country, led by the North Solomons Province. In response to these threats, constitutional provisions were inserted later for the establishment of provincial governments. The provincial government system in existence now is not a federal system but has been described as a "quasi-federal" or "devolved unitary system."

Part IV(A) of the Constitution, added by Constitutional Amendment No.1, provides for provincial governments. This part consists of ten sections, which provide for an organic law to make detailed provisions. The Organic Law on Provincial Governments (Chapter 1) does this.

Section 187(A) of the Constitution authorizes the establishment of provincial governments, and pursuant to this provision, all nineteen provinces have provincial governments. All provinces have their own provincial constitutions, which are given the status of organic laws. Pursuant to Section 187H(2) of the Constitution, a Premiers' Council has been established. The council, which is chaired by the Prime Minister, provides a forum for the settlement of intergovernmental disputes, thus avoiding legal proceedings.

All provincial governments have elective provincial legislatures as required by Section 187C of the Constitution, which provides for "an elective or mainly elective provincial legislature." Section 16 of the organic law sets the minimum number of legislative members at fifteen elected members, plus up to 3 appointed members or 10 percent of the elected memberships, whichever is the greater number. A number of provincial legislatures do have appointed or nominated members.

The Constitution provides under Section 187(C) for a provincial executive and head of provincial executive, and the organic law, under Section 17, establishes a provincial executive with a head and vests in it the province's executive power. Provincial executive heads are called Premiers. With the exception of Enga and the North Solomons provincial governments, whose Premiers are elected directly by the people in a presidential system, Premiers are elected by the provincial legislatures. All members of the executive of the provincial governments are members of the legislature. Elections of all provincial members are conducted following the same rules of the Organic Law on National Elections (Chapter 1) that apply to election of national legislators.

On fiscal matters, provincial governments' main source of revenue is grants from the national government. Provincial governments can impose taxes in a number of areas, including taxes on retail sales, public entertainments, and land; and fees for licensing of mobile traders and gambling or lottery operations.

A provincial government can be suspended on a number of grounds, as set out under Section 187(E) of the Constitution. The National Executive Council can suspend a provincial government in the following circumstances:

1. widespread corruption in the administration of the province;
2. gross mismanagement of the financial affairs of the province;
3. breakdown in the administration of the province;
4. deliberate and persistent frustration of or failure to comply with lawful directions of the national government; and
5. deliberate and persistent disobedience of an applicable law.

A provincial suspension can be confirmed or revoked by the national Parliament by a simple majority. During the period of suspension, the powers of the suspended government are vested in the National Executive Council. If the provisional suspension is confirmed, it is to be reestablished within nine months of the suspension. The establishment of the provincial government did not affect other local level governments.

Section 187(I) of the Constitution preserved the local and village governments that were in existence on the introduction of the provincial government system. Most of these local governments have been retained by the provincial governments.

Following the 1992 elections, Parliament began a comprehensive review of the provincial government system.

D. Emergency Powers

Part X of the Constitution deals with emergency powers. A public emergency can be declared in two instances. The first is when the country is at war (Section 227), and the second is when an emergency exists. An *emergency* is defined by Section 226 as (1) imminent danger of war between Papua New Guinea and another country or of warlike operations threatening national security; (2) an earthquake, volcanic eruption, storm, tempest, flood, fire, outbreak of pestilence or infectious disease, or other natural disaster; and (3) an individual's action or threat of action that would endanger public safety or human life.

The Head of State on the advice of the National Executive Council may declare a state of emergency for any of these reasons. An emergency can be declared for the whole of the country or a part of it. In the latter case, the Head of State is required to consult an emergency committee established by the Emergency Committees Act (Chapter 33A), passed pursuant to Section 240 of the Constitution, before the declaration of the emergency.

The Constitution authorizes a number of measures to be adopted to deal with an emergency. The first are emergency acts, which Parliament is empowered by Section 230 of the Constitution to enact either before or during a public emergency. In the absence of such act and especially when an emergency is declared by the Head of State before a Parliamentary sitting, the Head of State is empowered by Section 231 of the Constitution to make emergency regulations to deal with the emergency. These regulations must be forwarded immediately to the Speaker of the Parliament and to the emergency committee. Any emergency act or regulation can authorize any person to make emergency orders not inconsistent with such acts or regulations to deal with the emergency.

"Emergency laws" can, under Section 233 of the Constitution, make provision "for the peace, order and good government of the country to the extent reasonably required for achieving its purpose." These emergency laws can override some of the human rights provisions of the Constitution but not the right to life, the right to freedom from inhuman treatment and freedom of expression, and the right to vote and nominate for public office.

Emergency laws cease to be in force when revoked by Parliament or, in the case of emergency regulations, when the Head of State, acting on the advice of the National Executive Council, revokes them. Emergency laws terminate automatically when the period of emergency ends.

The executive arm of government initiates the declaration of public emergencies. The Constitution, however, provides a number of ways Parliament can supervise a declared emergency. First, Parliament must sanction an emergency if it was not Parliament that declared it. The period within which Parliament is required to give its sanction is fifteen days and at intervals of two months during the currency of an emergency if extended. Second, an emergency committee, consisting of members of Parliament, must be appointed by Parliament to oversee and monitor the operation of emergencies. The minimum membership of the committee is seven. No Cabinet minister can be a member. The committee's specific functions are, as provided under Section 242 of the Constitution, to receive copies of all emergency laws and to be consulted on the emergency by the Prime Minister. The committee is required to report to Parliament on "(a) whether or not the period of declared national emergency should continue; and (b) the justification for and the operation of the emergency laws, and (c) whether or not an emergency law should be altered." Third, Parliament must be kept informed by both the Prime Minister and the emergency committee on the general operation of the emergency.

The Constitution also provides for persons to be detained during periods of emergencies; however, strict safeguards are set for such internment. Internment during an emergency can be done only under an act of Parliament passed by an absolute majority vote. An interned person or his or her next of kin or other close relative must be informed of the reasons for the internment. Excepting an alien enemy, an interned person must be released at the end of two months after the commencement of the internment unless an independent and impartial tribunal determines after a review of the case that sufficient cause has been shown for the internment to continue. However, at the end of six months the person is to be released unless he or she is held under some law other than emergency laws.

A number of national emergencies have been declared to deal with natural disasters and law and order problems. The most significant emergency declared was in the North Solomons Province when the operation of the Bougainville copper mine was sabotaged, leading to an armed secession movement on that island.

E. Human Rights

In addition to the national goals and directive principles and the basic social obligations set out in the preamble to the Constitution, the Constitution declares in Part III certain basic rights for every individual. These rights and freedoms, which have their origin in the American Bill of Rights, were first contained in the pre-independence Human Rights Act of 1971. The Constitutional Planning Committee recommended that these be incorporated in the Constitution.

1. RIGHT TO FREEDOM

Under Section 32 of the Constitution,

> Every person has the right to freedom based on law, and accordingly has a legal right to do anything that (a) does not injure or interfere with the rights and freedoms of others, and (b)

is not prohibited by law, and no person (c) is obliged to do anything that is not required by law; and (d) may be prevented from doing anything that complies with the provisions of paragraph (a) and (b).

2. RIGHT TO LIFE

Except in cases of conviction for offenses specifically carrying the death penalty, such as treason or piracy, Section 35 of the Constitution guarantees every person the right to life. In 1991, Parliament enacted provisions authorizing the death penalty in certain cases of aggravated homicide, rape, and other crimes.

3. FREEDOM FROM INHUMAN TREATMENT

Every person is, under Section 36 of the Constitution, guaranteed the right to freedom from inhuman treatment, such as acts of torture or other forms of cruel or inhuman punishment. In a maximum security section of a prison, the following rules have been held to be inhuman treatment:

1. prohibition on talking;
2. serving food while detainees were holding night-soil buckets;
3. forcing detainees to get drinking water from toilets; and
4. total ban on visitors.[35]

4. RIGHT TO FULL PROTECTION OF LAW

The Constitution contains elaborate provisions aimed at protecting an accused person in the criminal process. Apart from the offense of contempt of court, a person cannot be charged for an offense that is not written. The Constitution also provides for the protection of a person on arrest; his or her rights in court, which include representation by a lawyer or by the Office of the Public Solicitor; and proper treatment of persons on conviction.

5. QUALIFIED RIGHTS

The fundamental rights named above may be altered only by a three-quarters absolute majority vote in Parliament. The other constitutional rights are the right to liberty; the right to freedom of employment; freedom from arbitrary search and entry; the freedom of conscience, thought, and religion; freedom of expression; freedom of assembly and association; freedom of employment; and the right to privacy. These provisions, being qualified rights, can be altered in accordance with Section 38 of the Constitution, which requires that they can be amended by an act of Parliament expressed for that purpose if it is in the public interest for reasons of defense, public safety, public order, public welfare, public health, the protection of children and persons under some disability, and the benefit of underprivileged people. Any such law passed qualifying the rights must be "justifiable in a democratic society." Constitutional amendments enacted in 1991 limit the right to liberty by (a) permitting detention of vagrants and (b) requiring defendants in criminal cases to prove certain elements of a criminal defense on an affirmative basis, rather than requiring the prosecution to prove all elements of its case.

6. CITIZEN-ONLY RIGHTS

The rights and freedoms conferred on citizens only are the right to equality, freedom of information, freedom of movement, and protection of property against unjust deprivation. Citizens also have the right to vote and stand for public office and to acquire freehold land.

7. ENFORCEMENT OF RIGHTS

All rights and freedoms are justiciable and thus enforceable by the courts. If the courts find an infringement of a right, they can order that compensation be awarded to the injured person.[36]

V. Administrative Organization and Law

A. Organization

The government bureaucracy consists of departments and statutory bodies. Each department is concerned with a specific area of government administration; for example, the Department of Minerals and Energy deals with mineral and energy exploration and development, and the Department of Justice is responsible for the administration of justice. It has, however, been held that constitutional offices like the Public Solicitor, the Public Prosecutor, the Committee of Mercy, and the Public Accounts Committee are independent bodies and therefore not arms of the government.[37] Apart from the national departments, each administrative unit of each province is also called a department.

Most of the public utility services are provided by statutory bodies. The postal, telecommunication, and electricity services, for instance, are provided by statutory corporations owned by the state. The Agriculture Bank of Papua New Guinea is another example of a statutory organization. This bank was established under the Agriculture Bank Act (Chapter 139) and funded by the government to lend money to Papua New Guinea businesses at concessional interest rates to encourage local business.

B. Public Service

The Constitution establishes the national public service, police force, defense force, and parliamentary service. All of these authorities, with the exception of the defense force, are civilian services.

The control of the public service is vested in the Public Services Commission. Its function is to keep under continuous review the state services (other than the defense force), the provincial services, and the services of other governmental bodies. More specifically, the commission is required to advise, either on its own initiative or on request, the national executive and any other authority responsible for any of those services, on organizational matters and the coordination of effort—especially on conditions of employment—with a view to avoiding wasteful duplication of effort and competition. The commission's powers do not, however, empower it to direct and control the public service.

The commission is comprised of four persons, all of whom are citizens appointed by the Head of State acting on the advice of the National Executive Council.

The disciplined forces—the police force and the defense force—are subject to the control and direction of the National Executive Council. The police force is headed by a commissioner of police and the defense force by a commander. These forces are both independent and are subject to control only by Cabinet collectively and not by individual ministers. For example, it has been held that the police force's function to prosecute charges is not subject to the control even of the Public Prosecutor.[38]

The executive is directed by the Head of State, who acts on the advice of the National Executive Council, which is headed by the Prime Minister. Ministers of the Cabinet are responsible for policy formulation and its implementation by their heads of department, who are in charge of the public service workforce in their respective departments. Public servants, including the head of department, come under the supervision and control of the Public Services Commission. Relations between departments are maintained and coordinated by the Public Services Commission, which reports to the Cabinet through the responsible minister. Individual ministers also report directly to the Cabinet on their departments.

The provincial government system further adds to this large bureaucracy their own provincial executives, a provincial secretariat, and public servants assigned to each province by the national government. Relations between individual provincial governments and the national government are maintained through consultation as provided by the Organic Law on Provincial Governments and through Premiers' council conferences held annually and chaired by the Prime Minister.

C. Public Finance and Audit

The Constitution states in Section 209, "Notwithstanding anything in this Constitution, the raising and expenditure of finance by the National Government, including the imposition of taxation and the raising of loans, is subject to the authorisation and control by Parliament." The provincial governments have limited taxation powers.

Expenditure of funds by all government bodies comes under the scrutiny of the Parliament through the parliamentary Public Accounts Committee. The office of the Auditor General audits all public bodies and is required to report at least once a year to Parliament. The Public Finances Management Act 1987 has detailed provisions on preparation of the national budget, collection of public revenue, and expenditure of funds by government departments and instrumentalities.

D. Rule Making

Numerous persons and authorities are given power to make rules on specific subjects by the Constitution and by different acts of Parliament. On the subdelegation of legislative power by Parliament, Section 100 of the Constitution, in vesting the legislative power of the people in the Parliament, expressly provides that this "does not prevent a law from conferring on an authority other than the Parliament legislative powers or functions (including, if the law so provides, a further power or further powers of delegation and sub-delegation)," subject to the qualification that such delegation or subdelegation does not enable "Parliament to transfer permanently, or divest itself of, legislative power." All subordinate legislative enactments made under acts of Parliament by such authorities are, however, required by Section 116 of the Constitution to be tabled in Parliament and are subject to disallowance by Parliament.

Many rules and regulations are made by the government—that is, by the National Executive Council—as part of its function of governing the country. Regulations or rules, whether promulgated by the National Executive Council or by individual ministers, generally require the assent of the Head of State to have effect.

Examples of other persons and bodies with rule-making powers are departmental heads, the Public Services Commission, the local government councils, the Papua New Guinea Law Society under the Lawyers Act (Chapter 91), and statutory bodies such as the Agriculture Bank. Section 184 of the Constitution provides for the making of rules of court. It provides, "the Judges of the Supreme Court and the National Court may make rules of court, not inconsistent with a constitutional law or an act of Parliament, with respect to the practice and procedure in relation to the Supreme Court or the National Court." Section 185 adds, "If in the circumstances of a particular case before a court no provision, or no adequate provision, is made in respect of a matter of practice or procedure, the court shall give ad hoc directions to remedy the lack or inadequacy."

E. Review of Administrative Action

The large and complex executive arm of government is subject to a number of controls. The first form of control and check is exercised by Parliament, to which the Cabinet is answerable on major issues through mandatory reports or through individual members' questions during question time in Parliament. Parliament has the ultimate power of overruling decisions of the executive.

The Constitution also deals with relations between this large bureaucracy and the citizen and provides relief to protect the latter from bureaucratic actions and decisions in a number of ways. First, the Constitution recognizes the application of the principles of natural justice developed at common law for the control of judicial and administrative proceedings as part of the underlying law when it states in Section 59, "The minimum requirement of natural justice is the duty to act fairly and, in principle, to be seen to act fairly." Further, the Constitution in Section 60 calls on the courts to give particular attention

> to the development of a system of principles of natural justice and of administrative law specifically designed for Papua New Guinea, taking special account of the National Goals and Directive Principles and the Basic Social Obligations, and typically Papua New Guinean procedures and forms of organization.

Sections 59 and 60 of the Constitution have been interpreted differently on a number of points. One issue relates to the bodies or authorities that are required to observe the principles of natural justice. Another issue is whether these provisions entrench the principles of natural justice as part of the principles to be observed or whether they are merely declaratory for developing appropriate principles as part of the underlying law. Both points have been addressed by the courts, but neither has been conclusively determined. In the *Premdas* case, the court held that the principles of natural justice apply only to decisions of judicial bodies or administrative bodies that are required to act judicially.[39] But that judgment (see especially the opinion of Prentice, C.J.) is based on outmoded English decisions. Even before *Premdas* was decided, English courts had adopted different criteria for the application of natural justice.[40] One such criterion is the test of "legitimate expectation" which was held by Wilson, J., in his dissenting judgment in *Premdas* to apply in Papua New Guinea. Prentice, C.J., was also of the opinion in *Premdas* that Section 59 did not entrench the natural justice principles as a guaranteed right. However, the Supreme Court has ruled differently in later cases.[41]

The second way the Constitution protects the citizen is in the overriding provision of Section 41, which provides that acts done under valid laws are nevertheless unlawful if (1) harsh or oppressive, (2) unwarranted by or disproportionate to the requirements of the particular case, or (3) not reasonably justifiable in a democratic society having a proper regard for the rights and dignity of mankind. The Supreme Court has held that Section 41 is not restricted to the enforcement of the qualified rights sections but is a general provision.[42] The onus is on a person invoking the provision to establish that it applies.

Third, the Constitution in Section 155 expressly gives the Supreme Court and the National Court power to review decisions of judicial authorities. In some cases, the courts have interpreted these review provisions to define their powers narrowly. For example, the Supreme Court has held that its review power does not extend to review of the decisions of administrative agencies.[43]

Finally, the Ombudsman Commission provides another venue for channeling complaints against public officers and public bodies. The commission is established to

1. ensure that all governmental bodies are responsive to the needs and aspirations of the people;
2. improve the work of governmental bodies and eliminate unfairness and discrimination by them;
3. help eliminate unfair or otherwise defective legislation and practices affecting or administered by governmental bodies; and
4. supervise enforcement of the Leadership Code.

The Constitution outlines the functions of the commission, which are further elaborated by the Organic Law on the Ombudsman Commission. It has powers to investigate, on its own initiative or on complaint by a person affected, the conduct of public bodies, agencies, officers, or statutory instrumentalities, as well as provincial governments and their agencies. The commission can also investigate defects in law or administrative practice and discriminatory practices of agencies or departments. The commission's findings in such investigations are reported to the National Executive Council for presentation to Parliament.

F. Official Secrets, Freedom of Information

The Constitution guarantees to every person the right to freedom of expression and to every citizen the right to freedom of information. The latter right is a right "of reasonable access to official documents." This right is made subject "to the need for such secrecy as is reasonably justifiable in a democratic society" (Constitution, Section 51).

The National Intelligence Organization Act (Chapter 405) provides for the collection of communication and other information for the security of the country by the National Intelligence Organization. This organization can intercept such information but only under a warrant issued by the National Security Council. The membership of this council consists of the Prime Minister (chairman); the Deputy Prime Minister; the ministers responsible for defense, foreign affairs and trade, provincial affairs, police, and finance. Various offenses are created for persons in the organization who use the information it obtains for unauthorized purposes.

VI. INTERNATIONAL OBLIGATIONS

Papua New Guinea has diplomatic ties with a number of countries. The Diplomatic and Consular Privileges and Immunities Act (Chapter 83) gives legislative force to the Vienna Convention on Diplomatic Relations, while the International Organizations (Privileges and Immunities) Act (Chapter 87) provides for privileges and immunities for international organizations and persons connected with them. The United Nations and Specialized Agencies (Privileges and Immunities) Act (Chapter 88) confers diplomatic privileges and immunities to United Nations agencies and persons connected with them.

Papua New Guinea has entered into a number of international, regional, multilateral, and bilateral agreements and treaties. The Supreme Court has held that Papua New Guinea also has international obligations independent of treaties; sending defense forces to quell a rebellion in Vanuatu was held to be the kind of obligation that does not require a treaty.[44]

Papua New Guinea is a party to the various Geneva Conventions relating to the amelioration of conditions for the wounded and sick in armed forces in the field and at sea, the treatment of prisoners of war, and the protection of civilian persons in times of war. The Geneva Conventions Act (Chapter 84) gives legal effect to the provisions of the various conventions.

A multilateral treaty to which Papua New Guinea is a party is the Pacific islands fisheries treaty with the United States, under which Pacific island countries allow U.S. fishing vessels to fish in Pacific island waters in return for a fee paid by the United States. The treaty is administered by the Forum Fisheries Agency (FFA).

Examples of bilateral treaties are the trade agreement between Papua New Guinea and Australia (PACTRA) made soon after independence and tax agreements with Australia and Canada. An investment protection agreement with Australia was concluded in 1991.

Papua New Guinea is a member of a number of international and regional organizations, including the United Nations, the Commonwealth, and the Asian Development Bank, as approved by the Asian Development Bank Act (Chapter 82). It has observer status in the General Agreement on Tariffs and Trade (GATT) and in the Association of South East Asian Nations (ASEAN). Within the Pacific, Papua New Guinea is a member of the South Pacific Forum. The International Financial Organization Act (Chapter 86) approved Papua New Guinea's membership in the International Monetary Fund, International Bank for Reconstruction and Development (World Bank), International Financial Corporation, and International Development Association. With the Solomon Islands and Vanuatu, Papua New Guinea is one of the three island countries making up the Melanesian Spear Head Group.

The Reciprocal Enforcement of Judgments Act (Chapter 50) provides for the enforcement of judgments of courts in countries that have reciprocal arrangements with Papua New Guinea, while the Extradition Act (Chapter 49) provides for the extradition of offenders of extraditable offenses in another country, based also on reciprocal arrangements. As a member of the Commonwealth, Papua New Guinea is party to the Commonwealth arrangements under which extradition and enforcement of judgments in the Commonwealth apply. A number of non-Commonwealth countries have separate extradition arrangements with Papua New Guinea.

VII. Revenue Law

The tax system is largely based on income tax on individuals and companies and import and excise duties. The general principles of tax law are similar to the taxation scheme in Australia. Although the government has introduced a number of revenue-raising measures recently, the basic legislation on taxation, the Income Tax Act 1959, still sets out the principles of taxation, such as the definitions of taxable income and allowable deductions.

Personal income tax in Papua New Guinea is progressive; the marginal rate of tax increases as a person's income rises. The minimum rate is no tax liability if the income is less than K3,000 per year; the maximum rate of tax for incomes exceeding K15,000 per year is 28 percent. Company tax, first introduced in 1959, has been at different rates. It was reduced from 30 percent to 25 percent in the 1992 budget; however, this reduction does not apply to mining and petroleum companies, whose rates are 35 and 50 percent, respectively. Successive governments in Papua New Guinea have attempted to expand the tax base by introducing the following new forms of taxes in addition to income tax on company profits:

1. Capital gains tax: The principles underlying this type of tax are similar to those of the tax introduced in Australia in 1985, except in the rate of tax on capital gains. For Papua New Guinea real estate, for example, the rate was 15 percent in 1989.
2. Royalties: The royalty withholding tax rate can be as high as 30 percent.
3. Foreign contractors: Rules under the Income Tax Act require that payments by a Papua New Guinea resident to foreign consultants operating outside the country are subject to tax.
4. Stamp duties: Stamp duties payable for documents and other transactions differ, depending on the type of document or transaction.
5. Customs or import duties: Apart from basic items such as rice and tinned fish, all other imports are subject to import tax ranging from 8.5 percent for machinery and construction materials to 75 percent duty on cars.
6. Export taxes: Taxes are imposed on exports of primary produce. In 1979, the applicable rate was 2.5 percent of export value of products.

The taxable income for both personal and company tax is income derived from all sources, whether from within or outside Papua New Guinea. This creates a situation in which foreign companies could be subject to double taxation unless their home country provides tax credits or other relief. To encourage investment, Papua New Guinea is in the process of entering into double tax treaties with a number of countries, including Canada, Australia, and the United Kingdom. Presently Australia extends a credit for foreign tax liability for income earned by Australian companies in foreign countries that is subject to tax in those countries. A similiar credit applies in the case of United States land investors.

VIII. Investment Law

Investment within the country, whether by individuals or companies, is encouraged. The Agriculture Bank of Papua New Guinea was established by the Agriculture Bank Act (Chapter 139) to help citizens and local companies establish and operate investment ventures by giving loans on more favorable terms than commercial banks. To encourage exports, the Tariff Advisory Committee Act (Chapter 121) was enacted. It establishes a Tariff Advisory Committee to advise the National Executive Council on assistance to industries established or to be established in the country and on temporary protective measures.

The government recently adopted policies aimed at directly encouraging industrial development. To this end, the Industrial Centres Development Corporation Act 1990 was enacted under which certain areas will be declared industrial centers where industrial development activities will be promoted. The act establishes the Industrial Centres Development Corporation with perpetual succession and as an entity that can sue and be sued. The corporation's functions are to plan and implement government policies on industrial centers, acquire land for the centers, prepare and coordinate finance for their development, and generally assist, manage, and promote industrial development in the industrial centers.

A Small Business Development Corporation was similarly established by the Small Business Development Corporation Act 1990. Its main function is to encourage small business development by Papua New Guineans by providing management and administrative assistance as well as incentives to encourage these businesses.

A third corporation called the Tourism Development Corporation was established by the Tourism Development Act 1990. Its main function is to formulate cultural and tourism policies, adopt measures to protect cultural rights and identities of individual groups, promote and encourage travel and tourism in the country, develop tourism products, provide tourism infrastructure, and generally promote tourism in the country.

Foreign investment was until recently regulated by the National Investment and Development Authority Act (Chapter 120). This act required registration of all "foreign enterprises" and placed stringent conditions on their operations. In 1991, the government made sweeping changes to the laws regulating foreign investment in the country. With the passage of the Investment Promotion Act 1991, the aim is no longer to regulate foreign investment but rather, as the act's title suggests, to promote foreign investment.

Under the 1991 act, a foreign investor desiring to invest in the country can apply to the Investment Promotion Authority, a body established under the act to administer its provisions, for a certificate. If the investment area sought is not reserved for citizens, the authority can issue a certificate, which must be done within thirty days of the application (Sections 28 and 29). The certificate will contain the name of the enterprise, the location and nature of the business activity, and the names and addresses of shareholders of the business.

A certificate will not be issued to an applicant if the area of business proposed is a reserved activity. The act provides for regulations to list business activities reserved either for the state or for "national enterprises"; the authority may amend the list every two years either by adding or removing activities. *National enterprises* are enterprises of which "50% or more [equity] is owned by citizens, unless the control of the enterprise exercisable by law or in practice is maintained by persons other than a governmental body or citizen" (Section 3).

The act contains other significant incentives to promote foreign investment. First, it gives the following guarantees under Section 37:

1. nationalization or expropriation is prohibited except when such measures are taken in accordance with law for a public purpose and upon payment of "full prompt and adequate . . . compensation";
2. the right of a foreign investor to repatriate (subject to the availability of foreign exchange reserves and after payment of appropriate taxes) all its profits and compensation payments (if property is expropriated); and
3. the foreign investor has the right to employ noncitizens in business enterprises in accordance with the Employment of Non-citizens Act (Chapter 374) if qualified citizens are not available to fill a position.

Second, if a dispute arises as to the interpretation of the act, the dispute may be referred to the World Bank's International Centre for the Settlement of Investment Disputes (ICSID) rather than to courts in Papua New Guinea. Third, the investment authority is made, in an important respect, the agent of a foreign investor, in that under Section 40 the authority is required to assist an investor in obtaining all necessary government permits, licenses, compliances, and approvals from other government agencies.

IX. Welfare Law

Papua New Guinea has no social security system. Its education system is largely publicly funded, although school fees are paid in primary schools, called community schools, and secondary schools. Tertiary education is mainly by government sponsorship, under a national scholarship scheme administered by the Commission for Higher Education. The two universities are the University of Papua New Guinea established by the University of Papua

New Guinea Act (Chapter 169) and located in Port Moresby, and the Papua New Guinea University of Technology established by the University of Technology Act (Chapter 170) and based in Lae.

Health services are also largely free in publicly run hospitals, clinics, and aid posts in rural areas. Only nominal fees are charged for outpatient treatment and for specified drugs. The Public Hospital (Charges) Act (Chapter 116) provides for these charges and vests in the responsible minister power to set or vary hospital charges. The minister can also exempt persons from hospital charges and fees for drugs and other medication.

Members of the public service and defense and disciplinary forces receive retirement, death, and disability benefits from a fund to which they and the government contribute. Parliament enacted legislation in 1990 increasing benefits and altering the proportions of employer and employee contributions. The National Provident Fund Act (Chapter 377) requires private sector employers to establish retirement funds for their employees as well.

X. Criminal Law

The Constitution, Section 37, provides that "nobody can be charged for an offence that is not defined by, and the penalty for which is not prescribed by, a written law."[45] There are two main statutes on the criminal law. The Criminal Code Act (Chapter 262), which had its origins in the Queensland Criminal Code, relates primarily to crimes and major misdemeanors, while the Summary Offences Act (Chapter 202) relates primarily to simple offenses.

Part V of the Criminal Code, dealing with criminal responsibility, provides freedom from criminal responsibility for offenses committed in the following situations:

1. Though ignorance of the law is stated to be no excuse, a person claiming an honest claim of right in property-related offenses is excused by Section 23.[46]
2. Subject to contrary provisions in any law, Section 24 provides that a person who did not have the requisite intent to commit an offense is not criminally responsible.[47]
3. Mistake of fact is excusable in the instances stipulated under Section 25.[48]
4. Section 26 excuses offenses committed in an emergency (this excuse does not affect the defenses of provocation and self-defense).[49]
5. If the person pleads and proves insanity, there is no criminal responsibility.[50]
6. Under Section 30, a person under the age of seven years is not criminally responsible, while a person under the age of fourteen years is presumed not to be criminally responsible for the offense of rape.[51]

The Criminal Code offenses are divided into the following categories:

1. offenses against public order, including treason, inciting to mutiny, assisting escaping prisoners of war, and sedition;
2. offenses against the executive and legislative power, such as interference with the Head of State and Parliament, giving false evidence, refusal by a witness to give evidence before Parliament, and bribing or receiving bribes from a member of Parliament;
3. unlawful assemblies and breaches of peace, including rioting, smuggling arms, forcible entry, challenge to a duel, threat of violence, and unlawful prosecutions;
4. offenses against the administration of law and justice, including disclosure of official secrets; corruption and abuse of office; corrupt and improper practice in elections; selling and trafficking in offices; judicial corruption; perjury or fabrication or destruction of evi-

dence; corrupting, deceiving, or preventing a witness from attending a hearing; conspiracy to bring false accusations or to defeat justice; attempting to pervert justice; escapes, rescues, and obstructing officers of court; offenses relating to currency; and offenses relating to posts and telegraphs;
5. acts injurious to the public in general, including offenses against religious worship; offenses against sexual morality including indecent treatment or abuse of children; indecent acts; incest; attempts to procure abortions and obscene publications and exhibitions; nuisance and misconduct relating to corpses; and offenses against public health;
6. offenses against persons, including assault; homicide covering willful murder, murder, and manslaughter; aiding suicide; assault and abduction of females including rape; bigamy; and kidnapping;
7. offenses relating to property, including stealing or theft; stealing with violence such as robbery, burglary and housebreaking, obtaining property by false pretenses and cheating, and receiving stolen or fraudulently obtained property;
8. other offenses in the code are forgery and counterfeiting trademarks and other documents, fraudulent debtors, and offenses relating to business associations.

The other major legislation dealing with criminal offenses—the Summary Offences Act—covers minor offenses such as drunkenness, simple assaults, breach of peace, unlawful trespass, escaping from lawful custody, indecent exposure and indecent writings, gaming and betting, and offenses relating to the police.

Other criminal offenses are created by statutes, such as the Motor Traffic Act (Chapter 243), which creates traffic offenses; the Employment Act, which addresses employers' failure to observe certain provisions of the act; and the Customs Act (Chapter 101), which creates a range of customs-related offenses.

The legislation that creates the different offenses also provides for the punishment to be imposed. Under the recently enacted Criminal Law (Compensation) Act 1991, the courts now have the power, in addition to any other punishment imposed, to order an offender to pay compensation in accordance with the criteria laid down in the act.

XI. JUDICIAL PROCEDURE

A. Civil Procedure

Village Courts and Land Courts are not bound by formal rules of evidence, and their proceedings have limited procedural guidelines and requirements.

The procedures for Local Courts and District Courts are found in their establishing statutes—the District Courts Act (Chapter 40) and the Local Courts Act (Chapter 41). The Local Court has jurisdiction under Section 12(1)(b) of the Local Courts Act over "all civil actions at law or in equity" except actions for divorce or for marriage other than customary marriages. Further, a Local Court can hear matters only if they arise within 33 kilometers of its boundary or where the defendant resides within this area.

Proceedings in the Local Court are commenced by a written or oral complaint under Section 22. Proceedings must be in open court, the complainant and defendant must be present at the hearing except if the defendant does not appear after service of summons, the complaint must be read to the defendant in a language the defendant understands, each party is entitled to cross-examine one another's witnesses, and the court can ask questions at any stage. Instead of a hearing, the Local Court can mediate a settlement at any stage of the proceedings.

The Local Court can award damages, order restitution of property, order specific performance of a contract other than a contract of service, or "make any other order which the justice of the particular case requires" (Section 15). The Local Court has power to award damages or compensation to a maximum value of K1,000.

The commencement of proceedings in the district court under the District Court Act is by way of information or complaint. The act provides for procedures similar to those in the Local Court. It requires the presence of the complainant and defendant and specifies the manner of adducing evidence and the summoning and appearance of witnesses.

The amount of compensation or damages that can be awarded by the District Court depends on the seniority of the presiding magistrate. A Magistrate Grade V has jurisdiction to award up to a maximum value of K10,000; Grade IV, K8,000; Grade III, K4,000; and Grade II, K2,000. The District Court does not have jurisdiction in actions involving infringement of trade names, defamation, dispute in land title, false imprisonment and malicious prosecution, validity and other disputes under a will, and seduction and breach of promise to marry. In cases where the District Court shares jurisdiction with the National Court, it can transfer a case to the latter.

The National Court and the Supreme Court's jurisdiction are provided for in the Constitution, as discussed in **IV C (d) Judiciary**. The civil procedure rules of the National Court are contained in the National Court Rules (Chapter 36). These rules make elaborate provisions for the commencement of proceedings, service of documents, filing of documents, pleadings, trial, evidence, judgment, orders, and enforcement of judgments. The rules, adopted in 1983 by the National Court, were to a large extent based on the Supreme Court Rules of New South Wales and a number of orders from the United Kingdom, the Australian Capital Territory, and the Victorian Rules of Court.

B. Criminal Procedure

The criminal jurisdiction of the different courts has been discussed in **X Criminal Law**. Criminal procedure in the Local Court is as set out under the Local Court Act. The proceedings are commenced by a complaint. The following procedure is required to be observed in a trial:

1. the hearing must be in open court;
2. the defendant must be present unless the court allows otherwise;
3. the particulars and nature of the complaint must be explained to the defendant at the commencement of the trial;
4. if the offense is also triable by a District Court, the defendant must be given a chance to make an election;
5. if the defendant pleads not guilty to the offense charged, the prosecution would lead evidence first, followed by the defendant (who cannot be compelled to give evidence) and his or her witnesses;
6. the court can ask questions in addition to cross-examination of witnesses by both the prosecution and defense; and
7. the court makes a decision.

The summary criminal procedure of the District Court is similar to the procedure in the Local Court. Proceedings are commenced by way of information or complaint, and the trial proceeds as in the Local Court. In the Local Court and District Court, the calling, summoning, and examination of witnesses follow similar procedures.

The District Court also hears committal proceedings for indictable offenses not triable summarily. If a person is charged with an indictable offense, he or she must be served a copy of the information charging him or her. There are now two procedures of conducting committal proceedings. In the older procedure, the court decides at a committal hearing whether there is a prima facie case to try the defendant. The new procedure, introduced recently by amendments to the District Court Act, permits the District Court to commit a defendant for trial without a hearing, if the court is satisfied that all material evidence is contained in written statements. However, this procedure is not available if the defendant has no legal representation or if the legal representative requests the court to consider a submission that the statements do not disclose sufficient evidence to try the defendant.

The procedure of the National Court in its original criminal jurisdiction is similar to that of the District Court in calling witnesses, adducing evidence, and in the general conduct of a criminal trial.

Two courts may share criminal jurisdiction over a number of offenses. Although the National Court has power to hear all criminal cases, in practice it hears only indictable offenses. The District Court has jurisdiction to hear some indictable offenses in addition to hearing all summary offenses. The District Court also shares jurisdiction over summary offenses with the Local Court. Defendants elect the court they wish to be tried by if they first appear before the Local Court.

A separate court called the Children's Court is created by the Child Welfare Act (Chapter 276). This court hears offenses committed by persons under the age of sixteen, except those charged with serious offenses, such as rape or homicide, that carry the maximum penalty of life imprisonment and are dealt with by the National Court. The jurisdiction of the Children's Court is exercised by a magistrate sitting with at least one lay member who would normally be a welfare officer. It is a court of summary jurisdiction and exercises the powers of such a court.

1. ARREST

An arrest, under the Arrest Act (Chapter 339), can be effected with or without a warrant. A police officer can arrest without warrant a person whom the officer believes is about to commit a crime, is committing a crime, or has committed a crime punishable by imprisonment. Members of the public may make a citizen's arrest.

The act, under Part III, makes further provision for arrest with a warrant, including the manner of effecting such arrests and the duties of the arresting officer and the officer in charge of the police station and the police over the arrested person.

2. SEARCHES AND SEIZURES

The Constitution, in Section 44, guarantees to every person freedom from being searched. However, this is a qualified right, and the section allows restriction of this right by law that makes reasonable provision for search under an order or warrant of a court or by an authorized public officer for tax and other purposes.

The Search Act (Chapter 341) provides for search in relation to criminal offenses. A search could be made in pursuant of a search warrant issued by a court other than the Local Court or a search could be made by a policeman without a warrant.

A search warrant issued by a court may be issued to a named person, to a particular police officer, or the whole police force naming the place to be searched and the offense to which the search is related. Search without a warrant can be made by a police officer if the officer believes on reasonable grounds that a person is in possession of anything that has been stolen or anything used or to be used in the commission of an offense.

In both cases, the person doing the search is allowed to touch the body and clothing of the person searched but this must be done with due regard to decency. If a female is searched, another adult female must be present. Any property found during the search can be seized if it is believed on reasonable grounds to have been stolen or used in the commission of an offense, or if it will provide evidence of an offense.

The National Intelligence Organization Act (Chapter 405) allows the National Intelligence Organization to carry out searches in the discharge of its functions.

3. RIGHTS OF DEFENDANTS

A person charged with an offense is accorded a number of protections under Part III of the Constitution, including the following:

1. a fair hearing within a reasonable time by an independent and impartial court;
2. the right to be presumed innocent until proven guilty according to law;
3. the right to be informed promptly in a language he or she understands, and in detail, of the nature of the offense he or she is charged with;
4. adequate time and facilities to prepare a defense;
5. the right to have an interpreter in the trial if required;
6. the right to defend himself or herself in person or by a legal representative of his or her choice or by the Public Solicitor if entitled to legal aid; and
7. the right to examine witnesses personally or through a legal representative.

If the person is convicted for the offense charged, a right of appeal against conviction or sentence is available; in detention, the prisoner is to be treated with humanity and with respect for human dignity.

4. BAIL

The Constitution, in Section 46, provides the right of liberty of every person, but it is a qualified right, and a number of exceptions are made. Under Subsection 2 "A person arrested or detained for an offence (other than treason or wilfull murder . . .) is entitled to bail at all times from arrest or detention until acquittal or conviction unless the interests of justice otherwise require." It is further provided under Subsection 7 that if bail is refused, the authority refusing bail must state in writing the reasons for refusing bail. The person is permitted to apply to the National or Supreme Court in a summary manner for his or her release.

Detailed provisions on bail are made by the Bail Act (Chapter 340), which provides that bail is to be granted by the police, or if the police refuse bail, the accused is to be taken to a magistrate as soon as practicable. Bail can be refused in the following circumstances:

1. the accused is unlikely to appear at the hearing;
2. the offense was committed when the accused was on bail for another offense;
3. the alleged offense was a serious assault, a threat of violence to another person, or involved the use or possession of a firearm, an imitation firearm, or other offensive weapon or explosive;
4. the accused is likely to commit an indictable offense if allowed bail;
5. the accused will interfere with witnesses; or
6. the accused needs protection.

5. TRIAL BY JURY

Papua New Guinea has no legislation either permitting or preventing trial by jury. The Constitution states in Section 186 that "Nothing in this Division prevents the establishment by or under an act of Parliament, of a system of juries or assessors." The National Court Assessors (TNG) Act (Chapter 42), which applies only to the area of the country that was formerly the Territory of New Guinea, allows assessors to be used; however, this procedure has rarely been used.

C. Appellate Review

Appeals from decisions of the Local Court lie to the National Court, which can entertain an appeal only if a substantial miscarriage of justice occurred. The National Court can receive fresh or additional evidence, whether orally or by affidavit, and can dismiss the appeal, reverse the decision, order a retrial, or substitute its own decision for the lower court's. In criminal cases, the state is precluded from appealing against the dismissal of a complaint. However, the Secretary for Justice can appeal or intervene in a criminal appeal if the matter is of public importance.

Appeals from the District Court also lie to the National Court, under procedures provided by Part XI of the District Court Act. A person aggrieved by a conviction, order, or adjudication can appeal within one month of the decision by filing a notice of appeal and by entering into a recognizance or by giving other security. On receiving a notice of appeal, the clerk of the court in which the decision is appealed is required to forward to the National Court all relevant files. Any condition precedent to the right of appeal required by law can be dispensed with by the National Court.

Detailed provisions on the procedure for appeals to the National Court and the service of documents is made under Order 68 of the National Court Rules. These rules provide for time limitation on lodging appeals, place for hearing of appeals, transmission of proceedings, inspection and copying of documents, and seeking leave to appeal (for example, by the Secretary for Justice).

As in the case of appeals from the Local Court, the state cannot appeal against the dismissal of a complaint by a District Court, but the Secretary for Justice can appeal or intervene in an appeal if the matter is of public importance. The Public Prosecutor can appeal against a sentence imposed by the District Court.

On hearing an appeal from the District Court, the National Court can receive fresh evidence on consent of both parties or by its own order. The National Court can make orders similar to those available on an appeal from the Local Court.

The Supreme Court has held that the National Court's power of review can be exercised not only over judicial bodies but over nonjudicial tribunals as well, and if its appeal powers are prohibited by a legislative enactment, it nevertheless has powers of review by way of a prerogative writ (see **IV, C (1) (d) Judiciary**).

Appeals from the National Court lie to the Supreme Court. The procedure for appeals is provided under the Supreme Court Act (Chapter 37). The Supreme Court is the final court of appeal. Appeals from the National Court fall into these two broad categories: first, appeals from a judge of the National Court sitting on appeal—that is, hearing an appeal from the District Court, Local Court, or other court; and second, appeals from decisions of the National Court itself at first instance. In the first category, appeals in both criminal and civil cases lie to the Supreme Court on a question of law, on a question of mixed fact and law, or with leave of the Supreme Court on a question of fact. The appeal is by way of rehearing; the Supreme Court has power to allow fresh evidence in the form of documents or other evidence and to draw its own inferences of fact.

In the second type of appeal, the grounds of appeal against a decision or order of the National

Court depend on whether the matter is criminal or civil. In civil matters, appeals to the Supreme Court from the National Court lie on questions of law, questions of mixed fact and law, or with leave of the Supreme Court on questions of fact. In criminal matters, a person convicted by the National Court can appeal against conviction on any ground involving a question of law; on a question of mixed fact and law; by leave of the Supreme Court or under certification by the National Court that the matter is a fit case for appeal, on the ground that it involves a question of fact alone; or with the leave of the Supreme Court, against sentence passed on conviction if the sentence is not fixed by law.

The Supreme Court also has an advisory role. In both civil and criminal cases, it can rule on questions of law referred to it by the National Court on application of a party or by the court itself at any stage of the proceedings.

On appeals, the Supreme Court in civil matters has powers to adjourn the hearing; affirm, reverse, or modify the judgment; give such judgment that ought to have been given in the first instance; remit the matter in whole or in part for further hearing; or order a new trial. In criminal appeals, the Supreme Court can make similar orders.

Further, the Constitution, in Section 155(4), declares that "Both the Supreme Court and the National Court have inherent power to make, in such circumstances as seem to them proper, orders in the nature of prerogative writs and such other orders as are necessary to do justice in the circumstances of a particular case." The latter part of this provision has been interpreted differently by the courts; in some cases, judges suggest that the court has power to make "such other orders as are necessary to do justice" according to law,[52] while in others judges suggest that the provision cannot be so strictly interpreted.[53]

XII. Land and Natural Resources

A. Land Tenure and Administration

Since colonial times, a dual land tenure system has existed in Papua New Guinea, consisting of (1) alienated land, regulated by statute and subject to common law; and (2) customary land, regulated by customary law.

After World War II, when both the territories of Papua and New Guinea were under the same administration, the customary land tenure system was seen as an important area needing reform for economic development. Legislative measures were introduced in the 1950s to bring about such reform. The Native Land Registration Ordinance 1952 established a Native Land Commission with powers to determine and record land rights of owners. This legislation was repealed a decade later, when it was realized that it could not achieve its objectives because customary landowners were uncooperative and suspicious of the administration's motives and also because the complicated rules of customary land ownership made implementation of the ordinance impractical.

The administration later adopted the Torrens registration system used in Australia and in parts of Africa. A number of laws were enacted. The Land Titles Commission Act 1974 established a Land Titles Commission with powers to adjudicate land rights under custom and to demarcate adjudicated land. Such land could then be converted, under the Land (Tenure Conversion) Ordinance 1963, from customary land to freehold estates, which were registerable under the Real Property Ordinance 1913 in Papua and the Land Registration Ordinance 1924 in New Guinea (the latter two statutes later were consolidated into the Land Registration Act 1981, Chapter 191). The amount of land actually converted and registered is small, due to the complicated process of determining ownership and the surveying expenses involved. Land tenure conversion and registration now come under the Lands Department.

B. Customary Land Tenure

Ninety-seven percent of land in Papua New Guinea is held under customary title. Specific rules on land use and land dealings differ from one customary group to another, but a few rules are common throughout the country. Land under custom is owned by a customary group, whether a lineal group, clan, or tribe. Specific individuals within the group then have the right to use land and things under and on the land. Land is seen as owned not only by those presently living, but also by those yet to be born and by the dead as well. Land also has great religious significance. Land transfers are therefore limited by custom to recognized customary situations, like settling customary obligations. The main rules of customary land tenure system are hence similar to those of other traditional societies of the Pacific, such as the Solomon Islands.

Attempts at reforming customary land tenure in Papua New Guinea did recognize some of these customary rules. The 1973 report of the Commission of Inquiry into Land Matters, for example, recommended the recognition of customary landowning groups and suggested the registration of group titles in line with the national goals on using Papua New Guinea forms of social, political, and economic organizations. The Land Groups Incorporation Act (Chapter 147) provided for the recognition by registration of customary groups. Under this act, the registrar may register the constitution of a customary group and issue a certificate of incorporation. The incorporated group then has all the attributes of a legal entity.

C. Government Taking of Land

The main statute regulating alienated land is the Land Act (Chapter 185), which vests all alienated land, apart from certain pre-independence freehold titles, in the state. It is, therefore, no longer possible for a person to hold freehold land. Section 4 states that "All estate, rights, title and interest other than customary rights in land at any time held by a person are held under the State."

The state can acquire land in three main ways. The first is through acquisition by agreement. The state is the only entity that can acquire customary land outside of customary land dealings.

Second, the state may declare land to be "waste and vacant" or "ownerless." Many land acquisitions by administrations in both Papua and New Guinea were made through such a declaration. The Crown Lands Ordinance of 1890 first empowered the Crown to acquire land that "was not used or reasonably likely to be required by Papuans." Successive legislation on land retained this provision; the Land Act 1962 preserved this power, as have the postindependence Revised Laws.

As might be expected, the acquisition of land in this way has not been unopposed. Customary owners have disputed the state's claims that land in Papua New Guinea was "waste and vacant" or "ownerless." A number of disputes reached the courts.[54]

Third, the state may acquire land by compulsory process, under Division 3 of Part IV of the Land Act. The Constitution permits such acquisition, but only for a "public purpose" and upon payment of "just compensation." Two other statutes, the Land Redistribution Act (Chapter 190) and the Land Acquisition (Development Purposes) Act (Chapter 192), gave further powers to the state to acquire alienated land. The former law permits state acquisition of land for the purpose of returning land to previous customary owners if there is a shortage of land in the customary group or for development purposes; the latter law permits acquisition for use by citizens for subsistence farming, economic development, or educational and other common welfare or community development purposes.

Land may also pass to the state by the operation of the doctrine of *bona vacantia* under Section 87 of the Wills, Probate and Administration Act (Chapter 291), if there are no heirs to intestate property.

D. National Parks and Reserves

The Minister for Lands is empowered by Section 5 of the Land Act to reserve land "by notice in the National Gazette . . . for a purpose specified in the notice, from lease or further lease by the State under this Act, Government land or land that is the subject of a State lease, that in his opinion is or may be required for that purpose." The minister can appoint trustees for such reserved land. Land reserved under this provision for the purpose of recreation and amusement of the public, a national park, a botanical or zoological garden, or a reserve or sanctuary for the protection of flora or fauna may be, by declaration in the *National Gazette*, committed to the Director of National Parks under Section 4 of the National Parks Act (Chapter 157). This act, which declares its aim in the preamble to "provide for the preservation [and management] of the environment and of the national cultural inheritance by . . . the conservation of sites and areas having particular biological, topographical, geological, historical, scientific or social importance" establishes the office of Director of National Parks. The director, who is appointed by the minister from the public service, controls, manages, and develops areas vested in the office of the director for the specified purpose. The national park regulations make detailed provisions on the use of the parks.

The Minister for Lands is empowered to accept a gift or bequest of land for a national park. If the land given is not suitable for a national park, the minister can dispose of the property.

The Land Act also empowers the minister to appoint trustees (other than the Director of National Parks) to control and manage other reserved land. A number of regulations have been made under this provision.

E. Agriculture, Forests, and Fisheries

1. AGRICULTURE

A number of statutes regulate agriculture, primarily cash crops such as coffee, cocoa, copra, palm oil, and rubber. The Coffee Industry Act (Chapter 208) makes provision for the control and regulation of production, processing, and export of coffee. It establishes a Coffee Industry Board, which controls and regulates the coffee industry, stabilizes coffee prices, and promotes the consumption of coffee.

The *Cocoa Act* (Chapter 388) makes similar provision for the cocoa industry. It establishes a Cocoa Board to act "in the best interest of cocoa growers" to control and regulate the growing, processing, marketing, and exporting of cocoa, cocoa beans, and cocoa products; manage prices; promote consumption, and sponsor research and development programs.

The Copra Act (Chapter 211) sets up a system for inspecting the production and sale of copra for export. Various offenses are created for contravention of standards required in the production of copra intended for export. The Copra Marketing Board Act (Chapter 212) establishes a board to purchase copra, determine the price to be paid by consumers, sell copra, and manage and control all matters connected with copra production and export.

The Rubber Act (Chapter 222) provides for the appointment of inspectors to inspect and grade rubber produced for export. Persons exporting rubber without inspection are guilty of a number of offenses under the act. A rubber board is created to hear appeals of an inspector's grading of rubber produced.

The one law dealing with the oil palm industry is the Palm Oil Industry (New Britain Agreement) Act (Chapter 219), which approved an agreement made between the state and Harrisons & Crossfield (ANZ) Limited, an Australian company, for the development of a palm oil industry in the Cape Hoskins area of West New Britain. The agreement sets up a joint venture project between the company and the state.

The Plant Disease and Control Act (Chapter 220) provides for the identification of diseased plants and the prohibition or restriction of the keeping or cultivation of such plants; the Animal Disease and Control Act (Chapter 206) does the same for animal diseases and their control. The Sale of Stolen Cattle Prevention Act (Chapter 223) provides for the remedy of restitution of stolen cattle in the possession of a buyer and for the latter to claim the purchase price from the seller.

2. FORESTRY

The Forestry Act 1991 repealed various prior legislation on forestry and replaced the department of forests with the Papua New Guinea Forest Authority.

Under the Act, there are three types of rights that may be issued, the timber permit, the timber authority, and a license. These rights may be issued over

(a) government land as approved by the National Forest Board;
(b) State leasehold land, where the lessee consents and subject to the terms of the lease; and
(c) customary land, where an agreement has been made between the customary owners and the Papua New Guinea Forest Authority.

The timber permit, which is granted by the minister responsible for forestry matters, is the main right for large-scale forestry developments. It will be granted on the recommendation of the National Forest Board, which in turn will be advised by a Provincial Management Committee. The timber authority is to be issued by provincial ministers responsible for forestry matters. It is limited to not more than 5,000 cubic meters of timber per annum for domestic processing. A timber authority may also be issued for the removal of trees for agricultural purposes or for the harvesting of other forests. The third right, the license, will be issued by the National Forest Board for purposes ancillary to forest development projects, including transporting, selling or purchasing, marketing, processing, grading, etc., of timber.

The 1992 act was passed following revelations of corruption in the management of forestry resources by civil servants and politicians and was aimed at improving the situation. A Commission of Inquiry that investigated the industry in 1989 recommended some of the changes found in the act.

3. FISHERIES

The Fisheries Act (Chapter 214) regulates fishing in Papua New Guinea waters. The responsible minister is empowered to control fishing by persons allowed to fish and regulate the areas and species of fish. Both Papua New Guineans (other than customary fishermen) and foreigners are required to be licensed. Fishing boats can also be licensed. The minister can restrict traditional fishing areas to licensed fishing. Foreign nationals or foreign boats licensed to fish in Papua New Guinea waters may be restricted by the minister from fishing in certain waters or from catching more than certain amounts of fish.

A Tuna Resources Advisory Council is established by the Tuna Resources Management Act

(Chapter 224) as an advisory body on the tuna fishing industry. It is to advise the minister, when called upon, on the total sustainable yield of tuna, the proposed levels of tuna catch, the licensing of vessels to take tuna in the offshore seas, and other aspects of the management and development of the tuna industry.

Papua New Guinea is a signatory to the tuna fishing treaty between a number of Pacific island states and the United States. The Treaty on Fisheries Between the Government of Certain Pacific Island States and the Government of the United States of America enables certain U.S. fishing boats to fish in specified waters of the Pacific island states on payment of licensing fees and a lump sum payment for the five-year treaty period. The treaty is administered by the Forum Fisheries Agency (FFA) of the South Pacific Forum. The treaty was signed following earlier objections by the United States to the 200-mile exclusive economic zones claimed by Pacific island states, which led to the confiscation in Papua New Guinea and the Solomon Islands of two U.S. fishing vessels.

The Crocodile (Trade) Act (Chapter 213) provides for the killing and trading of crocodile skins and licensing of their export. The Whaling Act (Chapter 225) deals with the regulation of whaling and requires observance of the International Whaling Convention of 1946 and the Protocol to the Convention of 1956.

F. Natural Resources

In 1992, Parliament enacted the Mining Act 1992, replacing the obsolete legislation that had been in effect since the 1920s. Under the new law, ownership of small alluvial gold operations is restricted to Papua New Guinea citizens, and large alluvial gold developments must be at least 51 percent Papua New Guinean owned. For large developments, the new act adopts a simplified system of exploration licenses, mining leases, and "special mining leases" (the last for the large-scale, multimillion dollar developments that have been typical of Papua New Guinea's mining industry in the 1970s and 1980s). Foreign investors are required to submit development plans to the government for approval and to consult with local landowners regarding the impact of their proposals, although the national government retains the right to approve a project despite the opposition of the landowners.

The 1992 act retains the relatively low level of royalty payments—1.25 percent of the value of the minerals produced—that has characterized the Papua New Guinea industry. The government's primary income from mining comes not from royalty, but from income tax, from an excess profits tax that applies once a project has earned more than a specified rate of return, and from the government's stake as an equity investor in most large projects.

The earliest large-scale projects in Papua New Guinea, the Bougainville and Ok Tedi copper and gold mines, were developed under comprehensive contractual agreements that were approved by Parliament and given the force of law, placing them outside the scope of the Mining Act. More recent projects, and those to be developed in the future, will also be the subject of comprehensive development contracts, but these contracts will not be given the force of law.

The Mining Development Act (Chapter 197) provides for a person to apply to the Department of Minerals and Energy for a loan to finance mining operations, particularly for determining the size and value of the orebody and for development work that will facilitate ore extraction. The loan is thus limited to persons who have already discovered the existence of an orebody.

Most of the major mining ventures in the country are not covered by the antiquated general legislation that was in force before 1991, but are regulated by comprehensive contracts between the mining companies and the state. Two of these contracts have been given legislative force. These are the Bougainville Copper Agreement, approved and given legislative force by the

Mining (Bougainville Copper Agreement) Act (Chapter 196), and the Ok Tedi Agreement, approved and given legislative force by the Mining (Ok Tedi Agreement) Act (Chapter 363). The other major mining ventures—the Porgera mine and the Misima mine—were established under the Porgera Development Contract and the Misima Development Contract, respectively. Neither has been given legislative sanction.

The Mineral Resources Stabilization Fund Act (Chapter 194) has the stated purpose of ensuring that

> (a) revenue accruing to the State from the development of the mineral resources of the country is dealt with in a manner that will promote national financial stability; and (b) wide fluctuations in revenue accruing to the State from year to year as a result of changing world prices for minerals do not interfere with the orderly progress of the Government's development programme.

The Mineral Resources Stabilization Fund Board is created by the act to manage this fund. Other provisions of the act provide for the rates of contribution and payments out of the fund.

Petroleum exploration and production in the country, including its foreshore areas, is regulated by the Petroleum Act (Chapter 198). It vests in the state ownership rights over petroleum found in the country and provides for rights, permits, and licenses for exploration and development. It also provides for the protection and payment of compensation to landowners of land used for these purposes. The Petroleum (Gulf of Papua) Agreements Act (Chapter 199) approved six agreements made between the state and a number of foreign oil companies concerning the exploration for petroleum in the Gulf of Papua and for development facilities to produce commercial quantities of petroleum discovered in the agreement areas.

The Continental Shelf (Living Natural Resources) Act (Chapter 210) seeks to protect the taking of "sedentary organisms" of the continental shelf of Papua New Guinea waters. The searching or taking of such organisms must be done under license. The taking by citizens and Papua New Guinea residents of such organisms for purposes other than sale or manufacture is excepted.

The use and management of water resources is regulated by the Water Resources Act (Chapter 205). It vests in the state the right of use, flow, and control of water. The use of water and acquisition of land for the taking of water can only be done with the approval of the state through the Water Resources Board. The board is also responsible for the allocation, quality, and conservation of water. Customary rights to the use of water for domestic and recreational purposes by others is exempted from the regulatory provisions of the act.

The Cultural Development Act (Chapter 153) establishes a number of bodies and cultural groups to encourage and assist the preservation of the national and local indigenous cultures and provides for the management of a number of institutions for these purposes. The National Cultural Council is established to "formulate and implement a program for the preservation and development of all aspects of culture and arts in the country" (Section 13). Other bodies established under the act are the National Arts School, National Theatre Company, Institute of Papua New Guinea Studies, Raun Raun Theatre Company, and trustees to museums. The National Museum and Art Gallery Act (Chapter 156A) provides for the continuance, extension, and the general management of the national museums and art galleries. The National Cultural Centre Trust is created by the National Cultural Centre Trust Act (Chapter 155) to control and manage a national cultural center.

The protection from sale and destruction of objects of cultural and historical importance and the compulsory acquisition of such objects by the responsible minister are provided for under the National Cultural Property (Prevention) Act (Chapter 156). The protection and control of fauna through the establishment of sanctuaries and the declaration of other protected areas is done under the Fauna (Protection and Control) Act (Chapter 154), which prohibits the removal or destruction of or other dealings in animals from protected areas.

XIII. Persons and Entities

Because the common law age of capacity of twenty-one was reduced to eighteen by statute in England before independence, there is disagreement as to the age of contractual capacity in Papua New Guinea.

The Companies Act (Chapter 146) provides for the incorporation of public and private companies. The act closely follows the United Kingdom Companies Act 1948. In England, the 1948 act has been amended in major respects, but the Papua New Guinea Act is in force without these amendments. Once incorporated, a company may sue and be sued.

XIV. Family Law

A. Marriage

The law recognizes two types of marriages in Papua New Guinea. The first is a marriage by custom and the second is a statutory marriage under the Marriage Act (Chapter 280).

The Marriage Act provides that a customary marriage entered into by a "native" in accordance with custom in the tribe or group to which the marriage partners belong "is valid and effective for all purposes." *Native* refers to an automatic citizen. This type of marriage raises a number of legal questions, one of which is whether or not a non-native person can validly enter into a customary marriage. Another is whether there could be a valid marriage if two or more customs on marriage conflict.

The Marriage Act makes elaborate provision for the statutory marriage, laying down the formalities required for a valid marriage, including witnesses and registration. The marriageable age is eighteen years for a male person and sixteen years for a female. The act permits persons within two years of marriageable age to apply to a court for permission to marry a person of marriageable age if there are exceptional or unusual circumstances.

B. Divorce, Separation, and Annulment

Separate rules of divorce apply to the two types of marriage. A divorce of a customary marriage can take place in accordance with custom, and the Local Court is, under the Local Court Act (Chapter 41), empowered to certify such a divorce.

The Matrimonial Causes Act (Chapter 282) provides that a statutory marriage can be dissolved by the National Court. The grounds for divorce in a statutory marriage are adultery, desertion, cruelty, and separation. Divorce in a statutory marriage is barred by condonation, connivance, and collusion. If the court finds that a case for divorce is established, it grants a decree nisi followed later by a decree absolute.

C. Custody

The same legal principles for determining a custody case apply to children born to a customary marriage and to those born to a statutory marriage. The considerations the court is to take into account are stipulated under Section 4 of the Matrimonial Causes Act: (1) the welfare of the child, (2) the conduct of the parents, and (3) the wishes of each parent.

The appropriate court to hear a custody proceeding depends on the legislation under which custody proceedings are brought. First, if divorce proceedings for dissolution of a statutory marriage are brought in the National Court under the Matrimonial Causes Act, if custody is also in issue, the National Court can decide on custody. This act cannot be used to bring a custody or maintenance claim on its own. Second, custody under customary marriages and custody without petitions for divorce of a statutory marriage can be brought under the Infants Act (Chapter 278). This can be heard in all courts including the Village Courts.

D. Maintenance

Maintenance can be claimed for both the spouse and children in the National Court under the Matrimonial Causes Act, together with a divorce petition in a statutory marriage. The terms of an order in such proceedings are at the discretion of the court. In a subsisting marriage (both customary and statutory), maintenance proceedings may be brought under the Deserted Wives and Children's Act (Chapter 277). The District Court is the proper court for maintenance proceedings under a statutory marriage under this act. In relation to a customary marriage, both the Local Court and District Court have jurisdiction under the act. A complaint for maintenance can be made if a husband has deserted his wife or children or left them without making adequate provision for their support. The court, where the claim is established, can make a reasonable award.

The third law under which a maintenance claim can be made is the Child Welfare Act (Chapter 276), which provides for maintenance for a child or children born out of lawful wedlock. The mother can seek maintenance from the father for the child but not for herself. These proceedings are commonly referred to as "affiliation proceedings," as paternity may also be contested. Jurisdiction under this act is in the Local Court and special Children's Courts.

E. Adoption

A child can be adopted in two ways—by customary adoption and by an adoption order of the National Court on application. A customary adoption, which is allowed by the Adoption of Children Act (Chapter 275), must be in accordance with custom.

The conditions a court must take into account in considering an adoption under the Adoption of Children Act are the welfare and best interest of the child. A person seeking to adopt must be over twenty-one years of age and, if male, eighteen years older than the child to be adopted and sixteen years older if female. A report from the Director of Child Welfare must be available with the court before an adoption order can be made. The consent of the natural parents is necessary, but if the consent is refused, the court has power to dispense with it if the circumstances require.

XV. Personal Property

The English common law principles of personal property law apply, subject to the limitations on the application of that system of law contained in Schedule 2 of the Constitution (**see III, G (2) Common Law and Equity**).

XVI. WILLS AND SUCCESSION

Two systems of succession exist in Papua New Guinea. The first is succession in accordance with custom or customary succession, and the second is succession under the Wills, Probate and Administration Act (Chapter 291). Which of the two succession rules apply depends on whether the testator is an "aboriginal native" or a "nonaboriginal native".

A. Aboriginal Native

An *aboriginal native*, or automatic citizen, can make a will under the Wills, Probate and Administration Act or a "customary will" under the Native Administrative Regulations (T.N.G.) (Chapter 315) and the Native Regulations (Papua) (Chapter 316). If there is no will at all, customary rules of succession apply. Succession under custom is not simple, especially if the testator owns property including noncustomary land and business interest that may be foreign to customary rules of succession.[55]

If there is a will under the Wills, Probate and Administration Act, property of the testator devolves according to the terms of the will. If there is a partial intestacy, that is, the will covers only part of the property, the part covered devolves according to the terms of the will and the part not covered is distributed according to the intestacy rules of the act and not in accordance with custom.[56] Customary land cannot be disposed by a will made under the Wills, Probate and Administration Act. Under a customary will, customary land can be disposed in New Guinea only if custom permits, as provided in the Native Administration Regulations (T.N.G.), but not in Papua, as this is expressly prohibited by the Native Regulations (Papua).

B. Nonaboriginal Native

A *nonaboriginal native*, anyone other than an automatic citizen, can make a will only under the Wills, Probate and Administration Act. If the person fails to make a will, there is an intestacy, and the intestacy rules apply under Section 81 of the act. In the case of a partial intestacy, the property covered by the will devolves in accordance with the terms of the will, and the rest are distributed applying the intestacy rules of the act.

A person over the age of twenty-one can make a will under the Wills, Probate and Administration Act. For a will to be valid, the formalities prescribed in the act—the execution of the will in the correct place and its attestation by two witnesses or by an authorized witness— must be complied with. However, failure to observe the formalities is not fatal, as Section 35 provides that a will is not invalid solely by reason of "any defect or want of formality" or "any failure to comply with [the] Act or any other law." This provision has been used to give effect to a number of wills that were not made following the stipulated formalities.[57] Wills made by soldiers, who may not be of the required age, do not require compliance with the formalities if the will is made while the soldier is in active service.

XVII. CONTRACTS

The English common law principles of contract law apply in Papua New Guinea. Provisions for specific types of contracts are made in a number of statutes. Examples are the Employment Act (Chapter 373), stipulating minimum terms of employment contracts; the Hire Purchase Act (Chapter 252) and the Goods Act (Chapter 251), providing for implied terms in hire purchase and sale of goods contracts respectively; the Insurance Act (Chapter 255) on insurance policies; and the Partnership Act (Chapter 148) concerning partnership agreements.

A number of contract cases have been decided by the courts. For the most part, they apply the common law and equity principles of England, although in a few cases the courts have held the English rule inapplicable to the circumstances of Papua New Guinea.[58] In deciding contract cases, the courts have not considered the possible applicability of customary law.

The power of the state to contract is conferred by the Constitution, and the Government Contracts Act (Chapter 34) further provides for the authority and extent of Cabinet Ministers to enter into contracts on behalf of the state. There is no statute providing for contractual capacity.

In 1977, the Law Reform Commission prepared and submitted to the Cabinet the Fairness of Transactions Bill, which proposed major changes to the common law principles of contract law to bring it more into line with customary notions of fairness and reciprocity in economic relations. However, this bill has not yet been enacted.

XVIII. Commercial Law

The English common law and equity rules largely apply in the area of commercial law. A number of statutes make provisions on particular subjects. On agency, for example, the Agents for Natives Regulations (T.N.G.) (Chapter 298) provide for persons to be licensed to act as agents for a "native" or automatic citizen in employment matters.

Because of the complex provisions of the Companies Act and the different regulatory compliance requirements under it, Parliament has enacted a number of other laws to allow Papua New Guineans and customary groups to be involved in the business sector.

The Land Groups Incorporation Act (Chapter 147) provides for customary landowning groups to be accorded corporate status to carry on business. The purpose of the act in particular is

> to encourage—(a) a greater participation by local people in the national economy by the use of the land; and (b) better use of such land; and (c) greater certainty of title; and (d) the better and more effectual settlement of certain disputes, by—(e) the legal recognition of the corporate status of certain customary and similar groups, and the conferring on them, as corporations, of power to acquire, hold, dispose of and manage land, and of ancillary powers; and (f) the encouragement of the self-resolution of disputes within such groups.

The Business Groups Incorporation Act (Chapter 144) allows other customary groups (not necessarily landowning groups) to be incorporated for business and other economic purposes and provides for their control and regulation. Once it is registered, the business group has the status of a corporation, has perpetual succession, and can sue and be sued.

The Business Names Act (Chapter 145) requires persons carrying on any type of business to register the business name. A failure to register the name carries criminal penalties. The Partnership Act (Chapter 148), again based on English legislation, regulates partnerships.

Provisions of the Insolvency Act (Chapter 253) apply to persons or entities other than companies incorporated under the Companies Act (Chapter 146) for which provision for liquidation is made under that act. It defines acts of insolvency and provides for petitioners and petitions for insolvency, adjudication of petitions by the National Court, election or appointment of trustees and the devolution of insolvents' property, the administration of such property by trustees, and the discharge of an insolvent.

Although no general legislation exists on consumer protection, there are a number of specific legislative provisions, for instance, on minimum standards of food quality and on regulation of prices. A provision under the Hire Purchase Act (Chapter 252) allows the courts to reopen unconscionable contracts. Some implied terms are made part of sales contracts under the Goods Act (Chapter 251), unless specifically excluded by the parties, and similar implied terms under the Hire Purchase Act cannot be excluded. There is no general legislation regulating unfair business practices.

XIX. Torts

The principles of law of tort in Papua New Guinea are the common law principles adopted as part of the underlying law, subject to the qualifications of Schedule 2.2 of the Constitution. Custom may also become relevant in particular instances, although the courts have generally applied English common law principles, turning to custom only when measuring the extent of damages.

A number of statutes make provision for specific subjects. The main statute applying to torts is the Wrongs (Miscellaneous Provisions) Act (Chapter 297), which contains provisions on the following tort issues:

1. The state is subject to all liabilities in tort as if it were a private person. The state can equally enforce an indemnity or contribution as a private person. The state is therefore responsible for liability in respect of motor vehicles and aircraft owned by the state or an instrumentality of the state. This liability is, however, limited to K30,000.
2. A husband and wife can sue one another as if they were not married.
3. In an action of seduction, the plaintiff (a parent or person in loco parentis) need not prove loss of service.
4. If a death occurs as a result of a wrongful act, neglect, or default of the defendant, the spouse, children, or brother, sister, uncle, aunt, or the issue of the deceased can claim damages from the defendant.
5. A plaintiff is entitled to claim damages for mental or nervous shock.
6. If there are joint tort-feasors, the plaintiff can bring action claiming damages severally or jointly. In the former case, the plaintiff can sue the other joint tort-feasor(s) separately, and in the latter case, the defendant is entitled to claim contribution from the other joint tort-feasor(s).
7. In cases of contributory negligence, the act provides that a plaintiff's claim is not defeated for that reason but damages recoverable are to be apportioned according to the share of responsibility for the damage.
8. If injury is caused by a flying aircraft either in trespass or nuisance or by falling articles or objects from it, the aircraft owners are liable without proof of intention or negligence.
9. If damage is done to a harbor or harbor works by a vessel, the owner of the vessel is liable. If the damage is caused by the willful act or negligence of the master, the master is jointly and severally liable.
10. The act provides for occupiers' liabilities, whereby an occupier of premises or landlord owes the common law duty of care to all visitors—which duty can be modified or excluded by agreement. This duty of care is to take reasonable steps to make the premises safe for the purpose of the visit.

11. Apart from a contractual obligation making a landlord liable, an action for damages for damage caused by accidental fire does not lie against a person in whose building or land the fire accidentally began.

The other relevant statutes are the Motor Vehicles (Third Party Insurance) Act (Chapter 295), making a statutory trust liable for injury or death caused by motor vehicles; the Civil Aviation (Aircraft Operators Liability) Act (Chapter 292), making private operators liable as are the state and state instrumentalities under the Wrongs (Miscellaneous Provisions) Act (Chapter 297); the Defamation Act (Chapter 293), providing criminal penalties as well as tortious liability for the publication of defamatory matters; the Sale of Cattle Prevention Act (Chapter 223), creating tortious liability for theft of cattle; and the Workers Compensation Act (Chapter 179), providing for compensation to dependents for injuries suffered by an employee arising out of or in the course of employment. The latter act establishes a workers' compensation commission to administer the act and workers' compensation tribunals to hear claims for injuries sustained, with powers to make awards. The Act also stipulates the amount of money payable as compensation for different types of injuries and for death.

XX. LABOR LAW

A number of legislative enactments regulate labor matters. The first is the Employment Act (Chapter 373), which includes the following provisions for contracts of employment and minimum conditions of employment:

1. The employment of casual workers is permitted under oral contracts that are to be reduced to writing by the employer. If not reduced to writing, the employee's version of the terms is conclusive.
2. Under certain circumstances, a contract can be terminated and the employer must meet certain minimum obligations.
3. When the contract expires or is terminated for other reasons outlined by the act, the act provides for repatriation of an employee and dependents by the employer.
4. Minimum conditions of employment cover areas such as maximum daily working hours (fixed at 12 hours with at least 50 minutes of break), overtime, minimum recreation, sick and other leave entitlements, payment and protection of wages, housing, and special restrictions and conditions applying to employment of females and young persons under the age of sixteen.
5. Certain forms of recruitment and licensing of employment agents are prohibited.

The second law is the Employment of Non-citizens Act (Chapter 374). This act provides machinery for the employment of noncitizens, including the requirement for work permit, government approval for recruitment, registration, and termination of employment.

The other statute in this area relates to industrial organizations and industrial relations. The statutes applying to the private sector are the Industrial Organisations Act (Chapter 173), Industrial Relations Act (Chapter 174), and Bureau of Industrial Organisations Act (Chapter 171). The statutes applying to the public sector are the Public Services Conciliation Act (Chapter 69) and Teaching Services Conciliation and Arbitration Act (Chapter 72).

The Industrial Organisations Act deals with the creation of registered industrial organizations and their officials, rights, and duties. This act also confers legal capacity on registered industrial organizations and protects them from criminal and civil prosecution of acts such as staging a stop-work action or going on strike. It allows for both employers and employees to form their respective organizations, which are to be registered in order to be recognized by industrial tribunals, especially in tribunal hearings relating to labor disputes.

The act gives registered industrial organizations the right to take industrial action for its members. The protections conferred on registered industrial organizations against criminal and civil liability are not available to organizations not registered under the act. It makes it an offense to act on behalf of an unregistered industrial organization except to register it, dissolve it, or bring legal proceedings.

The act is administered by an industrial registrar whose functions are to ensure the registration of industrial organizations, general enforcement of the act by inspectors, and compliance by registered organizations with the provisions of the act.

The Industrial Relations Act aims to encourage good industrial relations and free negotiations regarding conditions of employment between employer and employees. The act provides an orderly method of determining such conditions to prevent or settle industrial disputes by informal means. To this end, the act creates a number of authorities. The first are the industrial councils, which can be formed by employers and their registered organizations to discuss industrial matters under a chairman. Their objective is to prevent disputes from arising and, if they do arise, to negotiate and promote their peaceful settlement. If the council agrees to conditions of employment, such agreement can be registered as awards.

The second authority is the board of inquiry, appointed by the government to look into economic and industrial disputes. The board then submits a report to the Minister for Labor and Employment. It is an advisory body to the government.

The third body, the Minimum Wages Board, determines broad policy matters such as minimum rates of pay; allowable deductions for food and accommodation; deferred wages, allowances, and penalties; overtime rates; and hours of work and leave. Only the government can refer a matter for the board's consideration, although this would normally be as a result of a dispute. The board's determinations are filed with the industrial registrar and take effect when published in the *National Gazette*.

Instead of referring a dispute to the Minimum Wages Board, the government may appoint an arbitration tribunal. Such a tribunal is appointed ad hoc to deal with a specific dispute promptly and make an award.

The Bureau of Industrial Organisations Act establishes a bureau by that name separate from the government and funded by both the government and the private sector. It is an advisory body to advise employer or employee groups on forming industrial organizations and in assisting such organizations in their administration.

The Public Service Conciliation and Arbitration Act provides similar mechanisms to those under the Industrial Relations Act for the management and resolutions of industrial relations differences in the public service, with specific emphasis on conciliation and arbitration. Three authorities are created to carry out these functions—the Public Services Conciliation and Arbitration Tribunal, the registrar of that tribunal, and a board of inquiry.

The Teaching Services Conciliation and Arbitration Act deals with claims for changed conditions of employment of teachers employed in the teaching service. The general procedure on making, determining, and enforcing teachers' claims is done by the Teaching Services Conciliation and Arbitration Tribunal, a tribunal set up to hear teachers' claims separate from the Public Services Conciliation and Arbitration Tribunal.

XXI. Industrial and Intellectual Property Rights

There is no patent law. Section 123 of the Australian Patent Act of 1903–1973, which is adopted by Schedule 2.6 and Schedule 5 of the Constitution, states that there is no infringement of a patent if the patented invention is on board a foreign vessel that comes within the territorial waters. This is an odd provision as there is no patent law in the country.

There is a Trade Marks Act (Chapter 385), which provides for the registration of trademarks.

In the intellectual property law area, the law of passing off and breach of confidence, forming part of the common law, may exist in Papua New Guinea by virtue of the adoption of the common law as part of the underlying law of the country. There is no copyright legislation in force. A Copyright Act was passed in 1978, but it has not been brought into force, because the machinery for the depositing of materials for copyright protection has not been set up. It is unlikely that this legislation will be brought into force; however, there may be a copyright at common law.

XXII. Legal Education and Profession

The need for the training of lawyers for Papua New Guinea was debated in the early 1960s. The Law Council of Australia in 1963 recommended the establishment of a law school as part of a university in the Territory of Papua New Guinea. It also asked for the training of Papua New Guinean lawyers in the meantime in Australian universities. The Commission on Higher Education (the Currie commission) accepted this recommendation, and a law faculty was founded in 1968 with the establishment of the University of Papua New Guinea.

The duration of the degree course was initially five years after a preliminary year course, later reduced to four years. The law faculty graduated its first five Papua New Guineans in 1972. By 1989, over 470 law graduates had been produced by the law faculty, of whom 83 percent are Papua New Guinean.

Today's graduates attend a one year practical training program at the Legal Training Institute. On completion, they receive provisional admission, which qualifies them to hold a restricted practicing certificate, which is issued by the Papua New Guinea Law Society to those who are employed by a law firm or other organization.

Training of magistrates started at the Administrative College in 1966 and was later transferred to the University of Papua New Guinea. The university now offers a Diploma in Magisterial Studies, a two year program. Graduates are qualified to preside in Local Courts, beginning as Grade I magistrates and working their way up to Grade V. Magistrates with diplomas and practical experience can enroll for the L.L.B. degree program. It is now possible for a magistrate with a law degree and practical experience to be promoted to the position of judge of the National Court.

Legal practice was loosely regulated under the old Lawyers Act (Chapter 91). Under the revised Lawyers Act 1976, a system of registration and elaborate requirements for trust accounts has been set up. In order to practice in Papua New Guinea, a person must have either a restricted or an unrestricted practicing certificate. A restricted practicing certificate is issued to lawyers who are not practicing on their own account or in partnership with another lawyer and who do not hold trust monies. Hence, lawyers employed by law firms, the government, or other bodies hold only a restricted practicing certificate. Lawyers practicing on their own account or in partnership with another lawyer or other lawyers are required to hold unrestricted practicing certificates. This certificate will be issued only to those with considerable experience in practice and an approved professional indemnity insurance policy. The Papua New Guinea Law Society that issues these certificates must also be satisfied that the applicant for the certificates is a fit and proper person.

Papua New Guinea's Constitution, organic laws, and statutes are collected in the multivolume *Law of Papua New Guinea*, edited by the First Legislative Counsel and published by the Government Printer in Port Moresby. Selected judgments of the National Court and the Supreme Court are printed in the annual volumes of the *Papua New Guinea Law Reports* (PNGLR), published by the Law Book Company in Sydney, Australia. Unpublished judgments are available from the registrar of the courts in Port Moresby. A few cases are published in *South Pacific Law Reports*.

XXIII. Research Guide

Bayne, P., and J. Zorn, eds. *Foreign Investment, International Law and National Development.* Sydney: Butterworth's, 1975.

———. *Lo Bilong ol Manmeri: Crime, Compensation and Village Courts.* Port Moresby, University of Papua New Guinea, 1975.

Brown, B., ed. *Fashion of Law in New Guinea.* Sydney: Law Book Co., 1969.

Brunton, B., and D. Colquhoun-Kerr. *The Annotated Constitution of Papua New Guinea.* Port Moresby: University of Papua New Guinea Press, 1984.

Chalmers, D., and A. Paliwala. *An Introduction to the Law in Papua New Guinea*, 2d ed. Sydney: Law Book Co., 1984.

Chalmers, D., and D. Weisbrot. *Criminal Law and Practice in Papua New Guinea.* Sydney: Law Book Co., 1980.

DeVere, R., D. Colquhuon-Kerr, and J. Kaburise, eds. *Essays on the Constitution of Papua New Guinea.* Port Moresby: Government Printing Office, 1985.

Fitzpatrick, P. *Law and State in Papua New Guinea.* London: Academic Press, 1980.

Goldring, J. *The Constitution of Papua New Guinea.* Sydney: Law Book Co., 1978.

Griffin, J. *Criminal Procedure in Papua New Guinea.* Sydney: Law Book Co., 1977.

Hogbin, I., and P. Lawrence. *Studies in New Guinea Land Tenure.* Sydney: Sydney University Press, 1963.

James, R. *Land Law and Policy in Papua New Guinea.* Port Moresby: Law Reform Commission of Papua New Guinea, 1985.

Law Reform Commission of Papua New Guinea. "Consumer Protection." Working Paper No. 17, 1980.

———. "Customary Compensation," Report No. 11, 1980.

———. "Customary Marriage and Divorce in Selected Areas of Papua New Guinea." Occasional Paper No. 5, 1977.

———. "Fairness of Transactions." Report No. 6, 1977.

———. "Family Law." Working Paper No. 9, 1978.

———. "Forms and Functions of Business in Papua New Guinea." Occasional Paper No. 13, 1980.

———. "The Law of Succession." Working Paper No. 12, 1978.

Melanesian Law Journal. Vols. 1–18. Port Moresby: University of Papua New Guinea Law Faculty, 1971–present.

Ottley, B., and J. G. Zorn. "Code or Custom: Criminal Law in a New Nation." 31 *American J. of Comparative Law* 251 (1983).

O'Regan, R. *The Common Law in Papua New Guinea.* Sydney: Law Book Co., 1971.

Papua New Guinea Constitutional Planning Committee. Final Report. Port Moresby, 1974.

Roebuck, D., D. Srivastava, and J. Nonggorr. *The Context of Contract in Papua New Guinea.* Port Moresby: University of Papua New Guinea Press, 1984.

Sack, P. *Land Between Two Laws.* Canberra: Australian National University Press, 1973.

Scaglion, R., ed. *Customary Law in Papua New Guinea.* Port Moresby: Law Reform Commission of Papua New Guinea, 1982.

———. *Homicide Compensation in Papua New Guinea.* Port Moresby: Law Reform Commission of Papua New Guinea, 1981.

Strathern, M. "Official and Unofficial Courts." Canberra: Australian National University, *New Guinea Research Bull.* No. 47, 1971.

Weisbrot, D., A. Paliwala, and A. Sawyer. *Law and Social Change in Papua New Guinea.* Sydney: Butterworth's, 1982.

Young, L., ed. *Constitutional Development in Papua and New Guinea.* Port Moresby: University of Papua New Guinea, 1971.

Zorn, J. G. "Common Law Jurisprudence and Customary Law," in R. W. James, ed. *The Supreme Court and the Underlying Law.* Port Moresby: University of Papua New Guinea Press, 1991.

———. "Customary Law in the Papua New Guinea Village Courts," 2 *Contemporary Pacific* 279 (1990).

———. "Graun bilong Mipela: Local Courts and the Changing Customary Law of Papua New Guinea," 15(2) *Pacific Studies* (forthcoming, June 1992).

———. "Making Law in Papua New Guinea: the Influence of Customary Law on the Common Law," 4(4) *Pacific Studies* (1991).

9. Pitcairn Island

DHIRENDRA K. SRIVASTAVA

I. DATELINE

1767 Pitcairn Island visited by Captain Carteret of H.M.S. *Swallow*.
1790 Nine mutineers from British ship *Bounty* and nineteen Tahitians establish a settlement on Pitcairn Island.
1829 Pitcairn comes under authority of British Royal Navy.
1829 Pitcairn Island *Register*, main source of early history, begins publication.
1832 Joshua Hill seizes power and proclaims Pitcairn a Commonwealth, with himself as Governor or President.
1838 Regime of Joshua Hill ends. British Navy captain Elliott promulgates a simple Constitution and Code of Laws, providing for annual election of a Magistrate and formally acknowledging status of Pitcairn Island as British possession.
1856 The entire community leaves Pitcairn Island for Norfolk Island.
1859 Sixteen Pitcairners return to Pitcairn Island.
1863 Twenty-seven more Pitcairners return.
1864 Constitution and laws of 1838 are revived.
1893 Existing system of government replaced by new Constitution providing for parliamentary government. New set of laws introduced. Provision made for appointment of judges and for right of appeal from Island Court to Island Parliament.
1898 Pacific Order-in-Council 1893 applied to Pitcairn Island.
1904 Simplified Constitution adopted, providing for post of Chief Magistrate, establishment of two committees to take charge of internal and external affairs, and Council of Four.
1940 New code known as Pitcairn Island Regulations introduced.
1952 Pitcairn Order-in-Council transfers responsibility for administration of islands from Western Pacific High Commission to Governor of Fiji. Islands become a British colony.
1959 Jurisdiction of the High Commissioner's Court to hear island cases abolished and given to the Supreme Court of Fiji.
1970 On Fiji's independence, United Kingdom's High Commissioner to New Zealand appointed Governor of Pitcairn.

II. HISTORICAL, CULTURAL, AND ECONOMIC SURVEY

Pitcairn Island, one of the smallest and most remote of the world's inhabited islands, is the last remaining British colony in the Pacific. Approximately 2 miles long and 1 mile across, the island lies halfway between New Zealand and the Americas (latitude 25 degrees, 4 minutes south and longitude 130 degrees, 16 minutes west). The total number of the islanders residing in Pitcairn is around fifty-five, but many more live in other countries.

A. Political and Legal History

Pitcairn Island was visited in 1767 by Captain Carteret of H.M.S. *Swallow*. Numerous relics of Polynesian civilization were found, but the island was not then inhabited.

In 1790, the nine H.M.S. *Bounty* mutineers, along with six Tahitian men, twelve women, and a baby girl, landed on Pitcairn Island in search of an idyllic life-style. The descendants of those men and women inhabit the island today. The island was almost completely cut off from the rest of the world until 1808, when the presence of a community on the island was discovered by Captain Folger of the United States.

In 1832, Joshua Hill, claiming to represent the British government, seized power, proclaimed himself President of the Commonwealth of Pitcairn, and imposed arbitrary imprisonment and severe punishments. Hill's commonwealth was short-lived. He was removed in 1838, when Pitcairn Island received its first Constitution, drawn by British Navy captain Elliott of H.M.S. *Fly*. The reception of the Constitution from a British captain is regarded by the islanders as the formal incorporation of Pitcairn Island into the British empire.

Ten laws were enacted with the Constitution. They covered such subjects as the annual election and jurisdiction of the Magistrate; court procedure; control of dogs; punishment for the killing of cats; compensation for damage done by stray pigs; cultivation of land; cutting of timber; inspection of landmarks; prohibition of the importation, sale, or consumption of alcoholic liquor; and disallowing women from boarding any foreign vessel without the permission of the Magistrate. Some of the laws were innovative. Not only male but female suffrage was recognized in the election of the Magistrate. Compulsory education for children was introduced.

By 1850, the number of islanders exceeded 150. Food and water were becoming scarce. It was becoming clear that the island could not accommodate any further increases in population. The islanders were instructed by the British government to move to Norfolk Island. They did so in 1856, but by 1864, 43 of the islanders had returned to Pitcairn. The majority, however, remained on Norfolk, where their descendants still constitute a large proportion of the population.

In 1864, the 1838 Constitution and laws were revived. In 1893, that system of government was replaced by a parliamentary system, under a new Constitution. A Parliament of seven elected members was created, with authority to appoint from their number a President, Vice President, two judges, and a secretary. The duties of the Parliament included making laws, executing decisions of the Magistrate's Court, and hearing appeals from the court's decisions.

In 1898, the Pacific Order-in-Council 1893 was applied to Pitcairn, bringing the island under the administrative control of the High Commissioner for the Western Pacific in Fiji. Three other islands, Henderson, Oeno, and Ducie, which lie 105 miles east northeast, 75 miles north, and 293 miles west, respectively, were made dependencies of Pitcairn in 1902. These three islands are still uninhabited.

In 1904, the system of parliamentary government was abolished, and a simplified Constitution was adopted, with a Chief Magistrate as the principal official authority of the island. The Constitution established two committees to take charge of internal and external (marine) affairs. Both committees had power to make regulations. The Constitution also created a council, comprising the chairs of the committees and two assessors. The Chief Magistrate was given authority to hear minor cases alone, but cases involving a penalty of £5 or more were to be heard by the Magistrate with two annually elected assessors.

Most of the laws enacted in 1893, however, were continued in force and governed the islanders until 1940, when those laws were substantially amended by the introduction of a new code known as the Pitcairn Island Regulations. In 1953, the Pacific Order-in-Council 1893 ceased to have effect, and the Governor of Fiji was made the Governor of the Islands of Pitcairn, Henderson, Ducie, and Oeno. Pitcairn and its dependencies became a separate British colony. The Local Government Ordinance 1964 and the Justice Ordinance 1966 considerably restructured the system of law and government of Pitcairn Island (see **IV Constitutional System**). On Fiji's independence in 1970, the United Kingdom High Commissioner to New Zealand was appointed Governor of Pitcairn Island, and the administrative office was moved from Suva to Auckland. In 1971, the *Revised Edition of the Laws*, which consolidated in one volume the then existing laws, was published. A similar revision was published in 1985.

B. Economy

Subsistence farming, trade with visiting ships, sale of stamps, interest earned on money invested for the Pitcairners from past surpluses, and development grants from the British government under the Colonial Welfare Act 1959 support the island. New Zealand also provides various kinds of financial assistance.

The soil of Pitcairn Island is fertile, yielding fruits and vegetables in abundance. Pitcairn produces one of the best varieties of oranges. Export of oranges has been a source of income, and fruits and vegetables produced on the island are sold to visiting ships. Virtually every household makes souvenir handicrafts. Fish are plentiful.

Not many items are bought from the outside world; the main imports are flour, canned and dried goods, sugar, and fuel. Income from the sale of stamps and from interest on investments are the largest sources of revenue.

C. Culture

Today, most of the residents of Pitcairn can still trace their descent to the original 1790 settlers. Despite its isolation, Pitcairn Island is a modern place. The islanders live in reasonably good houses with electricity and telephones. Every child goes to school. The islanders have their own newspaper, the *Island Miscellany*.

The islanders' spoken language is a mixture of English and Tahitian. Seventh-Day Adventist John I. Tay, converted almost all islanders to his faith in the late 1880's. Even today, most islanders are Seventh-Day Adventists. The islanders still follow some of their old traditions. Their lives are regulated by the church bells, which are used to call people for prayer and public work, as well as to announce the arrival of ships.

III. Sources of Law

The laws applicable to Pitcairn consist of the following:

1. the Pitcairn Order 1970 and the Pitcairn Royal Instructions 1970;
2. ordinances proclaimed by the Governor;
3. subsidiary legislation enacted by the Island Council;
4. the common law and rules of equity and statutes of general application in force in England on January 1, 1983, so far as the local circumstances and the limits of local jurisdiction permit (Judicature Ordinance Chapter 2, Section 14);
5. rules and regulations made under ordinances proclaimed by the governor; and
6. custom.

The Revised Laws of Pitcairn, Henderson, Ducie and Oeno Islands 1985 include all legislation in force on December 31, 1984. Copies of the Revised Laws can be obtained from the office of the British High Commission in Auckland, New Zealand.

IV. Constitutional System

A. Legal Status

Pitcairn is a British colony and, for the purposes of the British Settlement Acts 1887 and 1945, a British settlement. The Pitcairn Order 1970, containing the main constitutional provisions, was made by virtue of the powers conferred under those acts.

B. Residency and Landing

The Landing and Residence Ordinance regulates the landing and residence of persons on the island. In most cases, a person who lands on the island without a license or fails to leave at the earliest opportunity after revocation or expiration of the license is guilty of an offense. The ordinance does not apply to the following:

1. public officers;
2. British Dependent Territories citizens;
3. British citizens, subjects or protected persons, within the meaning of the British Nationality Act 1981, who have ordinarily resided in Pitcairn Island for seven years or more;
4. persons or class of persons exempted by order of the governor;
5. persons who, before the commencement of the British Nationality Act 1981, were exempted from the provisions of the Landing and Residence Ordinance; and
6. the spouses or children of persons exempted as public officers.

The power to grant a license to reside in Pitcairn or to extend, renew or revoke a license already granted vests in the Governor, who may act with absolute discretion in such matters. The Island Magistrate (subject to directions of the Governor) has authority to grant a permit to any officer, member of the crew, or passenger of any vessel or aircraft visiting the island.

C. Government

The Pitcairn Order 1970 sets out the structure of government.

1. HEAD OF THE STATE

Because Pitcairn Island is British colony, the Queen is Head of State. But a Governor appointed by Her Majesty under the Pitcairn Order 1970 is directly responsible for the administration of the island. The Governor is normally the same person appointed British High Commissioner to New Zealand.

2. EXECUTIVE

Under the Pitcairn Order, the Governor may constitute courts for the island, make regulations for the proceedings in such courts and the administration of justice, and appoint all officers the Governor considers necessary. The Governor may also dismiss or suspend officers so appointed or take other disciplinary actions that may seem desirable. The Governor may, in Her Majesty's name and on Her Majesty's behalf, grant a pardon to any person convicted of any offense or grant a respite (either indefinite or for a specified period) of the execution of any punishment or may substitute a less severe form of punishment, penalty, or forfeiture.

While the Governor represents Her Majesty and holds the legislative and executive powers of the island, the most important officer in day-to-day terms is the Island Magistrate, who is the chief executive officer of the island, discharging duties assigned by the Governor. In addition, the Island Magistrate is also president of the Island Council, which wields considerable executive and legislative power under the Local Government Ordinance (Chapter 4). Subject to the directions of the Governor, the Island Council is responsible for the enforcement of ordinances and regulations. The structure of the council, under the Local Government Ordinance, is aimed at keeping the management of internal affairs in the hands of the islanders themselves. Apart from the Island Magistrate, the council consists of the chair of the Internal Affairs Committee, two elected councillors, the Island Secretary (an ex officio member), three nominated members (one appointed by the Governor and two by the elected members), and two nonvoting or advisory members (one appointed by the Governor and one by the council). The Island Magistrate, the chair of the Internal Affairs Committee and two councillors, collectively described as the Island Officers, are elected (see IV, C (3) Legislature).

The Local Government Ordinance also provides for the establishment of an Internal Affairs Committee to carry out the orders of the council. The committee is required to meet the first week of every month. Minutes of the proceedings and a report on the work done during the preceding month must be recorded by the Island Secretary.

3. LEGISLATURE

Under the Pitcairn Order 1970, the Governor is empowered to make laws for the peace, order, and good government of the island. Any law made by the Governor may, however, be disallowed by Her Majesty. Further, the Pitcairn Royal Instructions 1970 provide that certain laws made by the Governor require the prior approval of Her Majesty through a Secretary of State.

The Island Council has authority to make, amend, or revoke regulations for the good administration of the island; the maintenance of peace, order, and public safety, and the social and economic betterment of the islanders. These include regulations relating to public health and keeping the islands clean; town and country planning; use and control of public property; public works and other public activities; plant and animal quarantine; care and control of animals and wildlife; care of children and aged persons; conservation of land, soil, and food supplies; fishing and fishing rights; prisons; registration, use, care, and demarcation of land; control of explosives and firearms; trading by and between islanders and during visits to ships; and the appointment, powers, and duties of such officers, boards, and committees as the council considers necessary.

Under the Local Government Regulations made by the Island Council, no person may erect any building or add to or alter any existing building without the council's permission. No plants or animals can be imported into or exported from Pitcairn Island without a permit from the council. No goats can be kept on Pitcairn Island, except where the council may from time to time appoint. The council's approval is required for traveling by boat between Pitcairn and other islands and for connection to any public telephone or electricity.

Copies of all regulations made by the Island Council must be sent to the Governor, who may alter, vary, or revoke any regulation. In practice, however, the Island Council rarely exercises its legislative functions without consulting the Governor beforehand.

The Local Government Ordinance governs the election of Island Officers. A person over the age of twenty-one and whose name appears in the register of voters is eligible for election as Island Magistrate, chair of the Internal Committee, or councillor. In addition, a candidate for any elected office must be a native-born inhabitant or must have resided in Pitcairn Island for twenty-one years if standing for Island Magistrate or chair of the Internal Committee, or five years if standing for councillor. Until 1986, only males were eligible for election as Island Magistrate or chair of the Internal Committee. That discrimination was removed by Ordinance No. 1, 1986. A person of unsound mind may not hold any public office while unable to perform the duties of such office due to mental incapacity.

Every native-born inhabitant of Pitcairn and every person who has resided on Pitcairn for a period of three years or more is qualified to vote, provided he or she has attained age eighteen. The electoral roll is prepared by the Island Secretary in October each year; elections are held annually on a day between the first and fifteenth days of December. The Island Magistrate is elected in every third year on the election day appointed for that year.

4. JUDICIARY

At present, the courts exercising jurisdiction in relation to matters arising in Pitcairn are the Island Court and the Lands and Estates Court. The Governor may, however, appoint a judge to constitute a Supreme Court and a magistrate to conduct a Subordinate Court.

a. Island Court

The Justice Ordinance sets out the composition, jurisdiction, and powers of the Island Court The Island Court, a court of record, consists of the Island Magistrate and two assessors. The court sits at times and days as determined by resolution of the Island Council. The Island Magistrate may sit without assessors in minor civil and criminal cases where the penalty or amount of dispute does not exceed NZ$50, but in more serious matters the Island Magistrate must sit with assessors. In criminal cases, however, the penalty is decided by the Island Magistrate alone.

The civil jurisdiction of the Island Court is prescribed by the Justice Ordinance and extends to all suits between islanders where the amount in dispute does not exceed NZ$1,000. With the consent of all parties, the limit of jurisdiction may be raised to NZ$2,000.

The Island Court also has power to determine questions relating to guardianship, custody, and maintenance, but it cannot entertain any suit where the title to office, the ownership of land, or the legitimacy of any person is in question. Also the court cannot entertain any action for malicious prosecution, libel, slander, seduction, or breach of promise to marry.

The criminal jurisdiction of the court, as set out in the Justice Ordinance, covers all offenses committed within the island or in its territorial waters. But the maximum punishment that the court can impose is a fine of NZ$250 and imprisonment for not more than 100 days. Under the Justice Ordinance, Section 6, the Governor may by order increase the jurisdiction of the Island Court in any particular civil or criminal case.

The Island Court has also been given power to investigate death resulting from unnatural causes and causes of any fire that has damaged or destroyed property.

b. Land and Estates Court

The Lands and Estates Court was established by the Lands and Administration of Estates Ordinance. The court consists of the Island Magistrate as president and four other members appointed by the Island Council. Under the ordinance, the duties and functions of the court are to inquire and record the ownership and boundaries of lands on Pitcairn Island, to decide the manner in which land shall devolve, to hear and determine disputes about ownership of land, and to deal with applications for the administration of estates of deceased persons (**see XII, I Title to Land**).

c. Supreme Court and Subordinate Court

The Judicature Ordinance provides for the establishment of two other courts, a Supreme Court and a Subordinate Court. These courts may be created by the Governor as the need arises, but they do not currently operate.

The Supreme Court is to consist of a judge or judges appointed from time to time by the Governor. The jurisdiction of the Supreme Court is similar to the jurisdiction vested in Her Majesty's High Court of Justice in England or in any judge of that court. The Marriage Ordinance confers jurisdiction on the Supreme Court to decide all disputes relating to solemnification, dissolution, and annulment of any marriage.

The Subordinate Court is to exercise both criminal and civil jurisdiction. In criminal matters, the Judicature Ordinance confers on the court powers that are for the time being vested in Magistrates' Courts of England and, in civil matters, the jurisdiction and powers that are for the time being vested in Country Courts in England. Further jurisdiction and powers may be vested in the Subordinate Court by the Governor.

V. Administrative Organization and Law

Although the Governor is ultimately responsible for the administration of Pitcairn Island, the chief executive officer is the elected Island Magistrate, who is also president of the Island Council. The Island Magistrate discharges duties as assigned by the Governor. The Governor also appoints several public officers, including the Island Secretary, postmaster, radio officer, police officer, forester, and education officer.

VI. International Obligations

Since Pitcairn Island is a colony of England, it has no separate right to engage in international relations. Not all international conventions ratified by England, however, apply to Pitcairn. The Prevention of Collision at Sea Ordinance applies the International Regulations for Preventing Collisions at Sea 1972 (as amended by a resolution of the Inter-Governmental Maritime Consultative Organization of November 19, 1981), and the Trade Unions and Trade Disputes Ordinance seeks to implement the provisions of the International Labour Convention. The Post Office Ordinance declares that overseas mail is subject to any conventions in force for the time being.

VII. Revenue Law

There is no income tax. Until 1968, an annual license fee for the possession of firearms was Pitcairn's only tax. Now, a fee of fifty NZ cents a year is payable under the Local Government Regulations for each license to possess or to use any firearms. A license fee of fifty NZ cents is also charged by the police officer for issuing a driving license. The sale of postage stamps, however, is the single largest source of income and it is used to pay local officials for their services.

VIII. Investment Law

A. Foreign Investment

Foreigners are not encouraged to make investments in Pitcairn Island. Suggestions to build a tourist resort and facilities for passing ships and airplanes have not received any support from the island government.

B. Imports and Exports

The Local Government Regulations (Chapter 4) forbid importing plants or animals without a permit from the council. In some cases, permits must not be granted by the council without the prior approval of the Governor. Any person breaching these provisions is liable to a fine of NZ$100 or forty days' imprisonment.

IX. Welfare Law

Despite its limited resources, the government of Pitcairn Island pays social security benefits to eligible residents. The Social Welfare Benefits Ordinance (Chapter 11) provides for payment of pensions and widow and child benefits. Persons qualify for pensions when they are over sixty-five, if they have either resided on Pitcairn for at least five years during the immediately preceding twenty years and for the immediately preceding twelve months or have resided there for the immediately preceding three years. The Governor may, however, approve the grant of a pension to a person under age sixty-five if that person is incapable, because of mental or physical incapacity, of providing for himself or herself.

The council (subject to any directions of the Governor) can grant benefits to widows of permanent residents of Pitcairn Island. But a widow is eligible for the grant of a widow's benefit only if she has resided on Pitcairn for a continuous period of at least three years immediately prior to the death of her husband and is herself over age forty or, if under forty, has a dependent child residing with and supported by her. A widow's benefit is canceled on her remarriage or her qualifying for a pension.

Child benefits may be granted by the council to the resident parents or guardians of a child under the age of eighteen who resides with the parents or guardians. The parents or guardians of a child over fifteen and under eighteen will not be eligible for child benefits unless the child is attending a full-time course of education at the Pitcairn Island School.

X. Criminal Law

The sources of criminal law are (1) the common law and equity and statutes of general application in force in England on January 1, 1983, (2) ordinances enacted by the Governor, and (3) regulations made by the Island Council.

Under the Interpretation and General Clauses Ordinance, *offense* has been defined to include any crime, treason, felony, or misdemeanor and any contravention or other breach of, or failure to comply with, any provision of any law for which a penalty is provided. Although a Supreme Court or a Subordinate Court could be established by the Governor (**see IV, 4 Judiciary**), the court handling criminal cases today is the Island Court. The Island Court's jurisdiction is limited to imposing a fine of up to NZ$250 or 100 days' imprisonment.

Under the Justice Ordinance, offenses over which the Island Court has jurisdiction include contempt of court; perjury; escaping from, or rescuing a person escaping from, lawful custody; assaulting, resisting, or obstructing a police officer; assault; using threatening, profane, or abusive language; spreading false reports; being drunk or behaving indecently or in a riotous or disorderly manner in a public place; having unlawful carnal knowledge; adultery; stealing and receiving stolen property; failure to provide necessaries required by a person under the defendant's charge; failure by a person having the custody of any child to perform his or her duty of care and maintenance of the child; causing fires or causing malicious damage to property; removing, defacing, or otherwise mutilating or injuring prehistoric rock carvings; trespass; importing, manufacturing, selling, or supplying intoxicating liquor; importing drugs; importing or possessing obscene publications; smoking tobacco by any person under the age of eighteen; failure to vote; failure to furnish to the authorities any document that a citizen is required to file; refusal or neglect by any person to keep his or her child between five and fifteen years at regular attendance at the Pitcairn Island School; and aiding or abetting another to commit any offense.

XI. Judicial Procedure

A. Supreme Court and Subordinate Court

These courts have not yet been established. If and when they are, the Judicature Ordinance states that both civil and criminal trials before the Supreme Court are to be held by a judge, who may sit with or without assessors. The judge would be in no way bound by the opinion of the assessors. In matters of practice and procedure, both courts would be required to observe the practice and procedure followed by and before Courts of Justice in England, but only so far as local circumstances and the limits of local jurisdiction permit. The Governor has promulgated Supreme Court Rules, specifically adopting the Rules of the Supreme Court 1965 that are in force in England.

Appeals would lie to the Supreme Court from any judgment, sentence, or order of the Subordinate Court. The Supreme Court also has authority to review the proceedings of the Island Court. The Justice Ordinance permits the Governor, either *sua sponte* or on the application of any party, to direct that the record of proceedings in any case be submitted to the Supreme Court.

B. Island Court

The rules for civil and criminal trials are laid down in the Justice Ordinance and the Justice Regulations made under that ordinance.

1. CIVIL PROCEEDINGS

The Justice Ordinance provides that a civil proceeding before the court must commence by a writ of summons. Every writ of summons is issued by the Island Magistrate in writing at the request of the plaintiff. The procedure at hearings is similar to that in lesser trial courts throughout the Commonwealth. At the conclusion of a case, the court may dismiss the plaintiff's claim or make an order against either the plaintiff or the defendant. Where the court gives a judgment for the payment of money by any person, the Island Magistrate may order that the sum be paid immediately or in installments, or may levy on the real or personal property of the person and, in default, that the person may be imprisoned for a period not exceeding forty-two days.

2. CRIMINAL PROCEEDINGS

Normally, criminal proceedings are commenced by a police officer in the name of the Queen. Upon receipt of a complaint, the magistrate draws up a formal charge that must contain the details necessary to give reasonable information about the nature of the offense with which the accused person is charged. The magistrate may also issue a summons or a warrant (the latter is required only in cases of murder or treason). The magistrate can issue search warrants authorizing a police officer to search any building, ship, vehicle, box, receptacle, or place. Bail may be granted by the Island Court magistrate to any person not accused of committing murder or treason.

Where a date for hearing has been fixed and the defendant appears but the complainant does not, the court may either dismiss the charge or adjourn the hearing. If the defendant does not appear, the court may either issue a warrant to apprehend the defendant or hear and determine the case in the defendant's absence. Where the defendant has been convicted on the basis of trial held in his or her absence, that conviction may be set aside by the court if the defendant's absence was due to any cause beyond the defendant's control and the defendant has a possible defense on the merits of the case. If both parties appear and the defendant admits the truth of the charge, the court may convict unless there appears to be sufficient cause to the contrary. If the defendant does not admit the truth of the charge, the court may proceed to hear and determine the charge, with or without assessors. If the defendant is found guilty, the magistrate, after convicting the defendant, may pass sentence.

XII. LAND AND NATURAL RESOURCES

A. Land Tenure and Administration

Pitcairn Island's total area is less than 2 square miles, of which only 8 percent is flat land. Originally the whole of Pitcairn Island was divided among the families of the mutineers; it is unclear whether that land tenure system was based on individual or communal ownership. Pitcairn customs taken from Tahiti favored communal ownership, although individuals could dispose of their rights by gift or exchange, and on marriage the lands occupied by both husband and wife became merged in their joint occupancy. The concept of trusteeship came into existence after some of the Pitcairners returned from Norfolk Island; the returnees began to look after the lands of those who remained on Norfolk. Caretakers were frequently appointed for lands owned by Pitcairners leaving the island for long periods. Because of the shortage of land, there was also a practice of borrowing land for cultivation and for building houses.

At present, land rights in Pitcairn are largely regulated by the Lands and Administration of Estates Ordinance (Chapter 6), which gives statutory recognition to most of the customary rules of land tenure in existence at its enactment in 1967.

1. TITLE TO LAND

The ordinance establishes the Lands and Estates Court, which ordinarily comprises the Island Magistrate as president and four other members appointed by the Island Council. The Island Secretary is registrar of the court and is required to keep the lands register. The primary function of the court is to cause entries to be made in the lands register of all lands on Pitcairn Island for which ownership has been determined by the court or which are vested in the Island Council. A person claiming to be the owner of any land may apply to the court for registration. If the claimant had occupied a house on residential land for not less than three years without paying rent, the claimant may be registered as the owner. If the court decides that certain lands are not owned by any person or are lands for which no person applied to be registered as owner within five years after June 26, 1967, the Island Council is to be registered in the lands register as the owner. The effect of registration of a person as the owner is to vest in that person freehold title.

2. ABSENTEE LANDOWNERS, CARETAKERS, AND USUFRUCTUARY RIGHTS

Part V of the ordinance provides for the appointment by the court of a caretaker for land whose owner or lessee intends to leave the island for six months or more. A duly appointed caretaker may be registered in the lands register. The caretaker (subject to conditions imposed by the court) has the right to the use and enjoyment of that land, and to all crops, fruits, and other produce of the land and, if the caretaker has satisfactorily performed all required duties for three years or more, may be granted a lease or sublease by the court over any contiguous area not exceeding one-half the total area of the land under caretaking. If the owner or lessor is away from Pitcairn Island for a total of twelve months in any ten-year period and the caretaker has satisfactorily performed all required duties, the caretaker is entitled to succeed to the title of the absentee owner or lessor.

3. DEALINGS IN LAND

All dealings whether by sale, transfer, lease, mortgage, or otherwise are invalid unless approved by the Lands and Estates Court, which may in an appropriate case also direct that the transferee be registered as the owner. The court, however, must refuse to grant approval to any transfer if, as a result of that transfer, the transferor would not be left with sufficient land to support himself or herself and his or her dependents. Further, no lease of agricultural land or mortgage may be approved if such mortgage or lease is manifestly to the disadvantage of either party.

Agricultural leases may not be granted for less than ten years. The lessor of an agricultural lease who has complied with the conditions of the lease and cultivated the land in a manner consistent with the practice of good husbandry is entitled to two extensions of ten years each. Covenants usually implied at common law—such as the lessee's obligation to pay the rent and keep the building clean and in good repair, and the lessor's right, after giving reasonable notice to the lessee, to enter upon the land and view the state of maintenance and condition of the building—have been given statutory force. Other leases may be granted for any period up to ninety-nine years.

The owner or lessor of land may mortgage, create a charge, or otherwise transfer the land, but no mortgage, charge, or transfer may be approved by the court unless the court is satisfied that the terms of the mortgage, charge, or transfer are not manifestly to the disadvantage of either party and that any interest or consideration payable by the mortgagee, chargee, or transferee is fair and reasonable. In the case of land under a lease, the lessor and lessee's consent to dealings with the land must be obtained.

B. Acquisition of Unused Land by the Council

If agricultural land is not being used to agricultural advantage or a dwelling is subject to demolition order under the Local Government Regulations, the court may, on an application by the council, order cancellation of the ownership registration, and the registration of the council as the new owner, and payment by the council to the former owner of compensation at the rate of fifteen times the annual rental value of the land as determined by the court. Any order concerning cancellation of registration or payment of compensation made by the court may be varied by the governor.

C. Transfer or Lease of Lands Vested in the Council

Land of which the council is the owner may be transferred or leased by the council to any inhabitant of the island. To prevent favoritism or nepotism, the ordinance provides that no land may be transferred or leased to anyone except, in the case of a transfer, on payment of fifteen times the annual rental value of the land and, in the case of a lease, on payment of the annual rental value of the land as determined by the court.

D. Agriculture, Forests, and Fisheries

At the time of its discovery, almost the whole of Pitcairn Island was covered with trees, but now much of the land is under secondary bush and grass. Until recently, attempts at reforestation had proved abortive, particularly because of the presence of a large number of goats. The Local Government Regulations now provide that all goats kept on Pitcairn Island must be confined within fences or tethered so as to prevent them from straying. All other animals, except for dogs and cats, are also required to be fenced or tethered.

Fish are plentiful in the waters around Pitcairn Island. The Local Government Regulations forbid taking, hunting, or intentionally killing any blue whale, humpback whale, short-tailed albatross, cahow, dark-rumped petrel, green sea turtle, or leatherback turtle, unless authorized by the Conservation of Migratory Species of Wild Animals Committee. The committee may grant permission if the animal is required for scientific purposes, to enhance the survival or accommodate the needs of traditional subsistence users of the species, or under extraordinary circumstances.

The Fisheries Zone Ordinance provides for the establishment of a fisheries zone of up to 200 miles. If necessary or desirable for the conservation and management of fisheries resources, the governor may prohibit fishing within the limits of the territorial seas of the island or the fisheries zone without a license. Pitcairn boats also require a license for fishing outside those limits. For the regulation and conservation of fishing, the number of fishing boats or any class of fishing boats may be limited by the governor. A fishing boat may, however, enter the territorial seas of Pitcairn Island without a license for repairs, refueling, or any other purpose recognized by international law.

The Fisheries Zone Regulations forbid releasing into the territorial seas or the fisheries zone any living organism, article, or substance, other than fishing equipment or bait, which is likely to cause harm to any fish or marine mammal, obstruct fishing equipment, or become a hazard to navigation.

XIII. Persons and Entities

No legislation directly addresses the age of majority, but it is clear that a person attains full age for most purposes of the law of Pitcairn Island when that person attains the age of eighteen. The Interpretation and General Clauses Ordinance states that a person under that age is an "infant" or "minor." Further, the Local Government Ordinance declares that no person is qualified to vote for election of Island Officers unless he or she is eighteen.

Section 8 of the Local Government Ordinance confers legal personality on the Island Council, making the council a body corporate with perpetual succession and a seal. Under that section the council also has the power to hold land in accordance with the provisions of the Land and Administration of Estates Ordinance, to enter into contracts, to sue and be sued.

XIV. Family Law

A. Marriage

In matters of family law, the islanders are largely governed by the Marriage Ordinance (Chapter 10) and the Adoption of Infants Ordinance.

A registrar of marriages' certificate or Governor's license is a precondition to the solemnization of any marriage. The Marriage Ordinance requires that one of the parties to an intended marriage must give to the registrar a notice in the prescribed form. Such notice is then entered by the registrar in the marriage notice book. The registrar may issue a certificate that the notice was duly entered if the following conditions are satisfied:

1. one of the parties has been resident within Pitcairn, Henderson, Ducie, or Oeno Islands fifteen days immediately preceding the granting of the certificate;
2. each of the parties (not being a widower or widow) is eighteen years old or, if under that age, the requisite consent of the father, mother, or guardian of each of the parties has been obtained; and
3. there is no impediment of kindred or affinity or any other lawful hindrance.

In some cases the Governor may dispense with the notice and the issuing of the certificate by the registrar and may directly grant a license to the parties authorizing the celebration of their marriage.

Marriages may be celebrated by a registered minister or contracted before the registrar.

No marriage is valid that, if celebrated in England, would be null and void on the ground of kinship or affinity. Second, if either of the parties to a marriage is not of marriageable age (seventeen for males and sixteen for females), the marriage is void. Third, a marriage may be declared invalid if the parties to the marriage have knowingly and willfully acquiesced in its celebration in the following circumstances:

1. in the case of a marriage before the registrar, in any place other than the office of the registrar;
2. under a false name or names;
3. without the registrar's certificate or the Governor's license; or
4. by a person not a registered minister or the registrar of marriages.

The Supreme Court has jurisdiction to deal with any dispute arising in connection with a marriage.

B. Adoption

Under the Adoption of Infants Ordinance, the Supreme Court or the Island Court may authorize the adoption of a child under the age of eighteen years by an unmarried person, by two spouses jointly, or by the spouse of the mother or father of the child, subject to conditions regarding age, kinship, and consent of the natural parents that apply in most of the former

British colonies in the Pacific. The court will make an adoption order only if it is satisfied that the order will be for the welfare of the child. Further, the court may refuse to authorize an adoption where the applicant has received or been promised money or other reward in consideration of the adoption. The applicant can, however, accept a payment or reward if it is sanctioned by the court. After the adoption of an infant all rights, duties, obligations, and liabilities in relation to the future custody, maintenance, education, right to appoint a guardian, or give or refuse consent to marriage of the infant vests in the adopter. An adopted child has the same rights of inheritance from his adopter or adopters as if born to the adopter or adopters.

XV. Personal Property

Pitcairn has no law, other than the received common law, explicitly regulating the acquisition, use, or transfer of personal property (see **XVIII, A Sales and Consumer Protection**).

XVI. Wills and Succession

Under the Wills Ordinance, every person of sound mind, who is at least eighteen years of age, has the power to devise, bequeath, or dispose of by will or codicil all the property that person owns or is entitled to at the time of his or her death. A will or codicil is not valid unless the testator signs or affixes his or her signature or mark to it, or another person signs it in the presence of the testator according to the testator's direction, and unless it is witnessed by two or more persons. The devise, legacy, estate, interest, gift, or appointment of property to an attesting witness, the husband or wife of a witness, a person claiming under the witness or the wife or husband of the witness, is null and void. An obliteration, interlineation, or other alteration made in a will or codicil after its execution is invalid, unless executed in the same way as the will or codicil. No will or codicil or part of it that has been revoked can be revived except by reexecution. If a person marries after having made a will, the will is revoked by the marriage unless it was made in contemplation of that marriage or in exercise of a power of appointment.

Special provisions have been made for testamentary dispositions by soldiers, aviators, and mariners on active duty. Wills made by such persons may be in writing or by word of mouth. Because of the special circumstances in which such wills are likely to be made, their validity is not dependent upon the same strict rules as that of ordinary wills.

XVII. Contracts

Sale and exchange of vegetables and fruits by the islanders have been going on since the days of the first settlement by the mutineers. However, in contracts, Pitcairn Island is largely governed by the English common law.

XVIII. Commercial Law

A. Sales and Consumer Protection

Pitcairn has no sale of goods legislation nor anything resembling the Trade Practices Act of Australia or any other consumer protection act of the type found in the United States, England,

Australia, or New Zealand. Perhaps there is no need for any comprehensive consumer protection legislation for the small population of the island.

B. Corporations and Partnerships

There is no company or partnership legislation in Pitcairn Island, but the notion of artificial bodies having legal capacity or partnership is not unknown. By the Local Government Ordinance, the Island Council has been made a body corporate. The Pitcairn Souvenir Agency Ordinance, which establishes the Pitcairn Souvenir Agency, likewise declares that the agency is a body corporate having perpetual succession and common seal.

C. Regulated Businesses

The Dental and Medical Practitioners Ordinance makes it an offense to practice or perform dentistry, medicine, or surgery without being authorized to do so. A person licensed or otherwise authorized to practice dentistry, medicine, or surgery in the United Kingdom, Canada, Australia, or New Zealand is deemed to be licensed to practice that profession within Pitcairn Island. In exceptional cases a person who is not so licensed to practice may nevertheless be deemed to be so licensed. There is no specific legislation for regulation of other businesses and professions.

D. Financial Transactions

The pound sterling was Pitcairn Island's official currency until 1967, when it was replaced by the NZ dollar. American, Australian, and other currencies can usually be exchanged on the island, and British postal orders are sold and cashed and travelers' checks accepted.

XIX. TORTS

The English common law continues to be the main source of authority for dealing with tort cases. There has been little legislative activity in this area. The Trade Unions and Trade Disputes Ordinance grants immunity to trade unions from actions in tort. It also provides that an act done by a person in contemplation or furtherance of a trade dispute will not be actionable on the ground only that it induces some other person to break a contract of employment or that it interferes with the trade, business, or employment of such other person.

XX. LABOR LAW

The Trade Unions and Trade Disputes Ordinance, enacted to comply with the requirements of an international labor convention, governs the registration of trade unions and the actions a party to a trade dispute may take. The ordinance modifies the common law principle that a contract in restraint of trade is void. Section 4 categorically declares that the purposes of any trade union shall not, by reason merely that they are in restraint of trade, be deemed to be unlawful so as to render voidable any agreement or trust.

Every trade union must be registered within three months of its formation. An unregistered trade union or its members cannot legally perform any act in furtherance of the purposes of the trade union. The ordinance prescribes the rules of registration of trade unions and empowers the registrar of trade unions to refuse registration to a trade union if the prescribed formalities have not been complied with or if the purposes of the trade union are unlawful.

The ordinance defines "trade dispute" to mean any dispute between employer and worker and among workers. Any act by two or more persons in relation to a trade dispute is not triable as a conspiracy unless the act itself is punishable as a crime.

XXI. Intellectual Property Rights

Pitcairn has no law expressly governing trademarks, patents, or copyright protection. Should issues regarding these matters arise, the English common law would probably apply.

XXII. Legal Education and Profession

The Island Magistrate is elected and is not required to have legal qualifications. However, provision has been made for the appointment of a Legal Adviser under the Judicature Ordinance. The functions and powers exercised by the Legal Adviser are similar to those conferred upon the Attorney General of England.

XXIII. Research Guide

In 1971 D. H. McLoughlin, barrister and solicitor of Western Australia and Fiji and the then Legal Adviser, was appointed commissioner to prepare the 1971 Revised Laws of Pitcairn, Henderson, Ducie and Oeno Islands. D. J. Treadwell, barrister and solicitor of the High Court of New Zealand and the present Legal Adviser, prepared the 1985 edition.

Laws of Pitcairn, Henderson, Ducie and Oeno Islands. Rev. ed., 1971.
Laws of Pitcairn, Henderson, Ducie and Oeno Islands. Rev. ed., 1985.
Shapiro, H. L. *The Heritage of the Bounty*. New York: Simon & Schuster, 1936.
Waldegrave. "The Pitcairn Islanders," 3 *J. of the Royal Geographical Society* (London) 1833.
Young, R. A. *Mutiny of the Bounty and Story of Pitcairn Island, 1790–1894*. Wellington: Pastor David Nield, 1924.

10. Solomon Islands

JOHN NONGGORR

I. Dateline

1300–1000 B.C.	Radiocarbon dating provides evidence of Melanesian settlements in the Guadalcanal area during this period.
1568	Spanish expedition records first reported European sighting of the islands.
1800–1860s	European whalers trade tobacco, tools, salt, and other manufactured items for fresh food, tortoise shell, and other items of indigenous manufacture.
1892	Britain declares Solomon Islands a protectorate.
1896	First British Resident Commissioner for the Solomons appointed.
1942–1943	Japanese forces invade in 1942 and Solomons become scene of heavy fighting, involving more than 80,000 soldiers. By June 1943, Solomons recaptured by allied forces.
1945	British administration set up in Honiara.
1960	Local legislative council and executive council established.
1964	Local government councils established. Provision made for elected officials to sit in the Legislative Assembly.
1970	Legislative and executive councils replaced by a single Governing Council under the British Solomon Islands Order 1970.
1976	Solomon Islands granted self-government.
1978	Solomon Islands achieves independence on July 7 under British Solomon Islands Independence Order 1978.

II. Historical, Cultural, and Economic Survey

The Solomon Islands is an independent nation. It lies 2,000 kilometers north of Australia, and its neighbors include Papua New Guinea, Fiji, Kiribati, and Vanuatu. There are six large islands in the Solomons—New Georgia, Guadalcanal, Makira, Malaita, Isabel, and Choiseul—and at least eighty-six smaller islands, islets, and reefs. Geographically and culturally, the islands of Bougainville and Buka lie within the Solomon Islands group, although politically they are part of Papua New Guinea.

The indigenous population is predominantly Melanesian. There are, however, a few islands whose people are of Polynesian ancestry and culture. In addition, the British colonial administration resettled thousands of Micronesian Gilbertese (now Kiribati) near Honiara and Gizo between 1955 and 1971, and the Gilbertese now form part of the Solomons population. A few European and Chinese immigrants are also resident. The total population is 302,000.

The capital and main administrative center is Honiara, on Guadalcanal. After independence, a provincial government system was adopted setting up seven provincial governments covering the other islands.

The Solomons were probably settled by explorers from Southeast Asia traveling via New Guinea, as early as 2000 B.C. However, radiocarbon dating has established 1300 to 1000 B.C.

as the period of remains from Fotoruma Cave (near Poha River on Guadalcanal), the earliest settlement so far excavated. The first written confirmation of sighting of the islands by Europeans was made by a Spanish expedition led by explorer Alvaro de Mendana in 1568. He called the archipelago the Solomon Islands, implying that the islands were as rich as, or even the source of, King Solomon's treasure, a claim aimed at stimulating interest in the discovery.

Not until the end of the nineteenth century did traders and missionaries begin to arrive, although whalers and merchant ships visited regularly in the early part of that century. Late in the nineteenth century, large numbers of Solomon Islanders were recruited to work on sugar plantations in Fiji and Queensland. Because of reports of cruel treatment of recruited laborers, a number of European traders and missionaries in the Solomons were killed in retaliation.

The earliest colonial intervention in the Solomon Islands was by the British, through the Western Pacific High Commission in Fiji. The High Commission had extraterritorial authority over British subjects living in the Solomons by virtue of the Western Pacific Order-in-Council of 1877. Other Europeans and indigenous Solomon Islanders were not subject to this authority.

The late nineteenth century also saw a scramble by the European powers for colonies, markets, and natural resources in the Pacific. When Germany and France annexed territory neighboring the Solomons, Britain, with the additional intention of protecting Australia (a growing and important colony), established a protectorate in 1893 embracing the islands of Guadalcanal, Savo, Malaita, San Cristobal (or Makira), and New Georgia. The other islands of the Solomons, including the Santa Cruz group, were added later. The Shortland group, Santa Isabel (or Ysabel), Choiseul, and Ontong Java were transferred by treaty from Germany to Britain in the early 1890s.

The first resident administrator was sent by Britain in 1896. He set up office on the island of Tulagi, north of Guadalcanal. In keeping with Britain's policy of annexing colonies but refusing to incur any expenditure from them, the administrator, Charles Woodford, was ordered to raise sufficient local revenue to cover his own expenses and did so, in part, by encouraging traders to acquire large tracts of land. Later, the colonial administration acquired additional land by declaring it "waste and vacant."

British administration of the Solomons, by a Resident Commissioner answerable to the colonial office through the Western Pacific High Commission in Fiji, continued until April 1942 when, during World War II, Japanese forces took Guadalcanal. Some of the fiercest battles of World War II were fought on Guadalcanal between the Japanese and the allied forces before the Solomons were taken by the allies in June 1943.

After the war, the British administration returned, setting up headquarters in Honiara with infrastructure installed by the Americans during the war. All administrative and law-making powers were still vested in the High Commissioner. An advisory council was appointed, but the commissioner was under no obligation to follow its recommendations. A local government council system was introduced in Malaita in 1958 and extended to other regions of the Solomons by 1964. A local legislative council, consisting of the High Commissioner as president and eleven official and ten unofficial members, all twenty-one of whom were chosen by the High Commissioner, replaced the advisory council in 1960. In 1964, provision was made for an Assembly with membership consisting both of ex officio and elected members. With Britain anxious to relinquish colonial rule of the Solomons, discussions on self-government with a view to independence began in 1967. The Solomon Islands was granted self-government in 1976 and achieved independence on July 7, 1978, under the Solomon Islands Independence Order 1978.

During the long period of colonial rule, there was a lack of constructive economic development policies. The economy was dominated by coconut plantations in the hands of foreign traders. Indigenous people were first recruited to work in British controlled plantations in Queensland and Fiji and later in plantations established in the Solomon Islands.[1]

During the late 1950s, a number of major economic projects were initiated. Some mineral exploration was carried out. However, at independence the economic base was not developed enough to sustain the islands. Britain agreed to give financial assistance in the form of budgetary aid and to fund development projects as part of the independence agreement.

III. Sources of Law

At independence, the Solomon Islands adopted a Constitution, enacted as a schedule of the Solomon Islands Independence Order 1978. Section 75 of the Constitution authorizes the Solomon Islands Parliament to make provision for applicable laws, including custom. Schedule 3 of the Constitution applies until Parliament makes such a provision. The Solomon Islands Parliament has not as yet acted to provide for the applicable laws, and Schedule 3 therefore continues in effect. The laws as provided under that schedule include the Constitution, acts of the Solomon Islands parliament, certain pre-independence legislative enactments of the British Parliament, customary law, and the rules and principles of common law and equity of England.

A. Constitution

Section 2 of the Constitution declares that the Constitution "is the supreme law of the Solomon Islands and if any other law is inconsistent with this Constitution, that other law shall, to the extent of the inconsistency, be void." The Solomon Islands High Court applied the supremacy clause in holding that Section 226 of the Penal Code, which gives teachers a defense to a charge of assault when they administer "reasonable punishment" to their students, is ineffective to the extent that it conflicts with Section 7 of the Constitution, prohibiting degrading or inhuman punishment.[2]

The Constitution can be amended by Parliament by special majorities. Amendment of most of the provisions requires a vote of not less than two-thirds of all members of Parliament at the final voting, which is to be taken after two separate readings. Several provisions can be amended only by at least three-quarters of the members. These provisions include rights and freedoms, legal system, office of ombudsman, Parliament, and the office of the Auditor General.

B. Acts of Parliament

The Constitution confers on the Solomon Islands Parliament the power to make laws "for the peace, order and good government of Solomon Islands." Legislation passed by the Parliament is the next superior law.

C. Acts of the United Kingdom Parliament

The acts of the United Kingdom Parliament of general application in force on January 1, 1961, are adopted by Schedule 3 of the Constitution, subject to the provisions of the Constitution and to acts of the Solomon Islands Parliament. The High Court has held that the Homicide Act 1957 of the United Kingdom did not apply to reduce the offense of murder to manslaughter in a suicide pact, as it was inconsistent with the Penal Code.[3]

Legislative enactments in the form of rules or regulations made by the colonial administration and the pre-independence Assembly, though not specifically referred to by the Constitution, are also included in this category of law, as they were made pursuant to British enactments.

The Solomon Islands Independence Order 1978 provides in Section 5 that "the existing laws" that are in conformity with it and with the Constitution continue to apply. The expression "existing laws" is defined by Section 2 of the order to include

"Acts of the Parliament of the United Kingdom, Orders of Her Majesty in Council, Ordinances, rules, regulations, orders or other instruments having effect as part of the law of Solomon Islands (whether or not they have been brought into operation) immediately before the appointed day but does not include any order revoked by this Order."

D. Customary Law

Customary law, defined by Schedule 3.3(3) of the Constitution to mean "rules of customary law prevailing in an area of Solomon Islands" is next in the hierarchy of the laws. Schedule 3.3(2) provides that the customary laws to be applied must not be inconsistent with the Constitution or with acts of Parliament, including the United Kingdom statutes applying by adoption. The High Court has refused to mitigate the sentence of defendants accused of a payback killing, on the grounds that this custom is inconsistent with the Constitution and the Penal Code.[4]

Schedule 3 also provides for an act of Parliament to establish the proof and pleading of customary law, regulate the manner in which or the purposes for which customary law is to be recognized, and provide for the resolution of conflicts of customary law. There has not been any enactment on this to date, although a number of statutes provide for the recognition and application of custom in specific areas. Examples include the Islanders Marriage Act (Chapter 47), Islands Divorce Act (Chapter 48), Wills, Probate and Administration Act 1987, and Local Courts Act (Chapter 46).

E. Common Law

The principles and rules of common law and equity are adopted by Schedule 3.2 of the Constitution. Although the Constitution does not expressly spell out the provenance of the common law, the High Court has presumed it to be that of the United Kingdom.[5] The application of common law is subject to a number of qualifications. First, the common law rule must not be inconsistent with the Constitution or acts of Parliament; second, it must not be "inapplicable to or inappropriate in the circumstances of Solomon Islands;" and third, it must not be inconsistent with customary law.

The Constitution provides that statutory modifications of the principles and rules of common law and equity, made by the United Kingdom Parliament after the date that the Solomon Islands became independent, do not form part of the rules and principles received, unless the modifying statute has been expressly made applicable to the Solomons. The Constitution further stipulates that judicial pronouncements by English or other foreign courts made on or after independence do not bind the Solomon Islands courts. At least one (temporary) judge of the High Court has held that pre-independence decisions of the English courts are binding on the Solomon Islands courts.[6]

IV. Constitutional System

A. Nationality and Citizenship

During the negotiations leading up to independence, citizenship was one of the most controversial issues between the British and Solomon Islands governments. Controversy arose because some indigenous Solomon Islanders felt that nonindigenous people, including the resettled Gilbertese population, should not be allowed citizenship. The two governments agreed on two constitutional provisions for acquiring citizenship. The first is the acquisition of citizenship automatically on independence. This applies to all indigenous Solomon Islanders and persons who were born in the Solomon Islands before independence and who had two grandparents who belonged to a group or lineage indigenous to Papua New Guinea or the New Hebrides.

The second way citizenship is conferred is by registration. Persons qualified to apply for registration as citizens include women married to indigenous Solomon Islanders, citizens of the United Kingdom and its colonies or British protected persons born in the Solomon Islands, or naturalized British subjects. The expression "British protected person" refers to persons so described under the British Nationality Act 1948 (UK).

Persons born after independence become citizens under the constitutional provisions if either of their parents were or are citizens of Solomon Islands. Persons holding other citizenship must renounce it to acquire Solomon Islands citizenship.

The Constitution also permits Parliament to provide for the acquisition of citizenship by persons not qualifying under the Constitution. The Citizenship Act 1978 allows methods for three additional groups of people to acquire citizenship. The first group gains citizenship by adoption. The second group attains citizenship by naturalization, which involves an application made to the Citizenship Advisory Committee. The committee will grant citizenship if the applicant has been resident in the Solomon Islands for ten years; intends to continue to reside in the country; is of good character; can speak English, pidgin, or a local vernacular; understands the rights, privileges, responsibilities, and duties of citizenship; renounces other citizenship, and takes an oath of allegiance. The third group is noncitizen women marrying Solomon Islands citizens.

Loss of citizenship occurs if a citizen obtains another citizenship; takes an oath or makes a declaration or affirmation of allegiance to another country; serves in the armed forces of another country; votes or accepts electoral office in another country; or exercises rights exclusive to nationals of another country.

B. National Government

1. EXECUTIVE

   a. Head of State

   The Constitution declares that "the executive authority of the people of the Solomon Islands is vested in the Head of State." The English monarch is Head of State, represented by a Governor General. The Governor General, who must be a person eligible to be a member of the Solomon Islands Parliament, is appointed by the Queen on the advice of the Solomon Islands Parliament.

   The Constitution, Section 32, obliges the government to keep the Governor General informed of the conduct of the government and the country in general. The Governor General is not merely a figurehead. The Governor General is required to act and to exercise independent judgment in the following situations:

1. appointment of a minister to act as Prime Minister if the Prime Minister and the Deputy Prime Minister are ill or absent from the country, or if the Prime Minister is, in the opinion of the Governor General, unable to advise the latter on which minister should act in that office;
2. appointment of two members of the Committee on the Prerogative of Mercy;
3. removal of judges and acting judges in certain cases;
4. appointment of a member of the Judicial and Legal Services Commission;
5. removal of the commissioner of police; and
6. decisions on pensions for public officers, including constitutional officeholders.

b. Cabinet/Executive

The Constitution provides in Chapter V for a Cabinet that is responsible to Parliament. The Cabinet is headed by a Prime Minister who is elected by Parliament from among its members. The Prime Minister advises the Governor General on the appointment of other Cabinet ministers. The number of ministers in Cabinet is currently fixed by law at eleven. Each minister is responsible for overseeing the administration of a government department. The Cabinet is collectively responsible for decisions taken by the Cabinet or by individual ministers.

There are two ex officio members of the Cabinet. They are the Attorney General and the Permanent Secretary to Cabinet. Ministers of the Cabinet, including the Prime Minister, hold office until another general election or until a vote of no-confidence is successfully brought against the Prime Minister. Ministers can be removed by the Governor General on the advice of the Prime Minister.

2. LEGISLATURE

The Solomon Islands Parliament established under Chapter VI of the Constitution has the power to "make laws for the peace, order and good government of the Solomon Islands." Acts of Parliament may not alter the separation of powers of the three branches of government. An attempt by the legislature to usurp the powers and independence of the judiciary was thus held unconstitutional by the Court of Appeal.[7] Bills can be introduced by any member, apart from bills on taxation or other matters that would impose a charge on the consolidated fund or other fund, which must be supported by a recommendation of Cabinet. Bills passed by Parliament become law after the assent of the Governor General and operate on publication in the *Gazette*.

To qualify for election to Parliament, a person must be a citizen of the Solomon Islands, twenty-one years or older, and resident in the electorate. It has been held that Solomon Islands concepts of residence apply. For example, if people have a home in town or at their workplace and another in their village, both may be considered as the person's place of residence for this purpose.[8] Persons are disqualified from membership if they acknowledge allegiance to another state, hold public office, are bankrupt, are insane, are under sentence of death or imprisonment for more than six months, commit an election offense, or have responsibility for the conduct of elections.

Members of Parliament vacate their seats on dissolution of Parliament; on their resignation; if elected Speaker or appointed Governor General; if they are absent from two consecutive meetings of Parliament without permission, unless the Speaker determines otherwise; and if a condition of disqualification for membership exists.

Citizens of the Solomon Islands, eighteen years of age and older, are given the right to register and vote. Persons under imprisonment with sentences of six months or more or persons of unsound mind are disqualified from voting. A registered voter can vote in only one constituency, and that must be the one in which he or she is ordinarily resident.

Parliament is presided over by a Speaker, assisted by a Deputy Speaker, both of whom are elected by Parliament from among its members. The conduct of Parliament is in accordance with its standing orders and, if these do not provide for a particular matter, the usage and practice of the British House of Commons can be followed. It has been held that this includes a power in the Speaker to make rulings in answer to questions raising points of order that may have some bearing on the interpretation of constitutional provisions; and that this does not constitute a usurpation of the court's powers to interpret a constitutional law.[9]

Proceedings are open to the public unless otherwise provided by parliamentary rules of procedure. A quorum is half the sitting members. The Constitution provides for the Governor General, on the Speaker's advice, to appoint as leader of the official opposition a person who has the numerical support of opposition members of Parliament.

Parliament is dissolved every four years. By an absolute majority vote, Parliament can dissolve itself before the expiration of its four-year term. On dissolution, a general election must be held within four months.

Two commissions deal with electoral matters. The Electoral Boundaries Commission investigates and makes recommendations to Parliament on the number of electoral constituencies and their boundaries. The number of constituencies must not be less than thirty nor more than fifty, and is currently thirty-eight. The Electoral Commission supervises the registration and conduct of elections.

3. JUDICIARY

a. High Court and Court of Appeal

The Constitution establishes a High Court and a Court of Appeal. The High Court has unlimited jurisdiction in all cases and can hear appeals from all subordinate courts. It has original jurisdiction to determine constitutional questions raised by persons who allege that they have been harmed by the contravention of a constitutional provision. It was held that the leader of the parliamentary opposition has standing to challenge in the High Court by way of a constitutional reference the validity of a decision of the Committee on the Prerogative of Mercy.[10] If constitutional questions arise in the subordinate courts, they are to be referred to the High Court for its interpretation.

The High Court also has an advisory and supervisory jurisdiction. Its supervisory role is over subordinate courts for the purposes of ensuring that justice is duly administered by such courts.

The Court of Appeal hears appeals from the High Court in both civil and criminal matters. The Court of Appeal Act 1978 specifies in detail the grounds for and manner of appeal to the Court of Appeal, and the Court of Appeal Rules 1983 provide the appeal procedure.

The High Court is headed by a Chief Justice. Parliament is empowered to make provision for other judges. The Court of Appeal consists of a president, other justices of appeal as prescribed by Parliament, and the Chief Justice and other judges of the High Court sitting as ex officio members. All judges are appointed by the Governor General on the advice of the Judicial Services Commission. To qualify for appointment to these judicial positions a person must hold or have held high judicial office in a Commonwealth or other country prescribed by Parliament or be qualified to practice as a barrister or solicitor and have been practicing for at least five years.

Judges cease to hold office when their terms expire or they resign. They may be removed by the Governor General acting on advice from a tribunal established for the purpose of investigating allegations of inability to perform the duties. Judges may also be removed for misbehavior. Judges or justices of appeal who are citizens cannot hold office beyond the age of sixty years. If the office of the Chief Justice becomes vacant, a judge of the High Court can be appointed acting Chief Justice; and if there is a vacancy in the position of a judge, a person qualified to be a judge of the High Court can be appointed to act as judge. If the office of the president of the Court of Appeal is vacant, another member of the Court of Appeal or a person qualified to be a judge can be appointed to act as president. At present, the membership of the High Court consists only of the Chief Justice, and the Court of Appeal is constituted by three judges—one from Papua New Guinea, the second from New Zealand, and the third from Queensland.

b. Subordinate Courts

Three courts are subordinate to the High Court and the Court of Appeal. These are the Magistrates' Court, the Local Court, and the Customary Land Appeal Court.

The Magistrates' Courts Act (Chapter 3) confers both criminal and civil jurisdiction on Magistrates' Courts to hear and determine cases that arise in the area for which they are established. Magistrates' Courts are established by the Chief Justice, who can also, by warrant, confer extraterritorial jurisdiction on individual magistrates. The Chief Justice decides on the jurisdiction to be exercised by each court and can confer on a court specific jurisdiction to hear particular cases normally outside its jurisdiction.

Magistrates' Courts can be a Principal Magistrates' Court or, in order of hierarchy, a Magistrates' Court of the first or second class. A Principal Magistrates' Court exercises wider jurisdiction in terms of geographical area and amount of damages or compensation in a civil case and the penalty that can be imposed in a criminal case. It has jurisdiction throughout the country.

The Magistrates' Court has civil jurisdiction:

1. in all personal suits including counterclaims and set-offs arising in both tort and contract where the value of the claim does not exceed SI$1,000;
2. in all suits between landlord and tenant for possession of land or house where the annual rental value does not exceed SI$500;
3. to appoint guardians and make custody and maintenance orders for infants and wives;
4. to grant injunctions in proceedings instituted before it;
5. to order execution of judgment on land or other property if the value of such property does not exceed SI$500 in the case of a magistrate and SI$2,000 in the case of a principal magistrate;
6. to enforce attachments; and
7. to commit to imprisonment for up to six weeks persons who default in payment of judgment debts if the defaulter had the means to pay the debt.

The Magistrates' Courts of the first or second class have criminal jurisdiction to try offenses carrying a maximum penalty of imprisonment for a term of one year or a fine of SI$200 or both. The Chief Justice or a judge can confer on a particular Magistrates' Court jurisdiction to deal with other offenses. A Principal Magistrates' Court has jurisdiction to try offenses carrying a maximum of fourteen years' imprisonment or fine or both, but it cannot impose a prison sentence for a term exceeding five years or a fine in excess of SI$1,000 or both. The Magistrates' Courts Regulations (Chapter 3) specify the offenses that can be heard by the Magistrates' Courts. Magistrates' Courts also hear appeals on customary land matters from the Local Courts.

There are four Magistrates' Courts, one for each district of the Solomon Islands, presided over by qualified lawyers. There are plans to create more Magistrates' Courts in order to have a Magistrates' Court in every province.

The second set of subordinate courts are the Customary Land Appeal Courts, which hear appeals from the Local Courts on customary land matters and from Area Councils on timber rights permits. The Magistrates' Courts do not have power to hear appeals from Local Courts on customary land matters.[11]

The Customary Land Appeal Courts are presided over by at least four members of the community sitting with a person with some legal training (usually a magistrate) as clerk. The Customary Land Appeal Courts do not follow strict rules of procedure although they must observe the basic principles of an independent tribunal. The requirements of Section 10 of the Constitution, requiring civil courts to be impartial and independent, apply equally to the Customary Land Appeal Courts and therefore, if bias is proven, the decision of the court will be quashed.[12] The Customary Land Appeal Courts should give reasons for their decisions out of courtesy to the court whose decision is appealed.[13]

The courts apply customary law, for instance, in determining the line of descent for the purpose of inheritance of customary land.[14] Appeals from a Customary Land Appeal Court lie to the High Court, but the Land and Titles Act (Chapter 93) provides in Section 231B that the grounds of appeal cannot be on points of customary law.[15]

The third level of subordinate courts are the Local Courts, created under the Local Courts Act (Chapter 46). They are established in almost all provinces; their jurisdiction is exercised by three justices who are knowledgeable in customary law, with a government clerk providing advice and administrative support. The Chief Justice appoints the officials, including the justices and the court clerk.

Local Courts have jurisdiction in the geographic area for which they are established and can hear all customary law claims, and they have exclusive original jurisdiction in customary land matters. Local Courts have criminal jurisdiction over simple offenses created under bylaws made by the Area Councils (or, in the case of Honiara, the Honiara Town Council) if the offender is a Solomon Islander who has committed the offense in the area of the court. The Local Courts (Criminal Jurisdiction) Order 1978 limits their jurisdiction to prison sentences of up to six months or fines not exceeding SI$200. The act gives the Chief Justice power to confer special jurisdiction on Local Courts in both criminal and civil cases.

C. Provincial and Local Government

1. PROVINCIAL GOVERNMENT

Section 114 of the Constitution authorizes the division of the country into provinces and empowers Parliament to enact legislation for provincial governments. After demand for provincial governments with threats of secession from certain parts of the country, notably the Western Province, the Provincial Government Act 1981 was passed by Parliament, which set up seven provincial governments. These are Western, Isabel, Central, Guadalcanal, Malaita, Makira, and Temotu provinces.

Provincial governments are established under Part II of the act and are made up of a Provincial Assembly, a provincial executive, and a staff. Members of the Assembly are elected from electoral wards in the province. A Provincial Assembly can, by resolution, appoint nominated members. The provincial executive is headed by a Premier who is elected by and from the Assembly. All members of the Assembly must be present for the election of the Premier.[16] The

Premier in turn appoints the other members of the executive, who must also be members of the Assembly, with the approval of the national minister responsible for provincial affairs. A Speaker of the Assembly, also elected from the members of the Assembly, and is in charge of Assembly's operation and administration.

Provincial ordinances may be made by Provincial Assemblies but require the assent of the responsible minister to have effect. The minister must give the assent unless he or she is of the opinion that the proposed provincial law is beyond the province's powers or conflicts with government policy for the country as a whole. If assent is withheld on the second ground, the minister is required to table a copy of the proposed provincial ordinance, together with a statement of the policy in question, and move in Parliament for the proposed ordinance to be disallowed. The minister can withhold assent if the motion is carried but otherwise is required to give assent. Assent withheld on the first ground is referred to the High Court.

A number of functions of the national government can, as provided in the Provincial Government Act, be transferred to provincial governments. Statutory functions that can be transferred to provincial governments range from cultural and environmental matters to public holidays and liquor laws. Services that can be provided by a provincial executive include support of local trades and industries, oversight of cultural and environmental matters such as museums and libraries, authority over shipping, roads and aerodromes, agriculture and fishing, medical services and public health, forestry, provincial primary and secondary schools, and tourism.

The main source of revenue for provincial governments is national government grants. Provinces can borrow money from the government or other authorized lenders, but there are limitations on the amount.

2. LOCAL GOVERNMENT

The system of local government set up in the late 1950s has been retained after independence. The Local Government Act (Chapter 14) provides for the establishment of Area Councils. There is a town council in Honiara, and there are a number of Area Councils in each province. Area council representatives are elected by the people living in the council area. Their main functions are to promote health and welfare; maintain order and good government; prevent the commission of offenses; keep birth and death records; and make, amend, or cancel bylaws for their area.

The councils are given corporate status and are capable of suing and being sued, acquiring and disposing of personal and real property, accepting gifts, entering into contracts, and engaging council staff.

D. Emergency Powers

The Constitution provides at Section 16 for two types of public emergency—the first in which the Solomon Islands is at war and the second in which a public emergency is declared. A declaration of public emergency is made by a proclamation of the Governor General. The proclamation must be published immediately. Declarations exist for a period of seven days, unless revoked earlier, and may be extended if two-thirds of Parliament approves the declaration. If Parliament is not in session when an emergency declaration is made, it must convene within fourteen days, and the seven-day period commences on the day Parliament is convened.

If the declaration is approved by Parliament, it runs for a period of four months unless Parliament has in the resolution specified it to end earlier. Parliament retains the power to revoke its approval of the public emergency before the four months has ended.

Laws passed to deal with public emergencies or acts done in pursuance of those laws are valid even if inconsistent with or in contravention of the human rights provisions of the Constitution, provided however that such laws or acts are reasonably justifiable in the circumstances.

A person detained during an emergency must be informed in writing of the reasons for his or her detention. If the person is held beyond one month, an impartial tribunal must review the detention within a month and at least once every six months thereafter.

E. Human Rights

Chapter II of the Constitution contains a list of individual rights and freedoms that may generally not be interfered with. Some of the rights and freedoms are accorded to all individuals while others are conferred only on citizens. The rights and freedoms so conferred are as follows:

1. Right to life (except if death occurs as a result of reasonable force used to defend persons or property; to effect an arrest; to prevent an escape from lawful custody; to suppress a riot, insurrection, or mutiny; or to prevent the commission of an offence).
2. Right to personal liberty, except where detention is authorized by law.[17]
3. Freedom from slavery or other forced labor, except as required pursuant to a court conviction or work required to be done by members of the disciplined forces as part of their lawful duties.
4. Freedom from inhuman treatment, including inhuman or degrading punishment.[18]
5. Protection of one's property, except that compulsory acquisition may occur for a public purpose (in which event, reasonable compensation must be paid) or pursuant to court order or a law.
6. Full protection of the law for persons charged with criminal offenses, including the presumption of innocence until proven guilty; the right to be informed of the charge or charges in a language they understand; the right to defend themselves in person or by a legal representative and to examine and cross-examine witnesses; the right to have free of charge an interpreter if required; unless they consent otherwise, the right to have a trial conducted in their presence or the presence of their legal representative; and the right (under Section 10 of the Constitution) to a fair and proper hearing.[19]
7. Right to freedom of thought, religion, or belief and the right to exercise these rights.
8. Right to freedom of expression, although this right can be restricted by a law made in the public interest for defense; public safety; public order; public morality; public health; or for the protection of the reputation, rights, or freedoms of other people.
9. Freedom of assembly and association, subject to laws restricting it for reasons of public interest; for protection of other people's rights; and in the case of public officers. Such restrictions must be reasonably justifiable in a democratic society.
10. Right to freedom of movement within the Solomon Islands, restricted specified instances, but such restrictions must be justifiable in a democratic society.
11. Protection from discrimination on the grounds of race, place of origin, color, creed or sex, or political opinions.

Persons aggrieved by the contravention of Chapter II can apply to the High Court, which has the power to award compensation to the aggrieved person.[20] A number of these rights are suspended during periods of public emergencies (see **IV, D Emergency Powers**).

V. Administrative Organization and Law

A. Organization

The administrative departments of the government are each headed by a Permanent Secretary, who is responsible for the daily running of the department and for implementation of government policy. Each department is answerable to Parliament through a Cabinet minister. Section 40 of the Constitution gives the minister powers of general direction and control over his or her assigned department. The minister responsible for the public service is empowered by the Public Service Act 1988 to create, abolish, or amalgamate divisions of the public service, including reviewing the administration and approving the posting of public servants, in consultation with the Public Service Commission.

The government provides all public services and utilities through government departments, agencies, and statutory instrumentalities. These include health, education, electricity, and telecommunications. The government owns both the weekly newspaper and the radio station.

B. Public Service

Chapter XIII of the Constitution provides for the public service and establishes at Section 115 a Public Service Commission whose members and chair are appointed by the Governor General in accordance with advice from the Prime Minister. The commission is responsible for the appointment of officers to specified public offices and has the power to remove and exercise disciplinary control over them.

The Judicial and Legal Services Commission is separately established under Section 117 of the Constitution, with the Chief Justice as chair and other members appointed by the Governor General on the advice of the Prime Minister. It is empowered to make appointments and to remove and exercise control over those public officers who are required to have legal qualifications.

The Police and Prisons Services Commission is also separately established with powers to make appointments and to remove and exercise control over personnel in the police and prison services. The commission consists of the chairs of the Public Service Commission and Judicial and Legal Service Commission and a third person appointed by the Governor General on the advice of the Prime Minister (Constitution, Section 119).

The Constitution, in Sections 91 and 92, also establishes and prescribes the functions of the Director of Public Prosecutions and Public Solicitor. The Director of Public Prosecutions must be a qualified lawyer who is appointed by the Governor General on the advice of the Judicial and Legal Services Commission. The functions of this office are to institute and undertake criminal proceedings. The director is not subject to control from anyone, except in cases concerning defense, security, or international relations. In these cases, the director must act on directions given by the responsible minister.

The office of Public Solicitor is created "to provide legal aid, advice and assistance to persons in need" (Constitution, Section 92). This applies especially to persons charged with criminal offenses, but the High Court may order the Public Solicitor's office to assist other persons as well. Persons refused assistance by this office can apply to the High Court. The Public Solicitor can levy reasonable charges for services rendered, if authorized to do so by an act of Parliament. The Public Solicitor is not subject to direction or control. Appointment to the position is made by the Governor General on the advice of the Judicial and Legal Services Commission. The person appointed must be a lawyer qualified to practice in the Solomon Islands.

C. Public Finance and Audit

Chapter X of the Constitution provides for the raising and expenditure of public funds. All government revenue from all sources is required to be paid into the consolidated fund, except that Parliament can establish special funds for special purposes.

Most expenditures out of the consolidated fund can be made only pursuant to a warrant issued by the Minister of Finance. The minister cannot issue a warrant unless there is an appropriation act allowing such expenditure.

The Constitution does provide for the minister to authorize expenditures without an enabling act or subject to a supplementary appropriation act in special circumstances, such as unforeseen expenditure arising during a financial year not provided for under the appropriation act. If the provision is insufficient, a supplementary appropriation bill can remedy the need or shortfall. If it is not possible to pass an appropriation bill, the minister can be empowered by Parliament to cover necessary expenditure either by drawing on the fund or by appropriating money from the fund not in excess of the appropriation of the same period for the previous financial year.

The Auditor General is responsible for auditing the public accounts of the state, ministers, other bodies and authorities, provincial governments, and other bodies administering public funds. This annual audit is reported to Parliament through the Speaker (Constitution, Section 108).

D. Rule Making

Various statutes confer powers on authorities to promulgate rules on specified matters. A number of constitutional provisions also confer such powers on specified authorities. Authorities given rule-making powers include the Public Service Commission, under Section 4 of the Public Service Act 1988, and the Chief Justice under the Magistrates' Courts Act (Chapter 3), Court of Appeal Act 1978, Local Court Act (Chapter 46), and Legal Practitioners Act 1987.

E. Review of Administrative Action

The English common law rules apply to administrative actions; thus, the courts have held that the rules of natural justice (due process) apply to administrative hearings.[21] The Constitution does not expressly confer the power of judicial review over administrative action on any particular court, although at Section 83 it does give the High Court power to decide constitutional issues. Further, the general powers given to the High Court under Section 77 to "hear and determine any civil or criminal proceeding" implicitly authorize the court to review administrative decisions or actions, and the High Court has done so.[22]

The Constitution provides at Section 138 that where it requires a person or authority to be free from direction or control, the requirement does not preclude the courts from exercising their jurisdiction to determine whether the person or authority has performed its functions as provided by law. The courts also have power to inquire into matters in which the Crown claims a privilege, if the matter affects the rights of individuals—for example, in cases of deportation of aliens.[23]

Part IX of the Constitution establishes the office of ombudsman. The ombudsman is authorized to inquire into the conduct of officials and authorities, assist in the improvement of practices and procedures of public bodies, ensure the elimination of arbitrary and unfair decisions, and exercise additional powers conferred by Parliament. The ombudsman can investigate any public officer or agency, except the Governor General, the Director of Public Prosecutions, or persons acting under their instructions.

The ombudsman, as an independent authority, is not subject to direction or control by any person or authority, except where a matter concerns the security of the country and the Prime Minister gives notice to that effect. The proceedings of a commission of inquiry called by the ombudsman cannot be questioned in court. The ombudsman must furnish Parliament with annual reports.

The ombudsman is appointed by the Governor General on the advice of a committee constituted of the Speaker of the Parliament, the chair of the Public Service Commission, and the chair of the Judicial and Legal Services Commission. An ombudsman holds office for five years unless removed for misbehavior or for inability to perform his or her duties.

Complaints to the ombudsman can be made by residents of the Solomon Islands against government departments, including the police force and the prison services, Provincial Assemblies, authorities authorized to engage in contract negotiations on behalf of the government, statutory instrumentalities or authorities prescribed by Parliament, or officers of these bodies or authorities (Ombudsman [Further Provisions] Act 1980).

Chapter VIII of the Constitution provides for a leadership code. Persons to whom the code applies are under a duty to avoid placing themselves in a position in which they (1) have or could have a conflict of interest or in which the fair exercise of their public or official duties may be compromised; (2) demean their office or position; (3) allow their integrity to be called into question; or (4) endanger or diminish respect for and confidence in the integrity of the government of the Solomon Islands. Acts of corruption are prohibited. Family members and associates of office holders also are covered by the code. Nonobservance of these obligations constitutes misconduct in office.

F. Official Secrets, Freedom of Information

No legislation regulates public access to information. The Official Secrets Act (Chapter 23), on the other hand, creates numerous offenses for persons divulging official secrets to enemies of the state, including access by unauthorized persons to places designated as "prohibited places" under the act. These offenses include spying for an enemy; communication of secret codes, notes, documents, or other information; interfering with officers of the police; and attempts at inciting others to divulge official secrets. The act also requires the registration of persons carrying postal packages.

VI. INTERNATIONAL OBLIGATIONS

The Solomon Islands has diplomatic ties with a number of countries and has entered into bilateral and multilateral treaties. It is a member of the United Nations and the Commonwealth. It is also a member of a number of regional organizations, including the South Pacific Forum and, with Papua New Guinea and Vanuatu, the Melanesian Spear Head group. The Solomon Islands is also a signatory to the fisheries treaty of the Pacific island countries with the United States.

The Diplomatic Privileges Act (Chapter 113) authorizes the Governor General to confer on organizations and members of organizations certain immunities including immunity from legal suits and legal process and exemption from tax. The Consular Conventions Act (Chapter 114) provides similar privileges for officers of foreign states.

The Solomon Islands recognizes enforcement of foreign judgments by registration if reciprocal arrangements exist. The Foreign Reciprocal Enforcement of Judgments Act (Chapter 8) provides for the registration and enforcement of judgments obtained in the United Kingdom. The Foreign Judgments (Reciprocal Enforcement) Act (Chapter 9) provides for the registration and enforcement of foreign judgments obtained in other countries with which the Solomon Islands has reciprocal arrangements. At present, judgments of superior courts of all Commonwealth countries are enforceable under the act.

The Extradition Act 1987 requires specific extradition arrangements with other states if the Solomon Islands is to extradite offenders to those countries. The Solomons has extradition arrangements with the Commonwealth nations and the United States.

VII. Revenue Law

During the first four years of independence, a large part of the Solomon Islands budget was directly funded by Great Britain, which has continued to provide project grants and budgetary aid to the Solomons.

Revenues generated within the country are predominantly from customs and excise taxes, stamp duties, income tax, and sales tax. Income tax is payable on all income earned by residents of the Solomon Islands from gains or profits from business or employment, dividends other than dividends paid by resident companies to nonresident shareholders, pensions and annuities, and alimony or allowances received pursuant to court orders or separation agreements. Provision is made for certain allowable deductions and exemptions from income tax. Under the Sales Tax Act 1990, sales tax is payable by purchases of goods and services.

VIII. Investment Law

The government has recently enacted legislation aimed at promoting foreign investment. The new act supersedes existing legislation that was designed to control and regulate foreign investment. The Foreign Investment Act 1984 established an Investment Board to screen and regulate investments by foreigners and agreements concerning the licensing of industrial property rights, patents, and trademarks, and foreign technical management and marketing services. It has been replaced by the Investment Act 1990, which establishes a similar board (constituted by the same membership as under the 1984 act until new membership is determined) to receive, consider, and decide on foreign investment applications and, where approved, to grant certificates to approved investors. The criteria to be used in considering applications are to be provided for in regulations not yet promulgated.

Approved investors (i.e., those to whom certificates are issued) can apply to benefit from some of the incentives provided by the government under various statutes. One incentive is in income tax. Under the Income Tax (Amendment) (No. 2) Act 1990, an investor (both foreign and national) may be granted exemption from income tax and, in some cases, from dividend withholding tax for a period of up to five years. The incentives will be granted if the Investment Board considers that the investment will further the economic development of the country, increase employment opportunities in all levels of employment, include the use of local raw materials, promote exports or substitute imports, and transfer technology. The minister may exempt a Solomon Islander or Solomon Islands company if the minister believes this would help the business to get established.

In relation to foreign investors (defined to mean noncitizens and, in respect of corporations, where a noncitizen holds equity), the board is to consider two other factors as well: (1) the foreign capital input in the investment and (2) the value of tangible assets used or to be used in the investment project. The incentives granted to an investor may be extended for a further period of up to five years if a substantial additional investment is proposed and the investor had satisfied the conditions stipulated in the original investment.

The Investment Board can cancel a certificate granted to a foreign investor if the investment is not made within the period specified in the certificate or if any provision of the act is not complied with. Any variation of investment activity must have the approval of the board. An investor is guaranteed the right, subject to exchange control regulations in force, to transfer in foreign currency the proceeds of sale of the whole or part of its enterprise as well as profits and dividends.

Foreign investment is concentrated in the raw materials extraction industry. Fishing is the main form of foreign investment, notably by Japanese interests in joint ventures with the government. Logging and palm oil are the other areas of investment activity. Together with cocoa, gold, and copra, these represent the main exports of the country.

An Industrial Development Corporation was established by the Industrial Development Corporation Act 1991 to facilitate the development of industries in the Solomon Islands. The corporation, established with SI$100 million grant from the government, is authorized to issue shares to approved internal and external investors. The corporation's purposes are to promote, assist, and encourage local private sector industrial development by providing financial assistance; implement government policy on private sector participation in industrial ventures; coordinate private and public sector industrial growth; foster industrial research for the use of local resources; promote export of local products by providing financial assistance to relevant industries; and take all other measures including participating in regional cooperative activities in the field of international trade to promote industrial development in the Solomon Islands.

The Banking Ordinance 1976 regulates the banking industry in the Solomon Islands. The National Bank of Solomon Islands Act 1980 establishes and provides for the management of a reserve bank with power to regulate the banking industry. The Foreign Exchange Control Act 1976 confers on the responsible minister the power to make regulations concerning almost all matters relating to exchange control, including the foreign exchange reserves of the country, the protection of the currency or its credit, foreign investments within the Solomons, and Solomon Islands investments outside the country.

IX. Welfare Law

Solomon Islands has no social security system and no specific welfare legislation. Other social services, such as health and education, are provided by the government. The provision of health services and the administration of the responsible government department and agencies involved in health are regulated by the Health Services Act 1979. Although health services are generally free, the responsible minister is empowered to make regulations prescribing charges on patients. The Health Services (Hospitals) Regulations 1980 sets out a schedule of charges for private patients treated at public hospitals. These charges range from SI$2 for a ten-year-old private ward inpatient to SI$35 for specialist consultations.

Local authorities including the Honiara Town Council and provincial assemblies are required by the Environmental Health Act 1980 to make bylaws for the provision of health services in their areas. These services may include sanitation and education and publicity campaigns.

Education requires fees of up to SI$20 per school year in community primary schools and up to SI$140 for secondary schools. Tertiary education within the country is provided by the College of Higher Education, established under the College of Higher Education Act 1984. The college, which is governed by a council, includes schools of education, administration, industrial development, natural resources, nursing and paramedical studies, and marine studies. The college's purpose, under Section 6, is to "assist the government to meet the manpower needs of the Solomon Islands by

(i) providing preservice training to persons who have finished their primary or secondary education, in areas which are appropriate to the development needs of the country; and
(ii) improving the skills and knowledge of the existing work force through in-service education and training."

The government sponsors most students attending the college. Further education in overseas universities is funded by foreign governments, primarily Australia and New Zealand.

The Solomon Island National Provident Fund Act 1973 provides for the contribution by employers to a retirement fund for employees. The fund is managed by the National Provident Fund. For government employees and government instrumentalities, the Pensions Act (Chapter 110) establishes pensions, gratuities, or other allowances to officers at the retirement age of fifty-five or upon death or disability.

X. Criminal Law

The Penal Code Act (Chapter 5) codifies most of the major criminal offenses in Solomon Islands. The code covers both felonies and misdemeanors. If a person is found guilty of an offense, the court can impose a range of punishments provided under Part VI of the code, including imprisonment and fines. Upon a criminal conviction, the court has the power to order that compensation be paid by the defendant to any injured person.

XI. Judicial Procedure

Court procedure is modeled on the common law adversarial system. Although the conduct of a civil trial and a criminal trial is generally the same, there are significant differences in the procedural rules between the two.

A. Civil

The civil procedure rules of the different courts is found under their respective establishing statutes. The Local Courts are less formal and have very little or no procedural rules in civil trials.

The Crown or state can sue or be sued, invoking in most cases the same procedure as is available to or used against individuals. The right of action against the Crown in civil claims is expressly provided for under the Crown Proceedings Act (Chapter 7). The Crown is made vicariously liable for tortious acts, including cases of breach of statutory and common law duties committed by its servants or agents but excluding acts or omissions by persons performing judicial functions. In addition, members of the armed forces, acting in the line of duty, are not liable in tort.

Both the High Court and the Magistrates' Courts have jurisdiction to hear cases against the Crown. Judgment and costs can be awarded to and against the Crown in the same way as against any subject. Interest on judgments for general damages is generally 5 percent per year.[24]

The time limit for bringing a cause of action is six years. The Limitations Act 1984 also provides for limitations on the recovery of land (thirty years) and foreclosure of mortgages (twelve years).

B. Criminal

The Criminal Procedure Code Act (Chapter 4) provides that, unless required by another law, all offenses are to be investigated, tried, and otherwise dealt with according to its provisions. The code deals with investigation of crimes, search and seizure, arrest, bail, commencement of proceedings by complaint and summons, procedure for trial in both the Magistrates' Court and the High Court, and the taking and recording of evidence. Criminal procedure is also governed by Chapter II of the Constitution (**see IV, E Human Rights**).

1. ARREST

Arrests can be made with or without a warrant. An arrest may be made without a warrant by a police officer if a person is

1. suspected of having committed an offense or is committing an offense;
2. obstructing a police officer from his lawful duty;
3. escaping from lawful custody;
4. in possession of things reasonably suspected of having been stolen;
5. found in the night suspected of committing a felony;
6. in possession of housebreaking equipment; and
7. as a convicted person, released on recognizance and in breach of any condition of the recognizance.

Magistrates may make arrests, as may private citizens, if they believe on reasonable grounds that the person is committing or has committed a felony. An owner of property can also effect an arrest on persons committing property-related offenses.

2. SEARCH AND SEIZURE

For the purposes of an arrest, police are authorized to search premises under a warrant or under some other authority and to gain entry to the premises by using all reasonable means to effect an arrest, including breaking in and breaking out of such premises. On arrest, a person can be searched, and personal articles may be taken for safe keeping if the person is to be retained in custody.

3. BAIL

A person arrested without a warrant must be brought immediately before a magistrate or, if that is not practicable, the police officer in charge of a police station must inquire into the case. Unless the offense is of a serious nature, the person can be released with or without surety. The High Court has held that bail can be granted pending appeal against sentence only if there is a possibility that the sentence of imprisonment will be set aside or that the sentence is likely to be served before the hearing of the appeal or for other exceptional reasons.[25]

C. Appellate Review

Appeals from the Magistrates' Courts lie to the High Court as provided in the Magistrates' Courts Act (Chapter 3). In civil cases, a person can appeal from final or interlocutory orders, decisions, or judgments. The High Court has discretion to entertain appeals from Magistrates' Courts on any terms it thinks fit.

Criminal appeals are governed by the Criminal Procedure Code, which provides that decisions either of fact or of law may be appealed. Appeals are made by way of a petition to the Magistrates' Court that heard the case, which forwards it to the the High Court. The High Court can dismiss an appeal or may confirm, reverse, vary, or remit the case to the Magistrates' Court or make any other order that seems just. The Attorney General becomes a party to criminal appeals. An appeal against an acquittal of an accused can lie only with the approval of the Attorney General.

Decisions of the High Court may be appealed to the Court of Appeal. The procedure and grounds on which appeals can be instituted are contained in the Court of Appeal Act 1978 and the Court of Appeal Rules 1983.

Appeals from the Local Courts go to the Magistrates' Courts, except that decisions concerning customary land must be heard by the Customary Land Appeal Courts. Appeals to the Customary Land Appeal Courts need not be in any particular form.[26] A letter is sufficient; however, to be effective the appeal must be accompanied by the proper fee.[27] The Local Court Act (Chapter 46) requires an aggrieved person to appeal within thirty days from the date of the order of the Local Court. Appeals other than those concerning customary land are heard by a magistrate, who may be assisted by assessors. The magistrate may make an order or pass a sentence that the Local Court had power to make, or may order that the matter be reheard by the same court or by another Local Court. Decisions of the Customary Land Appeal Courts may be appealed to the High Court (**see IV, B (3) (b) Subordinate Courts**).

XII. LAND AND NATURAL RESOURCES

A. Land Tenure and Administration

The acquisition of land in the Solomon Islands by non-Solomon Islanders (some establishing trading stations and plantations, others for speculation) commenced as early as 1885. These land purchases were made directly from the customary holders. Trickery and cheating are reported to have been common on both sides.[28]

Colonial administration control of acquisition of land from customary owners was first introduced under Queen's Regulation No. 4, which required that the High Commissioner approve all sales of land to non-Solomon Islanders and further provided that only the Crown could acquire freehold title. Foreigners were limited to the acquisition of leasehold interests, held from the Crown, which were granted for periods ranging from ten to ninety-nine years.

The colonial administration made available to non-Solomon Islanders substantial tracts of land, some of which had been purchased and much of which was claimed by the Crown on the basis that it was "waste land," land not owned, cultivated, or occupied (Solomon Islands [Waste Lands] Regulations 1900). In some cases, land was acquired by mere possession.[29] The acquisition of land by the colonial administration through "waste land" declarations was later challenged by indigenous people. The early sales of land were also challenged on the grounds that payment had been inadequate, some land transfers were made by people other than the rightful customary owners, and some customary owners were excluded from receiving payment for such acquisitions.[30]

The Land and Titles Ordinance 1914, amended in 1959 and 1968, established a land registration system following the Australian Torrens title model and required the survey and registration of customary land. The concept of "waste land" acquisition was retained, although a significant proportion of land that had been acquired under the waste land regulations was returned to customary owners.

Land tenure was one of the major issues in the negotiations leading to independence. The Solomon Islands government wanted only automatic citizens of the Solomon Islands to own land and wanted the power to regain land that had been transferred to others. The British claimed that these rules would be discriminatory and that there must be proper and prompt compensation for land acquired from non-Solomon Islanders. The Land and Titles (Amendment) Act 1977 was enacted as a compromise. The act provides that only "Solomon Islanders" (defined as persons with at least two grandparents born in the Solomon Islands) may hold land in freehold or perpetual title. Other persons may hold leases of no more than seventy-five years. Existing freeholds held by non-Solomon Islanders were automatically converted to seventy-five-year leases with development and rental payment obligations. These limitations on land ownership by non-Solomon Islanders were adopted as Sections 110 and 111 of the Constitution.

B. Customary Land Tenure

Customary land forms more than 90 percent of the land in the Solomon Islands. Land to Solomon Islanders is not merely an economic asset; it has religious, political, and social significance. Under custom, land belongs to a community. Members of the community have rights to use the land.

> A person's right to use land comes from his membership of a line, tribe or clan that is descended from the first people to settle the land. The names of these Solomon Islanders are inherited by the elders and chiefs among their descendants. The names of the tribes, and the authority they gave, were passed from generation to generation by word of mouth, illustrated by symbols, from elders to youngsters. In this way, members of the same tribe know their land rights with simplicity, and without confusion.
>
> The right to use land is the entitlement of the members of the same tribe. Members of different lines, clans and tribes have no rights over other tribal land except through special arrangements such as compensation, marriage, warfare, or gifts. Uses of the land include: cultivation, hunting, building of houses, burying of the dead, collection of firewood, feeding of pigs, worshipping of forefathers, making of sacrifices, foretelling, collection of medicines, growing nali nuts and sago palms, knowledge of valuable trees, and knowledge about natural phenomena such as caves, rivers, rocks, harbours, reefs, and fish as sources of spiritual benefit.[31]

Most of the customary rules relating to land use and the transfer of customary land are closely associated with the religious beliefs of the people.

> . . . land was an ancestral trust committed to the living for the benefit of themselves and generations yet unborn. Land thus was the most valuable heritage of the whole community, and could not be lightly parted with. This is based on the belief that the departed ancestors superintended the earthly affairs of their living descendants, protecting them from disasters and ensuring their welfare, but demanding in return strict compliance with time-honoured

ethical prescriptions. Reverence for ancestral spirits was a cardinal point of traditional faith and such reverence dictated the preservation of land which the living shared with the dead.[32]

These principles of customary land tenure have made it difficult in the Solomon Islands to adopt the land tenure and land registration policies that are thought to lead to economic development. For example, attempts to use the Torrens system to register customary land have not been successful, mainly because the concept of land ownership by individuals is incompatible with customary concepts of communal land rights.

C. Government Taking of Land

Section 8 of the Constitution provides that the government may not acquire land by eminent domain except where the taking is necessary or expedient to promote public interests, where there is "reasonable justification for the causing of any hardship that may result," and where provision has been made by law for the prompt payment of reasonable compensation. Section 8 also provides for High Court review of compulsory acquisition. Section 112 of the Constitution further requires that, before the government compulsorily acquires customary land, it must negotiate with the owners, the owners must have access to independent legal advice, and, if practicable, the interest acquired should be for a fixed term, rather than freehold or permanent.

D. National Parks and Reserves

National parks or reserves can be created under the National Parks Act (Chapter 34) by compulsory process. The act also limits the activities that may be carried out on the park site. Persons may not reside in the park (unless permitted to do so) hunt, carry arms, or cause bush fires. Offenders are liable to imprisonment.

E. Agriculture, Forests, and Fisheries

The protection and advancement of the agricultural and livestock industries is dealt with in the Agriculture and Livestock Act (Chapter 80), which establishes an Agricultural Advisory Committee to make recommendations to the government. The responsible minister is empowered to order the eradication of noxious weeds and prohibit the importation of certain plants. Government inspectors can enter premises to inspect plants for this purpose. The act also restricts the importation of live animals, earth, and sand without satisfactory treatment. Inspectors can enter and examine vessels and prohibit the disposal of refuse from overseas vessels. Contravention of these regulations is a criminal offense.

The Cocoa Act (Chapter 81) provides for the processing, grading, and exporting of cocoa beans. Cocoa buyers must be licensed if they purchase for processing. Persons operating processing facilities must also be registered. The Cocoa Corporation Act (Chapter 82) creates a state corporation authorized to purchase, process, and sell cocoa beans; promote associations of cocoa growers; appoint persons or committees to advise it on the exercise of its functions; and sell machinery and other assets used in the cocoa industry.

The Copra Act (Chapter 83) makes provision for the licensing of copra processors, the grading of copra, and an inspection system.

Unlicensed fishing for trochus shell is restricted to "native" Solomon Islanders by the Trochus Shell Fishing Act (Chapter 87).

The Fisheries (United States of America) (Treaty) Act 1988 implements the treaty relating to fisheries entered into between the governments of the Pacific states and the United States government. The treaty recognizes that the tuna and other fisheries resources of the Pacific are the property of the Pacific states when they are within the 200-mile exclusive economic zones (EEZs) of those states. This reflects a change in the U.S. position, which had initially refused to recognize the 200-mile EEZ and had declared that, even within the zone, there could be no property rights in migratory species.

The original position of the United States had led to a number of incidents involving American fishing boats in the Pacific. For example, pursuant to the Fisheries Act 1972, the U.S. boat *Jeanette Diana* was arrested by Solomon Islands authorities for unlicensed fishing within the EEZ. The court ordered the captain and owner to pay fines and the boat to be forfeited to the Solomon Islands government.[33] The owners of the vessel, through the powerful U.S. Tuna Association, induced the U.S. government to retaliate with an embargo on the import of Solomon Islands tuna products into the United States. The incident was eventually settled by the release of the vessel on payment of compensation by the U.S. government.

The treaty now requires that U.S. vessels fishing in the EEZ waters of the member countries be licensed, and that royalties be paid to the treaty member countries through the Forum Fisheries Agency of the South Pacific Forum.

Forest and timber matters are regulated by the Forests and Timber Act (Chapter 90), which provides for the licensing of loggers and timber mills. The government is empowered to impose a levy for timber felled and exported from the country. The government may prohibit the extraction of timber from specified areas by declaring the land a state forest and may limit extraction to conserve water resources. It is an offense to contravene the act.

Most timber resources in the Solomon Islands are found on customary land. Any person wishing to acquire timber rights on customary land either for export or for saw milling in the country, must lodge an application with the Commissioner for Forest Resources under the Forest Resources and Timber Utilization (Amendment) Act 1990. The application is forwarded to the provincial government and Area Council of the area of the application. The Area Council is required to hold hearings involving the provincial government, the customary owners of the land, and the applicant. These hearings are intended to determine the owners of the area; whether the landowners wish to sell their timber rights, the nature of the rights to be granted to the applicant, the sharing of profits in the venture with landowners, and the participation of the provincial government in the venture. A recommendation for or against the application is then made to the commissioner who must act on such recommendation.

F. Natural Resources

All minerals in the Solomon Islands, whether on customary or freehold land, are, by virtue of Section 2 of the Mining Act 1990 vested in the people and the government of Solomon Islands. The act regulates prospecting and development of mineral deposits. Administration of the act is the responsibility of the Minerals Board established under Section 10. The granting of prospecting and mining licenses and other rights is done by the responsible minister.

A temporary permit to mine may be granted to a holder of a prospector's right or prospecting license. If minerals are found, the permit holder may apply for a mining lease, which allows the leaseholder to undertake mining operations. For large projects, if the general requirements of the act are inappropriate, special mining leases can be granted. The act also provides for access to land and for compensation for land used or damaged by mining.

Oil and gas prospecting, and extraction are regulated by the Petroleum (Production) Act (Chapter 92). All rights in petroleum are vested in the state. The responsible minister is authorized to grant rights and licenses for the search, exploration prospecting, and mining of petroleum.

The Protection of Wrecks and War Relics Act 1980 makes it an offense to remove or otherwise interfere with war wrecks and relics.

The Research Act 1982 requires persons wishing to enter the Solomon Islands to conduct research to obtain a permit. *Research* is defined to mean an "endeavour to discover new facts by careful search or enquiry, scientific study or critical investigation of a subject (a) which will result in a report, thesis, dissertation, academic article, book or manuscript or (b) with the purpose of making audio-visual recordings for academic or commercial purposes." Persons involved in research without a permit are liable to fines of up to SI$1,000.

XIII. Persons and Entities

The age of majority varies depending on the relevant statute. Bodies corporate may sue and be sued.

XIV. Family Law

A. Marriage

Marriages can be entered into in the Solomon Islands in three ways. First, marriages between persons other than "natives" are subject to the Births, Marriages and Deaths Act (Chapter 43), which provides that persons who would be competent to marry in England can marry and register their marriage under the act. The act further provides for the registration of ministers of religion to officiate and register marriages under it.

Second, marriages between indigenous Solomon Islanders may be performed under the Islanders Marriage Act (Chapter 47). Marriages by "non-native persons" under the act are also valid. The act requires that notice of the impending marriage be placed in the local church at least three weeks prior to the marriage. If there are no objections to the marriage, or if the objections are overruled, a minister may celebrate the marriage. Marriages may also be celebrated before the district registrar, in which case notice is not required. The marriageable age under the act is fifteen.

Third, Solomon Islanders may marry in accordance with local custom. The Islanders Marriage Act provides for voluntary registration of customary marriages. Two notable consequences follow from voluntary registration: first, the parties to the customary marriage commit the offense of bigamy if they enter into another marriage; and, second, the laws on divorce in marriages registered under the act apply.

B. Divorce, Separation, and Annulment

Divorce, in a customary marriage that was not registered, is regulated by custom. Divorce in a marriage under the Islanders Marriage Act or a registered customary marriage is regulated by the Islands Divorce Act (Chapter 48).

The procedure for obtaining a divorce is by petition to the High Court. The petition can be made on several grounds, including adultery; desertion for a period of at least three years; cruel treatment of the petitioner; and unsound mind of the respondent. A wife has additional grounds if the husband had been guilty of rape, sodomy, or bestiality. If the court is satisfied that the ground of the petition is proved, it can pronounce a decree of divorce. A husband petitioning for a divorce or judicial separation on the ground of adultery can claim damages from the person who committed adultery with his wife. A decree of judicial separation of a marriage to which the Islands Divorce Act applies can be granted by the High Court on the same grounds as a petition for divorce.

A purported marriage can be declared a nullity if the following conditions exist:

1. it is bigamous;
2. the marriage was induced by duress or mistake;
3. one of the parties was certified insane at the time of the marriage;
4. the parties were within the prohibited degrees of consanguinity or affinity; or
5. the proper formalities of a registered marriage were not complied with.

C. Custody

A court hearing a petition for divorce or judicial separation may in addition make, under the Islanders Marriage Act, "such orders as appear just and necessary with respect to the custody, maintenance and education of the children . . . and the maintenance of the wife." In custody proceedings before the High Court, the paramount consideration is the best interest of the child, which is usually presumed satisfied if custody is given to the mother, even if, under customary law, it would be presumed that the child's best interest would be best served by granting custody to the child's clan or lineage.[35]

XV. Personal Property

The English common law principles of personal property apply in the Solomon Islands.

XVI. Wills and Succession

Two systems of succession exist in the Solomon Islands—customary and statutory. The Wills, Probate and Administration Act 1987 states that its provisions do not apply to matters regulated by current customary usage or to customary land.

Property other than customary land may be transferred by will. Under the act, wills can be made by persons over the age of eighteen regardless of any current customary usage to the contrary. A number of formalities are required for a valid will, including attestation of the will by the testator and two witnesses, or in accordance with custom or the law of another state. Sailors and members of the armed forces on active military service need not comply with the formalities but their wills must demonstrate an intention on the part of the testator to dispose of property.

If a person dies without a will, the act provides for distribution of all property other than customary land mainly to the immediate family members of the deceased (spouse and children first and then parents and other relatives) unless custom provides other rules of distribution. The act also provides that children or spouses may apply to a Magistrates' Court for just provision to be made for them if the testator has not provided adequately under the will for their maintenance. If, under custom, an intestate leaves more than one wife, the property is to be distributed equally between them or their issue.

XVII. Contracts

There is little legislative activity in the area of contract law. The English common law of contract applies as part of the adopted common law and equity principles.

XVIII. Commercial Law

A. Sale of Goods

The English common law applies in most areas of commercial law, including bills of sale, hire purchase, agency, and sale of goods. Those statutes that are in force in the Solomon Islands, such as the Bills of Sale Act (Chapter 71), are taken from United Kingdom legislation.

B. Companies

Companies both private and public can be formed under the Companies Act (Chapter 66). Another form of business association introduced during the colonial period to encourage local people to participate in business, especially in the plantation sector, was the cooperative society (Co-operative Societies Act [Chapter 73]). A cooperative society, when registered, is a body corporate having perpetual succession with powers to hold property, enter into contracts, and sue and be sued. A cooperative may have limited or unlimited liability. To be registered, it must have as its object the promotion of the economic interests of its members and must have at least ten members, each of whom must be more than sixteen years of age and resident in the society area. A registered cooperative is in other respects like a registered company.

A business that is not registered under either the Companies Act or the Co-operative Societies Act must register its business name under the Registration of Business Names Act (Chapter 67), unless the business name consists of the names of the owner.

Trustees of an association for religious, educational, literary, scientific, social, or charitable purposes can register themselves as a corporate body under the Charitable Trusts Act (Chapter 115) if the Registrar of Companies is satisfied that the incorporation of the trustees as a corporation will be expedient for the trust.

XIX. Torts

The general English common law and equity principles of tort law apply as part of the received common law and equity rules, subject to conflicting statutory provisions. There are a number of such statutes. The common law defense of contributory negligence is displaced by the Law Reform (Contributory Negligence) Act 1945 (UK), which provides that the plaintiff's negligence is to be taken into account in determining damages, and such damages are to be reduced to the extent of the plaintiff's share of responsibility.

Other statutes modifying the common law include the Safety at Work Act 1982 and the

Workmen's Compensation Act (Chapter 77) (see **XX Labor Law, below**), Fatal Accidents Acts 1846–1959 (UK), and Law Reform (Miscellaneous Provisions) Act 1934 (UK).

XX. Labor Law

The Labor Act (Chapter 75) was enacted primarily to regulate recruitment and the conditions of employment of unskilled workers on plantations. The act authorized the responsible minister to set minimum wage rates and provided that employers could not make advances against wages. It established a six-day work week; required recruiters to hold licenses and prohibited the recruitment of persons under eighteen; provided that employment contracts exceeding one month were to be in writing and signed in the presence of the minister; prohibited women from working in mines; regulated child labor; and required employers to provide food, housing, and medical facilities.

Under the Unfair Dismissal Act 1982, employees cannot be dismissed without notice or unless the dismissal is justified. An unfair dismissal complaint is made to a Trade Disputes Panel established by the Trade Disputes (Settlement) Act 1981, which is empowered to dismiss the complaint or order reinstatement or compensation.

The Employment Act 1981 requires employers to keep records of the dates of employment, remuneration, holidays, sick leave, hours of work, terms for termination, and disciplinary procedures. Employers must hold insurance policies covering employment-related risks, including injuries and diseases. The act also makes provision for redundancy and long-service leave payments (for employee pension plans, see **IX Welfare Law**).

The Safety at Work Act 1981 requires that employers ensure the health and safety of both their workers and other persons who could be exposed to risks because of the nature of the business. Employees are also under a duty to take reasonable care when at work for the safety of themselves and others. A person who manages, designs, or constructs a work place or a substance at a work place is under a duty to ensure that it is safe. Breach of these duties carries criminal sanctions as well as civil liability.

The Workmen's Compensation Act (Chapter 77) requires employers to pay compensation to workers for injuries from accidents arising from or in the course of employment. The act excludes persons employed in nonmanual labor who earn more than SI$4,000 a year, casual laborers, outworkers, or members of the employer's family.

A trade union registered under the Trade Unions Act (Chapter 76) is immune from criminal liability for restraint of trade and from civil liability in both contract and tort for its lawful trade union activities. An agreement or trust created pursuant to its activities as a trade union is not void or voidable.

The Registrar of Trade Unions is responsible for the administration of the Trade Union Act, including registering trade unions, overseeing their administration, and ensuring compliance with the act. The registrar may cancel the registration of unions that breach the act. Unregistered trade unions are prohibited from carrying on business.

The Trade Dispute (Settlement) Act 1981 establishes a Trade Dispute Panel. A party to a trade dispute or the responsible minister can refer the dispute to the panel at any time. If the panel is of the opinion that the dispute can be settled by negotiation, it can offer its assistance to achieve this. If the negotiation succeeds, the settlement may be incorporated into an order. If a settlement is not achieved by negotiation, the panel can arbitrate the dispute. Once a dispute is before the Trade Dispute Panel, industrial action on the dispute is prohibited. Contravention of this prohibition can result in both criminal and civil liability. A person who suffers a loss as a result of an industrial action relating to a dispute that is before the panel can apply to the High Court for compensation. Compensation will not be awarded if the industrial action is over a matter not before the panel, even if it involves the same parties.[36]

XXI. Industrial and Intellectual Property Rights

The Copyright Act 1987 gives copyright protection to original literary, dramatic, musical, and artistic works; sound recordings; films; and broadcasts. Copyright protection exists for works in both published and unpublished form. If the work is unpublished, the author must be a "qualified person." A *qualified person* is defined as one who is a citizen of the Solomon Islands or domiciled, resident, or, if a company, incorporated in the Solomon Islands. Copyright protection is conferred for a published work if its first publication was in the Solomon Islands and the author is a qualified person.

Copyright in literary, dramatic, musical, and artistic works lasts for a period of fifty years from the death of the author if the work is not published, performed in public, offered for sale to the public, or broadcast. If the work is published, performed, offered for sale or broadcast, copyright exists for fifty years from the date of its first publication, performance, offer for sale, or broadcast.

Copyright protection is given to sound recordings, films, and broadcasts if the author is a qualified person, the work has been published, and its first publication or broadcast was in or from the Solomon Islands. The protection exists for fifty years from the date of first publication or broadcast.

The act empowers the responsible minister to extend its application to countries and international organizations if reciprocal protections are given to Solomon Islands copyright works.

Industrial patent legislation includes the Registration of United Kingdom Patents Act (Chapter 68) and the United Kingdom Designs (Protection) Act (Chapter 70), which provide for registration and protection of British registered patents, trademarks, and designs and confer the same rights as does British law.

XXII. Legal Education and Profession

The Legal Practitioners Act 1987 regulates the legal profession and legal practitioners. Admission or provisional admission to the Solomon Islands bar is by application to the Chief Justice. The Chief Justice will issue a certificate if satisfied that the applicant is qualified, is a fit and proper person, has complied with the rules relating to admission of legal practitioners, and has paid the required fee to the registrar. To qualify for provisional admission, an applicant must hold a law degree from a recognized university. For full admission, the applicant needs to have practical experience for a period of about two years. Persons admitted in other jurisdictions may be admitted to the Solomon Islands bar.

The act requires that a roll of practitioners be kept by the registrar, provides for the establishment of a disciplinary committee, and sets out penalties for practicing without being admitted and other offenses. The rules to be promulgated by the Chief Justice with the advice of a rules committee will give effect to most of the provisions of the act.

The legal profession at present consists of a number of Solomon Islanders trained in Papua New Guinea, Australia, and New Zealand and a few non-Solomon Islanders.

In-service courses have been conducted for paralegal personnel, including clerks of the Local

Courts, by the Chief Magistrate and the Director of Legal Education. The Law Faculty of the University of Papua New Guinea has conducted a number of paralegal courses with funding assistance from the Asia Foundation.

XXIII. RESEARCH GUIDE

Solomon Islands legislation through 1969 has been published in *Laws of the B.S.I.P.* (Honiara: British Solomon Islands Protectorate, 1971). No comprehensive set of statutes has been published since independence, although copies of individual laws are available from government offices and are published in annual bound volumes. Selected judgments are printed in *Solomon Islands Law Reports* (S.I.L.R.) (Honiara: High Court) for years after 1980, and a few Solomon Islands cases are reported in *South Pacific Law Reports* (Sydney, Oxford University Press), beginning in 1987.

Allardice, M. "Custom and Law in Malaita," [1984] *New Zealand Law J.* 283.

Brown, K. "The Public Solicitor's Office in Solomon Islands," in C. G. Powles and M. Pulea, eds. *Pacific Courts and Legal Systems*. Suva: University of the South Pacific, 1988.

———. "Criminal Law and Custom in Solomon Islands," 2 *Queensland Univ. Tech. Law J.* 133 (1986).

Corrin, J. C. "Constitutional Challenges in the Solomon Islands," 5 *Queensland Univ. Tech. Law J.* 145 (1989).

Daly, F. "Custom Bilong Yumi," 3(2) *Commonwealth Judicial J.* 26 (1979/81).

Hogbin, I. "Native Councils and Native Courts in the Solomon Islands," 14 *Oceania* 257 (1944).

Kenilorea, P. "The Executive in the Constitution," in P. Larmour, ed. *Solomon Islands Politics*. Suva: Institute of Pacific Studies, 1983.

Larmour, P. "Alienated Land and Independence in Solomon Islands," 12 *Melanesian Law J.* 101 (1984).

———, ed. *Land in Solomon Islands*. Suva: University of the South Pacific, 1979.

Paia, W.A. "Aspects of Constitutional Development in the Solomon Islands," 10(2) *J. Pacific History* 81 (1975).

Scheffler, H. W., and P. Larmour. "Solomon Islands: Evolving a New Custom," in R. G. Crocombe, ed. *Land Tenure in the Pacific*, 3d ed. Suva: University of the South Pacific, 1987.

Smiley, "Settling Land Disputes in Solomon Islands," 9(2) *Pacific Perspective* 24 (1980).

Takoa, I., and J. Freeman. "Provincial Courts in Solomon Islands," in C. G. Powles and M. Pulea, eds. *Pacific Courts and Legal Systems*. Suva: University of the South Pacific, 1988.

Tiffany, W. "Disputes in Customary Land Courts: Case Studies from the Solomon Islands," 7 *Melanesian Law J.* 99 (1979).

11. Tokelau

AH ANGELO

I. Dateline

1000 A.D.	First evidence of Polynesian settlement, probably from Samoa.
1765	First recorded sightings by Europeans.
1861–1863	Protestant mission established on Atafu and Fakaofo. Roman Catholic missions established on Nukunonu.
1863	Peruvian slave ships raid Tokelau and substantially diminish population.
1877	British jurisdiction extended to Tokelau.
1889	Each atoll formally placed under British protection.
1916	Order-in-Council annexes Union Islands (Tokelau) to the Gilbert and Ellice Islands Colony.
1925	Tokelau excluded from the Gilbert and Ellice Islands Colony.
1926	Administrative control for Tokelau transferred from Britain to New Zealand. Power to legislate delegated to Administrator of Western Samoa.
1946	Tokelau placed on the United Nations list of non-self-governing territories as a dependent territory administered by New Zealand.
1949	Tokelau becomes part of New Zealand.
1962	Tokelau, with New Zealand's agreement, placed on list of territories governed by the United Nations Declaration on the Granting of Independence to Colonial Countries and Peoples.
1976	First visit of a mission of the United Nations Special Committee on Decolonization.
1980	Treaty of Tokehega, delimiting the sea boundary between New Zealand and the United States in the area around Tokelau, signed in Tokelau.
1982	Existence of the General Fono (a joint meeting of representatives of each of the three islands of Tokelau) recognized in law.
1987	First Tokelauan heads Tokelau Public Service. A Tokelau mission visits the United Nations.

II. Historical, Cultural, and Economic Survey

By virtue of Section 3 of the Tokelau Act 1948 (NZ), Tokelau is an integral part of the state of New Zealand. Although Tokelau has a legal system distinct from that of metropolitan New Zealand, it has no independent legislature or executive. In international law, Tokelau is a non-self-governing dependent territory administered by New Zealand and is listed as a territory working toward self-determination under the aegis of the United Nations Committee on Decolonization.

A. History

Preliminary archaeological surveys indicate that the three small islands that constitute Tokelau have been inhabited for many centuries, at least since 1000 A.D., but details of early habitations are not known. It is likely, however, that the earliest settlers came from Samoa. The first contact with Europeans was in the eighteenth century, and most of the Tokelauan people were converted to Christianity in the early 1860s. The population was substantially diminished in 1863 by raiding Peruvian slave ships. The Western Pacific Order-in-Council of 1877, made under the Pacific Islanders Protection Acts (UK) and the Foreign Jurisdiction Acts (UK) extended British jurisdiction to Tokelau. This extension was followed in 1889 by a formal grant of protectorate status to each of Tokelau's three atolls. By an Order-in-Council of 1916, Tokelau, then known as the Union Islands, was annexed to Britain's Gilbert and Ellice Islands Colony.

Tokelau's relationship with New Zealand began in 1926, by virtue of the Union Islands (No. 1) Order in Council 1925 and the Union Islands (No. 2) Order in Council 1925, which respectively excluded Tokelau from the Gilbert and Ellice Islands Colony and (with effect from 1926) transferred administrative control for Tokelau from Great Britain to New Zealand. Then the New Zealand government, by virtue of the Union Islands (No. 1 of New Zealand) Order 1926, delegated the power to legislate for Tokelau to the Administrator of Western Samoa; Western Samoa was at that time also under New Zealand control.

In 1946, Tokelau was placed on the United Nations list of non-self-governing territories as a dependent territory administered by New Zealand. In 1949 Tokelau formally became part of New Zealand with the transfer of the territory from Great Britain.

The first team from the United Nations Special Committee on Decolonization visited Tokelau in 1976. The Committee of 24 has sent a special mission to Tokelau every five years since then. Since 1976, there has been little constitutional development at the legislative level, but a great deal of development in the practice of government. In particular, the General Fono, which is a joint meeting of representatives of each of the three islands of Tokelau, has taken over budgetary control for Tokelau and has also become the principal policy-making body. The most recent step in the evolution of local self-government has been the localization of the Tokelau Public Service in 1987 when, for the first time, a Tokelauan became the official secretary. Shortly after that, the official secretary and a representative of the General Fono visited the United Nations in New York.

B. Culture

Tokelau consists of three small coral atolls situated just south of the equator, approximately 300 miles north of Western Samoa. Each atoll has one village, which is situated on the west (and lee) side of the atoll. The atolls at their widest points measure 200 yards across and lie no more than 10 feet above sea level. The atolls are totally exposed to the elements and suffer occasional devastation by high seas, cyclones, and related phenomena.

The people of Tokelau are Polynesian; there is significant interchange with and intermarriage with people of Western Samoa and Tuvalu. The Tokelauan language closely resembles the Samoan and Tuvaluan languages; Samoan was until relatively recently the written language of Tokelau, because of the influence of the missionaries and the fact that the Bible used in Tokelau is written in Samoan.

The primary organizational features of Tokelauan society are the village, control by elders, and the churches. Tokelauans typically are either Roman Catholic or members of the Christian

Congregational Church of Samoa. The island of Atafu is Protestant, the island of Nukunonu is Roman Catholic, and the island of Fakaofo has both a Protestant and a Roman Catholic church and also a small group of Jehovah's Witnesses. The importance of the churches in the community is evident in the strict observance of Sunday, and religion plays a visible part in the regular daily activities of the communities.

C. Economy

The principal resources of Tokelau are its 1,629 people, coconut palms, breadfruit trees, and the fish of the lagoon, reef, and ocean. The islands lack soil, and two of them have no fresh water. They have little timber other than that of the coconut palms and breadfruit trees. It is a subsistence environment and economy.

The annual budgetary grant from the New Zealand government funds transport and government services. An increasing number of people are in paid employment, but they are almost exclusively civil servants and government and village officials. The schools, hospitals, essential services, and works departments are run by Tokelau Public Service employees. Other sources of individual income are copra and handicrafts. Remittances from abroad (principally New Zealand) are also a substantial source of income for the members of the communities. Those who have cash to spend buy consumer items from the village store. More substantial items such as aluminum dinghies and outboard motors are purchased abroad.

III. Sources of Law

Acts and regulations of New Zealand extended to Tokelau, the common law, custom, and village rules provide the official sources of law for Tokelau.

A. Legislation

The sources of law are set forth in the Tokelau Act 1948 (NZ). The preeminent source of Tokelau law is statutory—acts of the New Zealand Parliament that have been specifically extended to Tokelau. Of those acts, the most significant and the one that comes nearest to being a constitution for Tokelau, is the Tokelau Act 1948.

The second source is the body of regulations made under the acts of the New Zealand Parliament that are in force in Tokelau, including regulations made under Section 4 of the Tokelau Act 1948 specifically for Tokelau, under Section 9 of the Tokelau Amendment Act 1967 for the Tokelau Public Service, and under one of the other acts in force in Tokelau (regulations made expressly for Tokelau or part of a New Zealand law extended to Tokelau).

Regulations made under Section 4 of the Tokelau Act take two main forms: (1) regulations made specifically for Tokelau (for example, the Tokelau Divorce Regulations 1987) or (2) regulations that extend or adapt to Tokelau legislation existing elsewhere (for example, the Tokelau Crimes Regulations 1975, which transplant part of the law of Niue to Tokelau, or the Tokelau [New Zealand Laws] Regulations 1975, which extend to Tokelau various New Zealand statutes and the regulations made under them).

Section 5 of the Tokelau Act 1948 provides specifically for the continuance in force of laws that were operative in Tokelau before January 1, 1949 (the date on which Tokelau became part of New Zealand). A great range of law is potentially covered by Section 5; however, the laws that have been identified as still in force under Section 5 are inoperative, most are obsolete, and all are currently awaiting repeal as part of the Tokelau law reform project. For all practical purposes, legislation in force in Tokelau is restricted to that made after January 1, 1949.

B. Common Law

The other imported body of law applicable in Tokelau is described in Section 4A of the Tokelau Act 1948, which was added by amendment in 1969 as follows:

> The law of England as existing on the 14th day of January in the year 1840 (being the year in which the Colony of New Zealand was established) shall be in force in Tokelau, save so far as inconsistent with this Act or inapplicable to the circumstances of Tokelau: Provided that no Act of Parliament of England or of Great Britain or of the United Kingdom passed before the said 14th day of January in the year 1840 shall be in force in Tokelau, unless and except so far as it is in force in New Zealand at the commencement of this section.

This formula for receiving English common law is found throughout the Commonwealth, and its ambiguities are well known. There is no judicial practice in respect of it for Tokelau. The administrative practice, however, suggests that the common law of England is likely to be the body of law used to resolve a specific problem. The elders of Tokelau have recently resolved that the final source of law for Tokelau should be the law of England for the time being in force. This decision was made in order to resolve the difficulties surrounding the sources of law in Tokelau, and in particular the identification of the body of principle that should be used in the absence of specific legislation. The choice of the elders follows the pattern adopted by Section 112 of the Constitution of Western Samoa.

C. Custom and Village Rules

Custom is not specifically designated as a source of law, though the daily life of the village proceeds on the basis of custom. The prime areas of attention for custom are family relations, landholding, public order, and village organization—matters that have also been the subject of legislation; a task for the future is to bring the legislation into line with the customary practices.

Custom as a source of law in its own right has no official significance. However, custom remains central to an understanding of the operation of the Tokelau legal system, because legislation often refers to custom. This is the case, for instance, under the Tokelau Village Incorporation Regulations 1986 and the Tokelau Divorce Regulations 1987. In particular, all matters relating to land are subject to Tokelau custom as declared by decisions of the elders, by virtue of Tokelau Amendment Act 1967 (NZ).

The elders of each village make rules for their village by exercising the legislative power conferred on them by the Tokelau Village Incorporation Regulations 1986.

IV. Constitutional System

A. Territory

Tokelau is defined in the Tokelau Act 1948 as "the Islands of Fakaofo, Nukunonu and Atafu, together with all small islands, islets, rocks, and reefs depending on them." A 12-mile territorial sea is established by the Tokelau (Territorial Sea and Exclusive Economic Zone) Act 1977 (NZ), which also provides that the exclusive economic zone extends 200 nautical miles from the shore, except where otherwise agreed in the Treaty of Tokehega. The treaty sets the maritime boundary between the Tokelauan island of Fakaofo and Swains Island (part of American Samoa).

B. Nationality and Citizenship

There is no Tokelau nationality. Tokelau is part of New Zealand, and the only nationality that can be acquired under the law of Tokelau is that of New Zealand. The Citizenship Act 1977 (NZ) is part of Tokelau law and confers New Zealand citizenship on those born in Tokelau and on the first-generation descendants of persons born in Tokelau. Certain persons born abroad, such as the children of Tokelau public servants, may be registered as born in Tokelau, under the Tokelau Births and Deaths Registration Regulations 1969. New Zealand citizenship can be granted also to persons who have a specific connection with Tokelau, such as residence, marriage, or government service. Although the Citizenship Act is Tokelau law, the Passports Act 1980 of New Zealand is not. This means that Tokelauans, although New Zealand citizens, must apply for passports under New Zealand rather than Tokelauan law.

Residents of Tokelau do not vote in New Zealand elections and do not receive New Zealand social welfare benefits. New Zealand citizenship does, however, provide free access to metropolitan New Zealand, and people from Tokelau use this access readily for education, family, and employment purposes. Migration to New Zealand has at times resulted in a net population loss for Tokelau, but recent years have seen a slight reversal of this trend, with the return of some families to Tokelau after many years in metropolitan New Zealand.

The Tokelau Immigration Regulations 1991 prescribe a set of four permits for visitors to Tokelau. Tokelauans who are New Zealand citizens require no permit to enter, reside in, or work in Tokelau. Tokelauans who are not New Zealand citizens will be issued a special permit to enter, reside in, and work in Tokelau. Non-Tokelauan New Zealand citizens may enter Tokelau without a permit but require permits to reside or work in Tokelau. All other persons require a permit to enter, reside in, or work in Tokelau.

C. Government

1. TERRITORIAL (NEW ZEALAND) GOVERNMENT

a. Head of State

Because Tokelau is part of New Zealand, the Head of State of Tokelau is therefore the Head of State of the realm of New Zealand— the sovereign of the United Kingdom, who is represented in New Zealand by a Governor General. The Governor General acts on the advice of Her Majesty's ministers in the New Zealand Executive Council. The minister responsible for Tokelau affairs is the Minister of External Relations and Trade.

b. Executive

Executive organization for Tokelau as a whole is both internal and external. The external aspect of the organization of Tokelau is control from New Zealand. Although Tokelau's administration is ultimately under the control of the Minister of External Relations and Trade, its chief executive officer is the Administrator of Tokelau, who is appointed by the New Zealand government. The current Administrator is an assistant secretary in the Ministry of External Relations and Trade. The Administrator has the ultimate decision-making power on Tokelau administration. At law most of the governmental powers for Tokelau are vested in the Administrator, but there is power under the Tokelau Administration Regulations 1980 to delegate the exercise of those powers. The practice in recent years has been for the powers of day-to-day administration to be delegated to the official secretary (the head of the Tokelau Public Service based in Western Samoa). The result is that the Administrator is kept informed and makes occasional trips to Tokelau, but has little or nothing to do with its day-to-day governing. As a rule, key elders go to New Zealand for discussions with the Administrator and other officials once every two years.

c. Legislature

Legislative power over Tokelau is vested primarily in the New Zealand Parliament. Subordinate legislative power vests in the Governor General in council and may be exercised on the motion of the minister to the Executive Council. Additionally, the State Services Commission may make regulations in respect of the Tokelau Public Service; and under the Tokelau Village Incorporation Regulations 1986, each village may make rules on domestic matters.

d. Judiciary

Judicial power is set out in the Tokelau Amendment Act 1986, with three levels of courts. The lowest level, but the only one of any practical significance, is the village court, presided over by a commissioner. In the absence of a commissioner, the Faipule (the chair of the village council; see **IV, C (2) (a) Village Councils**) exercises the commissioner's powers. There are currently no commissioners, therefore the Faipule are the judicial officers. The jurisdiction of the commissioner is restricted to the island of appointment and by the nature of the offense (punishable by fine only or by imprisonment for not more than one year) in criminal matters or the value of the property in dispute (NZ$1,000) in civil matters. The maximum penalty the commissioner may impose is a fine of $150 or a term of imprisonment not exceeding three months.

The second court in the system is the High Court of New Zealand acting as a High Court for Tokelau. It acts at first instance for matters that are beyond the power of the commissioner, and on appeal from civil judgments and the more serious of criminal judgments of the commissioner. The High Court may sit in New Zealand or elsewhere as appropriate. It has not yet heard a case from Tokelau, but it is envisaged that a single judge would conduct any hearings and would make decisions on the papers. It is also anticipated that each island will establish an appeal committee to deal with appeals from the commissioner's court of less serious criminal matters.

From any judgments of the High Court, final appeal is to the Court of Appeal of New Zealand acting as a court of appeal for Tokelau.

Because very little exists in the written record of judicial activity in Tokelau, it is difficult to assess in Western terms precisely what volume of litigation there is or may be. An informed guess would suggest that each island has between twenty and thirty cases heard by the Faipule each year and that the bulk of these concern petty criminal matters, such as theft, adultery, fornication, rumor mongering, and assault. On the civil side, there are a number of land disputes each year, but land issues do not come before the court. They are decided under the Tokelau Amendment Act 1967 by the council of elders in accordance with custom. Other civil matters for which there is some evidence of litigation involve disputes as to possession of or title to chattels, such as fishing knives, roofing iron, and chickens. Matrimonial matters are now, by virtue of the Tokelau Adoption Regulations 1966, Tokelau Births and Deaths Registration Regulations 1969, Tokelau Marriage Regulations 1986, and Tokelau Divorce Regulations 1987, dealt with either by the Tokelau administration or by the elders; they are not judicial matters.

2. TOKELAUAN LOCAL GOVERNMENT

a. Village Councils

Although there are no regional divisions within Tokelau, geography creates significant divisions. Each of Tokelau's three islands is isolated from the others by high seas. Since 1992, physical communication is maintained among them by a motorized catamaran, specially built for the purpose, which carries freight and passengers. The geographical division is complemented by the autonomy of each of the villages. Each village has a legislative, administrative, and judicial organization independent of the other two in respect of its daily affairs.

The villages are controlled by representatives of each kaiga in the village. (A *kaiga* is an extended family group that consists of descendants of a common ancestor and holds land rights in common.) For instance, if there are thirty-nine families on the atoll, the village council will be made up of thirty-nine members. Among the chief officials of the village is the Faipule, who, as chair of the village council, deals with relations between the village and the outside world and, as a matter of practice, acts as the judicial officer on the island. The second official is the Pulenuku, who is often described as the village mayor; in matters of purely domestic and village concern, the Pulenuku is the most important of the village officers. The Pulenuku oversees the village workforce, the movement of boats, matters of village cleanliness, and the water supply. The third official, the Failautuhi, the village clerk and treasurer, is appointed by the village council. The Faipule and Pulenuku are elected once every three years by everyone in the village over the age of twenty-one.

The workings of the councils and election procedures differ slightly from island to island and from time to time. The most significant variation is in Fakaofo, where the village council is made up of a small group of senior leaders, approximately twenty-five out of the eighty or so kaiga representatives. This inner group of elders operates much as do the councils of the other two islands where all kaiga representatives are members.

The will of the village councils is executed principally by the able-bodied men of each village. The village council directs the men to, for instance, gather copra, clear plantations, go on fishing expeditions, or unload the monthly supply ship. The men then, under their own leader or (in Nukunonu) under the Pulenuku, perform the task. A parallel organization of women of the village has responsibility for house and village cleanliness and preparation of food for public gatherings.

b. General Fono

The General Fono is a group of elders from each of the three atolls that meets several times a year to discuss matters affecting Tokelau as a whole, including, in recent years, matters of law. Typically, each island sends fifteen representatives to the General Fono. The General Fono has a significant constitutional role but very limited legislative or executive powers. The current conventions are that all budgetary allocation is done by the General Fono and that no law will be made for Tokelau without the approval of the General Fono. Increasingly, major policy decisions are being taken by the General Fono. The next step in constitutional evolution would be for the General Fono to be given legislative powers.

c. Public Service

The Tokelau public service is controlled by the New Zealand State Services Commission and is based in Apia, Western Samoa. This means that the central executive authority of Tokelau is offshore.

The Tokelau public service has 180 members who are distributed approximately one-quarter in Apia and one-quarter in each of the three atolls. The head of the service is the official secretary, to whom report six directors (the Directors of Administration, Health, Education, Public Works, Agriculture and Fisheries, and Finance).

The Office for Tokelau Affairs has no specific legal status by the law of Tokelau, the law of New Zealand, or the law of Western Samoa. The Western Samoan government has before it a legislative proposal that would confer corporate personality on the Office for Tokelau Affairs under Western Samoan law and also extend certain of the diplomatic privileges and immunities to key officials in the Tokelau public service. In the meantime, the Tokelau administration operates simply as a private organization independent of the New Zealand High Commission and without the benefit of any of the privileges or immunities that typically attend government officials based in a foreign state.

D. Emergency Powers

There is no legislation on emergency powers, which are therefore governed, if at all, by the common law. The General Fono has approved a legislative proposal to formalize the administrative channels for the exercise of authority in emergencies and provide for compensation for private property in appropriate cases.

E. Human Rights

The International Covenant on Civil and Political Rights (including the Optional Protocol), the International Covenant on Economic, Social, and Cultural Rights; and the International Convention on the Elimination of All Forms of Discrimination against Women were ratified by New Zealand and apply to Tokelau. The due process requirements of international human rights are addressed in the draft Tokelau Crimes, Procedure and Evidence Regulations now under consideration by the New Zealand government.

V. Administrative Organization and Law

A. Tokelau Public Service

The Tokelau Amendment Act 1967 provides for the Tokelau public service and its control by the State Services Commission of New Zealand. The effect of this act has been to take the New Zealand public service administrative structure for the purposes of Tokelau law. The act provides, however, that laws relating to the terms of employment and pension funds do not apply to Tokelau. The result is that all matters of appointment, discipline, promotion, and dismissal are ultimately controlled by an independent service commission based in New Zealand. Section 4 of the Tokelau Amendment Act provides that the commission can appoint to the service of Tokelau the employees it considers necessary and can determine the conditions of service. The commission has a duty to ensure a proper standard of efficiency in the service and in the proper fulfillment of its role may issue instructions from time to time. The commission may make regulations as to the pay, allowances, discipline, control, and management of the public service. To date, no regulations have been made, and though the role of the State Services Commission is decisive in determining the pay and conditions of service of public servants, the General Fono has increasingly interacted with the State Services Commission to establish pay rates appropriate to the Tokelau public service.

The State Services Commission has, like the Administrator, delegated a substantial number of powers to the official secretary in Apia. Thus, in some matters, the secretary is responsible to the State Services Commission, in others to the Administrator, and in others to the representative of the General Fono.

B. Public Finance and Audit

The financial aspects of the Tokelau administration are provided for in the Tokelau Finance Regulations 1967, Tokelau Administration Regulations 1980, and Tokelau Copra Regulations 1952. All three sets of regulations are under review to take account of the localization of the Tokelau public service and the General Fono's increased role in financial matters. At the level of principle, the regulations are functional; however, at the level of detail they have for some time been found unduly restrictive and in a number of areas practice has gone ahead of changes in the law.

In matters of audit, Tokelau legislation is scant. In practice, New Zealand audit procedures still apply for Tokelau and New Zealand Treasury guidelines are used in financial matters. In terms of the Tokelau legal system, however, this has no more strength than that of a practice.

C. Rule Making

Subordinate legislation is made at a number of different levels for Tokelau. Most take the form of regulations made by Order-in-Council by the Governor General. This regulation making is either an exercise of the authority given under the Tokelau Act 1948 to make regulations for the "peace, order, and good government of Tokelau" (Section 4) or the exercise of a general regulation-making power in an act of the New Zealand Parliament that has been extended to Tokelau. Under the Tokelau Amendment Act 1967, the State Services Commission may make regulations for the Tokelau public service "with the approval of the Governor-General."

At the local level, each village has the power to make rules for the village, subject only to their compatibility with acts of the New Zealand Parliament that extend to Tokelau, regulations made for Tokelau, and international obligations binding on Tokelau (Regulation 18 of the Tokelau Village Incorporation Regulations 1986).

D. Review of Administrative Action

A New Zealand statute of significant administrative importance in New Zealand is the Ombudsman Act 1975. It does not, however, apply in Tokelau. While it has been argued that the ombudsman may investigate matters within the control of New Zealand agencies, including the State Services Commissions, even though they do not concern internal New Zealand affairs, the more widely accepted view is that the Ombudsman Act does not extend to Tokelau, and in practice the ombudsman has refrained from claiming jurisdiction in matters arising from the administration of Tokelau.

Apart from review procedures for employees of the Tokelau public service, there is no specific legislative provision for review of administrative action. Judicial review of the actions of individual officials is available under the common law. Tokelau has no legislative provision for suits against the government, and the English common law doctrine of sovereign immunity would probably be an effective bar to an action against the Crown.

The Tokelau Commissions of Inquiry Regulations 1991 provides, on the standard Common-

VI. International Obligations

A. Treaties and Conventions

International obligations that affect Tokelau are those entered into on its behalf by New Zealand. Of specific relevance to the Tokelau situation are the United Nations Covenant on Civil and Political Rights and the Convention on the Elimination of All Forms of Discrimination against Women. No specific reservations were made for Tokelau for either of these conventions.

The normal pattern is for the New Zealand government to sign treaties for New Zealand and for Tokelau to be bound as a result. The Treaty of Tokehega, which establishes New Zealand's boundary with American Samoa was signed for New Zealand by three elders of Tokelau.

In the Pacific region, Tokelau is represented directly in a number of forums. Tokelau deals directly with the South Pacific Commission, with the United Nations Development Program and with a number of other United Nations agencies.

The treaties that apply to Tokelau are in a number of respects different from those that affect metropolitan New Zealand, because Tokelau may still be subject to treaties concluded by the United Kingdom while Tokelau was under British jurisdiction. Each pre-1949 United Kingdom treaty would need to be examined to see if, on its wording, it had been made to encompass Tokelau. Conversely, not all treaties concluded by New Zealand, either before or since 1949, by their terms include Tokelau.

B. Diplomatic Privileges

The Consular Privileges and Immunities Act 1971 (NZ) and the Diplomatic Privileges and Immunities Act 1968 (NZ) have been extended to Tokelau and implement in Tokelau the relevant international conventions.

C. Reciprocal Enforcement and Extradition

There is no Tokelau legislation on reciprocal enforcement or extradition. The law of Tokelau is therefore the English common law on the recognition and enforcement of foreign judgments. Those rules also govern New Zealand judgments in Tokelau and Tokelau judgments in New Zealand.

The return of offenders to New Zealand from Tokelau is made possible by the Fugitive Offenders Act 1881 (UK) and the Commonwealth Countries Act 1977 (NZ). The return of offenders to Tokelau from New Zealand is also governed by the Fugitive Offenders Act. The return of offenders between Tokelau and countries other than New Zealand is probably covered by the Extradition Act 1870 (UK).

VII. Revenue Law

Two sets of legislation relate to taxes. The first and most significant is the Tokelau community services levy introduced by the Tokelau Amendment Act 1982. This legislation is significant for a number of reasons and at a number of levels. It marks the first occasion in the evolution of Tokelau government in which the General Fono made a specific legislative initiative. The levy establishes a balance in the relationship between members of the Tokelau public service and the traditional village community, in that its object is to restore to the village some money for services lost by the diversion of human resources from the village workforce to the government sector. Although the levy is an indication of the move into the world of money, it is far from being a general tax. Essentially it applies only to Tokelau public service employees, and the maximum tax rate is only 10 percent. There is no general tax on income earned in Tokelau.

The only other revenue legislation is the Tokelau Customs Regulations 1991, which establishes a customs regime of prohibited imports, imports requiring permits and exports requiring permits. There is a 10 percent *ad valorem* duty on commercial imports and a 65 percent duty on alcohol and tobacco products.

VIII. Investment Law

There is neither an investment incentive system nor significant investment potential in Tokelau. The community is small and homogeneous. There is no place of residence or special facility for non-Tokelauans. Tokelau does not present itself as an investment possibility, operating as it does at a subsistence level. No development of tourism or business in the international sense is envisaged, nor, with the present limited communication system with the outside world, could Tokelau realistically be seen as a tax haven. The jurisdiction is very stable politically and socially, but the communications infrastructure necessary for high-level offshore international business is totally lacking.

Tokelau has some trade with the outside, in the import of goods and materials from Western Samoa, American Samoa, New Zealand, and Fiji. Exports are few and consist mainly of copra and handicrafts; this trade is handled by the Tokelau administration, which subsidizes producers. The handicrafts are sold to the public through the Tokelau administration shop in Apia, along with Tokelau stamps and coins. The copra is sold to the copra mill in Western Samoa. Other limited opportunities for export trade that are being explored include trochus shell, palm syrup (kaleve), and fish products such as clams and coconut crabs.

IX. Welfare Law

A. Education

In Tokelau education is free and universal but not compulsory; most children attend school from the age of six to sixteen years and learn Tokelauan and English. The more academically successful students leave Tokelau before their school certificate year and study abroad as scholarship students in New Zealand, Western Samoa, Niue, the Cook Islands, Tonga, or Fiji. Local schooling ends at Form V (school certificate level), and successful scholars proceed to tertiary education in New Zealand, Australia, Fiji, or Western Samoa.

B. Social Services

Medical services are provided free of charge; there is a small hospital on each atoll.

The elderly receive a monthly cash payment of NZ$7. An accident compensation fund provides payments to the injured and disabled; the maximum sum payable is NZ$500.

The New Zealand social security system does not apply to Tokelau. The public welfare schemes that are in place are organized by the General Fono.

X. CRIMINAL LAW

The main body of criminal law of Tokelau is found in the Tokelau Crimes Regulations 1975, which derive from the Niue Act 1966 (NZ) and consequently are poorly adapted to Tokelau and little known or used there. The regulations provide a fairly standard range of offenses from murder and manslaughter through assaults, moral offenses, slander, theft, unlawful entry, arson, and lesser offenses against public order. Section 239 of the regulations provides that "no person shall be proceeded against for any criminal offence at common law." In addition to the offenses listed in the regulations, there are a small number of other Tokelau regulations, including assault, theft, drunkenness, and adultery. In 1985, the General Fono approved a new draft of Crimes, Procedure and Evidence Regulations, that would maintain most of the criminal offenses in a simplified form, add a number of customary offenses such as sexual intercourse between persons not married to each other, and redraft the definitions of a number of the existing offenses to take account of local conditions.

XI. JUDICIAL PROCEDURE

Judicial process is in principle regulated by the Tokelau Crimes Regulations 1975 and the Tokelau Amendment Act 1986. That legislation says very little about procedure or evidence, but to the extent that the matter is provided for it follows the standard common law pattern, presupposing an adversarial process.

The only judicial practice actually known to Tokelau is the procedure followed by the commissioner in Tokelau in handling the occasional criminal offense or rare civil matter. The most usual procedure is for an accused person to appear before the commissioner and assembled elders on an oral complaint presented by the police. The commissioner questions the accused and when the facts of the case are known the commissioner gives judgment. In criminal matters, the usual penalties are community service of a few weeks to three months or a fine of a few dollars.

The procedure still follows the oral tradition. There is no court documentation, offenders appear on request, and when convicted pay the penalties without necessity for execution. There are no prisons in Tokelau, nor is there any serious crime. The 1985 draft regulations for crimes, procedure, and evidence propose a blend of the common law and customary law procedures and in particular confirm Tokelau's commitment to an inquisitorial form of court procedure.

There is no provision in the law of Tokelau for the limitation of actions.

XII. LAND AND NATURAL RESOURCES

A. Land Tenure and Administration

All land is vested in the Crown as ultimate title holder. All land matters are governed by the Tokelau Amendment Act 1967 and most land is subject to custom, although three categories of land are identifiable under the act. They are land held by the Crown and not subject to any other interest, land held by the Crown subject to customary title, and land subject to an estate in fee simple.

1. LAND HELD BY THE CROWN NOT SUBJECT TO ANY OTHER INTEREST

The land in this category includes the following:

1. the foreshore, and the seabed and subsoil of the internal waters, the territorial sea, and the 200-mile economic zone, under Section 10 of the Tokelau (Territorial Sea and Exclusive Economic Zone) Act 1977;
2. land taken for public purposes under Section 24 of the Tokelau Amendment Act 1967; and
3. land alienated voluntarily to the Crown under Section 25 of the Tokelau Amendment Act 1967.

2. LAND HELD BY THE CROWN SUBJECT TO CUSTOMARY TITLE OF THE INHABITANTS

The second category applies to the following:

1. land held under pure custom;
2. land subject to noncustomary rights acquired before October 26, 1967 (Sections 20(1) and 23 of the Tokelau Amendment Act 1967); and
3. land subject to Crown lease (section 25(4) of the Tokelau Amendment Act 1967).

Land subject to custom may be:

1. nuku land: land owned by the village;
2. kaiga land: land owned by a family; or
3. church land: land "given" to a church by the village.

By Section 19 of the Tokelau Amendment Act 1967, all customary land is vested in the Crown and is held by the Crown subject to customary title. It is not lawful or competent for a Tokelauan to make any alienation or disposition of Tokelauan land or any interest in Tokelauan land other than to a Tokelauan in accordance with the customs and usages of the Tokelauan inhabitants or in favor of the Crown. Since the allocation of customary land among Tokelauans is under the control of the elders, it has, to date, not surfaced as a legal or governmental concern. Outside Tokelau customary land allocation has been of interest principally to anthropologists.

Church land is included within the "customary land" category because although the exact details of the gifts of the lands are unclear, the land is still regarded as "owned" by the village.

3. LAND SUBJECT TO AN ESTATE IN FEE SIMPLE THAT WAS OWNED BEFORE JANUARY 1, 1949

Section 18 of the Tokelau Amendment Act 1967 provides that any land in Tokelau owned in fee simple at January 1, 1949 by any person other than the Crown will be deemed to be held in fee simple by grant from the Crown and is not subject to customary law. About 40 acres of land is covered by this provision, and the land is now restricted as to alienation by the Tokelau Amendment Act 1986.

The Property Law Act 1952 (NZ) is in force in Tokelau and applies to land transactions by the Crown as well as by those holding fee simple land and those holding leases on other interests in Tokelauan land (Sections 23 and 25 of the Tokelau Amendment Act 1967). Such transactions must comply with provisions concerning formalities of deeds, covenants, mortgages, leases, and tenancies.

B. Customary Land Tenure

Most land is held in communal ownership by kaiga. Authority over the land is exercised by the senior male member of the kaiga in consultation with other members. Disputes about the land are mediated by the village council and typically relate to boundaries. There are no sales of Tokelauan customary land nor transfers by succession. The kaiga continues through time to reside on the land and live off its resources.

C. Government Taking of Land

Section 24 of the Tokelau Amendment Act 1967 (NZ) authorizes the Minister of External Relations and Trade to take any land in Tokelau for any public purpose; it thereupon becomes absolutely vested in the Crown free from all rights, or interests of other persons. All persons having any right, title, estate, or interest extinguished or divested are entitled to compensation from the Crown; dissatisfaction with the quantum of compensation is to be determined by arbitration.

No provision is made for reversion back to customary law at the end of the "public use."

D. Agriculture, Forests, and Fisheries

The Tokelau (Territorial Sea and Exclusive Economic Zone) Act 1977 became operative for the 200-mile zone in December 1988 with the promulgation of the Tokelau (Exclusive Economic Zone Fishing) Regulations 1988. It establishes a 200-mile exclusive economic zone and empowers the licensing of fishing within that zone. It also preserves inshore fishing for Tokelauans. It is, from the point of view of Tokelau, an essential complement to the tuna fishing agreement entered into between New Zealand and the United States in 1987 and effective for Tokelau in 1988. By amendment to the regulations in 1989, driftnet fishing is prohibited within the exclusive economic zone.

XIII. Persons and Entities

No special legislation relates to persons and entities. General common law rules would apply.

XIV. Family Law

Formally, family law in Tokelau is governed by the Tokelau Adoption Regulations 1966, Tokelau Births and Deaths Registration Regulations 1969, Tokelau Marriage Regulations 1986, and the Tokelau Divorce Regulations 1987. The status of illegitimacy was abolished by the Tokelau Amendment Act 1963.

In reality, the organization of the family is in accordance with Tokelauan custom, which provides for recognition of the extended family (the kaiga) as a landholding and labor-sharing organization. The kaiga has very strict and clear rules about personal relations within the group and with other groups, succession to land, and the roles of men and women within the family group. However, births, adoptions, marriages, and divorces are registered and performed in accordance with the regulations.

A. Marriage

The Tokelau Marriage Regulations 1969 were revised and repromulgated in 1986. They provide a minimum age for marriage of eighteen years for men and sixteen years for women, with parental consent required for a man under twenty-one or a women under nineteen. Among the prohibited degrees of relationship for marriage on the grounds of consanguinity or affinity is a first cousin bar, but these restrictions may be lifted on application to the Administrator. In deciding whether to lift the first cousin bar, the Administrator acts on the advice of the relevant village council. At least two days' public notice is required before celebration of a marriage. All marriages are celebrated by a warranted marriage officer.

B. Divorce, Separation, and Annulment

Tokelau is culturally against divorce, but there have been two or three Tokelau divorces this century. The rules relating to dissolution were reviewed in 1985, and the Tokelau Divorce Regulations 1987 introduced a new regime as from April 1, 1987. The grounds for divorce in Tokelau are now adultery, cruelty, or three years of living apart. There is jurisdiction to dissolve a marriage where one of the parties is a Tokelauan and one of the parties to the marriage ordinarily resides in Tokelau at the time of application. An application for divorce is made to the Administrator who, on being satisfied that due notice has been given to the respondent in any application for divorce, refers the matter to the relevant village council, which then advises whether the marriage should be dissolved. An order dissolving a marriage is made by the Administrator on the advice of the village council. The Administrator may, on or after the making of an order dissolving a marriage, make orders of an ancillary nature relating to custody, property, and maintenance.

C. Custody

Questions of child custody and access may be dealt with by the Administrator as an ancillary matter under the Tokelau Divorce Regulations 1987.

D. Adoption

The Tokelau Adoption Regulations 1966 supersede Tokelauan adoption custom and provide that the only valid local adoptions are those made under the regulations. Only a Tokelauan ordinarily resident in Tokelau may adopt a child. The adopted person must be a Tokelauan and under the age of twenty-one. The Administrator may vary or cancel a certificate of adoption. Where a certificate of adoption is canceled, the result is to restore the parties to their position immediately before the certificate of adoption was issued.

XV. Personal Property

Personal property has to date caused no significant problems or interest. There is very little of it in Tokelau, and even the most valuable item, an outboard motor, is unlikely in the contemporary environment to raise major issues.

Some statutes in force have a personal property aspect. They are the Property Law Act 1952 (NZ), Chattels Transfer Act 1924 (NZ), and Sale of Goods Act 1908 (NZ). The Chattels

Transfer Act and Sale of Goods Act, though in force in Tokelau, are poorly adapted to Tokelau and consequently do not operate there. The potentially most relevant provision for Tokelau of the Property Law Act is Section 4, relating to deeds, which provides that sealing is not necessary and a witnessed signature suffices.

XVI. Wills and Succession

Formally, succession law applicable to Tokelau is in the common law and, for intestacies, also partly in the sections of the Administration Act 1969 (NZ) that have been extended to Tokelau. These provide for distribution on intestacy first to a surviving spouse, then to children, and then to grandparents and siblings.

In practice, succession follows customary law. There has been no difficulty in practice about succession and little resort to statute or common law. The main asset is land, a family asset governed by custom. Other property appears to be dealt with by the relevant members of the family in accordance with customary expectations.

There is no pattern of will making in Tokelau. If there were wills, they would have to comply with common law requirements, and distribution would be in accordance with common law rules.

XVII. Contracts

To the extent regulation was necessary, contracts would be a matter of common law and village practice.

XVIII. Commercial Law

There is little commerce in Tokelau, and therefore little need for commercial law (**see XV, Personal Property**).

A. Business Licenses

Insurance, banking, and money-lending businesses are regulated by the Tokelau Business Restriction Regulations 1989. Administrative approval is required before anyone may engage in those businesses in Tokelau.

B. Consumer Protection

Consumer protection is not a matter of interest in Tokelau. The limited legal protection in place is found in the Chattels Transfer Act 1924 (NZ), Decimal Currency Act 1964 (NZ), Mercantile Law Act 1908 (NZ), and Sale of Goods Act 1908 (NZ), none of which is currently used in Tokelau.

C. Business Associations

There are no business associations in Tokelau. There are, however, stores on each island, under the control of the village elders. The village adds a fixed percentage to the retail sales price of all goods as a profit margin.

D. Transport

The only means of transport to Tokelau is the charter supply ship which runs about ten times each year. Carriage of goods by sea between Tokelau and other places is governed by the Hague Rules by virtue of the Sea Carriage of Goods Act 1940 (NZ). The carriage of passengers by sea is governed by the common law of contract. Parts of the Marine Pollution Act 1974 (NZ) and all of the Marine Insurance Act 1908 (NZ) are Tokelau law.

XIX. TORTS

The law of torts is primarily a matter of common law and custom. However, the villages have established an accident compensation scheme, with a maximum award in any one case of NZ$500 to deal with personal injury claims. It is not customary for injured persons to get compensation from the person who has done the harm, and legislation has been requested by the elders to abrogate the common law right to damages in tort claims for personal injury. The law of tort is likely to be restricted in future to property claims.

XX. LABOR LAW

There is only one body of salaried persons in Tokelau, the members of the Tokelau public service. Their employment arrangements are dealt with by the Tokelau Amendment Act 1967 (**see V, A Tokelau Public Service**).

At the village level, some employment is arranged by the villages and the terms of such employment are principally customary. The most significant labor relations at the village level are those between the village council and the able-bodied men. This is a traditional relationship and typically one that would not be regarded by the common law as an employment relationship. Certainly no money passes to the men for the work done for the village. The villages are communal cooperative ventures in which everyone plays his or her part. The customary perception of the men's group is closely related to a corporate body, but at law the grouping has no corporate personality.

Until recently, the principal source of revenue for the men's group was the fee received from the Tokelau administration for the unloading and loading of the monthly supply ship. The operation is under the control of the village elders, but the men may hold the money in their own right and use it for their own purposes.

Relatively new to Tokelau are public works contracts arranged between the Tokelau administration and village councils. These arrangements, borrowing from Western Samoan terminology, are called *konkelate* and have evolved in the context of reducing the tension that from time to time occurs between the public service and village elders. The typical pattern of these work contracts is for the official secretary to arrange with the village council for the performance of a development project, such as the building of a house or the addition of a classroom to a school, and for the administration to agree to pay the village a fixed sum of money on completion of the work. The government provides the materials and sometimes the tools, and the village elders, by directing the men's group, provide the labor. The village council organizes the local labor as it sees fit in order to meet the deadlines. The money will also be dealt with as the village elders think fit.

XXI. Industrial and Intellectual Property Rights

The New Zealand Copyright Act 1962, Patents Act 1953, Trade Marks Act 1953, and Merchandise Marks Act 1954 are all in force in Tokelau. To date none of them has had any practical significance and for the foreseeable future, perhaps only the Copyright Act may have any role to play in the legal system. The potential for the Copyright Act is in the field of protection of Tokelauan culture, and the relationship of Tokelau government documents to the New Zealand archival system.

XXII. Legal Education and Profession

There are no Tokelauan lawyers and no lawyers in Tokelau. One Tokelauan is in law training in New Zealand. There is no provision in Tokelau law for a legal profession, but legislation will provide for suitably qualified Commonwealth lawyers to practice in Tokelau courts.

The Tokelau Law Project is an integral part of Tokelau's legal development. The project, funded by the United Nations Development Program, began in 1981 in response to Tokelau's wish to develop a workable and relevant legal system that would take into account the culture and needs of Tokelau. An important part of the project involves drafting laws consistent with Tokelau's wishes and conditions. Frequently this involves repealing inappropriate New Zealand laws. The process begins with the elders of Tokelau considering various legal problems and proposing suggestions for a legislative solution to them. Legislation is then drafted following the guidelines given and presented to the General Fono for debate. Examples of areas in which laws have been promulgated and translated are family law matters such as marriage and divorce, affidavits and declarations, and village incorporation. The goal is that the law that is promulgated will be relevant to Tokelau, informative, and linguistically accessible.

XXIII. Research Guide

The Tokelau Law Project (**described in XXII Legal Education and Profession**) has undertaken the publication of Tokelauan laws. In addition, much early legislation and regulations have been collected in *Tokelau Subdelegated Legislation 1877–1948* (2d ed., Tokelau Administration & Victoria University of Wellington, Wellington, 1989). Because no local cases are appealed to courts of record in New Zealand (**see IV, C (1) (d) Judiciary**), there are no reported Tokelau decisions.

Angelo, A. H. "The Common Law in NZ and Tokelau," 16 *Melanesian Law J.* 1 (1988).
———. "Tokelau: Its Legal System and Recent Legislation," 6 *Otago Law Review* 477 (1987).

Angelo, A. H., and H. Kirifi, "The Treaty of Tokehega: An Exercise in Law Translation," 17 *Victoria Univ. of Wellington Law Rev.* 125 (1987).

Hooper, A., and J. W. Huntsman. "Male and Female in Tokelau Culture" 84 *J. Polynesian Society* 415 (1975).

———. "Tenure, Society and Economy," in R. G. Crocombe, ed. *Land Tenure in the Atolls.* Suva: Institute of Pacific Studies, University of the South Pacific, 1987, 117.

Report of the Administrator for Tokelau for the Year Ended 30 June 1990. Wellington: New Zealand Government, Ministry of External Relations and Trade, 1990.

Report of the U.N. Visiting Mission to Tokelau 1986. (U.N. General Assembly A/AC 109/877 & Add 1.)

12. Tonga

C. GUY POWLES

I. Dateline

10th century B.C.	Tongan archipelago settled by people who are to become the Tongans of today. Tongan and Samoan explorers subsequently discover and settle other Polynesian islands.
1500–1700 A.D.	Tongans invade and briefly rule Samoa and Fiji.
1616–1643	Dutch navigators visit, including two in 1616 and Abel Tasman in 1643.
1773–1797	British visitors begin with James Cook (1773 and 1777) and William Bligh (1789). First missionaries arrive in 1797.
1822	Methodist missionary work begins, including local printing, in Tongan, of Bible, rules of church government, and school books.
1838	Codes of laws promulgated by Taufa'ahau for island groups of Vava'u and Ha'apai.
1845	After years of warfare, Taufa'ahau becomes Tu'i Kanokupolu, effective ruler, and is named King George Taufa'ahau Tupou I.
1850	Code of laws for Tonga promulgated by King.
1855	Treaty signed between Tonga and France.
1862	Code of laws instituted, declaring Tongans free from serfdom under chiefs.
1875	The Constitution of Tonga granted by king and adopted by Legislative Assembly.
1876	Treaty signed between Tonga and Germany.
1879	Treaty signed between Tonga and Great Britain.
1886	Treaty signed between Tonga and United States.
1891	*Consolidated Laws of Tonga* published in Tongan and English.
1900	Under Treaty of Friendship with Great Britain and Proclamation of Protection, Tonga becomes British Protected State.
1905	King Tupou II signs supplementary agreement giving Great Britain powers of intervention in Tongan affairs. First expatriate Chief Justice appointed.
1918	Queen Salote Tupou III comes to throne.
1958	Treaty with United Kingdom revokes 1900 treaty and 1905 agreement and acknowledges Tonga's complete responsibility for internal affairs and greater responsibility for foreign affairs.
1965	King Taufa'ahau Tupou IV crowned.
1968	Treaty signed with United Kingdom, leading way to full sovereignty.
1970	Full responsibility for foreign affairs and defense reverts to Tonga on June 4. Tonga resumes international status as sovereign nation and becomes full member of the Commonwealth.
1990	Court of appeal is constituted to hear appeals in all cases except the determination of nobles' hereditary estates and titles (which continue to be handled by the Tongan Privy Council).

II. HISTORICAL, CULTURAL, AND ECONOMIC SURVEY

The Kingdom of Tonga is an independent state. It comprises some 150 islands and islets, about 40 of which are inhabited and divided among three main groups, namely Tongatapu (site of the capital), Haʻapai and Vavaʻu. Including uninhabited islands and internal waters, the total land area is approximately 269 square miles.

The Tongan nation today, with a population of almost 100,000, is homogeneous in language and culture. It has been almost entirely Christian for over 100 years.

A. History and Culture

Tonga was settled over 3,000 years ago, and, together with Samoa, is at the historical base and traditional heart of the growth and spread of Polynesian civilization. It was from these two archipelagoes that, about 1,700 years ago, the great sailing canoes made their way first to the Marquesas and thence to Hawaii, Tuvalu, the Cook Islands, and New Zealand. Although the Polynesian states still have much in common, long periods of isolation between groups of islands fostered distinctive language and cultural development. In the sixteenth and seventeenth centuries, Tonga wielded power in other archipelagoes, particularly Samoa and the Fiji group.

Like other parts of Polynesia, Tonga had a traditional hierarchical organization and extensive kinship groupings and allegiances that were conducive to the formation of broad bases of power. Disruptive warfare and conquest within Tonga, between competing dynasties of mainly hereditary chiefs, caused the severance of many of the ties linking groups of people with their leaders and the land. Thus, classes developed and in the last century Tonga's chiefly system became highly centralized. With the support of missionaries, Taufaʻahau, the inheritor of a powerful regional chiefdom, established his claim to the title Tuʻi Kanokupolu, high chief of the then most powerful Tongan lineage. By 1845 he had unified Tonga under his leadership as King George Taufaʻahau Tupou I.

A measure of Taufaʻahau's success was the early international recognition of his sovereignty in the form of treaties with France, Germany, Great Britain, and the United States. Further, the Constitution of Tonga of 1875, now one of the world's oldest extant constitutions, relegated all rival chiefs to a status subordinate to the monarch. At the same time the Constitution entrenched the powers of thirty-three of them as hereditary nobles to control parliament and, together with a further six hereditary estate-holding chiefs, to control much of the land. Today, the first King's great-great-great-grandson, Taufaʻahau Tupou IV, rules through basically the same constitutional structure.

The form of government under the King was intended to reflect the Westminster model of responsible cabinet and independent judiciary. Initially, advisers, administrators, and clerks were from Britain, Australia, and New Zealand, as were the Protestant missionaries. Some traders were German. Inevitably, the legal system assumed a very British appearance, which was enhanced in 1891 and again in 1903 by the consolidation of the laws into codes in both Tongan and English. Financial instability and dissension between church groups brought British intervention in 1887, and the proclamation of Tonga as a British "protected state" in 1900.

During the early period of British involvement, British policy required British-appointed Europeans in key positions in the Cabinet and public service and as Chief Justice and Treasurer. Read together, the treaty of 1900 and supplementary agreement of 1905, which the British forced Tupou II to sign, supplanted the Constitution as supreme law. The British government, which could always provide the ultimate sanction, was beyond the jurisdiction of the Tongan monarch and the Tongan courts. However, Great Britain chose for the most part not to interfere directly, and Tonga by and large administered its own affairs.

During Queen Salote's reign, British influence diminished. The 1900 treaty and 1905 agreement were revoked in 1958, and Tonga regained full sovereignty and independence in 1970.

B. Economy

The basis of Tonga's economy is agriculture, the primary products being copra, bananas, vanilla beans, and vegetable crops. Cattle, pigs, and poultry are well established. The major export is coconut oil. Tourism is growing as an income earner. Other industries encouraged by government under the Industrial Development Incentives Act include garment manufacture, dried coconut, jewelry, and fiberglass products (**see VIII, C Investment and Enterprise Incentives**). Tonga imports flour, canned meat and fish, textiles, fuel, and manufactured goods.

As is common among developing countries that lack mineral resources and nearby markets, Tonga is unlikely to be able to sustain a policy of rational economic growth based on limited agricultural exports whose international market prices fluctuate greatly. The economy is assisted by invisible earnings from tourism, remittances from Tongans overseas, donations, and aid grants. Tonga receives financial and technical assistance from Australia, New Zealand, the United Kingdom, Japan, and other countries. It also receives grants, loans, and technical assistance from the Asian Development Bank and other international agencies.

III. Sources of Law

The sources of law of Tonga's legal system are the Constitution, statutes, and subsidiary legislation of Tonga; and English common law and (where necessary) English statutes.

Over the past 150 years, Tonga has been engaged in the formation and then in the preservation of key institutions. Initially, the successful ordering of a Tongan nation required the adoption of compatible concepts from two legal cultures. There evolved a powerful combination of the authoritarian elements of Tongan chiefly law with the command theory of English jurisprudence. These forces, together with the Christian notions of individual responsibility and morality, eroded other characteristics of Tongan legal culture, such as reciprocity of obligation and primacy of the kinship group, to the point where such characteristics are scarcely reflected in the legal framework of the state and must operate outside it.

The Constitution of 1875 tied together threads of Tongan and English law and initiated an active process of law making that acknowledged the Constitution as the source of its legitimacy. A host of laws and the 850-section Code of Laws of 1891 provided a central legal foundation for modern Tonga. Courts were active early this century in implementing law and securing compliance.

Today, little in Tongan law can be discerned as based solely on traditional Tongan norms or customs. The structure of central government and the law relating to land tenure and local government reflect an amalgam of traditional and introduced thinking. Nevertheless, these longstanding statutory provisions are now regarded as legitimately Tongan. (**See III, D Traditional Law and Custom and IV, F Traditional Authority and the Law.**)

A. Constitution

The Constitution is the supreme law (Clause 82, as amended by the Constitution Amendment Act 1990). The Constitution itself may be changed (as it has, on numerous occasions) by an amending act passed through the Assembly, accepted unanimously by the Privy Council and approved by the sovereign (Clause 79).

The Constitution protects the succession to the throne and the titles and hereditary estates of the nobles, as well as of "the law of liberty" (referring to the Declaration of Rights that begins the Constitution). On the face of it, the Assembly is not permitted to amend the law affecting these matters (Clause 79). However, the likely intention of the framers of the Constitution was that the sovereign and nobles could waive the protection (**as discussed in IV, C (1) (c) Legislature**), and, indeed, amendments affecting nobles' estates have been made.

The Constitution provides no formal guidance on the reception of legal concepts from Tongan tradition or from elsewhere. It commences, however, with a Declaration of Rights that sets out certain introduced legal principles applicable in the kingdom.

B. Common Law and Equity

In 1966, the Civil Law Act provided that Tongan courts "shall apply the common law of England and the rules of equity, together with statutes of general application in force in England at the date on which this Act shall come into force," and in 1983 the reference to the date was removed. The imported law is to be applied only so far as no other provision has been made in the Kingdom and "as the circumstances of the Kingdom and of its inhabitants permit and subject to such qualifications as local circumstances render necessary."

However, even prior to 1966, the English common law had been applied in Tonga. The Chief Justices and judges of the Supreme Court, the powers of which "extend to all cases in law and equity arising under the Constitution and laws of this Kingdom" (Constitution, Clause 90), had adopted without question the view that English common law extended to Tonga. It was to be applied where Tongan law was silent—for example, to confer inherent jurisdiction on the Supreme Court to issue prerogative writs in the name of the sovereign; to give guidance on the hearing of appeals, and to provide law, such as the law of torts and the principles of natural justice.

C. English Statute Law

The Civil Law Act as amended in 1983 has now made it clear that, in the absence of Tongan law in a particular area, current English statutes may be drawn upon, subject to the "circumstances" and "qualifications" referred to above. In this way, for example, the Guardianship of Minors Act 1971 and 1973 (UK)[1] and the Representation of the People Act 1983 (UK)[2] have been applied by the Tongan courts, but it has been doubted whether an English criminal law statute could be applied[3] (**see also XI, A Civil Procedure and B Criminal Procedure**).

D. Traditional Law and Custom

The formal law of Constitution and statute recognizes no informal Tongan customary law. Clear precedence is attached to the written word, which seems to cover most areas to which Tongan custom once applied. English common law is seldom, if ever, confronted with unwritten custom, which does not play a significant role in the courts except occasionally as to kinship relations and mitigation of sentence, and rarely as to land matters not encompassed by legislation (such as the control of village cemeteries, which may be determined according to custom.)[4]

Tongan custom in relation to the authority of chiefs and the holding of property, as a body of traditional law, was long ago transformed into a codified amalgam of local and introduced law. English common law and statute and any unwritten custom defer to this code.

E. Statute Law Consolidation

The Constitution, acts, ordinances, and subsidiary legislation have been consolidated and revised up to December 31, 1988 by a Law Revision Commissioner appointed to the task in 1988. The resulting *Revised Edition of the Laws of Tonga* in ten loose-leaf volumes (five in English and five in Tongan) are deemed for all purposes to be the law of Tonga at that date (Laws Consolidation Act 1988). In this chapter, references to statutes are to the 169 chapters of the 1988 Revised Edition.

IV. CONSTITUTIONAL SYSTEM

A. Territory

By royal proclamation dating from 1889, Tonga's domestic legislation defines the boundaries and limits of the kingdom as a rectangle—that is, "the total area" bounded by 15 degrees and 23 degrees 30 minutes south latitude and 173 degrees and 177 degrees west longitude—to which is added the islands proclaimed in 1972 as Teleki Tokelau and Teleki Tonga (Interpretation Act, Chapter 1.) The criminal law and petroleum, mining, and minerals legislation is extended to such areas of seabed as Tonga is entitled (Continental Shelf Act Chapter 63), but Tonga has not yet brought into operation its Territorial Sea and Exclusive Economic Zone Act, enacted in 1978. Therefore Tonga does not conform to the usual international claims of 12-mile territorial sea and 200-mile exclusive economic zone.

B. Nationality and Citizenship

A person is deemed a Tongan subject who is born in Tonga of a Tongan father (or, if out of wedlock, of a Tongan mother) and if born abroad of a Tongan father who was born in Tonga. An alien woman who marries a Tongan is entitled to become naturalized by taking steps within twelve months of marriage. There are provisions for the status of children of aliens and for the loss of nationality. The grant of naturalization, which is at the absolute discretion of the sovereign, requires that the applicant meet standards of residence (five years), good character, and knowledge of the Tongan language; and take an oath of allegiance. Naturalization confers all the rights of a natural-born subject except in relation to the grant of hereditary land allotment (Nationality Act, Chapter 59).

No person may enter or remain in Tonga without a valid permit unless a Tongan subject or exempt from holding a permit (Immigration Act, Chapter 62).

Every Tongan wishing to leave the kingdom must apply for a passport or identity certificate, which may be issued at the discretion of the Minister of Police after detailed requirements have been met. Under the Passports Act (Chapter 61), the category of "Tongan protected person" enables a person who is not a Tongan subject to purchase a Tongan passport for up to ten years on certain conditions, including payment to the Tonga Trust Fund (**see VIII, A Banking**).

This scheme—the sale of Tongan passports to foreigners for revenue-earning purposes—has provoked public protest. In February 1991, the government responded to litigation attempting to test the validity of the scheme by amending the Constitution to safeguard it.

C. Government

1. NATIONAL GOVERNMENT

   a. Sovereign

By legal as well as traditional status and by constitutional function, the sovereign is preeminent.

The Tongan monarchy has secured perpetual succession. The Constitution provides at Clause 31, "The form of Government for this Kingdom is a Constitutional Government under His Majesty King Taufa'ahau Tupou IV, his heirs and successors." Succession is to be through the male line and, if there is no male heir, through the female line. The royal line is protected by the requirement that the sovereign's consent be given to the marriage of any member of the royal family, which includes all persons related by descent either lineally or collaterally to the sovereign up to twenty times removed. The present King has, by proclamation followed by act of Parliament, annulled the marriages of a niece (1970) and son (1980) and has proclaimed that a nephew who wished to marry without consent would cease to possess royal status, rights, and privileges (1983). There are three sons, a daughter, and several grandchildren in direct line of succession.

In the absence of a lawful heir, the sovereign may appoint a successor subject to the approval of the nobles of the Legislative Assembly, who may, as a last resort, choose the successor to the throne "as the first of a new dynasty" (Constitution, Clause 32).

To the royal title are permanently attached lands reserved by the Constitution in each of the island groups for the sovereign and the heir apparent. In addition, royal lands are similarly reserved to be granted for life as the sovereign thinks fit (Constitution, Clause 48; Land Act, Chapter 132; Royal Estates Act, Chapter 6).

The sovereign, descendants by royal succession, and royal estates and lands are immune from impeachment or legal challenge in that there is no provision for interference or removal in the Constitution that guarantees them, and there can be no amendment to the Constitution (nor any law) without the sovereign's consent (Constitution, Clauses 41, 56, 68, and 79).

Since 1875, when traditional leadership and control of land were converted into the constitutional concepts of an intermediate noble status and hereditary land estates, the sovereign has retained authority in relation to appointment to noble titles, trusteeship of estates during a noble heir's minority, and the reversion of interests in the absence of an heir (Constitution, Clauses 44, 104, and 112; Land Act, Chapter 132).

The sovereign is head of state, head of the executive, and commander-in-chief of the forces (Constitution, Clauses 31, 36, 41, and 50).

   b. Executive

The Privy Council presided over by the sovereign constitutes the highest executive authority. Members of the Privy Council are appointed by the sovereign and comprise the ministers of the Cabinet, the Governors of Vava'u and Ha'apai and any other persons the sovereign sees fit to appoint. The Cabinet consists of the Prime Minister and such other ministers as the sovereign may be pleased to appoint (currently a Cabinet of ten), who hold office at the sovereign's pleasure. By Privy Council decision and increasingly pursuant to statute, ministers are responsible for specified government ministries and departments, they are answerable in Privy Council, and they are required to report annually to the sovereign and the Legislative Assembly. Both the Privy Council and Cabinet meet regularly, usually weekly.

The sovereign with the consent of Cabinet appoints a Governor to each of the Haʻapai and Vavaʻu groups of islands to represent the government and supervise administration.

The Privy Council has certain legislative powers between meetings of the Legislative Assembly, when it may pass ordinances that take effect as law but must be laid before the next meeting of the Assembly for confirmation, amendment, or rescission (Constitution, Clauses 50–55; Government Act, Chapter 3).

c. Legislature

An essential part of the law-making process is the Legislative Assembly, composed of the members of the Privy Council (ten ministers and two Governors), nine representatives of the nobles, and nine representatives of the people. The privy councillors sit "as nobles" (Constitution, Clauses 38 and 56–83; Legislative Assembly Act, Chapter 4). Subject to the power of the sovereign to convoke or dissolve the Assembly at any time, the life of the Assembly is three years.

Separate simultaneous general elections for representatives of the nobles and of the people are held in five electoral districts. The approximately thirty adult holders of noble titles are entitled to vote for nobles' representatives. Every Tongan subject of twenty-one years or older who is not a noble is qualified to be an elector and a representative of the people. The requirement that no person holding salaried office as a public servant may enter the Assembly as an elected representative has been held by the Supreme Court to apply to nobles and people alike, despite the fact that there is only a small pool of nobles for electoral purposes.[5] The Electoral Act 1989 provides for an electoral roll for the people and for the conduct of elections for representatives of both nobles and people. Voting, which is by secret ballot, is not compulsory. Bribery is extensively defined and has been interpreted by the court of appeal.[6] A candidate is not permitted to spend more than T$10,000 on an election campaign. Electoral petitions may be taken to the Supreme Court by electors or candidates.

The sovereign appoints the Speaker of the Legislative Assembly, which makes its own rules of procedure. Subject to local practices and certain limitations on matters that may be dealt with in the Assembly (see below), the single-chamber Assembly owes the general form of its procedure to Westminster. The privilege of parliament as established under English common law has been applied by the Privy Council (sitting as the highest court) in two recent cases in order to deny jurisdiction to the courts to inquire into the validity of the Assembly's internal proceedings where there has been no breach of the Constitution.[7] Members are immune from arrest (except for indictable offenses) and judgment while the Assembly is sitting and are not liable for what they say or publish in the Assembly. The Assembly may punish anyone who speaks or acts disrespectfully in the Assembly or publishes any libel on the Assembly (Constitution, Clauses 61, 62, 70, 73).

The Assembly may impeach any privy councillor, minister, Governor, or judge for breach of the law, Assembly resolutions, maladministration, incompetency, and other "offences." The Assembly is required to conduct a trial, presided over by the Chief Justice. If found guilty, the impeached person may be dismissed from office (Constitution, Clause 75).

Despite this autonomy, the Legislative Assembly lacks full control over the law-making process, and the ministers of the Cabinet appear to be responsible to the sovereign rather than to the elected members of the legislature.

The sovereign and the Legislative Assembly have the power to enact laws. When a bill has been read and passed by a majority of members three times, it is presented to the sovereign for approval. Once signed by the sovereign, it becomes law upon publication. While the sovereign has seldom withheld approval, there appears to be no convention that it must be given. If the approval is withheld, the Assembly is not permitted to discuss the matter further until the following session (Constitution, Clauses 56, 68).

The support of the executive is essential to the law-making process in two further ways. The rules of the Assembly require that bills be prepared and presented to the House by ministers of the Cabinet. While there is provision for private members' petitions to be lodged, debated, and endorsed as recommendations or rejected by the Assembly, there is none for private members' bills. Then, although the practice is for the wishes of the majority of the Assembly to be respected, the sovereign retains ultimate authority through royal powers of dissolution (of the Assembly) and dismissal (of ministers and Governors) (**see part IV, F** for further discussion of traditional authority).

The principal power of the Legislative Assembly in relation to the executive is that it may delay or decline to pass the appropriation bills.

The legal status of the sovereign and nobles is protected against changes in the law generally and against constitutional change (**see IV, C (1) (a) Sovereign**). Only the nobles of the Legislative Assembly are permitted to discuss or vote on laws relating to the sovereign, the royal family, or the titles and inheritances of the nobles. In practice, the nobles have not insisted that the peoples' representatives be excluded from the voting process (Constitution Clause 67).

Pressure appears to have grown for the reform of the Legislative Assembly and greater accountability of the executive to it. In the general elections of 1987 and 1990, the questions raised were critical issues for voters, and the pro-reform candidates were elected as representatives of the people.

d. Judiciary

The judicial power of the kingdom is vested in the Court of Appeal, Supreme Court, the Magistrates' Courts, and the Land Court, with limited appeal to the Tongan Privy Council (Constitution, Clauses 84–103; Court of Appeal Act, Chapter 9 as amended 1990; Supreme Court Act, Chapter 10; Magistrates' Courts Act, Chapter 11; Land Act, Chapter 132; Inquests Act, Chapter 20).

The bulk of the judicial work is carried out by a Chief Police Magistrate and ten magistrates (locally trained Tongans) of the Magistrates' Courts, sitting in nine locations, who deal with most criminal and civil matters. The magistrates, who are appointed by the Prime Minister with the consent of the Cabinet, have the same tenure as public servants. Criminal jurisdiction extends to offenses punishable by three years' imprisonment or a fine of T$1,000, and the trial of more serious offenses by consent. Magistrates have a civil jurisdiction (excluding land cases) to a value of T$1,000 and may make maintenance orders. The Chief Police Magistrate exercises jurisdiction over offenses punishable by up to three years' imprisonment or a fine of T$1,500 and in civil matters up to a value of T$2,000.

The Land Court, established to hear all disputes and questions of title affecting land or any interest in land, is presided over by a Supreme Court judge appointed by the Privy Council and an assessor selected from a panel of assessors similarly appointed. The members of the Land Court hold office during the pleasure of the Privy Council. (The function of the Land Court is discussed further in **XI, C Land Court and XII, B Administration of Land.**)

The Supreme Court has jurisdiction "in all cases in law and equity arising under the Constitution and laws of the Kingdom" except land cases, and in all cases involving treaties and maritime cases. There is a right of trial by jury in the Supreme Court in civil cases and for indictable offences. The Chief Justice and other judges of the Supreme Court (there is currently a Chief Justice and one puisne judge) are appointed by the sovereign with the consent of the Privy Council and hold office "during good behaviour." Their salaries, which are determined by the legislature, may not be reduced during their terms of office. They are responsible for the court's rules of procedure (see **XI Judicial Procedure**).

Right of appeal from the Supreme Court and the Land Court lies to the Court of Appeal,[8] except that, in matters in the Land Court relating to the determination of hereditary estates and titles, appeal lies to the Privy Council of Tonga.

The Chief Justice is president of the Court of Appeal and he or she or the senior judge present presides at sittings of the court, which is constituted by at least three judges who may be judges of the Supreme Court or other judges qualified and appointed in the same manner as Supreme Court judges (**see also XI, D Appellate Procedure**).

For appeal hearings in the Privy Council, the sovereign generally appoints as ad hoc judicial adviser to the Privy Council a senior judge normally a resident of Fiji or New Zealand.

2. LOCAL GOVERNMENT

The hierarchy of executive government emanates from the Privy Council and Prime Minister at the center to Governors for each of the island groups of Ha'apai and Vava'u, who hold office during the sovereign's pleasure. The Governors are responsible for enforcement of the law, supervision of government officers, and annual reports to the Prime Minister (Constitution, Clauses 54, 55; Government Act, Chapter 3).

The kingdom is divided into twenty-three districts, each with a district officer, and specified towns under the jurisdiction of town officers. The officers are elected every three years to carry out responsibilities such as the maintenance of law and order, health and sanitation, agricultural inspections, the operation of business licenses, and the payment of taxes. (District and Town Officers Act, Chapter 43.) Nobles and chiefs with estates are also regarded, by unwritten custom, as having responsibilities in relation to people living on their lands.

The means by which government communicates its wishes to the people is the *fono* or public meeting, summoned by the district officer, the noble, the Governor, or the Prime Minister, depending on the size and importance of the occasion. Where proper notice has been given, there are penalties for nonattendance at such meetings (Fonos Act, Chapter 50).

Local government is assisted by regulatory acts, in addition to the Criminal Offences Act and the Order in Public Places Act (**see X Criminal Law**). It is an offense to fail to support near relatives; to plant insufficient food to keep oneself and dependents; and to neglect dwellings, frontages, and cemeteries. Tongan custom is reflected in requirements that a traveler "to a distant place upon a government road, if he be thirsty may peel and drink coconuts growing by the roadside . . . but only to relieve thirst"; and that it is unlawful to pass any of the nobles on horseback or in a vehicle "without stopping until the noble is passed and saluting by raising the hand" (Town Regulations Act, Chapter 44).

D. Emergency and Public Order Powers

In an emergency (not defined), the sovereign in council may make regulations "for securing the public safety, the defence of the Kingdom, the maintenance of public order and for the maintaining of supplies and services essential to the life of the community." Such regulations may provide for arrest and trial, detention, or the taking of property—notwithstanding any enactment to the contrary, and without affecting the prerogative of the sovereign (Emergency Powers Act, Chapter 45).

The Tonga police force is under the command and direction of the Minister of Police, who may delegate to the superintendent but who remains responsible to Cabinet for carrying out the Police Act (Chapter 35). The Tonga Defence Services, consisting of regular and territorial forces, and comprising infantry, royal guards, and maritime units, are under the command of the sovereign and administered by the Tonga Defence Board, comprising the sovereign and members of the Privy Council (Tonga Defence Services Act, Chapter 55).

Special powers may be assumed by government in relation to any area in the kingdom where it is considered that public order in the area is seriously threatened or disturbed. If the Prime Minister on the advice of the Minister of Police, or a Governor to whom authority is delegated, considers it necessary to do so, he or she may proclaim a "state of danger" to exist in the area. A proclamation is valid for one month and renewable but subject to annulment by the Privy Council. Within a proclaimed area, additional powers of search, arrest, and seizure are conferred on members of the police force and Defense Services, and special offenses are created (Public Order (Preservation) Act, Chapter 38). Under the Criminal Offences Act (**X Criminal Law**) it is an offense to belong to or assist any society declared by the sovereign in council to be a threat or danger to the peace, order, and good government of the kingdom.

E. Human Rights

The thirty clauses of the Declaration of Rights (Constitution, Clauses 1–29) prohibit slavery, punishment without trial, search without warrant, double jeopardy, retrospective laws, and confiscation of property except for public purposes; and they protect freedom of worship, sanctity of the Sabbath, freedom of speech and press, the writ of habeas corpus, impartial trial by jury, and the taxpayer's right to vote (Clauses 1–29). The wording of the declaration, much of it adopted in 1875 from the Hawaii and U.S. Constitutions, appears very different from more recent formulations of civil and political rights, but significant safeguards are placed in the hands of the judiciary. The notion of equality before the law—"There shall be but one law in Tonga for chiefs and commoners" (Clause 4)—has been held capable of limitation only by constitutional direction[9] or by law which is constitutionally justifiable and not arbitrary.[10]

F. Traditional Authority and the Law

Tonga's governmental structure is today an amalgam of traditional and imported concepts (**see III Sources of Law**). In the absence of conventions of the type that limit the power of the British Crown, the Constitution preserves the ultimate authority of the Tongan sovereign and the restricted privileges of the hereditary chiefs (**III, A Constitution and IV, C (a) Sovereign**). Of course, the sovereign is seldom called upon to rely on residual powers, and the formalities of consultation and delegation are generally observed. The form of monarchy that the Tupou dynasty demonstrates is today regarded as a traditional Tongan institution representing a past of which people are proud and a source of leadership and authority on which many Tongans are willing to rely.

The noble title was fashioned last century after the style of the English baronetcy—that is to say, it is an honor or dignity held from the monarch; it is inalienable (except for treason), hereditary, and permanently associated with land estates (**see XII, C Noble Titles**).

Accordingly, much traditional authority is enshrined in the law. Beyond Constitution and statute, the Tongan people observe many traditional obligations in relation to the sovereign, royal family, and nobility. There is thus an awareness that, as far as authority and obedience are concerned, there are always two dimensions to be considered—legal sanctions and unwritten obligations.

V. Administrative Organization and Law

A. Organization

The government of Tonga is led by ten ministers appointed to the Cabinet by the sovereign and who sit with him in the Privy Council. As their membership of the Legislative Assembly is by appointment and not election, and as the ministers hold their portfolios by appointment from the sovereign, their responsibility appears directed to the Privy Council rather than to the Assembly. The ministries, departments and offices are headed by senior civil servants responsible to their ministers. Some of the major Ministries are established or guided by statute, such as the Education Act (Chapter 86), Police Act (Chapter 35), Public Health Act (Chapter 74), Land Act (Chapter 132), and Post Office Act (Chapter 95). A Cabinet portfolio was created in 1988 for the newly combined positions of Minister of Justice and Attorney General. The new privy councillor heads both the Ministry of Justice (which administers the courts) and the Crown Law Department (where the senior salaried lawyer is designated Solicitor General).

Much government activity is carried on by statutory agencies, such as the boards and commissions under the Commodities Board Act (Chapter 115), Electric Power Board Act (Chapter 93), Broadcasting Commission Act (Chapter 100), Tonga Defence Services Act (Chapter 55), Tonga Development Bank Act (Chapter 106), and Tourism Act (Chapter 117).

Government powers of regulation are extended through the operation of officials and bodies appointed under legislation such as the Price and Wage Control Act (Chapter 113), Intoxicating Liquor Act (Chapter 84), Medical Registration Act (Chapter 75), and Companies Act (Chapter 27).

Offenses are created in the Official Secrets Act (Chapter 5) to protect government documents and information and prevent breach of official trust. There is no statutory scheme whereby members of the public may apply for details of information on government files. However, the Supreme Court will make orders for discovery against the government in appropriate cases.[11]

B. Public Service

The civil service is under the authority of the Prime Minister, who, with the consent of the Cabinet, may appoint, dismiss, or discipline all government officers, including magistrates. The Prime Minister may delegate these powers, and the Cabinet may approve regulations for the administration of the civil service (Government Act, Chapter 3). In the absence of Tongan law on the subject, the Supreme Court has held that the principles of natural justice require that a senior civil servant be accorded a hearing prior to dismissal, and damages may be awarded for breach of natural justice.[12]

C. Public Finance and Audit

The government is required to obtain prior approval for expenditure and borrowing by appropriation legislation submitted to the Legislative Assembly (Constitution, Clause 19; Public Revenue Act, Chapter 64; Public Finance Administration Act, Chapter 65; General Loan and Stock Act, Chapter 109). The National Reserve Bank of Tonga is responsible for currency, reserves, interest rates, and exchange control (National Reserve Bank Act, Chapter 102; **see also VIII Investment Law**). The Auditor General's annual report on government financial transactions and property is submitted to the Prime Minister, Privy Council, and thence to the Assembly (Public Audit Act, Chapter 66).

D. Rule Making

Statutes from time to time confer regulation-making powers on the Privy Council, Cabinet, or individual ministers. Regulations must be placed before the next session of the Assembly for confirmation, amendment, or rescission.

E. Review of Administrative Action

In the absence of a statutory basis for review, government action may be challenged only by invoking the common law jurisdiction of the Supreme Court. The Court has inherent power to issue prerogative writs[13] and will apply the principles of natural justice.[14]

There is no official complaints procedure. The Privy Council may initiate a government inquiry internally or by appointing a commission to inquire into a matter "for the public welfare" (Royal Commissions Act, Chapter 41). Recent major inquiries have been into land administration and the Commodities Board.

The Kingdom of Tonga may sue and be sued in Tongan courts in accordance with court rules, and the state is liable in tort as if it were a private person, subject to statutory limitations (Crown Proceedings Act, Chapter 13).

VI. INTERNATIONAL OBLIGATIONS

A. Treaties and Conventions

Tonga is a party to a number of international and regional treaties and conventions and a member of the United Nations and the South Pacific Forum. Entering into such obligations is the prerogative of the sovereign (Constitution, Clause 39). Treaties do not become domestic law until implemented by statute.

Commencing in 1900, Great Britain had responsibility for the external affairs of Tonga. By exchange of letters on June 4, 1970, the United Kingdom ceased to have such responsibility and the relevant articles of the 1968 treaty between the two countries ceased to have effect. Tonga became a full member of the Commonwealth and accepted the Queen of England as a symbol of the free association of members and head of the Commonwealth. The United Kingdom is now represented in Tonga by a High Commissioner.

Conduct of Tonga's foreign affairs is the responsibility of the minister and Ministry of Foreign Affairs.

B. Diplomatic Privileges

Tonga has implemented portions of the Vienna Conventions on Diplomatic and Consular Relations and the New York Convention on Special Missions in order to confer the usual privileges and immunities on personnel from overseas representing foreign governments. Such privileges, including immunity from suit and process and exemption from taxation are extended to specified international organizations. (Diplomatic Relations Act, Chapter 158; Consular Relations Act, Chapter 159; Consular Conventions Act, Chapter 160; Diplomatic Privileges Act, Chapter 161; Special Missions Privileges Act, Chapter 162; International Organisations Act, Chapter 163; British High Commissioner to Tonga Act, Chapter 164). To clarify the position of the immunity of foreign governments, the State Immunity Act of 1978 (UK) has been applied.[15]

C. Reciprocal Enforcement and Extradition

The Reciprocal Enforcement of Judgments Act (Chapter 14) provides for the registration and enforcement in Tonga of superior court civil judgments given in foreign countries that afford reciprocal treatment to such judgments given in Tonga, and for facilitating the enforcement of Tongan judgments. Judgments must be for a sum of money and final and conclusive. Challenges to registration may be made on the ground of fraud, public policy, and lack of jurisdiction. Judgments made or registered in accordance with the act may be executed in the ordinary way.

The Extradition Act (Chapter 22) provides for the extradition of offenders to designated countries that extend reciprocal arrangements to Tonga. A person found in Tonga who is accused or convicted of a relevant offense (one that is described in the act and would also constitute an offense in Tonga) in a designated country may be arrested and returned to that country. The offense may not be of a political character, the accused may not be proceeded against or prejudiced on account of race, religion, nationality, or political opinions. Procedures for request, arrest, committal, and extradition and safeguards for the person subject to extradition proceedings are laid down by the act.

VII. REVENUE LAW

A. Income Tax

An annual levy on personal and corporate incomes is the principal method of taxation. The Income Tax Act (Chapter 68) provides for the collection of income tax by requiring annual returns of income and deduction of employees' taxes at the source by employers. Following assessment by the Commissioner of Inland Revenue of the tax payable, objection may be made to the commissioner, appeal to the court of review appointed by the Privy Council and final appeal to the Supreme Court.

Exemptions and deductions are allowed from gross income for such purposes as industrial incentives, new industry, the export of goods, and the promotion of tourism. Every individual has a personal exemption of T$2,000 plus T$350 per dependent. The act deals with income derived from overseas by Tongan residents and in Tonga by nonresidents and with relief from double taxation.

The rates of tax and exemptions are amended from time to time by the Assembly. Legislation in 1987 fixed the resident company rate at 15 percent, increased to 30 percent for income in excess of T$100,000; the nonresident company rate at 37.5 percent, increased to 42.5 percent for income in excess of T$50,000; and the individual basic rate at 10 percent.

B. Sales Tax

In 1986, Tonga introduced a sales tax of 5 percent on the retail sale of all goods and services payable by customers at the time of sale, and recoverable monthly by the government from vendors. Goods and services subject to the tax include commodities of all kinds, provision of food, accommodation, entertainment, and international travel. Sales of local produce in the markets and by street vendors, the sale of bread and flour, and all export sales are exempt (Sales Tax Act, Chapter 69). On the sale of motor spirit, kerosene, and gas oil there is a tax of two seniti per liter (Fuel Sales Tax Act, Chapter 72).

C. Estate, Gift, and Stamp Duties

There is no tax, as such, on inherited property or gifts in Tonga. However, probate and administration fees are payable of T$12.50 on the first T$1,000 of the estate and T$6.00 on each remaining T$500 of value. Also, stamp duty is recovered under the Stamp Duties Act (Chapter 70) on documents such as agreements, bills of lading, checks, leases, conveyances, mortgages, and receipts. On the gift of a lease or sublease, stamp duty of 12.5 percent is charged on the balance of rent payable.

D. Customs and Excise Taxes

Under the Customs and Excise Act (Chapter 67), revenue is obtained from imports and exports according to tariffs fixed from time to time.

VIII. Investment Law

A. Banking

The National Reserve Bank of Tonga (which in May 1989 held its first meeting under the National Reserve Bank Act, Chapter 102) is, in effect, the government's bank. Its functions are to regulate the issue of currency and the supply, availability, and international exchange of money; manage Tonga's external reserves; license and regulate trading banks and financial institutions; and generally act as the government's principal adviser and instrument of policy in the management of the economy. The Tonga Development Bank, a government agency under its act (Chapter 106), promotes economic expansion by making loans to local enterprises and encouraging joint ventures with foreign investors. Under the Bretton Woods Agreements Act (Chapter 104), Tonga is a member of the International Monetary Fund and related international institutions, while the Asian Development Bank Act (Chapter 111) confirms Tonga's membership of that bank. The General Loan and Stock Act (Chapter 109) authorizes the issue by government of stocks and bonds for borrowing for public purposes.

The Bank of Tonga, a statutory corporation under its Act (Chapter 105), remains the principal trading bank. All financial institutions are required to maintain the local asset ratios and provide the banking information the Reserve Bank stipulates.

Tonga has enacted the Off-Shore Banking Act (Chapter 110) but has not yet provided the facilities for its operation. The Tonga Trust Fund Act (Chapter 112) establishes a government reserve fund to accumulate and invest revenue from the sale of Tongan protected persons passports **(see IV, B Nationality and Citizenship)** and other foreign sources; this fund is available for national development projects.

B. Credit Unions

Credit unions may be formed by a group of fifteen or more residents who desire to become a body corporate with limited liability to promote thrift among members by receiving the savings of members and making loans to them for provident and productive purposes. The registrar under the Credit Union Act (Chapter 107) is responsible for registration and supervision.

C. Investment and Enterprise Incentives

The government encourages foreign investment through tax, customs, and other exemptions; leasehold arrangements; and joint venture participation (see discussion of Tonga Development Bank in **VIII, A Banking**).

Since 1978, the Ministry of Labor, Commerce and Industries has promoted local and foreign investment through the issue of licenses under the Industrial Development Incentives Act (Chapter 114). Licenses for processing, manufacturing, or providing prime facilities to the tourist industry carry relief from income tax, customs, and port duties, and license holders may receive protection from competition under the act.

D. Foreign Exchange and Import/Export Control

The flow of money and goods into and out of Tonga is regulated by the National Reserve Bank and the government through the Foreign Exchange Control Act (Chapter 103) and the 1965 regulations made thereunder, the Customs and Excise Act (Chapter 67) and the National Reserve Bank Act (Chapter 102). For example, goods may not be imported, and money may not leave the country to pay for them, without government approval. Currency and exchange rates are regulated by the National Reserve Bank.

IX. Welfare Law

The Tongan family system provides support for the young, elderly, and incapacitated. Further, near relatives commit a statutory offense if they desert an indigent person, and they may be ordered by the court to maintain their relation (Town Regulations Act, Chapter 44). The government has no universal sickness, aged persons, or social security schemes, nor is there any workers' compensation or motor accident coverage, other than private insurance.

X. Criminal Law

A large number of statutes create offenses, but the major criminal laws are the Criminal Offences Act (Chapter 18), Order in Public Places Act (Chapter 37), Town Regulations Act (Chapter 44), and Traffic Act (Chapter 156). No common law or customary offenses are recognized by the courts. As to criminal responsibility, no child under seven years may be convicted, nor may a child between seven and twelve years be convicted unless he or she was aware of the nature and consequences of the conduct; and no person is responsible who can, in accordance with the act, prove insanity or intoxication. Provision is made for attempts to commit offenses, the abetting of crime, and the harboring of offenders. Offenses against the state include treason (which carries the death penalty or life imprisonment), sedition, bribery, and extortion. Offenses against "justice, public peace and public morals" include perjury and interference with the course of justice, forming or assisting an unlawful society (see **IV, D Emergency and Public Order Powers**), unlawful assembly, riot, bigamy, and prostitution. Detailed provisions define culpable homicide, murder (which carries the death penalty or life imprisonment), manslaughter, and provocation. Other serious offenses against the person include grievous bodily harm, rape, indecent assault, abduction, incest, and sodomy. The principal offenses relating to property are theft, robbery, embezzlement, obtaining credit by false pretenses, forgery, housebreaking, arson, and willful damage.

The Order in Public Places Act and Town Regulations Act set out a wide range of lesser offenses relating to order, cleanliness, and convenience in or near public places. Constitutional protection of the Sabbath (Chapter 6) is given effect by the offenses of practicing one's trade or profession on the Sabbath, gardening, fishing, or engaging in sport or games whether organized or not. Certain essential services are permitted on Sundays.

Certain offenses have their origin in Tongan concern for the interests of the family and for traditional authority (**IV, C (2) Local Government**). On the other hand, a person who follows the "former Tongan custom" of taking anything belonging to a relative without permission and with intent to deprive permanently is liable to punishment for theft (Criminal Offences Act, Chapter 18, Section 147).

The Defamation Act (Chapter 33) creates the offenses of defaming the character of the sovereign, royal family, Cabinet ministers, nobles, and other dignitaries. The defense of truth must be established on the balance of the probabilities.[16]

Special offenses relate to the exercise by government of its emergency and public order powers (**see IV, D**).

Contemporary concerns are reflected in the Drugs and Poisons Act (Chapter 79) and the Arms and Ammunition Act (Chapter 39).

Punishments provided for in the Criminal Offences Act as amended in 1990 (and other statutes) are payment of compensation (which, on conviction, may be ordered paid to any person injured or suffering loss), fine (with mandatory imprisonment for failure to pay), whipping, community service, imprisonment, and death (by hanging, with approval of the sovereign and Privy Council). The court has power to suspend all or part of a prison sentence. Young males between seven and sixteen years may, on conviction for any offense, be ordered whipped by a police officer "with a light cane," instead of other punishment. Males of sixteen years and over may be sentenced to be whipped by a jailer "with a cat," on conviction for offenses prescribed in 1987 as including bodily harm, rape, incest, sodomy, robbery and housebreaking. Approval of the Cabinet is required in the case of males of sixteen and over.

XI. Judicial Procedure

The jurisdiction and powers of the courts have been outlined above (**IV, C (d) Judiciary**). The Constitution requires lack of bias in the courts (Clause 15).

A. Civil Procedure

The Supreme Court Rules 1958 were made by a Supreme Court judge for that Court. Although a judge is empowered to make rules for the Magistrates' Courts, these courts are governed largely by the detailed provisions of their act (Chapter 11). Civil proceedings are instituted in the Supreme Court as an action by a writ of summons; divorce proceedings are initiated by petition.

The statute of limitations for bringing proceedings for debt or damages is five years from the date on which liability was incurred. There is no provision for extension of the period (Supreme Court Act, Chapter 10).

The trial of civil cases in the Supreme Court is before a judge and jury of seven unless the parties consent to trial by judge alone. At the conclusion of the evidence, the judge sums up and directs the jury on the law. The jury's verdict may be a majority of five. Jury service is the responsibility of all adults of twenty-one years or more, who may be required by summons to attend the court (Constitution, Clause 28).

In the Magistrates' Courts, civil actions are brought by way of summons issued over a magistrate's seal and are tried by a single magistrate.

Evidentiary rules governing civil matters are contained in the Evidence Act (Chapter 15).

The Supreme Court has held that, as Tongan law is silent on the accrual of interest on civil judgments awarded, jurisdiction to order the payment of interest exists under the relevant United Kingdom statute.[17]

B. Criminal Procedure

The Constitution guarantees no punishment without conviction; certain minimum rights for the accused in relation to the indictment, search of premises, and the right not to be a witness; and protection against retrospective offenses and being tried twice for the same offense (Clauses 10–16, and 20).

Prosecution is the responsibility of the Attorney General. Detailed rules in the Magistrates' Courts Act, Evidence Act, Bail Act 1990, and Police Act deal with arrest, search, proceedings by way of summons or indictment, preliminary inquiry before a magistrate, committal for trial, and bail. Abuse of police powers of arrest and detention may give rise to actions for damages.[18] The Tongan Evidence Act as to the admissibility of confessions and the English "judges rules" are inconsistent, and the incompleteness of the former allows the court to apply the United Kingdom Police and Criminal Evidence Act 1984[19] (**see III, C English Statute Law**). By and large, the Evidence Act (Chapter 15) constitutes a remarkable code of the law of evidence, setting out the main principles in simplified form.

The Supreme Court tries indictable offenses with a jury of seven (the verdict of which must be unanimous), although the accused may elect to be tried by a judge alone.

C. Land Court

Under the Land Act (Chapter 132), the Land Court Rules 1927 are made by a judge of the court and provide for proceedings by way of summons on the application of the Minister of Lands or of any person claiming an interest in land. The court possesses the enforcement powers of the Supreme Court and may punish for contempt. The judge is assisted by an assessor, appointed from a panel, to advise on the relevant Tongan usages and custom.

The statute of limitations under the Land Act is ten years from when the action accrued to the person bringing the claim or to the person through whom such person claims. The question of time limitation is solely for the Land Court, with no prospect of review in the Supreme Court.[20] The Crown is not bound by the limitation period.[21]

D. Appellate Procedure

Appeals lie as of right from Magistrates' Courts to the Supreme Court in both civil and criminal matters, but further appeal in these matters to the Court of Appeal lies only on a point of law with leave of the Supreme Court or the Court of Appeal.

Legislation passed in 1966 establishing a court of appeal was brought into operation in 1990 and amended that year. The Court of Appeal now hears appeals from the Supreme Court in all matters and from the Land Court in all matters except determinations of nobles' hereditary estates and titles. Rules of procedure are made by the Chief Justice. The court has indicated that it will adopt the conventional British approach when reviewing a question of fact decided by the judge alone.[22]

In the cases remaining within its jurisdiction the Privy Council, joined by the Chief Justice or a judge appointed by the sovereign, will review the cases and give its judgment. The council does not rehear the evidence.

XII. LAND AND NATURAL RESOURCES

A. Principles of Land Tenure and Succession

All land in Tonga is vested in the Crown—that is to say, in the sovereign on behalf of the kingdom. All other interests in land are, in formal terms, life interests in favor of individual persons, but most of these interests may be inherited. There is no provision for freehold in fee simple, and although limited leasing or mortgaging of life interests is permitted, alienation by way of sale or devise by will is prohibited (Constitution, Clause 104). Life interests are of three types—tofi'a, royal estates, and api.

1. TOFI'A

Holders of the thirty-three noble titles and six hereditary chiefships (**see II, A History and Culture; IV, F Traditional Authority and the Law; and XII, B Administration of Land**) have life interests in the tofi'a, inherited estates associated with their titles. Titles and estates were originally granted and guaranteed by the sovereign. Succession to titles and estates passes, according to the Constitution (Clause 111) and Land Act (Chapter 132), only to a legitimate descendant, the eldest male (and the male line to the second generation) being preferred. In the absence of male children possessing male children, the eldest female inherits and may pass the interest to her sons. Failing direct heirs, the rights pass to brothers, and failing them to sisters. In the absence of an heir, the rights revert to the Crown, and the sovereign may determine to whom they should be granted.

Certain titles and estates associated with the royal family, namely Tungi, Tu'ipelehake (currently the present King's brother), and Tupouto'a (the heir apparent, the King's eldest son) are treated as tofi'a (Royal Estates Act, Chapter 6; Land Act, Chapter 132, Schedule I).

2. ROYAL ESTATES

Royal estates for the use of the sovereign for the time being and royal family estates from which the sovereign may grant life interests from time to time, are set aside from Crown lands (Land Act, Chapter 132, Schedules II and III).

3. API

Every adult Tongan male is, in principle, entitled to the grant of two api, an agricultural allotment of 8.25 acres and a small town allotment for use as a residence. The grant is to be made from the tofi'a, or hereditary estate, where he is residing or, if he is residing on Crown land, from Crown land. On the death of the api holder, his widow has a life interest unless she remarries or is found guilty by the Land Court of fornication or adultery. Subject to the widow's interest, the api passes to the holder's eldest son or his male heir or, if there is none, to the next eldest son of the original holder, and so on. If there is no heir through sons, an unmarried daughter may acquire a life interest, which she cannot pass on. If there are no daughters, succession passes to the original holder's brothers and their sons (Land Act, Chapter 132). Thus, unlike succession to tofi'a and to the royal line, succession to api cannot be traced through females. If succession through the male line fails, the api reverts to the tofi'a holder or the Crown, as the case may be.

The balance of land not granted as tofi'a, royal estates, or api, is Crown land, much of which is leased by the Ministry of Lands and Survey.

B. Administration of Land

The law relating to land tenure and administration is contained in a single statute which, subject to the Constitution, is generally exclusive of other sources of law. The Land Act (Chapter 132) originated in a farsighted scheme, the fundamentals of which were introduced in 1882. The present law, which has changed little since the comprehensive Land Act of 1927, is administered by the Ministry of Lands and Survey under the minister, who has extensive powers.

The act provides for applications by resident Tongan males for api allotments and grants of allotments by the minister. No person may hold more than one agricultural allotment. Once the procedures have been completed, including, in the case of land on a tofi'a, the approval of the tofi'a holder, the applicant is entitled to registration of the life interest, inheritable in accordance with the act. Registration provides statutory protection, and the api holder cannot lose his interest other than through court action. A small annual rental is payable to the tofi'a holder or the Crown.

The Land Court and Privy Council have developed a body of jurisprudence surrounding the application of the Land Act. The act is interpreted strictly as an exhaustive code.[23] The court will upset the grant of an allotment only if it can be shown that the minister acted contrary to statute, in breach of natural justice, or in breach of a clear promise by him and the tofi'a holder in favor of someone else.[24] The court will review where the minister's decision is shown to have been exercised on wrong principles,[25] but there is concern over the lack of principles governing decisions on competing claims to an allotment.[26]

Despite the apparent intent of the act and views of the Privy Council[27] that no interest in land can be acquired other than in accordance with the strict application of the statute, recent decisions indicate a willingness on the part of the land court to apply common law principles. For example, the court may recognize equitable defenses such as estoppel[28] and even a constructive trust in favor of a claimant.[29]

The principle of every adult male having his own allotment is far from achieved, due to population pressure and lack of land. Other factors include some reluctance on the part of tofi'a holders to approve registration and preference by some families for informal arrangements. Official figures for 1987 show that 44 percent of the total area of Tonga (including lakes and uninhabited land) is subject to registered allotments, 18.5 percent is allocated but approval has not been given for registration, and 7 percent is retained by the nobles and hereditary chiefs. Slightly more than half the adult males have registered allotments. The number of registrations annually has recently increased.

Subject to Cabinet approval, an allotment holder may lease the allotment to a Tongan or a foreigner for up to twenty years. Tofi'a and allotments may be mortgaged in favor of the government or the Bank of Tonga or Development Bank. The mortgage is created by a "mortgage lease" for a period not exceeding thirty years. On default by the mortgagor, the mortgagee may not sell the land but may take possession for the balance of the period, and may sublease the land and may sell buildings. The land tenure system permits no other power of sale.

C. Noble Titles

As a customary concept, the noble title, like the royal title and the titles of lesser chiefs, has an existence independent of the holder. The title is a dignity, a status from which rights and obligations flow **(see IV, F Traditional Authority and the Law)**. However, as a matter of law, the rights and status of lesser chiefs have been abolished, and the courts look to the Constitution, Government Act (Chapter 3), and Land Act (Chapter 132) to determine the legal attributes of royal **(see IV, C (1) (a) Sovereign)** and noble titles. In English common law terms, the noble title is like an English baronetcy—an incorporeal hereditament, inalienable (except for treason), permanently associated with land estates (tofi'a) and inheritable according to the terms imposed by the conferring authority, that is to say, by the sovereign in conformity with the Constitution and Land Act.

Although noble titles are held "from the Sovereign," succession is strictly governed by law **(see XII, A above)**. Despite much earlier litigation, the Privy Council was not prepared until 1961 to question the antecedents of a noble whose direct ancestor had been appointed at the original granting of constitutional honors in 1880.[30] Because of evidentiary difficulties such an inquiry is still rare, even though the English common law rule against hearsay has long been held not to exclude evidence relating to ancestors.

The holder of a noble title today has authority in relation to the hereditary estates and has privileges in the Legislative Assembly **(IV, C (1) (c) Legislature)**. The noble's influence is traditional, and much depends on his or her relationship with the royal family.

D. Government Taking of Land

Subject to the constitutional obligation to pay "the fair value" (Clause 18), the process by which the government, by decision of the Privy Council, may resume any land compulsorily for public purposes is entirely administrative. The Minister of Lands is required to give thirty days' notice of intention to resume possession, and the rates of compensation payable in respect of crops, buildings, and land are determined by Privy Council regulations (Land Act, Chapter 132).

E. Minerals and Mining

All minerals are reserved as the property of the Crown and all mining activity is regulated by the Minerals Act (Chapter 133) and the Petroleum Mining Act (Chapter 134).

F. Parks and Reserves

The Privy Council may declare areas of land or sea to be parks or reserves to be administered by the Ministry of Lands for the benefit and enjoyment of the people of Tonga.

G. Forests, Birds, and Fish Protection

Areas desirable for forestry may be reserved (Forests Act, Chapter 126). Species of birds, fish, and whales and the Tongatapu lagoon are protected (Fisheries Regulation Act, Chapter 122; Whaling Industry Act, Chapter 124; Birds and Fish Preservation Act, Chapter 125).

H. Cultural Resources

The Tongan Traditions Committee appointed by the sovereign has control over archaeological explorations under the Preservation of Objects of Archaeological Interest Act (Chapter 90). The removal from Tonga of any such objects or articles of Tongan culture listed in customs regulations is prohibited without consent. The King of Tonga is party to the Polynesian Heritage Trust Deed (by the act of 1984, Chapter 91), under which representatives of Fiji, New Zealand, Western Samoa, and Tonga, as a trust board, undertake projects to foster the values, heritage, and culture of Polynesia.

XIII. PERSONS AND ENTITIES

A. Persons

1. STATUS

The status of being a Tongan is required for a number of purposes, including holding a landallotment and voting in elections. The status of holding a noble title confers rights and privileges (**XII, C Noble Titles**). While the Constitution protects such statuses, it also declares that there is but one law for chiefs and commoners, for non-Tongans and Tongans (Clause 4).

2. MAJORITY AND OTHER CAPACITIES

The age required for voting in elections and jury service is twenty-one years; the minimum age for marriage is fifteen, but consent is required for marriage under eighteen years, up to which age parents can be held responsible for maintaining their children. It is difficult to determine an "age of majority" because sixteen years is the required age for many important purposes including holding land, entering into an enforceable contract, making a will, and being sentenced to "whipping with the cat" (**see X Criminal Law**). Children born out of wedlock are legitimated by the subsequent marriage of their parents (Legitimacy Act, Chapter 32). Mental incapacity is provided for under the Lunatics Detention Act (Chapter 80).

B. Entities

1. INCORPORATION

Companies incorporated under the Companies Act (Chapter 27), as well as nonprofit organizations incorporated under the Incorporated Societies Act (Chapter 28), cooperatives incorporated under the Co-operative Societies Act (Chapter 118) and credit unions organized under the Credit Union Act (Chapter 107) are legal entities and may sue and be sued.

2. PARTNERSHIP

Partnership, as the relationship between persons who do not wish to become an incorporated body, carrying on a business in common with a view to profit, is governed by the common law[31] and the United Kingdom Partnership Act 1890.

XIV. Family Law

A. Births and Marriages

Births and marriages are registered with clerks of the Magistrates' Courts and Supreme Court under the Births, Deaths and Marriages Act (Chapter 42). A valid form of marriage in Tonga requires solemnization by a minister of religion (registered for the purpose) in the presence of two witnesses, after the issue of a marriage license, for which six months' residence is required. There is no recognition of any other form of celebration of marriage in Tonga. Marriage of persons within the prohibited degrees of consanguinity is illegal. The minimum age for marriage is fifteen years, and consent of a parent or guardian is required under the age of eighteen years.

B. Divorce and Annulment

The principal grounds for divorce are adultery, sentence of five years' imprisonment, bigamy, willful and continuous desertion for two years, affliction with incurable contagious disease, unsound mind for five years, incapacity (on limited grounds) to consummate the marriage, continuous separation for two years without intention to resume normal marital relations, and behavior by the respondent such that the petitioner cannot reasonably be expected to live with the respondent (Divorce Act, Chapter 29). There is no jurisdiction for a court to order nullity or separation. Annulment may be obtained by act of Parliament, as in the case of the marriage without the sovereign's consent of a member of the royal family.[32] Divorce may be sought by a husband or wife domiciled in Tonga at the date of the petition.

C. Maintenance and Affiliation

The Supreme Court may make orders for maintenance in conjunction with divorce proceedings or at any time, in favor of parties or children (Divorce Act, Chapter 29). The Magistrates' Courts and Supreme Court may make orders in favor of deserted wives (Maintenance of Deserted Wives Act, Chapter 31).

In the case of an illegitimate child, a magistrate may make an affiliation order adjudging a person to be the father and requiring payment to the mother of birth expenses and maintenance (Maintenance of Illegitimate Children Act, Chapter 30).

D. Custody

In divorce proceedings, the Supreme Court may make orders on the custody of children (Divorce Act, Chapter 29). There is no other statutory provision for custody, so that the Court looks to English statute (Guardianship of Minors Acts 1971 and 1973 and common law for guidance. The child's welfare is the paramount consideration.[33]

E. Adoption

The only statutory authority on adoption is the Maintenance of Illegitimate Children Act (Chapter 30) under which letters of adoption may be granted by the Supreme Court to an approved person in respect of an illegitimate person under twenty-one years, with the consent of the mother unless unreasonably withheld. The effect of letters of adoption is to render the adopting adult the legal guardian of the young person and to change that person's name. No other legal consequences appear to flow from the Court's order.

XV. Personal Property

There is no Tongan law governing the sale of goods, hire purchase, or chattel securities. Generally, the law of personal property is governed by the English common law and statute, so far as the circumstances of Tonga permit (Civil Law Act, Chapter 25) and subject to the Tongan statutes providing for contracts (**see XVII Contracts**) and bills of exchange and carriage of goods (**see XVIII Commercial Law**). Noble titles have been dealt with in **XII, C**.

XVI. Wills and Succession

A. Wills

A person of sixteen years or more who is of sound mind may dispose of property (other than hereditary allotments or estates) by a will in writing signed by that person in the presence of two witnesses. Rules for attestation and construction of wills are contained in the Probate and Administration Act (Chapter 16). Wills are revoked by subsequent marriage.

B. Succession

Succession to hereditary agricultural allotments and estates is determined by the Land Act (**see XII, A Principles of Land Tenure and Succession**). In the case of a town allotment, the widow is entitled to the dwelling whether or not the deceased left a will (Probate and Administration Act, Chapter 16). In other respects, the terms of a will apply, and if there is no will, property passes in accordance with intestacy rules. The surviving spouse without children takes all the property. While a widow with children takes one-third (plus the dwelling) and the children two-thirds, a husband with children takes all the property.

The probate and administration of deceased persons' estates is supervised by the Supreme Court. There is no statutory provision for empowering the court to override the wishes of a testator in order to provide for a deserving or needy relative.

C. Trusts

No statute governs the general powers and obligations of trusteeship, nor is there a public trust office. English common law and equity apply, so far as the circumstances of Tonga permit.

XVII. Contracts

As indicated in **XV Personal Property**, there are few statutory provisions in the area of contracts. The English common law of contract applies, subject to the Contract Act (Chapter 26), which was enacted in 1921 "to regulate dealings upon credit with Tongan subjects." The act requires all contracts by Tongans of sixteen years or more for goods, services, or loans to be evidenced in writing. No action may be brought on such a contract where the amount involved is T$500 or less unless receipts and invoices are produced; where the amount exceeds T$500, no action may be maintainable unless supported by an agreement witnessed and registered in the Magistrates' Courts. The magistrate may refuse to register an agreement that appears to be contrary to law or "beyond the power of either party to perform." Appeal from refusal lies to the Supreme Court. This form of consumer protection is not available to Tongan companies.[34]

The only statutory provision for insurance is that which deals with marine risks. The Marine Insurance Act (Chapter 144) applies the insurance principles adopted internationally. Generally, insurance is governed by the law of contract.

XVIII. Commercial Law

A. Regulation of Commerce

1. BUSINESS LICENSES

All persons and companies carrying on a business or calling listed in a comprehensive schedule to the Licences Act (Chapter 47) are required to hold licenses issued each year at the discretion of the Ministry of Labour, Commerce and Industries. Conditions are attached, depending on the type of license.

2. PRICE CONTROL

The competent authority appointed under the Price and Wage Control Act (Chapter 113) may control the prices of goods and services, and wage rates, in order to secure availability at fair prices. There is provision for investigation and appeal, subject to final determination by the Cabinet.

3. REGULATORY AGENCIES

The roles of statutory agencies, bodies, and officials have been referred to in **V, A Organization**. For example, delegated government powers under the Commodities Board Act (Chapter 115) extend to control of the quality, quantity, and marketing of specified agricultural and marine produce.

B. Consumer Protection

The requirement that contracts for goods and loans be supported in writing, and for registration, affords a limited measure of protection (Contracts Act, **see XVII Contracts**), as do the Price and Wage Control Act (**XVIII, A (2) above**) and the Weights and Measures Act (Chapter 119). There is no statutory protection in trade practices or consumer contracts.

C. Business Associations

Companies are incorporated in Tonga and overseas companies registered under the Companies Act (Chapter 27). In every case, the memorandum and articles of association of the company, which govern the duties of directors and rights of shareholders, are referred to the Privy Council for approval, amendment, or rejection. On issue by the registrar of the certificate of incorporation, the members are deemed to be a corporate body having perpetual succession. The act and rules provide for management, supervision, and dissolution.

The three other principal methods of incorporation are societies formed by five or more persons for purposes other than pecuniary gain, under the Incorporated Societies Act (Chapter 28); cooperatives for the promotion of the economic interests of its members in accordance with cooperative principles, under the Cooperative Societies Act (Chapter 118); and credit unions with the object of promoting thrift under the Credit Union Act (Chapter 107, **see VIII, B Credit Unions**). In each case, the appointed registrar supervises the incorporated bodies.

D. Insolvency

Incorporated bodies are dissolved and their assets distributed to creditors and members under the statutes and rules governing their incorporation (**see XIII, B Entities**). In particular, insolvent companies are dissolved under the supervision of the Supreme Court and its Winding Up Practice Directions (*Gazette* 1986, p. 199). There is no statutory provision for the bankruptcy of individuals.

E. Bills of Exchange

Orders for payment of money, such as bills of exchange, checks, and promissory notes, are governed by rules detailed in the Bills of Exchange Act (Chapter 108).

XIX. Torts

The courts apply the English common law of tortious liability for intentional or negligent harm so far as the circumstances of Tonga and its inhabitants permit (Civil Law Act, Chapter 25). Special statutory provision is made for civil and criminal defamation. Rules relating to truth as a defense and certain defamatory matter that does not require proof of actual loss are contained in the Defamation Act (Chapter 33), leaving to the common law such matters as innuendo.[35]

Fault causing death may give rise to a statutorily based cause of action for the benefit of the dependents of the deceased (Fatal Accidents Act, Chapter 34).

XX. Labor Law

Employment and industrial relations are the responsibility of the Ministry of Labour, Commerce and Industries. There are no general statutory provisions for conditions of employment or the handling of industrial disputes. The Trade Unions Act (Chapter 48) contains machinery for the formation and registration of unions that may act in restraint of trade and enjoy immunity from tort, but the legislation has not been implemented.

The Price and Wage Control Act (Chapter 113) authorizes wage orders. To date, such orders have been limited to the fixing of maximum rates to prevent abuses due to competition (**see XVIII, A and B**). The position of seamen is governed by the Shipping Act (Chapter 136).

XXI. Industrial and Intellectual Property Rights

The law relating to inventions and patents is not subject to statute in Tonga, with the result that English law applies. Trademark registration in Tonga may be obtained only by prior registration in the United Kingdom. The Trade Marks Act (Chapter 120) enables the proprietor of a trademark registered in the United Kingdom under English law to have it registered in Tonga by the Tongan registrar. The Copyright Act (Chapter 121) permits authors in Tonga to obtain copyright protection of original literary, artistic, and scientific works.

XXII. Legal Education and Profession

The practice of law in Tonga is regulated by the Law Practitioners Act 1989, which provides for a roll of law practitioners, the issuing of annual practicing certificates, a Tongan Law Society with disciplinary and rule-making powers, and the supervising jurisdiction of the Supreme Court. Under the 1989 act, prior to enrollment, the Chief Justice may require evidence of sufficient professional knowledge, experience, and training. Practicing certificates may be issued subject to conditions or restrictions.

A distinctive feature of the legal system is the licensing of local practitioners to act as advocates for fees approved by the court. Since 1916, advocates have handled cases of all types. Advocates are not required to have law degrees. At times they have been required to study general legal principles and Tongan law and to pass a local examination, but this requirement has not been constantly imposed. Some twenty-five advocates are currently licensed. In addition, several degree-qualified lawyers are licensed to practice, two as residents and some as temporary licensees from overseas (mainly New Zealand). The Attorney General, the Solicitor General, the senior Crown counsel and the Crown counsel are degree-qualified Tongans who graduated in New Zealand.

XXIII. Research Guide

The Tongan Constitution statutes, and subsidiary legislation, up to date through December 31, 1988, have been published in the ten-volume *Revised Edition of the Laws of Tonga* by the Government Printer in Nuku'alofa, pursuant to the Laws Consolidation Act 1988. Selected cases are published in the *Tongan Law Reports* (TLR), and a few cases from 1987 onward are reprinted in the *South Pacific Law Reports* (SPLR), published by Oxford University Press, Melbourne. Most cases are unreported, and copies are available directly from the court.

Afeaki, E. "Tonga: The Last Pacific Kingdom," in R. G. Crocombe and A. Ali, eds. *Politics in Polynesia.* Suva: University of the South Pacific, 1983.
Ghai, Y. "Systems of Government" and "Political Consequences of Constitutions," in Y. Ghai, ed. *Law, Politics and Government in the Pacific Island States.* Suva: University of the South Pacific, 1988.
Helu, H. "Independence of Adjudicators and Judicial Decision-Making in Tonga," in C. G. Powles and M. Pulea, eds. *Pacific Courts and Legal Systems.* Suva: University of the South Pacific, 1988.
———. "The Judiciary and Tongan Society," 4(4) *Commonwealth Judicial.* 11–14 (1982).
Latukefu, S. *Church and State in Tonga.* Canberra: Australian National University Press, 1974.
———. *The Tongan Constitution.* Nuku'alofa: Traditions Committee, 1975.
Manu, T. "Lawyers in Tonga: A Personal View," in C. G. Powles and M. Pulea, eds. *Pacific Courts and Legal Systems.* Suva: University of the South Pacific, 1988.
Marcus, G. E. *The Nobility and the Chiefly Tradition in Tonga.* Wellington: Polynesian Society, 1980.

Maude, A., and F. Sevele. "Tonga: Equality Overtaking Privilege," in R. G. Crocombe, ed. *Land Tenure in the Pacific*. 3d ed. Suva: University of the South Pacific, 1987.

Nayacakalou, R. "Land Tenure and Social Organisation in Tonga," 68 *J. of Polynesian Society* 93–114 (1959).

Niu, L. "The Constitution and Traditional Political System in Tonga," in Y. Ghai, ed. *Law, Politics and Government in the Pacific Island States*. Suva: University of the South Pacific, 1988.

Powles, C. G. "The Common Law as a Source of Law in the South Pacific: The Experiences of Western Samoa and Tonga" 10(1) *Univ. of Hawaii Law Rev.* 105–135 (1988).

———. "The Early Accommodation of Tongan and English Law," in P. Herda, ed. *Tongan History and Culture*. Canberra: Australian National University, 1990.

———. "Law, Courts and Legal Services," in C. G. Powles and M. Pulea, eds. *Pacific Courts and Legal Systems*. Suva: University of the South Pacific, 1988.

———. "Traditional Institutions in Pacific Constitutional Systems: Better Late or Never?" in P. Sack, ed. *Pacific Constitutions*. Canberra: Australian National University, 1982.

Powles, C. G., and M. Pulea, eds. *Pacific Courts and Legal Systems*. Suva: University of the South Pacific, 1988.

Qalo, R. "Tonga," in P. Larmour and R. Qalo, eds. *Decentralisation in the South Pacific*. Suva: University of the South Pacific, 1985.

Rutherford, N., ed. *Friendly Islands: A History of Tonga*. Melbourne: Oxford University Press, 1977.

Taumoepeau, A. "The Land Court of Tonga," in C. G. Powles and M. Pulea, eds. *Pacific Courts and Legal Systems*. Suva: University of the South Pacific, 1988.

Wood Ellem, E. "Chief Justices of Tonga 1905–1940," 24(1) *J. of Pacific History* 21–37 (1989).

13. Tuvalu

MARTIN TSAMENYI

I. Dateline

1400 A.D.	Initial settlement, probably from Samoa.
1837	First European settlers arrive.
1892	British protectorate declared over the Gilbert and Ellice Islands.
1915	United Kingdom proclaims the Gilbert and Ellice Islands Order-in-Council November 10, making the islands a British Crown colony under administration of British High Commissioner.
1963	Executive Council formed to advise Resident Commissioner.
1966	Island Councils recognized under Local Government Act.
1967	Gilbert and Ellice Islands Order promulgated, replacing Executive Council with governing council and establishing House of Assembly.
1972	Line Islands become part of Gilbert and Ellice Islands colony.
1973	Commission appointed to study future political relations between Gilbert and Ellice Islands.
1975	Advisory council on Ellice Islands affairs established. Ellice Islands separated from Gilbert Islands and renamed Tuvalu. Constitution promulgated for Tuvalu.
1976	Tuvalu becomes separate colony.
1978	Tuvalu independence Constitution promulgated; Tuvalu becomes independent October 1.
1986	Independence Constitution replaced by revised Constitution.

II. Historical, Cultural, and Economic Survey

Tuvalu was a British colony administered together with the Gilbert Islands (now Kiribati) as part of the Gilbert and Ellice Islands colony. Tuvalu became an independent state on October 1, 1978.

Tuvalu comprises nine atolls, eight of which are inhabited. The total land area of the country is about 10 square miles, composed of rock and sand. There is no surface water or forest vegetation on the islands. Tuvalu's biggest asset is its 200-mile exclusive economic zone (EEZ), covering some 900,000 square kilometers of sea.

A. History and Culture

Polynesians make up 97 percent of the population of Tuvalu, which is estimated at about 10,500 (including 1,400 living temporarily overseas, especially in Nauru). The language of Tuvalu has Polynesian origins and is closely related to Samoan. English, which is spoken throughout the country, is used in government, law, business, and commerce.

Precolonial Ellice Islands (Tuvaluan) society was homogeneous. A common ethnic identity and language facilitated cultural unity. The family unit was the basis of political allegiance, and chiefs and village elders exercised political and judicial authority in appropriate circumstances. Breaches of social norms were punished by customary penalties. The advent of missionaries and later British colonial rule transformed the fundamental basis of the Tuvaluan legal system, based on custom, to a foreign one.

The first outside influence on Tuvalu's legal system was Christianity. The London Missionary Society arrived in Tuvalu in the 1860s. By the early 1870s, mission stations were established throughout the Ellice Islands group. Sabbath observance became obligatory, traditional standards of dress were discouraged, and traditional dancing was banned. Christian doctrines also had significant effects on customary family relations. Infanticide, abortion, and all sexual relationships outside the confines of monogamous marriage were discouraged. Polygamous marriage relations were terminated.

Two significant changes in the legal system of the Ellice Islands occurred during the early phase of colonial rule. First was the introduction of the English common law and statutory law. English law determined the basis of criminality. At the same time, the concepts and vocabulary of the common law were also introduced. Second were structural changes in the administration of justice, including the introduction of common law procedures for civil and criminal matters. More importantly, magistrates emerged as the dominant figures in the administration of the islands in place of the chiefs and village elders.

The 1960s witnessed significant constitutional developments in the Gilbert and Ellice Islands Colony (GEIC). A series of advisory and legislative bodies prepared the GEIC for self-government. As self-government approached, the controversial issue became whether the Ellice Islands should secede from the Gilberts. In a 1984 referendum, over 90 percent of the Ellice Islands voters favored separation from the Gilbert Islands. The main argument for separate status for the Ellice Islands was that the Gilbertese, comprising about 86 percent of the population of the GEIC, would dominate the Ellice Islanders at independence. This argument was reinforced by the cultural differences of the two groups; the Ellice Islanders are predominantly Polynesians whilet the Gilbertese are Micronesians. In October 1975, the Ellice Islands under the precolonial name of Tuvalu (meaning "eight standing together") became a separate British dependency. The eight Ellice Islands representatives to the GEIC House of Assembly became the first elected members of the new Tuvalu House of Assembly.

Tuvaluan constitutional development has gone through several phases since separation from the Gilbert Islands. The first Constitution created a ministerial form of government short of full internal self-government. Executive authority was retained by the colonial administration, but a legislative assembly was created, composed of eight members who elected a chief minister. The second constitutional phase began in 1977. The Tuvalu Order 1977 amended the 1975 Constitution by giving more executive powers to elected Tuvaluans and increasing to twelve the membership of the House of Assembly. A general election was held in August 1977, and an independence Constitution promulgated for Tuvalu by the United Kingdom in 1978, among other things, changing the title of the legislature from House of Assembly to Parliament. Tuvalu attained independence under this Constitution in May 1978. In 1986, Tuvaluans approved a new, autochthonous Constitution In 1991, Parliament approved a study of the possibility of making Tuvalu a republic, thus ending the Queen's status as head of State.

B. Economy

The economy of Tuvalu is predominantly a subsistence economy, with about 70 percent of the population operating outside the cash economy. Tuvalu's economic problems arise from its lack of natural resources. Until recently, copra production constituted the main foreign-exchange earner for the country. Since 1983, with the declaration of an exclusive economic zone by Tuvalu, fisheries resources have been significant in economic terms. Apart from copra and fisheries, other significant foreign exchange is earned from foreign aid and from remittances sent home by Tuvaluans working overseas, especially on Nauru and on foreign ships.

In 1987, the governments of Australia, New Zealand, and the United Kingdom in conjunction with the government of Tuvalu established the Tuvalu Trust Fund, under which the three donor nations contributed A$24.7 million. This money has been placed in portfolio investments, and the net income each year is paid to Tuvalu to meet its recurrent budget.

III. Sources of Law

As declared by the Laws of Tuvalu Act 1987, the five sources of law in Tuvalu are the Constitution, acts of Parliament, customary law, applied laws, and the common law. In addition, international law applies in Tuvalu.

A. Constitution

According to the 1986 Constitution and the Laws of Tuvalu Act 1987, the Constitution is the supreme law of Tuvalu. Any law inconsistent with the Constitution is, to the extent of the inconsistency, void. Further, all other laws are to be interpreted and applied subject to the Constitution and, as far as practicable, in such a way as to conform with the Constitution.

B. Acts of Parliament

The second source of law in Tuvalu is legislation enacted by the Tuvaluan Parliament, including subsidiary legislation made under an act. After a number of years of little legislative activity, the pace of enactments increased markedly in 1991, when Parliament enacted statutes on company formation and dissolution, rehabilitation of offenders, plant quarantine, water and sanitation, civil aviation, and public finance.

The Attorney General and the Parliamentary Counsel completed a law revision project in 1991, compiling all the statutes in force as of December 31, 1990. These statutes are available from the office of the Parliamentary Counsel.

C. Customary Law

The third source of law in Tuvalu is customary law. The preamble to the Constitution affirms "that the stability of Tuvaluan Society and the happiness and welfare of the people of Tuvalu, both present and future, depend very largely on the maintenance of Tuvaluan values, culture and tradition," although the Constitution makes no attempt to define these terms. The Laws of Tuvalu Act defines Tuvaluan customary law as the customs and usages of the people of Tuvalu, except those that are inconsistent with acts or applied laws. In practice, customary law rules are recognized and applied only in connection with land matters, succession, adoption, and personal law. Schedule I to the Laws of Tuvalu Act provides procedures for ascertaining customary rules of law. Customary law is to be recognized, enforced by, and pleaded in all courts unless, in a particular case, the recognition and enforcement of customary law would, in the opinion of the court, result in injustice or be contrary to the public interest.

Different rules apply to the recognition of customary law in criminal and civil cases. In criminal matters, customary law may be taken into account only for the following purposes:

1. ascertaining the existence of a state of mind of a person;
2. deciding the reasonableness of an act, default, or omission by a person;
3. deciding the reasonableness of an excuse;
4. deciding whether to proceed to the conviction of a guilty party; or
5. deciding the penalty to be imposed on a guilty party.

The real significance of a customary law in Tuvalu is in relation to civil matters. The Laws of Tuvalu Act stipulates that the following matters must be regulated by customary law:

1. all matters pertaining to the ownership and use by custom of land, including rights of hunting on, and gathering and taking minerals from native land;
2. ownership by custom of and customary navigation and fishing rights over any part of the territorial sea, lagoon, inland waters, foreshore, and seabed;
3. the ownership by custom of water, or of rights in or over water;
4. the devolution of native land or rights in, over, or in connection with native land;
5. defamation;
6. the legitimacy, legitimation, and adoption of children;
7. the rights of married persons arising out of their marriage in relation to the termination of their marriage by nullity, divorce, or death;
8. the right of a member of a family to support by other members of that family, or the right to custody or guardianship of infants;
9. the duty of members of a community to contribute to projects for the welfare of that community; and
10. any transaction that the parties intend should be or which justice requires should be regulated wholly or partly by custom and not by any other law.

The Laws of Tuvalu Act also provides guidance as to the proof of custom. All questions of the existence and nature of custom and its application or relevance to any particular circumstance are to be determined as questions of law. The courts have a duty to apply custom, and custom may be raised by the court on its own volition. To find custom, the court should first consider submissions of the parties, then consult cases, legal textbooks, or similar sources; if the court entertains any doubt as to the existence and scope of custom after these steps, it is required to hold an inquiry. Where there is a conflict of customs in a particular case, the court should adopt those rules that the justice of the case requires. Where a court cannot resolve the conflict of customs, it may apply the rules of the common law, with any modifications it may consider necessary.

D. Applied Laws

The fourth source of law in Tuvalu consists of "applied laws," defined in the Laws of Tuvalu Act 1987 as "those imperial enactments which have effect as part of the law of Tuvalu." The Attorney General may effect amendments to any applied law that appear necessary or expedient for bringing the law into conformity with the Constitution, any act of Parliament, or customary law. A project for the "patriation" of inherited laws, through their enactment by Tuvalu's Parliament, has begun, and three commercial statutes, dealing with sale of goods, arbitration, and partnership, were introduced in 1991.

E. Common Law

The final source of law in Tuvalu mentioned in the Laws of Tuvalu Act is the common law. The English common law and doctrines of equity are to be administered concurrently, but in the event of conflict, equity prevails. Any rule inappropriate or inapplicable in the circumstances pertaining in Tuvalu is to be disregarded as part of the common law of Tuvalu.

F. International Law

Neither the Constitution of Tuvalu nor the Laws of Tuvalu Act mentions international law as a source of law in Tuvalu. However, under the English common law, customary international law rules form part of the common law. The Constitution of Tuvalu has also indirectly incorporated some customary international law rules. The enumeration of the fundamental rights enjoyed by Tuvaluans reflect the provisions of the United Nations Charter and the various United Nations pronouncements on human rights. The Constitution is also silent on the status of treaty rules. The approach taken by nearly all common law countries is that treaties form part of the domestic law when they have been implemented by acts of Parliament. The Tuvalu Parliament has adopted this approach, for example, by enacting statutes ratifying international marine pollution and driftnet conventions.

IV. Constitutional System

Section 1 of the Constitution describes Tuvalu as a sovereign democratic state governed in accordance with the Constitution and the principles outlined in the preamble. The preamble acknowledges the existence of Tuvalu as part of a community of nations and recognizes that

> the stability of Tuvaluan society and the happiness and welfare of the people of Tuvalu, both present and future, depend very largely on the maintenance of Tuvaluan values, culture and tradition, including the vitality and the sense of identity of island communities and attitudes of co-operation, self-help and unity within and amongst those communities.

A. Territory

Section 2 of the Constitution defines the territory of the country as comprising the land area within the rectangle bounded by the 5 and 11 degrees south latitude and 176 and 180 degrees east longitude, and including the territorial sea and the inland waters declared by law to be part of the land area of Tuvalu.

The constitutional provisions must be read together with the Marine Zone (Declaration) Act 1983, which provides that the sovereignty of Tuvalu extends beyond its land territory and internal waters and its archipelagic waters, over its territorial sea, to the airspace over them, the seabed and subsoil under them, and the resources contained in them. The act declares a 12-mile territorial sea and a 200-mile exclusive economic zone, in accordance with current international practice.

B. Nationality and Citizenship

Part III of the Constitution makes detailed provisions on citizenship. There are four categories of citizens. First, citizenship is granted automatically to "initial citizens," people who became citizens under the independence Constitution and the Citizenship Ordinance 1979. The second group of automatic citizens includes anyone born in Tuvalu after independence, except those whose fathers are diplomatic agents, or neither of whose parents possesses Tuvaluan citizenship or whose fathers are citizens of a country with which Tuvalu is at war. Third, people born outside Tuvalu after independence are automatic citizens if one of their parents is a citizen of Tuvalu.

Finally, the independence Constitution gave Parliament the power to make additional provisions for the acquisition of Tuvaluan citizenship. The Citizenship Act 1979 provides for the acquisition of Tuvaluan citizenship by registration or naturalization. To qualify, a person must be ordinarily resident in Tuvalu for seven years immediately prior to the date of application, intend to settle permanently in Tuvalu, have a means of financial support at the time of application and in the future, be familiar with the laws and customs of Tuvalu, and be of good character and free of communicable diseases.

C. National Government

1. HEAD OF STATE

Queen Elizabeth II of the United Kingdom is designated by Section 48 of the Constitution as Head of State, represented in Tuvalu by a Governor General who is appointed by and may be removed by the sovereign, acting with the advice of the Prime Minister. The Prime Minister is required to consult Parliament about any such appointment or removal.

To be Governor General, a person must be a citizen of Tuvalu, be eligible to be elected a member of Parliament, and be at least fifty years old. The Governor General has the power to summon, prorogue, and dissolve Parliament, on the advice of the Prime Minister. No bill becomes law until assented to by the Governor General.

2. EXECUTIVE

The executive comprises the sovereign, represented by the Governor General, and the Cabinet, which is headed by a Prime Minister elected by the members of Parliament from among themselves. The Cabinet is collectively responsible to Parliament for the performance of the executive authority of government. Part V of the Constitution establishes the office of Prime Minister and such number of other ministers as determined by the Head of State on the advice of the Prime Minister.

3. LEGISLATURE

The Parliament of Tuvalu consists of a single chamber with twelve elected members. Four islands send two members each, two vote together for one member, and the other three islands send one member each. A speaker, elected by members of Parliament, presides at sittings. The normal life of Parliament is four years.

Only citizens of Tuvalu who have attained the age of twenty-one years qualify to be elected to Parliament. The Constitution disqualifies anyone who owes allegiance or obedience to a foreign power; has been declared bankrupt; has been certified to be insane or of unsound mind; is under sentence of death or serving a sentence of imprisonment for a term of or exceeding twelve months; commits offenses against the electoral laws; or holds any public office, other than those offices specifically not exempted under any law.

Members of Parliament lose their seats on dissolution of Parliament. Individual members also lose their seats if they are absent from the sittings of Parliament, if they resign their seat, if they have pecuniary interests in any matter under discussion in Parliament but vote on that matter without first disclosing the full nature of the interest to Parliament, or if they are sentenced to death or imprisonment for a term of at least exceeding twelve months.

Electors must be citizens, aged eighteen or older; and must not have been sentenced to death or to imprisonment for a term exceeding twelve months, which term is still continuing or ended less than three years before the election. Nor may persons vote if they have been certified to be insane or of unsound mind or have violated electoral laws in force in Tuvalu.

The Constitution gives to the legislature the power to make laws for the governance of Tuvalu. These laws may have extraterritorial effect and may apply retrospectively. The legislature may also delegate its law-making powers to any person or authority. The law-making powers of the legislature are exercised by means of bills. Every member of Parliament is competent to introduce a bill in Parliament. Except for appropriation bills and bills certified by the Head of State to be urgent or not of general public importance, every bill must pass through two sessions of Parliament, so that local governments will have an opportunity to comment on it. A bill becomes an act of Parliament when it is assented to by the Governor General.

The Constitution gives immunity to members of Parliament. No civil or criminal proceedings can be instituted against a member of Parliament for words spoken in or included in a report to Parliament or a committee of Parliament, or for any matter or thing brought by the member in Parliament or a committee.

4. JUDICIARY

The court system consists of the sovereign in council, Court of Appeal and the High Court, which are courts of general trial and appellate jurisdiction, and the Magistrates' Courts, Island Courts, and Land Courts, lower courts with limited jurisdiction.

a. Island and Land Courts

At the bottom of the Tuvaluan court system are the eight Island Courts and the Land Courts. The Island Courts, regulated by the Island Courts Act (Chapter 3), are courts of summary jurisdiction within the island on which each is situated.

Each Island Court is composed of three lay magistrates, and every criminal and civil proceeding in an Island Court must be heard and determined by the three members sitting together. Decisions of the court are by a majority.

The civil jurisdiction of the courts includes divorces, where both parties are resident or normally resident in Tuvalu; civil actions where the value of the property, debt, or damage claimed is under A$60 dollars; and applications for maintenance or custody of children. The criminal jurisdiction of the Island Courts includes offenses in which the maximum penalty is a fine of A$100, six months' imprisonment, or both.

Civil appeals go to a Magistrates' Court in relation to any divorce matter or any matter in which the value of the property, debt, or damage claimed exceeds A$10. Criminal appeals go to the Magistrates' Courts in respect of a conviction to undergo any term of imprisonment without the option of a fine, to pay any fine in excess of A$10, or to undergo imprisonment for a term exceeding seven days in default of the payment of all or any part of a fine.

A separate system of Land Courts has been established under the Native Lands Act to determine customary land disputes. Each island has a Land Court composed of six members. The jurisdiction of a Land Court covers all cases concerning rights to customary land, land boundaries, transfers of titles to customary land, and disputes on the use and possession of such land. A Land Court also acts as a probate court for customary wills and all cases arising from the administration of customary succession. Matters relating to customary adoption and customary fishing rights also fall within the jurisdiction of a Land Court. Appeals from the decisions of a Land Court lie in the first instance to a Land Court Appeals Panel consisting of three members and then to the Senior Magistrates' Court.

b. Magistrates' Courts

The Senior Magistrates' and Magistrates' Courts are established under the Magistrates' Court Act (Chapter 2) and headed by a senior magistrate. Magistrates' Courts have original jurisdiction in all civil matters except those under the jurisdiction of a Land Court. In matrimonial proceedings, the jurisdiction of the Magistrates' Court is limited to cases that have not already been commenced in an Island Court.

In criminal matters, Senior Magistrates' Courts have jurisdiction over any offense for which the maximum punishment does not exceed fourteen years' imprisonment or fine of A$1,000 or both. A Magistrates' Court has criminal jurisdiction over any offense for which the maximum penalty does not exceed imprisonment for one year, a fine of A$200, or both. The Chief Justice has power under the Magistrates' Courts Act to invest the Senior Magistrates' Court and any Magistrates' Court with jurisdiction to try summarily any offense that would otherwise be beyond its jurisdiction. Appeals from civil and criminal decisions of a Magistrates' Court go to the Senior Magistrates' Court. Appeals from a Senior Magistrates' Court go to the High Court. A Magistrates' Court also has power to review any judgment, sentence, or order of any Island Court within the district in which the Magistrates' Court is situated.

At present, there are no Senior Magistrates' Courts. A resident magistrate, who does not have a law degree, tours the islands.

c. High Court

The High Court of Tuvalu is established under Part VII of the Constitution and consists of the Chief Justice. The Head of State has power, upon advice of the Cabinet, to appoint additional judges. To qualify for appointment as a High Court judge, a person must have been a judge of a court of unlimited jurisdiction in civil and criminal matters in some country with a legal system similar to that of Tuvalu or of a court having jurisdiction in appeals from such a court. The person also must have been qualified to practice as a barrister or solicitor in a country whose legal system is similar to that of Tuvalu for at least five years. The present Chief Justice, who is also Chief Justice of Nauru, sits in the Tuvalu High Court about once a year, although interlocutory matters and appeals may be dealt with by the Chief Justice at any time outside Tuvalu.

The original jurisdiction of the High Court, under Sections 130–132 of the Constitution, includes enforcement of the bill of rights, questions on the membership of Parliament, and interpretation or application of the Constitution. The High Court also hears appeals from the lower courts.

d. Court of Appeal

The Court of Appeal, established under Sections 134 and 135 of the Constitution, is to be regulated by an act of Parliament, which has not yet acted to establish the Court of Appeal. If established, it would have jurisdiction to determine all appeals from the High Court.

e. Sovereign in Council

Appeals from decisions of the Court of Appeal may be made to the sovereign in council, but only in cases involving interpretation or application of the Constitution; appeals relating to the enforcement of the bill of rights; and final or interlocutory decisions of the Court of Appeal which, in the opinion of the Court of Appeal, are of public importance.

D. Local Government

The Local Government Act (Chapter 19), as amended by the Local Government Amendment Act 1985, regulates the composition, operation, and functions of local governments. All the inhabited Islands except Funafuti atoll (which has a town council) are administered by Island Councils. The councils are linked to the central government through the Prime Minister's office which provides assistance in the form of skilled manpower, finance, and technical advice. The Prime Minister's office also supervises and coordinates the activities of the councils, particularly with regard to development programs.

Each of the councils is composed of six elected members who serve four-year terms. In addition, members of Parliament whose electorates lie wholly or partly within the area of authority of a particular council and every medical officer ordinarily resident in the area of authority of a council are ex officio members. In the case of a town council, ex officio membership is restricted to the elected members of Parliament for an electoral district all or part of which lies within the area of authority of the council.

The island and town councils have responsibility over agriculture, education, housing, environmental protection, health, trade, and commerce. They also have power to finance their programs by borrowing money and raising revenues through the imposition of head tax, land tax, license fees, and rent. The councils also serve as law enforcement agencies at the local level. The councils may make subordinate legislation. Under the Constitution, every bill before Parliament must be considered and commented on by the local councils. Although the councils cannot prevent the passage of a bill, their comments are taken into account by Parliament.

E. Emergency Powers

The declaration of public emergencies is regulated by Part II, Division 4 of the Constitution. The power to declare emergencies is vested in the Head of State, acting on the advice of the Prime Minister. A public emergency includes war or any circumstance deemed by the Head of State to be an emergency. A proclamation declaring a state of emergency lapses after three days or, if made when Parliament was not sitting, fourteen days—unless Parliament approves it, in which case it remains in force for up to six months. It may be extended by further resolution for periods each not exceeding six months.

During public emergencies, Parliament can impose restrictions on the rights, granted under the Constitution, to life, personal liberty, privacy of home and property, freedom of belief, freedom of expression, freedom of assembly and association, freedom of movement, and freedom from discrimination. Persons detained during an emergency must be given, within eighteen days, a statement of the reason for their detention, and the detention must be reviewed within one month (and every six months thereafter) by a one-person tribunal appointed by the Chief Justice.

F. Human Rights

The Constitution enshrines certain rights and fundamental freedoms, including the following:

1. the right not to be deprived of life;
2. the right to personal liberty;

3. freedom from slavery and forced labor;
4. freedom from inhuman treatment;
5. protection of property;
6. privacy of the home and property;
7. freedom of belief;
8. freedom of movement; and
9. freedom from discrimination.

Every law of Tuvalu must be enacted and interpreted to take account of these rights and freedoms. Any law is unlawful that is harsh or oppressive or not reasonably justified in a democratic society having a proper respect for human rights and dignity. To determine whether a law is reasonably justified, the courts must consider Tuvalu's traditional standards, values, and practices and its previous laws and judicial decisions. The courts must also take into account the laws, practices, and judicial decisions of other countries that the court reasonably regards as democratic, as well as international conventions, declarations, recommendations, and judicial decisions concerning human rights, and any other matters that the court thinks relevant.

V. Administrative Organization and Law

A. Organization

Under Part V of the Constitution, the Tuvaluan central government administration is divided into ministries, including Finance; Social Services, Works and Communications; Commerce and Natural Resources; Foreign Affairs, and Civil Service Administration. The day-to-day administration of the ministries is the responsibility of Permanent Secretaries appointed by the Public Service Commission. There are also a number of statutory bodies, including the Island Councils, the National Loans Board, and the National Bank of Tuvalu.

B. Public Service

The government is the main employer of labor in Tuvalu, so particular attention is given to issues relating to public employment. Part VIII of the Constitution establishes a Public Service Commission, consisting of a chairperson and three other members, appointed by the Head of State, acting on the advice of the Cabinet.

The functions of the commission include the efficient management and control of the public service in relation to appointment, promotion, transfer, discipline, suspension and termination of employment, and all personnel matters. In the exercise of these functions, the commission is limited only by general policy directions given by the Cabinet.

One of the principal constitutional objectives of the Public Service Commission is localization, defined as preference in public employment for citizens of Tuvalu, persons whose usual places of residence are in Tuvalu, or persons having some other special connection with Tuvalu. People adversely affected by the localization policies of the government are entitled to termination benefits and compensation.

C. Public Finance and Audit

Part IX of the Constitution governs public finance. The Constitution requires the government to present a national budget each financial year, including estimates of revenue and expenditure. The Constitution provides that Parliament cannot legislate on taxation; the imposition, increase, or alteration of any charge on public funds; or the compounding or remission of any debt due to the government.

The Constitution establishes the Office of the Auditor General. The Auditor General is responsible for inspecting and auditing public accounts, for the control of public money and property of the state, and for auditing all transactions with or concerning public money or property of the state.

D. Rule Making

The Constitution provides for the law-making powers of Parliament to be delegated to any person or authority. These persons or authorities can make regulations and other subsidiary laws. All statutory bodies and Island Councils have power to make regulations. The rule-making powers of these authorities are circumscribed by the legislation establishing them.

E. Review of Administrative Action

A Tuvaluan public or statutory body is required to act in accordance with its governing statute. The executive and public or statutory bodies are subject to judicial review by the Tuvaluan courts. The common law rules of administrative law apply where there is evidence that public officials have acted improperly or failed to act. In a leading case, plaintiffs were public servants who argued that they had been dismissed without notice or hearing, contrary to natural justice.[1] The Court held that, as there is no legislation in Tuvalu that restricts the common law right of the Crown to dismiss at pleasure, the Governor General was entitled to exercise this discretion. The court further held that natural justice was satisfied because the Governor General had sought and received the advice of the Public Service Commission before he dismissed the plaintiffs. The Governor General had therefore acted in accordance with the sole prerequisite laid down for the lawful exercise of the power to dismiss.

VI. INTERNATIONAL OBLIGATIONS

Tuvalu has assumed a number of international obligations through treaties and is a member of international and regional organizations, including the Commonwealth, World Health Organization, and South Pacific Forum. Under Section 2 of the Constitution, to be binding on Tuvalu, international agreements must be approved by Parliament. Tuvalu has entered into a number of bilateral and multilateral treaties, the most significant of which are the Chicago Convention on International Civil Aviation, the Vienna Convention on Diplomatic Immunities, the United Nations Convention on the Status of Refugees, and the convention banning driftnet fishing.

VII. REVENUE LAW

A. Income Tax

Income tax is governed by the Income Tax Act (Chapter 52). Income tax is levied on chargeable income on a sliding scale from 9 percent of the first A$500 to 50 percent of income over

A$6,000. Companies pay 25 percent on all chargeable incomes. The use of taxation policies as investment incentives has so far received very little attention in Tuvalu.

B. Import Duties

Import levy is also imposed on most goods imported into Tuvalu under the Import Levy (Special Fund) Act. This levy is a fixed rate calculated according to the weight or volume of the goods. A special fund, the Import Levy Fund, has been established under the Import Levy (Special Fund) Act for the purpose of subsidizing the transport of goods to the various islands in Tuvalu. All monies raised from import levies are credited to the Import Levy Fund.

VIII. INVESTMENT LAW

Financial transactions are regulated by the Currency Act and the Exchange Control Act. The Currency Act provides that Australian currency notes and coins and Tuvaluan coins are legal tender.

The Exchange Control Act governs all transactions involving gold, foreign currency, and securities and provides that all transactions involving foreign currencies require the authorization of the relevant minister. For the purpose of the act, the pound sterling, Fijian, Australian, and New Zealand dollars are not foreign currencies. Any person resident in Tuvalu who contravenes the Exchange Control Act is guilty of an offense and liable, on summary conviction, to a fine and imprisonment for three months. In the case of a contravention by a body corporate, the maximum penalty is, on summary conviction, $1,000 and on conviction on indictment, $2,000. The court may also order forfeiture to the state where the offense involves gold, foreign currency, security, or goods.

IX. WELFARE LAW

No legislation deals with social security and pensions; however, various laws address the welfare of children. For example, under the Matrimonial Proceedings Act, in granting a divorce, the court considers the welfare of the children of the parties as of prime importance. The court can refuse to grant a divorce or defer the grant unless it is satisfied that adequate arrangements have been or will be made for the welfare of the children. Similarly, under the Custody of Children Act, the courts are required to regard the welfare of the child as of paramount importance. As a result, the maintenance provisions of the act require any person having custody of a child or any person with whom the child is living to maintain that child.

The Native Land Act contains provisions dealing with the maintenance and custody of children born out of wedlock. The act provides that in any case in which a single woman delivers a child, the Land Court is required to summon the woman together with any other persons the court may deem necessary for inquiry into the paternity of the child. Where the father is a Tuvaluan and accepts paternity, the mother is entitled to have custody of the child until the child reaches the of age of two years. Thereafter, custody is to be transferred to the father, and the child is entitled to inherit land and other property from the father in the same way as his legitimate children. Where the putative father does not accept paternity of the child, but the court is nevertheless satisfied that he is the father of the child, it may grant custody to the mother. In such a case, the court may transfer to the child title to any such portion or other property owned by the putative father as is necessary for the maintenance of the child. Where the putative father does not own any land or property, the court may order maintenance to be paid by the father to the mother until the child reaches age twenty-one.

X. Criminal Law

Serious crimes are rare in Tuvalu. The majority of criminal offenses are minor, primarily assaults or infringements of the traffic or liquor laws. The more serious criminal offenses are contained in the Penal Code. Criminal cases can be heard in the Island Courts or Magistrates' Courts, depending on the seriousness of the offense. Sentencing takes a variety of forms, the most severe of which is imprisonment.

XI. Judicial Procedure

A. Civil Procedure

1. ISLAND COURTS

Civil matters before the Island Courts must follow the procedure laid down in the Island Courts Act. A civil action before an Island Court is commenced by a writ of summons stating the particulars of the claim. The writ is served on the defendant. The hearing begins by the defendant's entering a plea of "indebted" or "not indebted." If the defendant enters a plea of "indebted," the court gives judgment. Where defendant enters a plea of "not indebted," the court hears the evidence. Both plaintiff and defendant have the right to cross-examine each other and their respective witnesses. On completion of the hearing the court gives a judgment.

2. LAND COURTS

The procedure of the Land Courts is contained in the Native Land Act (Chapter 22). The court, either of its own motion or on the application of any party, may commence a case by issuing a summons. Where any party fails to obey a summons, the court may summon a relative of the party who may reasonably be expected to have knowledge about the land under dispute. Where there is an applicant, the court hears the witnesses brought by the parties. Where there is no applicant, the court may call such witnesses as it deems fit. The parties may cross-examine each other and their witnesses; the court may also question witnesses. After hearing all the evidence, the court discusses the customary laws rules applicable to the matter in issue and reaches a decision by majority vote.

3. MAGISTRATES' COURTS AND HIGH COURT

Civil procedure in the Magistrates' Court and the High Court is regulated by the Western Pacific High Court (Civil Procedure) Rules 1964.

Every civil action in the High Court must commence by a writ of summons, which must be endorsed with a statement of the nature of the claim and the relief or remedy required in the action. A writ of summons must be served on the defendant.

Every defendant on whom a writ is served must appear. If the defendant fails to do so, a default judgment may be entered. If a defendant who fails to appear is an infant or a person of unsound mind, the plaintiff must ask the court for an order that a guardian be appointed for the defendant before a default judgment can be entered.

B. Criminal Procedure

1. ISLAND COURTS

The rules governing criminal procedure of the Island Courts are contained in the Island Courts Act. The court may issue a summons that is served by a police officer or any other authorized person, by delivering the summons personally to the person to be served. Alternatively, the court may issue a warrant of arrest if it deems that the circumstances warrant an immediate arrest. Where a person duly served with a summons fails to appear before the court, the court is required to issue a warrant for arrest. Committals may not exceed seven days. Except where a longer time is allowed by law, no offense can be tried by an Island Court unless the charge relating to the offense is brought within six months from the time the offense was committed. At a hearing, the court is required to hear the evidence of the person making the charge. The accused person and the person making the charge may cross-examine each other and their witnesses.

2. MAGISTRATES' COURTS AND HIGH COURT

Criminal procedure before the Magistrates' Courts and the High Court is regulated by the Criminal Procedure Code.

The High Court or a Magistrates' Court may, in its discretion, issue either a summons or a warrant to compel the accused person to appear before the court. Every summons must be served personally on the person summoned. If the accused fails to appear in court at the time and place appointed in the warrant, the Court may issue a warrant for the arrest of the accused.

Bail is readily available except for people charged with treason or murder. Bail may be granted with or without a surety. The amount of bail, which must not be excessive, is fixed by the trial judge with regard to the circumstances of the case. Recognizance bail may also be granted.

The court may, at any stage of the trial, summon any person as a witness. All witnesses are examined on oath. The witnesses may be cross-examined and reexamined. At the end of the trial, judgment must be pronounced in open court and the substance of the judgment explained.

C. Appellate Procedure

Appeals in criminal cases are governed by the Criminal Procedure Code. Appeals in Civil cases are governed by the Island Courts Act and the Magistrates' Court Act. For appeals from Land Courts, see IV, C (1) (d) Court of Appeal. Every appeal must be in the form of a petition containing the grounds upon which it is alleged the lower court erred. On receipt of the petition, if it appears to the judge that the appeal ought to be allowed and the respondent gives notice of intent not to oppose, the appeal may be summarily allowed without a hearing. Where the appeal is not allowed or dismissed summarily, a hearing is held at which the court hears arguments from the appellant and respondent. After the hearing, the court may make orders to confirm, reverse, or vary the decision of the lower court or remit the matter to the lower court for rehearing.

XII. Land and Natural Resources

A. Land Tenure and Administration

With a population of about 7,000 people sharing a land area of 10 square miles, land is a central focus for Tuvalu and probably the most significant thing in the lives of Tuvaluans. Tuvaluans view their land not simply as an economic asset, but also as a possession that secures status. The administration of all land titles comes under the Native Land Commission, which is set up under the Native Land Act (Chapter 22).

B. Customary Land Tenure

Virtually all land in Tuvalu is held by Tuvaluans either jointly or individually for subsistence cultivation. The constant subdivision of customary land holdings through succession has fragmented land and increased land disputes. The customary land tenure rules have been codified under the Native Land Act, which requires all titles to be registered with the Native Land Commission; prohibits the alienation of native land whether by sale, gift, or lease to a person who is not a native (except for alienation of land to the Crown, a local council, or a registered cooperative society); and provides that leases and subleases are invalid unless approved by the minister. No lease or sublease may be granted for a period exceeding ninety-nine years or for any parcel of land larger than 10 acres, although the minister may waive these limits. Customary owners of land on all the islands except Nanumea, Nukufetau, and Funafuti, may sell their land to other Tuvaluans, subject to the approval of the Land Court. On Nanumea, Nukufeteau, and Funafuti, the sale of land is forbidden.

C. Government Taking of Land

The Crown Acquisition of Land Act vests in the minister power to acquire private land for public purposes, which include any acquisition (1) for exclusive use by the government; (2) for or in connection with any new township, government station, or government housing scheme; (3) in connection with sanitary improvement, and (4) in connection with any port, railway, or roads. The acquisition may be absolute or for a term of years. Jurisdiction over compensation is vested in the High Court, which is obliged to take into account the market value of the land and the economic damage sustained by the landowner as a result of the acquisition.

The Neglected Lands Act authorizes the minister to purchase neglected lands for the settlement of "indigent natives," that is, those Tuvaluans who have insufficient land for the support of themselves and their families. Land is considered to be neglected if it is suitable for agricultural use but is not being fully and efficiently utilized for that purpose.

D. Agriculture, Forests, Fisheries, and Mining

Tuvalu is disadvantaged agriculturally. Vegetation is limited to coconuts, bananas, and breadfruit. The only significant natural asset Tuvalu possesses is the marine resources in its 200-nautical-mile exclusive economic zone, which covers some 9 million square kilometers of sea. The most important of these resources is fisheries. Manganese nodules have also been discovered within the exclusive economic zone. The Marine Zones Declaration Act 1983 declares the exclusive economic zone. The Fisheries Act 1978 governs both local and fishing activities within the exclusive economic zone. It is an offense to fish within Tuvalu's exclusive economic zone without a license from the minister in charge of fisheries. The Mineral Development Licensing Act 1977 regulates minerals extraction. Grants of prospecting and exploration licenses and mining leases are subject to the discretion of the Minister for Natural Resources. Royalties are payable under the act.

XIII. Persons and Entities

Individuals and business entities such as corporations, business associations, and cooperative societies constitute legal persons under the laws of Tuvalu. Under the Constitution, the age of majority is eighteen years. In 1991, Parliament enacted a statute providing for the formation and dissolution of companies.

XIV. Family Law

Family law in Tuvalu is regulated by statutes that to a large extent codify customary law—in particular, the Marriage Act (Chapter 29), Custody of Children Act (Chapter 20), Adoption of Children Act 1985, and Matrimonial Proceedings Act 1984. Under customary principles, polygamy is permitted although, because of the influence of Christianity, it is rare in practice.

A. Marriage

All marriages in Tuvalu are regulated by the Marriage Act, which provides for the solemnization of all marriages by registered celebrants. A marriage within proscribed degrees of kinship is void. The prohibited degrees of relationship cover the immediate family as well as spouses of the immediate family and grandparents. Marriages are also void if either party is still in a valid marriage, if either party is under the age of sixteen, if the marriage is solemnized by a person other than a marriage officer, or if either party has married under a false name. Where either party to an intended marriage is under the age of twenty-one years, the written consent of the father is required. Where the father is dead, of unsound mind, or absent from the district, the mother or a guardian may give the written consent. The Registrar General may dispense with the requirements for consent where a person has no father, mother, or guardian or if the person whose consent is required unreasonably refuses to give it. Widowers and widows are exempt from the parental consent requirement.

The Marriage Act also makes provisions on marriage by proxy, where a person over the age of twenty-one resident outside Tuvalu desires to enter into a contract of marriage with a person resident in Tuvalu.

B. Divorce

Divorce is regulated by the Matrimonial Proceedings Act 1984. The act allows for divorce in only three cases: where one party to a marriage has willfully refused to consummate the marriage; where the marriage has been induced by fraud, duress, or mistake; and where the marriage has broken down. Evidence of marital breakdown includes adultery, desertion, cruelty, insanity, and circumstances in which it would be unreasonable to expect one party to continue in the marriage relationship with the other.

In proceedings based on marital breakdown, the court will adjourn the proceedings for three months or more to allow the parties to attempt reconciliation, unless the court is satisfied that no attempt to reconcile the parties is likely to succeed. The court may refuse to grant a divorce if the court believes that adequate arrangements have not been made or will not be made for the welfare of the children.

C. Maintenance and Custody

Maintenance and custody of children are regulated by the Custody of Children Act (Chapter 20). Before making an order, the court is obliged to inquire into all the circumstances. The courts must put the welfare of the child first and paramount. The maintenance provisions of the act require any person having custody of a child or any person with whom the child is living to maintain that child.

D. Adoption

The law on adoption is contained in the Native Land Code and the Adoption of Children Act 1985. The former act regulates customary adoption. All customary adoptions must be approved and registered before the Land Court. The court may approve an adoption only when it is satisfied that the adoptive parent's real issue or family will not suffer economic hardship as a result of the adoption. Adopted children do not lose their natural parentage but are entitled to receive inheritance from their natural father and mother as if they were not adopted. They also receive rights to a share of the estate of the adoptive parent. On most islands, such share reverts to the donor's family if the adopted child dies without issue.

The Adoption of Children Act makes provision for the legal adoption of children in circumstances in which customary procedures are not appropriate. Only children under the age of twelve may be adopted under the act. An adoption order can be made only in favor of a husband and wife jointly unless the court is satisfied that exceptional circumstances justify the making of the order in favor of a single person. The adoptive parents must be of good repute and fit and proper persons to fulfill the responsibilities of parents of the adopted child. In judging their suitability, the cout must consider the age, state of health, education, and religious upbringing of the child and the prospective parents; any wishes expressed by a parent or guardian of the child; and the welfare and interest of the child, which are regarded as paramount.

The consent of the natural parents of a child is required before an adoption order can be made, but the court may dispense with this requirement if it is satisfied that there is no appropriate person to give consent; if the person whose consent is required cannot be found or identified; if the person has, for a period of not less than one year, failed without reasonable cause to discharge the obligations of a parent or guardian; or if there are other special circumstances. An order for the adoption of a child who has attained the age of ten years also requires the consent of the child.

Unlike customary adoption, adoption under the Adoption of Children Act terminates the parental relationship between the child and the natural parents.

XV. Personal Property

The limitations imposed on the alienation of real property under the Land Code also apply to personal property (**see XII, B Customary Land Tenure**). Under the Administration of Native Estates Regulations, the disposal of the personal and real property of a deceased person are governed by the same rules. The Wills Act also applies equally to personal and real property (**see XVI Wills and Succession**).

XVI. WILLS AND SUCCESSION

Customary succession in Tuvalu is based on patrilineal descent. Every Tuvaluan must have an identified paternity to be able to inherit property, particularly land. The Native Land Act empowers the Land Court to identify the father of any person born out of wedlock (**see IX Welfare Law**).

A. Testate Succession

The law on wills is governed by the Wills Act and the Tuvalu Land Code. The Wills Act does not prescribe any formalities for a valid will. The formalities are prescribed by the Land Code. A valid will can be written on any paper (although the practice is to use a standard form supplied by the Land Court). It must be signed in the presence of two witnesses, who must also sign it. The signatures of the witnesses must be witnessed by two other persons who are neither members of the testator's family nor beneficiaries under the will. Oral wills are valid provided they are witnessed.

Land is at the center of the law of succession in Tuvalu. As such, much of the law of succession and wills is contained in the Tuvalu Land Code. As a general rule, every owner of property controls its use. A property owner may dispose of his or her property subject to certain limitations. First, the majority of the adult children, brothers, and sisters of the testator must consent to the disposal. The Land Court must in turn approve the distribution. Second, a property owner cannot distribute his or her property (other than property received as a reward for work or property bought or received in exchange for a canoe) to anyone except a child or sibling unless these next of kin have deliberately neglected the owner or the majority of them agree to the disposition.

The act also allows a property owner to make a testamentary gift to a person who nursed or cared for the testator, subject to the approval of the Land Court. The gift may be given to nonfamily members only if the testator's own family refused to nurse him or her. Spouses may also give each other such gifts. On some of the islands, the gift reverts to the donor's family on the death of the recipient.

B. Intestate Succession

Where a Tuvaluan dies intestate, the Administration of Native Estates Regulations vest in the lands officer the powers of administrator of the estates of the deceased. The land officer is authorized to receive all movable and immovable properties of the deceased person and hold them in trust pending a final distribution. Distribution of the property of person who dies intestate is governed by the Tuvalu Land Code, which allows the next of kin to agree on a distribution formula. Failing their agreement, the Land Court distributes the property according to the act. Where the deceased has more than one spouse, the issue of the first spouse ordinarily receive more lands than the issue of the second spouse. However, the Land Court may disregard this rule if some of the issue will suffer hardship as a consequence. The eldest son's share of the estate usually must exceed that of his brothers, and the shares of sons usually exceed those of daughters. Where there are no sons, the share of the eldest daughter usually exceeds that of the other daughters. Where an issueless owner of property dies intestate, the property is distributed among next of kin. To maintain equity, only those who received smaller shares from previous distributions are entitled to inherit from the estate. No distinction is made between men and women. Where the deceased has no issue and no siblings, property inherited from the deceased's father will revert to the father's brothers and sisters or their issue, and property inherited from the mother reverts to the mother's brothers and sisters.

XVII. Contracts

The common law of England is the basis, directly or indirectly, of the law of contract in Tuvalu.

XVIII. Commercial Law

A. Business Associations

All companies, businesses, and partnerships that establish places of business in Tuvalu are required to be incorporated under the Companies and Business Registration Act. After incorporation, every company or partnership is required to file an annual balance sheet with the minister. Where a company operating in Tuvalu is a limited liability company and uses that description as part of its name, it is required to (1) state the country of incorporation in every prospectus inviting subscription for its shares or debentures; (2) conspicuously exhibit on every place where it carries on business in Tuvalu the name of the company and the name of the country of incorporation; and (3) display the name of the country of incorporation on all bills, letterheads, advertisements, and other official publications of the company.

External companies operating in Tuvalu are regulated by the External Companies (Registration Control) Act 1987. The act defines an "external company" as an incorporated company formed outside Tuvalu but which either sets up an office or a place of business in Tuvalu or in any way carries on business in Tuvalu. The act prescribes procedures for the registration of external companies. The application must disclose the company name, its objects, the location of its principal office in the country of incorporation, the names of its directors, its balance sheet, its principal places of business in Tuvalu, and the name of its local manager. The minister has a discretionary power to refuse the registration of an external company that the minister deems undesirable or unacceptable. Once registered, the external company can be struck off the register only by an order of the High Court. A registered external company operating in Tuvalu is also required to display the name of the country of incorporation conspicuously. The name of a local person appointed as local manager of an external company must be shown on all business letters. The local manager is required to consent in writing to the appointment.

B. Sole Traders

Under the Companies and Business Registration (Amendment) Act 1985, sole traders—that is, individuals carrying on a business enterprise (otherwise than in partnership) with a view to profit—are required to file with the minister such documents as may be prescribed.

C. Cooperative Societies

The formation and operation of cooperative societies are governed by the Co-operative Societies Act (Chapter 64). The act requires cooperative societies to be registered. To qualify for registration, a society must have at least ten persons as members. The registration of a society renders it a body corporate with power to hold property, enter into contracts, institute and defend suits and other legal proceedings, and perform all acts necessary for the purposes set out in its constitution.

XIX. TORTS

As in the case of contract law, the common law of England is the basis for tort law in Tuvalu. In practice there are few if any tort actions, as disputes are resolved at the communal level by resort to customary dispute settlement mechanisms such as conciliation, mediation, and arbitration.

XX. LABOR LAW

A. Employment

Most Tuvaluans are active in the village economy. The government employs most of the people working in the cash economy, and a small number are employed in the private sector. Conditions of employment in both the private and public sectors are governed by the Employment Act, which provides for a Commissioner for Labour to administer all issues relating to employment and to regulate wages, working hours, recruitment, and contracts of employment. The act requires that contracts for longer than a month be in writing and prohibits dismissal of an employee prior to termination of the contract except upon notice and for cause. The act provides that a contract involving travel within Tuvalu or to Nauru (where many Tuvaluans are employed) cannot exceed twelve months if the employee is not accompanied by family or twenty-four months if the family goes along. The act also regulates contracts for employment outside Tuvalu and Nauru. Any such contract is void if the employee is a minor, and the term of the contract cannot exceed two years unless the employee is accompanied by family. If the laws of the place of employment are substantially the same as the laws of Tuvalu, the conditions of employment are to be determined by the place of employment; but if the laws of the place of employment differ from the laws of Tuvalu in respect of repatriation, the Commissioner for Labour may require a deposit or security from the employer.

Special provisions of the Employment Act regulate the employment of women and children. With some exceptions, employers may not require women and children to work at night or in mines. The act prohibits employment of children under fifteen and sets minimum age limits for dangerous work.

B. Trade Unions

Under Section 11 of the Constitution, every Tuvaluan is entitled to freedom of assembly and association. The Trade Unions Act (Chapter 82) provides that no employer shall make it a condition of employment that a worker not join a trade union.

Trade unions must be registered. At least seven members are required to form a trade union. The Trade Unions Act also protects trade unions and their members in pursuing the objectives of the union. An agreement or combination in furtherance of a lawful trade union goal cannot be tried as a conspiracy. Acts done in connection with trade disputes to induce some other person to break a contract of employment or that interfere with the trade, business, or employment of some other person are also not offenses.

Trade unions and their officials, however, can be sued in relation to the property of the union. The members of a trade union can also be prosecuted for riots, unlawful assembly, breach of the peace, sedition, or offenses against the state. Illegal or wrongful use of authority by persons in connection with trade disputes are also actionable. Picketing is permitted, but picketing that is not peaceful is punishable as a crime.

Industrial relations are further regulated by the Industrial Relations Code (Chapter 85), which requires industrial disputes to be settled peacefully. The code also prescribes the circumstances in which strike action may be used in the settlement of industrial disputes.

C. Workers' Compensation

Tuvaluans who suffer injury or death arising out of their employment are entitled to compensation under the Workmen's Compensation Act (Chapter 83). The act covers persons who work under a contract of employment or apprenticeship, whether or not the contract conforms to the Employment Act. A contract provision in which employees renounce their right to compensation for injuries is void. Compensation is payable to employees for personal injuries or accidents arising out of and in the course of the employment, or for accidents that occur while the employee is traveling to or from work.

Employers are not liable to pay compensation in the following circumstances:

1. if the injury does not incapacitate the employee for more than three days;
2. if an injury that does not result in death or serious permanent incapacity is attributable to willful misconduct of the employee;
3. if the injury, even one resulting in permanent incapacity or death, resulted from deliberate self-injury; or
4. if the injury was occasioned by other employment.

The amount of compensation for temporary or permanent injury depends on whether the injured employee needs ongoing care and whether the injury results in partial or total incapacity. Compensation for death depends upon the number of dependents. Awards may be determined in a negotiation between employer and employee. Failing agreement within fifteen days, the employee may apply to the Magistrates' Court for a determination of compensation.

XXI. Industrial and Intellectual Property Rights

A. Copyright

Under the Copyright Act, it is an offense for any person knowingly to do the following:

1. make for sale or hire any infringing copy of a work in which copyright subsists;
2. sell or let for hire or by way of trade expose or offer for sale or hire any such work;

3. distribute any such work either for the purposes of trade or to such an extent as to affect prejudicially the owner of the copyright;
4. exhibit in public by way of trade any infringing copy of any such work; or
5. import for sale any infringing copy of any such work.

The Copyright Act makes Section 22 of the Copyright Act of the United Kingdom applicable in Tuvalu. This section regulates the importation of literary, dramatic, or musical work.

B. Patents

Patent rights are protected under United Kingdom Patents Act. Grantees of patent or persons deriving rights from grantees are required to apply within three years of grant of the patent in the United Kingdom to have it registered in Tuvalu. Registration confers on the applicants all the rights they are entitled to under United Kingdom law.

C. Designs and Trademarks

The registered proprietor of a design registered in the United Kingdom enjoys protection for the design in Tuvalu under the United Kingdom Designs Protection Act. Similarly, under the Registration of United Kingdom Trade Marks Act, registered proprietors of trademarks in the United Kingdom may apply to have such trademarks registered in Tuvalu, and upon registration the protection accorded in the United Kingdom is duplicated in Tuvalu.

XXII. Legal Education and Profession

Tuvalu has no institutions for training lawyers. Legal qualifications are obtained by Tuvaluan lawyers from the University of Papua New Guinea and universities in Australia and New Zealand. There are currently fewer than half a dozen national qualified lawyers in Tuvalu. There is no bar association and no legislation regulating the legal profession in Tuvalu.

An office of People's Lawyer has been established and its independence from direction by other agencies guaranteed by statute. The People's Lawyer represents criminal defendants and gives advice in civil matters. There is no charge for the services of the People's Lawyer.

XXIII. Research Guide

In 1991, Tuvalu's Attorney General and Parliamentary Counsel completed a law revision project, compiling all statutes in force as of December 31, 1990. These statutes are available from the office of the Parliamentary Counsel in Funafuti. Some Tuvalu cases are included, beginning in 1987, in *South Pacific Law Reports*, published by Oxford University Press in Melbourne.

Atkinson, B. "Regional Cooperation in the Courts: a Tuvalu View," in C. G. Powles and M. Pulea, eds. *Pacific Courts and Legal Systems*. Suva: University of the South Pacific, 1988.
Isala, T. "Tuvalu: Island Nation," in R. G. Crocombe and A. Ali, eds. *Politics in Polynesia*. Suva: Institute of Pacific Studies, 1983.
Kaitu, L. "Functions and Standards of Adjudicators in Tuvalu," in C. G. Powles and M. Pulea, eds. *Pacific Courts and Legal Systems*. Suva: University of the South Pacific, 1988.
Laloniu, S. *Land in Tuvalu: A History*. Suva: University of the South Pacific, 1983.

Leupena, T., and K. Lutelu. "Providing for the Multitude," in R. G. Crocombe, ed. *Land Tenure in the Atolls*. Suva: Institute of Pacific Studies, University of the South Pacific, 1987.

Macdonald, B. *Cinderellas of the Empire: Towards a History of Kiribati and Tuvalu*. Canberra: Australian National University Press, 1982.

———. "Current Developments in the Pacific: The Separation of the Gilbert and Ellice Islands," 10 *J. of Pacific History* 84 (1975).

———. "The Making of Tuvalu: A Postscript," 16(2) *Pacific Viewpoint* (1975).

———. "Succession in the Defense of Identity: The Making of Tuvalu," 16(1) *Pacific Viewpoint* 26 (1975).

———. "Constitutional Development in the Gilbert and Ellice Islands Colony," 5 *J. of Pacific History* 139 (1970).

14. Vanuatu

DON PATERSON

I. DATELINE

1000 B.C.	Melanesians inhabit islands of the archipelago later known as New Hebrides.
1606 A.D.	First European sighting of archipelago by Spanish explorer Pedro Fernandez de Quiros, who attempted unsuccessfully to establish European settlement.
1768	French explorer Louis Antoine de Bougainville sails around northern islands of the archipelago.
1774	British navigator James Cook sails around and maps central and southern islands.
1886	Britain and France establish joint naval commission to protect their citizens who settled in archipelago.
1906	Initial Anglo-French agreement to establish joint administration, the Condominium.
1914	Anglo-French protocol signed to expand powers of the Condominium.
1957	Advisory council of New Hebrideans appointed to advise British and French Resident Commissioners; council later elected on restricted suffrage.
1975	Representative Assembly established with power to recommend regulations to Resident Commissioners, but National (later called Vanua'aku) party withdraws from Assembly in 1977, objecting to composition of Assembly.
1978	Internal self-government established and New Hebridean elected Chief Minister.
1979	Constitutional Planning Committee appointed by the government to draft Constitution.
1980	Britain and France accept independence Constitution; New Hebrides becomes independent as state of Vanuatu on July 30; attempted secession by French-dominated islands is suppressed with the aid of Papua New Guinea troops.
1991	Walter Lini, Prime Minister since independence, is removed as leader of the Vanua'aku party and as Prime Minister. At general elections, francophone Union of Moderate Parties wins largest number of seats and forms a coalition government with National United party, formed by Lini. Maxim Carlot Korman, leader of UMP, becomes prime minister.

II. HISTORICAL, CULTURAL, AND ECONOMIC SURVEY

Vanuatu is composed of some 80 islands that lie in a double chain formation between 12 and 21 degrees south latitude and 166 and 171 degrees east longitude. The largest island is the northern island of Santo, but the capital, Vila, is situated on an island in the center of the group, Efate.

A. History

It is believed that the archipelago now known as Vanuatu had been inhabited by Melanesian people for several thousand years before their first sighting by Europeans in 1606, when the

Spanish explorer Pedro Fernandez de Quiros attempted unsuccessfully to establish an extensive settlement there. In 1769, the French navigator Louis Antoine de Bougainville landed briefly in some of the northern islands, and five years later British captain James Cook explored most of the central and southern islands, mapped them, and named the group the New Hebrides.

The nineteenth century saw increasing numbers of sandalwood traders, "blackbirder" labor recruiters, missionaries, traders, and planters, especially from Britain and France, arriving in the islands. In 1886, Britain and France agreed to set up a joint naval commission to protect the lives and property of their respective citizens. This arrangement was succeeded in 1906 by a convention that established a Condominium providing the two European countries with greater power over their respective citizens and others living in the New Hebrides. In 1914, a protocol containing more elaborate arrangements for government of the islands was signed by Britain and France; this protocol remained, after ratification in 1922 and with later amendments, the basis for the government of the islands until 1980.

In 1957, an advisory council was appointed by the two administering powers. In succeeding years, the proportion of elected members of the advisory council was increased, and the council was replaced in 1975 by a representative Assembly in which most, but not all, of the members were elected. The National party, which sought independence, was successful at the election in 1975, but in 1977, protesting the continued presence in the Assembly of appointed members and the form of the franchise adopted for the election, the National party withdrew from the Assembly, boycotted the elections held later that year, and set up a separate provisional government. The administering powers allowed for internal self-government in 1978 under a government headed by George Kalsakau, a New Hebridean.

Later in 1978, the National party, now called the Vanua'aku party, returned to the Assembly and participated in a government of national unity headed by Father Gerard Leymang, the leader of the moderate parties.

In 1979, the government of national unity appointed a Constitutional Planning Committee that, with the assistance of advisers appointed by Britain and France, completed a draft that provided for independence. This draft was accepted by the government of national unity, and by Britain and France. Elections were held later in 1979; the Vanua'aku party achieved a substantial majority. Its leader, Father Walter Lini, became Chief Minister and, after independence on July 30, 1980, Prime Minister. Opposition to the government and to independence was strong in two islands, Santo and Tanna, but was eventually suppressed with the assistance of military forces from Papua New Guinea.

After independence, the Vanua'aku party retained a majority in the Parliament and provided the government until 1991. In early 1988, Father Lini's leadership was challenged unsuccessfully by Barak Sope, and the opposition parties boycotted Parliament, with the result that their seats were vacated. Later in the year, the president, Ati George Sokomanu, attempted to intervene by suspending Parliament and appointing an interim government pending new general elections. His efforts were declared unconstitutional by the Supreme Court; he and the five members of his interim government were tried by the Supreme Court for sedition and incitement to mutiny. They were convicted, but these convictions were later overturned by the Court of Appeal.

In 1991, Father Lini was removed as party leader by a special congress of the Vanua'aku party and, following a no-confidence vote in Parliament, was replaced as Prime Minister by Donald Salpokas, also of the Vanua'aku party. At general elections held in December 1991, the francophone Union of Moderate Parties won the largest number of seats in Parliament, but not a majority. It formed a coalition government with the National United party, which had been established by former Prime Minister Walter Lini. The UMP leader, Maxim Carlot Korman, became prime minister.

B. Culture

The population of Vanuatu, which numbers about 142,000, is mainly Melanesian, with many different local cultural patterns. There are also small minorities of European, Vietnamese, and Chinese people. About 120 different Melanesian languages are spoken. Persons indigenous to Vanuatu are called ni-Vanuatu. The three official languages are English, French, and Bislama (the Vanuatu variant of Melanesian pidgin). Most Melanesians speak Bislama as well as their local language; about half of the educated Melanesians speak English and about half speak French, with some overlap. The bulk of the population lives in the rural areas, but approximately 20,000 live in the capital, Vila, and about 7,000 live in the second largest town, Luganville.

C. Economy

The economy is basically a subsistence economy, but copra, beef, and cocoa are exported. There is also a growing trade and international finance center in Vila. Local sources, mostly import and export duties, makes up approximately 70 percent of the recurrent revenue, but aid from Britain and France is necessary to cover the remainder of recurrent budget requirements. Development expenditure is financed almost entirely by overseas aid.

III. Sources of Law

Vanuatu has a variety of sources of law as a result of its joint administration by Britain and France before independence in 1980.

A. Constitution

The Constitution of Vanuatu was brought into force in 1980 by an exchange of notes between Britain and France. Its provisions provide the basic structure of the government of Vanuatu and also the fundamental rights, freedoms, and duties of individuals. Article 2 of the Constitution provides that the Constitution is the supreme law of Vanuatu.

Parliament may amend the Constitution by the vote of not less than two-thirds of all members at a special meeting attended by at least three-quarters of members in the first instance, or two-thirds of the members one week later—provided that any amendment regarding the status of the three official languages, the electoral system, or the parliamentary system shall not come into effect unless supported at a national referendum (Constitution, Chapter 14).

B. Statutory Law

The Constitution provides at Article 16 that Parliament "may make laws for the peace, order and good government of Vanuatu." Article 16 further stipulates that laws may not be inconsistent with the Constitution.

Acts of Parliament, as well as those pre-independence regulations that are still in force, are compiled in the *Laws of Vanuatu*, which was published in a revised edition in 1988. In the revised edition, each law is designated by chapter number.

C. British and French Laws

The Constitution provides, at Article 93, that the British and French laws in force or applied in New Hebrides immediately before independence continue to apply to the extent that they are neither expressly revoked by Parliament nor incompatible with the independent status of Vanuatu.

The Anglo-French Protocol of 1914, which came into force in 1922 and regulated the government of the New Hebrides, provided that the laws of Britain and France were to apply to the nationals of each country and also to nationals of other countries who chose, or opted, to be subject to such laws.

This meant that much of French law was applied to French nationals and optants. So far as British nationals and optants were concerned, the Pacific Order-in-Council 1893, which established a High Commissioner's Court for British dependencies in the Pacific, provided that "the substance of the law for the time being in force in and for England" was to be applied. The Western Pacific (Courts) Order 1961, which replaced the High Commissioner's Court with the High Court of the Western Pacific, provided that the court was to apply "(a) the statutes of general application in force in England on the 1st day of January 1961 and (b) the substance of the English common law and equity . . . so far only as the circumstances of any particular territory and its inhabitants and the limits of Her Majesty's jurisdiction permit." After the abolition of the High Court of the Western Pacific by the New Hebrides Order 1975 and its replacement in the New Hebrides by the High Court of the New Hebrides, the High Court of the New Hebrides Regulation 1976 provided that "so far as circumstances admit . . . the statutes of general application in force in England on the 1st day of January 1976" were to be applied as well as the principles of common law and equity. In addition, the Pacific Order-in-Council 1893 authorized the British High Commissioner of the Western Pacific to make regulations for the peace, order, and good government of those subject to British jurisdiction. Accordingly, British nationals and optants were, prior to independence, subject to statutes of general application in force in England on January 1, 1976, to the substance of English common law and equity (so far as appropriate to the circumstances of the country), and to the regulations that under the revised edition of the laws of Vanuatu are now designated as acts. These nationals were also subject to any particular British acts of Parliament and subsidiary legislation expressly stated to apply in the New Hebrides.

D. Joint Regulations

The Anglo-French Protocol of 1914 authorized the Resident Commissioners of Britain and France to act together to make joint regulations that were binding on all inhabitants. A large number of joint regulations were made, some of which authorized the making of rules or orders by public officers and bodies—that is, subsidiary legislation.

The Constitution provides at Article 93 that, until otherwise specified by Parliament, all joint regulations (now called acts) and subsidiary legislation in force immediately before independence will continue in force and will be construed with adaptations necessary to bring them into conformity with the Constitution.

E. Common Law

The Constitution makes no express provision for the reception of the common law. However, Article 93 of the Constitution provides that British and French laws in force immediately before independence continue to apply to the extent that they are neither expressly revoked by Parliament nor incompatible with the independent status of Vanuatu. Prior to independence, French nationals and optants were not subject to the English common law, but, under the High Court of the New Hebrides Regulation 1976, the common law was received for British nationals and optants, so far as it was appropriate to the circumstances of the country (**see III, C British and French Laws**). It is therefore to be assumed that British nationals and optants are still subject to the English common law.

F. Customary Law

The Constitution recognizes customary law in a number of ways. It provides at Article 72 that "the rules of custom shall form the basis of ownership and use of land in the Republic." Article 93 of the Constitution provides in general terms that "customary law shall continue to have effect as part of the law of the Republic." Article 45 directs the judiciary "to resolve proceedings according to law," and *law*, according to Article 93, includes custom. Article 45 continues: "If there is no rule of law applicable to a matter before it, a court shall determine the matter according to substantial justice and whenever possible in conformity with custom." Article 49 authorizes Parliament to "provide for the manner of the ascertainment of relevant rules of custom," which would assist the courts in applying custom.

IV. CONSTITUTIONAL SYSTEM

A. Territory

The Anglo-French Protocol of 1914 referred only in general terms to "the group of the New Hebrides, including the Banks and Torres Islands," and the Constitution refers to "New Hebrides," later amended to "Vanuatu." There is no statutory definition of these terms.

B. Nationality and Citizenship

The Constitution provides in Chapter 3 that on the day of independence, persons with four grandparents indigenous to Vanuatu and persons of a lesser degree of ni-Vanuatu ancestry who did not hold citizenship, nationality, or the status of an optant of a foreign state automatically became citizens. (*Ni-Vanuatu* is not defined the the Constitution but means indigenous to Vanuatu.)

Persons who at independence were ni-Vanuatu but held citizenship, nationality, or the status of an optant of a foreign state were nonetheless entitled to Vanuatu citizenship if they made application within three months of independence and renounced their other citizenship or nationality within three months of receiving Vanuatu citizenship.

Persons born after Independence Day, whether in Vanuatu or abroad, are citizens if at least one of their parents is a Vanuatu citizen.

Nationals of foreign states or stateless persons may apply to be naturalized as citizens of Vanuatu if they have lived in Vanuatu continuously for a period of ten years before the date of application.

C. National Government

Vanuatu is a unitary state with a parliamentary type of government based on the Westminster model.

1. HEAD OF STATE

The Constitution provides at Chapter 6 and Schedule 1 that the Head of State, to be known as the President, must be an indigenous ni-Vanuatu citizen qualified to be elected to Parliament. The President is to be elected in a secret ballot by an electoral college comprising the members of Parliament and chairs of local government councils. A two-thirds majority vote is required, and the vote may take place only if a quorum of three-fourths is present at the first meeting of the college. If that quorum is not present, the college must meet forty-eight hours later and may then vote if two-thirds of the members are present. The term of office is five years; the President can be removed by a two-thirds majority of the electoral college for gross misconduct or incapacity. There is no express provision for the suspension or resignation of the President, although a President has in fact resigned on one occasion.

The President has a general function to symbolize the unity of the nation, and a number of more specific functions. The President has a duty to assent to all bills passed by the Parliament, unless the President considers a bill unconstitutional, in which case it will be referred to the Supreme Court for its opinion. The President is authorized, on the advice of the council of ministers, to dissolve Parliament but not to summon or adjourn it.

With regard to the executive, the President has the right to be kept fully informed by the Prime Minister of the general conduct of government of the Republic and the power to refer any regulation made by ministers to the Supreme Court if the President considers it unconstitutional. The President has no power to appoint or dismiss ministers, except that if the Prime Minister dies and there is no Deputy Prime Minister, the President may appoint a minister to act as Prime Minister until a new one is elected.

With regard to public administration, the President has power to appoint the five members of the Public Service Commission after consultation with the Prime Minister and to appoint a chair each year from among the members of the commission. The President also has the power to appoint but no express power to suspend or remove the ombudsman, after consultation with the Prime Minister, leaders of the political parties represented in Parliament, the Speaker of Parliament, the president of the National Council of Chiefs, the chairs of the local government councils, and the chairs of the Public Service Commission and Judicial Service Commission.

2. EXECUTIVE

The executive power of the people of the Republic, which Chapter 7 of the Constitution vests in the Prime Minister, and the Council of Ministers, is to be exercised as provided by the Constitution or a law.

The Prime Minister is elected by an absolute majority of the members of Parliament voting by secret ballot. The Prime Minister may appoint, from members of Parliament, ministers not exceeding a quarter of the number of members of Parliament, and may designate one of them as Deputy Prime Minister. Ministers remain members of Parliament. The Prime Minister assigns responsibilities for conduct of government to ministers and may remove them from office.

The Council of Ministers, including the Prime Minister, is collectively responsible to Parliament; which may by an absolute majority pass a motion of no confidence in the Prime Minister. This motion will cause the Prime Minister and other ministers to cease to hold office, although they are to continue to exercise their functions until a new Prime Minister is elected by Parliament.

The Council of Ministers ceases to hold office when the Prime Minister resigns or dies, but they continue to exercise their functions until a new Prime Minister is elected. If, on the death of the Prime Minister, there is no Deputy Prime Minister, the President may appoint a minister to act as Prime Minister until a new one is elected. A minister, including the Prime Minister, ceases to hold office when after a general election Parliament meets to elect a new Prime Minister; if the minister ceases to be a member of Parliament for any reason other than dissolution of Parliament, or if the minister is elected President or Speaker.

3. PARLIAMENT

As provided in Chapter 4 of the Constitution, Parliament consists of a single chamber, the members of which are elected by universal suffrage through an electoral system that includes an element of proportional representation. Any citizen of Vanuatu who is at least twenty-five years of age is eligible to stand for election, subject to certain disqualifications provided by the Representation of People Act 1982, and every citizen of Vanuatu at least eighteen years of age is eligible to vote.

The Constitution provides that Parliament is to meet twice a year in ordinary session and may meet in extraordinary session if requested by a majority of its members, the Speaker, or the Prime Minister. Parliament normally makes decisions by a public vote of a simple majority of the members voting; a quorum is two-thirds of the members, unless fewer are present at the first sitting in which case the session may begin three days later, at which point a simple majority of members, can constitute a quorum.

Parliament has power to make laws for the peace, order, and good government of the country, to approve the budget of the government, and to ratify certain treaties entered into by the government.

Parliament also has power to pass, by an absolute majority of members, a motion of no confidence in the Prime Minister, which will cause the Prime Minister and other ministers to cease to hold office, although they may continue to exercise their functions until a new Prime Minister is elected by Parliament.

Parliament normally continues for four years from the date of election but may be dissolved earlier by the president, on the advice of the Council of Ministers. Parliament may also be dissolved by the vote of an absolute majority of members at a special sitting when at least three-quarters of members are present. Neither kind of dissolution can occur within the first twelve months after a general election.

The general responsibility for the registration of voters and the conduct of elections to Parliament (as well as to the National Council of Chiefs and to local government councils) vests in an electoral commission, consisting of three persons appointed by the President on the advice of the Judicial Service Commission. In the exercise of its functions, the electoral commission is not subject to direction or control by any person.

4. NATIONAL COUNCIL OF CHIEFS

Chapter 5 of the Constitution establishes a National Council of Chiefs, composed of traditional chiefs elected by their peers sitting in district councils of chiefs. The council chooses its own president from among its members. The council is required to meet at least once a year. Additional meetings may be called by the council itself, Parliament, or the Cabinet.

The council has no legislative authority. It is empowered only "to discuss all matters relating to custom and tradition and [to] make recommendations for the preservation and promotion of ni-Vanuatu culture and languages" (Article 28). Article 28 also provides that the council "may be consulted on any question, particularly any question relating to tradition and custom, in connection with any bill before Parliament," but the article does not specify who will do the consulting, nor does it require that other branches of government adopt the council's advice.

5. JUDICIARY

Chapter 8 of the Constitution establishes a Supreme Court with unlimited jurisdiction in civil and criminal proceedings. The Constitution also gives the Supreme Court jurisdiction over the following matters:

1. claims that the Constitution has been contravened;
2. questions as to whether a person has been validly elected to Parliament, to the National Council of Chiefs, or to a local government council, or has vacated his or her seat in such bodies, or has become disqualified to hold it;
3. the validity of emergency regulations made by the Council of Ministers, and the validity of any bill or regulation referred to the court by the President; and
4. appeals from Island Courts as to the ownership of land.

The Chief Justice is appointed by the President after consultation with the Prime Minister and leader of the opposition, and other judges of the Supreme Court are appointed by the President on the advice of the Judicial Service Commission.

The Constitution also provides for a Court of Appeal, to be made up of two or more judges of the Supreme Court sitting together. Decisions of the Court of Appeal are final.

Magistrates' Courts are not referred to in the Constitution but are established by the Courts Act (Chapter 122). In criminal proceedings, an ordinary Magistrates' Court has jurisdiction to try offenses punishable by imprisonment not exceeding two years; however, a Magistrates' Court presided over by a senior magistrate has jurisdiction to try offenses punishable by imprisonment not exceeding five years, but with power to impose a sentence of not more than two years' imprisonment. In civil proceedings, all Magistrates' Courts have jurisdiction to try claims where the amount claimed or the subject matter in dispute does not exceed VT200,000, disputes between landlord and tenant where the amount claimed does not exceed VT500,000, claims for maintenance not exceeding VT2,000,000, and uncontested petitions for divorce or nullity of marriage. Magistrates' Courts also have jurisdiction to hear appeals from decisions of Island Courts, except decisions as to the ownership of land, which must be heard by the Supreme Court. Magistrates are appointed by the President, acting on the advice of the Judicial Service Commission.

The Constitution states at Article 50 that Parliament should provide for the establishment of Village Courts or Island Courts, with jurisdiction over customary and other matters. Article 50 stipulates that chiefs should have a role in these courts. The Island Courts Act (Chapter 167) establishes Island Courts, which have jurisdiction over criminal offenses occurring within their district and specified in their warrants of appointment (usually minor offenses such as assault, trespass, health offenses, and offenses under regional bylaws). The Island Courts can impose fines not exceeding VT24,000 or imprisonment not exceeding six months. In civil matters, Island Courts are usually authorized by their warrants to determine all claims to ownership of land, claims in contract or tort where the amount claimed or the value of the subject does not exceed VT50,000, claims for compensation under regional bylaws not exceeding VT50,000, and claims for maintenance not limited in amount. The act also provides at Section

10 that Island Courts "shall administer the customary law" of their localities "so far as the same is not in conflict with any written law and is not contrary to justice, morality and good order."

D. Provincial and Local Government

The Constitution contains a chapter that expressly recognizes the importance of decentralization to the people's full participation in the government of their regions. Chapter 13 provides for Parliament to enact legislation to give effect to that ideal, by enacting legislation dividing the country into regions, each of which may have a local government council. Representatives of customary chiefs are to sit on each coucil.

The Decentralization Act (Chapter 127) provides for the election of local government councils every four years. These councils are to have responsibility for the location, construction, and maintenance of schools, clinics, dispensaries, health centers, bridges, roads, (other than those for which the national government has responsibility), water supplies, wharves, markets, libraries, museums, and cultural centers. The act also authorizes local government councils to regulate and control markets; to license cinemas, business premises, and premises for sale of liquor or for trading; to control dogs, pigs, and other livestock; to supervise and control area and village councils; to supervise fishing within one nautical mile of the low water line; and to provide staff for village courts and information services.

Local government councils are authorized by the act to levy and collect various kinds of taxes (head tax, liquor licensing tax, trading tax, dog tax, cinema tax, entertainment tax, gaming and lottery tax); control vehicular traffic, and register births, deaths, and marriages. A local government council can make regional laws for the good government of the region and welfare of its people, but such regional laws must not conflict with the Constitution or with any act, joint regulation, or order that expressly or implicitly applies throughout Vanuatu.

E. Emergency Powers

The Constitution provides at Chapter 11 that the Council of Ministers may make regulations for dealing with a public emergency whenever the Republic is at war or the President, acting on the advice of the Council of Ministers, declares a state of emergency by reason of natural calamity, or to prevent a threat to or to restore public order.

Emergency regulations made by the Council of Ministers have effect notwithstanding the provisions in the Constitution relating to fundamental rights, freedoms, and duties, except that no regulation shall derogate from the right to life and the freedom from inhuman treatment and forced labor. Neither shall any such regulation provide for the detention of a person without trial for more than one month unless the person is an enemy alien. Emergency regulations should be reasonably necessary in the circumstances of the emergency and justifiable in a democratic society. Any person aggrieved by an emergency regulation may challenge its validity in the Supreme Court.

A state of emergency declared by the President shall, if Parliament is in session, terminate after one week unless approved by resolution of two-thirds of the members of Parliament, and if Parliament is not in session, terminate after two weeks. Parliament may approve a state of emergency for up to three months but may approve further extensions of that period. Parliament may at any time terminate a state of emergency by a resolution supported by an absolute majority of its members.

During a state of emergency, Parliament may meet whenever it decides, and it shall not be dissolved during a state of emergency. If the life of Parliament comes to an end during a state of emergency, Parliament may meet to consider the state of emergency until the new Parliament first meets.

F. Human Rights

The Constitution recognizes that, subject to certain exceptions, all persons are entitled, without discrimination on the ground of race, place of origin, religion or traditional beliefs, political opinions, language, or sex, to the following fundamental rights and freedoms:

1. life, liberty, security of the person;
2. protection of the law;
3. freedom from inhuman treatment and forced labor;
4. freedom of conscience and worship;
5. freedom of expression;
6. freedom of assembly and association;
7. freedom of movement;
8. protection for the privacy of the home and other property and from unjust deprivation of property; and
9. equal treatment under the law or administrative action.

These rights and freedoms are not defined or described in further detail, except for protection of the law, which includes the following rights:

1. a fair hearing to be held within a reasonable time by an independent and impartial court;
2. provision of a lawyer if the defendant is charged with a serious offense;
3. innocence of the defendant to be presumed until guilt is established;
4. the defendant to be promptly informed of the offense charged in language the defendant understands;
5. interpreter to be provided if defendant does not understand the language of the proceedings;
6. person not to be tried in absentia without consent unless the person's conduct makes it impossible for the trial to proceed;
7. no one to be convicted for conduct that was not an offense at the time of the conduct;
8. no one to be punished with a greater penalty than existed at the time of the conduct;
9. no one to be tried for the same offense for which that person has been already convicted, acquitted, or pardoned.

The exceptions to these fundamental rights and freedoms are restrictions imposed by law on noncitizens; respect for the rights and freedoms of others; and the legitimate public interest in defense, safety, public order, welfare, and health. In the case of the fundamental right to equal treatment under the law or administrative action, an exception is provided for laws that provide for the special benefit, welfare, protection, or advancement of females, children, and young persons, members of underprivileged groups, or inhabitants of less developed areas.

Article 6 of the Constitution provides that anyone who considers that any of the rights guaranteed by the Constitution has been, is being, or is likely to be infringed, may, apart from any other possible legal remedy, apply to the Supreme Court to enforce that right. The Supreme Court is given power to make such orders, issue such writs, and give such directions, including the payment of compensation, as it considers appropriate to enforce the right.

In addition to the fundamental rights and freedoms, the Constitution also provides in Chapter 2 that every person has the following fundamental duties:

1. to respect and act in the spirit of the Constitution;
2. to participate actively in the development of the national community;
3. to exercise the rights guaranteed under the Constitution and participate fully in the government of Vanuatu;
4. to safeguard the national wealth, resources, and environment of Vanuatu;
5. to work in socially useful employment;
6. to respect the rights and freedom of others;
7. to contribute to the revenues required for the advancement of the republic;
8. in the case of a parent, to support, assist, and educate children; and
9. in the case of a child, to respect one's parents.

These fundamental duties are stated by Article 8 of the Constitution, however, to be nonjusticiable, unless specifically provided by law. Nevertheless, all public authorities are under a duty to encourage compliance with them insofar as lies within their powers.

V. Administrative Organization and Law

A. Organization

The administration of Vanuatu is provided for in Chapter 9 of the Constitution, which establishes the public service and the Public Service Commission.

The Public Service Commission consists of five members appointed for three years by the President after consultation with the Prime Minister, and the President may also each year appoint one of the members the chairperson. The commission is responsible for the appointment, promotion, and discipline of public servants and the selection of those to undergo training courses but has no authority over members of the judiciary, the armed forces, or the police and teaching services. In the exercise of its functions, the commission is not subject to direction or control by any other person or body. The teaching service and the police service are established as separate services under the control of their own service commissions under the Teaching Service Act (Chapter 171) and the Police Act (Chapter 105), respectively.

The Reserve Bank of Vanuatu and the Vanuatu Commodities Marketing Board are the major statutory bodies or quasi-governmental organizations in Vanuatu.

B. Public Service

Public servants, who must be citizens, are appointed by the Public Service Commission and may not be removed from their positions, so long as the positions exist, except in accordance with the Constitution. The Constitution provides that public servants will leave the service upon reaching retirement age or upon being dismissed by the Public Service Commission and may not be demoted without consultation with the commission.

The security of tenure provisions do not apply to the personal political advisers of the Prime Minister and ministers. Senior public servants in ministries may be transferred by the Prime Minister to other posts of equivalent rank. Public servants are subject to such compulsory early retirement as the law may provide.

The Constitution further provides that the Prime Minister or, in urgent cases, the Public Service Commission in place of the Prime Minister, may make provision for the recruitment of staff for a specified period to meet unforeseen needs.

C. Public Finance and Audit

Article 23 of the Constitution requires that every year the government present a budget bill for Parliament's approval and that no taxation be imposed or altered and no public funds expended except in accordance with a law passed by Parliament. Article 23 also provides that no motion for levying or increasing taxation or for the expenditure of public funds shall be introduced unless supported by the government.

The office of Auditor General, appointed by the Public Service Commission, is established by Article 23 of the Constitution, with responsibility to audit and report to Parliament and the government on the public accounts of Vanuatu. In the exercise of official functions, the Auditor General is not subject to direction or control by any other person or body.

D. Rule Making

There are no constitutional requirements on the manner in which rules or subsidiary laws are to be made, but the Interpretation Act (Chapter 132) contains some general provisions on the topic. The common law principle that subsidiary legislation must be made in accordance with the terms of the authorizing statute is applied by the courts.

E. Review of Administrative Actions

1. JUDICIAL REVIEW

The Supreme Court of Vanuatu applies the common law principles of judicial review—that is, decisions of public officials may be reviewed on grounds of lack or excess of jurisdiction, breach of principles of natural justice, error of law, and fraud.

The procedures for applying for judicial review are contained in the Rules of the High Court of the Western Pacific 1964, which are applied by the Supreme Court of Vanuatu. Leave must be first obtained from the Court for the issue of proceedings for judicial review. The rules provide also for the granting of the prerogative remedies of certiorari, prohibition, mandamus, and habeas corpus, as well as the making of a declaration of rights.

2. OMBUDSMAN

The Constitution provides at Chapter 9 for an ombudsman to be appointed by the President, after consultation with the Prime Minister and leaders of political parties in Parliament, the Speaker, the president of the National Council of Chiefs, chairpersons of the local government councils, and of the Public Service and Judicial Service Commissions. A person who is a member of Parliament, the National Council of Chiefs, or a local government council; holds any other public office; or exercises a position of responsibility within a political party is disqualified from appointment as ombudsman.

The ombudsman, who serves a five-year term, is not subject to direction or control from any other person or body. The ombudsman may inquire into the conduct of any public servant, public authority and ministerial department except the President, the Judicial Service Commission, the Supreme Court, and other judicial bodies, but the person or body complained of must be given an opportunity to reply to the complaints. The ombudsman may find that the complaint is unjustified or that the conduct was contrary to law, based on error of law or fact, unjustifiably delayed, unjust, or blatantly unreasonable. The findings of the ombudsman shall be made known to the complainant, the Prime Minister, and the public department or authority concerned.

Another function of the ombudsman is to investigate a complaint by a citizen that the citizen has been denied the service which he or she may rightfully expect from the Republic's administration in the official language that he or she uses. The ombudsman is also required each year to make a special report to Parliament about observance of multilingualism and the measures likely to ensure its respect.

3. COMMISSION OF REVIEW

There is no provision in Vanuatu for review of administrative action by a standing commission of review. The Commission of Enquiry Act (Chapter 85) does, however, provide for the appointment of a commission of inquiry to enquire into any matter that in the opinion of the minister should be investigated for the public welfare.

4. LEADERSHIP CODE

Chapter 10 of the Constitution requires political leaders (the President, the Prime Minister, other ministers, members of Parliament, and such other public servants or government officers as the law may prescribe) to conduct themselves, in both their public and private lives, so as not to be in positions where they have or could have a conflict of interest, demean their offices, allow their integrity to be called into question, or endanger or diminish respect for and confidence in the integrity of the government. In particular, Article 64 prohibits leaders from using their office for personal gain and from entering into any transaction or engaging in any enterprise that might be expected to give rise to doubt in the public mind as to whether they are carrying out their offices in the manner required by Chapter 10.

VI. INTERNATIONAL OBLIGATIONS

A. Treaty Making

Article 24 of the Constitution requires treaties negotiated by the government to be presented to Parliament for ratification if they concern international organizations, trade, or peace; commit the expenditure of public funds; affect the status of people; require the amendment of the laws of Vanuatu; or provide for the transfer, exchange, or annexing of territory.

The treaties that have been presented for ratification by Parliament since independence involve loans the government has negotiated from overseas agencies and countries, including loan agreements with the Asian Development Bank, Barclays Bank, and the Republic of China.

Vanuatu entered into a fishing agreement with the Soviet Union in 1987 for one year but it expired in 1988 without renewal. This treaty was not presented for ratification since it did not commit public funds or in any other respect fall within the categories of treaties for which ratification by Parliament is required.

B. Diplomatic Privileges

The Diplomatic Privileges and Immunities Act (Chapter 143) provides that the articles contained in Schedule 1 of the Vienna Convention on Diplomatic Relations 1961 have the force of law in Vanuatu, subject to the power of the minister to withdraw certain privileges from a state if the minister considers that the privileges and immunities accorded to a mission of Vanuatu by that state are less than those conferred by the act on a mission of that state. The act authorizes the minister to order that any international organization may have such of the privileges and immunities set out in the act as are specified in the order.

C. International Organizations

Vanuatu is a member of the United Nations and hosts the Pacific operations office of the U.N. Economic and Social Commission for Asia and the Pacific. Vanuatu is also a member of the Commonwealth, the French cultural association, the Association de Co-operation Culturelle et Technique, the South Pacific Forum group, the Spear Head Group of Melanesian countries, and the Non-Aligned Movement.

D. Reciprocal Enforcement of Judgments

There is no Vanuatu legislation for the reciprocal enforcement of judgments, and the occasion for such legislation had not arisen. Presumably the Foreign Judgements (Reciprocal Enforcement) Act 1933 (UK) would be applicable to British citizens and optants under the terms of the New Hebrides Order 1975, as amended by the High Court of the New Hebrides Regulations 1976; and the provisions of the French Code Civil would apply to French citizens and optants.

E. Extradition

The Extradition Act (Chapter 199) applies to those Commonwealth countries designated by the minister and other countries with which Vanuatu has an extradition arrangement (treaty states).

The act provides that a person may be extradited under the act for offenses in a Commonwealth country of the kind described in the schedule to the act if punishable by imprisonment of not less than one year, offenses in a treaty state of the kind described in the treaty, and offenses that would be offenses under Vanuatu law if they occurred in Vanuatu. However, under the act a person may not be extradited if the offense is of a political character; if the purpose of the proposed extradition is to punish the person on account of race, religion, nationality, or political opinions; or if the person, if extradited, might be prejudiced at trial or punished, detained, or restricted in personal liberty by reason of race, religion, nationality, or political opinions. The act also provides that a person may not be extradited if the person would be entitled, if charged with the offense in Vanuatu, to be discharged under the rule of law relating to previous acquittal or conviction.

VII. Revenue Law

There is no income tax legislation in Vanuatu. There is a tax, currently 10 percent, charged on the amount paid by guests in hotels and licensed premises for goods and services supplied by virtue of the Hotel and Licensed Premises Tax Act (Chapter 141).

The Export Duties Act (Chapter 31), as amended, authorizes the imposition of export duty on certain goods and products. The Import Duties (Consolidation) Act (Chapter 91), as amended, authorizes the imposition of import duty on the items set out in the customs import duties tariff at the rates therein specified, with power in the minister to exempt specified items.

A tax on properties, currently 5 percent of rental value, was introduced by the municipalities of Vila and Luganville in 1977. A tax, presently ranging from 5 percent to 15 percent, is imposed upon rents received, under the Taxation Act (Chapter 196). The act exempts some rental income, in particular as regards customary owners.

VIII. INVESTMENT LAW

A. Banking

The Banking Act (Chapter 63) provides that no banking business can be carried on in Vanuatu unless licensed by the minister. A license may be granted in the discretion of the minister, but if the Minister is of opinion that it would not be in the public interest to grant the license, the minister may refuse it and need not give any reason. The regulation also provides that a license will not be granted unless the applicant has a paid-up capital of not less than VT12.5 million if its head office is situated in Vanuatu, and not less than VT50 million if its head office is situated outside Vanuatu.

At present there are six licensed banks operating in Vanuatu.

B. Investment funds

A finance center has been set up as an association between banks, trust companies, chartered accountants, and solicitors to facilitate and encourage investment in Vanuatu to take advantage of the absence of company or personal income tax, capital gains tax, and death and estate duties. The association is a business grouping and has no statutory basis.

The Trust Companies Act (Chapter 69) provides that no company shall carry on the business of acting as trustee, executor, or administrator unless licensed by the minister. The minister may refuse to grant a license whenever the minister considers it in the public interest. The minister need not give any reason. The regulation also provides that a license shall not be granted unless the applicant company has a paid-up capital of not less than VT2.5 million if its head office is situated in Vanuatu, and not less than VT50 million if its head office is located outside Vanuatu.

At present there are five licensed trust companies operating in Vanuatu.

C. Credit Unions

Some credit unions currently operate in Vanuatu, but no specific legislation is designed for the registration of credit unions. It is believed that they can be registered under the cooperative societies legislation, but none has so far been so registered.

D. Foreign Exchange Control

There is no foreign exchange control in Vanuatu. The New Hebrides Joint Defence (Finance) Regulation 1941, which provided for the exercise of control over movements of foreign exchange into and out of New Hebrides, has not been operative for some years.

E. Imports and Exports

The Import of Goods (Control) Act (Chapter 176) authorizes the minister responsible for industry to make orders prohibiting the importation into Vanuatu of goods of any description for the purpose of protecting and stimulating local industry. The Animal Importation and Quarantine Act (Chapter 201) authorizes the prohibition of the import of animals and animal products.

There is no corresponding act generally authorizing the prohibition of exports. However, the export of green snail, trochus, bêche de mer, coral, and crustacean is prohibited without the permission of the minister, and the export of turtle and turtleshell is totally prohibited by regulations made under the Fisheries Act (Chapter 158). The Vanuatu Commodities Marketing Board Act (Chapter 133) prohibits the export, except by the board, of any product that has been prescribed by the minister after consultation with the board chairperson. At present, copra is the major product to have been prescribed.

F. Exemption from Customs Duties

The Import Duties (Consolidation) Act (Chapter 176) as amended, provides for exemptions from import duties to be granted by the minister for articles imported for new enterprises.

IX. Welfare Law

A. National Provident Fund

The Vanuatu National Provident Fund Act (Chapter 189) established a National Provident Fund composed of contributions forwarded by employers for their employees. Contributions consist of 6 percent of the remuneration paid to employees, of which half is to be paid by deductions from the employee's salary and half by the employer. Moneys of the fund are then to be invested by the Provident Fund Board, in accordance with policy guidelines approved by the Minister for Finance and the Central Bank of Vanuatu. The board is required to declare a rate of interest of 3 percent each year.

The Vanuatu Provident Fund Board consists of seven members, six appointed by the minister, of whom two are government employees, two are representatives of employers, and two are representatives of employees. The general manager of the fund is the seventh member of the board.

A person is entitled to receive payment of the moneys to his or her credit in the fund at age fifty-five, when the person has become permanently incapable of further employment, or when he or she is about to leave Vanuatu permanently. If a person dies before reaching age fifty-five, the fund account may be paid to that person's heirs or estate.

There is provision for existing provident schemes to be registered as an alternative to the Vanuatu National Provident Fund. Noncitizens who are contributing to a social security scheme of some other country, the benefits of which are at least comparable to those of the Vanuatu National Provident Fund, are exempt from contributing to the fund.

B. Workers' Compensation

A Workmen's Compensation Act was passed in 1987 to provide for employers to make payments of compensation to employees injured in the course of their work, but was not yet in force as of early 1992.

X. Criminal Law

The Penal Code Act (Chapter 135) provides general principles of jurisdiction in criminal matters and general principles of criminal liability, as well as descriptions of the main criminal offenses in Vanuatu.

Jurisdiction of the courts of Vanuatu extends to criminal offenses committed wholly or partly within Vanuatu (including its territorial waters and the airspace); offenses against the external security of the republic; counterfeiting of currency; and the international offenses of piracy, hijacking of aircraft, traffic in persons, slave trading, and traffic in narcotics, wherever committed. In addition, any citizen of Vanuatu who does something outside Vanuatu, which, if it had been committed in Vanuatu, would have been a criminal offense, may, subject to certain limitations, be convicted of such offense upon return to the country.

The Penal Code provides that a person shall not be guilty of a criminal offense unless that person intentionally or recklessly does a prohibited act or omission and unless there is an express statement or necessary and distinct implication to the contrary in the statute. Consent of the victim is a defense to criminal liability, except where the purpose of the defendant's act was to inflict serious physical or mental injury incompatible with the well-being of the victim. Insanity is a complete defense, as is an honest and reasonable mistake of fact, but mistake of law is not. Voluntary intoxication is a defense only if it is so gross as to deprive the accused of the capacity to form the necessary criminal intention. Self-defense or defense of property are defenses if not disproportionate to the danger threatened. Submission to superior orders is a defense unless the order was manifestly or known to be unlawful. Criminal liability remains, but punishment may be reduced, if the defendant was suffering from abnormality of the mind not amounting to insanity; was acting under threats of death or grievous harm or under coercion from a person having authority over the defendant; was provoked beyond normal self-control, provided the response was not disproportionate to the provocation.

Among criminal offenses provided for in the Penal Code are treason, sedition, riot, unlawful assembly, perjury and false statements, escapes and rescues, insult to religion, rape, unlawful sexual intercourse, homosexual acts with persons under eighteen, slavery, kidnapping, abortion, criminal defamation, theft, fraud, arson, robbery, forgery, counterfeiting, piracy, and hijacking.

A person is also criminally liable if that person aids, counsels, or procures the commission of an offense; shelters another person who is known or believed to have commited a criminal offense; or has possession of or disposes of anything taken during the offense or used in committing the offense.

XI. Judicial Procedure

A. Civil Proceedings

The procedure for civil proceedings in Island Courts is regulated by the Island Courts (Civil Procedure) Rules 1984, which require that civil proceedings be started by the filing in the court office of a statement of claim, which must be served on the defendant. The defendant may give notice of a counterclaim or set-off. Either party may give notice admitting the claim of the other and may apply to the court to settle issues, but there is no other provision for pleadings or interlocutory proceedings.

The procedures for civil proceedings in a Magistrates' Court are regulated by the Magistrate's

Courts (Civil Procedure) Rules 1976. Civil proceedings in Magistrates' Courts are commenced by a writ of summons issued upon oral or written application. The court may at any time before trial settle the issues.

The procedure for civil proceedings in the Supreme Court is very closely modeled on the rules that apply in Supreme Court of England. Civil proceedings are commenced by a writ of summons, upon which is endorsed a summary of the claim and to which may be attached a full statement of claim (or this may be filed later). The defendant must, within the time specified in the writ, file an entry of appearance and also a statement of defense, or risk a default judgment or summary judgment. The same rules about pleadings and procedure at hearings apply as in civil proceedings in the High Court in England.

B. Criminal Proceedings

The procedure for criminal proceedings in the Island Courts is regulated by the Islands Court (Criminal Procedure) Rules 1984, which provide for such proceedings to be commenced by a charge filed by the police with the clerk of the court, who then issues a summons to the accused to attend on a stipulated day. If the court has reason to believe that the accused is avoiding service of the summons or is unlikely to obey the summons, a warrant for arrest may be issued. The procedure at hearings is similar to that of courts throughout the Commonwealth.

The court is authorized to promote reconciliation of offenses that are of a personal nature and punishable by a fine only or imprisonment for less than two years.

Criminal proceedings in a Magistrates' Court are regulated by the Criminal Procedure Code Act (Chapter 136), which provides for criminal proceedings to be commenced by a charge filed in the court office by the police or a complaint made on oath to a magistrate. A summons is then issued, with power for the court to issue an arrest warrant if there is reason to believe the accused is avoiding service or is unlikely to attend.

Criminal proceedings in the Supreme Court are regulated by the Criminal Procedure Code Act. Criminal proceedings are commenced in the Supreme Court by the filing of an information by the Public Prosecutor, after a preliminary inquiry in the Magistrates' Court to ascertain the sufficiency of the evidence to justify a trial in the Supreme Court. At the hearing, the procedure is basically the same as in the Island Courts and Magistrates' Courts, except that the prosecution and then the accused can address the court at the conclusion of all the evidence and before the court renders its decision.

C. Appellate Proceedings

Appeals lie, under the Island Courts Act (Chapter 167), from decisions of Island Courts directly to the Supreme Court in land claims and to a Magistrates' Court in all other cases. The act requires that appeals be lodged within thirty days from the date of the decision appealed against, but neither the act nor the Island Court (Civil Procedure) Rules 1984 nor the Criminal Procedure Code Act make express provision for procedures to be followed in such appeals.

The supervising magistrate may also revise any of the proceedings of an Island Court in civil or criminal matters and make any order that the court might have made or order the proceedings to be reheard by the same or another Island Court.

The Island Courts Act requires that, in the exercise of its appellate jurisdiction from Island Courts, the Magistrates' Court appoint two or more assessors knowledgeable in custom to sit with the court; the act authorizes the court to consider any records relevant to the decision and to receive evidence and make any inquiries it thinks fit. The Court Act 1980 provides that the

Magistrates' Court may review all the findings of the Island Court and substitute its own opinion for that of the Island Court, except that it cannot interfere with the exercise of discretion by the Island Court unless it was manifestly wrong.

The Island Courts Act requires that the Supreme Court, in the exercise of its appellate jurisdiction in land cases, appoint two or more assessors knowledgeable in custom, consider the records of the Island Court, and receive evidence and make any inquiries it thinks fit. In dealing with appeals from Island Courts, the Supreme Court and the Magistrates' Court may review all findings of the Island Court and substitute its own opinion upon them, except that it may not interfere with the exercise of discretion unless it is manifestly wrong.

Appeals from decisions of Magistrates' Court in civil proceedings lie, by virtue of the Courts Act (Chapter 122), to the Supreme Court. The procedure for appeals in civil proceedings from the Magistrates' Courts to the Supreme Court is regulated by the Rules of the High Court of the Western Pacific 1964. These rules require that a notice of appeal be filed in the Magistrates' Court within fourteen days from the date of a decision in an interlocutory matter and within three months from the date of a final decision.

Appeals are by way of rehearing of the evidence recorded in the Magistrates' Court. No new evidence may be adduced without the leave of the Supreme Court. The Courts Act provides that the Supreme Court shall have all the powers of the court appealed from but shall not interfere with the exercise of discretion by that court unless it was manifestly wrong.

Appeals from decisions of Magistrates' Courts in criminal proceedings may, under the provisions of the Criminal Procedure Code Act, be brought to the Supreme Court by any person who has been convicted on any ground, and by the Public Prosecutor on a point of law only. The code provides that notice in writing of the appeal must be lodged within fourteen days of the decision, and, within a further fourteen days, a memorandum of appeal must be lodged setting out the matters of fact or law on which the Magistrates' Court is alleged to have erred. The Criminal Procedure Code Act provides that the Supreme Court, in the exercise of its appellate jurisdiction from Magistrates' Courts in criminal proceedings, may reject an appeal summarily if, after perusing the memorandum of appeal, it considers that there is insufficient ground for interfering with the decision.

Appeals from decisions of the Supreme Court in the exercise of its original jurisdiction in civil proceedings lie, under the Courts Act, to the Court of Appeal. There is no appeal from decisions of the Supreme Court made in its appellate jurisdiction on appeal from the Island Courts or from the Magistrates' Courts in civil matters. The procedure for appealing from decisions of the Supreme Court is regulated by the Court of Appeal Rules 1973 made under the Western Pacific (Courts) Order in Council 1961. These rules require that the appeal must be by way of written notice of motion setting out that part of the decision appealed from and the order the appellant seeks from the Court of Appeal. The notice of appeal must be filed with the registrar of the Supreme Court within thirty days from the date of the decision appealed from, and a copy must be served on every person directly affected by the appeal.

The procedure for hearing appeals is prescribed by the Court of Appeal Rules and proceeds on the basis of the evidence given before the Supreme Court; new evidence is not admitted except on special grounds. The Courts Act provides that the Court of Appeal may dismiss the appeal or amend or reverse the decision but may not interfere with the exercise of discretion by the Supreme Court unless it was manifestly wrong.

Appeals in criminal proceedings lie from decisions of the Supreme Court to the Court of Appeal, under the Criminal Procedure Code Act, which provides that any person who has been convicted in a trial in the Supreme Court may appeal on any ground, and the Public Prosecutor may appeal on any question of law arising in original or appellate proceedings in the Supreme

Court. The act requires that appeals be by notice in writing, which must be filed with the Supreme Court within fourteen days from the decision appealed from. Within fourteen days from filing of the notice of appeal, the appellant must file a memorandum of appeal setting out the matters in respect of which the court is alleged to have erred.

The same procedures are prescribed by the Criminal Procedure Code Act to be followed in the case of appeals from the Supreme Court to the Court of Appeal as are to be followed in appeals from Magistrates' Courts to the Supreme Court.

Decisions of the Court of Appeal, in both civil and criminal proceedings, are final, and there is no provision for further appeal.

XII. LAND AND NATURAL RESOURCES

A. Land Tenure and Administration

The Constitution, provides, in Articles 71 to 73, that all land in the Republic belongs to the "indigenous custom owners and their descendants," that "the rules of custom shall form the basis of ownership and use of land in the Republic," and that "only indigenous citizens . . . who have acquired their land in accordance with a recognised system of land tenure shall have perpetual ownership of their land."

The Constitution also provides, however, at Articles 78 and 79, that the government may own land acquired by it in the public interest and may buy land from customary owners for the purpose of transferring ownership to indigenous citizens or communities from over populated islands.

Under the Land Reform Act (Chapter 123) and the Land Leases Act (Chapter 163), land may be leased by customary owners to other persons for periods up to seventy-five years and may be mortgaged.

All land transactions between an indigenous citizen and either a nonindigenous citizen or a noncitizen must be approved by the government, but such approval shall be granted unless the transaction is prejudicial to the interests of the customary owners of the land; the indigenous citizen, if not the customary owner; the community in which the land is situated; or the republic (Constitution, Article 77).

The administration of land in the Republic is undertaken by the Department of Lands under the control of the Minister of Lands. At one time, corporate bodies were established in the urban areas of Vila and Luganville to exercise functions delegated to them by the minister, but these were abolished in 1988, and their functions are now exercised by staff of the Department of Lands.

B. Customary Land Tenure

Pursuant to Article 76 of the Constitution, the Land Reform Act provides for the President to establish special courts to determine disputes about the ownership of customary land. However, the Island Courts Act established Island Courts authorized by their warrant of appointment to determine such disputes. The act also provides that appeals from the Island Courts on land matters be heard by the Supreme Court, whose decision is final.

C. Government Taking of Land

The Constitution declares at Article 78 that the government may own land acquired by it in the public interest. The Constitution also provides at Article 5 that—subject to respect for the rights and freedoms of others and to the legitimate public interest in defense, public order, welfare, and health—all persons are entitled to the fundamental right of protection from unjust deprivation of property.

The Land Reform Act provides that all land owned on January 1, 1980, by the British government, the French government, the Condominium, or a municipality is, on Independence Day, July 31, 1980, automatically vested in the government of Vanuatu, as public land held for the benefit of the Republic.

Under the Land Reform Act the minister may, on the advice of the Council of Ministers, by order vest any public land in indigenous citizens or communities in accordance with Article 79 of the Constitution, subject to the payment of compensation to the customary owners. So far no such order has been made. The Land Reform Act also provides that the government must give the customary owners six months' notice of its intention to use public land for development or public purposes and must agree upon compensation to be paid to the customary owners. The minister may, at any time, on the advice of the Council of Ministers and after consultation with the customary owners, declare any land to be public land.

D. National Parks and Reserves

There is no legislation relating to national parks.

E. Agriculture, Forests, and Fisheries

There is no legislation relating to agriculture generally.

The Fisheries Act (Chapter 158) creates the office of Director of Fisheries, and requires the director to prepare and keep under review plans for the management and development of fisheries in Vanuatu waters. The act also requires foreign fishing vessels in Vanuatu waters to be registered and licensed. Vanuatu waters are defined as including the territorial sea, archipelagic waters, and a 200-mile exclusive economic zone. Regulations made under the act prohibit interference of any kind with turtles and prohibit the export of green snail, trochus, bêche de mer, coral, or crustachean without the permission of the minister.

The Forestry Act (Chapter 147) provides that forest areas may be set aside where the minister considers it in the public interest that forest land should be protected, exploited, developed, or utilized in accordance with principles of good forestry or should be subject to provision for reforestation. When a forest area has been declared, the owners and persons cutting timber must comply with certain requirements.

In addition, the Forestry Act provides for the establishment of forestry reserves where the minister considers that the public interest requires that any land remain permanently under forest.

XIII. Persons and Entities

The law of Vanuatu recognizes adult human beings as persons having full legal capacity. But capacity to vote at elections is restricted by the Representation of People Act (Chapter 146) to persons age eighteen or over. Criminal responsibility is restricted by the Penal Code Act (Chapter 135) to persons aged ten years or over, but persons between ten and fourteen are criminally responsible only if it is proved that they are able to distinguish between right and wrong.

No Vanuatu legislation prescribes legal capacity to enter into contracts or the effect on a contract of the fact that one of the parties is a child. So far as British citizens or optants are concerned, it would seem that the Family Law Reform Act 1969 (UK) would apply, while French citizens and optants would be regulated by the provisions of the French Code Civil.

The Companies Act (Chapter 191) provides that a registered company has the capacity of a natural person of full capacity. The act states that actions not authorized by the memorandum and articles of association of a company may be prohibited by order of a court, but they are not otherwise void.

XIV. Family Law

A. Marriage

The Civil Status (Registration) Act (Chapter 61) requires that all births, deaths, marriages, and dissolutions or nullifications of marriage be recorded by district registrars.

The Marriage Act (Chapter 60) provides that marriages may be celebrated before a district registrar or a minister approved for celebrating marriages. Marriages may also be made in accordance with custom, provided the requirements of the regulation are fulfilled as to age (males over eighteen, females over sixteen); as to parental consent for any party under twenty-one, and as to prior notice, procedure, witnesses, and formalities after ceremony.

B. Divorce, Annulment, and Separation

The Matrimonial Causes Act (Chapter 192) provides that a marriage is void on one of the following grounds:

1. the marriage was induced by duress or mistake;
2. at the time of the marriage one of the parties was, by reason of unsoundness of mind, unable to understand the nature of the ceremony;
3. the parties were within prohibited degrees of consanguinity; or
4. the ceremony was not celebrated in proper form.

A marriage shall be voidable on the following grounds:

1. lack of consummation by the respondent;
2. unsoundness of mind or recurrent fits of insanity or epilepsy of either party;
3. venereal disease of the respondent;
4. pregnancy of the respondent by some man other than the spouse.

In the case of the last three grounds, the petitioner must have been unaware of the relevant facts at the time of the marriage, must have commenced proceedings within twelve months of becoming aware of them, and must have had no sexual relations with the respondent since becoming aware of them. Any child of the marriage is to be regarded as legitimate.

The act provides that parties to a marriage celebrated by custom may be separated or the marriage dissolved in accordance with the rules of custom. A marriage celebrated by a district registrar or a minister may be dissolved on grounds of adultery by the respondent, desertion by the respondent for three years or more without just cause, persistent cruelty by the respondent, incurable unsoundness of mind of the respondent for at least five years, and absence of the respondent for at least seven years without any communication. A petition for dissolution of marriage may not be presented within the first two years of the marriage, unless exceptional hardship has been suffered by the petitioner or exceptional depravity practiced by the respondent.

The court may not proceed with a petition for dissolution unless it is satisfied that reconciliation is impossible and must dismiss the petition if it is satisfied that the petitioner has aided, connived at, or condoned the adultery complained of; or has condoned the cruelty complained of; or has acted in collusion with the respondent; or that proper arrangements have not been made for the care and upbringing of any child of the marriage under age sixteen. The decree of the court dissolving the marriage takes effect absolutely three months after it is made.

C. Maintenance

The Matrimonial Causes Act (Chapter 192) provides that a court, when making a decree of divorce or annulment, may make an order for the husband to pay a reasonable sum for the maintenance and support of the wife and children.

The Maintenance of Family Act (Chapter 42) provides that a married man who fails, for over one month, to make adequate provision for the maintenance of his wife or legitimate children under eighteen years of age may be fined and ordered to make adequate provision for them as the court thinks fit, unless he is financially incapable of doing so by reason of illness or injury, imprisonment, or any other circumstances beyond his control.

The Maintenance of Children Act (Chapter 46) provides that a ni-Vanuatu woman who gives birth to a child when she is unmarried or married without witnesses or without the presence of a resident agent may apply to the court that the father be ordered to pay for the maintenance and upbringing of the child. The application must be made by the parent or guardian of that woman if she is under twenty-one years, and within twelve months of the child's birth, or within that period the man must have contributed to the child's maintenance and upbringing. During the normal period of conception there must have been an offer of marriage, the parties must have lived together as man and wife, the man contributed to the maintenance of the child in a parental capacity, or the man admitted paternity of the child. The act also provides that an order may not be made if, during the normal period of conception the mother was of notorious loose behavior or had sexual intercourse with another man, or the man was physically incapable of being the father of the child.

British subjects and optants are presumably subject to the statutes relating to maintenance in force in England on January 1, 1976, and French subjects and optants to the relevant laws of France.

D. Custody

The Matrimonial Causes Act (Chapter 192) provides that a court when making a decree of divorce or annulment may make an order for the custody of the children of the marriage.

E. Adoption

There is no joint regulation or act of Parliament providing for adoption. Adoption by British citizens and optants would therefore be regulated by statutes of general application in force in

England on January 1, 1976, while adoption by French citizens and optants would be regulated by the provisions of the French Code Civil.

XV. Personal Property

Vanuatu has no legislation providing generally for the acquisition of rights in personal property or for the changing or transfer of such rights. Presumably, for British subjects and optants, personal property is regulated by the principles of common law and equity and British statutes of general application in force in England on January 1, 1976, and, for French subjects and optants, it is regulated by the French Code Civil.

XVI. Wills and Succession

There is no act generally regulating the devolution of property upon the death of the owner.

The Constitution provides at Articles 71 to 72 that land may be owned only by ni-Vanuatu as determined in accordance with principles of custom. It is believed that succession to movable property owned by ni-Vanuatu is also determined in accordance with principles of custom.

Succession to property owned by British citizens and optants is regulated by the Succession, Probate and Administration Regulation 1972. Succession to property owned by French citizens and optants is regulated by the French Code Civil.

XVII. Contracts

No Joint Regulation or postindependence act of Parliament regulates contracts. Accordingly, the making and effect of contracts by British citizens and optants is regulated by the English common law and equity and statutes of general application in force in England on January 1, 1976, and the making and effect of contracts by French citizens and optants is regulated by the French Code Civil.

XVIII. Commercial Law

A. Sale of Goods

Vanuatu has no legislation relating to the sale of goods, consumer protection, or trade regulation.

B. Business Associations

The Companies Act (Chapter 85), which replaces previous British and French laws, provides that seven or more persons, or two or more persons in the case of a private company, may apply to the minister for a permit to form an incorporated company, which may be limited by shares or by guarantee or may be of unlimited liability. The application for incorporation must be accompanied by a memorandum of association setting out the full names of the persons applying to form a company and any restrictions on the powers of the company when it is formed, and by Articles of Association setting out the rules for internal administration of the company. The minister may grant or refuse a permit at the minister's discretion and without giving reasons. If a permit to form a company is granted, the person subscribing the memorandum of association may, within six months, file the memorandum with the Registrar of Companies, who issues a certificate of incorporation entitling the company to have perpetual succession and to exercise all the functions of an incorporated company.

An incorporated company has the capacity of a natural person of full capacity, but it may not carry out any business or act prohibited by the memorandum or articles or exercise any of its powers in a way inconsistent with them. A company may be ordered by the court not to do any such business or act, but such business or act shall not otherwise be invalid.

Contracts that have been made by a person on behalf of a company before it is incorporated bind that person but may be adopted by the company within a reasonable time after incorporation, whereupon they become binding on the company and cease to be binding on that person, unless the court orders otherwise.

A prospectus cannot be issued without the permission of the minister and must contain matters set out in the Fourth Schedule to the act unless it is proposed to offer shares or debentures generally, application is made to an approved stock exchange to deal in those shares or debentures on that stock exchange, and a certificate is issued on behalf of the stock exchange that compliance with the requirements of the Fourth Schedule would be unduly burdensome. A copy of each prospectus must be lodged with the registrar, and civil and criminal liability is imposed in respect of any untrue statement in the prospectus.

Companies may be dissolved by the court in a variety of circumstances and also may be dissolved voluntarily.

Companies incorporated outside Vanuatu may establish a place of business within Vanuatu, provided a permit from the minister has been first obtained. Any such company must file with the registrar a certified copy of its memorandum and articles of association, and a copy of its annual balance sheet and profit and loss account.

Companies registered in Vanuatu and carrying on business outside Vanuatu, or in some limited cases inside Vanuatu, may apply to the minister for a permit to be registered as an exempted company. The provisions of the act generally apply to an exempt company, except that no information need be disclosed about the affairs of the company, unless authorized by the act or by a decision of the court. Private companies other than banks, trust companies, or insurance companies may issue bearer shares and shares without par value; they do not have to file all the annual returns required.

Companies previously incorporated under French law must reregister under the act by filing with the registrar a certified copy of the constitution; a list of members and directors; and a statement of amount of capital, different categories of shareholders, and indebtedness of the company. Upon reregistration under the act, the parts of its constitution corresponding to memorandum or to articles of association shall be deemed to be memorandum and articles of association. No further companies can be formed under French law after the commencement of the act.

There is no postindependence legislation dealing with partnership, so British and French laws continue to apply, which means presumably that for British citizens and optants the provisions of the British Partnership Act 1890 apply insofar as appropriate to the circumstances of Vanuatu. For French citizens and optants, the provisions of the French Code Civil relating to such matters apply.

C. Cooperative Societies

Cooperative societies have been operating in Vanuatu for some time, regulated initially by the Cooperatives Joint Regulation 1962 and more recently by the Cooperatives Societies Act (Chapter 152), which provides that any society carrying on any business, industry, or trade in accordance with cooperative principles and comprising at least seven persons or a lesser number, together with an existing registered society, may apply to the Registrar of Co-operatives for registration as a cooperative society. If the registrar is satisfied that the proposed society and its proposed bylaws are not inconsistent with the act or any other law, the society is registered as a cooperative society.

Upon registration, a cooperative society becomes a body corporate. It may amend its bylaws, but the amendments are not to take effect until registered by the registrar, who may refuse registration if the amendment is contrary to the act or any other law.

The act provides that a registered society cannot generally make loans to a person who is not a member or lend money on the security of any movable property other than produce or goods in which it is authorized to deal. However, a registered society may invest or deposit its funds in any bank approved by the registrar, in government securities, or in any other registered society approved by the registrar.

Not less than one quarter of the net profits of a registered society must be placed annually in a statutory reserve fund, and the remainder of the profits must be divided among the members as provided by the bylaws—except that, with the approval of the registrar, an amount not exceeding 10 percent may be contributed to any charitable purpose or to a common-good fund.

Registered societies are required to make annual returns to the registrar, together with a copy of the balance sheet and profit and loss account for each year. The registrar must ensure that the accounts of every registered society are audited at least once a year.

D. Agency

No postindependence legislation deals with agency, so the British and French laws continue to apply; for British citizens and optants, then, the principles of common law and equity and statutes of general application in force in England on January 1, 1976, apply in Vanuatu, insofar as appropriate to the circumstances of Vanuatu. French subjects and optants are regulated by the Code Civil.

E. Bills of Exchange and Checks

There are no preindependence joint regulations or postindependence acts of Parliament relating to bills of exchange and checks. As a result, the Bills of Exchange Act 1882 (UK) would seem to apply to British citizens and optants, while the Code Civil applies to French citizens and optants.

F. Insolvency

No preindependence joint regulation nor any postindependence act of Parliament deals with insolvency, so British citizens and optants are presumably regulated by the Bankruptcy Act 1914 (UK), while French citizens and optants are regulated by the Code Civil of France.

G. Business License Fees

The Business Licence Act (Chapter 173), as amended, provides that all occupations carried on for profit, with certain exceptions, must be licensed, for which prescribed fees must be paid.

XIX. Torts

No joint regulation or postindependence legislation regulates tort liability in Vanuatu. Accordingly, liability in torts for British citizens and optants is regulated by the English common law and equity and statutes of general application in force in England on January 1, 1976, and liability in torts for French and optants is regulated by the French Code Civil.

XX. Labor Law

Five statutes make up the labor legislation in force in Vanuatu: the Employment Act (Chapter 160), Trade Unions Act (Chapter 161), Trade Disputes Act (Chapter 162), Minimum Wage and Minimum Wages Board Act (Chapter 182), and Health and Safety at Work Act 1986. A sixth, the Workers' Compensation Act 1987, was not in force as of early 1992.

The Employment Act 1983 provides for the appointment of a Labour Advisory Board consisting of an equal number of employers' and employees' representatives and public servants to advise the minister on labor matters, and a Commissioner of Labour and a labor officer to give effect to the act. The act prohibits forced labor and sex discrimination, certain kinds of work for women and young children, and unsanitary and unsafe conditions of work. The act also prescribes the maximum hours of work (that is, eight hours per day, six days per week with a break of one hour for a meal and two tea breaks of ten minutes), annual leave of at least one day for each month of employment, and overtime to be paid for hours of work exceeding those prescribed. Maternity leave of six weeks before and six weeks after confinement is also prescribed by the act.

The Trade Unions Act provides for the registration of a trade union if its objects are not unlawful and if its rules are consistent with certain principles described in the act. A decision of the registrar refusing registration may be appealed to the Supreme Court. Upon registration, a trade union becomes a body corporate and is given by the act immunity from liability for certain acts that would otherwise constitute torts or breaches of contract.

The act prescribes the purposes for which the funds of a registered trade union are to be used and expressly prohibits the use of funds for political purposes. Other provisions prohibit employers and other persons from putting pressure upon employees to be or not to be members of a union. The act is to apply to members of the public service, but not members of the armed forces, police force, or prison service.

The Trade Disputes Act provides that where a trade dispute exists and the agreed procedures have failed to resolve the dispute, the Commissioner of Labor, if there appears to be a reasonable chance of resolving the dispute by conciliation, may appoint a conciliator. The conciliator may require the parties to set out the issues between them and the efforts they have made to resolve the dispute. If the conciliator brings about a settlement of the dispute, a memorandum setting out the terms of the settlement is prepared to be signed by the parties and to have effect as an award made by a board of arbitration.

If the conciliator fails to achieve an agreed settlement the Commissioner of Labour may, subject to the written approval of the parties, recommend to the minister that the dispute be referred to a board of arbitration, consisting of a sole arbitrator or a chairperson and equal representatives of employers and workers. The board of arbitration shall have power to make awards, and in doing so shall have regard not only for the rights and interests of the parties to the dispute, but also for the social and economic development of Vanuatu. A settlement made by a conciliator or an award made by a board of arbitration is binding on the parties for a period of not less than one year as is specified in the settlement or award.

When, in the opinion of the minister, a trade dispute produces serious disruption or threatens serious disruption to essential services as described in the act or as declared by the minister, the minister may take such action and issue such directives as appear necessary to bring about a settlement of the dispute. Pending settlement, the President may on the advice of the Prime Minister issue a proclamation of emergency for a period of one month, during which the minister may make orders prohibiting the strike and directing action to maintain the essential service.

A trade dispute is defined by the act as a dispute between employer(s) and worker(s) or between workers which is connected with terms and conditions of employment; engagement, suspension, or dismissal of worker(s); allocation of work; matters of discipline; membership or nonmembership in a trade union; facilities for officials of a trade union; and machinery for negotiation and settlement of disputes.

Where a dispute between an employer and a worker does not involve a trade dispute, either party may require a labor officer to assist to bring about a settlement by conciliation; if the officer thinks there is a reasonable chance of success, he or she shall endeavor to settle the dispute.

The Minimum Wage and Minimum Wages Board Act provides for the declaration of a minimum wage and authorizes the minister to increase the amount, either generally or in particular areas, and for the Minimum Wage Board to make recommendations to the minister as to an appropriate minimum wage, whether generally or in particular parts of the country or in particular occupations.

The Health and Safety at Work Act imposes a duty on employers to ensure, so far as is reasonably practicable, the health, safety, and welfare of their employees and also of others who may be affected by the work. There is also a duty upon Employees have a duty to take reasonable care for the health and safety of themselves and of any others who might be affected. A duty is also imposed on the manufacturers or suppliers of things to be used at work to ensure, so far as is reasonably practicable, that they are safe when properly used.

The minister may make regulations for securing the health, safety, and welfare of workers and may also approve a code of practice for such purposes. An inspector may issue an improvement notice to require a person to remedy a breach of the act or regulations. If an inspector considers that there is a risk of serious personal injury from a breach of the act or regulations, he or she may issue a prohibition notice directing that specified activities not be carried out and may seize and render harmless any substance considered a cause of imminent danger of serious personal injury.

XXI. Industrial and Intellectual Property Rights

The Registration of United Kingdom Patents Act (Chapter 80) provides that United Kingdom patents and registered trademarks may, at the discretion of the registrar, be reregistered in Vanuatu by British citizens or optants. There is similar provision for the registration of British trademarks contained in the United Kingdom Trade Marks Act (Chapter 81). French citizens or optants can rely on the provisions for the registration of patents and trademarks in the French Code Civil.

XXII. LEGAL EDUCATION AND PROFESSION

The legal profession in Vanuatu is not large. At present five legal practitioners are in government service, and about the same number of firms are in private practice, each with only one or two partners. Most of the legal practitioners in government service are ni-Vanuatu, but only one practitioner in private practice is ni-Vanuatu.

The Legal Practitioners' Act (Chapter 119) established a Law Council, composed of the Chief Justice, the Attorney General, and one legal practitioner nominated by the Minister of Justice. The Law Council has general responsibility for the control and supervision of the legal profession and is required in particular to prescribe the qualifications for legal practitioners; keep a register of legal practitioners; be responsible for the discipline, legal education, and training of legal practitioners; and control the registration of notaries public. The Law Council is authorized to establish a disciplinary committee consisting of not fewer than five members, made up of a judicial officer, not fewer than two legal practitioners nominated by the attorney general, at least one other legal practitioner, and such other persons as the Law Council considers suitable.

Students at present wishing to obtain a law degree must travel to a law school in Australia, New Zealand, or Papua New Guinea or enroll for an external law degree. The University of the South Pacific Law Unit, located in Vila, is responsible for providing programs by extension for a certificate (five subjects) and diploma (ten subjects) in legal studies, not only for citizens of Vanuatu but also for citizens of other countries within the University's region. The University recently approved the establishment of a law degree program to begin in 1994.

XXIII. RESEARCH GUIDE

A revised edition of the *Laws of Vanuatu* was published in 1988. In the revised edition, all legislation (including laws enacted by Parliament and those pre-independence regulations that are still in force) are designated as acts. Each act is assigned a chapter number. A few Vanuatu cases are reprinted in *South Pacific Law Reports*, published by Oxford University Press, Melbourne, beginning in 1987.

Arutangai, S. "Vanuatu: Overcoming the Colonial Legacy," in R. Crocombe, ed. *Land Tenure in the Pacific*. 3d ed. Suva: University of the South Pacific, 1987.

Bakeo, T. "Land Disputes in Vanuatu," in C. G. Powles and M. Pulea, eds. *Pacific Courts and Legal Systems*. Suva: University of the South Pacific, 1988.

Bulu, H. "The Judiciary and the Court System in Vanuatu," in C. G. Powles and M. Pulea, eds. *Pacific Courts and Legal Systems*. Suva: University of the South Pacific, 1988.

———. "Law and Custom in Vanuatu," 2 *Queensland Institute of Technology Law J.* 129 (1986).

Corrin, J. C. "Sources of Law Under the Constitution of Vanuatu," 1 *Queensland Institute of Technology Law J.* 225 (1985).

Ghai, Y. "Vanuatu," in P. Larmour, ed. *Decentralisation in the Pacific*. Suva: University of the South Pacific, 1985.

Government of the Republic of Vanuatu. *Investing in Vanuatu: A Guide to Entrepreneurs*. Vila, 1983.

———. *Acts*. Vila, 1980–1990.

Hubbard, K. "Registration of a Vessel Under Vanuatu Law," 13 *J. of Maritime Law and Commerce* 235 (1982).

Larmour, P., ed. *Land Tenure in Vanuatu*. Suva: Institute of Pacific Studies, 1984.

Lynch, C. J. "The Constitution of Vanuatu," 62 *Parliamentarian* 46 (1981).

O'Connell, D. "Condominium of the New Hebrides," 43 *British Yearbook of International Law*. 71 (1968–1969).

Oliver, S. "Land in the Vanuatu Courts," in C. G. Powles and M. Pulea, eds. *Pacific Courts and Legal Systems*. Suva: University of the South Pacific, 1988.

Paterson, D. "Vanuatu Penal Code," 2 *Queensland Institute of Technology Law J.* 119 (1986).

Powles, C. G. "Prosecution and Defence in Vanuatu," in C. G. Powles and M. Pulea, eds. *Pacific Courts and Legal Systems*. Suva: University of the South Pacific, 1988.

Rodman, W. L. " 'A Law Unto Themselves': Legal Innovation in Ambae, Vanuatu," 12 *American Ethnologist* 603 (1985).

Theroux, E. A. "Transferred Corporate Domicile: A New Hebrides Refuge from War and Other Calamities," 25 *American J. of Comparative Law*. 405 (1977).

Weisbrot, D. "Custom, Pluralism and Realism in Vanuatu: Legal Development and the Role of Customary Law," 13 *Pacific Studies* 65 (1989).

15. Western Samoa

C. GUY POWLES

I. DATELINE

10th century B.C.	Samoan archipelago settled by people from the west who eventually become Polynesian Samoans.
1721–1768	First Europeans to visit Samoa are Roggeveen (Dutch, 1721) and Bougainville (French, 1768), who names the group "Navigator Islands."
1830	London Missionary Society teachers arrive.
1850–1900	British, American, and German interests compete in Samoa through commercial, consular, and military representatives.
1873–1887	Constitutions and laws are adopted in 1873, 1875, 1880, and 1887 but, due to internal and international turmoil, are short-lived.
1889	Under Treaty of Berlin, laws introduced to control foreign interests and assist Samoan internal government.
1900	Samoa partitioned; Germany assumes control of Western Samoa.
1914	German interests seized by New Zealand forces at outbreak of World War I; military administration established.
1919	Western Samoa declared a mandate under League of Nations, administered by New Zealand.
1926–1936	Extensive periods of civil disobedience and alternative government.
1946	Mandate replaced by United Nations trusteeship, again administered by New Zealand.
1947	Legislative Assembly established.
1954	Constitutional convention held to study proposals for political development.
1959	Working committee begins to prepare draft constitution. Cabinet government inaugurated; Fiame Mata'afa elected first Prime Minister.
1960	Second constitutional convention adopts Constitution under which Tupua Tamasese Mea'ole and Malietoa Tanumafili II, two of Western Samoa's highest chiefs, become joint Heads of State.
1961	Following a plebiscite in which people vote for independence, United Nations dissolves trusteeship and New Zealand enacts legislation terminating its powers over Western Samoa.
1962	On January 1, Western Samoa becomes independent. Treaty of Friendship between Western Samoa and New Zealand entered into.
1990	Following a plebiscite, universal suffrage is introduced prior to 1991 elections.

II. HISTORICAL, CULTURAL, AND ECONOMIC SURVEY

Western Samoa is an independent state. It comprises nine islands, totaling some 1,090 square miles, dominated by Savai'i (660 square miles) and 'Upolu (430 square miles).

Western Samoa's population of about 162,000 is homogeneous in terms of the language and culture that it shares with American Samoa, from which it was partitioned at the beginning of this century. It has been almost entirely Christian for over 100 years. The principal urban area of some 50,000 people is the capital of Apia on 'Upolu.

A. History

Samoa was settled over 3,000 years ago. Along with Tonga, Samoa was the base from which Polynesian civilization developed and spread. From these two archipelagoes about 1,700 years ago, canoes traveled east to the Marquesas and then to Hawaii, Tuvalu, the Cook Islands, and New Zealand. Long periods of isolation between groups of islands fostered distinctive language and cultural development, resulting today in several Polynesian nation-states. However, the Polynesian territories and cultures still have much in common.

Throughout the latter half of the nineteenth century, the high chiefs of Samoa were embroiled in an international rivalry that saw the consuls of Germany, Great Britain, and the United States endeavoring to manipulate local politics while at the same time being manipulated by Samoan chiefs. Samoa's first constitution, which was adopted by chiefs in 1873, owed much to American thinking. This document and subsequent constitutions were short-lived. Foreign interests wanted to impose a model of "king and government" unsuited to Samoan political organization at the time. Eventually, under the protection of the Treaty of Berlin, international competition was contained, although the treaty led to partition of the Samoan archipelago in 1900, when the United States took the eastern islands and Western Samoa became a German colony.

Commercial interests, land claims, and the growth of a European enclave in Apia, the capital city, had exposed Samoa to new concepts and had entrenched an imported system of law that would thereafter compete with traditional Samoan law.

A feature of the German colonial administration was the introduction in 1903 of a land and titles commission (later renamed a "court") to decide disputes relating to customary land and chiefly titles. After the outbreak of World War I in 1914, New Zealand occupied Western Samoa. Military administration gave way to civilian government in 1919 when New Zealand was granted a League of Nations C class mandate for Western Samoa. Samoans expressed their opposition to some New Zealand policies and methods of administration over the period 1926–1936, through civil disobedience and the formation of the Mau, an organization of alternative government. After the end of World War II, Western Samoa became a United Nations Trust Territory with New Zealand as administering authority.

The period from 1947 to 1961 saw a series of planned constitutional advances that introduced self-government and, finally, independence. The main features of the process were the creation of a Legislative Assembly in 1947; a Constitutional Convention in 1954, the recommendations of which were largely adopted by New Zealand; the formation of cabinet government in 1959; and a second convention in 1960, which adopted the draft Constitution, leading to the 1961 plebiscite of all adult Samoans that approved independence under the Constitution. The United Nations promptly terminated the trusteeship, and New Zealand passed legislation ending its authority. Western Samoa became independent on January 1, 1962. In the same year, under a Treaty of Friendship, New Zealand agreed to act as agent in foreign affairs when requested to do so by Western Samoa.

B. Culture

At the heart of Samoan society is the 'aiga (or extended family), which, as the basic descent group, constitutes the means by which all Samoans relate to their ancestors, their matai (or chief), their land, and their descendants. Political organization is founded on chiefly leadership, the matai system. The matai, holders of chiefly titles, are the heads of the 'aiga groups, which have rights in respect of both the chiefly title and the area of land associated with it **(for titles and land tenure, see XII)**.

The basic unit of traditional Samoan politics is the village to which the chiefly titles of the constituent family descent groups belong. The matai meet regularly in fono (council) where every title has its own rank. As a traditional institution of government, the village fono functioned as executive, legislative, and judiciary. It remains largely intact today **(see III, D Samoan Custom and Usage; IV, C (2) Local Government)**.

Above 'aiga and village, there exist large-scale district and lineage allegiances that divide the islands into factions without, however, forming the basis for a national political system. Struggles for national leadership were frustrated last century by foreign intervention, and German and New Zealand administrators discouraged the notion of a single paramount chief or monarch. In accordance with longstanding political rules, there were four tama'aiga titles (literally, sons of the major lineages), namely Malietoa, Tupua Tamasese, Mata'afa, and Tuimaleali'ifano. The desire for formal recognition of these paramount titles persisted. The position of fautua was created by the Germans for the highest ranking leaders of the day, and the two tama'aiga who held this office during preparations for independence under the New Zealand administration ultimately became the first joint Heads of State **(see IV, C (1) (a))**.

C. Economy

Agriculture forms the basis for Western Samoa's economy. It has been largely of subsistence type, with little money accruing to the average Samoan planter. Today, the three major cash crops are coconut (for oil, cream, and copra), cocoa, and taro; together with timber and tropical fruits these constitute the main exports. Tourism is a growing income earner. Other industries encouraged by government under the Enterprises Incentives Act 1984 include the production of foodstuffs and beverages, manufacture of garments and footwear, saw milling, and a brewery. Western Samoa's imports are concentrated on foodstuffs, textiles, fuel, and manufactured goods. Western Samoa is currently offering itself as an offshore financial center under offshore banking legislation **(see VIII, C Offshore Banking)**.

In common with many developing countries that lack mineral resources and nearby markets, Western Samoa finds it difficult to sustain a policy of rational economic growth against a background of limited agricultural exports and wide fluctuations in international market prices. The economy is assisted greatly by private remittances from Samoans living and working in New Zealand and elsewhere. Western Samoa also receives financial and technical assistance from New Zealand, Australia, and other countries and from United Nations programs and agencies.

III. SOURCES OF LAW

The sources of law discernible today are constitutional and statutory, English common law (as developed in common law jurisdictions), and Samoan customary law. The Constitution determines which matters are to be governed by customary law and which by common law. It also determines priorities among sources of law.

A. Constitution

Effective January 1, 1962, the Constitution is supreme law, rendering void any preexisting or subsequent law that is inconsistent with its terms.

The Constitution may normally be amended by an act approved by two-thirds of the total number of members of the Legislative Assembly after ninety days have elapsed between second and third readings. Article 102, prohibiting the alienation of customary land beyond limited lease or license, may not be amended without the additional step of a referendum of territorial electors (**see IV, C (1) (c) ii Electoral Law**) in which the amendment receives at least two-thirds of votes cast (Article 109).

B. Statute Law

The statute law component of pre-independence law that was brought forward included New Zealand statutes made applicable to Western Samoa. To clarify the position, the Reprint of Statutes Act 1972 repealed all New Zealand and United Kingdom statutes except those listed in the schedule to the act. After subsequent deletions, only four New Zealand statutes (Bankruptcy Act 1908, Companies Act 1955, Property Law Act 1952, and Samoa Act 1921) and certain regulations now remain in force in Western Samoa. However, the law that such New Zealand statutes and regulations represent in Western Samoa is the law they represented in New Zealand immediately prior to independence in 1962, without subsequent New Zealand amendments. All German law was repealed in 1920.

The Constitution, acts, ordinances, and subsidiary legislation were consolidated and reprinted as at January 1, 1978. They are published in English in six bound volumes under the title *Western Samoa Statutes Reprint 1920–1977*.

C. Common Law

Prior to independence, the law of England existing on January 14, 1840 (the date New Zealand became a British colony), and the rules of English common law and equity as developed in English and New Zealand courts—except where inconsistent with statute or inapplicable to the circumstances of Western Samoa—were followed in Western Samoa. The Constitution brought forward existing law, subject to its provisions, one of which was a new definition of law.

Included in the definition of law are "the English common law and equity for the time being insofar as they are not excluded by any other law in force in Western Samoa" (Constitution Article 111). Although the common law referred to is English, the courts since independence have continued to demonstrate their affinity with New Zealand, as well as attaching particular weight to decisions of the Australian and United Kingdom courts. In relation to fundamental rights provisions of the Constitution, the courts have examined decisions of United States courts.[1] In 1980, the Chief Justice expressed the view that the Constitution's reference to "the English common law" did not require Western Samoan courts to apply the law of England itself, but instead referred to a body of law originally exported from England and not necessarily being applied there at the time of reception, which is whenever Western Samoa chooses to apply it.[2] English common law may thus be developed elsewhere and borrowed later. Western Samoan courts also find other Pacific jurisdictions helpful in developing the common law.[3]

All courts, within the limits of their jurisdiction, administer common law and equity concurrently, and where there is conflict the rules of equity prevail (Judicature Ordinance 1961).

D. Samoan Custom and Usage

1. EXPRESS CONSTITUTIONAL RECOGNITION

The Constitution establishes custom and usage as a source of law in two ways. Matai titles and customary land are declared to be "held in accordance with Samoan custom and usage" (Constitution, Articles. 100, 101). Further, the definition of law includes "any custom or usage which has acquired the force of law in Western Samoa or any part thereof under the provisions of any Act or under a judgment of a Court of competent jurisdiction" (Constitution, Article 111).

The Constitution also recognizes "the law relating to" Samoan custom and usage, which appears to refer to procedural rather than substantive law. It envisages legislation providing for the registration of interests and resolution of disputes, such as the Land and Titles Act 1981, which gives effect to the constitutional requirement that there be a Land and Titles Court in relation to matai titles and customary land (Article 103). The court's jurisdiction is exclusive.

Custom that has acquired the force of law under a court judgment appears to take priority over any rule of the English common law that is inconsistent with it (Constitution, Article 111). Similarly, no statute may encroach upon the domain of such substantive customary law.

2. CUSTOM AND USAGE DEFINED

In the absence of a constitutional definition, the Land and Titles Act 1981 provides a working one—"the customs and usages of Western Samoa accepted as being in force at the relevant time"—and includes both the principles accepted "by the people of Western Samoa in general" and the customs and usages accepted as being in force "in respect of a particular place or matter."

3. TRADITIONAL AUTHORITY OF CHIEFS

While the Constitution makes no mention of chiefly authority as such, its reference at Articles 100 and 101 to the "holding" of matai titles and customary land in accordance with custom appears to encompass the necessary attributes of the traditional authority of chiefs in relation to such matters.

4. AUTHORITY OF VILLAGE COUNCILS

In 1990, the national government decided to provide statutory support for the traditional authority of the village councils (the fono), for the first time incorporating the fono into the formal structure of local government and the administration of justice. The Village Fono Act 1990 purports to "validate and empower" the village council in the exercise of its "power and authority in accordance with the custom and usage" of the village. The village perspective, held by many matai, is that their authority requires no validation by the national legislature.

E. Duality of Legal Systems

The structural separation of court jurisdictions according to subject matter and source of law does not prevent conflict between the common law and customary systems. In 1982, the Court of Appeal reversed a Supreme Court ruling that matai suffrage was void because discriminatory.[4]

Common law damages have been claimed for harm caused by the actions of matai in enforcing their council decisions, which may also be tested against the "fundamental rights" provisions of the Constitution, such as the freedoms of religion and movement.[5]

Conflict also occurs when customary law is pleaded in the Supreme Court and Magistrates' Courts. Despite the popularly recognized "law and order" functions of the village councils (**see IV, C (1) (d) ii Magistrates' Court and Village Councils; (2) Local Government**), the absence of a statutory basis for the councils has denied the courts any legal justification for accepting council decisions as conclusive or for enforcing village council orders. Under the Village Fono Act 1990, the courts are required to take village punishments into account in mitigation of sentence, but the determination of guilt by a council does not bar court action in respect of the same behavior. Similarly, the formal acceptance of a ritual public apology (ifoga) does not preclude a civil action for damages at common law.[6] Uncertainty in the area leaves the situation open to abuse.

IV. Constitutional System

A. Territory

Western Samoa consists of the islands of Upolu, Savai'i, Manono, and Apolima together with other adjacent islands lying between 13 and 15 degrees south latitude and between 171 and 173 degrees west longitude (Constitution, Article 1). The territorial sea extends 12 nautical miles from the statutory baseline, and the seabed, subsoil, and land up to high water mark are vested in the state (Territorial Sea Act 1971). The exclusive economic zone extends to 200 nautical miles from the baseline, and jurisdiction over the zone is governed by statute (Exclusive Economic Zone Act 1977, operative December 1, 1980; Fisheries Act 1988).

B. Citizenship

The principal rules confer citizenship by birth on every person born in Western Samoa and by descent on every person born outside Western Samoa if, at the time of birth, the father (or, if born out of wedlock, the mother), was a citizen by birth. Citizenship may be granted by registration to the wives and minor children of Western Samoan citizens. Registration may also be granted to approved citizens of Commonwealth countries who have resided in Western Samoa for over three years. Naturalization may be applied for by an alien of more than five years' residence (Citizenship Act 1972). Only a Western Samoan citizen who possesses some Samoan blood may hold a matai title or rights in customary land, other than by lease, license, or mortgage (Samoan Status Act 1963). No sale or long-term lease of freehold land is permitted without the consent of the Head of State to anybody who is not a resident citizen or to an overseas corporation (Alienation of Freehold Land Act 1972).

A citizen of Western Samoa does not lose that citizenship on taking citizenship in another country, so that dual citizenship is possible,[7] but there are procedures whereby the government may move to deprive a person of citizenship on public interest grounds (Citizenship Act 1972). The rights of Western Samoans in relation to New Zealand are determined by the law of that country (**see VI, A Treaties and Conventions**).

No person may enter or remain in Western Samoa without a valid permit unless a citizen or exempted from holding a permit (Immigration Act 1966).

Every person who has been in Western Samoa for three months or more must obtain a permit

C. Government

1. NATIONAL GOVERNMENT

a. Head of State and Council of Deputies

On independence in 1962, two holders of the highest tama'aiga titles (see II, B Culture) were made joint Heads of State under the Constitution. Tupua Tamasese Mea'ole died in 1963, and constitutional procedures for election of a single Head of State by the Legislative Assembly will come into operation when the present Head of State dies (Constitution, Articles 17, 18, First Schedule).

The question whether the office should be reserved for one of the highest traditional title holders has not been resolved. Although the Legislative Assembly may by resolution require such qualifications as it thinks fit, it has not done so. Nevertheless, certain features of Western Samoa's highest constitutional office are clear:

1. The office bears a newly created honorific title "O le Ao o le Malo," thereby establishing a status distinct from all preexisting titles.
2. The Head of State is not permitted to hold any other office for reward but may retain traditional authority over customary land.
3. The term of office is for five years, and the holder of the office is eligible for reelection.
4. The Head of State may be removed from office by motion of the Legislative Assembly supported by two-thirds of the total membership, on ground of misbehavior or infirmity.
5. Salary is determined by statute.
6. While the Head of State must generally act on advice and possesses only limited discretionary power, the Head of State is required to be kept informed of all Cabinet documents and business and may summon meetings of the Executive Council, where the head of state presides, and generally exercise considerable influence.

The Council of Deputies is associated with the office of Head of State. Membership in the council may also be regarded as an office with a status suitable for the holders of highest titles such as the tama'aiga. The council may consist of one, two, or three persons who are eligible to be Head of State and are elected by the Assembly for five years. To date, all members of the council have been tama'aiga.

The council acts as "deputy" Head of State during vacancy or absence of the Head of State from Western Samoa. Also, on the declaration of the Chief Justice that certain requirements are met, the council may perform the functions of Head of State if the incumbent is incapable on health grounds or unavailable to perform the functions of office (Constitution, Part III).

b. Executive

The executive power of Western Samoa is vested in the Head of State to be exercised in accordance with the Constitution, which means, with certain limited exceptions, in accordance with the advice of the Prime Minister, the Cabinet, or the appropriate Minister.

(i) Prime Minister

The Head of State is required to appoint as Prime Minister to preside over Cabinet the member of Parliament who "commands the confidence" of a majority of the other members. This means that the practice has been for the Legislative Assembly to convene after a general election and "elect" the leader of government. The Prime Minister chooses a Cabinet of twelve other members of Parliament and may revoke appointments and make replacements. The Prime Minister holds office for the term of the Legislative Assembly (five years unless earlier dissolved). The Prime Minister's appointment is terminated if the Assembly passes a motion of no confidence in the Cabinet. However, the Prime Minister may request that, instead of termination of the Prime Minister's appointment, the Assembly be dissolved and a general election be called. The Head of State is not obliged to dissolve the Legislative Assembly on the request of the Prime Minister unless the Head of State acting in his or her discretion, is satisfied that, in tendering the request, the Prime Minister commands the confidence of the majority of members. Constitutional rules also govern the absence or incapacity of the Prime Minister (Constitution, Articles 32, 33, 63).

(ii) Cabinet

The ministers in Cabinet have the general direction and control of the executive government and are collectively responsible to Parliament of which they are members. Subject to the Prime Minister's power of revocation of appointment, ministers hold office as long as the Prime Minister does. Ministers undertake departmental responsibilities assigned by the Prime Minister. The Prime Minister convenes the Cabinet, which determines its own procedure.

(iii) Cabinet Decisions and Executive Council

Cabinet decisions take effect in accordance with a formula that enables the Head of State to apply a brake to the process by requiring reconsideration. Except where the Cabinet has declared an issue to be of extreme urgency, a Cabinet decision will not take effect for four days unless earlier approved by the Head of State, acting in his or her discretion, or unless an earlier meeting of the Executive Council is held. The Head of State and the Prime Minister each has the power to call a meeting of the Executive Council, which comprises the Head of State and members of Cabinet sitting together. If the Head of State opposes a decision of Cabinet in the Executive Council, Cabinet is immediately reconvened. After reconsideration, the Cabinet may reaffirm its decision, which shall then take effect (Constitution, Articles 37–40).

Cabinet also possesses wide regulation-making powers under various statutes; such regulations are made in the name of the Head of State, acting on the advice of Cabinet.

(iv) Discretion of Head of State

In addition to the powers mentioned in relation to dissolution of the Legislative Assembly and reconsideration of Cabinet decisions, the Head of State's own discretion may be involved in the proclamation of a state of emergency or the granting of pardons and remissions of sentence (Constitution, Articles 105–108, 110).

c. Legislature

(i) Composition

The Parliament of Western Samoa comprises the Legislative Assembly and the Head of State (who is not a member of the Assembly). The Legislative Assembly currently consists of forty-nine members, who must be citizens of Western Samoa and qualified in accordance with electoral law **(see (ii) Electoral Law, below)**. The Constitution divides the country into forty-one territorial constituencies. Two members are elected from each of the six largest constituencies and one from each of the remainder.

In addition, the Constitution provides for the election of other members to represent the small segment of the population who regard themselves as being of European or part-European origin (called "individual voters"). The number of such members (currently two) is determined every five years by constitutional formula (Second Schedule).

Members of Parliament hold office from election until dissolution of the Assembly, which, unless earlier dissolved by the Head of State on the advice of the Prime Minister, occurs five years after the preceding general election. Parliament amended the Constitution in November 1991 to extend the term from three to five years. Members choose one of their number to be Prime Minister and form a Cabinet of ministers and also elect members to hold the offices of Speaker and Deputy Speaker of the Assembly (Constitution, Articles 32, 42, 44–46, 49, 50, 63).

(ii) Electoral Law

Electors and candidates for election to the Assembly are recorded on either the territorial constituency electoral roll or the individual voters' roll, pursuant to the Electoral Act 1963.

Until the 1991 general election, only the matai of Western Samoa, whose names (currently some 20,000) appear on the Register of Matai and electoral roll, were entitled to vote for and be elected to the Legislative Assembly from any of the forty-one territorial constitutencies. Only a person possessing some Samoan blood may hold a matai title (Samoan Status Act 1963). Persons of European or part-European descent may be registered on the individual voters' roll to elect the two non-Samoan members if those Europeans or part-Europeans neither hold a matai title or rights to customary land nor are married to a person who does. In 1982, in a significant constitutional decision, the Court of Appeal concluded that this split electoral system, which predated the Constitution, was not rendered void by the antidiscrimination provisions of Article 15 of the Constitution.[8]

In 1990, the government tested public opinion in a plebiscite of adult citizens (twenty-one years or older), a majority of whom voted in favor of universal suffrage to elect matai representatives. The Legislative Assembly then enacted the Electoral Amendment Acts 1990 and 1991. Candidates for election in the territorial constituencies must be adult citizens holding a matai title in the constituency they wish to represent. Eligibility to vote is open to all adult citizens who are linked to the constituency by residence, service, or family ties.

In addition to the above qualifications, electors and candidates are required to be a Western Samoan citizen of twenty-one years of age and must not be an undischarged bankrupt, of unsound mind, or serving sentence for a serious offense (Electoral Act 1963).

Election is by secret ballot under the control of the chief returning officer to whom the Head of State gives at least fifty days' notice of the polling day. The officer gives forty-five days' public notice of polling day and calls for nominations of candidates. In addition to the many offenses relating to electoral rolls, nominations, and political activities on polling day, the Electoral Act proscribes corrupt practices (such as impersonation, bribery, treating, and undue influence) and illegal practices (such as the conduct of a candidate who, during the forty-five-day notice period prior to the election, directly or indirectly presents food, beverage, money, or anything valuable to an elector at a ceremony or activity other than a funeral).

Petitions contesting the validity of elections are tried in the Supreme Court, where the decision of the Court, communicated to the Speaker of the Assembly, is final. Election petitions alleging corrupt practices (the finding of which renders the candidate's election void or may nullify individual votes) are not an uncommon feature of Western Samoan elections. It has often been difficult for the Court to distinguish between corrupt practices and the traditional presentation of food and money that is required of matai in the course of frequent activities unrelated to elections.[9] Such presentations by a matai candidate during the notice period, made regardless of proof of corrupt intent, were rendered illegal in 1984. The standard of proof required of corrupt and illegal practices in election cases is the criminal test of proof beyond reasonable doubt.[10] On occasion the Supreme Court has had to exercise its electoral jurisdiction to investigate the validity of a matai's claim to hold a title, an investigation normally the exclusive function of the Land and Titles Court[11] (**see XII, C Matai Titles**).

(iii) Law-Making Process

A bill becomes law after it has been passed at three readings in the Assembly and assented to by the Head of State acting on the advice of the Prime Minister. Known as an act of Parliament, the legislation comes into force either on the day it is assented to or on a date specified in the act. If the Prime Minister should advise the Head of State not to assent to a bill, the Prime Minister may face a motion of no confidence in the Assembly, which could precipitate loss of office or dissolution of the Assembly (Constitution, Articles 33, 43, 60).

(iv) Procedure and Privileges

So long as it meets at least once a year and its term does not exceed five years, the Legislative Assembly may be prorogued and dissolved, and its meeting times and places may be fixed, as determined by the Head of State acting on the Prime Minister's advice, unless the Prime Minister fails to command the confidence of the Assembly (**see IV, C (1) (b) i Prime Minister**).

The Legislative Assembly has passed standing orders regulating its procedure, which is generally of the Westminster type. The Constitution requires that proceedings be presided over by the Speaker or Deputy Speaker, no business be transacted without a quorum of one-half the total number of members, and except as otherwise provided (as for constitutional amendment), questions can be decided by a majority of votes of members present. Subject to standing orders, any member may initiate a bill, motion, or petition, except that "money" bills require the approval of the Cabinet. The clerk is appointed the administrative servant of the Assembly (Constitution, Articles 51–53, 55, 57–59, 63).

The Legislative Assembly Powers and Privileges Ordinance 1960 confers on members immunities from civil or criminal proceedings in relation to Assembly speeches, debates, and written reports; imprisonment for minor offenses; and service of civil process in the precincts of the Assembly. The ordinance also provides for powers of committees of the Assembly, the conduct of members, and offenses committed by strangers in the precincts.

d. Judiciary

(i) Constitutional Power and Judicial Service Commission

The Constitution establishes two courts of original jurisdiction—the Supreme Court as a superior court of record, with certain constitutional functions and further jurisdiction provided by statute, and the Land and Titles Court with such jurisdiction "in relation to matai titles and customary land" as is provided by statute. Parliament also provides for the jurisdiction of the Court of Appeal, established by the Constitution, and for subordinate courts.

The Judicial Service Commission, consisting of the Chief Justice, the Attorney General, and a nominee of the Minister of Justice, is responsible for the appointment of all judicial officers other than the Chief Justice (who is appointed by the Head of State on the advice of the Prime Minister) and for the dismissal of all such officers other than the Chief Justice and other judges of the Supreme Court (Constitution, Articles 65, 72–75, 79).

(ii) Magistrates' Courts and Village Councils

The bulk of formal court work is handled in the Magistrates' Courts, which are in two divisions. The higher jurisdiction of the magistrate (a barrister or solicitor of not less than five years' experience, or registrar of the Supreme Court of not less than fifteen years' experience) includes civil matters to a value of WS$1,000 (or higher, by agreement), criminal offenses where the maximum penalty does not exceed five years' imprisonment, and maintenance and affiliation proceedings. The magistrate is also the coroner, responsible for inquests and related functions consequent upon unnatural deaths. The Magistrates' Courts possess no jurisdiction in relation to customary land and matai titles.

A Magistrates' Court may also be presided over by a fa'amasino fesoasoani, assistant magistrate, who is not required to have legal training. A court so constituted has jurisdiction in civil matters up to WS$40 (unless extended by certificate to WS$200) and in criminal matters to impose a fine of up to WS$40 (extendable to WS$100 or six months' imprisonment) where the offense carries a maximum penalty of a WS$200 fine or one year's imprisonment or, in the case of theft, where the value of the property stolen does not exceed WS$40. (Magistrates' Courts Act 1969; Coroners Ordinance 1959).

In some 200 villages, the fono, councils of matai, deal regularly with offenses under locally prescribed village rules and generally with civil disputes and other conduct that may threaten village harmony. By the Village Fono Act 1990, village councils are incorporated into the formal legal structure. The power of each council to exercise customary authority is validated and deemed to include (but is not limited to) the imposition of fines and work orders in respect of "village misconduct," which, in addition to conduct traditionally regarded as punishable, includes breach of council rules governing hygiene and village land. The council of a village, which may delegate its powers to a committee, is defined as the assembly of the chiefs and orators of that village "meeting in accordance with the custom of the village." A person "adversely affected" by a fono decision may appeal by petition to the Land and Titles Court. The court may allow or dismiss the appeal or refer the decision back for reconsideration, but it may not vary the fono decision or substitute its own, nor may it entertain a further appeal after reconsideration **(see II, B Culture; III, D Samoan Custom and Usage and E Duality of Legal Systems; IV, C (2) Local Government)**.

(iii) Land and Titles Court

The Land and Titles Court is a court of record possessing exclusive jurisdiction in all matters relating to Samoan names and titles and in all claims and disputes relating to customary land. It applies Samoan custom and usage. The court consists of the president, who is the Chief Justice or a judge of the Supreme Court, and Samoan judges and assessors who are matai of character, ability, standing, and reputation appointed on the advice of the Judicial Service Commission. Samoan judges, who are usually also fa'amasino fesoasoani, are appointed for three-year terms, and assessors are selected for each sitting of the court from a panel of not less than ten. One or more of the Samoan judges are appointed deputy presidents. Original jurisdiction is exercised by the court comprising the president or a deputy president and a total of at least four Samoan judges and assessors. Appeals, with the leave of the president, are heard by the court comprising the president and two Samoan judges appointed by the president. There is no further appeal (Land and Titles Act 1981).

(iv) Supreme Court: Appointment and Functions

The Supreme Court is comprised of a Chief Justice, appointed by the Head of State on the advice of the Prime Minister, and other judges appointed by the Head of State on the advice of the Judicial Service Commission. The Court of Appeal has recently expressed its disapproval of a decision by the executive to appoint the Attorney General as acting Chief Justice.[12] A judge must have been in practice as a barrister in Western Samoa or an approved country (New Zealand, Australia, or the United Kingdom) for at least eight years. Citizens of Western Samoa hold office to age sixty-two, while expatriate judges are appointed for a term of years. Currently, both the Chief Justice and puisne (deputy) judge are expatriates. Judges may not be removed except by the Head of State on a resolution supported by two-thirds of the total of members of the Legislative Assembly on the ground of stated misbehavior or infirmity of body or mind. Judicial salaries are determined by statute, and the Assembly may not diminish such salaries unless as part of a general reduction of all salaries (Constitution, Articles 65, 68, 69).

The powers of the Supreme Court may be exercised by any one or more of the judges. The Judicature Ordinance 1961 confers on the court "all the jurisdiction, power and authority which may be necessary to administer the laws of Western Samoa." The Supreme Court has inherent jurisdiction, for example, to punish for contempt,[13] subject to right of appeal.[14] The Constitution also gives the Supreme Court responsibility in three areas—enforcement of the fundamental rights provisions of the Constitution, interpretation of the Constitution on the application of a party to any court proceedings, and interpretation of the Constitution in an opinion requested by the Head of State on the advice of the Prime Minister[15] (Constitution, Articles 4, 66, 73).

(v) Court of Appeal

The Constitution establishes, as a superior court of record, the Court of Appeal of Western Samoa. The three judges of the Court of Appeal may be the Chief Justice, other judges of the Supreme Court, and such other persons qualified to be Supreme Court judges who are appointed on the advice of the Judicial Service Commission. In practice, judges, lawyers, and academics from New Zealand have been appointed to deal with cases as required. A "pool" of South Pacific judicial personnel is now being established to assist Western Samoa and other countries.

The Court of Appeal hears appeals from the Supreme Court with leave and as of right as described in **XI Judicial Procedure**. It has no jurisdiction in relation to Land and Titles Court matters (Constitution, Articles 75, 76; Judicature Ordinance 1961).

2. LOCAL GOVERNMENT

a. Village Government

The formal structure of government of Western Samoa established by Constitution and statute makes no provision for the government of municipalities or districts and, until 1990, extended only limited recognition to villages. The Village Fono Act 1990 acknowledges the customary law basis of local government by the village fono as the traditional political unit that administers the village through its own rules, punishes local offenders, and resolves disputes on a regular basis **(see II, B Culture; IV, C (1) (d) ii Magistrates' Courts and Village Councils)**. The act confers additional powers to make rules in relation to hygiene and development of village land and to direct persons to do work pursuant to such rules. In the past, chiefs feared that statutory provision establishing village councils would diminish their authority.

b. Pulenu'u and Central Administration

Since its introduction by the German administration, the idea of appointing a village chief the representative of central government in each village has persisted. Today, a chief nominated by the village council is appointed pulenu'u for a three-year term by the Head of State on the advice of the Prime Minister. The pulenu'u meets with government officials, acts as liaison between apia and village, and carries out functions imposed by statute. Although paid a salary, the pulenu'u is not a member of the public service (Pulenu'u and Sui O Le Malo Act 1978). Central government has established a department to deal with internal affairs and rural development, requiring closer relationships with village councils and women's committees.

D. Emergency Powers

If the Head of State is satisfied, acting in his or her discretion after consultation with the Cabinet, that a grave emergency exists whereby the security or economic life of Western Samoa or any part is threatened, whether by war, external aggression, internal disturbance, or natural catastrophe, the Head of State may issue a proclamation of emergency for up to thirty days and further such proclamations. While a proclamation remains in force, the Head of State may make such emergency orders as appear necessary or expedient for securing public safety and maintaining public order, supplies and services, and related matters. Emergency orders may take effect notwithstanding the fundamental rights provisions of Part II of the Constitution. Safeguards lie in the requirements for laying proclamations and orders before the Legislative Assembly and in certain restrictions on detention (Constitution, Part X). Western Samoa has no armed forces or military-style units. The police service is under the command of the commissioner, a public servant responsible to the Minister of Police in Cabinet (Police Service Act 1977).

E. Human Rights

Part III of the Constitution contains a bill of "fundamental rights" expressed, in each case, with certain derogations. The bill includes the rights to life, personal liberty, property,[16] and fair trial, and concerning criminal law,[17] freedom from forced labor and inhuman treatment; and freedoms of religion, speech, assembly, association, movement, and residence. In relation to the right to a fair trial, the Supreme Court has confirmed the presumption of innocence and the accused's right not to be compelled to give evidence[18] (as to legal representation, see **XI, B Criminal Procedure**).

The bill of rights acknowledges traditional obligations in one respect. The right to freedom from forced labor does not apply to work or service required by Samoan custom. However, the courts have been reluctant to allow village matai to use force,[19] and actions by village councils that interfere with a village member's freedom of religion have incurred judicial censure.[20] A difficult issue is the traditional village sanction of banishment and its potential for denial of freedom of residence. The Land and Titles Court has attempted to discourage council banishment orders.[21]

The bill of rights concludes with Article 15 on freedom from discrimination, which nullifies any state law or action that discriminates adversely on grounds including descent, sex, language, religion, political opinion, social origin, place of birth, and family status. This article has been used to strike down the requirement that enforcement of a security over property given by a Samoan requires the consent of the Supreme Court.[22] The Chief Justice's reliance on the same article in 1982 in order to declare void the dual electoral system was overturned by the Court of Appeal.[23]

Article 4 of the Constitution provides direct access to the Supreme Court, which may make "all such orders as may be necessary and appropriate to secure to the applicant the enjoyment of the rights conferred" under Part II.

V. Administrative Organization and Law

A. Organization

The government of Western Samoa is led by the Prime Minister and up to twelve ministers who are members of Parliament **(IV, C (1) (b) Executive)**. The Prime Minister assigns to ministers responsibility for ministries, departments, and offices, which are in turn headed by senior public servants, or permanent heads, responsible to their ministers. Most of the major departments are established or guided by statute, such as the Health Ordinance 1959, Education Ordinance 1959, Public Works Ordinance 1959, Land Ordinance 1959, Agriculture, Forests and Fisheries Ordinance 1959, Judicature Ordinance 1961, Economic Development Act 1965, Prisons Act 1967, Post Office Act 1972, Police Service Act 1977, and Customs Act 1977.

Much government activity is carried on by statutory agencies under related legislation, such as the Western Samoa Trust Estates Corporation Act 1977, Handicrafts Industry Corporation Act 1965, National Provident Fund Board Act 1972, Special Projects Development Corporation Act 1972, Electric Power Corporation Act 1980, National Investment Corporation Act 1981, Western Samoa Visitors' Bureau Act 1984, Central Bank of Samoa Act 1984, National University of Samoa Act 1984, Copra Board Act 1988, and Cocoa Board Act 1988.

Government powers of regulation are extended through the operation of officials and bodies appointed under legislation such as price control and trade practices under the Commerce Act 1978, liquor manufacture and sale under the Liquor Act 1971, doctors under the Medical Practitioners Act 1975, lawyers under the Law Practitioners Act 1976, and companies under the Companies Act 1955 (NZ). (The regulation of commerce is also considered in **XVIII Commercial Law**.)

B. Public Service

The Public Service Commission established under Part VII of the Constitution and operating under the Public Service Act 1977 is responsible for the appointment, promotion, dismissal, and disciplinary control of public servants in "the service of Western Samoa." The commission of three members, appointed by the Head of State on the advice of the Prime Minister, takes into account general Cabinet policy and any policy decisions conveyed to it by the Prime Minister; otherwise the commission acts independently of government. Appeals from its decisions lie to the Public Service Board of Appeal chaired by the Chief Justice or a judicial officer nominated by the Chief Justice. Public servants obtain benefits under the Government Superannuation Act 1972.

In the case of permanent heads of departments (other than the Attorney General and the controller and chief auditor), powers of appointment and dismissal are vested in the Head of State on the advice of the Cabinet after the Cabinet has consulted the commission. Certain posts, such as Speaker, judges, Attorney General, police officers, pulenu'u, and clerk of the Assembly, are beyond the jurisdiction of the Public Service Commission. Employees of many statutory corporations are subject not to the Public Service Act but to the Labour and Employment Act 1972.[24]

C. Public Finance and Audit

The government is required to obtain parliamentary approval for taxation, expenditure, and borrowing. Appropriation and loan authorization bills are presented annually to the Assembly.

Appropriations for salaries of ministers, members of Parliament, the Head of State, and the judiciary are done under the Civil List Act 1964, Head of State Act 1965, and Judicature Ordinance 1961, respectively. Government finances are administered by the Treasury under a financial secretary responsible to the Minister of Finance. (Constitution, Part VIII; Public Money Act 1964; Financial Powers Act 1964). The Central Bank of Samoa is responsible for currency, reserves, interest rates, and exchange control (**see also VIII Investment Law**).

The controller and chief auditor, appointed by the Head of State on advice of the Prime Minister, has constitutional responsibilities for the audit of public funds and accounts and for annual reports to the Assembly (Constitution, Articles 97–99; Audit Office Ordinance 1961).

D. Rule Making

Statutes from time to time confer regulation-making powers on the Head of State (acting on the advice of ministers), Prime Minister, Cabinet, or individual ministers. Regulations come into force either on the specified date or when made. They must be laid before the Legislative Assembly within twenty-eight days after having been made or within twenty-eight days after the commencement of the next session of the Legislative Assembly. Regulations are printed and sold in Samoan and English in the same manner as acts. (Regulations Ordinance 1953).

E. Review of Administrative Action

1. JUDICIAL REVIEW

In the absence of statutory provision, review of administrative decisions lies with the Supreme Court exercising its inherent common law powers. The Court may order habeas corpus, mandamus, certiorari, or prohibition and may issue injunctions and declaratory judgments. Administrative decisions may be challenged for breach of the common law rules of natural justice and the duty to act fairly.[25]

2. OMBUDSMAN

The komesina o sulufaiga (the ombudsman) is appointed for three years by the Head of State on the recommendation of the Legislative Assembly. The ombudsman may not be a member of Parliament or a public servant or hold other office or occupation. On the complaint in writing of any person or on the ombudsman's own initiative, the ombudsman is to investigate any decision or recommendation (including a recommendation to a minister) or act done or omitted, relating to "matters of administration" in or by government departments, organizations, or their employees. The schedule to the Komesina o Sulufaiga (Ombudsman) Act 1988 lists the government departments and includes the statutory agencies, boards, and corporations. The ombudsman may also investigate matters referred by Assembly committees or the Prime Minister. The ombudsman may not proceed where the complainant has a right of appeal or objection to a court or tribunal or where the decision concerned is that of a trustee. Wide discretions are vested in the ombudsman.

Investigations are in private, with power to require evidence on oath and production of documents and to enter departmental premises. The Attorney General may deny information to the ombudsman on grounds of prejudice to the security or international relations of Western Samoa, to the investigation of offenses, or that such information might disclose the deliberations or proceedings of the Cabinet.

If in the ombudsman's opinion the decision or act under review appears to be contrary to law, unreasonable, unjust, oppressive, improperly discriminatory, based on mistake of law or fact, or wrong, the ombudsman may recommend the action to be taken. The recommendation goes to the department or agency and minister concerned. If appropriate action is not taken within a reasonable time, the ombudsman may report the matter to the Prime Minister; the final sanction is a report to the Legislative Assembly. The ombudsman also reports annually to the Assembly.

3. COMMISSIONS OF INQUIRY

The Commissions of Inquiry Act 1964 both empowers the Cabinet to establish commissions of inquiry and defines the powers and procedures available to commissions. The Head of State on the advice of the Cabinet may appoint one or more persons to inquire into and report to the Cabinet on questions arising out of government administration, the working of law or the necessity for new law, or a disaster or accident involving citizens. Under this act numerous matters have been investigated including parliamentary salaries, superannuation, the Cocoa Board, the Health Department (twice), and the Lands and Survey Department—and sometimes major restructuring of administration has been recommended.

A commission is empowered to hold its inquiry in public or private; to admit any evidence that appears relevant, whether strictly admissible or not; and to exercise the powers of a Supreme Court judge in citing parties, summoning witnesses, hearing evidence, and conducting the inquiry. Other legislation has conferred the powers of a commission of inquiry on other bodies, such as the Accident Compensation Board, Civil Aviation Board of Inquiry, Poisons Appeal Committee, and Law Society Council. In 1973, the Supreme Court discussed the powers of a commission of inquiry in relation to its terms of reference and decided that commissions must observe the rules of natural justice.[26]

4. PROCEEDINGS AGAINST THE STATE

Under the Government Proceedings Act 1974, civil proceedings may be taken by or against the government as if it were a private person of full capacity, subject to limitations in relation to judicial functions and to procedural requirements. Interrogatories and the discovery of documents should not be ordered against the government until it has had the opportunity to consider whether the public interest might be affected.[27]

VI. INTERNATIONAL OBLIGATIONS

A. Treaties and Conventions

Western Samoa is party to a number of treaties and conventions. Entering into such obligations is the prerogative of the executive, and no consideration by the legislature is required. However, treaties do not become domestic law unless implemented by statute. For example, the 1982 Protocol to the Treaty of Friendship between Western Samoa and New Zealand, which followed litigation in New Zealand courts and New Zealand legislation on the rights of citizenship of Western Samoans in relation to New Zealand, was not justiciable in Western Samoan courts.[28] Western Samoa joined the Commonwealth of Nations as a full member in 1970 and the United Nations in 1976; it is also a member of the South Pacific Forum.

The conduct of Western Samoa's foreign affairs is the responsibility of the minister, the secretary, and overseas representatives (Foreign Affairs Act 1972).

B. Diplomatic Privileges

Western Samoa has implemented portions of the Vienna Conventions on Diplomatic Relations and Consular Relations in order to confer the usual privileges and immunities on personnel from overseas representing foreign governments. Such privileges, including immunity from suit and process, inviolability of premises, and exemption from taxation, are extended to specified international organizations and representatives attending international conferences in Western Samoa (Diplomatic Privileges and Immunities Act 1978).

C. Reciprocal Enforcement and Extradition

The Reciprocal Enforcement of Judgments Act 1970 provides for the registration and enforcement in Western Samoa of superior court civil judgments given in foreign countries that afford reciprocal treatment to such judgments given in Western Samoa. The act also facilitates the enforcement of Western Samoan judgments. Judgments must be for a sum of money and must be final and conclusive. Challenges to registration may be made on the grounds of fraud, public policy, and lack of jurisdiction. Judgments made or registered in accordance with the act may be executed in the ordinary way. Western Samoa has reciprocal arrangements with New Zealand and Western Australia.

Similarly, the Maintenance and Affiliation Act 1967 provides for the registration of orders requiring the payment of maintenance, usually in favor of children. The scheme relates primarily to Commonwealth countries, but others may be included.

The Extradition Act 1974 makes provision for the extradition of offenders to designated Commonwealth countries (Pacific member countries have been designated) and to foreign countries with which Western Samoa has an extradition treaty. A person found in Western Samoa who is accused or convicted of an extradition offense in a Commonwealth or treaty country may be arrested and returned to that country. An extradition offense must be one that would also constitute an offense in Western Samoa. Restrictions on extradition include requirements that the offense not be of a political character and that the accused not be proceeded against or prejudiced on account of race, religion, nationality, or political opinions. Procedures for request, arrest, committal, and extradition, as well as safeguards for the person subject to extradition proceedings, are laid down by the act.

VII. REVENUE LAW

A. Income Tax

The principal method of taxation is an annual levy on personal and corporate incomes, administered through three statutes. The Income Tax Administration Act 1974 establishes the Inland Revenue Department and the machinery for collection of tax through the requirements of annual returns of income, deduction of employees' tax at source by employers, and payment of provisional tax by self-employed taxpayers. Following assessment by the department of the tax payable, objection to the assessment may be made to the Commissioner of Inland Revenue. Appeal lies to the Supreme Court.

The Income Tax Act 1974 imposes the tax on taxable income and provides in detail for exemptions and deductions allowed from gross income before tax is levied. The act deals with income derived overseas by Western Samoan residents and in Western Samoa by nonresidents, taxation of companies and trusts, and penalties for tax evasion.

Schedules to the Income Tax Rate Act 1974, amended from time to time, fix rates of tax and deductions. Legislation in 1988 fixed the company tax rate at 39 percent on all taxable income and fixed the maximum rate for individuals at 50 percent on income over WS$10,000. A capital gains tax of 30 percent was introduced in 1989.

B. Estate, Gift, and Stamp Duties

There is no tax on inherited property or gifts in Western Samoa. Legislation providing for estate and gift duties was repealed in 1986.

Stamp duty is recovered under the Stamp Duty Ordinance 1932 on instruments such as agreements, conveyances, deeds, bills of exchange, bills of lading, leases, and mortgages.

C. Goods and Services Tax

The Inland Revenue Department administers a 10 percent tax under the Goods and Services Tax Act 1986 on payments made by consumers for specified goods and services, being principally admission charges to films, theaters and entertainment; video hire; and the provision of accommodation, meals, refreshments, and alcoholic beverages. The tax has survived a constitutional challenge.[29]

D. Customs, Excise, and Export Taxes

Goods imported or exported are subject to the control of the Customs Department under the comptroller of customs pursuant to the Customs Act 1977. Tariffs are fixed from time to time by amendments to the Customs Tariff Act 1975, and excise duty is also imposed by the Excise Tax (Import Administration) Act 1984 at rates fixed under the Excise Tax Rate Act 1984. The Customs Department also collects a tax on the export of cocoa and copra under the Export Levies Act 1977.

The manufacture of goods in Western Samoa is taxed under the Excise Tax (Domestic Administration) Act 1984. To assist in the collection of tax, manufacturers are required to be licensed annually by the Inland Revenue Department and to pay the tax on the price paid or payable for the goods at the rates specified in the Excise Tax Rate Act 1984.

VIII. Investment Law

A. Banking

The principal adviser to government and instrument of government policy in relation to money supply, monetary stability, and the supervision of financial institutions is the Central Bank of Samoa. In addition to its wide powers of regulation under the Central Bank of Samoa Act 1984, this bank is, in effect, the government's bank. The Development Bank, a government agency under the Development Bank Act 1974, promotes economic expansion by making loans to local enterprises. Under the International Finance Agreements Act 1971, Western Samoa is a member of the International Monetary Fund and related international institutions.

Under its act and under Part VII of the Monetary Board of Western Samoa Act 1974, the Central Bank is responsible for licensing and regulating Western Samoan trading banks and financial institutions, which include the Bank of Western Samoa, a statutory corporation under its 1959 ordinance. All financial institutions are required to maintain the local assets ratios and to provide the banking information required by the Central Bank. In the course of trading, banks are required to keep records (Banking Ordinance 1960). Offshore banking is beyond the reach of most of the above legislation **(see C Offshore Banking, below).**

B. Credit Unions

Credit unions may be formed by a group of twelve or more residents who desire to become a body corporate with limited liability for the purpose of promoting thrift among members by receiving their savings and making loans to them "for provident and productive purposes." Credit unions are registered and supervised by a registrar under the Credit Union Ordinance 1960.

C. Offshore Banking, Insurance, and International Trusts

Western Samoa has established an international offshore financial center. Under recent legislation, Western Samoa offers exemption from income tax and other duties on the transactions and profits of—and the dividends or interest paid by or to—the international or foreign companies registered or licensed under the scheme. There are no currency or exchange controls, restrictions, or levies on the taking or sending of foreign currency out of Western Samoa by such companies or on their offshore transactions. Western Samoa, which has entered into no taxation treaties with other countries, derives revenue from fees paid under the scheme for registrations, licenses, and annual renewals. Confidentiality and nondisclosure of information are secured by secrecy provisions and heavy penalties for their breach.

The International Companies Act 1987 (revised in 1989) governs the incorporation of international companies and the registration of foreign companies that desire a Western Samoan domicile. Such companies are prohibited from investing domestically or using Western Samoan currency. They may be licensed to carry on offshore banking business under the Off-Shore Banking Act 1987 (revised in 1989) or insurance outside Western Samoa under the International Insurance Act 1988. Such operations are facilitated by the International Trusts Act 1987 (revised in 1989), which applies to registered international trusts the English common law and equity without statutory variation, and also by the Trustee Companies Act 1987 (revised in 1989), which provides for the one domestic entity necessary to service the "international" companies under the scheme.

D. Investment and Enterprise Incentives

The Department of Economic Development, its minister, director, and board, have broad responsibilities under the Economic Development Act 1965, as does the Development Bank under its 1974 act. In order to encourage new export industries, the Industrial Free Zone Act 1974 provides for the granting of leases of public land to licensed enterprises whose manufacturing and processing operations for export purposes are entitled to customs and income tax exemptions. In order to encourage participation by Western Samoan citizens and citizen-owned companies in economic enterprises, the National Investment Corporation under its act of 1981 is empowered to invest in local enterprises and for that purpose to borrow and lend money and to buy and issue shares for subscription.

Since 1965, both domestic and foreign enterprises, have been established or expanded through legislation now termed the Enterprises Incentives Act 1984. The Incentives Board recommends to the Cabinet the granting of approval for relief from income tax, excise tax, and customs duty for enterprises that will benefit the economy without unduly affecting any existing enterprise producing similar products in Western Samoa. The board is bound to act fairly in considering its recommendations.[30]

E. Foreign Exchange and Import/Export Control

The flow of money and goods into and out of Western Samoa is regulated by the Central Bank through the Central Bank of Samoa Act 1984 and the Exchange Control Regulations 1961. Money may not leave the country, for example to pay for imports, without bank approval, and goods may not be exported unless the bank is satisfied with regard to the repatriation of the proceeds of the sale. Currency and exchange rates are regulated by the Central Bank. A levy on foreign currency sold in Western Samoa is payable by banks under the Foreign Exchange Levy Act 1977.

IX. WELFARE LAW

Government provides no universal sickness, unemployment, or aged persons benefits. Support for the young, elderly, and incapacitated is provided by the traditional 'aiga (family) system. Schemes have been introduced in the areas of employee retirement and motor vehicle and industrial accident compensation.

A. Employee Superannuation

Employees are covered under either the Government Superannuation Act 1972, for public servants, or the National Provident Fund Act 1972, for all other employees under contracts of service. The principle of the two schemes is that both government and private employers are required to pay into the National Provident Fund an amount equal to 10 percent of the employee's wages (at higher rates for long service, in the case of the government scheme), one-half of which is recoverable by the employer out of the employee's wages. The fund pays benefits on death, at fifty-five years of age, on permanent incapacity, or on permanent departure from Western Samoa. The benefits include payment on death or monthly pension and limited lump-sum rights.[31]

B. Accident Compensation

The Accident Compensation Act 1978 and the Accident Compensation Board Act 1989 provide compensation for personal injury or death in road or industrial accidents. The scheme is funded by a levy on all employers of 1 percent of wages paid and by a customs levy of five sene (WS cents) per gallon on all imported gasoline. A person who suffers personal injury by accident is entitled to be paid compensation by the Accident Compensation Board, and if death results from the injury dependents are entitled to such compensation, where either

1. the injury was caused by or in connection with the use of a motor vehicle in Western Samoa; or
2. the injury to an employee of an employer liable to contribute to the scheme arose out of and in the course of employment.

Benefits under the scheme, which leave unaffected any civil claims for negligence or breach of statutory duty, include compensation payments for death (to dependents) to a maximum of WS$9,000; for economic loss due to incapacity weekly payments of 60 percent of gross earnings to a maximum of WS$90 per week for up to four years; lump-sum payment for permanent incapacity according to a schedule of injuries, to a maximum of WS$3,000; and medical expenses up to WS$400. Decisions by the board are subject to appeal to the Supreme Court.

X. Criminal Law

Offenses are created by a large number of statutes, but primarily by the Crimes Ordinance 1961, Police Offences Ordinance 1961, Road Traffic Ordinance 1960, and Narcotics Act 1967. There are no common law or customary offenses. Statutory jurisdiction extends to offenses by citizens or residents on board ships or aircraft anywhere and to any persons on Western Samoan ships or aircraft.

All common law rules of justification or excuse are available. Ignorance of the law is no excuse. No child under eight years may be convicted nor of eight years and under fourteen unless he or she knew the act was wrong. No person may be convicted who can prove insanity, compulsion, self-defense, or defense of land or buildings, provided that justification for self-defense is measured by the gravity of the threat. The defense of provocation to murder must be proved having regard to the standard of control of a reasonable Samoan.[32] Provision is made for accessories and attempts.

Offenses against the public order include treason (which carries the death penalty), sedition, unlawful assembly, and riot. Offenses affecting public and judicial administration include official corruption, perjury, conspiring to defeat justice, and escape from imprisonment. Offenses against morality and public welfare include blasphemous libel, drug-related offenses, rape (the penalty is life imprisonment), incest, and other sexual offenses. Of the offenses against person and reputation, the more serious are murder (which carries the death penalty), manslaughter (life imprisonment), procuring abortion, bigamy, grievous bodily harm, kidnapping, abduction, and defamatory libel. Theft, conversion, receiving stolen property, burglary, obtaining credit by fraud, forgery, arson, and willful damage constitute the offenses against property.

The Police Offences Ordinance 1961 sets out a wide range of lesser offenses relating to order, cleanliness, and convenience in public places and meetings. Two offenses originate in the traditional Samoan concern for the maintenance of public order. First is the offense of speaking or writing to any other person any insulting or derogatory words concerning the genealogy or parentage of any person with intent to insult, taunt, annoy, or offend. The truth of such words is no defense. Secondly, it is an offense to originate or repeat a false rumor (whether believed to be true or not) if such rumor is likely to agitate, distress, or divide the population of Western Samoa or any section of it.

The village councils establish and enforce their own codes of village conduct (**see III, E Duality of Legal Systems; IV, C (1) (d) ii Magistrates' Courts and Village Councils, and (2) Local Government**). Pursuant to the Village Fono Act 1990, they try and punish persons for "village misconduct." It remains an open question whether village convictions are offenses "defined by law" as required by the Constitution (Article 10).

XI. Judicial Procedure

A. Civil Procedure

The Constitution requires "a fair public hearing within a reasonable time by an independent and impartial tribunal established under the law" (Article 9). The Supreme Court (Civil Procedure) Rules 1980, made by the Head of State on the advice of the Prime Minister and the rules committee under the Judicature Ordinance 1961, provide for the Supreme Court; while the Magistrates' Courts Rules 1971, made in the same manner under the Magistrates' Courts Act 1969, provide for the Magistrates' Courts.

Civil proceedings are generally instituted by way of action or motion. While a different mode of initiating proceedings may not necessarily be a nullity, the existence of a sufficient number of deficiencies and irregularities in the documents may constitute failure to disclose a cause of action, causing the proceedings to be dismissed.[33]

Discretionary prerogative proceedings may be issued for review of government action (**V, E (1) Judicial Review**). Proceedings for a declaration may be brought under the Declaratory Judgments Act 1988.

The Limitation Act 1975 defines the periods during which actions must be brought but does not apply to customary land or matai titles. The limitation period is six years from accrual of cause of action in the case of actions founded on simple contract or tort and twelve years in the case of actions on a deed, to contest a will, or to recover land. Where action is brought in respect of bodily injury, the limitation period is two years but may be extended up to six years on grounds of justice and lack of prejudice. Disability, fraud, and mistake may also extend limitation periods.

There is no provision for jury or assessor trials in civil matters. Rules of evidence, verbal and documentary, are to be found in the court rules and also in the Evidence Ordinance 1961 and the Oaths, Affidavits and Declarations Act 1963. The standard of proof in civil matters is generally "on the balance of the probabilities." In the case of election petitions in the Supreme Court, the standard required is proof beyond reasonable doubt.[34]

Where damages are the appropriate remedy, the court may award exemplary damages in addition to other forms of relief.[35] When judgment is given, interest on damages awarded and unpaid is then recoverable, but not on damages prior to judgment.[36] Judgments may be enforced under court rules and also under the Judgment Summonses Act 1965, which limits imprisonment for debt.

B. Criminal Procedure

The Constitution requires a fair trial (**see IV, E Human Rights; XI, A Civil Procedure**) and stipulates that the accused is innocent until proved guilty according to law and cannot be compelled to be a witness; has certain minimum rights in relation to arrest and detention, the accusation or charge, and the preparation and conduct of the defense; the accused is entitled to legal assistance of his or her own choosing, but the obligation of the state to provide free legal assistance where the accused lacks sufficient means to pay and the interests of justice require it does not extend to choice of counsel.[37] The Justice Department has recently begun to provide the services of a Public Defender. The accused is also protected against retrospective offenses and from being tried twice for the same offense[38] (Constitution Articles 6, 9, 10).

The Criminal Procedure Act 1972 deals with the prosecution of offenses (for which the Attorney General has ultimate discretion under Article 41 of the Constitution), arrest, search, the laying of information, trial, pleas, witnesses, adjournments, and bail. The common law rules as to admissibility of statements apply.[39] In its criminal jurisdiction, the Supreme Court sits with four assessors on trials involving imprisonment for more than five years and five assessors for the offense carrying the death penalty. Assessors are persons who, in the opinion of the Judicial Service Commission, are qualified by reason of character, education, ability, and reputation. If the accused pleads guilty or if the accused in cases other than murder or manslaughter so chooses, the case proceeds before a judge alone. On a trial with assessors, a conviction requires the concurrence of three out of four or four out of five assessors, as well as the concurrence of the presiding judge.

Penalties, powers of discharge, and retrials are governed by the Criminal Procedure Act 1972. The Head of State has power to commute the death sentence under Article 110 of the Constitution, and has invariably done so in recent years.

The Village Fono Act 1990 empowers each village council to exercise its authority "in accordance with the custom and usage of that village." No records need be kept (although they usually are). The potential for conflict between traditional procedures and the constitutional "fair trial" requirements have not been tested since passage of the act. There is limited review by the Land and Titles Court of village fono actions (**see IV, C (1) (d) ii Magistrates' Courts and Village Councils**).

C. Appellate Procedure

Appeal lies from Magistrates' Court to the Supreme Court, and from the Supreme Court to the Court of Appeal. Appeals to the Court of Appeal in both civil and criminal matters are governed by the Judicature Ordinance 1961 and the Court of Appeal Rules 1961. Appeal lies in civil matters as of right where the matter in dispute is of over WS$400 in value, and with leave of the court where the matter is of public importance or where the interests or question involved are substantial. The Court of Appeal also exercises appellate functions under Articles 80 and 81 of the Constitution relating to issues of constitutional interpretation and fundamental rights. In criminal cases, appeal lies as of right on ground of law alone or against fixed sentence, and with leave of the court on a ground involving facts or against sentence other than one fixed by law. Appeal also lies in contempt cases.[40] The courts have frequently considered the burden of proof on appeal and the principles applicable to appellate review of findings of fact.[41] The Court of Appeal has declared that it is not bound to follow its previous decisions where changed circumstances require a new rule.[42]

D. Land and Titles Court

The procedure of the Land and Titles Court is governed by its act of 1981. Proceedings are commenced by way of petition and summons prepared by the registrar, the petitioner, or his or her solicitor. In addition to service on known parties, publication in the government newspaper of petition details and date of court sitting is required in order that all persons having an interest in the land or matai title in question will be bound by the court's decision.

Hearings follow procedures that are a combination of Samoan custom and court convention. Parties are required to submit written summaries of their arguments in advance, and court officials seek to mediate. Witnesses may not be cross-examined except by members of the court. Lawyers are not permitted to appear. The court applies custom and usage and law relating to the application of custom and usage, and, where such custom and usage does not apply, the court acts as it considers fair and just.

The decision of the court is that of the majority of its members, and reasons for the decision are issued. The decision is subject to appeal by way of rehearing by the court (reconstituted for appeals) with the leave of the president, on prescribed grounds, such as new evidence, misconduct of party or witness, error of law or custom, or a decision that was manifestly against the weight of evidence. On appeal, the court's decision is final.

XII. Land and Natural Resources

A. Land Tenure and Administration

1. THREE CLASSES: TWO SYSTEMS

All land is vested in the state and is classified as customary land, freehold land, or public land. There are two systems of land tenure, customary and freehold; the former is applicable to 80 percent of the land in Western Samoa and the latter to 4 percent. Public or government land, which has attributes of freehold, constitutes the balance. The Constitution not only confirms the three classes and two systems but highlights the importance of land classification by entrenching the protection of customary land against alienation (Constitution, Articles 101, 102, 109; and **see XII, B (2) Alienation: Leases and Licenses**). The distinction between freehold and customary is critical, and the history of land dealings is often confusing and misunderstood.[43] There is no town planning or land use law apart from health and safety requirements and rules for the taking of land for public purposes.

2. CHANGE OF STATUS

The Land and Titles Court may be petitioned, under its act of 1981, to have title to land that is freehold or in doubt declared to be customary. In view of the prohibition on alienation of customary land, it is difficult to sustain a claim that title to land that is in doubt should be freehold. The Commission under the Land Titles Investigation Act 1966 may investigate such claims and determine the status of land.

3. FREEHOLD LAND

Legal title to freehold interests in fee simple is protected by registration under the Samoa Land Registration Order 1920 (NZ). Instruments of title, such as a conveyance, transfer, lease, and mortgage, must be registered by the Registrar of Land on the land register in the Department of Lands and Survey, in priority of application and after payment of charges under the Fees for Land Registration Ordinance 1952. The general law of real property at common law applies to freehold land, as modified and extended, particularly in relation to leases and mortgages, under the Property Law Act 1952 (NZ). This act, with its amendments prior to independence in 1962, is still part of the law of Western Samoa. Title by adverse possession is possible in the case of freehold land.[44] Imprisonment for nonpayment of rent has been abolished (Samoa Act 1920, NZ).

The sale (or lease for more than twenty years) of freehold land to persons who are not resident citizens of Western Samoa is prohibited without the consent of the Head of State on the advice of the Prime Minister. Alienation is similarly prohibited to a corporation registered outside Western Samoa or to a local one in which more than 25 percent of shareholders are not resident citizens. A transaction attempted without such consent is unlawful and of no effect (Alienation of Freehold Land Act 1972).

4. PUBLIC LAND

Sometimes called "Crown" or "Government" land, public land may also be registered under the 1920 order and is administered by the Department of Lands and Survey under the Lands and Environment Act 1989. Substantial areas are leased to individuals and corporations under the supervision of the Director of Lands. Public land includes all land lying around the coast below the line of the high water mark (Constitution, Article 104).

B. Customary Land

Customary land is held from the state in accordance with Samoan custom and usage and with the law relating to custom and usage, such as the Land and Titles Act 1981 (Constitution, Article 101). There is no codification or official description of customary law, which is, instead, articulated in the decisions of the Land and Titles Court.

1. PRINCIPLES OF TENURE

   a. Eligibility and Pule

Only Western Samoan citizens who have some Samoan blood (almost all citizens satisfy this qualification) may hold an interest in customary land (Samoan Status Act 1963). In customary law terms, an interest in customary land is held by an individual through the 'aiga of which he or she is a member. Membership of the group, which might include several nuclear families, is determined by heredity, relationship by marriage, and personal service to the group and matai. Thus, land is vested beneficially in that group of family members who are for the time being living or working on it, or contributing to it, and who are serving the pule, or authority, of the chiefly title to which the land pertains. Land is regarded as appurtenant to the title of the matai of the family, who is responsible for administering the land on behalf of the family. The matai's pule in relation to land is extensive and exclusive **(see also XII, C, Matai Titles)**. In practice, land for housing and crops is subdivided and allocated to family members. With rapidly increasing matai numbers, family subdivisions are headed by lesser chiefs.

   b. Succession, Acquisition, and Alienation

Land, as the inheritance of the descent group, is held for its successors and cannot be permanently alienated. The sale, passing by will, or other divesting of interests in customary land is impossible (although exchanges have been recognized). Additional rights can be acquired by those who clear and cultivate land not previously developed, but such lands are subject to the pule of the matai of the cultivator.

   c. Village Land and Buildings

The customary land of Western Samoa is divided into traditional districts, within which run the boundaries between villages, usually from the mountain ridges down to the shore and out to the reef. There is no part of the country that does not belong to one village or another. Within the village territory are lands for house sites and crops that are held under the pule of specific village matai. Common land in the vicinity of the village is controlled by the village council. A third category is land not yet developed, which may be cleared and cultivated subject to village approval and then becomes appurtenant to the matai of the cultivator. Today, the concept of individual ownership, particularly in relation to cash crops, can be seen in the increasing tendency of such "acquired" rights to be recognized as capable of being retained by the cultivator's nuclear family and even passed to immediate successors.

Traditionally, house sites are lava rock constructions on which a wooden house is built. The right to build, occupy, and remove the house was distinct from the right to the land on which it stood. Prior to independence, the High Court was, on one occasion, prepared to exercise jurisdiction over a church building separate from the customary land under it.[45] More recently, the Supreme Court has held that, unless the building is designed to be removable, it is part of the land and subject to the exclusive jurisdiction of the Land and Titles Court.[46]

2. ALIENATION: LEASES AND LICENSES

As indicated in earlier sections, (**III, A Constitution; XII, A Land Tenure and Administration**), no person may make any alienation or disposition of customary land, whether by sale, mortgage, or otherwise; nor may customary land be taken for debt. Alienation is permitted by the Constitution only by legislation authorizing leases and licenses and the taking of land for public purposes (Constitution, Article 102).

The Alienation of Customary Land Act 1965 empowers the Minister of Lands, as trustee for beneficial owners of customary land and with their consent, to grant for an authorized purpose a lease or license of the land for up to two thirty-year terms in the case of hotel or industrial use and for up to two twenty-year terms in other cases. Rent is collected by the Lands Department and paid to the owners. The act requires that beneficial owners be consulted. The only purposes authorized are public, hotel, industrial, commercial, business (including agricultural), and religious. In order for a Samoan to be granted a lease or license of customary land for agricultural purposes he or she must be a matai.

C. Matai Titles

As a customary law concept, a chiefly title has an existence independent of its holder. The title is a dignity, a status at law from which rights and obligations flow. It is associated with a particular village, and certain land is appurtenant to the title (**see XII, B Customary Land**). Decisions of the court in relation to titles are, accordingly, judgments in rem (**see XI, D Land and Titles Court**). In English common law terms, the matai title is similar to a baronetcy—an incorporeal hereditament, inalienable, and descendible according to the terms imposed by the conferring authority.

The Land and Titles Court has held that the following customary law principles apply to titles:

1. The holder of the title has pule, or authority, over the group and the land appurtenant to the title.
2. Untitled members living or working on the land render service to the matai.
3. The matai has responsibilities to family and village.
4. The authority to appoint a person to a title is vested in the core of the extended family, except where the rules relating to the particular title require otherwise. Frequently the village council is consulted, and the new holder of a title is not recognized until the ceremony of appointment traditional to the village has been performed.
5. In determining succession to title (and appurtenant land), hereditary blood lines, age and experience, and service to the group can be considered, but no single factor alone is conclusive.
6. The land appurtenant to the title is vested beneficially in the family members who are living or working on it and serving the matai.
7. Collectively, the holders of village titles, meeting in council, exercise authority over village land and village affairs (**see IV, C (2) Local Government**). All village titles are ranked, one against the other, according to traditional status.

As in the case of customary land, the law applicable to matai titles is custom and usage (Constitution, Article 100) subject to the procedural provisions of the Land and Titles Act 1981. A register of matai maintained by the registrar under the act records all title holders whose appointment ceremonies have been certified by the village and accepted by the registrar and who are thus eligible to be elected to the Legislative Assembly. Only Western Samoan citizens who have some Samoan blood may hold a matai title (Samoan Status Act 1963). Currently, some 24,000 titles are registered. A person may hold more than one title, and many do, but must elect which title to use for election purposes. Some 20,000 matai are eligible for election. Existing titles may be split and allocated among heads of subbranches or distantly related branches of the family. The practice of splitting titles in order to secure more votes has been regarded as a problem for the Land and Titles Court rather than the Supreme Court on election petitions.[47] As matai numbers grow, the holding of a title has become usual for senior public servants and business people.

D. Government Taking of Land

Governmental powers in relation to the compulsory taking of land, whether freehold or customary, for public purposes and on the payment of compensation are regulated by the Taking of Land Act 1964. Public purposes include aerodromes, public health, education, recreation, telephone services, roads, harbors and any lawful purposes or function of government. These may be added to by order of the Head of State on the advice of the Cabinet. Procedures for taking, such as notice and determination of ownership, depend on whether the land is freehold or customary.

The Constitution requires that the law relating to the compulsory taking of land must provide for "the payment within a reasonable time of adequate compensation" and for access to the Supreme Court to determine interests in the land and the amount of compensation (Constitution, Article 14). The Taking of Land Act 1964 confers the right to "full and just compensation" from the Minister of Lands on every person having an interest in land taken for a public purpose, injuriously affected thereby, or suffering any damage from the exercise of powers under the act. If the minister's offer of compensation is not accepted, a claim may be filed in the Supreme Court. The Court's assessment of compensation may be appealed, as of right, to the Court of Appeal. In the case of customary land, special provisions require the minister to deal with and pay all compensation direct to the matai who has pule over the land.

E. National Parks and Reserves: Environmental Protection

Under the National Parks and Reserves Act 1974, public land may be set aside and declared by the Head of State on the advice of Cabinet to be a national park or a nature, recreation, or historic reserve. A national park is required to be preserved in its natural state in perpetuity for the benefit and enjoyment of the people of Western Samoa and may be revoked only by act of the Legislative Assembly. Nature reserves for the protection of plants and wildlife may include the territorial sea, subject to customary fishing rights. For environmental protection purposes, those parts of Western Samoa specified by order may be brought under the purview of the Lands and Environment Act 1989.

F. Agriculture, Forests, and Fisheries

The Agriculture, Forests and Fisheries Ordinance 1959, Forests Act 1967, the Fisheries Act 1988, and the Exclusive Economic Zone Act 1977 give government extensive powers over certain uses of land, sea, and natural resources and the behavior of persons who enter prescribed areas. For example, the Forests Act establishes state forest land, provides for the granting of forestry licenses, and creates machinery for the control of all forestry exploitation, replanting operations, and conduct on forest land.

G. Cultural Resources

Land of national, historic, legendary, or archaeological significance may be declared a historic reserve under the National Parks and Reserves Act 1974. The Samoan Antiquities Ordinance 1954 prohibits the removal from Western Samoa, without written permission of the Minister of Customs, of any Samoan antiquities, including Samoan relics, articles, and things of historic, anthropological, or scientific value or of interest relating to Samoa. Under the National Cultural Centre Trust Act 1978 and the Youth, Sports and Cultural Affairs Act 1976, government agencies have been established with responsibilities for the promotion of culture.

XIII. Persons and Entities

A. Persons

1. STATUS

The status of being of Samoan blood is required for the purpose of holding a matai title or an interest in customary land. The status of holding a matai title carries rights and privileges (**XII, B Customary Land and XII, C Matai Titles**). While the Constitution protects such status, it also prohibits discriminatory law and practice on grounds such as descent, sex, social origin, and family status (Article 15; **see IV, E Human Rights**).

2. MAJORITY AND OTHER CAPACITIES

A person must be twenty-one years or older to vote in general elections, enter into contracts without the supervision of the court, or purchase liquor. In order to make a will or inherit directly, a person must be eighteen years, while a driving license may be obtained at age seventeen. (**For capacity to marry, see XIV, A Births and Marriages**). The legal capacity of married women is the same as that of unmarried women. Mental incapacity is provided for under the Mental Health Ordinance 1961.

B. Entities

Companies incorporated under the Companies Order 1935 (NZ) or the Companies Act 1955 (NZ), as well as organizations formed under the Incorporated Societies Ordinance 1952, the Co-operative Societies Ordinance 1952, the Credit Union Ordinance 1960, and the Industrial and Provident Societies Act 1968 are legal entities, with capacity to sue and be sued.

Partnership is governed by the Partnership Act 1975 and the common law. The act enunciates such principles as the power of a partner to bind the firm and the liability of a partner for all its debts. Dissolution by the court is provided for.

The Secret Commissions Act 1975 establishes offenses in relation to giving or receiving gifts whereby an agent might be induced to act in relation to the principal's affairs without the latter's consent.

XIV. Family Law

A. Births and Marriages

Births, adoptions, marriages, and deaths are registered with the Registrar General in the Justice Department under the Births and Deaths Registration Ordinance 1961 and the Marriage Ordinance 1961.

A valid form of marriage within Western Samoa requires solemnization, after ten days' notice, in the presence of a marriage officer (a minister of religion or registrar appointed by the Head of State) and two witnesses. There is no provision for the recognition of customary marriages, although such marriages entered into prior to the establishment of formal government may be recognized.[48] Marriage of persons within the degrees of relationship prohibited by the Marriage Ordinance 1961 is void. The minimum age of marriage is eighteen years for a husband and sixteen for a wife, while consent of a parent, unless exempted by a magistrate, is required for a husband under twenty-one years and a wife under nineteen.

B. Divorce, Separation, and Nullity

The principal grounds for divorce are adultery; willful and continuous desertion without just cause for three years; habitual drunkenness and cruelty for three years; separation agreement or order in full force for three years; living apart and improbability of reconciliation for five years;[49] unsound mind for five years; convictions for murder, rape, or bodily harm; or sentence of seven years' imprisonment. Grounds for a separation order are cruelty, adultery, or desertion without just cause for two years.

A marriage is void where either party is already married or on grounds of lack of consent, prohibited degrees of consanguinity, or lack of solemnization in due form. A marriage can be declared void for nonconsummation and on other grounds.

The Divorce and Matrimonial Causes Ordinance 1961 provides that divorce may be sought in any marriage on the petition to the Supreme Court of a person domiciled in Western Samoa (at least two years' residence being required in most cases). The nullity jurisdiction may be exercised on the basis of either domicile or the celebration of the marriage in Western Samoa. Decrees of divorce and nullity may be enforced as judgments of the Supreme Court. There is no right of appeal. Overseas decrees may be recognized.

C. Maintenance and Affiliation

The Supreme Court may make orders for maintenance in conjunction with divorce or nullity proceedings. The principal jurisdiction for the maintenance of destitute persons by near relatives, of wives and husbands, and of children, is vested in the Magistrates' Court presided over by a magistrate under the Maintenance and Affiliation Act 1967.

In the case of an illegitimate child, a magistrate may make an affiliation order adjudging a person to be the father of the child and requiring payment to the mother of birth expenses and maintenance.

D. Custody

While the custody of children in relation to divorce or nullity proceedings is dealt with in the Supreme Court, custody and access orders generally may be made by a judge or a magistrate in proceedings brought under the Infants Ordinance 1961. In any proceedings where the custody or upbringing of a child is in question, the court regards the welfare of the child to be of paramount importance.[50] Courts may also commit neglected children to the care of child welfare officers.

E. Adoption

The Infants Ordinance 1961 also empowers a magistrate to make adoption orders in respect of infants (under twenty-one years) with the consent of the natural parents where the magistrate is satisfied that the welfare and interests of the infant will be promoted and the adopting parent or parents have sufficient credentials and ability. An adoption order has the effect of changing the infant's name, and the infant is deemed for most legal purposes to be the child born in lawful wedlock of the adopting parents.

XV. Personal Property

Generally, personal property is governed by the English common law, subject to the codification of certain principles in the Property Law Act 1952 (NZ). (A number of statutes regulate transactions in personal property; **see XVIII Commercial Law.**)

XVI. Wills and Succession

A. Wills

A person of eighteen years or older may dispose of any personal property and any real property other than customary land, by a will in writing signed by that person in the presence of two witnesses who are required to sign their names in the presence of that person and of each other. Wills are deemed revoked by subsequent marriage and may be varied by codicil. Common law principles of construction are applied to wills.[51]

B. Succession

Succession to property on the death of the proprietor is determined by customary law in the case of customary land (**see XII, B (1) Principles of Tenure**), by the terms of any will in the case of other property, and by Part III of the Administration Act 1975 in the absence of a valid will. On intestacy, the principal rules require the estate to pass to the surviving spouse if there are no children or parents of the deceased; if there are children, the surviving spouse receives the personal property, the first WS$5,000, and one-third of the residue, if any, while the children receive two-thirds; if there are parents but no children, the spouse receives two-thirds of the residue and the parents one-third.

Administration or probate of the estate of a deceased person is subject to the supervision of the Supreme Court. Powers and procedures of administrators and the Court are set out in the Administration Act 1975. Under the act, a spouse, child, or parent of the deceased may receive further provision from the estate if it seems to the Court that such person has been insufficiently provided for.

C. Trusts

The general rules governing powers and duties of trustees and the supervisory role of the Supreme Court are set out in the Trustee Act 1975. In a wide range of matters, the public trustee is empowered to act as trustee under wills and for persons of less than full capacity, under the Public Trust Office Act 1975. Property may be vested in trustees for charitable purposes (which include religious and educational purposes) under the Charitable Trusts Act 1965.

XVII. Contracts

The courts apply the English common law of contract, subject, in the case of contracts relating to personal property, to the statutes referred to in **XV Personal Property, above and XVIII Commercial Law, below**. Specific performance of a contract of employment has been held to be unavailable.[52] Damages may be awarded for breach of a bailment contract.[53] The Frustrated Contracts Act 1975 provides relief in the event that a contract has become impossible to perform. However, there is no statutory provision permitting harsh, oppressive, or unfair contracts to be reopened.

XVIII. Commercial Law

A. Incorporation

Companies are incorporated in Western Samoa under the Samoa Companies Order 1935 (NZ) and the Companies Act 1955 (NZ) as amended prior to 1962. The registrar of the Supreme Court is also the Registrar of Companies, with powers in relation to the approval of documentation, issue of certificates of incorporation, and supervision of the annual obligations of companies. The company is governed by its memorandum and articles of association, which impose duties on elected directors and confer rights on shareholders. (For international and trustee companies associated with the offshore financial center, see **VIII, C Offshore Banking**.)

The four other principal methods of incorporation are societies formed for purposes other than pecuniary gain, under the Incorporated Societies Ordinance 1952; cooperatives for the promotion of the economic interests of its members in accordance with cooperative principles, under the Co-operative Societies Ordinance 1952; credit unions with the object of promoting thrift under the Credit Union Ordinance 1960 (see **VIII, B Credit Unions**); and societies under the Industrial and Provident Societies Act 1968. In each case, there is a registrar responsible for supervision of the incorporated bodies.

B. Regulation of Commerce

1. SALE OF GOODS

The Sale of Goods Act 1975 regulates contracts in goods, particularly with regard to the formation of the contract, its subject matter, the price, conditions, and warranties implied in the contract, rules for the passing of property and transfer of title in the goods, duties of seller and buyer, and the rights and remedies of the parties. The Mercantile Law Act 1975 prescribes rules for goods handled through agents, bills of lading, and warehousing generally. The Chattels Transfer Act 1975 provides the means whereby bills of sale, mortgages, liens, and other instruments that deal in chattels may be registered. Covenants are implied in all instruments by way of security.

2. BUSINESS LICENCES ORDINANCE 1960

All persons and companies carrying on a business, calling, trade, or profession are required to hold business licenses issued each year by the Commissioner of Inland Revenue. In issuing or renewing licenses the government may have regard to such matters as the public interest and the economic welfare of other licensees.

3. PRICE CONTROL

The Commerce Board under the Commerce Act 1978 controls and stabilizes the prices of certain goods and services in the public interest under general or special price orders published and enforced by the Customs Department.

4. REGULATORY AGENCIES

Statutory agencies set export standards for certain goods. For example, under the Banana Board Act 1975, Copra Act 1988, Cocoa Act 1988, and Produce Marketing Act 1977, applicable agencies regulate the quality, quantity, price, and overseas marketing of produce.

C. Consumer Protection

The Commerce Act 1978, Measures Ordinance 1960, Consumer Information Act 1988 and Decimal Currency Act 1966 afford protection against hoarding and profiteering, unfair practices in conditional sales, as well as regulating weights and measures, the information that must be provided to consumers, prices, and currency. Apart from these, there is no statutory protection in relation to trade practices or consumer contracts other than the Sale of Goods, Mercantile Law, and Chattels Transfer Acts, as discussed above in **A (1) Sales of Goods**.

D. Insolvency

Persons who cannot pay debts may be declared bankrupt by the Supreme Court, on their own or a creditor's petition, under the Bankruptcy Act 1908 (NZ) and Samoa Bankruptcy Order 1922 (NZ). The official assignee exercises powers in relation to the bankrupt's property for the benefit of creditors, and the bankrupt is prohibited from carrying on business while subject to the Court's order. Incorporated bodies are dissolved and their assets distributed to creditors and members under the statutes governing their incorporation (**see XIII, B Entities**).

E. Bills of Exchange

Orders for payment of money, such as bills of exchange, checks, and promissory notes, are governed by rules detailed in the Bills of Exchange Act 1976.

F. Transport and Insurance

1. TRANSPORT

The registration of ships, collisions at sea, wrecks, salvage, and harbors are provided for in the Shipping Act 1972 and associated regulations. For aircraft registration and licensing, airport services, and accident inquiries, the Civil Aviation Act 1963, Airport Authority Act 1984, and New Zealand Civil Aviation Regulations apply.

As to the carriage of goods, the Sea Carriage of Goods Ordinance 1960, Mercantile Law Act 1975, and Carriage By Air Act 1964 (incorporating the Warsaw Convention and Hague Protocol) govern rights and liabilities.

The liability of carriers of passengers and goods within Western Samoa is limited by the Carriers Act 1975.

2. INSURANCE

The insurance business in Western Samoa is required to be licensed by the Minister of Finance under the Insurance Act 1976. The minister must be satisfied as to reputation, means, and adequacy of deposits. The Western Samoan Life Assurance Corporation is established under its act of 1976 as a statutory agency to carry out life insurance business. For marine risks, the Marine Insurance Act 1975 applies the marine insurance principles widely adopted internationally. Subject to the above statutory provisions, the common law of contract applies to insurance.

XIX. TORTS

The courts apply the English common law of tortious liability for intentional or negligent harm. For example, the principles in relation to libel, proof of "truth"[54] and fair comment,[55] and breach of statutory duty,[56] have been adopted. The defense of common employment does not apply, and persons liable for the same damage may be jointly and severally liable but are able to claim contribution from each other (Law Reform Act 1964). In cases where the person causing and the person suffering damage have both been at fault, the courts may apportion liability (Contributory Negligence Act 1964).

The traditional Samoan ifoga, or public apology, is customarily offered and accepted as a means of healing relations between families where a member of one has caused harm to a member of the other. Despite the fact that money and ceremonial goods may pass between the families in the ifoga, the courts have, to date, been unwilling to hold that an apology that is accepted represents full settlement of a claim for damages brought by the injured party.[57]

Causes of action for or against a person survive that person's death (Law Reform Act 1964) and fault causing death may give rise to a statutorily based cause of action for the benefit of the dependents of the deceased (Fatal Accidents Act 1974). Compensation provided under the Accident Compensation Act 1978 is taken into account in respect of but is not a bar to common law actions in negligence (**see IX, B Accident Compensation**).

XX. LABOR LAW

The Commissioner of Labour and Labour Department administer the Labour and Employment Act 1972, which provides for the protection of wages; the fixing of a minimum hourly wage by order; rules for the termination of contracts of service; holidays, leave, and overtime; and working conditions and safety. The Shops Ordinance 1961 provides protection for shop workers in relation to hours of employment and wage records. Under the Accident Compensation Act 1978, workers injured in the course of their employment receive weekly and lump-sum benefits (**see IX, B Accident Compensation**).

The power of dismissal in accordance with the express terms of a contract of employment is not subject to an implied obligation of a nongovernmental employer to act fairly or in conformity with the rules of natural justice.[58]

There is no statutory provision for the formation and registration of trade unions. Parties to an industrial dispute may request the Minister of Labour to appoint a conciliation committee representing the parties, and the commissioner has conciliation responsibilities. If conciliation fails, the minister may refer the dispute to a judge of the Supreme Court with two assessors, one appointed by each side. The Court hears and determines the dispute, and its decision is final.

The Labour and Employment Act does not apply to persons rendering service to matai under the 'aiga system nor to persons in the service of Western Samoa who are governed by public service law. However, the act does apply to statutory corporations unless service of the corporation is expressly deemed to be in the "service of Western Samoa."[59]

XXI. Industrial and Intellectual Property Law

Local and overseas inventions are protected by the issue of letters patent and the registration of overseas patents by the registrar of the Supreme Court under the Patents Act 1972. The creator of an industrial design is protected by registration and the regulation of licensing procedures under the Industrial Designs Act 1972. The Trade Marks Act 1972 requires the registrar to maintain a register of trademarks listing local and overseas trademarks for goods or classes of goods that have been registered in accordance with the act. There is no statutory provision for the protection of copyright.

XXII. Legal Education and Profession

Legal practitioners in Western Samoa may be barristers or solicitors or both. The Law Practitioners Act 1976, which governs the affairs of the legal profession, does not define the terms but states that a person who draws and prepares conveyances, deeds, or tenancy agreements is practicing as a solicitor. Legal practitioners are usually both barristers and solicitors and either work in the offices of the attorney general and Justice Department or practice in one of the eight or nine private law firms in Apia. Twenty-three practitioners are in private practice.

Legal practitioners must be admitted by order of the Supreme Court as barristers or solicitors or both and entered on the Court roll. For admission, a practitioner must be a citizen of Western Samoa of good character, holding the qualifications prescribed by the Law Society Council. At a minimum, these qualifications must be equivalent to an academic or professional qualification in law in a country that, in the council's opinion, has a legal system similar to that of Western Samoa. There is no law school in Western Samoa. Qualifications from New Zealand, Australia, the United Kingdom, and the United States are currently recognized.

The act requires solicitors to hold clients' money in audited trust accounts and confers on the elected Law Society Council disciplinary powers over professional misconduct, with appeal to the Supreme Court. The Supreme Court retains its inherent supervisory role in relation to the legal profession.

XXIII. Research Guide

The Constitution, acts, ordinances, and subsidiary legislation as in force on December 31, 1977, have been published in the six-volume *Western Samoa Statutes Reprint 1920–1977* by the government of Western Samoa. More recent statutes and regulations are available from the Justice Department. Selected cases are published in the *Western Samoa Law Reports* (WSLR), and a few significant cases, beginning in 1987, are reprinted in *South Pacific Law Reports* (SPLR), published by Oxford University Press, Melbourne.

Aikman, C. C. "Constitutional Development," in A. Ross, ed. *New Zealand's Record in the Pacific Islands*. Auckland: Longman Paul, 1969.

Aiono, Fana'afi. "Western Samoa: the Sacred Covenant," in C. Bolabola and others, *Land Rights of Pacific Women*. Suva: University of the South Pacific, 1986.

Ala'ilima, F.C. and V.J. "Consensus and Plurality in a Western Samoan Election," 25 *Human Organisation* 240 (1966).

Anesi, Taulapapa, and Auelua Enari. "The Land and Chiefly Titles Court of Western Samoa," in C. G. Powles and M. Pulea, eds. *Pacific Courts and Legal Systems*. Suva: University of the South Pacific, 1988.

Bayne, P. "The Constitution and the Franchise in Western Samoa," 1 *Queensland Institute of Technology Law J.* 201–223 (1985).

Boyd, M. *New Zealand and Decolonisation in the South Pacific*. Wellington: New Zealand Institute of International Affairs, 1987.

Davidson, J. W. *Samoa Mo Samoa*. Melbourne: Oxford University Press, 1967.

Epati, Aeau S. "Lawyers and the Customary Law Court," in C. G. Powles and M. Pulea, eds. *Pacific Courts and Legal Systems*. Suva: University of the South Pacific, 1988.

Ghai, Y. "Constitution-Making and Decolonisation," "Systems of Government," and "Political Consequences of Constitutions," in Y. Ghai, ed. *Law, Politics and Government in the Pacific Island States*. Suva: University of the South Pacific, 1988.

Gilson, R. P. *Samoa 1830–1900: Politics of a Multicultural Community*. Melbourne: Oxford University Press, 1970.

Lockwood, B. *Samoan Village Economy*. Melbourne: Oxford University Press, 1971.

Marsack, C. C. *Notes on the Practice of the Land and Titles Court*. Apia: Justice Department of Western Samoa, 1961.

Meleisea, M. *The Making of Modern Samoa: Traditional Authority and Colonial Administration*. Suva: University of the South Pacific, 1987.

Meleisea, M., and P. Schoeffel, eds. *Lagaga: a Short History of Western Samoa*. Suva: University of the South Pacific, 1987.

———. "Western Samoa: Like a Slippery Fish," in R. G. Crocombe and A. Ali, eds. *Politics in Polynesia*. Suva: University of the South Pacific, 1983.

O'Meara, T. "Samoa: Customary Individualism" in R. G. Crocombe, ed. *Land Tenure in the Pacific*. 3d ed. Suva: University of the South Pacific, 1987.

Pitt, D. *Tradition and Economic Progress in Samoa*. Oxford: Clarendon Press, 1970.

Powles, C. G. "The Common Law as a Source of Law in the South Pacific: The Experiences of Western Samoa and Tonga" 10 (1) *University of Hawaii Law Rev.* 105–135 (1988).

———. "Law, Courts and Legal Services," in C. G. Powles and M. Pulea, eds. *Pacific Courts and Legal Systems*. Suva: University of the South Pacific, 1988.

———. "Legal Systems and Political Cultures: Competition for Dominance in Western Samoa," in P. Sack and E. Minchin, eds. *Legal Pluralism.* Canberra: Australian National University, 1986.

———. *The Status of Customary Law in Western Samoa.* Wellington: Victoria University of Wellington, 1973.

———. "Traditional Institutions in Pacific Constitutional Systems: Better Late or Never?" in P. Sack, ed. *Pacific Constitutions.* Canberra: Australian National University, 1982.

Powles, C. G., and M. Pulea, eds. *Pacific Courts and Legal Systems.* Suva: University of the South Pacific, 1988.

Pulea, M. *The Family, Law and Population in the Pacific Islands.* Suva: University of the South Pacific, 1986.

Quentin-Baxter, A. "The Independence of Western Samoa: Some Conceptual Issues" 17 (4) *Victoria U. of Wellington Law Rev.* 345–372 (1987).

Sapolu, F. "Adjudicators in Western Samoa," in C. G. Powles and M. Pulea, eds. *Pacific Courts and Legal Systems.* Suva: University of the South Pacific, 1988.

Schuster, S. A. "Training for Police Prosecutors in Western Samoa," in C. G. Powles and M. Pulea, eds. *Pacific Courts and Legal Systems.* Suva: University of the South Pacific, 1988.

Shore, B. *Sala'ilua: A Samoan Mystery.* New York: Columbia University Press, 1982.

Stevenson, T. W. "Samoan Legal Profession: Some History and Background" [1986] *New Zealand Law J.* 49–50.

Thomas, P. "Society, Land and Law: Land Policy in Western Samoa" 12 *Melanesian Law J.* 129–148 (1984).

———. "Western Samoa," in P. Larmour and R. Qalo, eds. *Decentralisation in the South Pacific.* Suva: University of the South Pacific, 1985.

Tiffany, S. W. "The Land and Titles Court and the Regulation of Customary Title Succession and Removals" 83 *J. of Polynesian Society* 35–57 (1974).

———. "Politics of Land Disputes in Western Samoa" 50 (3) *Oceania* 176–208 (1980).

Va'ai, Al. S. "The Western Samoan Legal Profession," in C. G. Powles and M. Pulea, eds. *Pacific Courts and Legal Systems.* Suva: University of the South Pacific, 1988.

PART TWO

The Presidential Model

16. American Samoa

MARY McCORMICK

I. DATELINE

1000 B.C.	First settlement of Samoa by people from Tonga and Fiji.
300 A.D.	Rapid expansion of population and settlement of inland areas.
1000	Tongan raids and evolution of Samoan society into a more hierarchical structure.
1878	Treaty of Friendship and Commerce made and ratified between the United States and the Government of the American Samoa Island but annulled by the Treaty of Berlin of 1899.
1899	Eastern islands of the Samoan group allocated to the United States by the Treaty of Berlin.
1900–1904	Chiefs of Tutuila cede rights to the United States.
1925	United States sovereignty extended to Swains Island.
1929	Deeds of Cession ratified by U.S. Congress.
1930	Bill of Rights adopted for American Samoa by U.S. Congress.
1948	Fono becomes official legislature of American Samoa.
1951	Administration of American Samoa transferred from the U.S. Secretary of the Navy to Secretary of the Interior.
1960	Constitution granted to American Samoa by U.S. Secretary of the Interior.
1966	Revised American Samoa Constitution adopted.
1977	U.S. Congress adopts legislation permitting local election of Governor and Lieutenant Governor.
1978	U.S. Congress adopts legislation permitting local election of nonvoting delegate to U.S. House of Representatives.

II. HISTORICAL, CULTURAL, AND ECONOMIC SURVEY

A. History

American Samoa is an unincorporated and unorganized territory of the United States.[1] The seven islands of American Samoa, lying about 2,300 miles southwest of Hawaii and 1,600 miles northeast of New Zealand, are the only U.S. possession south of the equator. The population is approximately 47,000.

The Samoan islands were originally settled about 1000 B.C. by Polynesians who probably came by way of Fiji and Tonga. From Samoa and Tonga, the Polynesians discovered and settled much of the Pacific. Early European visitors to Samoa called it the Navigator Islands because of the Samoans' navigational and sailing skills. During the nineteenth century, the United States, Great Britain, and Germany each established a presence in Samoa and became involved in the social and political affairs of the islanders as a means of pursuing their own commercial and political interests. During the initial period of foreign involvement, there was continuous interisland warfare, with foreign powers supplying all parties with weaponry. The high chiefs of Tutuila received assistance from the United States in return for undertaking commercial and treaty obligations.

An agreement of the concerned major powers in 1899 allocated Tutuila and certain other eastern islands of the Samoan group to the United States and 'Upolu, Savai'i, and certain other western islands to Germany. The chiefs of Tutuila and Manu'a, in 1900 and 1904 respectively, ceded their rights over the islands of eastern Samoa to the United States. The islands were thereafter administered as a U.S. naval station, although the Articles of Cession were not ratified by the U.S. Congress until 1929. In 1925, U.S. sovereignty was extended to Swains Island, an 800-acre coral atoll 280 miles east of the other islands with a small, ethnically Tokelauan native population. Swains Island is still owned by descendants of Eli Jennings, a nineteenth-century New Yorker; special legislation applies to it.

The U.S. Navy ruled American Samoa until after World War II, the naval commander being advised by the fono of matais (a traditional council of chiefs). In 1930, a bill of rights was adopted for Samoa by the U.S. authorities, and the judicial and executive functions were split. In 1948, the bicameral Fono became the official legislature. In 1951, administration of the islands was transferred to the U. S. Department of the Interior, which in 1960 promulgated a Constitution for American Samoa. This Constitution was revised by a constitutional convention in 1966. In 1967, after approval by the voters of American Samoa in a referendum, the revised Constitution was acceded to by the Secretary of the Interior. Legislation allowing local election of a Governor and Lieutenant Governor was passed by the U.S. Congress in 1977. In 1980, American Samoa began to elect a nonvoting delegate to the U.S. House of Representatives.

American Samoa has received relatively little attention from the U.S. Congress since Congress ratified the Cession in 1929. Congress has never acted on the 1929 joint resolution intended to keep American Samoa under the authority of the executive branch only until Congress enacted further legislation. The 1983 congressional statute, 48 USC Sec. 1662, permitting modification of Samoa's Revised Constitution only by an act of Congress, amounts to implicit acceptance by Congress of the American Samoa Constitution.

B. Culture and Change

The basic social unit in American Samoa is the 'aiga, an extended family group. The chief matai and lesser matais (the 'aiga heads) administer 'aiga property and are significant voices in allocating 'aiga land to family members for houses and cultivation; assigning labor, goods, and money for 'aiga-sponsored projects and ceremonial redistribution; acting as custodians of other 'aiga assets; mediating and arbitrating intra- and inter-'aiga disputes; and representing the 'aiga in district and local councils.[2]

Today, the matai system is undergoing change, caused in part by the changing economic and political system. The introduction of a wage economy in World War II, the migration of many Samoans to the American mainland, the development of cash crops, and the election of legislators have been among the factors producing changes in the traditional system. The primary sources of matai authority today include the matais' role in the disposition of communally owned land and in the upper house of the Fono (the Samoan legislature), which consists entirely of matais.

III. SOURCES OF LAW

Congress has not set out sources of law for American Samoa. A statement of the sources of law established by the Fono is contained in Title 1 of American Samoa's Code. These sources of law are the American Samoa Constitution, the U.S. Constitution, U.S. and Samoan statutes, the common law, and custom.

A. American Samoa Constitution

The 1966 Revised Constitution grants certain rights to the people of American Samoa, discussed below (**IV, D Human Rights**), and establishes legislative, executive, and judicial branches of government for American Samoa. Article V of the Revised Constitution permits proposal of constitutional amendments in either house of the Fono. If agreed to by three-fifths of all members of each house, voting separately, the Governor must submit the amendment to the voters at the next general election. Once the amendment has been approved, the Governor must submit it to the Secretary of the Interior for approval or disapproval within four months after its receipt. Since 1983, Article V has been subject to an additional requirement that the Constitution be modified only by an act of the U.S. Congress (**see II, A History**). References herein to the Constitution are to the Revised Constitution of American Samoa.

B. U.S. Constitution

Because American Samoa is an unincorporated territory, only "fundamental provisions" of the U.S. Constitution apply to it.[3] It is up to the Samoan and U.S. courts to determine, on a case-by-case basis, which provisions of the U.S. Constitution are fundamental. In cases arising in other U.S. territories, the United States courts have defined the right to the writ of habeas corpus, protection against unreasonable searches and seizures, and the right to just compensation as fundamental.[4] In cases arising in American Samoa, the right to a jury trial has been defined as fundamental (**see XI, B Criminal Procedure**).[5]

C. United States Statutes

Those U.S. statutes and treaties that expressly state that they apply to territories of the United States are part of the law of American Samoa.

D. American Samoa Statutes

The Fono may enact laws on matters of local application, and regulations may be issued pursuant to those laws, provided that the laws are consistent with the Constitution of American Samoa, fundamental provisions of the U.S. Constitution, and applicable laws of the United States. The statutory law of American Samoa has been organized into the *American Samoa Code Annotated*, initially published in 1981, and regularly updated, in which statutes are grouped into titles and chapters by topic. Acts are cited here by name, title, and chapter number. Provisions of earlier American Samoa codes and other laws not inconsistent with the provisions of the Annotated Code are part of American Samoa law until repealed or superseded.

E. Common Law

Only that part of the Anglo-American common law applied and modified by the courts of the United States since 1961, suitable to conditions in American Samoa, and not inconsistent with other adopted laws is part of American Samoa law. Normally, the appropriate common law is the rule codified in the *Restatements of the Law* of the American Law Institute.[6]

F. Customary Law

The Constitution of American Samoa does not expressly declare that custom is a source of law, although Section 3 does provide that the state is responsible for protecting Samoans against destruction of *fa'a Samoa* (the Samoan way of life). The code (Title 1, Chapter 2) makes it clear that custom is to be considered a source of law but does not clearly delineate custom's rank in relation to common law. On the one hand, Section 1.0202 of the Code reiterates the constitutional declaration that Samoan custom be preserved, and Section 1.0201 provides that courts can use the common law only if it is "suitable to conditions in American Samoa." This suggests that custom should rank above the imported common law. However, Section 1.0202 further provides that custom is a source of law only to the extent that it does not conflict with the "laws" of American Samoa or "laws" of the United States that concern American Samoa. Whether this places custom above or below the imported common law depends upon the meaning that the drafters of the code intended to convey by their use of the word *laws*. If the word refers only to statutes, then custom is above the common law, but if the word refers both to statutes and to the common law, then custom has a ranking inferior to the common law.

For the relation of American Samoan customary law to the Bill or Rights of the U.S. Constitution, **see IV, D Human Rights and XI, B Criminal Procedure.**

IV. CONSTITUTIONAL SYSTEM

A. Territory

American Samoa consists of 76.2 square miles. The United States has proclaimed a 200-mile exclusive economic zone for itself and each of its territories.

B. Nationality and Citizenship

American Samoa, including Swains Island, is an "outlying possession" of the United States. Under Title 8, Sections 1101 and 1436 of the U.S. Code, persons born to native residents of an outlying possession are noncitizen nationals of the United States; they can carry U.S. passports and travel freely throughout the United States. They may become U.S. citizens by migrating to the United States and becoming resident in a state. A five-year residency is generally required of aliens who wish to take up U.S. citizenship, but American Samoans meet the residency requirement by residency in American Samoa.

Because American Samoans are not citizens of a state, they have no right to vote in U.S. elections. Since 1978, however, American Samoa has been represented in the U.S. Congress by a nonvoting delegate to the House of Representatives elected for a term of two years. The U.S. Code requires that candidates be twenty-five years of age, have been U.S. citizens for at least seven years before the date of the election, be inhabitants of American Samoa, and not be candidates for any other office.

C. Government

1. NATIONAL GOVERNMENT

The 1966 Revised Constitution establishes a tripartite system of government similar to that of the United States. It permits the Fono to enact laws on matters of local application, subject to the U.S. Constitution and to veto by the Governor and Secretary of the Interior.

a. Executive Branch

Matters pertaining to the executive branch are found in Article IV of the Revised Constitution and Title 4 of the American Samoa Code.

A decade after the Revised Constitution was adopted, the Secretary of the Interior, in response to a referendum, provided by order for an elected Governor and Lieutenant Governor, each of whom serves a four-year term.[7] Candidates for the two offices are jointly elected by a majority of the votes cast by qualified electors.

The Secretary's order specifies the manner in which the Governor and Lieutenant Governor are elected. The qualifications of nominees, nominating procedures, terms of office, recall, method of impeachment, and compensation are set out in Title 4 of the American Samoa Code. A candidate for either office must be a U.S. citizen or national, thirty-five years of age or older, and a bona fide American Samoa resident for five years immediately preceding the election. Absence from American Samoa in connection with service in the U.S. armed services, the United States or American Samoa government, or in pursuit of an education does not preclude an otherwise qualified person from nomination. A person is ineligible for election to either office if convicted of a felony under the laws of American Samoa, the United States, or any of its states, unless pardoned, or if separated from the U.S. armed forces under other than honorable conditions. A government employee seeking nomination to either office must resign before commencing active campaigning and in any event no later than sixty days before the election.

The Governor is subject to recall if two-thirds of the number of persons who voted for Governor in the preceding election and who constitute a majority in the referendum election vote in favor of recall. Both the Governor and Lieutenant Governor may be impeached for conviction of felonies and for conduct amounting to gross abuse of power.

The Governor has general supervision and control of all executive institutions and the power to issue regulations not in conflict with American Samoa laws, its Constitution, or U.S. laws applicable to American Samoa. The Governor appoints directors of Cabinet departments and heads of bureaus or offices whose appointments are subject to confirmation by the Fono; officers whose appointments are not otherwise provided for; boards, commissions, and executives he or she deems advisable; and a leading registered matai as Secretary of Samoan Affairs to be head of the Department of Local Government and, in conjunction with the district governors, to coordinate the administration of district, county, and village affairs and supervise ceremonial functions as provided by law.

The Governor has power to call out the militia to prevent or suppress violence, invasion, insurrection, or rebellion; to remit fines and forfeitures; commute sentences and grant reprieves and pardons after conviction for offenses against the laws of American Samoa; and to attend or depute another person to attend meetings of the Fono and express his or her views before that body.

The Governor also has the following constitutionally imposed duties:

1. to make each year a comprehensive financial report to the U.S. Congress and the Secretary of the Interior;
2. to report governmental transactions to the Secretary of the Interior and the Fono after the close of each fiscal year;
3. to give the Fono information on the state of the government and recommend measures he or she deems necessary and expedient; and
4. to make provision for publishing laws within fifty-five days after the close of each session of the Fono for distribution to public officials and for sale to the public.

The Lieutenant Governor has no legislative duties or functions but acts as Secretary of American Samoa and functions as Governor when that office is vacant or the incumbent is ill, absent, or temporarily disabled.

b. Legislative Branch

Article II of the Constitution establishes a legislature, the Fono, composed of a Senate and House of Representatives. Elections are held biennially in even-numbered years. Reapportionment must occur at intervals of not less than five years. There are two regular sessions of the Fono each year; the Governor may call a special session.

The Senate has eighteen members, each of whom is a registered matai who fulfills his or her customary obligations in the county from which elected. Three senators are elected from the Manu'a District, six from the Western District and nine from the Eastern District. A candidate for the Senate must be a U.S. national, at least thirty years of age at the time of election, who has lived in American Samoa at least five years and been a bona fide resident for at least one year preceding the election. Senators are elected in accordance with Samoan custom by councils of the counties they are to represent and hold office for a term of four years.

The House of Representatives has twenty members. A representative must be a U.S. national, at least twenty-five years of age at the time of election, who has lived in American Samoa for a total of at least five years and been a resident of the district from which elected for at least one year immediately before the election. Representatives are chosen by secret ballot of the qualified electors of the representative district and hold office for a term of two years.

The adult permanent residents of Swains Island who are U.S. nationals elect a nonvoting delegate to the House of Representatives at an open meeting. The delegate must have the qualifications of a representative except that, in lieu of residence in a district, the person must have been a resident of Swains Island for at least one year preceding the election. The delegate holds office for a term of two years.

Each house is the judge of the elections, returns, and qualifications of its own members. A house does not have power, however, to determine whether its procedures for selection of members conform to constitutional requirements; those decisions are judicial rather than political and are matters of constitutional interpretation for the court.[8] Each house chooses its officers and determines its rules of procedure, although the business of each house and of the committee of the whole must be transacted in open and not in secret session. Each house has power to punish its members for disorderly behavior and may expel a member with the consent of two-thirds of its entire membership. A person who has been expelled from the Fono for giving, receiving, or being an accessory to a bribe is ineligible to sit in the Fono. A person convicted of a felony under the laws of American Samoa, the United States, or the law of any state of the United States must have been pardoned and had his or her civil rights restored before being eligible to sit in the Fono. No employee or public officer of the government may sit in the Fono while in that employment or office.

Members of the Fono are privileged from arrest during any of its sessions except in cases of treason, felony, or breach of the peace. A member of the Fono may not be held to answer before any other tribunal for any speech or debate in the Fono.

Enactments of the Fono are restricted to subjects of local legislation. No law may be inconsistent with the American Samoa Constitution, fundamental provisions of the U.S. Constitution, or U.S. laws applicable in American Samoa, including treaties or international obligations of the United States. An act may embrace only one subject and matters properly connected with that subject, which must be expressed in the title. Matters in an act not expressed in the title are void. Money bills may not appropriate funds in excess of revenues raised, unless revenue measures to provide the needed funds are included in the bill.

A bill or joint resolution must be passed by a majority of all the members of each house. Once a bill has passed both houses, it is signed by the President of the Senate and the Speaker of the House and presented to the Governor for approval. A bill signed by the Governor becomes law and must be deposited in the office of the Secretary of American Samoa. A vetoed bill is returned with the Governor's objections to the House in which it originated. The Governor may veto part and approve part of a bill appropriating money. If not returned within ten days, a vetoed bill becomes law unless the Fono has by its adjournment prevented the bill's return. In that case, the bill becomes law only if the Governor signs it within thirty days after adjournment. A vetoed bill may become law if two-thirds of the entire Fono override the veto not later than fourteen months after the veto. A repassed bill must be presented to the Governor for approval. If the Governor does not approve the bill within fifteen days, it must be sent to the Secretary of the Interior together with the Governor's comments. The bill will become law only if the Secretary of the Interior approves it within ninety days after its receipt.

Any U.S. national who is at least eighteen years old, has lived in American Samoa for a total of at least two years, has been a resident of the proposed voting district for at least one year preceding the election, and meets any registration requirements is eligible to vote in elections for the House of Representatives. Excluded are persons under guardianship, those who are insane, and those who have been convicted of a felony unless the person's civil rights have been previously restored or he or she has maintained good behavior for 2 years following the date of conviction or release from prison, whichever is later. Elections for the Fono are held biennially in even-numbered years. The date of election for territorial offices is set by the chief election officer.

Provisions relating to the registration of voters, the conduct of elections, form and content of ballots, voting procedures, election contests, absentee voting, creation of election offenses, and reporting of election contributions and expenses are contained in Title 6 of the Annotated Code.

c. Judicial Branch

Provisions relating to the judiciary are found in Article III of the Constitution and Title 3 of the Code. The Constitution vests the judicial power in a High Court, District Courts, and such other courts as may from time to time be created by law and declares that the judicial branch shall be independent of the executive and legislative branches. Village Courts have been created by statute under this provision.

There are no appeals from the decisions of the American Samoa courts to appellate courts in the United States. The decision not to provide this appeal process has been held to have a rational purpose in that it helps to preserve the Fa'a Samoa (Samoan Way) by respecting Samoan traditions, such as those concerning land ownership.[9] However, even when alternative remedies are available in the American Samoa courts, a collateral attack on decisions of the American Samoa courts may be made by bringing suit against the Secretary of the Department of the Interior in a U.S. District Court, provided the appellant can raise a valid question under U.S. law.[10]

The Chief Justice and the necessary number of Associate Justices are appointed by the Secretary of the Interior (Constitution, Article III). Title 3 of the Code provides that justices must be learned in the law and that they hold office during good behavior. Each justice is a member of the High Court, and one or the other presides at all its divisions. The Chief Justice supervises the judicial branch of government, has power to make rules regulating the pleading, practice, procedure, and conduct of business in the courts of American Samoa, and to admit qualified persons to the practice of law. Because there are at present only a Chief Justice and one Associate Justice, each sits as a trial court and, as a member of the appellate court, reviews the other's decisions.

The Governor may also appoint as associate judges Samoans who are not legally qualified and who are recommended by the Chief Justice and confirmed by the Senate, each of whom holds office during good behavior until age sixty-five. Associate judges are typically traditional Samoan leaders with a knowledge of local customs. One associate judge is designated by the Chief Justice as chief associate judge. Associate judges may be heard on all questions before any division of the court, examine any party or witness in the proceedings, and advise the court on questions the court may refer to them (Code, Title 3, Chapter 2).

All courts in American Samoa exercise personal jurisdiction in civil cases over any person residing or found in American Samoa or who has been duly summoned or voluntarily appears. The courts also have jurisdiction over any person, firm, or corporation, whether or not a citizen or resident of the territory, who transacts business; commits a tortious act; makes a contract to insure any person, property, or risk within American Samoa; or owns, uses, or possesses any real estate there. Criminal cases may be prosecuted and tried only in a court having territorial jurisdiction over the place where the crime was committed (Code, Title 3, Chapter 1).

(i) High Court

The High Court is a court of record, with appellate, trial, and land and titles divisions. The trial and land and titles divisions have power to give declaratory relief. The High Court's jurisdiction extends throughout American Samoa, including Swains Island and Rose Island. The Court sits at any appropriate place in American Samoa where the interest of justice or the convenience of the parties, witnesses, or the Court requires. Any case brought in the High Court or in a District Court may, in the interest of justice and for the convenience of the parties and witnesses, be transferred to any court in which it might have been brought originally (Code, Title 3, Chapter 2).

The Trial Division of the High Court is a court of general jurisdiction. Its jurisdiction includes civil cases in which the amount in controversy exceeds US$5,000 (except land and titles cases), criminal felony cases, juvenile cases, probate and administration of estates, and domestic relations. The Land and Titles Division of the High Court has exclusive jurisdiction in all controversies relating to matai titles and to land.

The Chief Justice, the Associate Justice, and all of the associate judges sit in the trial and land and titles divisions, sessions of which are held before a justice and two associate judges. The presence of a justice and one associate judge is necessary to constitute a quorum. However, cases relating to matai titles must be heard by a justice and four associate judges, and a justice and three associate judges constitute a quorum. If, after conference, any difference of opinion remains between the justice and the associate judges, the opinion of the justice prevails.

The appellate division, which consists of the Chief Justice and Associate Justice, acting Associate Justices appointed by the Secretary of the Interior, and all the associate judges, has jurisdiction to review final decisions of the Trial Division, the Land and Titles Division, the District Court, administrative decisions, and other matters provided for by statute. Sessions of the Appellate Division are held before three justices and two associate judges, and the presence of two of the justices and one associate judge is necessary to constitute a quorum. If after conference any difference of opinion among panel members remains, the opinion of two of the justices shall prevail. If in the determination of any land or matai title case any difference among panel members remains, the majority of the five panel members shall prevail.

(ii) District and Village Courts

The District Court (governed by Title 3, Chapter 3 of the Code) is an inferior court of limited jurisdiction with power to hear minor criminal and civil cases other than actions involving land or matai titles, traffic cases except those involving a felony, initial appearances and preliminary examinations in all criminal cases, adoptions, and public health offenses. District Court judges must be learned in the law and are appointed by the Governor on recommendation of the Chief Justice and confirmation by the Senate. They hold office during good behavior and preside at all sessions of the District Court.

Each village has a Village Court, presided over by an associate judge of the High Court, which has exclusive jurisdiction over matters arising under the regulations of the village, except that appeals from the Village Court may be retried before the District Courts.

2. LOCAL GOVERNMENT

Local government is recognized by Article IV of the Constitution and regulated under Title 5 of the Code. American Samoa is divided into three political districts, each having five counties. Counties are further divided into villages. The Governor appoints district, county, and village officials, after consultation with local officials.

a. District Government

The Secretary for Samoan Affairs heads the Department of Local Government; coordinates the administration of district, county, and village affairs; and supervises all ceremonial functions in conjunction with the district governors.

A district governor, who holds office for four years, must be a U.S. national and leading matai of the district for which appointed, must have maintained customary responsibilities, and must be a resident of the district. A district governor is responsible for the welfare and good order of the people in the district and presides at meetings of the district council. The district governor may be removed for misconduct, incompetence, or neglect of duties (Code, Title 5, Chapter 1).

A district council is chosen in each area in accordance with Samoan custom. It is responsible for supervising the cleanliness of an area, the planting of lands by the people, the making and clearing of roads, and all local matters.

b. County Government

The county chief, or pulenuu, serves a four-year term under the district governor unless removed for misconduct, incompetence, or neglect of duty. The pulenuu is responsible for the welfare and good order of the people of the county. The county council is chosen in accordance with Samoan custom (Code, Title 5, Chapter 2).

c. Village Government

Every two years, the Governor appoints a chief who resides in a village as the pulenuu. The pulenuu is responsible for the welfare and good order of the people of the village and for enforcement of all village regulations. The village council consists of all chiefs and heads of families resident in the village. At its monthly meetings the council may enact village regulations concerning the cleanliness of the village, planting of village lands, making and cleaning of roads, and any other local matters. Village regulations take effect only after approval by the Department of Samoan Affairs. Neither the pulenuu nor the village council may inflict punishment on an offender, who must be taken before the court. The councils retain their own forms of meeting to discuss their affairs according to Samoan custom (Code, Title 5, Chapter 3).

d. Swains Island

The local government for Swains Island consists of a government representative who represents the Governor on the island, a village council, a pulenuu, and village policemen. The village council consists of all resident male persons over twenty-four years of age. Neither the proprietor of Swains Island nor any employee of the proprietor is eligible for appointment as government representative, although the Swains Island delegate to the Fono may be (and at present is) a relative of the proprietor. The government representative mediates disputes between employees and their employer; enforces the laws of the United States and American Samoa applicable on the island and village regulations; keeps the Governor advised as to the state of affairs on the island, particularly as to the health, education, safety, and welfare of its people; ensures that the people of Swains Island continue to enjoy the rights, privileges, and immunities accorded to them by the laws of the United States and American Samoa; and ensures that the proprietary authority of the proprietor is respected (Code, Title 5, Chapter 4).

D. Human Rights

Individual civil rights in American Samoa are predicated both upon the rights provisions of the Constitution of American Samoa (Article I) and, where a court has determined them to be applicable to the unincorporated territories, certain provisions of the Bill of Rights of the U.S. Constitution. (see III Sources of Law).

Article I of the Constitution of American Samoa establishes the separation of church and state; freedom of religion, speech, assembly, and the press; and the right to petition the government for redress of grievances. It also prohibits the establishment of religion. A due process (natural justice) clause prohibits the deprivation of life, liberty, or property without due process of law and requires just compensation when private property is taken for public use.

Despite this enumeration of individual rights, Article I also recognizes and supports the chiefly and communitarian aspects of Fa'a Samoa (Samoan Way). Section 3 states that it is the policy of the government of American Samoa to protect persons of Samoan ancestry against alienation of their lands and the destruction of the Samoan way of life and language contrary to their best interests. The policy is enforceable through laws designed to protect the lands, customs, culture, and traditional family organization of persons of Samoan ancestry and to encourage business enterprises by such persons. No change in the law respecting the alienation or transfer of land or any interest in land is effective unless the governor and two-thirds of the entire membership of each house in two successive legislatures approve the measure. The High

Court has held that these restrictions on non-Samoan ownership of customary lands do not violate the U.S. Constitution's equal protection provisions (see **XII Law and Natural Resources**), but the matter has not been adjudicated in a U.S. court.

The Bill of Rights requires that the dignity of the individual be respected. It also prohibits "malicious and unjustifiable attacks on a person's name, reputation, or honour or that of the person's family" (Article I, Section 4); unreasonable searches and seizures; and issuance of warrants other than on probable cause. An accused is protected against double jeopardy and compulsory self-incrimination. The accused also has the following rights:

1. not to have his or her failure to testify commented upon or taken against him or her;
2. to a speedy and public trial;
3. to be informed of the nature and cause of the accusation and to have a copy of it;
4. to be confronted with the witnesses against him or her;
5. to have compulsory process for obtaining favorable witnesses; and
6. to have the assistance of defense counsel.

A person is presumed innocent until pronounced guilty by law, and no act of severity that is not reasonably necessary to secure the arrest of an accused person is permitted. All persons are bailable by sufficient sureties, except where the judicial authorities determine that the presumption is great that an infamous crime (murder and rape) has been committed and that a grant of bail would constitute a danger to the community. Excessive bail is prohibited, as are excessive fines and cruel or unusual punishments.

The privilege of the writ of habeas corpus must be granted without delay and free of costs. The quartering of soldiers or members of the militia in time of peace without the consent of the owner or lawful occupant or in time of war except in a manner prescribed by law is prohibited. The military authority is always subordinate to the civil authority in time of peace.

Prohibited are imprisonment for debt except in cases of fraud; slavery and involuntary servitude, except as a punishment for crime; bills of attainder; ex post facto laws; laws impairing the obligation of contracts or abridging the privileges or immunities of citizens of American Samoa; and convictions for treason except on the testimony of two witnesses to the same overt act or a confession in open court. No person who advocates or who aids or belongs to any group that advocates the overthrow by force or violence of the American Samoa government or that of the United States may hold any public office of trust or profit under that government.

Laws may be enacted for the protection of the health, safety, morals, and general welfare of the people of American Samoa. The government is required to operate a system of free and nonsectarian public education and to encourage qualified persons of good character to acquire further education, locally and abroad, both general and technical, and thereafter to return to American Samoa to benefit the people of American Samoa.

V. Administrative Organization and Law

Title 4, Chapter 10 of the Code establishes rule-making and decision-making processes for governmental agencies.

A. Organization

The executive branch has twelve departments: legal affairs, health, agriculture, port administration, local government, administrative services, parks and recreation, public safety, human resources, public works, education, and the Treasury. Other independent offices within the executive branch include program planning and budget development, the power authority, territorial planning, health planning and development, Registrar of Vital Statistics, Archivist, Public Defender, Territorial Registrar, Territorial Auditor, and Director of Manpower Resources.

B. Public Service

Provisions relating to the public service are found in Title 7 of the Code. American Samoa has a career public service that includes all employees of the government except contract employees; federal employees; district, county, and village officials; members and employees of the Fono, and judges. The policy of American Samoa is that all appointments and promotions to positions in the career service are to be made solely on the basis of merit, fitness, and length and quality of previous service; whenever practicable, merit and fitness are to be ascertained by competitive examination. Administrators are required, when they prepare examinations or select incumbents in the absence of examinations to take cognizance of the trend in American Samoa toward a greater degree of self-determination and the need for training opportunities for American Samoans in furthering that transition. Whenever possible, standards for employment should give due recognition to practical experience in the function and probable aptitude for learning on the job, rather than relying in the main on formalized education and training.

The Government Employees' Retirement Fund provides retirement annuities to government employees. American Samoa has also adopted a deferred compensation plan that permits government employees to defer taxation on income until received.

C. Public Finance and Audit

The Secretary of the Interior oversees the government of American Samoa. The executive and judicial budgets must each be approved by the secretary.[11] The Inspector General of the U. S. Department of the Interior has comprehensive audit powers. The integrity of the judiciary is maintained because funds allocated to the courts are beyond the control of the department once they have been awarded.[12] In addition, Title 4, Chapter 4 of the Code establishes a territorial audit office, under the control of an auditor, appointed by the Governor and confirmed by the Fono. The auditor can be removed prior to the expiration of a four-year term only by the Governor with the consent of two-thirds of the members of each house of the Fono (Code, Title 4, Chapter 5).

D. Rule Making

All government agencies other than the legislature or the courts are required to adopt rules of practice and procedure, as well as rules stating the general course and method of operation and the method by which the public may obtain information or make requests or submissions. Before a rule is adopted, amended, or repealed, the public must be given notice of the intended action and an opportunity to present argument orally or in writing. In the case of substantive rules, an oral hearing must be held if twenty-five people, a governmental division or agency, or an association having not less than twenty-five members, so request. All adopted rules must be published (Code, Title 4, Chapter 10).

E. Review of Administrative Action

Parties in a contested administration case must be given an opportunity to present evidence and argument and conduct such cross-examination as is necessary for a full and true disclosure of the facts. A person who has exhausted all administrative remedies available within an agency and who is aggrieved by a final decision in a contested case is entitled to judicial review by the High Court, Appellate Division. The review is confined to the record. If a party requests, the Court will receive briefs and hear oral argument and may in its discretion receive any evidence necessary to supplement the record. The Court, under Code, Title 4, Chapter 10, may reverse or modify an agency's decision or remand the case for further proceedings if substantial rights of the petitioner have been prejudiced or if the agency's decision

1. violates applicable constitutional or statutory provisions;
2. exceeds its statutory authority;
3. was made on unlawful procedure or is affected by other error of law;
4. is clearly erroneous in view of the reliable, probative, and substantial evidence in the whole record; or
5. is arbitrary, capricious, or characterized by abuse of discretion.

VI. INTERNATIONAL OBLIGATIONS

As a territory of the United States, American Samoa has no authority to enter into international obligations, although it is obliged to comply with the provisions of obligations entered into by the United States.

VII. REVENUE LAW

The only provision in the Constitution relating to revenue law is Article II, Section 1, which requires a balanced budget. Other provisions are found in the Income Tax Act, contained in Title 11, Chapter 4 of the Code. American Samoa imposes an income tax, an alternative minimum tax, a sales tax, excise taxes on imports and exports, and a tax on secondhand imported items. In addition to those taxes, the Governor may at any time, either on the request of a district, county, or village chief or on the Governor's own initiative, authorize and direct the chief to levy a special tax for a special purpose.

American Samoa has adopted those portions of the U.S. Internal Revenue Code that are not clearly inapplicable or incompatible with the intent of American Samoa's Income Tax Act. The provisions adopted include but are not limited to those relating to the collection of income tax at source on wages and those concerning crimes, other offenses, and forfeitures. The administration and enforcement of the American Samoa income tax is the responsibility of the Treasurer of American Samoa under the supervision of the Governor. The High Court has exclusive original jurisdiction over criminal and civil American Samoa income tax proceedings. The requirements for taxpayer suits to recover erroneously or illegally assessed or collected income tax, unauthorized penalties, or overpayments of income tax are those applicable to suits for the recovery of such amounts maintained against the United States in the U.S. District Courts with respect to U.S. income tax (Code, Title 11, Chapter 5).

American Samoa imposes a sales tax on all tangible personal property sold or leased to the ultimate consumer. Bona fide wholesalers are not responsible for collection of the tax when they are wholesaling to a licensed retailer (Code, Title 11, Chapter 3).

In 1967, American Samoa abolished customs duties on all imports and imposed an excise tax on the purchase price of imported alcoholic beverages, tobacco products and smoking accessories, firearms and firearm ammunition, motor vehicles and parts, motor bicycles, construction materials, and soft drinks and nonalcoholic carbonated beverages. It imposes an excise tax by volume on imported petroleum products. It also imposes an additional special tax on all secondhand motor vehicles, machinery, and household appliances imported into American Samoa for retail sale (Code, Title 11, Chapter 10).

During the first ten days of any calendar year, but not thereafter during that year, the Governor may, after prior consultation and discussion with the exporters substantially affected, impose an export duty—not to exceed that imposed on like articles imported into the United States from foreign countries generally—on any article exported from American Samoa and destined for importation into the U.S. customs area (Code, Title 11, Chapter 15).

VIII. INVESTMENT LAW

American Samoa government policy is to promote economic development and capital investment in American Samoa by tax incentives to establish a firm foundation for self-government and assist the American Samoan people in improving their living standards and prospects for employment (Code, Title 11, Chapter 16), although, in fact, there has been little industrial or economic development.

The Governor, assisted by an advisory tax exemption board, has authority to grant, deny, amend, renew, and revoke tax exemptions to enterprises owned by a person who is or a partnership one of whose members is an American Samoa resident. The governor also has such authority over corporations created under the laws of American Samoa or foreign corporations authorized by American Samoa law to do business in American Samoa. A resident for these purposes is a person who has resided continuously in American Samoa for not less than five years immediately before the date of application for employment, or who was born in American Samoa and has resided therein not less than one year immediately prior to the application. At least 75 percent of the total workforce of the enterprise must be American Samoan residents, who must be employed at the prevailing wage rate or at not less than the minimum wage rate (Code, Title 11, Chapter 16).

To encourage foreign export trade by U.S. companies, the U.S. Congress in 1984 established various tax incentives, such as tax-favored foreign sales corporations (FSCs), which could be established in U.S. possessions, including American Samoa. No tax could be imposed on foreign trade income derived by an FSC before January 1, 1987. American Samoa has enacted legislation permitting the creation of qualifying American Samoa foreign sales corporations (QASFSCs), an FSC created or organized under the laws of American Samoa that at all times during the taxable year, maintains a bank account in American Samoa from which it disburses all dividends, legal and accounting fees, and salaries of officers and members of the board of directors. A QASFSC may not engage in the manufacture, production, or processing of products for sale in American Samoa, but it is not subject to American Samoa customs duties or income, excise, or withholding taxes for a period of ten years after incorporation if the incorporation occurred before January 1, 1987. Shareholders of a QASFSC are exempt from paying tax on income realized from sources within American Samoa from QASFSCs. A franchise tax of US$2,500 per year is imposed on each QASFSC.

In an effort to improve its economic and fiscal position, the welfare and property of its people, and its export balance, American Samoa established an economic development authority in 1986. The authority issues revenue bonds and enters into other obligations to acquire real estate and to finance housing projects, utilities, health care, agricultural businesses, industrial and commercial enterprises, and educational and governmental facilities. American Samoa also can issue industrial development bonds that are exempt from all taxes (Code, Title 11, Chapter 19).

IX. Welfare Law

American Samoa has consistently rejected application of most U.S. welfare programs, in the belief that to do so would be to undermine its traditional family structure. In 1988, US$11,604,000 was paid by the federal government directly to individuals, almost entirely in social security disability, retirement, and survivors' insurance payments and in veterans' pensions and disability payments.[13]

X. Criminal Law

Crimes in American Samoa are divided by Title 46 of the Code into felonies and misdemeanors, each having four grades. Attempts to commit a felony are classified one degree below the substantive offense. Conspiracies are punishable in the same manner as attempts.

Criminal liability is based on conduct that includes a voluntary act accompanied by a culpable mental state. A culpable mental state is not required for an infraction if the statute creating it so specifies or for an offense if the statute defining it clearly dispenses with that requirement. The defenses of entrapment, duress, intoxicated or drugged condition, infancy and mental duress or defect are recognized, as are those of self-defense and defense of others, defense of property, and use of force to arrest or prevent escape from imprisonment or by a person with responsibility for the care, safety, or discipline of others. Ignorance of the law is not recognized as an excuse.

Offenses are classified as follows: those against the person, family, the public order, property, and the administration of justice; sexual offenses; offenses involving prostitution, abortion, gambling, pornography, and weapons; offenses affecting government; and miscellaneous offenses.

Criminal offenses are found in other parts of the Code as well. Controlled substances are regulated in Title 13, Chapter 10. Penalties are provided for unlawful possession, delivery, dispensation, distribution, production, and manufacture of listed controlled substances in a variety of categories. Driving rules and penalties for violation are contained in Title 22 of the Code.

A. Sentencing

Sentencing policies are set out in Title 46, Chapters 19 to 27 of the Code. Persons convicted of murder in the first degree may be sentenced to death. All death sentences are reviewed by the High Court, with a further right of review by the Secretary of the Interior.

A person convicted of a felony or misdemeanor may be sentenced to imprisonment; a fine; suspension of imposition of sentence, with or without probation; suspended execution of sentence with probation; detention as a condition of probation; or ordinary labor. A person guilty of an infraction may be sentenced to any of the above except imprisonment or detention. Presentence investigations are made in all felony cases unless waived by the defendant and in all other cases as directed by the court.

An able-bodied person sentenced to imprisonment may be required to perform labor (ordinary labor for men and light labor for women) during the sentence unless the sentence provides otherwise. Prisoners may be placed in solitary confinement for discipline upon written order of the Attorney General for not more than ten days for any one offense. If there has been some semblance of due process, a prisoner placed in solitary confinement may also be put on bread and water with a full ration every third day, unless a medical doctor considers other food necessary for the preservation of the prisoner's health.

Section 1910 of Title 46 provides that, in sentencing an accused, the court may reduce the extent or duration of the sentence or the level of the crime if an ifoga ceremony (the Samoan custom of public apology) has been performed. The ifoga presented to the family of a deceased or an injured person by the family of a wrongdoer is not meant as compensation for the family of the deceased but primarily as an expression of sorrow and apology. Despite the statutory requirements, judges have recently refused to grant significant reductions in sentences on account of the ifoga ceremony because the ceremony is performed by the family of the accused, not by the accused personally, and therefore cannot be considered a penalty.

Parole is available to prisoners serving a term longer than six months—other than juvenile delinquents or committed youth offenders—who have served the minimum of the prison term imposed on them.

B. Juvenile Justice

The Juvenile Justice Act of 1980, based primarily on Title 19 of the State of Colorado Revised Statutes (1973), establishes three categories of children subject to the High Court's exclusive control—delinquent children, children in need of supervision, and neglected and dependent children. The High Court trial division also has exclusive jurisdiction to

1. determine legal custody of such children;
2. terminate the legal parent-child relationship;
3. issue orders of support;
4. determine paternity;
5. grant a contested adoption;
6. judicially consent to marriage, employment, or enlistment of a child; and
7. grant temporary orders for protection, support, or medical or surgical treatment.

Children alleged delinquent have a right to trial by jury. Hearings are closed to the public and conducted informally. Publications may not identify any parties to juvenile proceedings. The Court may appoint referees, including nonlawyers, to hear all but contested delinquency jury trials. A verbatim record is made of all proceedings. A social study is required before disposition of a case, and the author of the report is subject to cross-examination.

The Court may terminate parental rights where one or both parents voluntarily relinquish their parental rights or where the Court has determined the child to be neglected by one or both parents or to be independent. The Court's primary interest is the best interest of the child.

Paternity proceedings must be initiated before a child is five years of age unless paternity has been acknowledged by the father in writing or by furnishing support. Upon a finding of paternity, the court may order the father to provide fixed periodic sums for the support and education of the child until the child is eighteen years of age or twenty-one years of age at the discretion of the court. The court may order payment after the child reaches twenty-one years of age if the child is unable to care for himself or herself by reason of mental or physical handicap or other reason justifiable in the opinion of the Court. The father may also be required to pay for the mother's confinement and expenses in connection with her pregnancy.

XI. Judicial Procedure

A. Civil Procedure

The High Court follows, as closely as is practical, the U.S. Federal Rules of Civil Procedure. Rules concerning service of process by publication, prejudgment attachment, orders in aid of judgment, execution upon judgment, and garnishment are contained in Title 43 of the Code. The Uniform Enforcement of Foreign Judgments Act, Title 43, Chapter 17, applies to judgments, decrees, and orders of a U.S. court or any other court entitled to full faith and credit in American Samoa. The act is not exclusive, and a judgment creditor may bring an action to enforce the judgment instead of proceeding under the act.

Special rules protect a Samoan's real property, which is not subject to sale under a writ of court to satisfy any judgment other than a judgment foreclosing a valid mortgage. The Court may appoint a receiver to gather produce lying and being on the property belonging to a Samoan debtor. In this context, the term *Samoan* includes American Samoans of at least one-half Samoan blood and persons born on other islands in the Pacific Ocean who are of at least one-half Polynesian, Melanesian, or Micronesian blood and who reside in American Samoa.

Special rules also govern proceedings in the Lands and Titles Division (Code, Title 3, Chapter 2). No action relating to controversies over communal land or matai titles may be commenced unless a certificate signed and attested by the Secretary of Samoan Affairs or the secretary's deputy is filed with the complaint showing that an effort has been made to resolve the controversy, although this provision is applied with some flexibility.[14] Before proceedings are commenced, the Chief Justice or an Associate Justice may, if necessary, restrain any Samoan from remaining in possession of or entering upon any Samoan land, holding or using any Samoan name or title, or exercising any right or doing anything concerning or affecting Samoan land or a Samoan name or title. Such an order may be made ex parte.

Limitation periods for commencing civil actions are as follows:

1. six months for actions to set aside a will;
2. two years for actions for injuries to the person or reputation, including tort claims against American Samoa, and wrongful death actions;
3. three years for actions on written contracts, injuries to property, and actions for which no limitation period is prescribed;
4. five years for actions to set aside a judgment quieting title to real estate;
5. ten years for actions founded on a written contract or judgment of a court of record; and
6. twenty years for actions brought for recovery of real property.

But in actions for trespass to property and where fraud or mistake is alleged, the limitation period runs from the date of discovery of the fraud, mistake, or trespass. When there is a continuous, open, concurrent account, the cause of action is deemed to have accrued on the date of the last item therein, as proved on the trial. Minors and insane persons have one year from the termination of disability to commence any action that would otherwise be beyond the applicable limitation period. Special rules apply where a plaintiff or defendant dies before an action has been commenced. Any period during which a defendant is a nonresident of American Samoa is not included in the computation of a limitation period.

Causes of action founded on contract are revived by an admission in writing, signed by the party to be charged, that the debt is unpaid or by a new written promise to pay the debt. All actions, causes of actions, or defenses do not abate by death or other disability of a party or by the transfer of any interest therein. The action may be begun or maintained or a defense may be set up by the party's successors in interest or representative.

Title 43 also governs remedies, including declaratory and injunctive relief, summary proceedings to recover possession of premises, and forcible entry of property. On matters relating to communal or 'aiga land or to matai titles within a family, no one but the sa'o of a family (the family head) may request injunctive relief. Only if the matai title of the sa'o is vacant or the sa'o is incapacitated may other members of the family bring such an application (Code, Title 43, Chapter 13).

B. Criminal Procedure

Criminal procedure in the High Court and district court conforms as nearly as may be practical to the U.S. Federal Rules of Criminal Procedure (Code, Title 46, Chapters 5 to 27). Criminal prosecutions are brought in the name of the Government of American Samoa. The Attorney General prosecutes all criminal offenses before the High Court. Prosecution of felonies may be initiated only by criminal information, but misdemeanors may be prosecuted by complaint or by criminal information.

Generally, no arrest may be made without a duly issued warrant, although a police officer or private person may arrest without a warrant under a variety of circumstances. Immediately after a warrantless arrest is made, the person making the arrest must apply to a judge of the High Court for a warrant of arrest and commitment of the arrested person. However, a person lawfully arrested by a police officer may be detained for up to twenty-four hours when the arresting officer deems the detention necessary for the safety of the person arrested or of the public.

The provisions of the U.S. Constitution requiring a jury trial have been held to apply to criminal trials in American Samoa.[15] Unless the right is waived, a person charged with an offense carrying a maximum possible punishment of over six months' imprisonment will be tried by a jury of six persons whose verdict must be unanimous. Two associate judges sit with one of the justices, who presides and rules on all questions of law.

In addition to the protections in the bills of rights of the U.S. and American Samoa Constitutions (**see IV, D Human Rights**), every defendant in a criminal case before an American Samoa court is entitled to the following:

1. a copy of the charge in advance of trial;
2. consultation with counsel before trial and assistance of a representative of the defendant's choosing in the defense at trial;
3. adjournment to allow more time to prepare a defense, if the court is satisfied the defendant will otherwise be substantially prejudiced in the defense;
4. right to call or have the court summon material witnesses;
5. right to testify, subject to cross-examination, although not compelled to do so;
6. right to appeal; and
7. right to a speedy, public trial.

In juvenile proceedings, all children and their parents or legal guardians have a right to be represented by counsel.

Free legal representation is available on request or, without objection from the defendant, on the court's own motion, to any indigent person under arrest for or charged with committing a felony, a misdemeanor, or an immigration or traffic violation; and to a person held in any institution against his or her will by process or otherwise for the treatment of any disease or disorder or confined for the protection of the public. Counsel will be appointed in proceedings against children alleged delinquent or in need of supervision, where termination of parental rights is stated as a possible remedy in the summons, or where the child is in any way restrained by court order, process, or otherwise. The court has discretion to appoint counsel in other cases if necessary to protect the interests of the child or of other parties.

American Samoa has adopted the Uniform Criminal Extradition Act (Code, Title 46, Chapter 9).

C. Village Court Procedures

The village pulenuu prosecutes offenses before the Village Court. A pulenuu who has evidence that a village regulation has been violated may file a written complaint with the Village Court and serve a copy of the complaint on the accused prior to arraignment. No trial may be held sooner than seven days after the accused has been served with a copy of the complaint.

An accused before a Village Court has the same rights as any defendant in any other criminal case. The court may enter a finding of guilty and sentence a defendant who pleads guilty on arraignment to the penalty provided in the village regulations. An accused who pleads not guilty may be found guilty only after a public trial in the Village Court. At trial the court may consider only the evidence presented before it under oath or stipulated to; no other written statements of witnesses or other hearsay may be presented. The Village Court has power to impose a fine or require the defendant to perform labor for the village. If an accused fails to appear for trial or fails to perform a sentence, the matter must be referred to the District Court. An accused found guilty by a Village Court may have the case retried de novo before the District Court by requesting a retrial within ten days of pronouncement of judgment. There is otherwise no appeal from or review of Village Court proceedings; neither is there right of appeal from a judgment of the District Court after a trial de novo (Code, Title 46, Chapter 18).

D. Appellate Review

The High Court, Appellate Division, has power to affirm, modify, set aside, or reverse a judgment or order appealed from or to remand the case with directions for a new trial or for entry of such judgment as may be just (Code, Title 43, Chapter 8). Findings of fact of the trial, probate, and land and titles divisions of the High Court or a series of legal conclusions unsupported by meaningful discussion may be set aside only if "clearly erroneous," as that phrase has been defined by the U.S. Supreme Court.[16]

The filing of a motion for new trial within ten days after announcement of the judgment or sentence, setting out the grounds of error, is a jurisdictional prerequisite to the filing of a civil or criminal appeal. It is improper to raise as error in the motion an issue that could have been but was not raised at trial.[17] In a criminal case, a notice of appeal must be filed within ten days after denial of the motion for new trial. Execution of a final judgment or order is not stayed pending the determination of an appeal unless the court orders a stay.

Criminal appeals are governed by Title 46, Chapter 24 of the Code. The government may appeal in a criminal case (1) from a decision based upon the invalidity or construction of the statute upon which the prosecution is founded; and (2) from a decision suppressing or excluding evidence or requiring the return of seized property. If a defendant has not been put in jeopardy before the decision is made, the Attorney General must certify at the time the appeal is filed that it is not taken for the purpose of delay and—when evidence has been suppressed, excluded, or returned—that the evidence is substantial proof of a fact material in the proceedings. If the defendant has been put in jeopardy before the decision is made, there may be no further prosecution. The court on review may make its determination of the issue raised as a matter of law. The government must file a notice of appeal within ten days after entry of the decision.

XII. LAND AND NATURAL RESOURCES

In 1964, about 13,000 acres, or 26 percent, of the total land area of American Samoa was under cultivation; the remainder was rugged mountain, heavily forested. Over 90 percent of all the land is held communally under Samoan customary law. Sixty-six parcels, consisting of less than 600 acres, were acquired by papalagis (outsiders) before 1900. Much of this land has been converted back to communal land.[18] The Instruments of Cession of 1900 and 1904 required the United States to respect and protect the rights of the Samoan people to their lands and other property, although the government was granted the power of eminent domain upon payment of fair compensation. The Constitution continues these safeguards. The High Court has held that protection of Samoan ownership of their lands is a permissible governmental objective and does not violate the equal protection clause of the U.S. Constitution.[19] Whether a U.S. court would agree has yet to be tested.[20]

In the early years of American occupation, the High Court sought to apply English property concepts to local patterns of land use. In recent years, however, the Court has acted diligently to protect communal land. Today, the court begins by presuming that since all land was once communal land, it is still communal. Any entity asserting that a given parcel is anything other than communal land must overcome this presumption.[21]

A. Land Tenure and Administration

The categories of land in American Samoa are freehold land, individually owned native land and family-owned communal land (Code, Title 37, Chapter 1). Freehold land may be alienated to a person who has less than one-half native blood, but communal land, which is theoretically under the control of the matai, may be alienated only to persons with more than one-half native blood and then only with the consent of the Governor. Communal land may be alienated to a person with any non-native blood only if the person was born in American Samoa, is descended from a Samoan family, lives with Samoans as a Samoan, has lived in American Samoa for more than five years, and has officially declared an intent to remain in American Samoa for life.

Individually owned native land is a hybrid concept created by the High Court. The Court's definition of individually owned land is that the individual cleared it on his or her own initiative, cultivated it, and occupied it.[22] Such land may be used by an individual without consultation with the family or approval by the matai but may not be alienated except in accordance with the requirements for alienating communal land. The term *native* in this context means full-blooded Samoan, including both Western Samoans and American Samoans.[23] A native owner of individual native land may provide for children who do not meet the land ownership requirements by establishing a trust for their use or the use of their issue (Code, Title 37, Chapter 2).

If the Governor approves, native land of sufficient size on which to erect a church or dwelling house for the pastor may be conveyed to an authorized, recognized religious society. This provision is consistent with the Samoan custom that permits a matai to assign a parcel of communal land for use by an assignee so long as the assignee exists and serves the matai. Service may consist, for example, of the provision of a religious program. Once the property ceases to be used for the particular purpose or the service is no longer being rendered, the property reverts to the family. Reconveyance and retransfer of the land may be made only to native Samoans and in the discretion and by approval of the Governor (Code, Title 37, Chapter 2).

In order to facilitate development of communally or individually owned native land, fixtures may be separated from the real estate on which they are attached. Family members or a majority of male members of the family over eighteen years of age may agree in writing with any person that any existing or later erected structure on such lands will not be part of the real estate but will remain separate and distinct therefrom, subject to ownership separate from the land and removal by the owner of the structure. The agreement must be filed with the territorial registrar. The person or persons who must execute any such agreement are specified and public notice given. If an objection is filed, the matter is set down for hearing as a civil matter in the High Court. At trial, the Court must find that the requirements of law have been met; that the separation agreement will not unduly interfere with the use of lands by the family, if it has such right of use; and that the cost of the building is to be borne by the person who erects or erected it (Code, Title 37, Chapter 15).

The doctrine of adverse possession was first applied to land by the High Court. Early High Court judges used the concept to determine when a family had exercised sufficient rights over property previously cleared for use by another family to justify the Court's recognition of title in the family that now exercised control of the land. The Code now requires actual, open, notorious, hostile, exclusive, and continuous occupancy of freehold land for thirty years for title to be conferred (Code, Title 37, Chapter 1).

The Governor may approve a lease of land to any person for a term not exceeding fifty-five years for any purpose except the working of minerals and cutting of timber. Such leases must be conditioned on occupation or cultivation of at least one-tenth of the area leased. Failure to comply with this condition or to occupy or cultivate the land for any period of five years after the approval date may result in forfeiture of the lease. Leases of ten years or longer are not effective until thirty days have expired without disapproval by concurrent resolution of the Fono. Leases of government property for longer than four years must contain a provision for altering the lease price or rentals to adjust for inflation. Leases of government property for longer than six years must also permit the rental to be renegotiated at three-year intervals to adjust for changed circumstances (unrelated to inflation) that increase or decrease the value of the leasehold. Changed circumstances might be governmental actions that increase or decrease the value of leases. Native land may be leased for school purposes for a renewable period of thirty years with approval of the Governor. The school must be subject to governmental supervision and must regularly offer instruction in the English language as the Governor directs (Code, Title 37, Chapter 2).

Swains Island became a part of American Samoa after the restrictions on alienation were enacted. The children of the present record title holder and their lineal descendants born in American Samoa are deemed to have inheritance rights with respect to any or all of Swains Island. An otherwise valid devise of any or all of the island to such a child or descendant does not violate the rules against alienation of native land (Code, Title 37, Chapter 2).

B. Customary Land Tenure[24]

Traditional Samoan society is based on intertwined communal landowning and social obligations. The system of communal property ownership provides the basis of and justification for the continued existence of the matai system, although the matai and communal land systems are no longer as inextricably linked as they are in Western Samoa. Each family, which may consist of several clans, has a head or matai who has considerable powers of control over family land and who also wields substantial political power and power over the lives of family members who live according to Samoan custom. Although the inevitable effect of U.S. colonialism has been to alter the power and responsibilities of the matais, the matai structure remains significant. Samoan custom permits the matai to distribute family land to family members and outsiders who serve the matai. However, alienation of customarily held land is strictly regulated by statute (Code, Title 37, Chapter 2; **see XII, A Land Tenure and Administration**).

Matai titles are bestowed by a family on the family member considered best capable of providing leadership and maintaining family harmony. The method by which a person becomes and remains a matai has been institutionalized by statute (Code, Title 1, Chapter 4). The only matais recognized by law are those registered before January 1, 1969, and their lawfully chosen successors. To be a matai, a person must be at least one-half Samoan, have been born on American Samoa soil (with exceptions for families traveling abroad or temporarily resident elsewhere at the time of a birth), be chosen by the family for the title, and live with Samoans as a Samoan. Women may be matais. A daughter who otherwise qualified could become matai in preference to a grandson. To claim or object to succession to a matai title, a person must have resided in American Samoa for one calendar year immediately preceding the date of the claim or objection or be absent from American Samoa for one of several permitted reasons, such as education or missionary work.

Disputed claims of succession to titles are heard and determined by the High Court. The Code lists the following five factors that the Court must consider:

1. the best hereditary right;
2. the wish of the majority or plurality of customary family clans;
3. the forcefulness, character, and personality of the persons under consideration;
4. the person's knowledge of Samoan customs;
5. the value of the holder of the title to the family, village, and country.

To these, the High Court has added the personal demeanor, presence of mind, clarity, speed and correctness of answers, candidness, ability to withstand cross-examination, education, self-confidence, and speech and behavior of the candidate.[25] In the event of a dispute, a panel of the trial division of the High Court consisting of four associate judges and either the Chief Justice or Associate Justice, who has a vote only in the event of a tie among the associate judges.

C. Government Taking of Land

Both the United States and American Samoa governments may acquire native land for governmental purposes if fair compensation is paid to those deprived of their property by the taking (Constitution, Article I). Title vests in fee simple and does not revert to the original owner if the government fails to use the property for the purpose for which it was taken.[26] When the government wants to acquire any property interest, it files a petition in the High Court, Trial Division, and may file a declaration that the lands or other property rights sought are taken for the use of the government, depositing in the Court the amount of estimated compensation stated in the declaration. The Court's role is restricted to reviewing the amount of compensation after compulsory arbitration has taken place (Code, Title 37, Chapter 20).

XIII. Persons and Entities

The age of majority in American Samoa for males and females is eighteen years (Code, Title 45, Chapter 1).

The law relating to corporations is in Title 30 of the Code. Three or more persons of full age, at least two-thirds of whom must be U.S. nationals and at least one an American Samoan resident, may form a corporation by adopting articles of incorporation containing information about the corporation. A resident or foreign corporation may not buy or acquire any interest in land unless the Governor approves the transaction.

Any three or more adults, a majority of whom are U.S. nationals, may incorporate to establish a charitable institution.

XIV. Family Law

A. Marriage

Provisions relating to marriage, annulment, and divorce are in Title 42 of the Code. To enter into a valid marriage contract, the parties must not be related to each other nearer than the fourth degree of consanguinity. A male must be at least eighteen years old, and a female must be at least fourteen years old or have the consent of one parent or her guardian. Neither party may have a lawful spouse living at the time of marriage. A marriage ceremony must be performed by a minister of any Christian religion registered as such with the Registrar of Vital Statistics, or by an associate judge, or the Chief Justice or Associate Justice. Customary marriages are not recognized by the Code.

B. Divorce, Separation, and Annulment

The High Court may annul any illegally contracted marriage. It may dissolve a marriage contract and grant a decree of divorce or judicial separation only for adultery, habitual cruelty, or ill usage; desertion for six months or more; a sentence to imprisonment for ten or more years or for life; or voluntary continuous separation for five years or more. One party to the action must be a bona fide and continuous resident of American Samoa for at least one year preceding the commencement of the action. The Court must dismiss a petition if it finds the petitioner

1. has failed to prove the charge alleged;
2. is found to have been, during the marriage, an accessory to or to have connived with the respondent in the offense alleged;
3. is guilty of collusion with the respondent in presenting the petition or in the trial of the action or proceeding;
4. is guilty of any of the grounds for divorce or separation; or
5. has condoned the act or acts complained of in the petition.

Condonation may be presumed by the voluntary cohabitation of the parties with the knowledge of the offense charged.

When a decree for divorce, separation, or annulment is granted, the Court may also order maintenance for the other party; divide the property of either or both of the parties as it deems fair and proper; make orders for the custody, care, maintenance, and support of minor children of the parties; and restore to the woman the name she used before the marriage. American Samoa has adopted the Uniform Reciprocal Enforcement of Support Act, Title 42, Chapter 4, to improve the enforcement of duties for support of children.

C. Custody

The High Court, Trial Division, has sole jurisdiction to appoint a guardian of the person and/or estate of a minor or a person who is mentally or physically incompetent to manage his or her own property. Under Title 40 of the Code, such a guardian must be age twenty-one or older, a resident of American Samoa, and mentally competent to execute the duties of such trust.

D. Adoption

Any person at least twenty-one years of age or a minor, with High Court approval, may, under Title 45 of the Code, petition the court to decree an adoption. Any person under the age of eighteen who is legally available for adoption may be adopted, and a person between the ages of eighteen and twenty-one may be adopted on Court approval. The legal effect of a final decree of adoption is that the adoptive parent and adopted child have toward each other the legal relation of parent and child, including the rights of inheritance from each other. They also have all the rights and are subject to all the duties as if the child were born in lawful wedlock to the petitioner. The natural parents are divested of all legal rights and obligations with respect to the child, and the adopted child is free from all legal obligations of obedience and maintenance with respect to the natural parents. The Court will not grant adoption where it is the apparent purpose of the adoption to increase the amount of social security payments to the proposed adoptive parents—usually the child's grandparents.

XV. Personal Property

American Samoa has not adopted legislation governing the inter vivos disposition of personal property. It must be assumed that the common law rules relating to the disposal of personal property apply in American Samoa, except for property the disposition of which is regulated by custom.

XVI. Wills and Succession

The statutory provisions relating to succession and the administration of estates (Code, Title 40) do not apply to communal property held under Samoan custom.

Any person of full age and sound mind may dispose by will of all noncommunal property, subject to the right of dower in the surviving spouse and subject to the statutory provisions restricting alienation of land. A will involving personal property with a total value of more than US$300 must be in writing signed by the testator or by some person in his or her presence and by his or her express direction. The signature must be witnessed by two competent persons who sign their names as attesting witnesses (Code, Title 40, Chapter 1).

Dower is one-third of all the legal or equitable estate in real or personal property possessed by a decedent at the time of death set apart to the surviving spouse in fee simple, subject to the statutory provisions restricting alienation of land. When the surviving spouse is named as a devisee or legatee in a will, it is presumed that the devise or legacy is in lieu of dower, but the presumption may be overcome by clear and explicit evidence of the testator's contrary intention. A surviving spouse may elect to take dower instead of property devised or bequeathed to the spouse. The election must be made by filing with the clerk of the High Court within ninety days after admission of the will to probate a written notice of intention to take dower.

The personal property of a person who dies without disposing of it by will is succeeded to and distributed, subject to the payment of debts and to dower, to the children of the intestate and such persons as legally represent any deceased children and, in the absence of a surviving spouse, children, or legal representative of any deceased children, to the intestate's next of kin. Distribution of real property belonging to an intestate is distributed by lineal descent forever to the intestate's issue. If there are no lineal descendants, distribution goes first to the brothers and sisters of the intestate or their issue *per stirpes*; next, to the father if living and, if not, to the mother, if living; and finally, when none of the above rules vest the real property in an heir, to the surviving spouse. Where no one is capable of succeeding to the real or personal property of an intestate, that property escheats to the government (Code, Title 40, Chapter 2).

XVII. Contracts

The general common law rules relating to contract apply, with some statutory modifications contained in Title 27 of the Code. American Samoa has adopted special rules regarding warranty coverage of consumer goods and the return of defective goods or specially ordered goods that do not conform to the special order to an automobile dealer or retailer of major appliances when such goods are covered by a warranty (Code, Title 27, Chapter 7).

No merchant, trader, storekeeper, or other person may sell goods to a Samoan on credit for more than the current cash selling price of like goods at the place where the credit transaction took place, but a Samoan may agree in writing to pay interest of not more than 8 percent per year on overdue accounts growing out of credit transactions (Code, Title 27, Chapter 15).

XVIII. Commercial Law

American Samoa has not adopted the Uniform Commercial Code, which is in force in most states and territories of the United States. The currency of the United States at its face value is the only legal tender in American Samoa for the payment of public and private debts and obligations. All checks drawn upon the Treasurer by the government are negotiable at par, and it is illegal to charge a fee for cashing an American Samoa government check. American Samoa has, in Title 27 of the Code, adopted the Uniform Negotiable Instruments Law as proposed by the U.S. National Conference of Commissioners on Uniform State Laws and as construed by a majority of the courts in the United States regarding certain commercial transactions. U.S. bankruptcy law applies in American Samoa. Provisions relating to interest on loans are contained in Title 28 of the Code.

A foreign company desiring to do business in American Samoa must file with the Treasurer its articles of incorporation, a request for a permit to transact business in American Samoa, and a statement verified on oath by the head and secretary of the corporation of the information required in the articles of a newly formed Samoan corporation. The application must also contain a statement subscribed and sworn to by at least two of the corporation's principal officers, setting forth certain facts about the corporation. A permit, when issued, states specifically the business the corporation may transact; it may transact no business in American Samoa other than that specified. Criminal penalties are provided for violation by a foreign corporation of the sections enumerated in its permit or by an agent, officer, or employee who transacts business for a foreign corporation, knowing it does not have a valid permit.

XIX. TORTS

American Samoa follows the general principles of tort law applicable in the United States. It has adopted the doctrine of comparative negligence and permits a wrongful death action to be brought on behalf of the surviving spouse, parents, children, or other next of kin of a decedent. A deceased's legal representative may recover on behalf of the estate the reasonable expenses of the deceased's last illness and burial. Under the Code, Title 43, Chapter 50; the court may give as damages fair and just compensation, with reference to the pecuniary injury and loss of love and affection, including the following:

1. loss of society, companionship, comfort, consortium, or protection;
2. loss of marital care, attention, advice, or counsel;
3. loss of parental care, training, guidance, or education, suffered as a result of the death of the person by the surviving spouse, children, father, mother, or by a person wholly or partly dependent upon the deceased person.

Pecuniary injury means losses for which a monetary amount can be readily attached and does not include loss of consortium and damages suffered by the deceased.[27] The damages awarded are allocated to the persons entitled to them and do not, apart from the reasonable expenses of last illness and burial, become a part of the estate of the deceased.

The American Samoa government has waived some of its sovereign immunity to permit suit against it to the same extent as a private individual under like circumstances. Excluded from the waiver provisions are the following:

1. liability for prejudgment interest and for punitive damages in most cases;
2. claims based on the act or omission of a governmental employee exercising due care in the execution of the law;
3. claims based on the exercise or failure of an officer or employee to exercise a discretionary function or duty, whether or not the discretion is abused;
4. claims regarding the assessment or collection of any tax or customs duty or the detention of any goods or merchandise;
5. claims for which there is a remedy elsewhere in the laws of the government;
6. claims arising out of assault, battery, false imprisonment, false arrest, malicious prosecution, abuse of process, libel, slander, misrepresentation, deceit, or interference with contract rights; and
7. claims arising in a foreign country.

The government's sovereign immunity has been limited so as to permit suit for action or inaction at the operational level but not at the executive or administrative level of government (Code, Title 43, Chapter 12). The government may also be liable when it is the plaintiff's landlord and breaches a duty owed to the plaintiff in the government's proprietary capacity.[28]

Trespass to timber is a statutorily created tort that permits an award of treble damages to the landowner or village against a person who damages trees on land of another person; on the street or highway fronting another person's house or a village; on cultivated grounds; or on the common public grounds of a village without lawful authority or permission (Code, Title 43, Chapter 50).

American Samoa has codified its law of defamation at Title 43, Chapter 52. Four grounds of privilege are recognized for publications made in the following circumstances:

1. in the proper discharge of an official duty;
2. in any legislative or judicial proceeding or other official proceeding authorized by law;
3. in a communication without malice to an interested person by one who is also interested or by one who may have a reasonable ground for supposing the motive for the communication innocent or who is requested by the person interested to give the information; and
4. by a fair and true report without malice of a judicial, legislative, or other public official proceeding or of anything said in the course thereof.

Public media facility owners and operators who make those facilities available to any person, whether a candidate for public office or any other person, for discussion of controversial or other subjects, in the absence of proof of malice are exempted from liability. An owner, operator, or broadcaster is not relieved from liability where the broadcast is prepared or made in the course of the person's employment.

A newspaper, periodical, or radio or television station must be given a week to correct defamatory matter before a civil action for defamation may be commenced. A retraction is the only acceptable means of correction where the true facts are, with reasonable diligence, ascertainable with certainty. Otherwise the publication of the libeled person's statement of the facts—or so much thereof as is not libelous of another, scurrilous, or otherwise improper for publication—constitutes a correction. If it appears upon trial that the publication was made under an honest mistake or misapprehension, then a correction published in a timely fashion without comment in a position and type as prominent as the alleged libel or broadcast at the same time of day as the broadcast complained of and of equal duration shall constitute a defense against the recovery of any damages except actual damages. It is also competent and material in mitigation of actual damages to the extent the correction published does in fact mitigate them.

XX. Labor Law

Labor legislation is contained in Title 32 of the Code. American Samoa policy is that the right to work cannot be denied or abridged because of membership or nonmembership in a labor organization. Any practice that makes membership or nonmembership in or support or nonsupport of a labor organization a condition of employment is illegal and void. Also illegal and void are compulsory fees, dues, or other charges to a labor organization as a condition of employment. Violations by an employer or labor organization are punishable by criminal sanctions and give rise to claims for the actual damages sustained by a person injured by a violation or to injunctive relief.

American Samoa maintains a wage and hours board to set minimum wages payable to employees and maximum hours employees may be employed without payment of overtime compensation.

Every employer of more than two employees in nonhazardous occupations is liable to pay compensation, according to a schedule, for injury to or death of an employee arising out of and in the course of employment. Liability attaches without regard to fault as to cause of the injury or death, except where an injury is occasioned by intoxication or willful intention to injure or kill the worker or another. Each employer liable to pay compensation under the scheme must carry workers' compensation insurance. The workers' compensation scheme is an exclusive remedy that replaces an employer's liability to an employee and others entitled to recover damages from the employer at law or in admiralty. Only if an employer cannot secure payment of compensation may the employee bring an action at law or in admiralty against the employer, who may not raise as defenses the fellow servant rule, assumption of risk, or contributory negligence. The employer is liable to furnish medical, surgical, and nursing care and any necessary medical apparatus if no other provision is made and to pay compensation to a surviving spouse and children if the employee dies.

A workers' compensation commission has been created to administer the scheme. The commissioner is not bound by common law or statutory rules of evidence or by technical or formal rules of procedure. A party aggrieved by the decision may apply to the High Court to suspend or set aside an order that violates applicable constitutional or statutory provisions; is in excess of the commissioner's authority; is made on unlawful procedure; is affected by other error of law; is clearly erroneous in view of the reliable, probative, and substantial evidence in the whole record; or is arbitrary, capricious, or characterized by abuse of discretion.[29]

An injured employee who accepts compensation from the employer may still maintain an action against a third party. If compensation is accepted, a suit not filed within six months of the award operates as an assignment of an employee's rights to recover damages against a third party. Payment where the employee is deceased also operates as an assignment of all rights of the legal representative of the deceased employee to recover damages against the third party. The employer may retain attorney's fees, cost of benefits furnished, amounts paid as compensation, present value of amounts payable in future as compensation, and one-fifth of any excess. The remaining excess must be paid to the individual entitled to compensation or that person's legal representative.

XXI. INDUSTRIAL AND INTELLECTUAL PROPERTY RIGHTS

American Samoa provides trademark protection for registered prints, labels, trademarks, or trade names (Code, Title 27, Chapter 3). American Samoa is covered by the treaties entered into by the United States concerning copyright and patent law and by federal copyright and patent legislation.

XXII. LEGAL EDUCATION AND PROFESSION

American Samoa has no law school. Most of its lawyers receive their legal education in law schools in the United States. The Chief Justice is responsible for establishing admission rules and rules of conduct for the legal profession.

XXIII. RESEARCH GUIDE

American Samoa's Constitution and statutes can be found in the *American Samoa Annotated Code*, published since 1981 and updated by the Book Publishing Company of Seattle. High

Court cases are published in the *American Samoa Reporter*, 1st and 2d series (ASR and ASR 2d) (the latter for post-1983 cases) by the High Court of American Samoa in Pago Pago. Certain relevant decisions of U.S. courts appear in the *Federal Supplement* (F. Supp.) for District Court cases; *Federal Report*, 2d series (F.2d) for Court of Appeals cases; and *United States Reports* (U.S.) for U.S. Supreme Court cases.

Laughlin, S. "The Application of the Constitution in United States Territories: American Samoa, A Case Study," 2 *Univ. of Hawaii Law Rev.* 337 (1980–1981).

———. "The Constitutional Structure of the Courts of the United States Territories: the Case of American Samoa," 13 *Univ. of Hawaii Law Rev.* 379 (1991).

———. "United States Government Policy and Social Stratification in American Samoa," 53 *Oceania* 29 (1982–1983).

Liebowitz, A. H. "American Samoa: Decline of a Culture," 10 *California Western J. of International Law.* 220 (1989).

Lutuli, A. P., and N. J. Stewart. "A Chiefly System in Twentieth-Century America: Legal Aspects of the Matai and Land Tenure Systems in the Territory of American Samoa," 4 *Georgia J. International & Comparative Law.* 388 (1973).

McBride, M. H. "The Application of the American Constitution to American Samoa," 9 *J. of International Law & Economics.* 325 (1975).

McKibben, L. A. "The Political Relationship Between the United States and Pacific Islands Entities," 11 *Harvard International Law J.* 257 (1990).

Schwartz, R. "The Status of American Samoa," 2 *Samoan Pacific Law J.* 111 (1974).

Stewart, W. J. "Land Tenure in American Samoa," 10 *Hawaii Bar J.* 52 (1973–74).

Tagupa, W. E. H. "Judicial Intervention in Matai Title Succession Disputes in American Samoa," 54 *Oceania* 23 (1983–84).

Tiffany, S. "The Cognatic Descent Groups of Contemporary Samoa," 1 *MAN* (new series) 430 (1975).

Tiffany, W. "The Applicability of Western Judicial Concepts to Polynesian Land Disputes: High Court Use of the Adverse Possession Principle in American Samoa," 7 *Samoan Pacific Law J.* 75 (1981).

———. "High Court Influences on Land Tenure Patterns in American Samoa," 49 *Oceania* 258 (1979).

———. "The Role of the High Court in Matai Succession Disputes in American Samoa," 5 *Samoan Pacific Law J.* 11 (1979).

Tuiteleleapaga, N. "The Criminal Offender: Alternatives to Prison Sentencing," 2 (3/4) *Samoan Pacific Law J.* 171 (1974).

17. The Federated States of Micronesia

JEAN G. ZORN

I. Dateline

3000–500 B.C. Islands collectively referred to as Micronesia settled by people who probably originated in Southeast Asia and Malaysia.
1565 Micronesia claimed by Spain.
1800s Micronesia visited by traders, whalers, and missionaries from various European countries, Japan, the United States, and Russia. Germany, in particular, disputes Spain's territorial claims to Micronesia.
1870 Impelled by the presence of an American warship, some Ponapean chiefs sign a treaty permitting missionaries to operate on their island and agreeing to alienate land in fee simple to foreigners.
1885 Dispute between Spain and Germany submitted to Pope Leo XIII, who affirms Spain's dominion over most of Micronesia but permits Germany to continue to use other ports in Micronesia as trading stations.
1899 Spain sells its Micronesian interests to Germany.
1914 Japan takes the territory from Germany.
1920 The League of Nations mandates Micronesia to Japan as class C mandate.
1944 U.S. forces capture Micronesia from Japanese. U.S. Navy administers islands under military rule.
1947 United Nations designates all Micronesian islands except Guam as Trust Territory of the Pacific Islands, a "strategic trust" under administration of United States.
1951 Administrative authority over Trust Territory transferred by U.S. president from U.S. Navy to Department of Interior.
1965 By order of U.S. Secretary of Interior, Congress of Micronesia, an elected bicameral body, established as legislature for Trust Territory. At first intended as advisory body, it later is granted limited legislative powers.
1967 Congress of Micronesia begins to formulate policies for the post-Trusteeship status of Micronesia, as well as for future relations of Micronesia with United States, and creates a commission to negotiate with United States for independence.
1969 Negotiations on change of status begin in October.
1975 Between July and November, representatives from each of the six districts of Trust Territory (Ponape, Truk, Yap, the Marianas, Palau, and the Marshalls) meet in constitutional convention to draft Constitution for an independent Micronesia. Representatives attend from each district, even though Marianas and Marshalls have already determined to seek separate political status. Draft Constitution is completed November 8.

1977	By vote of Congress of Micronesia, Kusiaie, formerly part of Ponape, becomes separate district under the name Kosrae.
1978	In April at a meeting in Hawaii, United States and representatives of Congress of Micronesia, Palau, and Marshalls agree to the Hilo Principles, which establish free association as guiding principle for future relationship between United States and Micronesia. The FSM Constitution ratified in July 12 referendum by majority vote in Yap, Ponape (which would adopt Pohnpei as the official spelling of its name as a state), Truk (now Chuuk), and Kosrae; these states form Federated States of Micronesia.
1979	Elections held in Ponape (now officially Pohnpei), Yap, Truk (now Chuuk), and Kosrae in March to choose members of new Congress of the Federated States of Micronesia, which convenes May 10, effective date of FSM Constitution. U.S. Secretary of Interior promulgates Secretarial Order No. 3039, providing for transition of governmental powers and functions from Trust Territory Administrative Authority to federal and state governments of FSM.
1981	FSM Supreme Court comes into existence May 5.
1982	Representatives of governments of United States, FSM, Marshall Islands, and Palau sign Compacts of Free Association on October 1.
1983	Compact approved by overall majority vote of people of FSM in June 21 plebiscite observed (but not supervised) by the United Nations. Three of FSM's four state legislatures (Pohnpei against) then approve the compact.
1985–1986	Compacts approved by a Joint Resolution of U.S. Congress in December 1985 and signed by U.S. President on January 14, 1986. Secretarial Order No. 3039 ceases to be applicable, as do earlier U.S. executive and secretarial orders.
1986	The United Nations Trusteeship Council approves Compact of Free Association on May 26, by vote of 3 to 1. On November 3 (Independence Day), U.S. president by proclamation declares Trust Territory dissolved, and President of the FSM by proclamation declares independence of FSM.
1987	Office of High Commissioner for Trust Territory closed on July 10.
1989	FSM voters approve establishment of constitutional convention to consider revising or amending FSM Constitution.
1990	On December 22, by vote of 14 to 1, the United Nations Security Council votes to ratify compacts of the FSM and the Marshalls, thereby dissolving Trusteeship. The FSM's status as an independent nation will now be internationally recognized.
1990–1991	In August 1990, constitutional convention proposes amendments to the Constitution. Four amendments approved by FSM voters in referendum on July 2, 1991.

II. Historical, Cultural, and Economic Survey

The Federated States of Micronesia (the FSM) is a federal republic in free association with the United States. The FSM is part of Micronesia, whose atolls and volcanic islands occupy about 3 million square miles in the western Pacific just north of the equator. The territory of the FSM consists of 607 islands, with an aggregate land area of approximately 271 square miles, spread across 30 square miles of ocean. Its population is estimated at 86,000. The climate is tropical, and mineral resources (other than phosphate) are few. The monetary economy is heavily dependent on foreign aid (primarily from the United States), remittances from Micronesians working abroad, and government employment. Much of the population continues to be engaged, either wholly or partly, in subsistence agriculture and fishing. In the FSM, two-thirds of those drawing wages or salaries are government employees, and the unemployment rate may be as high as 80 percent.

The people of the FSM are predominantly Micronesian; there has been some immigration, primarily from Polynesia. Micronesian societies tend to be matrilineal (although the island of Yap is patrilineal). Land tenure and rank derive in large part from lineage membership. Most societies are divided into royal and commoner lineages. Traditionally, chiefs of the royal lines had considerable (although not unlimited) authority over land allocation and use, services, and the titles and authority of lesser chiefs. Colonialism made significant changes to the traditional system. In some areas (most notably, Ponape), land ownership was individualized and succession to land made patrilineal. The powers of chiefs were circumscribed, their functions altered, and the means of chiefly succession sometimes changed. But membership in a matrilineage is still important; chiefly rank and authority still play significant roles; and traditional culture remains a major influence on the politics, economy, and life of Micronesia.

As a colony, the islands that are now the FSM were ruled successively by Spain, Germany, Japan, and the United States. The Micronesians benefited little from any of their colonial rulers. The Spanish focused primarily on conquest and religious conversion. Germany, which concentrated its attention on trade, copra production, and phosphate mines, paid Micronesian laborers very low wages for their work on the plantations and in the mines. Germany's major impact was its attempt to convert land tenure to titles that were similar to freehold and held by males. Japan's economic development of the islands was considerably more extensive than that of either of its predecessor administrations, but its economic policies, including the importation into Micronesia of a substantial population of Japanese and Okinawans, tended to favor expatriates over the indigenous population. Nevertheless, there was sufficient spill-over of economic benefits to Micronesians during the Japanese administration for this to be remembered as a time of relative economic prosperity.

The United States has been primarily interested in Micronesia as a Pacific military installation. Of the eleven trusteeships established under United Nations jurisdiction after World War II, this was the only one designated a "strategic trust" and jointly supervised by the Security and Trusteeship Councils.[1] Especially in the early years of American occupation, economic development of the islands tended to occur, where it occurred at all, as on offshoot of U.S. military needs, rather than as an end in itself. Beginning in the 1960s, the United States introduced an intensive program of political development following an American model and made substantial financial contributions to Micronesia. These contributions tended to be as wages for government employment and as welfare payments, rather than for economic development projects, however, so they have not led to significant economic growth. Micronesia was closed to U.S. private investment until the mid-1960s and to third-country investment until the mid-1970s.

In 1969, the Congress of Micronesia, a locally elected body, began negotiations with the United States for termination of the Trusteeship. In 1975, the Congress established a constitutional convention to draft a constitution for an independent Micronesia. In both the drafting of the Constitution and the negotiations for termination of the Trusteeship, the two issues of paramount political concern in Micronesia were the future relationship of the islands to the United States and the relations of the people of the FSM to one another.[2] By the end of 1975, the constitutional convention had produced the document that eventually became the Constitution of the Federated States of Micronesia. In 1978, it was ratified by the four Trust Territory districts (Ponape [Pohnpei], Kosrae, Yap, and Truk [Chuuk]) that thereby became the four states of the FSM. The Constitution did not receive the approval of majorities in Palau and the Marshalls, and these districts would therefore not become part of the FSM. The Northern Marianas, having earlier determined to become a commonwealth of the United States, did not participate in the referendum.

Negotiations to end the Trusteeship took longer. The Compact of Free Association, ending the FSM's colonial status, was not approved by all parties until 1986. The major question prolonging negotiations for an end to the Trusteeship was the form that future relations between Micronesia and the United States should take. Although many Micronesians desired full political independence, they also recognized that economic underdevelopment (in large part caused by U.S. Trusteeship policies) would require continuing financial reliance on the United States. Nor was the United States willing entirely to sever its relationship with Micronesia, believing that the national security interests of the United States necessitated a continuing presence.

The Compact of Free Association between the United States and the FSM limits the FSM's authority over defense and international relations in exchange for a U.S. promise of fifteen years of economic support (**see III, E Treaties; VI International Obligations**). The compact's guarantee of a continuing U.S. role in FSM affairs caused some nations to doubt that the FSM had achieved the status of a fully independent entity. Although the United Nations Trusteeship Council voted in 1986 to dissolve the Trust Territory, the Security Council, whose approval is also needed to end a "strategic trust," did not formally take up the matter until 1990. In the interim, although all the Pacific states, as well as a number of other nations, recognized the FSM's independence, a number of countries (including the United Kingdom and the Soviet Union) did not. However, with the December 22, 1990, vote of the Security Council, the FSM's status as an independent state is now internationally accepted.

At the same time that negotiations with the United States for an end to the Trusteeship were proceeding, the peoples of Micronesia were discussing among themselves whether they would form one or several nations and what the governmental structure of each nation would be. The impetus toward separatism—or at least federalism—had several causes. The cultural diversity of the peoples of Micronesia and the vast geographical distances separating the islands militated against the creation of a unitary state. Large states were not characteristic of precolonial Micronesia. Smaller politics were preferred. Colonialsim also had an influence. The differential treatment that the districts had received from the United States under the Trusteeship and were likely to receive after independence decreased any sense of common purpose. Most importantly, Micronesia's long experience of authoritarian colonial rule has left its peoples with a deep distrust of centralized power and a consequent bias in favor of decentralization. As a result, the former Trusteeship has divided itself into four self-governing nations or commonwealths—the Republics of the Marshall Islands and of Palau, the Commonwealth of the Northern Marianas, and the Federated States of Micronesia—with varying kinds of relationships to the United States.

The internal governmental structure of the FSM also reflects this distrust of centralism. The FSM Constitution establishes a federal system of sovereign states. The FSM comprises those districts of the Trust Territory that ratified the Constitution by the required vote of a majority of the people residing in that district (FSM Constitution, Article I, Section 1). The FSM Constitution provides, at Article VIII, Section 1, that the national government exercise only those powers that are expressly delegated to it by the Constitution or are "of such an indisputably national character as to be beyond the power of a state to control." Some of the national government's express powers (such as foreign affairs and defense) are exclusive to the national government, other express powers (such as public welfare) are shared concurrently with the states, and all powers not expressly delegated or necessary to the national government reside exclusively in the states (FSM Constitution, Article VIII and Article IX, Sections 2 and 3).

The people and governments of the FSM continue to seek the proper balance of powers and responsibility between the national government and the states. A second constitutional convention was convened from July to August 1990. Many of the convention's proposed amendments to the Constitution would have shifted more power to the states. Examples of such proposals were that the states receive half of governmental revenues from fishing and all from taxes on fuel, that jurisdiction over land matters be taken from the FSM Supreme Court, that the state courts be given concurrent jurisdiction in diversity cases, and that states have exclusive authority over permits for foreign investment in their territories. The voters, in a referendum on July 22, 1991, did not adopt any of these proposals. Of the twenty-six proposals submitted to popular vote, only four were adopted. These will give the states greater jurisdiction in criminal matters (see **X Criminal Law**) and more authority over health and education (see **IX Welfare Law**). The other amendments set limits on leasing land to noncitizens (**XII Land and Natural Resources Law**) and instruct the FSM Supreme Court to follow FSM precedents in interpreting the Constitution (see **III, A FSM Constitution**).

III. Sources of Law

A. FSM Constitution[3]

The FSM Constitution was meant to be self-executing and to take effect one year after its ratification on July 12, 1978, unless the Congress of Micronesia specified an earlier date. The FSM Congress was elected in March 1979 and declared the Constitution effective on May 10, 1979, less than twelve months after ratification. The Constitution is, by its terms, the supreme law of the Federated States of Micronesia. Any act of the government in conflict with the Constitution is invalid to the extent of the conflict (Article II, Section 1). The Constitution's supremacy is based, as stated in its preamble, on the premise that the Constitution was adopted by the people of Micronesia in whom "inherent sovereignty" resides. The Constitution recognizes other sources of law—state constitutions, legislation (local, state, and national), and treaties, "the traditions of the people of the Federated States of Micronesia" (Article V, Section 2), the decisional law of Micronesian courts (common law), and certain statutes of the Trust Territory—but these are valid only to the extent that they do not conflict with the Constitution.[4]

The FSM Supreme Court has held that the Constitution gives to it the power to review laws, treaties, and other acts of the FSM government, and to declare invalid those that conflict with the FSM Constitution.[5] In exercising its power of judicial review, the Court interprets the Constitution in accordance with the Judicial Guidance Clause (FSM Constitution, Article XI, Section 11), which, as initially adopted, required courts to conform their decisions to the provisions of the Constitution itself, to the customs and traditions of Micronesia, and to the social and geographical configuration of the FSM. In 1991, the Judicial Guidance Clause was amended to add that the courts must also consult and apply FSM sources. Even before the 1991 amendments, the FSM Supreme Court had held that interpretations by U.S. courts of similar provisions in the U.S. Constitution are not binding on the FSM courts but may be persuasive if the provisions in the two constitutions are substantially similar, the decisions of the U.S.

courts were issued before adoption of the FSM Constitution, and the decisions are in accord with Micronesian customs and conditions.[6]

Amendments to the FSM Constitution may be proposed by a constitutional convention, by popular initiative, or by Congress. Proposed amendments are submitted to the electorate and become part of the Constitution if approved by 75 percent of votes cast in at least three of the four states. The Constitution is subject to revision every ten years, when Congress must submit to the voters the question of whether to have a convention to amend or revise the Constitution. If a majority of those voting approve the calling of a convention, then delegates must be selected no later than the next regular election (Article XIV, Sections 1 and 2). As this provision requires, the question was submitted to the voters in 1989; more than 70 percent of those voting were in favor of a convention, which was called for July 1990. On July 2, 1991, voters approved four amendments (see II Historical, Cultural, and Economic Survey). One of the proposals that was not approved by a sufficient margin would have changed from seventy-five percent to 50 percent the vote required to adopt a proposed amendment.

B. State Constitutions

The FSM Constitution provides at Article VII, Section 2, that "each state shall have a democratic constitution."[7] In anticipation of this provision, the states enacted charters that were approved by the Congress of Micronesia and the Trust Territory High Commissioner (who made numerous amendments) in 1977 and 1978. At independence, these charters became the states' interim constitutions, until new constitutions could be drafted and ratified. All four states have now adopted constitutions.

Each state constitution is by its terms the supreme law of that state (subject only to the FSM Constitution). The constitutions of Yap (at Article I) and Pohnpei (at Article 2), for example, each provide that it is the supreme law of the state and that any act of the state government in conflict with it is invalid to the extent of the conflict. The power of State Courts to review state and local legislation and to overturn those that violate the state or FSM constitutions is not expressly set forth in the state constitutions, but this power is implicit in their supremacy clauses. It is also implicit in their judicial guidance clauses, such as that in Article 10 of the Pohnpei Constitution, which provides that decisions of the State Courts must be consistent with the Pohnpei Constitution and with "the concepts of justice of the people of Pohnpei." The Pohnpei Constitution provides that no appeal on any matter relating to the Pohnpei Constitution, to Pohnpei law, customs, or traditions may be taken to any court other than the Pohnpei Supreme Court, a provision that might conflict with the FSM Constitution if it were read to prohibit appeals from the Pohnpei Supreme Court.

Unlike the FSM Constitution, which exists only in English, a number of the state constitutions exist both in an English and a local language version. This chapter is based on the English-language versions of the state constitutions, but because many concepts are impossible to translate precisely into English, there are likely to be significant differences between what the state constitutions are reported here as providing and the sense that local people have of what those constitutions provide.

Each state constitution provides that amendments must be submitted to the people for approval. The Yap Constitution, for example, states at Article X that approval of proposed amendments is by a majority of votes cast in an election in which all registered voters may participate. Amendments to the Yap Constitution may be proposed by an initiative signed by 25 percent of registered voters or by a resolution of 75 percent of the legislature. At least every ten years, the voters must decide whether to hold a constitutional convention. The Yap Constitution went into effect in 1982, so voters may be asked to approve a constitutional convention in 1992.

C. National Legislation

The legislative power of the national government is vested by Article IX of the FSM Constitution in the Congress of the Federated States. The scope of Congress' law-making authority is limited by the constitutional requirement that the national government has only those powers that are expressly delegated to it by the Constitution or that are inherently national in character. By Article IX, Section 2, as amended in 1991, Congress is vested with the following expressly delegated powers, exclusive of the states:

1. to provide for the national defense;
2. to ratify treaties;
3. to regulate immigration, nationalization, and citizenship;
4. to impose duties and tariffs;
5. to impose income taxes;
6. to issue and regulate currency;
7. to regulate banking, foreign and interstate commerce, insurance, bankruptcy, and patents and copyrights;
8. to regulate navigation and shipping;
9. to establish usury limits;
10. to provide for a postal system;
11. to acquire and govern new territory;
12. to govern the national capital area;
13. to regulate maritime resources (except that states have the power over maritime resources within 12 miles of island baselines);
14. to regulate the national public service;
15. to impeach and remove the President, Vice President, and Supreme Court justices;
16. to define and prescribe penalties for national crimes; and
17. to override a presidential veto by not less than a three-fourths vote of all state delegations.

Congress and the states have concurrent power in the following areas:

1. appropriating public funds;
2. borrowing money on public credit;
3. promoting education and health; and
4. establishing systems of social security and public welfare.

(For limits on Congress' powers over education and health, see **X Welfare Law**.)

All other legislative powers are reserved exclusively to the states.

The legislation of the FSM has been codified. The Revised Code (cited here as FSM Code or the Code) was published in 1982, and a supplement was published in 1987. All acts that are in the Code are cited here by title and sometimes by section number.

D. State and Local Legislation

The states, as sovereign entities, may provide for themselves and for local bodies within their boundaries the democratic forms of government they choose. The states may make laws on all matters other than those exclusively delegated to the national government, subject only to the national and state constitutions. The FSM Supreme Court has held that state legislation is an act of the government, and thus invalid if in conflict with the FSM Constitution.[8] Certain states have codified their laws. Yap, for example, has published a Yap State Code (sometimes referred to here as YSC).

E. Treaties

Among the express powers delegated exclusively to the national government is the power to make and ratify treaties (FSM Constitution, Article IX, Section 2; Article X, Section 2). Treaties normally are not major sources of law. In the FSM's situation, however, its treaty with the United States, the Compact of Free Association, has a major impact on the nation and on its laws. By Section 311 of the compact, the United States has assumed "full authority and responsibility for security and defense matters in or relating to . . . the Federated States of Micronesia." This authority includes the U.S. obligation to defend the FSM "from attack or threats thereof as the United States and its citizens are defended" and the option of the United States to "establish and use military areas and facilities" in the FSM. Further, in the conduct of its foreign relations, the FSM must consult with the United States (Compact, Section 123). In return, the United States is obliged to serve as the FSM's primary source of financial support for fifteen years; the compact establishes the nature and amount of financial and program assistance that the United States will provide to the FSM.

The compact may be terminated by mutual agreement; it may also be terminated unilaterally—if by the United States, upon six months' notice and if by the FSM, after a plebiscite and upon three months' notice (Compact, Sections 442 and 443). Upon termination, however, the authority of the United States over the FSM's security and defense would continue, as would the requirement that the United States provide financial assistance to the FSM (Compact, Sections 451 and 452). (For a discussion of other treaties and international obligations of the FSM, **see VI International Obligations**).

F. Customary Law

The customary norms and dispute settlement processes of the peoples of Micronesia are the earliest and most enduring sources of law in the FSM, but the position of custom as a source of law in the FSM's new legal system is ambiguous. On the one hand, the constitutions and statutes establish a governmental structure and a system of norms, values, and processes that depart significantly from customary law. On the other hand, both national and state constitutions expressly recognize custom as a source of decisional law (**see III, H Common Law**). Custom is also intended to be a source of legislation. The FSM Constitution provides at Article V, Section 2, that the traditions of the people of the FSM may be protected by statute. The Pohnpei state Constitution contains a similar provision at Article 5, Section 2, and the Yap Constitution provides at Article XV, Section 1 that the legislature must codify traditional law within a reasonable time. The Yap legislature has yet to do this, however.

G. Trust Territory Laws

The FSM and state constitutions provide that statutes of the Trust Territory, which are not amended or repealed, continue in effect to the extent that they are consistent with the Constitution (FSM Constitution, Article XV, Section 1; Yap Constitution, Article XV, Section 2).

Some Trust Territory statutes continued only as instructions to the Trust Territory High Court and only for so long as it continued to operate, but they have no application to FSM national or state courts. Some of the surviving Trust Territory statutues are deemed to be national laws, and some are now viewed as state laws. Whether a Trust Territory statute is deemed to be national or state law depends on the content of the statute. Only those that relate to matters within the powers of the national government are considered national laws; all others are state laws.[9]

H. Common Law

Many colonies and some newly independent nations receive, as their common law, that which is in effect in another country. For example, the Trust Territory Code required that American common law, as expressed in the American Law Institute's Restatements[10] or as generally understood and applied in the United States, should be the common law of the Trust Territory.[11]

The FSM national and state constitutions, however, do not receive the common law either of the United States or of Trust Territory courts.[12] The Judicial Guidance Clause, Article XI, Section 11, of the FSM Constitution, provides that judicial decisions of FSM national courts must be consistent with the "Constitution, Micronesian customs and traditions, and the social and geographical configuration of Micronesia" and, as the clause has been amended, with FSM sources. The FSM Supreme Court interpreted the clause, prior to its amendment, to require FSM courts to fashion a uniquely Micronesian common law, looking first to the Constitution, then to custom, and—only if neither were applicable—to the common law of other jurisdictions.[13] The Court recommends that, in choosing among the common law of other jurisdictions, FSM courts give special regard to American law, because it is familiar to the FSM judiciary, but the Court expects common law precedents from other jurisdictions to be cited as well, and none—including those of the Trust Territory courts—are to be binding upon an FSM court. In applying the common law of any jurisdiction, including the United States, courts must evaluate it as to its applicability to the society and customs of the FSM.[14] The Court has also held that the Judicial Guidance Clause effectively overrules Trust Territory statutes which recognized only those customs not in conflict with the written laws.[15]

The Judicial Policy Clause in the Pohnpeian Constitution (Article 10, Section 11) requires that court decisions conform to it and to the sense of justice of the Pohnpeian people. The Pohnpeian State Supreme Court has held that this clause is substantially similar in effect to the Judicial Guidance Clause of the FSM Constitution.[16]

The Yap Constitution's Judicial Guidance Clause (Article VII, Section 7) is similar, but the Yap Constitution also provides (Article III, Section 2) that not even the Yap Constitution may be construed to limit or invalidate custom (which leaves doubtful the relation of this provision to the Supremacy Clause). The Yap Constitution also states explicitly (Article XV, Section 3) that decisions of Trust Territory courts are not binding upon the Yap courts.

The Kosrae Constitution provides that "Court decisions shall be consistent with this Constitution, State traditions and customs, and the social and geographical configurations of the State" (Kosrae Constitution, Article VI, Section 9).

IV. CONSTITUTIONAL SYSTEM

As a federal system, FSM's national and state governments each have a constitution establishing the structure, duties, and powers of government. The constitutions follow, with some modifications, the U.S. model of a tripartite system in which the powers of government are separated into executive, legislative, and judicial branches, each of which provides checks on the power of the other branches.

There are three major differences from the United States model. First, the Micronesian constitutions provide potential roles for traditional leaders (see IV, C (1) **National Government and (2) State Government**). Second, the division of power between the FSM national and state governments is, in some ways, different from that in the United States (**see, for example, VIII, A (2) Foreign Investment and X Criminal Law**). Third, in practice, the duties and powers of the FSM national executive and legislative branches sometimes overlap in ways that would be considered violations of the separation of powers doctrine in the United States (**see, for example, V, A (1) Organization**). Whether the FSM courts would consider these overlaps to be violations of the FSM Constitution has yet to be decided.[17]

A. Territory

The territory of the FSM comprises those former districts of the Trust Territory that ratified the FSM Constitution. Each state is made up of the islands of each district, as defined by Trust Territory laws in effect immediately prior to the effective date of the FSM Constitution. The marine boundaries between adjacent states are determined by law, applying the principle of equidistance. State boundaries may be changed by the FSM Congress with the consent of the state legislatures involved. Territory may be added to the FSM upon approval of Congress and by vote of the inhabitants of the area and of the state of which the area would become a part. New states may be formed and admitted (FSM Constitution, Article I).

The waters connecting the islands of the FSM are internal waters, regardless of dimensions; the jurisdiction of the FSM extends 200 miles outward from the baselines (which are, depending upon whether an island is fringed by a reef, either the low water mark of the island or the seaward side of the reef) and includes the seabed, subsoil, water column, insular or continental shelves, airspace, "and any other territory or waters belonging to Micronesia by historic right, custom or legal title" (FSM Constitution, Article I, Section 2; see also FSM Code, Title 18). The national government has exclusive power over navigation and shipping except within lagoons, lakes, and rivers. It also has exclusive power to regulate the ownership, exploration, and exploitation of natural resources beyond 12 miles from island baselines. The states have exclusive power over marine resources within the 12-mile limit (FSM Constitution, Article IX, Section 2; FSM Code, Title 18). The FSM Code, Title 18, preserves traditionally recognized fishing rights in submerged reef areas. The Yap Constitution is potentially in conflict with the FSM Constitution, declaring at Article XIII, Section 5, that no action may be taken to impair traditional rights and ownership of natural resources and areas within and beyond the 12-mile limit.

B. Nationality, Citizenship, and Elections

1. NATIONALITY AND CITIZENSHIP

a. National

The FSM Constitution provides four ways persons may become citizens of the FSM. Automatically citizens and nationals of the FSM are, first, persons who were both citizens of the Trust Territory immediately before the effective date of the FSM Constitution and domiciliaries of a district ratifying the Constitution and, second, persons born of parents one or both of whom are citizens of the FSM. In addition, persons who were citizens of the Trust Territory immediately prior to the effective date of the FSM Constitution and domiciliaries of a district that did not ratify the Constitution may become citizens and nationals of the FSM by applying to an FSM court within six months after the later of the effective date of the Constitution or their eighteenth birthday. Finally, persons who were citizens of the Trust Territory and who become nationals of the United States under the terms of the Northern Mariana Islands Covenant may become citizens and nationals of the FSM by applying to an FSM court within six months of the date they became United States nationals (FSM Constitution, Article III).

The FSM Citizenship and Naturalization Act (FSM Code, Title 7, Sections 201–207) provides a fifth means of obtaining citizenship. Persons may become naturalized citizens if they have lawfully resided within the FSM for five years, are children or spouses of FSM citizens or nationals, renounce previous citizenships and allegiances, take an oath of allegiance to the FSM, and have competence in at least one of the indigenous languages of the FSM.

The Constitution provides that persons who are citizens both of the FSM and of another nation will lose their FSM citizenship (although they will remain FSM nationals) unless they renounce their other citizenship within three years after the later of the effective date of the FSM Constitution or their eighteenth birthday (FSM Constitution, Article III). The FSM Citizenship and Naturalization Act provides, in addition, that citizenship may be lost in the following ways: if an FSM citizen obtains naturalization in or takes an oath of allegiance to a foreign state, serves in the armed forces of any foreign state other than the United States, votes in the elections of a foreign state, or formally renounces FSM citizenship.

b. State

For the most part, citizens of the FSM are considered citizens of the states in which they are domiciled. For example, Article XIV, Section 8, of the Yap Constitution provides that a citizen of the FSM domiciled in Yap is a citizen of Yap. Article 3 of the Pohnpeian Constitution, however, provides three classes of Pohnpeian citizenship. Persons are "citizen[s] and pweldak" of Pohnpei if either of their parents was such, or if immediately prior to the effective date of the Pohnpei Constitution, they were citizens or pweldak of a local government. (A pweldak—also rendered as pwilidak; see **XII, A Land Tenure and Administration**—is very roughly translated as a child of the soil of Pohnpei, thus a true native.) A person is merely a "citizen of Pohnpei" if he or she was a citizen or legal resident of Pohnpei on the effective date of the Pohnpei Constitution.

2. ELECTIONS

a. National

Article VI, Section 1, of the FSM Constitution provides that voting must be secret; that a citizen eighteen years of age may vote in national elections; and that Congress shall prescribe a residency period, provide for voter registration, and establish disqualification guidelines for criminal convictions or for mental incompetence. Congress has provided that every citizen of the FSM is eligible to vote in national elections if eighteen years of age or older on the day of the election; a resident or domiciliary of and a registered voter for at least thirty days in any of the states of the FSM; not currently under a judgment of mental incompetency or insanity; and not currently under parole, probation, or sentence for any felony conviction by any court of the FSM, the Trust Territory, or the United States (FSM Code, Title 9 [1987]).

b. State

Voting in Pohnpeian state elections is open to any citizen of Pohnpei who is at least eighteen years of age and has not committed a felony for which he or she is on parole or probation or under sentence. Although other qualifications may be prescribed by statute, the Constitution prohibits property qualifications or the imposition of voting taxes or fees (Pohnpei Constitution, Article 6).

In Yap, elections occur every four years, voting is by secret ballot and is open to citizens of the FSM who are eighteen or older; registered to vote; not currently incompetent or insane; and not currently under parole, probation, or sentence. Registration is limited to persons who have resided in the FSM for nine months and in the election district for three months immediately prior to registering (Yap Constitution, Article IV; Yap Election Act of 1978 [7 YSC 102 ff.]).

Voters in Yap and Pohnpei may also engage in initiatives and recall votes. In Pohnpei, initiatives are submitted to the legislature on a petition signed by 35 percent of the qualified voters. In Yap, the petition, which must be signed by 25 percent of registered voters, goes to the next general election, where it may be passed by a majority of votes cast. In Pohnpei, a recall of the governor, lieutenant governor, or a member of the legislature may occur upon the presentation of a petition signed by 35 percent of the affected registered voters followed by an election in which 60 percent of the affected registered voters vote for recall. In Yap, a recall requires a petition signed by 25 percent of voters qualified to vote for that official. A special election must follow within sixty days, and the recall will be effective if approved by a majority of votes cast. There may be only one recall vote per term and none in an official's first year in office. Pohnpei also permits referenda, which become law if approved by 60 percent of votes cast (Yap Constitution, Article XIV, Sections 7 and 9; Pohnpei Constitution, Article 6, Section 5, and Article 13, Section 7).

C. Government

1. NATIONAL GOVERNMENT

The FSM Constitution establishes a tripartite governmental structure with executive, legislative, and judicial branches (FSM Constitution, Articles IX, X and XI) and places limits on the power of the national government by permitting it only the functions expressly delegated to it or those of indisputably national character (FSM Constitution, Article IX).

The FSM Constitution makes possible (but does not require) a continuing role for traditional leaders in the new polity, first by stating that nothing in the Constitution takes away any of the customary functions of traditional leaders, and second by providing that the Constitution or a statute may give traditional leaders formal or functional roles at any level of government (Article V, Section 1). Resolution No. 32, adopted by the first Micronesian Constitutional Convention in 1975 and ordered appended to all copies of the Constitution, provides, "It is not the intention of the Delegates to the Micronesian Constitutional Convention to affect adversely any of the relationships which prevail between traditional leaders and the people of Micronesia, nor to diminish in any way the full honor and respect to which they are entitled." The FSM Congress is empowered to establish "when needed" a Chamber of Chiefs, consisting of traditional leaders, and state constitutions may provide an active, functional role for traditional leaders (FSM Constitution, Article V, Section 3). However, the FSM Congress has not established a Chamber of Chiefs, and in 1991 voters did not approve a proposed constitutional amendment that would have mandated establishment of the chamber.

a. Head of State

The President of the FSM is both chief executive and Head of State. As Head of State, the President receives all ambassadors, conducts foreign affairs and the national defense (but Congress has the power to ratify treaties and to provide for the national defense), and appoints ambassadors with the advice and consent of Congress.

b. Executive

Article X of the FSM Constitution establishes the executive branch of the national government. It follows the U.S. model in providing for the election of a President and a Vice President to serve for not more than two consecutive terms of four years each. The FSM departs from the U.S. model, however, and approximates the Westminster model in providing that the President and Vice President (who may not be from the same state) are to be chosen by a majority vote of the Congress from among members of Congress who were elected at large to represent the states. Once Congress has chosen the President and Vice President, their congressional seats are declared vacant and filled by a special election. A proposal to amend the Constitution to provide for direct election of the President was presented to the 1990 Constitutional Convention but was not adopted.

Only persons who are at-large members of Congress, citizens by birth of the FSM, and who have resided in the FSM for at least fifteen years may be President or Vice President. To be elected to a second term, a President or Vice President must be reelected to Congress. If the President vacates the office or is unable to perform its duties, the Vice President assumes the presidency. If both offices become vacant, Congress must provide for the succession by statute.

The President has the following constitutionally enumerated duties:

1. to execute and implement the provisions of the Constitution and all national laws;
2. to receive ambassadors and to conduct foreign affairs and national defense;
3. to grant pardons and reprieves; and
4. with the advice and consent of Congress, to make ambassadorial, judicial, and executive appointments.

The President is required to submit the annual budget of the executive branch to Congress in May of each year; although the President appoints the heads of all executive departments and offices, those choices are subject to the advice and consent of Congress.

c. Legislature

Article IX of the Constitution vests the legislative power of the national government in a unicameral Congress of the Federated States of Micronesia. Article IX, Section 8, attempts to apportion congressional constituencies so that there will be representation both of the people and of the states, by providing that one member be elected at large from each state and "additional members elected from congressional districts in each state apportioned by population." State members serve for four-year terms, and district members serve for two-year terms. There must be at least one district member from each state, in addition to the member elected at large, and (in recognition that representation of the people means taking account of the cultural and linguistic diversity of the FSM) each district "shall be approximately equal after giving due regard to language, cultural and geographical differences." Congress must reapportion itself at least every ten years.

A member of Congress must be at least thirty years old, must have been a citizen of the FSM for at least fifteen years and a resident of the state from which he or she is elected for at least five years, and may not have been convicted of a felony. Members of Congress may not hold other public office or employment. In the first Congress, in addition to the four at-large members, there were ten members elected on the basis of population—one from Kosrae, one from Yap, three from Pohnpei, and five from Chuuk.

The goal of representing the interests both of the states and of the people is reflected as well in the process by which legislation is enacted. To become law, a bill must pass two readings on separate days. To pass the first reading, a two-thirds vote of all members of Congress is required. On the second reading, the voting is by states, with each state entitled to one vote. To pass, the bill must have the votes of two-thirds of the states. A bill passed by Congress must be presented to the President. If the President disapproves of the bill, it is returned to Congress within ten days or, if Congress has fewer than ten days remaining in its session, within thirty days. A bill that is not so returned is deemed approved. Congress may override presidential disapproval of a bill by the vote of three-fourths of the state delegations. (So long as there are four states in the FSM, the requirement of a vote of three-fourths of the states to override a presidential veto is the same as the requirement of a vote of two-thirds of the states to pass a bill. A proposal for a constitutional amendment to require a higher vote to override presidential vetoes was defeated in 1991.)

Article IX of the Constitution grants Congress the power to conduct hearings in support of its legislative powers, and for this purpose Congress may compel the attendance and testimony of witnesses and the production of documents. Congress has by legislation provided for the establishment, membership, and procedural rules governing legislative investigating committees (FSM Code, Title 3). Certain of the powers expressly delegated to Congress by Article IX of the Constitution assist in providing checks and balances among the branches of government. Thus, Congress by a two-thirds vote of its members, has the power to remove from office the President, Vice President, or a justice of the Supreme Court for treason, bribery, or conduct involving corruption in office. The removal of a justice, however, is reviewable by a special tribunal, called by the President and composed of one judge from each state court. Further, although appointments of ambassadors, justices, and the principal officers of executive departments are within the purview of the President, such appointments may be made only with the advice and consent of Congress.

Article IX of the Constitution limits certain of Congress' legislative powers in deference to the interests of the states. Thus, Congress has the power by a two-thirds vote of its members to ratify treaties, but treaties, such as the Compact of Free Association, delegating major powers of the government of the FSM to another government, require, in addition, majority approval by the legislatures of two-thirds of the states. Similarly, Congress has the power to levy taxes, but at least 50 percent of the resulting revenues must be paid into the treasury of the state where collected. Finally, Congress has the power to regulate the ownership, exploration and exploitation, of marine resources that are beyond 12 miles from island baselines, but net revenues derived from ocean floor mineral resources must be divided equally between the national government and the appropriate state governments.

Except for treason, felony, or breach of the peace, members of Congress are privileged from arrest during attendance at Congress and while going to and from sessions of Congress. A member may not be held liable for statements made in Congress. Congress itself is the sole judge of the elections and qualifications of members and may discipline members and by a two-thirds vote may suspend or expel a member. Congress establishes its own rules of procedure (including the choice of a presiding officer from among its members), except that sessions of Congress must be regular and public. Congress has provided for two regular sessions per year, each to last for thirty calendar days. Special sessions may be called by the President or the presiding officer of

Congress on the written request of two-thirds of the members (FSM Constitution, Article IX; FSM Code, Title 3).

d. Judiciary

Article XI of the Constitution vests the judicial power of the national government in a Supreme Court (which is to have both a trial and an appellate division) and in such inferior courts as Congress may establish by statute. At present, no inferior national courts have been established. The membership of the Supreme Court is to consist of a Chief Justice and not more than five associate justices, who are to be appointed by the President with the approval of two-thirds of Congress. Justices serve during good behavior. Trials may be conducted by one justice, but a panel of at least three of the justices, none of whom was the trial judge, must hear appeals. Until 1992, the court consisted only of the Chief Justice and one Associate Justice, both Americans. In 1992, the Chief Justice announced his departure, two Micronesians were appointed to the Court, and additional appointments of Micronesians were expected. Under the power given by Article XI, Section 9(b), to give special assignments to retired judges and judges of other courts, the Chief Justice has staffed appellate panels with justices from other Micronesian nations, from the United States, and from the FSM state courts (see FSM Judiciary Act of 1979, FSM Code, Title 4, Section 104).

The Constitution provides at Article XI, Section 5, that the qualifications and compensation of justices and other judges are to be set by statute and may not be reduced during their terms of office unless all salaries set by statute are reduced by the same percentage. Congress has provided that justices of the Supreme Court must be at least thirty years of age, and either (1) graduates of an accredited law school and admitted to practice in any jurisdiction, or (2) "a person of equivalent and extraordinary legal ability gained through at least five years of experience practicing law" (FSM Constitution, Article XI, Section 5; Judiciary Act of 1979, FSM Code, Title 4, Section 107). This provision permits the appointment of justices who are not citizens or residents of the FSM. Beginning under the Trust Territory and continuing into the present, Micronesians without law degrees have served as trial advocates and have gained considerable experience and expertise; this statutory provision permits their appointment to Supreme Court justiceships as well. A number of distinguished state court judges are nonlawyers.

The Chief Justice is the administrative head of the national judicial system. As such, the Chief Justice may make rules governing the national courts, divide the Supreme Court and inferior courts into geographical or functional divisions, may assign judges among the divisions, establish rules of procedure and evidence, govern the transfer of cases between the state and national courts, and govern the admission to practice and discipline of attorneys and the retirement of judges (FSM Constitution, Article XI, Section 9). The Chief Justice has established rules of procedure and evidence and has made rules, including the passing of an examination, governing admission to practice before the Supreme Court. Rules made by the Chief Justice may be amended by statute (FSM Constitution, Article XI, Section 9).

Article XI, Section 2 of the Constitution declares that the Supreme Court is "the highest court in the nation." The Trial Division of the Supreme Court has original and exclusive jurisdiction in cases involving officials of foreign governments; disputes between states, admiralty or maritime cases; and in cases in which the national government is a party, except where an interest in land is at issue. In addition, the national courts have original jurisdiction in cases arising under the FSM Constitution, national laws or treaties, and in diversity cases (civil disputes between a state and citizen of another state; between citizens of different states; and between a state or a citizen thereof and a foreign state, citizen, or subject).

2. STATE GOVERNMENTS

Like the national government, the state governments consist of an executive (headed by a popularly elected Governor), a legislative, and a judicial branch. Some state constitutions provide that the customary roles of traditional leaders are to be recognized and that the legislature may give traditional leaders new roles in government (for example, the Chuuk Constitution, Article IV). However, only in Yap have traditional leaders been given new governmental roles. The Yap Constitution, Article III, established councils of traditional leaders from Yap Island (the Council of Pilung) and the outer islands (the Council of Tamol). The councils determine their own membership. While their greatest power lies in their ability to veto legislation (see **IV, C (2) (c) Legislature**), their other responsibilities include giving advice on custom to the Governor, legislature, and government departments (such as the Historic Preservation Office); resolving problems and assisting in matters concerning custom in municipalities; and promoting and preserving tradition and custom (5 YSC 102, 409).

a. Head of State

Although the states are sovereign entities, power over foreign relations resides with the national government, and the President is the FSM's Head of State.

b. Executive

Each of the states places executive authority in a Governor who is chosen by popular vote for a four-year term. The constitutions of Yap and Pohnpei provide that no person may serve more than two full consecutive terms as Governor. Each state also provides for the office of Lieutenant Governor, who would become Governor were the office to fall vacant. In Yap and Pohnpei, candidates for Governor and Lieutenant Governor run on a single ticket. If no candidate for Governor receives a sufficient percentage of the votes cast, a runoff election is held between the two candidates who received the highest number of votes. In Yap, candidates must receive 45 percent, in Pohnpei a majority.

In Yap, the Governor and Lieutenant Governor must be thirty years old; citizens of the FSM by birth; and residents of the state for fifteen years, at least five years of which must be immediately prior to the election. They must have had no felony convictions. One must be from Yap Island and the other from the Outer Islands. In Pohnpei, the Governor must be a citizen of Pohnpei by birth and at least thirty-five years old and must never have been convicted of a felony.

As chief executive of the state, the Governor is responsible for the faithful execution of the laws. The Governor may grant reprieves and pardons. Subject to the approval of the legislature, the Governor appoints the chief officers of executive departments and agencies who serve at the Governor's pleasure (except that, in Yap, the removal of the Attorney General requires approval of the legislature). The Governor must report to the legislature at the beginning of each regular session on the condition of the state (Pohnpei State Constitution, Article IX; Yap State Constitution, Article VI; see also Chuuk Constitution, Article VI).

c. Legislature

Yap and Pohnpei place legislative power in unicameral legislatures, which are apportioned so that election districts have roughly approximate populations and, at the same time, represent the social configuration of the state. Thus, in Pohnpei, the initial legislature consisted of twenty-three members, with at least one from each local government district and more from districts with greater populations. In Yap, there were ten senators, six from the main island of Yap and one from each of the outlying districts. The Chuuk Constitution, on the other hand, creates a bicameral legislature, in which the ten senators are chosen on the basis of regional equality and the twenty-eight members of the House of Representatives on the basis of population and geography. Most state constitutions provide for reapportionment every ten years (Yap Constitution, Article V; Pohnpei Constitution, Article VIII; Chuuk Constitution, Article V).

Members of the Yap and Pohnpei legislatures serve for four-year terms; in Chuuk, senators serve four years and representatives two years. Qualifications emphasize residence in the state and in the electoral district. In Pohnpei, members must have been citizens of Pohnpei for at least twenty-five years and citizens of the local government that they represent for at least three years. In Yap, members must have been citizens of the FSM for ten years and residents of Yap for five years and of their district for one year. In Chuuk, legislators must be born Chuukese and must have been residents and registered voters of their districts for at least five years prior to the election (Pohnpei Constitution, Article VIII; Yap Constitution, Article V; Chuuk Constitution, Article V).

Legislatures meet in regular sessions at times specified in state constitutions. Special sessions may, in addition, be convened by the Governor, by the presiding officer of the legislature, or on the petition of legislators. In Pohnpei, a quorum consists of three-fourths of the membership. To become law, a bill must pass two readings on separate days, and passage on the second reading requires the affirmative roll-call vote of a majority of the membership regardless of vacancies. Resolutions, however, may be adopted on one reading by the affirmative vote of a majority of the membership. Every bill passed by the legislature must be presented to the Governor, who has ten days to consider bills presented ten or more days before a recess or adjournment and thirty days to consider all other bills. If the Governor disapproves of a bill, it must be returned to the legislature with objections. The Governor may exercise an item veto over appropriation bills but must disapprove other bills only in their entirety. Any bill not returned by the time specified becomes law. The legislature may override the Governor's veto upon a single reading by the affirmative vote of two-thirds of the membership regardless of vacancies (Pohnpei Constitution, Article VIII).

In the Yap legislature, a quorum consists of two-thirds of the membership; votes require a majority of those present, except that final votes on bills require two-thirds of all members. To become law, a bill must pass two readings. After passage, all bills are submitted to the Councils of Pilung and Tamol, which may disapprove any bill concerning custom or customary leadership roles. The councils have thirty days to disapprove a bill. A disapproved bill may be amended to meet the councils' objections (an amended bill requires only one reading to pass the legislature) and must then be submitted to the councils again. (There is disagreement as to whether disapproval by either council requires amendment, or whether disapproval by both councils is necessary.) If not disapproved, a bill is submitted to the Governor who may veto any item in an appropriations bill but can veto other bills only as a whole. The Governor has ten days to exercise a veto during legislative sessions and thirty days out of session. If the Governor does not act, the bill becomes law. Legislators can pass a vetoed bill on one reading by a two-thirds vote of the membership. If the legislature amends a bill to meet the Governor's objections, it must be presented to the Governor again (Yap Constitution, Article V).

State legislatures have the power to conduct investigations, hold public hearings, subpoena witnesses and documents, and administer oaths. They are also empowered to impeach or remove the Governor, Lieutenant Governor, and certain other state officials for cause. The Pohnpei legislature has the power (and the duty) to enact a code of ethical conduct for officials and employees of the state government. Except for felony or breach of the peace, members of state legislatures are privileged from arrest during and while going to or returning from sessions; a member may not be held liable for statements made in the legislature. Legislatures are the sole judges of the qualifications of their members and may punish members by censure, suspension, or expulsion (Yap Constitution, Article V; Pohnpei Constitution, Article VIII; Chuuk Constitution, Article V).

d. Judiciary

Article 10 of the Pohnpei Constitution vests the judicial power of Pohnpei in the Pohnpei Supreme Court and in such inferior courts as are established by statutes. Local courts with limited jurisdiction exist in most of the local government districts of Pohnpei. The Pohnpei Supreme Court consists of a Chief Justice and up to four Associate Justices. The Supreme Court is the highest court in Pohnpei and is divided into the Trial Division and the Appellate Division. The Trial Division has original jurisdiction over all civil and criminal cases within the jurisdiction of Pohnpei and appellate jurisdiction over the decisions of all inferior courts and adjudicatory bodies. The Appellate Division has jurisdiction over all matters in the Trial Division.

Each justice of the Pohnpei Supreme Court is a member of both the Trial Division and the Appellate Division. A single justice may hear a case in the Trial Division, but no fewer than three justices may form an appellate panel, and the justice who heard a case at trial may not participate in the appeal.

All judges and members of adjudicatory bodies are nominated by the Governor with the approval of a majority of the members of the legislature. Justices serve for twelve-year terms, and may be reappointed to additional terms. To be a justice of the Pohnpei Supreme Court, a person must be at least thirty-five years of age and must never have been convicted of a felony; a justice need not have a law degree. There were, in 1989, four justices of the Pohnpei Supreme Court. Although none was a lawyer, two had significant experience as trial advocates before the Trust Territory High Court, the third was a traditional leader and a former Trust Territory District Court judge, and the fourth had served as an administrator of the Trust Territory court system. The nomination and qualifications of temporary justices are also subject to the approval of the legislature.

In Yap, the State Court, which may have a Chief Justice and at least two Associate Justices, is the highest court. The State Court has a Trial Division and an Appellate Division. One justice may hear a case in the Trial Division, but appeals must be heard by at least three justices, none of whom may be the trial judge. The State Court's jurisdiction extends to the whole state. The Trial Division has original jurisdiction over all cases (except those exclusive to the FSM Supreme Court) and rehears cases appealed from municipal courts. The Appellate Division has jurisdiction over all cases heard in the Trial Division.

Justices of the State Court are appointed by the Governor, with the advice and consent of the legislature, and serve for six years. In addition, the Chief Justice may appoint temporary justices. Justices must be citizens of the FSM by birth, thirty-five years or older, residents of Yap for at least twenty-five years and for the five years immediately preceding appointment, and "learned in the law" (a requirement that does not necessitate a degree in law, although in 1989 one of the Yap State Court justices had a law degree). Justices must be residents of different municipalities (Yap Constitution, Article VII; State Judiciary Act, 4 YSC 102–157).

Yap law provides for a court in each municipality, although not all municipalities have as yet established courts. Presiding judges of Municipal Courts are the traditional leaders representing the municipality in the Council of Pilung or Tamol, and associate judges are other traditional leaders appointed by the presiding judge. Municipal Courts have jurisdiction over civil cases involving persons who reside in the municipality and who voluntarily appear, as well as over certain minor criminal offenses. The procedure of Municipal Courts is intended to be consistent with customary means of resolving disputes, and, before bringing a case to the Municipal Court, the parties are supposed to try to resolve it in accordance with custom within the family or village. The Trial Division of the State Court can order any pending case transferred to it, and any party can cause a case to be removed to the State Court on a showing that the municipal court is unable or unwilling to decide the case. Appeals from municipal courts are to the Trial Division of the State Court for a trial de novo (State Judiciary Act, 4 YSC 161–167).

3. LOCAL GOVERNMENTS

The division of powers between state and local governments varies from state to state. The Pohnpei and Yap Constitutions, for example, both presume that the powers of local governments are derived from the state but handle the state's grant of power to local governments differently. Although both constitutions authorize local governments to draft charters establishing their own governmental structures, the Pohnpei Constitution (Article 14) provides that local governments may exercise all authority not prohibited under state law, whereas the Yap Constitution (Article VIII) provides that local governments may exercise only those powers conferred by state law. The Yap Municipal Government Act of 1979 (Yap State Code, Title 6) defines these powers as promoting natural beauty and places of historic and cultural interest, promoting the public welfare, constructing and operating public facilities, preserving custom, and imposing taxes.

The local governments of Pohnpei are the eleven local government districts that existed on the effective date of the state constitution. Areas currently outside the boundaries of any local government are to be administered by the state government until they are, by statute, either incorporated into existing local governments (which may not be done without the consent of the affected local governments) or are established as separate local governments. Pohnpei local governments may also provide a functional role for traditional leaders. The local governments of Yap consist of those municipalities that existed at the effective date of the Municipal Government Act, with their boundaries drawn according to custom.

D. Emergency Powers

The President of the FSM has the power to declare a national emergency "if required to preserve public peace, health or safety, at a time of extreme emergency caused by civil disturbance, natural disaster or immediate threat of war or insurrection." Within thirty days after the declaration, Congress must meet to consider revocation, amendment, or extension of the declaration. Unless Congress has acted either to revoke or extend, the declaration of emergency automatically expires after thirty days. The declaration of emergency will be free from judicial interference for that thirty-day period, though it otherwise may not impair the power of the judiciary. A declaration of emergency may infringe upon a civil right "only to the extent actually required for the preservation of peace, health or safety" (FSM Constitution, Article 10, Section 9). During a state of emergency, the President may set curfews, prohibit the use or transport of firearms or explosives, close off roads, forbid the sale of alcohol, and make other orders (11 FSM Code 802).

State governors may also declare states of emergency. However, the provisions permitting them to impair civil rights can apply only to rights granted by state constitutions, since the FSM Constitution can be suspended only by the President.

E. Human Rights

1. NATIONAL

The FSM Constitution contains at Article IV a Declaration Rights, which focuses primarily on the civil or political rights of individuals and, as such, closely resembles the Bill of Rights of the

U.S. Constitution. The FSM Constitution, however, contains brief explanations of these provisions that are probably intended to clear up inconsistencies or ambiguities discovered in the 200 years that U.S. courts have been interpreting the Bill of Rights. The rights set forth in Article IV are as follows:

1. No law may deny or impair freedom of expression, peaceable assembly, association, or petition.
2. No law may be passed respecting an establishment of religion or impairing the free exercise of religion, except that nonreligious assistance may be provided to church-related schools.
3. No person may be deprived of life, liberty, or property without due process of law or be denied the equal protection of laws.
4. Equal protection of the laws may not be denied or impaired on account of gender, race, ancestry, national origin, language, or social status.
5. The right of the people to be secure in their persons, houses, papers, and other possessions against unreasonable search, seizure, or invasion of privacy may not be violated, nor may a warrant be issued except on probable cause.
6. Defendants in criminal cases have the right to a speedy public trial, to be informed of the nature of the accusation against them, to have counsel, to confront witnesses, and to compel the attendance of witnesses.
7. No persons may be compelled to give evidence against themselves in a criminal case or be subject to double jeopardy.
8. Excessive bail may not be required, excessive fines imposed, nor cruel and unusual punishments inflicted.
9. Capital punishment is prohibited.
10. Slavery and involuntary servitude are prohibited except to punish crimes.
11. A bill of attainder or ex post facto law may not be passed.
12. A citizen of the FSM may freely travel and migrate within the FSM.
13. Imprisonment for debt is prohibited.

By setting forth only the same kind of essentially civil and political rights as are contained in the United States Constitution, the drafters of the FSM Constitution missed an opportunity to give constitutional protection to other kinds of rights, in particular to economic rights, such as rights to subsistence, work, and shelter, which are recognized in international human rights conventions.

However, the FSM Constitution does differ from its U.S. model in recognizing "the right of the people to education, health care, and legal services" and promising that the national government "shall take every step reasonable and necessary to provide these services." But the placement of this provision in Article XIII, Section 1, rather than in Article IV raises the question as to whether these rights to basic services are to be treated differently by the legislature and the courts than are the rights to civil liberty.

Because the Declaration of Rights is premised upon individualism, it is in many respects contrary to customary values. However, Article IV is to be read in conjunction with Article V, Section 2, which provides that the customs of Micronesia may be protected by statute and that, if a statute is challenged as violating the Declaration of Rights "protection of Micronesian tradition shall be considered a compelling social purpose warranting such governmental action." This phrasing was probably derived from American judicial decisions, which hold that a statute that has a "compelling social purpose" passes constitutional muster more easily than do other statutes, although it can be struck down as unconstitutional.

2. STATE

Each state constitution contains a list of civil rights very similar to those in the FSM Constitution, although there are some important differences. Article 4, Section 1, of the Pohnpei Constitution, for example, limits the right to free speech, as follows: "A person may be held responsible for untruthful statements injuring other persons without privilege, and for statements creating a clear and immediate danger of unlawful conduct or substantial injury to the public." These qualifications to the right of free speech are similar to those imputed by U.S. courts into the Free Speech Clause of the U.S. Constitution. The Pohnpei Constitution also differs from the FSM Constitution in that the Pohnpei Constitution contains a contract rights provision. Article 4, Section 5, of the Pohnpei Constitution provides that "No law may impair an existing contractual obligation, except for the protection of an essential public interest." One assumes that the qualifying phrase is intended to avoid a repetition of the sorry history of "liberty of contract" in the United States, where the constitutional protection of contract rights was used to destroy the civil liberties and fundamental economic rights of the common people. It might have been safer to follow the example of the FSM Constitution and omit a contract provision entirely.

Like the FSM Constitution, state constitutions also support tradition in providing that, in the case of a conflict between custom and a constitutionally protected civil right, custom might prevail. The Pohnpeian Constitution seems, at first, to be stronger in its support of custom than is the FSM Constitution. For example, the Pohnpei Constitution contains, in Article 4, no protection for free religious exercise, although Article 4, Section 3, does provide that government may not deny equal protection on account of religion (nor on account of gender, race, ancestry, national origin, language, or social status—a clause that in many respects contravenes Pohnpeian custom). The Pohnpei Constitution, at Article 5, Section 1, "upholds, respects, and protects the customs and traditions of the traditional kingdoms in Pohnpei." However, the Constitution of Pohnpei states that any statute that supports custom may be upheld only "upon proof of the existence and regular practice of the custom or tradition and the reasonableness of the means established for its protection, as determined by the Pohnpei Supreme Court" (Article 5, Section 2). This is a more difficult standard for custom to meet than is the "compelling social purpose" test of the FSM Constitution. It requires, first, that custom's existence be proven as a factual matter and, second, that the statute upholding the customary norm or practice must be reasonable (i.e., must not unnecessarily abridge a fundamental right). The Yap Constitution provides the strongest protection for custom, asserting at Article III, Section 2, that "nothing in this Constitution shall be construed to limit or invalidate any recognized tradition or custom."

V. Administrative Organization and Law

A. *Organization*

1. NATIONAL

Article X of the FSM Constitution vests the executive power of the national government in the President and provides for executive departments to be established by statute. The FSM Code, at Title 2, Sections 203 to 204 (1987), provides for the establishment in the executive branch of four departments (Finance, External Affairs, Resources and Development, and Transportation) and eight offices (Attorney General, Budget, Information, Personnel, Planning and Statistics, Public Defender, Education and Health Services). The secretary of each department, the head of each office, and the deputies of each, are nominated by the President and appointed with the advice and consent of the Senate. Secretaries, who may not be members of Congress, have Cabinet rank. Although not required to do so by law, Presidents generally try to balance nominees for high offices among the states. The President may appoint lesser officers and employees without the advice and consent of Congress (2 FSM Code 207 [1987]).

In addition to the departments and offices of the executive branch, the FSM government includes government corporations and agencies (see **VIII Investment Law and IX Welfare Law**). Authority for the management of a number of these corporations and agencies resides in boards of directors, some of whose members are chosen by the FSM President, with the advice and consent of Congress, and some by state Governors. The FSM Airline Corporation, for example, which is to be the flag carrier of the FSM, will have a seven-member board of directors, two of whom to be appointed by the President with the advice and consent of Congress, four to be appointed by the Governors of each state, and one to be the chief executive officer of the corporation, who serves ex officio and is appointed by the board of directors (20 FSM Code 201–208 [1987]). Governmental corporations and agencies with similarly hybrid sources of authority include the Telecommunications Corporation; Coconut Development Authority; National Fisheries Corporation; Environmental Protection Board; Institute for Micronesian History and Culture; FSM Board of Education; Medical Health Care Licensing Board, which has five members appointed by the President, four of whom are each supposed to represent a state; and Federated Development Authority, which has a five-member policy board, consisting of the chief executives of the state and national governments of FSM (21 FSM Code 209; 22 FSM Code 203; 24 FSM Code 709 [1987]; 25 FSM Code 601 [1987]; 26 FSM Code 203; 40 FSM Code 103; 41 FSM Code 204 [1987]; 55 FSM Code 326 [1987]).

While the makeup of these agencies demonstrates an interest in sharing authority between the national and state governments, the membership of the governing boards of other agencies demonstrates an interest in sharing authority within the national government between Congress and the executive. The Micronesian Maritime Authority, for example, which is charged with regulating the exploitation of resources within the extended fisheries limits of the FSM, is composed of seven members, four from Congress, one of whom is appointed by the President in consultation with the presiding officer of Congress, and two of whom are the Secretary of External Affairs and the Secretary of Resources and Development or their designees (24 FSM Code 301 [1987]).[18] Similar agencies include the Banking Board (composed of one member appointed by the President and two members appointed by Congress) and the Foreign Investment Board (composed of three members appointed by the President and two members appointed by the presiding officer of Congress). A few agencies (such as the FSM Development Bank, the Postal Service, and the Social Security Board) have members, heads of agency or boards of directors entirely appointed by the President, with the advice and consent of Congress (29 FSM Code 201; 32 FSM Code 206; 30 FSM Code 107 [1987]).

2. STATE

State constitutions vest executive power in state governors and provide that governmental departments are to be established by statute. Article VI of the Yap Constitution, for example, provides that each government department must be under a single department head, that all department heads are responsible to the Governor, who appoints them with the advice and consent of the legislature to serve at the Governor's pleasure (except that removal of the Attorney General requires consent of the legislature). The Yap Executive Branch Organization Act of 1979 (Yap State Code, Title 3) establishes the Departments of Education, Health, Public

Utilities and Contracts, Resources and Development, Public Affairs, Administrative Services, Attorney General, and Planning and Budget; and stipulates that, if a gubernatorial appointment has not achieved legislative consent within 180 days, the nomination is deemed withdrawn.

Article 9 of the Pohnpei Constitution vests executive power in the Governor and provides that members of all policy-making boards, the chief officers of executive departments and agencies, and other executive officers are appointed by the Governor, with the approval of a majority of the membership of the legislature. Appointees may be removed either at the pleasure of the Governor or by an impeachment process begun by the legislature. The Governor may reorganize the executive branch at any time, but executive reorganization plans require legislative approval.

B. Public Service

1. NATIONAL

The national and state governments are both concerned to establish a public service system based upon merit and ensuring security of tenure. The National Public Service System Act (FSM Code, Title 52) establishes a system of tenure, a salary schedule, and merit increases for employees of the national government. Preference in employment in the national public service is given to citizens of the FSM. The act provides for hearings for any employee who is suspended for more than three working days, demoted, or dismissed. An employee must exhaust administrative remedies before seeking judicial review.

2. STATE

State constitutions similarly provide that the civil service will operate on merit (see, for example, the Yap Constitution, Article XIV, Section 2), and state statutes give state employees protections similar to those enjoyed by national employees. The Yap State Public Service System Act (Yap State Code, Title 8), for example, requires equal opportunity in hiring, job security, and promotion in the public service, no discrimination on account of physical disabilities, impartial selection based on tests, and fair and reasonable grievance procedures for employees. However, like the National Public Service System Act, the Yap act gives preference to FSM citizens in public service employment, notwithstanding its merit and antidiscrimination provisions.

C. Public Finance and Audit

A number of provisions in both national and state constitutions and laws are aimed at ensuring the financial stability of the new nation and preventing mismanagement, overspending, or corruption. The state laws are very similar to those of the national government.

The FSM Constitution provides, at Article XII, that public money raised by the national government must be deposited in accounts or funds within the national Treasury and may not be withdrawn except on enactment of appropriations statutes. The President must submit a proposed budget to Congress each year. Congress may alter the budget in any respect but may pass no specific appropriation bills until the budget has been enacted. The President may item veto an appropriation in any bill passed by Congress, and the veto may be overturned by a vote of three-fourths of all state delegations.

The state constitutions require that public moneys be spent only as appropriated by the legislature and that the Governor prepare an annual budget for submission to the legislature

(Pohnpei Constitution, Article 11; Yap Constitution, Article IX). State statutes also require that construction and purchase contracts with the government be chosen by competitive bidding (see, for example, 9 YSC 501).

Article XII of the FSM Constitution creates the office of Public Auditor, an official appointed by the President with the advice and consent of Congress. The Public Auditor is to serve for a four-year term, and duties of the office include the inspection and audit of accounts in every part of the national government and in other entities receiving funds from the national government. It is not clear whether these powers would extend to audits of states, which receive funds from the national government from national taxation and the division of foreign assistance funds. The Public Auditor is answerable not to the President but to Congress and must report annually to Congress and submit a budget to Congress. The Public Auditor can be removed by Congress for cause by a two-thirds vote, in which case the Chief Justice appoints an acting Public Auditor.

State law also provides for independent public audits (Pohnpei Constitution, Article 11; Yap Constitution, Article IX; Yap Public Auditor Act, 13 YSC 701–713). The Yap Public Auditor Act also protects whistle-blowers.

D. Rule Making

The FSM, at both the national and state levels, has followed the U.S. model in placing significant rule-making and enforcement powers in governmental agencies. Statutes define broad areas of policy and create agencies with the power to carry out these policies by promulgating and enforcing regulations. Title 17 of the FSM Code lays out general standards for the rule-making procedures of government agencies. It applies to all authorities of the national government, except the Congress, the courts, and the Micronesian Maritime Authority (but probably does not apply to government corporations). Title 17 requires that, prior to the adoption, amendment, or repeal of any regulation, the agency must publish a notice of its intended action for at least thirty days in each state capital, communicate information about the regulation by radio in English and the language or languages of each state, afford to all interested persons the opportunity to submit their views on the regulation, and transmit copies of the proposal to Congress. Certified copies of all regulations adopted by an agency must be filed in a number of state and national governmental offices, which maintain copies for public inspection. When adopted in compliance with Title 17, these regulations have the force of law. State statutes lay out similar standards for agency rule making (see, for example, the Yap State Administrative Procedure Act, 10 YSC 111–142).

Title 17 of the FSM Code permits any interested person to petition an agency for adoption, amendment, or repeal of a regulation or for an agency advisory opinion on the applicability of any statutory provision or regulation; the agency must respond in writing within thirty days. Any interested person requesting agency action may petition the agency for an order, and the agency must issue the order or explain its refusal within thirty days. State law, while substantially similar, contains some differences. In Yap, for example, the Administrative Procedure Act requires state agencies to hold hearings on the issuance, amendment, or repeal of regulations, if requested by twenty-five persons, by another government agency, or by an association with at least twenty-five members.

E. Review of Administrative Action

Both national and state laws provide agency hearings and judicial review of those hearings to persons aggrieved by agency action (see, for example, FSM Code, Title 17; Yap State Code,

Title 10). Title 17 of the FSM Code provides that any person aggrieved by the action of an agency is entitled to a hearing before the highest administrative official of the department or office of which that agency is a part. The hearing must be held within thirty calendar days after the aggrieved party has submitted a petition requesting it, unless the petitioner requests a delay. All parties, as well as other persons with an interest in the controversy, are entitled to personal and timely notice of the time, place, and nature of the hearing, the legal authority and jurisdiction under which the hearing is being held, the statutes and regulations involved, and the issues presented. Hearings must be public, unless the petitioner requests otherwise.

The hearing is an adjudicatory proceeding, and Title 17 vests the hearing officer with quasi-judicial powers, including the authority to issue subpoenas for witnesses and tangible evidence, administer oaths and affirmations, take dispositions, regulate the course of the hearing, hold conferences for the settlement or simplification of the issues, dispose of procedural requests, and take other actions necessary to serve the ends of justice.

Although the hearing is adjudicatory, it is not as formal as a court trial, and the technical rules of evidence applicable to courts do not apply. However, Title 17 does set some rules of evidence applicable to agency hearings. For example, privileges relating to evidence in the courts do apply to the conduct of hearings, and parties are entitled to present their cases or defenses by oral or documentary evidence, submit rebuttal evidence, and conduct cross-examinations. Further, the hearing officer is authorized to rule on the admissibility of evidence and, although any oral or documentary evidence may be received, the hearing officer is required as a matter of policy to exclude irrelevant, immaterial, unreliable, or unduly repetitious evidence.

The decision of a hearing officer constitutes final agency disposition of the action. A person adversely affected or aggrieved by the action of an agency is entitled to judicial review in the FSM Supreme Court. The Court conducts a de novo trial of the matter, although it may receive in evidence any or all of the evidence from the administrative hearing. It can compel the agency to take action that the agency was unlawfully refusing or delaying. It also has the power to set aside agency actions or decisions that it finds arbitrary, capricious, an abuse of discretion, or otherwise not in accordance with law; contrary to constitutional right, power, privilege, or immunity; in excess of statutory jurisdiction or authority; a denial of legal rights; without substantial compliance with the procedures required by law; or unwarranted by the facts. An aggrieved party may obtain a review by the appellate division of a final judgment of the Trial Division; the basis for review is whether the finding of the trial court was justified by substantial evidence of record.

VI. INTERNATIONAL OBLIGATIONS

The FSM Constitution provides, at Article IX, that the power to ratify treaties is exclusive to the national government and allocates the power over foreign affairs to the executive and the legislature. Treaties are negotiated by the President but must be ratified by a vote of two-thirds of the members of Congress (and treaties, such as the compact, that delegate major powers of government to another nation require majority approval of the legislatures of two-thirds of the states). Under Article X of the Constitution, the President is delegated the powers to receive all ambassadors, conduct foreign affairs and the national defense, and appoint ambassadors with the advice and consent of Congress. By statute, the duties and powers of the President also include entry into diplomatic relations with foreign governments, consent to the establishment in the FSM of diplomatic missions, and the approval of foreign affairs policies. The conduct of foreign affairs, subject to the President's ultimate authority, resides with the Department of

External Affairs, under the direction of the secretary of the department. The duties and powers of the Secretary of External Affairs include formulating foreign affairs policies for review by the President; executing approved foreign affairs policies; establishing diplomatic and consular missions and offices; supervising diplomatic and consular staff; receiving heads of missions and representatives to be accredited to the FSM, approving the staffs of missions and regional or international organizations; and representing the FSM in negotiating, adopting, or authenticating treaties (FSM Code, Title 10[1987]).

The FSM's most important treaty is the Compact of Free Association, which requires, at Section 123, that the government of the FSM consult in the conduct of its foreign affairs with the United States (**see III, E Treaties**). The FSM has established diplomatic relations with a number of nations, both in the Pacific and elsewhere, and is a member of the United Nations, the South Pacific Forum, and other international and regional organizations. The FSM recognizes the diplomatic immunities of members of international organizations.

VII. Revenue Law

A. National

In 1989, almost 90 percent of the FSM's annual budget consisted of aid from the United States under the Compact of Free Association, but that proportion is intended to decrease as U.S. aid amounts gradually drop over a fifteen-year period.[19] Much of this aid is for particular programs, so it is impossible to place a precise value upon it, but it probably amounts to at least US$1 billion over the fifteen-year life (dating from 1986, when the compact was approved) of the compact's financial provisions, and some level of funding from the United States is likely to continue beyond that date. The remainder of the annual FSM budget comes primarily from income, business revenue, and import-export taxes. The FSM Constitution requires, at Article IX, Section 5, that national taxes be uniformly imposed. The FSM Income Tax Law (54 FSM Code 111–156) and the FSM laws on import and export taxes (54 FSM Code 201–203) provide for taxation of the wages and salaries of employees earned wholly or in part from employment within the FSM, the gross revenues of businesses derived from activities conducted wholly or in part within the FSM, and imports.

The tax on wages and salaries is equal to 6 percent of the first US$11,000 of wages and salaries and 10 percent on all amounts over US$11,000, except that any employee whose gross wages or salary is under US$5,000 may deduct US$1,000 from wages and salaries subject to taxation. Resident employers are required to withhold the tax imposed on wages and salaries. The tax on gross business revenues is US$80 per year on the first US$10,000 of gross revenues and 3 percent on amounts above US$10,000. Businesses with gross revenues of US$2,000 or less are exempt from taxation.

All imports are subject to a 3 percent value-added tax; there are higher tax rates, some of which were imposed to promote import substitution, on laundry bar soap, cigarettes, tobacco, perfume, cosmetics, toiletries, soft drinks, alcoholic beverages, food, gasoline, and diesel fuel (54 FSM Code 201). In late 1991, Congress passed a bill increasing import duties on fresh citrus fruits from 1 to 100 percent, and raising the duty on cigarettes by 160 percent, on soft drinks by 176 percent, and on beer by 139 percent. The increased duties are intended both to raise revenue and to protect local industry from less expensive foreign competition. By shifting from a set rate to a percentage basis, the bill also enables tax revenue to rise as the prices of goods increase.

B. States

The FSM Constitution, Article XII, requires that at least 50 percent of the revenues from national taxes be paid into the treasury of the state where collected. The Code gives the states higher proportions of some revenues. For example, 80 percent of the revenues from fuel taxes is distributed to the states.

Article XII of the Constitution permits state and local governments to levy taxes, although it stipulates that no tax may be levied or money appropriated by states except for public purposes; Article IX, Section 2, places all authority to levy income or import taxes in the national government. State governments therefore may levy taxes only on sales or property, and municipalities are further limited.[20] The Yap State Tax Act of 1979 (13 YSC 101–113), for example, levies excise taxes on meat and animal products, vegetables, beverages, spirits, tobacco, chemicals, plastics and synthetics, leather products, wood, paper, textiles, footwear, precious metals, and works of art. It also mandates a 10 percent hotel occupancy tax and a 10 percent tax on motor vehicle rentals. The FSM Constitution permits municipal governments to levy a surtax of up to 20 percent of taxes levied by the state government and gives municipal governments sole authority to levy business license fees. The national government does not tax real property. The Yap Constitution at Article IX provides that only municipal governments may levy taxes on real property. The Chuuk Constitution at Article VIII prohibits taxes on real property.

VIII. INVESTMENT LAW

A. Economic Development

Like most new nations, the FSM faces the need to use its limited resources to create and maintain infrastructure and public services, and to foster economic development. An aim of the United States in its compact negotiations was to change the FSM from "a government economy to a private sector economy,"[21] and the FSM seems to have chosen a free market economic model, so the production and distribution of many goods and services will depend on the market rather than on national needs-based planning. Government, in the market economy model, does supply some goods and services: it may take responsibility for large-scale capital projects or ongoing infrastructural services (such as communications and travel facilities), and it may offer some of the services (such as education) needed to sustain and reproduce the workforce. For the most part, however, in this economic model, government does not define and meet socioeconomic needs, but serves primarily to regulate the activities of the market and to provide the legal rules and mechanisms by which market decisions are made and enforced.

Although the FSM has opted generally to rely on a market economy to produce and distribute goods and services, the laws act in a number of ways to define economic development needs, to channel the activities of the market toward economic development, and to protect Micronesian interests. First, the national and state governments have set up agencies to establish and implement development plans, as well as funds earmarked for development programs. Second, government not only regulates, but also owns copra and fish processing plants, the key resource industries of Micronesia (see **XII, D Agriculture and Fisheries**). Third, there are limits on participation by non-Micronesians in the economy.

1. DEVELOPMENT PLANNING AND FUNDING

The national government has established the Federated Development Authority to establish overall development goals, policies, and strategies for the FSM and to coordinate development efforts so that state and national programs will be mutually supportive (55 FSM Code 321–328 [1987]). The Federated Development Authority is managed by a policy board, consisting of representatives of the chief executives of the FSM and of each of the four states. One of its major tasks, in conjunction with the Secretary of Finance, is the investment of compact funds. The Compact of Free Association requires at Section 211 that spending by the FSM of grants contributed pursuant to the compact must be in accordance with official overall economic development plans. In particular, 25 percent of compact funds are earmarked for economic development. Although the FSM Congress approved the first national development plan, covering the years 1985 to 1989 (see 42 FSM Code, Sec. 101 ff [1987]), approximately US$12 million of compact moneys lay fallow until November 1988 when, after much prodding by the President and the Federated Development Authority, the FSM Congress authorized the establishment of an Investment Development Fund. At the same session, Congress passed the Compact Financing Act, which permits states to borrow money on bonds backed by their future compact funds.

The FSM has also established the FSM Development Bank. The bank is managed by a five-member board of directors, appointed by the President with the advice and consent of Congress. The bank makes long-term, low-interest loans to FSM citizens. Interest on loans may not be less than one-half of 1 percent nor more than 5 percent per year, and each loan has a grace period, during which no interest accrues, equal to the time required before a project can be reasonably expected to yield a sufficient return to enable the borrower to make interest payments and repayments of principal. Funding for the loans comes from the FSM Revolving Economic Development Loan Fund, established by Congress, and from principal and interest payments (30 FSM Code 102–121 [1987]).

Economic development is a responsibility of both the national and state governments. The President must annually submit to each state governor a planning estimate, setting forth in detail compact and other funding available to each state for that fiscal year and in general the funding available for the next two fiscal years. In addition, the President must by May 15 of each year submit to Congress a comprehensive executive budget, containing annual program plans for compact and other funds for each state and for the national government and including an analysis of funding sources, spending emphases, staff levels, and programs (FSM Code, Title 55 [1987]).

The constitutions of Pohnpei (Article 7) and Yap (Article XIII) recognize the responsibility of the state government to promote economic and natural resource development. The Yap legislature has established planning commissions to create and implement master plans and land use requirements. One commission serves Yap Island proper and consists of one resident of each of the ten Yap Island municipalities, appointed by the chair of the Council of Pilung. The other commission serves the outer islands and consists of thirteen members who are residents of the area and appointed by the chiefs of the atolls. Commission members may not be members of the Councils of Pilung or Tamol (20 YSC 101–122).

Economic development may be a responsibility of municipalities as well. For example, Article 11, Section 3, of the Pohnpei Constitution requires that not less than 30 percent of all taxes received by the state government from sources within the state be appropriated to local governments for development projects and, if the local government has after public hearings adopted a local plan then for the operations identified in the local plan as well.

2. FOREIGN INVESTMENT

All national and state constitutions prohibit a noncitizen or a corporation not wholly owned by citizens from acquiring title to land or waters in Micronesia (**see XII, Land and Natural Resources Law**). The national and state governments also attempt to limit and regulate investment or business activities in the FSM by foreigners. The FSM Foreign Investment Act (32 FSM Code 201–232), provides that a noncitizen may engage in a business in the FSM or may acquire an interest in a business operating in the FSM only after obtaining a foreign investment permit.

Permit applications for businesses that will operate in more than one state are submitted to the FSM Foreign Investment Board. The board consists of five members, three of whom are appointed by the President and two by the Speaker of the FSM Congress. The board makes its determinations on the following bases:

1. the economic, social, or environmental need for the business;
2. the degree to which the business will effect change in exports or imports;
3. the extent to which the business will deplete a nonrenewable natural resource or disturb or pollute the environment;
4. the extent of participation by citizens in the ownership and management of the business;
5. the intent of the applicant to give employment preference to citizens and to train citizens for management positions;
6. the extent to which the capital, managerial, and technical skills for such a business are available among FSM citizens;
7. the extent to which the business will contribute to the overall economic well-being of the FSM; and
8. recommendations by the governments of all affected states.

The President may reverse an action taken by the board that the President determines would adversely affect a compelling national interest. Both the applicants and the state authorities have a right of appeal of board or presidential decisions. Any noncitizen who intentionally engages in business activities in the FSM without a permit, fails to comply with the limitations in a permit, or who obtains a permit by fraud or misrepresentation is subject to imprisonment for up to one year or a fine of not more than US$2,000, or both. Citizens who aid or abet noncitizens in the above activities are subject to similar penalties.

After a decision by the FSM Supreme Court that the Foreign Investment Act did not apply to the practice of law by noncitizen lawyers, Congress amended the act to require noncitizen lawyers to obtain foreign investment permits in order to practice law in the FSM.[22]

The power to regulate foreign and interstate commerce has been delegated exclusively to the national government by the FSM Constitution, Article IX, Section 2. However, states have enacted legislation intended to regulate and direct foreign businesses within their borders. Whether such enactments are in derogation of national powers has not been decided by the courts. The duties of the Yap Business License Board (established under the Yap State Business License Act, 22 YSC 201–281; **see XVIII Commercial Law**) include reviewing applications from non-Yapese and from corporations with less than majority Yapese ownership who wish to conduct business in Yap. In determining whether to grant a license, the board must take into account traffic safety; the availability of water and sewerage; the effect on land resources and on economic opportunities for resident Yapese; the effect on Yap customs, culture, and traditions; and conformity of the business to Yap's master plans. The penalty for failure to obtain a license is imprisonment for not more than six months, a fine of US$100 to US$500, or both.

There are some incongruities between the national and state legislation. For example, the FSM Foreign Investment Act provides that permit applications for businesses that will operate in only one state are to be submitted to the authorities in that state and not to the FSM Foreign

Investment Board. Meanwhile, the Yap State Business License Act provides that, prior to submission of an application for a Yap business license, foreign applicants must have obtained a permit under the FSM Foreign Investment Act.

Both national and state legislation gives preference in government contracts to FSM citizens. The FSM Public Contracts Act (55 FSM Code 401–418 [1987]), gives preference in construction and sales contracts with the FSM government to "citizen bidders," defined as businesses in which at least 51 percent of the ownership interest is held by citizens of the FSM, that have been resident in the FSM for at least one year immediately prior to the bidding, and that have paid gross revenue taxes to the FSM for the year immediately preceding the bidding. The states also give preference to their citizens and residents. In Yap, for example, preference in bidding on government contracts is given to corporations that are 51 percent owned by citizens and in which a substantial proportion of the labor force are citizens of the FSM and residents of Yap (9 YSC 530). Preference is also given in the public service and in private employment to FSM citizens (see **V, B Public Service and XX Labor Law**).

B. Banking

The power to regulate banking is delegated to the national government (FSM Constitution, Article IX, Section 2). The Federated States of Micronesia Bank Act of 1980 (FSM Code, Title 29) applies to all banks operating a branch or office in the FSM, both domestic and foreign. The act establishes a banking board (consisting of two members appointed by the President and one by Congress) that regulates and supervises all banks and banking operations, reviews applications for the organization of domestic banks, grants permits for the operation of branches of foreign banks, and issues the annual licenses required of all banks. The act prohibits the operation of a banking business without a license and provides that any entity operating as a licensed bank may engage in no other business. The act sets as goals of the FSM that executive positions be occupied by citizens and residents, that at least 75 percent of deposits be loaned to citizens and local businesses, and that no bank discriminate unfairly.

Domestic banks may be organized by any five or more persons with good character and banking or commercial ability and experience. The application to organize a domestic bank must establish the need in the locality for banking services. In determining whether to approve operations, the board should also consider whether the bank will be of benefit to the general public. A domestic bank must have capital stock of at least US$500,000, half of which must be paid in cash before the bank can start operating. Two-thirds of the capital stock must be owned by citizens of the FSM who have resided in the FSM for at least one year. The Bank of the Federated States of Micronesia, the country's first domestic commercial bank, opened in 1988. More than 90 percent of the bank's capital is owned by Micronesians, with the FSM Development Bank the largest shareholder.

To establish an office in the FSM, a foreign bank must have capital of at least US$20 million, except that a member bank of the United States Federal Deposit Insurance Corporation needs capital of only US$1 million. The application of the foreign bank must state the benefit to the public expected from its operation, and the board, in granting the application, should also consider the overall financial condition of the applicant, and the character and banking or commercial experience of its officers, and the investment the bank has made in the FSM.

All banks must be licensed annually by the board. In reviewing license applications, the board should consider (in addition to the development goals outlined above) whether the bank has served community needs by hiring, training, and promoting citizens of the FSM, whether loans made by the bank bear a prudent relation to deposits, and whether the bank has engaged in unfair discrimination.

IX. Welfare Law

The power to provide for public health and welfare is shared by the national and state governments. The FSM Constitution (Article IX, Section 3) was amended in 1991 to restrict Congress' power over education and health to setting minimum standards, coordinating state activities relating to foreign assistance, and supporting postsecondary education. The FSM Constitution, at Article XIII, Section 1, recognizes "the right of the people to education, health care and legal services," but requires the national government only to "take every step reasonable and necessary to provide these services," which is something less than a guarantee of all services possible. State constitutions contain similar provisions. The Pohnpei and Yap constitutions, for example, each mandate the state government to provide educational and health care services (Pohnpei Constitution, Article 7; Yap Constitution, Article XII). None of the constitutions include these as fundamental rights, however.

A. National

According to legislation initially passed under the Trusteeship, school attendance is required of all children between the ages of six and fourteen or until completion of elementary school (40 FSM Code 242). The FSM has educational facilities, both public and private, through high school, although places for students beyond the eighth grade are few. University education in the FSM is limited, and most FSM students seeking higher education attend universities in the United States. They can be supported up to a total of US$16,000 per eligible student by the Student Loan Revolving Fund (40 FSM Code 324–334 [1987]); in addition, FSM students are eligible for grants from the United States government.

The FSM Board of Education consists of five members—the chief of the Office of Education and one member from each state (appointed by the President, after discussion and consultation with the Governor of each state, and with the advice and consent of Congress). The board's primary responsibilities are to advise the national government in formulating national educational objectives and policies; establishing minimum uniform national standards for curricula, textbooks, teacher certification, and school licensing; and evaluating educational expenditures and recommending budgets. (40 FSM Code 121–128).

National laws set policies and minimum standards for health services, and establish agencies to carry out statutory policies and enforce statutory standards. The 1991 constitutional amendment will reduce the powers granted under these statutes. The Medical Health Care Licensing Act of 1986 (FSM Code, Title 41 [1987]) provides for licensing medical personnel (including doctors, nurses, optometrists, dentists, and pharmacists) and medical facilities. No persons (except citizens of the FSM who are practicing the traditional healing arts) may engage in the practice of medicine unless they are licensed by the FSM Health Care Licensing Board, are participating as students in a controlled residency program, or are licensed by a foreign jurisdiction and approved by the Health Care Licensing Board. The board has the power to set licensing requirements that comply with the five-year health plan. Similarly, under the Health Care Certificate of Need Act of 1982 (FSM Code, Title 41 [1987]), no health care facility or service may be constructed, expanded, or altered without first obtaining a certificate of need from the

Micronesia Health Planning and Development Agency, which may adopt regulations that comply with the five-year health plan.

B. State

The constitutions of the various states show minor but interesting variations in their approaches to the duty to provide education and health care. In education, for example, the Pohnpei Constitution, at Article 7, focuses on achieving universal primary education. To that end, the state government is required to establish free, compulsory education through a grade to be set by statute and to limit fees for education above those grades to the ability to pay. The government is also required to set minimum standards for educational achievement, which will be applicable to all public and private schools.

The Yap Constitution, at Article XII, while also stating that primary education is free, focuses on custom, providing that the traditions and customs of the people are to be taught in the schools. Legislation permits local school boards to employ "culture teachers" (16 YSC 101). Primary school education is made compulsory by statute in Yap (16 YSC 203). The states also provide scholarships and loans for students in postsecondary courses that are necessary to the state's development (see, for example, 16 YSC 502). The Yap State Educational and Recreational TV Act of 1978 (16 YSC 1001–1005) empowers the Governor to acquire equipment to construct a television station that will be operated either by the government or under lease; the equipment has not yet been purchased.

The state constitutions and laws also differ somewhat in relation to health care. The Pohnpei Constitution, Article 7, requires the state government to provide and regulate health care services for the public (although there is no requirement that these be free) and mandates the government to establish and execute comprehensive plans for health care improvement. The Yap Constitution, Article XII, again focuses on custom, providing that the state's support for public health care must include support for traditional medicine. The Yap State Code also requires that drug labels include warnings in both English and Yapese (15 YSC 302).

X. Criminal Law

A. National

Until 1991, Article IX, Section 2, of the FSM Constitution provided that the national government had jurisdiction over "major" crimes and gave to Congress the exclusive power "to define major crimes and prescribe penalties, having due regard for local custom and tradition." Thus, the distinction between national and state criminal jurisdiction was founded not on whether the crime has a national or state nexus but on the severity of the crime.

The National Criminal Code (FSM Code, Title 11) originally defined major crimes as those punishable by three or more years' imprisonment or those resulting in loss or theft of property or services in the value of US$1,000 or more, as well as any attempt to commit such crimes. In 1987, Title 11 was amended to give the states jurisdiction over a larger proportion of offenses. The amended Code provided that major crimes would be those punishable by ten or more years' imprisonment.

However, in 1991, Article IX, Section 2, of the Constitution was amended to give the national government jurisdiction not over "major" crimes, but over "national" crimes (**see II Historical, Cultural, and Economic Survey**). This change means that jurisdiction of the national courts will depend not on the severity of the offense but, according to the committee reports of the 1990 constitutional convention, on whether the matter is "inherently national [in] character":

> [A] repeal of the major crimes power is needed at this time. . . . [T]he state courts are well-established and fully-functioning, unlike when the Constitution was first approved. The Committee is fully confident in the ability of these courts to guarantee the due process rights of the accused, and provide speedy and impartial decisions in all criminal proceedings, regardless of the severity of the crime or the identity of the defendant. Also . . . each state can best decide how to give due regard to local custom and tradition in defining crimes and their punishments.[23]

The 1987 amendment to the National Criminal Code made much of that Code redundant and required the states to expand the coverage in their codes. The constitutional amendment gives to the states exclusive jurisdiction over yet more offenses now defined only in the National Criminal code. The states have not yet enacted revisions to their codes. On the presumption that state criminal codes will roughly track the now-redundant provisions of the National Criminal Code, this section will summarize its major provisions.

The FSM Code classifies a felony as an offense that may be punished by imprisonment for more than one year, a petty misdemeanor as an offense that may be punished by imprisonment for not more than thirty days, and all other crimes as misdemeanors. There is no statutory time limitation on prosecutions for murder. The statute of limitations for an offense punishable by imprisonment for more than ten years is six years, for any other felony is three years, for a misdemeanor is two years, and for a petty misdemeanor is six months.

The National Criminal Code requires courts to recognize and consider generally accepted customs prevailing within the FSM relating to crimes and to criminal liability, but the Code itself detracts from the force of its support of custom by providing that, whenever there is a dispute as to the existence or effect of customary law, the party asserting applicability has the burden of proving by a preponderance of the evidence the existence, applicability, and effect of the customary law.

The FSM Supreme Court has had mixed reactions to the recognition of custom in criminal cases. The Court has interpreted Articles V and XI of the Constitution and the National Criminal Code to require that it consider and apply customary law, even when custom conflicts with provisions of the Code.[24] However, the Court has refused to take a traditional Pohnpeian forgiveness ceremony into account in determining criminal liability. The Court based this decision on a review of the differing goals served by customary rules and the criminal law. Customary forgiveness ceremonies, the Court said, repair the breach between the victim and the defendant and restore harmony to the community; whereas criminal law serves the interest of the state in deterring crime, promoting respect for its laws, and maintaining the social order—aims that cannot be met by customary forgiveness ceremonies.[25] But, the Court has held that customary punishments must be taken into account in sentencing.[26]

A person who has been convicted of a national offense may, in addition to or instead of imprisonment, be sentenced to pay a fine that, depending upon the offense, could be as high as US$100,000. There are no mandatory sentences. Courts may impose imprisonment or a fine for less than the maximum term, suspension, probation, restitution or service to the victim or the victim's family, confinement to a particular geographical area, or community service. Restitution and service to the victim or the victim's family are customary responses to criminal acts in Micronesia, and the Code provides that this should be the sentence imposed whenever appropriate.

B. State

The states now have exclusive jurisdiction over all crimes, except those of an inherently national character. Although redrafts of the state criminal codes that take account of the recent change in their criminal jurisdiction are not yet available, earlier versions of state criminal codes suggest that the state legislatures may treat custom differently than does the National Criminal Code. For example, the Yap State Crimes Act (Yap State Code, Title 11) recognizes the existence of crimes that are such solely by generally respected native custom and provides a maximum penalty for these offenses of six months' imprisonment, a US$100 fine, or both. In Yap, custom must also be taken into account in sentencing. The State Crimes Act requires the courts, in making sentencing decisions, to give due recognition to custom. Instead of or in addition to other penalties, a court may order a defendant to establish residence at a specific place and to remain there for a period not to exceed the maximum time for the offense. A court may also order restitution or compensation for the victim of the crime. State courts have occasionally dropped the charges or mitigated sentences when customary forgiveness ceremonies have been held, and the Kosrae court has held that since by custom short-term crops belong to the farmer rather than to the land holder, a person who grew crops is not liable for theft for harvesting them on someone else's land.[27]

XI. JURISDICTION AND JUDICIAL PROCEDURE

A. Civil Procedure

Article XI of the FSM Constitution and the Judiciary Act of 1979, (FSM Code, Title 4) govern the structure, jurisdiction, and powers of the national courts. The FSM Supreme Court has the power to make declaratory judgments;[28] issue writs and other process, make rules and orders, and do all acts not inconsistent with law or with rules of procedure and evidence established by the Chief Justice;[29] and to punish those in contempt of court.[30]

Title 6, Chapter 8, of the FSM Code establishes statutory limitations on bringing actions. Actions upon court judgments and actions for the recovery of land must be brought within twenty years after the cause of action accrues. Actions for assault and battery, false imprisonment or slander, actions against a police officer, actions for malpractice, and actions for wrongful death or injury caused by the wrongful act or negligence of another must be brought within two years. All other actions must be brought within six years. The FSM Supreme Court permits tolling of the statute of limitations in wrongful death actions.[31]

Under Article XI, Section 9 of the FSM Constitution, the Chief Justice is authorized to establish rules of civil procedure. Revised rules were issued in 1990, based on U.S. models. The formal rules do not give much scope for the flexibility of customary processes.

The states may be somewhat more open to customary process. The Pohnpei State Court, denying a motion for a default judgment, has held that rules of civil procedure and the adversary system must be mitigated in line with the less rigid views and practices of custom.[32] The Yap State Judiciary Act (Yap State Code, Title 4) provides that the procedure of Municipal Courts must be consistent with customary means of resolving disputes. Before bringing a case to the Municipal Court, the parties are supposed to try to resolve it in accordance with custom within the family or village. However, the Kosrae State Code provides at Section 6.303 that the State Court cannot consider custom unless counsel produce evidence of its existence.

B. Criminal Procedure

Pursuant to Article XI, Section 9 of the Constitution, the FSM Supreme Court has adopted rules of criminal procedure, amended in 1990, that are similar to the U.S. Federal Rules of Criminal Procedure, except that there are no arraignments. In addition, Title 12 of the FSM Code, initially promulgated under the Trusteeship, remains in effect and is applicable both to the FSM Supreme Court and to the states until they enact new criminal procedure codes or other laws in conflict with it.

Under Title 12, a person may not be arrested without a warrant, unless a breach of the peace or other criminal offense has been committed, and the offender is trying to escape; the offender is in the act of committing a criminal offense; a criminal offense has been committed, and a policeman has reasonable grounds to believe that the person to be arrested has committed it; or persons are found under circumstances that justify a reasonable suspicion that they have committed or intend to commit a felony. In every case in which the arrested person refuses to submit or attempts to escape, the degree of force necessary to compel submission (but no greater degree of force) may be used. Force may be used to enter premises in order to make an arrest, but before force is used entry must be demanded, and the reason for it given, in a loud voice and, if practicable, in a local language.

Any person making an arrest must, at or before the time of the arrest, make every reasonable effort to inform the arrested person as to the cause and authority of the arrest.[33] Persons arrested have the following rights:

1. the right to see counsel once, at any time, for a reasonable period of time at the place of detention and afterward at reasonable intervals and for reasonable periods of time;
2. the right to see at reasonable intervals and for reasonable periods of time family members and employers;
3. the right to have a message sent to counsel, family members, and employers;
4. the right to be released or charged within a reasonable time, which cannot exceed twenty-four hours;
5. the right either to be released or to be brought before a court for a bail hearing within a reasonable period of time, which cannot exceed twenty-four hours;
6. the right to remain silent, to confer with counsel before being questioned and to have counsel present during questioning, and to have the services of the Public Defender; and
7. the right to be informed of all these rights before being questioned.

Searches and seizures may not be made without a warrant, except in connection with an arrest, in which case the arrested person may be searched for weapons, and his or her person and the premises where the arrest was made may be searched for the instruments, fruits, and evidence of the criminal offense for which the arrest was made. The warrant may be issued only upon a showing of probable cause, supported by an affidavit describing the place to be searched and the persons or things to be seized. Unlawfully seized property may be suppressed or excluded from evidence.[34]

Any person arrested for a criminal offense other than murder is entitled to be released on bail before conviction. The amount of bail must be such as, in the judgment of the court or official fixing it, will ensure the presence of the arrested person at further proceedings, and no more.

Defendants have the following rights in connection with their trials:

1. to have in advance of trial a copy of the charge;
2. to consult counsel before trial and to have representation at trial;[35]
3. to have additional time to prepare a defense;

4. to present witnesses of their choice;
5. to give evidence on their own behalf, but a defendant may not be compelled to give evidence;
6. to have proceedings interpreted; and
7. to have an assessor appointed.

C. Jurisdiction

The FSM Constitution's allocation of civil jurisdiction between the national and state courts attempts to strike a balance between uniformity on national issues and decentralization of decision-making authority to the states. But the balance seems weighted in favor of the national courts. The Constitution provides at Article XI, Section 6, that the FSM Supreme Court has original (although not necessarily exclusive) jurisdiction where cases involve national laws and where there is diversity among the parties. In addition, the Constitution provides at Article XI, Section 8, that state courts must certify to the Appellate Division of the FSM Supreme Court questions involving substantial issues of national law. In interpreting these constitutional provisions, the FSM Supreme Court has struck the balance in favor of the states where questions of national law are concerned but toward the national courts in diversity cases.

The FSM Supreme Court has stated that, although the certification of national questions to the national courts is important in developing a nationally uniform law, it is also important that courts have the benefit of one another's opinions. Therefore, noting that its jurisdiction over national questions is not exclusive, the Court has held that it will normally remand to the state courts cases certified to it under Article XI, Section 8, unless definite reasons not to do so appear.[36]

The Court has also decided that the national courts should generally abstain from taking cases that are important to the states. Considerations that should lead a national court to abstain include the interest of the state in developing a coherent policy on the issue, the risk of costly or duplicative litigation, and cases in which the plaintiff is seeking monetary damages from the state. Considerations weighing against abstention include the prevention of delay or injustice and the presence of national interests.[37]

But the FSM Supreme Court's willingness to defer to state courts is not manifest in its decisions on diversity jurisdiction under Article XI, Section 6, of the FSM Constitution. The Court has held that parties have an unconditional right to invoke diversity jurisdiction and that there need not be complete diversity among the parties for diversity jurisdiction to be invoked.[38]

A potential conflict exists between the Court's diversity jurisdiction and constitutional limitations on its jurisdiction over land matters. Intending to limit the role of the national government in land matters, the drafters of the Constitution provided in Article XI that the FSM Supreme Court does not have jurisdiction over land matters where the government is a party to the case. The Court has held, however, that national courts do have jurisdiction over land matters arising under diversity jurisdiction.[39] These decisions could deprive state courts of what was probably intended to be exclusive jurisdiction over land matters. Partially resolving the problem, the Court has held that the FSM Constitution does not bar state courts from hearing cases that arise under national law and that, except where a substantial constitutional question is at issue, national courts should abstain, permitting state courts to decide the case under state law.[40]

State laws generally provide that the state's highest court has original trial jurisdiction over all cases arising within the state. The Yap State Judiciary Act (Yap State Code, Title 4), for example, gives to the State Court subject matter jurisdiction over all cases in the state, except those exclusive to the FSM Supreme Court. It gives the State Court personal jurisdiction in civil cases over persons residing or found in the state, and over persons who transact any business within the state, operate a vehicle in the state or a boat in the state fishery zone, or commit a tort within the state.

If a national court hears a dispute that involves state law issues, it should decide those issues on the basis of state law. State court decisions are still relatively scarce, however, and if no state law exists, a national court must decide the issues based upon its understanding of what the ruling of the state's highest court would probably be. If the state court subsequently decides the issue differently in a different case, the national courts will follow that state decision in future cases. A national court may, rather than decide a state issue itself, certify that issue to a state court for decision. The FSM Supreme Court has held that certification should be preferred in order to promote federalism and judicial harmony and is especially recommended when the state is a defendant in the case. The Court further held, however, that an issue should not be certified to a state court if it is insignificant, if it is an issue of fact rather than law, if the state's law regarding the issue is settled, or if the issue is not part of the case or controversy between the parties.[41]

The national courts have decided a number of cases, particularly in contracts and torts, without mentioning that state law controls. These cases have been decided with reference to the Judicial Guidance Clause (Article XI, Section 11, of the FSM Constitution), which requires that decisions of the national courts be congruent with the Constitution, with Micronesian custom, and with the social and geographical conditions of Micronesia. The state courts seem to be adopting a similar approach to the development of the common law, so the general tenor of decisions may not differ significantly (see III, H Common Law). Despite their general similarities, however, the differing sensitivities of the national and state judiciaries to customary law may lead to specific differences in judicial decisions that will only be resolved as state courts issue decisions in more cases.

D. Appellate Jurisdiction and Procedure

At both the national and state levels, appeals are heard by the Appellate Division of the highest court, except that the Trial Division of that court hears appeals from lower courts. Appeals in the FSM Supreme Court's appellate division must be heard by a panel of at least three justices, none of whom was the trial judge (FSM Constitution, Article XI, Section 2), but fewer than three justices may decide a national question certified to the Appellate Division by a state court.[42] In 1991, the FSM Supreme Court issued revised rules of appellate procedure, pursuant to the rule-making authority granted to the Chief Justice by Article XI, Section 9, of the Constitution. The rules are similar to U.S. models.

XII. LAND AND NATURAL RESOURCES

A. Land Tenure and Administration

Land is scarce in Micronesia. It is also an important economic and cultural resource, serving in traditional cultures as a source of subsistence and as a basis for chiefly titles and clan prestige. During the colonial period, land also became, for those operating in the imported sector (a group that included some Micronesians and many expatriates), a source of capital and a commodity. As a result, much land passed out of clan control and into individual or governmental ownership. Recognizing the overwhelming power that a centralized administration can bring to bear on land issues, the Constitutional Convention pointedly excluded any power over land tenure and administration from the national government, leaving issues of land law to be determined by the states.[43]

Fears that more land would pass from traditional or Micronesian ownership also led to the adoption of Article XIII, Sections 4 and 5, of the FSM Constitution, as amended, which prohibit noncitizens or corporations not wholly owned by citizens from acquiring title to land or waters in the FSM and also prohibit lease agreements for the use of land for an indefinite term by such persons or by any government.

State constitutions similarly protect land from alienation to or perpetual occupation by noncitizens. The Pohnpeian Constitution, for example, provides at Article 12 that permanent interests in real property may be acquired only by "Pohnpeian citizens who are also pwilidak of Pohnpei." (*Pwilidak* —also rendered in the Pohnpeian Constitution as *pweldak*; see IV, B (1) (b) Nationality and Citizenship— is roughly translated as a true citizen, a child of the soil of Pohnpei.) The Pohnpeian-language version of the state Constitution is stronger than the English version, in that the Pohnpeian text denies to other than pwilidak not only the ownership of land, but all the rights that are caught up in customary notions of relations to land, including the right to work or use it and the right to inherit it. The Pohnpeian Constitution also provides that no lease of land may exceed twenty-five years or purport to grant the use of the land indefinitely, except leases granted by the Pohnpeian government or as provided by statute. The Yap Constitution provides, at Article XIII, that noncitizens and corporations not wholly owned by citizens may acquire the use of land for periods not to exceed fifty years. The Trust Territory High Court decided many disputes over land ownership according to titles recorded by the German or Japanese colonial administrations, rather than according to customary title. Article XV, Section 3, of the Yap Constitution, which provides that the opinions of the Trust Territory High Court are not precedent in Yap State Courts, may be a reaction to this.

The states vary in the extent to which customary law is recognized in their land tenure laws, a variation resulting in large part from the different experiences of the states during the colonial period. On the island of Pohnpei, for example, where land was held under customary law by matrilineages, the Germans instituted between 1912 and 1914 a massive conversion to conditional freehold titles and patrilineal succession. German land laws provided that land could be owned only by male heads of extended families (although they were required to provide use rights to sisters and younger brothers), sold only with the consent of the Nanmwarki (the paramount chief) and the German Governor, and passed at death only to the eldest male heir. During later colonial administrations, new laws permitted land to be owned by women and to be sold, donated, or willed but did not revive customary rules of ownership (in fact, the authority of chiefs over land sales was eliminated). The clarification of interests in land continues to be a major problem in Pohnpei, despite the existence of German titles. Many of the German land documents had no clearly stipulated boundaries, land was reclassified or sold without registration under subsequent colonial administrations, and many documents were destroyed during World War II. The Pohnpei Constitution now provides, at Article 12, that land may be transferred only according to statute.

The Pohnpei Land Commission was created in the 1970s to investigate, adjudicate, and register ownership and other interests in all lands, both public and private, whether or not the interests were disputed. Its determinations, made after hearings, could be appealed to the trial and then to the appellate division of the Trust Territory High Court (later to state courts). Francisco Castro, Chief Land Commissioner, reported in 1984 that (in addition to registering undisputed interests) the commission had adjudicated more than 4,000 disputed cases, of which

106 had been appealed. Of the appeals heard by 1984, the commission's ruling had been upheld in 48 cases and reversed in 3.[44]

In Yap, most land is still held under customary tenure, and the Yap Constitution provides, at Article XIII, Section 3, that title to land may be acquired only in a manner consistent with tradition and custom. In Yap, too, the clarification of titles and boundaries remains problematic, as suggested by the legislative attempt to establish a land survey system that will be "permanent and lasting" (10 YSC 501) and by the Yap Land Surveyors Registration Act (Yap State Code, Title 22), which creates a state board to register land surveyors so that land surveys and maps can be attested by registered surveyors. The Yap legislature has established planning commissions to create and implement master plans and land use requirements (20 YSC 101–122).

The Real Property Security Instruments Act of 1977 (FSM Code, Title 33), which applies only in those states that have adopted it, provides for the creation of deeds of trust in real property securing the performance of an obligation or the payment of a debt. The act requires that a foreclosure sale of the real property may occur only on the filing of a notice of default and service of the notice upon the debtor. The act also provides that a debtor may cure the default prior to foreclosure. To date, no state has adopted it.

B. Customary Land Law[45]

Traditional land tenure systems vary considerably among the Micronesian islands, and colonialism, population growth, and economic change have introduced further variations. (This brief summary will, for the most part, focus on traditional land tenure, as if the changes wrought by colonialism had not occurred.) In most Micronesian societies, customary land tenure is part of the hierarchic structure of society, so that land is viewed as held at the pleasure of the paramount chief. Even in precolonial times, however, there were many restrictions on a chief's ability to influence land tenure—contests for succession, the need to retain the loyalty of followers, the inherited relationship of clans or kin groups to defined areas of land—and colonial authorities did much to weaken or destroy chiefly authority over land. Nevertheless, it is still true of most areas to say that politics and land rights are interrelated.

Any piece of usable land is subject to numerous overlapping interests or rights. Most Micronesian societies are divided into royal and commoner clans or lineages. In some areas, commoners hold use rights to land, subject to the right of the landholding nobility to receive a portion of the land's produce; in other areas, royal clans hold the better land. Micronesian societies are segmental, with clans or lineages identified with certain territory. This identification is both political (the lineage head may administer the group's lands) and usufructuary (clan membership is the normative basis for rights to resources). Although clans and lineages are the ultimate landholders, however, the basic landholding and land-working unit tends to be a smaller matrilineal kin group (but on Yap Island, it is patrilineal), usually a household unit or extended family. Each family needs a variety of land types for different purposes—including taro gardens, other gardens, fruit trees, house plots, and ceremonial areas. In some societies, this is accomplished by giving each family a contiguous strip of land that runs from the hills to the sea; in other societies, estate holders have a variety of small, widely separated plots of land. Different persons or groups may have simultaneous interests in the same plot of land. While the estate holders maintain the right to build houses or plant gardens, for example, others may be free (with or without permission) to gather uncultivated plants or fruits, to hunt, or even to plant gardens. A person gardening on another's land has sole right to the fruits of his or her labor, but the land reverts to the estate holder after harvest. Men's houses, dance grounds, or other community areas may be constructed on land nominally held by one family or may be viewed as clan property. In an atoll culture, the sea, reef, and lagoon are resources as important as land, and use rights as carefully divided. In some societies, clan members can fish anywhere (perhaps with the requirement that a part of the catch go to the rights holder); in others, rights to areas of the reef are divided among estate-holding groups.

Rights to land are contingent upon membership in a kin group, but land tenure and succession to land are flexible. Members of the clan can expect to receive a portion of the household's land when they mature or marry, although title to that land may not be secure until the death of the elder generation. Because the clan holds residual title to all land, transfers of land to nonmembers are usually transfers only of temporary use rights. However, in earlier times, when a smaller population and the absence of cash crops meant less pressure on land, persons without land could usually obtain it through gift, trade, or marriage. Land also changed ownership in precolonial times by war and conquest. A person whose matrilineage did not have sufficient land could obtain land from patrilineal relatives. Land thus could be transferred outside the clan, although this was usually viewed as extending clan membership to a former outsider rather than as alienating land from the clan.

C. Government Taking of Land

During the colonial period, much land passed into government hands. The German government purported to purchase land, although few customary land tenure systems recognized the concept of permanent alienation of land to strangers. The Japanese government declared itself the owner of all uncultivated land, although most of it was clan hunting or fallow territory. It has been estimated that, by 1933, approximately 73 percent of the total land area of Micronesia was claimed by the colonial administration.[46] During World War II, the American military occupied much private land for war purposes. After the war, the military government continued to occupy much of the land, although it did attempt to determine the owners and to pay compensation.

These experiences convinced many Micronesians that the central government ought not to have the power to take land. In a compromise worked out at the Constitutional Convention, all reference to eminent domain powers was omitted from the FSM Constitution. The Constitution does not expressly forbid the national government from seizing land, but it does not expressly permit the government to do so. While the Constitution gives the national government no express rights, it does give the government a duty. Article XIII, Section 6, obligates the national government to seek renegotiation of any agreement for the use of land to which the government of the United States is a party.

Unlike the FSM Constitution, state constitutions contain express grants of power to state governments to take land, but this power is circumscribed. The Pohnpei Constitution (Article 12) requires that land be taken only for a public purpose and only after consultation with the relevant local government and good faith negotiation with the owners of the interests. Negotiation must include an offer either to exchange the land for land of comparable value or to pay just compensation. Under the Pohnpei Public Lands Distribution Act of 1980, the Ponape Land Commission had by 1984 adjudicated 658 claims of interests in public lands.[47]

The Yap Constitution (Article II, Section 11) permits the state to take land by eminent domain but makes the limitations on the state's eminent domain powers one of the fundamental rights. Under Article II, the state may take land only for a public purpose and must engage in good faith negotiations with its owners, pay just compensation, and consult with the local government.. The Yap State Code adds that the government may transfer its interest in public lands, but any sale, grant, or lease for more than ten years requires legislative consent. Any contract for the sale, grant, or lease of public lands must certify that it is consistent with Yap's official state plans (9 YSC 103).

The Chuuk Constitution, at Article XI, Section 2, provides that the government may take land only "for a specified purpose of general public interest, as prescribed by statute." Just compensation must be given before the land is taken, and the government can unilaterally set the compensation only after "negotiations with the owner for voluntary lease, sale, or exchange [have been] fully exhausted." The courts may determine not only the adequacy of compensation, but also the good faith of the negotiations and the "reasonable necessity of the acquisition." If the purpose for which the land was taken ends, the state must return the land to the original owner or the owner's successor.

D. Agriculture and Fisheries

1. NATIONAL

Among the powers expressly delegated to Congress by Article IX of the FSM Constitution are regulation of foreign and interstate commerce; of navigation and shipping except within lagoons, lakes, and rivers; and of ownership, exploration, and exploitation of marine resources beyond 12 miles from island baselines. Congress has exercised these powers to assist copra production and fishing, the FSM's two major export industries. Congress' aims are to sustain prices, assist the industries to become more efficient and productive, preserve land and marine resources, and discourage foreign competition.

The Coconut Development Authority is both a regulator of coconut prices and itself a producer. As a producer, it is authorized to engage in the manufacture and processing of coconut products; to buy, sell, and export coconut products; and to purchase and maintain production facilities. It also has the power to stabilize the price of coconut products by fixing the prices to be paid to producers or sellers. The government, in addition, regulates the export of copra by requiring that no person or entity may purchase copra for export without first obtaining a license from the Secretary of Resources and Development (FSM Code, Title 22).

In the fisheries industry, the government's ownership interest and its interest in promoting the fisheries industry are vested in the National Fisheries Corporation, established under the FSM National Fisheries Corporation Act of 1983 (FSM Code, Title 24 [1987]), as a public corporation authorized to engage in all commercial activities that further the development of the fishing and fisheries industries in FSM. The corporation has the power to enter into joint venture and other agreements with foreign persons and governments, participate as owner or other interest holder in commercial fishing ventures, manage or operate commercial fishing projects, provide technical assistance and services to the fisheries industry, promote the training of Micronesian citizens in the fisheries industry, and invest in the expansion and improvement of the fisheries industry in FSM.

The government's interests in regulating fishing by private parties and in strictly limiting the access of foreign fishing vessels to the FSM extended fishery zone are carried out by the Micronesian Maritime Authority. The authority's powers include adopting regulations for the conservation, management, and exploitation of living resources in the extended fishery zone; concluding agreements with foreign persons wishing to fish in the FSM's extended fishery zone; and issuing permits for foreign fishing in the zone. In addition, the authority participates in planning and executing programs of the National Fisheries Corporation. The Code requires foreign fishing vessels to obtain permits before fishing in the FSM's fishery zone and imposes severe penalties for violations of this requirement (FSM Code, Title 24 [1987]).

Title 23 of the FSM Code, much of which was enacted under the Trusteeship, sets limits on the exploitation of certain scarce marine resources, primarily in order to ensure that there will be a continuing economic supply of these resources and that their exploitation is limited to Micronesian citizens. Included are sea turtles, artificially cultivated sponges, mother-of-pearl oysters, and trochus. Penalties for violation of these limits include fines of up to US$100 or imprisonment for up to six months, or both. Exceptions to the prohibitions and limits are made when the exploitation is for traditional purposes or by traditional methods.

2. STATE

The state governments have also acted to support agriculture and fishing. The Yap Constitution provides, at Article XIII, Section 1, that the state government should promote conservation and the development of resources. The Yap legislature has provided for the appointment of agricultural extension agents to assist local farmers in coconut planting and copra, vegetable, and fruit production (21 YSC 101–106). The Yap Fishing Authority Act of 1979 (18 YSC 101–182) created the Yap Fishing Authority to promote and support commercial utilization of marine resources, guide the state government in establishing a marine resources development policy, adopt regulations governing the exploitation of marine resources, make loans and otherwise support commercial fisheries development by locally owned private enterprise, act as an agent for the sale of supplies, and carry on fisheries businesses.

The Yap Constitution also provides, at Article XIII, Section 5, for state recognition of traditional rights and ownership of natural resources and areas both within and beyond Yap's 12-mile jurisdictional limit. This may conflict with the FSM Constitution's delegation to the national government of exclusive authority beyond the 12-mile limit. Section 5 of the Yap Constitution further declares that no action may be taken to impair these traditional rights except that the state may provide for conservation of natural resources within the 12-mile limit. Although the national government has the exclusive power to regulate foreign commerce (and, thus, perhaps to regulate foreign fishing), the Yap Constitution, Article XIII, Section 6, provides that no foreign fishing may take place within the state's marine space unless permitted by persons exercising traditional rights or persons who have acquired ownership by statute. The Yap State Fishery Zone Act of 1980 (Yap State Code, Title 18) establishes the state fishery zone as extending 12 miles from island baselines; provides that traditionally recognized fishing rights on submerged reefs are to be preserved; forbids foreign fishing in internal waters and requires permits for foreign fishing in the state fishery zone; and creates additional duties for the Yap Fishing Authority, including adoption of regulations regarding marine resources conservation, issuance of fishing permits (including those for foreign vessels), and negotiation (with the advice and consent of the Micronesian Maritime Authority) of foreign fishing contracts.

F. Other Natural Resources

1. THE ENVIRONMENT

The FSM Environmental Protection Act (FSM Code, Title 25 [1987]) recognizes "the critical importance of restoring and maintaining environmental quality for the overall welfare and development of man" and declares at Section 520 that

> it is the continuing policy of the Federated States of Micronesia . . . to use all practicable means and measures . . . to foster and promote the general welfare, to create and maintain conditions under which man and nature can exist in productive harmony, and fulfill the

social, economic, and other requirements of present and future generations of the Federated States of Micronesia.

This less than resounding support for the environment is to be carried out by an Environmental Protection Board, with the power to promulgate regulations "to protect the environment, human health, welfare, and safety and to abate, control, and prohibit pollution or contamination of air, land and water" in accordance with the act. This broad power is limited, however, by the requirement that the board "balance the needs of economic and social development against those of environmental quality" (25 FSM Code 609 [1987]). The board may require the national government (but not state governments or private parties) to prepare an environmental impact statement before taking action that would significantly affect the environment. Penalties for violations of the act can include an order to clean up or abate the effects of any pollutant, a civil penalty of up to US$10,000 for each day of the violation, and a civil action for damages.

State legislation on environmental protection has not gone even so far as national legislation. Thus, while Article XIII, Section 1, of the Yap Constitution requires the state to promote conservation and natural resources, the only solely conservationist legislation protects certain endangered species—wild pigeons, coconut crabs, wild turtles, clams, and fruitbats (8 YSC 1001). (See also Pohnpei Constitution, Article 7, Section 1.)

2. HISTORICAL AND CULTURAL RESOURCES

The FSM Institute for Micronesian History and Culture was established under the Trusteeship to "protect and preserve the diverse cultural heritage of the peoples of Micronesia" (26 FSM Code 101). The powers and duties of the institute include assisting the states in cultural and historic preservation programs, advising the executive branch and Congress about the potential effects of public and private actions on historic and cultural properties, and administering research grants. The institute can suspend any activity by any party operating with government funding or permission, if the institute determines that the action threatens immediate and irreparable harm to a historical or cultural artifact. The activity may not be resumed until approved by the President. A recent amendment (26 FSM Code 401 [1987]) makes it an offense to willfully transport, deface, or destroy any historic property without governmental authority.

State constitutions and legislation also provide for the conservation of traditional cultural artifacts. The Pohnpei Constitution, for example, provides at Article 7, Section 5, that the government of Pohnpei must establish plans for the identification and preservation of places, artifacts, and information of historical and cultural importance and, at Article 7, Section 3, for the establishment of a library, museum, and archives. Similarly, the Yap Historic Preservation Act (5 YSC 401–411) establishes the Historic Preservation Office to preserve sites, structures, buildings, objects, areas, traditions, crafts, arts, stories, and songs. The act requires agencies of the government to notify the Historic Preservation Office before commencing any activity that may have an impact on historic properties or culture. If agreement cannot be reached on how to minimize adverse impact, the Governor makes a binding decision, balancing the value of the activity to Yap's social and economic development against the value of the historic property or culture.

3. NUCLEAR SUBSTANCES

Both national and state constitutions prohibit the use or storage of nuclear or other harmful substances. The FSM Constitution, at Article XIII, Section 2, forbids the use or storage of nuclear materials in the FSM. "Radioactive, toxic chemical, or other harmful substances may not be tested, stored, used, or disposed of within the jurisdiction of the Federated States of Micronesia without the express approval of the national government of the Federated States of Micronesia." State constitutional provisions are in potential conflict with the FSM Constitution. The Pohnpei Constitution (Article 13) prohibits the introduction, storage, use, testing, or disposal within the territory of Pohnpei of nuclear, chemical, gas or biological weapons, nuclear power plans, or the waste materials therefrom, unless specifically and expressly permitted to do so by a majority of votes cast in a referendum by the people of Pohnpei. The Pohnpei Constitution further provides that the introduction, storage, use, testing, or disposal of all harmful substances other than the above shall be limited to activities declared by statute to be necessary for the enhancement of public health, public safety, and economic development. The Yap Constitution (Article XIII, Section 4) bans all radioactive or nuclear substances from the state.

XIII. Persons and Entities

FSM statutes do not define persons and do not state whether corporations or other business associations possess the legal attributes of persons. Title 36 of the FSM Code, which contains the requirements for corporate formation (see **XVIII, B Business Organizations**), does not describe the purposes and powers of corporations

The age of maturity is generally eighteen, although it is somewhat differently defined in various statutes, depending upon the subject matter. For example, voting is open to citizens who are eighteen, although the President and members of Congress must be at least thirty (Constitution, Articles VI and IX). To contract a valid marriage under the Trust Territory Code (Title 39, Chapter 2) a male must be eighteen and a female sixteen, and females between sixteen and eighteen require parental consent (see **XIV, A Marriage**). In criminal cases, offenders under the age of eighteen may be held criminally liable but are to receive special treatment from the courts, such as informal hearings in closed session and detention apart from adult offenders (FSM Code, Title 12). Offenders between sixteen and eighteen, however, may be treated as adults "if in the opinion of the court [the offender's] physical and mental maturity so justifies" (FSM Code, Title 12, Section 1101).

XIV. Family Law

The FSM Constitution leaves all matters of personal and family law to the exclusive jurisdiction of the states (FSM Constitution, Article VIII, Section 2, and Article IX, Section 2). However, none of the states has enacted family law legislation, perhaps because citizens of the FSM may choose whether to marry and divorce one another and may adopt children, according to custom or according to statute, and customary laws are viewed as satisfactory in this area. In the absence of new legislation, the applicable provisions of Title 39 of the Trust Territory Code remain in force (see, for example, Yap Constitution, Article XV, Section 2).

A. Marriage

In most customary societies, the commencement of marriage is a gradual process, probably not complete until the first child is born. The process may begin when the couple choose to live together (where they live will depend upon whether their society is patrilocal or matrilocal and upon how much land each family has available) and will probably include feasts, ceremonies, and gift giving, either when the couple establish their residence or when the wife becomes pregnant. In most Micronesian societies, clans are exogamous, so a marriage creates links between two lineages or clans and also creates a new set of mutual obligations, not just for the couple but for clan and lineage members as well. A couple is expected to be of sufficient maturity to marry, but this is more a matter of physical development and behavior than of a precise numerical age.

Title 39, Chapter 2, of the Trust Territory Code, which applies in the states until they enact new family laws, recognizes as valid marriages that are "solemnized in accordance with recognized customs" (39 TTC 55 [1980]). The Trust Territory Code permits citizens of the FSM to choose whether to marry one another under custom or statute but requires that marriages in which either partner is a noncitizen take place according to the Code. To contract a valid statutory marriage, a male must be eighteen years old and a female sixteen (but a female under eighteen requires the consent of a parent or guardian), and neither of the parties may have a living spouse. The marriage ceremony must be performed by a member of the clergy, judge, or anyone authorized to perform marriages, and must be witnessed by at least two persons. Notice of both statutory and customary marriages must be registered.

B. Divorce, Separation, and Annulment

Title 39, Section 4 of the Trust Territory Code recognizes the validity of any divorce or annulment "effected in accordance with local custom" and provides that no restrictions or limitations may be imposed upon the granting of annulments or divorces in accordance with local custom. This implies that FSM citizens may obtain customary divorces or annulments, even if their marriage took place under the Code.

In the customary law of most Micronesian societies, separation and divorce are essentially synonymous. In some Micronesian societies, such as those on Chuuk, a divorce may be obtained at any time, at will, merely by one spouse announcing that he or she is renouncing the other.[48] In contrast, the Trust Territory Code (Title 39, Chapter 3) sets stringent limitations on annulments or divorces obtained under the Code. A statutory annulment will be granted only if the marriage, at the time it was entered into, was illegal and void or voidable. The court may in its discretion refuse to grant a statutory annulment if the parties voluntarily cohabited after the obstacle to the validity of the marriage had been removed, unless the public interest requires annulment of the marriage. No statutory annulment may be granted unless one of the parties has resided in the FSM for at least three months immediately prior to filing the complaint. The children of an annulled marriage are legitimate.

A statutory divorce will be granted only on the following grounds:

1. adultery;
2. cruelty (defined as neglect or personal indignities that make the life of the other spouse burdensome and intolerable and their further living together intolerable);
3. desertion for one year or more;
4. habitual drunkenness or drug use for at least one year;
5. a prison sentence of three years or more;
6. insanity for three years or more;
7. leprosy;
8. separation without cohabitation for two consecutive years; or
9. willful failure of the husband to provide support.

No statutory divorce will be granted if the ground for the divorce has been forgiven by the injured spouse, but such "forgiveness implies a condition that the forgiving party must be treated with conjugal kindness" (39 TTC 203 [1980]). An action for statutory divorce may be brought only if one of the parties has resided in the FSM for two years immediately preceding the action.

C. Custody and Support

Determinations about the custody of minor children and about support for spouses and children may be made either by the parties and their community under customary law or by the courts under applicable statutory law. Under customary law, the right to custody of and the duty to support children resides in the lineage. In a matrilineal society like those on Chuuk, where children belong to their mother's lineage, a man is expected to care for his sister's children, whether or not a divorce has occurred. In a patrilineal society, such as those on Yap, where children are members of the patriclan, they might remain with their father should a divorce occur. Since land is ultimately the property of the lineage or clan, there is seldom much question as to the division of property between spouses upon divorce, although disputes can occur. Customary law is flexible, however, and the parties (including the family and clan, as well as the parents) can agree to variations in custody, support, and property division arrangements.

Under Title 39, Chapter 3, of the Trust Territory Code, which applies until a state adopts new legislation, courts are empowered, as part of an action for statutory divorce or annulment, to make orders for custody of minor children, support for spouses and children, and distribution of marital property. In interpreting these provisions, the Trust Territory courts held that determinations about the custody of children should be made on the basis of the best interests of the child and that the mother should usually have custody of children under twelve where this is consistent with local customs. However, the decisions of Trust Territory courts are not binding upon FSM courts (see III, H Common Law), and the FSM Supreme Court, applying state law, has held that custom, which once favored the father, now considers that both parents have authority and responsibility for their children.[49] The FSM has maintained reciprocal and uniform support and custody legislation, originally enacted as Title 39, Chapter 4, of the Trust Territory Code, in order to avoid conflict and promote cooperation with United States and other jurisdictions.

D. Adoption

Adoption by FSM citizens may occur either under customary law or under applicable state statutes (until the states enact their own legislation, the applicable provisions are found in the Trust Territory Code, Title 39, Chapter 4). Customary adoptions tend to occur within the clan, and the adoptive parents tend to be childless or to have excess land. An adopted person is theoretically entitled to all the inheritance and other rights that would accrue to a biological child. The adopted person may, in addition, maintain ties with his or her biological family and has residual rights to the land of the biological family's clan or lineage.

Under Title 39, Chapter 4, of the Trust Territory Code, an adoption may be granted only if the person to be adopted is a child, if the child appears before the court and the court is satisfied that the adoption is in the best interests of the child, if the adopting parent or parents are "suitable persons" (39 TTC 252 [1980]), and if the biological parents have received notice or given written consent (unless the biological parents are dead or unknown, have abandoned the child for at least six months, or have been judged insane or incompetent). The statutory adoption of a child over age twelve requires the consent of the child. Adoption relieves the biological parents of all parental duties and responsibilities toward the child, as well as all rights over the child, but the child may still inherit from biological parents.

A child adopted under the Code has the same inheritance rights as a person adopted according to recognized custom at the place where the land is situated in the case of real estate and at the place where the decedent resided at the time of death in the case of personal property (39 TTC 255 [1980]). Where there is no recognized custom as to the inheritance rights of adopted children, a child adopted under the Code inherits from the adopting parents as if the child were their biological child and may also inherit from the biological parents and kindred.

XV. Personal Property

The law in the FSM concerning title to personal property, gifts, bailments, and liens is a matter of state law—to date primarily of state common law—and, as such, is governed by the judicial guidance clauses of the state constitutions. Generally, these constitutional provisions require that, in the absence of applicable statutes, the courts develop a law appropriate to the FSM by looking first to custom. If no appropriate custom can be found, the courts are to utilize such of the common law of other jurisdictions as is applicable to Micronesian social conditions and not antithetical to Micronesian customary law (see III, H Common Law). Traditionally, personal property in Micronesia consists not only of chattels, but also of intangibles, such as songs, rituals, and lore. Chiefly and lesser titles are the most important personal and political property in Micronesian societies. Ownership of titles resides in paramount chiefs, who can bestow and take them away at will, although chiefs tend to follow general rules as to which lineages get which titles. Nor is it usual for a recipient to be awarded a title until he is considered a mature member of the community.

XVI. Wills and Succession

Responsibility for testate and intestate succession is reserved to the states (FSM Constitution, Articles VIII and IX). State laws provide that succession may be in conformity either with custom or with statute.

A. Customary Succession[50]

While customary succession rules vary among Micronesian societies, there are certain similarities. Since land is at the basis of clan and lineage identity, customary succession rules tend to emphasize the retention of land within the clan, as well as provision of adequate land for members of each household. Although customary land can be acquired in a variety of ways (see XII, B Customary Land Law), inheritance is the usual mode. Traditionally, a commoner's right to inherit land is nominally subject to the rights of the chief, but it is unusual for a chief to deny the estate to the expected heirs. On Ponape and Kosrae, where customary inheritance rules were changed during the colonial period (see XII, A Land Tenure and Administration), and on Yap Island land is inherited patrilineally and tends to pass from the father to his sons, although the rules are flexible enough to permit daughters to inherit as well. On Chuuk, matrilineages are the landholding groups, but children can inherit from their father, in which case they then form the basis of a new matrilineal landholding group. In many Micronesian societies, the actual transfer of land occurs before the death of the testator. On Yap and Kosrae, for example, the estate head (usually the father) will parcel land out to his sons (or, if there are no sons, to his daughters) as they mature and marry, usually saving the homestead for his oldest son. This division of land may not be deemed final until after the testator's death. At that time, on Kosrae, the eldest son is expected to oversee the ultimate division, following his father's wishes.

Personal property (including intangibles such as songs and rituals) are given by the holder during his or her lifetime to people of the giver's choice (although it is expected that in a matrilineal society a man will give significant property to his sister's children and in a patrilineal society, to his own children), but certain personal property is strictly speaking, not inheritable (for instance, only the chief may determine who receives titles).

B. Statutory Intestate Succession

Some states (Yap, for example) have not enacted succession legislation, probably on the presumption that customary succession is the usual and preferred mode. Where new legislation does not exist, the laws of the Trust Territory remain in force (Yap Constitution, Article XV, Section 2). In Pohnpei, however, where much land had been converted under the German administration to individual freehold tenure, it was found necessary to enact laws governing intestate succession. The laws introduced during the period of German rule enforced primogeniture and forbade the making of wills. In 1979, the Pohnpei law of intestate succession was altered to provide that, in the absence of a will, property passes, in equal and undivided shares, to all children of the intestate living at the time of the intestate's death; in the absence of children, to the testator's parents; if they were deceased, to grandparents; and, if they were deceased, to great-grandparents. The Pohnpei statute also provides that a spouse, if alive at the time of the testator's death, receives one-third of the personal property and a life estate in the real property.

C. Wills

Any person over eighteen years may make a will enforceable pursuant to provisions enacted as part of the Trust Territory Code. A will must be signed by the testator and by two witnesses. The signature of a witness who receives property under the will does not invalidate the will, but the witness forfeits so much of the bequest as exceeds what the witness would have taken had the testator died intestate, unless there were two other, disinterested witnesses. Wills may also be handwritten or oral. A holographic will does not require a witness, but two persons must testify that the body and signature of the will are in the testator's handwriting. An oral will is enforceable for personal property only up to US$1,000, may not revoke or change an earlier written will, and is valid only if the testator is in imminent peril of death and dies as a result.

XVII. CONTRACTS

Contract disputes are a matter of state law, usually of state common law,[51] and will normally be within the jurisdiction of state courts, although the FSM Supreme Court has decided some contracts cases (see XI, C Jurisdiction). The judicial guidance clauses of national and state constitutions provide that, in developing the common law, the courts are to look first to the constitutions and to Micronesian custom (see III, H Common Law). The judges of the Pohnpei

State Courts are more familiar than are the judges of the FSM Supreme Court with customary law principles and seem more confident in applying custom to contract disputes. Conversely, the judges of the FSM Supreme Court may too easily take it for granted that, because a contract dispute arises in a business or governmental context, custom is not applicable.[52] However, the national and state courts are alike in that both seem to have accepted that the common law will provide the general framework in which customary or common law principles will operate.

The Pohnpei Supreme Court has interpreted a car rental agreement, using a mixture of Pohnpeian custom (the maxim that a person must reap the fruit of his misdeeds), the common law duty to mitigate damages, and interpretation of the applicable provision of the rental agreement.[53] The FSM Supreme Court has held that an ambiguous indemnification provision in a contract will be interpreted against the drafter of the agreement, basing its holding on the policy of strictly construing contracts in favor of the party that did not draft the agreement. Although the Court professed that no customary law principles were applicable and thus looked to the common law of United States jurisdictions for guidance, the Court did note that its holding was in accord with Micronesian values.[54] The Court also noted that care should generally be taken in interpreting contracts in the FSM because Micronesians will read contracts differently, based on their lack of facility with English, lack of experience in business, and fewer legal resources.[55]

XVIII. Commercial Law

A. Commercial Transactions

Commercial transactions within states are matters of state law, but interstate and foreign commerce is reserved by Article IX, Section 2, of the FSM Constitution to the national government. For the most part, statutes relating to sales of real and personal property, commercial paper, letters of credit, bulk transfers, warehouse receipts, and bills of lading have not been enacted. The FSM Code does include at Title 33 provisions enacted under the Trusteeship on secured transactions.

B. Business Organizations

Both the states and the national government have the power to incorporate business associations. Most large corporations are chartered under Title 36, Chapters 1 and 2 of the FSM Code, which provides that the President may grant charters of incorporation for profit and nonprofit corporations. The President may also create public corporations, subject to the approval of Congress. An association of persons seeking a corporate charter must submit both the articles of incorporation (containing essential information about the organization, management, purposes, and capitalization of the corporation) and the bylaws for approval by the President. Corporations must comply with regulations promulgated by the Registrar of Corporations, who is an officer of the Department of Resources and Development and is appointed by the President. Anyone wishing to sell shares of stock in FSM corporations to the public must furnish all material information relating to the stock offering to the registrar, who will make the information available to the public. In addition, no security in any corporation may be issued, sold, exchanged, or transferred until a registration statement has been filed with the registrar and approval of the registration statement has been obtained.

C. Regulated Businesses

The FSM Code provides at Title 32 that any person or entity engaged in importing, exporting, the sale of securities, insurance, or banking must be licensed. State legislation also requires business licensing. The Yap State Code, Title 22, for example, creates the Business License Board to issue regulations defining the categories of business licenses and the payment of licensing fees and to approve license applications on the basis of payment of fees, the public interest, state development plans, the conduct of the business in the past, and the opinion of the chief of the island as to the desirability of the business. Provision is made for judicial review for any person aggrieved by an action of the board. Licenses are also required of foreign businesses (see VIII Investment Law).

D. Unfair Business Practices

Anticompetitive agreements and practices (such as restricting trade or commerce, preventing competition in manufacture or sale, fixing prices, discriminating in price between different purchasers, or agreeing to pool interests connected with the sale or transportation of commodities) are unlawful, subject to fines of US$50 to US$5,000. In addition, persons injured by another's anticompetitive agreement or practices may sue for treble damages (FSM Code, Title 32).

E. Consumer Protection

The FSM Consumer Protection Act (FSM Code, Title 34) deems unlawful the following unfair methods of competition and unfair or deceptive acts or practices in the conduct of trade:

1. passing off goods or services as those of another;
2. representing that goods or services have approval, characteristics, ingredients, uses, benefits, or qualities that they do not have;
3. representing that used goods are new;
4. disparaging the goods, services, or business of another by false or misleading representations;
5. using advertisements that are misleading as to the goods that will be sold or the quantity of goods available for sale;
6. making false or misleading statements as to the reasons for price reductions; and
7. engaging in any other act or practice that is unfair or deceptive to the consumer.

Legal action against persons engaging in deceptive practices may be brought by the Attorney General (seeking an injunction and, for willful violations of the act, civil damages of up to US$1,000 per violation) or by injured parties (for damages). Persons who violate the terms of an injunction are liable for civil damages of up to US$10,000 per violation. The Consumer Protection Act also provides that installment contracts for the sale or lease of consumer goods or services, entered into between a retail seller and a retail buyer, are non-negotiable, and, should such contracts be assigned, the assignee is subject to all the claims and defenses of the buyer against the seller.

The setting of usury limits on major loans is a responsibility of the national government (FSM Constitution, Article IX, Section 2). The FSM's usury law (FSM Code, Title 34 [1987]) provides that, in consumer credit transactions in which the principal amount exceeds US$300, the rate of interest may not exceed an annual percentage rate of 15 percent. In commercial credit transactions, no maximum interest rate is imposed if the principal amount exceeds US$1 million. If the principal amount is less than US$500,000, the rate of interest may not exceed an annual percentage rate of 2 percent in excess of the prime rate on the day before the transaction; if the principal amount is between US$500,000 and US$1 million, the rate of interest may not exceed an annual percentage rate of 2.25 percent in excess of the prime rate on the day before the transaction. Notwithstanding the above, in commercial credit transactions of less than US$1 million, the rate of interest may not exceed an annual percentage rate of 23 percent. The law does not apply to interest on credit cards, if the principal place of business of the issuer of the card is in another jurisdiction.

XIX. TORTS

The Micronesian Constitutional Convention intended law-making power in torts to lie with the states, rather than with the national government.[56] Thus, the Trust Territory wrongful death statutes are matters of state rather than national law, even though they are contained in the FSM Code.[57]

As state law, cases involving torts are within the jurisdiction of state courts. The national courts will hear torts cases only when diversity jurisdiction is involved or the national government is a party, and the national court is expected to apply state law in diversity cases (see **XI, C Jurisdiction**). The judicial guidance clauses of the national and state constitutions require that court decisions be congruent with the constitution, with Micronesian custom, and with the social and geographical conditions of Micronesia (see **III, H Common Law**). The former Trust Territory rule mandating the American Law Institute's *Restatement* as the source of tort law has been held not to apply.[58] Thus, in contravention of decisions of the Trust Territory courts, the FSM Supreme Court has recommended that comparative rather than contributory negligence be the FSM rule,[59] and the Pohnpei State Supreme Court has also suggested discomfort with the harshness of the contributory negligence standard.[60]

In developing tort law, the national and state courts are following similar paths, although there are differences in outlook and emphasis. Both the national and state courts seem to have accepted that, although they will look to custom for particular rules, the common law will provide the general framework for tort law. However, the different sensitivities of the national and state judiciaries as to the content and relative importance of custom and common law may lead to differences in their decisions on specific issues.

The Pohnpei Supreme Court has held that, because the FSM is new to industrial development, there is a duty on the owner, seller, or controller of machinery to educate and inform Pohnpeians as to its dangers before they buy or use it and has imposed liability for failure to warn.[61] The Pohnpei Supreme Court recognizes employer liability and has refused at this time to permit piercing the corporate veil, stating that too many Micronesians currently run their businesses as family affairs to make this a reasonable rule.[62] The Pohnpei Supreme Court has held that, in collecting damages, multiple defendants are not jointly and severally liable, but should pay according to the proportion of plaintiff's injuries that each caused. The court cites, for this holding, Pohnpeian custom, as well as the recent movement in many common law jurisdictions away from joint and several liability.[63]

The FSM Supreme Court has ruled on the one hand that, because large water-filled holes are inherently dangerous, a defendant cannot escape liability for having left one uncovered by getting an independent contractor to do the work, and on the other hand that employer liability does not extend to a defendant who had relinquished to another all control over his workers, the workplace, and their work.[64] The Court has also held that it will permit recovery for tortious interference with a contractual relationship.[65] But the Court has recognized custom in holding that an adult daughter will be considered a child for purposes of wrongful death actions brought by parents.[66]

The sovereign immunity of the FSM national government has been waived by statute (6 FSM Code 701–702) in the following instances:

1. claims for recovery of any tax erroneously or illegally collected;
2. claims for damages or other relief arising out of improper administration of law;
3. claims upon an express or implied contract;
4. claims, up to a recovery of US$20,000, for injury or loss of property or personal injury or death caused by the wrongful act or negligence or omission of an employee of the national government acting within the scope of his employment; and
5. claims, up to a recovery of US$20,000, for injuries suffered if a national government employee violates any of the rights secured under Article IV of the Constitution.

The Yap Constitution includes among the fundamental rights set forth in Article II the right of persons to sue the state for redress for the illegal acts of public officials. The Yap Government Liability Act of 1986 (31 YSC 101–109) provides that sovereign immunity is waived for illegal or erroneous tax collection; improper administration of laws or regulations; contract claims; claims for injury or loss to property or personal injury or death by the wrongful act or omission of an official acting within the scope of the official's employment if a private person would be liable for the same act; and violations of Article II, the fundamental rights provisions of the Yap Constitution. The act limits damages for wrongful death to US$20,000 and for injuries to persons or property to US$40,000.

The FSM Supreme Court has held that the state of Pohnpei is not immune from suit, basing its decision on custom, the common law, and statute.[67]

XX. Labor Law

Labor legislation in the FSM gives preference to citizens and permanent residents in employment, provides a system of retirement insurance, and establishes governmental agencies to promote the development of labor. There is no legislation setting minimum wages and regulating working conditions for workers in private industry. However, the FSM's largest employer is the government, and legislation sets salaries and other conditions of employment for public servants (see V, B Public Service).

The FSM Protection of Resident Workers Act (FSM Code, Title 51) gives preference in employment to persons who are citizens of the FSM and to persons admitted to the FSM as nonresident aliens seeking permanent residence. The act requires that employers in every industry or occupation give preference to resident workers if qualified and available. The act permits the hiring of nonresident workers only to supplement the labor force. Any employer who wants to import alien workers must file an application with the FSM employment service, which will first try to fill the position with resident workers. If no qualified resident workers are available, the employment service may still deny the application, if it is determined that employment of nonresident workers is not in the best interests of the FSM. In accepting an application, the service may set conditions, such as the period of time for which nonresidents may be employed. No nonresident worker may be employed by another employer in the FSM without first leaving the country. Any employer who violates the act is liable for a fine of not more than US$2,000 or imprisonment for up to six months or both.

The Federated States of Micronesia Social Security Act (FSM Code, Title 53 [1987]) is a comprehensive insurance scheme, providing retirement, disability, and survivors' benefits to workers and their dependents. The system is administered by the Social Security Board, consisting of five members, representing public and private sector employers and employees. Coverage extends to all employees of any employer incorporated or doing business in the FSM (including the FSM government) and to self-employed persons with more than US$10,000 of gross annual revenue. Family employees are exempted. Contributions from employers and employees fund the system. Employees pay an annual tax, which equaled 2 percent of wages through June 30, 1985, rising gradually to 6 percent of wages by June 30, 2000. Employers contribute equivalent amounts per employee. Every insured individual is entitled to retirement benefits at age sixty and to disability benefits after three months for any disability that prevents the person from working for twelve months or more. Upon the death of an insured individual, the spouse and children are entitled to benefits.

The Micronesia Labor Development Act of 1975, which has become part of FSM Code, Title 51, authorizes the chief of the Labor Division, FSM Department of Resources and Development, to enter into programs such as the exchange with other Pacific nations of labor administration personnel for training and experience, to evaluate and obtain for the FSM programs of the U.S. Department of Labor, and to establish an apprentice program.

The states may also implement programs to improve the conditions and skills of labor. The Pohnpei Constitution, for example, at Article 7, makes this a responsibility of the government of Pohnpei. Pohnpei has enacted a Wages and Hours Law, providing for a forty-hour work week and a US$1.35 per hour minimum wage. Discrimination in employment on the basis of race, religion, or gender is prohibited.

XXI. INDUSTRIAL AND INTELLECTUAL PROPERTY RIGHTS

The regulation of patents and copyrights is among the exclusive powers of the national government (FSM Constitution, Article IX, Section 1). Under the FSM copyright law (FSM Code, Title 35 [1987]), copyright protection exists for all unpublished works and for those published works of which one or more of the authors is a national or domiciliary of the FSM or of a country that is a party to a copyright treaty with the FSM. Copyright endures for the life of the author plus fifty years. For the owner of a copyright to receive protection, notice of the copyright, as provided in the statute, must be affixed to the work. Copyright may be registered with the office of the FSM Attorney General, but registration is not necessary. Fair use of copyrighted works is permitted. Ownership of a copyright may be transferred by any means. Anyone who infringes a copyright is liable for an injunction, and for actual and punitive damages. Anyone who willfully and for commercial advantage or private gain infringes a copyright may be fined US$10,000 or imprisoned for up to one year or both. No legislation has been enacted in the FSM governing patents or trademarks.

XXII. LEGAL EDUCATION AND PROFESSION

FSM lawyers are trained in law schools in the United States and in Papua New Guinea. Currently only about ten FSM citizens are lawyers, with about thirty lawyers in all in the FSM, most of whom work for government. The justices of the FSM Supreme Court, as well as many of the lawyers in the Office of the Attorney General and the private bar, are noncitizens. The FSM Congress recently enacted an amendment to the Foreign Investment Law requiring noncitizen lawyers to obtain business licenses before practicing law in the FSM (see **VIII Investment Law**). Nonlawyer trial advocates are permitted to practice before the national and state courts, and nonlawyers who have had experience as trial advocates may be judges of state courts. Persons who cannot afford legal assistance may be represented by lawyers and trial advocates of the Micronesian Legal Services Corporation, which is funded by grants from the U.S. government.

The FSM Supreme Court has adopted rules of practice that require lawyers who practice before it to pass an examination covering FSM constitutional, statutory, and customary law. Graduates of law schools and persons who have served as trial advocates are eligible to sit for the examination.

XXIII. RESEARCH GUIDE

The *FSM Revised Code* was published in 1982. It includes all laws enacted up to the publication date, and arranges them by title and section. A supplement adds all the laws enacted between 1982 and 1987. The *Revised Code* and the supplement are referred to in this chapter as the FSM Code, and all acts that are in the *Revised Code* or supplement are cited to in this chapter by title number (for example, FSM Code, Title 12) or by title and section numbers (for example, 4 FSM Code 44).

Some states have also codified their legislation. State laws are cited to in this chapter either by their name alone or, where codified laws exist, by title number (for example, Yap State Code, Title 12) or by title and section numbers (for example, 4 YSC 44).

A few Trust Territory statutes are still in effect in the FSM. The laws of the Trust Territory were last codified in 1980, and references in this chapter to Trusteeship laws are to the Trust Territory Code (or TTC) and, where appropriate, to the title and section numbers of cited provisions.

The FSM Supreme Court publishes its trial and appellate opinions in a loose-leaf service entitled *FSM Interim Reports* (cited as FSM Intrm.). The reporter also includes selected decisions of the state courts. Cases are cited to here by volume and page number.

A. Law, Politics, and Culture of the FSM

Alkire, W. "Land Tenure in the Woleai," in H. P. Lundsgaarde, ed. *Land Tenure in Oceania*. ASAO Monograph No. 2, Honolulu: University Press of Hawaii, 1974, 18–38.

Arnett, A. "The American Legal System and Micronesian Customary Law: The Legal Legacy of the United States to the New Nations of the Trust Territory," 4 *UCLA Pacific Basin Law J.* 161 (1985).

Bowman, A. "Judicial Seminars in Micronesia," 9 *Univ. of Hawaii Law Rev.* 533 (1987).

―――. "Legitimacy and Scope of Trust Territory High Review of Court Power to Review Decisions of Federated States of Micronesia Supreme Court: The Otokichy Cases," 5 *Univ. of Hawaii Law Rev.* 57 (1983).

Castro, F. "Ponape: Land Tenure and Registration," in B. Acquaye and R. G. Crocombe, eds. *Land Tenure and Rural Productivity in the Pacific Islands*. Suva: University of the South Pacific, 1984.

Crocombe, R. G., and A. Ali, eds. *Politics in Micronesia*. Suva: Institute of Pacific Studies, University of the South Pacific, 1988.

Dator, J. "Inventing a Judiciary for the State of Ponape," 34 *Political Science* 92 (1982).

Defngin, F. "The Nature and Scope of Customary Land Rights of the Yapese Community," in Trust Territory of the Pacific Islands, Office of the High Commissioner. *Land Tenure Patterns: Trust Territory of the Pacific Islands*, 1958.

Fischer, J. "Contemporary Ponape Island Land Tenure," in Trust Territory of the Pacific Islands, Office of the High Commissioner. *Land Tenure Patterns*, 1958.

———. "Native Land Tenure in the Truk District," in Trust Territory of the Pacific Islands Office of the High Commissioner. *Land Tenure Patterns*, 1958.

Goodenough, W. H. *Property, Kin and Community on Truk*. Publications in Anthropology, No. 46. New Haven: Yale University Press, 1951.

Hanlon, D. *Upon a Stone Altar*. Honolulu: University of Hawaii Press, 1988.

Howe, K. R. *Where the Waves Fall*. Sydney: Allen & Unwin, 1984.

Hughes, D., and S. Laughlin, Jr., "Key Elements in the Evolving Political Culture of the Federated States of Micronesia," 6 *Pacific Studies* 71 (1983).

Hussey, R. "The Evolution of Land Inheritance on Pohnpei Island, FSM." University of Hawaii, Honolulu, Mimeo, 1989.

JK Report on Micronesia (Kolonia, Pohnpei, published monthly).

Lingenfelter, S. *Yap: Political Leadership and Culture Change in an Island Society*, Honolulu: University of Hawaii Press, 1975.

McGrath, W., and W. S. Wilson. "The Marshall, Caroline and Mariana Islands: Too Many Foreign Precedents," in R. G. Crocombe, ed. *Land Tenure in the Pacific*, 3d ed. Suva: University of the South Pacific, 1987, 190.

Mahoney, J. "Land Tenure Patterns on Yap Island," in Trust Territory of the Pacific Islands, Office of the High Commissioner. *Land Tenure Patterns*, 1958.

Marshall, M. *Weekend Warriors: Alcohol in a Micronesian Culture*. Mountain View, Calif.: Mayfield Publishing Co., 1979.

Olsen, D. "Piercing Micronesia's Colonial Veil," 15 *Columbia J. of Transnational Law* 473 (1976).

Peoples, J. *Island in Trust: Culture Change and Dependence in a Micronesian Economy*. Boulder, Colo.: Westview Press, 1985.

Petersen, C. G. *One Man Cannot Rule a Thousand*. Ann Arbor: University of Michigan Press, 1989.

Powles, C. G., and M. Pulea, eds. *Pacific Courts and Legal Systems*. Suva: University of the South Pacific, 1988.

Sack, P., ed. *Pacific Constitutions*. Canberra: Australian National University, 1982.

Stewart, R. J. "The Legal System of Micronesia," in K. Redden, *Modern Legal Systems Cyclopedia*. Buffalo, N.Y.: Hein, 1984.

Tamanaha, B. "A Proposal for the Development of a System of Indigenous Jurisprudence in the Federal States of Micronesia," 13 *Hastings International & Comparative Law Rev.* 71 (1989).

———. "The Role of Custom and Traditional Leaders under the Yap Constitution," 10 *Univ. of Hawaii Law Rev.* 81 (1988).

Turcott, B. "The Beginnings of the Federated States of Micronesia Supreme Court," 5 *Univ. of Hawaii Law Rev.* 361 (1983).

———. "Constitutional Jurisprudence of the Federated States of Micronesia Supreme Court," 6 *UCLA Pacific Basin Law J.* 103 (1989).

B. Constitutional and Compact Development

Armstrong, A. J. "The Emergence of the Micronesians into the International Community: A Study of the Creation of a New International Entity," 5 *Brooklyn J. of International Law* 207 (1979).

———. "The Island Nations of the Pacific Basin: Their Emerging Independence and Regionalism," in R. Rosendahl, ed. *Current Legal Aspects of Doing Business in the Pacific Basin*. New York: American Bar Association, 1987.

———. "The Negotiations for the Future Political Status of Micronesia," 74 *American J. of International Law* 689 (1980).

———. "Strategic Underpinnings of the Legal Regime of Free Association: The Negotiations for the Future Political Status of Micronesia," 7 *Brooklyn J. International Law* 179 (1981).

Armstrong, A. J., and H. L. Hills. "The Negotiations for the Future Political Status of Micronesia (1980–1984)," 78 *American J. of International Law* 484 (1984).

Burdick, A. "The Constitution of the Federated States of Micronesia," 8 *Univ. of Hawaii Law Rev.* 419 (1986); also in Y. Ghai, ed. *Law, Politics and Government in the Pacific Island States*. Suva: University of the South Pacific, 1988.

Hirayasu, N. "The Process of Self-Determination and Micronesia's Future Political Status under International Law," 9 *Univ. of Hawaii Law Rev.* 487 (1987).

Hughes, D., and S. Lingenfelter. eds. *Political Development in Micronesia*. Columbus: Ohio State University Press, 1974.

Isenberg, D. "Reconciling Independence and Security: The Long Term Status of the Trust Territory of the Pacific Islands," 7 *UCLA Pacific Basin Law Journal* 210 (1985).

Macdonald, J. R. "Termination of the Strategic Trusteeship: Free Association, the United Nations and International Law," 7 *Brooklyn J. of International Law* 235 (1981).

Meller, N. *Constitutionalism in Micronesia*. Honolulu: Institute for Polynesian Studies, Brigham Young University, 1985.

Petersen, G. "A Cultural Analysis of the Ponapean Independence Vote in the 1983 Plebiscite," 9 *Pacific Studies* 13 (1985).

Van Dorn, W. G., Jr. "The Compact of Free Association: An End to the Trust Territory of the Pacific Islands," 5 *Boston Univ. International Law J.* 213 (1987).

18. Guam

MARY MCCORMICK

I. Dateline

2000 B.C.–500 A.D.	Guam settled by proto-Malays, later known as Chamorros.
1565	Spain claims Guam as a royal possession.
1898	U.S. forces capture Guam; pursuant to the Treaty of Paris of 1898, Spain cedes Guam to United States.
1917	First Guam Congress convened.
1941	One month before Pearl Harbor, all American military dependents evacuated from Guam.
1942	Guam occupied by Japanese forces.
1945	U.S. forces retake Guam.
1950	Administration of Guam transferred from U.S. Secretary of Navy to U.S. Secretary of Interior. Congress enacts Organic Act for Guam.
1968	Organic Act amended to permit local election of Governor and Lieutenant Governor.
1972	U.S. Congress approves nonvoting delegate from Guam to House of Representatives.
1976	Enabling Act passed by U.S. Congress permits a Constitution for Guam.
1977–1979	Guam Constitutional Convention's draft Constitution defeated by Guam voters by a margin of 5 to 1.

II. Historical, Cultural, and Economic Survey

Guam, the largest and southernmost of the Mariana Islands, is an unincorporated territory of the United States. Its population, including non-Chamorros, is about 133,000.

The Marianas were settled during the great waves of Pacific migration from 2000 B.C. to 500 A.D. Proto-Malays, later known as the Chamorros, settled in Guam and established what became a class society. By the time Spain seized Guam as a royal possession in 1565, there were three distinct classes of Chamorros within the population of 50,000 to 100,000: chiefs and main landowners (matua), junior branches of the matua (atachaot), and commoners (manachang). Descendants of the nobility aligned themselves with the Spanish to form a new upper class. Foreign diseases and a series of internecine conflicts and wars with the Spanish reduced the population to less than 3,000 by the late 1700s.

The year 1898 brought major changes to Guam. American forces captured the Spanish governor and garrison during the Spanish-American War; Spain and the United States ratified the Treaty of Paris by which Spain ceded Guam to the United States; President William McKinley designated Guam as a naval station and a senior naval officer as Governor of Guam. The Treaty of Paris was proclaimed in 1899.

Between 1898 and the outbreak of hostilities in the Pacific during World War II, the United States fostered an Americanization program in Guam. A local congress met from 1917 until World War II. Beginning in 1922, Guam's educational system was modeled on California's system; children were forbidden to speak Chamorro at school, and Chamorro dictionaries were seized and burned.

In 1931, all military installations were removed from the island, leaving Guam defenseless. All dependents of American military personnel were evacuated in November 1941 as war with Japan became likely. The Japanese invaded in 1942 and remained in control of Guam until its recapture by American forces in 1945.

At the close of the war, the U.S. Navy resumed its administration of the island. The governmental structure included a legislature; an Attorney General; a Judiciary Department; departments of Education, Health, Internal Affairs, Public Works, Civil Police, Records and Accounts; a Fire Marshal; a Land and Claims Commission; a City Planning Commission; the Bank of Guam; the U.S. Post Office; and commissioners for each municipality. In a referendum in June 1946, Guamanians voted in favor of holding a general election for members of both houses of the Congress. The first postwar congressional election was held on July 13, 1946. One of its first acts was to change its name from the Eleventh Guam Congress to the First Guam Legislature.

In 1950 the administration of Guam was transferred from the U.S. Secretary of the Navy to the Secretary of the Interior, ending fifty years of military rule on Guam. On August 1, 1950, President Harry S Truman signed into law the Organic Act of Guam, declared effective as of July 21, 1950, the anniversary of the retaking of Guam by American forces in World War II. Guamanians were made United States citizens. Guam's administration was vested in a Governor appointed for a four-year term by the President of the United States with the advice and consent of the U.S. Senate. The Governor was required to be a civilian or retired officer of the U.S. armed forces. The Guam Legislature was given more power to legislate over local matters.

In 1968, the U.S. Congress amended the Organic Act to permit popular election of the Governor and Lieutenant Governor. The same amendment, however, removed some powers from the Governor's office and vested them in a federally appointed Comptroller (now, the Inspector General of the U.S. Department of the Interior). A provision giving preference to Chamorros in hiring was also deleted. The first elected Governor took office in 1971, and in the following year Guam was given authority to elect a nonvoting delegate to the U.S. House of Representatives.

During the 1970s, Guam was granted authority to adopt a locally drafted constitution. A constitutional convention met and drafted a constitution, but it was overwhelmingly defeated by the voters in a referendum; some voters wished closer ties with the United States, some wanted to retain the status quo, and others wanted to completely sever ties with the United States. Today, the United States still has air force and navy bases on Guam, and Guam is still trying to determine the type of relationship it wants with the United States.

III. Sources of Law

The Organic Act of 1950 establishes the sources of law applicable to Guam as those in force on August 1, 1950, except as amended by the Organic Act or modified or repealed by the Congress of the United States or the Legislature of Guam. These sources of law are the Treaty of Paris, the U.S. Constitution, U.S. laws, Guam laws, custom, and the common law:

A. Treaty of Paris

The treaty that ceded Guam to the United States in 1898 is the ultimate source of authority for U.S. control of Guam.

B. U.S. Constitution

Because Guam is an "unincorporated territory" of the United States, only "fundamental provisions" of the U.S. Constitution apply to Guam of their own force.[1] Those provisions of the U.S. Constitution that have been held by U.S. courts to be fundamental include the prohibition against post facto laws,[2] protection against unreasonable searches and seizures, the right to just compensation for qovernmental acquisition of property, the right to the writ of habeas corpus, the right to a jury trial and the due process clause of the Fourteenth Amendment.[3] Provisions that have been deemed not fundamental include the right to indictment only by a grand jury[4] and the right to confront witnesses.[5]

C. U.S. Laws

The Organic Act makes applicable to Guam those U.S. laws that are applicable to the Northern Marianas, on the same terms and conditions as they apply to the Northern Marianas. Included are laws that provide federal services and financial assistance programs, the federal banking laws as they apply to Guam, and the U.S. Public Health Services Act as it applies to the Virgin Islands. Not included in these applicable laws, however, are supplemental security income provisions and benefits for elderly uninsured individuals under the U.S. Social Security Act and the Micronesian Claims Act as it applied to the former Trust Territory of the Pacific Islands. U.S. laws are codified in the U.S. Code, referred to herein as USC.

D. Guam Laws

Guam has power to legislate on all subjects of local application not inconsistent with the provisions of the Organic Act and the laws of the United States applicable to Guam. The Governor has power to issue executive orders and regulations pursuant to the Organic Act and to acts of the Legislature. When the Organic Act was passed, pre-Organic Act laws of Guam not amended by the Organic Act continued in force, subject to modification or repeal by the U.S. Congress or the Guam Legislature, except that all laws of Guam inconsistent with the provisions of the Organic Act were repealed at the time of its enactment to the extent of the inconsistency.

The official record of Guam laws, other than laws of the United States, is contained in the Guam Code Annotated (referred to herein as GCA or the Code) and in public laws, session laws, and current laws.

E. Custom

Custom is not recognized as a source of law in the Organic Act or in the Code. The courts have not taken custom into consideration in their published opinions.

F. Common Law

The Guam statute that provides for adoption of the common law was unintentionally omitted from the *Guam Code Annotated*. It is therefore uncertain whether the common law has been adopted for Guam, although Guam courts continue to issue judgments as though the common law and equity are in force (see GCA, Title 6, Section 4205, Comment).

Guam's hierarchy of law is set out in Title 1 of the Code: (1) the Constitution, treaties, and laws of the United States applicable to Guam; (2) acts of the Guam legislature; (3) executive orders of the Governor; (4) U.S. Supreme Court decisions ruling on the portions of the U.S. Constitution, treaties, and laws applicable to Guam, or on cases and controversies involving Guam; (5) decisions of the appellate courts that have jurisdictions to hear cases involving matters applicable to Guam; and (6) in individual cases, decisions of the Guam Superior Court.

IV. Constitutional System

A. Territory

The United States acquired a 3-mile territorial sea around Guam when it acquired Guam from Spain. Under Title 1 of the Code, Guam claims an exclusive economic zone 200 miles seaward from the low water mark of the outermost of its islands or reefs. Guam claims exclusive rights to determine the conditions and terms of scientific research, management, exploration, and exploitation of ocean resources and sources of energy and prevention of pollution within this economic zone, including pollution from outside the zone that poses a threat within the zone.

B. Nationality and Citizenship

Citizens of Guam are citizens of the United States but do not have the right to vote in presidential elections, a right dependent on state residency.[6] Citizens of the United States who move to Guam are eligible to vote in local elections after a short period of residence but also retain their right to vote in presidential elections.

Pursuant to 48 USC 1711, Guam is represented in the U.S. House of Representatives by an elected nonvoting delegate who must be at least twenty-five years of age on the date of the election; a citizen of the United States for at least seven years prior to that time; an inhabitant of Guam; and on the date of election, not a candidate for any other office.

Guam has had customs authority since Congress excluded all territories and possessions of the United States from the definition of "United States" in the Tariff Act of 1930. That exclusion operated as a delegation of customs authority to Guam.[7] It remains unclear, however, whether Guam has authority to administer only its own customs laws or whether it also has authority to administer U.S. customs laws.

C. Government

The U.S. government's power to legislate for Guam stems from four sources: (1) the U.S. Constitution, Article IV, which gives the U.S. Congress power to legislate directly for a territory or to establish a government for it subject to congressional control; (2) congressional war and treaty powers;[8] (3) the broad foreign affairs and military powers of the presidency;[9] and (4) the inherent powers of a national government.

As a territory, Guam has no inherent right to govern itself.[10] Congress has given Guam the powers set out in the Organic Act, subject to applicable laws of the United States but has retained for itself the power to veto the Organic Act or any legislation passed by the Guam Legislature, including a local Constitution.[11] Although Guam has the appearance of a body politic, it is essentially an instrumentality of the U.S. government,[12] under the administrative supervision of the Secretary of the Interior. It is not, however, considered to be the equivalent of a federal agency.[13]

1. EXECUTIVE

Provisions relating to the Guam executive are contained in 48 USC Section 1422. The executive power of Guam is vested in a Governor who is elected jointly with a Lieutenant Governor in elections held every four years. No person who has been elected Governor for two full successive terms is eligible to hold that office again until a full term has intervened. A candidate for either office must be an eligible voter, at least thirty years old, who has been a U.S. citizen and a bona fide resident of Guam for five years immediately preceding the election. The Governor must reside in Guam during his or her tenure of office.

The Governor is responsible for the faithful execution of the laws of Guam and U.S. laws applicable in Guam and has general supervision and control of all instrumentalities of the executive branch. The Governor has the power to pardon and reprieve for offenses against local laws; to veto legislation, subject to legislative override; to issue orders and regulations not in conflict with a law; to appoint and remove officers and employees of the executive branch except as otherwise provided; and to declare martial law in emergencies.

The Lieutenant Governor has powers and duties assigned by the Governor or prescribed by the Organic Act or Guam laws and, if the Governor is temporarily disabled or absent, has the Governor's powers. If the Governor's office becomes permanently vacant, the Lieutenant Governor becomes Governor for the unexpired term. The Speaker of the Legislature acts as Lieutenant Governor if the Lieutenant Governor is temporarily disabled or absent. In the event the Lieutenant Governor's office becomes permanently vacant, the Governor appoints a new Lieutenant Governor with the advice and consent of the Legislature.

2. LEGISLATURE

The main provisions relating to the Guam Legislature are in 48 USC 1423 and in Chapters 2 and 3 of the Guam Code. The unicameral Legislature has a maximum of twenty-one members, known as senators, elected at large for a term of two years. General elections are held biennially in even-numbered years. A qualified voter is a U.S. citizen and Guam resident, eighteen years or older, who complies with voter registration requirements. He or she must not be confined to a mental institution, nor judicially declared insane nor committed under a sentence of imprisonment. Reapportionment of the Legislature may occur at not less than ten-year intervals and must be based on the most recent population census.

A senator must be a U.S. citizen at least twenty-five years old, domiciled in Guam for at least five years immediately preceding the sitting of the Legislature in which election is sought, who has not been convicted, unless pardoned, of a felony or crime involving moral turpitude. The Legislature judges the selection and qualification of its own members; chooses officers from its members; determines its rules and procedure; and determines how vacancies will be filled, except that no one filling a vacancy may hold office longer than for the remainder of the term for which his or her predecessor was elected. A person who holds a position requiring legislative confirmation is ineligible to be a candidate or senator, and a senator may not be appointed, either during the term elected or for the year following the expiration of that term, to any office created or the salary or emoluments of which have been increased during that term. Senators are privileged from arrest during attendance at and in going to and returning from the Legislature except in cases of treason, felony, or breach of the peace. A senator may not be held to answer before any other tribunal for any speech or debate in the Legislature.

Regular sessions of the Legislature, which must be open to the public, are held annually and continue for the term set by the Legislature. The Governor may call special legislative sessions.

No legislation may be considered at a special session other than that specified in the call or in a special message by the Governor to the Legislature while it is in special session.

The Legislature has law-making powers over all subjects of legislation of local application not inconsistent with U.S. laws applicable to Guam. It has power to tax and issue bonds and other obligations and may pass laws in respect of federal laws applicable to Guam in order to assist the Governor in enforcing those laws.[14] The Legislature has no power to reappropriate funds provided directly to the government of Guam by the U.S. Congress.[15] Bills introduced must receive a public hearing unless emergency conditions involving danger to the public health or safety exist. Although the Organic Act provides that no bill may become law unless passed at a meeting with a quorum (consisting of eleven members) by the affirmative vote of a majority of the members present and voting, the Guam Code prohibits passage of a law with fewer than eleven affirmative votes.

A bill passed by the Legislature must be presented to the Governor. A bill vetoed by the Governor may become law if repassed by two-thirds of all the members of the Legislature. A bill not vetoed by the Governor or repassed by the Legislature becomes law and is sent to the head of the agency designated by the U.S. President for final action. The U.S. Congress reserves the power and authority to annul any enacted law.

The people of Guam retain the right to exercise the power of initiative and referendum with regard to legislative matters, including the removal from office of the Governor, Lieutenant Governor, or a member of the Legislature by a referendum election. The Legislature may also submit a measure to the voters for approval if it has received a vote of fourteen members of the Legislature.

3. JUDICIARY

Provisions relating to the judicial branch are found in 48 USC 1424. The judicial power in Guam is vested in a U.S. District Court for Guam and in local courts established by Guam law. The U.S. District Court, created under Article IV of the U.S. Constitution, is a court of record and has original jurisdiction in all cases arising under the U.S. Constitution and treaties and laws of the United States, regardless of the sum or value of the matter in controversy.[16] The District Court also has diversity, bankruptcy, and appellate jurisdiction. It has exclusive jurisdiction over all criminal and civil proceedings respecting the Guam territorial income tax. Questions relating to the applicability of indictment by a grand jury or trial by jury are determined by Guam law.

The U.S. District Court is staffed by a judge, appointed by the President with the advice and consent of the U.S. Senate, who holds office for eight years, unless removed by the President for cause. The judge's salary is paid by the United States at the same rate as that paid to U.S. District Court judges. The President also appoints, by and with the advice and consent of the Senate, a U.S. Attorney and U.S. Marshal.

The Organic Act gives the U.S. District Court jurisdiction not only in cases arising under U.S. laws, but also in all cases under Guam law that were not vested by the Legislature in some other court. The Court Reorganization Act of 1974 removed jurisdiction over cases involving Guam law from the District Court; abolished the Island Court and Police Court, which before 1974 had original jurisdiction over minor civil and criminal matters; and created a Guam Superior Court. Except where a U.S. law gives the District Court jurisdiction, the act vests the Guam Superior Court with jurisdiction of every legal or administrative matter under the laws of Guam, including common law cases,[17] and suits that were previously heard by the Island Court and Police Court. In 1985, the composition of the Superior Court was a presiding judge and five additional judges.

All appeals from the Superior Court are to a three-judge appellate panel of the U.S. District Court, with the District Court judge presiding. The other judges are designated by the presiding judge from among judges of the Superior Court, U.S. Circuit Court judges, and judges of the former Trust Territory High Court. The concurrence of two judges is necessary to any decision on the merits of an appeal, but the presiding judge alone can make appropriate orders prior to the hearing. The U.S. Court of Appeals for the Ninth Circuit has jurisdiction over appeals from all decisions of the appellate division of the District Court.

In 1984, Guam was given authority to create an appellate court to hear appeals from the Superior Court. The Guam legislature has not yet established such a court.[18] Until Guam establishes an appellate court, the U.S. Court of Appeals for the Ninth Circuit will continue to act as Guam's "Supreme Court."

D. Emergency Powers

The Governor has power to declare martial law in a state of emergency (see **IV, C (1)**).

E. Human Rights

Not all civil and political rights provided by the U.S. Constitution have been extended to Guam (see **III, B U.S. Constitution**). However, the Organic Act contains a number of provisions that could be considered a bill of rights for Guam. For example, the act forbids the following:

1. imprisonment for debt;
2. imposition of a voting qualification with respect to property, income, political opinion, or any other matter apart from citizenship, civil capacity, and residence;
3. discrimination against any person on account of race, language, or religion;
4. denial of the equal protection of the laws;
5. conviction of treason against the United States except on the testimony of two witnesses to the same overt act or on confession in open court;
6. the spending of any public money or property for any religious purpose;
7. the employment of children under the age of fourteen years in any occupation injurious to health or morals or hazardous to life or limb; and
8. imposition of any religious test as a qualification to any office or public trust under the government of Guam.

The act makes education compulsory for all children between the ages of six and sixteen years.

In 1968, Congress applied to Guam additional civil rights provisions of the U.S. Constitution and reapplied some provisions already in the Organic Act, including habeas corpus; prohibitions against bills of attainder and ex post facto laws; freedom of speech, association, and religion; the right to be free from unlawful search and seizure; the prohibition on cruel and unusual punishment; the right to counsel; the rights to due process and equal protection of the laws; and a prohibition on involuntary servitude. Title 8 of the Guam Code also codifies some of the constitutional rights applicable to a defendant in a criminal trial.

V. Administrative Organization and Law

A. Organization

In addition to its administrative agencies, Guam has autonomous agencies overseeing its airport and port, visitors, housing and urban renewal, telephone, power, mass transit, education, telecommunications, housing, economic development and public defender services. Of these, the telephone, airport, port, and power authorities are instrumentalities of the government. Because the Guam visitors' bureau is a public corporation, not a governmental entity,[19] an employee of the bureau may be discharged for political reasons without violating any civil rights protections against patronage discharge.[20] Presumably, this is also true of the other autonomous agencies not specially designated as governmental instrumentalities.

An Office of Suruhanu (ombudsman), created under Title 2 of the Guam Code, overviews government agencies. The Suruhanu is responsible for correcting problems citizens have with the government and providing access to an expert in dealing with the government, so that citizen complaints will be investigated.

B. Public Service

The Organic Act requires the Legislature to establish a merit system for appointments and promotions in the public service. Rules relating to the merit system are in Title 4 of the Code. The government's personnel policy is implemented by the Civil Service Commission, whose members are appointed by the governor with legislative consent. Guam policy supports an affirmative action program to ensure that physically and mentally handicapped persons have an opportunity to obtain government employment; forbids the employment of persons who habitually use intoxicating beverages or who unlawfully use narcotic or other mind-altering drugs; and prohibits the appointment of more than two members of the same family to the public service, except in the medical, paramedical, and teaching professions. People who advocate or who aid or belong to any party, organization, or association that advocates the overthrow by force or violence of the government of Guam or of the United States are not qualified to hold any public office of trust or profit under the government of Guam.

C. Public Finance and Audit

Independent audit oversight of the government of Guam is provided by the Inspector General of the Department of the Interior. The Governor must submit an annual financial report to Congress and to the Secretary of the Interior. Guam also has its own auditor.

D. Rule Making

Guam has established a uniform method for the making and publishing of rules by all administrative agencies. Agencies may make nonrenewable emergency regulations that are effective for 180 days. Before any other rule is adopted, amended, rescinded, or repealed by an agency, the time and manner in which a hearing regarding it will be held must be published in a newspaper of general circulation in Guam. At the hearing, interested parties must be given adequate opportunity to help formulate any proposed rule. Any interested person may petition an agency requesting promulgation, amendment, or repeal of any rule.

E. Review of Administrative Action

The validity of an agency rule may be challenged by petition for a declaratory judgment in the Superior Court. The agency is a required party to the proceeding. The court will declare a rule invalid that violates provisions of law, exceeds the statutory authority of the agency, or was adopted without compliance with statutory rule-making procedures. The Administrative Adjudication Act governs proceedings in which legal rights, duties, or privileges of specific parties must be determined after an agency hearing.

VI. International Obligations

As a territory of the United States, Guam has no right to engage in international relations. Guam is a member of the Asian Pacific Parliamentary Union and the Pacific Conference of Legislators.

VII. Revenue Law

The Organic Act adopted the U.S. Internal Revenue Code, Title 26, USC, as the territorial tax law. Revenue from the tax accrues to the territorial government, which relieves the U.S. Treasury from making direct appropriations.[21] Guam also receives revenue from U.S. government grants. Other matters concerning taxation are contained in Title 11 of the Guam Code. General revenue authority is placed in the Legislature. The Department of Revenue and Taxation is responsible for the administration and enforcement of laws relating to taxes on income, real property, use, excise and admission, occupancy of hotel and lodging houses, and business (on gross receipts, alcoholic beverages, liquid fuel, automotive surcharges, and tobacco). The department is also responsible for business licenses, insurance, vehicle registration, weights and measures, alcoholic beverage control, corporations, narcotics, gaming, savings and loan associations, securities, and greyhound racing.

All public property, all buildings and land used solely for education, religion, or officially approved charities, and all land used for government-approved cemetery purposes are exempt from taxation.

VIII. Investment Law

Guam has sought to attract U.S. and foreign business investment in order to increase domestic income and provide local employment, but the provisions adopted have not been much used to date.

Corporations engaged in eligible businesses may apply for a qualifying certificate, which entitles them to tax rebates. Tax abatements are available to a qualifying corporation on real property taxes; taxes on income derived from lease of land, buildings, machinery, or equipment; and gross receipts taxes from the sale of petroleum products and alcoholic beverages manufactured in Guam and sold to U.S. or Guam governmental agencies. A 75 percent rebate on corporate income tax is also available. To qualify for these abatements, a corporation must employ a stated percentage of residents of Guam who are U.S. citizens or permanent residents and must maintain a management training program for such employees.

Guam also offers inducements to attract U.S. companies engaged in export trade to establish foreign sales corporations in Guam. Guam income tax is not levied on foreign trade income. Neither is there income tax on investment income or carrying charges related to the sale or lease of property outside Guam or effectively connected with the trade or business of the foreign sales corporation that produces foreign trade income.

IX. Welfare Law

A number of U.S. health, welfare, and educational assistance programs apply to Guam (see III, C U.S. Laws). In addition, under Title 10, Chapter 1, of the Code, Guam has authorized public assistance programs for those people who do not have sufficient income or other resources to provide a subsistence compatible with decency and health and who are sixty-five years of age or older, blind, permanently and totally disabled, or under the age of eighteen. To receive assistance, a child under the age of eighteen must be living with a relative and be deprived of parental support or suitable care because of the father's unemployment or death; continued absence from home; physical or mental incapacity; or the cruelty, neglect, or depravity of a parent. Guam has implemented the U.S. food stamp program. Guam also provides free dental care to all preschool and school-age children through age sixteen; medical assistance to those who are unable, by themselves or through third-party payments, to pay the cost of necessary medical care; and a health maintenance organization to offer health services to the people of Guam at the lowest possible cost.

X. Criminal Law

Guam has adopted the Model Penal Code, promulgated by the U.S. National Conference of Commissioners on Uniform State Laws, as Title 9 of its Code. A major source of Guam's criminal law, however, is the California Penal Code. Cases decided by the California courts are considered persuasive. Although some U.S. federal criminal statutes apply to Guam, references in such statutes to a "state" will not be considered to apply to Guam in the absence of express Congressional intent.[22]

A. Classes of Crimes

No conduct, except contempt, constitutes an offense in Guam unless it is a crime or violation under the Criminal Code or under another statute of Guam. Crimes are classified as felonies, misdemeanors, petty misdemeanors, and violations. Felonies are divided into the first, second, and third degree. A felony that does not specify the degree is of the third degree. A misdemeanor or petty misdemeanor is a crime that does not specify the grade or the sentence authorized upon conviction. A violation is an offense for which no sentence other than a fine, fine and forfeiture, or other civil penalty is authorized upon conviction. A violation is not a crime, and conviction of a violation does not give rise to any disability or legal disadvantage based on conviction for a criminal offense.

B. Principles of Liability

Criminal liability is based on conduct that includes a voluntary act or the omission of an act of which a person is physically capable. Except where the definition of a violation or offense indicates a purpose to dispense with a culpable mental state, a person is not guilty of a crime unless acting intentionally, knowingly, recklessly, or with criminal negligence. Qualified exemptions from criminal liability exist for juvenile status; ignorance or mistake as to law or fact; intoxication; or where as a result of mental illness, disease, or defect, a person lacked at the time substantial capacity to know or understand what he or she was doing, to know or understand that the conduct was wrongful, or to control those actions. Other defenses include entrapment; duress; consent; self-defense; force in defense of third persons or property in law enforcement and by a person having a special care, duty, or responsibility for another; and abandonment in a prosecution for attempt, criminal facilitation, or conspiracy. The Criminal Code permits a person to be granted "use" immunity, but not "transactional" immunity.

C. Offenses

The Criminal Code has adopted the inchoate offenses of attempt, solicitation, and conspiracy. Substantive crimes and offenses are divided into the categories of crimes against the person; offenses of public indecency; offenses against the family; offenses against property; offenses of a fraudulent nature; and miscellaneous offenses. Guam has adopted the Uniform Controlled Dangerous Substances Act.

Criminal offenses are found in other statutes as well. Most offenses relating to elections and election fraud are contained in Title 3, Chapters 8 and 14, of the Guam Code. Penalties for violation of the Vehicle Code are found in Title 16, Chapter 9, of the Code. Guam's 1990 statute imposing criminal penalties for abortion has been declared unconstitutional by the U.S. District Court for Guam.[23]

Because Guam has concurrent civil and criminal jurisdiction with the United States with regard to property owned, reserved, or controlled by the United States, a judgment regarding such property under the laws of Guam or the United States is a bar to any prosecution under the criminal laws of the other jurisdiction for the same act or acts.

D. Sentencing

Title 9, Chapter 80, of the Code permits a court to suspend the imposition of a sentence; order a person committed in lieu of sentence; or sentence a person to imprisonment for a term required by law or to imprisonment and an additional parole, to probation, to pay a fine, or to specified combinations of those sentences. Restitution may also be required but may not exceed the victim's loss. When a person has been convicted of an offense, a court may enter judgment for a lesser included offense and impose sentence accordingly, if the court thinks sentencing the offender in accordance with the Code would be unduly harsh. The court may dismiss the prosecution and civilly commit a chronic alcoholic, narcotic addict, or person suffering from mental abnormality who is charged with a third-degree felony or lesser offense.

XI. Judicial Procedure

A. Civil Procedure

The U.S. District Court uses the Federal Rules of Civil Procedure and other rules authorized under 48 USC 1424. The Guam Code of Civil Procedure (Guam Code, Title 7), adopted in 1933 from the California Civil Code, governs actions in the Guam Superior Court.

1. EVIDENCE

Title 6 of the Code contains a unified Evidence Code. Additional rules of evidence, promulgated by the Judicial Council of Guam and subsequently codified by the Legislature, are also in Title 6. Where there is a conflict between the Code and the rules, the rules generally control. The rules, patterned after the U.S. Federal Rules of Evidence, govern proceedings in the Superior Court of Guam. There are a few differences; for example, Guam has adopted the modern view that if one spouse is willing to testify against the other, the marriage has so thoroughly broken down as to be beyond the protection of the marital privilege.

2. LIMITATION PERIODS

General limitation provisions are found in Chapter 1 of the Code of Civil Procedure. Most actions relating to real property must be brought within five years of the accrual of the action. Actions founded on a written instrument must generally be brought within four years, and other contractual actions must be brought within two years. Most tort actions relating to property must be brought within three years, while those relating to the person must generally be brought within one year. An action to recover goods or the value of goods seized by the tax collector, to recover stock sold for a delinquent assessment, or to set aside or invalidate any action taken by a majority of the trustees of any corporation dissolved by operation of law must be brought within six months. There is no limitation to actions brought to recover money or other property deposited with any bank, banker, trust company, building and loan association, or savings and loan society, so long as they have not become insolvent.

Claims alleging civil rights violations under 42 USC 1983, must be brought within the two-year period allowed by the Guam Civil Procedure Code for recovery of damages for personal injury in a tort action.[24] The limitation period for actions for a breach of the duty of fair representation by a union is six months.[25]

B. Criminal Procedure

Guam uses the Federal Rules of Criminal Procedure. Additional rules in Title 8 of the Guam Code also govern criminal proceedings.

1. PRETRIAL PROCEDURE

Prosecutions for felonies (including those joined with misdemeanors) must be commenced by grand jury indictment unless the defendant waives this right. Other offenses are prosecuted by complaint. Private prosecutions are no longer permitted, and all prosecutions are initiated by the prosecuting attorney.

Where a prosecution is begun by complaint, the judge must first find probable cause to believe the defendant has committed an offense and then issue a summons for the defendant's appearance unless a valid reason is shown for issuance of an arrest warrant. An arrested person may be released on bail or on recognizance, with or without conditions. If an arrest has been made other than upon a warrant, an officer may release the person upon a notice to appear. An arrested person must be taken without unnecessary delay before a judge of the Superior Court. The defendant must be advised of the following:

1. the nature of the complaint;
2. the right to counsel;
3. the circumstances under which pretrial release can be obtained;
4. the right to prosecution by indictment, if applicable;

5. the right to a preliminary examination; and
6. the privilege against self-incrimination.

After indictment and after the filing of a complaint or information, an accused must be arraigned. The court must inform the defendant of the nature of the charge, of the right to plead not guilty or to persist in that plea if it has already been made, of the fact that upon a plea of guilty or nolo contendere there will not be a further trial of any kind, and of the maximum penalty that can be imposed.

Title 8, Chapter 70, of the Code permits wide discovery by the accused in a criminal case but also requires the accused to appear in a lineup; speak for identification by witnesses to an offense; be fingerprinted; pose for photographs not involving reenactment of a scene; try on articles of clothing; provide handwriting specimens; permit the taking of samples of blood, hair, and other bodily materials that involve no unreasonable bodily intrusion; and submit to a reasonable physical or medical inspection.

Title 9, Chapter 7, of the Code permits a court to dismiss a prosecution if, having regard to the nature of the conduct and the attendant circumstances, it finds that the defendant's conduct was not unlawful.

Guam has adopted the Uniform Extradition and Rendition Act of 1983.

2. TRIAL PROCEDURE

Under the Civil Procedure Code, a defendant is entitled to a jury trial in all criminal cases where the authorized punishment consists of confinement for more than sixty days or a fine of more than US$500. Other procedural matters are covered in Title 8, Chapter 80, of the Code. Speedy trial provisions require the court to dismiss a criminal action if trial has not commenced within forty-five days after arraignment for a defendant in custody or sixty days after arraignment for a defendant not in custody, unless good cause is shown. The defendant may waive a jury trial with the approval of the court and consent of the government. Juries consist of six members, except that a defendant is entitled to a jury of twelve in a felony prosecution.

3. POST-TRIAL PROCEDURE

After the close of trial, the court may, on motion of a defendant, grant a new trial if one is required in the interests of justice. The court has no power to order a new trial on its own motion.[26] The granting of the motion places the parties in the same position as if no trial had been held.

Where a general verdict or finding by the court is made in favor of the defendant, a judgment of acquittal must be given immediately and the defendant discharged, unless detained for any other legal cause. Where the finding or verdict is against the defendant, the court must order the person detained or released and appoint a time for pronouncing judgment.

A presentence investigation and report is required before sentence is imposed unless the court otherwise directs. The court must allow counsel an opportunity to speak on the defendant's behalf and must ask the defendant personally whether he or she wishes to make a statement and present any information in mitigation of punishment. After imposing sentence in a case that has been tried on a plea of not guilty, the court must advise the defendant of the right to appeal.

The court may correct an illegal sentence at any time. It may correct a sentence imposed in an illegal manner or reduce a sentence within 120 days after sentence is orally pronounced.[27] Clerical mistakes and errors in the record arising from oversight or omission may be corrected by the court at any time. Although the Guam Code permits special sentencing of offenders aged

18 to 25, no special facilities have been established, and no one has been sentenced under this act.[28]

4. LIMITATION PERIODS

A prosecution for murder may be commenced at any time. A prosecution for any felony other than murder must be commenced within three years after it is committed, and all other offenses must be prosecuted within one year after commission; however, a prosecution against a public officer or employee based on misconduct in office or any person acting in complicity with that person may be commenced at any time while the public officer continues in public office or within three years thereafter. The limitation periods do not run while a criminal action against the defendant for the same conduct is pending in Guam.

C. Appellate Procedure

1. CIVIL APPEALS

Where an appeal is authorized to the Ninth Circuit Court of Appeals from a judgment of the U.S. District Court, Appellate Division, the Ninth Circuit has adopted a strict standard of review that accords no deference to interpretations of local law by the Appellate Division.[29] The Ninth Circuit relies on California cases interpreting that state's Civil Code to interpret the Guam Code[30] and on its own decisions to interpret Guam rules of civil procedure that track U.S. federal rules of civil procedure.[31]

2. CRIMINAL APPEALS

An appeal may be taken by the defendant in any criminal case in the Guam Superior Court. Appeals by the prosecution from the Superior Court to the District Court, Appellate Division, and from that court to the U.S. Court of Appeals for the Ninth Circuit are governed by 48 U.S.C., Section 1493. Guam's local statute on appeals, 8 Guam Code Annotated, Section 130.20, may be preempted by this U.S. federal statute.[32]

An appeal is taken by filing a timely notice of appeal with the clerk of the Superior Court. The appellate court may reverse, affirm, or modify a judgment or order appealed from or reduce the degree of the offense or the punishment imposed; may set aside, affirm, or modify any or all the proceedings subsequent to or dependent upon such judgment or order; and may order a new trial or remand the cause to the trial court for such proceedings as may be just under the circumstances.

XII. LAND AND NATURAL RESOURCES

Early naval governors took the position that all land in Guam was the property of the United States because the inhabitants of Guam were unable to prove their title under Spanish law. Frequently, landholders were able to find only records of possessory rights, which were used as a basis for paying compensation to people from whom the territorial administration took land.[33] After World War II, which destroyed nearly all buildings and survey markers, the U.S. Navy took possession of large land areas. In rebuilding, the Navy ignored old property boundaries, thereby causing even greater problems for landholders seeking compensation.

In response to protests that the United States dealt unfairly with Guamanian landowners in acquiring land through condemnation for use as military bases during the last years of World

War II and the early postwar years, the Organic Act was amended in 1977 and 1980 to give the U.S. District Court exclusive jurisdiction to review land claims where the issue of compensation had been adjudicated in the U.S. District Court between July 21, 1944 and August 23, 1963. The District Court has power to award fair compensation where less than fair market value was paid as a result of duress, unfair influence, or other unconscionable actions of the United States. Many of the claims filed under this amendment are still pending.

The United States has, subject to valid existing rights, conveyed to Guam to be administered in trust for the benefit of the people of Guam all right, title, and interest in the tidelands of Guam; in submerged lands within 3 miles of the shore; and in artificially made, filled-in, or reclaimed lands. Excepted from the transfer were all deposits of oil, gas, and other minerals (not including coral, sand, and gravel) and a wide variety of submerged lands adjacent to property owned or administered by the United States or designated by the President. The United States retained the right to establish naval defensive sea areas and airspace reservations deemed necessary for national defense and U.S. constitutional rights over navigable waters. A 1975 U.S. Executive Order exempted some submerged lands from the transfer. Under the Submerged Lands and Concurrent Jurisdiction Act, the Guam courts have concurrent civil and criminal jurisdiction with U.S. courts with regard to property owned, reserved, or controlled by the United States in Guam, unless Guam's jurisdiction has been excluded by an order of the President. As of 1986, such an order had not been issued.

Guam's property law is in Division II of its Civil Code (GCA, Title 1). Guam has a modified Torrens system, adopted in 1933 from California's land title registration law.[34] The starting date for determining title is January 1, 1935. All property within the boundaries of Guam that does not belong to any person or to which title fails for want of heirs or next of kin vests to the government of Guam. The government of Guam—but not of the United States—has power to acquire property by eminent domain.

Guam's statute of frauds requires that any transfer of real property, other than an estate at will or for a term not exceeding one year, be effective by operation of law or be in writing and be subscribed by the party disposing of the property or an agent authorized in writing. A transfer of real property is presumed to pass a fee simple title and passes all easements attached to the property.

Any person, including an alien, may own or lease residential property. An attempted lease to aliens of other real property in Guam for a period longer than five years is prohibited and void. Penalty for a violation of that provision is a fine of 50 percent of the value of the lease for each year over five years, one-half payable by the lessee and one-half by the lessor, and an additional fine not exceeding US$100.00 to be paid by the lessor.

XIII. Persons and Entities

Guam's general domestic corporation law is in the Civil Code, which also regulates the incorporation of religious and other nonprofit corporations and institutions of learning.

XIV. Family Law

Provisions relating to marriage, annulment, and divorce are contained in the Civil Code.

A. Marriage

A valid marriage requires solemnization by the Governor or a substitute, a judge of the District Court or Superior Court, or ordained clergy and priests. Noncompliance with the Code's provisions by others than the parties to a marriage does not invalidate the marriage. The husband is the head of the family and may choose any reasonable place or mode of living to which the wife must conform.

Neither party to a contract to marry is bound by a promise made in ignorance of the other's want of personal chastity, and either is released from the marriage by unchaste conduct on the part of the other unless both parties participate. Females above the age of eighteen years and males above the age of twenty-one are capable of consenting to and consummating marriage. Females between the ages of sixteen and eighteen and males between the ages of eighteen and twenty-one who live under parental authority must present the written consent of a parent or guardian. Females between the ages of fourteen and sixteen and males between the ages of sixteen and eighteen must have the written consent of a parent or guardian and an order of the Superior Court.

Marriages between parents and children, ancestors and descendants of every degree, between brothers and sisters of the half as well as the whole blood, and between uncles and nieces or aunts and nephews are incestuous and void.

A marriage must be annulled or dissolved before a valid subsequent marriage can be entered into unless the former spouse has been absent and believed dead for five years. Guam does not recognize the validity of a marriage contracted within one year after the entry of an interlocutory decree in divorce proceedings. A marriage contracted in violation of these provisions is valid, however, until declared nullified by a competent tribunal.

B. Divorce, Separation, and Annulment

Either party to an incestuous or void marriage may proceed, by action in the Superior Court, to have it so declared. A marriage may be annulled in the following circumstances:

1. at the time of the marriage, the person in whose behalf the annulment is sought was under age and the marriage was contracted without the consent of a parent or guardian;
2. a previous marriage of one of the parties was still in force;
3. a party was of unsound mind;
4. the consent of a party was obtained by fraud or force; or
5. a party was physically incapable of entering into the marriage state, and the incapacity continues and appears to be incurable.

In the case of a person under age or of unsound mind or of a marriage contracted by fraud or force, an annulment will not be granted if that party freely cohabits with the other as husband or wife after the removal of the impediment. An action for a decree of nullity of marriage must be commenced within four years of the removal of the impediment where the party was under age or in the case of fraud, force, or incapacity; and during the life of either party where there was a former valid marriage or where one of the parties is of unsound mind. A judgment of nullity of marriage does not affect the legitimacy of children conceived or born before the judgment. The judgment is conclusive only as against the parties to the action and those claiming under them.

A dissolution of marriage may be granted for adultery, extreme cruelty, willful desertion, willful neglect, habitual intemperance, or conviction of felony. A decree of dissolution of marriage must be denied upon a showing of connivance, collusion, condonation, recrimination, or limitation and lapse of time. An action based on adultery must be commenced within two years after the commission of the act or its discovery by the injured party. When the cause is conviction of a felony, the action must be commenced before the expiration of two years from conviction and sentence. In all other cases a divorce will be denied when there is an unreasonable lapse of time before the commencement of the action.

A dissolution of marriage may not be granted unless the plaintiff has been a resident of Guam for one year preceding the commencement of the action. The court may not grant a dissolution of marriage upon the defendant's default or the uncorroborated statement, admission, or testimony of the parties but must require proof of the facts alleged. If the court determines no dissolution of marriage should be granted, the judgment entered will be final. If it determines a dissolution should be granted, the judgment entered is interlocutory and becomes final at the expiration of one year.

C. Support and Maintenance

The Superior Court can hear suits for maintenance of a spouse and children whether or not grounds for the dissolution of the marriage exist and whether or not a dissolution of the marriage is sought. Foreign-created alimony and support obligations are enforceable in Guam.

In determining issues of child support and maintenance, the court must resort first to community property and then to the separate property of the husband. When the wife has a separate estate or community property is sufficient to give her alimony or proper support, the court in its discretion may withhold any allowance to her out of the husband's separate property. The community and separate property may be used for the support and education of the children in such proportions as the court deems just.

In rendering a decree of dissolution of marriage, the court must dispose of the community property and the family home as required by law and if necessary may order a partition or sale of the property and a division or other disposition of the proceeds. The community property and home are assigned as follows:

1. if the decree is based on adultery or extreme cruelty, community property is assigned to the parties in proportions the court deems just;
2. if the decree is rendered on any other ground, the community property is divided equally between the parties;
3. a home may be assigned to the innocent party or the proceeds of its sale may be divided as the court deems just.

Guam adopted the Uniform Reciprocal Enforcement of Support Act in 1954.

D. Custody

In actions for divorce, separation, annulment, separate maintenance or any other proceeding where the custody of a minor child is disputed, the court may, during the minority of the child, make custody orders that seem necessary or proper. In awarding custody, the court is guided by the best interest of the child. Custody may be awarded to either parent or to some other persons whenever such an award serves the child's best interest. If a child is of sufficient age and capacity to reason to form an intelligent preference, the court will consider and give due weight to the child's wishes. Any custody award is subject to alteration whenever the best interest of the child requires. Reasonable visitation rights must be awarded to parents and to any person interested in the welfare of the child in the discretion of the court, unless it is shown that such rights are detrimental to the child's best interest.

E. Legitimacy

A child is considered legitimate for all purposes if the parents of the child were married at the conception of the child or at any time after the conception of the child and before the child's eighteenth birthday; the child is legitimate under the laws of the place of birth; or the parents have jointly executed an affidavit before the child's eighteenth birthday, affirming they are the natural, biological parents of the child, stating the child's birth date and affirming their desire to legitimate the child. A child is also considered legitimate if, before the child's eighteenth birthday, a court has determined the child's paternity in a divorce action, paternity action, or action for support.

XV. Personal Property

The mode of transferring personal property is contained in Division III of the Civil Code. Title to personal property, whether sold or exchanged, passes to the buyer when the parties agree on a present transfer and the thing itself is identified whether separated from other things or not. Title is transferred by an executory agreement for the sale or exchange of personal property only when the buyer has accepted the thing or when the seller has completed it, prepared it for delivery, and offered it to the buyer with intent to transfer the title in the manner prescribed by law. Where possession of personal property, together with a power to dispose of it, is transferred by its owner to another person, an executed sale by the latter, while in possession, to a second buyer in good faith and in the ordinary course of business, for value, transfers to that second buyer the title of the original owner.

Gifts are also regulated by the Civil Code. A verbal gift must be actually or symbolically delivered to the donee, unless the means of obtaining possession and control of the thing are given. A gift, other than a gift made in contemplation, fear, or peril of death, with intent that it shall take effect only in case of death, cannot be revoked by the giver. Guam has adopted the Uniform Gift to Minors Act.

XVI. Wills and Succession

Succession law is found in Title 15 of the Guam Code. Every adult person of sound mind may dispose of his or her real and personal property and his or her share of community property and make gifts of body parts to certain institutions, by a will written in any language. Title 15 has no provision for an oral will. To be valid, a will must be in writing. Every will other than a holographic will must be signed at the end by the testator or by some person in the testator's presence and by his or her direction. The signature must be made in the presence of two attesting witnesses, present at the same time, each of whom must sign the instrument as a witness. A holographic will is one that is written, dated, and signed by the hand of the testator. No formalities are necessary for its making or execution; it need not be witnessed.

A will made before marriage is automatically revoked after marriage as to the spouse and any issue of the marriage, unless provision for the spouse has been made by marriage contract or unless the spouse is provided for or mentioned in the will in a way that shows an intention not to make such provision. A will is also automatically revoked as to a divorced spouse, unless the will shows a specific intent to the contrary. If a child or the issue of a deceased child is unintentionally omitted from a will, that child or issue succeeds to the same share in the testator's estate as if the testator had died intestate. A will may be revoked by a subsequent written will or by the destruction of the will with the intent to revoke it.

A will executed outside of Guam is valid in Guam if executed according to the provisions of Title 15 of the Code or according to the law where it was executed or where the testator was domiciled at death or at the time of the wills execution.

Guam is a community property jurisdiction. Upon the death of any married person, one-half of any community property belongs to the surviving spouse. The other one-half is subject to testamentary disposition of the decedent. The separate property of a person who dies without disposing of it by will is distributed to the surviving spouse and the decedent's children unless there are no issue, in which case one-half goes to the surviving spouse and one-half to the decedent's parents. If there is neither issue nor surviving spouse, the decedent's separate estate goes to the decedent's parents and if both parents are dead, to the decedent's siblings and to the descendants of the siblings. If there is neither issue, spouse, parent, sibling, nor descendant of a sibling, the separate estate goes to the next of kin.

Because Guam is a community property jurisdiction, it has no "widow's election" provision as to separate property of the deceased. However, an exception is made in the case of a married person not domiciled in Guam who dies leaving a valid will disposing of real property in Guam that is not the community property of the decedent and surviving spouse. The surviving spouse has the same right to elect to take a portion of or interest in such property against the will of the decedent as though the property were situated in the decedent's domicile at death.

XVII. Contracts

The Organic Act permits the government of Guam to be sued on any contract entered into with respect to the exercise by the government of any of its lawful powers, with the consent of the Legislature evidenced by enacted law.

Guam's version of the Uniform Commercial Code (UCC) is found in Title 13 of the Guam Code. Unless displaced by particular provisions of the UCC, the principles of law and equity—including the mercantile law and the law relative to capacity to contract, principal and agent, estoppel, fraud, misrepresentation, duress, coercion, mistake, bankruptcy, or other validating or invalidating cause—supplement its provisions.

Guam has adopted a working draft of the Uniform Consumer Credit Code, which applies to consumer credit sales; consumer loans; and insurance supplied in connection with a consumer credit sale, lease, or loan. The Code also restricts a creditor's remedies, while giving remedies to debtors and imposing criminal penalties for willful violation of provisions of the act.

XVIII. Commercial Law

As an unincorporated territory of the United States, Guam is not subject to constitutional restrictions on its regulation of interstate commerce (see II, B U.S. Constitution). The government of Guam, including its public corporations, is immune from antitrust liability to the same extent as is the U.S. government.[35] Guam is subject to the U.S. bankruptcy laws.

Domestic corporations, which include Northern Marianas corporations, may be formed by the voluntary association of three or more persons. Executed articles of incorporation containing information about the corporation must be signed by the directors and filed in the Department of Revenue and Taxation after the corporation has received a certificate of approval from the Governor. The articles must be accompanied by a sworn statement of the treasurer that at least 20 percent of the entire capital stock has been subscribed and at least 25 percent of the subscription paid to the treasurer for the benefit and to the credit of the corporation. The corporation must adopt a code of bylaws within one month after filing articles of incorporation.

Foreign corporations must obtain a foreign corporation license and certificate of registration from the Director of Revenue and Taxation before transacting business in Guam and must show they are solvent, sound financially, and established according to the laws of the place where incorporated.

Special rules govern the registration of religious, educational, and other nonprofit corporations. Most such corporations are required to file annual reports showing a statement of income and expenditures for the preceding year and a balance sheet showing assets and liabilities.

Industrial development corporations may be formed by ten or more residents of Guam to promote, develop, and advance the prosperity and economic welfare of Guam. At least three banks, federal savings and loan associations, insurance companies, domestic building and loan associations, or other approved lending institutions authorized to do business in Guam must be members of the corporation. Any corporation organized as an industrial development corporation is a territorial development company as defined in the Small Business Investment Act of 1958.

Professional corporations may be formed to render any type of professional services that may be lawfully rendered only pursuant to a license, certification, or registration authorized by the Business License Law. Provisions of the general corporation law apply to professional corporations, except where they conflict with the Professional Corporation Act.

XIX. Torts

Tort law in Guam is primarily a common law matter. Compensation in wrongful death actions is limited to the pecuniary loss suffered by the plaintiff; injuries to a decedent's estate, punitive damages, and damages based on pain and suffering are not recoverable.[36] U.S. common law principles such as the borrowed servant rule apply to Guam.[37]

Some statutory modifications of the common law relating to tort have been adopted by the U.S. Congress and the Guam Legislature. For example, under Title 16, Chapter 17, of the Code, liability is imputed to the owner of a motor vehicle that, while driven by another with the owner's permission, causes death or injury. A direct action is permitted by an injured person against an insurer.[38]

The Civil Code codifies Guam's law pertaining to defamation. Libel and slander are prohibited except where publication is privileged. These laws, enacted in 1953, must be read in light of later First Amendment decisions of the U.S. Supreme Court.

The laws relating to public and private nuisance have been codified in the Civil Code. A public nuisance may be abated by any authorized public body or officer or by a private person, where the nuisance is specially injurious to that person. The Department of Public Health and Social Services has power to order the immediate abatement of any public nuisance, defined as anything that is dangerous to life or injurious to health or that renders soil, air, water, or food impure or unwholesome. Maintenance of a public nuisance is a misdemeanor. Injunctive or other civil relief is available, as is the right of the department to abate the nuisance, whether on private or public property, and charge the property owner for the costs of abatement.

Although the government of Guam has inherent sovereign immunity,[39] the Organic Act permits Guam to be sued on any tort committed incident to the exercise by the government of Guam of any of its lawful powers, with the consent of the Legislature evidenced by enacted law. The Government of Guam Claims Act creates a limited waiver of governmental immunity from suit and requires the filing of a claim with the Attorney General before suit is filed. Statutory bodies, such as the Guam Power Authority, that have power to sue and be sued have generally waived their immunity from suit.[40]

Under Title 4 of the Code officers of the government of Guam and of its political subdivisions are liable for damage or injury to persons or property resulting from the defective or dangerous condition of public property only in the following circumstances:

1. the injury sustained was the direct and proximate result of the defective or dangerous condition;
2. the officer had notice of the defective or dangerous condition or that condition was directly attributable to his or her work or work done under his or her direction in a negligent, careless, or unworkmanlike manner;
3. the officer had authority and the duty to remedy the condition at the expense of the local governing body and funds for that purpose were immediately available;
4. within a reasonable time after receiving notice and being able to remedy the condition, the officer failed to take reasonable steps to give adequate warning of the condition; and
5. the damage or injury was sustained while the public property was being carefully used, and due care was being exercised to avoid the danger due to the condition.

Public property in this context means public streets, highways, bridges, buildings, parks, grounds, works, or property.

A local government officer is not liable for moneys stolen from his or her custody unless the loss was sustained because the officer failed to exercise due care. Local government officers employed on a salary established by the Legislature or local government are personally liable for the negligence of deputies or employees serving under them performing the duties of an office whose appointment has been approved by the local body only where the officers fail to exercise due care in the selection, appointment, or supervision of the employees or negligently fail to suspend or discharge the employees after knowledge or notice of their inefficiency or incompetency.

Because Guam is a territory, neither the government of Guam nor its officers acting in their official capacities are persons chargeable in a U.S. court with violations of U.S. laws.[41] Guam's officers may be sued in their personal capacities.[42] Prospective injunctive relief is available against an official acting in his or her official capacity.[43]

XX. Labor Law

Guam's Workmen's Compensation Act is modeled upon and substantially the same as the U.S. Longshoremen's and Harbor Workers' Act.

XXI. Industrial and Intellectual Property Rights

The Organic Act adopts the copyright laws of the United States.

XXII. Legal Education and Profession

Most lawyers practicing in Guam received their legal education in the United States. Admission to the bar is within the jurisdiction of the Superior Court, which also has power to disbar, suspend, or otherwise discipline members of the Bar of Guam for misconduct under the Superior Court Rules Governing Discipline, which are based on the Supreme Court of New Mexico's rules. Under the Government Code, an ethics committee hears disciplinary matters. Discipline may be imposed for conviction of a crime other than a nonserious traffic offense, for violation of a rule of professional conduct in effect in Guam, because discipline has been imposed in another jurisdiction, or for violation of any disciplinary or disability rule or order of any court having jurisdiction in Guam or of any law imposing a rule of professional conduct upon lawyers. A lawyer will be immediately suspended from practice if found to be incompetent or incapacitated from practicing law or convicted of a crime other than a nonserious traffic offense. A lawyer may be suspended if the lawyer is under investigation for violation of the American Bar Association's *Model Rules of Professional Conduct* or has violated a court rule, statute, or other law or if a criminal complaint, information, or indictment has been filed against the lawyer.

XXIII. Research Guide

Guam statutes are contained in the *Guam Code Annotated*, published by the Guam Law Revision Commission, Agana, and in annual volumes of public laws, session laws, and current laws, available from the government offices in Guam. Decisions of the Guam courts are reported in the *Guam Reports* (Guam), published by Equity Publishing Company, Oxford, New Hampshire, since 1955. Certain relevant decisions of U.S. courts appear in the *Federal Supplement* (F. Supp.) for District Court cases, *Federal Reporter*, 2d series (F. 2d) for Court of Appeals cases, and *United States Reports* (U.S.) for U.S. Supreme Court cases.

Guam Bar Journal. Agana, Guam, Guam Bar Association, 1981–.

Liebowitz, A. H. "The Applicability of Federal Law to Guam," 16 *Virginia J. of International Law* 21 (1975).

———. "United States Federalism: The States and the Territories," 28 *American Univ. Law Rev.* 449 (1979).

McKibben, L.A. "The Political Relationship Between the United States and the Pacific Islands Entities: The Path to Self-Government in the Northern Marianas Islands, Palau and Guam," 31 *Harvard International Law J.* 257 (1990).

Souder, P. "Guam: Land Tenure in a Fortress," in R. G. Crocombe, ed., *Land Tenure in the Pacific*. 3d ed. Suva: University of the South Pacific, 1987.

19. The Commonwealth of the Northern Mariana Islands

BRUCE L. OTTLEY

I. Dateline

1500 B.C. Mariana Islands first settled by Chamorros, immigrants of Southeast Asian descent.
1565 A.D. Mariana Islands officially claimed by Spain.
1700 Spanish move most of Chamorro population to Guam, leaving Northern Mariana Islands, except for Rota, essentially uninhabited.
1820 Spanish begin to permit islanders from Caroline Islands to settle in Northern Mariana Islands.
1885 Pope Leo XIII confirms Spain's sovereignty over Northern Mariana Islands. Chamorros on Guam encouraged to move back to Northern Mariana Islands.
1899 Following its defeat in Spanish-American War, Spain sells Northern Mariana Islands to Germany, which administers them until 1914, when Japan takes control.
1920 The League of Nations mandates Northern Mariana Islands to Japan as class C mandate. Japanese immigration and development of large sugar cane plantations radically change traditional Chamorro culture.
1944 United States forces capture Mariana Islands from Japanese. The U.S. Navy administers islands under military rule until 1947.
1947 United Nations Security Council authorizes United States to administer Northern Mariana Islands, Palau, Federated States of Micronesia, and Marshall Islands as Trust Territory of the Pacific Islands. Trusteeship Agreement for the Former Japanese Mandated Islands designates the area a "strategic trust." During the next fifteen years the Trust Territory governed by the U.S. Navy and Department of the Interior pursuant to series of Executive Orders.
1962 Full authority over Northern Mariana Islands delegated to Department of the Interior. Secretary of the Interior vests governing authority in High Commissioner and judicial authority in High Court.
1965 Congress of Micronesia, popularly elected bicameral legislature, established for the Trust Territory.
1969 United States begins negotiations with Congress of Micronesia on political future of Trust Territory.
1975 United States and Marianas Political Status Commission conclude a Covenant to Establish a Commonwealth of the Northern Mariana Islands in Political Union with the United States of America. The Covenant is ratified in a plebiscite in June 1975 and signed into law by the U.S. President in March 1976. Certain sections of Covenant become effective in 1976 and 1978.
1978 Constitution of Northern Mariana Islands takes effect.

1984 Commonwealth Code adopted.
1986 United Nations Trusteeship Council concludes that United States satisfactorily discharged its obligations under Trusteeship Agreement, that people of Northern Mariana Islands freely exercised their right of self-determination, and that Trusteeship Agreement is terminated. The Covenant becomes fully effective on November 3.

II. Historical, Cultural, and Economic Survey

The Commonwealth of the Northern Mariana Islands, an archipelago of sixteen islands, has an estimated population of 43,300, over half of whom are foreign workers. Of the Marianas' indigenous inhabitants, most are Chamorros who, as voyagers originating from Southeast Asia, first settled in the islands approximately 3,500 years ago. The Chamorros established a matrilineal society based on extended families. Their social system consisted of nobles and lesser nobles (who owned the land and were warriors, sailors, artists, and fishermen) and commoners (who worked the land). Approximately 30 percent of the indigenous people of the Commonwealth are Micronesians of Carolinian descent, who settled in the Marianas later than the Chamorros and consider themselves culturally and ethnically different from the Chamorro majority.

During the past 400 years, the Northern Mariana Islands have been under the control of four foreign powers—Spain, Germany, Japan, and the United States. European diseases and rebellions against the Spanish reduced the original Chamorro population from about 100,000 to less than 5,000 by the end of the seventeenth century. During the eighteenth century the Spanish forcibly removed most of the remaining population to Guam, where they intermarried with Spanish and other Asian groups. Seventy percent of the present indigenous inhabitants of the Commonwealth are Chamorros, while the remaining inhabitants are Carolinians, descendants of people who migrated from the Carolines during the nineteenth century. Because of the long period of colonization and intermarriage with foreigners, very little of the traditional Chamorro and Caroline cultures remain.

From 1947 until 1986, the United States administered the Northern Mariana Islands as part of the Trust Territory of the Pacific Islands. Article 3 of the United Nations Trusteeship Agreement gave the United States "full powers of administration, legislation, and jurisdiction" over the Trust Territory and permitted it to apply those laws of the United States that it considered "appropriate to local conditions and requirements." Article 6 of the Trusteeship Agreement committed the United States to "promote the development of the inhabitants of the Trust Territory toward self-government or independence as may be appropriate to the particular circumstances of the Trust Territory and its people and the freely expressed wishes of the peoples concerned."

In 1975, the United States and the Marianas concluded a Covenant to Establish a Commonwealth of the Northern Marianas Islands in Political Union with the United States of America. With the termination of the United Nations Trusteeship Agreement in 1986, the Northern Mariana Islands became, as provided in the Covenant (Section 101), "a self-governing commonwealth . . . in political union with and under the sovereignty of the United States of America." The political union can be dissolved only with the consent both of the United States and of the Commonwealth. The Covenant gives the people of the Commonwealth the right of local self-government and control over their internal affairs according to the provisions of their own constitution. Defense and foreign affairs remain the responsibility of the United States.

The economy of the Commonwealth relies heavily on federal programs and other services available to United States territories and on the financial assistance guaranteed by Article VII of the Covenant. In recent years, the Commonwealth, particularly Saipan, has become heavily dependent upon the tourist industry.

III. Sources of Law

Because the Commonwealth is both "self-governing" and "in political union with and under the sovereignty of the United States," its legal system is a mixture of the laws of the United States and local legislation. The Covenant, specified provisions of the United States Constitution, and treaties and laws of the United States applicable to the Commonwealth are the supreme law of the land.

In addition to these supreme sources of law, the Constitution of the Commonwealth, pre-Commonwealth laws, legislation enacted by the Commonwealth legislature, custom, decisions of Commonwealth courts, and the common law as applied in the United States are sources of law in the Commonwealth.

A. Covenant

The Covenant governs relations between the Commonwealth and the United States and cannot be changed without mutual consent. It provides for citizenship and nationality, judicial authority, laws of the United States applicable to the Commonwealth, revenue and taxation, United States financial assistance, title to real property, and a resident representative to the United States.

B. U.S. Constitution

Section 501 of the Covenant makes the following provisions of the United States Constitution applicable to the Commonwealth:

1. Article I, 9, Clauses 2, 3, and 8, restricting the situations in which the writ of habeas corpus may be suspended and prohibiting bills of attainder, ex post facto laws, and titles of nobility;
2. Article I, 10, Clauses 1 and 3, prohibiting the Commonwealth from, among other things, entering into treaties or alliances, coining money, impairing the obligation of contracts, keeping troops, or engaging in war;
3. Article IV, 1 and 2, Clauses 1 and 2, requiring the Commonwealth to give full faith and credit to the acts, records, and judicial proceedings of the states and stating that citizens of the Commonwealth are entitled to all the privileges and immunities of citizens of the states);
4. Amendments I–IX, freedom of religion, speech, the press, and assembly; the right to keep and bear arms; a prohibition on quartering soldiers in private homes during peacetime; protection against unreasonable search and seizure; the privilege against self-incrimination; the right to a jury trial; and a prohibition of excessive bail and cruel and unusual punishment;
5. Amendment XIII, prohibiting slavery;
6. Amendment XIV, 1, prohibiting the Commonwealth from abridging the privileges and

immunities of citizens of the United States or denying them due process and equal protection of the law;
7. Amendment XV, the right to vote;
8. Amendment XIX, prohibiting a denial of the right to vote based upon sex; and
9. Amendment XXVI, establishing the right to vote at age eighteen.

However, trial by jury and indictment by grand jury are not required in civil actions or criminal prosecutions based upon local law unless required by local law.

C. Treaties and Laws of the United States

The Covenant specifies a number of U.S. laws applicable to the Commonwealth and provides, in addition, that the United States may enact legislation applicable to the Commonwealth. However, the authority of the United States to legislate for the Commonwealth is limited by the right of self-government granted by Section 105 of the Covenant.

D. Constitution of the Northern Mariana Islands

As required by the Covenant, the Commonwealth adopted a Constitution in 1978. The Constitution specifies the personal rights of individuals; governs the legislative, executive, and judicial branches of government; provides for representation in the United States, local governments, the eligibility to vote, elections, taxation and public finance, public lands, eminent domain, and education; and restricts alienation of land. (In this chapter, references to the "Constitution" refer to the Northern Marianas Constitution.)

Article XVIII of the Constitution sets out three methods by which the Constitution may be amended. First, an initiative petition may submit to the voters the question of a constitutional convention to propose amendments to the Constitution. The petition must be signed by at least 25 percent of the persons qualified to vote in the Commonwealth or by at least 75 percent of the persons qualified to vote in a senatorial district. An initiative petition must be filed with the Attorney General for certification. If certified, the initiative petition must be submitted to the voters at the next general election. If two-thirds of the votes cast in that election are affirmative, the legislature must convene a constitutional convention promptly. The delegates to the convention must be equal to the number of members of the legislature.

Second, the legislature may propose amendments to the Constitution by the affirmative vote of three-fourths of the members of each house.

Finally, amendments to the Constitution may be proposed by popular initiative signed by at least 50 percent of the qualified voters in the Commonwealth and at least 25 percent of the qualified voters in each senatorial district. A petition must be filed with the Attorney General for certification. If certified, it must be submitted to each house of the legislature. If the proposal is approved by the affirmative vote of a majority of the members of each house, the proposed amendment must be submitted for ratification in the same manner as an amendment proposed by legislative initiative.

E. Pre-Commonwealth Laws

Section 505 of the Covenant provides for the continued enforcement of the laws of the Trust Territory, the Mariana Islands district, and its local municipalities and all other executive and district orders of a local nature applicable to the Commonwealth on the date the Covenant became effective insofar as these laws and orders are not inconsistent with the Covenant or with those provisions of the U.S. Constitution or treaties or laws of the United States applicable to the Commonwealth.

F. Legislation

Article II of the Commonwealth Constitution extends the power of the Commonwealth legislature "to all rightful subjects of legislation." This phrasing suggests that legislation cannot be inconsistent with treaties and international agreements of the United States, the Covenant, the U.S. Constitution, laws of the United States applicable to the Commonwealth, or the Commonwealth Constitution, but the legislature can alter pre-Commonwealth laws and make new laws.

Article IX of the Constitution also provides for the enactment of legislation by initiative and the rejection of laws by referendum. An initiative petition must contain the full text of the proposed law and must be signed by at least 20 percent of the persons qualified to vote in the Commonwealth. The petition must be filed with the Attorney General for certification. If certified, the initiative must be submitted to the voters at the next general election. Laws enacted by the legislature may be rejected by referendum. The procedure for a referendum vote is the same as for an initiative.

Commonwealth legislation has been gathered into the Commonwealth of the Northern Marianas Code (cited in this chapter as "CMC" or "the Code"), which is divided into titles according to subject matter. Most titles include several related acts.

G. Custom

Although the Constitution makes no mention of traditional law, the Code gives legal recognition to "recognized custom" in a number of areas: adoption, annulment, and divorce; marriage; and the settlement of estates of limited value (see **XIV Family Law and XVI Wills and Succession**). In order for a custom to be legally recognized, it must be "a law established by long usage and . . . [must be] . . . such usage as by common consent and uniform practice has become the law of the place, or the subject matter, to which it relates."[1] The few reported judicial decisions involving custom have related to the traditional practice of distributing family land before the death of the head of the household[2] (see **XVI Wills and Succession**).

H. Common Law

The Code (Title 7, Section 3401) provides that in the absence of written law or customary law, the rules of common law, as expressed in the *Restatements* prepared by the American Law Institute or as generally understood and applied in the United States are the rules of decision in the courts of the Commonwealth.

The function of the Commonwealth Law Reform Commission is to examine customary law, common law, statutes enacted by the legislature, laws in force, and court decisions and recommend draft legislation to establish a cohesive body of law in each area of the Commonwealth (CMC, Title 1).

IV. Constitutional System

A. Territory

The Commonwealth of the Northern Mariana Islands is an archipelago of sixteen islands with a land area of approximately 477 square kilometers.

B. Nationality and Citizenship

Under Article III of the Covenant, persons born in the Commonwealth are citizens of the United States and are entitled to all the privileges and immunities of citizens of the United States. However, they do not have the right to vote for the President of the United States or to elect representatives or senators to the United States Congress.

C. Government

The Commonwealth has adopted a form of government modeled on that of the states of the United States. Under this system, the Commonwealth government consists of an executive (headed by an elected Governor), a legislature, and a judicial system and local governments headed by Mayors.

1. COMMONWEALTH GOVERNMENT

a. Executive

Article III of the Constitution vests the executive power of the Commonwealth in a Governor and a Lieutenant Governor, each of whom must be a qualified voter in the Commonwealth who is at least thirty years old and has been a resident and domiciliary of the Commonwealth for at least seven years prior to taking office. The Governor and Lieutenant Governor are elected jointly for a four-year term. No person can be elected Governor more than three times. The Governor and Lieutenant Governor may be impeached for treason, the commission of a felony, corruption, or neglect of duty.

In the event of the death, removal, or resignation of the Governor, the Lieutenant Governor becomes Governor. If both offices become vacant, the president of the Senate becomes acting Governor. If the Governor is physically absent from the Commonwealth or is unable to discharge the duties of the office because of physical or mental disability, the Lieutenant Governor becomes the acting Governor.

Article III also specifies the functions and powers of the Governor. The Governor must submit an annual proposed budget to the legislature, describing anticipated revenues and recommending expenditures. The Governor must make an annual report to the legislature regarding the affairs of the Commonwealth and measures that are necessary or desirable. The Governor has the power to grant reprieves, commutations, and pardons after conviction for offenses.

Article III requires the Governor to appoint an executive assistant for Carolinian affairs who is "acceptable to the Carolinian community within the Commonwealth." This assistant reviews the application of government policies and the availability and quality of government services to persons of Carolinian descent. The assistant also investigates complaints and conducts hearings regarding matters affecting persons of Carolinian descent.

b. Legislature

Article II of the Constitution vests the legislative power of the Commonwealth in a Senate and House of Representatives. The Senate consists of nine members, with three members elected at large from each of three senatorial districts. Senators are elected for four-year terms and must be qualified voters in the Commonwealth who are at least twenty-five years old and have been residents and domiciliaries of the Commonwealth for at least five years prior to taking office. The House of Representatives consists of fifteen members who are elected for two-year terms. Representatives must be qualified to vote in the Commonwealth, at least twenty-one years old, and residents and domiciliaries of the Commonwealth for at least three years prior to taking office.

A vacancy in the legislature must be filled by a special election if one-half or more of the term remains. If less than one-half of the term remains, the Governor appoints the unsuccessful candidate in the last election or, if no candidate is available, a qualified person from the district.

Every ten years the legislature must reapportion the seats in the House of Representatives or revise the districts for electing representatives. If the legislature fails to act, the Governor must reapportion or redistrict. Voters have the right to petition the courts to review and amend the reapportionment plan so that it complies with the Constitution or to establish a reapportionment plan if the governor fails to act.

The legislative power of the Commonwealth extends "to all rightful subjects of legislation" (Constitution, Article II). Although appropriation and revenue bills must originate in the House of Representatives, other bills may be introduced either in the Senate or the House. To be enacted, bills require the approval of a majority of votes cast in each house of the legislature.

Under the Constitution and the Local Law Act of 1983 (CMC, Title 1), the legislature also has the power to enact "local bills" that relate exclusively to matters within one senatorial district. Such laws require the review and comment of the local mayor and the approval of the legislature or the majority of the members representing the local legislative delegation. A member of the legislature who has a financial or personal interest in a bill must disclose that interest and may not vote on the bill.

Every bill enacted by the legislature must be signed by the presiding officer of the house in which it originated and sent to the Governor. If the Governor signs the bill, it becomes law. If the Governor vetoes the bill, it is returned to the presiding officer of each house of the legislature with a statement of the reasons for the veto. The Governor may veto an item or section in an appropriation bill and sign the remainder of the bill. If the Governor fails to sign or veto a bill within the prescribed time, it becomes law. The legislature may override a veto by a two-thirds vote.

The legislature has two other important powers described in Title 1 of the Code. First, the Senate and House may conduct legislative investigations and have power to issue subpoenas to require the attendance of witnesses and the production of evidence. Witnesses have the right to counsel, and testimony may be taken. A person who fails to cooperate may be held in contempt. The legislature also has the power to impeach members of the executive and judicial branches who are subject to impeachment. The House of Representatives must initiate the impeachment by a vote of two-thirds of its members, and the Senate must convict after a hearing by a vote of two-thirds of its members.

Members of the legislature enjoy two important privileges. First, they may not be questioned in any other place for any written or oral statement made in the legislature. Second, they cannot be arrested while going to or coming from a meeting of the legislature except for treason, a felony, or a breach of the peace.

Each house of the legislature is the final judge of the election and qualifications of its members; it may compel the attendance of absent members, discipline members, and expel members. Each house must choose its presiding officers from among its members and must establish committees necessary for the conduct of business. The meetings of the legislature and its committees must be public unless authorized by two-thirds of the members of the house.

Article VIII of the Constitution requires that regular general elections in the Commonwealth be held on the first Sunday of November. Other elections may be held as provided by law. The Northern Mariana Islands Election Act (CMC, Title 1) creates a board of elections to administer and supervise elections and establishes the procedures and requirements for the eligibility to vote, the registration of voters, voting and absentee voting, the nomination of candidates, the conduct of elections, and the resolution of contested elections.

Article IX of the Constitution also provides for the recall of public officials. Elected public officials are subject to recall by the voters of the Commonwealth or of the island or district from which elected. A recall petition must identify by name and office the public official whose recall is sought, state the grounds for the recall, and have signatures of at least 40 percent of the persons qualified to vote for the office occupied by the official. The petition must be filed with the Attorney General for certification. If certified, it must be submitted to the voters at the next regular general election. A petition may not be filed against a public official more than once in any year or during the first six months in office.

c. Judiciary

Article IV of the Constitution vests the judicial power in a Commonwealth Trial Court and a Commonwealth appeals court. While a trial court was established, no appeals court was created until the Commonwealth Judicial Reorganization Act of 1989 created the Supreme Court of the Commonwealth of the Northern Mariana Islands to hear appeals from the Trial Court, which was then named the Commonwealth Superior Court. The Superior Court now has original jurisdiction over all civil, criminal, and land actions in the Commonwealth.

The Supreme Court is composed of a Chief Justice and two Associate Justices. The Superior Court consists of a Chief Judge and at least two associate judges. All judges are appointed by the Governor with the advice and consent of the Senate. Judges are appointed for an initial term of six years and terms of twelve years if reappointed. They must be at least thirty years old, citizens or nationals of the United States, and graduates of accredited law schools. They must have been admitted to practice in the highest appellate court of a state or possession of the United States and have practiced for at least five years or have served as a judge for at least three years. Judges may not hold another government position, practice law, make financial contributions to a political organization, hold an executive office in a political organization, participate in a political campaign, or become a political candidate without resigning judicial office at least six months before becoming a candidate. Judges must disqualify themselves in cases in which they are a party or are primarily interested, are a relative to either party, or have been counsel to any party in a prior action. They must also disqualify themselves in cases in which they are biased or prejudiced. Judges are subject to impeachment for treason, commission of a felony, corruption, or neglect of duty.

Article IV of the Covenant creates a U.S. District Court for the Northern Mariana Islands that is part of the judicial courts of the United States. This court hears cases arising under the U.S. Constitution, U.S. statutes, and cases in which one party is a resident of the Commonwealth and the other resides elsewhere. The U.S. Court of Appeals for the Ninth Circuit exercises appellate jurisdiction over decisions of the District Court.

d. Representation in the United States

Although the citizens of the Commonwealth are United States citizens, they are not entitled to vote in elections in the United States nor do they have representation in the U.S. Senate and House of Representatives. The only representation the Commonwealth has in the United States is a representative elected for a term of two years. The representative must be at least twenty-five years old, a qualified voter in the Commonwealth, a citizen of the United States, and a resident of the Commonwealth for at least seven years prior to taking office. The function of the representative is to present to Congress the views of the Commonwealth on issues affecting it. The representative must also submit an annual report to the Governor and legislature of the Commonwealth detailing his activities for the year and outlining matters that require the attention of the government of the Commonwealth (Covenant, Article IX; Constitution, Article V; CMC, Title 1).

2. LOCAL GOVERNMENT

Article VI of the Constitution provides for the creation of local governments headed by Mayors on the islands of Rota, Tinian, Aguiguan, and the islands north of Saipan. A mayor must be qualified to vote in the Commonwealth, at least twenty-five years old, and a resident and domiciliary of the Commonwealth for at least three years immediately preceding taking office. Among the constitutional and statutory duties (Constitution, Article IV; CMC, Title 1) of the Mayors are the following:

1. to serve on the Governor's Council to advise on government operations and local matters;
2. to review and recommend local services and appropriations;
3. to investigate complaints and conduct hearings concerning local matters;
4. to recommend and review items for inclusion in the budget;
5. to spend on local public purposes the funds that have been allocated by the legislature for those purposes;
6. to appoint, supervise, and remove local employees;
7. to be responsible for Commonwealth programs and activities at the local level; and
8. to act as the principal local official for mobilizing resources during a state of emergency.

Article VI of the Constitution also provides for municipal councils on Rota, Tinian, Aguiguan, and Saipan; the councils' members are elected on a nonpartisan basis.

D. Emergency Powers

Article III of the Constitution provides that, in the event of civil disturbance, invasion, natural disaster, or other calamity, the Governor may declare a state of emergency. In order to provide assistance in the event of an emergency and clarify the roles of the Governor and Mayors in disaster relief, the legislature enacted the Commonwealth Disaster Relief Act of 1979 (CMC, Title 1). The legislature has also created a civil defense Coordinator to prepare an administrative plan for the civil defense and emergency needs of the Commonwealth (CMC, Title 3).

E. Human Rights

Article I of the Constitution contains an extensive statement of "Personal Rights":

1. No law can be enacted that is a bill of attainder, an ex post facto law, a law impairing the obligation of contracts, or a law prohibiting the traditional art of healing;

2. No law can be enacted that establishes a religion, prohibits the free exercise of religion; or abridges the freedom of speech, the press, or peaceable assembly to petition the government;
3. The people have a right to be secure in their persons, houses, papers, and belongings against unreasonable searches and seizures. A warrant cannot be issued without probable cause supported by an oath or affirmation. Electronic eavesdropping and other forms of surveillance require a warrant. A person who has been subject to an illegal search or seizure has a right of action against the government;
4. In all criminal cases, the accused has the following rights:
    a. to be assisted by counsel,
    b. to be confronted with adverse witnesses and to have compulsory process for obtaining favorable witnesses,
    c. to be free from compulsion to give self-incriminating testimony,
    d. to be given a speedy and public trial,
    e. to be free of double jeopardy,
    f. to be free of excessive bail,
    g. to be free of cruel and unusual punishment and free of capital punishment;
    h. to be protected, if under eighteen years of age, in criminal judicial proceedings and in conditions of imprisonment;
5. No person may be deprived of life, liberty, or property without due process of law;
6. No person can be denied the equal protection of the laws or discriminated against because of race, color, religion, ancestry, or sex;
7. Soldiers may not be quartered in peacetime in any house without the consent of the owner or in time of war except as provided by law;
8. The legislature may provide for trial by jury in civil and criminal cases;
9. Everyone has the right to a clean and healthful environment;
10. The right to privacy may not be infringed except upon a showing of compelling interest.

V. Administrative Organization and Law

A. Organization

The major departments of the executive branch of the Commonwealth government are set out in the Executive Branch Organization Act (CMC Title 1). These are the Office of the Governor; Office of the Lieutenant Governor, Office of the Attorney General, Office of the Public Defender, Department of Education, Office of the Public Auditor, Department of Community and Cultural Affairs, Department of Public Works, Department of Commerce and Labor, Department of Public Safety, Department of Finance, Department of Public Health and Environmental Protection, and Department of Natural Resources.

The act also provides that each department of the executive branch must be under the supervision of an executive appointed by the Governor with the advice and consent of the Senate. A department head and a member of a board or commission must be a resident of the Commonwealth and a citizen or national of the United States who is at least eighteen years old. The Governor may delegate to a Mayor responsibility for the execution of Commonwealth laws and administration of public services on the island in which the Mayor has been elected.

B. Public Sector

The Commonwealth Civil Service Act (CMC, Title 1) creates a career civil service system and a seven-member Civil Service Commission, appointed by the Governor with the advice and consent of the Senate, to propose personnel policies and hear and decide appeals of employees for disciplinary actions. Within the Civil Service Commission is a personnel officer who serves as the principal adviser to the Governor on matters of personnel administration; administers the personnel administration system for the executive branch; and develops programs on employee efficiency, classification, compensation, recruitment, qualifications, training, and housing. The act also makes it a policy of the Commonwealth to administer the personnel system according to merit principles and to give preference to resident citizens in filling positions within the government. The Commonwealth Salary Act of 1982 (CMC, Title 1) establishes a uniform salary schedule that determines the base salary to be paid to government employees covered by the civil service system.

C. Public Finance and Audit

The Planning and Budgeting Act of 1983 (CMC, Title 1) sets out the procedures for the preparation of the proposed annual budget, which must contain a detailed estimate of all anticipated revenues and expenditures and proposed appropriations to agencies for the fiscal year. The Governor must submit a balanced budget proposal to the legislature. No Commonwealth funds may be spent unless authorized by the legislature in annual appropriation acts. These acts may not exceed the total Commonwealth financial resources without additional taxation, revenues, or resources.

Article X of the Constitution provides that public debt may not be authorized or incurred without the affirmative vote of two-thirds of the members in each house of the legislature. Public debt, other than bonds or other obligations of the government payable solely from the revenues derived from a public improvement or undertaking, may not be authorized in excess of 10 percent of the aggregate assessed valuation of the real property in the Commonwealth. Public indebtedness may not be authorized for operating expenses of the Commonwealth government or its political subdivisions.

The Executive Branch Organization Act and the Commonwealth Auditing Act (CMC, Title 1) also create the Office of Public Auditor as an independent agency. The Office is headed by a Public Auditor, appointed by the Governor with the advice and consent of each house of the legislature. The Public Auditor audits the receipt, possession, and disbursement of public funds by agencies of the Commonwealth government and submits an annual report to the Governor and presiding officer of each house of the legislature.

D. Rule Making

The Administrative Procedure Act (CMC, Title 1) is concerned with the procedure for protecting and enforcing the rights of individuals. One aspect of the act focuses on the rule-making process for government agencies. A government agency is defined, in 1 CMC, Section 9101, as "each authority of the Commonwealth government" excluding the legislature and the courts.

Under the act, a proposal to adopt, amend, or repeal a rule may be made by a government agency or by individual petition to an agency. The agency must respond to an individual petition within thirty days, either denying the petition or initiating the rule-making proceedings. An agency must give at least thirty days public notice of the adoption, amendment, or repeal of any regulation. The notice must contain the substance of the proposed regulation or change; reference to the authorities under which that action is proposed; and the time, place, and manner in which interested persons may present their views. A public hearing must be held if requested by the legislature, one of its committees, or a government subdivision or agency.

The Registrar of Corporations must publish a monthly register of proposed and newly adopted regulations, rules, and orders; and other notices and orders. No agency rule, order, or decision is valid against any person until it has been published in the register and a certified copy filed with the Registrar of Corporations and the Governor. The Attorney General must prepare a compilation of the rules adopted by each agency, which must be available for public inspection and copying.

E. Review of Administrative Action

The Administrative Procedure Act is also concerned with the adjudication of disputes between private parties and government agencies. In administrative proceedings where a sanction may be imposed, the persons involved must be informed of the time, place, and nature of the hearing; the legal authority and jurisdiction under which the hearing is held; the statute and rules involved; and the matters under contention. They are also entitled to be represented by counsel. The agency or a hearing officer appointed by the agency must preside at the hearing and take evidence. Persons presiding at the hearing must be impartial. They have the power to issue subpoenas, rule on offers of proof, take depositions, regulate the hearing, hold conferences, dispose of procedural requests, and make or recommend orders.

The record in the hearing must include all pleadings, motions and rulings, evidence, questions and offers of proof, proposed findings, decisions, opinions and reports by the presiding officer, and all staff memoranda or data submitted to the presiding officer. The record must also include a statement of matters officially noticed and a transcript or summary of the testimony.

A person who has exhausted all administrative remedies and who has suffered "a legal wrong because of agency action" is entitled to judicial review of the action in the Commonwealth Superior Court. The court must decide all relevant questions of law, interpret constitutional and statutory provisions, and determine the meaning or applicability of the terms of the agency action. The court may compel agency action if it has been unlawfully withheld or hold unlawful and set aside agency action. An appeal may be taken from the decision of the Commonwealth Superior Court to the Commonwealth Supreme Court.

VI. International Obligations

Because the Northern Mariana Islands is a Commonwealth of the United States, the United States Constitution prohibits it from entering into treaties with other countries. Instead, the Covenant (Section 104) delegates to the United States "complete responsibility for and authority with respect to matters relating to foreign affairs and defense." However, Section 904 of the Covenant permits the Commonwealth to participate in international organizations concerned with social, economic, educational, scientific, technical, and cultural matters.

VII. Revenue Law

Article VI of the Covenant establishes the basic tax structure of the Commonwealth and governs its fiscal relations with the United States. Section 601 makes the "income tax laws in force in the United States" applicable to the Commonwealth as a "local territorial income tax" in the same manner as they are in force in Guam. Section 602 permits the Commonwealth to impose additional taxes by local law. The Commonwealth may also rebate any taxes received by it on income derived from sources within the Commonwealth but not on income derived from sources outside the Commonwealth. Section 603 exempts the Commonwealth from the customs territory of the United States and allows it to impose duties on imports and exports. Imports from the Commonwealth into the United States must be treated in the same manner as those imported from Guam. In the United States the individual states have no right to a return of tax money collected in the states, but Section 703(b) of the Covenant requires that all customs duties and federal income taxes derived from the Commonwealth, all import taxes collected by the United States on articles produced in the Commonwealth, and all other taxes Congress may levy on the inhabitants of the Commonwealth must be paid into the Treasury of the Commonwealth government.

Although the Covenant permits the Commonwealth to levy its own local taxes, Article X of the Constitution states that the government may not impose a tax or appropriate public money except for a public purpose. Every five years the Governor must report to the legislature on the social, fiscal, and economic impact of tax exemptions provided by law. All revenue raised under the tax laws and revenue laws and all moneys received by the Commonwealth must be deposited in the general fund. The Director of Finance may make payments from the general fund only as authorized by appropriation laws (Revenue and Taxation Act of 1982, CMC, Title 4).

The Revenue and Taxation Act specifies the local taxes and fees the Commonwealth may collect; these are a wage and salary tax, a tax on the gross revenues of businesses, excise taxes, a bar tax, a hotel occupancy tax, business license fees, a tax on amusement machines, and user fees. A person who fails to file a timely tax return or pay a required tax is subject to civil suit, criminal penalties, and interest.

VIII. INVESTMENT LAW

The Commonwealth Banking Code of 1984 (CMC, Title 4) establishes a comprehensive code for the regulation of the banking industry within the Commonwealth. The Code creates a Director of Banking who is responsible for issuing, denying, suspending, and revoking applications for a banking license; conducting an annual audit of the banking operations of licensees; restricting the withdrawal of deposits and requesting the appointment of a receiver to take possession of a bank that is not in sound financial condition. The director may also issue rules regulating the Commonwealth and foreign banks.

IX. WELFARE LAW

Article XV of the Constitution provides that every person in the Commonwealth has the right to free, compulsory, and public elementary and secondary education. This article is implemented by the Education Act of 1983 (CMC, Title 3), which establishes a public school system, including elementary and secondary levels and a college, and governs nonpublic elementary and secondary education. The act also establishes public health requirements for school children by requiring immunization and regular examinations.

The Northern Mariana Islands Social Security Act (CMC, Title 4) creates a retirement fund supported by mandatory employee and employer contributions. The act provides disability and survivors' insurance to wage earners and their dependents. The program is administered by a social security administrator, who is nominated by the United States social security administrator after consultation with the Commonwealth legislature and appointed by the Governor. Title 1 of the Code also establishes a Northern Mariana Islands Retirement Fund to provide retirement annuities and disability benefits to Commonwealth employees and annuities to the survivors of employees.

To remedy the shortage of suitable and affordable rental housing in the Commonwealth for persons with low and moderate incomes, the legislature established the Mariana Islands Housing Authority to develop and operate affordable housing.

X. Criminal Law

The Commonwealth Criminal Code (CMC, Title 6), classifies offenses as either felonies (offenses punishable by more than one year in jail) or misdemeanors. Criminal responsibility attaches to "principals" and to "accessories after the fact" and to the attempt, solicitation, and conspiracy to commit an offense.

The Code classifies offenses into the following categories:

1. homicide: murder, which is divided into first-degree murder, second-degree murder, and manslaughter (which is classified as voluntary and involuntary);
2. assault and related offenses;
3. sexual offenses: rape, sodomy, oral copulation, sexual assault of an animal, indecent exposure, and sexual abuse of a child;
4. other crimes against the person: robbery, kidnapping, false arrest, criminal coercion, usurping control of aircraft, mutiny, and resisting arrest;
5. theft and related offenses;
6. forgery, fraud, and counterfeiting;
7. other property offenses: burglary, arson, criminal mischief, and criminal trespass;
8. offenses against public peace, safety, and morals: disturbing the peace, riot, bigamy, nuisance, failing to report wounds, littering, possessing fireworks, excavating for or removing human remains, using potassium cyanide, and furnishing tobacco to minors;
9. gambling;
10. offenses against the Commonwealth: bribery, misconduct in public office, escape, and rescue of prisoner;
11. offenses against public administration: compounding an offense, obstructing justice, tampering with judicial records, jury tampering, perjury, and contempt;
12. offenses against government property: possession or removal of government property and tampering with the mail;
13. child abuse or neglect and failure to report child abuse or neglect.

The Commonwealth Controlled Substance Act (CMC, Title 6) prohibits the manufacture, distribution, or dispensing of designated controlled substances without registering and complying with the act. The Commonwealth Weapons Control Act (CMC, Title 6) prohibits the manufacture, purchase, sale, possession, and carrying of firearms, dangerous devices, or ammunition except as provided by the act.

The Criminal Code requires that in sentencing for an offense, a court must take into account the local customs of the people of the Commonwealth to the extent that they may provide mitigating or aggravating factors. Although there is mandatory sentencing for some offenses, in most cases courts may choose between imposition of a fine, alternative sentences, suspension of a sentence, orders requiring the person to reside in a specific place for a period of time, restitution, compensation or forfeiture, closure of a business, community service, or probation. Before imposing or suspending a sentence, a court may consider evidence of good and bad character and any prior criminal record. Any person convicted of an offense may be pardoned by the Governor on recommendation of the board of parole or paroled by the board of parole.

Persons who have been judged insane and children under the age of ten are conclusively presumed to be incapable of committing any crime. Children between the ages of ten and fourteen are also presumed to be incapable of committing any crime, except murder and rape, in which case the presumption is rebuttable. A person under the age of eighteen may be punished as a delinquent child.

XI. JUDICIAL PROCEDURE

A. Civil Procedure

The rules of civil procedure for the Commonwealth Superior Court are contained in Title 7 of the Code and the Rules of Practice and the Rules of Civil Procedure promulgated by the court.

1. JURISDICTION

Any person who, in person or through an agent, does any one of the following acts within the Commonwealth submits to the jurisdiction of the courts of the Commonwealth for a cause of action arising from the act: the transaction of any business;[3] contracting to supply goods or services; contracting to insure any person, property, or risk; causing tortious injury or damage; holding or having interest in real property; any act done outside the Commonwealth that causes injury or damage within the Commonwealth; or any other act done within or outside the Commonwealth from which a cause of action arises and for which it would not be unreasonable or unjust to hold the person doing the act legally responsible in the Commonwealth.

If a person subject to jurisdiction is outside the Commonwealth, service of process is made by leaving a certified copy with the Attorney General and service on the defendant wherever found or sent by certified or registered mail to the defendant.

2. ABSENT DEFENDANTS

In actions involving annulment, divorce, adoption, liens, or real or personal property against a defendant who cannot be served within the Commonwealth, the court may order service on the defendant wherever found, by mail to the defendant's last known address or by posting a copy of the order in a conspicuous place. If the defendant fails to appear, the court may proceed as if the defendant had been served within the Commonwealth. However, any order of the court can affect only the property or the status that is the subject of the action.

3. DECLARATORY JUDGMENTS

In any case involving an actual controversy within its jurisdiction, a court may issue a declaratory judgment setting out the rights and other legal relations of the party seeking the declaration, regardless of whether other relief is or could be sought. A declaratory judgment has the force of a final judgment and is reviewable.

4. CONCILIATION PROCEEDINGS

The Code provides in Title 7 for "an amicable settlement" of civil disputes by permitting a court, at the request of a party, to invite the other parties to appear before a judge for an informal hearing. If a settlement is reached, the judge must reduce the agreement to writing and have it signed by the parties. It then has the force of a judgment.

5. LIMITATION OF ACTIONS

Under Title 7 of the Code, a civil action must be commenced within two years, six years, or twenty years from the date the cause of action accrued, depending on the particular cause of action. The time limit for the commencement of an action against a minor or a person who is insane or imprisoned does not begin to run until the disability is removed. The time limit does not run while a person is outside the Commonwealth. If a person fraudulently conceals a cause of action, the time limit does not begin to run until the person entitled to bring the action knows of the cause of action or has reasonable opportunity to discover it.

6. JURY TRIALS

Title 7 of the Code provides a right to trial by a jury of six persons on all legal issues in civil actions where the amount in controversy exceeds US$1,000. Any citizen of the Commonwealth or the United States who is at least eighteen years old and who has resided within the Commonwealth for a period of one year prior to the jury service is competent to serve as a juror unless he or she has been convicted of a felony; is unable to read, write, speak, or understand English, Chamorro, or Carolinian; is incapable by reason of physical or mental infirmities to serve on a jury; or is exempted from jury service by law. A judge may also excuse or exclude a person from jury service for good reason. A serious problem with the jury system is that most prospective jurors claim relationships either with the parties or the attorneys or insist they will be unable to render an unbiased opinion. In one case, 107 prospective jurors were examined over two days but only 3 qualified jurors were found.

7. ENFORCEMENT OF JUDGMENTS

Title 7 of the Code sets out the procedures for enforcing money judgments, judgments affecting land, and other judgments. It also defines the procedure for obtaining writs of attachment, writs of execution, and orders in aid of a judgment.

8. EVIDENCE

The rules of evidence in the Commonwealth Superior Court are contained in the Rules of Evidence promulgated by the court. These rules cover judicial notice; presumptions; relevancy; privileges; witnesses; opinions and expert testimony; hearsay; authentication and identification; and the contents of writings, recordings, and photographs.

B. Criminal Procedure

The rules of criminal procedure for the U.S. District Court of the Northern Mariana Islands are set out in the United States Federal Rules of Criminal Procedure. Criminal procedure in the Commonwealth courts is governed by Title 6 of the Code and the Rules of Criminal Procedure promulgated by the court pursuant to Article IV of the Constitution. Jury trials in criminal cases are provided for in Title 7 of the Code.

1. ARREST

A person may not be arrested without a warrant except in the following circumstances:

1. a criminal offense has been committed and the offender attempts to escape;
2. a criminal offense is being committed;
3. a criminal offense has been committed and a policeman has reasonable grounds to believe that the person to be arrested has committed it; or
4. a policeman finds a person in a situation that justifies a reasonable suspicion that the person has committed or intends to commit a felony.

Force may be used in making an arrest when a person refuses to submit or attempts to escape. An arrested person has the right to see his or her counsel, family members, or employer; to send messages to any of those people; to be released or charged with a criminal offense within twenty-four hours; to be informed of the right to remain silent; and to be informed that the police will, if requested, call private counsel or the public defender.

2. SEARCHES AND SEIZURES

No warrant is required to seize offensive weapons from a person incident to an arrest or to search the premises controlled by the person incident to an arrest for evidence of the criminal offense. Reasonable force may be used to enter a building to execute a search warrant.

3. RIGHTS OF DEFENDANTS

Every defendant in a criminal case has the right to have, in advance of trial, a copy of the charge; to consult counsel before trial and be represented by counsel of choice at trial; to have sufficient time to prepare a defense; to have material witnesses; to give evidence at trial but not to be compelled to give evidence; and to have the proceedings interpreted if the defendant cannot understand them.

4. PRELIMINARY HEARINGS

A preliminary hearing must be held for an arrested person unless he or she waives it. If a hearing is waived, or if the evidence presented at the hearing indicates probable cause that a criminal offense has been committed and that the arrested person has committed it, the arrested person must be committed for trial on the charge and either released on bail or personal recognizance or held in jail pending the trial.

5. BAIL

A person arrested for a criminal offense other than murder in the first degree has a right to be released on bail before conviction. A person arrested for murder in the first degree may be released on bail by a judge. The amount of bail must be designed to ensure the presence of the accused in court. A court may increase or decrease bail in a pending case. When the punishment for an offense does not exceed US$100 or six months' imprisonment or both, a person may be released on personal recognizance.

6. WITNESSES

A court may issue a witness summons to compel the presence of a witness at a trial. If a court believes that a witness may be intimidated or become unavailable for trial, the witness may be detained as a material witness for up to twenty-one days. The witness has the right to be released on bail.

7. EXTRADITION

The Governor may have arrested and extradited to any state in the United States or any of its territories and possessions any person charged with a crime in one of those jurisdictions who has fled to the Commonwealth. The Code sets out the procedure for a demand for extradition, the warrant of arrest, bail, and the hearing. The Code also prescribes the procedure for the extradition to the Commonwealth of persons who have committed offenses in the Commonwealth and fled to other states.

8. HABEAS CORPUS

A person unlawfully imprisoned or detained or any person on behalf of such a person may apply to a judge of the Commonwealth Trial Court for a writ of habeas corpus to determine the reasons for the imprisonment or detainment. The court must then issue a writ directing the person against whom it is directed to show cause why the person detained should not be released. Based on the evidence presented to it, the court must then issue or deny the writ. Such a determination is appealable to the District Court for the Northern Mariana Islands.

9. TRIAL BY JURY

A person accused of committing a felony punishable by more than five years' imprisonment or by more than a US$2,000 fine or both has a right to a trial by a jury of six persons. Because of the problems of impartiality in such a small population, there have been few jury trials in the Commonwealth.

10. JUVENILES

For offenders under the age of eighteen, the Superior Court sits as a juvenile court with a flexible procedure based on the Rules of Juvenile Delinquency Practice, which were promulgated by the court. Although a finding that a youth is a delinquent is not a criminal conviction, the court may make an order under Title 6 of the Code requiring the delinquent to be confined for the same period as if convicted of an offense. If a child is placed on probation and the court determines that the delinquency resulted from the failure of the parents to subject the child to reasonable parental control, the parents may be subject to a bond for the period of the probation and forfeiture of the bond if the child is again found delinquent.

XII. LAND AND NATURAL RESOURCES

A. Public Land and Administration

Because approximately 80 percent of the land in the Commonwealth is public land, Article XI of the Constitution creates the Marianas Public Land Corporation to manage these lands. The directors of the corporation, who are appointed by the Governor with the advice and consent of the Senate, must represent the various geographic and ethnic groups within the Commonwealth. The corporation must make available some portion of the public lands for a homestead program; may not transfer a leasehold interest in public lands that exceeds twenty-five years, including renewal rights; may not transfer an interest in more than five hectares of public land for use for commercial purposes without the approval by a majority of the members of the legislature; may not transfer an interest in public lands located within 150 feet of the high water mark of a sandy beach; must adopt a comprehensive land use plan with respect to the public lands, including priority of uses, and may amend the plan as appropriate. Article XI of the

Constitution also creates the Marianas Public Land Trust to manage the money received from public lands.

B. Land Tenure and Administration

During the periods of Spanish, German, and Japanese rule, the traditional landholding systems of the Chamorros were abolished, private ownership of land was instituted, and considerable amounts of land were transferred to foreigners. Because of the shortage of land in the Commonwealth, Article XII of the Constitution restricts the "acquisition of permanent and long-term interests in real property within the Commonwealth" to "persons of Northern Marianas descent." An acquisition includes transfer "by sale, lease, gift, inheritance or other means." An exception to this restriction is made for a transfer to a spouse by inheritance and a foreclosure on a mortgage if the mortgagee disposes of its interest in the real property within five years to a person of Northern Marianas descent. "Permanent and long-term interests in real property" include freehold interests and leasehold interests of more than forty years, including renewal rights.

A "person of Northern Marianas descent" is defined by Article XII of the Constitution as a person who is a citizen or national of the United States and who is of at least one-quarter Northern Marianas Chamorro or Northern Marianas Carolinian blood or a combination thereof or an adopted child of a person of Northern Marianas descent if adopted while under the age of eighteen. A corporation is considered a "person of Northern Marianas descent" if it is incorporated in the Commonwealth, has its principal place of business in the Commonwealth, has directors at least 51 percent of whom are persons of Northern Marianas descent, and has voting shares at least 51 percent of which are owned by persons of Northern Marianas descent.

Under the statute of frauds (CMC, Title 2), no estate or interest in real property and no trust or power over real property, except for leases of less than one year, is valid unless by deed of conveyance or other instrument in writing signed by the party creating the interest or an agent.

The Real Estate Mortgage Law (CMC, Title 2) permits lenders to take realty as security for commercial and residential loans and protects persons who execute mortgages by requiring that the mortgage be in writing and filed with the clerk of courts. The act also provides remedies, including judicial foreclosure, for the mortgagee in the event of default by the mortgagor.

Because of the shortage of land in the Commonwealth, the Land Commission Act of 1983 (CMC, Title 2) creates a land commission to make surveys and plats in connection with the determination of title to land, to hold hearings on disputed land claims, and to issue and record certificates of title to land.

C. Government Taking of Land

Article XIII of the Constitution gives the Commonwealth the power of eminent domain to acquire private property to carry out public purposes. Under Titles 1 and 2 of the Code, private property may be taken only if no suitable public land is available and just compensation paid.

D. Natural Resources

Article XIV of the Constitution requires that marine resources in waters off the coast of the Commonwealth over which the Commonwealth has jurisdiction must be managed, controlled, protected, and preserved for the benefit of the people. Under the Marine Sovereignty Act of 1980 (CMC, Title 2) the Commonwealth claims sovereignty over its land area and internal waters and 12-mile territorial sea (regardless of their depth or distance from the coast), as well as their airspace, seabed, subsoil, and resources. It also claims sovereignty in a 200-mile exclusive economic zone for the purpose of exploring, exploiting, conserving, and managing the natural resources of the seabed, subsoil, and adjacent waters of the zone. The territorial sea and exclusive economic zone are measured by straight archipelagic baselines joining the outermost islands and drying reefs of the Commonwealth as drawn by the Director of Natural Resources.

The Commonwealth has also sought to protect its natural resources by enacting the Submerged Lands Act, Commonwealth Nuclear and Chemical Free Zone Act, Coastal Resources Management Act of 1983, Commonwealth Environmental Protection Act, and Fish, Game, and Endangered Species Act, all of which are included in Title 2 of the Code.

Article XIV of the Constitution also requires that certain islands be maintained as uninhabited islands for cultural and recreational purposes. Places of cultural, traditional, and historical importance must be protected and preserved. To carry out this constitutional mandate, the legislature has enacted the Historic Preservation Act of 1982 (CMC, Title 2).

XIII. Persons and Entities

The definition of a "person" in Title 4 of the Code includes natural persons, corporations, trusts, partnerships, and incorporated and unincorporated associations.

The legal age for all persons residing in the Commonwealth is age eighteen. This is the legal age for marriage and for entering into a contract (CMC, Title 8; U.S. *Restatement (Second) of Contracts*). In addition, Article VII of the Constitution provides that a citizen or national of the United States who is at least eighteen years old, who is not insane or serving a sentence for a felony, and who is domiciled and resident in the Commonwealth is eligible to vote. A person may not be denied the right to vote because of an inability to read or write. While neither the Code nor the *Restatement* mention a minimum age for liability for an intentional tort, Section 213A of the *Restatement (Second) of Torts* provides that the standard of care required for negligence is that of "a reasonable person of like age, intelligence, and experience under like circumstances."

XIV. Family Law

Family law is governed by Title 8 of the Code.

A. Marriage

A marriage between two citizens of the Commonwealth may be performed by a minister, a judge, the Governor, or anyone authorized by law to perform marriages and must be witnessed by at least two persons. A marriage between two citizens of the Commonwealth will be valid if it conforms either to "recognized custom" or to the rules for marriages of noncitizens. Notice of a customary marriage must be registered with the clerk of Courts.

In order for two noncitizens (or a noncitizen and a citizen) to marry, the male must be at least eighteen years old and the female at least sixteen years old. However, because the age of majority in the Commonwealth is eighteen, the female must have the consent of at least one of her parents or her guardian if she is less than eighteen years old. The marriage ceremony may be performed by the same persons authorized to perform marriages between citizens of the Commonwealth.

B. Divorce, Separation, and Annulment

Title 8 of the Code sets out the grounds and procedures for annulment and divorce, but the provisions do not apply to annulments or divorces granted according to local custom. However, if the validity of a customary annulment or divorce is questioned or property rights are disputed, any of the parties or their children may seek confirmation of the annulment or divorce by the Superior Court.

An annulment may be granted on any ground that, at the time of the marriage, made it illegal and void or voidable. A court may refuse to annul a marriage that has been ratified by voluntary cohabitation after the obstacle to the validity to the marriage has ceased. The children of an annulled marriage are legitimate.

The only grounds for divorce are adultery; cruel treatment, neglect, or personal indignities making life burdensome and intolerable; willful desertion for at least one year; habitual intemperance in the use of intoxicating liquor or drugs for at least one year; a prison sentence of three years or more; insanity that has existed for at least three years; leprosy; separation for two years without cohabitation; and willful failure of the husband to provide support. No divorce can be granted where the ground for the divorce has been forgiven by the injured spouse. All decrees for annulment or divorce are subject to appeal and do not become absolute until the time for appeal has expired.

C. Custody and Support

Decrees for annulment or divorce may contain orders for the custody of minor children, support, and the distribution of property. Title 8 of the Code also provides reciprocal and uniform legislation for the criminal and civil enforcement of support orders. The Northern Mariana Islands Uniform Child Custody Jurisdiction Act (CMC, Title 8) was adopted to avoid conflict and promote cooperation and consistency with other states in matters of child custody.

D. Adoption

Although Title 8 of the Code sets out restrictions and limitations on the adoption of children, those provisions do not apply to an adoption according to "local custom." According to 8 CMC, Section 1401, any "suitable person" may adopt a child not theirs by birth. A single person, a person married to the father or mother of a child, or a husband and wife jointly may be suitable persons. A Code adoption requires the written consent of or notice to known living legal parents who have not been judged insane or incompetent or who have not abandoned the child. The adoption under the Code of a child over the age of twelve requires the consent of the child. An adoption can be granted only if it is in the best interests of the child.

An adoption decree is subject to appeal and does not become absolute until the time for appeal has expired. Once absolute, the decree relieves the natural parents of all duties and responsibilities toward the child. Those duties pass to the adopting parents. A child adopted according to the provisions of the Code has the same inheritance rights as a person adopted according to the custom of the place where the land is located (in the case of real property) or the place where the decedent was a resident at the time of death (in the case of personal property). If there is no recognized custom as to the inheritance rights of adopted children, a child adopted according to the Code inherits from the adopting parents as if the child were the natural child of the adopting parents and may also inherit from the natural parents as if no adoption had taken place.

XV. Personal Property

The Commonwealth has no legislation dealing with personal property. The Commonwealth Trial Court (now the Superior Court) has also held that there is no customary law governing the distribution of personal property at death.[4] Thus, the law concerning title to personal property, gifts of chattels, bailments, liens, and fixtures is governed by the common law as applied by courts in the United States and the Commonwealth.

XVI. Wills and Succession

The law of wills and intestate succession is found at Title 8 of the Code. Any person who is of sound mind and at least eighteen years old may make a will under Title 8. The will may dispose of property that, at the time of death, the testator had a right to dispose of without the consent of any other person. A will may also be made in accordance with customary law.

A will made according to Title 8 of the Code must be signed by the testator and witnessed by two persons. If the will gives a witness a personal or beneficial interest in property, the interested witness forfeits the will's provisions made for him or her that exceed in value at the time of the testator's death what the witness would have taken had the testator died intestate, unless the will is also witnessed by two disinterested persons.

Under the Code a holographic (handwritten) will does not require a witness. However, the signature and provisions of such a will must be in the handwriting of the testator and proved by two witnesses.

A nuncupative (oral) will is valid under the Code only if a person is in imminent peril of death and dies as a result of the peril. It may not revoke or change an existing written will. A nuncupative will may dispose only of personal property with an aggregate value under US$1,000.

A will made outside the Commonwealth that is valid according to the laws of the Commonwealth, the place of its execution, or the law of the testator's domicile at the time of execution is valid in the Commonwealth.

A source of litigation in the Commonwealth is the Chamorro custom of *partida*.[5] According to this custom, a father should, at some time before his death, call his family together and designate a division of all family lands and ancestral lands, including those brought in by the wife, among his children. In dividing the land, the father is expected to act fairly and according to Chamorro customs and standards. He may turn over formal ownership and control of the lands at once or retain ownership and control until some later date or until he dies. Recently, efforts have been made to encourage the elderly to make formal wills instead of oral dispositions of their property.

Probate in the Commonwealth is governed by the Northern Marianas Probate Law (CMC, Title 8) and the Rules of Probate Procedure promulgated by the Commonwealth Superior Court. These rules cover the procedures for the probate of wills and intestate estates, summary administration, and guardianship.

XVII. Contracts

The making, effect, and enforcement of contracts in the Commonwealth is determined according to the United States *Restatement (Second) of Contracts* and the common law of contracts followed by courts in the United States.[6] In addition, Article 2 of the Uniform Commercial Code, enacted as Title 5 of the Commonwealth Code, governs contracts for the sale of goods **(see XVIII, E Commercial Transactions)**.

XVIII. Commercial Law

A. Consumer Protection

The Consumer Protection Act (CMC, Title 4) makes it unlawful to engage in unfair methods of competition and unfair or deceptive practices in the conduct of any trade or commerce. Among the unlawful acts are the following:

1. passing off goods or services as those of another;
2. causing confusion about the source, approval, sponsorship, approval, or certification of goods or services;
3. deceptive representations as to the origin of goods;
4. disparaging goods or services;
5. misrepresenting used goods as new; and
6. false advertising.

The act may be enforced by the Attorney General, individuals' suits, or class actions. Violators are subject to civil and criminal penalties.

B. Unfair Business Practices

It is a criminal offense in the Commonwealth to create or use an existing combination of capital, skill, or acts to restrict trade or commerce; limit the production or increase the price of commodities; prevent competition in the manufacture or sale of goods; fix prices; or discriminate in price between different purchasers. Criminal and civil penalties are imposed for commission of any of the prohibited acts (CMC, Title 4).

C. Business Organizations

The Governor may grant charters of incorporation to business organizations, nonprofit associations, cooperatives, and credit unions. The Governor may also create public corporations with the approval of the legislature. Persons seeking a charter for a private corporation must submit the following information for approval by the Governor:

1. proposed name of the corporation;
2. place of business;
3. duration;
4. purposes;
5. powers;
6. capitalization;

7. names of incorporators;
8. names and number of directors;
9. provisions for management, voting, and shareholding;
10. disposition of financial surplus;
11. liquidation;
12. articles of incorporation; and
13. bylaws.

All documents required by the government relating to a business association are held by the Registrar of Corporations, who may convene special meetings and order the production of accounts and documents of any association (CMC, Title 4).

Section 6 of the Schedule on Transitional Matters in the Constitution provides that corporations incorporated or qualified to do business in the Commonwealth on the date the Constitution took effect continue to be incorporated or qualified until provided otherwise by law.

D. Regulated Businesses

A number of businesses, occupations, and professions that are regulated in the Commonwealth require a license or registration. These include health care professionals, nurses, architects, engineers, surveyors, plumbers, electricians, carpenters, ship's officers, barbers and beauticians, notaries public, and insurance providers (see the Medical Practice Act of 1982, CMC, Title 3; Nurse Practice Act of 1982, CMC, Title 3; Land Surveyors Registration Act, CMC, Title 4; and, generally, CMC, Title 4).

Section 6 of the Schedule on Transition Matters in the Constitution provides that licenses in effect on the day the Constitution took effect are valid until changed by law. However, no license possessed by a land surveyor, ship's officer, health professional, or practicing trial assistant may be amended or revoked except for incompetence or unethical conduct.

E. Commercial Transactions

The Commonwealth has adopted the Uniform Commercial Code, which has been enacted in every state in the United States except Louisiana. The Uniform Commercial Code, enacted in the Commonwealth as Title 5 of the CMC, covers sales (the sale, lease, rental, and gift of tangible personal property); commercial paper (drafts, checks, certificates of deposits, and notes); bank deposits and collections; letters of credit; bulk transfers; warehouse receipts, bills of lading, and other documents of title; investment securities; and secured transactions.

XIX. TORTS

The general tort law of the Commonwealth is the common law of torts as expressed in the United States *Restatement (Second) of Torts* and applied by courts in the United States.[7] The Government Liability Act of 1983 (CMC, Title 7) makes the Commonwealth liable in tort for damages resulting from the negligent act of employees of the Commonwealth who are acting within the scope of their employment. However, the liability of the Commonwealth and its employees is limited to US$50,000 in wrongful death actions and US$100,000 in other tort actions, and the Commonwealth is not liable for interest before judgment, court fees, witness fees, or punitive damages.[8] The act also places limits on attorney fees in actions against the Commonwealth.

The act gives the Commonwealth immunity for liability from a broad range of claims:

1. acts or omissions in the execution of a statute or regulation or a discretionary function or duty;
2. assault, battery, false imprisonment, false arrest, malicious prosecution, abuse of process, libel, slander, misrepresentation, deceit, or interference with contract rights;
3. damages caused by the fiscal operations of the Treasury or the regulation of the monetary system;
4. the failure to make a medical referral to a medical faculty outside the Commonwealth;
5. the detention of goods by a law enforcement officer; or
6. the establishment of a quarantine.

Libel, slander, and invasion of privacy actions are governed by the Uniform Single Publication Act (CMC, Title 7). This act permits only one cause of action for each publication, exhibition, or edition of material in a book, magazine, or broadcast on radio or television.

The Commonwealth has also enacted legislation permitting a cause of action based upon tort to survive the death of the plaintiff, defendant, or other person liable. The action may be brought by or against the personal representative of the deceased (CMC, Title 7).

The Contribution Among Joint Tort-Feasors Act (CMC, Title 7) creates a right of contribution among tort-feasors who are jointly or severally liable. The right exists for a defendant who has paid more than his or her pro rata share of the common liability and does not apply to a defendant who intentionally, willfully, or wantonly contributed to the injury or death.

XX. Labor Law

Labor legislation in the Commonwealth (CMC, Titles 3 and 4) gives residents a preference in employment, protects seamen, and establishes minimum wages and maximum hours of employment.

Under the Nonresident Workers Act (CMC, Title 3), "residents [are to] be given preference in employment and . . . any necessary employment of nonresident workers in the Commonwealth [may] not impair the wages and working conditions of resident workers." Nonresident workers should be employed only to supplement the available resident workforce. The Chief of Labor must establish a system of employment services to assist potential resident workers in obtaining employment and to aid employers in locating resident workers.

An employer who seeks to employ nonresident workers must notify the Chief of Labor of the number of workers desired, the qualifications of the workers, their wages, and the date and place the workers are required. If, thirty days after notification of the positions, no qualified residents are available, the Chief of Labor may enter into a nonresident agreement with the employer specifying the wages, conditions, and period of time under which nonresident workers may be employed.

The Seamen's Protection Act (CMC, Title 4) governs the minimum age of employment, working hours, wages, vacations, benefits, discharge, repatriation, and punishable offenses of crew and officers employed on vessels. It also gives sailors and their employers the right to establish and join organizations of their choosing.

The Minimum Wages and Hours Act (CMC, Title 4) establishes a minimum hourly wage and maximum hours of employment before overtime compensation must be paid.

XXI. Industrial and Intellectual Property Rights

No legislation has yet been enacted in the Commonwealth governing copyrights, patents, or trademarks.

XXII. Legal Education and Profession

There are no law schools in the Commonwealth. Most Commonwealth lawyers received their legal education in the United States, although some have been educated in Papua New Guinea. Approximately 100 persons are admitted to practice in the Commonwealth, although many of those persons maintain their offices in Guam. Persons admitted to practice before the High Court of the Trust Territory of the Pacific Islands before January 9, 1978, are entitled to automatic admission to practice before the Commonwealth Trial Court. Title 1 of the Code and the Rules of Admission promulgated by the court provide that other persons of good moral character who have not been convicted of a felony, who have graduated from law school, and who have passed the bar examination administered by the Commonwealth Supreme Court are entitled to admission to practice law in the Commonwealth.[9] Attorneys who are employed by the Commonwealth or the Micronesian Legal Services Corporation may practice for four years without being admitted to practice if they are acting within the scope of their employment and are admitted to practice in another American jurisdiction.

Article I of the Constitution guarantees the right to counsel in criminal cases. A defendant who is indigent may be represented by the Public Defender or court-appointed counsel. In civil cases, legal aid is provided by the Micronesian Legal Services Corporation.

Public Law No. 1-5 and the Constitution give the Commonwealth Supreme Court the power to prescribe Rules of Court for disciplinary cases. Such cases are heard by a disciplinary panel of the Commonwealth Superior Court with a right of appeal to the Commonwealth Supreme Court.

XXIII. Research Guide

Statutes in force in the Marianas are compiled in the Commonwealth of the Northern Marianas Code, which is referred to in this chapter as CMC or the Code. The Code organizes the law into titles according to subject matter, with one or more acts in each title. Citations to acts in this chapter are to the title where the act may be found in the Code and, sometimes, to a relevant section number of the act.

Decisions of the Commonwealth courts are published in Commonwealth Reports, cited as CR. Decisions printed in CR may be those of the Commonwealth Trial court (CTC), Superior Court, or Supreme Court (**IV, C (1) (c) Judiciary**) or of the U.S. District Court. Judicial decisions applicable to the Commonwealth are also found in Trust Territory Reports (TTR).

Armstrong, A. J. "The Emergence of the Micronesians into the International Community: A Study of the Creation of a New International Entity," 2 *Brooklyn J. of International Law* 207 (1979).

Edwards, D. *United States Naval Administration of the Trust Territories of the Pacific Islands*. Washington, D.C.: Office of Chief of Naval Operations, 1957.

King, V. "The Commonwealth of the Northern Mariana Islands' Rights under United States and International Law to Control its Exclusive Economic Zone," 13 *Univ. of Hawaii L. Rev.* 477 (1991).

Kluge, P. *The Edge of Paradise: America in Micronesia.* New York: Random House, 1991.

McHenry, D. *Micronesia: Trust Betrayed.* New York: Carnegie Endowment, 1975.

McShane, J. "Is the Jury System Suitable for the Commonwealth of the Northern Mariana Islands?" 34 *Political Science* 66 (1982).

Meller, N. *The Congress of Micronesia.* Honolulu: University of Hawaii Press, 1969.

Tagupa, W.E.H. "The Constitution of the Northern Mariana Islands: Special Issues in Constitutional Law and Governance," 5 *Melanesian Law J.* 285 (1977).

20. The Republic of Palau

BRUCE L. OTTLEY

I. Dateline

1000 B.C. Islands of Palau settled by immigrants from Southeast Asia.

1783 A.D. Regular contact between Palauans and Europeans begins after English explorer Henry Wilson is shipwrecked on a reef in Palau. During the next century, diseases introduced by Europeans decrease population of Palau from 40,000 to 4,000.

1885 A dispute between Germany and Spain over control of the Caroline Islands, including Palau, is submitted to Pope Leo XIII for arbitration. He confirms Spanish sovereignty over Palau.

1899 Following its defeat in the Spanish-American War, Spain sells Palau to Germany, which administers the islands until 1914, when Japan takes control.

1920 League of Nations mandates Palau to Japan as class C mandate. Japan makes Palau administrative center for its Micronesian possessions. Large-scale Japanese immigration, mining, plantation agriculture, and commercial fishing radically change traditional Palauan culture.

1944 United States forces capture Palau from Japan.

1947 United Nations Security Council authorizes United States to administer Palau, Federated States of Micronesia, Northern Mariana Islands, and Marshall Islands as "Trust Territory of the Pacific Islands." Trusteeship Agreement for the Former Japanese Mandated Islands designates the area a "strategic trust."

1951 Administration of Palau transferred from U.S. Secretary of Navy to Secretary of Interior. Islands are governed by a High Commissioner appointed by U.S. President.

1965 Congress of Micronesia, a popularly elected bicameral legislature, established for the Trust Territory.

1969 United States begins negotiations with Congress of Micronesia on political future of Trust Territory.

1981 Palau achieves semi-self-government when Constitution of Republic of Palau is adopted by referendum.

1982 Palau and United States sign Compact of Free Association. Because provisions of compact conflict with Palau's Constitution, compact has not yet been ratified.

1985 Republic of Palau National Code adopted by Olbiil Era Kelulau.

II. Historical, Cultural, and Economic Survey

The Republic of Palau is an archipelago of 343 islands with a land area of approximately 488 square kilometers. The country lies seven degrees north of the equator and almost 500 miles east of the Philippines and has a population of 14,000 people.

Palau is a United Nations Mandated Trust Territory of the United States. In 1947, Article 3 of the United Nations Trusteeship Agreement gave the United States "full powers of administration, legislation, and jurisdiction" over Palau and permitted it to apply those laws of the United States that it considered "appropriate to local conditions and requirements." Article 6 of the Trusteeship Agreement committed the United States to "promote the development of the inhabitants of the Trust Territory toward self-government or independence as may be appropriate to the particular circumstances of the Trust Territory and its peoples and the freely expressed wishes of the peoples concerned."

Despite the Trusteeship Agreement, the United States stressed its own economic and political interests and until the 1960s did little to involve the Palauan people in the government or develop the Palauan economy. Palau now earns less than US$5 million a year from tourism, fish, and handicrafts while importing more than US$30 million a year in foodstuffs and manufactured goods. This makes the country almost entirely dependent on U.S. aid.

Traditional Palauan culture has undergone change as a result of the years of control by the Japanese and the United States. Most Palauans are now employed by the government. Although the clan and the system of chiefs are still important, these traditional sources of authority are being superseded by that of elected officials. Article V of the Constitution attempts to preserve traditional culture by prohibiting the government from interfering with those customary functions of traditional leaders that are not inconsistent with the Constitution. A number of state constitutions also provide for a council of traditional chiefs to safeguard and promote traditional ways of life.

With the adoption of the Palauan Constitution in 1981, the signing of the Compact of Free Association in 1982, and the enactment of the National Code in 1985, Palau is on the verge of a new political status. The compact gives Palau full internal autonomy and the authority to conduct its own foreign affairs in "free association" with the United States. The United States assumes full responsibility for the security and defense of the country for up to fifty years. The compact also requires the United States to provide substantial economic assistance and technical services.

Termination of the United Nations Trusteeship Agreement has been prevented by a conflict between provisions of the compact and the Palauan Constitution. Title Three of the compact gives the United States the right to operate nuclear-capable or nuclear-propelled vessels and aircraft in Palauan territory "without either confirming or denying the presence or absence of such weapons." Article II, 3, of the Constitution states that an international agreement "which authorizes use, testing, storage or disposal of nuclear, toxic chemical, gas or biological weapons intended for use in warfare shall require approval of not less than three-fourths (3/4) of the votes cast in [a] referendum." Article XIII, 6, of the Constitution further provides:

> Harmful substances such as nuclear, chemical, gas or biological weapons intended for use in warfare, nuclear power plants, and waste materials therefrom, shall not be used, tested, stored, or disposed of within the territorial jurisdiction of Palau without the express approval of not less than three-fourths (3/4) of the votes cast in a referendum submitted on this specific question.

The Constitution requires that the compact be approved by a referendum. However, on the eight occasions in which a referendum has been held, voters have failed to approve the compact by the three-fourths required by the Constitution. After an attempt in 1986 by the then President of Palau to certify approval of the compact, the Supreme Court of Palau upheld the Constitution and stated that the compact cannot be ratified without a three-fourths approval by the voters.[1]

In 1987 the legislature approved a bill calling for a special referendum to amend the Constitution. On August 4, 1987, a constitutional amendment to replace the three-fourths vote needed to override the antinuclear materials provisions with the requirement of a simple majority was passed by 73 percent of the Palauan voters. On August 21, 1987, Palau conducted its seventh compact referendum, in which 73 percent of the voters approved the compact. However, the Supreme Court of Palau upheld a lower court ruling that the August 21 referendum was insufficient to approve the compact since the legislature had not complied with the Constitution in holding the special referendum to amend the Constitution.[2] In November 1992, voters approved holding a referendum that would allow amendment of the nuclear-free provisions by a simple majority instead of 75 percent.

III. Sources of Law

Although Palau is still a United Nations Trust Territory, it exercises substantial powers of internal and external self-government. There are five sources of law for the country's legal system.

A. Constitution

Article II of the Constitution makes the Constitution "the supreme law of the land." No law, act of the government, or agreement to which the government is a party may conflict with the Constitution. Under Article XIV, an amendment to the Constitution may be proposed by a constitutional convention, a popular initiative signed by 25 percent of the voters, or a resolution adopted by at least three-fourths of the members of the Olbiil Era Kelulau (the Palauan legislature). An amendment so proposed will be adopted if it obtains a majority of the votes cast in a general election.

B. Republic of Palau National Code

The Palau National Code, adopted in 1985 and referred to in this chapter as the Code or PNC, codifies all national laws applicable to the Republic. The Code is a compilation of the following:

1. the laws of the Palau District Code, which is a compilation of those laws of the Palau legislature in effect in the Palau district in March 1971;
2. the Trust Territory Code, which is a compilation and codification of the laws of the Congress of Micronesia in effect throughout the Trust Territory;
3. the laws of the Fifth, Sixth, and Seventh Palau legislatures; and
4. the Republic of Palau public laws of the Olbiil Era Kelulau.

Section 301 of the National Code also gives the effect of law in Palau to the following:

1. the United Nations Trusteeship Agreement;
2. laws of the United States that are applicable to Palau, including Executive Orders of the President of the United States and orders of the Secretary of the Interior;
3. laws of the Trust Territory and amendments to them, to the extent they have not been repealed by the Olbiil Era Kelulau;
4. district orders and emergency district orders promulgated by the district administrator of the Palau district and in accordance with the Trust Territory Code;
5. the acts of the Olbiil Era Kelulau; and
6. state laws.

The Code repeals all laws, regulations, and ordinances enacted by the Spanish, Germans, and Japanese except those concerning the ownership, use, inheritance, and transfer of land that were in effect on December 1, 1941, and that have not been changed by express written agreement.

Since its publication in 1985, two supplements have been issued to the Code. Supplement One contains all laws enacted from the initial publication of the Code up to March 1, 1986. Supplement Two contains all laws enacted between March 1, 1986, and April 1, 1987. The Code is divided into titles according to subject matter, so most titles incorporate several acts of the legislature.

C. Initiative

Article XIII of the Constitution permits citizens to enact or repeal national laws by initiative. An initiative petition must be submitted to voters at the next general election if signed by 10 percent of the voters.

D. Custom

The Constitution and Code take different approaches to the weight to be given to customary law in Palau's legal system. Article V of the Constitution makes "statutes and traditional law . . . equally authoritative." When statutes and traditional law conflict, a statute prevails only to the extent that it does not conflict with "the underlying principles of the traditional law." These principles are not defined by the Constitution. The Code (Title 1, Section 302), however, resolves conflicts in favor of written law:

> The customs of the people of Palau not in conflict with the legal authority set out in section 301 [of the Code] shall be preserved. The recognized customary law of the Republic shall have the full force and effect of law so far as such customary law is not in conflict with such legal authority.

Unfortunately, the difference between the Constitution and the Code has never been resolved by the courts.

In order for custom to be legally binding, it must have "existed long enough to have become generally known and have been peacefully and fairly uniformly acquiesced in by those whose rights would naturally be affected."[3] Normally, an expert witness assists the court by tracing the historical application of the custom to the facts. A court will frequently appoint an assessor to resolve any conflict in the expert testimony.[4] Although custom has been rejected as a defense in criminal cases,[5] and in cases of intentional tort,[6] custom has been applied to questions of land ownership, disputes over the ownership of traditional money,[7] claims to the title to chief,[8] and the contribution of money for clan purposes.[9]

E. Common Law

In the absence of written law or customary law, the rules of common law, as expressed in the *Restatements* prepared by the American Law Institute or as applied in the United States, are the rules of decisions in the courts of Palau (PNC, Title 1).

IV. Constitutional System

A. Territory

Under Article I of the Constitution, Palau asserts "jurisdiction and sovereignty" over the land of the Palauan archipelago and its territorial waters extending "two hundred nautical miles from a straight archipelagic baseline, the seabed, subsoil, water column, insular shelves, and airspace over land and water, unless otherwise limited by international treaty obligations." The 200-nautical-mile limit is measured from the baselines connecting the outer limits around the islands and reefs of Palau. This claim of jurisdiction does not limit the right of innocent passage and internationally recognized freedom of the high seas. Article I also gives each state exclusive ownership of all living and nonliving resources from the land to 12 nautical miles seaward from the traditional baselines.

B. Nationality and Citizenship

Palauan citizenship is governed by Article III of the Constitution and the Citizenship Act (PNC, Title 13). Anyone who was a citizen of the Trust Territory immediately prior to January 1, 1981, and had at least one parent of "recognized Palauan ancestry" is a citizen of Palau. A person born of parents one or both of whom are citizens of Palau is also a Palauan citizen so long as the person does not become a citizen of another country. A citizen of Palau who has dual citizenship must, within three years after his or her eighteenth birthday, renounce citizenship in the other country and register an intent to remain a citizen of Palau. Failure to do so results in the loss of Palauan citizenship. A citizen of another country may become a naturalized Palauan citizen only if one or both of the person's parents are of "recognized Palauan ancestry" and the person renounces citizenship in the other country.

C. Government

Palau has adopted a modified federal system of government. Under the Constitution, governmental responsibilities are shared by a national government and sixteen states. All powers not expressly delegated to the states or denied the national government are powers of the national government. The national government may also delegate powers to the state governments.

1. NATIONAL GOVERNMENT

   a. Executive

   Palau has chosen the presidential form of government. Under Article VIII of the Constitution, the executive branch is headed by a President and Vice President. Any citizen of Palau who is at least thirty-five years old and who has resided in Palau for the five years immediately preceding the election is eligible to be President or Vice President. The President and Vice President are elected for four-year terms, and the President may not serve for more than two consecutive terms. If the office of President becomes vacant and 180 days or less remain in the term, the Vice President succeeds to the presidency for the remaining term. If more than 180 days remain in the term, a special election is held. The President and Vice President may be impeached for treason, bribery, or other serious crimes by a vote of at least two-thirds of the members of each house of the Olbiil Era Kelulau. The President and Vice President may also be removed from office by a recall referendum.

In addition to the President and Vice President, the executive branch consists of a Cabinet of ministers who are not members of the legislature. Ministers are appointed by the President with the advice and consent of the Senate. In 1989 the Senate used its power to reject the entire Cabinet submitted by the President. The Constitution also establishes a Council of Chiefs, composed of a traditional chief from each of the states, which advises the President on matters concerning traditional laws, customs, and their relation to the Constitution and laws of Palau.

Article VIII of the Constitution gives the President the power and duty to enforce the law of the land; to conduct negotiations with foreign nations and make treaties with the advice and consent of the legislature; to appoint ambassadors and other national officers with the advice and consent of the legislature; to appoint judges; to grant pardons, commutations, and reprieves; to spend money pursuant to appropriations and collect taxes; to represent the national government in all legal actions; and to propose the annual budget.

The President is also required to appoint, with the advice and consent of the Olbiil Era Kelulau, a special prosecutor. Among the functions of the special prosecutor is to receive complaints, investigate, and prosecute all allegations of violations of the Constitution and the laws of Palau by elected or appointed officials of the national or state governments (PNC, Title 2).

b. Legislature

Article IX of the Constitution vests the legislative power of the national government in the Olbiil Era Kelulau, composed of the House of Delegates and the Senate. The House of Delegates consists of one delegate elected from each of Palau's sixteen states. The number of senators is determined by the Congressional Reapportionment Commission.[10] Currently there are eighteen senators. Members of both houses are elected for a four-year term. They must be citizens who are at least twenty-five years old. They must have been resident in Palau for at least five years immediately preceding the election and in the district they wish to represent for at least one year immediately prior to the election.

Article IX of the Constitution gives the Olbiil Era Kelulau power to do the following:

1. levy and collect taxes;
2. borrow money;
3. regulate commerce;
4. regulate immigration and naturalization;
5. establish uniform laws on bankruptcy;
6. provide a monetary and banking system and national currency;
7. ratify treaties;
8. approve presidential appointments;
9. establish diplomatic immunities;
10. regulate banking, insurance, securities, patents, and copyrights;
11. provide a national postal system;
12. regulate natural resources;
13. regulate navigation and shipping;
14. regulate the use of airspace;
15. delegate authority to the states and administrative agencies;
16. impeach and remove the President, Vice President, and justices of the Supreme Court;
17. provide for the national defense;

18. create or consolidate states;
19. confirm or disapprove a state of emergency;
20. provide for the general welfare, peace, and security;
21. and enact laws.

A bill must be approved by both houses of the Olbiil Era Kelulau and signed by the President in order to become law. The President may veto a bill, but the veto may be overridden by the vote of two-thirds of the members of each house. No approval by the Council of Chiefs is required for a bill to become law.

Under Article VII of the Constitution, a citizen of Palau who is at least eighteen years of age may vote in all national and state elections. A prerequisite for voting is registration as a voter. The Olbiil Era Kelulau establishes residency and voter registration requirements for national elections, while the states set the requirements for state elections. The right and requirements to vote are also governed by the Voting Rights Act (PNC, Title 23).

The Code establishes procedures for conducting national and state elections and imposes penalties for intimidation or bribery of voters. Nomination of candidates for elections is by petition initiated by a candidate, voters, or a political party. The election process is supervised and administered by a five-person election commission (appointed by the President) and a board of election for each election district.

c. Judiciary

Article X of the Constitution vests the judicial power of Palau in a judiciary consisting of a Supreme Court, a National Court, and inferior courts of limited jurisdiction. The judicial power extends to all matters in law and equity and to all persons physically within Palau (PNC, Title 4). Courts, except for the Supreme Court, may be divided geographically, but they have not been so divided, and there are no state courts. The structure of the judicial system and the qualifications of the judiciary are governed by Article X of the Constitution and Title 4 of the Code.

The Supreme Court consists of a Trial Division and an Appellate Division. It is composed of a Chief Justice, three full-time Associate Justices and three part-time Associate Justices. The Trial Division has "original and exclusive jurisdiction over all matters affecting Ambassadors, other Public Ministers and Consuls, admiralty and maritime cases, and those in which the national government or a state government is a party." The appellate division has jurisdiction to review all decisions of the trial division and all decisions of lower courts. Matters in the trial division are heard by one justice while appeals are heard by three justices.

All trials not falling within the jurisdiction of the trial division of the Supreme Court are conducted by the National Court, which consists of a presiding judge.

The only court of limited jurisdiction in Palau is the Court of Common Pleas, which consists of a senior judge and an associate judge. In practice, the Court of Common Pleas hears all civil cases where the amount claimed does not exceed US$1,000. However, the court may not hear cases involving title to or an interest in land; these are reserved for the National Court. The Chief Justice of the Supreme Court may assign criminal cases to the Court of Common Pleas if the maximum fine does not exceed US$2,000 or five years' imprisonment or both.

A justice of the Supreme Court or judge of the National Court must have been admitted to practice law before the highest court of the state or country in which he or she is admitted to practice for at least five years preceding appointment. A judge of the Court of Common Pleas must have been a judge in the District Courts of the Trust Territory, an attorney or trial assistant licensed to practice before the courts of the Trust Territory or the courts of Palau, or a citizen of Palau with a wide knowledge of Palauan custom.

All judges hold office during good behavior. A justice of the Supreme Court may be impeached for cause by a two-thirds vote of the members of each house of the Olbiil Era Kelulau. Judges of the National Court and Court of Common Pleas may be impeached for cause by a majority vote of the members of each house of the Olbiil Era Kelulau.

A justice of the Supreme Court, a judge of the National Court, or a judge of the Court of Common Pleas may appoint assessors to assist at trial on matters of local law, custom, or matters requiring specialized knowledge. However, the assessor cannot participate in the determination of the case. The President must also appoint for a definite term at least two special judges of the Supreme Court to sit with the justice assigned to try murder cases in the trial division. The special judges participate in voting on questions of fact and sentence, but only the presiding justice can decide questions of law.

2. STATE GOVERNMENTS

Article XI of the Constitution provides that the "structure and organization of the state governments must follow democratic principles, traditions of Palau, and shall not be inconsistent with the Constitution." Although some of the states have fewer than 100 residents and the largest state, Koror, has just over 9,000 residents, each of the sixteen states has a constitution providing for a Governor and state government.

Article XIII of the Constitution prohibits any state from seceding from Palau and provides that a new state may be created with the approval of three-fourths of the states.

D. Emergency Powers

Article VIII of the Constitution provides that, in the event that war, external aggression, civil rebellion, or natural catastrophe threatens the lives or property of the people of Palau, the President may declare a state of emergency and temporarily assume legislative powers. However, the President must first be given approval by the Olbiil Era Kelulau for the state of emergency and may not assume emergency powers for more than ten days without the further approval of the Olbiil Era Kelulau.

E. Human Rights

Article IV of the Constitution contains an extensive statement of "fundamental rights":

1. freedom of conscience and philosophical and religious belief;
2. freedom of expression and the press;
3. freedom of peaceful assembly, association, and petition of the government for redress of grievances;
4. the right to be secure in person, house, papers, and effects against entry, search, and seizure;
5. equality under the law, equal protection, and freedom from discrimination based on sex, race, place of origin, language, religion or belief, social status, or clan affiliation;
6. freedom from the deprivation of life, liberty, or property without due process of law; protection against the taking of private property except for "a recognized public use" and for just compensation; freedom from criminal liability for an act that was not a legally recognized crime at the time of its commission; freedom from double jeopardy for the

same offense; a prohibition on the impairment of contracts by legislation; no imprisonment for debt; a requirement that a warrant for search and seizure be issued only by a judge on a showing of probable cause;

7. a presumption of innocence in criminal cases until proof of guilt is established beyond a reasonable doubt; the right of an accused to be informed of the nature of the accusation, to have a speedy public trial, to examine all witnesses, and to be protected against self-incrimination; the right to counsel and to reasonable bail; a recognition of the writ of habeas corpus that cannot be suspended; the liability of the national government for damages for unlawful arrest or damage to private property;
8. the right of a victim of a criminal offense to compensation by the government or at the discretion of a court;
9. a prohibition on torture, cruel, inhumane, or degrading treatment or punishment and excessive fines;
10. a prohibition of slavery and involuntary servitude;
11. the right of citizens to examine any government document and to observe the official deliberations of any government agency;
12. equality between men and women concerning marital and related parental rights, privileges, and responsibilities.

V. Administrative Organization and Law

A. Organization

The major departments of the executive branch of the national government are specified in the Executive Branch Organization Act (PNC Title 2). They are the ministries of State, Justice, Natural Resources, Social Services, and Administration. Each is headed by a minister. Although ministers are appointed by the President with the advice and consent of the Senate, they serve at the pleasure of the President. In addition, the President may establish offices and agencies within the executive Branch and prescribe their duties, responsibilities, and functions by executive order. The heads of these offices and agencies are appointed by the President and serve at his will.

B. Public Service

The national government is the largest employer in Palau. The National Public Service System Act (PNC, Title 33) creates a National Public Service System and a five-member National Civil Service Board. The board formulates policies and regulations concerning recruitment, examinations, filling job vacancies, tenure, resignations, job classification, compensation, performance ratings, reduction in force, dismissal, and the outside employment of members of the public service. The Pension Plan and Retirement Fund Act of 1987 (PNC Supp.) establishes a civil service pension trust fund.

C. Public Finance and Audit

Article XII of the Constitution requires the President to submit an annual budget to the Olbiil Era Kelulau. The chief executive of each state must also submit an annual budget to the state legislature for approval.

The Unified National Budget Procedure Act of 1981 (PNC, Title 40) sets out procedures for the preparation of the national budget, which details all proposed revenues, expenditures, and obligations for the fiscal year. The President must submit a balanced budget to the Olbiil Era Kelulau, which may amend the budget in its authorization bill, setting out the maximum allocations available for each budget activity. The President must then submit to the Olbiil Era Kelulau specific legislation to appropriate funds. This legislation must follow the allocations reflected in the Olbiil Era Kelulau's authorization bill; however, the President may veto or reduce an item in an appropriation bill.

The Public Auditing Act of 1985 (PNC, Title 40) creates an Office of the Public Auditor to conduct audits of all national and local government agencies and activities of the government. The Public Auditor has the authority to receive and investigate confidential complaints concerning fraud, waste, and abuse in the collection and expenditure of public funds. The Public Auditor must report to the Attorney General any reasonable grounds to believe that criminal laws have been violated and may also institute civil recovery proceedings where appropriate.

D. Rule Making

The Administrative Procedure Act (PNC, Title 6) is concerned with the procedure for protecting and enforcing the rights of individuals. One aspect of the act focuses on the rule-making process for government agencies; a government agency is defined at Section 102 of Title 6 as "a ministry, bureau, division, board, commission or department, officer or other administrative unit of the national government."

Under the act, government agencies have rule-making powers that are legislative in character. Agencies must adopt rules describing their organization, method of operations, and the procedures for the public to obtain information or to make submissions to them. Agencies must also make available for public inspection all rules and written policy statements, final orders, decisions, and opinions of general applicability. No agency rule, order, or decision is valid against any person until it has been made available for public inspection.

A proposal to adopt, amend, or repeal any rule may be made by a government agency or by individual petition to an agency. The agency must respond to an individual petition within thirty days, either denying the petition or initiating the rule-making proceedings. An agency must give at least thirty days' public notice of the adoption, amendment, or repeal of a rule. Although a public hearing on a proposed rule is not required, one may be held at the discretion of the agency or the request of the Olbiil Era Kelulau or another government agency.

Each agency must send a copy of each rule adopted to the President on the day of its adoption. The President has twenty days in which to approve or disapprove of the rule. If the President either does not act within twenty days or approves the rule, it becomes effective thirty days after its adoption by the agency.

A rule adopted by an agency may become invalid in one of three ways. First, the validity or applicability of any rule may be determined in an action for a declaratory judgment in the Supreme Court if it is alleged that the rule interferes with or impairs the legal rights of the plaintiff. Second, the President may rescind or suspend all or part of a rule of an agency by executive order. Finally, any rule or part of a rule may be rendered void by the joint resolution of both houses of the Olbiil Era Kelulau within 120 days after the rule's adoption.

E. Review of Administrative Action

The Administrative Procedure Act also deals with the adjudication of disputes between private parties and government agencies. Individuals may contest an agency rule or action on the grounds that their legal rights have been directly and adversely affected. All parties to a contested case must be given an opportunity for a hearing after reasonable notice. Notice includes statements of the time, place, and nature of the hearing; the legal authority and jurisdiction under which the hearing is held; the statute and rules involved; and the matters under contention.

The record in a contested case must include all pleadings, motions and rulings, evidence, matters officially noticed, questions and offers of proof, proposed findings, decisions, opinions and reports by the presiding officer, and all staff memoranda or data submitted to the presiding officer. Oral proceedings must be recorded and transcribed on request of any party at the party's expense. In all contested cases, the Republic of Palau Rules of Evidence must be followed. A final decision (or an order in a contested case that is adverse to a party) must be in writing and include findings of fact and conclusions of law.

A person who has exhausted all administrative remedies and who is aggrieved by a final decision in a contested case is entitled to judicial review of the decision in the Trial Division of the Supreme Court. The review by the Court must be limited to the record. The Court cannot substitute its judgment for that of the agency as to the weight of the evidence or the finding of facts. The Court may affirm the decision or remand it for further proceedings. The Court may also reverse or modify the decision if substantial rights of the person have been prejudiced because the administrative finding violates the constitution or a statute or the express statutory authority of the agency. An appeal may be taken from the decision of the Trial Division of the Supreme Court to the Appellate Division of the Supreme Court.

VI. International Obligations

Since Palau is still technically a United Nations Mandated Trust Territory, it has not been able to enter into diplomatic relations with other countries or assume the international obligations of an independent country. However, if the compact is approved, Palau will have limited authority to conduct its own foreign affairs, subject to approval by the United States. Article VIII of the Constitution gives the President of Palau the power to conduct negotiations with foreign nations, to make treaties, and to appoint ambassadors with the advice and consent of the Olbiil Era Kelulau.

Despite its current limitations, Palau has demonstrated attributes of sovereignty. It has negotiated commercial treaties and agreements with several nations on a government-to-government basis and has joined several international organizations.

VII. Revenue Law

The Unified Tax Act (PNC, Title 40) specifies the taxes and license fees the national government may collect:

1. a wages and salary tax on employees, withheld by every employer and paid to the director of the Bureau of the National Treasury;
2. a gross revenue tax on persons engaged in any retail or wholesale business or trade or in a profession and a net income tax on persons engaged in operating a financial institution;
3. an import tax on products imported into Palau for resale;

4. a hotel room tax, an amusement device tax, a traveler's head tax, a road use tax, and a foreign water vessel tax; and
5. business license fees as a condition precedent to engaging or continuing to engage in business.

A person who fails to file a tax return, a timely tax return, or an employer statement or fails to pay a required tax or license fee is liable for criminal penalties, interest, or the revocation of a business license.

Title 40 of the Code also establishes a national Treasury of the Republic of Palau, under a director of the Bureau of the National Treasury, for the deposit of all national revenues.

VIII. Investment Law

Article VI of the Constitution imposes a duty on the national government to promote economic development. In order to meet this responsibility, the government established the Economic Planning and Coordinating Council, whose nine members are appointed by the President with the advice and consent of the Olbiil Era Kelulau (PNC, Title 36). It is the function of the council to determine the economic goals of the country, conduct studies to determine the economic base and potential of the country, develop plans and programs to meet those objectives, and coordinate efforts to implement the plans. In order to encourage the export of goods and services, the Olbiil Era Kelulau enacted the Export Incentive Act (PNC, Title 11), which exempts export producers and brokers from the gross revenue tax and from any sales or profits tax.

The National Development Bank Act (PNC, Title 26) establishes the National Development Bank of Palau, a public corporation managed by a board of directors appointed by the President, to guarantee loans and direct financing to persons for the development of industrial or commercial projects. Priority for loans is given to the development of new enterprises and import substitutes. The corporation is a development bank, not a commercial bank, and receives its funds from the national government, borrowing, and the issuance of bonds rather than from time deposits. Before making a loan, the corporation must first attempt to guarantee the loan through commercial banks. If an enterprise receives a loan or loan guarantee from the corporation, the corporation may acquire an interest in the enterprise and take part in its management if necessary to ensure its continued viability.

The National Government Private Borrowing Authority Act (PNC, Title 40) permits the national government to borrow funds for development projects from private financial institutions and persons at reasonable rates and under reasonable terms. Such borrowing is conditioned on the issuance of sufficient bonds or securities to permit the government to meet the conditions normal to private borrowing.

The Foreign Investors Business Permit Act (PNC, Title 28) requires noncitizens who wish to conduct business in Palau to obtain a permit from the Foreign Investment Board. The decision to grant a permit depends upon the economic contribution of the operation; its effect on imports and exports; the impact of the activity on natural resources and the environment; and the extent of participation by citizens in ownership and employment. If a permit is issued, the board may place conditions based upon the length of time of the permit, the scope of activity, and employment preferences for citizens in the operation.

The Off-Shore Banking Act (PNC, Title 11) sets guidelines for the establishment and operation of banks within Palau that receive money from and lend money to noncitizens.

IX. Welfare Law

Article VI of the Constitution imposes a number of duties on the national government to promote the welfare of the people. These include protection of the safety and security of persons and property; promotion of the health and social welfare of citizens through the provision of free or subsidized health care; and the provision of public education for citizens which shall be free and compulsory as prescribed by law.

The government has sought to fulfill its constitutional obligations through extensive legislation regulating health, sanitation, plants and animals, and controlled substances; requiring the maintenance of vital statistics; providing for police, fire protection, water safety, and disaster relief; establishing a commission to work with juvenile delinquents; and providing housing to low-income families (see Title 34 of the Code).

The government has also enacted legislation promoting education. It establishes a Palau board of education and state or community boards of education; sets educational standards for public and private schools; provides for transportation, residence, and scholarship assistance to students, and special assistance to handicapped students. School attendance is compulsory for children between the ages of six and fourteen or until graduation from elementary school (PNC, Title 22). The Programs and Services for Handicapped Children Act of 1989 (PNC Supp.) commits the national government to provide financial, material, and human resources to help handicapped children.

The Social Security Act of 1987 (PNC Supp.) creates a retirement and disability fund supported by compulsory employee and employer contributions. The act also provides survivors' benefits for the spouse and children of wage earners. The act is administered by the Republic of Palau Social Security Administration.

X. Criminal Law

Substantive criminal law is governed by Title 17 of the Code. Crimes are classified either as felonies (offenses punishable by more than one year in prison) or misdemeanors (all other crimes). Criminal liability attaches to "principals," "accessories," and for attempts to commit a crime set out in the Code. No person who is judged insane can be convicted of any crime. Children under the age of ten are conclusively presumed to be incapable of committing any crime. Children between the ages of ten and fourteen are also presumed to be incapable of committing any crime except murder and rape, in which case the presumption is rebuttable. A person under the age of eighteen may be punished as a delinquent child.

The Code makes the following acts a crime: abortion; abuse of process; arson; assault and battery; bigamy; bribery; burglary; conspiracy; contempt of court; counterfeiting; disturbing the peace, rioting, drunken and disorderly behavior, and fighting in a public place; escape and rescue; false arrest; forgery; gambling; homicide; kidnapping; larceny; libel; malicious mischief; mayhem; misconduct in public office; nuisance; obstructing justice; perjury; robbery; sex crimes (incest, rape, sodomy, carnal knowledge, adultery, indecent assault); trespass; and certain other crimes (compounding a crime, mail tampering, unauthorized disposition of certain foods, possession or removal of government property, theft of electricity). In addition, the National Firearms Control Act and the Trust Territory Weapons Control Act (both of which are also in Title 17) prohibit the private ownership of firearms, ammunition, and "dangerous devices" in Palau. At Section 108 of Title 17, the Code recognizes and permits the punishment of acts that are crimes "solely by generally respected native custom."

Sentencing is also governed by Title 17 of the Code. In determining the sentence for a crime, a court must take into account the customs of the people of Palau, evidence of good and bad character, and prior criminal record. Depending on the crime for which a person has been convicted, a court may impose a fine; order the person to reside in a specific place for a period of time; order restitution, compensation, or forfeiture; order the closure of a business for a period of time; order hard labor in lieu of imprisonment; suspend a sentence; or place the person on probation. If an act is made a crime solely by custom, the maximum penalty cannot exceed US$100 or six months in prison or both. A person convicted of a criminal offense may petition the President for an executive pardon, commutation, reprieve, or for suspension and remission of fines (Executive Clemency Act of 1989, PNC Supp).

XI. Judicial Procedure

A. Civil Procedure

The rules governing civil proceedings are set out in Title 14 of the Code and the Courts of the Republic of Palau Rules of Civil Procedure, promulgated by the Supreme Court under Article X of the Constitution. These rules govern proceedings in the Supreme Court, National Court, and Court of Common Pleas.

1. LONG-ARM JURISDICTION

Under the Long-Arm Jurisdiction and Service of Process Act of 1982 (PNC, Title 14), any person, corporation, or legal entity, whether a resident of Palau or not, who in person or through an agent does any one of a series of acts submits to the jurisdiction of the courts of Palau for a cause of action arising from the act. The following are acts included:

1. the transaction of any business within Palau;
2. the operation of a motor vehicle within Palau;
3. the operation of a vessel or craft within the territorial waters or airspace of Palau;
4. the commission of a tort within Palau;
5. contracting to insure any person, property, or risk located within Palau at the time of contracting;
6. the ownership, use, or possession of any property within Palau;
7. entering into an express or implied contract with a resident of Palau to be performed by either party in Palau;
8. acting within Palau as a director or officer of any corporation organized under the laws of Palau or having its principal place of business in Palau;
9. acting as the administrator or executor of an estate within Palau;
10. causing injury to persons or property within Palau as the result of an act committed outside Palau; and
11. living in a marital relationship within Palau.

If a person covered by the act is outside Palau, service of process may be by personal service on the person, by certified mail to the person's last known address, or by certified mail to the appropriate government body of the country where the person resides. If the person fails to respond to the summons, a default judgment may be entered after the expiration of at least thirty days from the date of service.

2. ABSENT DEFENDANTS

In actions involving annulment, divorce, adoption, liens, or real or personal property within Palau against a defendant who cannot be served within Palau, the court may order service on the defendant wherever found, by mail to the defendant's last known address or by posting a copy of the order in a conspicuous place. If the defendant does not appear, the court may proceed as if the defendant had been served within Palau. However, any order of the court can affect only the property or status that is the subject of the action.

3. VENUE

Since Palau has a unified judicial system, all civil actions must be brought in the National Court or Court of Common Pleas.

4. LIMITATION OF ACTIONS

The period of time during which a civil action must be commenced is two years, six years, or twenty years from the date the cause of action accrued, depending on the particular cause of action. However, the time limit for the commencement of an action against a minor or a person who is insane or imprisoned does not begin to run until the disability is removed. Similarly, the time limit does not run while a person is outside Palau. In addition, if a person fraudulently conceals a cause of action, the time limit does not begin to run until the person entitled to bring the action knows of the cause of action or had reasonable opportunity to discover it.

5. ACTIONS AGAINST THE REPUBLIC

Certain claims against the Republic of Palau must be brought in the Trial Division of the Supreme Court. These are actions to recover taxes alleged to have been erroneously collected; civil actions or claims based on a law or regulation of Palau or a contract with the government; and civil actions for money damages for personal injury or death caused by the negligent or wrongful act of a government employee. The trial division of the Supreme Court does not have jurisdiction over other claims against the government.

6. DECLARATORY JUDGMENTS

In any case involving an actual controversy within its jurisdiction, a court may issue a declaratory judgment setting out the rights and other legal relations of any party seeking such a declaration, regardless of whether other relief is or could be sought. A declaratory judgment has the force of a final judgment and is reviewable.

7. CONCILIATION PROCEEDINGS

Section 1101 of Title 14 of the Code provides for "an amicable settlement" of a controversy by permitting a court, at the request of a party to any civil action, to invite the parties to appear before a judge for an informal hearing. If a settlement is reached, the judge must reduce the agreement to writing and have it signed by the parties. It then has the force of a judgment.

8. ENFORCEMENT OF JUDGMENTS

Title 14 of the Code sets out procedures for enforcing money judgments, judgments affecting land, and other judgments. It also defines procedures for obtaining writs of attachment, writs of execution, and orders in aid of a judgment.

9. CONTEMPT OF COURT

The Contempt of Courts Act (PNC, Title 14, Section 2202) permits a court to punish for criminal or civil contempt "any conduct that offends the dignity of and respect towards the court or of any judicial office in the performance of a judicial function."

Acts that may be punished as criminal contempt are disorderly, contemptuous, or insolent behavior before a court; a disturbance directly tending to interrupt court proceedings; willful disobedience or resistance to the lawful orders of a court; unlawful refusal to be sworn as a witness; or publication of a false or grossly inaccurate report of a court proceeding.

A court may punish with civil contempt an attorney or other person appointed to perform a judicial function for misbehavior in office, neglect of a duty, or disobedience of a court order; a party for putting in a fictitious bail or surety or abuse of a proceeding of a court; a party for nonpayment of a sum of money ordered to be paid by a court; a person for impersonating an officer of a court; a person for refusing or neglecting to obey a subpoena or answer as a witness; or a juror for improperly conversing with a party to an action or with any other person about the merits of that action or receiving communication from any person about the action.

A person accused of civil or criminal contempt has the right to notice of the charges and an opportunity to present a defense. If the contempt is committed in the presence of the court, it may be punished summarily. The maximum penalty for criminal or civil contempt is a fine of not more than US$1,000 or imprisonment for not more than six months or both. If a person is held in contempt for refusing to obey an order of a court, the person may be imprisoned until he obeys the order. A finding of contempt is subject to appeal to the Appellate Division of the Supreme Court.

10. EVIDENCE

In civil actions, courts are bound by the Courts of the Republic of Palau Rules of Evidence, promulgated by the Supreme Court pursuant to Article X of the Constitution.

B. Criminal Procedure

The rules governing criminal procedure are contained in Article IV of the Constitution, Title 18 of the Code, and the Courts of Republic Palau Rules of Criminal Procedure, promulgated by the Supreme Court pursuant to Article X of the Constitution.

1. ARREST

A person may not be arrested without a warrant except in the following circumstances:

1. a criminal offense has been committed and the offender is attempting to escape;
2. a criminal offense is being committed; or
3. a criminal offense has been committed and a policeman has reasonable grounds to believe that the person to be arrested has committed it; or
4. a policeman finds a person under circumstances that justify a reasonable suspicion that the person has committed or intends to commit a felony.

A warrant can be issued by a judge, the clerk of court (subject to limitations), or any other person authorized in writing by the President upon a complaint filed by an individual or an information signed by the Attorney General and after a showing of probable cause that the offense has been committed by the person named in the complaint or information. If the punishment for an offense does not exceed a fine of US$100 or six months' imprisonment or both, a penal summons to appear before a court may be issued instead of a warrant. A judge may issue an oral order instead of a warrant or a penal summons if the judge determines that the public interest requires it.

Force may be used in making an arrest to prevent a person from resisting or escaping. A person arrested by a private individual must be turned over to a policeman and persons arrested by a policeman must be brought before a court without unnecessary delay. Arrested persons have the right to see their counsel, members of their family, or their employer; to send messages to any of these people; to be released or charged with a criminal offense within twenty-four hours; and to be advised of their right to remain silent; and to be informed that the police will, if requested, call private counsel or the public defender.

2. SEARCH AND SEIZURE

Article IV(4) of the Constitution provides that "[e]very person has the right to be secure in his person, house, papers and effects against entry, search and seizure." However, Title 18 of the Code provides that no warrant is required to seize offensive weapons from a person incident to an arrest or to search the premises controlled by the arrested person for evidence of the offense. In all other instances a search warrant is required. A warrant can be issued only to search and seize property where possession is prohibited by law; stolen, embezzled, or fraudulently appropriated property; forged instruments or counterfeit coins or the instruments for making them; arms or munitions for insurrection or riot; property necessary for evidence at a trial; or property that has been used or is intended to be used for a crime. In an emergency, an oral order may be issued instead of a search warrant.

3. RIGHTS OF DEFENDANTS

A person accused of a criminal offense is presumed innocent until proven guilty beyond a reasonable doubt (Constitution, Article IV). Under Title 18 of the Code, defendants have a right to be informed before trial of the charge; to consult counsel before trial and be represented by counsel of choice at trial; to have sufficient time to prepare a defense; to examine all witnesses and compel witnesses and evidence on their behalf; to give evidence on their own behalf at trial but not to be compelled to give evidence; to have the proceedings interpreted if they cannot understand them; and to request the appointment of an assessor if one is not appointed by the court.

4. PRELIMINARY HEARING

A preliminary hearing must be held for arrested persons unless they waive it. If an arrested person waives the hearing—or if the evidence presented at the hearing indicates probable cause that a criminal offense has been committed and that the arrested person has committed it—the arrested person must be committed for trial on the charge and either released on bail or personal recognizance or held in jail pending the trial.

5. BAIL

Title 18 of the Code provides that any person arrested for a criminal offense other than murder in the first degree has a right to be released on bail before trial. Persons arrested for murder in the first degree may be released on bail by a judge. This provision appears to conflict with Article IV of the Constitution, which provides that "bail may not be unreasonably excessive nor denied those accused and detained before trial."

Under Title 18, the amount and form of bail must be designed to ensure the presence of the accused in court. A court may increase or decrease bail in a pending case. When the punishment for an offense does not exceed US$100 or six months' imprisonment or both, a person may be released on personal recognizance.

6. WITNESSES

A summons may be issued by a court to compel the presence of a witness at a trial. If a court believes that a witness may be intimidated or become unavailable for trial, the witness may be detained as a material witness for up to twenty-one days. Such a person has the right to release on bail.

7. EXTRADITION

The President may have arrested and extradited to any state in the United States and its possessions, the Commonwealths of Puerto Rico and the Northern Mariana Islands, American Samoa, and Guam any person charged with a crime in that state who has fled from that state to Palau.

8. HABEAS CORPUS

Article IV of the Constitution provides for the writ of habeas corpus, which may not be suspended. Any person unlawfully imprisoned or detained or any person on behalf of that person may apply to the Trial Division of the Supreme Court or other judge designated by the Chief Justice for a writ of habeas corpus to determine the reasons for the imprisonment or detainment. The court must then issue an order directing the person against whom the writ is directed to show cause why the person detained should not be released. Based on the evidence presented to the court, it must then issue or deny the writ. Such a determination is appealable to the appellate division of the Supreme Court (PNC, Title 18).

C. Appellate Procedure

The rules of appellate procedure are governed by Title 14 of the Code and by the Courts of the Republic of Palau Rules of Appellate Procedure, promulgated by the Supreme Court pursuant to Article X of the Constitution. An appeal may be taken by filing a notice of appeal (within the required period from the date of the judgment, order, or decree appealed from) with the presiding judge or justice of the court from which the appeal is taken or with the clerk of courts.

An Appellate Court has the power to affirm, modify, set aside, or reverse the judgment or order appealed from and to remand the case for a new trial or for entry of judgment. The findings of fact of the Trial Division of the Supreme Court may not be set aside on appeal unless they were clearly erroneous. In all other cases, the Appellate Court may review findings of facts as well as law.

XII. LAND AND NATURAL RESOURCES

A. Land Tenure and Administration

Land in Palau may be held according to freehold or custom. Palauans place great importance on land. One reason for the rejection of the compact is that it gives the United States the right to take as much as one-third of the islands' land for military bases. According to Title 39 of the Code, only citizens of Palau or corporations wholly owned by Palauan citizens may own land in

Palau. In addition, the Palau Lands Registration Act (PNC, Title 35) provides for the registration of all lands within Palau, the determination of ownership of lands, and the return to the original owners of lands wrongfully taken during the colonial period.

1. FREEHOLD LAND

Land held in fee simple may be transferred, sold, or disposed of as the owner wishes, regardless of local customs (PNC, Title 39). However, no transfer or encumbrance upon title to real estate, other than a lease for less than one year, is valid until recorded with the clerk of courts. Under the statute of frauds, no estate or interest in real property and no trust or power over real property, except a lease for less than one year, is valid unless by a deed of conveyance or other instrument in writing signed by the person creating the interest or the person's agent and executed as required by law (PNC, Title 39).

The Mortgage Act of 1981 (PNC, Title 39) permits lenders to take realty as security for commercial and residential loans and protects persons who execute mortgages by requiring that the mortgage be in writing and filed with the clerk of courts. The act also provides remedies, including judicial foreclosure, for the mortgagee in the event of default by the mortgagor.

2. CUSTOMARY LAND TENURE

The administration of land tenure laws in Palau is complicated by the fact that, over the centuries, a complex system of customary land tenure based on clan and lineage ownership has developed. The shortage of land and the value Palauans place on it has made disputes over customary title, as well as statutory title determinations, the largest source of litigation.

B. Government Taking of Land

Title 35 of the Code defines as *public lands* those lands that were owned by the Japanese government or the Trust Territory administration, as well as other land that the Palauan government may acquire. The Code establishes the Palau Public Lands Authority to administer those lands.

The national government has the right to acquire land by the exercise of eminent domain. It may, through proceedings in the Trial Division of the Supreme Court, condemn private property for public use and appropriate the ownership and possession of such property by paying the owner "a fair value for the land" (PNC, Title 35). The Code (Title 35, Section 303) defines a *public use* as any use determined by the President to be a public use.

Under Title 35 of the Code, the national government, a state government, or any agency of the government may also acquire real property for use in any program. The government body must make every effort to acquire the property by negotiation based upon just compensation for the land. If the negotiations fail, the government may then seek to exercise its power of eminent domain. Persons displaced by the acquisition of land for national government land acquisition programs may seek relocation assistance.

C. Natural Parks and Reserves

The Code provides at Title 24 for the creation of the Ngerukewid Islands Wildlife Preserve and at Title 34 for a Palau Recreation and Parks Board to promote athletic, cultural, social, and other recreational activities and programs for the public and to establish and govern parks and other recreational areas in the country. The Historical and Cultural Preservation Act (PNC, Title 19) seeks to preserve and foster the country's historical and cultural heritage.

D. Agriculture, Forests, and Fisheries

Few Palauans are still engaged in full-time agriculture. However, the Code at Title 9 creates an Agricultural Commission to assist persons in the villages in establishing farmers' cooperatives and developing commercial agriculture and to manage the Palau Central Produce Market.

Because of the importance of fishing to Palauans, Title 27 of the Code regulates foreign fishing in its territorial waters. It creates exclusive and extended fishery zones around islands and atolls contiguous to the territorial sea. Within these zones, the national government has sovereign rights to the living resources. The Code establishes the Palau Maritime Authority to manage and regulate the fishery zones and to negotiate fishing agreements with foreign governments which must be approved by the Olbiil Era Kelulau. Any foreign party fishing in the Palauan territorial sea or internal waters without the requisite permit is subject to criminal and civil penalties; its ship may be forfeited to the national government. However, a lack of patrol boats has made it extremely difficult for Palau to protect its waters from illegal fishing by foreign ships.

Title 27 gives the state governments the power to promote, develop, and support domestic commercial fishing and cooperative associations. It also establishes a national Palau Fishing Authority for the same purposes.

E. Natural Resources

Article VI of the Constitution imposes a duty on the national government to take "positive action to attain . . . a beautiful, healthful and resourceful national environment." The government has attempted to carry out this constitutional responsibility by enacting the Environmental Quality Protection Act, Trust Territory Environmental Quality Protection Act, Endangered Species Act, and other laws protecting sea and land life, all of which are collected at Title 19 of the Code.

An essential part of protecting the environment and natural resources is the regulation of land use. The Land Planning Act (PNC, Title 31) establishes planning commissions, comprehensive planning programs, and zoning. Pursuant to this act, land use planning commissions have been established in each of the states, and regulations have been adopted that divide Koror state into detailed use zones and control land subdivision in that state. Under Title 35 of the Code, all land in Palau must be registered with the Palau Land Commission, whose function is also to hear cases concerning interests and disputes in land.

XIII. PERSONS AND ENTITIES

The definition of a *person* in the Code (Title 11) includes individuals, corporations, firms, partnerships and any other associations permitted by the laws of Palau.

The age of majority for all persons residing in Palau is age eighteen. This age determines the legal age for marriage and for entering into a contract (PNC, Title 21; *Restatement (Second) of Contracts*, Section 14).

XIV. Family Law

A. Marriage

Under Title 21 of the Code, a marriage between two citizens of Palau may be performed by a minister, a judge, the President, or anyone authorized by law to perform marriages and must be witnessed by at least two persons. Title 21 provides that marriage between two citizens of Palau that is solemnized in accordance with recognized custom is also valid. Notice of a customary marriage must be sent to the clerk of courts.

For two noncitizens of Palau or a noncitizen and a citizen to make a valid marriage contract, the male must be at least eighteen years of age and the female at least sixteen years of age. However, since the age of majority both for males and females residing in Palau is eighteen, the female must have the consent of at least one parent or her guardian if she is less than eighteen years old. Such a marriage may be performed in the same way as noncustomary marriages between citizens.

B. Divorce, Separation, and Annulment

Although Title 21 of the Code sets out the grounds and procedures for annulment and divorce, the Code does not apply to annulments or divorces granted according to local custom. However, if the validity of a customary annulment or divorce is questioned or property rights are disputed, any of the parties or their children may seek confirmation of the annulment or divorce from the Trial Division of the Supreme Court.

A divorce under the Code provisions may be granted to persons married according to law or recognized custom. The only grounds for divorce under the Code are adultery; cruel treatment, neglect, or personal indignities that make life burdensome and intolerable; willful desertion for at least one year; habitual intemperance in the use of intoxicating liquor or drugs for at least one year; a prison sentence of three years or more; insanity that has existed for at least three years; leprosy; separation for two years without cohabitation; or willful failure of the husband to provide support. However, no divorce can be granted where the ground for the divorce has been forgiven by the injured spouse.

An annulment may be granted on any ground that, at the time of the marriage, made it illegal and void or voidable. The children of an annulled marriage are legitimate. All decrees for annulment or divorce are subject to appeal and do not become absolute until the time for appeal has expired.

C. Custody and Support

Decrees for annulment and divorce may contain orders for the custody of minor children, support, and distribution of property.[11] A person who is the cause of a divorce must provide support ordered by a court for the natural and adopted children of the marriage until they reach age eighteen.[12] Title 21 of the Code also provides reciprocal and uniform legislation for the criminal and civil enforcement of support orders.

D. Adoption

Adoption is very common in Palau. An adoption may be according to custom or according to Title 21 of the Code. Under the Code, any "suitable person"—whether a single person, a person married to the father or mother of a child, or a husband and wife jointly—may adopt a child not theirs by birth. An adoption requires the written consent or notice to the known living legal parents who have not been adjudged insane or incompetent or who have not abandoned the child. The adoption of a child over the age of twelve requires the consent of the child. An adoption can be granted only if it is in the best interests of the child.

An adoption decree is subject to appeal and does not become absolute until the time for appeal has expired. Once absolute, an adoption decree relieves the natural parents of all duties and responsibilities toward the child. Those duties pass to the adopting parents. A child adopted according to the provisions of Title 21 of the Code has the same inheritance rights as a person adopted according to the custom of the place where the land is located (in the case of real property) or the place where the decedent was a resident at the time of death (in the case of personal property). If there is no recognized custom as to the inheritance rights of adopted children, a child adopted according to the Code inherits from the adopting parents as if the natural child of the adopting parents and may also inherit from the natural parents as if no adoption had taken place.

XV. Personal Property

Palau has no legislation dealing with personal property. The law concerning title to personal property, gifts of chattels, bailments, liens, and fixtures is governed by custom or by the common law as applied by the courts in the United States. In particular, disputes over ownership of traditional Palauan money have been resolved according to custom.[13]

XVI. Wills and Succession

Any person who is of sound mind and at least eighteen years of age may make a will under Title 25 of the Code. The will may dispose of property that, at the time of the death, the person has a right to dispose of without the consent of any other person. A will may also be made in accordance with customary law.

A will made according to the Code must be signed by the person making it and witnessed by two persons. If the will gives a witness a personal or beneficial interest in property, the interested witness forfeits the provisions made in the will for him or her that exceed in value at the time of the person's death what the witness would have taken had the person died intestate, unless the will is also witnessed by two disinterested persons.

A holographic (handwritten) will does not require a witness. However, the signature and provisions of such a will must be in the handwriting of the testator and proved by two witnesses.

A nuncupative (oral) will is valid only if a person is in imminent peril of death and dies as a result of the peril. It may not revoke or change an existing written will. A nuncupative will may dispose only of personal property that has an aggregate value of less than US$1,000.

A will made outside Palau that is valid according to the laws of Palau, the place of its execution, or the law of the testator's domicile at the time of execution is valid in Palau.

Land held in fee simple may also be devised by will. If there is no will, land held in fee simple is inherited by the owner's oldest legitimate living male child of sound mind, whether natural or adopted. If there is no male heir, land is inherited by the oldest legitimate living female child of sound mind, natural or adopted. If the owner of fee simple land dies without issue or a will, the land is disposed of according to the desires of the immediate maternal or paternal lineage to which the deceased was related by birth or adoption and that was actively and primarily responsible for the deceased prior to death.

XVII. Contracts

The making, effect, and enforcement of contracts is determined according to the *Restatement (Second) of Contracts* and the common law of contracts followed by courts in the United States.[14] There are no Palauan statutes regulating contracts between private individuals.

XVIII. Commercial Law

A. Securities

It is a crime to issue, sell, exchange, or transfer any security in Palau until it has been registered with the Registrar of Corporations. The President may issue a stop order against the trading of any securities if, after approval by the registrar, it is discovered that the registration contained material misrepresentations of fact or omissions. A person injured by such an order may seek review in the Trial Division of the Supreme Court. Persons who suffer damages as a result of a material misrepresentation or omission in a registration application may sue the issuer and every person who signed the application for the difference between the amount paid for the security and its value at the time of suit. Securities issued or guaranteed by the United States or the Republic of Palau are exempt from the provisions on securities regulation (PNC, Title 12).

B. Business Organizations

The basic law governing public and private corporations is contained in Title 12 of the Code. The President has the power to create nonprofit public corporations with the approval of the Olbiil Era Kelulau. Persons seeking a charter for a private corporation must submit for approval by the President information concerning the corporation's name; place of business; purposes; powers; capitalization; incorporators; names and number of directors; provisions for management, voting, and shareholding; articles of incorporation; and bylaws. All documents required by the government relating to a corporation are held by the Registrar of Corporations, who has the power to convene special meetings and order the production of accounts and documents of any corporation.

C. Unfair Business Practices

It is a criminal offense in Palau to engage in an unfair business practice, defined as the combination of capital, skill, or acts to restrict trade or commerce; limit the production or increase the price of commodities; prevent competition in the manufacture or sale of goods; fix prices; or discriminate in price between different purchasers. The Consumer Protection Act (PNC, Title 11) imposes criminal and civil penalties on individuals and corporations that engage in unfair methods of competition and unfair or deceptive practices in the conduct of a business. The Usurious Interest Act (PNC, Title 11) limits the maximum interest rate on loans of US$15 million or less to 18 percent per annum. The maximum interest rate on loans above US$15 million cannot exceed an annual interest rate of 2 1/4 percentage points above the most recently announced prime rate on the date credit was extended.

D. Debtor-Creditor Relations

Title 11 of the Code deals with the rights and remedies of a debtor and creditor where a security interest in personal property has been given. If a creditor fails to comply with the provisions of this act, disposition of the property may be ordered by a court on such terms and conditions as the court deems appropriate. If property has been taken by a creditor in violation of the Code provisions, the debtor may recover his or her actual damages with a minimum recovery of one-quarter of the total of all payments made by the debtor, together with 6 percent interest per year, without consideration of the value of the collateral.

If, at a nonjudicial foreclosure, a debtor has paid at least 50 percent of the principal due, the creditor must sell the property at public auction with not fewer than ten days' written notice of the sale to the debtor. If the debtor has paid less than 50 percent of the principal due, the creditor has the option of retaining the property without any obligation to account to the debtor (after notice to the debtor), which results in full discharge of the debtor's obligations, or selling the property with a right to recover any deficiency.

E. Regulated Businesses

A number of occupations and activities in Palau are regulated and require a license or registration. These include general wholesalers, solicitors, peddlers, land surveyors, notaries public, taxi drivers, tour operators, the sale of alcoholic beverages, operating vessels, shipping within territorial waters, exporting or transshipping imported commodities, and the copra trade (PNC, Titles 7, 11 and 28).

XIX. Torts

The general law of torts in Palau is based on the common law of torts applied by courts in the United States.[15] Title 14 of the Code makes the government of Palau liable in tort to the same extent as a private individual. However, the government is not liable for interest before judgment or for punitive damages.

The Survival and Death Act of 1982 (PNC, Title 14) permits a cause of action based on tort to survive the death of the plaintiff or the defendant or other person liable. In such a case, the action may be brought by or against the personal representative of the decedent. Damages are limited to those that accrued before death and exclude punitive damages. If the tort resulted in a death, the personal representative may recover medical and burial expenses incident to the death; the present monetary value of support, services, and financial contributions the decedent would have made to the survivors; compensation for the decedent's pain and suffering, loss of consortium and companionship, and mental anguish; and attorneys' fees and expenses.

The Contribution Among Joint Tort-Feasors Act (PNC, Title 14) creates a right of contribution among tort-feasors who are jointly or severally liable. The right exists only for defendants who have paid more than their pro rata share of the common liability and does not apply to a defendant who intentionally, willfully, or wantonly contributed to the injury or death.

Palau has also adopted the Uniform Single Publication Act (PNC, Title 14) for libel, slander, and invasion of privacy actions. This act permits only one cause of action for each publication,

XX. LABOR LAW

Labor legislation in Palau is designed to give citizens a preference in employment and to protect seamen.

The stated purpose of the Protection of Resident Workers Act (PNC, Title 30) is to give "workers who are citizens of the Republic . . . preference in employment in occupations and industries in the Republic" for which they are qualified and available. Nonresident workers may be employed only to supplement the labor force of resident workers. An exception is made for temporary employees who cannot be employed for more than 180 days. Resident workers are further protected by a requirement that the national government not enter into any contract for the construction of a building, airport, road, harbor, or other project unless the contract provides that the benefits for nonresident workers are the same as for resident workers.

An employer who seeks to employ nonresident workers in Palau must file an application with the employment service of the Division of Labor setting out the number of workers desired, the occupational qualifications of the workers, their wages, and the date and place the workers are required. If, thirty days after notification of the positions, no qualified resident workers are available, nonresident workers may be employed if the Chief of the Division of Labor determines that it is "in the best interests of the Republic."

The Seamen's Protection Act (PNC, Title 7) governs the minimum age of employment, working hours, wages, vacations, benefits, discharge, repatriation, and punishable offenses of crew and officers employed on vessels. It also gives sailors and their employers the right to establish and become members of organizations of their choosing.

XXI. INDUSTRIAL AND INTELLECTUAL PROPERTY RIGHTS

Article IX of the Constitution gives the Olbiil Era Kelulau the power "to regulate . . . patents and copyrights." No legislation has yet been enacted governing these subjects.

XXII. LEGAL EDUCATION AND PROFESSION

Palau has no law schools. There are, however, approximately ten Palauan lawyers who have graduated from law schools in the United States. Admission to practice is governed by the Palau Rules of Admission. In addition, a number of trial counselors who do not have law degrees are permitted to practice law under conditions specified by the Palau Rules of Admission.

For those unable to afford legal services in criminal cases, representation is provided by the Office of the Public Defender. The Micronesian Legal Services Corporation provides legal aid in civil matters.

XXIII. RESEARCH GUIDE

The national laws of Palau are contained in the *Palau National Code*, referred to here as the Code or PNC, which was published in 1985 and supplemented in 1986 and 1987. In the Code and its supplements, laws are arranged into numbered titles according to subject matter. References to acts in this chapter are to the title under which they may be found and, where relevant, to sections within that title.

The courts of Palau publish their decisions in the Republic of Palau Interim Reports (ROP Intrm.), a loose-leaf service. In addition, many decisions applicable to Palau are found in the Trust Territory Reports (TTR).

Butler, W., G. Edwards, and M. Kirby. *Palau: A Challenge to the Rule of Law in Micronesia*. New York: American Association for the International Commission of Jurists, 1988.

Clark, R., and S. Roff. *Micronesia: The Problem of Palau*. Rev. ed.: London: Minority Rights Group, 1987.

Edwards, D. *United States Naval Administration of the Trust Territories of the Pacific Islands*. Washington, D.C.: U.S. Office of Chief of Naval Operations, 1957.

Kluge, P. *The Edge of Paradise: America in Micronesia*. New York: Random House, 1991.

McHenry, D. *Micronesia: Trust Betrayed*. New York: Carnegie Endowment, 1975.

Meller, N. *The Congress of Micronesia*. Honolulu: University of Hawaii Press, 1969.

Parmentier, R. *The Sacred Remains: Myth, History and Polity in Belau*. Chicago: University of Chicago Press, 1987.

Smith, D. *Palauan Social Structure*. New Brunswick: Rutgers University Press, 1983.

PART THREE

The French Territories

21. New Caledonia

MICHAEL A. NTUMY

I. Dateline

2000 B.C.	First evidence of Melanesian settlement in New Caledonia, earliest recorded use of pottery in Oceania.
500 A.D.	Evidence of advanced agricultural techniques, using irrigation and terracing.
1774	Captain James Cook lands on Grand Terre, the main island of New Caledonia.
1843	First settlement of Protestants of London Missionary Society, followed by French Catholic missionaries.
1853	France annexes Grand Terre and the Isle of Pines, which are placed under authority of French naval governor at Papeete.
1859	Policy of moving Melanesians into land designated as native reserves instituted.
1860	New Caledonia and its dependencies become separate French colony.
1863	Discovery of gold leads to large influx of European immigrants.
1868–1894	New Caledonia becomes penal colony of about 30,000 convicts from France.
1875	Nickel discovered, followed by immigration of large number of European and Asian laborers.
1878	Kanak rebellion organized by Chief Atai.
1885	General Council created, elected by island's male French citizens.
1917	Second major Kanak revolt.
1946	New Caledonia classified as non-self-governing territory and included in United Nations decolonization list. France unilaterally revokes this designation in 1947, when New Caledonia becomes French Overseas Territory and French citizenship is conferred on inhabitants.
1951	Melanesians enfranchised.
1953	A progressive Melanesian party, the Caledonian Union, created to articulate Melanesian interests.
1957	New institutions created; greater autonomy guaranteed to territory.
1958	By referendum, New Caledonia approves new French Constitution of 1958 and opts to remain part of the French Republic. Territorial Assembly then chooses to maintain status of Overseas Territory.
1962–1974	Changes in territory's administrative structure, resulting in reduction of territory's autonomy.
1966–1972	Nickel boom brings new immigrants, reducing Kanak population to minority.
1975	Declaration for independence made for the first time by the Multiracial Union for New Caledonia.
1977	An anti-independence party, the Rally for Caledonia, founded (later renamed Rally for New Caledonia within the Republic (RPCR)).
1979	Caledonian Union also declares for independence; Territorial Assembly is dissolved. New elections held and RPCR brought to power.

1981	Change of government in France. General Secretary of the Caledonian Union, Pierre Declercq, assassinated. French government introduces reforms aimed at recognizing Melanesian identity and participation in management of New Caledonia. Land reforms also introduced to return ancestral lands to Melanesians.
1983	Conference of Nainville les Roches recognizes legitimacy of Kanak people's seeking independence through territorial self-determination process and pursuing autonomy.
1984	Greater autonomy conferred on territory and new institutions created to prepare for self-determination in 1989. New coalition party, Front de Libération Nationale Kanake et Socialiste (FLNKS), founded to demand Kanaky independence. Fight for Kanaky independence erupts into violence.
1985	French government plan outlines new status for territory.
1986	South Pacific Forum calls for inclusion of New Caledonia in the U.N. list of non-self-governing territories; draft resolution to this effect adopted by U.N. General Assembly.
1987	FLNKS opposes French constitutional proposals and votes to boycott referendum.
1988	Matignon Accord between French government, RPCR, and FLNKS outlines new plans for future status of New Caledonia.
1989	Provincial elections held, followed by implementation of Matignon Accord.

II. Historical, Cultural, and Economic Survey

New Caledonia is a cluster of islands in the Pacific Ocean. Its population of about 165,000 is spread across many islands but concentrated in Grande Terre, the Loyalty Islands, and the Isle of Pines. Many languages are spoken in this French territory, reflecting different ethnic origins, but the official language is French. Its capital is Noumea. Before European contact, the islands' only inhabitants were Melanesians and Polynesians, estimated at around a total of 40,000.

The existence of New Caledonia (Caledonia is the Roman name for Scotland, after which the island was named) became known to the Western world in the late eighteenth century through the explorations of James Cook, who landed on the main island, Grande Terre, in 1774. The territory was explored further between 1792 and 1793 by the French admiral Bruni d'Entrecasteaux. From the late eighteenth century to the beginning of the nineteenth century, a series of exploratory and trading missions were organized by English explorers from Port Jackson (now Sydney) to the Loyalty Islands. The strong resistance of the indigenous inhabitants of these islands to foreign missions resulted in the first skirmishes between them and the Europeans.

The discovery of sandalwood in 1841 transformed the coastal areas of the islands into the rendezvous of all types of traffickers, merchants, and adventurers, some more honorable than others. This group of Europeans was later joined by more permanent groups of Westerners— the Christian missionaries—in the mid-nineteenth century. First to arrive were the Protestants of the London Missionary Society (LMS), operating out of Tahiti, followed by the French Catholic missionaries. Through persuasion and force, the Grande Terre, the Loyalty Islands, and the Isle of Pines were effectively Christianized.

Christianization paved the way for the political conquest that soon followed. In 1853, France annexed Grand Terre and the Isle of Pines, and the chiefs of both islands were persuaded to sign treaties with France that greatly reduced their powers. In 1854, Captain Tardy de Montravel was given charge of New Caledonia under the general supervision of the French naval governor at Papeete. In 1860, the territory became a French colony administered by the Governor of the French Establishments of Oceania (E.F.O.), the Marquis de Bouzet.

The first Governor for the territory, Rear Admiral Guillain, was appointed in 1862. During his incumbency, the first group of convicts landed on the territory in pursuance of the French policy of converting the territory to a penal colony. The annexation of the Loyalty Islands followed, and a judicial and administrative framework was created for the colony.

The discovery of gold in 1863 and nickel in 1875 lured many white settlers to the colony. The French colonial administration granted these settlers land concessions to encourage them to become permanent members of the society. Land was acquired for this purpose by expropriation of Kanak tribal land and resettlement of the tribes on native reserves. Inside the reserves, the system of land ownership and distribution flagrantly disregarded the traditions and customs of the Kanak people. The imposition of alien institutions and practices on the Kanaks undermined the traditional system of authority and hastened the disintegration of tribal society.

The large influx of European, Asian, and other alien intruders aggravated the Kanak unrest that had been seething since the French colonial administration instituted the policy of native reserves. In protest, the Kanaks, led by Chief Atai, rebelled against French policies and authority. This revolt, as well as the prevailing environment of a penal colony, discouraged potential colonists from coming to New Caledonia.

The convict system was abolished in 1898 by Paul Feillet, the first civilian Governor, and an active propaganda campaign then invited white settlers from France. To pacify the colonists who were now deprived of cheap convict labor, Feillet promoted the immigration of Asians as indentured labor on the farms and in the mines. The success of this policy led to a marked increase in the number of French and other immigrants. It is estimated that between 1895 and 1902, 525 French families and 1,500 Indians, Tonkinese, Javanese, and Melanesians from the New Hebrides (now Vanuatu) migrated to the colony. To provide land for these new settlers, Feillet retrieved land from the penitentiary authorities and, alleging a decrease in the Kanak population, reduced the land allocated to the Kanaks as native reserves.

The economic growth and population expansion that marked the end of the nineteenth century were halted by the economic crisis of 1903 and later by World War I. The colony entered a long and difficult period of inactivity and isolation that lasted until World War II. During this period, the Melanesian population, whose growth had been stunted by French colonial policies, started to increase again.

Three important ramifications of the end of World War II led to the decline of the original colonial system. First, in 1946, New Caledonia's status as a colony was changed to that of a French Overseas Territory, and the *indigenat* (a regime of disciplinary penalties that deprived the Kanaks of the protection of the law and placed them under the arbitrary authority of administrators who could sentence offenders to imprisonment, fines, or confiscation of their property) was abolished. Secondly, because of the entry of the United States into the war in the South Pacific, the island after the war became an important market for American exports, thus stimulating economic activity once again. Finally, the extension of the universal franchise to the Kanaks in 1951 signaled a definite end to the old colonial system.

During the thirty-year period 1945–1974, the economic and social conditions of New Caledonia were greatly transformed. The productive capacity of the territory increased immensely through the active intervention of the French state, which embarked on a policy of industrial expansion based on nickel exploitation. The demographic structure of the island also underwent significant changes. The spread of industrial activity and the development of a tertiary sector led to migration from the rural areas to the urban center. The population of Noumea, which was 25,000 in 1956, increased to 65,000 in 1983. During the same period the Kanak population grew from 3,800 to 16,600 and the European population from 16,500 to 42,800.

In response to these social and economic changes, French policy listed as one of its goals the integration of ethnic groups on the island. More specifically, French policy was to transform Melanesians into French citizens, embracing French culture. This policy led to varied reactions among the Melanesians. While a minority tried to adopt French culture and become part of the European middle class in New Caledonia, a sizable group that had been absorbed into the industrial network as workers remained little affected by the changes. The majority, however, remained on the reserves without any contact with the modern sector and resisted any attempts to adulterate their culture. On the whole, the reaction of the Kanaks to the French policy of integration was a reawakening of the consciousness of Kanak cultural and political identity.

The manifestation of this consciousness took three different forms. First, claims for land were spearheaded by the Palika, a new political party created in 1976 to fight for the return of all tribal land to the Kanaks. To control this demand, the French government initiated a land reform program in 1977 and created a fund for buying back tribal land from white settlers to return it to the Kanaks. The poor administration of this program condemned it to failure.

The second manifestation of Kanak consciousness was expressed in the claim to sovereignty. This started in 1970, with the territorial elections that led to the division of the Caledonian Union party. Yann Uregei, who lost the election for the presidency of the Territorial Assembly, left the Caledonian Union and created a new party, the Multiracial Union for New Caledonia. This party proposed a motion demanding autonomy for New Caledonia. The rejection of the proposal by the Territorial Assembly culminated in the formation of the Group of 1878, which launched the struggle for independence.

From 1977, this struggle received the broad support of all the political parties. In 1979, the Caledonian Union, led by Jean-Marie Tjibaou, recognized the legitimacy of the independence claims and joined the Front de Libération Nationale Kanake et Socialiste (FLNKS) created by the small independence parties. Autonomy, which until then had been the main objective of these political parties, was now regarded as only a step towards independence.

Finally, Kanak consciousness was manifested in the affirmation of Kanak cultural identity and the demand for official recognition of customary institutions and law. The French government's reaction to this, which hardly satisfied the Kanaks, was the establishment of an administrative office for Melanesian culture.

In 1981, a change of government in France created a certain anxiety in the territory. To respond to the rift developing between the two communities of the white population and the Kanaks, the French government promoted the idea of a roundtable conference with the participation of all political parties. This led to the July 1983 Conference of Nainville Les Roches.

In 1984, a new status was conferred on the territory by the French government. This status conceded broader autonomy to the territory and proposed the creation of new institutions. A special committee was created and entrusted with the preparation of the territory for self-determination in 1989. The Independence Front (now the Front de Libération Nationale Kanake et Socialiste, or FLNKS), however, adopted a more militant posture and boycotted the November elections. Violence broke out, followed by a stormy period of fighting between those who wanted independence and those who opposed it.

The new status was subsequently amended to include a referendum on self-determination to be held before the end of 1987; the creation of four regions governed by regional councils to be elected in June 1985; economic, social, and cultural reforms; and the reinforcement of the French military presence. As a result of the regional elections, the FLNKS assumed control of three out of the four regions.

French policy toward New Caledonia was modified again in 1986, following a change of government in France. The institutions dealing with land, cultural, and regional affairs were altered, and an economic revival plan was designed for the territory. In 1987, the French Parliament passed a bill granting the people of New Caledonia the choice of determining whether to become independent or to remain part of France. By referendum, the majority opted to remain part of France.

Between 1987 and 1988, tension and violence became the order of the day in New Caledonia. There was a shift in the FLNKS strategy from conciliation to confrontation as was evidenced by the hostage crisis that marred the French presidential elections in May 1988. Immediately after the elections, the reelected socialist President of France opted for rapprochement to avert an escalation of the New Caledonia crisis. A dialogue initiated by the French government between the leaders of the pro- and anti-independence parties culminated in the 1988 Matignon Accord on the future status of New Caledonia. The main features of the accord are as follows:

1. strategies for the gradual decolonization of the territory;
2. a self-determination referendum in 1998 after a transitional ten-year period of limited self-government with one year of French direct rule in the beginning; and
3. political and economic reforms during the transitional period to enable the Kanaks to prepare themselves for self-government by 1998.

This agreement forms the basis of the current Territorial Statute of New Caledonia. It was proclaimed by Law No. 88-1028 of 9 November 1988, relating to the Statutory Dispositions and Preparations for the Autonomy of New Caledonia. The provisions of the Statute (except for those on indemnity and amnesty for those involved in the 1988 hostage crisis and the elections to the Territorial Assembly, which took effect immediately after publication of the law) came into force in July 1989, following the provincial elections. This law provides the legal basis for the current structure, organization, and powers of all territorial institutions.

The following account of the legal system of New Caledonia presents only the general principles of public law as they apply to all the French Overseas Territories. Within this broad framework, the minor variations necessitated by the specific organization of New Caledonia will be highlighted. For an account of the private law aspects of the legal system, **see Chapter 22, Wallis and Futuna.**

III. SOURCES OF LAW

The sources of law in the legal system of New Caledonia follow very closely those of the French legal system. In French law, a fundamental distinction is made between primary sources, which are binding, and secondary sources (also known as authorities), which become operative only when primary sources are absent, unclear, or incomplete. Secondary sources are not binding and they are neither necessary nor sufficient as the basis for a judicial decision. The following is the hierarchical order of the primary sources of law:

1. the 1958 Constitution of the French Republic, which has general and full binding effect;
2. international treaties signed by France on matters relating to the territory;
3. legislation, (or *la loi*), a term that includes statute law (parliamentary and executive legislation) and the French Codes;

4. general principles of law, derived either from constitutional and legislative writings or from case law; and
5. administrative regulations, which are binding only on the individual concerned.

The secondary sources of law are case law emanating from the higher courts and custom, which is allowed to supplement but not to abrogate the written law. Since custom is the basis of Kanak identity, it plays a very significant role in the legal system of New Caledonia, despite its secondary importance as a source of law (see **XII, B Application of Customary Law**).

IV. Constitutional System

A. Territory

New Caledonia is a French Overseas Territory situated between 18 degrees and 23 degrees south latitude and between 158 degrees and 172 degrees west longitude. It comprises Grand Terre, Isle of Pines, the Belep Archipelago, the Huon and Surprise Islands, the Chesterfield Islands and the Bellone coral reefs, the Loyalty Islands (Mare, Lifou, Tiga, and Ouvea), the Walpole Islands, the islands of Beautemps Beaupre and Astrolabe, and the Matthew and Fearn or Hunter Islands.

Under Article 6 of the Territorial Statute, the territory is divided into three Provinces, the Northern Province, the Southern Province, and the province of the Loyalty Islands.

According to Law No. 71-1060 of 24 December 1971, which is applicable to the Overseas Territories as well, the French territorial waters extend to a limit fixed at 12 nautical miles measured from the baselines of each territory.

B. Nationality and Citizenship

Article 77 of the French Constitution proclaims that there shall be only one citizenship in the Republic, and all citizens are equal before the law whatever may be their origin, race, or religion. Citizenship confers on all French nationals, including the peoples of the Overseas Territories, equal rights and duties.

The French law of nationality is governed by the Code of Nationality passed in 1945. Under this law, nationality is based on the *jus soli*, the *jus sanguinis*, or the *jus voluntatis*. The tendency is to attribute French nationality to all persons who have a substantial connection with France, subject to permitting persons whose connection is relatively remote to repudiate it in six months before attaining majority.

According to the criterion of *jus sanguinis*, anyone born anywhere of a French father or mother is French. Citizenship under the *jus soli* criterion is acquired by anyone born in France or in a French territory of a father or mother born in France or in a French territory, anyone born in France or in a French territory of unknown parents, and anyone born in France or in a French territory of foreign parents who have habitually resided there since the age of sixteen. No distinction is generally made between father and mother or between legitimate and illegitimate children.

Foreigners may, according to the *jus voluntatis* criterion, be naturalized if they meet certain prescibed conditions, and minors born in France or in a French territory may claim French citizenship by declaration, subject to certain family consents.

French citizenship may be forfeited in the following cases:

1. voluntary acquisition of a foreign nationality;
2. failure to comply with an order to resign from the service of a foreign government;
3. habitual residence abroad for more than fifty years; or
4. in the case of a naturalized citizen, commission of certain crimes or acting for a foreign state in a manner incompatible with the character of a French citizen and prejudicial to French interests.

Unless the forfeiture is due to a voluntary act of expatriation, it is the result of proceedings instituted by government in a civil court.

C. Territorial Government

The legal status of New Caledonia as a French Overseas Territory is defined by the 1958 Constitution of the French Republic,[1] which determines the legal relationship between the French Republic and the French Overseas Territories. The basic principle underlying this relationship is expressed in Article 76 of the Constitution, which states that Overseas Territories form an integral part of the Republic of France.

Article 72 of the Constitution confers responsibility for national interests, administrative supervision, and respect for the laws on the government delegate (that is, the High Commissioner) appointed by the President of the Republic. In addition, it declares that an elected council within the territory is free to organize the local administration of the territory. To promote this freedom, Article 74 concedes to each territory a special organization determined by its Territorial Statute, which takes into account its territorial interests within the context of the general interest of the French Republic. Finally, Article 77 grants each territory autonomy, while Article 86 provides for the possibility of the territory's becoming independent of France through a referendum.

Notwithstanding the concessions that the Constitution makes to the Overseas Territories, these provisions clearly indicate that the territories are under the total legal control of the French state. This control is symbolized in the person of the High Commissioner, who can question the legality of all acts of the territorial authorities.

The control function also extends to the Council of State (Conseil d'Etat) in metropolitan France. Since the legislative framework within which the territorial authorities operate is determined and restricted by French public law, the Council of State, as the highest public law court, can veto by decree any territorial decision on the grounds of excess of power, illegality, national defense, public order, security, and liberties. In fact, this control mechanism has proved a decisive instrument in suppressing political moves for independence.

The legal relationship of the territories and the state has, however, been modified lately by the interpretation of Article 74 of the Constitution by the Constitutional Council (Conseil Constitutionnel), the highest constitutional court. According to this council, while Overseas Territories have no law-making powers, Article 74 requires that the local congress or Territorial Assembly in any overseas territory be consulted before certain laws affecting the internal organization of the territory can be applied to them.[2]

The procedure for consultation begins with a request from Parliament for the Territorial Assembly's approval of a bill. After a debate in the Assembly, the bill is either approved or rejected (rejection is rare). The approval may also be given with recommendations, but Parliament is not bound by such recommendations. Once approval is given, Parliament may proceed to pass the original bill with or without Parliament's own amendments and extend its application to the overseas territories. Parliament is under no obligation to refer amendments to the Territorial Assembly for its approval.

In practice, the application of a law passed by the French Parliament to New Caledonia is signified by the subsequent publication of the law in the territory's official gazette (*Journal Officiel*). In the absence of such publication, even though publication in the French metropolitan official gazette validates the law, the law does not apply to the territory unless and until the Territorial Assembly specifically requests Parliament to extend the application of the law to the territory. This procedure recognizes a traditional principle, *la spécialité de la législation*, which means that the laws and decrees of France do not automatically apply to the territories unless the intention of the legislature, whether expressly or by implication, so indicates. This principle is not included in the Constitution but is recognized as a general legal principle.

1. HEAD OF STATE

The Head of State of the territory is the President of the French Republic, who is elected by universal suffrage for seven years and represented in the Overseas Territories by the High Commissioner of the Republic. Citizens in the Overseas Territories who are registered to vote participate in the election of the President.

2. EXECUTIVE

The chief executive of the territory, according to Title IV of the Territorial Statute, is the French High Commissioner, who also represents the state as the delegate of the French government.

As the executive head of the territory, the High Commissioner represents the territory and in this capacity prepares and executes the decisions of the Territorial Congress and its Permanent Commission and signs and executes the territorial budget. The High Commissioner, who is in charge of the services of the territory, has power to appoint the personnel of the territorial services, the directorate of public agencies, and the representatives of the Bank of France. The commissioner has the power of budgetary control over the territorial and provincial budgets and, whenever these budgets are not balanced, can propose the changes required to balance them. The High Commissioner also controls the legality of the acts of the public territorial and provincial institutions and can refer to the Administrative Tribunal any acts that are contrary to the law.

The High Commissioner decides the order of public works, proposes for congressional approval the prices of services, and can decide to suspend or reduce (for a short period of time) customs excise to protect local production. Such decisions must, however, be submitted for congressional approval immediately.

In the execution of the duties of the office, the High Commissioner is assisted by the consultative committee, which comprises the chairman and the deputy chairman of the three Provincial Assemblies, as well as the chairman and the deputy chairman of the Territorial Congress. This committee meets once every month to consider and advise on budgetary bills and other decisions that the law requires be referred to it. In all other matters, the High Commissioner is represented in each province by a delegated Commissioner of the Republic.

In the capacity of delegate of the French government, the High Commissioner is responsible for promoting the national interests of the Republic, supervising the administration in each province, and ensuring that the laws are respected; the Commissioner is in charge of public order and must maintain law and order in the territory and ensure respect for public freedom and individual and public rights. The High Commissioner has power to control public or private organizations that benefit from public funds and to declare a state of emergency under conditions determined by law.

The High Commissioner can attend every session of the Territorial Congress or the Provincial Assemblies and has the right to address them. He or she is in charge of the publication of national laws and decrees, ordinances of Congress, and povincial assembly orders and decisions in the local gazette.

3. LEGISLATURE

According to Article 34 of the 1958 Constitution, the competent body to legislate for the Republic of France is the French Parliament. Consequently, Overseas Territories have no lawmaking powers of their own. They are subject to the overall jurisdiction of the French Parliament whose laws, subject to the principle of *la spécialité de la législation*, have general applicability to them as well. As a concession, they are entitled to be represented in the French Parliament, whose laws, because of the absence of the principle of judicial review in French constitutional law, cannot be questioned in any court of law on the grounds of unconstitutionality.

Accordingly, New Caledonia has representation in the two houses of the French Parliament as provided by Article 24 of the Constitution.[3] In the National Assembly, the territory is represented by two deputies elected by direct universal suffrage; one senator represents the territory in the French Senate. The senator is elected by an electoral college of representatives from the municipal councils and all members of the Territorial Congress.

Representatives elected to the French Parliament must be French citizens of at least twenty-three years of age who are in possession of their civil and political rights and not otherwise disqualified from voting. They must also have completed the one-year compulsory national service in the French army required of all males between the ages of eighteen and twenty.

a. Powers of the National Government

Article 8 of the Territorial Statute of New Caledonia confers on the French state the competence to legislate on a variety of issues of vital interest to the French Republic. The areas reserved for France's exclusive legislative competence are external relations, foreign investment authorizations, international trade, control of immigration and foreign nationals, external communications, navigation and management of the maritime economic zone, air traffic control, post and telecommunications, police powers and security control of internal flights.

Other areas under French national control include currency, treasury, and foreign exchange; finance, credit, and interest rates; defense, arms, and ammunition control; law and order and external security; citizenship; registration of births, deaths, marriages, divorces, and adoptions; civil law and commercial law, with the exception of customary law; mining regulations and taxation of mining exports; the main principles of land law and real property; the main principles of industrial law; and the control of labor relations.

Finally, France also has exclusive jurisdiction to legislate on matters relating to justice, organization of the judiciary, and the legal profession; criminal law and judicial procedure; legal aid; prisons, juvenile delinquency, and child abuse; state civil service; administrative and financial control of public agencies within the provinces and communes; verification of the legality of communal administration; secondary and higher education; television and satellite communications; and sovereignty over airspace, private and public lands, and the maritime zone.

b. Powers of the Territorial Government

Subject to the exclusive power of the state to legislate on the above matters, the internal administration of the territory is entrusted to the following territorial institutions created by the Territorial Statute: the Provincial Assemblies, the Territorial Congress, the executive of the territory, the Economic and Social Council, the Territorial Consultative Council on Customary

Affairs, and the municipal councils. The first two of these institutions participate in law making in areas within their compétence. Their decisions are promulgated in the form of ordinances.

c. Territorial Congress

The Territorial Congress is made up of fifty-four members and formed by the union of the three Provincial Assemblies. Its members are elected by universal suffrage for a period of six years to run concurrently with the life of the Provincial Assemblies. However, if a Provincial Assembly is dissolved, members of the Territorial Congress from that Assembly retain their positions until the next election.

The members elect from among themselves a President, a Vice President, and a Permanent Commission consisting of seven to eleven members. The commission considers matters referred to it by the Territorial Congress and advises the Congress. All decisions of the Territorial Congress and its Permanent Commission are automatically executory as soon as published and after notification to the High Commissioner.

The Congress holds two ordinary sessions (administrative and budgetary sessions) and one extraordinary session every year. The ordinary sessions are called by the President, who determines the agenda for all meetings; the extraordinary session is called upon written request by the majority of the members or the High Commissioner addressed to the President. During the administrative session, the High Commissioner reports on the situation of the territory and the activity of territorial public services. Every year before the first of September, the High Commissioner also presents the current year's financial report and informs the Territorial Congress on matters that will be presented to it. All the meetings of the Congress are public unless special circumstances require in camera meetings.

The Territorial Congress is assigned responsibility under Article 9 of the Territorial Statute for voting the budget and approving the financial report. It also has enumerated powers over imports and taxes, medical and social services, public hygiene, social security, internal public transport and driving rules, local public servants employed by the territorial institutions, professional organizations, insurance, rules and procedures regarding public tender, civil procedure, legal aid, and child welfare.

Other areas within the competence of the Territorial Congress are weights and measures, price control, the main principles of urban law, veterinary service, quarantine services, territorial public service (with regard to recruitment, nomination, and status), census and statistics, territorial public buildings, maintenance of territorial roads, shipping services, dams, and the production of electricity for territorial consumption.

The Territorial Congress can also make decisions regarding abbatoires; domestic meteorological services, domestic posts and telecommunications; sports and cultural activities of territorial interest; rules of industrial law (excepting the main principles); and industrial organization, without prejudice to the powers of the provinces over professional training of workers.

Finally, the legislative competence of the Territorial Congress extends to the power to vote its standing orders and impose fines for violations of its orders, and the right to request Parliament (with regard to matters within the state's competence) to extend the application of state laws to the territory or modify the application of the rules to it.

The Territorial Congress also has the right to be consulted on the following matters: extension of state laws to the territory, legislative proposals authorizing the ratification of international conventions on matters within the competence of the territory or provinces, and all matters within the state's competence and in which the High Commissioner seeks the advice of Congress. Whenever the Congress is consulted on the above issues, it must respond within one month unless requested by the High Commissioner to do so in two weeks. After the expiration of the two weeks, if the Congress does not respond, the answer is presumed to be affirmative.

d. Provincial Assemblies

Provinces are defined as territorial collectivities of the Republic that, according to the Territorial Statute, have the legal right to administer themselves freely through elected assemblies. Consequently, each of the three provinces has an elected Assembly composed of fifteen members in the Northern Province, thirty-two in the Southern Province, and seven in the Loyalty Islands. Members of the assemblies are elected for six years.

Each Provincial Assembly elects from among its members a president, a first vice president, and a second vice president who constitute the bureau of the Assembly. The Provincial Assemblies are required to sit at least once every two months at a venue chosen by the High Commissioner and at a time when the Territorial Congress is not in session. All meetings must be open to the public, unless special circumstances make publicity undesirable. The quorum for meetings is 50 percent of the membership of the Assembly. If the quorum is not reached at a session, the meeting is automatically postponed for three days, after which the quorum requirement is waived. All decisions require the absolute majority of the votes, and the presidents have casting votes.

Article 7 of the Territorial Statute confers on the provinces competence in all matters not specifically assigned to the state or the territory. The most important of these residual powers is the power to approve the budget plans and vote the provincial budget, to approve the accounts and expenditures of the province, and to authorize the management of provincial resources. The other areas of provincial competence are economic development, promotion of local cultures, and teaching of vernacular languages. In addition, the Provincial Assemblies have power to control and manage investments, roads, and airports in their provinces.

The Provincial Assemblies also can make standing orders to supplement existing laws and can delegate their powers to enable the executive bureau to vote a budget. Ordinances emanating from the assemblies become valid after publication and notification to the High Commissioner. Such notification must list all acts or decisions made by the bureau under delegated authority, the general and individual decisions made by the presidents when exercising powers given to them as provincial executive heads, general acts voted by the province, tender and loan agreements, decisions regarding individual persons employed by the province, and specific decisions made by the province before a congressional or state decision on investment in the province. If the High Commissioner rejects any of these decisions, the matter is referred to the administrative tribunal for a determination of their legality.

Article 466 of the Penal Code of 1814 empowers the Provincial Assemblies to impose a penalty on those who violate their general orders. This penalty may take the form of a fine (up to 50,000 CFPF, which is paid into the provincial account) or correctional means. The imposition of criminal punishment (imprisonment) is permitted only for particular acts with the approval of the French Parliament. The Assemblies can also opt to settle out of court, except that if the matter will normally lead to a criminal trial then the approval of the Procureur (the representative of the Ministry of Justice) must be sought.

The presidents of the Provincial Assemblies are, according to Article 25 of the Territorial Statute, the executive heads of the respective provincial governments. In this capacity, they have the following responsibilities: preparation and implementation of bills passed by the Assemblies, signing and executing provincial budgets and expenditures, and administration of provincial assets.

The presidents decide the order of issues discussed in the Assemblies, provided that they oblige the High Commissioner's requests at all times. They must sign all minutes approved by the Assemblies and circulate the agenda for meetings at least eight days in advance. While the Assemblies are in session, the presidents have police powers and can request the removal and arrest of persons who engage in disorderly conduct. They also can appoint officials to various administrative positions and create special positions and fill them without regard to the state civil service procedure.

In the preparation and execution of the decisions of the Assemblies, the presidents can utilize personnel and services of the state or territorial agencies with the approval of the High Commissioner or the director of the agency concerned.

The presidents are required to submit to the Assemblies a financial account of the last budget before the first of September every year and to report on the activity of public services in their provinces during every budgetary session.

e. Consultative Councils

Title III, Chapters III and IV of the Territorial Statute regulate two important consultative councils whose basic function is to advise the Provincial Assemblies and the Territorial Congress in their law-making roles.

The first is the Economic and Social Council, which must be consulted on all important social, economic, and cultural matters concerning the territory. Its membership reflects a broad representation of the whole territory as well as all branches of the economy. Out of a total membership of thirty-one, eight are elected from the Northern Province, sixteen from the Southern Province, and four from the Loyalty Islands. The remaining three members are drawn from the Chamber of Agriculture, Chamber of Commerce and Industry, and Chamber of Artisans.

The second council, the Territorial Consultative Council on Customary Affairs, consists of representatives from all the customary areas of New Caledonia. This council must be consulted on all matters pertaining to the law of particular civil status and customary land law proposed by the Provincial Assemblies and the Territorial Congress. It may also be consulted on matters relating to economic, social, and cultural development, as well as planning and budget. On its own initiative, the Territorial Consultative Council may refer all matters on the regulation of customary law or the native reserves to the Territorial Congress or the Provincial Assemblies. It also advises the High Commissioner, the Provincial Assemblies, and the Territorial Congress on any other matter referred to it.

Each of the customary areas listed above has a customary council whose composition is determined by the area's customary law. The function of these councils is to assist the Territorial Consultative Council and to advise the Provincial Assemblies on local customary law and customary land law.

The activities of the Territorial Consultative Council and the other councils are financed with funds allocated by the territorial budget.

4. JUDICIARY

Justice and the organization of the judiciary, as stipulated by Article 8 of the Territorial Statute, are matters within the exclusive competence of the state. Consequently, the judicial authority of the territory, as provided by the Constitution, is the President of the French Republic, and the judicial structure and personnel of the territory form part and parcel of the judicial system and service of metropolitan France. Within the territory, however, the judicial institutions are placed under the authority of the first president of the Court of Appeal of Noumea and the Public Prosecutor of Noumea.

The structural organization of the courts in New Caledonia, as in metropolitan France, reflects the traditional division between private law and public law. The private law courts and the public law courts (administrative tribunals) form two separate and independent hierarchies, with the Court of Cassation (Cour de Cassation) at the apex of the former while the Council of State (Conseil d'Etat) heads the latter (see **Chapter 22, Wallis and Futuna**, for a more detailed discussion of private law in the French Overseas Territories).

In keeping with the French legal tradition of referring to only the private law courts as judicial courts, we describe the administrative tribunals under Administrative Organization and Law (**see V, E**). Jurisdictional conflicts between the two systems of court are referred to the tribunal of conflicts.

The private law courts are divided into the civil courts and the criminal courts, both of which are based on the principle of a two-tier jurisdiction. At the first level of ordinary jurisdiction are the Courts of First Instance, such as the Civil Court, which deals with minor civil cases, and the Police Court and the Summary Court, which handle petty criminal offenses and misdemeanors respectively. The Court of Assizes has original and appellate jurisdiction in all the more serious criminal matters (that is, felonies), and cases before this court are heard by three judges and a jury. In addition, at this level several specialized courts coexist with the regular civil and criminal courts. For example, matters arising under the Commercial Code are heard by the Joint Commercial Court, disputes between employers and employees by the Labour Court, and juvenile cases by the Juvenile Tribunal.

Since the decentralization of the administration of justice, Courts of First Instance have been established in the provinces as well. These courts normally sit with only one judge or with the president and two assessors (who are also judges), depending on the nature of the case. But when they deal with matters concerning the law of particular civil status (that is, customary law), they are required to co-opt two customary assessors.

Appeals from the Courts of First Instance go to the second level of appellate jurisdiction, which is the Court of Appeal. This court sits only in Noumea with a President and two other judges called Councillors of the Court of Appeal.

Decisions of the Court of Appeal and the Court of Assizes may be challenged only on a point of law before the Court of Cassation in France.

D. Local Government

At the local government level, the territory is divided into four administrative subdivisions, each with a head. The administrative subdivisions are further divided into thirty-two communes[5] or municipalities, each representing an electoral constituency. The communes are administered by an elected municipal council that comprises the Mayor as the head, two or more deputy mayors, and other elected members.

The capital city of the territory, Noumea, is administered separately as a municipal government with an elected Mayor at the head.

In addition, the tribe[6] is recognized as the basic unit of Melanesian traditional organization.

1. MUNICIPAL COUNCILS

The municipal councils are the administrative organs of the communes or municipalities. Under the 1987 Code of Communes applicable to New Caledonia and its dependencies, the councils are competent to deal with all matters that concern the communes. They vote on their annual budget, determine what installations are necessary, and decide on the creation and maintenance of services that will benefit the commune. Their administrative units assist in the organization of disaster relief and are therefore required by law to be consulted in budgetary discussions on relief money. They also advise the High Commissioner on matters referred to them. All decisions of the councils are, however, controlled by the High Commissioner, whose approval is required in, for example, decisions to obtain bank loans or buy shares in a private organization.

All members of the councils are elected collectively on a party basis, and voters have no right to change the order in which the candidates are listed on the ballot paper. The right to contest elections to the councils is open to every voter who is at least eighteen years of age and has been resident in the commune for at least six months. The total number of members in each council may vary between nine and forty-five.

The councils meet at least once a year; however, the Mayors, as the chief executives of the commune, can summon them at will. The High Commissioner can also direct the Mayors to summon the council, and the council must then meet within one month following such direction. The quorum for meetings is 50 percent of the membership. Should there be no quorum at a meeting, the meeting is postponed for three days, after which the quorum requirement is waived. Decisions are made by absolute majority through secret voting unless a public vote is requested by at least four members. One proxy vote is allowed for each member and the Mayors have casting votes. All decisions take effect two weeks after they have been deposited with the High Commissioner and posted on the town hall notice board for one week.

2. MAYORS

As chief executives of the communes, the Mayors are in charge of the assets and the civil and general administration of the commune. They are responsible for the public works and the maintenance of communal roads, cemeteries, and mortuaries and the construction of new classroom blocks. They prepare and execute the budget and sign all tender agreements; they can revise the electoral roll as well as create public agencies to provide utilities to the communes. They have power to publish and execute laws that concern the communes without reference to any other authority. Together with their deputies, they administer the registration of civil law marriages, births, deaths, divorces, and adoptions. They have the duty to publicize laws that are not respected, control the national patrol police force in their communes, and provide education for their people.

The Mayors also function as representatives of the state in the communes. In this capacity, they authenticate signatures and publicize the laws of the Republic.

E. Emergency Powers

The emergency powers of the territory are governed by the Law of April 3, 1955. Under this law, the French Council of Ministers can, by decree, declare a state of emergency in any part or the whole of the territory whenever public order is seriously endangered or the nature or gravity of events represents a public disaster or calamity. The decree must define the area of the territory under emergency and the duration of the state of emergency. The normal period for a state of emergency is twelve days, a period that can be extended only by law.

The declaration of a state of emergency empowers the High Commissioner, as the representative of the French government, to

1. restrict the movement of persons or vehicles in specific areas and at specific times;
2. declare certain areas as protection or security zones and regulate residency in those areas; and

3. forbid actions that interfere with measures to control the emergency.

During a state of emergency, the civil authorities (as opposed to the military) retain the competence to maintain order unless the military authorities decide that the situation warrants military intervention. On account of the chaotic political situation in New Caledonia, the military has often exercised this competence to maintain order during periods of emergency as occurred, for example, in 1987.

F. Human Rights

Under the preamble to the 1958 Constitution, the peoples of the Overseas Territories are guaranteed the right to self-determination and democratic development based on the principles of liberty, equality, and fraternity. Accordingly, Article 75 maintains the right for indigenous peoples of the Overseas Territories to keep their own status and does not allow the French Parliament to legislate on matters pertaining to the law of particular civil status that applies only to indigenous people (see **XII, A Status of Customary Law**).

Article 2 of the preamble guarantees to all French citizens equality before the law without distinction as to origin, race, or religion. The application of this constitutional principle in practice means that uniform rules of law must be applied to all citizens throughout the Republic. Consequently, laws of common application (those relating to constitutional matters, elections, civil status, and civil servants) passed by the French Parliament automatically apply to the Overseas Territories without the requirement for local publication or promulgation.

Article 3 guarantees to all French citizens of both sexes who have attained the age of majority (eighteen years) and are in possession of their civil and political rights the right to suffrage on the basis of equality.

Other constitutional liberties guaranteed by the Constitution are incorporated from the Declaration of the Rights of Man and the Citizen (1789) and the preamble to the 1946 Constitution. These rights include the following:

1. the freedom to do everything not expressly prohibited by law;
2. freedom of expression, communication, movement, and association;
3. the right to work and to seek employment;
4. the right to belong to a trade union; and
5. the rights of workers to obtain further education, organize legal strikes, and enjoy the benefits of social security.

The declaration prohibits discrimination at work on the basis of political or religious opinion or belief and the retroactive application of law in criminal matters. Finally, the declaration guarantees the equality of men and women; the inviolability of the individual's body, home, and vehicle; compulsory education for children between the ages of six and sixteen; leisure hours for children, mothers, and old people; and the right of foreigners to seek political asylum in France.

In principle, these guaranteed liberties can be limited only by law in the public interest. However, in the Melanesian context, even with formal civil equality of the Kanaks and those of European origin, inequalities that are more open in the political and economic arena still persist. In fact, until the tenacious attitudes and prejudices that characterize the relationship between the two communities are altered and a more equitable distribution of land, wealth, and opportunity is introduced, the guaranteed liberties will continue to have little meaning for the Kanaks.

V. Administrative Organization and Law

A. Organization

The public service is responsible to the High Commissioner through a general secretary. In addition, there are assistant secretaries for administration and for economic affairs, and a large number of government departments, bureaus, and statutory bodies. Certain officials, including the Public Prosecutor, the heads of the juridical department and treasury, and the administrative tribunal, are independent of this administrative structure and report directly to the High Commissioner, while the police, intelligence and military services report to the High Commissioner through a principal private secretary, and not through the general secretary of the administration.

B. Public Service

There are two categories of the civil service in New Caledonia: the national civil service operates in matters reserved to the exclusive competence of the state, and the local civil service is limited to the territorial or municipal levels.

C. Public Finance and Audit

Since finance is an area reserved exclusively to state competence, the accounting system and administrative personnel are under the Ministry of Economy and Finance in metropolitan France. This control is exercised by the minister in charge of the budget, who appoints the accountant of the territory and one accountant for each province to carry out the actual work of financial administration. These administrative personnel are subject to the checks of the Territorial Chamber of Accounts, which certifies the work of the accountants.

D. Rule Making

The same general principles and procedure of the French system of administrative law (*droit administratif*) are applicable in New Caledonia and all the other Overseas Territories.

In consonance with the traditional division between private and public law, administrative law within the French legal system is recognized as an autonomous branch of public law with a separate jurisdiction and court system. The legal principles and procedure of the French system of administrative law are also distinctively public law principles that are applied only by the administrative tribunals to secure justice for the individual in dealings with the administration.

For example, with regard to the law of contract, the French legal system distinguishes between a contract of private law and a contract of public law. The determination as to whether a contract is one of public law or not depends on two conditions. First, one of the parties must be a public body or at least a body providing a public service. Secondly, the object of the contract must be performed entirely by each party, one of which must be a public body and the other a private person. The contract must also contain provisions not usually found in a private contract of a similar kind.

While contracts of private law are governed by the ordinary rules of contract and fall within the jurisdiction of the regular civil courts, contracts of public law are regulated by the principles of *contrat administratif* and fall within the exclusive jurisdiction of the administrative tribunals. The principles of *contrat administratif* stipulate that in contracts of public law, the administration has the power of direction, control, and sanctions; the private contractor has a right to financial

E. Review of Administrative Action

The review of administrative action is carried out by the Administrative Tribunals (Tribunaux Administratifs), which form a separate hierarchy of courts apart from the regular civil courts. This hierarchy of courts comprises the Council of State at the top, followed by the Tribunal of Administrative Appeals (Cour des Appels Administratifs) and then the Administrative Tribunal. The jurisdiction of these tribunals extends to all executive and administrative acts with the exception of acts directly or partially connected with the legislative process, acts related to diplomatic relations of the government with foreign states or international organizations, and cases dealing with private property and fundamental liberties.

The single Administrative Tribunal in New Caledonia is based in Noumea. This court was created in 1984 as part of the French state's attempt to decentralize the administration of justice. Appeals from this court go to the Tribunal of Administrative Appeals in Paris.

The main categories of cases brought before the Administrative Tribunal are ultra vires proceedings to quash administrative decisions and full jurisdiction proceedings to obtain damages. Persons initiating these processes must have locus standi, which is liberally interpreted to mean direct interest, and must have exhausted all available administrative remedies.

The procedure adopted by this court consists mostly of the use of written memoranda. The whole process is open to the public, and the judge, as is typical in civil law countries, plays an active role. The judge is in charge of all preliminary investigation and conducts the procedure with little or no initiative from the parties. All parties are entitled to legal representation and inexpensive legal aid is available on request. A summary procedure is available to enable an aggrieved citizen to obtain urgent relief from the court in emergencies.

The court is composed of three judges and one commissioner of the government. All decisions are collegial and based on majority vote. Judgment is executed against the public accounts of the administration; if after four to six months the administration fails to honor the judgment order for compulsory payment of damages, the public accountant is obligated to pay on presentation of the judgment order.

The main principles of *droit administratif*, derived from the decisions[7] of the Council of State, are the following:

1. *légalité*—the administration's acts run the risk of annulment unless they conform with the law;
2. *responsabilité*—the administration is responsible for its mistakes as well as for other acts (for example, administrative risk and the use of dangerous methods) that might not be mistakes and will be liable to indemnify any citizen whose rights have been infringed through such unlawful administrative acts;
3. *égalité*—this means that in recognition of the constitutional guarantee of equality, all citizens must be treated equally by the administration with regard to taxation, public burdens, access to public services, and so forth (any administrative act that imposes a special and important burden on an individual over and above the general public is regarded as a breach of equality and entitles the individual to damages);
4. *le droit de la différence*—the right of all citizens to have access to their files in the administration and to have an explanation; and
5. nonretroactivity of administrative decisions.

The grounds for review are the following:

1. *incompétence*—want of authority;
2. *vice de forme*—procedural ultra vires;
3. *violation de la loi*—the basis of the examination of the actual content of the administrative act to determine whether it conforms with the legal conditions for administrative action in the particular case; and
4. *détournement de pouvoir*—abuse of power.

The *droit administratif* provides two principal remedies. The first is the *recours en annulation*, that is, proceedings to quash an administrative decision on the ground of violating the principle of legality. The second remedy is *recours indemnité*. This proceeding involves recourse to the full jurisdiction of the court to indemnify an aggrieved citizen on the ground of the principle of administrative liability. These two proceedings are not exclusive of one another and may therefore be combined together.

The main difference between the two forms of remedies is that the locus standi required for the former is much wider and more liberal, whereas only the party to the contract or the victim of the tort can sue for an indemnity. Also, the decision of the court in proceedings to quash is valid with respect to all persons whereas in proceedings for indemnity the decision takes effect only as between the parties.

VI. INTERNATIONAL OBLIGATIONS

Article 78 of the Constitution provides that responsibility for foreign affairs lies on the French community—that is, the French state. The state's monopoly of power in this area is reinforced by Article 8 of the Territorial Statute, which places matters relating to external affairs, financial relations with foreign countries, and international trade within the exclusive competence of the state. The territory of New Caledonia and other Overseas Territories therefore have no international personality and cannot enter into any legally binding international negotiations or treaties with a foreign country. Indeed, French sovereignty over its Overseas Territories is regarded as a fundamental principle of law. The territories, ipso facto, become members of all the international bodies that France accedes to, including the European Community. New Caledonia does not, however, consider itself bound by the Treaty of Rome.

Subject to the above restrictions, the Territorial Congress and the Provincial Assemblies have the right under Article 88 of the Territorial Statute to propose to the French government to enter into international negotiations with any state or territory within the Pacific on matters of interest to the territory. During such negotiations, one representative of the Territorial Congress or the Provincial Assemblies may be allowed to participate in the debates. Similarly, when issues of international aviation or maritime relations are the subject of an international agreement whose objective is to provide services to New Caledonia, representatives of the Territorial Congress or the Provincial Assemblies may participate in the negotiations.

A special concession is made with regard to agreements with Pacific regional organizations and the United Nations and its specialized agencies. In such cases, in addition to the state representative, the President of the Territorial Congress may be authorized to participate in the negotiations as the representative of the territory if the subject of the agreement falls within the competence of the territory or the provinces. Where the agreement is with an international body within the South Pacific (for example, the South Pacific Commission, of which New

Caledonia is member), the concessions are even greater. In such a case, the state may entrust the presidents of the Territorial Congress and the Provincial Assemblies with the power to negotiate on behalf of the state provided the subject of the agreement is within the competence of the territory or the provinces. Any agreement negotiated by them is, however, subject to ratification by the French President or Parliament.

Extradition is governed by the European Convention on Human Rights, which was made applicable to the Overseas Territories of France by the Act of 27 June 1983. However, the Act of 31 December 1973 makes reservations on the application of Protocols No. 1 and 4 as well as some provisions of Protocol No. 7 to the Overseas Territories in order to guarantee the sovereignty of the state. The 1983 act sets the conditions, procedures, and effects of extradition.

VII. Revenue Law

The main source of revenue is taxation, a matter within the competence of the Territorial Congress. The existing laws on taxation are, however, inspired by French laws and derived from various legislations of the French Parliament. Currently, the following forms of taxation are applicable in the territory: income tax, real estate tax, customs duty on imports and exports, land tax, business tax (on patents), entertainment tax (on games and gambling), mining tax, and special tax on drivers.

An agreement between the French government and New Caledonia enables all French citizens to pay taxes where they live and not at the source of their income.

Apart from taxes, the territory also derives a substantial amount of revenue from aid from the French government. The various forms of aid are development aid, investment and operating expenditure grants, subventions for judicial and administrative functionaries, and educational grants. These are regulated by specific legislation of the French Parliament and the budget provisions of the Territorial Statute.

VIII. Investment Law

The regulation and control of foreign investment in New Caledonia falls within the exclusive competence of the state. Consequently, the territory cannot enter into international trade agreements except in cases of direct foreign investment projects below the value of 80 million CFPF. The state exercises its authority in this area through special bills that provide aid and spell out the conditions for investment. These bills control investment activity for only a specified period of time. A new bill to implement the economic reforms proclaimed by the current Territorial Statute is yet to be passed.

New Caledonia offers an open-door policy toward direct foreign investment projects. Except for French citizens (who, of course, are not considered foreigners), all foreigners including those from European Community countries are treated equally. It is a requirement for all foreigners who wish to establish any kind of business in New Caledonia to have a certain minimum capital—the amount of which varies with the type of company—and to obtain a residence permit and an authorization from the local administration. In addition, all companies must be registered with the Registre du Commerce et des Sociétés in Noumea. The particular form of the company and the rules governing such a company are provided in the French Code of Commerce, which is applicable to New Caledonia as well (see **XIII, A Business Associations, Chapter 22**).

Foreign investments are divided into the following two categories:

1. those that benefit from the Territorial Development Aid Program, including hotels, transportation relating to tourism, agriculture, forestry, and fisheries; and
2. those that do not enjoy any benefit from the aid program, including commercial activities, restaurants not integrated within tourism, engineering, construction, and services.

The benefits provided by the Aid Program include the following:

1. protection from external competition;
2. state contribution toward social expenditure;
3. temporary subsidy to assist in the recruitment of workers;
4. rebates on licenses, patents, and contracts during the formative years of the enterprise; and
5. various tax concessions.

To qualify for these benefits, the investor must be professionally qualified, possess the necessary management skills and capital, and undertake to recruit local workers and utilize local materials.

The territory operates an import substitution economy. To encourage investment, special tax regulations apply to investments in the following activities: industry, fisheries, hotels, tourism, new forms of energy, agriculture, building and public works, transportation, and crafts. For these enterprises, the total amount of investments and subscriptions made to their share capital may be deductible from their taxes. The only condition for the enjoyment of these tax benefits is that the investment should concern new products and be directly related to the professional operations of the enterprise.

Foreigners can purchase any kind of property (except tribal land); there are neither currency exchange regulations nor limitations on the transfer of profits.

IX. Welfare Law

New Caledonia does not have a comprehensive social security system. Nevertheless, several private organizations provide social security and health care for the people. Among these organizations, the following are notable:

1. Caisse de Compensation des Prestations Familiales, des Accidents du Travail et de Prévoyance des Travailleurs de la Nouvelle Caledonie et Dépendances, an agency that pays family allowances, provides compensation for industrial accidents, and maintains a reserve fund for workers in the private sector and workers in the administratiom other than civil servants;
2. Mutuelle des Fonctionnaires, a mutual insurance agency for civil servants;
3. Mutuelle de Commerce, a mutual insurance agency for people in trade and commerce; and
4. Aide Médicale, an agency that provides medical insurance for people with insufficient income or no income at all.

Generally, most of the inhabitants of the territory have a health insurance policy; it is also possible to contribute to complementary health insurance funds in metropolitan France.

X. LAND AND NATURAL RESOURCES

A. Land Tenure and Administration

The three main systems of land tenure in New Caledonia are these:

1. Public property (public or private domain) which belongs to the territory or the state and is governed by the Civil Code (see **Chapter 22, X Personal Property**;
2. Native reserves, areas of land delimited for the Kanaks and governed by customary law (see **X, B Customary Land Tenure**); and
3. Civil property, land governed by property law as defined in the French Civil Code (see **XV, Chapter 22, X Personal Property**).

The land tenure systems of New Caledonia have been characterized in the past twenty years by the systematic individualization of the land. This has taken various forms, from the repurchase of colonial properties to the development of rental properties with the option to purchase and private land grants. Of equal importance, since it aims toward the same goal, is the individual appropriation of inherited land, a factor considered essential for the integration of the Melanesians into the modern individualistic and capitalist society.

The repurchase of European properties is not a new phenomenon in New Caledonia. As early as 1930 the French colonial administration had authorized the acquisition of land by indigenous people with the same title as by Europeans. This policy, however, remained for a long time unrealized because the Melanesians lacked the capital, credit, and collateral to take advantage of the opportunity.

The policy was nevertheless significant because it opened the way for the first land acquisitions by Melanesians outside the reserves. This right to acquire land was first exercised in 1970 through the extension of credit facilities by the Société Immobilière de Crédit de la Nouvelle Caledonie (a real estate agency/building society) to the Melanesians. A few Melanesians have since acquired land through this process, but the repurchases are still relatively exceptional because of competition from other modes of land acquisition, such as rental with the option to purchase and the grant of free concessions.

Before World War II, only the European planters held estates. Shortly after the War and for the next twenty years, a few Melanesians acquired land sporadically from the Europeans for cattle pasture. These land acquisitions were held as rented estates. From the 1960s the practice developed whereby Europeans holding lands they were not using would rent them to Melanesians living on neighboring reserves.

Initially, the tenancy formula for these rented estates prevented any extensive development by the Melanesians because the Europeans, being loath to tie up their lands through leases, preferred free loans they remained in control of. With the generalization of the practice over the next two decades, the terms and conditions of the contract for the rented estates have partially changed. Today, they tend to be more liberal, allowing for more control by the Melanesians with even the option to purchase. The importance of this process of land acquisition, which far outweighs concessions, is surpassed only by direct appropriation.

Until the 1960s, apart from a few land concessions granted to former servicemen, Melanesians, even those who had adopted the civil status, were excluded from certain rights to land. In 1955, the Mission des Terres (the Sorin Lands Commission) denounced "this aberrant administration of free land concessions to the profit of only one category of citizens" and concluded that the administration of land grants must be extended to the Melanesians as well.

Following the commission's recommendation, in 1959 the first land grants were awarded to

Melanesians who had not been servicemen. Today, Melanesians have the right to solicit a free land grant. Even though the number of urban allotments awarded to them remains modest compared to that made to Europeans, rural Melanesian concessions have increased significantly.

This free grant is given initially under provisional title for five years. The grant is subject to a development program whose execution is a condition for obtaining a definitive title. Normally, a plan for the development program is drawn up by the Agence de Développement Rural et d'Aménagement Foncier (ADRAF), the agency for rural and land development, and it is accompanied by a report on the economic possibilities offered by the concession. These documents serve as the basis for the Lands Commission's guarantee of the project.

To satisfy the conditions for a definitive title, the grantee generally is required to engage in cultivation (subsistence or speculative) of a minimal area or in reforestation or in pastoral improvements such as sowing fodder, clearing, enclosure, and partitioning of pasture. This development program is spaced out over a period of five years, through successive annual steps.

Finally, the accession of the Melanesian planter class to individual property has also been one of the important forms of the systematic individualization of landed property in New Caledonia. In pursuance of the assimilationist policy that aims at making Melanesians citizens like the others, the administration has encouraged conversion projects involving the partition of land within the native reserves with allotments to individuals under individual titles. This conversion of communal property into individual property frees the land of any customary encumbrances and confers on the individual the right to freely dispose of his or her allotment either through outright sale or mortgage.

The introduction of individual interest as an incentive factor is viewed by the Administration as a guarantee for modernization, productivity, and development. At the same time, the acquisition of property under this policy imposes the renunciation or forfeiture of the historical rights of the customary owners over part of their patrimony and creates a new arbitrarily constituted landed aristocracy—a Melanesian planter class.

Young Melanesians, eager to assert their individual existence within the communal society and seeking emancipation from the burdens of the extended family without a total dislocation from the group, have seized this opportunity. This desire for individual appropriation is found particularly among public servants and others in regular employment who have acquired a European-type life-style.

B. Customary Land Tenure

The traditional Melanesian concept of property regards land as sacred, the very foundation of life and society. Its value transcends material wealth and profit. According to this concept, the land belongs to the descendants of its first occupants and is owned communally by the clan.

Since the clan is the landowning unit, the individual's interest in it is based on membership of the clan. The proprietary right of the clan is vested in the clan chief, who exercises control and supervision over the land (not the tribal chief, who wields only political power.) Individual members of the clan have usufructuary rights over land allocated to them and are entitled to the enjoyment of the fruits of their cultivation. Because of the sacred nature of the land, it is inalienable. User rights can be transferred to strangers only with the approval of the clan chief. Such transfers, however, do not constitute a sale nor do they necessarily include the plants on the land, and the transferee is obliged to reciprocate the gesture of the transferor through offerings of gifts.

The Decree of 21 May 1980 gives legal recognition to this concept of *propriété clanique* by declaring that "The land of the clan is the common property of the family groups of which it is composed." The decree also recognizes the clan council as the appropriate body for administering clan property and proclaims customary law as the law regulating clan property.

Although the French government recognizes the Kanaks' right of ownership over occupied lands,[8] it rejects their claim over land not occupied at the inception of the system of native reserves. This has confined the traditional lands of the Kanaks (that is, lands subject to customary law) to lands delimited as reserves. As Article 2 of the Lands Ordinance of 1985 clearly states,

> no customary rights of usage may be recognized over the public domain; urban areas; existing establishments for public works, civil and military, as well as existing establishments necessary for the functioning of the public service; and areas reserved for public works to be established within 5 years.

The reserves have been proclaimed as "inalienable, imprescriptible, and sacrosanct collective property."[9] Their ownership and control are vested in the tribal chief (*grand chef*), who traditionally had no such authority. Individual rights in land include use rights, rights to crops, and rights to leave the land fallow. Furthermore, reserve lands cannot be the object of lease agreements and are protected from all forms of seizure except through a procedure commenced by the customary authorities and expropriation by the state for construction of private dwellings.

The validity of the concept of collective property imposed by the French government under the system of native reserves has never been recognized by the Melanesians who have persistently maintained the inviolability of their traditional system of land tenure.[10] The result of this impasse is a complex situation of contradictory and overlapping concepts of land ownership.

C. Government Taking of Land

The power of expropriation is vested in the state, the territory, and the communes by the Land Reform Act of 12 December 1980. Articles 2 to 5 of this law require the necessary land to be acquired, if possible, by agreement. The criterion for determining land to be expropriated is the special need of the Melanesians in the context of general agrarian reform. This means that the law can be applied to any property, developed or undeveloped, whenever the needs of Melanesians are deemed serious.

Under the law, the Territorial Assembly can issue a declaration of public need and expropriation. Unless challenged, the declaration takes effect and the expropriated land is allocated under either civil or customary law, as determined by the Territorial Assembly. The law limits the extent of any single property expropriated to 50 percent of the affected property. Whenever the declaration of public need and expropriation is challenged, the issue is referred to a commission of inquiry consisting of a presiding magistrate and representatives of the state, the territory, the commune, the Melanesian authorities, and rural proprietors and farmers. If the commission's recommendation is affirmative, the declaration is then promulgated by the High Commissioner. Any expropriated land not used within three years for the purposes defined in the act may be returned to the former owner on application to the High Commissioner.

The High Commissioner also has the power to declare any estate abandoned or uncultivated. The owner of such an estate is then given a period of time within which to develop the land or lose it to the state.

The act provides for the payment of compensation to the proprietors of expropriated land and also allows the payment of pensions to farmers of fifty years or more who voluntarily cede their land to the state in furtherance of the land reform program. In the case of voluntary ceding of land, the territory has the right of preemption for three months. After the expiration of this period, if the territory and the proprietor fail to agree on the price of the land, the issue is referred to the Court of First Instance for judicial determination.

D. Fisheries

Fishing is a matter within the competence of the state. Decree No. 67-451 of June 7, 1967, which extends the territorial fishing zone of New Caledonia and Wallis and Futuna, prohibits foreign boats from fishing within the 12-mile limit of the territorial waters of these territories without special permission from the French authorities. Once a fishing agreement with France is obtained, the territory may enter into direct negotiations (if the value of the fishing concession is below 70 million CFPF) and may issue fishing licenses subject to the agreement.

New Caledonia and Wallis and Futuna have a fishing agreement with Japan (the France-Japan Fishing Agreement of 1991) that permits Japanese industrial fishing boats to fish in the exclusive 188-mile economic zone of their territories. This agreement (worth 36 million CFPF) was negotiated directly by the territories.

XI. Legal Education and Profession

All the lawyers and judges in New Caledonia are trained in the French system of legal education. To qualify as an advocate (*avocat*), requires a university degree (*maîtrise*) in law, which corresponds to an LL.B. degree. The degree course takes four years of study. After the first two years, the candidate is awarded the Diploma of General Studies (D.E.U.G.) that, since the establishment of the French University of the South Pacific in Noumea and Papeete in 1987, can be obtained in New Caledonia or French Polynesia. At the end of the third year, the student obtains a license in law, followed in the fourth year by the degree. The last two years of the degree program are available only in metropolitan France. In addition to the degree, the student is required to have a Certificate of Aptitude to the Profession of Advocate (C.A.P.A.), which is awarded on the basis of a special examination after a compulsory one-year preparation. The candidate is then admitted as an apprentice advocate and becomes a full advocate after three to five years of apprenticeship.

Magistrates or judges follow a similar course of training. After obtaining the *maîtrise* in law, the student is qualified to take a competitive examination for the National Magistracy School. Upon admission, the student attains the status of a law clerk and from then on is part of the magistrature. At the end of three years of study, the law clerk takes another examination and then becomes a full-fledged magistrate.

There are twenty advocates practicing in Noumea, all of whom are either from metropolitan France or of European origin. Of the sixteen judges, only one is Melanesian.

XII. Customary Law

A. Status of Customary Law

At the basis of customary law is the tribe, which is recognized by a prefectoral decision of 29 December 1867. At present there are 336 tribes; each consists of related clans grouped together into 58 districts. The tribes are represented by a chief designated by the council of elders and called the *grand chef*. Each district belongs to one of the eight *pays* (counties) or customary zones.

Since 1866 when the French Civil Code was made applicable to New Caledonia, the Kanaks have been exempted from Code provisions relating to personal status. As a result of this exemption, the personal status of almost all the Melanesian population is regulated by the law of particular civil status—that is, customary law. This exemption is based upon the Kanak's right to be different, a principle affirmed by the 1946 Constitution and reproduced in Article 75 of the 1958 Constitution. These constitutional provisions state that citizens of the Republic who do not have common law civil status (status governed by the French civil law) shall retain their personal status (customary law status) as long as they do not renounce it.

In spite of this constitutional guarantee of the Kanak's right to be different and the fact that about 70,000 Melanesians have the particular or special civil status (which means that their personal status is regulated by customary law), customary law has not been elevated to the level of a primary source of law, nor has there been an express recognition or official documentation of it. In the courts, the only legal basis for its application is inferred from Ordinance No. 82-877 of 1982, which established the customary assessors of the Court of First Instance and the Court of Appeal in Noumea. Under this ordinance, the proof of customary law is subject to declaration by customary assessors.

As a result of the above situation, customary law remains essentially an unwritten law with no precise institutionalization of its organs, structures, and procedures. Knowledge about it, apart from oral accounts from Melanesian elders, inevitably is based on fragmented information provided by sociologists, legal anthropologists, and a few legal texts. Customary rules are thus not only variable and blurred but tend to disappear, leaving more space to civil law (**see also X, B Customary Land Tenure**).

B. Application of Customary Law

The application of customary law in New Caledonia is permitted only to the extent warranted by the particular civil status. This status is granted only to Melanesians who are born in New Caledonia. Its application implies that Kanak customary law is substituted for French civil law in the areas of family law, traditional land tenure, and succession. Also, persons of particular civil status are exempted from military service abroad. Below is a brief account of the applicable rules and established practices of Kanak customary law.

C. Family Law

The family is recognized as an important unit of social organization. Although its legal status has been reduced today to that of an accessory to other forms of collective authority such as the clan and the tribe, family ties with either the uterine uncle or the eldest brother are still of considerable importance, especially in succession cases.

Article 40 of the Territorial Resolution of 3 April 1967 provides that marriages of citizens of particular civil status are to be governed by customary law. Such marriages must be confirmed within thirty days by the mayor of the commune. A mixed marriage, however, produces civil law effects and carries with it a partial renunciation of status by the spouse with the particular civil law status.

Divorce proceedings can only be initiated by the husband, and the clans of the spouses have exclusive jurisdiction in divorce cases.

Adoption is also governed by customary law; its basic requirement is the consent of the families concerned.

D. Succession

The preamble of Resolution No. 11 of 20 June 1962 authorizes the distribution of property of deceased citizens with particular civil status to be regulated by customary law. Because the family structure of the Melanesians is matrilineal, succession under Kanak customary law is established principally through the maternal uncle rather than the father. The only exception to this rule, according to the Territorial Assembly Resolution of 8 September 1980, is with regard to real property acquired in conformity with the civil law; these may be subject to patrilineal succession.

The procedure for succession under customary law requires that, after the death of a person with particular civil status, anyone who has an interest in the matter may apply to the appropriate administrative department (the Territorial Service of the General Administration) for authority to hold a family or clan meeting to discuss the distribution of the deceased's property. A record of the discussion, which may be challenged within thirty days, is drawn up by the officer of Melanesian affairs, setting out the wishes of the family, clan, or council of elders. After the thirty-day period, a certificate of inheritance or a certificate of title is drawn up by the Territorial Service of the General Administration, which designates the person or persons (persons of civil law status may be included) entitled to inherit and the property involved.

E. Registration of Particular Civil Status

The civil status of persons of particular civil status is administered by the Office of Melanesian Affairs, which controls the registry of all births, deaths, marriages, divorces, and adoptions of such persons. The option exists for all Melanesians who have attained the age of eighteen years to renounce their particular civil law status in favor of the civil law status. However, if this option is exercised, the resulting civil law status becomes irrevocable and hereditary.

F. Conflict of Laws

The applicable law in a matter involving persons of different civil status is determined as follows:

1. in a dispute between two persons of civil law status, the civil law alone applies;
2. in a dispute between two persons with different civil status, the civil law takes precedence and therefore applies exclusively; and
3. in a dispute between two persons of particular civil status, the dispute can be resolved by the customary authorities without resort to the civil law courts.

XII. Research Guide

Cornell, J. *New Caledonia or Independent Kanaky? The Political History of a French Colony.* Canberra: Australian National University, 1986.

Crabb, J., and J. A. Sigler. "France: French Overseas Territories: New Caledonia," in A. P. Blaustein and P. M. Blaustein, eds. *Constitutions of Dependencies and Special Sovereignties.* Dobbs Ferry, N.Y.: Oceana, 1989.

Crocombe, R. G., ed. *Land Tenure in the Pacific*. Suva: University of the South Pacific, 1987.
Dornoy, M. *Politics in New Caledonia*. Sydney: Sydney University Press, 1984.
"New Caledonia." *Taxes and Investments in Asia and the Pacific*. Amsterdam: International Bureau of Fiscal Documentation, 1985.
Saussol, A. *L'Heritage*. Paris: Société des Oceanistes, 1979.
Ward, A. W. *Land and Politics in New Caledonia*. Canberra: Australian National University, 1982.

22. Wallis and Futuna

MICHAEL A. NTUMY

I. Dateline

300 A.D.	Possible settlement of Uvea (Wallis) and Futuna by Polynesians from Tonga and Samoa.
1616	Dutch navigators Lemaire and Schouten sail to Futuna.
1767	British navigator Samuel Wallis sails to Wallis archipelago.
1837	The Roman Catholic Society of Mary arrives on the islands.
1842	King of Wallis requests French protection, which is granted in principle.
1870	Constitution adopted and Roman Catholic bishop appointed adviser to monarch.
1886	Treaty between France and islands establishes French Resident with seat on Council of Ministers.
1887	Treaty formally ratified.
1888	Futuna becomes French protectorate.
1909	French administration formalized.
1910	French Resident persuades the King to sign an order expelling head of Catholic mission. The order, which leads to political uproar, is revoked.
1913	King of Wallis requests that kingdom be attached to France.
1933	French judicial system established on Wallis and Futuna.
1959	Following a referendum, status of territory changed from protectorate to Overseas Territory.
1961	Status of Overseas Territory formally conferred on islands.

II. Historical, Cultural, and Economic Survey

Wallis and Futuna islands are two separate archipelagoes in the Pacific Ocean. Wallis is 200 kilometers northeast of Futuna. The main island of Wallis, Uvea (not to be confused with the island of the same name in the Loyalty Islands), is surrounded by about twenty islets. The main town of the island, Mata-Utu, is also the administrative center of the territory. It is 16,065 kilometers from metropolitan France. The Futuna archipelago (not to be confused with the island of the same name in Vanuatu) is situated at 179 degrees east longitude and 14 degrees 20 minutes south latitude, north of the Fiji Islands. It consists of Futuna itself and Alofi, which together form the Horn islands. The two islands have an estimated population of 13,000 people of Polynesian descent. The main town of Futuna is Sigave.

Uvea and Futuna are relatively close to Tonga and Samoa, and archaeological evidence suggests the earliest settlers of Uvea and Futuna were from those centers of Polynesian culture. The first European contact with Futuna was recorded in 1616 by the Dutch navigators Lemaire and Schouten, while Wallis became known to the Western world in 1767 through the efforts of the British navigator Samuel Wallis, after whom the island was named.

Long before European contact, these islands had a well-developed sociopolitical system based on tradition. However, as elsewhere in the Pacific, following the first European contacts, Wallis and Futuna islands became the target of Christian evangelizing missions and imperialism in the nineteenth century. In 1837, the Roman Catholic Society of Mary landed on the islands and founded a theocracy based on customary kingdoms. Under this new arrangement, a Roman Catholic bishop was appointed the King's adviser.

Following the evangelization of the islands, the French king, Louis Philippe, moved in to give French support to the kings of the islands. A formal treaty was signed between France and the islands on November 19, 1886, stipulating that a French Resident be appointed on the islands with a seat on the Council of Ministers. Under the terms of the treaty, the French Resident was to be a Roman Catholic father or assisted by a father as an interpreter in his dealings with the King. The treaty was formally ratified in 1887, the year Wallis became a French protectorate. Protectorate status was conferred on Futuna in 1888. By an order of June 1909, French administration was established on the islands, and in 1910 the 1886 treaty was revised to ensure that only the French government could appoint the French Resident, who could not be a member of the Catholic mission. In June 1913, the kingdom of Wallis, at the King's request, was attached to France.

Notwithstanding the various political vicissitudes of European contact, the traditional socio-political system survives today. In fact, the present internal administrative organization of the territory integrates the customary kingdoms into the institutional framework imposed by the French administration.

In 1959, the people voted in a referendum for the status of Overseas Territory of the French Republic. This decision was formalized by the Act of 29 July 1961, which has since remained the Territorial Statute of the territory.

Since Wallis and Futuna came under French control, the islands have never had the economic resources necessary for independent development. Most of the islands' population is engaged in subsistence farming and fishing. For this reason, until 1959, when Wallis and Futuna attained autonomy under the status of an Overseas Territory, they were placed under the charge of a Resident Administrator responsible to the Governor of New Caledonia. The administrative link engendered by this historical event persists today and plays a dominant role in the administrative and judicial organization of the territory. Most of the cost of the islands' government is paid for by French subventions.

This link—in addition to the fact that all Overseas Territories of France are subject to the laws of France, have the same legal attributes, and operate under a uniform constitutional system—make the legal system of Wallis and Futuna virtually identical to that of New Caledonia. The only differences relate to the organization of Wallis and Futuna as provided by its Territorial Statute.

Because the general principles of public law described in **Chapter 21, New Caledonia**, are applicable to Wallis and Futuna as well, the following account of the legal system of Wallis and Futuna only highlights the minor details of public law that are peculiar to the territory. Private law principles applicable to Wallis and Fortuna as well as New Caledonia are discussed fully in this chapter.

III. SOURCES OF LAW

The sources of law of Wallis and Futuna correspond exactly to those of New Caledonia. However, in order to clarify the pre-autonomy laws that are still applicable to the territory, the Territorial Statute specifically lists the sources of law. According to Clause 4 of the statute, the following are the applicable laws of the territory:

1. laws of the French Republic as well as decrees and ministerial orders expressly declared to be applicable to Overseas Territories or to Wallis and Futuna in particular;
2. rulings of the High Commissioner and the chief administrator of the territory;
3. rulings of the High Commissioner or the French Resident Commissioner in Wallis and the delegate in Futuna before local promulgation of the Territorial Statute; and
4. laws and statutes relating to New Caledonia (with the exception of those relating to the particular organization of the territory) that were in force in that territory at the time of local promulgation of the Territorial Statute and that have been extended by decree to Wallis and Futuna.

IV. Constitutional System

A. Nationality and Citizenship

Clause 2 of the Territorial Statute proclaims that all Wallisians are of French nationality and confers on them the rights, prerogatives, and freedoms, as well as the obligations of citizenship.

B. Government

1. NATIONAL/TERRITORIAL GOVERNMENT

    a. Executive

Clause 9 of the Territorial Statute confers the executive power of the territory on the Chief Administrator, who functions as head of the territory and representative of the French government. The Chief Administrator is entrusted with the power to take all statutory measures necessary to ensure the execution of the Territorial Assembly's deliberations and all prescribed or statutory actions arising from the position of head of the territory. The Chief Administrator's decisions must be based on the advice of the Territorial Council and must be within the terms prescribed by laws, decrees, and regulations.

The Chief Administrator has charge of the territorial budget and publication of the Territorial Assembly's resolutions, represents the territory in judicial and civil matters, and can enforce the Territorial Assembly's resolutions by decree.

Any infringements of the head of the territory's decrees can be sanctioned by the courts according to a scale of penalties set up by the High Commissioner for the Republic in the Pacific. These penalties, however, cannot exceed the maximum laid down for ordinary police penalties.

    b. Legislature

Following the French pattern of administering the Overseas Territories, Clause 7 of the Territorial Statute lists a number of areas in which the state has exclusive competence. These areas are defense, public order and security, respect for law, rulings and decisions of the courts, external relations and communications, education, civil status, treasury, customs, administrative and financial control, and justice. Since the French Parliament's laws have general applicability for the territory, under Clause 1 of the Territorial Statute the territory is represented in both houses of the French Parliament. In the National Assembly it is represented by a deputy, while a senator represents it in the Senate. Both representatives are elected by French citizens in Wallis and Futuna and have full voting power.

Subject to the state's powers of general control, Clause 7 of the Territorial Statute provides for the establishment of three Territorial Constituencies, the head of territory, the Territorial Council, and the Territorial Assembly and its Permanent Commission. These are the territorial institutions responsible for the internal administration of the territory. In their various capacities, they participate in the law-making function.

(i) Powers of the Territorial Assembly

The Territorial Assembly is composed of twenty members elected by universal suffrage for five years. The rules relating to their election and mode of functioning, as well as the jurisdiction of the Territorial Assembly, are determined by various laws of the Republic.

The Assembly is an advisory body whose main function is to provide advice on fiscal and penal sanctions on matters referred to it.

(ii) Powers of the Permanent Commission

A Permanent Commission of four members is appointed from the ranks of the Assembly in such a way as to be representative of the territory and its constituencies. It performs some of the functions of the Territorial Assembly. This commission can meet at any time of the year in the capital of the territory but can only deliberate on matters referred to it by the Territorial Assembly. In times of emergency, the commission has the power to make decisions and issue notices in all matters within the competence of the Territorial Assembly that are referred to it by the head of the territory on the advice of the Territorial Council.

(iii) Powers of the Territorial Council

Clause 10 of the Territorial Statute institutes a Territorial Council whose main function is to examine all proposals of law to be submitted to the Territorial Assembly. In addition, the council assists the head of the territory in administration of the territory.

The council is made up of the head of the territory as president of the council, the three traditional chiefs or their deputies, and three members nominated by the chief administrator with approval of the Territorial Assembly.

(iv) Powers of the Territorial Constituencies

The Territorial Constituencies acquire legal personality by virtue of Clause 18 of the Territorial Statute, which confers on them the power to operate their own budgets. Their organization is subject to the orders of the Chief Administrator, acting on the advice of the Territorial Assembly, and their substantive powers are determined by the Territorial Council within the limits prescribed by laws and decrees. The Chief Administrator functions as head of the constituency in Wallis while the delegate of the Chief Administrator heads the constituencies in Futuna.

The heads of the constituencies are responsible for the constituencies' budgets. In addition, they have statutory power to represent their constituencies in civil matters.

Each constituency has a council whose members are elected according to custom. The number of members in the constituency council is determined by an order of the Chief Administrator. The president of this council, who must be one of the vice presidents of the Territorial Council in the constituency, represents the constituency in legal matters.

c. Judiciary

The Courts of First Instance have jurisdiction in all civil and less serious criminal cases, as well as matters arising out of customary law. They sit with a panel of one judge and two lay assessors whose expertise in custom is invaluable in customary law cases. All the decisions of these courts are collegial. More serious criminal cases are heard by the Court of Assizes, which sits with a judge and jury. In cases where the resident judge is unable to preside because the judge has acted as the *juge d'instruction* at the investigatory stage of the proceedings, a different judge is sent from Noumea to complete the trial. Noumea barristers also visit occasionally to represent parties in serious criminal cases.

All appeals from these courts lie to the Court of Appeal in Noumea.

2. PROVINCIAL/LOCAL GOVERNMENT

Clause 7 of the Territorial Statute divides the territory into three territorial constituencies, Uvea, Alo, and Sigave. These divisions at the local government level correspond to the kingdoms of the territory.

The island of Wallis is organized as a kingdom with a Lavelu (King), who is assisted by a Kivalu (Prime Minister) and five ministers. This kingdom is divided into three districts, each of which is under the control of a Faiopule (district chief). The districts are further divided into nineteen villages with a pule (village chief) at the head of each village. Futuna is divided into two kingdoms: Sigave and Alo, the latter also covering the island of Alofi. Each kingdom is governed by a King (Tuiaigaifo in Alo and Tuisigave in Sigave), assisted by five ministers and village chiefs.

C. Human Rights

Clause 3 of the Territorial Statute provides that the French Republic guarantees the people of Wallis and Futuna religious freedom as well as respect for their beliefs and customs insofar as they are not contrary to the general principles of law or to the provisions of this law. Under Clause 2 of the statute, those who have not expressly renounced their particular civil status are allowed to retain it.

V. PRIVATE LAW

The principles of private law described here are generally applicable to all French citizens in the Overseas Territories except with regard to specific derogations made in the interest of those who retain their particular civil status (**see Chapter 21, XII, A Status of Customary Law**, for an explanation of particular civil status).

The major branches of private law are civil law (which in French law is only one branch of private law), criminal law, commercial law, labor law, and industrial and intellectual property law. The French concept of civil law comprises the following areas of law regulated by the French Civil Code of 1804:

1. the law of persons;
2. family law (domestic relations and matrimonial property relations);
3. property law;
4. the law of obligations (contracts and torts);
5. the law of succession;
6. some rules of private international law;
7. formalities of promulgation and publication of status;

8. regulations affecting civil registers; and
9. numerous aspects of the law of evidence and judicial procedure.

VI. Criminal Law

The source of criminal law in Wallis and Futuna and all the French Overseas Territories is the French Penal Code of 1811. Under the code, penal offenses (infractions) are classified as crimes, *délits*, and contraventions. Each of these classifications corresponds to the severity of the penalty attached to it. Crimes are serious infractions punishable by imprisonment of over five years; these correspond to felonies. *Délits* and contraventions are essentially misdemeanors and petty offenses respectively.

VII. Judicial Procedure

A. Civil Procedure

The basic source of law on civil procedure in Wallis and Futuna and all the French Overseas Territories is the Code of Civil Procedure of 1806. The code requires that judicial proceedings be public. A civil case starts with a preliminary hearing in which the issues of security for costs, jurisdiction, and other dilatory pleas are decided by interlocutory judgment. The facts of the case are then developed by a prehearing judge (*juge des mises en état*), who prepares the case and issues an *ordonnance de cloture* terminating the first stage. Then a *juge rapporteur* consolidates the case for hearing.

The trial consists of a series of motions, pleadings, and incidental hearings during which the judge plays an active role in questioning witnesses and framing or reformulating the issues. Proof by witnesses plays a minor role, and the police report usually forms part of the dossier produced at the end of the case. A judgment on the merit of the case is generally executed out of the defeated party's property.

Because there are few legal personnel in the territory, disputes are often resolved through an informal mediation process. The resulting agreement reached with the parties is then validated by a court order. On appellate review, since the dossier is the record, the appeal does not involve any new consideration of facts or law. The procedure in the Court of Appeal is basically the same as that before the Courts of First Instance, including the power to order additional proof before rendering judgment. Ultimate review in the Court of Cassation (*Cour de Cassation*) is available only in metropolitan France and is limited to issues of law only.

B. Criminal Procedure

The procedure for criminal trials is laid down in the Code of Criminal Procedure of 1811. This Code provides a different court and procedure for each class of offenses.

The first phase of the criminal proceeding is an extensive pretrial investigation conducted by the *juge d'instruction*. This official decides whether there is sufficient evidence to warrant formal charges after interrogating witnesses, collecting other evidence, and questioning the suspect. The accused has the right to be represented by counsel during the interrogation and the right to remain silent.

If the examining magistrate determines that there is reasonable cause, a judicial warrant is issued for the arrest and confinement of the suspect, and the dossier compiled during the preliminary investigation is forwarded to the criminal court. Except in cases of crimes or *délits flagrants*, no police officer may arrest, search, or seize on his own authority. Release on bail is subject to the discretion of the *juge d'instruction*. In French law, penal and civil fault merge to a greater extent. For example, simple negligence is regarded as a penal offense. Consequently, provision is made for a private party who has suffered from the injury or loss resulting directly from the infraction to constitute himself into a civil party in the penal action.

The trial begins with the interrogation of the accused based on the criminal complaint or indictment and the dossier. The decision on both guilt and sentence is collegial and reached by secret ballot after joint consultation.

Convictions for crimes in the Court of Assizes are reviewable only by the Court of Cassation in metropolitan France and then only for errors of law. The Court of Appeal in France hears appeals from the Police Court for contraventions and from the Summary Court for *délits* can make new findings of fact and law, and can reverse any acquittal by the lower courts.

VIII. PERSONS AND ENTITIES

Persons can be natural persons and juristic or moral persons. Natural persons are normal persons enjoying unrestricted legal capacity or persons under incapacity (*les incapables*). All persons of either sex who have reached the age of eighteen and are of sound mind have unrestricted legal capacity. Persons under incapacity are minors and the mentally incompetent. The moral persons recognized by French law are classified into three categories:

1. moral persons of public law, for example, the state, territorial units, provinces, communes, and professional organizations;
2. moral persons of a mixed public and private character, for example, nationalized banks and railways that are essentially public but treated as private and committees of enterprises that are essentially private but treated as public; and
3. moral persons of private law, for example, commercial and civil companies, trade unions, and friendly societies and associations.

The capacity of moral persons is determined by specific laws.

IX. FAMILY LAW

Family law, as understood in common law legal systems, combines what in French law are two different branches of civil law, namely, the law of domestic relations and the law of matrimonial property relations. Only the principles of the former, which more closely approximate the common law notion of family law, are described here (**see Chapter 21, XII, D Succession**).

A. Marriage

The legal conditions of marriage under the civil law require that the bridegroom be not less than eighteen years of age and the bride not less than fifteen years. Both parties must not be within the prohibited degrees of relationship, and in the case of persons under eighteen years of age, the law requires parental consent. Notice of every contemplated marriage must be posted on the door of the town hall of the commune where the marriage is to be celebrated and of the domicile or residence of each party for at least ten days before the marriage ceremony. At the same time, each party must submit a medical certificate indicating that he or she has been medically examined with a view to marriage.

The law recognizes the following reciprocal duties between the spouses as the effects of marriage:

1. fidelity;
2. responsibility for the family;
3. support;
4. assistance; and
5. cohabitation, which includes the recognition of conjugal rights.

B. Divorce, Separation, and Annulment

Divorce is permitted on any of the following grounds:

1. the adultery of either party (on equal terms);
2. the condemnation of either spouse to a death penalty or long-term imprisonment;
3. physical violence or moral cruelty, if either constitutes a grave or renewed violation of the obligations resulting from the marriage and makes the maintenance of the conjugal bond intolerable; or
4. mutual agreement.

The annulment of marriages is rare but may arise from the following circumstances:

1. lack of parental consent, in the case of persons marrying before the ages of eighteen (or fifteen);
2. defects in the consent of the spouses themselves, due to mistake or duress;
3. where one or both parties is below the age of consent;
4. where the parties are within the prohibited degrees of relationship; or
5. where the marriage is bigamous.

C. Custody

The parentage of a legitimate child is proved by the act of his birth. An illegitimate child may be legitimated by the subsequent marriage of his parents. However, the affiliation of an illegitimate child, whether to his or her father or mother, can only be established by the parent's recognition, recorded in an authentic document, or by judicial decree given at the suit of the child. Once the illegitimate filiation is established, parental authority is governed by the same rules as in the case of legitimate children. This means that the mutual obligations of support that exist between natural children and their parents and the mutual rights of intestate succession of natural children and their parents apply. The child subsequently takes the surname of that parent whose parenthood is first established.

D. Adoption

Adoption is permitted under conditions laid down by law and is made by an order from the civil division of the Court of Appeal.

X. Personal Property

Property, or bien, is something that is appropriated and has an owner. Biens are classified as either movable or immovable. The main principle with regard to movable property is that possession creates a presumption of ownership. Immovables are further classified as immovables by nature, by destination, or by the object to which they apply. Immovables that have no other owner belong to the state and are thus public property. Public property may be either public domain, which is characterized by the fact that things included in that category are inalienable and imprescriptible, or private domain, which comprises all state property not possessing this special character.

French law recognizes the following rights in rem: ownership, usufruct (usage and habitation), servitudes, and hypothecs. A fundamental principle of French property law is the unity of ownership: there can be no distinction between legal and equitable ownership. Ownership confers the right to enjoy and dispose of things in the most absolute way, provided that no use is made of them that is prohibited by law. Consequently, prescription does not merely extinguish adverse titles but confers a positive title on the person prescribing.

The principal ways in which property may be acquired are

1. contract inter vivos;
2. inheritance, *intestat* or by will;
3. prescription;
4. judgment, as in proceedings for execution; and
5. operation by law.

All interests in immovable property are subject to a system of registration of deeds under which the public register records only conveyances and makes no pretense of guaranteeing the title of the grantor.

XI. Wills and Succession

Succession may be either by operation of law when the deceased person dies intestate (*succession intestat*) or by the will, expressed in legal form, of the deceased (*succession testamentaire*).

The devolution of the succession on intestacy depends upon kindred or blood relationship in either the direct or collateral line. The order in which the succession devolves (provided that they succeed, do not renounce the succession, and are not excluded as unworthy) is as follows:

1. descendants;
2. privileged ascendants and privileged collaterals;
3. ordinary ascendants;
4. the surviving spouse;
5. ordinary collaterals; and
6. the state.

A testamentary succession occurs whenever the deceased has made a valid disposition by will of all or part of his estate. The code defines a will as a revocable instrument by which the testator disposes, for the time when he will no longer be living, of the whole or a part of his estate. A will remains revocable during the lifetime of the testator and may be revoked either expressly or tacitly.

The will must be made in one of the forms prescribed by law, all of which involve writing.

An oral will is therefore a nullity. The will of only one person at a time must be expressed in a prescribed form, as French law does not recognize joint wills. The prescribed forms of the will are

1. holograph will, the simplest and most commonly used, written entirely by the hand of the testator, dated, and signed;
2. authentic will, a will made in the presence of a notary and two witnesses, all of whom must sign the will after the testator has done so;
3. mystic will, a secret will written privately by the testator and presented in a sealed envelope to a notary and two witnesses, all of whom must sign an endorsement by the notary that the envelope contains the last will of the testator; and
4. privileged will, in which, because of special circumstances, the ordinary rules, or some of them, are relaxed.

To have testamentary capacity, the testator must have reached the age of majority; be of sound mind; and not be the victim of force, fraud, or undue influence. A person condemned to penal servitude for life loses testamentary capacity, and any existing will is revoked. A married woman has full testamentary capacity.

XII. CONTRACTS

Contracts of private law are governed by the French Civil Code. The code defines a contract of private law as an agreement by which one or several persons bind themselves, in favor of one or several persons, to give, to do, or not to do something. The expression *to give* connotes the transfer of property and therefore implies that the parties have the necessary capacity and also that they intend to create legal obligations. Two types of contracts of private law may be distinguished: a civil contract and a commercial contract, in which one of the parties must be a merchant and goods must be bought for resale or hire (see **Chapter 21, V, D Rule Making** for a discussion that distinguishes contracts of private and public law).

A contractual obligation is valid only if there is an offer and acceptance, agreement on the object (which must be determined or determinable), and agreement on the cause (motivating reason, purpose, or end) of the obligation. The cause must be legal.

Contracts are classified into the following categories:

1. Synallagmatic (bilateral) contracts and unilateral contracts. A synallagmatic contract creates reciprocal obligations, each party having both rights and obligations, as in contract of sale.
2. Gratuitous and onerous contracts. This distinction is based on the purposes pursued by the parties. Gratuitous contracts confer the advantage with the intention of obtaining no such advantage; that is, they have an *intention libérale*.
3. Commutative and aleatory contracts. This is a distinction within the category of onerous contracts. A contract is commutative when the extent of the presentations owed to each of the parties is immediately apparent; it is aleatory when the extent of one party's performance depends on some future uncertain event while the other party's performance does not vary correspondingly.
4. Nominate and innominate contracts. Nominate contracts have specific names in the Code, while innominate contracts are the result of the theory of the autonomy of the will.

5. Consensual, formal, and real contracts. The general rule is that all contracts in French law are consensual. No writing is required to constitute a valid contract, with the exception of the following cases known as *contrats solennels*, which must be expressed in notarial instrument: donations, marriage contracts, hypothecs, subrogation to wife's hypothecs, subrogation to the right of a creditor with the consent of the debtor, and the assignment in whole or in part of a patent.

The standard remedy for a breach of a contractual obligation is an action for damages permitting the creditor to obtain a sum of money as an equivalent satisfaction. Specific performance is not always available, but the creditor may also be able to have the contract rescinded. Such rescission may be either with or without a claim for damages.

XIII. Commercial Law

Commercial law in Wallis and Futuna and all the Overseas Territories is governed by the French Code of Commerce of 1807 as supplemented by the Civil Code.

A. Business Associations

Business associations are classified as either *société* (commercial company) or *association* (civil company). The former, which can only be the result of a *contrat de société* (company and partnership), is defined by the Civil Code as an agreement between two or more persons to constitute a common stock with a view to sharing the resultant profit. The latter arises from a contract to combine for some purpose other than profit, such as the promotion of charity or the organization of a social club. Whereas the *société* is endowed with full legal personality, the *association* has only some attributes of a legal person depending on whether or not it has been recognized by ministerial decree as an *association d'utilité publique*. The general principles of the law of contract, as set out in the Civil Code, apply equally to commercial contracts and civil contracts. Civil and commercial companies are, however, treated differently for tax purposes. Commercial companies are subject to the commercial law and the jurisdiction of the commercial courts while the civil companies are not. Commercial companies alone are bound by the general obligations of merchants and, like them, are liable to be made bankrupt. They must also comply with the rules of publicity.

French law recognizes these five types of commercial company:

1. *société en nom collectif* (partnership);
2. *société en commandite simple* (limited partnership);
3. *société à responsabilité limitée* (private limited company);
4. *société anonyme* (public company); and
5. *société en commandite par actions* (stock partnership).

B. The Sale of Goods

French law does not make a clear distinction between sales of goods and sales of other kinds of property. Instead, all sales are considered under the single head of *vente* and governed by the Civil Code. Some particular kinds of property, such as *ventes de fonds de commerce* and *ventes de valeurs mobilières*, however, do have special rules that are contained in separate legislation distinct from the Civil Code. In addition, a commercial contract of sale will be subject to certain special rules in the Code of Commerce.

C. Negotiable Instruments

The French Code of Commerce recognizes three forms of negotiable instruments:

1. bearer instruments, which are transferable by simple delivery;
2. order instruments, which are transferable by endorsement; and
3. nominative instruments, which are transferable by whatever more formal means may be appropriate for the particular instrument involved.

The character of negotiability, where the holder in good faith receives a title free from any defects in the titles of prior parties, is conferred on a wide variety of instruments, such as bonds, bills of lading, bills of exchange, promissory notes, and checks.

XIV. Torts

The classical theory of French law is that fault is a necessary condition of civil liability (*la responsabilité civile*). The conditions of liability in tort are that the plaintiff must show that he or she suffered damage and that the damage was caused by an act or omission for which the defendant was responsible. This responsibility may arise because the defendant was personally at fault or vicariously liable for another's fault or because the damage was caused by a thing in the defendant's care.

French law recognizes the following defenses to a tortious act in the absence of which the plaintiff must be compensated:

1. private defense of one's person and property;
2. necessity;
3. superior orders;
4. statutory exclusion; and
5. prescription after thirty years from the date of the tortious act.

XV. Labor Law

Industrial relations in Wallis and Futuna and all the French Overseas Territories are regulated by the French Labour Code. This code provides the basic legal rules for labor contracts, wages and hours of work, workers' and employers' organizations, court proceedings, and conciliation and arbitration. Other matters such as industrial accident insurance, social security insurance, and social welfare are dealt with by specific laws.

Two categories of labor contracts are recognized. First, contracts for an unfixed period of time, which is the normal contract agreement, and contracts for a fixed period of time (for example, for casual or temporary work). In a normal contract agreement, both parties can terminate the contract, provided the worker gives notice and the employer gives reasons for the termination. At the termination of the contract, the worker must be given a certificate describing the type of job done, the length of service, and so forth, without specifying the reasons for the termination. Both parties must also sign a document to the effect that the worker does not owe the employer. The agreement can be suspended for certain purposes, such as enabling the worker to fulfill the requirements of compulsory military national service. In such a case, there is an obligation to reemploy the worker after the national service.

In all enterprises where there are more than twenty workers, the employer is under an obligation to write a standard order explaining in detail the disciplinary rules and sanctions and the application of legal machinery for security and health within the organization. The employer has the right of dismissal. However, in the exercise of this right, unless the worker is guilty of a serious fault, the employer must give the worker notice (the duration of which varies according to the length of time the employee has worked for the employer). The decision to dismiss the worker must meet the fair hearing requirements of the principle of natural justice and provide reasons for the dismissal. Otherwise, the labor court may invalidate the decision, and the employer must reopen the procedure and pay the worker six months' wages as damages.

Provisions are made for the layoff of workers. Under these provisions, the employer has the right, subject to collective agreements, to break the contract for economic reasons. The procedure for the exercise of this right requires a meeting of the employer, the Inspector of Labour, and the representatives of the workers in order to determine the criteria (for example, age, marital status, years of employment) to be used as the basis for and the order of laying off the workers. The workers have the right to apply to the Inspector of Labor to challenge the decision if they have cause to believe that the layoff was not for economic reasons. In such a case, the inspector must institute an inquiry to ensure that the workers laid off are not replaced by other people, and if within one year a similar position lost by a worker is created within the enterprise, the laid off worker must be reinstated.

Under the provisions of the code, the minimum wage is fixed at 61,000 CFPF and the number of working hours at thirty-nine per week. All employers are legally required to provide free medical service and leave with pay for family events, recreation, and maternity. An employer can neither refuse to employ a woman simply because she is pregnant nor dismiss her for that reason. Neither can he try to find out if she is pregnant unless it is necessary for the purpose of relocating her for health reasons. A pregnant worker can stop work fifteen minutes earlier than the normal closing time daily, and is entitled to a special room and an hour each day for breastfeeding.

The Code establishes a Consultative Commission of Labour comprising the High Commissioner as chairman and an equal number of employers and employees. The role of this commission is to advise the High Commissioner on all industrial matters. Consulting this commission is a necessary condition of validity for all acts relating to industrial matters.

In addition to the statutory rights of workers laid down in the Labour Code, workers have a constitutional right to belong to a trade union of their choice and the right to engage in legal strikes. They are also entitled to accident leave and special leave without pay. The resolution of disputes arising from individual employment contracts between the worker and the employer fall within the jurisdiction of the specialized Labour Court.

The Labour Code also provides for collective labor agreements between workers' organizations and employers. A collective agreement is defined as an agreement to fix the rules that permit workers to collectively negotiate their conditions of employment and social guarantees within the employment. Collective agreements may cover only one enterprise or several enterprises within the same sector, but the terms of the agreement can be extended by the High Commissioner to other enterprises.

Individual contracts are subject to the terms of the collective agreement and cannot be less advantageous than the collective agreement. Sympathy strikes are legally permitted if the demands of the striking workers will benefit the sympathizers. However, where a sympathy strike is aimed at protecting against the breakup of a contract or pressuring an employer who has a problem with his employee (who is not a trade union representative), it is not allowed.

The two parties to the agreement must meet once a year to discuss wages and once every five years to amend the terms of the agreement, if necessary.

Disagreements between parties to a collective agreement may be settled through the following process. The first stage is conciliation, in which the parties try to resolve the dispute by themselves. If after five days they fail to settle their differences, the case is referred to the Inspector of Labour for mediation. In case of a successful resolution of the disagreements, the decision of the mediator has the effect of a collective agreement. If, however, after two weeks there is no progress through mediation, the case then becomes the subject of voluntary arbitration and the results have the same effect as a collective agreement.

XVI. Industrial and Intellectual Property Rights

Industrial and intellectual property rights in Wallis and Futuna and the French Overseas Territories are governed by the French Law of 11 March 1957. This law applies to literary, musical, and artistic compositions of all kinds. Under the law, copyright continues during the lifetime of the author and for the benefit of heirs and assigns for fifty years after death. During this period, the author's spouse is also entitled to the profits of the copyrighted work.

The contract between the author and the publisher is regulated by the 1957 law in such a way as to guard against unconscionable terms. Hence, in addition to a proprietary right that is assignable, the author has a moral right which enables the author to refrain from publication and to insist on due respect being paid to the work. Thus the author can sue anyone that plagiarizes or garbles the work and can insist on the right to alter the work or even revoke an assignment of a copyright on terms of indemnifying the assignee against loss.

Artists and their heirs have a right to share in an unforeseen rise in the commercial value of their work and retain an inalienable right to a share in the price of their work during the entire period of the copyright.

XVII. Legal Education and Profession

There are only two legally qualified officers in the territory, a judge who is appointed from metropolitan France and a Wallisian prosecutor.

XVII. Research Guide

Cornell, J. *Migration, Employment and Development in the South Pacific*. Noumea: South Pacific Commission, 1985.
David, R., and H. de Vries. *The French Legal System*. Dobbs Ferry, N.Y.: Oceana, 1958.
Pacific Constitutions, Vol. 1. Suva: University of the South Pacific, 1988.
Powles, G., and M. Pulea, eds. *Pacific Courts and Legal Systems*. Suva: University of the South Pacific and Faculty of Law, Monash University, 1988.

Price, J., and D. B. Epstein. "French Overseas Territory: Wallis and Futuna," in A. P. Blaustein and P. M. Blaustein, eds. *Constitutions of Dependencies and Special Sovereignties*. Dobbs Ferry, N.Y.: Oceana, 1986.

Virginia, T., and R. Adolff. *The French Pacific Islands*. Berkeley: University of California Press, 1971.

23. French Polynesia

MICHAEL A. NTUMY

I. DATELINE

1595	First European to see Marquesas Islands is Spanish navigator Alvarez de Mendana.
1767–1769	Visits to Tahiti by Samuel Wallis of the British navy, the Frenchman Bougainville, and the British navigator James Cook.
1796	Arrival and settlement of members of London Missionary Society in Tahiti.
1819	Tahiti brought under Christian influence following conversion of King Pomare II by English Protestants. Pomare Code of Laws promulgated.
1825	All islands except Marquesas Islands converted to Christianity.
1842	Marquesas colonized by France.
1847	Tahiti, Moorea, the Tuamotu Islands, and two of the Austral Islands become French protectorates.
1858	Clipperton Island claimed for France.
1880	King Pomare V cedes kingdom to France; French citizenship conferred on his subjects.
1881	Gambier Islands annexed by France.
1885	General Council created, with members elected by all the island's male French citizens.
1888	Leeward Islands annexed by France.
1899	Marquesas, Tuamotus, Gambiers, Tubuai, and Rapa established as separate administrative units.
1946	French Polynesia acquires status of French Overseas Territory.
1984	New Territorial Statute adopted.

II. HISTORICAL, CULTURAL, AND ECONOMIC SURVEY

French Polynesia is situated in the south central Pacific between 7 degrees and 27 degrees latitude and 134 degrees and 155 degrees west longitude. The territory comprises about 130 islands grouped into the following divisions: the Society Islands (the Windward and Leeward groups), the Tuamotu Islands, the Marquesas Islands, the Gambier Islands, the Austral or Tubuai Islands, and Clipperton Island, which, though uninhabited, is administratively part of French Polynesia.

The majority of the 176,000 people who live on the islands are Polynesians and speak Polynesian languages; however, the official language is French. The capital of the territory, Papeete, is about 15,713 kilometers from the metropolitan capital, Paris.

The Marquesas Islands had its first European contact in 1595 through the efforts of the Spanish navigator Alvarez de Mendana. This sailor named the islands after the Marquise of Mendoza, the wife of the tenant governor of Peru. Tahiti was not known to the Europeans until 1767 when Captain Samuel Wallis of the British navy sailed to the island. He named the island King George III Island. In 1768 this island was visited by Louis-Antoine de Bougainville, who claimed it for France. In the following year, James Cook, an English navigator, also visited it and drew the first map of the island.

The first permanent European settlers were the members of the Protestant London Missionary Society who arrived in 1796. These missionaries helped the local Pomare family gain political control over the entire island. After Pomare I had conquered the islands and extended his sovereignty over them, his successor, Pomare II, consolidated this politico–religious triumph by establishing a missionary kingdom, which was ruled according to a missionary-inspired code of law promulgated in 1819. The code prohibited polygamy, adultery, human sacrifice, and infanticide, and also compelled observance of the Sabbath.

In 1824, an English missionary called George Pritchard arrived on the island and quickly became a dominant force in local politics. Under his influence, the first French missionaries were expelled from the island in 1836. In 1842, following a show of armed force, France was able to assert its ascendancy over Queen Pomare IV, who consequently allowed the French government to establish a protectorate over her kingdom. In 1846, the French government negotiated British recognition of a French protectorate over Tahiti, Moorea, the Tuamotus, and two of the Austral Islands.

In 1880, King Pomare V ceded his kingdom to France, thus allowing Tahiti to become a French colony. This status, however, was not extended to the Marquesas, which had been taken over by France in 1842, nor to the other islands that eventually became part of the new colony called the French Establishments of Oceania (E.F.O.).

In the following five decades, France systematically colonized the other islands one after the other. Tuamotu, which was a fief under the King of Tahiti, was transferred to France by the same treaty of 1880 that converted Tahiti into a colony. The Tubuai or Austral Islands, which had been a French protectorate since 1880, was annexed in 1900. Similarly, the protectorates established over the Gambiers and Rapa were followed by outright annexation in 1881 and 1901 respectively. Finally, Clipperton Island, taken over by France in 1858, was awarded to France in 1931 by the Italian King, Victor-Emmanuel III, as a result of an arbitration between France and Mexico.

The colonial administration of the colony was initially under the charge of a naval governor. In 1883, a civilian governor was named and an eighteen-member elected General Council was created by the Decree of 28 December 1885. In the outer islands, many of the functions that had been performed by the district councils under the protectorate were handed over to the *gendarmerie* in 1877. Thereafter, the *gendarmerie*, assisted by the native police (*mutoi*), was in charge of supervising road maintenance, tax collection, and registration of vital statistics and land transfers. In 1903, following criticisms leveled against it by the outer islanders, the council was abolished and replaced by a consultative council of administration. This left the overall administration of the colony in the hands of the Governor, who combined executive with legislative powers.

After World War II, a representative assembly, modeled after the General Councils of France, was instituted in the E.F.O. This Assembly was elected by adult suffrage of all the newly enfranchised citizens and placed under French penal law. The powers of the Assembly were confined largely to economic matters, the most important of which was the power to vote the local budget. This budget, however, was to be drafted by the Governor-in-Council and included obligatory expenditures over which the Assembly had no control. Debates on political issues were prohibited, but the Assembly had to be consulted on specific subjects and it could pass resolutions on matters of general administration.

This legal framework preserved the Governor's authority and the control exercised by the French government until 1946 when the colony became an Overseas Territory. This status was reaffirmed by Law 84-820 of 6 September 1984, relating to the Territorial Statute of French Polynesia. The Overseas Territory status has meant that the constitutional regime and legal system of the territory are virtually the same as that of the other French Overseas Territories with which it shares a common legal status.

For this reason, the following account of the legal system of the territory presents only the noteworthy differences that are occasioned by *spécificité locale*, that is, local conditions specified by the territory's Territorial Statute.

For details of the public law aspects of the legal system, see **Chapter 21, New Caledonia**; for details of private law, see **Chapter 22, Wallis and Futuna**.

III. SOURCES OF LAW

The sources of law of French Polynesia are the same as that of New Caledonia. In addition, the adaptation of French law to the local conditions of the territory has been remarkably successful due to the absence of a local customary law.

A specialist of the Polynesian legal system, Judge Gire, attributes the absence of a local customary law in French Polynesia to two reasons. The first is the fact that the traditional ways of the Polynesians were never taken into account by the French administration. Around 1840, after France imposed monarchy in Tahiti with King Ponare I, a feeble attempt to codify the Tahitian customary law failed. Thereafter, in 1866, the French Civil Code was made applicable to French Polynesia.

Secondly, unlike New Caledonia, French Polynesia has no customary or tribal land. With the establishment of the land registry (*cadastre*) in 1830, all land titles in French Polynesia were registered and any remaining unclaimed land was deemed public property. Since then, all local land disputes have been brought under the jurisdiction of the Lands Tribunal.

IV. CONSTITUTIONAL SYSTEM

A. Territory

Under Article 1 of the Territorial Statute, the territory is divided into the Leeward Islands, the Windward Islands, the Austral Islands, the Tuamotu Islands, the Gambier Islands, and the Marquesas Islands.

B. Government

1. HEAD OF STATE

The Head of State, the President of France, is represented in the territory by the resident French High Commissioner. The High Commissioner also acts as the state representative and delegate of the French government.

The High Commissioner is in charge of public order and law and order and is responsible for ensuring respect for public freedom and individual and public rights. The High Commissioner controls the legality of the decisions of the government of the territory as well as the deliberations of the Territorial Assembly and can refer any decisions of these bodies to the Administrative Court for a determination of their legality.

The High Commissioner also has power to control public and private organizations that benefit from public funds, declare a state of emergency under conditions determined by law, and issue regulations in matters in which the commissioner is competent. In addition, the High Commissioner is in charge of the publication in the local gazette of national laws and decrees and territorial government and Territorial Assembly decisions.

2. EXECUTIVE

The chief executive of the territory is the President of the government of the territory, who is also the chief of the territorial administration. In the former capacity, the President represents the territory, defines the role of each minister, and distributes the corresponding portfolio. The President directs and coordinates the actions of all ministers and prepares and executes the deliberations of the Territorial Assembly and its Permanent Commission.

The government of the territory can delegate to the President the power to decide on the following matters:

1. administration of the assets of the territory, including acquisitions, sales, exchanges, and rentals;
2. acceptance or rejection of gifts and donations made to the territory;
3. legal actions and commercial transactions undertaken on behalf of the territory;
4. agreements relating to private airstrips; and
5. the codification of territorial rules and annual updating of codes.

Decisions on the above matters must, however, be taken in conjunction with the minister in charge.

As the chief of the territorial administration, the President of the government of the territory is charged with responsibility for the territorial budget. The President can employ the services of state agencies in the execution of projects within the competence of the territory and can engage the services of the state in the preparation and execution of the deliberations of the Territorial Assembly and the Council of Ministers. Together with the High Commissioner, the President coordinates the services of the state and the territory and signs on behalf of the territory the conventions between the state and the territory that determine the areas in which to deploy state agencies and services.

3. LEGISLATURE

Following the general French pattern of distributing power between the state and the overseas territories, Article 3 of the Territorial Statute of French Polynesia confers on the state the exclusive competence to legislate on exactly the same matters enumerated under New Caledonia's Territorial Statute (see **Chapter 21, IV, C (3) Legislature**).

Subject to the state's power to legislate on the matters reserved to its competence, the following territorial institutions that are responsible for administering the territory and implementing measures designed to realize its internal autonomy participate in the law-making process:

1. the government of the territory,
2. the Territorial Assembly, and
3. the Economic and Social Council.

4. GOVERNMENT OF THE TERRITORY

The government of the territory is composed of a President and a Council of Ministers comprising six to ten ministers. The ministers, one of whom is appointed the Vice President, are responsible to the Council of Ministers. The members of the council may be chosen from the Territorial Assembly or outside it, and under Section III of the Territorial Statute, are charged with the collective responsibility for preparing the legislative proposals and measures that require the deliberation of the Territorial Assembly.

The specific powers of the council include the power to do the following:

1. determine the annual program of imports and the amount of foreign exchange required annually from the state;
2. determine the type of tariffs to be attached to public territorial services;
3. determine the purpose and mode of execution of territorial public works and the order in which public works are to be executed;
4. create and organize the structures that promote the economic interests of the territory;
5. study the statistical programs and data of the territory;
6. authorize agreements between the territory and farmers and other contractors;
7. accord landing rights to aircraft;
8. administer the acquisitions, sales, exchanges, and rentals of territorial assets according to limits set by the Territorial Assembly;
9. accept or reject gifts and donations on behalf of the territory;
10. exercise control over the transfer of property in cases where the purchaser is not resident in the territory;
11. exercise control over all foreign investment projects below 80 million French francs;
12. participate in the negotiations of international air and maritime agreements that affect the interests of the territory;
13. negotiate economic, scientific, technical, and cultural agreements within the competence of the territory (subject to delegation by the state and to ratification or approval by the French President or Parliament); and
14. nominate the chiefs of territorial services and the directors and commissioners of public institutions.

In addition to the above, the council can determine the rules applicable to the following matters:

1. organization of public territorial services;
2. educational matters within the competence of the territory;
3. teaching of local languages;
4. scholarships and educational grants charged to the local budget;
5. regulation of weights and measures and control of fraud;
6. organization of fares and markets of territorial interest;
7. regulation of prices, tariffs, and internal commerce;
8. recovery of taxes paid for services rendered;
9. quantitative restriction of imports; and
10. agreements relating to private airstrips.

Under exceptional circumstances, the Council of Ministers can decide to suspend or reduce all customs excise for a period of time in order to protect local production. Such an action, however, has to be ratified by the Territorial Assembly or its Permanent Commission if the Assembly is in recess. If the decision is approved, it takes effect from the date it was made by the Council of Ministers. However, if the decision is not ratified, its application ceases on the date of the Territorial Assembly's deliberation.

The Council of Ministers can, under Article 466 of the Penal Code of 1811, impose a penalty on those who violate its decisions. This penalty may take the form of a fine (up to 50,000 CFPF, which is paid into the territorial account) or correctional means. The imposition of criminal punishment (imprisonment) is permitted only for particular acts with the approval of the French Parliament. With regard to administrative and economic matters within its competence, the council may opt to settle out of court, except that if the matter will normally lead to a criminal trial then the approval of the Procureur (the representative of the Ministry of Justice) must be sought.

Under Article 31 of the Territorial Statute, the Council of Ministers has the right to be consulted by the minister in charge of Overseas Territories or the High Commissioner on questions relating to the following matters:

1. changes in the tariff for internal postage, telephone, and international telecommunications;
2. definition of the state educational system and its adaptation to pedagogical programs;
3. security matters relating to civilians;
4. decisions on direct foreign investment projects in the territory not within the competence of the Territorial Assembly;
5. fishing agreements and the terms of operating international air and maritime services in the territory;
6. control of immigration and visits to the territory lasting longer than three months;
7. legislative framework for registration of births, deaths, marriages, and civil status; and
8. creation and modification of administrative subdivisions of the territory and the nomination of the subdivision chiefs by the French government.

Whenever the council is consulted on the above issues, it must respond within one month.

The council is statutorily required to meet at least three times every month in the capital of the territory; its acts and decisions become effective after publication or notification to the interested parties and communication of the decision by the President to the High Commissioner.

5. TERRITORIAL ASSEMBLY

Article 62 of the Territorial Statute confers on the Territorial Assembly competence in all matters that are within the territory's competence and not specifically assigned to the Council of Ministers or the President of the government of the territory. These residual powers include voting the territorial budget, economic development, promotion of local cultures, and the teaching of vernacular languages.

In all matters within its competence, the Territorial Assembly has the power to adopt resolutions to extend application of laws of the French Parliament to the territory or abridge, modify, or complement the application of existing laws to the territory. It oversees all administrative, fiscal, customs, and economic matters within its competence. Consequently, it can interfere in all acts dealing with such cases. However, if any such act constitutes an infringement of a law in the public domain, the Territorial Assembly can act only with the consent of the Attorney General of the territory.

The Assembly must be consulted on ratification of international conventions that relate to matters within its competence. When consulted, it must respond within three months unless the High Commissioner requests a shorter period. The Assembly can impose a penalty for the violation of its decisions, provided the sanction imposed corresponds with that laid down for similar offenses in the Penal Code.

The Territorial Assembly holds two ordinary sessions each year in the capital of the territory. The first session (the administrative session) opens between March 1 and April 30. Once every year during this session, the President of the Territorial Assembly must address the Assembly and report on the state of the territory and the public services. The second session, the budgetary session, opens between September 1 and October 30. During this session, the President must report on the activities of the government in the preceding year.

If for any reason a meeting is not scheduled during these two periods, the High Commissioner can, following the advice of the President of the government of the territory, modify the normal period of Assembly sessions by decree and convene an ordinary session of the Assembly. The Territorial Assembly itself determines the date and duration of its sessions. The duration of the session, however, cannot exceed two months. If it goes on recess without fixing the date for the next session, its Permanent Commission may do so on its behalf. All meetings must be open to the public, unless special circumstances make publicity undesirable. The quorum for meetings is 50 percent of the members. If there is no quorum at a session, the meeting is automatically postponed for three days, after which the quorum requirement is waived. All decisions require an absolute majority vote and the president has a casting vote.

6. ECONOMIC AND SOCIAL COUNCIL

Chapter III of the Territorial Statute creates an Economic and Social Council whose main function is to offer advice on social and economic matters referred to it by the government of the territory or the Territorial Assembly. The council must be consulted on all important social, economic, and cultural matters concerning the territory. Its membership is drawn from professional organizations; trade unions; and other social, economic, and cultural organizations. Its operative costs are charged on the territorial budget.

7. JUDICIARY

Article 3 of the Territorial Statute reserves to the state matters relating to justice and the organization of the judiciary. Hence, like all other overseas territories, the principles of justice and jurisdictional organization are practically identical with that of New Caledonia. The territory, however, has its own Courts of First Instance, Court of Appeal, Court of Assizes, and specialized courts.

The Courts of First Instance have general jurisdiction in all matters not expressly stated to be within the jurisdiction of other courts. In civil cases, they sit with three professional judges and a representative of the Ministère Public, and their jurisdiction extends to contracts, torts, and matters relating to civil status. In criminal cases, they have jurisdiction as a Police Court to deal with petty criminal offenses and as a Criminal Court to hear misdemeanors. Decisions in the Police Court are made by a single judge; the criminal jurisdiction is exercised by a panel of three judges. Appeals from this court go to the Court of Appeal, which has jurisdiction over all cases decided by the Courts of First Instance, including petty criminal offenses and misdemeanors. Decisions of the Court of Appeal may be challenged only on a point of law before the Court of Cassation in metropolitan France.

The Court of Assizes has jurisdiction in cases involving the most serious criminal offenses. This court is composed of three judges who sit together with a jury. The decision of the court is final and cannot be appealed. The only recourse to a dissatisfied party is to the Court of Cassation in metropolitan France. The Court of Cassation exercises ultimate limited review over all cases in the French legal system after all other methods of review have been exhausted.

There are two specialized courts in French Polynesia. The first is the Labour Court, which settles disputes between employers and employees. This court is composed of a professional judge who presides over the proceedings and two assessors, one representing the employers and the other the employees. Union representatives are permitted to represent their members in all proceedings; there is no requirement for representation by legal counsel. Appeals from this court are heard by the Court of Appeal.

The second court with special jurisdiction is the Mixed Commercial Court, whose function is to settle disputes arising in commercial transactions. Its composition is one professional judge (who is the chairman) and merchant judges elected by traders from the business community. Appeals from this court also go to the Court of Appeal.

The territory also has an Administrative Tribunal with jurisdiction in all matters involving the administration. This court was created in 1984 as a replacement for the Council for Administrative Disputes, which was established in 1881. The composition of the court is one president and several other members, one of which functions as the commissioner of government. Appeals from this court go to the Council of State (Conseil d'Etat) in metropolitan France.

V. International Obligations

Within the limits of the applicable laws relating to international relations (**see Chapter 21, VI, International Obligations**), the President of the government of the territory has considerable powers in the field of international law. The President can propose to the French government to enter into international negotiations with any state or territory within the Pacific region on economic, scientific, technical, and cultural matters of interest to the territory; during such negotiations, the President or a representative can participate in the debates. The President also represents the French state (jointly with the High Commissioner) at meetings of Pacific regional organizations.

VI. Legal Education and Profession

Approximately twenty-five lawyers of French Polynesian origin practice in the territory. However, their appearance is not obligatory in all cases, as private persons or their close relatives are allowed to represent themselves or their relatives. A system of free legal aid enables all indigent citizens, especially in criminal cases, to obtain free legal representation.

VII. Research Guide

Cornell, J. *Migration, Employment and Development in the South Pacific.* Noumea: South Pacific Commission, 1985.
Houghton, G., and J. Wakefield. *French Polynesia.* Melbourne: Macmillan, 1987.
Milnes, Barry B., and E. Jehle. *Tahiti (French Polynesia) Taxes and Investments in Asia and the Pacific.* Amsterdam: International Bureau of Fiscal Documentation, 1985.
The Pacific Guide, 3d ed. Essex: World of Information, 1986.
Sigler, J. A., and R. Henry. "French Overseas Territories: French Polynesia," in A. P. Blaustein and P. M. Blaustein, eds. *Constitutions of Dependencies and Special Sovereignties.* Dobbs Ferry, N.Y.: Oceana, 1986.

Notes

ABBREVIATIONS

AC	Appeal Cases (U.K.)
ALJR	Australian Law Journal Reports
ASR	American Samoa Reporter
CA	Court of Appeal
CLR	Commonwealth Law Reports (Australia)
CTC	Commonwealth Trial Court
F. 2d	Federal Reporter, 2d Series (U.S.)
F. Supp.	Federal Supplement (U.S.)
FLR	Fiji Law Reports
FLR	Federal Law Reports (Australia) (Chap. 7)
FSM Intrm.	Federated States of Micronesia, Interim Reporter
GILR	Gilbert Islands Law Reports
Guam	Guam Reports
HC	High Court
LC	Land Court
LRC	Law Reports of the Commonwealth (U.K.)
LT	Land and Titles Division of High Court (American Samoa)
MIRC	Marshall Islands Revised Code
PC	Privy Council
PNC	Palau National Code
PNGLR	Papua New Guinea Law Reports
ROP Intrm.	Republic of Palau, Interim Reporter
SC	Supreme Court
SCR	Supreme Court Reference
SILR	Solomon Islands Law Reports
SPLR	South Pacific Law Reports
TLR	Tongan Law Reports
TTR	Trust Territory (U.S.) Reports
U.S.	United States Supreme Court Reports
WSLR	Western Samoa Law Reports

CHAPTER 1. THE COOK ISLANDS

1. *Graham v. Graham*, Divorce Action No. 5 of 1986, mimeo decision (1986).

CHAPTER 2. FIJI

1. *Bose Levu Vakaturaga* is used in the Constitution, rather than the term *Great Council of Chiefs*, which is used in the English-language versions of Fiji's laws and regulations. The Fijian term also has connotations of "functioning in a chiefly and Fijian fashion." The Fijian term is generally used in this chapter

where the reference is to constitutional issues and *Great Council of Chiefs* in reference to a specific statutory provision.

2. Throughout this chapter, *Fiji* is used to refer to the country as a whole, while *Fijian* is used to refer only to ethnic indigenous Fijians, using the definition in the 1990 Constitution—namely, those who can trace their ancestry through the male line to indigenous inhabitants of Fiji. *Indian* is used to refer to those who can trace their ancestry through the male line to indigenous inhabitants of the Indian subcontinent.

3. *Ratu* is an honorific generally used by those holding Fijian chiefly titles.

4. B. Knapman, *Fiji's Economic History, 1874–1939: Studies of Capitalist Colonial Development*, Pacific Research Monograph No. 15 (Canberra: Australian National University, 1987), 1.

5. *Pacific Economic Bull.* (Canberra, National Centre for Development Studies, July 1986), 1.

6. *R. v. Mohammed Hanif*, Supreme Court Criminal Case No. 12 of 1972 (evidence obtained in illegal search need not be excluded from trial); *Mam Chand v. R.*, 17 FLR 86 (Supreme Court, 1971) (constitutional guarantee of adequate time to prepare defense does not apply where the accused pleads guilty); *R. v. Butadroga*, Supreme Court, August 9, 1977 (unreported) (constitutional rights of freedom of expression, assembly, and association are not infringed by statutory ban on racially inflammatory statements). But, in *Sundarjee Bros. Ltd. v. Coulter*, Supreme Court Civil Action No. 756 of 1986, a statutory provision authorizing the arrest of debtors believed about to flee the country was held to be an unconstitutional deprivation of liberty.

7. In this chapter, the first substantive reference to an act will identify the act by title, date of initial enactment, and, if applicable, the chapter number in the 1985 edition of the *Revised Laws*. Post-1985 acts and decrees are identified only by title and date.

8. *State v. Afasio Mua and Ors.*, High Court of Fiji, judgment of June 9, 1988 (unreported; the text of the judgment is printed in the *Fiji Times*, June 10, 1988, 12).

9. Under Section 68 of the 1970 Constitution, the nine acts listed above could not be amended at all unless the amendment was supported by a three-fourths majority in the House of Representatives and, if the amendment affected Fijian land, customs, or customary rights, by at least six of the eight senators nominated by the Bose Levu Vakaturaga.

10. The Privy Council has itself recognized that English precedents are not to be applied mechanically to cases arising in jurisdictions that have adopted English common law as of some specific date. See, e.g., *Jamil Bin Harun v. Yang Kamsiah* [1984] 1 *Modern Law J.* 217, holding that modern English case law has only persuasive and not precedential effect in such situations.

11. *Timoci Bavadra v. Native Land Trust Board*, Supreme Court, Feb. 11, 1986 (unreported). See also *Namasiu Dikau No. 1 and Ors. v. Native Land Trust Board*, Supreme Court, Civil Action No. 801 of 1984 (individual members of a *mataqali*, the Fijian landowning group, do not have standing to sue to enforce customary land rights).

12. Under the Magistrates' Courts (Chapter 14) Amendment Decree 1987, resident magistrates may be appointed without formal legal qualifications.

13. Under Legal Notice No. 75, *Fiji Republic Gazette Supplement* No. 20, July 1, 1988, judges may be appointed from Fiji, most Commonwealth countries, the Philippines, or the United States.

14. For a discussion of Fijian administrative organization, **see IV, C, 3 Fijian Affairs**.

15. The Fijian Affairs Act defines *Fijian* for this purpose to include other Pacific islanders who have elected to live in a traditional fashion in a Fijian village.

16. T. J. MacNaught, "Chiefly Civil Servants: Ambiguity in a District Administration and the Preservation of the Fijian Way of Life," 9 *J. Pacific Histtory* 3 (1976).

17. *Attorney General v. Langon*, 16 FLR 43 (Supreme Court 1973) (*Traffic Ordinance* does not apply on Rabi Island, because roads there are vested in the council and are therefore not public roads).

18. This provision was held, in *R. v. Butadroka*, Supreme Court, August 9, 1977 (unreported), not to violate the freedom of speech guarantees contained in the 1970 Constitution. For a discussion of the case, see Aikman, "Public Order and the Bill of Rights in Fiji: *R. v. Butadroka*," 11 *Victoria Univ. of Wellington Law Rev.* 169 (1981) and Mataitoga, "Human Rights and the Supreme Court in Fiji: *Butadroka* Revisited," [1985] *New Zealand Law J.* 58.

19. The Fijian predominance dates to World War II, when most of the Indian community declined to

serve in support of British interests. See T. J. MacNaught, *The Fijian Colonial Experience*, Pacific Research Monograph No. 7 (Canberra: Australian National University, 1982), 149.

20. *Director of Public Prosecutions v. Isimeli Bili*, Supreme Court Criminal Appeal No. 30 of 1986 (Suva City Council bylaw purporting to grant arrest powers is ultra vires).

21. See Office of the Ombudsman, *Fourteenth Annual Report of the Ombudsman* (Suva, Parliamentary Paper No. 21 of 1986), 3–5.

22. *Schramm v. Attorney General of Fiji*, Fiji Court of Appeal, Civil Appeal No. 72 of 1981.

23. *Fiji Republic Gazette Supplement* No. 30 (September 7, 1990), 439.

24. For details of reciprocal enforcement in these areas, **see XIV Family Law and XVI Wills and Succession** later in this chapter.

25. For example, the 1990 tax treaty with Australia limits Fiji withholding tax on amounts paid to residents of Australia to 20 percent for dividends, 15 percent for royalties, and 10 percent for interest.

26. See Hotel Turnover Tax Act (Amendment) Decree 1990, 4 *Fiji Republic Gazette* 221 (March 28, 1990). Turnover Tax (Miscellaneous Services) Act (Amendment) Decree 1990, 4 *Fiji Republic Gazette* 222 (March 28, 1990).

27. See *Ali Mohammed v. Azad Wali*, Fiji Court of Appeal, Civil Appeal No. 49 of 1982 (landlord's need for the dwelling must be bona fide; desire to provide a dwelling for the landlord's adult son is not sufficient).

28. *Carter v. State*, High Court Criminal Appeal No. 71 of 1990.

29. See *Virendra Singh v. R.*, Supreme Court Criminal Appeal No. 36 of 1986 (in the case of noncognizable offenses, a mere belief, no matter how well-founded, is insufficient; the officer must actually have observed the person committing the offense).

30. *R. v. Mohammed Hanif*, Supreme Court Criminal Case No. 12 of 1972.

31. Chief Justice's Practice Direction of April 14, 1983; but see *David Ram Singh v. R.*, Supreme Court Criminal Appeal No. 5 of 1986, and *Uiesa Tuituba v. State*, High Court Criminal Appeals Nos. 48, 49, and 50 of 1990 (despite the lack of requirement for a formal evidentiary hearing, the court must conduct a sufficient inquiry so that it can be satisfied that the statement is voluntary, and this inquiry must be reflected in the record).

32. *Shiu Prasad v. R.*, 18 FLR 68 (Court of Appeal, 1972).

33. The *Interpretation (Amendment) Decree* of 1989 substituted the word *State* for *Crown* in all laws.

34. See generally P. France, *The Charter of the Land* (Melbourne: Oxford University Press, 1969).

35. See *In the matter of Bulou Eta Kacalaini Vosailagi and Others*, Judicial Review No. 19 of 1988, High Court of Fiji.

36. *Aznat Ali v. Mohammed Janil and Another*, Court of Appeal, Civil Appeal No. 111 of 1985.

37. Other relevant laws are the Sugar Cane Growers Fund Authority Act 1984 (Chapter 207), establishing a statutory body to make loans to cane farmers; the Loans (Cane Crop Rehabilitation Scheme) Act 1983 (Chapter 208), relating to payments to farmers made by the Fiji Sugar Corporation in the drought year 1983; and the Fiji Sugar Corporation Limited Act 1972 (Chapter 209), by which the government nationalized the sugar-milling operations of the Colonial Sugar Refining Company.

38. M. Pulea, *The Family, Law and Population in the Pacific Islands* (Suva: Institute of Pacific Studies, 1986), 124.

39. Pulea, 136.

40. Pulea, 145.

41. See *Jayantilal v. Kalawati Ukabhai Parmar*, 17 FLR 15 (Supreme Court, 1971) (husband's potential future earnings as well as merely his current salary may be taken into account in fixing maintenance).

42. Pulea, 145.

43. See *R. v. Emberson*, Supreme Court, Criminal Action No. 16 of 1976 (elaborating on the "good faith" requirement).

44. Pulea, 111.

45. See, for example, *Ratu Sir Kamisese Mara v. Fiji Times Ltd.*, Fiji Court of Appeal, Civil Appeal No. 7 of 1984.

46. *Coulam v. Fiji Law Society*, 18 FLR 175 (Fiji Court of Appeal, 1972).

47. The last four countries were added by Legal Notice No. 106, *Fiji Republic Gazette Supplement* No. 36 (November 25, 1988).

48. See *Re Handley*, 20 FLR 58 (Supreme Court, 1978) (Fiji Law Society takes the position that foreign counsel should be permitted to appear only in constitutional or political cases or matters requiring specialized expertise, such as taxation).

49. Byrne, "The Desirability of a Public Solicitor in Fiji," 2(2) *Fiji Law Talk* 21 (June 1991).

CHAPTER 3. KIRIBATI

1. See, for example, *Taribia Burau Tuwava v. Kaikai Timau* (Civ. A 5/85). This was an appeal against an award of A$50 in damages for slander, where the magistrate applied local custom rather than the common law of slander. On appeal, the High Court, per Jones C.J., upheld the decision.

2. [1977] GILR 119.

3. A similar conclusion was reached in the case of *Tebao Tokia v. R.* [1977] GILR 124.

4. *Kiribati Co-operative Wholesale Society v. Nei Tangitana*, unreported High Court judgment, July 16, 1982.

5. *Nei Teburenga v. Nei Tera Kennang Teekabu and Aberaam Obera* [1979] Kiribati Law Reports 78.

6. *Karere Irata and Others v. Nei Emi Bobu* [1979] Kiribati Law Reports 27.

CHAPTER 4. THE REPUBLIC OF THE MARSHALL ISLANDS

1. For discussions of the development and content of the Constitution, see C. J. Lynch, "The 1979 Constitution of the Marshall Islands—A Hybrid?" 61 *Parliamentarian* 230 (1980); Lynch, "Traditional Leadership in the Constitution of the Marshall Islands" (Working Papers Series, Pacific Islands Studies, Center for Asian and Pacific Studies, Social Science Research Institute, University of Hawaii, 1984; A. Quentin-Baxter, "The Constitutions of Niue and the Marshall Islands: Common Traits and Points of Difference," in P. Sack, ed., *Pacific Constitutions* (Canberra, Australian National University, Department of Law, Research School of Social Sciences, 1982).

2. *Jacklick v. Jejo*, Civ. Act. No. 1983-42 (1983).

3. Quoted in Lynch, "The 1979 Constitution of the Marshall Islands."

4. Lynch, "Traditional Leadership in the Constitution of the Marshall Islands," vi.

5. Lynch, "Traditional Leadership in the Constitution of the Marshall Islands," 9.

6. *Levi v. Kumtak*, TTR (1986).

7. *Iroij Laplap Kabua Kabua v. Kwajalein Atoll Corp.*, Civil Action No. 1984-102 (1985).

8. *Reimers v. Helkena*, Civ. Act. No. 1983-59 (1983).

9. The description here of customary land law and changes to it is drawn primarily from L. Mason, "The Marshall Islands: Tenures from Subsistence to Star Wars," in R. G. Crocombe, ed., *Land Tenure in the Atolls* (Suva: Institute of Pacific Studies, 1987); W. McGrath and W. S. Wilson, "The Marshall, Caroline and Mariana Islands: Too Many Foreign Precedents," in R. G. Crocombe, ed., *Land Tenure in the Pacific*, 3d ed. (Suva: University of the South Pacific, 1987); and M. Neas, "Land Ownership Patterns in the Marshall Islands," 85 *Atoll Research Bull.* 17 (1961).

10. *Limet Mojilong v. Atol*, Civ. Act. No. 1982-76 (1982).

11. McGrath and Wilson, "The Marshall, Caroline and Mariana Islands."

12. *Lorennij v. Muller*, Civ. Act. No. 1983-57 (1983); *Ebot v. Jablotok*, Civ. Act. No. 1982-49 (1982).

13. C. J. Lanham, "Manual on How to Do a Divorce Case in the Marshall Islands" (Majuro, 1983, Mimeographed).

14. *Iroij Laplap Kabua Kabua v. Kwajalein Atoll Corp.*

CHAPTER 7. NORFOLK ISLAND

1. *Newberg v. The Queen* (1965) 7 FLR 34; *Berwick Ltd. v. Gray* (1976) 133 CLR 603.

CHAPTER 8. PAPUA NEW GUINEA

1. See *Geita Sabea v. Territory of Papua* (1943) 67 CLR 543.
2. *Peter v. South Pacific Brewery Ltd.* [1976] PNGLR 537.
3. See, e.g., J. G. Zorn, "Common Law Jurisprudence and Customary Law," in R. W. James, ed. *The Supreme Court and the Underlying Law* (Port Moresby: University of Papua New Guinea Press, 1991); Zorn, "Making Law in Papua New Guinea," 4(4) *Pacific Studies* (1991).
4. *Supreme Court Reference No. 2 of 1982: Re Organic Law* [1982] PNGLR 214.
5. *State v. Independent Tribunal; ex parte Moses Sasakila* [1976] PNGLR 491.
6. *Peter v. South Pacific Brewery Ltd.*
7. *The Ship Federal Huron v. Ok Tedi Mining Ltd.* [1986] PNGLR 5.
8. *Supreme Court Reference No. 4 of 1980: Re Petition of M. T. Somare* [1981] PNGLR 265.
9. *State v. Aubafo Feama and Ors.* [1978] PNGLR 301.
10. As pointed out by Kidu, C.J., in *State v. Paul Pokolou* (1983) (Unreported) N404.
11. *State v. Aubafo Feama and Ors.* (holding that acts of cannibalism were repugnant to the general principles of humanity); and *Sanguma Wauta v. State* [1978] PNGLR 326 (holding that to treat a custom that regards sexual intercourse between a customary adopting father and an adopted daughter as equivalent to "incest" coming within the definition of that offense under the Criminal Code would be inconsistent with the code).
12. *Constitutional Reference No. 1 of 1978* [1977] PNGLR 295; and *The Ship Federal Huron v. Ok Tedi Ltd.*
13. Expressed by Kearney, J., in *State v. Allan Woila* [1978] PNGLR 99.
14. See, in particular, works by Roebuck et al. and Brunton and Colquhoun-Kerr in **XXIII Research Guide**.
15. This Blackstonian view of the law is stated in a number of Judge Kapi's decisions including *Wahgi Savings and Loans Society Ltd. v. Bank of South Pacific* (1980) (Unreported) S.C. 185, at 19; *State v. Bisket Urranquae Pokia* [1980] PNGLR 97; and *Supreme Court Reference No. 4 of 1980 Re Petition of M. T. Somare*. Miles, J., in *Vian Guatal v. Papua New Guinea* [1981] PNGLR 230, took the same view as Kapi.
16 At least one judge (Wilson, J.) suggests that the Supreme Court must accept this responsibiity. *P.L.A.R. No. 1 of 1980* [1980] PNGLR 326, at 334.
17. See *State v. Kaupa Ungi* [1980] PNGLR 199, in respect of a trial judge's power to recall a sentence imposed and sentence afresh before the formal closure of a circuit; and *State v. Joseph Tapa* [1978] PNGLR 134, which states the principles to be applied when considering the evidence of accomplices.
18. *James Mopio v. Speaker of the National Parliament* [1977] PNGLR 420.
19. *Supreme Court Reference No. 1 of 1982: Re Bouraga* [1982] PNGLR 178, 186, and 187.
20. *Peter v. South Pacific*, supra (per Frost, C.J., at 298); and *Supreme Court Reference No. 1 of 1977* [1977] PNGLR 362 (per Prentice, Dep. C.J., at 377).
21. *Re Moresby North East Election No. 2* [1977] PNGLR 448.
22. *John Jaminan v. State* [1983] PNGLR 318.
23. *In re Joseph Auna* [1980] PNGLR 500; and *Supeme Court Reference No. 2 of 1982; Re Opai Kunangel Amin* (1982) (Unreported) SC 231.
24. *Supreme Court Reference No. 4 of 1982: Re Delba Biri v. Bill Ginbogl Ninkama* [1982] PNGLR 342.
25. *Supreme Court Reference No. 1A of 1981: Re Motor Traffic Act* [1982] PNGLR 122; but see *Avia Aihi v. State* [1981] PNGLR 81 (Greville Smith, J., dissenting).
26. *State v. Independent Tribunal; Ex parte Sasakila, Reva Mase v. State* (1980) (Unreported) N260.
27. *Constitutional Reference No. 3 of 1978: Re Inter-Group Fighting Act of 1977* [1978] PNGLR 421;

Supreme Court Reference No. 1 of 1981: Re Inter-Group Fighting Act of 1977 [1981] PNGLR 151 and *Supreme Court Reference No. 2 of 1982: Re Organic Law on National Elections* [1982] PNGLR 214.

28. *Supreme Court Reference No. 5 of 1982: Hugo Berghauser and Ors. v. Joseph Aoae* (1982) PNGLR 379, and *Supreme Court Reference No. 3 of 1982: Re Sections 57 and 155(4) of the Constitution* [1982] PNGLR 405.

29. *Cory v. Blyth (No. 1)* [1976] PNGLR 274. See also *Hetura Paz Development Co. Pty. Ltd. v. Niugini Nius Pty. Ltd.* [1982] PNGLR 250 (in which Kapi, J., suggested that the constitutionality of the Defamation Act might be a proper matter for referral); *Peter v. South Pacific* (title of an act too trivial to be referred); and *State v. Kaputin (No. 1)* [1979] PNGLR 532 (question of sufficiency of complaint too trivial for referral).

30. *Supreme Court Reference No. 4 of 1980; Re Petition of Somare.*

31. *Application by Wili Wili Goiya* (1991) (Unreported) (No. SC 408).

32. See *Rumints and Ors* (1972) (Unreported) No. 728 (District Court may sit only in a place that has been declared for holding court hearings); *Wat v. Kari* (1975) (Unreported) No. 839 (sitting in a building away from the courthouse is permissible so long as in the gazetted area); *R. v. McEachern* [1967–1968] PNGLR 48 (venue limitations apply to summary hearings only).

33. *Iapnava v. Moyas* [1971–1972] PNGLR 266.

34. *Madum Towei v. Kepas Tundual* (1972) (unreported) No. 719.

35. *Tom Amaiu v. Commissioner of Corrective Institutions and the State* [1983] PNGLR 87.

36. The decision in *Re Heni Pauta and Kenneth Susuve (No. 2)* (1982) (Unpublished) N337, held that the principles applicable in calculating compensation are the same as the principles on damages, and the court can, as was done in *Amaiu v. Commissioner of Corrective Institutions and the State* [1983] PNGLR 87, award exemplary damages.

37. *Constitutional Reference No. 1 of 1978* [1978] PNGLR 345.

38. *State v. Principal Magistrate District Court of Port Moresby; Ex parte the Public Prosecutor* [1983] PNGLR 43.

39. *Premdas v. Independent State of Papua New Guinea* [1979] PNGLR 329; *Falscheer v. Iambakey Okuk* [1980] PNGLR 101; and *Iambakey Okuk v. Falscheer* [1980] PNGLR 274.

40. *Ridge v. Baldwin* [1964] AC 40, and *Durapyappah v. Fernando* [1967] 2 AC 337.

41. Miles, J., and Pratt, J., in *Iambakey Okuk v. Falscheer.*

42. *Premdas v. State;* and *Perryman v. Minister of Foreign Affairs and Trade* [1982] PNGLR 339.

43. *Premdas v. State.*

44. *Supreme Court Reference No. 4 of 1980: Re Petition of Somare.*

45. On this provision, see *Supreme Court Reference No. 1 of 1981: Re Inter-Group Fighting Act of 1977* [1981] 153–156; *Sanguma Wauta v. State* [1978], at 33; *Supreme Court Reference No. 1 of 1981: In the Matter of Section 19(1)(f) of the Criminal Code* [1982] PNGLR 150, 173.

46. See *Tiden v. Tokavanamur-Topaparik* [1967–1968] PNGLR 231, 236; *State v. Aubafu Feama, Nama Auri, Kafidiri Kudedebe* [1978] PNGLR 301; *Sebulon Wat v. Peter Kari* [1975] PNGLR 325; and *Prosecutor's Request No. 4 of 1974* [1975] PNGLR 365.

47. See *Momote-Kulang of Temogat v. R.* (1964) 111 CLR 64; *Timba-Kolian v. R.* [1967–1968] PNGLR 320; and *R. v. Hatenave-Tete* [1965–1966] PNGLR 336.

48. See *R. v. Philip Boike Ulel* [1973] PNGLR 254; *R. v. Timba-Kolian;* and *R. v. K. J. & Anor.* [1973] PNGLR 93.

49. See *R. v. Pius Piane* [1975] PNGLR 52.

50. See *R. v. Koiyari-Igeva* [1965–1966] PNGLR 284; *R. v. Brigitta Asamaken* [1964] PNGLR 193, and *R. v. Hatevave-Tete.*

51. See *R. v. Iakapo & Rapirikila* [1965–1966] PNGLR 147, and *R. v. David Bradley* (1948) (Unreported) No. 5.

52. *Supreme Court Reference No. 2 of 1981: Re Section 19 of the Criminal Code* [1982] PNGLR 150 (per Kapi, J.).

53. *Avia Aihi v. State* (per Kearney, Dep. C.J.).

54. See, for example, *Agevu v. Government* [1977] PNGLR 99; *Administration v. Guba* (1973) ALJR 621

and [1973] PNGLR 603; *Tolain v. Administration* [1965–1966] PNGLR 232; *First Assistant Secretary v. Administration* (1974) F.C. 55.

55. The decision in *Re Doa Minch* [1973] PNGLR 558 illustrates the problems that can arise. The decedent was an indigenous Papua New Guinean, but his estate consisted of property and business interests including noncustomary land of considerable value. The potential heirs, the customary group and the decedent's spouse, also disagreed on who were the beneficiaries and who should administer the estate. The court decided that the property should go to the customary heirs.

56. *Peter Timereke v. Ferrie and Johns* (1982) (Unreported) N379.

57. See, for example, *Public Curator of Papua New Guinea v. Public Trustee of New Zealand* [1976] PNGLR 427 (will admitted although there was only one witness and no attestation by the testator); *Public Curator of Papua New Guinea v. Rei Reinou and Others* [1978] PNGLR 253 (will admitted although altered without witnesses); *Re Breckenridge Deceased* [1974] PNGLR 90 (lost will admitted to probate); *Re Johns* [1971–1972] PNGLR 110 (will destroyed by fire admitted to probate).

58. See, for example, *Tonolei Development v. Lucas Waka* (1983) (Unreported) N404 (although this case turns on a misconception by the National Court of the rule relating to acceptance by post).

CHAPTER 10. SOLOMON ISLANDS

1. For a full historical account, see Bennett, *Wealth of the Solomons*.
2. *R. v. Stephen Rose*, Criminal Case No. 43 of 1987.
3. *R. v. Ngena* [1983] SILR 1.
4. *R. v. Loumia and Or.* [1984] SILR 51.
5. *Cheung v. Tanda* [1984] SILR 108 per Kapi, J.A.
6. *Cheung v. Tanda*.
7. *Kenilorea v. Attorney General* [1984] SILR 179.
8. *Tegavota v. Bennet*, Civil Case No. 104 of 1982.
9. *Nathaniel Waena v. Attorney General*, Civil Case No. 42 of 1989.
10. *Kenilorea v. Attorney General* [1983] SILR 61.
11. *Manubili & Or. v. Fenda* [1984] SILR 1.
12. *Manedetea v. Kulagoe* [1984] SILR 20.
13. *Haikiu v. Akuila* [1983] SILR 109.
14. *Maerua v. Kahanatarou* (1983) SILR 96.
15. See also *Cambell v. Mafuara* [1984] SILR 4.
16. *In Re Application by the Minister for Western Provincial Affairs* [1983] SILR 141.
17. See *Jamakana v. Attorney General and Ano.* [1983] SILR 12, holding that a ministerial order restraining the plaintiff for no valid reason was in breach of the right to freedom of movement.
18. It was, for example, held in *R. v. Stephen Rose*, Criminal Case No. 43 of 1987, that corporal punishment by a teacher on a pupil is not inherently inhuman but could become so by the manner of its execution, for instance, by caning a student in front of other students.
19. It was held in *DPP v. Glass, DPP v. Kupper*, and *Kupper v. DPP*, [1984] SILR 28, that a proper hearing requires the court to properly conclude the hearing.
20. *Jamakana v. Attorney General and Ano.* at 127.
21. *Temasuu v. Toupongi* [1983] SILR 103; *R. v. Public Services Commission ex parte Tiare* [1984] SILR 80.
22. *Lopez v. Attorney General* (No.2) [1983] SILR 240.
23. *Lopez v. Attorney General* (No.1) [1983] SILR 232.
24. *Liliau v. Trading Company (Solomons)* (No.2) [1983] SILR 10.
25. *Inito v. R.* [1983] SILR 177.
26. *Nano and Ano. v. Riringi, Katovai v. Lumukana* [1984] SILR 9.
27. *Patatoa v. Talauai* [1983] SILR 112.

28. B. Ulufa'alu, "Colonial and Customary Land Tenure" in *Land in the Solomon Islands* (Suva: University of the South Pacific, 1979), 10.
29. See, for example, *Uma v. Registrar of Titles* [1983] SILR 265.
30. *Uma v. Registrar of Titles*.
31. G. Zoleveke, "Traditional Ownership and Land Policy" in *Land in Solomon Islands* (Suva: University of the South Pacific 1979), 1–2.
32. Ibid., p. 4.
33. *R. v. Jose Francisco Silva Finete and C & F Fishing Ltd.*, Criminal Case No. 4 of 1984.
34. *Mahon v. Mahon; Reid v. Reid* [1984] SILR 86.
35. *Sukutaona v. Hounihou* [1982] SILR 13; *In Re B.* [1983] SILR 223.
36. *Solomon Island Navigation Services Ltd. v. National Union of Workers* [1983] SILR 117.

CHAPTER 12. TONGA

1. *Muller v. Muller*, PC 1986 No. 1 (April 21, 1986).
2. *Sanft and Siale v. Paasi*, PC 1987 Nos. 7, 8 and 9 (August 3, 1987); [1987] SPLR 359; but see now Electoral Act 1989, No. 21.
3. *Lolohea v. Police*. PC 1987 No. 6.
4. *Vaitulala v. Smith*, LC 1989 No. 4 (August 18, 1989).
5. *Hon. Tu'ivakano v. Holani*, SC 1987 No. 2; [1987] SPLR 382.
6. *Fasi v. Pohiva*, CA 1990 No. 10 (September 5, 1990).
7. *Hon. Kalaniuvalu Fotofili and others v. Siale*. PC 1987 Nos. 1 and 2 (August 3, 1987); [1987] SPLR 339; [1988] LRC (Const.) 103; *Sanft and Fuko v. Hon. Kalaniuvalu Fotofili and others*, PC 1987 No. 3 (August 3, 1987); [1987] SPLR 354; [1988] LRC (Const.) 110.
8. Legislation establishing a Court of Appeal was passed in 1966 but not brought into operation until 1990.
9. *Hon. Tu'ivakano v. Holani*.
10. *Tu'itavake v. Porter and Government of Australia*, SC 1989 No. 24 (November 2, 1989).
11. *Pohiva v. Prime Minister*, SC 1986 No. 7 (Decision on discovery application February 11, 1988).
12. *Pohiva v. Prime Minister*, SC 1986 No. 7 (May 6, 1988); [1988] LRC (Const.) 949; *'Uta'atu v. Commodities Board*, SC 1989 No. 40 (October 19, 1989).
13. *Afuha'amango v. Minister of Finance* (1954) I TLR 70.
14. *Pohiva v. Prime Minister*.
15. *Tu'itavake v. Porter and Government of Australia*.
16. *R. v. Pohiva*, SC 1987 No. 11.
17. *Travis v. Kingdom of Tonga*, SC 1986 No. 81.
18. *Saokai v. Taulua*. PC 1983 No. 6; *Fifita v. Moata'ane*, SC 1985 Criminal Appeal No. 7; *Teaupa v. Tu'ihalangingie*, SC 1987 Criminal Appeal No. 3.
19. *R. v. Pailate*, SC 1988 No. 120; *R. v. Fainga'anuku*, SC 1988 No. 38 (April 10, 1989).
20. *Isaloi v. Nuku* PC 1988 No. 1 (reversing *'Etu v. Nuku*, PC (1958) II TLR 161).
21. *Minister of Lands v. Leger*, LC 1987 No. 1; [1987] SPLR 352.
22. *Brown and Others v. Tali 'Ofa*, CA 1990 No. 1 (September 3, 1990).
23. *Baron Tuita v. Vete, Lolohea and others*, LC 1987 Nos. 12 and 13 (March 4, 1988).
24. *Havea v. Hon. Tu'i'afitu*. PC 1977 No. 5; *Hausia v. Vaka'uta*. PC 1978 No. 5.
25. *Makalofi To'ofohe v. Minister of Lands*, PC (1958) II TLR 157; *Finau v. Vea and others*, LC 1983, No. 8 (June 14, 1985).
26. *V. M. Tauelangi v. T. Tauelangi and Minister of Lands*, LC 1978 No. 12 (July 22, 1985).
27. *Sanft v. Tonga Tourist Co*, PC 1981 No. 2.
28. *Veikune v. To'a*, LC 1978 No. 8 (October 3, 1988); *Matavalea v. Uata*, PC 1988 No. 3.
29. *Mokena v. Sitani*, LC 1985 No. 13 (March 10, 1989).
30. *Hon. Fulivai v. Kaianuanu*, PC (1961) II TLR 178.

NOTES TO PAGES 335–414   653

31. *Tangitau v. Paunga*, PC 1978 No. 7; *Fua v. Fua*, SC 1984 No. 244.
32. Mele Siulikutapu New Zealand Marriage Annulment Act 1970 No. 4; Fatafehi Tuku'aho Marriage Annulment Act 1980 No. 7.
33. *Muller v. Muller*. **Note 1 above.**
34. *Sanft v. Tonga Tourist Co.*, PC 1981 No. 2; *Ullric Exports Ltd. v. Teta Ltd.*, SC 1982 No. 63 (June 15, 1984).
35. *Kingdom of Tonga and Editor of Chronicle v. Mataele*, PC 1974 No. 1.

CHAPTER 13. TUVALU

1. *Pula Toafa and Ors. v. Attorney General of Tuvalu* (High Court, No. 1 of 1987).

CHAPTER 15. WESTERN SAMOA

1. *Ti'a Si'omia v. Police* (1971) [1970] WSLR 21.
2. *Fao Avau v. Va'ai Kolone*, SC 1982 No. 5979.
3. *Opeloge Olo v. Police*, SC 1980 No. 5092, followed in M. *Ilalio v. Police*, SC 1988 No. 8545.
4. *Attorney General v. S. Olomalu*, CA August 26, 1982, reported in 14(3) *Victoria University of Wellington Law Rev.* 275-293 (1984).
5. *Tariu Tuivaiti v. F. Sila*, SC December 17, 1980.
6. *P. Lemalu v. F. Jessop* (1960) [1960–1969] WSLR 214.
7. *Election Petition re Palauli (Le Falefa) No. 41* (1979) [1970–1979] WSLR 281.
8. *Attorney General v. S. Olomalu*.
9. *Election Petition re Aleipata (Itupa I Lalo) No. 19* (1979) [1970–1979] WSLR 247.
10. *Election Petition re Gagaifomauga No. 2* (1967) [1960–1969] WSLR 169; *Election Petition re Safata No. 13* (1979) [1970–1979] WSLR 239.
11. *Election Petitions re Palauli North No. 41* (1973) [1970–1979] WSLR 68; *Election Petition re Fa'asalelega No. 2* (1979) [1970–1979] WSLR 254.
12. *Uelese Petaia v. Supreme Court of Western Samoa*, CA, December 19, 1990.
13. *In re Tapu Leota* (1964) [1960–1969] WSLR 106.
14. *Uelese Petaia v. Supreme Court of W.S.*
15. *In the Matter of a Reference to the Supreme Court* (on legal aid), SC October 18, 1988.
16. *W.S. National Provident Fund Board v. Samoa Holdings Ltd.* (1977) [1970–1979] WSLR 170.
17. *Police v. Siaki Tuala* (1969) [1960–1969] WSLR 239.
18. *Ailafo Ainu'u v. Police* (1969) [1960–1969] WSLR 203; *Ti'a Si'omia v. Police*.
19. *E. Sale v. Police* (1978) [1970–1979] WSLR 177.
20. *Tariu Tuivaiti v. F. Sila*.
21. Direction by Donne, President, to Samoan Judges of the Land and Titles Court, April 17, 1980.
22. *Chu Ling v. Bank of Western Samoa* [1987] SPLR 413.
23. *Attorney General v. S. Olomalu*.
24. *Commission of Labour v. Electric Power Corporation* (1977) [1970–1979] WSLR 130.
25. *Apia Bottling Co Ltd. v. Attorney General* (1979) [1970–1979] WSLR 227.
26. *In Re Commission of Inquiry and T. Tauvaga* (1973) [1970–1979] WSLR 95.
27. *New Samoa Industries Ltd. v. Attorney General* (1978) [1970–1979] WSLR 222.
28. *Lesa v. Attorney General of New Zealand* [1982] 3 *Weekly Law Reports* 898; Citizenship (Western Samoa) Act of 1982 (NZ); *Father Ioana Vito and Ors. v. Attorney General of Western Samoa* SC September 19, 1988.
29. *Western Samoa Hotel Co. Ltd. v. Commissioner of Inland Revenue* [1987] SPLR 429.
30. *Apia Bottling Co. Ltd. v. Attorney General*.
31. *W.S. National Provident Fund Board v. Samoa Holdings Ltd.*

32. *A. Tolovaʻa v. Police*, CA, (1974) [1970–1979] WSLR 105.
33. *T. Atoa and Ors. v. G. T. Jackson and Ors.*, SC December 29, 1986.
34. *Election Petition re Gagaifomauga No. 2.*
35. *Matatumua M. v. Public Service Commission*, SC September 7, 1988.
36. *Western Samoa Trust Estates Corporation v. S. Atioo*, SC May 15, 1986.
37. *In the Matter of a Reference to the Supreme Court.*
38. *Police v. Siaki Tuala.*
39. *M. Tumanuvao v. Police* (1978) [1970–1979] WSLR 192.
40. *Uelese Petaia v. Supreme Court of W.S.*
41. *Wesley, S. v. Police* (1971) [1970–1979] WSLR 29; *Ah Mu, H. R. v. Ah Mu, I.* (1977) [1970–1979] WSLR 165; *Samoa Iron & Steel Ltd. v. Breckwoldt & Co. Ltd.* (1978) [1970–1979] WSLR 213.
42. *Uelese Petaia v. Supreme Court of W.S.*
43. *P. Ao v. P. Leota and L.D.S. Church* (1978) [1970–1979] WSLR 202.
44. *Western Samoan Trust Estates Corporation v. Faisaovale, L.* (1977) [1970–1979] WSLR 138.
45. *Methodist Church v. Vaeau* (1960) [1960–1969] WSLR 10.
46. *Suʻa T. v. Suʻa T.C.* (1978) [1970–1979] WSLR 179.
47. *Election Petition re Vaisigano No. 1* (1967) [1960–1969] WSLR 179.
48. *Samoan Public Trustee v. Annie Collins and Ors.* (1961) [1960–1969] WSLR 52.
49. *Y. Hing v. U. Y. Hing* (1969) [1960–1969] WSLR 236; *Ng Lam v. Ng Lam* (1972) [1970–1979] WSLR 46.
50. *S. Tuiletufuga v. F. Tuiletufuga and C. Weaver.* (1979) [1970–1979] WSLR 273.
51. *In re Will of O. F. Nelson* (1964) [1960–1969] WSLR 109.
52. *H. J. Keil v. Polynesian Airlines Ltd.*, SC 28, May 28, 1987.
53. *Lone, T. v. Kalati, T.A.* (1979) [1970–1979] WSLR 284.
54. *Matatumua v. Samoa Times (Apia) Ltd.* (1977) [1970–1979] WSLR 144.
55. *Rankin v. Samoa Printing & Publishing Co. Ltd.* (1961) [1960–1969] WSLR 38.
56. *Lauofo Meti Properties Ltd. v. Morris Hedstrom Samoa Ltd.*, SC June 10, 1988.
57. *P. Lemalu v. F. Jessop* (1960) [1960–1969] WSLR 214; *Samoan Public Trustee v. Pila Patu* (1972) [1970–1979] WSLR 35.
58. *H. J. Keil v. Polynesian Airlines Ltd.*, CA, January 8, 1991.
59. *Commissioner of Labour v. Electric Power Corporation.*

Chapter 16. American Samoa

1. An "unorganized" United States territory is one for which the U.S. Congress has not enacted an Organic Act; an "unincorporated" territory is one that is not considered an integral part of the United States and to which Congress has not extended all the privileges and benefits of states.
2. See S. Laughlin, "The Application of the Constitution in United States Territories: American Samoa, A Case Study," 2 *Univ. of Hawaii Law Rev.* 337, 363–364 (1980–1981); S. Tiffany, "The Cognatic Descent Groups of Contemporary Samoa," 10 MAN (new series) 430 (1975).
3. Laughlin, 372–381.
4. See, for example, *Best v. United States*, 184 F.2d 131, 138 (1950); *Mitchell v. Harmony*, 54 U.S. 115, 134 (1852); *Turney v. United States*, 115 F. Supp. 457, 464 (1953).
5. *King v. Andrus*, 452 F. Supp. 11 (D.D.C. 1977).
6. *Tung v. Ah Sam*, 4 ASR 746 (1971).
7. United States Department of the Interior, Secretary's Order No. 3009, September 13, 1977.
8. *Meredith v. Mola*, 4 ASR 773 (1973).
9. *Church of Jesus Christ of the Latter-Day Saints v. Hodel* 837 F.2d 374, 386 (1987).
10. *King v. Morton*, 520 F.2d 1140 (1975).
11. U.S. Department of the Interior, Secretary's Order No. 2657 (August 29, 1951, as amended 1972).

NOTES TO PAGES 444–467

12. Office of the Controller General, "Matter of Expenditure Incurred by the Government of American Samoa for the American Samoa Judiciary," March 14, 1980.
13. U.S. Bureau of the Census, *Federal Expenditure by State for Fiscal Year 1989*. Washington, D.C.: Government Printing Office, 1990.
14. *Fa'atupu v. Malepaeai*, 2 ASR 2d 58 (1985).
15. *King v. Andrus*, 450 F. Supp. 11 (1977).
16. See *Taufaasou v. Manuma*, 4 ASR 947 (1977).
17. *Olotoa Overland Manuma v. Bartley*, 3 ASR 2d 21 (1986).
18. Speech of High Chief Lutali A. P. Lauvao, "Land, Fine Mats and Dollars," cited in A. H. Leibowitz, "American Samoa: Decline of a Culture", 10 *California Western International Law J.* 220, 239 (1980).
19. *Craddick and Craddick v. Territorial Registrar of American Samoa*, 1 ASR 2d 10 (1980).
20. Laughlin.
21. *Reid v. Tavete*, 1 ASR 85 (1983).
22. *Fanene v. Talio* (1977) LT No. 64-77 (1977).
23. *Moon v. Falemalama*, 4 ASR 836 (1975).
24. This discussion of customary land tenure is based on S. Laughlin; T. O'Meara, "Customary Individualism," in R. G. Crocombe, ed., *Land Tenure in the Pacific*, 3d. ed. (Suva: University of the South Pacific, 1987); and A. P. Lutuli and W. J. Stewart, "A Chiefly System in Twentieth-Century America: Legal Aspects of the Matai and Land Tenure Systems in the Territory of American Samoa," 4 *Georgia J. of International & Comparative Law* 388 (1973).
25. *Asuega v. Manuma*, 4 ASR 616 (1965); see W. Tiffany, "The Role of the High Court in Matai Succession Disputes," 5 *Samoan Pacific Law J.* 11 (1979).
26. *Meredith v. American Samoa Government*, 2 ASR 2d 66 (1985).
27. *Logoa'i v. South Pacific Island Airways, Inc.*, 6 ASR 2d 28 (1987).
28. *Savage v. American Samoa Government*, 2 ASR 2d 6 (1984).
29. *Hartford Fire Insurance Co. v. Workmen's Compensation Commission*, No. 76-74 (High Court, 1977).

CHAPTER 17. FEDERATED STATES OF MICRONESIA

1. Trusteeship Agreement for the Former Japanese Mandated Islands, July 18, 1947, 61 Stat. 3301; TIAS 1665.
2. This discussion draws upon the works listed in **XXIII, B Research Guide**, particularly A. J. Armstrong, "The Negotiations for the Future Political Status of Micronesia," 74 *American J. of International Law* 689 (1980); A. J. Armstrong and H. L. Hills, "The Negotiations for the Future Political Status of Micronesia (1980–1984)," 78 *American J. of International Law* 484 (1984); N. Meller, *Constitutionalism in Micronesia* (Honolulu: Institute for Polynesian Studies, Brigham Young University, 1985); and G. Petersen, "A Cultural Analysis of the Ponapean Independence Vote in the 1983 Plebiscite," 9 *Pacific Studies* 13 (1985).
3. This discussion draws upon the works listed in **XXIII, B Research Guide**, particularly A. Burdick, "The Constitution of the Federated States of Micronesia," 8 *Univ. of Hawaii Law Rev.* 419 (1986); N. Meller, *Constitutionalism in Micronesia*; B. Tamanaha, "A Proposal for the Development of a System of Indigenous Jurisprudence in the Federated States of Micronesia," 13 *Hastings International & Comparative Law Rev.* 71 (1989); and B. Turcott, "Constitutional Jurisprudence of the Federated States of Micronesia Supreme Court," 6 *UCLA Pacific Basin Law J.* 103 (1989).
4. *Truk v. Hartman*, 1 FSM Intrm. 174, 176–177 (Truk 1982); *Suldan v. FSM*, 1 FSM Intrm. 339, 345 (Pon. 1983); *Edwards v. State of Pohnpei*, 3 FSM Intrm. 350, 357 (Pon. 1988); *Bank of Guam v. Semes*, 3 FSM Intrm. 370, 378 (Pon. 1988).
5. *Suldan v. FSM* (II), 1 FSM Intrm. 339, 343–344 (Pon. 1983).
6. *Alaphonso v. FSM*, 1 FSM Intrm. 209, 213–216 (App. 1981); *Sohl v. FSM*, 4 FSM Intrm. 186 (Pon. 1990); *Paul v. Celestine*, 4 FSM Intrm. 205 (App. 1990); *Federal Business Development Bank v. S/S Thorfinn*, 4 FSM Intrm. 368 (App. 1990); *Etscheit v. Santos*, 5 FSM Intrm. 35 (App. 1991).

7. One state court has interpreted this to mean that state constitutions must provide for separation of powers. *People of Kapingamarangi v. Pohnpei Legislature*, 3 FSM Intrm. 5 (Pon. S. Ct. Tr. 1985).

8. *Etpison v. Perman*, 1 FSM Intrm. 405, 428 (Pon. 1984).

9. *Edwards v. State of Pohnpei*, at 355; *Lonno v. Trust Territory*, 1 FSM Intrm. 53, 72 (Kos. 1982); *Pohnpei v. Mack*, 3 FSM Intrm. 45 (Pon. S. Ct. Tr. 1987).

10. The American Law Institute (ALI) is a nongovernmental body, made up of judges, lawyers, and law professors. The *Restatements* of the common law, published by the ALI, are intended to reflect the general rules of common law in force in most states of the United States. Although U.S. courts often cite to the *Restatements*, they do not have the force of law and are not considered binding precedent in any state in the United States.

11. See *Rauzi v. FSM*, 2 FSM Intrm. 8 (Pon. 1985), holding that this provision of the Trust Territory Code applies to Trust Territory courts and not to FSM courts.

12. *Alaphonso v. FSM*; at 213.

13. *Alaphonso v. FSM*; *Semens v. Continental Airlines, Inc.*, 2 FSM Intrm. 131, 140–141 (Pon. 1985).

14. *Semens v. Continental Airlines, Inc.*

15. *FSM v. Mudong*, 1 FSM Intrm. 135, 139 (Pon. 1982).

16. *Koike v. Ponape Rock Products, Inc.*, 3 FSM Intrm. 57 (Pon. S. Ct. Tr. 1986).

17. This discussion draws upon the works cited in **XXIII, B Research Guide**, particularly Burdick, "The Constitution of the Federated States of Micronesia."

18. Congressional membership in executive agencies may be in violation of Article IX, Section 13 of the Constitution, which prohibits members of Congress from holding other public offices, but the issue has not come before the FSM courts. Burdick, "The Constitution of the Federated States of Micronesia," at 446–450.

19. *Wall Street Journal*, January 3, 1989, 1 and 8.

20. *Gimnang v. Yap*, 4 FSM Intrm. 212 (Yap 1990); *Bruton v. Moen Municipality*, 5 FSM Intrm. 9 (Chk. 1990).

21. A. J. Armstrong, "The Island Nations of the Pacific Basin: Their Emerging Independence and Regionalism," in R. Rosendahl, ed., *Current Legal Aspects of Doing Business in the Pacific Basin* (New York: American Bar Association, 1987), 385.

22. *Carlos v. FSM*, 4 FSM Intrm. 17 (App. 1989).

23. Committee on Governmental Structure and Functions, Constitutional Convention of the Federated States of Micronesia, Standing Report No. 20–90, August 22, 1990.

24. *FSM v. Mudong*, at 139–140; *FSM v. Ruben, 1 FSM Intrm. 34 (Truk 1981)*.

25. *FSM v. Mudong*, at 144–146.

26. *Tammed v. FSM, 4 FSM Intrm. 266 (App. 1990)*.

27. *Kosrae v. Tolenoa*, 4 FSM Intrm. 201 (Kos. St. Tr. Ct. 1989).

28. *Ponape Chamber of Commerce v. Nett Municipal Government*, 1 FSM Intrm. 389, 400 (Pon. 1984).

29. *Nix v. Ehmes*, 1 FSM Intrm. 114, 118 (Pon. 1984).

30. *In re Robert*, 1 FSM Intrm. 18, 20 (Pon. 1981).

31. *Luda v. Maeda Road Construction Co., Ltd.*, 2 FSM Intrm. 107, 113 (Pon. 1985).

32. *Hadley v. Trustees*, 3 FSM Intrm. 14 (Pon. S. Ct. Tr. 1985).

33. *Loch v. FSM*, 1 FSM Intrm. 566, 569 (App. 1984).

34. *FSM v. Tipen*, 1 FSM Intrm. 79, 92 (Pon. 1982).

35. *FSM v. Edward*, 3 FSM Intrm. 224 (Pon. 1987).

36. *Bernard's Retail Store v. Johnny*, 4 FSM Intrm. 33 (App. 1989).

37. *Gimnang v. Yap*, 4 FSM Intrm. 212 (Yap 1990); *Ponape Transfer and Storage v. Federated Shipping*, 4 FSM Intrm. 37 (Pon. 1989).

38. *Ponape Transfer and Storage v. Federated Shipping; Bank of Guam v. Semes; In re Nahnsen*, 1 FSM Intrm. 97 (Pon 1982).

39. *In re Nahnsen*.

40. *Gimnang v. Yap*, 5 FSM Intrm. 13 (App. 1991).

41. *Edwards v. State of Pohnpei*, at 360–364.

42. *Bernard's Retail Store v. Johnny.*

43. This discussion draws upon works cited in **XXIII, A Research Guide**, including R. Hussey, "The Evolution of Land Inheritance on Pohnpei Island, FSM" (University of Hawaii, Honolulu, 1989 mimeo); W. McGrath and W. S. Wilson, "The Marshall, Caroline and Mariana Islands: Too Many Foreign Precedents," in R. G. Crocombe, ed., *Land Tenure in the Pacific*, 3d ed. (Suva: University of the South Pacific, 1987), 190; D. Olsen, "Piercing Micronesia's Colonial Veil," 15 *Columbia J. of Transnational Law* 473 (1976)

44. F. Castro, "Ponape: Tenure and Registration" in B. Acquaye and R. G. Crocombe, eds., *Land Tenure and Rural Productivity in the Pacific Islands* (Suva: University of the South Pacific, 1984), 190.

45. This discussion draws on works cited in **XXIII, A Research Guide**, including F. Defngin, "The Nature and Scope of Customary Land Rights of the Yapese Community," in Trust Territory of the Pacific Island, Office of the High Commissioner, *Land Tenure Patterns: Trust Territory of the Pacific Islands*, 1958; J. Fischer, "Contemporary Ponape Island Land Tenure" and "Native Land Tenure in the Truk District," in Trust Territory of the Pacific Islands, Office of the High Commissioner, *Land Tenure Patterns: Trust Territory of the Pacific Islands*, 1958; W. H. Goodenough, *Property, Kin and Community on Truk*. Publications in Anthropology, No. 46 (New Haven: Yale University Press, 1951); McGrath and Wilson, "The Marshall, Caroline and Mariana Islands.

46. McGrath and Wilson, "The Marshall, Caroline and Mariana Islands."

47. F. Castro, "Ponape: Tenure and Registration."

48. For discussions of customary divorce norms and practices, see *Aisea v. Trust Territory*, 1 TTR 245 (1955); *Yamada v. Yamada*, 2 TTR 66 (1959); *Lornis v. Trust Territory*, 2 TTR 114 (1959); *Solomon v. Alfons*, 2 P.S. Ct. R. 111 (Tr. 1986).

49. *Yamada v. Yamada*; *Pernet v. Aflague*, 4 FSM Intrm. 222 (Pon. 1990).

50. See McGrath and Wilson, "The Marshall, Caroline and Mariana Islands."

51. But, in *Bank of Hawaii v. Jack*, 4 FSM Intrm. 216 (Pon. 1990), the court held that cases regarding promissory notes issued by banks are a matter of national law.

52. See, for example, *FSM v. Ocean Pearl*, 3 FSM Intrm. 87, 90–91 (Pon. 1987); *Falcam v. FSM Postal Service*, 3 FSM Intrm. 112 (Pon 1987).

53. *Phillip v. Aldis*, 3 FSM Intrm. 28 (Pon. S. Ct. Tr. 1987).

54. *Semens v. Continental Airlines, Inc.*, at 147.

55. *Semens v. Continental Airlines, Inc.*

56. *Edwards v. State of Pohnpei*, 3 FSM Intrm. 350, 356-357 (Pon. 1988); *Semens v. Continental Airlines, Inc.*, at 137.

57. *Edwards v. State of Pohnpei*, at 359.

58. *Rauzi v. FSM*, at 14; *Koike v. Ponape Rock Products, Inc.*, at 64.

59. *Ray v. Electrical Contracting Corp.*, 2 FSM Intrm. 21, 23 (App. 1985).

60. *Koike v. Ponape Rock Products, Inc.*, at 68–69.

61. *Koike v. Ponape Rock Products, Inc.*

62. *Koike v. Ponape Rock Products, Inc.* at 70.

63. *Koike v. Ponape Rock Products, Inc.*

64. Compare *Ray v. Electrical Contracting Corp.*, at 25, with *Semens v. Continental Airlines, Inc.*, at 144.

65. *Federated Shipping Co. v. Ponape Transfer and Storage*, 4 FSM Intrm. 3 (Pon. 1989).

66. *Leeruw v. FSM*, 4 FSM Intrm. 350 (Yap 1990).

67. *Panuelo v. Pohnpei*, 2 FSM Intrm. 150 (Pon. 1986).

Chapter 18. Guam

1. An "unorganized" United States territory is one for which the U.S. Congress has not enacted an Organic Act, and an "unincorporated" territory is one that is not considered an integral part of the United States and to which Congress has not extended all the privileges and benefits of states.

2. *Johnson v. Eisentrager*, 339 U.S. 763, 770–1 (1950).

3. *Reid v. Covert*, 354 U.S. 1, 8–9, fn. 10 (1957); see also *Ralpho v. Bell*, 569 F. 2d 607 (D.C. Cir. 1977).

4. *Ocampo v. United States*, 234 U.S. 91 (1914); *United States v. Seagraves*, 100 F. Supp. 424 (D. Guam App. Div., 1951).

5. *Dowdell v. United States*, 221 U.S. 325 (1911).

6. *Attorney General of Guam v. U.S.*, 738 F.2d 1017 (9th Cir. 1984), cert. denied, 469 U.S. 1209 (1985).

7. *People of the Territory of Guam v. Sugiyama*, 846 F.2d 570 (9th Cir. 1988), cert. denied, 490 U.S. 1010 (1989).

8. See *American Insurance Co. v. 365 Bales of Cotton*, 26 U.S. 511, 542 (1828); and Leibowitz, "The Applicability of Federal Law to Guam," 16 *Virginia J. of International Law* 21, 34 (1975).

9. See Leibowitz, "United States Federalism: The States and the Territories," 28 *American University Law Rev.* 449 (1979).

10. *Rodriguez v. Gaylord*, 429 F. Supp. 797 (Hawaii, 1977).

11. See *National Bank v. County of Yankton*, 101 U.S. 129, 133 (1879).

12. Leibowitz, "The Applicability of Federal Law to Guam." See also *Ngiraingas v. Sanchez*, 495 U.S. 182 (1990).

13. *Blas v. Government of Guam*, 941 F.2d 778 (9th Cir. 1991), cert. denied, 112 S. Ct. 1295 (1992).

14. *People v. Salas* (Sup. Ct. Guam 1982) CR No. 47F-82.

15. *Wong v. Camina*, 2 Guam 132 (D. Guam App. Div. 1978).

16. *People v. Okada*, 694 F. 2d 565, 569 (9th Cir. 1982), cert. denied, 469 U.S. 1021 (1984).

17. *Samuel v. St. Pierre*, 1 Guam 299 (Sup. Ct. 1975).

18. *People v. Ulloa*, 903 F. 2d 1283 (9th Cir. 1990).

19. *Bordallo v. Reyes*, 763 F.2d 1098 (9th Cir. 1985).

20. *Laguana v. Guam Visitors Bureau*, 725 F.2d 519 (9th Cir. 1984).

21. *Bank of America v. Chaco*, 539 F.2d 1226 (9th Cir. 1976).

22. *U.S. v. Bordallo*, 857 F.2d 519 (9th Cir. 1988), amended and rehearing denied, 872 F.2d 334, cert. denied, 493 U.S. 818 (1989).

23. *Guam Society of Obstetricians and Gynecologists v. Ada*, 776 F. Supp. 1422 (D. Guam 1990); affirmed, 962 F. 2d 1366 (9th Cir. 1992).

24. *Wilson v. Garcia*, 471 U.S. 261 (1985); *Ngiraingas v. Sanchez*, 849 F.2d 372 (9th Cir. 1988), aff'd 495 U.S. 182 (1990); *Owens v. Okure*, 488 U.S. 235 (1989).

25. *Gardner v. International Telegraph Employees Local No. 9*, 850 F.2d 518 (9th Cir. 1988).

26. *People v. Fergurgur*, D.C. App. Guam 1981, Cr App #79-00062A.

27. *People v. Cepeda*, D.C. Guam App. Div., DC Cr 86-00014A (1986).

28. *People v. Ibanez*, 935 F.2d 275 (9th Cir. 1991).

29. *People v. Yang*, 850 F.2d 507 (1988), an en banc decision overturning earlier decisions of the Ninth Circuit in *Electrical Construction & Maintenance Co., Inc. v. Maeda Pacific Corporation*, 764 F.2d 619 (9th Cir. 1985) and *Laguana v. Guam Visitors Bureau*, 725 F.2d 519 (9th Cir. 1984).

30. *Guam Hakubotan, Inc. v. Furusawa Investment Corp.*, 947 F.2d 398 (9th Cir. 1991).

31. *Unpingao v. Hong Kong Macau Corp.*, 935 F.2d 1043 (9th Cir. 1991).

32. *People v. Ulloa*, 903 F.2d 1283 (9th Cir. 1990).

33 *In re Application of Iglesias*, 1 Guam 129 (D. Guam App. Div. 1963).

34. *Taitague v. First Island Industry, Inc.*, 942 F.2d 794 (9th Cir. 1991).

35. *Sakamoto v. Duty Free Shoppers, Ltd.*, 764 F.2d 1285 (9th Cir. 1985), cert. denied, 475 U.S. 1081 (1986); *IT&E Overseas, Inc. v. RCA Global Communications, Inc.*, 747 F. Supp. 6 (D.D.C. 1990).

36. *Lawrence v. Barker*, 1 Guam 625 (Sup. Ct. 1979).

37. *Parker v. Joe Lujan Enterprises, Inc.* 848 F.2d 118 (9th Cir. 1988).

38. *Sani-System, Inc. and Anor. v. Capital Insurance & Surety Co. Inc.*, 1 Guam 168 (D. Guam App. Div. 1967).

39. *Marx v. Government of Guam*, 866 F.2d 294 (9th Cir. 1989).

40. *Chang Soo Chong v. Guam Power Authority*, 1 Guam 595 (Sup. Ct. 1979).
41. *Ngiraingas v. Sanchez*. 495 U.S. 182 (1990).
42. *Guam Society of Obstetricians and Gynecologists v. Ada* 776 F. Supp. 1422 (D. Guam 1990), aff'd, 962 F. 2d 1366 (9th Cir. 1992).
43. Ibid.

CHAPTER 19. THE COMMONWEALTH OF THE NORTHERN MARIANA ISLANDS

1. *In re Estate of Antonio Roberto Camacho*, 1 CR 395, 402 (CTC 1983).
2. See *Pangelinan v. Tudela*, 1 CR 708 (District Court 1983), *In re Estate of Antonio Roberto Camacho*; *In re Estate of Jose Diaz Torres and Ascuncion Ada Torres*, 1 CR 237 (District Court 1981); *Palacios v. Coleman*, 1 CR 34 (District Court 1980).
3. See *Sirok v. ROTEC Engineering Co.*, 2 CR 179 (CTC 1985); the court applied the "most liberal standard available so long as due process requirements are met" in interpreting "transacting business within the Commonwealth."
4. *In re Estate of Edward Calub Refugia*, 1 CR 219 (CTC 1981).
5. *Pangelinan v. Tudela*, 1 CR 708 (District Court 1983).
6. See *Taimanao v. Young*, 2 CR 285 (District Court 1985).
7. See *Guerrero v. L & T International Corp.*, 2 CR 1068 (CTC 1987) (negligence); *Candelaria v. Yano Enterprises*, 2 CR 220 (District Court 1985) (false imprisonment); *Arriola v. Insurance Company of North America*, 2 CR 113 (CTC 1985) (followed the *Restatement* and denied a claim for negligent infliction of emotional harm absent bodily harm); and *Tenorio v. Santos*, 1 CR 48 (District Court 1980) (defamation).
8. See *Gower v. Commonwealth of Northern Mariana Islands*, 2 CR 413 (District Court 1985), upholding the limitation on Commonwealth liability when the government consents to be sued in tort.
9. See *Abrams v. Trust Territory High Commissioner Disciplinary Panel*, 7 TTR 517 (1977).

CHAPTER 20. THE REPUBLIC OF PALAU

1. *Gibbons v. Salii*, 1 ROP Intrm. 333 (App. Div. 1986).
2. *Fritz v. Salii*, App. No. 8-88, August 29, 1988.
3. *Ngirmekur v. Municipality of Airai*, 7 TTR 477, 483 (1986).
4. *Chief Uoruyos Udiu and Uodelchad Irorow v. Dirrecheteet*, 1 ROP Intrm. (App. Div. 1984).
5. *Figir v. Trust Territory*, 4 TTR 368 (Tr. Div. 1969).
6. *Ngirmekur v. Municipality of Airai*, 1 ROP Intrm. 22 (High Ct. 1982).
7. See *Takawo v. Sechelong*, 1 ROP Intrm. 130 (Tr. Div. 1984).
8. See *Tet Ra Ollei Uehara v. Obeketang*, 1 ROP Intrm. 267 (Tr. Div. 1985) (dispute concerning the title of "Tet"); *Chief Uoruyos Udui and Uodelchad Irorow v. Dirrecheteet*, 1 ROP Intrm. 114 (App. Div. 1984) (suit to determine traditional title of chief); and *Acting High Chief Reklai v. Isimang*, 1 ROP Intrm. 30 (Tr. Div. 1982) (dispute over the removal of one of the two paramount chiefs of Palau).
9. See *Ksau v. Kuskus*, 6 TTR 629 (1974).
10. See *In re Eriich v. Reapportionment Commission*, 1 ROP Intrm. 150 (App. Div. 1984), which upheld the 1984 reapportionment and redistricting plan with slight modifications.
11. *Ikeda v. Ngirachelbaed*, 5 TTR 204 (1970).
12. *Ngiraroro v. Martin*, 7 TTR 310 (1976).
13. *Takawo v. Sechelong*.
14. *Armaluuk v. Mereb*, 7 TTR 459 (1975).
15. *Antonio v. Trust Territory*, 7 TTR 123 (1974), *Obak v. Tulop*, 6 TTR 240 (1973); *Demei v. Sungino*, 6 TTR 499 (1974); *Baiei v. Bilamang*, 5 TTR 389 (1971); and *Mechol v. Kyos*, 5 TTR 262 (1970).

Chapter 21. New Caledonia

1. See *Pacific Constitutions*, Vol. 1, *Polynesia* (Suva: University of the South Pacific, 1988), 107–130.

2. See the decision of the Constitutional Council of July 2, 1965. For a full discussion of the Constitutional Council's decision, see Lampue, P., "Le Regime Constitutionnel des Territoires d'Outre-Mer," 100 *Revue du Droit Public et de la Science Politique* (1984), 7–20.

3. New Caledonia was first represented in the French Parliament in 1945. See Ordinances of August 17 and 22, 1945.

4. This power is reenacted in Article 24 of the Territorial Statute.

5. These communes, similar to those in metropolitan France, were created in 1969. Before then, Noumea was the only commune.

6. The *tribe* in New Caledonia, in contrast to traditional homogeneous organizations referred to by the same term in sociology, is an amorphous artificial creation of French colonial policies. Essentially, it consists of a few hundred people, without any necessary ancestral links, who have been brought together in the native reserves.

7. The main source of *droit administratif* is judicial decisions, it being the only notable major branch of law in the French legal system that is not codified.

8. This recognition was enacted in Ordinance No. 82-877 of October 15, 1982, and No. 85-1185 of November 13, 1985, relating to the orientation of economic development and land reform respectively.

9. For a detailed discussion of the native reserves and the problems associated with them, see M. Dornoy, *Politics in New Caledonia* (Sydney: Sydney University Press, 1984), 119–153; A. Saussol, *New Caledonia: Colonization and Reaction*, in R. G. Crocombe, ed., *Land Tenure in the Pacific* (Suva: University of the South Pacific, 1987), 240–260; and A. Ward, *Land and Politics in New Caledonia* (Canberra: Australian National University, 1982).

10. The province of the Loyalty Islands, particularly, is notable for the preservation of its traditional system of land tenure.

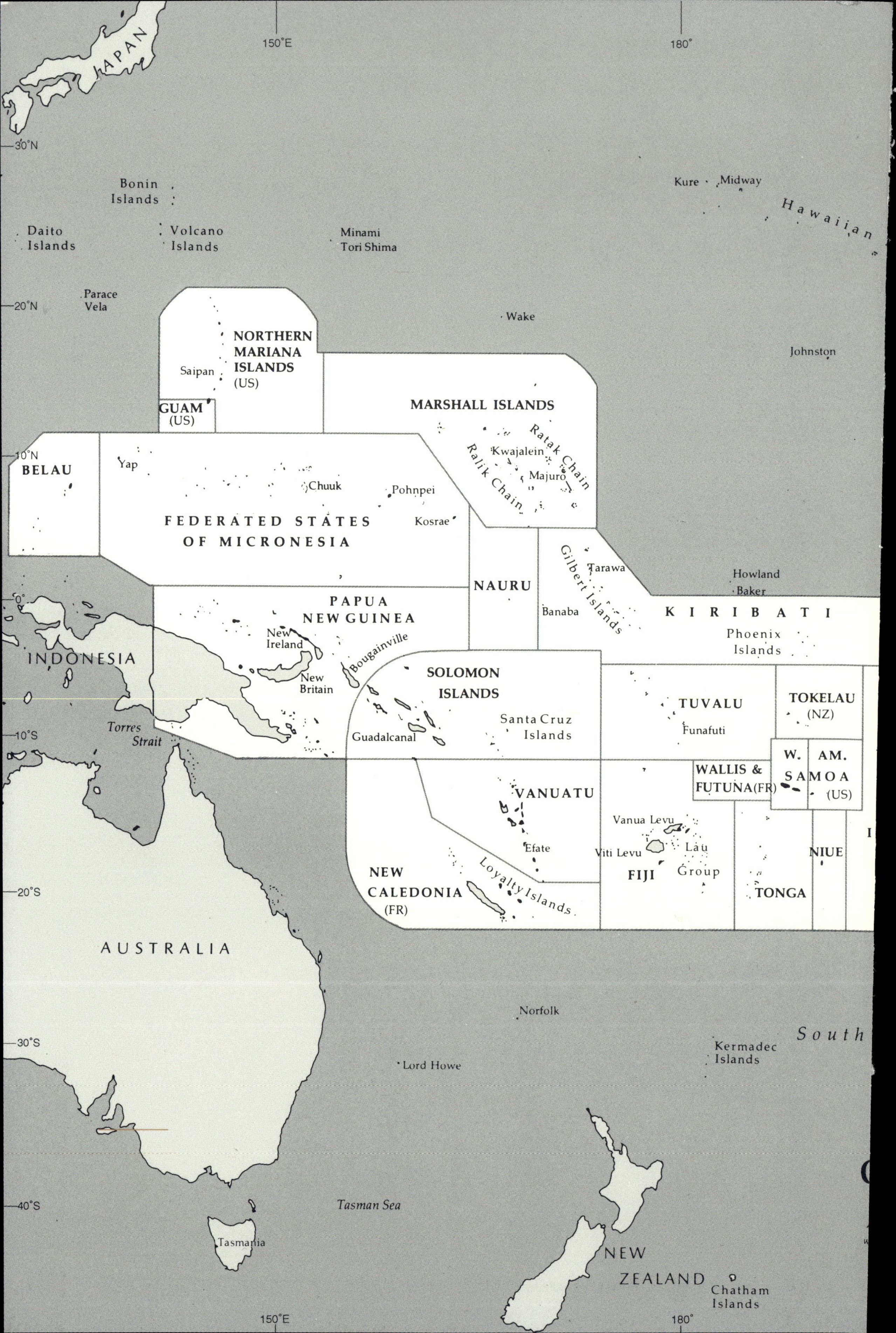
JAPAN
150°E
180°
30°N
Bonin Islands
Daito Islands
Volcano Islands
Minami Tori Shima
Kure
Midway
Hawaiian
Parace Vela
20°N
Wake
Johnston
NORTHERN MARIANA ISLANDS (US)
Saipan
GUAM (US)
MARSHALL ISLANDS
Ratak Chain
Ralik Chain
Kwajalein
Majuro
10°N
BELAU
Yap
Chuuk
Pohnpei
Kosrae
FEDERATED STATES OF MICRONESIA
Tarawa
Gilbert Islands
Howland
Baker
NAURU
Banaba
KIRIBATI
0°
PAPUA NEW GUINEA
New Ireland
New Britain
Bougainville
Phoenix Islands
INDONESIA
SOLOMON ISLANDS
Guadalcanal
Santa Cruz Islands
TUVALU
Funafuti
TOKELAU (NZ)
Torres Strait
10°S
W. SAMOA
AM. SAMOA (US)
WALLIS & FUTUNA (FR)
VANUATU
Efate
Vanua Levu
Viti Levu
Lau Group
FIJI
NIUE
TONGA
NEW CALEDONIA (FR)
Loyalty Islands
20°S
AUSTRALIA
Norfolk
30°S
South
Kermadec Islands
Lord Howe
40°S
Tasman Sea
Tasmania
NEW ZEALAND
Chatham Islands